Building Code
of New York State

New York State
Department of State
Division of Code Enforcement and Administration

2010

David A. Paterson Governor
Lorraine Cortés-Vázquez Secretary of State

2010 Building Code of New York State

Publication Date: August 2010

ISBN: 978-1-60983-000-7

COPYRIGHT © 2010
by

International Code Council, Inc.
500 New Jersey Avenue, NW, 6th Floor
Washington, D.C. 20001

and

New York State
Department of State
99 Washington Avenue
Albany, NY 12231

Cover Photo Credits: Courtesy of New York State Office of Parks, Recreation and Historic Preservation.

Darwin Martin House State Historic Site: The Darwin Martin House, located in Buffalo, New York, is one of Frank Lloyd Wright's most celebrated Prairie style homes. Constructed for the Martin family in the early 1900s, the house features Wright's signature low, horizontal design and free-flowing plan. This National Historic Landmark property, which includes several interconnected buildings and landscape features, is being meticulously restored to its 1907 appearance.

Olana State Historic Site: Olana, located in Hudson, New York, is the spectacular 19th-century estate of Hudson River School painter Frederic Edwin Church. The magnificent Persian style house and studio as well as the surrounding landscape were designed by Church. The property, a National Historic Landmark, offers dramatic views of the Hudson Valley that inspired Church's paintings.

PRINTED IN THE U.S.A.

ACKNOWLEDGMENTS

The Department of State gratefully acknowledges the following individuals who contributed to the development of the Building Code of New York State:

STATE FIRE PREVENTION AND BUILDING CODE COUNCIL

Lorraine A. Cortés-Vázquez	Chair - Secretary of State, NYS Department of State
Ronald E. Piester, AIA	designee - Director, NYS Department of State Division of Code Enforcement & Administration
Floyd Madison	State Fire Administrator - NYS Office of Fire Prevention & Control
John F. Mueller	designee - Deputy State Fire Administrator NYS Office of Fire Prevention & Control
Richard F. Daines, M. D.	Commissioner - NYS Department of Health
Richard W. Svenson, P.E.	designee - Director, NYS Department of Health Division of Environmental Health Protection
M. Patricia Smith	Commissioner - NYS Department of Labor
Blaise Thomas, P.E.	designee - NYS Department of Labor Associate Engineer, Engineering Services
Michael R. Bloomberg	Mayor - City of New York
John H. Lee, R.A.	designee - New York City Buildings
Matthew J. Driscoll	Mayor - City of Syracuse
Nicholas Altieri	designee - City of Syracuse, Code Enforcement Inspection Office
Randolph F. Bateman	Mayor - City of Oswego
Neal Smith	designee - Director of Code Enforcement
Michael W. Behling	Legislator - County of Jefferson
David Ross	designee - Code Enforcement Official
Robert E. Olson	Councilman - Town of Horicon
L. Stephen Brescia	Mayor - Village of Montgomery
Carmen R. Dubaldi, Jr.	designee - Orange County, Division of Risk Management
Joseph F. Sauerwein	Fire Service Official Blue Point Fire District
Gary B. Higbee, AIA	Registered Architect - Director of Industry Development The Steel Institute of New York
Thomas B. Vanderbeek, P.E.	Professional Engineer
John H. Flanigan	Code Enforcement Official
Robert Hankin	Builders' Representative
John J. Torpey	Trade Union Representative
Richard M. Vargas	Persons with Disabilities Representative NYS Commission on Quality of Care and Advocacy for Persons with Disabilities

DEPARTMENT OF STATE

Lorraine A. Cortés-Vázquez	Secretary of State
Daniel Shapiro	First Deputy Secretary of State
Ronald E. Piester, AIA	Director - Division of Code Enforcement & Administration
Thomas P. Mahar	Deputy Director - Division of Code Enforcement & Administration
Raymond J. Andrews, R.A.	Assistant Director for Code Development - Division of Code Enforcement & Administration
Joseph P. Ball, Esq.	Office of Counsel

BUILDING CODE TECHNICAL SUBCOMMITTEE

Mark Blanke, P.E. (Chair), Edward Haher, Gerard Hathaway, R.A., Brian Tollisen, P.E. - Department of State Staff, Mark Dedrick, Frank Golon, P.E., William Gregory, Timothy DeRuyscher, P.E., Joseph Razza, P.E., Joseph Reich, Thomas Robert, R.A., Thomas Tyson, P.E.

Content

The Building Code of New York State combines language from the 2006 International Building Code®, and New York modifications developed by the State Fire Prevention and Building Code Council and its Building Code Technical Subcommittee.

Marginal Markings

Solid vertical lines in the margins within the body of the code indicate a technical change from the requirements of the 2007 Edition. Deletion indicators (➡) are provided in the margin where a paragraph or item has been deleted.

Letter Designations in Front of Section Numbers

The content of sections in this code which begin with a letter designation are maintained by another code development committee in accordance with the following: [B] Building Code; [F] Fire Code; [M] Mechanical Code and [P] Plumbing Code.

TABLE OF CONTENTS

CHAPTER 1   GENERAL REQUIREMENTS 1

Section

101   Title, Scope and Purpose 1

102   Applicability............................. 1

103   Materials, Equipment and Methods of
          Construction 2

104   Service Utilities 3

105   Temporary Structures...................... 3

106   Modular Buildings 3

107   Administration and Enforcement 3

CHAPTER 2   DEFINITIONS 5

Section

201   General 5

202   Definitions 5

**CHAPTER 3   USE AND OCCUPANCY
                CLASSIFICATION 17**

Section

301   General 17

302   Classification 17

303   Assembly Group A 17

304   Business Group B 18

305   Educational Group E 18

306   Factory Group F 18

307   High-Hazard Group H 19

308   Institutional Group I 27

309   Mercantile Group M...................... 28

310   Residential Group R 29

311   Storage Group S 29

312   Utility and Miscellaneous Group U 30

**CHAPTER 4   SPECIAL DETAILED
                REQUIREMENTS BASED ON
                USE AND OCCUPANCY 31**

Section

401   Scope 31

402   Covered Mall Buildings 31

403   High-Rise Buildings...................... 34

404   Atriums................................. 35

405   Underground Buildings 36

406   Motor-Vehicle-Related Occupancies 37

407   Group I-2 41

408   Group I-3 42

409   Motion Picture Projection Rooms 44

410   Stages and Platforms 44

411   Special Amusement Buildings.............. 46

412   Aircraft-Related Occupancies 47

413   Combustible Storage 49

414   Hazardous Materials 49

415   Groups H-1, H-2, H-3, H-4 and H-5 53

416   Application of Flammable Finishes.......... 65

417   Drying Rooms 66

418   Organic Coatings 66

419   Group I-1, R-1, R-2, R-3 66

420   Hydrogen Cutoff Rooms 66

**CHAPTER 5   GENERAL BUILDING
                HEIGHTS AND AREAS........... 69**

Section

501   General................................. 69

502   Definitions 69

503   General Height and Area Limitations 69

504   Height.................................. 71

505   Mezzanines.............................. 71

506   Area Modifications 72

507   Unlimited Area Buildings 73

508   Mixed Use and Occupancy 74

509   Special Provisions 76

CHAPTER 6   TYPES OF CONSTRUCTION 79

Section

601   General................................. 79

602   Construction Classification 79

603   Combustible Material in Type I and II
          Construction........................... 81

**CHAPTER 7   FIRE-RESISTANCE-RATED
                CONSTRUCTION............... 83**

Section

701   General................................. 83

702   Definitions 83

703   Fire-Resistance Ratings and Fire Tests 84

704   Exterior Walls 85

705	Fire Walls	88
706	Fire Barriers	90
707	Shaft Enclosures	91
708	Fire Partitions	94
709	Smoke Barriers	95
710	Smoke Partitions	95
711	Horizontal Assemblies	95
712	Penetrations	96
713	Fire-Resistant Joint Systems	98
714	Fire-Resistance Rating of Structural Members	99
715	Opening Protectives	100
716	Ducts and Air Transfer Openings	104
717	Concealed Spaces	107
718	Fire-Resistance Requirements for Plaster	109
719	Thermal- and Sound-Insulating Materials	109
720	Prescriptive Fire Resistance	131
721	Calculated Fire Resistance	131

CHAPTER 8   INTERIOR FINISHES 159

Section

801	General	159
802	Definitions	159
803	Wall and Ceiling Finishes	159
804	Interior Floor Finish	161
805	Combustible Materials in Type I and II Construction	162
806	Decorative Materials and Trim [F]	162

CHAPTER 9   FIRE PROTECTION SYSTEMS... 165

Section

901	General	165
902	Definitions	165
903	Automatic Sprinkler Systems	168
904	Alternative Automatic Fire-Extinguishing Systems	172
905	Standpipe Systems	174
906	Portable Fire Extinguishers	176
907	Fire Alarm and Detection Systems	176
908	Emergency Alarm Systems	184
909	Smoke Control Systems	185
910	Smoke and Heat Vents	192
911	Fire Command Center	193
912	Fire Department Connections	194

CHAPTER 10   MEANS OF EGRESS 195

Section

1001	Administration	195
1002	Definitions	195
1003	General Means of Egress	196
1004	Occupant Load	197
1005	Egress Width	199
1006	Means of Egress Illumination	199
1007	Accessible Means of Egress	200
1008	Doors, Gates and Turnstiles	201
1009	Stairways	206
1010	Ramps	209
1011	Exit Signs	210
1012	Handrails	211
1013	Guards	211
1014	Exit Access	212
1015	Exit and Exit Access Doorways	214
1016	Exit Access Travel Distance	215
1017	Corridors	216
1018	Exits	217
1019	Number of Exits and Continuity	217
1020	Vertical Exit Enclosures	218
1021	Exit Passageways	220
1022	Horizontal Exits	220
1023	Exterior Exit Ramps and Stairways	221
1024	Exit Discharge	221
1025	Assembly	222
1026	Emergency Escape and Rescue	227

CHAPTER 11   ACCESSIBILITY 229

Section

1101	General	229
1102	Definitions	229
1103	Scoping Requirements	229
1104	Accessible Route	230
1105	Accessible Entrances	231
1106	Parking and Passenger Loading Facilities	232
1107	Dwelling Units and Sleeping Units	233
1108	Special Occupancies	236
1109	Other Features and Facilities	238
1110	Signage	241

CHAPTER 12   INTERIOR ENVIRONMENT..... 243

Section

1201	General	243

1202	Definitions	243
1203	Ventilation	243
1204	Temperature Control	244
1205	Lighting	244
1206	Yards or Courts	245
1207	Sound Transmission	245
1208	Interior Space Dimensions	245
1209	Access to Unoccupied Spaces	246
1210	Surrounding Materials	246

CHAPTER 13   ENERGY EFFICIENCY 247

Section

1301	General	247

CHAPTER 14   EXTERIOR WALLS 249

Section

1401	General	249
1402	Definitions	249
1403	Performance Requirements	249
1404	Materials	250
1405	Installation of Wall Coverings	251
1406	Combustible Materials on the Exterior Side of Exterior Walls	254
1407	Metal Composite Materials (MCM)	255

CHAPTER 15   ROOF ASSEMBLIES AND ROOFTOP STRUCTURES 257

Section

1501	General	257
1502	Definitions	257
1503	Weather Protection	257
1504	Performance Requirements	258
1505	Fire Classification	259
1506	Materials	259
1507	Requirements for Roof Coverings	260
1508	Roof Insulation	268
1509	Rooftop Structures	268
1510	Reroofing	269

CHAPTER 16   STRUCTURAL DESIGN 271

Section

1601	General	271
1602	Definitions and Notations	271
1603	Construction Documents	272

1604	General Design Requirements	273
1605	Load Combinations	276
1606	Dead Loads	277
1607	Live Loads	277
1608	Snow Loads	282
1609	Wind Loads	283
1610	Soil Lateral Loads	287
1611	Rain Loads	287
1612	Flood Loads	288
1613	Earthquake Loads	289

CHAPTER 17   STRUCTURAL TESTS AND SPECIAL INSPECTIONS 295

Section

1701	General	295
1702	Definitions	295
1703	Approvals	296
1704	Special Inspections	296
1705	Statement of Special Inspections	305
1706	Contractor Responsibility	306
1707	Special Inspections for Seismic Resistance	307
1708	Structural Testing for Seismic Resistance	308
1709	Structural Observations	309
1710	Design Strengths of Materials	309
1711	Alternative Test Procedure	309
1712	Test Safe Load	309
1713	In-Situ Load Tests	309
1714	Preconstruction Load Tests	310
1715	Material and Test Standards	311

CHAPTER 18   SOILS AND FOUNDATIONS 313

Section

1801	General	313
1802	Foundation and Soils Investigations	313
1803	Excavation, Grading and Fill	314
1804	Allowable Load-Bearing Values of Soils	315
1805	Footings and Foundations	316
1806	Retaining Walls	326
1807	Dampproofing and Waterproofing	326
1808	Pier and Pile Foundations	328
1809	Driven Pile Foundations	333
1810	Cast-in-Place Concrete Pile Foundations	336
1811	Composite Piles	339
1812	Pier Foundations	340

CHAPTER 19   CONCRETE................ **343**

Section

1901   General..................................... 343

1902   Definitions 343

1903   Specifications for Tests and Materials 343

1904   Durability Requirements 343

1905   Concrete Quality, Mixing and Placing....... 345

1906   Formwork, Embedded Pipes and
        Construction Joints..................... 345

1907   Details of Reinforcement 346

1908   Modifications to ACI 318.................. 346

1909   Structural Plain Concrete 349

1910   Minimum Slab Provisions 350

1911   Anchorage to Concrete—Allowable
        Stress Design 350

1912   Anchorage to Concrete—Strength Design..... 350

1913   Shotcrete................................... 351

1914   Reinforced Gypsum Concrete 352

1915   Concrete-Filled Pipe Columns 352

CHAPTER 20   ALUMINUM **355**

Section

2001   General 355

2002   Materials.................................. 355

CHAPTER 21   MASONRY................... **357**

Section

2101   General 357

2102   Definitions and Notations................. 357

2103   Masonry Construction Materials 361

2104   Construction 364

2105   Quality Assurance 367

2106   Seismic Design............................ 368

2107   Allowable Stress Design................... 369

2108   Strength Design of Masonry............... 370

2109   Empirical Design of Masonry 371

2110   Glass Unit Masonry 377

2111   Masonry Fireplaces 378

2112   Masonry Heaters.......................... 381

2113   Masonry Chimneys........................ 381

CHAPTER 22   STEEL...................... **387**

Section

2201   General 387

2202   Definitions 387

2203   Identification and Protection of Steel
        for Structural Purposes.................. 387

2204   Connections 387

2205   Structural Steel........................... 387

2206   Steel Joists 388

2207   Steel Cable Structures 388

2208   Steel Storage Racks 389

2209   Cold-Formed Steel........................ 389

2210   Cold-Formed Steel Light-Framed
        Construction.......................... 389

CHAPTER 23   WOOD **391**

Section

2301   General.................................... 391

2302   Definitions 391

2303   Minimum Standards and Quality 392

2304   General Construction Requirements 396

2305   General Design Requirements for
        Lateral-Force-Resisting Systems 405

2306   Allowable Stress Design 412

2307   Load and Resistance Factor Design......... 422

2308   Conventional Light-Frame Construction 422

CHAPTER 24   GLASS AND GLAZING......... **465**

Section

2401   General.................................... 465

2402   Definitions 465

2403   General Requirements for Glass 465

2404   Wind, Snow, Seismic and
        Dead Loads on Glass 465

2405   Sloped Glazing and Skylights 467

2406   Safety Glazing 468

2407   Glass in Handrails and Guards............. 470

2408   Glazing in Athletic Facilities 470

2409   Glass in Elevator Hoistway 470

**CHAPTER 25   GYPSUM BOARD
             AND PLASTER**................. **471**

Section

2501   General................................... 471

2502   Definitions 471

2503   Inspection................................. 471

2504   Vertical and Horizontal Assemblies 471

2505   Shear Wall Construction 471

2506   Gypsum Board Materials 471

2507   Lathing and Plastering 472

2508	Gypsum Construction	472
2509	Gypsum Board in Showers and Water Closets	473
2510	Lathing and Furring for Cement Plaster (Stucco)	474
2511	Interior Plaster	474
2512	Exterior Plaster	475
2513	Exposed Aggregate Plaster	475

CHAPTER 26   PLASTIC 477

Section

2601	General	477
2602	Definitions	477
2603	Foam Plastic Insulation	477
2604	Interior Finish and Trim	480
2605	Plastic Veneer	481
2606	Light-Transmitting Plastics	481
2607	Light-Transmitting Plastic Wall Panels	482
2608	Light-Transmitting Plastic Glazing	482
2609	Light-Transmitting Plastic Roof Panels	483
2610	Light-Transmitting Plastic Skylight Glazing	484
2611	Light-Transmitting Plastic Interior Signs	484

CHAPTER 27   ELECTRICAL 485

Section

2701	General	485
2702	Emergency and Standby Power Systems	485

CHAPTER 28   MECHANICAL SYSTEMS 487

Section

2801	General	487

CHAPTER 29   PLUMBING SYSTEMS 489

Section

2901	General	489
2902	Minimum Plumbing Facilities	489

CHAPTER 30   ELEVATORS AND CONVEYING SYSTEMS 493

Section

3001	General	493
3002	Hoistway Enclosures	493
3003	Emergency Operations	493
3004	Hoistway Venting	494
3005	Conveying Systems and Lifts	494
3006	Machine Rooms and Machinery Spaces	495

CHAPTER 31   SPECIAL CONSTRUCTION 497

Section

3101	General	497
3102	Membrane Structures	497
3103	Temporary Structures	498
3104	Pedestrian Walkways and Tunnels	498
3105	Awnings and Canopies	499
3106	Marquees	500
3107	Signs	500
3108	Radio and Television Towers	500
3109	Swimming Pool Enclosures and Safety Devices	500

CHAPTER 32   ENCROACHMENTS INTO THE PUBLIC RIGHT-OF-WAY 505

Section

3201	General	505
3202	Encroachments	505

CHAPTER 33   SAFEGUARDS DURING CONSTRUCTION 507

Section

3301	General	507
3302	Construction Safeguards	507
3303	Demolition	507
3304	Site Work	507
3305	Sanitary	507
3306	Protection of Pedestrians	507
3307	Protection of Adjoining Property	509
3308	Temporary Use of Streets, Alleys and Public Property	509
3309	Fire Extinguishers	509
3310	Exits	509
3311	Standpipes	509
3312	Automatic Sprinkler System	510

CHAPTER 34   RESERVED 511

CHAPTER 35   REFERENCED STANDARDS 513

APPENDIX A   RESERVED 533

APPENDIX B   RESERVED 535

APPENDIX C   RESERVED 537

APPENDIX D   RESERVED 539

APPENDIX E   SUPPLEMENTARY ACCESSIBILITY
REQUIREMENTS................ 541

Section

E101   General 541

E102   Definitions 541

E103   Accessible Route 541

E104   Special Occupancies..................... 541

E105   Other Features and Facilities 541

E106   Telephones 542

E107   Signage................................ 543

E108   Bus Stops 543

E109   Transportation Facilities and Stations 544

E110   Airports................................ 544

E111   Referenced Standards.................... 545

APPENDIX F   RODENTPROOFING............ 547

Section

F101   General 547

APPENDIX G   RESERVED 549

APPENDIX H   RESERVED 551

APPENDIX I   PATIO COVERS 553

Section

I101   General 553

I102   Definitions 553

I103   Exterior Openings........................ 553

I104   Structural Provisions 553

APPENDIX J   RESERVED 555

APPENDIX K   RESERVED 557

APPENDIX L   ASSISTIVE LISTENING
SYSTEMS PERFORMANCE
STANDARDS.................. 559

Section

L101   General 559

L102   Induction Loop System.................... 559

L103   Infrared System 559

L104   FM System 560

APPENDIX S   NEW YORK STATE AGENCIES
WITH CONSTRUCTION
REGULATIONS OR
CONSTRUCTION AUTHORITY.. 561

INDEX.. 585

CHAPTER 1

GENERAL REQUIREMENTS

SECTION 101
TITLE, SCOPE AND PURPOSE

101.1 Title. These provisions shall be known as the *Building Code of New York State* and shall be cited as such and will be referred to herein as "this code."

101.2 Scope. The provisions of this code shall apply to the construction, alteration, movement, enlargement, replacement, repair, equipment, use and occupancy, location, maintenance, removal and demolition of every building or structure or any appurtenances connected or attached to such buildings or structures.

Exceptions:

1. Detached one-and two-family dwellings and multiple single-family dwellings (townhouses) not more than three stories in height above grade with separate means of egress and their accessory structures shall comply with the *Residential Code of New York State*.

2. Agricultural buildings, including barns, sheds, poultry houses and other buildings and equipment on the premises used directly and solely for agricultural purposes.

3. Construction trailers used as a temporary office for the purpose of monitoring construction at a construction site.

4. Structures such as radio and television transmission, communication and wind generation towers not attached to buildings.

101.3 Purpose. This code is intended to provide minimum requirements to safeguard public safety, health and general welfare through structural strength, means of egress facilities, stability, sanitation, adequate light and ventilation, energy conservation and safety to life and property from fire and other hazards attributed to the built environment.

101.4 Referenced codes. The other codes listed in Sections 101.4.1 through 101.4.8 and referenced elsewhere in this code shall be considered part of the requirements of this code to the prescribed extent of each such reference.

101.4.1 Electrical. The provisions of Chapter 27 of this code shall apply to the installation of electrical systems, including alterations, repairs, replacement, equipment, appliances, fixtures, fittings and appurtenances thereto.

101.4.2 Fuel gas. The provisions of the *Fuel Gas Code of New York State* shall apply to the installation of gas piping from the point of delivery, gas appliances and related accessories as covered in this code. These requirements apply to gas piping systems extending from the point of delivery to the inlet connections of appliances and the installation and operation of residential and commercial gas appliances and related accessories.

101.4.3 Mechanical. The provisions of the *Mechanical Code of New York State* shall apply to the installation, alterations, repairs and replacement of mechanical systems, including equipment, appliances, fixtures, fittings and/or appurtenances, including ventilating, heating, cooling, air-conditioning and refrigeration systems, incinerators and other energy-related systems.

101.4.4 Plumbing. The provisions of the *Plumbing Code of New York State* shall apply to the installation, alteration, repair and replacement of plumbing systems, including equipment, appliances, fixtures, fittings and appurtenances, and where connected to a water or sewage system and all aspects of a medical gas system.

101.4.5 Property maintenance. The provisions of the *Property Maintenance Code of New York State* shall apply to existing structures and premises; equipment and facilities; light, ventilation, space heating, sanitation, life and fire safety hazards; responsibilities of owners, operators and occupants; and occupancy of existing premises and structures.

101.4.6 Fire prevention. The provisions of the *Fire Code of New York State* shall apply to matters affecting or relating to structures, processes and premises from the hazard of fire and explosion arising from the storage, handling or use of structures, materials or devices; from conditions hazardous to life, property or public welfare in the occupancy of structures or premises; and from the construction, extension, repair, alteration or removal of fire suppression and alarm systems or fire hazards in the structure or on the premises from occupancy or operation.

101.4.7 Energy. The provisions of the *Energy Conservation Construction Code of New York State* shall apply to all matters governing the design and construction of buildings for energy efficiency.

101.4.8 Existing buildings. The provisions of the *Existing Building Code of New York State* shall apply to all matters governing the repairs, alterations, change of occupancy, additions and relocation of existing buildings.

SECTION 102
APPLICABILITY

102.1 General. Where, in any specific case, different sections of this code specify different materials, methods of construction or other requirements, the most restrictive shall govern. Where there is a conflict between a general requirement and a specific requirement, the specific requirement shall be applicable.

102.2 Other laws and regulations. This code is part of the State Uniform Fire Prevention and Building Code (the Uniform Code) promulgated pursuant to Article 18 of the Executive Law. The provisions of the Uniform Code shall not be deemed to nullify any federal, state or local law, ordinance, administrative code, rule or regulation relating to any matter as to which the Uniform Code does not provide. However:

(1) Pursuant to section 383(1) of the Executive Law, and except as otherwise provided in paragraphs a, b and c of section 383 of the Executive Law, the provisions of the Uniform Code supersede any other provision of a general, special or local law, ordinance, administrative code, rule or regulation inconsistent or in conflict with the Uniform Code;

(2) Pursuant to section 379(3) of the Executive Law, no city, town, village, county or other municipality shall have the power to supersede, void, repeal, or make less restrictive any provision of the Uniform Code; and

(3) The ability of any city, town, or village, or the County of Nassau, to enact or adopt, and to enforce, a local law or ordinance imposing higher or more restrictive standards for construction within the jurisdiction of such city, town, village, or county than are applicable generally to such city, town, village, or county in the Uniform Code is subject to the provisions and requirements of section 379 of the Executive Law.

Nothing in this section 102.2 shall be construed (1) as affecting the authority of the State Labor Department to enforce a safety or health standard issued under provisions of sections 27 and 27-a of the Labor Law; (2) to relieve a person from complying with a stricter standard issued pursuant to the Occupational Safety and Health Act of 1970, as amended; (3) as superseding, limiting, impairing or otherwise affecting any provision in Parts 1219 to 1228 of Title 19 of the New York Codes, Rules and Regulations, as now in effect and as hereafter amended from time to time.

102.3 Change of use or occupancy. No change shall be made in the use or occupancy of any structure that would place the structure in a different division of the same group or occupancy or in a different group of occupancies, unless such structure is made to comply with the requirements of the *Existing Building Code of New York State.*

102.4 Application of references. References to chapter or section numbers, or to provisions not specifically identified by number, shall be construed to refer to such chapter, section or provision of this code.

102.5 Referenced standards. The standards referenced in this code shall be considered part of the requirements of this code to the prescribed extent of each such reference. Where differences occur between provisions of this code and referenced standards, the provisions of this code shall apply.

102.6 Appendices. The following appendices have been adopted and are made part of this code:

Appendix E - Supplemental Accessibility Requirements

Appendix F - Rodent Proofing

Appendix I - Patio Covers

Appendix L - Assistive Listening Systems Performance Requirements

Appendix S - New York State Agencies with Construction Regulations or Construction Authority

102.7 Partial invalidity. In the event that any part or provision of this code is held to be illegal or void, this shall not have the effect of making void or illegal any of the other parts or provisions.

102.8 Existing structures. The legal occupancy of any structure existing on the date of adoption of this code shall be permitted to continue without change, except as is specifically covered in this code, the *Property Maintenance Code of New York State,* the *Fire Code of New York State* or the *Existing Building Code of New York State.*

SECTION 103
MATERIALS, EQUIPMENT AND METHODS OF CONSTRUCTION

103.1 Approved materials and equipment. Materials, equipment and devices approved by the code enforcement official for use shall be constructed and installed in accordance with such approval. Materials, equipment and devices tested by an approved testing laboratory shall be permitted to be constructed and installed in accordance with such approval.

103.2 Used materials and equipment. Material, equipment and devices shall not be reused unless they meet the requirements of this code for new materials.

103.3 Alternate materials, design and methods of construction and equipment. This code is not intended to prevent the use of any material not specifically prescribed by this code or to prohibit any design or method of construction not specifically prescribed by this code, provided that any such alternative material, design or method of construction has been approved by the code enforcement official or the State Fire Prevention and Building Code Council. An alternative material, design or method of construction may be approved only when the code enforcement official or the State Fire Prevention and Building Code Council shall have determined, in writing, that such alternative material, design or method of construction (1) complies with the intent of the provisions of this code and (2) is at least equivalent of that prescribed in this code in quality, strength, effectiveness, fire resistance, durability and safety. Nothing in this section 103.3 shall be construed as permitting any code enforcement official, or any town, village, city, county, or state agency charged with the administration and enforcement of the Uniform Code, to waive, vary, modify or otherwise alter any provision or requirement of this code or any other provision or requirement of the Uniform Code. Provisions or requirements of the Uniform Code may be varied or modified only pursuant to procedures established by the Secretary of State pursuant to section 381(1)(f) of the Executive Law.

103.4 Safeguards during construction. All construction work covered in this code, including any demolition, shall comply with the requirements of the *Fire Code of New York State* and Chapter 33 of this code.

103.5 Workmanship. Repairs, maintenance work, alterations or installations which are caused directly or indirectly by the enforcement of this code shall be executed and installed in a workmanlike manner and installed in accordance with this code and the manufacturer's installation instructions.

SECTION 104
SERVICE UTILITIES

104.1 Connection of service utilities. Connections from a utility, source of energy, fuel or power to any building or system which is regulated by this code shall be made in accordance with the regulations of the public utility or other authority having jurisdiction.

104.2 Temporary power. Temporary power shall comply with the requirements of Chapter 27 of this code.

SECTION 105
TEMPORARY STRUCTURES

105.1 Conformance. Temporary structures shall conform to Chapter 31 of this code and Chapter 24 of the *Fire Code of New York State.*

SECTION 106
MODULAR BUILDINGS

106.1 Modular buildings. Such buildings shall be constructed and installed in accordance with the requirements of this code and shall bear the Insignia of Approval by the Secretary of State.

Exception: An Insignia of Approval shall not be required for the following buildings:

1. Modular buildings with structural components that cannot be inspected at the installation site but can be inspected in accordance with Section 1704 of this code at the manufacturing facility in which it was built.

2. Buildings of Group S or U occupancy having an area not exceeding 400 square feet and not customarily used for human occupancy.

SECTION 107
ADMINISTRATION AND ENFORCEMENT

107.1 107.1 Administration and enforcement. Administration and enforcement of the *New York State Uniform Fire Prevention and Building Code* shall be in accordance with local law, subject to the minimum requirements set forth in the "Official Compilation of Codes Rules and Regulations of the State of New York," 19 NYCRR Part 1203, "Minimum Standards for Administration and Enforcement." State agencies shall comply with the minimum requirements set forth in 19 NYCRR Part 1204, "Administration and Enforcement by State Agencies."

107.2 107.2 Modification. No town, village, city or county, nor any state agency charged with the administration and enforcement of this code may waive, modify or otherwise alter any provision of this code unless approved by the State Fire Prevention and Building Code Council in accordance with Section 379 of Article 18 of the Executive Law.

107.3 Application for variance or appeal. Variance or appeal of any provision of this code shall be in accordance with the provisions of the "Official Compilation of Codes Rules and Regulations of the State of New York," 19 NYCRR Part 1205, "Variance Procedures."

CHAPTER 2

DEFINITIONS

SECTION 201
GENERAL

201.1 Scope. Unless otherwise expressly stated, the following words and terms shall, for the purposes of this code, have the meanings shown in this chapter.

201.2 Interchangeability. Words used in the present tense include the future; words stated in the masculine gender include the feminine and neuter; the singular number includes the plural and the plural, the singular.

201.3 Terms defined in other codes. Where terms are not defined in this code and are defined in the *Fuel Gas Code of New York State, Fire Code of New York State, Mechanical Code of New York State* or *Plumbing Code of New York State,* such terms shall have the meanings ascribed to them as in those codes.

201.4 Terms not defined. Where terms are not defined through the methods authorized by this section, such terms shall have ordinarily accepted meanings such as the context implies.

SECTION 202
DEFINITIONS

AAC MASONRY. See Section 2102.1.

ACCESSIBLE. See Section 1102.1.

ACCESSIBLE MEANS OF EGRESS. See Section 1002.1.

ACCESSIBLE ROUTE. See Section 1102.1.

ACCESSIBLE UNIT. See Section 1102.1.

ACCREDITATION BODY. See Section 2302.1.

ADDITION. An extension or increase in floor area or height of a building or structure.

ADHERED MASONRY VENEER. See Section 1402.1.

ADOBE CONSTRUCTION. See Section 2102.1.

    Adobe, stabilized. See Section 2102.1.

    Adobe, unstabilized. See Section 2102.1.

[F] AEROSOL. See Section 307.2.

    Level 1 aerosol products. See Section 307.2.

    Level 2 aerosol products. See Section 307.2.

    Level 3 aerosol products. See Section 307.2.

[F] AEROSOL CONTAINER. See Section 307.2.

AGRICULTURAL, BUILDING. A structure designed and constructed to house farm implements, hay, grain, poultry, livestock or other horticultural products, excluding any structure designed, constructed or used, in whole or in part, for human habitation, as a place of employment where agricultural products are processed, treated or packaged, or as a place used by the public.

AIR-INFLATED STRUCTURE. See Section 3102.2.

AIR-SUPPORTED STRUCTURE. See Section 3102.2.

    Double skin. See Section 3102.2.

    Single skin. See Section 3102.2.

AISLE. See Section 1002.1.

AISLE ACCESSWAY. See Section 1002.1.

[F] ALARM NOTIFICATION APPLIANCE. See Section 902.1.

[F] ALARM SIGNAL. See Section 902.1.

[F] ALARM VERIFICATION FEATURE. See Section 902.1.

ALLOWABLE STRESS DESIGN. See Section 1602.1.

ALTERATION. Any construction or renovation to an existing structure other than repair or addition.

ALTERNATING TREAD DEVICE. See Section 1002.1.

ANCHOR. See Section 2102.1.

ANCHOR BUILDING. See Section 402.2.

ANCHORED MASONRY VENEER. See Section 1402.1.

ANNULAR SPACE. See Section 702.1.

[F] ANNUNCIATOR. See Section 902.1.

APPROVED. Acceptable to the code enforcement official as determined to meet the requirements of this code.

APPROVED AGENCY. See Section 1702.1.

APPROVED FABRICATOR. See Section 1702.1.

APPROVED SOURCE. An independent person, firm or corporation, approved by the code enforcement official, who is competent and experienced in the application of engineering principles to materials, methods or systems analyses.

ARCHITECTURAL TERRA COTTA. See Section 2102.1.

AREA. See Section 2102.1.

    Bedded. See Section 2102.1.

    Gross cross-sectional. See Section 2102.1.

    Net cross-sectional. See Section 2102.1.

AREA, BUILDING. See Section 502.1.

AREA OF REFUGE. See Section 1002.1.

AREAWAY. A subsurface space adjacent to a building open at the top or protected at the top by a grating or guard.

202.1 ASSISTIVE LISTENING DEVICE. A permanent system that reinforces sound transmission within an area from a source to a receiver/transducer to be used by the hearing impaired within that area.

ASSISTED LIVING FACILITIES. See Section 310.2, "Residential Care/Assisted living facilities."

ATRIUM. See Section 404.1.1.

ATTIC. The space between the ceiling beams of the top story and the roof rafters.

[F] AUDIBLE ALARM NOTIFICATION APPLIANCE. See Section 902.1.

202.2 AUTHORITY HAVING JURISDICTION. The local government, county government or state agency responsible for the administration and enforcement of an applicable regulation or law.

AUTOCLAVED AERATED CONCRETE (AAC). See Section 2102.1.

[F] AUTOMATIC. See Section 902.1.

[F] AUTOMATIC FIRE-EXTINGUISHING SYSTEM. See Section 902.1.

[F] AUTOMATIC SPRINKLER SYSTEM. See Section 902.1.

[F] AVERAGE AMBIENT SOUND LEVEL. See Section 902.1

AWNING. An architectural projection that provides weather protection, identity or decoration and is wholly supported by the building to which it is attached. An awning is comprised of a lightweight, rigid skeleton structure over which a covering is attached.

BACKING. See Section 1402.1.

BALCONY, EXTERIOR. See Section 1602.1.

BALED COTTON. See Section 307.2.

BALED COTTON, DENSELY PACKED. See Section 307.2.

[F] BARRICADE. See Section 307.2.

    Artificial barricade. See Section 307.2.

    Natural barricade. See Section 307.2.

BASE FLOOD. See Section 1612.2.

BASE FLOOD ELEVATION. See Section 1612.2.

BASEMENT. See Section 502.1 and 1612.2.

BED JOINT. See Section 2102.1.

BLEACHERS. See Section 1002.1.

BOARDING HOUSE. See Section 310.2.

[F] BOILING POINT. See Section 307.2.

BOND BEAM. See Section 2102.1.

BOND REINFORCING. See Section 2102.1.

BRACED WALL LINE. See Section 2302.1.

BRACED WALL PANEL. See Section 2302.1.

BRICK. See Section 2102.1.

    Calcium silicate (sand lime brick). See Section 2102.1.

    Clay or shale. See Section 2102.1.

    Concrete. See Section 2102.1.

BUILDING. Any structure used or intended for supporting or sheltering any use or occupancy.

BUILDING LINE. The line established by law, beyond which a building shall not extend, except as specifically provided by law.

BUILDING OFFICIAL. The officer or other designated authority charged with the administration and enforcement of this code, or a duly authorized representative.

BUILT-UP ROOF COVERING. See Section 1502.1.

BUTTRESS. See Section 2102.1.

CABLE-RESTRAINED, AIR-SUPPORTED STRUCTURE. See Section 3102.2.

CANOPY. An architectural projection that provides weather protection, identity or decoration and is supported by the building to which it is attached and at the outer end by not less than one stanchion. A canopy is comprised of a rigid structure over which a covering is attached.

[F] CARBON DIOXIDE EXTINGUISHING SYSTEMS. See Section 902.1.

CAST STONE. See Section 2102.1.

[F] CEILING LIMIT. See Section 902.1.

CEILING RADIATION DAMPER. See Section 702.1.

CELL. See Section 2102.1.

CEMENT PLASTER. See Section 2502.1.

CERAMIC FIBER BLANKET. See Section 721.1.1.

CERTIFICATE OF COMPLIANCE. See Section 1702.1.

CHIMNEY. See Section 2102.1.

CHIMNEY TYPES. See Section 2102.1.

    High-heat appliance type. See Section 2102.1.

    Low-heat appliance type. See Section 2102.1.

    Masonry type. See Section 2102.1.

    Medium-heat appliance type. See Section 2102.1.

CIRCULATION PATH. See Section 1102.1.

[F] CLEAN AGENT. See Section 902.1.

CLEANOUT. See Section 2102.1.

[F] CLOSED SYSTEM. See Section 307.2.

202.3 CODE ENFORCEMENT OFFICIAL. The officer or other designated authority charged with the administration and enforcement of this code.

COLLAR JOINT. See Section 2102.1.

COLLECTOR. See Section 2302.1.

COLUMN, MASONRY. See Section 2102.1.

COMBINATION FIRE/SMOKE DAMPER. See Section 702.1.

[F] COMBUSTIBLE DUST. See Section 307.2.

[F] COMBUSTIBLE FIBERS. See Section 307.2.

[F] COMBUSTIBLE LIQUID. See Section 307.2.

    Class II. See Section 307.2.

Class IIIA. See Section 307.2.

Class IIIB. See Section 307.2.

COMMON PATH OF EGRESS TRAVEL. See Section 1002.1.

COMMON USE. See Section 1102.1.

COMPOSITE ACTION. See Section 2102.1.

COMPOSITE MASONRY. See Section 2102.1.

[F] COMPRESSED GAS. See Section 307.2.

COMPRESSIVE STRENGTH OF MASONRY. See Section 2102.1.

CONCRETE, CARBONATE AGGREGATE. See Section 721.1.1.

CONCRETE, CELLULAR. See Section 721.1.1.

CONCRETE, LIGHTWEIGHT AGGREGATE. See Section 721.1.1.

CONCRETE, PERLITE. See Section 721.1.1.

CONCRETE, SAND-LIGHTWEIGHT. See Section 721.1.1.

CONCRETE, SILICEOUS AGGREGATE. See Section 721.1.1.

CONCRETE, VERMICULITE. See Section 721.1.1.

CONGREGATE LIVING FACILITIES. See Section 310.2.

CONNECTOR. See Section 2102.1.

[F] CONSTANTLY ATTENDED LOCATION. See Section 902.1.

CONSTRUCTION DOCUMENTS. Written, graphic and pictorial documents prepared or assembled for describing the design, location and physical characteristics of the elements of a project necessary for obtaining a building permit.

CONSTRUCTION TYPES. See Section 602.

Type I. See Section 602.2.

Type II. See Section 602.2.

Type III. See Section 602.3.

Type IV. See Section 602.4.

Type V. See Section 602.5.

[F] CONTINUOUS GAS-DETECTION SYSTEM. See Section 415.2.

[F] CONTROL AREA. See Section 307.2.

CONTROLLED LOW-STRENGTH MATERIAL. A self-compacted, cementitious material used primarily as a backfill in place of compacted fill.

CONVENTIONAL LIGHT-FRAME WOOD CONSTRUCTION. See Section 2302.1.

CORRIDOR. See Section 1002.1.

CORROSION RESISTANCE. The ability of a material to withstand deterioration of its surface or its properties when exposed to its environment.

[F] CORROSIVE. See Section 307.2.

COURT. An open, uncovered space, unobstructed to the sky, bounded on three or more sides by exterior building walls or other enclosing devices.

COVER. See Section 2102.1.

COVERED MALL BUILDING. See Section 402.2.

CRIPPLE WALL. See Section 2302.1.

CRYOGENIC FLUID. See Section 307.2.

DALLE GLASS. See Section 2402.1.

DAMPER. See Section 702.1.

DAY BOX. See Section 307.2.

DEAD LOADS. See Section 1602.1.

DECK. See Section 1602.1.

DECORATIVE GLASS. See Section 2402.1.

[F] DECORATIVE MATERIALS. All materials applied over the building interior finish for decorative, acoustical or other effect (such as curtains, draperies, fabrics, streamers and surface coverings), and all other materials utilized for decorative effect (such as batting, cloth, cotton, hay, stalks, straw, vines, leaves, trees, moss and similar items), including foam plastics and materials containing foam plastics. Decorative materials do not include floor coverings, ordinary window shades, interior finish and materials 0.025 inch (0.64 mm) or less in thickness applied directly to and adhering tightly to a substrate.

[F] DEFLAGRATION. See Section 307.2.

[F] DELUGE SYSTEM. See Section 902.1.

DESIGN DISPLACEMENT. See Section 1908.1.3.

DESIGN EARTHQUAKE GROUND MOTION. See Section 1613.2.

DESIGN FLOOD. See Section 1612.2.

DESIGN FLOOD ELEVATION. See Section 1612.2.

DESIGN STRENGTH. See Section 1602.1.

DESIGNATED SEISMIC SYSTEM. See Section 1702.1.

[F] DETACHED BUILDING. See Section 307.2.

DETAILED PLAIN CONCRETE STRUCTURAL WALL. See Section 1908.1.3.

DETECTABLE WARNING. See Section 1102.1.

[F] DETECTOR, HEAT. See Section 902.1.

[F] DETONATION. See Section 307.2.

DIAPHRAGM. See Sections 1602.1 and 2102.1.

Diaphragm, blocked. See Sections 1602.1.

Diaphragm, boundary. See Section 1602.1.

Diaphragm, chord. See Section 1602.1.

Diaphragm, flexible. See Section 1602.1.

Diaphragm, rigid. See Section 1602.1.

Diaphragm, unblocked. See Section 2302.1.

DIMENSIONS. See Section 2102.1.

Actual. See Section 2102.1.

Nominal. See Section 2102.1.

Specified. See Section 2102.1.

DISPENSING. See Section 307.2.

DOOR, BALANCED. See Section 1002.1.

DORMITORY. See Section 310.2.

DRAFTSTOP. See Section 702.1.

DRAG STRUT. See Section 2302.1.

[F] DRY-CHEMICAL EXTINGUISHING AGENT. See Section 902.1.

DRY FLOODPROOFING. See Section 1612.2.

DURATION OF LOAD. See Section 1602.1.

DWELLING. A building that contains one or two dwelling units used, intended or designed to be used, rented, leased, let or hired out to be occupied for living purposes.

DWELLING UNIT. A single unit providing complete, independent living facilities for one or more persons, including permanent provisions for living, sleeping, eating, cooking and sanitation.

DWELLING UNIT OR SLEEPING UNIT, MULTI-STORY. See Section 1102.1.

DWELLING UNIT OR SLEEPING UNIT, TYPE B. See Section 1102.1.

EFFECTIVE HEIGHT. See Section 2102.1.

EGRESS COURT. See Section 1002.1.

[F] EMERGENCY ALARM SYSTEM. See Section 902.1.

[F] EMERGENCY CONTROL STATION. See Section 415.2.

EMERGENCY ESCAPE AND RESCUE OPENING. See Section 1002.1.

[F] EMERGENCY VOICE/ALARM COMMUNICATIONS. See Section 902.1.

EMPLOYEE WORK AREA. See Section 1102.1.

EQUIPMENT PLATFORM. See Section 502.1.

ESSENTIAL FACILITIES. See Section 1602.1.

[F] EXHAUSTED ENCLOSURE. See Section 415.2.

EXISTING CONSTRUCTION. See Section 1612.2.

EXISTING STRUCTURE. A structure erected prior to the date of adoption of the appropriate code, or one for which a legal building permit has been issued. See also Section 1612.2.

EXIT. See Section 1002.1.

EXIT, HORIZONTAL. See Section 1002.1.

EXIT ACCESS. See Section 1002.1.

EXIT DISCHARGE. See Section 1002.1.

EXIT DISCHARGE, LEVEL OF. See Section 1002.1.

EXIT ENCLOSURE. See Section 1002.1.

EXIT PASSAGEWAY. See Section 1002.1.

EXPANDED VINYL WALL COVERING. See Section 802.1.

[F] EXPLOSION. See Section 902.1.

[F] EXPLOSIVE. See Section 307.2.

High explosive. See Section 307.2.

Low explosive. See Section 307.2.

Mass detonating explosives. See Section 307.2.

UN/DOTn Class 1 Explosives. See Section 307.2.

Division 1.1. See Section 307.2.

Division 1.2. See Section 307.2.

Division 1.3. See Section 307.2.

Division 1.4. See Section 307.2.

Division 1.5. See Section 307.2.

Division 1.6. See Section 307.2.

EXTERIOR SURFACES. See Section 2502.1.

EXTERIOR WALL. See Section 1402.1.

EXTERIOR WALL COVERING. See Section 1402.1.

EXTERIOR WALL ENVELOPE. See Section 1402.1.

F RATING. See Section 702.1.

FABRIC PARTITIONS. See Section 1602.1.

FABRICATED ITEM. See Section 1702.1.

[F] FABRICATION AREA. See Section 415.2.

FACILITY. See Section 1102.1.

FACTORED LOAD. See Section 1602.1.

FIBER CEMENT SIDING. See Section 1402.1.

FIBERBOARD. See Section 2302.1.

FIRE ALARM BOX, MANUAL. See Section 902.1.

[F] FIRE ALARM CONTROL UNIT. See Section 902.1.

[F] FIRE ALARM SIGNAL. See Section 902.1.

[F] FIRE ALARM SYSTEM. See Section 902.1.

FIRE AREA. See Section 702.1.

FIRE BARRIER. See Section 702.1.

[F] FIRE COMMAND CENTER. See Section 902.1.

FIRE DAMPER. See Section 702.1.

[F] FIRE DETECTOR, AUTOMATIC. See Section 902.1.

FIRE DOOR. See Section 702.1.

FIRE DOOR ASSEMBLY. See Section 702.1.

FIRE EXIT HARDWARE. See Section 1002.1.

[F] FIRE LANE. A road or other passageway developed to allow the passage of fire apparatus. A fire lane is not necessarily intended for vehicular traffic other than fire apparatus.

FIRE PARTITION. See Section 702.1.

FIRE PROTECTION RATING. See Section 702.1.

[F] FIRE PROTECTION SYSTEM. See Section 902.1.

FIRE RESISTANCE. See Section 702.1.

FIRE-RESISTANCE RATING. See Section 702.1.

FIRE-RESISTANT JOINT SYSTEM. See Section 702.1.

[F] FIRE SAFETY FUNCTIONS. See Section 902.1.

FIRE SEPARATION DISTANCE. See Section 702.1.

FIRE WALL. See Section 702.1.

FIRE WINDOW ASSEMBLY. See Section 702.1.

FIREBLOCKING. See Section 702.1.

FIREPLACE. See Section 2102.1.

FIREPLACE THROAT. See Section 2102.1.

FIREWORKS. See Section 307.2.

FIREWORKS, 1.3G. See Section 307.2.

FIREWORKS, 1.4G. See Section 307.2.

FLAME SPREAD. See Section 802.1.

FLAME SPREAD INDEX. See Section 802.1.

[F] FLAMMABLE GAS. See Section 307.2.

[F] FLAMMABLE LIQUEFIED GAS. See Section 307.2.

[F] FLAMMABLE LIQUID. See Section 307.2.

    Class IA. See Section 307.2.

    Class IB. See Section 307.2.

    Class IC. See Section 307.2.

[F] FLAMMABLE MATERIAL. See Section 307.2.

[F] FLAMMABLE SOLID. See Section 307.2.

[F] FLAMMABLE VAPORS OR FUMES. See Section 415.2.

[F] FLASH POINT. See Section 307.2.

FLEXURAL LENGTH. See Section 1808.1.

FLOOD OR FLOODING. See Section 1612.2.

FLOOD DAMAGE-RESISTANT MATERIALS. See Section 1612.2.

FLOOD HAZARD AREA. See Section 1612.2.

FLOOD HAZARD AREA SUBJECT TO HIGH VELOCITY WAVE ACTION. See Section 1612.2.

FLOOD INSURANCE RATE MAP (FIRM). See Section 1612.2.

FLOOD INSURANCE STUDY. See Section 1612.2.

FLOODWAY. See Section 1612.2.

FLOOR AREA, GROSS. See Section 1002.1.

FLOOR AREA, NET. See Section 1002.1.

FLOOR FIRE DOOR ASSEMBLY. See Section 702.1.

FLY GALLERY. See Section 410.2.

[F] FOAM-EXTINGUISHING SYSTEMS. See Section 902.1.

FOAM PLASTIC INSULATION. See Section 2602.1.

FOLDING AND TELESCOPIC SEATING. See Section 1002.1.

FOOD COURT. See Section 402.2.

FOUNDATION PIER. See Section 2102.1.

[F] GAS CABINET. See Section 415.2.

[F] GAS ROOM. See Section 415.2.

[F] GASEOUS HYDROGEN SYSTEM. See Section 420.2.

GLASS FIBERBOARD. See Section 721.1.1.

GLASS UNIT MASONRY. See Section 2102.1.

GLUED BUILT-UP MEMBER. See Section 2302.1.

GRADE FLOOR OPENING. A window or other opening located such that the sill height of the opening is not more than 44 inches (1118 mm) above or below the finished ground level adjacent to the opening.

GRADE (LUMBER). See Section 2302.1.

GRADE PLANE. See Section 502.1.

GRANDSTAND. See Section 1002.1.

GRIDIRON. See Section 410.2.

GROSS LEASABLE AREA. See Section 402.2.

GROUTED MASONRY. See Section 2102.1.

    Grouted hollow-unit masonry. See Section 2102.1.

    Grouted multiwythe masonry. See Section 2102.1.

GUARD. See Section 1002.1.

GYPSUM BOARD. See Section 2502.1.

GYPSUM PLASTER. See Section 2502.1.

GYPSUM VENEER PLASTER. See Section 2502.1.

HABITABLE SPACE. A space in a building for living, sleeping, eating or cooking. Bathrooms, toilet rooms, closets, halls, storage or utility spaces and similar areas are not considered habitable spaces.

[F] HALOGENATED EXTINGUISHING SYSTEMS. See Section 902.1.

[F] HANDLING. See Section 307.2.

HANDRAIL. See Section 1002.1.

HARDBOARD. See Section 2302.1.

[F] HAZARDOUS MATERIALS. See Section 307.2.

[F] HAZARDOUS PRODUCTION MATERIAL (HPM). See Section 415.2.

HEAD JOINT. See Section 2102.1.

HEADER (Bonder). See Section 2102.1.

[F] HEALTH HAZARD. See Section 307.2.

HEIGHT, BUILDING. See Section 502.1.

HEIGHT, STORY. See Section 502.1.

HEIGHT, WALLS. See Section 2102.1.

HELIPORT. See Section 412.5.1.

HELISTOP. See Section 412.5.1.

[F] HIGHLY TOXIC. See Section 307.2.

HORIZONTAL ASSEMBLY. See Section 702.1.

[F] HPM FLAMMABLE LIQUID. See Section 415.2.

[F] HPM ROOM. See Section 415.2.

HURRICANE-PRONE REGIONS. See Section 1609.2.

[F] HYDROGEN CUTOFF ROOM. See Section 420.2.

IMMEDIATELY DANGEROUS TO LIFE AND HEALTH (IDLH). See Section 415.2.

IMPACT LOAD. See Section 1602.1.

INCOMPATIBLE MATERIALS. See Section 307.2.

[F] INITIATING DEVICE. See Section 902.1.

INSPECTION CERTIFICATE. See Section 1702.1.

INTENDED TO BE OCCUPIED AS A RESIDENCE. See Section 1102.1.

INTERIOR FINISH. See Section 802.1.

INTERIOR FLOOR FINISH. See Section 802.1.

INTERIOR SURFACES. See Section 2502.1.

INTERIOR WALL AND CEILING FINISH. See Section 802.1.

INTERLAYMENT. See Section 1502.1.

JOINT. See Section 702.1.

JURISDICTION. The governmental unit that has adopted this code under due legislative authority.

LABEL. See Section 1702.1.

LIGHT-DIFFUSING SYSTEM. See Section 2602.1.

LIGHT-FRAME CONSTRUCTION. A type of construction whose vertical and horizontal structural elements are primarily formed by a system of repetitive wood or light gage steel framing members.

LIGHT-TRANSMITTING PLASTIC ROOF PANELS. See Section 2602.1.

LIMIT STATE. See Section 1602.1.

[F] LIQUID. See Section 415.2.

[F] LIQUID STORAGE ROOM. See Section 415.2.

[F] LIQUID USE, DISPENSING AND MIXING ROOMS. See Section 415.2.

LISTED. See Section 902.1.

LIVE LOADS. See Section 1602.1.

LIVE LOADS (ROOF). See Section 1602.1.

LOAD AND RESISTANCE FACTOR DESIGN (LRFD). See Section 1602.1.

LOAD EFFECTS. See Section 1602.1.

LOAD FACTOR. See Section 1602.1.

LOADS. See Section 1602.1.

LOT. A portion or parcel of land considered as a unit.

LOT LINE. A line dividing one lot from another, or from a street or any public place.

[F] LOWER FLAMMABLE LIMIT (LFL). See Section 415.2.

LOWEST FLOOR. See Section 1612.2.

MAIN WINDFORCE-RESISTING SYSTEM. See Section 1702.1.

MALL. See Section 402.2.

[F] MANUAL FIRE ALARM BOX. See Section 902.1.

MANUFACTURER'S DESIGNATION. See Section 1702.1.

MARK. See Section 1702.1.

MARQUEE. A permanent roofed structure attached to and supported by the building and that projects into the public right-of-way.

MASONRY. See Section 2102.1.

   Ashlar masonry. See Section 2102.1.

   Coursed ashlar. See Section 2102.1.

   Glass unit masonry. See Section 2102.1.

   Plain masonry. See Section 2102.1.

   Random ashlar. See Section 2102.1.

   Reinforced masonry. See Section 2102.1.

   Solid masonry. See Section 2102.1.

   Unreinforced (plain) masonry. See Section 2102.1.

MASONRY UNIT. See Section 2102.1.

   Clay. See Section 2102.1.

   Concrete. See Section 2102.1.

   Hollow. See Section 2102.1.

   Solid. See Section 2102.1.

MAXIMUM CONSIDERED EARTHQUAKE GROUND MOTION. See Section 1613.2.

MEAN DAILY TEMPERATURE. See Section 2102.1.

MEANS OF EGRESS. See Section 1002.1.

MECHANICAL-ACCESS OPEN PARKING GARAGES. See Section 406.3.2.

MECHANICAL EQUIPMENT SCREEN. See Section 1502.1.

MECHANICAL SYSTEMS. See Section 1613.2.

MEMBRANE-COVERED CABLE STRUCTURE. See Section 3102.2.

MEMBRANE-COVERED FRAME STRUCTURE. See Section 3102.2.

MEMBRANE PENETRATION. See Section 702.1.

MEMBRANE-PENETRATION FIRESTOP. See Section 702.1.

MERCHANDISE PAD. See Section 1002.1.

METAL COMPOSITE MATERIAL (MCM). See Section 1402.1.

METAL COMPOSITE MATERIAL (MCM) SYSTEM. See Section 1402.1.

METAL ROOF PANEL. See Section 1502.1.

METAL ROOF SHINGLE. See Section 1502.1.

MEZZANINE. See Section 502.1.

MICROPILES. See Section 1808.1.

MINERAL BOARD. See Section 721.1.1.

MINERAL FIBER. See Section 702.1.

MINERAL WOOL. See Section 702.1.

MODIFIED BITUMEN ROOF COVERING. See Section 1502.1.

MODULAR BUILDING. A building wholly or in substantial part manufactured in a manufacturing facility, intended or designed for permanent installation or assembly on a building site, and whereby all portions may not be reasonably inspected at the installation site without disassembly or destruction thereof.

MORTAR. See Section 2102.1.

MORTAR, SURFACE-BONDING. See Section 2102.1.

MULTILEVEL ASSEMBLY SEATING. See Section 1102.1.

[F] MULTIPLE-STATION ALARM DEVICE. See Section 902.1.

[F] MULTIPLE-STATION SMOKE ALARM. See Section 902.1.

MULTISTORY UNITS. See Section 1102.1.

NAILING, BOUNDARY. See Section 2302.1.

NAILING, EDGE. See Section 2302.1.

NAILING, FIELD. See Section 2302.1.

NATURALLY DURABLE WOOD. See Section 2302.1.

    Decay resistant. See Section 2302.1.

    Termite resistant. See Section 2302.1.

NOMINAL LOADS. See Section 1602.1.

NOMINAL SIZE (LUMBER). See Section 2302.1.

NONCOMBUSTIBLE MEMBRANE STRUCTURE. See Section 3102.2.

[F] NORMAL TEMPERATURE AND PRESSURE (NTP). See Section 415.2.

NOSING. See Section 1002.1.

[F] NUISANCE ALARM. See Section 902.1.

OCCUPANCY CATEGORY. See Section 1602.1.

OCCUPANT LOAD. See Section 1002.1.

OCCUPIABLE SPACE. A room or enclosed space designed for human occupancy in which individuals congregate for amusement, educational or similar purposes or in which occupants are engaged at labor, and which is equipped with means of egress and light and ventilation facilities meeting the requirements of this code.

OPEN PARKING GARAGE. See Section 406.3.2.

[F] OPEN SYSTEM. See Section 307.2.

OPERATING BUILDING. See Section 307.2.

ORDINARY PRECAST STRUCTURAL WALL. See Section 1908.1.3.

ORDINARY REINFORCED CONCRETE STRUCTURAL WALL. See Section 1908.1.3.

ORDINARY STRUCTURAL PLAIN CONCRETE WALL. See Section 1908.1.3.

[F] ORGANIC PEROXIDE. See Section 307.2.

    Class I. See Section 307.2.

    Class II. See Section 307.2.

    Class III. See Section 307.2.

    Class IV. See Section 307.2.

    Class V. See Section 307.2.

    Unclassified detonable. See Section 307.2.

ORTHOGONAL. See Section 1613.2.

OTHER STRUCTURES. See Section 1602.1.

OWNER. Any person, agent, firm or corporation having a legal or equitable interest in the property.

[F] OXIDIZER. See Section 307.2.

    Class 4. See Section 307.2.

    Class 3. See Section 307.2.

    Class 2. See Section 307.2.

    Class 1. See Section 307.2.

[F] OXIDIZING GAS. See Section 307.2.

PANEL (PART OF A STRUCTURE). See Section 1602.1.

PANIC HARDWARE. See Section 1002.1.

PARTICLEBOARD. See Section 2302.1.

PENETRATION FIRESTOP. See Section 702.1.

PENTHOUSE. See Section 1502.1.

PERMIT. An official document or certificate issued by the authority having jurisdiction which authorizes performance of a specified activity.

PERSON. An individual, heirs, executors, administrators or assigns, and also includes a firm, partnership or corporation, its or their successors or assigns, or the agent of any of the aforesaid.

PERSONAL CARE SERVICE. See Section 310.2.

[F] PHYSICAL HAZARD. See Section 307.2.

[F] PHYSIOLOGICAL WARNING THRESHOLD LEVEL. See Section 415.2.

PIER FOUNDATIONS. See Section 1808.1.

    Belled piers. See Section 1808.1.

PILE FOUNDATIONS. See Section 1808.1.

    Auger uncased piles. See Section 1808.1.

    Caisson piles. See Section 1808.1.

    Concrete-filled steel pipe and tube piles. See Section 1808.1.

    Driven uncased piles. See Section 1808.1.

Enlarged base piles. See Section 1808.1.

Steel-cased piles. See Section 1808.1.

Timber piles. See Section 1808.1.

PINRAIL. See Section 410.2.

PLASTIC, APPROVED. See Section 2602.1.

PLASTIC GLAZING. See Section 2602.1.

PLASTIC HINGE. See Section 2102.1.

PLATFORM. See Section 410.2.

POSITIVE ROOF DRAINAGE. See Section 1502.1.

PREFABRICATED WOOD I-JOIST. See Section 2302.1.

PRESERVATIVE-TREATED WOOD. See Section 2302.1.

PRESTRESSED MASONRY. See Section 2102.1.

PRISM. See Section 2102.1.

PROSCENIUM WALL. See Section 410.2.

PUBLIC ENTRANCE. See Section 1102.1.

PUBLIC-USE AREAS. See Section 1102.1.

PUBLIC WAY. See Section 1002.1.

[F] PYROPHORIC. See Section 307.2.

[F] PYROTECHNIC COMPOSITION. See Section 307.2.

RAMP. See Section 1002.1.

RAMP-ACCESS OPEN PARKING GARAGES. See Section 406.3.2.

[F] RECORD DRAWINGS. See Section 902.1.

REFERENCE RESISTANCE (D). See Section 2302.1.

REGISTERED DESIGN PROFESSIONAL. An individual who is a Registered Architect (RA) in accordance with Article 147 of the New York State Education Law or a licensed Professional Engineer (PE) in accordance with Article 145 of the New York State Education Law.

REINFORCED PLASTIC, GLASS FIBER. See Section 2602.1.

RELIGIOUS WORSHIP, PLACE OF. A building or portion thereof intended for the performance of religious services.

REPAIR. The reconstruction or renewal of any part of an existing building for the purpose of its maintenance.

REQUIRED STRENGTH. See Sections 1602.1 and 2102.1.

REROOFING. See Section 1502.1.

RESIDENTIAL AIRCRAFT HANGAR. See Section 412.3.1.

RESIDENTIAL CARE/ASSISTED LIVING FACILITIES. See Section 310.2.

RESISTANCE FACTOR. See Section 1602.1.

RESTRICTED ENTRANCE. See Section 1102.1.

RETRACTABLE AWNING. See Section 3105.2.

ROOF ASSEMBLY. See Section 1502.1.

ROOF COVERING. See Section 1502.1.

ROOF COVERING SYSTEM. See Section 1502.1.

ROOF DECK. See Section 1502.1.

ROOF RECOVER. See Section 1502.1.

ROOF REPAIR. See Section 1502.1.

ROOF REPLACEMENT. See Section 1502.1.

ROOF VENTILATION. See Section 1502.1.

ROOFTOP STRUCTURE. See Section 1502.1.

RUBBLE MASONRY. See Section 2102.1.

Coursed rubble. See Section 2102.1.

Random rubble. See Section 2102.1.

Rough or ordinary rubble. See Section 2102.1.

RUNNING BOND. See Section 2102.1.

SCISSOR STAIR. See Section 1002.1.

SCUPPER. See Section 1502.1.

SEISMIC DESIGN CATEGORY. See Section 1613.2.

SEISMIC-FORCE-RESISTING SYSTEM. See Section 1613.2.

SELF-CLOSING. See Section 702.1.

SELF-SERVICE STORAGE FACILITY. See Section 1102.1.

[F] SERVICE CORRIDOR. See Section 415.2.

SERVICE ENTRANCE. See Section 1102.1.

SHAFT. See Section 702.1.

SHAFT ENCLOSURE. See Section 702.1.

SHEAR WALL. See Sections 2102.1 and 2302.1.

Detailed plain masonry shear wall. See Section 2102.1.

Intermediate prestressed masonry shear wall. See Section 2102.1.

Intermediate reinforced masonry shear wall. See Section 2102.1.

Ordinary plain masonry shear wall. See Section 2102.1.

Ordinary plain prestressed masonry shear wall. See Section 2102.1.

Ordinary reinforced masonry shear wall. See Section 2102.1.

Perforated shear wall. See Section 2302.1.

Perorated shear wall segment. See Section 2302.1.

Special prestressed masonry shear wall. See Section 2102.1.

Special reinforced masonry shear wall. See Section 2102.1.

SHELL. See Section 2102.1.

SINGLE-PLY MEMBRANE. See Section 1502.1.

[F] SINGLE-STATION SMOKE ALARM. See Section 902.1.

SITE. See Section 1102.1.

SITE CLASS. See Section 1613.2.

SITE COEFFICIENTS. See Section 1613.2.

SKYLIGHT, UNIT. A factory-assembled, glazed fenestration unit, containing one panel of glazing material that allows for natural lighting through an opening in the roof assembly while preserving the weather-resistant barrier of the roof.

SKYLIGHTS AND SLOPED GLAZING. Glass or other transparent or translucent glazing material installed at a slope of 15 degrees (0.26 rad) or more from vertical. Glazing material in skylights, including unit skylights, solariums, sunrooms, roofs and sloped walls, are included in this definition.

SLEEPING UNIT. A room or space in which people sleep, which can also include permanent provisions for living, eating, and either sanitation or kitchen facilities but not both. Such rooms and spaces that are also part of a dwelling unit are not sleeping units.

[F] SMOKE ALARM. See Section 902.1.

SMOKE BARRIER. See Section 702.1.

SMOKE COMPARTMENT. See Section 702.1.

SMOKE DAMPER. See Section 702.1.

[F] SMOKE DETECTOR. See Section 902.1.

SMOKE-DEVELOPED INDEX. See Section 802.1.

SMOKE-PROTECTED ASSEMBLY SEATING. See Section 1002.1.

SMOKEPROOF ENCLOSURE. See Section 902.1.

[F] SOLID. See Section 415.2.

SPECIAL INSPECTION. See Section 1702.1.

   Special inspection, continuous. See Section 1702.1.

   Special inspection, periodic. See Section 1702.1.

SPECIAL FLOOD HAZARD AREA. See Section 1612.2.

SPECIFIED. See Section 2102.1.

SPECIFIED COMPRESSIVE STRENGTH OF MASONRY (f'_m). See Section 2102.1.

SPLICE. See Section 702.1.

SPRAYED FIRE-RESISTANT MATERIALS. See Section 1702.1.

STACK BOND. See Section 2102.1.

STAGE. See Section 410.2.

STAIR. See Section 1002.1.

STAIRWAY. See Section 1002.1.

STAIRWAY, EXTERIOR. See Section 1002.1.

STAIRWAY, INTERIOR. See Section 1002.1.

STAIRWAY, SPIRAL. See Section 1002.1.

[F] STANDPIPE SYSTEM, CLASSES OF. See Section 902.1.

   Class I system. See Section 902.1.

   Class II system. See Section 902.1.

   Class III system. See Section 902.1.

[F] STANDPIPE, TYPES OF. See Section 902.1.

   Automatic dry. See Section 902.1.

   Automatic wet. See Section 902.1.

   Manual dry. See Section 902.1.

   Manual wet. See Section 902.1.

   Semiautomatic dry. See Section 902.1.

START OF CONSTRUCTION. See Section 1612.2.

STEEL CONSTRUCTION, COLD-FORMED. See Section 2202.1.

STEEL JOIST. See Section 2202.1.

STEEL MEMBER, STRUCTURAL. See Section 2202.1.

STEEP SLOPE. A roof slope greater than two units vertical in 12 units horizontal (17-percent slope).

STONE MASONRY. See Section 2102.1.

   Ashlar stone masonry. See Section 2102.1.

   Rubble stone masonry. See Section 2102.1.

[F] STORAGE, HAZARDOUS MATERIALS. See Section 415.2.

STORY. That portion of a building included between the upper surface of a floor and the upper surface of the floor or roof next above (also see "Mezzanine" and Section 502.1). It is measured as the vertical distance from top to top of two successive tiers of beams or finished floor surfaces and, for the topmost story, from the top of the floor finish to the top of the ceiling joists or, where there is not a ceiling, to the top of the roof rafters.

STORY ABOVE GRADE PLANE. Any story having its finished floor surface entirely above grade plane, except that a basement shall be considered as a story above grade plane where the finished surface of the floor above the basement is:

1. More than 6 feet (1829 mm) above grade plane; or

2. More than 12 feet (3658 mm) above the finished ground level at any point.

STRENGTH. See Section 2102.1.

   Design strength. See Section 2102.1.

   Nominal strength. See Sections 1602.1 and 2102.1.

   Required strength. See Sections 1602.1 and 2102.1.

STRENGTH DESIGN. See Section 1602.1.

STRUCTURAL COMPOSITE LUMBER. See Section 2302.1.

   Laminated veneer lumber (LVL). See Section 2302.1.

   Parallel strand lumber (PSL). See Section 2302.1.

STRUCTURAL GLUED-LAMINATED TIMBER. See Section 2302.1.

STRUCTURAL OBSERVATION. See Section 1702.1.

STRUCTURE. That which is built or constructed.

SUBDIAPHRAGM. See Section 2302.1.

SUBSTANTIAL DAMAGE. See Section 1612.2.

SUBSTANTIAL IMPROVEMENT. See Section 1612.2.

SUNROOM ADDITION. See Section 1202.1.

[F] SUPERVISING STATION. See Section 902.1.

[F] SUPERVISORY SERVICE. See Section 902.1.

[F] SUPERVISORY SIGNAL. See Section 902.1.

[F] SUPERVISORY SIGNAL-INITIATING DEVICE. See Section 902.1.

SWIMMING POOLS. See Section 3109.2.

T RATING. See Section 702.1.

TENT. Any structure, enclosure or shelter which is constructed of canvas or pliable material supported in any manner except by air or the contents it protects.

THERMAL ISOLATION. See Section 1202.1.

THERMOPLASTIC MATERIAL. See Section 2602.1.

THERMOSETTING MATERIAL. See Section 2602.1.

THIN-BED MORTAR. See Section 2102.1.

THROUGH PENETRATION. See Section 702.1.

THROUGH-PENETRATION FIRESTOP SYSTEM. See Section 702.1.

TIE-DOWN (HOLD-DOWN). See Section 2302.1.

TIE, LATERAL. See Section 2102.1.

TIE, WALL. See Section 2102.1.

TILE. See Section 2102.1.

TILE, STRUCTURAL CLAY. See Section 2102.1.

[F] TIRES, BULK STORAGE OF. See Section 902.1.

TOWNHOUSE. A single-family dwelling unit constructed in a group of three or more attached units in which each unit extends from the foundation to roof and with open space on at least two sides.

[F] TOXIC. See Section 307.2.

TRANSIENT. See Section 310.2.

TREATED WOOD. See Section 2302.1.

TRIM. See Section 802.1.

[F] TROUBLE SIGNAL. See Section 902.1.

TYPE A UNIT. See Section 1102.1.

TYPE B UNIT. See Section 1102.1.

UNDERLAYMENT. See Section 1502.1.

[F] UNSTABLE (REACTIVE) MATERIAL. See Section 307.2.

    Class 4. See Section 307.2.

    Class 3. See Section 307.2.

    Class 2. See Section 307.2.

    Class 1. See Section 307.2.

[F] USE (MATERIAL). See Section 415.2.

VAPOR-PERMEABLE MEMBRANE. A material or covering having a permeance rating of 5 perms (52.9×10^{-10} kg/Pa $\cdot$ s $\cdot$ m^2) or greater, when tested in accordance with the des-

sicant method using Procedure A of ASTM E 96. A vapor-permeable material permits the passage of moisture vapor.

VAPOR RETARDER. A vapor-resistant material, membrane or covering such as foil, plastic sheeting or insulation facing having a permeance rating of 1 perm (5.7×10^{-11} kg/Pa $\cdot$ s $\cdot$ m^2) or less, when tested in accordance with the dessicant method using Procedure A of ASTM E 96. Vapor retarders limit the amount of moisture vapor that passes through a material or wall assembly.

VEHICLE BARRIER SYSTEM. See Section 1602.1.

VENEER. See Section 1402.1.

VENTILATION. The natural or mechanical process of supplying conditioned or unconditioned air to, or removing such air from, any space.

VINYL SIDING. See Section 1402.1.

[F] VISIBLE ALARM NOTIFICATION APPLIANCE. See Section 902.1.

WALKWAY, PEDESTRIAN. A walkway used exclusively as a pedestrian trafficway.

WALL. See Section 2102.1.

    Cavity wall. See Section 2102.1.

    Composite wall. See Section 2102.1.

    Dry-stacked, surface-bonded wall. See Section 2102.1.

    Masonry-bonded hollow wall. See Section 2102.1.

    Parapet wall. See Section 2102.1.

WALL, LOAD-BEARING. Any wall meeting either of the following classifications:

    1. Any metal or wood stud wall that supports more than 100 pounds per linear foot (1459 N/m) of vertical load in addition to its own weight.

    2. Any masonry or concrete wall that supports more than 200 pounds per linear foot (2919 N/m) of vertical load in addition to its own weight.

WALL, NONLOAD-BEARING. Any wall that is not a load-bearing wall.

WALL PIER. See Section 1908.1.3.

[F] WATER-REACTIVE MATERIAL. See Section 307.2.

    Class 3. See Section 307.2.

    Class 2. See Section 307.2.

    Class 1. See Section 307.2.

WATER-RESISTIVE BARRIER. See Section 1402.

WEATHER-EXPOSED SURFACES. See Section 2502.1.

WEB. See Section 2102.1.

[F] WET-CHEMICAL EXTINGUISHING SYSTEM. See Section 902.1.

WHEELCHAIR SPACE. See Section 1102.1.

WIND-BORNE DEBRIS REGION. See Section 1609.2.

WINDER. See Section 1002.1.

WIRE BACKING. See Section 2502.1.

[F] WIRELESS PROTECTION SYSTEM. See Section 902.1.

WOOD SHEAR PANEL. See Section 2302.1.

WOOD STRUCTURAL PANEL. See Section 2302.1.

    Composite panels. See Section 2302.1.

    Oriented strand board (OSB). See Section 2302.1.

    Plywood. See Section 2302.1.

[F] WORKSTATION. See Section 415.2.

WYTHE. See Section 2102.1.

YARD. An open space, other than a court, unobstructed from the ground to the sky, except where specifically provided by this code, on the lot on which a building is situated.

[F] ZONE. See Section 902.1.

CHAPTER 3

USE AND OCCUPANCY CLASSIFICATION

SECTION 301
GENERAL

301.1 Scope. The provisions of this chapter shall control the classification of all buildings and structures as to use and occupancy.

SECTION 302
CLASSIFICATION

302.1 General. Structures or portions of structures shall be classified with respect to occupancy in one or more of the groups listed below. A room or space that is intended to be occupied at different times for different purposes shall comply with all of the requirements that are applicable to each of the purposes for which the room or space will be occupied. Structures with multiple occupancies or uses shall comply with Section 508. Where a structure is proposed for a purpose that is not specifically provided for in this code, such structure shall be classified in the group that the occupancy most nearly resembles, according to the fire safety and relative hazard involved.

1. Assembly (see Section 303): Groups A-1, A-2, A-3, A-4 and A-5

2. Business (see Section 304): Group B

3. Educational (see Section 305): Group E

4. Factory and Industrial (see Section 306): Groups F-1 and F-2

5. High Hazard (see Section 307): Groups H-1, H-2, H-3, H-4 and H-5

6. Institutional (see Section 308): Groups I-1, I-2, I-3 and I-4

7. Mercantile (see Section 309): Group M

8. Residential (see Section 310): Groups R-1, R-2, R-3 and R-4

9. Storage (see Section 311): Groups S-1 and S-2

10. Utility and Miscellaneous (see Section 312): Group U

SECTION 303
ASSEMBLY GROUP A

303.1 Assembly Group A. Assembly Group A occupancy includes, among others, the use of a building or structure, or a portion thereof, for the gathering of persons for purposes such as civic, social or religious functions; recreation, food or drink consumption; or awaiting transportation.

Exceptions:

1. A building or portion of a building used for nonaccessory assembly purposes with an occupant load of less than 50 persons shall be classified as a Group B occupancy.

2. A room or space used for assembly purposes with an occupant load of less than 50 persons and accessory to another occupancy shall be classified as a Group B occupancy or as part of that occupancy.

3. A room or space used for assembly purposes that is less than 750 square feet (70 m^2) in area and is accessory to another occupancy shall be classified as a Group B occupancy or as part of that occupancy.

Assembly occupancies shall include the following:

A-1 Assembly uses, usually with fixed seating, intended for the production and viewing of the performing arts or motion pictures including, but not limited to:

Motion picture theaters

Symphony and concert halls

Television and radio studios admitting an audience

Theaters

A-2 Assembly uses intended for food and/or drink consumption including, but not limited to:

Banquet halls

Night clubs

Restaurants

Taverns and bars

A-3 Assembly uses intended for worship, recreation or amusement and other assembly uses not classified elsewhere in Group A including, but not limited to:

Amusement arcades

Art galleries

Bowling alleys

Places of religious worship

Community halls

Courtrooms

Dance halls (not including food or drink consumption)

Exhibition halls

Funeral parlors

Gymnasiums (without spectator seating)

Indoor swimming pools (without spectator seating)

Indoor tennis courts (without spectator seating)

Lecture halls

Libraries

Museums

Waiting areas in transportation terminals

Pool and billiard parlors

A-4 Assembly uses intended for viewing of indoor sporting events and activities with spectator seating including, but not limited to:

Arenas

Skating rinks

Swimming pools

Tennis courts

A-5 Assembly uses intended for participation in or viewing outdoor activities including, but not limited to:

Amusement park structures

Bleachers

Grandstands

Stadiums

SECTION 304
BUSINESS GROUP B

304.1 Business Group B. Business Group B occupancy includes, among others, the use of a building or structure, or a portion thereof, for office, professional or service-type transactions, including storage of records and accounts. Business occupancies shall include, but not be limited to, the following:

Airport traffic control towers

Animal hospitals, kennels and pounds

Banks

Barber and beauty shops

Car wash

Civic administration

Clinic-outpatient

Dry cleaning and laundries: pick-up and delivery stations and self-service

Educational occupancies for students above the 12th grade

Electronic data processing

Laboratories: testing and research

Motor vehicle showrooms

Post offices

Print shops

Professional services (architects, attorneys, dentists, physicians, engineers, etc.)

Radio and television stations

Telephone exchanges

Training and skill development not within a school or academic program

SECTION 305
EDUCATIONAL GROUP E

305.1 Educational Group E. Educational Group E occupancy includes, among others, the use of a building or structure, or a portion thereof, by six or more persons at any one time for educational purposes through the 12th grade. Religious educational rooms and religious auditoriums, which are accessory to places of religious worship in accordance with Section 508.3.1 and have occupant loads of less than 100, shall be classified as A-3 occupancies.

305.2 Day care. The use of a building or structure, or portion thereof, for educational, supervision or personal care services for more than five children older than $2^1/_2$ years of age, shall be classified as a Group E occupancy.

SECTION 306
FACTORY GROUP F

306.1 Factory Industrial Group F. Factory Industrial Group F occupancy includes, among others, the use of a building or structure, or a portion thereof, for assembling, disassembling, fabricating, finishing, manufacturing, packaging, repair or processing operations that are not classified as a Group H hazardous or Group S storage occupancy.

306.2 Factory Industrial F-1 Moderate-Hazard Occupancy. Factory industrial uses which are not classified as Factory Industrial F-2 Low Hazard shall be classified as F-1 Moderate Hazard and shall include, but not be limited to, the following:

Aircraft

Appliances

Athletic equipment

Automobiles and other motor vehicles

Bakeries

Beverages; over 12-percent alcohol content

Bicycles

Boats

Brooms or brushes

Business machines

Cameras and photo equipment

Canvas or similar fabric

Carpets and rugs (includes cleaning)

Clothing

Construction and agricultural machinery

Disinfectants

Dry cleaning and dyeing

Electric generation plants

Electronics

Engines (including rebuilding)

Food processing

Furniture

Hemp products

Jute products

Laundries

Leather products

Machinery

Metals

Millwork (sash & door)

Motion pictures and television filming (without spectators)

Musical instruments

Optical goods

Paper mills or products

Photographic film

Plastic products

Printing or publishing

Recreational vehicles

Refuse incineration

Shoes

Soaps and detergents

Textiles

Tobacco

Trailers

Upholstering

Wood; distillation

Woodworking (cabinet)

306.3 Factory Industrial F-2 Low-Hazard Occupancy. Factory industrial uses that involve the fabrication or manufacturing of noncombustible materials which during finishing, packing or processing do not involve a significant fire hazard shall be classified as F-2 occupancies and shall include, but not be limited to, the following:

Beverages; up to and including 12-percent alcohol content

Brick and masonry

Ceramic products

Foundries

Glass products

Gypsum

Ice

Metal products (fabrication and assembly)

SECTION 307
HIGH-HAZARD GROUP H

[F] 307.1 High-Hazard Group H. High-hazard Group H occupancy includes, among others, the use of a building or structure, or a portion thereof, that involves the manufacturing, processing, generation or storage of materials that constitute a physical or health hazard in quantities in excess of those allowed in control areas constructed and located as required in Section 414. Hazardous uses are classified in Groups H-1, H-2, H-3, H-4 and H-5 and shall be in accordance with this section, the requirements of Section 415 and the *Fire Code of New York State*.

Exceptions: The following shall not be classified in Group H, but shall be classified in the occupancy that they most nearly resemble:

1. Buildings and structures that contain not more than the maximum allowable quantities per control area of hazardous materials as shown in Tables 307.1(1) and 307.1(2), provided that such buildings are maintained in accordance with the *Fire Code of New York State*.

2. Buildings utilizing control areas in accordance with Section 414.2 that contain not more than the maximum allowable quantities per control area of hazardous materials as shown in Tables 307.1(1) and 307.1(2).

3. Buildings and structures occupied for the application of flammable finishes, provided that such buildings or areas conform to the requirements of Section 416 and the *Fire Code of New York State*.

4. Wholesale and retail sales and storage of flammable and combustible liquids in mercantile occupancies conforming to the *Fire Code of New York State*.

5. Closed piping system containing flammable or combustible liquids or gases utilized for the operation of machinery or equipment.

6. Cleaning establishments that utilize combustible liquid solvents having a flash point of 140°F (60°C) or higher in closed systems employing equipment listed by an approved testing agency, provided that this occupancy is separated from all other areas of the building by 1-hour fire barriers or 1-hour horizontal assemblies or both.

7. Cleaning establishments that utilize a liquid solvent having a flash point at or above 200°F (93°C).

8. Liquor stores and distributors without bulk storage.

9. Refrigeration systems.

10. The storage or utilization of materials for agricultural purposes on the premises.

11. Stationary batteries utilized for facility emergency power, uninterrupted power supply or telecommunication facilities, provided that the batteries are provided with safety venting caps and ventilation is provided in accordance with the *Mechanical Code of New York State*.

12. Corrosives shall not include personal or household products in their original packaging used in retail display or commonly used building materials.

13 Buildings and structures occupied for aerosol storage shall be classified as Group S-1, provided that such buildings conform to the requirements of the *Fire Code of New York State*.

14. Display and storage of nonflammable solid and nonflammable or noncombustible liquid hazardous materials in quantities not exceeding the maximum

allowable quantity per control area in Group M or S occupancies complying with Section 414.2.5.

15. The storage of black powder, smokeless propellant and small arms primers in Groups M and R-3 and special industrial explosive devices in Groups B, F, M and S, provided such storage conforms to the quantity limits and requirements prescribed in the *Fire Code of New York State.*

307.1.1 Hazardous materials. Hazardous materials in any quantity shall conform to the requirements of this code, including Section 414, and the *Fire Code of New York State.*

[F] 307.2 Definitions. The following words and terms shall, for the purposes of this section and as used elsewhere in this code, have the meanings shown herein.

AEROSOL. A product that is dispensed from an aerosol container by a propellant.

Aerosol products shall be classified by means of the calculation of their chemical heats of combustion and shall be designated Level 1, 2 or 3.

Level 1 aerosol products. Those with a total chemical heat of combustion that is less than or equal to 8,600 British thermal units per pound (Btu/lb) (20 kJ/g).

Level 2 aerosol products. Those with a total chemical heat of combustion that is greater than 8,600 Btu/lb (20 kJ/g), but less than or equal to 13,000 Btu/lb (30 kJ/g).

Level 3 aerosol products. Those with a total chemical heat combustion that is greater than 13,000 Btu/lb (30 kJ/g).

AEROSOL CONTAINER. A metal can or a glass or plastic bottle designed to dispense an aerosol. Metal cans shall be limited to a maximum size of 33.8 fluid ounces (1,000 ml). Glass or plastic bottles shall be limited to a maximum size of 4 fluid ounces (118 ml).

BALED COTTON. A natural seed fiber wrapped in and secured with industry accepted materials, usually consisting of burlap, woven polypropylene, polyethylene or cotton or sheet polyethylene, and secured with steel, synthetic or wire bands or wire; also includes linters (lint removed from the cottonseed) and motes (residual materials from the ginning process).

BALED COTTON, DENSELY PACKED. Cotton made into banded bales with a packing density of at least 22 pounds per cubic foot (360 kg/m³), and dimensions complying with the following: a length of 55 inches (1397 ± 20 mm), a width of 21 inches (533.4 ± 20 mm) and a height of 27.6 to 35.4 inches (701 to 899 mm).

BARRICADE. A structure that consists of a combination of walls, floor and roof, which is designed to withstand the rapid release of energy in an explosion and which is fully confined, partially vented or fully vented; or other effective method of shielding from explosive materials by a natural or artificial barrier.

Artificial barricade. An artificial mound or revetment a minimum thickness of 3 feet (914 mm).

Natural barricade. Natural features of the ground, such as hills, or timber of sufficient density that the surrounding exposures that require protection cannot be seen from the magazine or building containing explosives when the trees are bare of leaves.

BOILING POINT. The temperature at which the vapor pressure of a liquid equals the atmospheric pressure of 14.7 pounds per square inch (psi) (101 kPa) gage or 760 mm of mercury. Where an accurate boiling point is unavailable for the material in question, or for mixtures which do not have a constant boiling point, for the purposes of this classification, the 20-percent evaporated point of a distillation performed in accordance with ASTM D 86 shall be used as the boiling point of the liquid.

CLOSED SYSTEM. The use of a solid or liquid hazardous material involving a closed vessel or system that remains closed during normal operations where vapors emitted by the product are not liberated outside of the vessel or system and the product is not exposed to the atmosphere during normal operations; and all uses of compressed gases. Examples of closed systems for solids and liquids include product conveyed through a piping system into a closed vessel, system or piece of equipment.

COMBUSTIBLE DUST. Finely divided solid material that is 420 microns or less in diameter and which, when dispersed in air in the proper proportions, could be ignited by a flame, spark or other source of ignition. Combustible dust will pass through a U.S. No. 40 standard sieve.

COMBUSTIBLE FIBERS. Readily ignitable and free-burning materials in a fibrous or shredded form, such as cocoa fiber, cloth, cotton, excelsior, hay, hemp, henequen, istle, jute, kapok, oakum, rags, sisal, Spanish moss, straw, tow, wastepaper, certain synthetic fibers or other like materials. This definition does not include densely packed baled cotton.

COMBUSTIBLE LIQUID. A liquid having a closed cup flash point at or above 100°F (38°C). Combustible liquids shall be subdivided as follows:

Class II. Liquids having a closed cup flash point at or above 100°F (38°C) and below 140°F (60°C).

Class IIIA. Liquids having a closed cup flash point at or above 140°F (60°C) and below 200°F (93°C).

Class IIIB. Liquids having a closed cup flash point at or above 200°F (93°C).

The category of combustible liquids does not include compressed gases or cryogenic fluids.

COMPRESSED GAS. A material, or mixture of materials which:

1. Is a gas at 68°F (20°C) or less at 14.7 pounds per square inch atmosphere (psia) (101 kPa) of pressure; and

2. Has a boiling point of 68°F (20°C) or less at 14.7 psia (101 kPa) which is either liquefied, nonliquefied or in solution, except those gases which have no other health- or physical-hazard properties are not considered to be compressed until the pressure in the packaging exceeds 41 psia (282 kPa) at 68°F (20°C).

[F] TABLE 307.1(1)

MAXIMUM ALLOWABLE QUANTITY PER CONTROL AREA OF HAZARDOUS MATERIALS POSING A PHYSICAL HAZARD[a, j, m, n, p]

MATERIAL	CLASS	GROUP WHEN THE MAXIMUM ALLOWABLE QUANTITY IS EXCEEDED	STORAGE[b]			USE-CLOSED SYSTEMS[b]			USE-OPEN SYSTEMS[b]	
			Solid pounds (cubic feet)	Liquid gallons (pounds)	Gas (cubic feet at NTP)	Solid pounds (cubic feet)	Liquid gallons (pounds)	Gas (cubic feet at NTP)	Solid pounds (cubic feet)	Liquid gallons (pounds)
Combustible liquid[c, i]	II	H-2 or H-3	N/A	120[d,e]	N/A	N/A	120[d]	N/A	N/A	30[d]
	IIIA	H-2 or H-3	N/A	330[d,e]	N/A	N/A	330[d]	N/A	N/A	80[d]
	IIIB	N/A	N/A	13,200[e,f]	N/A	N/A	13,200[f]	N/A	N/A	3,300[f]
Combustible fiber	Loose	H-3	(100)	N/A	N/A	(100)	N/A	N/A	(20)	N/A
	Baled[o]		(1,000)			(1,000)			(200)	
Consumer fireworks (Class C, Common)	1.4G	H-3	125[d,e,l]	N/A	N/A	N/A	N/A	N/A	N/A	N/A
Cryogenics flammable	N/A	H-2	N/A	45[d]	N/A	N/A	45[d]	N/A	N/A	10[d]
Cryogenics, oxidizing	N/A	H-3	N/A	45[d]	N/A	N/A	45[d]	N/A	N/A	10[d]
Explosives	Division 1.1	H-1	1[e,g]	(1)[e,g]	N/A	0.25[g]	(0.25)[g]	N/A	0.25[g]	(0.25)[g]
	Division 1.2	H-1	1[e,g]	(1)[e,g]	N/A	0.25[g]	(0.25)[g]	N/A	0.25[g]	(0.25)[g]
	Division 1.3	H-1 or 2	5[e,g]	(5)[e,g]	N/A	1[g]	(1)[g]	N/A	1[g]	(1)[g]
	Division 1.4	H-3	50[e,g]	(50)[e,g]	N/A	50[g]	(50)[g]	N/A	N/A	N/A
	Division 1.4G	H-3	125[d,e,l]	N/A	N/A	N/A	N/A	N/A	N/A	N/A
	Division 1.5	H-1	1[e,g]	(1)[e,g]	N/A	0.25[g]	(0.25)[g]	N/A	0.25[g]	(0.25)[g]
	Division 1.6	H-1	1[d,e,g]	N/A	N/A	N/A	N/A	N/A	N/A	N/A
Flammable gas	Gaseous	H-2	N/A	N/A	1,000[d,e]	N/A	N/A	1,000[d,e]	N/A	N/A
	liquefied		N/A	30[d,e]	N/A	N/A	30[d,e]	N/A	N/A	N/A
Flammable liquid[c]	1A	H-2 or H-3	N/A	30[d,e]	N/A	N/A	30[d]	N/A	N/A	10[d]
	1B and 1C		N/A	120[d,e]	N/A	N/A	120[d]	N/A	N/A	30[d]
Combination flammable liquid (1A, 1B, 1C)	N/A	H-2 or H-3	N/A	120[d,e,h]	N/A	N/A	120[d,h]	N/A	N/A	30[d,h]
Flammable solid	N/A	H-3	125[d,e]	N/A	N/A	125[d]	N/A	N/A	25[d]	N/A
Organic peroxide	UD	H-1	1[e,g]	(1)[e,g]	N/A	0.25[g]	(0.25)[g]	N/A	0.25[g]	(0.25)[g]
	I	H-2	5[d,e]	(5)[d,e]	N/A	1d	(1)	N/A	1[d]	(1)[d]
	II	H-3	50[d,e]	(50)[d,e]	N/A	50[d]	(50)[d]	N/A	10[d]	(10)[d]
	III	H-3	125[d,e]	(125)[d,e]	N/A	125[d]	(125)[d]	N/A	25[d]	(25)[d]
	IV	N/A	NL	NL	N/A	NL	NL	N/A	NL	NL
	V	N/A	NL	NL	N/A	NL	NL	N/A	NL	NL

(continued)

[F] TABLE 307.1(1)—continued
MAXIMUM ALLOWABLE QUANTITY PER CONTROL AREA OF HAZARDOUS MATERIALS POSING A PHYSICAL HAZARD[a, j, m, n, p]

Material	Class	Group When the Maximum Allowable Quantity Is Exceeded	Storage — Solid pounds / Liquid gallons	Storage — Gas cubic feet at NTP	Use-Closed Systems — Solid pounds	Use-Closed Systems — Liquid gallons	Use-Closed Systems — Gas cubic feet at NTP	Use-Open Systems — Solid pounds	Use-Open Systems — Liquid gallons
Oxidizer	4	H-1	1[e,g]	N/A	0.25[g]	(0.25)[g]	N/A	0.25[g]	(0.25)[g]
	3[k]	H-2 or H-3	10[d,e]	N/A	2[d]	(2)[d]	N/A	2[d]	(2)[d]
	2	H-3	250[d,e]	N/A	250[f]	(250)[d]	N/A	50[f]	(50)[d]
	1	N/A	4,000[e,f]	N/A	4,000[f]	(4,000)[f]	N/A	1,000[f]	(1,000)[f]
Oxidizing gas	Gaseous	H-3	N/A	1,500[d,e]	N/A	N/A	1,500[d,e]	N/A	N/A
	liquefied		15[d,e]	N/A	N/A	15[d,e]	N/A	N/A	N/A
Pyrophoric material	N/A	H-2	4[e,g]	50[e,g]	1[g]	(1)[g]	10[e,g]	0	0
Unstable (reactive)	4	H-1	1[e,g]	10[e,g]	0.25[g]	(0.25)[g]	2[e,g]	0.25[g]	(0.25)[g]
	3	H-1 or H-2	5[d,e]	50[d,e]	1[d]	(1)[d]	10[d,e]	1[d]	(1)[d]
	2	H-3	50[d,e]	250[d,e]	50[d]	(50)[d]	250[d,e]	10[d]	(10)[d]
	1	N/A	NL	NL	NL	NL	NL	NL	NL
Water reactive	3	H-2	5[d,e]	N/A	5[d]	(5)[d]	N/A	1[d]	(1)[d]
	2	H-3	50[d,e]	N/A	50[d]	(50)[d]	N/A	10[d]	(10)[d]
	1	N/A	NL	N/A	NL	NL	N/A	NL	NL

For SI: 1 cubic foot = 0.023 m3, 1 pound = 0.454 kg, 1 gallon = 3.785 L.

NL = Not Limited; N/A = Not Applicable; UD = Unclassified Detonable

a. For use of control areas, see Section 414.2.

b. The aggregate quantity in use and storage shall not exceed the quantity listed for storage.

c. The quantities of alcoholic beverages in retail and wholesale sales occupancies shall not be limited providing the liquids are packaged in individual containers not exceeding 1.3 gallons. In retail and wholesale sales occupancies, the quantities of medicines, foodstuffs, consumer or industrial products, and cosmetics containing not more than 50 percent by volume of water-miscible liquids with the remainder of the solutions not being flammable, shall not be limited, provided that such materials are packaged in individual containers not exceeding 1.3 gallons.

d. Maximum allowable quantities shall be increased 100 percent in buildings equipped throughout with an automatic sprinkler system in accordance with Section 903.3.1.1. Where Note e also applies, the increase for both notes shall be applied accumulatively.

e. Maximum allowable quantities shall be increased 100 percent when stored in approved storage cabinets, day boxes, gas cabinets, exhausted enclosures or safety cans. Where Note d also applies, the increase for both notes shall be applied accumulatively.

f. The permitted quantities shall not be limited in a building equipped throughout with an automatic sprinkler system in accordance with Section 903.3.1.1.

g. Permitted only in buildings equipped throughout with an automatic sprinkler system in accordance with Section 903.3.1.1.

h. Containing not more than the maximum allowable quantity per control area of Class IA, IB or IC flammable liquids.

i. Inside a building, the maximum capacity of a combustible liquid storage system that is connected to a fuel-oil piping system shall be 660 gallons provided such system complies with the *Fire Code of New York State*.

j. Quantities in parenthesis indicate quantity units in parenthesis at the head of each column.

k. A maximum quantity of 200 pounds of solid or 20 gallons of liquid Class 3 oxidizers is allowed when such materials are necessary for maintenance purposes, operation or sanitation of equipment. Storage containers and the manner of storage shall be approved.

l. Net weight of the pyrotechnic composition of the fireworks. Where the net weight of the pyrotechnic composition of the fireworks is not known, 25 percent of the gross weight of the fireworks, including packaging, shall be used.

m. For gallons of liquids, divide the amount in pounds by 10 in accordance with Section 2703.1.2 of the *Fire Code of New York State*.

n. For storage and display quantities in Group M and storage quantities in Group S occupancies complying with Section 414.2.5, see Tables 414.2.5(1) and 414.2.5(2).

o. Densely packed baled cotton that complies with the packing requirements of ISO 8115 shall not be included in this material class.

p. The following shall not be included in determining the maximum allowable quantities:
1. Liquid or gaseous fuel in fuel tanks on vehicles.
2. Liquid or gaseous fuel in fuel tanks on motorized equipment operated in accordance with this code.
3. Gaseous fuels in piping systems and fixed appliances regulated by the *Fuel Gas Code of New York State*.
4. Liquid fuels in piping systems and fixed appliances regulated by the *Mechanical Code of New York State*.

[F] TABLE 307.1(2)
MAXIMUM ALLOWABLE QUANTITY PER CONTROL AREA OF HAZARDOUS MATERIAL POSING A HEALTH HAZARD[a, b, c, j]

MATERIAL	STORAGE[d]			USE-CLOSED SYSTEMS[d]			USE-OPEN SYSTEMS[d]	
	Solid pounds[e, f]	Liquid gallons (pounds)[e, f]	Gas (cubic feet at NTP)[e]	Solid pounds[e]	Liquid gallons (pounds)[e]	Gas (cubic feet at NTP)[e]	Solid pounds[e]	Liquid gallons (pounds)[e]
Corrosive	5,000	500	810[f, g]	5,000	500	810[f, g]	1,000	100
Highly toxic	10	(10)[i]	20[h]	10	(10)[i]	20[h]	3	(3)[i]
Toxic	500	(500)[i]	810[f]	500	(500)[i]	810[f]	125	(125)[i]

For SI: 1 cubic foot = 0.028 m3, 1 pound = 0.454 kg, 1 gallon = 3.785 L.

a. For use of control areas, see Section 414.2.

b. In retail and wholesale sales occupancies, the quantities of medicines, foodstuffs, consumer or industrial products, and cosmetics, containing not more than 50 percent by volume of water-miscible liquids and with the remainder of the solutions not being flammable, shall not be limited, provided that such materials are packaged in individual containers not exceeding 1.3 gallons.

c. For storage and display quantities in Group M and storage quantities in Group S occupancies complying with Section 414.2.5, see Tables 414.2.5(1) and 414.2.5(2).

d. The aggregate quantity in use and storage shall not exceed the quantity listed for storage.

e. Quantities shall be increased 100 percent in buildings equipped throughout with an approved automatic sprinkler system in accordance with Section 903.3.1.1.
Where Note f also applies, the increase for both notes shall be applied accumulatively.

f. Quantities shall be increased 100 percent when stored in approved storage cabinets, gas cabinets or exhausted enclosures as specified in the *Fire Code of New York State*. Where Note e also applies, the increase for both notes shall be applied accumulatively.

g. A single cylinder containing 150 pounds or less of anhydrous ammonia in a single control area in a nonsprinklered building shall be considered a maximum allowable quantity. Two cylinders, each containing 150 pounds or less in a single control area, shall be considered a maximum allowable quantity provided the building is equipped throughout with an automatic sprinkler system in accordance with Section 903.3.1.1.

h. Allowed only when stored in approved exhausted gas cabinets or exhausted enclosures as specified in the *Fire Code of New York State*.

i. Quantities in parenthesis indicate quantity units in parenthesis at the head of each column.

j. For gallons of liquids, divide the amount in pounds by 10 in accordance with Section 2703.1.2 of the *Fire Code of New York State*.

The states of a compressed gas are categorized as follows:

1. Nonliquefied compressed gases are gases, other than those in solution, which are in a packaging under the charged pressure and are entirely gaseous at a temperature of 68°F (20°C).

2. Liquefied compressed gases are gases that, in a packaging under the charged pressure, are partially liquid at a temperature of 68°F (20°C).

3. Compressed gases in solution are nonliquefied gases that are dissolved in a solvent.

4. Compressed gas mixtures consist of a mixture of two or more compressed gases contained in a packaging, the hazard properties of which are represented by the properties of the mixture as a whole.

CONTROL AREA. Spaces within a building where quantities of hazardous materials not exceeding the maximum allowable quantities per control area are stored, dispensed, used or handled. See also the definition of "Outdoor control area" in the *Fire Code of New York State*.

CORROSIVE. A chemical that causes visible destruction of, or irreversible alterations in, living tissue by chemical action at the point of contact. A chemical shall be considered corrosive if, when tested on the intact skin of albino rabbits by the method described in DOTn 49 CFR, Part 173.137, such a chemical destroys or changes irreversibly the structure of the tissue at the point of contact following an exposure period of 4 hours. This term does not refer to action on inanimate surfaces.

CRYOGENIC FLUID. A liquid having a boiling point lower than -150°F (-101°C) at 14.7 pounds per square inch atmosphere (psia) (an absolute pressure of 101 kPa).

DAY BOX. A portable magazine designed to hold explosive materials constructed in accordance with the requirements for a Type 3 magazine as defined and classified in Chapter 33 of the *Fire Code of New York State*.

DEFLAGRATION. An exothermic reaction, such as the extremely rapid oxidation of a flammable dust or vapor in air, in which the reaction progresses through the unburned material at a rate less than the velocity of sound. A deflagration can have an explosive effect.

DETACHED BUILDING. A separate single-story building, without a basement or crawl space, used for the storage or use of hazardous materials and located an approved distance from all structures.

DETONATION. An exothermic reaction characterized by the presence of a shock wave in the material which establishes and maintains the reaction. The reaction zone progresses through the material at a rate greater than the velocity of sound. The principal heating mechanism is one of shock compression. Detonations have an explosive effect.

DISPENSING. The pouring or transferring of any material from a container, tank or similar vessel, whereby vapors, dusts, fumes, mists or gases are liberated to the atmosphere.

EXPLOSIVE. Any chemical compound, mixture or device, the primary or common purpose of which is to function by explosion. The term includes, but is not limited to, dynamite, black powder, pellet powder, initiating explosives, detonators, safety fuses, squibs, detonating cord, igniter cord, igniters and display fireworks, 1.3G (Class B, Special).

The term "explosive" includes any material determined to be within the scope of USC Title 18: Chapter 40 and also includes any material classified as an explosive other than consumer fireworks, 1.4G (Class C, Common) by the hazardous materials regulations of DOTn 49 CFR.

High explosive. Explosive material, such as dynamite, which can be caused to detonate by means of a No. 8 test blasting cap when unconfined.

Low explosive. Explosive material that will burn or deflagrate when ignited. It is characterized by a rate of reaction that is less than the speed of sound. Examples of low explosives include, but are not limited to, black powder; safety fuse; igniters; igniter cord; fuse lighters; fireworks, 1.3G (Class B, Special) and propellants, 1.3C.

Mass-detonating explosives. Division 1.1, 1.2 and 1.5 explosives alone or in combination, or loaded into various types of ammunition or containers, most of which can be expected to explode virtually instantaneously when a small portion is subjected to fire, severe concussion, impact, the impulse of an initiating agent or the effect of a considerable discharge of energy from without. Materials that react in this manner represent a mass explosion hazard. Such an explosive will normally cause severe structural damage to adjacent objects. Explosive propagation could occur immediately to other items of ammunition and explosives stored sufficiently close to and not adequately protected from the initially exploding pile with a time interval short enough so that two or more quantities must be considered as one for quantity-distance purposes.

UN/DOTn Class 1 explosives. The former classification system used by DOTn included the terms "high" and "low" explosives as defined herein. The following terms further define explosives under the current system applied by DOTn for all explosive materials defined as hazard Class 1 materials. Compatibility group letters are used in concert with the division to specify further limitations on each division noted (i.e., the letter G identifies the material as a pyrotechnic substance or article containing a pyrotechnic substance and similar materials).

Division 1.1. Explosives that have a mass explosion hazard. A mass explosion is one which affects almost the entire load instantaneously.

Division 1.2. Explosives that have a projection hazard but not a mass explosion hazard.

Division 1.3. Explosives that have a fire hazard and either a minor blast hazard or a minor projection hazard or both, but not a mass explosion hazard.

Division 1.4. Explosives that pose a minor explosion hazard. The explosive effects are largely confined to the package and no projection of fragments of appreciable size or range is to be expected. An external fire must not cause virtually instantaneous explosion of almost the entire contents of the package.

Division 1.5. Very insensitive explosives. This division is comprised of substances that have a mass explosion hazard, but that are so insensitive there is very little probability of initiation or of transition from burning to detonation under normal conditions of transport.

Division 1.6. Extremely insensitive articles which do not have a mass explosion hazard. This division is comprised of articles that contain only extremely insensitive detonating substances and which demonstrate a negligible probability of accidental initiation or propagation.

FIREWORKS. Any composition or device for the purpose of producing a visible or audible effect for entertainment purposes by combustion, deflagration or detonation that meets the definition of 1.4G fireworks or 1.3G fireworks as set forth herein.

FIREWORKS, 1.3G. (Formerly Class B, Special Fireworks.) Large fireworks devices, which are explosive materials, intended for use in fireworks displays and designed to produce audible or visible effects by combustion, deflagration or detonation. Such 1.3G fireworks include, but are not limited to, firecrackers containing more than 130 milligrams (2 grains) of explosive composition, aerial shells containing more than 40 grams of pyrotechnic composition, and other display pieces which exceed the limits for classification as 1.4G fireworks. Such 1.3G fireworks are also described as fireworks, UN0335 by the DOTn.

FIREWORKS, 1.4G. (Formerly Class C, Common Fireworks.) Small fireworks devices containing restricted amounts of pyrotechnic composition designed primarily to produce visible or audible effects by combustion. Such 1.4G fireworks which comply with the construction, chemical composition and labeling regulations of the DOTn for fireworks, UN0336, and the U.S. Consumer Product Safety Commission (CPSC) as set forth in CPSC 16 CFR: Parts 1500 and 1507, are not explosive materials for the purpose of this code.

FLAMMABLE GAS. A material that is a gas at 68°F (20°C) or less at 14.7 pounds per square inch atmosphere (psia) (101 kPa) of pressure [a material that has a boiling point of 68°F (20°C) or less at 14.7 psia (101 kPa)] which:

1. Is ignitable at 14.7 psia (101 kPa) when in a mixture of 13 percent or less by volume with air; or

2. Has a flammable range at 14.7 psia (101 kPa) with air of at least 12 percent, regardless of the lower limit.

The limits specified shall be determined at 14.7 psi (101 kPa) of pressure and a temperature of 68°F (20°C) in accordance with ASTM E 681.

FLAMMABLE LIQUEFIED GAS. A liquefied compressed gas which, under a charged pressure, is partially liquid at a temperature of 68°F (20°C) and which is flammable.

FLAMMABLE LIQUID. A liquid having a closed cup flash point below 100°F (38°C). Flammable liquids are further categorized into a group known as Class I liquids. The Class I category is subdivided as follows:

Class IA. Liquids having a flash point below 73°F (23°C) and a boiling point below 100°F (38°C).

Class IB. Liquids having a flash point below 73°F (23°C) and a boiling point at or above 100°F (38°C).

Class IC. Liquids having a flash point at or above 73°F (23°C) and below 100°F (38°C).

The category of flammable liquids does not include compressed gases or cryogenic fluids.

FLAMMABLE MATERIAL. A material capable of being readily ignited from common sources of heat or at a temperature of 600°F (316°C) or less.

FLAMMABLE SOLID. A solid, other than a blasting agent or explosive, that is capable of causing fire through friction, absorption or moisture, spontaneous chemical change, or retained heat from manufacturing or processing, or which has an ignition temperature below 212°F (100°C) or which burns so vigorously and persistently when ignited as to create a serious hazard. A chemical shall be considered a flammable solid as determined in accordance with the test method of CPSC 16 CFR; Part 1500.44, if it ignites and burns with a self-sustained flame at a rate greater than 0.1 inch (2.5 mm) per second along its major axis.

FLASH POINT. The minimum temperature in degrees Fahrenheit at which a liquid will give off sufficient vapors to form an ignitable mixture with air near the surface or in the container, but will not sustain combustion. The flash point of a liquid shall be determined by appropriate test procedure and apparatus as specified in ASTM D 56, ASTM D 93 or ASTM D 3278.

HANDLING. The deliberate transport by any means to a point of storage or use.

HAZARDOUS MATERIALS. Those chemicals or substances that are physical hazards or health hazards as defined and classified in this section and the *Fire Code of New York State*, whether the materials are in usable or waste condition.

HEALTH HAZARD. A classification of a chemical for which there is statistically significant evidence that acute or chronic health effects are capable of occurring in exposed persons. The term "health hazard" includes chemicals that are toxic or highly toxic, and corrosive.

HIGHLY TOXIC. A material which produces a lethal dose or lethal concentration that falls within any of the following categories:

1. A chemical that has a median lethal dose (LD_{50}) of 50 milligrams or less per kilogram of body weight when administered orally to albino rats weighing between 200 and 300 grams each.

2. A chemical that has a median lethal dose (LD_{50}) of 200 milligrams or less per kilogram of body weight when administered by continuous contact for 24 hours (or less if death occurs within 24 hours) with the bare skin of albino rabbits weighing between 2 and 3 kilograms each.

3. A chemical that has a median lethal concentration (LC_{50}) in air of 200 parts per million by volume or less of gas or vapor, or 2 milligrams per liter or less of mist, fume or dust, when administered by continuous inhalation for 1 hour (or less if death occurs within 1 hour) to albino rats weighing between 200 and 300 grams each.

Mixtures of these materials with ordinary materials, such as water, might not warrant classification as highly toxic. While this system is basically simple in application, any hazard evaluation that is required for the precise categorization of this type of material shall be performed by experienced, technically competent persons.

INCOMPATIBLE MATERIALS. Materials that, when mixed, have the potential to react in a manner that generates heat, fumes, gases or byproducts which are hazardous to life or property.

OPEN SYSTEM. The use of a solid or liquid hazardous material involving a vessel or system that is continuously open to the atmosphere during normal operations and where vapors are liberated, or the product is exposed to the atmosphere during normal operations. Examples of open systems for solids and liquids include dispensing from or into open beakers or containers, dip tank and plating tank operations.

OPERATING BUILDING. A building occupied in conjunction with the manufacture, transportation or use of explosive materials. Operating buildings are separated from one another with the use of intraplant or intraline distances.

ORGANIC PEROXIDE. An organic compound that contains the bivalent -O-O- structure and which may be considered to be a structural derivative of hydrogen peroxide where one or both of the hydrogen atoms have been replaced by an organic radical. Organic peroxides can pose an explosion hazard (detonation or deflagration) or they can be shock sensitive. They can also decompose into various unstable compounds over an extended period of time.

Class I. Those formulations that are capable of deflagration but not detonation.

Class II. Those formulations that burn very rapidly and that pose a moderate reactivity hazard.

Class III. Those formulations that burn rapidly and that pose a moderate reactivity hazard.

Class IV. Those formulations that burn in the same manner as ordinary combustibles and that pose a minimal reactivity hazard.

Class V. Those formulations that burn with less intensity than ordinary combustibles or do not sustain combustion and that pose no reactivity hazard.

Unclassified detonable. Organic peroxides that are capable of detonation. These peroxides pose an extremely high explosion hazard through rapid explosive decomposition.

OXIDIZER. A material that readily yields oxygen or other oxidizing gas, or that readily reacts to promote or initiate combustion of combustible materials. Examples of other oxidizing gases include bromine, chlorine and fluorine.

Class 4. An oxidizer that can undergo an explosive reaction due to contamination or exposure to thermal or physical shock. Additionally, the oxidizer will enhance the burning rate and can cause spontaneous ignition of combustibles.

Class 3. An oxidizer that will cause a severe increase in the burning rate of combustible materials with which it comes in contact or that will undergo vigorous self-sustained decomposition due to contamination or exposure to heat.

Class 2. An oxidizer that will cause a moderate increase in the burning rate or that causes spontaneous ignition of combustible materials with which it comes in contact.

Class 1. An oxidizer whose primary hazard is that it slightly increases the burning rate but which does not cause spontaneous ignition when it comes in contact with combustible materials.

OXIDIZING GAS. A gas that can support and accelerate combustion of other materials.

PHYSICAL HAZARD. A chemical for which there is evidence that it is a combustible liquid, compressed gas, cryogenic, explosive, flammable gas, flammable liquid, flammable solid, organic peroxide, oxidizer, pyrophoric or unstable (reactive) or water-reactive material.

PYROPHORIC. A chemical with an autoignition temperature in air, at or below a temperature of 130°F (54.4°C).

PYROTECHNIC COMPOSITION. A chemical mixture that produces visible light displays or sounds through a self-propagating, heat-releasing chemical reaction which is initiated by ignition.

TOXIC. A chemical falling within any of the following categories:

1. A chemical that has a median lethal dose (LD_{50}) of more than 50 milligrams per kilogram, but not more than 500 milligrams per kilogram of body weight when administered orally to albino rats weighing between 200 and 300 grams each.

2. A chemical that has a median lethal dose (LD_{50}) of more than 200 milligrams per kilogram but not more than 1,000 milligrams per kilogram of body weight when administered by continuous contact for 24 hours (or less if death occurs within 24 hours) with the bare skin of albino rabbits weighing between 2 and 3 kilograms each.

3. A chemical that has a median lethal concentration (LC_{50}) in air of more than 200 parts per million but not more than 2,000 parts per million by volume of gas or vapor, or more than 2 milligrams per liter but not more than 20 milligrams per liter of mist, fume or dust, when administered by continuous inhalation for 1 hour (or less if death occurs within 1 hour) to albino rats weighing between 200 and 300 grams each.

UNSTABLE (REACTIVE) MATERIAL. A material, other than an explosive, which in the pure state or as commercially produced, will vigorously polymerize, decompose, condense or become self-reactive and undergo other violent chemical changes, including explosion, when exposed to heat, friction or shock, or in the absence of an inhibitor, or in the presence of contaminants, or in contact with incompatible materials. Unstable (reactive) materials are subdivided as follows:

Class 4. Materials that in themselves are readily capable of detonation or explosive decomposition or explosive reaction at normal temperatures and pressures. This class includes materials that are sensitive to mechanical or localized thermal shock at normal temperatures and pressures.

Class 3. Materials that in themselves are capable of detonation or of explosive decomposition or explosive reaction but which require a strong initiating source or which must be heated under confinement before initiation. This class includes materials that are sensitive to thermal or mechanical shock at elevated temperatures and pressures.

Class 2. Materials that in themselves are normally unstable and readily undergo violent chemical change but do not detonate. This class includes materials that can undergo chemical change with rapid release of energy at normal temperatures and pressures, and that can undergo violent chemical change at elevated temperatures and pressures.

Class 1. Materials that in themselves are normally stable but which can become unstable at elevated temperatures and pressure.

WATER-REACTIVE MATERIAL. A material that explodes; violently reacts; produces flammable, toxic or other hazardous gases; or evolves enough heat to cause autoignition or ignition of combustibles upon exposure to water or moisture. Water-reactive materials are subdivided as follows:

Class 3. Materials that react explosively with water without requiring heat or confinement.

Class 2. Materials that react violently with water or have the ability to boil water. Materials that produce flammable, toxic or other hazardous gases or evolve enough heat to cause autoignition or ignition of combustibles upon exposure to water or moisture.

Class 1. Materials that react with water with some release of energy, but not violently.

[F] 307.3 High-Hazard Group H-1. Buildings and structures containing materials that pose a detonation hazard shall be classified as Group H-1. Such materials shall include, but not be limited to, the following:

Explosives:

    Division 1.1

    Division 1.2

    Division 1.3

        Exception: Materials that are used and maintained in a form where either confinement or configuration will not elevate the hazard from a mass fire to mass explosion hazard shall be allowed in H-2 occupancies.

    Division 1.4

        Exception: Articles, including articles packaged for shipment, that are not regulated as an explosive under Bureau of Alcohol, Tobacco and Firearms regulations, or unpackaged articles used in process operations that do not propagate a detonation or deflagration between articles shall be allowed in H-3 occupancies.

    Division 1.5

    Division 1.6

Organic peroxides, unclassified detonable

Oxidizers, Class 4

Unstable (reactive) materials, Class 3 detonable and Class 4

Detonable pyrophoric materials

[F] 307.4 High-Hazard Group H-2. Buildings and structures containing materials that pose a deflagration hazard or a hazard from accelerated burning shall be classified as Group H-2. Such materials shall include, but not be limited to, the following:

Class I, II or IIIA flammable or combustible liquids which are used or stored in normally open containers or systems, or in closed containers or systems pressurized at more than 15 psi (103.4 kPa) gage.

Combustible dusts

Cryogenic fluids, flammable

Flammable gases

Organic peroxides, Class I

Oxidizers, Class 3, that are used or stored in normally open containers or systems, or in closed containers or systems pressurized at more than 15 psi (103 kPa) gage

Pyrophoric liquids, solids and gases, nondetonable

Unstable (reactive) materials, Class 3, nondetonable

Water-reactive materials, Class 3

[F] 307.5 High-Hazard Group H-3. Buildings and structures containing materials that readily support combustion or that pose a physical hazard shall be classified as Group H-3. Such materials shall include, but not be limited to, the following:

Class I, II or IIIA flammable or combustible liquids that are used or stored in normally closed containers or systems pressurized at 15 pounds per square inch gauge (103.4 kPa) or less

Combustible fibers, other than densely packed baled cotton

Consumer fireworks, 1.4G (Class C, Common)

Cryogenic fluids, oxidizing

Flammable solids

Organic peroxides, Class II and III

Oxidizers, Class 2

Oxidizers, Class 3, that are used or stored in normally closed containers or systems pressurized at 15 pounds per square inch gauge (103 kPa) or less

Oxidizing gases

Unstable (reactive) materials, Class 2

Water-reactive materials, Class 2

[F] 307.6 High-Hazard Group H-4. Buildings and structures which contain materials that are health hazards shall be classified as Group H-4. Such materials shall include, but not be limited to, the following:

Corrosives

Highly toxic materials

Toxic materials

[F] 307.7 High-Hazard Group H-5 structures. Semiconductor fabrication facilities and comparable research and development areas in which hazardous production materials (HPM) are used and the aggregate quantity of materials is in excess of those listed in Tables 307.1(1) and 307.1(2) shall be classified as Group H-5. Such facilities and areas shall be designed and constructed in accordance with Section 415.8.

[F] 307.8 Multiple hazards. Buildings and structures containing a material or materials representing hazards that are classified in one or more of Groups H-1, H-2, H-3 and H-4 shall conform to the code requirements for each of the occupancies so classified.

SECTION 308
INSTITUTIONAL GROUP I

308.1 Institutional Group I. Institutional Group I occupancy includes, among others, the use of a building or structure, or a portion thereof, in which people are cared for or live in a supervised environment, having physical limitations because of health or age are harbored for medical treatment or other care or treatment, or in which people are detained for penal or correctional purposes or in which the liberty of the occupants is restricted. Institutional occupancies shall be classified as Group I-1, I-2, I-3 or I-4.

308.2 Group I-1. This occupancy shall include buildings, structures or parts thereof housing more than 16 persons, on a 24-hour basis, who because of age, mental disability or other reasons, live in a supervised residential environment that provides personal care services. The occupants are capable of responding to an emergency situation without physical assistance from staff. This group shall include, but not be limited to, the following:

Residential board and care facilities

Assisted living facilities

Halfway houses

Group homes

Congregate care facilities

Social rehabilitation facilities

Alcohol and drug centers

Convalescent facilities

A facility such as the above with five or fewer persons shall be classified as a Group R-3 or shall comply with the *Residential Code of New York State* in accordance with Section 101.2. A facility such as above, housing at least six and not more than 16 persons, shall be classified as Group R-4.

308.3 Group I-2. This occupancy shall include buildings and structures used for medical, surgical, psychiatric, nursing or custodial care on a 24-hour basis for more than five persons who are not capable of self-preservation. This group shall include, but not be limited to, the following:

Hospitals

Nursing homes (both intermediate care facilities and skilled nursing facilities)

Mental hospitals

Detoxification facilities

A facility such as the above with five or fewer persons shall be classified as Group R-3 or shall comply with the *Residential Code of New York State* in accordance with Section 101.2.

308.3.1 Child care facility. A child care facility that provides care on a 24-hour basis to more than five children $2^1/_2$ years of age or less shall be classified as Group I-2.

308.4 Group I-3. This occupancy shall include buildings and structures that are inhabited by more than five persons who are under restraint or security. An I-3 facility is occupied by persons who are generally incapable of self-preservation due to security measures not under the occupants' control. This group shall include, but not be limited to, the following:

Prisons

Jails

Reformatories

Detention centers

Correctional centers

Prerelease centers

Buildings of Group I-3 shall be classified as one of the occupancy conditions indicated in Sections 308.4.1 through 308.4.5 (see Section 408.1).

308.4.1 Condition 1. This occupancy condition shall include buildings in which free movement is allowed from sleeping areas, and other spaces where access or occupancy is permitted, to the exterior via means of egress without restraint. A Condition 1 facility is permitted to be constructed as Group R.

308.4.2 Condition 2. This occupancy condition shall include buildings in which free movement is allowed from sleeping areas and any other occupied smoke compartment to one or more other smoke compartments. Egress to the exterior is impeded by locked exits.

308.4.3 Condition 3. This occupancy condition shall include buildings in which free movement is allowed within individual smoke compartments, such as within a residential unit comprised of individual sleeping units and group activity spaces, where egress is impeded by remote-controlled release of means of egress from such a smoke compartment to another smoke compartment.

308.4.4 Condition 4. This occupancy condition shall include buildings in which free movement is restricted from an occupied space. Remote-controlled release is provided to permit movement from sleeping units, activity spaces and other occupied areas within the smoke compartment to other smoke compartments.

308.4.5 Condition 5. This occupancy condition shall include buildings in which free movement is restricted from an occupied space. Staff-controlled manual release is provided to permit movement from sleeping units, activity spaces and other occupied areas within the smoke compartment to other smoke compartments.

308.5 Group I-4, day care facilities. This group shall include buildings and structures occupied by persons of any age who receive custodial care for less than 24 hours by individuals other than parents or guardians, relatives by blood, marriage or adoption, and in a place other than the home of the person cared for. A facility such as the above with five or fewer persons shall be classified as a Group R-3 or shall comply with the *Residential Code of New York State* in accordance with Section 101.2. Places of worship during religious functions are not included.

308.5.1 Adult care facility. A facility that provides accommodations for less than 24 hours for more than five unrelated adults and provides supervision and personal care services shall be classified as Group I-4.

Exception: A facility where occupants are capable of responding to an emergency situation without physical assistance from the staff shall be classified as Group A-3.

308.5.2 Child care facility. A facility that provides supervision and personal care on less than a 24-hour basis for more than five children $2^1/_2$ years of age or less shall be classified as Group I-4.

Exception: A child day care facility that provides care for more than five but no more than 100 children $2^1/_2$ years or less of age, when the rooms where such children are cared for are located on the level of exit discharge and each of these child care rooms has an exit door directly to the exterior, shall be classified as Group E.

SECTION 309
MERCANTILE GROUP M

309.1 Mercantile Group M. Mercantile Group M occupancy includes, among others, buildings and structures or a portion thereof, for the display and sale of merchandise, and involves stocks of goods, wares or merchandise incidental to such purposes and accessible to the public. Mercantile occupancies shall include, but not be limited to, the following:

Department stores

Drug stores

Markets

Motor fuel-dispensing facilities

Retail or wholesale stores

Sales rooms

309.2 Quantity of hazardous materials. The aggregate quantity of nonflammable solid and nonflammable or noncombustible liquid hazardous materials stored or displayed in a single control area of a Group M occupancy shall not exceed the quantities in Table 414.2.5(1).

SECTION 310
RESIDENTIAL GROUP R

310.1 Residential Group R. Residential Group R includes, among others, the use of a building or structure, or a portion thereof, for sleeping purposes when not classified as an Institutional Group I or when not regulated by the *Residential Code of New York State* in accordance with Section 101.2. Residential occupancies shall include the following:

R-1 Residential occupancies containing sleeping units where the occupants are primarily transient in nature (transient multiple dwellings), including:

Boarding houses (transient)

Hotels (transient)

Motels (transient)

R-2 Residential occupancies containing sleeping units or more than two dwelling units where the occupants are primarily permanent in nature (permanent multiple dwellings), including:

Apartment houses

Boarding houses (not transient)

Convents

Dormitories

Fraternities and sororities

Hotels (nontransient)

Monasteries

Motels (nontransient)

Vacation timeshare properties

Congregate living facilities with 16 or fewer occupants are permitted to comply with the construction requirements for Group R-3.

R-3 Residential occupancies where the occupants are primarily permanent in nature and not classified as Group R-1, R-2, R-4 or I, including:

Buildings that do not contain more than two dwelling units.

Adult facilities that provide accommodations for five or fewer persons of any age for less than 24 hours.

Child care facilities that provide accommodations for five or fewer persons of any age for less than 24 hours.

Congregate living facilities with 16 or fewer persons.

Adult and child care facilities that are within a single-family home are permitted to comply with the *Residential Code of New York State.*

R-4 Residential occupancies shall include buildings arranged for occupancy as residential care/assisted living facilities including more than five but not more than 16 occupants, excluding staff.

Group R-4 occupancies shall meet the requirements for construction as defined for Group R-3, except as otherwise provided for in this code, or shall comply with the *Residential Code of New York State.*

310.2 Definitions. The following words and terms shall, for the purposes of this section and as used elsewhere in this code, have the meanings shown herein.

BOARDING HOUSE. A building arranged or used for lodging for compensation, with or without meals, and not occupied as a single-family unit.

CONGREGATE LIVING FACILITIES. A building or part thereof that contains sleeping units where residents share bathroom and/or kitchen facilities.

DORMITORY. A space in a building where group sleeping accommodations are provided in one room, or in a series of closely associated rooms, for persons not members of the same family group, under joint occupancy and single management, as in college dormitories or fraternity houses.

PERSONAL CARE SERVICE. The care of residents who do not require chronic or convalescent medical or nursing care. Personal care involves responsibility for the safety of the resident while inside the building.

RESIDENTIAL CARE/ASSISTED LIVING FACILITIES. A building or part thereof housing persons, on a 24-hour basis, who because of age, mental disability or other reasons, live in a supervised residential environment which provides personal care services. The occupants are capable of responding to an emergency situation without physical assistance from staff. This classification shall include, but not be limited to, the following: residential board and care facilities, assisted living facilities, halfway houses, group homes, congregate care facilities, social rehabilitation facilities, alcohol and drug abuse centers and convalescent facilities.

TRANSIENT. Occupancy of a dwelling unit or sleeping unit for not more than 30 days.

SECTION 311
STORAGE GROUP S

311.1 Storage Group S. Storage Group S occupancy includes, among others, the use of a building or structure, or a portion thereof, for storage that is not classified as a hazardous occupancy.

311.2 Moderate-hazard storage, Group S-1. Buildings occupied for storage uses that are not classified as Group S-2, including, but not limited to, storage of the following:

Aerosols, Levels 2 and 3

Aircraft repair hangar

Bags: cloth, burlap and paper

Bamboos and rattan

Baskets

Belting: canvas and leather

Books and paper in rolls or packs

Boots and shoes

Buttons, including cloth covered, pearl or bone

Cardboard and cardboard boxes

Clothing, woolen wearing apparel

Cordage

Dry boat storage (indoor)

Furniture

Furs

Glues, mucilage, pastes and size

Grains

Horns and combs, other than celluloid

Leather

Linoleum

Lumber

Motor vehicle repair garages complying with the maximum allowable quantities of hazardous materials listed in Table 307.1(1) (see Section 406.6)

Photo engravings

Resilient flooring

Silks

Soaps

Sugar

Tires, bulk storage of

Tobacco, cigars, cigarettes and snuff

Upholstery and mattresses

Wax candles

311.3 Low-hazard storage, Group S-2. Includes, among others, buildings used for the storage of noncombustible materials such as products on wood pallets or in paper cartons with or without single thickness divisions; or in paper wrappings. Such products are permitted to have a negligible amount of plastic trim, such as knobs, handles or film wrapping. Storage uses shall include, but not be limited to, storage of the following:

Aircraft hangar

Asbestos

Beverages up to and including 12-percent alcohol in metal, glass or ceramic containers

Cement in bags

Chalk and crayons

Dairy products in nonwaxed coated paper containers

Dry cell batteries

Electrical coils

Electrical motors

Empty cans

Food products

Foods in noncombustible containers

Fresh fruits and vegetables in nonplastic trays or containers

Frozen foods

Glass

Glass bottles, empty or filled with noncombustible liquids

Gypsum board

Inert pigments

Ivory

Meats

Metal cabinets

Metal desks with plastic tops and trim

Metal parts

Metals

Mirrors

Oil-filled and other types of distribution transformers

Parking garages, open or enclosed

Porcelain and pottery

Stoves

Talc and soapstones

Washers and dryers

SECTION 312
UTILITY AND MISCELLANEOUS GROUP U

312.1 General. Buildings and structures of an accessory character and miscellaneous structures not classified in any specific occupancy shall be constructed, equipped and maintained to conform to the requirements of this code commensurate with the fire and life hazard incidental to their occupancy. Group U shall include, but not be limited to, the following:

Aircraft hangars, accessory to a one- or two-family residence (see Section 412.3)

Barns

Bathhouse

Carports

Fences more than 6 feet (1829 mm) high

Grain silos, accessory to a residential occupancy

Greenhouses

Livestock shelters

Private garages

Retaining walls

Sheds

Stables

Tanks

Toilet facilities

Towers

CHAPTER 4

SPECIAL DETAILED REQUIREMENTS BASED ON USE AND OCCUPANCY

SECTION 401
SCOPE

401.1 Detailed use and occupancy requirements. In addition to the occupancy and construction requirements in this code, the provisions of this chapter apply to the special uses and occupancies described herein.

SECTION 402
COVERED MALL BUILDINGS

402.1 Scope. The provisions of this section shall apply to buildings or structures defined herein as covered mall buildings not exceeding three floor levels at any point nor more than three stories above grade plane. Except as specifically required by this section, covered mall buildings shall meet applicable provisions of this code.

Exceptions:

1. Foyers and lobbies of Groups B, R-1 and R-2 are not required to comply with this section.

2. Buildings need not comply with the provisions of this section when they totally comply with other applicable provisions of this code.

402.2 Definitions. The following words and terms shall, for the purposes of this chapter and as used elsewhere in this code, have the meanings shown herein.

ANCHOR BUILDING. An exterior perimeter building of a group other than H having direct access to a covered mall building but having required means of egress independent of the mall.

COVERED MALL BUILDING. A single building enclosing a number of tenants and occupants such as retail stores, drinking and dining establishments, entertainment and amusement facilities, passenger transportation terminals, offices, and other similar uses wherein two or more tenants have a main entrance into one or more malls. For the purpose of this chapter, anchor buildings shall not be considered as a part of the covered mall building.

FOOD COURT. A public seating area located in the mall that serves adjacent food preparation tenant spaces.

GROSS LEASABLE AREA. The total floor area designed for tenant occupancy and exclusive use. The area of tenant occupancy is measured from the centerlines of joint partitions to the outside of the tenant walls. All tenant areas, including areas used for storage, shall be included in calculating gross leasable area.

MALL. A roofed or covered common pedestrian area within a covered mall building that serves as access for two or more tenants and not to exceed three levels that are open to each other.

402.3 Lease plan. Each covered mall building owner shall provide both the building and fire departments with a lease plan showing the location of each occupancy and its exits after the certificate of occupancy has been issued. No modifications or changes in occupancy or use shall be made from that shown on the lease plan without prior approval of the code enforcement official.

402.4 Means of egress. Each tenant space and the covered mall building shall be provided with means of egress as required by this section and this code. Where there is a conflict between the requirements of this code and the requirements of this section, the requirements of this section shall apply.

402.4.1 Determination of occupant load. The occupant load permitted in any individual tenant space in a covered mall building shall be determined as required by this code. Means of egress requirements for individual tenant spaces shall be based on the occupant load thus determined.

402.4.1.1 Occupant formula. In determining required means of egress of the mall, the number of occupants for whom means of egress are to be provided shall be based on gross leasable area of the covered mall building (excluding anchor buildings) and the occupant load factor as determined by the following equation.

$$OLF = (0.00007)\,(GLA) + 25 \quad \textbf{(Equation 4-1)}$$

where:
OLF = The occupant load factor (square feet per person).
GLA = The gross leasable area (square feet).

402.4.1.2 OLF range. The occupant load factor (OLF) is not required to be less than 30 and shall not exceed 50.

402.4.1.3 Anchor buildings. The occupant load of anchor buildings opening into the mall shall not be included in computing the total number of occupants for the mall.

402.4.1.4 Food courts. The occupant load of a food court shall be determined in accordance with Section 1004. For the purposes of determining the means of egress requirements for the mall, the food court occupant load shall be added to the occupant load of the covered mall building as calculated above.

402.4.2 Number of means of egress. Wherever the distance of travel to the mall from any location within a tenant space used by persons other than employees exceeds 75 feet (22 860 mm) or the tenant space has an occupant load of 50 or more, not less than two means of egress shall be provided.

402.4.3 Arrangements of means of egress. Assembly occupancies with an occupant load of 500 or more shall be so located in the covered mall building that their entrance will be immediately adjacent to a principal entrance to the mall and shall have not less than one-half of their required means of egress opening directly to the exterior of the covered mall building.

402.4.3.1 Anchor building means of egress. Required means of egress for anchor buildings shall be provided independently from the mall means of egress system. The occupant load of anchor buildings opening into the mall shall not be included in determining means of egress requirements for the mall. The path of egress travel of malls shall not exit through anchor buildings. Malls terminating at an anchor building where no other means of egress has been provided shall be considered as a dead-end mall.

402.4.4 Distance to exits. Within each individual tenant space in a covered mall building, the maximum distance of travel from any point to an exit or entrance to the mall shall not exceed 200 feet (60 960 mm).

The maximum distance of travel from any point within a mall to an exit shall not exceed 200 feet (60 960 mm).

402.4.5 Access to exits. Where more than one exit is required, they shall be so arranged that it is possible to travel in either direction from any point in a mall to separate exits. The minimum width of an exit passageway or corridor from a mall shall be 66 inches (1676 mm).

Exception: Dead ends not exceeding a length equal to twice the width of the mall measured at the narrowest location within the dead-end portion of the mall.

402.4.5.1 Exit passageways. Where exit passageways provide a secondary means of egress from a tenant space, doorways to the exit passageway shall be protected by 1-hour fire door assemblies that are self- or automatic closing by smoke detection in accordance with Section 715.4.7.3.

402.4.6 Service areas fronting on exit passageways. Mechanical rooms, electrical rooms, building service areas and service elevators are permitted to open directly into exit passageways, provided the exit passageway is separated from such rooms with not less than 1-hour fire-resistance-rated fire barriers and 1-hour opening protectives.

402.5 Mall width. For the purpose of providing required egress, malls are permitted to be considered as corridors but need not comply with the requirements of Section 1005.1 of this code where the width of the mall is as specified in this section.

402.5.1 Minimum width. The minimum width of the mall shall be 20 feet (6096 mm). The mall width shall be sufficient to accommodate the occupant load served. There shall be a minimum of 10 feet (3048 mm) clear exit width to a height of 8 feet (2438 mm) between any projection of a tenant space bordering the mall and the nearest kiosk, vending machine, bench, display opening, food court or other obstruction to means of egress travel.

402.6 Types of construction. The area of any covered mall building, including anchor buildings, of Type I, II, III and IV construction, shall not be limited provided the covered mall building and attached anchor buildings and parking garages are surrounded on all sides by a permanent open space of not less than 60 feet (18 288 mm) and the anchor buildings do not exceed three stories in height. The allowable height and area of anchor buildings greater than three stores in height shall comply with Section 503, as modified by Sections 504 and 506. The construction type of open parking garages and enclosed parking garages shall comply with Sections 406.3 and 406.4, respectively.

402.7 Fire-resistance-rated separation. Fire-resistance-rated separation is not required between tenant spaces and the mall. Fire-resistance-rated separation is not required between a food court and adjacent tenant spaces or the mall.

402.7.1 Attached garage. An attached garage for the storage of passenger vehicles having a capacity of not more than nine persons and open parking garages shall be considered as a separate building where it is separated from the covered mall building by a fire barrier having a fire-resistance rating of at least 2 hours.

Exception: Where an open parking garage or enclosed parking garage is separated from the covered mall building or anchor building a distance greater than 10 feet (3048 mm), the provisions of Table 602 shall apply. Pedestrian walkways and tunnels which attach the open parking garage or enclosed parking garage to the covered mall building or anchor building shall be constructed in accordance with Section 3104.

402.7.2 Tenant separations. Each tenant space shall be separated from other tenant spaces by a fire partition complying with Section 708. A tenant separation wall is not required between any tenant space and the mall.

402.7.3 Anchor building separation. An anchor building shall be separated from the covered mall building by fire walls complying with Section 705.

Exception: Anchor buildings of not more than three stories above grade plane that have an occupancy classification the same as that permitted for tenants of the covered mall building shall be separated by 2-hour fire-resistive fire barriers complying with Section 706.

402.7.3.1 Openings between anchor building and mall. Except for the separation between Group R-1 sleeping units and the mall, openings between anchor buildings of Type IA, IB, IIA and IIB construction and the mall need not be protected.

[F] 402.8 Automatic sprinkler system. The covered mall building and buildings connected shall be equipped throughout with an automatic sprinkler system in accordance with Section 903.3.1.1, which shall comply with the following:

1. The automatic sprinkler system shall be complete and operative throughout occupied space in the covered mall building prior to occupancy of any of the tenant spaces. Unoccupied tenant spaces shall be similarly protected unless provided with approved alternate protection.

2. Sprinkler protection for the mall shall be independent from that provided for tenant spaces or anchors. Where tenant spaces are supplied by the same system, they shall be independently controlled.

Exception: An automatic sprinkler system shall not be required in spaces or areas of open parking garages constructed in accordance with Section 406.2.

402.8.1 Standpipe system. The covered mall building shall be equipped throughout with a standpipe system as required by Section 905.3.3.

402.9 Smoke control. A smoke control system shall be provided where required for atriums in Section 404.

402.10 Kiosks. Kiosks and similar structures (temporary or permanent) shall meet the following requirements:

1. Combustible kiosks or other structures shall not be located within the mall unless constructed of any of the following materials:

    1.1. Fire-retardant-treated wood complying with Section 2303.2.

    1.2. Foam plastics having a maximum heat release rate not greater than 100kW (105 Btu/h) when tested in accordance with the exhibit booth protocol in UL 1975.

    1.3. Aluminum composite material (ACM) having a flame spread index of not more than 25 and a smoke-developed index of not more than 450 when tested as an assembly in the maximum thickness intended for use in accordance with ASTM E 84.

2. Kiosks or similar structures located within the mall shall be provided with approved fire suppression and detection devices.

3. The minimum horizontal separation between kiosks or groupings thereof and other structures within the mall shall be 20 feet (6096 mm).

4. Each kiosk or similar structure or groupings thereof shall have a maximum area of 300 square feet (28 m²).

402.11 Children's playground structures. Structures intended as children's playgrounds that exceed 10 feet (3048 mm) in height and 150 square feet (14 m²) in area shall comply with the following.

402.11.1 Materials. Children's playground structures shall be constructed of noncombustible materials or of combustible materials that comply with the following:

1. Fire-retardant-treated wood.

2. Light-transmitting plastics complying with Section 2606.

3. Foam plastics (including the pipe foam used in soft-contained play equipment structures) having a maximum heat-release rate not greater than 100 kW when tested in accordance with UL 1975.

4. Aluminum composite material (ACM) meeting the requirements of Class A interior finish in accor-

dance with Chapter 8 when tested as an assembly in the maximum thickness intended for use.

5. Textiles and films complying with the flame propagation performance criteria contained in NFPA 701.

6. Plastic materials used to construct rigid components of soft-contained play equipment structures (such as tubes, windows, panels, junction boxes, pipes, slides and decks) meeting the UL 94 V-2 classification when tested in accordance with UL 94.

7. Ball pool balls, used in soft-contained play equipment structures, having a maximum heat release rate not greater than 100 kW when tested in accordance with UL 1975. The minimum specimen test size shall be 36 inches by 36 inches (914 mm by 914 mm) by an average of 21 inches (533 mm) deep, and the balls shall be held in a box constructed of galvanized steel poultry netting wire mesh.

8. Foam plastics shall be covered by a fabric, coating or film meeting the flame propagation performance criteria of NFPA 701.

9. The floor covering placed under the children's playground structure shall exhibit a Class I interior floor finish classification, as described in Section 804, when tested in accordance with NFPA 253.

402.11.2 Fire protection. Children's playground structures located within the mall shall be provided with the same level of approved fire suppression and detection devices required for kiosks and similar structures.

402.11.3 Separation. Children's playground structures shall have a minimum horizontal separation from other structures within the mall of 20 feet (6090 mm).

402.11.4 Area limits. Children's playground structures shall not exceed 300 square feet (28 m²) in area, unless a special investigation has demonstrated adequate fire safety.

402.12 Security grilles and doors. Horizontal sliding or vertical security grilles or doors that are a part of a required means of egress shall conform to the following:

1. They shall remain in the full open position during the period of occupancy by the general public.

2. Doors or grilles shall not be brought to the closed position when there are 10 or more persons occupying spaces served by a single exit or 50 or more persons occupying spaces served by more than one exit.

3. The doors or grilles shall be openable from within without the use of any special knowledge or effort where the space is occupied.

4. Where two or more exits are required, not more than one-half of the exits shall be permitted to include either a horizontal sliding or vertical rolling grille or door.

402.13 Standby power. Covered mall buildings exceeding 50,000 square feet (4645 m²) shall be provided with standby power systems that are capable of operating the emergency voice/alarm communication system.

[F] 402.14 Emergency voice/alarm communication system. Covered mall buildings exceeding 50,000 square feet (4645 m²) in total floor area shall be provided with an emergency voice/alarm communication system. Emergency voice/alarm communication systems serving a mall, required or otherwise, shall be accessible to the fire department. The system shall be provided in accordance with Section 907.2.12.2.

402.15 Plastic signs. Plastic signs affixed to the storefront of any tenant space facing the mall shall be limited as specified in Sections 402.15.1 through 402.15.5.2.

402.15.1 Area. Plastic signs shall not exceed 20 percent of the wall area facing the mall.

402.15.2 Height and width. Plastic signs shall not exceed a height of 36 inches (914 mm), except if the sign is vertical, the height shall not exceed 96 inches (2438 mm) and the width shall not exceed 36 inches (914 mm).

402.15.3 Location. Plastic signs shall be located a minimum distance of 18 inches (457 mm) from adjacent tenants.

402.15.4 Plastics other than foam plastics. Plastics other than foam plastics used in signs shall be light-transmitting plastics complying with Section 2606.4 or shall have a self-ignition temperature of 650°F (343°C) or greater when tested in accordance with ASTM D 1929, and a flame spread index not greater than 75 and smoke-developed index not greater than 450 when tested in the manner intended for use in accordance with ASTM E 84 or meet the acceptance criteria of Section 803.2.1 when tested in accordance with NFPA 286.

402.15.4.1 Encasement. Edges and backs of plastic signs in the mall shall be fully encased in metal.

402.15.5 Foam plastics. Foam plastics used in signs shall have flame-retardant characteristics such that the sign has a maximum heat-release rate of 150 kilowatts when tested in accordance with UL 1975 and the foam plastics shall have the physical characteristics specified in this section. Foam plastics used in signs installed in accordance with Section 402.14 shall not be required to comply with the flame spread and smoke-developed indexes specified in Section 2603.3.

402.15.5.1 Density. The minimum density of foam plastics used in signs shall be not less than 20 pounds per cubic foot (pcf) (320 kg/m³).

402.15.5.2 Thickness. The thickness of foam plastic signs shall not be greater than $^1/_2$ inch (12.7 mm).

[F] 402.16 Fire department access to equipment. Rooms or areas containing controls for air-conditioning systems, automatic fire-extinguishing systems or other detection, suppression or control elements shall be identified for use by the fire department.

SECTION 403
HIGH-RISE BUILDINGS

403.1 Applicability. The provisions of this section shall apply to buildings with an occupied floor located more than 75 feet (22 860 mm) above the lowest level of fire department vehicle access.

Exception: The provisions of this section shall not apply to the following buildings and structures:

1. Airport traffic control towers in accordance with Section 412.

2. Open parking garages in accordance with Section 406.3.

3. Buildings with an occupancy in Group A-5 in accordance with Section 303.1.

4. Low-hazard special industrial occupancies in accordance with Section 503.1.1.

5. Buildings with an occupancy in Group H-1, H-2 or H-3 in accordance with Section 415.

[F] 403.2 Automatic sprinkler system. Buildings and structures shall be equipped throughout with an automatic sprinkler system in accordance with Section 903.3.1.1 and a secondary water supply where required by Section 903.3.5.2.

Exception: An automatic sprinkler system shall not be required in spaces or areas of:

1. Open parking garages in accordance with Section 406.3.

2. Telecommunications equipment buildings used exclusively for telecommunications equipment, associated electrical power distribution equipment, batteries and standby engines, provided that those spaces or areas are equipped throughout with an automatic fire detection system in accordance with Section 907.2 and are separated from the remainder of the building by fire barriers consisting of not less than 1-hour fire-resistance-rated walls and 2-hour fire-resistance-rated floor/ceiling assemblies.

403.3 Reduction in fire-resistance rating. The fire-resistance-rating reductions listed in Sections 403.3.1 and 403.3.2 shall be allowed in buildings that have sprinkler control valves equipped with supervisory initiating devices and water-flow initiating devices for each floor.

403.3.1 Type of construction. The following reductions in the minimum construction type allowed in Table 601 shall be allowed as provided in Section 403.3:

1. For buildings not greater than 420 feet (128 m) in height, Type IA construction shall be allowed to be reduced to Type IB.

   Exception: The required fire-resistance rating of columns supporting floors shall not be allowed to be reduced.

2. In other than Groups F-1, M and S-1, Type IB construction shall be allowed to be reduced to Type IIA.

3. The height and area limitations of the reduced construction type shall be allowed to be the same as for the original construction type.

403.3.2 Shaft enclosures. For buildings not greater than 420 feet (128 m) in height, the required fire-resistance rating of the fire barriers enclosing vertical shafts, other than exit enclosures and elevator hoistway enclosures, shall be reduced to 1 hour where automatic sprinklers are installed within the shafts at the top and at alternate floor levels.

403.4 Emergency escape and rescue. Emergency escape and rescue openings required by Section 1026 are not required.

[F] 403.5 Automatic fire detection. Smoke detection shall be provided in accordance with Section 907.2.12.1.

[F] 403.6 Emergency voice/alarm communication systems. An emergency voice/alarm communication system shall be provided in accordance with Section 907.2.12.2.

[F] 403.7 Fire department communications system. A two-way fire department communications system shall be provided for fire department use in accordance with Section 907.2.12.3.

[F] 403.8 Fire command. A fire command center complying with Section 911 shall be provided in a location approved by the fire department.

403.9 Elevators. Elevator operation and installation shall be in accordance with Chapter 30.

[F] 403.10 Standby power. A standby power system complying with Section 2702 shall be provided for standby power loads specified in Section 403.10.2.

403.10.1 Special requirements for standby power systems. If the standby system is a generator set inside a building, the system shall be located in a separate room enclosed with 2-hour fire barriers constructed in accordance with Section 706 or horizontal assemblies constructed in accordance with Section 711, or both. System supervision with manual start and transfer features shall be provided at the fire command center.

[F] 403.10.2 Standby power loads. The following are classified as standby power loads:

1. Power and lighting for the fire command center required by Section 403.8;

2. Electrically powered fire pumps; and

3. Ventilation and automatic fire detection equipment for smokeproof enclosures.

Standby power shall be provided for elevators in accordance with Sections 1007.4 and 3003.

[F] 403.11 Emergency power systems. An emergency power system complying with Section 2702 shall be provided for emergency power loads specified in Section 403.11.1.

[F] 403.11.1 Emergency power loads. The following are classified as emergency power loads:

1. Exit signs and means of egress illumination required by Chapter 10;

2. Elevator car lighting;

3. Emergency voice/alarm communications systems;

4. Automatic fire detection systems; and

5. Fire alarm systems.

403.12 Stairway door operation. Stairway doors other than the exit discharge doors shall be permitted to be locked from stairway side. Stairway doors that are locked from the stairway side shall be capable of being unlocked simultaneously without unlatching upon a signal from the fire command center.

403.12.1 Stairway communications system. A telephone or other two-way communications system connected to an approved constantly attended station shall be provided at not less than every fifth floor in each required stairway where the doors to the stairway are locked.

403.13 Smokeproof exit enclosures. Every required stairway serving floors more than 75 feet (22 860 mm) above the lowest level of fire department vehicle access shall comply with Sections 909.20 and 1020.1.7.

403.14 Seismic considerations. For seismic considerations, see Chapter 16.

SECTION 404
ATRIUMS

404.1 General. In other than Group H occupancies, and where permitted by Exception 5 in Section 707.2, the provisions of this section shall apply to buildings or structures containing vertical openings defined herein as "Atriums."

404.1.1 Definition. The following word and term shall, for the purposes of this chapter and as used elsewhere in this code, have the meaning shown herein.

ATRIUM. An opening connecting two or more stories other than enclosed stairways, elevators, hoistways, escalators, plumbing, electrical, air-conditioning or other equipment, which is closed at the top and not defined as a mall. Stories, as used in this definition, do not include balconies within assembly groups or mezzanines that comply with Section 505.

404.2 Use. The floor of the atrium shall not be used for other than low fire hazard uses and only approved materials and decorations in accordance with the *Fire Code of New York State* shall be used in the atrium space.

Exception: The atrium floor area is permitted to be used for any approved use where the individual space is provided with an automatic sprinkler system in accordance with Section 903.3.1.1.

[F] 404.3 Automatic sprinkler protection. An approved automatic sprinkler system shall be installed throughout the entire building.

Exceptions:

1. That area of a building adjacent to or above the atrium need not be sprinklered, provided that portion of the building is separated from the atrium portion by not less than a 2-hour fire-resistance-rated fire barrier or horizontal assembly, or both.

2. Where the ceiling of the atrium is more than 55 feet (16 764 mm) above the floor, sprinkler protection at the ceiling of the atrium is not required.

404.4 Smoke control. A smoke control system shall be installed in accordance with Section 909.

> **Exception:** Smoke control is not required for atriums that connect only two stories.

404.5 Enclosure of atriums. Atrium spaces shall be separated from adjacent spaces by a 1-hour fire barrier constructed in accordance with Section 706 or a horizontal assembly constructed in accordance with Section 711, or both.

> **Exceptions:**
>
> 1. A glass wall forming a smoke partition where automatic sprinklers are spaced 6 feet (1829 mm) or less along both sides of the separation wall, or on the room side only if there is not a walkway on the atrium side, and between 4 inches and 12 inches (102 mm and 305 mm) away from the glass and designed so that the entire surface of the glass is wet upon activation of the sprinkler system without obstruction. The glass shall be installed in a gasketed frame so that the framing system deflects without breaking (loading) the glass before the sprinkler system operates.
>
> 2. A glass-block wall assembly in accordance with Section 2110 and having a $^3/_4$-hour fire protection rating.
>
> 3. The adjacent spaces of any three floors of the atrium shall not be required to be separated from the atrium where such spaces are included in the design of the smoke control system.

[F] 404.6 Standby power. Equipment required to provide smoke control shall be connected to a standby power system in accordance with Section 909.11.

404.7 Interior finish. The interior finish of walls and ceilings of the atrium shall not be less than Class B with no reduction in class for sprinkler protection.

404.8 Travel distance. In other than the lowest level of the atrium, where the required means of egress is through the atrium space, the portion of exit access travel distance within the atrium space shall not exceed 200 feet (60 960 mm).

SECTION 405
UNDERGROUND BUILDINGS

405.1 General. The provisions of this section apply to building spaces having a floor level used for human occupancy more than 30 feet (9144 mm) below the lowest level of exit discharge.

> **Exceptions:**
>
> 1. One- and two-family dwellings, sprinklered in accordance with Section 903.3.1.3.
>
> 2. Parking garages with automatic sprinkler systems in compliance with Section 405.3.

3. Fixed guideway transit systems.

4. Grandstands, bleachers, stadiums, arenas and similar facilities.

5. Where the lowest story is the only story that would qualify the building as an underground building and has an area not exceeding 1,500 square feet (139 m^2) and has an occupant load less than 10.

405.2 Construction requirements. The underground portion of the building shall be of Type I construction.

[F] 405.3 Automatic sprinkler system. The highest level of exit discharge serving the underground portions of the building and all levels below shall be equipped with an automatic sprinkler system installed in accordance with Section 903.3.1.1. Water-flow switches and control valves shall be supervised in accordance with Section 903.4.

405.4 Compartmentation. Compartmentation shall be in accordance with Sections 405.4.1 through 405.4.3.

> **405.4.1 Number of compartments.** A building having a floor level more than 60 feet (18 288 mm) below the lowest level of exit discharge shall be divided into a minimum of two compartments of approximately equal size. Such compartmentation shall extend through the highest level of exit discharge serving the underground portions of the building and all levels below.
>
> > **Exception:** The lowest story need not be compartmented where the area does not exceed 1,500 square feet (139 m^2) and has an occupant load of less than 10.
>
> **405.4.2 Smoke barrier penetration.** The compartments shall be separated from each other by a smoke barrier in accordance with Section 709. Penetrations between the two compartments shall be limited to plumbing and electrical piping and conduit that are firestopped in accordance with Section 712. Doorways shall be protected by fire door assemblies that are automatic closing by smoke detection in accordance with Section 715.4.7.3 and are installed in accordance with NFPA 105 and Section 715.4.3. Where provided, each compartment shall have an air supply and an exhaust system independent of the other compartments.
>
> **405.4.3 Elevators.** Where elevators are provided, each compartment shall have direct access to an elevator. Where an elevator serves more than one compartment, an elevator lobby shall be provided and shall be separated from each compartment by a smoke barrier in accordance with Section 709. Doors shall be gasketed, have a drop sill and be automatic closing by smoke detection in accordance with Section 715.4.7.3.

[F] 405.5 Smoke control system. A smoke control system shall be provided in accordance with Sections 405.5.1 and 405.5.2.

> **[F] 405.5.1 Control system.** A smoke control system is required to control the migration of products of combustion in accordance with Section 909 and the provisions of this section. Smoke control shall restrict movement of smoke to the general area of fire origin and maintain means of egress in a usable condition.

405.5.2 Compartment smoke control system. Where compartmentation is required, each compartment shall have an independent smoke control system. The system shall be automatically activated and capable of manual operation in accordance with Section 907.2.18.

[F] 405.6 Fire alarm systems. A fire alarm system shall be provided where required by Section 907.2.19.

[F] 405.7 Public address. A public address system shall be provided where required by Section 907.2.19.1.

405.8 Means of egress. Means of egress shall be in accordance with Sections 405.8.1 and 405.8.2.

405.8.1 Number of exits. Each floor level shall be provided with a minimum of two exits. Where compartmentation is required by Section 405.4, each compartment shall have a minimum of one exit and shall also have an exit access doorway into the adjoining compartment.

405.8.2 Smokeproof enclosure. Every required stairway serving floor levels more than 30 feet (9144 mm) below its level of exit discharge shall comply with the requirements for a smokeproof enclosure as provided in Section 1020.1.7.

[F] 405.9 Standby power. A standby power system complying with Section 2702 shall be provided standby power loads specified in Section 405.9.1.

405.9.1 Standby power loads. The following loads are classified as standby power loads.

1. Smoke control system.

2. Ventilation and automatic fire detection equipment for smokeproof enclosures.

3. Fire pumps.

Standby power shall be provided for elevators in accordance with Section 3003.

405.9.2 Pick-up time. The standby power system shall pick up its connected loads within 60 seconds of failure of the normal power supply.

[F] 405.10 Emergency power. An emergency power system complying with Section 2702 shall be provided for emergency power loads specified in Section 405.10.1.

[F] 405.10.1 Emergency power loads. The following loads are classified as emergency power loads:

1. Emergency voice/alarm communications systems.

2. Fire alarm systems.

3. Automatic fire detection systems.

4. Elevator car lighting.

5. Means of egress and exit sign illumination as required by Chapter 10.

[F] 405.11 Standpipe system. The underground building shall be equipped throughout with a standpipe system in accordance with Section 905.

SECTION 406
MOTOR-VEHICLE-RELATED OCCUPANCIES

406.1 Private garages and carports.

406.1.1 Classification. Buildings or parts of buildings classified as Group U occupancies because of the use or character of the occupancy shall not exceed 1,000 square feet (93 m²) in area or one story in height except as provided in Section 406.1.2. Any building or portion thereof that exceeds the limitations specified in this section shall be classified in the occupancy group other than Group U that it most nearly resembles.

406.1.2 Area increase. Group U occupancies used for the storage of private or pleasure-type motor vehicles where no repair work is completed or fuel is dispensed are permitted to be 3,000 square feet (279 m²) when the following provisions are met:

1. For a mixed occupancy building, the exterior wall and opening protection for the Group U portion of the building shall be as required for the major occupancy of the building. For such a mixed occupancy building, the allowable floor area of the building shall be as permitted for the major occupancy contained therein.

2. For a building containing only a Group U occupancy, the exterior wall shall not be required to have a fire-resistance rating and the area of openings shall not be limited when the fire separation distance is 5 feet (1524 mm) or more.

More than one 3,000-square-foot (279 m²) Group U occupancy shall be permitted to be in the same building, provided each 3,000-square-foot (279 m²) area is separated by fire walls complying with Section 705.

406.1.3 Garages and carports. Carports shall be open on at least two sides. Carport floor surfaces shall be of approved noncombustible material. Carports not open on at least two sides shall be considered a garage and shall comply with the provisions of this section for garages.

Exception: Asphalt surfaces shall be permitted at ground level in carports.

The area of floor used for parking of automobiles or other vehicles shall be sloped to facilitate the movement of liquids to a drain or toward the main vehicle entry doorway.

406.1.4 Separation. Separations shall comply with the following:

1. The private garage shall be separated from the dwelling unit and its attic area by means of a minimum $^1/_2$-inch (12.7 mm) gypsum board applied to the garage side. Garages beneath habitable rooms shall be separated from all habitable rooms above by not less than a $^5/_8$-inch Type X gypsum board or equivalent. Door openings between a private garage and the dwelling unit shall be equipped with either solid wood doors or solid or honeycomb core steel doors not less than $1^3/_8$ inches (34.9 mm) thick, or doors in compliance with Section 715.4.3. Openings

from a private garage directly into a room used for sleeping purposes shall not be permitted. Doors shall be self-closing and self-latching.

2. Ducts in a private garage and ducts penetrating the walls or ceilings separating the dwelling unit from the garage shall be constructed of a minimum 0.019-inch (0.48 mm) sheet steel and shall have no openings into the garage.

3. A separation is not required between a Group R-3 and U carport, provided the carport is entirely open on two or more sides and there are not enclosed areas above.

406.2 Parking garages.

406.2.1 Classification. Parking garages shall be classified as either open, as defined in Section 406.3, or enclosed and shall meet the appropriate criteria in Section 406.4. Also see Section 509 for special provisions for parking garages.

406.2.2 Clear height. The clear height of each floor level in vehicle and pedestrian traffic areas shall not be less than 7 feet (2134 mm). Vehicle and pedestrian areas accommodating van-accessible parking required by Section 1106.5 shall conform to ICC/ANSI A117.1.

406.2.3 Guards. Guards shall be provided in accordance with Section 1013 at exterior and interior vertical openings on floor and roof areas where vehicles are parked or moved and where the vertical distance to the ground or surface directly below exceeds 30 inches (762 mm).

406.2.4 Vehicle barriers. Parking areas shall be provided with exterior or interior walls or vehicle barriers, except at pedestrian or vehicular accesses, designed in accordance with Section 1607.7. Vehicle barriers not less than 2 feet (607 mm) high shall be placed at the end of drive lanes, and at the end of parking spaces where the difference in adjacent floor elevation is greater than 1 foot (305 mm).

> **Exception:** Vehicle storage compartments in a mechanical access parking garage.

406.2.5 Ramps. Vehicle ramps shall not be considered as required exits unless pedestrian facilities are provided. Vehicle ramps that are utilized for vertical circulation as well as for parking shall not exceed a slope of 1:15 (6.67 percent).

406.2.6 Floor surface. Parking surfaces shall be of concrete or similar noncombustible and nonabsorbent materials.

> **Exception:** Asphalt parking surfaces are permitted at ground level.

The area of floor used for parking of automobiles or other vehicles shall be sloped to facilitate the movement of liquids to a drain or toward the main vehicle entry doorway.

406.2.7 Mixed separation. Parking garages shall be separated from other occupancies in accordance with Section 508.3.

406.2.8 Special hazards. Connection of a parking garage with any room in which there is a fuel-fired appliance shall be by means of a vestibule providing a two-doorway separation.

> **Exception:** A single door shall be allowed provided the sources of ignition in the appliance are at least 18 inches (457 mm) above the floor.

406.2.9 Attached to rooms. Openings from a parking garage directly into a room used for sleeping purposes shall not be permitted.

406.3 Open parking garages.

406.3.1 Scope. Except where specific provisions are made in the following subsections, other requirements of this code shall apply.

406.3.2 Definitions. The following words and terms shall, for the purposes of this chapter and as used elsewhere in this code, have the meanings shown herein.

MECHANICAL-ACCESS OPEN PARKING GARAGES. Open parking garages employing parking machines, lifts, elevators or other mechanical devices for vehicles moving from and to street level and in which public occupancy is prohibited above the street level.

OPEN PARKING GARAGE. A structure or portion of a structure with the openings as described in Section 406.3.3.1 on two or more sides that is used for the parking or storage of private motor vehicles as described in Section 406.3.4.

RAMP-ACCESS OPEN PARKING GARAGES. Open parking garages employing a series of continuously rising floors or a series of interconnecting ramps between floors permitting the movement of vehicles under their own power from and to the street level.

406.3.3 Construction. Open parking garages shall be of Type I, II or IV construction. Open parking garages shall meet the design requirements of Chapter 16. For vehicle barriers, see Section 406.2.4.

406.3.3.1 Openings. For natural ventilation purposes, the exterior side of the structure shall have uniformly distributed openings on two or more sides. The area of such openings in exterior walls on a tier must be at least 20 percent of the total perimeter wall area of each tier. The aggregate length of the openings considered to be providing natural ventilation shall constitute a minimum of 40 percent of the perimeter of the tier. Interior walls shall be at least 20 percent open with uniformly distributed openings.

> **Exception:** Openings are not required to be distributed over 40 percent of the building perimeter where the required openings are uniformly distributed over two opposing sides of the building.

406.3.4 Uses. Mixed uses shall be allowed in the same building as an open parking garage subject to the provisions of Sections 508.3, 402.7.1, 406.3.13, 509.3, 509.4 and 509.7.

406.3.5 Area and height. Area and height of open parking garages shall be limited as set forth in Chapter 5 for Group

S-2 occupancies and as further provided for in Section 508.3.

406.3.5.1 Single use. When the open parking garage is used exclusively for the parking or storage of private motor vehicles, with no other uses in the building, the area and height shall be permitted to comply with Table 406.3.5, along with increases allowed by Section 406.3.6.

Exception: The grade-level tier is permitted to contain an office, waiting and toilet rooms having a total combined area of not more than 1,000 square feet (93 m²). Such area need not be separated from the open parking garage.

In open parking garages having a spiral or sloping floor, the horizontal projection of the structure at any cross section shall not exceed the allowable area per parking tier. In the case of an open parking garage having a continuous spiral floor, each 9 feet 6 inches (2896 mm) of height, or portion thereof, shall be considered a tier.

The clear height of a parking tier shall not be less than 7 feet (2134 mm), except that a lower clear height is permitted in mechanical-access open parking garages where approved by the building official.

406.3.6 Area and height increases. The allowable area and height of open parking garages shall be increased in accordance with the provisions of this section. Garages with sides open on three-fourths of the building's perimeter are permitted to be increased by 25 percent in area and one tier in height. Garages with sides open around the entire building's perimeter are permitted to be increased by 50 percent in area and one tier in height. For a side to be considered open under the above provisions, the total area of openings along the side shall not be less than 50 percent of the interior area of the side at each tier and such openings shall be equally distributed along the length of the tier.

Allowable tier areas in Table 406.3.5 shall be increased for open parking garages constructed to heights less than the table maximum. The gross tier area of the garage shall not exceed that permitted for the higher structure. At least three sides of each such larger tier shall have continuous horizontal openings not less than 30 inches (762 mm) in clear height extending for at least 80 percent of the length of the sides and no part of such larger tier shall be more than 200 feet (60 960 mm) horizontally from such an opening. In addition, each such opening shall face a street or yard accessible to a street with a width of at least 30 feet (9144 mm) for the full length of the opening, and standpipes shall be provided in each such tier.

Open parking garages of Type II construction, with all sides open, shall be unlimited in allowable area where the height does not exceed 75 feet (22 860 mm). For a side to be considered open, the total area of openings along the side shall not be less than 50 percent of the interior area of the side at each tier and such openings shall be equally distributed along the length of the tier. All portions of tiers shall be within 200 feet (60 960 mm) horizontally from such openings or other natural ventilation openings as defined in Section 406.3.3.1. These openings shall be permitted to be provided in courts with a minimum width of 30 feet (9144 mm) for the full width of the openings.

406.3.7 Fire separation distance. Exterior walls and openings in exterior walls shall comply with Tables 601 and 602. The distance to an adjacent lot line shall be determined in accordance with Table 602 and Section 704.

406.3.8 Means of egress. Where persons other than parking attendants are permitted, open parking garages shall meet the means of egress requirements of Chapter 10. Where no persons other than parking attendants are permitted, there shall not be less than two 36-inch-wide (914 mm) exit stairways. Lifts shall be permitted to be installed for use of employees only, provided they are completely enclosed by noncombustible materials.

406.3.9 Standpipes. Standpipes shall be installed where required by the provisions of Chapter 9.

406.3.10 Sprinkler systems. Where required by other provisions of this code, automatic sprinkler systems and standpipes shall be installed in accordance with the provisions of Chapter 9.

406.3.11 Enclosure of vertical openings. Enclosure shall not be required for vertical openings except as specified in Section 406.3.8.

406.3.12 Ventilation. Ventilation, other than the percentage of openings specified in Section 406.3.3.1, shall not be required.

TABLE 406.3.5
OPEN PARKING GARAGES AREA AND HEIGHT

TYPE OF CONSTRUCTION	AREA PER TIER (square feet)	HEIGHT (in tiers)		
			Mechanical access	
			Automatic sprinkler system	
		Ramp access	No	Yes
IA	Unlimited	Unlimited	Unlimited	Unlimited
IB	Unlimited	12 tiers	12 tiers	18 tiers
IIA	50,000	10 tiers	10 tiers	15 tiers
IIB	50,000	8 tiers	8 tiers	12 tiers
IV	50,000	4 tiers	4 tiers	4 tiers

For SI: 1 square foot = 0.0929 m².

406.3.13 Prohibitions. The following uses and alterations are not permitted:

1. Vehicle repair work.

2. Parking of buses, trucks and similar vehicles.

3. Partial or complete closing of required openings in exterior walls by tarpaulins or any other means.

4. Dispensing of fuel.

406.4 Enclosed parking garages.

406.4.1 Heights and areas. Enclosed vehicle parking garages and portions thereof that do not meet the definition of open parking garages shall be limited to the allowable heights and areas specified in Table 503 as modified by Sections 504, 506 and 507. Roof parking is permitted.

406.4.2 Ventilation. A mechanical ventilation system shall be provided in accordance with the *Mechanical Code of New York State*.

406.5 Motor fuel-dispensing facilities.

406.5.1 Construction. Motor fuel-dispensing facilities shall be constructed in accordance with the *Fire Code of New York State* and this section.

406.5.2 Canopies. Canopies under which fuels are dispensed shall have a clear, unobstructed height of not less than 13 feet 6 inches (4115 mm) to the lowest projecting element in the vehicle drive-through area. Canopies and their supports over pumps shall be of noncombustible materials, fire-retardant-treated wood complying with Chapter 23, wood of Type IV sizes or of construction providing 1-hour fire resistance. Combustible materials used in or on a canopy shall comply with one of the following:

1. Shielded from the pumps by a noncombustible element of the canopy, or wood of Type IV sizes;

2. Plastics covered by aluminum facing having a minimum thickness of 0.010 inch (0.30 mm) or corrosion-resistant steel having a minimum base metal thickness of 0.016 inch (0.41 mm). The plastic shall have a flame spread index of 25 or less and a smoke-developed index of 450 or less when tested in the form intended for use in accordance with ASTM E 84 and a self-ignition temperature of 650°F (343°C) or greater when tested in accordance with ASTM D 1929; or

3. Panels constructed of light-transmitting plastic materials shall be permitted to be installed in canopies erected over motor vehicle fuel-dispensing station fuel dispensers, provided the panels are located at least 10 feet (3048 mm) from any building on the same lot and face yards or streets not less than 40 feet (12 192 mm) in width on the other sides. The aggregate areas of plastics shall not exceed 1,000 square feet (93 m²). The maximum area of any individual panel shall not exceed 100 square feet (9.3 m²).

406.5.2.1 Canopies used to support gaseous hydrogen systems. Canopies that are used to shelter dispensing operations where flammable compressed gases are located on the roof of the canopy shall be in accordance with the following:

1. The canopy shall meet or exceed Type I construction requirements.

2. Operations located under canopies shall be limited to refueling only.

3. The canopy shall be constructed in a manner that prevents the accumulation of hydrogen gas.

406.6 Repair garages.

406.6.1 General. Repair garages shall be constructed in accordance with the *Fire Code of New York State* and this section. This occupancy shall not include motor fuel-dispensing facilities, as regulated in Section 406.5.

406.6.2 Mixed uses. Mixed uses shall be allowed in the same building as a repair garage subject to the provisions of Section 508.3.

406.6.3 Ventilation. Repair garages shall be mechanically ventilated in accordance with the *Mechanical Code of New York State*. The ventilation system shall be controlled at the entrance to the garage.

406.6.4 Floor surface. Repair garage floors shall be of concrete or similar noncombustible and nonabsorbent materials.

> **Exception:** Slip-resistant, nonabsorbent, interior floor finishes having a critical radiant flux not more than 0.45 W/cm², as determined by NFPA 253, shall be permitted.

406.6.5 Heating equipment. Heating equipment shall be installed in accordance with the *Mechanical Code of New York State*.

[F] 406.6.6 Gas detection system. Repair garages used for repair of vehicles fueled by nonodorized gases, such as hydrogen and nonodorized LNG, shall be provided with an approved flammable gas-detection system.

[F] 406.6.6.1 System design. The flammable gas-detection system shall be calibrated to the types of fuels or gases used by vehicles to be repaired. The gas detection system shall be designed to activate when the level of flammable gas exceeds 25 percent of the lower explosive limit. Gas detection shall also be provided in lubrication or chassis repair pits of garages used for repairing nonodorized LNG-fueled vehicles.

[F] 406.6.6.2 Operation. Activation of the gas detection system shall result in all of the following:

1. Initiation of distinct audible and visual alarm signals in the repair garage.

2. Deactivation of all heating systems located in the repair garage.

3. Activation of the mechanical ventilation system, where the system is interlocked with gas detection.

[F] 406.6.6.3 Failure of the gas detection system. Failure of the gas detection system shall result in the deactivation of the heating system, activation of the mechanical ventilation system when the system is interlocked with the gas detection system and cause a trouble signal to sound in an approved location.

SECTION 407
GROUP I-2

407.1 General. Occupancies in Group I-2 shall comply with the provisions of this section and other applicable provisions of this code.

407.2 Corridors. Corridors in occupancies in Group I-2 shall be continuous to the exits and separated from other areas in accordance with Section 407.3 except spaces conforming to Sections 407.2.1 through 407.2.4.

407.2.1 Spaces of unlimited area. Waiting areas and similar spaces constructed as required for corridors shall be permitted to be open to a corridor, only where all of the following criteria are met:

1. The spaces are not occupied for patient sleeping units, treatment rooms, hazardous or incidental use areas as defined in Section 508.2.

2. The open space is protected by an automatic fire detection system installed in accordance with Section 907.

3. The corridors onto which the spaces open, in the same smoke compartment, are protected by an automatic fire detection system installed in accordance with Section 907, or the smoke compartment in which the spaces are located is equipped throughout with quick-response sprinklers in accordance with Section 903.3.2.

4. The space is arranged so as not to obstruct access to the required exits.

407.2.2 Nurses' stations. Spaces for doctors' and nurses' charting, communications and related clerical areas shall be permitted to be open to the corridor, when such spaces are constructed as required for corridors.

407.2.3 Mental health treatment areas. Areas wherein mental health patients who are not capable of self-preservation are housed, or group meeting or multipurpose therapeutic spaces other than incidental use areas as defined in Section 508.2, under continuous supervision by facility staff, shall be permitted to be open to the corridor, where the following criteria are met:

1. Each area does not exceed 1,500 square feet (140 m^2).

2. The area is located to permit supervision by the facility staff.

3. The area is arranged so as not to obstruct any access to the required exits.

4. The area is equipped with an automatic fire detection system installed in accordance with Section 907.2.

5. Not more than one such space is permitted in any one smoke compartment.

6. The walls and ceilings of the space are constructed as required for corridors.

407.2.4 Gift shops. Gift shops less than 500 square feet (46.5 m^2) in area shall be permitted to be open to the corridor provided the gift shop and storage areas are fully sprinklered and storage areas are protected in accordance with Section 508.2.

407.3 Corridor walls. Corridor walls shall be constructed as smoke partitions in accordance with Section 710.

407.3.1 Corridor doors. Corridor doors, other than those in a wall required to be rated by Section 508.2 or for the enclosure of a vertical opening or an exit, shall not have a required fire protection rating and shall not be required to be equipped with self-closing or automatic-closing devices, but shall provide an effective barrier to limit the transfer of smoke and shall be equipped with positive latching. Roller latches are not permitted. Other doors shall conform to Section 715.4.

407.3.2 Locking devices. Locking devices that restrict access to the patient room from the corridor, and that are operable only by staff from the corridor side, shall not restrict the means of egress from the patient room except for patient rooms in mental health facilities.

407.4 Smoke barriers. Smoke barriers shall be provided to subdivide every story used by patients for sleeping or treatment and to divide other stories with an occupant load of 50 or more persons, into at least two smoke compartments. Such stories shall be divided into smoke compartments with an area of not more than 22,500 square feet (2092 m^2) and the travel distance from any point in a smoke compartment to a smoke barrier door shall not exceed 200 feet (60 960 mm). The smoke barrier shall be in accordance with Section 709.

407.4.1 Refuge area. At least 30 net square feet (2.8 m^2) per patient shall be provided within the aggregate area of corridors, patient rooms, treatment rooms, lounge or dining areas and other low-hazard areas on each side of each smoke barrier. On floors not housing patients confined to a bed or litter, at least 6 net square feet (0.56 m^2) per occupant shall be provided on each side of each smoke barrier for the total number of occupants in adjoining smoke compartments.

407.4.2 Independent egress. A means of egress shall be provided from each smoke compartment created by smoke barriers without having to return through the smoke compartment from which means of egress originated.

[F] 407.5 Automatic sprinkler system. Smoke compartments containing patient sleeping units shall be equipped throughout with an automatic fire sprinkler system in accordance with Section 903.3.1.1. The smoke compartments shall be equipped with approved quick-response or residential sprinklers in accordance with Section 903.3.2.

[F] 407.6 Automatic fire detection. Corridors in nursing homes (both intermediate care and skilled nursing facilities), detoxification facilities and spaces permitted to be open to the corridors by Section 407.2 shall be equipped with an automatic fire detection system. Hospitals shall be equipped with smoke detection as required in Section 907.2.

Exceptions:

1. Corridor smoke detection is not required where patient sleeping units are provided with smoke detectors that comply with UL 268. Such detectors shall provide a visual display on the corridor side of each patient sleeping unit and an audible and visual alarm at the nursing station attending each unit.

2. Corridor smoke detection is not required where patient sleeping unit doors are equipped with automatic door-closing devices with integral smoke detectors on the unit sides installed in accordance with their listing, provided that the integral detectors perform the required alerting function.

407.7 Secured yards. Grounds are permitted to be fenced and gates therein are permitted to be equipped with locks, provided that safe dispersal areas having 30 net square feet (2.8 m²) for bed and litter patients and 6 net square feet (0.56 m²) for ambulatory patients and other occupants are located between the building and the fence. Such provided safe dispersal areas shall not be located less than 50 feet (15 240 mm) from the building they serve.

SECTION 408
GROUP I-3

408.1 General. Occupancies in Group I-3 shall comply with the provisions of this section and other applicable provisions of this code (see Section 308.4).

408.2 Mixed occupancies. Portions of buildings with an occupancy in Group I-3 that are classified as a different occupancy shall meet the applicable requirements of this code for such occupancies. Where security operations necessitate the locking of required means of egress, provisions shall be made for the release of occupants at all times.

Means of egress from detention and correctional occupancies that traverse other use areas shall, as a minimum, conform to requirements for detention and correctional occupancies.

Exception: It is permissible to exit through a horizontal exit into other contiguous occupancies that do not conform to detention and correctional occupancy egress provisions but that do comply with requirements set forth in the appropriate occupancy, as long as the occupancy is not a high-hazard use.

408.3 Means of egress. Except as modified or as provided for in this section, the provisions of Chapter 10 shall apply.

408.3.1 Door width. Doors to resident sleeping units shall have a clear width of not less than 28 inches (711 mm).

408.3.2 Sliding doors. Where doors in a means of egress are of the horizontal-sliding type, the force to slide the door to its fully open position shall not exceed 50 pounds (220 N) with a perpendicular force against the door of 50 pounds (220 N).

408.3.3 Spiral stairs. Spiral stairs that conform to the requirements of Section 1009.8 are permitted for access to and between staff locations.

408.3.4 Exit discharge. Exits are permitted to discharge into a fenced or walled courtyard. Enclosed yards or courts shall be of a size to accommodate all occupants, a minimum of 50 feet (15 240 mm) from the building with a net area of 15 square feet (1.4 m²) per person.

408.3.5 Sallyports. A sallyport shall be permitted in a means of egress where there are provisions for continuous and unobstructed passage through the sallyport during an emergency egress condition.

408.3.6 Exit enclosures. One of the required exit enclosures in each building shall be permitted to have glazing installed in doors and interior walls at each landing level providing access to the enclosure, provided that the following conditions are met:

1. The exit enclosure shall not serve more than four floor levels.

2. Exit doors shall not be less than ³/₄-hour fire door assemblies complying with Section 715.4

3. The total area of glazing at each floor level shall not exceed 5,000 square inches (3 m²) and individual panels of glazing shall not exceed 1,296 square inches (0.84 m²).

4. The glazing shall be protected on both sides by an automatic fire sprinkler system. The sprinkler system shall be designed to wet completely the entire surface of any glazing affected by fire when actuated.

5. The glazing shall be in a gasketed frame and installed in such a manner that the framing system will deflect without breaking (loading) the glass before the sprinkler system operates.

6. Obstructions, such as curtain rods, drapery traverse rods, curtains, drapes or similar materials shall not be installed between the automatic sprinklers and the glazing.

408.4 Locks. Egress doors are permitted to be locked in accordance with the applicable use condition. Doors from an area of refuge to the exterior are permitted to be locked with a key in lieu of locking methods described in Section 408.4.1. The keys to unlock the exterior doors shall be available at all times and the locks shall be operable from both sides of the door.

408.4.1 Remote release. Remote release of locks on doors in a means of egress shall be provided with reliable means of operation, remote from the resident living areas, to release locks on all required doors. In Occupancy Conditions 3 or 4, the arrangement, accessibility and security of the release mechanism(s) required for egress shall be such that with the minimum available staff at any time, the lock mechanisms are capable of being released within 2 minutes.

Exception: Provisions for remote locking and unlocking of occupied rooms in Occupancy Condition 4 are not required provided that not more than 10 locks are necessary to be unlocked in order to move occupants from one smoke compartment to a refuge area within 3 minutes. The opening of necessary locks shall be accomplished with not more than two separate keys.

408.4.2 Power-operated doors and locks. Power-operated sliding doors or power-operated locks for swinging doors shall be operable by a manual release mechanism at the door, and either emergency power or a remote mechanical operating release shall be provided.

Exception: Emergency power is not required in facilities with 10 locks or less complying with the exception to Section 408.4.1.

408.4.3 Redundant operation. Remote release, mechanically operated sliding doors or remote release, mechanically operated locks shall be provided with a mechanically operated release mechanism at each door, or shall be provided with a redundant remote release control.

408.4.4 Relock capability. Doors remotely unlocked under emergency conditions shall not automatically relock when closed unless specific action is taken at the remote location to enable doors to relock.

408.5 Vertical openings. Vertical openings shall be enclosed in accordance with Section 707.

Exception: A floor opening between floor levels of residential housing areas is permitted without enclosure protection between the levels, provided that both of the following conditions are met:

1. The entire normally occupied areas so interconnected are open and unobstructed so as to enable observation of the areas by supervisory personnel.

2. Means of egress capacity is sufficient to provide simultaneous egress for all occupants from all interconnected levels and areas.

The height difference between the highest and lowest finished floor levels shall not exceed 23 feet (7010 mm). Each story, considered separately, has at least one-half of its individual required means of egress capacity provided by exits leading directly out of that story without traversing another story within the interconnected area.

408.6 Smoke barrier. Occupancies in Group I-3 shall have smoke barriers complying with Section 709 to divide every story occupied by residents for sleeping, or any other story having an occupant load of 50 or more persons, into at least two smoke compartments.

Exception: Spaces having a direct exit to one of the following, provided that the locking arrangement of the doors involved complies with the requirements for doors at the smoke barrier for the use condition involved:

1. A public way.

2. A building separated from the resident housing area by a 2-hour fire-resistance-rated assembly or 50 feet (15 240 mm) of open space.

3. A secured yard or court having a holding space 50 feet (15 240 mm) from the housing area that provides 6 square feet (0.56 m²) or more of refuge area per occupant, including residents, staff and visitors.

408.6.1 Smoke compartments. The maximum number of residents in any smoke compartment shall be 200. The travel distance to a door in a smoke barrier from any room door required as exit access shall not exceed 150 feet (45 720 mm). The travel distance to a door in a smoke barrier from any point in a room shall not exceed 200 feet (60 960 mm).

408.6.2 Refuge area. At least 6 net square feet (0.56 m²) per occupant shall be provided on each side of each smoke barrier for the total number of occupants in adjoining smoke compartments. This space shall be readily available wherever the occupants are moved across the smoke barrier in a fire emergency.

408.6.3 Independent egress. A means of egress shall be provided from each smoke compartment created by smoke barriers without having to return through the smoke compartment from which means of egress originates.

408.7 Subdivision of resident housing areas. Sleeping areas and any contiguous day room, group activity space or other common spaces where residents are housed shall be separated from other spaces in accordance with Sections 408.7.1 through 408.7.4.

408.7.1 Occupancy Conditions 3 and 4. Each sleeping area in Occupancy Conditions 3 and 4 shall be separated from the adjacent common spaces by a smoke-tight partition where the travel distance from the sleeping area through the common space to the corridor exceeds 50 feet (15 240 mm).

408.7.2 Occupancy Condition 5. Each sleeping area in Occupancy Condition 5 shall be separated from adjacent sleeping areas, corridors and common spaces by a smoke-tight partition. Additionally, common spaces shall be separated from the corridor by a smoke-tight partition.

408.7.3 Openings in room face. The aggregate area of openings in a solid sleeping room face in Occupancy Conditions 2, 3, 4 and 5 shall not exceed 120 square inches (77 419 mm²). The aggregate area shall include all openings including door undercuts, food passes and grilles. Openings shall be not more than 36 inches (914 mm) above the floor. In Occupancy Condition 5, the openings shall be closeable from the room side.

408.7.4 Smoke-tight doors. Doors in openings in partitions required to be smoke tight by Section 408.7 shall be substantial doors, of construction that will resist the passage of smoke. Latches and door closures are not required on cell doors.

408.8 Windowless buildings. For the purposes of this section, a windowless building or portion of a building is one with nonopenable windows, windows not readily breakable or without windows. Windowless buildings shall be provided with an engineered smoke control system to provide ventilation (mechanical or natural) in accordance with Section 909 for each windowless smoke compartment.

SECTION 409
MOTION PICTURE PROJECTION ROOMS

409.1 General. The provisions of this section shall apply to rooms in which ribbon-type cellulose acetate or other safety film is utilized in conjunction with electric arc, xenon or other light-source projection equipment that develops hazardous gases, dust or radiation. Where cellulose nitrate film is utilized or stored, such rooms shall comply with NFPA 40.

409.1.1 Projection room required. Every motion picture machine projecting film as mentioned within the scope of this section shall be enclosed in a projection room. Appurtenant electrical equipment, such as rheostats, transformers and generators, shall be within the projection room or in an adjacent room of equivalent construction.

409.2 Construction of projection rooms. Every projection room shall be of permanent construction consistent with the construction requirements for the type of building in which the projection room is located. Openings are not required to be protected.

The room shall have a floor area of not less than 80 square feet (7.44 m²) for a single machine and at least 40 square feet (3.7 m²) for each additional machine. Each motion picture projector, floodlight, spotlight or similar piece of equipment shall have a clear working space of not less than 30 inches by 30 inches (762 mm by 762 mm) on each side and at the rear thereof, but only one such space shall be required between two adjacent projectors. The projection room and the rooms appurtenant thereto shall have a ceiling height of not less than 7 feet 6 inches (2286 mm). The aggregate of openings for projection equipment shall not exceed 25 percent of the area of the wall between the projection room and the auditorium. Openings shall be provided with glass or other approved material, so as to close completely the opening.

409.3 Projection room and equipment ventilation. Ventilation shall be provided in accordance with the *Mechanical Code of New York State*.

409.3.1 Supply air. Each projection room shall be provided with adequate air supply inlets so arranged as to provide well-distributed air throughout the room. Air inlet ducts shall provide an amount of air equivalent to the amount of air being exhausted by projection equipment. Air is permitted to be taken from the outside; from adjacent spaces within the building, provided the volume and infiltration rate is sufficient; or from the building air-conditioning system, provided it is so arranged as to provide sufficient air when other systems are not in operation.

409.3.2 Exhaust air. Projection rooms are permitted to be exhausted through the lamp exhaust system. The lamp exhaust system shall be positively interconnected with the lamp so that the lamp will not operate unless there is the required airflow. Exhaust air ducts shall terminate at the exterior of the building in such a location that the exhaust air cannot be readily recirculated into any air supply system. The projection room ventilation system is permitted to also serve appurtenant rooms, such as the generator and rewind rooms.

409.3.3 Projection machines. Each projection machine shall be provided with an exhaust duct that will draw air from each lamp and exhaust it directly to the outside of the building. The lamp exhaust is permitted to serve to exhaust air from the projection room to provide room air circulation. Such ducts shall be of rigid materials, except for a flexible connector approved for the purpose. The projection lamp or projection room exhaust system, or both, is permitted to be combined but shall not be interconnected with any other exhaust or return system, or both, within the building.

409.4 Lighting control. Provisions shall be made for control of the auditorium lighting and the means of egress lighting systems of theaters from inside the projection room and from at least one other convenient point in the building.

409.5 Miscellaneous equipment. Each projection room shall be provided with rewind and film storage facilities.

SECTION 410
STAGES AND PLATFORMS

410.1 Applicability. The provisions of this section shall apply to all parts of buildings and structures that contain stages or platforms and similar appurtenances as herein defined.

410.2 Definitions. The following words and terms shall, for the purposes of this section and as used elsewhere in this code, have the meanings shown herein.

FLY GALLERY. A raised floor area above a stage from which the movement of scenery and operation of other stage effects are controlled.

GRIDIRON. The structural framing over a stage supporting equipment for hanging or flying scenery and other stage effects.

PINRAIL. A rail on or above a stage through which belaying pins are inserted and to which lines are fastened.

PLATFORM. A raised area within a building used for worship, the presentation of music, plays or other entertainment; the head table for special guests; the raised area for lecturers and speakers; boxing and wrestling rings; theater-in-the-round stages; and similar purposes wherein there are no overhead hanging curtains, drops, scenery or stage effects other than lighting and sound. A temporary platform is one installed for not more than 30 days.

PROSCENIUM WALL. The wall that separates the stage from the auditorium or assembly seating area.

STAGE. A space within a building utilized for entertainment or presentations, which includes overhead hanging curtains, drops, scenery or stage effects other than lighting and sound.

410.3 Stages. Stage construction shall comply with Sections 410.3.1 through 410.3.7.

410.3.1 Stage construction. Stages shall be constructed of materials as required for floors for the type of construction of the building in which such stages are located.

Exceptions:

1. Stages of Type IIB or IV construction with a nominal 2-inch (51 mm) wood deck, provided

that the stage is separated from other areas in accordance with Section 410.3.4.

2. In buildings of Type IIA, IIIA and VA construction, a fire-resistance-rated floor is not required, provided the space below the stage is equipped with an automatic fire-extinguishing system in accordance with Section 903 or 904.

3. In all types of construction, the finished floor shall be constructed of wood or approved noncombustible materials. Openings through stage floors shall be equipped with tight-fitting, solid wood trap doors with approved safety locks.

410.3.1.1 Stage height and area. Stage areas shall be measured to include the entire performance area and adjacent backstage and support areas not separated from the performance area by fire-resistance-rated construction. Stage height shall be measured from the lowest point on the stage floor to the highest point of the roof or floor deck above the stage.

410.3.2 Galleries, gridirons, catwalks and pinrails. Beams designed only for the attachment of portable or fixed theater equipment, gridirons, galleries and catwalks shall be constructed of approved materials consistent with the requirements for the type of construction of the building; and a fire-resistance rating shall not be required. These areas shall not be considered to be floors, stories, mezzanines or levels in applying this code.

Exception: Floors of fly galleries and catwalks shall be constructed of any approved material.

410.3.3 Exterior stage doors. Where protection of openings is required, exterior exit doors shall be protected with fire door assemblies that comply with Section 715. Exterior openings that are located on the stage for means of egress or loading and unloading purposes, and that are likely to be open during occupancy of the theater, shall be constructed with vestibules to prevent air drafts into the auditorium.

410.3.4 Proscenium wall. Where the stage height is greater than 50 feet (15 240 mm), all portions of the stage shall be completely separated from the seating area by a proscenium wall with not less than a 2-hour fire-resistance rating extending continuously from the foundation to the roof.

410.3.5 Proscenium curtain. Where a proscenium wall is required to have a fire-resistance rating, the stage opening shall be provided with a fire curtain of approved material or an approved water curtain complying with Section 903.3.1.1. The fire curtain shall be designed and installed to intercept hot gases, flames and smoke and to prevent a glow from a severe fire on the stage from showing on the auditorium side for a period of 20 minutes. The closing of the fire curtain from the full open position shall be accomplished in less than 30 seconds, with the last 8 feet (2438 mm) of travel requiring 5 or more seconds for full closure.

410.3.5.1 Activation. The curtain shall be activated by rate-of-rise heat detection installed in accordance with Section 907.10 operating at a rate of temperature rise of 15 to 20°F per minute (8 to 11°C per minute), and by an auxiliary manual control.

410.3.5.2 Fire test. A sample curtain with a minimum of two vertical seams shall be subjected to the standard fire test specified in ASTM E 119 for a period of 30 minutes. The curtain shall overlap the furnace edges by an amount that is appropriate to seal the top and sides. The curtain shall have a bottom pocket containing a minimum of 4 pounds per linear foot (5.9 kg/m) of batten. The exposed surface of the curtain shall not glow, and flame or smoke shall not penetrate the curtain during the test period. Unexposed surface temperature and hose stream test requirements are not applicable to the proscenium fire safety curtain test.

410.3.5.3 Smoke test. Curtain fabrics shall have a smoke-developed rating of 25 or less when tested in accordance with ASTM E 84.

410.3.5.4 Tests. The completed proscenium curtain shall be subjected to operating tests prior to the issuance of a certificate of occupancy.

410.3.6 Scenery. Combustible materials used in sets and scenery shall meet the fire propagation performance criteria of NFPA 701, in accordance with Section 806 and the *Fire Code of New York State*. Foam plastics and materials containing foam plastics shall comply with Section 2603 and the *Fire Code of New York State*.

410.3.7 Stage ventilation. Emergency ventilation shall be provided for stages larger than 1,000 square feet (93 m²) in floor area, or with a stage height greater than 50 feet (15 240 mm). Such ventilation shall comply with Section 410.3.7.1 or 410.3.7.2.

410.3.7.1 Roof vents. Two or more vents constructed to open automatically by approved heat-activated devices and with an aggregate clear opening area of not less than 5 percent of the area of the stage shall be located near the center and above the highest part of the stage area. Supplemental means shall be provided for manual operation of the ventilator. Curbs shall be provided as required for skylights in Section 2610.2. Vents shall be labeled.

[F] 410.3.7.2 Smoke control. Smoke control in accordance with Section 909 shall be provided to maintain the smoke layer interface not less than 6 feet (1829 mm) above the highest level of the assembly seating or above the top of the proscenium opening where a proscenium wall is provided in compliance with Section 410.3.4.

410.4 Platform construction. Permanent platforms shall be constructed of materials as required for the type of construction of the building in which the permanent platform is located. Permanent platforms are permitted to be constructed of fire-retardant-treated wood for Type I, II, and IV construction where the platforms are not more than 30 inches (762 mm) above the main floor, and not more than one-third of the room floor area and not more than 3,000 square feet (279 m²) in area. Where the space beneath the permanent platform is used for storage or any other purpose other than equipment, wiring or plumbing, the floor construction shall not be less than 1-hour fire-resistance-rated construction. Where the space beneath the permanent platform is used only for equipment, wiring or plumbing, the underside of the permanent platform need not be protected.

410.4.1 Temporary platforms. Platforms installed for a period of not more than 30 days are permitted to be constructed of any materials permitted by the code. The space between the floor and the platform above shall only be used for plumbing and electrical wiring to platform equipment.

410.5 Dressing and appurtenant rooms. Dressing and appurtenant rooms shall comply with Sections 410.5.1 through 410.5.3.

410.5.1 Separation from stage. Where the stage height is greater than 50 feet (15 240 mm), the stage shall be separated from dressing rooms, scene docks, property rooms, workshops, storerooms and compartments appurtenant to the stage and other parts of the building by a fire barrier with not less than a 2-hour fire-resistance rating with approved opening protectives. For stage heights of 50 feet (15 240 mm) or less, the required stage separation shall be a fire barrier with not less than a 1-hour fire-resistance rating with approved opening protectives.

410.5.2 Separation from each other. Dressing rooms, scene docks, property rooms, workshops, storerooms and compartments appurtenant to the stage shall be separated from each other by fire barriers with not less than a 1-hour fire-resistance rating with approved opening protectives.

410.5.3 Stage exits. At least one approved means of egress shall be provided from each side of the stage and from each side of the space under the stage. At least one means of escape shall be provided from each fly gallery and from the gridiron. A steel ladder, alternating tread stairway or spiral stairway is permitted to be provided from the gridiron to a scuttle in the stage roof.

[F] 410.6 Automatic sprinkler system. Stages shall be equipped with an automatic fire-extinguishing system in accordance with Chapter 9. Sprinklers shall be installed under the roof and gridiron and under all catwalks and galleries over the stage. Sprinklers shall be installed in dressing rooms, performer lounges, shops and storerooms accessory to such stages.

Exceptions:

1. Sprinklers are not required under stage areas less than 4 feet (1219 mm) in clear height that are utilized exclusively for storage of tables and chairs, provided the concealed space is separated from the adjacent spaces by not less than $^5/_8$-inch (15.9 mm) Type X gypsum board.

2. Sprinklers are not required for stages 1,000 square feet (93 m^2) or less in area and 50 feet (15 240 mm) or less in height where curtains, scenery or other combustible hangings are not retractable vertically. Combustible hangings shall be limited to a single main curtain, borders, legs and a single backdrop.

3. Sprinklers are not required within portable orchestra enclosures on stages.

[F] 410.7 Standpipes. Standpipe systems shall be provided in accordance with Section 905.

SECTION 411
SPECIAL AMUSEMENT BUILDINGS

411.1 General. Special amusement buildings having an occupant load of 50 or more shall comply with the requirements for the appropriate Group A occupancy and this section. Amusement buildings having an occupant load of less than 50 shall comply with the requirements for a Group B occupancy and this section.

Exception: Amusement buildings or portions thereof that are without walls or a roof and constructed to prevent the accumulation of smoke.

For flammable decorative materials, see the *Fire Code of New York State.*

411.2 Special amusement building. A special amusement building is any temporary or permanent building or portion thereof that is occupied for amusement, entertainment or educational purposes and that contains a device or system that conveys passengers or provides a walkway along, around or over a course in any direction so arranged that the means of egress path is not readily apparent due to visual or audio distractions or is intentionally confounded or is not readily available because of the nature of the attraction or mode of conveyance through the building or structure.

[F] 411.3 Automatic fire detection. Special amusement buildings shall be equipped with an automatic fire detection system in accordance with Section 907.

[F] 411.4 Automatic sprinkler system. Special amusement buildings shall be equipped throughout with an automatic sprinkler system in accordance with Section 903.3.1.1. Where the special amusement building is temporary, the sprinkler water supply shall be of an approved temporary means.

Exception: Automatic sprinklers are not required where the total floor area of a temporary special amusement building is less than 1,000 square feet (93 m^2) and the travel distance from any point to an exit is less than 50 feet (15 240 mm).

[F] 411.5 Alarm. Actuation of a single smoke detector, the automatic sprinkler system or other automatic fire detection device shall immediately sound an alarm at the building at a constantly attended location from which emergency action can be initiated including the capability of manual initiation of requirements in Section 907.2.11.2.

[F] 411.6 Emergency voice/alarm communications system. An emergency voice/alarm communications system shall be provided in accordance with Sections 907.2.11 and 907.2.12.2, which is also permitted to serve as a public address system and shall be audible throughout the entire special amusement building.

411.7 Exit marking. Exit signs shall be installed at the required exit or exit access doorways of amusement buildings. Approved directional exit markings shall also be provided. Where mirrors, mazes or other designs are utilized that disguise the path of egress travel such that they are not apparent, approved low-level exit signs and directional path markings shall be provided and located not more than 8 inches (203 mm) above the walking surface and on or near the path of egress travel. Such markings shall become visible in an emergency. The directional exit marking shall be activated by the automatic fire detection system and the automatic sprinkler system in accordance with Section 907.2.11.2.

411.8 Interior finish. The interior finish shall be Class A in accordance with Section 803.1.

SECTION 412
AIRCRAFT-RELATED OCCUPANCIES

412.1 Airport traffic control towers.

412.1.1 General. The provisions of this section shall apply to airport traffic control towers not exceeding 1,500 square feet (140 m^2) per floor occupied only for the following uses:

1. Airport traffic control cab.

2. Electrical and mechanical equipment rooms.

3. Airport terminal radar and electronics rooms.

4. Office spaces incidental to the tower operation.

5. Lounges for employees, including sanitary facilities.

412.1.2 Type of construction. Airport traffic control towers shall be constructed to comply with the height and area limitations of Table 412.1.2.

TABLE 412.1.2
HEIGHT AND AREA LIMITATIONS FOR AIRPORT TRAFFIC CONTROL TOWERS

TYPE OF CONSTRUCTION	HEIGHT[a] (feet)	MAXIMUM AREA (square feet)
IA	Unlimited	1,500
IB	240	1,500
IIA	100	1,500
IIB	85	1,500
IIIA	65	1,500

For SI: 1 foot = 304.8 mm, 1 square foot = 0.0929 m^2.

a. Height to be measured from grade plane to cab floor.

412.1.3 Egress. A minimum of one exit stairway shall be permitted for airport traffic control towers of any height provided that the occupant load per floor does not exceed 15. The stairway shall conform to the requirements of Section 1009. The stairway shall be separated from elevators by a minimum distance of one-half of the diagonal of the area served measured in a straight line. The exit stairway and elevator hoistway are permitted to be located in the same shaft enclosure, provided they are separated from each other by a 4-hour fire barrier having no openings. Such stairway shall be pressurized to a minimum of 0.15 inch of water column (43 Pa) and a maximum of 0.35 inch of water column (101 Pa) in the shaft relative to the building with stairway doors closed. Stairways need not extend

to the roof as specified in Section 1009.11. The provisions of Section 403 do not apply.

Exception: Smokeproof enclosures as set forth in Section 1020.1.7 are not required where required stairways are pressurized.

[F] 412.1.4 Automatic fire detection systems. Airport traffic control towers shall be provided with an automatic fire detection system installed in accordance with Section 907.2.

[F] 412.1.5 Standby power. A standby power system that conforms to Section 2702 shall be provided in airport traffic control towers more than 65 feet (19 812 mm) in height. Power shall be provided to the following equipment:

1. Pressurization equipment, mechanical equipment and lighting.

2. Elevator operating equipment.

3. Fire alarm and smoke detection systems.

412.1.6 Accessibility. Airport traffic control towers need not be accessible as specified in the provisions of Chapter 11.

412.2 Aircraft hangars. Aircraft hangars shall be in accordance with Sections 412.2.1 through 412.2.6.

412.2.1 Exterior walls. Exterior walls located less than 30 feet (9 144 mm) from property lines, lot lines or a public way shall have a fire-resistance rating not less than 2 hours.

412.2.2 Basements. Where hangars have basements, the floor over the basement shall be of Type IA construction and shall be made tight against seepage of water, oil or vapors. There shall be no opening or communication between the basement and the hangar. Access to the basement shall be from outside only.

412.2.3 Floor surface. Floors shall be graded and drained to prevent water or fuel from remaining on the floor. Floor drains shall discharge through an oil separator to the sewer or to an outside vented sump.

Exception: Aircraft hangars with individual lease spaces not exceeding 2,000 square feet (186 m^2) each in which servicing, repairing or washing is not conducted and fuel is not dispensed shall have floors that are graded toward the door, but shall not require a separator.

412.2.4 Heating equipment. Heating equipment shall be placed in another room separated by 2-hour fire-resistance-rated construction. Entrance shall be from the outside or by means of a vestibule providing a two-doorway separation.

Exceptions:

1. Unit heaters and vented infrared radiant heating equipment suspended at least 10 feet (3048 mm) above the upper surface of wings or engine enclosures of the highest aircraft that are permitted to be housed in the hangar and at least 8 feet (2438 mm) above the floor in shops, offices and

other sections of the hangar communicating with storage or service areas.

2. A single interior door shall be allowed, provided the sources of ignition in the appliances are at least 18 inches (457 mm) above the floor.

412.2.5 Finishing. The process of "doping," involving use of a volatile flammable solvent, or of painting, shall be carried on in a separate detached building equipped with automatic fire-extinguishing equipment in accordance with Section 903.

[F] 412.2.6 Fire suppression. Aircraft hangars shall be provided with fire suppression as required by NFPA 409.

> **Exception:** Group II hangars as defined in NFPA 409 storing private aircraft without major maintenance or overhaul are exempt from foam suppression requirements.

412.3 Residential aircraft hangars. Residential aircraft hangars as defined in Section 412.3.1 shall comply with Sections 412.3.2 through 412.3.6.

412.3.1 Definition. The following word and term shall, for the purposes of this chapter and as used elsewhere in this code, have the meaning shown herein.

RESIDENTIAL AIRCRAFT HANGAR. An accessory building less than 2,000 square feet (186 m²) and 20 feet (6096 mm) in height, constructed on a one- or two-family residential property where aircraft are stored. Such use will be considered as a residential accessory use incidental to the dwelling.

412.3.2 Fire separation. A hangar shall not be attached to a dwelling unless separated by a fire barrier having a fire-resistance rating of not less than 1 hour. Such separation shall be continuous from the foundation to the underside of the roof and unpierced except for doors leading to the dwelling unit. Doors into the dwelling unit must be equipped with self-closing devices and conform to the requirements of Section 715 with at least a 4-inch (102 mm) noncombustible raised sill. Openings from a hanger directly into a room used for sleeping purposes shall not be permitted.

412.3.3 Egress. A hangar shall provide two means of egress. One of the doors into the dwelling shall be considered as meeting only one of the two means of egress.

[F] 412.3.4 Smoke alarms. Smoke alarms shall be provided within the hangar in accordance with Section 907.2.21.

412.3.5 Independent systems. Electrical, mechanical and plumbing drain, waste and vent (DWV) systems installed within the hangar shall be independent of the systems installed within the dwelling. Building sewer lines shall be permitted to be connect outside the structures.

> **Exception:** Smoke detector wiring and feed for electrical subpanels in the hangar.

412.3.6 Height and area limits. Residential aircraft hangars shall not exceed 2,000 square feet (186 m²) in area and 20 feet (6096 mm) in height.

[F] 412.4 Aircraft paint hangars. Aircraft painting operations where flammable liquids are used in excess of the maximum allowable quantities per control area listed in Table 307.7(1) shall be conducted in an aircraft paint hangar that complies with the provisions of Section 412.4.

[F] 412.4.1 Occupancy group. Aircraft paint hangars shall be classified as Group H-2. Aircraft paint hangars shall comply with the applicable requirements of this code and the *Fire Code of New York State* for such occupancy.

412.4.2 Construction. The aircraft paint hangar shall be of Type I or II construction.

[F] 412.4.3 Operations. Only those flammable liquids necessary for painting operations shall be permitted in quantities less than the maximum allowable quantities per control area in Table 307.1(1). Spray equipment cleaning operations shall be conducted in a liquid use, dispensing and mixing room.

[F] 412.4.4 Storage. Storage of flammable liquids shall be in a liquid storage room.

[F] 412.4.5 Fire suppression. Aircraft paint hangars shall be provided with fire suppression as required by NFPA 409.

412.4.6 Ventilation. Aircraft paint hangars shall be provided with ventilation as required in the *Mechanical Code of New York State*.

412.5 Heliports and helistops. Heliports and helistops shall be permitted to be erected on buildings or other locations where they are constructed in accordance with this section.

412.5.1 Definitions. The following words and terms shall, for the purposes of this chapter and as used elsewhere in this code, have the meanings shown herein.

HELIPORT. An area of land or water or a structural surface that is used, or intended for use, for the landing and taking off of helicopters, and any appurtenant areas that are used, or intended for use, for heliport buildings and other heliport facilities.

HELISTOP. The same as a "Heliport," except that no fueling, defueling, maintenance, repairs or storage of helicopters is permitted.

412.5.2 Size. The landing area for helicopters less than 3,500 pounds (1588 kg) shall be a minimum of 20 feet (6096 mm) in length and width. The landing area shall be surrounded on all sides by a clear area having a minimum average width at roof level of 15 feet (4572 mm) but with no width less than 5 feet (1524 mm).

412.5.3 Design. Helicopter landing areas and the supports thereof on the roof of a building shall be noncombustible construction. Landing areas shall be designed to confine any flammable liquid spillage to the landing area itself and provisions shall be made to drain such spillage away from any exit or stairway serving the helicopter landing area or from a structure housing such exit or stairway. For structural design requirements, see Section 1605.5.

412.5.4 Means of egress. The means of egress from heliports and helistops shall comply with the provisions of Chapter 10. Landing areas located on buildings or structures shall have two or more means of egress. For landing areas less than 60 feet (18 288 mm) in length, or less than 2,000 square feet (186 m²) in area, the second means of egress may be a fire escape or ladder leading to the floor below.

412.5.5 Rooftop heliports and helistops. Rooftop heliports and helistops shall comply with NFPA 418.

SECTION 413
COMBUSTIBLE STORAGE

413.1 General. High-piled stock or rack storage in any occupancy group shall comply with the *Fire Code of New York State*.

413.2 Attic, under-floor and concealed spaces. Attic, under-floor and concealed spaces used for storage of combustible materials shall be protected on the storage side as required for 1-hour fire-resistance-rated construction. Openings shall be protected by assemblies that are self-closing and are of noncombustible construction or solid wood core not less than $1^3/_4$ inch (45 mm) in thickness.

Exceptions:

1. Areas protected by approved automatic sprinkler systems.

2. Group R-3 and U occupancies.

SECTION 414
HAZARDOUS MATERIALS

[F] 414.1 General. The provisions of this section shall apply to buildings and structures occupied for the manufacturing, processing, dispensing, use or storage of hazardous materials.

[F] 414.1.1 Other provisions. Buildings and structures with an occupancy in Group H shall also comply with the applicable provisions of Section 415 and the *Fire Code of New York State*.

[F] 414.1.2 Materials. The safe design of hazardous material occupancies is material dependent. Individual material requirements are also found in Sections 307 and 415, and in the *Mechanical Code of New York State* and the *Fire Code of New York State*.

[F] 414.1.2.1 Aerosols. Level 2 and 3 aerosol products shall be stored and displayed in accordance with the *Fire Code of New York State*. See Section 311.2 and the *Fire Code of New York State* for occupancy group requirements.

[F] 414.1.3 Information required. Separate floor plans shall be submitted for buildings and structures with an occupancy in Group H, identifying the locations of anticipated contents and processes so as to reflect the nature of each occupied portion of every building and structure. A report identifying hazardous materials including, but not limited to, materials representing hazards that are classified in Group H to be stored or used, shall be submitted and the methods of protection from such hazards shall be indicated on the construction documents. The opinion and report shall be prepared by a qualified person, firm or corporation approved by the building official and shall be provided without charge to the enforcing agency.

[F] 414.2 Control areas. Control areas shall comply with Sections 414.2.1 through 414.2.5 and the *Fire Code of New York State*.

414.2.1 Construction requirements. Control areas shall be separated from each other by fire barriers constructed in accordance with Section 706 or horizontal assemblies constructed in accordance with Section 711, or both.

[F] 414.2.2 Percentage of maximum allowable quantities. The percentage of maximum allowable quantities of hazardous materials per control area permitted at each floor level within a building shall be in accordance with Table 414.2.2.

[F] 414.2.3 Number. The maximum number of control areas within a building shall be in accordance with Table 414.2.2.

414.2.4 Fire-resistance-rating requirements. The required fire-resistance rating for fire barriers shall be in accordance with Table 414.2.2. The floor construction of the control area and the construction supporting the floor

[F] TABLE 414.2.2
DESIGN AND NUMBER OF CONTROL AREAS

FLOOR LEVEL		PERCENTAGE OF THE MAXIMUM ALLOWABLE QUANTITY PER CONTROL AREAª	NUMBER OF CONTROL AREAS PER FLOOR	FIRE-RESISTANCE RATING FOR FIRE BARRIERS IN HOURSᵇ
Above grade plane	Higher than 9	5	1	2
	7-9	5	2	2
	6	12.5	2	2
	5	12.5	2	2
	4	12.5	2	2
	3	50	2	1
	2	75	3	1
	1	100	4	1
Below grade plane	1	75	3	1
	2	50	2	1
	Lower than 2	Not Allowed	Not Allowed	Not Allowed

a. Percentages shall be of the maximum allowable quantity per control area shown in Tables 307.1(1) and 307.1(2), with all increases allowed in the notes to those tables.

b. Fire barriers shall include walls and floors as necessary to provide separation from other portions of the building.

of the control area shall have a minimum 2-hour fire-resistance rating.

Exception: The floor construction of the control area and the construction supporting the floor of the control area is allowed to be 1-hour fire-resistance rated in buildings of Type IIA, IIIA and VA construction, provided that both of the following conditions exist:

1. The building is equipped throughout with an automatic sprinkler system in accordance with Section 903.3.1.1, and

2. The building is three stories or less in height.

[F] 414.2.5 Hazardous material in Group M display and storage areas and in Group S storage areas. The aggregate quantity of nonflammable solid and nonflammable or noncombustible liquid hazardous materials permitted within a single control area of a Group M display and storage area, a Group S storage area or an outdoor control area is permitted to exceed the maximum allowable quantities per control area specified in Tables 307.1(1) and 307.1(2) without classifying the building or use as a Group H occupancy, provided that the materials are displayed and stored in accordance with the *Fire Code of New York State* and quantities do not exceed the maximum allowable specified in Table 414.2.5(1).

In Group M occupancy wholesale and retail sales uses, indoor storage of flammable and combustible liquids shall not exceed the maximum allowable quantities per control area as indicated in Table 414.2.5(2), provided that the materials are displayed and stored in accordance with the *Fire Code of New York State*.

The maximum quantity of aerosol products in Group M occupancy retail display areas, storage areas adjacent to retail display areas and retail storage areas shall be in accordance with the *Fire Code of New York State*.

[F] 414.3 Ventilation. Rooms, areas or spaces of Group H in which explosive, corrosive, combustible, flammable or highly toxic dusts, mists, fumes, vapors or gases are or may be emitted due to the processing, use, handling or storage of

[F] TABLE 414.2.5(1)
MAXIMUM ALLOWABLE QUANTITY PER INDOOR AND OUTDOOR CONTROL AREA IN GROUP M AND S OCCUPANCIES
NONFLAMMABLE SOLIDS AND NONFLAMMABLE AND NONCOMBUSTIBLE LIQUIDS [d,e,f]

CONDITION		MAXIMUM ALLOWABLE QUANTITY PER CONTROL AREA	
Material[a]	Class	Solids pounds	Liquids gallons
A. Health-hazard materials-nonflammable and noncombustible solids and liquids			
1. Corrosives[b, c]	Not Applicable	9,750	975
2. Highly toxics	Not Applicable	20[b, c]	2[b, c]
3. Toxics[b, c]	Not Applicable	1,000	100
B. Physical-hazard materials-nonflammable and noncombustible solids and liquids			
1. Oxidizers[b, c]	4	Not Allowed	Not Allowed
	3	1,150[g]	115
	2	2,250[h]	225
	1	18,000[i, j]	1,800[i, j]
2. Unstable (reactives)[b, c]	4	Not Allowed	Not Allowed
	3	550	55
	2	1,150	115
	1	Not Limited	Not Limited
3. Water (reactives)	3[b, c]	550	55
	2[b, c]	1,150	115
	1	Not Limited	Not Limited

For SI: 1 pound = 0.454 kg, 1 gallon = 3.785 L.

a. Hazard categories are as specified in the *Fire Code of New York State*.

b. Maximum allowable quantities shall be increased 100 percent in buildings that are sprinklered in accordance with Section 903.3.1.1. When Note c also applies, the increase for both notes shall be applied accumulatively.

c. Maximum allowable quantities shall be increased 100 percent when stored in approved storage cabinets, in accordance with the *Fire Code of New York State*. When Note b also applies, the increase for both notes shall be applied accumulatively.

d. See Table 414.2.2 for design and number of control areas.

e. Allowable quantities for other hazardous material categories shall be in accordance with Section 307.

f. Maximum quantities shall be increased 100 percent in outdoor control areas.

g. Maximum amounts are permitted to be increased to 2,250 pounds when individual packages are in the original sealed containers from the manufacturer or packager and do not exceed 10 pounds each.

h. Maximum amounts are permitted to be increased to 4,500 pounds when individual packages are in the original sealed containers from the manufacturer or packager and do not exceed 10 pounds each.

i. The permitted quantities shall not be limited in a building equipped throughout with an automatic sprinkler system in accordance with Section 903.3.1.1.

j. Quantities are unlimited in an outdoor control area.

materials shall be mechanically ventilated as required by the *Fire Code of New York State* and the *Mechanical Code of New York State*.

Ducts conveying explosives or flammable vapors, fumes or dusts shall extend directly to the exterior of the building without entering other spaces. Exhaust ducts shall not extend into or through ducts and plenums.

Exception: Ducts conveying vapor or fumes having flammable constituents less than 25 percent of their lower flammable limit (LFL) are permitted to pass through other spaces.

Emissions generated at workstations shall be confined to the area in which they are generated as specified in the *Fire Code of New York State* and the *Mechanical Code of New York State*.

The location of supply and exhaust openings shall be in accordance with the *Mechanical Code of New York State*. Exhaust air contaminated by highly toxic material shall be treated in accordance with the *Fire Code of New York State*.

A manual shutoff control for ventilation equipment required by this section shall be provided outside the room adjacent to the principal access door to the room. The switch shall be of the break-glass type and shall be labeled: VENTILATION SYSTEM EMERGENCY SHUTOFF.

[F] 414.4 Hazardous material systems. Systems involving hazardous materials shall be suitable for the intended application. Controls shall be designed to prevent materials from entering or leaving process or reaction systems at other than the intended time, rate or path. Automatic controls, where provided, shall be designed to be fail safe.

[F] 414.5 Inside storage, dispensing and use. The inside storage, dispensing and use of hazardous materials in excess of the maximum allowable quantities per control area of Tables 307.1(1) and 307.1(2) shall be in accordance with

Sections 414.5.1 through 414.5.5 of this code and the *Fire Code of New York State*.

[F] 414.5.1 Explosion control. Explosion control shall be provided in accordance with the *Fire Code of New York State* as required by Table 414.5.1 where quantities of hazardous materials specified in that table exceed the maximum allowable quantities in Table 307.1(1) or where a structure, room or space is occupied for purposes involving explosion hazards as required by Section 415 or the *Fire Code of New York State*.

[F] 414.5.2 Monitor control equipment. Monitor control equipment shall be provided where required by the *Fire Code of New York State*.

[F] 414.5.3 Automatic fire detection systems. Group H occupancies shall be provided with an automatic fire detection system in accordance with Section 907.2.

414.5.4 Standby or emergency power. Where mechanical ventilation, treatment systems, temperature control, alarm, detection or other electrically operated systems are required, such systems shall be provided with an emergency *or standby power system in accordance with Chapter 27* of the *Building Code of New York State*.

Exceptions:

1. Storage areas for Class I and II oxidizers.

2. Storage areas for Class III, IV and V organic peroxides.

3. Storage, use and handling areas for highly toxic or toxic materials as provided for in the *Fire Code of New York State*.

4. Standby power for mechanical ventilation, treatment systems and temperature control systems shall not be required where an approved fail-safe engineered system is installed.

[F] TABLE 414.2.5(2)
MAXIMUM ALLOWABLE QUANTITY OF FLAMMABLE AND COMBUSTIBLE LIQUIDS IN WHOLESALE AND RETAIL SALES OCCUPANCIES PER CONTROL AREA[a]

TYPE OF LIQUID	MAXIMUM ALLOWABLE QUANTITY PER CONTROL AREA (gallons)		
	Sprinklered in accordance with Note B densities and arrangements	Sprinklered in accordance with Tables 3404.3.6.3(4) through 3404.3.6.3(8) and Table 3404.3.7.5.1 of the *Fire Code of New York State*	Nonsprinklered
Class IA	60	60	30
Class IB, IC, II and IIIA	7,500[c]	15,000[c]	1,600
Class IIIB	Unlimited	Unlimited	13,200

For SI: 1 foot = 304.8 mm, 1 square foot = 0.0929 m^2, 1 gallon = 3.785 L, 1 gallon per minute per square foot = 40.75 L/min/m^2.

a. Control areas shall be separated from each other by not less than a 1-hour fire barrier wall.

b. To be considered as sprinklered, a building shall be equipped throughout with an approved automatic sprinkler system with a design providing minimum densities as follows:

    1. For uncartoned commodities on shelves 6 feet or less in height where the ceiling height does not exceed 18 feet, quantities are those permitted with a minimum sprinkler design density of Ordinary Hazard Group 2.

    2. For cartoned, palletized or racked commodities where storage is 4 feet 6 inches or less in height and where the ceiling height does not exceed 18 feet, quantities are those permitted with a minimum sprinkler design density of 0.21 gallon per minute per square foot over the most remote 1,500-square-foot area.

c. Where wholesale and retail sales or storage areas exceed 50,000 square feet in area, the maximum allowable quantities are allowed to be increased by 2 percent for each 1,000 square feet of area in excess of 50,000 square feet, up to a maximum of 100 percent of the table amounts. A control area separation is not required. The cumulative amounts, including amounts attained by having an additional control area, shall not exceed 30,000 gallons.

[F] TABLE 414.5.1
EXPLOSION CONTROL REQUIREMENTS[a]

MATERIAL	CLASS	EXPLOSION CONTROL METHODS	
		Barricade construction	Explosion (deflagration) venting or explosion (deflagration) prevention systems[b]
HAZARD CATEGORY			
Combustible dusts[c]	-	Not Required	Required
Cryogenic flammables	-	Not Required	Required
Explosives	Division 1.1	Required	Not Required
	Division 1.2	Required	Not Required
	Division 1.3	Not Required	Required
	Division 1.4	Not Required	Required
	Division 1.5	Required	Not Required
	Division 1.6	Required	Not Required
Flammable gas	Gaseous	Not Required	Required
	Liquefied	Not Required	Required
Flammable liquid	IA[d]	Not Required	Required
	IB[e]	Not Required	Required
Organic peroxides	U	Required	Not Permitted
	I	Required	Not Permitted
Oxidizer liquids and solids	4	Required	Not Permitted
Pyrophoric gas	-	Not Required	Required
Unstable (reactive)	4	Required	Not Permitted
	3 Detonable	Required	Not Permitted
	3 Nondetonable	Not Required	Required
Water-reactive liquids and solids	3	Not Required	Required
	2[g]	Not Required	Required
SPECIAL USES			
Acetylene generator rooms	-	Not Required	Required
Grain processing	-	Not Required	Required
Liquefied petroleum gas- distribution facilities	-	Not Required	Required
Where explosion hazards exist[f]	Detonation	Required	Not Permitted
	Deflagration	Not Required	Required

a. See Section 414.1.3.

b. See the *Fire Code of New York State*.

c. As generated during manufacturing or processing. See definition of "Combustible dust" in Chapter 3.

d. Storage or use.

e. In open use or dispensing.

f. Rooms containing dispensing and use of hazardous materials when an explosive environment can occur because of the characteristics or nature of the hazardous materials or as a result of the dispensing or use process.

g. A method of explosion control shall be provided when Class 2 water-reactive materials can form potentially explosive mixtures.

[F] 414.5.5 Spill control, drainage and containment. Rooms, buildings or areas occupied for the storage of solid and liquid hazardous materials shall be provided with a means to control spillage and to contain or drain off spillage and fire protection water discharged in the storage area where required in the *Fire Code of New York State*. The methods of spill control shall be in accordance with the *Fire Code of New York State*.

[F] 414.6 Outdoor storage, dispensing and use. The outdoor storage, dispensing and use of hazardous materials shall be in accordance with the *Fire Code of New York State*.

[F] 414.6.1 Weather protection. Where weather protection is provided for sheltering outdoor hazardous material storage or use areas, such areas shall be considered outdoor storage or use when the weather protection structure complies with Sections 414.6.1.1 through 414.6.1.3.

[F] 414.6.1.1 Walls. Walls shall not obstruct more than one side of the structure.

Exception: Walls shall be permitted to obstruct portions of multiple sides of the structure, provided that the obstructed area does not exceed 25 percent of the structure's perimeter.

[F] 414.6.1.2 Separation distance. The distance from the structure to buildings, lot lines, public ways or means of egress to a public way shall not be less than the distance required for an outside hazardous material storage or use area without weather protection.

[F] 414.6.1.3 Noncombustible construction. The overhead structure shall be of approved noncombustible construction with a maximum area of 1,500 square feet (140 m²).

Exception: The increases permitted by Section 506 apply.

[F] 414.7 Emergency alarms. Emergency alarms for the detection and notification of an emergency condition in Group H occupancies shall be provided as set forth herein.

[F] 414.7.1 Storage. An approved manual emergency alarm system shall be provided in buildings, rooms or areas used for storage of hazardous materials. Emergency alarm-initiating devices shall be installed outside of each interior exit or exit access door of storage buildings, rooms or areas. Activation of an emergency alarm-initiating device shall sound a local alarm to alert occupants of an emergency situation involving hazardous materials.

[F] 414.7.2 Dispensing, use and handling. Where hazardous materials having a hazard ranking of 3 or 4 in accordance with NFPA 704 are transported through corridors or exit enclosures, there shall be an emergency telephone system, a local manual alarm station or an approved alarm-initiating device at not more than 150-foot (45 720 mm) intervals and at each exit and exit access doorway throughout the transport route. The signal shall be relayed to an approved central, proprietary or remote station service or constantly attended on-site location and shall also initiate a local audible alarm.

[F] 414.7.3 Supervision. Emergency alarm systems shall be supervised by an approved central, proprietary or remote station service or shall initiate an audible and visual signal at a constantly attended on-site location.

SECTION 415
GROUPS H-1, H-2, H-3, H-4 AND H-5

[F] 415.1 Scope. The provisions of this section shall apply to the storage and use of hazardous materials in excess of the maximum allowable quantities per control area listed in Section 307.1. Buildings and structures with an occupancy in Group H shall also comply with the applicable provisions of Section 414 and the *Fire Code of New York State*.

[F] 415.2 Definitions. The following words and terms shall, for the purposes of this chapter and as used elsewhere in the code, have the meanings shown herein.

[F] CONTINUOUS GAS-DETECTION SYSTEM. A gas detection system where the analytical instrument is maintained in continuous operation and sampling is performed without interruption. Analysis is allowed to be performed on a cyclical basis at intervals not to exceed 30 minutes.

[F] EMERGENCY CONTROL STATION. An approved location on the premises where signals from emergency equipment are received and which is staffed by trained personnel.

[F] EXHAUSTED ENCLOSURE. An appliance or piece of equipment that consists of a top, a back and two sides providing a means of local exhaust for capturing gases, fumes, vapors and mists. Such enclosures include laboratory hoods, exhaust fume hoods and similar appliances and equipment used to locally retain and exhaust the gases, fumes, vapors and mists that could be released. Rooms or areas provided with general ventilation, in themselves, are not exhausted enclosures.

[F] FABRICATION AREA. An area within a semiconductor fabrication facility and related research and development areas in which there are processes using hazardous production materials. Such areas are allowed to include ancillary rooms or areas such as dressing rooms and offices that are directly related to the fabrication area processes.

[F] FLAMMABLE VAPORS OR FUMES. The concentration of flammable constituents in air that exceed 25 percent of their lower flammable limit (LFL).

[F] GAS CABINET. A fully enclosed, noncombustible enclosure used to provide an isolated environment for compressed gas cylinders in storage or use. Doors and access ports for exchanging cylinders and accessing pressure-regulating controls are allowed to be included.

[F] GAS ROOM. A separately ventilated, fully enclosed room in which only compressed gases and associated equipment and supplies are stored or used.

[F] HAZARDOUS PRODUCTION MATERIAL (HPM). A solid, liquid or gas associated with semiconductor manufacturing that has a degree-of-hazard rating in health, flammability or reactivity of Class 3 or 4 as ranked by NFPA 704 and which is used directly in research, laboratory or production processes that have as their end product materials that are not hazardous.

[F] HPM FLAMMABLE LIQUID. An HPM liquid that is defined as either a Class I flammable liquid or a Class II or Class IIIA combustible liquid.

[F] HPM ROOM. A room used in conjunction with or serving a Group H-5 occupancy, where HPM is stored or used and which is classified as a Group H-2, H-3 or H-4 occupancy.

[F] IMMEDIATELY DANGEROUS TO LIFE AND HEALTH (IDLH). The concentration of air-borne contaminants which poses a threat of death, immediate or delayed permanent adverse health effects, or effects that could prevent escape from such an environment. This contaminant concentration level is established by the National Institute of Occupational Safety and Health (NIOSH) based on both toxicity and flammability. It generally is expressed in parts per million by volume (ppm v/v) or milligrams per cubic meter (mg/m^3). If adequate data do not exist for precise establishment of IDLH concentrations, an independent certified industrial hygienist, industrial toxicologist, appropriate regulatory agency or other source approved by the code official shall make such determination.

[F] LIQUID. A material that has a melting point that is equal to or less than 68°F (20°C) and a boiling point that is greater than 68°F (20°C) at 14.7 pounds per square inch absolute (psia) (101 kPa). When not otherwise identified, the term "liquid" includes both flammable and combustible liquids.

[F] LIQUID STORAGE ROOM. A room classified as a Group H-3 occupancy used for the storage of flammable or combustible liquids in a closed condition.

[F] LIQUID USE, DISPENSING AND MIXING ROOMS. Rooms in which Class I, II and IIIA flammable or combustible liquids are used, dispensed or mixed in open containers.

[F] LOWER FLAMMABLE LIMIT (LFL). The minimum concentration of vapor in air at which propagation of flame will occur in the presence of an ignition source. The LFL is sometimes referred to as "LEL" or "lower explosive limit."

NORMAL TEMPERATURE AND PRESSURE (NTP). A temperature of 70°F (21°C) and a pressure of 1 atmosphere [14.7 psia (101 kPa)].

[F] PHYSIOLOGICAL WARNING THRESHOLD LEVEL. A concentration of air-borne contaminants, normally expressed in parts per million (ppm) or milligrams per cubic meter, that represents the concentration at which persons can sense the presence of the contaminant due to odor, irritation or other quick-acting physiological response. When used in conjunction with the permissible exposure limit (PEL) the physiological warning threshold levels are those consistent with the classification system used to establish the PEL. See the definition of "Permissible exposure limit (PEL)" in the *Fire Code of New York State*.

[F] SERVICE CORRIDOR. A fully enclosed passage used for transporting HPM and purposes other than required means of egress.

[F] SOLID. A material that has a melting point, decomposes or sublimes at a temperature greater than 68°F (20°C).

[F] STORAGE, HAZARDOUS MATERIALS.

1. The keeping, retention or leaving of hazardous materials in closed containers, tanks, cylinders or similar vessels, or

2. Vessels supplying operations through closed connections to the vessel.

[F] USE (MATERIAL). Placing a material into action, including solids, liquids and gases.

[F] WORKSTATION. A defined space or an independent principal piece of equipment using HPM within a fabrication area where a specific function, laboratory procedure or research activity occurs. Approved or listed hazardous materials storage cabinets, flammable liquid storage cabinets or gas cabinets serving a workstation are included as part of the workstation. A workstation is allowed to contain ventilation equipment, fire protection devices, detection devices, electrical devices and other processing and scientific equipment.

[F] 415.3 Fire separation distance. Group H occupancies shall be located on property in accordance with the other provisions of this chapter. In Groups H-2 and H-3, not less than 25 percent of the perimeter wall of the occupancy shall be an exterior wall.

Exceptions:

1. Liquid use, dispensing and mixing rooms having a floor area of not more than 500 square feet (46.5 m²) need not be located on the outer perimeter of the building where they are in accordance with the *Fire Code of New York State* and NFPA 30.

2. Liquid storage rooms having a floor area of not more than 1,000 square feet (93 m²) need not be located on the outer perimeter where they are in accordance with the *Fire Code of New York State* and NFPA 30.

3. Spray paint booths that comply with the *Fire Code of New York State* need not be located on the outer perimeter.

[F] 415.3.1 Group H occupancy minimum fire separation distance. Regardless of any other provisions, buildings containing Group H occupancies shall be set back to the minimum fire separation distance as set forth in Items 1 through 4 below. Distances shall be measured from the walls enclosing the occupancy to lot lines, including those on a public way. Distances to assumed lot lines established for the purpose of determining exterior wall and opening protection are not to be used to establish the minimum fire separation distance for buildings on sites where explosives are manufactured or used when separation is provided in accordance with the quantity distance tables specified for explosive materials in the *Fire Code of New York State*.

1. Group H-1. Not less than 75 feet (22 860 mm) and not less than required by the *Fire Code of New York State*.

Exceptions:

1. Fireworks manufacturing buildings separated in accordance with NFPA 1124.

2. Buildings containing the following materials when separated in accordance with Table 415.3.1:

   2.1. Organic peroxides, unclassified detonable.

   2.2. Unstable reactive materials, Class 4.

   2.3. Unstable reactive materials, Class 3 detonable.

   2.4. Detonable pyrophoric materials.

2. Group H-2. Not less than 30 feet (9144 mm) where the area of the occupancy exceeds 1,000 square feet (93 m²) and it is not required to be located in a detached building.

3. Groups H-2 and H-3. Not less than 50 feet (15 240 mm) where a detached building is required (see Table 415.3.2).

4. Groups H-2 and H-3. Occupancies containing materials with explosive characteristics shall be separated as required by the *Fire Code of New York State*. Where separations are not specified, the distances required shall not be less than the distances required by Table 415.3.1.

[F] 415.3.2 Group H-1 and H-2 or H-3 detached buildings. Where a detached building is required by Table 415.3.2, there are no requirements for wall and opening protection based on fire separation distance.

TABLE 415.3.1
MINIMUM SEPARATION DISTANCES FOR BUILDINGS CONTAINING EXPLOSIVE MATERIALS

QUANTITY OF EXPLOSIVE MATERIAL[a]		MINIMUM DISTANCE (feet)		
		Lot lines[b] and inhabited buildings[c]		
Pounds over	Pounds not over	Barricaded[d]	Unbarricaded	Separation of magazines[d, e, f]
2	5	70	140	12
5	10	90	180	16
10	20	110	220	20
20	30	125	250	22
30	40	140	280	24
40	50	150	300	28
50	75	170	340	30
75	100	190	380	32
100	125	200	400	36
125	150	215	430	38
150	200	235	470	42
200	250	255	510	46
250	300	270	540	48
300	400	295	590	54
400	500	320	640	58
500	600	340	680	62
600	700	355	710	64
700	800	375	750	66
800	900	390	780	70
900	1,000	400	800	72
1,000	1,200	425	850	78
1,200	1,400	450	900	82
1,400	1,600	470	940	86
1,600	1,800	490	980	88
1,800	2,000	505	1,010	90
2,000	2,500	545	1,090	98
2,500	3,000	580	1,160	104
3,000	4,000	635	1,270	116
4,000	5,000	685	1,370	122
5,000	6,000	730	1,460	130
6,000	7,000	770	1,540	136
7,000	8,000	800	1,600	144
8,000	9,000	835	1,670	150
9,000	10,000	865	1,730	156
10,000	12,000	875	1,750	164
12,000	14,000	885	1,770	174
14,000	16,000	900	1,800	180
16,000	18,000	940	1,880	188
18,000	20,000	975	1,950	196
20,000	25,000	1,055	2,000	210
25,000	30,000	1,130	2,000	224
30,000	35,000	1,205	2,000	238
35,000	40,000	1,275	2,000	248
40,000	45,000	1,340	2,000	258
45,000	50,000	1,400	2,000	270

(continued)

TABLE 415.3.1—CONTINUED
MINIMUM SEPARATION DISTANCES FOR BUILDINGS CONTAINING EXPLOSIVE MATERIALS

QUANTITY OF EXPLOSIVE MATERIAL[a]		MINIMUM DISTANCE (feet)		
		Lot lines[b] and inhabited buildings[c]		
Pounds over	Pounds not over	Barricaded[d]	Unbarricaded	Separation of magazines[d, e, f]
50,000	55,000	1,460	2,000	280
55,000	60,000	1,515	2,000	290
60,000	65,000	1,565	2,000	300
65,000	70,000	1,610	2,000	310
70,000	75,000	1,655	2,000	320
75,000	80,000	1,695	2,000	330
80,000	85,000	1,730	2,000	340
85,000	90,000	1,760	2,000	350
90,000	95,000	1,790	2,000	360
95,000	100,000	1,815	2,000	370
100,000	110,000	1,835	2,000	390
110,000	120,000	1,855	2,000	410
120,000	130,000	1,875	2,000	430
130,000	140,000	1,890	2,000	450
140,000	150,000	1,900	2,000	470
150,000	160,000	1,935	2,000	490
160,000	170,000	1,965	2,000	510
170,000	180,000	1,990	2,000	530
180,000	190,000	2,010	2,010	550
190,000	200,000	2,030	2,030	570
200,000	210,000	2,055	2,055	590
210,000	230,000	2,100	2,100	630
230,000	250,000	2,155	2,155	670
250,000	275,000	2,215	2,215	720
275,000	300,000	2,275	2,275	770

For SI: 1 pound = 0.454 kg, 1 foot = 304.8 mm, 1 square foot = 0.0929 m^2.

a. The number of pounds of explosives listed is the number of pounds of trinitrotoluene (TNT) or the equivalent pounds of other explosive.

b. The distance listed is the distance to lot line, including lot lines at public ways.

c. For the purpose of this table, an inhabited building is any building on the same lot that is regularly occupied by people. Where two or more buildings containing explosives or magazines are located on the same lot, each building or magazine shall comply with the minimum distances specified from inhabited buildings and, in addition, they shall be separated from each other by not less than the distance shown for "Separation of magazines," except that the quantity of explosive materials contained in detonator buildings or magazines shall govern in regard to the spacing of said detonator buildings or magazines from buildings or magazines containing other explosive materials. If any two or more buildings or magazines are separated from each other by less than the specified "Separation of Magazines" distances, then such two or more buildings or magazines, as a group, shall be considered as one building or magazine, and the total quantity of explosive materials stored in such group shall be treated as if the explosive were in a single building or magazine located on the site of any building or magazine of the group, and shall comply with the minimum distance specified from other magazines or inhabited buildings.

d. Barricades shall effectively screen the building containing explosives from other buildings, public ways or magazines. Where mounds or revetted walls of earth are used for barricades, they shall not be less than 3 feet in thickness. A straight line from the top of any side wall of the building containing explosive materials to the eave line of any other building, magazine or a point 12 feet above the centerline of a public way shall pass through the barricades.

e. Magazine is a building or structure, other than an operating building, approved for storage of explosive materials. Portable or mobile magazines not exceeding 120 square feet in area need not comply with the requirements of this code, however, all magazines shall comply with the *Fire Code of New York State*.

f. The distance listed is permitted to be reduced by 50 percent where approved natural or artificial barriers are provided in accordance with the requirements in Note d.

TABLE 415.3.2
REQUIRED DETACHED STORAGE

DETACHED STORAGE IS REQUIRED WHEN THE QUANTITY OF MATERIAL EXCEEDS THAT LISTED HEREIN			
Material	Class	Solids and Liquids(tons)[a,b]	Gases(cubic feet)[a,b]
Explosives	Division 1.1	Maximum Allowable Quantity	Not Applicable
	Division 1.2	Maximum Allowable Quantity	
	Division 1.3	Maximum Allowable Quantity	
	Division 1.4	Maximum Allowable Quantity	
	Division 1.4[c]	1	
	Division 1.5	Maximum Allowable Quantity	
	Division 1.6	Maximum Allowable Quantity	
Oxidizers	Class 4	Maximum Allowable Quantity	Maximum Allowable Quantity
Unstable (reactives) detonable	Class 3 or 4	Maximum Allowable Quantity	Maximum Allowable Quantity
Oxidizer, liquids and solids	Class 3	1,200	Not Applicable
	Class 2	2,000	Not Applicable
Organic peroxides	Detonable	Maximum Allowable Quantity	Not Applicable
	Class I	Maximum Allowable Quantity	Not Applicable
	Class II	25	Not Applicable
	Class III	50	Not Applicable
Unstable (reactives) nondetonable	Class 3	1	2,000
	Class 2	25	10,000
Water reactives	Class 3	1	Not Applicable
	Class 2	25	Not Applicable
Pyrophoric gases	Not Applicable	Not Applicable	2,000

For SI: 1 ton = 906 kg, 1 cubic foot = 0.02832 m^3, 1 pound = 0.454 kg.

a. For materials that are detonable, the distance to other buildings or lot lines shall be as specified in Table 415.3.1 based on trinitrotoluene (TNT) equivalence of the material. For materials classified as explosives, see Chapter 33 the *Fire Code of New York State*. For all other materials, the distance shall be as indicated in Section 415.3.1.

b. "Maximum Allowable Quantity" means the maximum allowable quantity per control area set forth in Table 307.7(1).

c. Limited to Division 1.4 materials and articles, including articles packaged for shipment, that are not regulated as an explosive under Bureau of Alcohol, Tobacco and Firearms (BATF) regulations or unpackaged articles used in process operations that do not propagate a detonation or deflagration between articles, providing the net explosive weight of individual articles does not exceed 1 pound.

[F] 415.4 Special provisions for Group H-1 occupancies. Group H-1 occupancies shall be in buildings used for no other purpose, shall not exceed one story in height and be without a basement, crawl spaces or other under-floor spaces. Roofs shall be of lightweight construction with suitable thermal insulation to prevent sensitive material from reaching its decomposition temperature.

Group H-1 occupancies containing materials which are in themselves both physical and health hazards in quantities exceeding the maximum allowable quantities per control area in Table 307.1.(2) shall comply with requirements for both Group H-1 and H-4 occupancies.

[F] 415.4.1 Floors in storage rooms. Floors in storage areas for organic peroxides, pyrophoric materials and unstable (reactive) materials shall be of liquid-tight, noncombustible construction.

[F] 415.5 Special provisions for Group H-2 and H-3 occupancies. Group H-2 and H-3 occupancies containing quantities of hazardous materials in excess of those set forth in Table 415.3.2 shall be in buildings used for no other purpose, shall not exceed one story in height and shall be without basements, crawl spaces or other under-floor spaces.

Group H-2 and H-3 occupancies containing water-reactive materials shall be resistant to water penetration. Piping for conveying liquids shall not be over or through areas containing water reactives, unless isolated by approved liquid-tight construction.

Exception: Fire protection piping.

[F] 415.5.1 Floors in storage rooms. Floors in storage areas for organic peroxides, oxidizers, pyrophoric materials, unstable (reactive) materials and water-reactive solids and liquids shall be of liquid-tight, noncombustible construction.

[F] 415.5.2 Waterproof room. Rooms or areas used for the storage of water-reactive solids and liquids shall be constructed in a manner that resists the penetration of water through the use of waterproof materials. Piping carrying water for other than approved automatic fire sprinkler systems shall not be within such rooms or areas.

[F] 415.6 Group H-2. Occupancies in Group H-2 shall be constructed in accordance with Sections 415.6.1 through 415.6.4 and the *Fire Code of New York State*.

[F] 415.6.1 Combustible dusts, grain processing and storage. The provisions of Sections 415.6.1.1 through 415.6.1.6 shall apply to buildings in which materials that produce combustible dusts are stored or handled. Buildings that store or handle combustible dusts shall comply with the applicable provisions of NFPA 61, NFPA 120, NFPA 484, NFPA 654, NFPA 655, NFPA 664 and NFPA 85, and the *Fire Code of New York State*.

[F] 415.6.1.1 Type of construction and height exceptions. Buildings shall be constructed in compliance with the height and area limitations of Table 503 for Group H-2; except that where erected of Type I or II construction, the heights and areas of grain elevators and similar structures shall be unlimited, and where of Type IV construction, the maximum height shall be 65 feet (19 812 mm) and except further that, in isolated areas, the maximum height of Type IV structures shall be increased to 85 feet (25 908 mm).

[F] 415.6.1.2 Grinding rooms. Every room or space occupied for grinding or other operations that produce combustible dusts shall be enclosed with fire barriers that have not less than a 2-hour fire-resistance rating where the area is not more than 3,000 square feet (279 m²), and not less than a 4-hour fire-resistance rating where the area is greater than 3,000 square feet (279 m²).

[F] 415.6.1.3 Conveyors. Conveyors, chutes, piping and similar equipment passing through the enclosures of rooms or spaces shall be constructed dirt tight and vapor tight, and be of approved noncombustible materials complying with Chapter 30.

[F] 415.6.1.4 Explosion control. Explosion control shall be provided as specified in the *Fire Code of New York State*, or spaces shall be equipped with the equivalent mechanical ventilation complying with the *Mechanical Code of New York State*.

[F] 415.6.1.5 Grain elevators. Grain elevators, malt houses and buildings for similar occupancies shall not be located within 30 feet (9144 mm) of interior lot lines or structures on the same lot, except where erected along a railroad right-of-way.

[F] 415.6.1.6 Coal pockets. Coal pockets located less than 30 feet (9144 mm) from interior lot lines or from structures on the same lot shall be constructed of not less than Type IB construction. Where more than 30 feet (9144 mm) from interior lot lines, or where erected along a railroad right-of-way, the minimum type of construction of such structures not more than 65 feet (19 812 mm) in height shall be Type IV.

[F] 415.6.2 Flammable and combustible liquids. The storage, handling, processing and transporting of flammable and combustible liquids shall be in accordance with the *Mechanical Code of New York State* and the *Fire Code of New York State*.

[F] 415.6.2.1 Mixed occupancies. Where the storage tank area is located in a building of two or more occupancies, and the quantity of liquid exceeds the maximum allowable quantity for one control area, the use shall be completely separated from adjacent fire areas in accordance with the requirements of Section 508.3.3.

[F] 415.6.2.1.1 Height exception. Where storage tanks are located within only a single-story building, the height limitation of Section 503 shall not apply for Group H.

[F] 415.6.2.2 Tank protection. Storage tanks shall be noncombustible and protected from physical damage. A fire barrier wall or horizontal assemblies or both around the storage tank(s) shall be permitted as the method of protection from physical damage.

[F] 415.6.2.3 Tanks. Storage tanks shall be approved tanks conforming to the requirements of the *Fire Code of New York State*.

[F] 415.6.2.4 Suppression. Group H shall be equipped throughout with an approved automatic sprinkler system, installed in accordance with Section 903.

[F] 415.6.2.5 Leakage containment. A liquid-tight containment area compatible with the stored liquid shall be provided. The method of spill control, drainage control and secondary containment shall be in accordance with the *Fire Code of New York State*.

> **Exception:** Rooms where only double-wall storage tanks conforming to Section 415.6.2.3 are used to store Class I, II and IIIA flammable and combustible liquids shall not be required to have a leakage containment area.

[F] 415.6.2.6 Leakage alarm. An approved automatic alarm shall be provided to indicate a leak in a storage tank and room. The alarm shall sound an audible signal, 15 dBa above the ambient sound level, at every point of entry into the room in which the leaking storage tank is located. An approved sign shall be posted on every entry door to the tank storage room indicating the potential hazard of the interior room environment, or the sign shall state: WARNING, WHEN ALARM SOUNDS, THE ENVIRONMENT WITHIN THE ROOM MAY BE HAZARDOUS. The leakage alarm shall also be supervised in accordance with Chapter 9 to transmit a trouble signal.

[F] 415.6.2.7 Tank vent. Storage tank vents for Class I, II or IIIA liquids shall terminate to the outdoor air in accordance with the *Fire Code of New York State*.

[F] 415.6.2.8 Room ventilation. Storage tank areas storing Class I, II or IIIA liquids shall be provided with mechanical ventilation. The mechanical ventilation system shall be in accordance with the *Mechanical Code of New York State* and the *Fire Code of New York State*.

[F] 415.6.2.9 Explosion venting. Where Class I liquids are being stored, explosion venting shall be provided in accordance with the *Fire Code of New York State*.

[F] 415.6.2.10 Tank openings other than vents. Tank openings other than vents from tanks inside buildings shall be designed to ensure that liquids or vapor concentrations are not released inside the building.

[F] 415.6.3 Liquefied petroleum gas-distribution facilities. The design and construction of propane, butane, propylene, butylene and other liquefied petroleum gas-distribution facilities shall conform to the applicable provisions of Sections 415.6.3.1 through 415.6.3.5.2. The storage and handling of liquefied petroleum gas systems shall conform to the *Fire Code of New York State*. The design and installation of piping, equipment and systems that utilize liquefied petroleum gas shall be in accordance with the *Fuel Gas Code of New York State*. Liquefied petroleum gas-distribution facilities shall be ventilated in accordance with the *Mechanical Code of New York State* and Section 415.6.3.1.

[F] 415.6.3.1 Air movement. Liquefied petroleum gas-distribution facilities shall be provided with air inlets and outlets arranged so that air movement across the floor of the facility will be uniform. The total area of both inlet and outlet openings shall be at least 1 square inch (645 mm²) for each 1 square foot (0.093 m²) of floor area. The bottom of such openings shall not be more than 6 inches (152 mm) above the floor.

[F] 415.6.3.2 Construction. Liquefied petroleum gas-distribution facilities shall be constructed in accordance with Section 415.6.3.3 for separate buildings, Section 415.6.3.4 for attached buildings or Section 415.6.3.5 for rooms within buildings.

[F] 415.6.3.3 Separate buildings. Where located in separate buildings, liquefied petroleum gas-distribution facilities shall be occupied exclusively for that purpose or for other purposes having similar hazards. Such buildings shall be limited to one story in height and shall conform to Sections 415.6.3.3.1 through 415.6.3.3.3.

[F] 415.6.3.3.1 Floors. The floor shall not be located below ground level and any spaces beneath the floor shall be solidly filled or shall be unenclosed.

[F] 415.6.3.3.2 Materials. Walls, floors, ceilings, columns and roofs shall be constructed of noncombustible materials.

[F] 415.6.3.3.3 Explosion venting. Explosion venting shall be provided in accordance with the *Fire Code of New York State*.

[F] 415.6.3.4 Attached buildings. Where liquefied petroleum gas-distribution facilities are located in an attached structure, the attached perimeter shall not exceed 50 percent of the perimeter of the space enclosed and the facility shall comply with Sections 415.6.3.3 and 415.6.3.4.1. Where the attached perimeter exceeds 50 percent, such facilities shall comply with Section 415.6.3.5.

[F] 415.6.3.4.1 Fire separation. Separation of the attached structures shall be provided by fire barriers having a fire-resistance rating of not less than 1 hour and shall not have openings. Fire barriers between attached structures occupied only for the storage of LP-gas are permitted to have fire door assemblies that comply with Section 715. Such fire barriers shall be designed to withstand a static pressure of at least 100 pounds per square foot (psf) (4788 Pa),

except where the building to which the structure is attached is occupied by operations or processes having a similar hazard.

[F] 415.6.3.5 Rooms within buildings. Where liquefied petroleum gas-distribution facilities are located in rooms within buildings, such rooms shall be located in the first story above grade plane and shall have at least one exterior wall with sufficient exposed area to provide explosion venting as required in the *Fire Code of New York State*. The building in which the room is located shall not have a basement or unventilated crawl space and the room shall comply with Sections 415.6.3.5.1 and 415.6.3.5.2.

[F] 415.6.3.5.1 Materials. Walls, floors, ceilings and roofs of such rooms shall be constructed of approved noncombustible materials.

[F] 415.6.3.5.2 Common construction. Walls and floor/ceiling assemblies common to the room and to the building where the room is located shall be fire barriers with not less than a 1-hour fire-resistance rating and without openings. Common walls for rooms occupied only for storage of LP-gas are permitted to have opening protectives complying with Section 715. The walls and ceilings shall be designed to withstand a static pressure of at least 100 psf (4788 Pa).

Exception: Where the building, within which the room is located, is occupied by operations or processes having a similar hazard.

[F] 415.6.4 Dry cleaning plants. The construction and installation of dry cleaning plants shall be in accordance with the requirements of this code, the *Mechanical Code of New York State*, the *Plumbing Code of New York State* and NFPA 32. Dry cleaning solvents and systems shall be classified in accordance with the *Fire Code of New York State*.

[F] 415.7 Groups H-3 and H-4. Groups H-3 and H-4 shall be constructed in accordance with the applicable provisions of this code and the *Fire Code of New York State*.

[F] 415.7.1 Gas rooms. When gas rooms are provided, such rooms shall be separated from other areas by not less than a 1-hour fire barrier.

[F] 415.7.2 Floors in storage rooms. Floors in storage areas for corrosive liquids and highly toxic or toxic materials shall be of liquid-tight, noncombustible construction.

[F] 415.7.3 Separation-highly toxic solids and liquids. Highly toxic solids and liquids not stored in approved hazardous materials storage cabinets shall be isolated from other hazardous materials storage by a fire barrier having a fire-resistance rating of not less than 1 hour.

[F] 415.8 Group H-5.

[F] 415.8.1 General. In addition to the requirements set forth elsewhere in this code, Group H-5 shall comply with the provisions of Section 415.8 and the *Fire Code of New York State.*

[F] 415.8.2 Fabrication areas.

[F] 415.8.2.1 Hazardous materials in fabrication areas.

[F] 415.8.2.1.1 Aggregate quantities. The aggregate quantities of hazardous materials stored and used in a single fabrication area shall not exceed the quantities set forth in Table 415.8.2.1.1.

Exception: The quantity limitations for any hazard category in Table 415.8.2.1.1 shall not apply where the fabrication area contains quantities of hazardous materials not exceeding the maximum allowable quantities per control area established by Tables 307.1(1) and 307.1(2).

[F] 415.8.2.1.2 Hazardous production materials. The maximum quantities of hazardous production materials (HPM) stored in a single fabrication area shall not exceed the maximum allowable quantities per control area established by Tables 307.1(1) and 307.1(2).

[F] 415.8.2.2 Separation. Fabrication areas, whose sizes are limited by the quantity of hazardous materials allowed by Table 415.8.2.1.1, shall be separated from each other, from corridors and from other parts of the building by not less than 1-hour fire barriers.

Exceptions:

1. Doors within such fire barrier walls, including doors to corridors, shall be only self-closing fire door assemblies having a fire protection rating of not less than $^3/_4$ hour.

2. Windows between fabrication areas and corridors are permitted to be fixed glazing listed and labeled for a fire protection rating of at least $^3/_4$ hour in accordance with Section 715.

[F] 415.8.2.3 Location of occupied levels. Occupied levels of fabrication areas shall be located at or above the first story above grade plane.

[F] 415.8.2.4 Floors. Except for surfacing, floors within fabrication areas shall be of noncombustible construction.

Openings through floors of fabrication areas are permitted to be unprotected where the interconnected levels are used solely for mechanical equipment directly related to such fabrication areas (see also Section 415.8.2.5).

Floors forming a part of an occupancy separation shall be liquid tight.

[F] 415.8.2.5 Shafts and openings through floors. Elevator shafts, vent shafts and other openings through floors shall be enclosed when required by Section 707.

Mechanical, duct and piping penetrations within a fabrication area shall not extend through more than two floors. The annular space around penetrations for cables, cable trays, tubing, piping, conduit or ducts shall be sealed at the floor level to restrict the movement of air. The fabrication area, including the areas through which the ductwork and piping extend, shall be considered a single conditioned environment.

[F] 415.8.2.6 Ventilation. Mechanical exhaust ventilation at the rate of not less than 1 cubic foot per minute per square foot (0.044 L/s/m^2) of floor area shall be provided throughout the portions of the fabrication area where HPM are used or stored. The exhaust air duct system of one fabrication area shall not connect to another duct system outside that fabrication area within the building.

A ventilation system shall be provided to capture and exhaust gases, fumes and vapors at workstations.

Two or more operations at a workstation shall not be connected to the same exhaust system where either one or the combination of the substances removed could constitute a fire, explosion or hazardous chemical reaction within the exhaust duct system.

Exhaust ducts penetrating occupancy separations shall be contained in a shaft of equivalent fire-resistance-rated construction. Exhaust ducts shall not penetrate fire walls.

Fire dampers shall not be installed in exhaust ducts.

[F] 415.8.2.7 Transporting hazardous production materials to fabrication areas. HPM shall be transported to fabrication areas through enclosed piping or tubing systems that comply with Section 415.8.6.1, through service corridors complying with Section 415.8.4, or in corridors as permitted in the exception to Section 415.8.3. The handling or transporting of HPM within service corridors shall comply with the *Fire Code of New York State.*

[F] 415.8.2.8 Electrical.

[F] 415.8.2.8.1 General. Electrical equipment and devices within the fabrication area shall comply with Chapter 27 of the *Building Code of New York State.* The requirements for hazardous locations need not be applied where the average air change is at least four times that set forth in Section 415.8.2.6 and where the number of air changes at any location is not less than three times that required by Section 415.8.2.6. The use of recirculated air shall be permitted.

[F] 415.8.2.8.2 Workstations. Workstations shall not be energized without adequate exhaust ventilation. See Section 415.8.2.6 for workstation exhaust ventilation requirements.

TABLE 415.8.2.1.1
QUANTITY LIMITS FOR HAZARDOUS MATERIALS IN A SINGLE FABRICATION AREA IN GROUP H-5[a]

HAZARD CATEGORY		SOLIDS (pounds per square feet)	LIQUIDS (gallons per square feet)	GAS (feet^3 @ NTP/square feet)
PHYSICAL-HAZARD MATERIALS				
Combustible dust		Note b	Not Applicable	Not Applicable
Combustible fiber	Loose	Note b	Not Applicable	Not Applicable
	Baled	Notes b, c		
Combustible liquid	II	Not Applicable	0.01	Not Applicable
	IIIA		0.02	
	IIIB		Not Limited	
Combination Class I, II and IIIA			0.04	
Cryogenic gas	Flammable	Not Applicable	Not Applicable	Note d
	Oxidizing			1.25
Explosives		Note b	Note b	Note b
Flammable gas	Gaseous	Not Applicable	Not Applicable	Note d
	Liquefied			Note d
Flammable liquid	IA	Not Applicable	0.0025	Not Applicable
	IB		0.025	
	IC		0.025	
Combination Class IA, IB and IC			0.025	
Combination Class I, II and IIIA			0.04	
Flammable solid		0.001	Not Applicable	Not Applicable
Organic peroxide			Not Applicable	Not Applicable
Unclassified detonable		Note b		
Class I		Note b		
Class II		0.025		
Class III		0.1		
Class IV		Not Limited		
Class V		Not limited		
Oxidizing gas			Not Applicable	1.25
	Gaseous	Not Applicable		1.25
	Liquefied			1.25
Combination of gaseous and liquefied				
Oxidizer	Class 4	Note b	Note b	Not Applicable
	Class 3	0.003	0.03	
	Class 2	0.003	0.03	
Combination	Class 1	0.003	0.03	
	Class 1, 2, 3	0.003	0.03	
Pyrophoric material		Note b	0.00125	Notes d and e
Unstable reactive	Class 4	Note b	Note b	Note b
	Class 3	0.025	0.0025	Note b
	Class 2	0.1	0.01	Note b
	Class 1	Not Limited	Not Limited	Not Limited
Water reactive	Class 3	Note b	0.00125	Not Applicable
	Class 2	0.25	0.025	
	Class 1	Not Limited	Not Limited	
HEALTH-HAZARD MATERIALS				
Corrosives		Not Limited	Not Limited	Not Limited
Highly toxic		Not Limited	Not Limited	Note d
Toxics		Not Limited	Not Limited	Note d

For SI: 1 pound per square foot = 4.882 kg/m^2, 1 gallon per square foot = 40.7 L/m^2, 1 cubic foot @ NTP/square foot = 0.305 m^3 @ NTP/m^2, 1 cubic foot = 0.02832 M^3.

a. Hazardous materials within piping shall not be included in the calculated quantities.

b. Quantity of hazardous materials in a single fabrication shall not exceed the maximum allowable quantities per control area in Tables 307.1(1) and 307.1(2).

c. Densely packed baled cotton that complies with the packing requirements of ISO 8115 shall not be included in this material class.

d. The aggregate quantity of flammable, pyrophoric, toxic and highly toxic gases shall not exceed 9,000 cubic feet at NTP.

e. The aggregate quantity of pyrophoric gases in the building shall not exceed the amounts set forth in Table 415.3.2.

[F] 415.8.3 Corridors. Corridors shall comply with Chapter 10 and shall be separated from fabrication areas as specified in Section 415.8.2.2. Corridors shall not contain HPM and shall not be used for transporting such materials, except through closed piping systems as provided in Section 415.8.6.3.

Exception: Where existing fabrication areas are altered or modified, HPM is allowed to be transported in existing corridors, subject to the following conditions:

1. Corridors. Corridors adjacent to the fabrication area where the alteration work is to be done shall comply with Section 1017 for a length determined as follows:

    1.1. The length of the common wall of the corridor and the fabrication area; and

    1.2. For the distance along the corridor to the point of entry of HPM into the corridor serving that fabrication area.

2. Emergency alarm system. There shall be an emergency telephone system, a local manual alarm station or other approved alarm-initiating device within corridors at not more than 150-foot (45 720 mm) intervals and at each exit and doorway. The signal shall be relayed to an approved central, proprietary or remote station service or the emergency control station and shall also initiate a local audible alarm.

3. Pass-throughs. Self-closing doors having a fire protection rating of not less than 1 hour shall separate pass-throughs from existing corridors. Pass-throughs shall be constructed as required for the corridors and protected by an approved automatic fire-extinguishing system.

[F] 415.8.4 Service corridors.

[F] 415.8.4.1 Occupancy. Service corridors shall be classified as Group H-5.

[F] 415.8.4.2 Use conditions. Service corridors shall be separated from corridors as required by Section 415.8.2.2. Service corridors shall not be used as a required corridor.

[F] 415.8.4.3 Mechanical ventilation. Service corridors shall be mechanically ventilated as required by Section 415.8.2.6 or at not less than six air changes per hour, whichever is greater.

[F] 415.8.4.4 Means of egress. The maximum distance of travel from any point in a service corridor to an exit, exit access corridor or door into a fabrication area shall not exceed 75 feet (22 860 mm). Dead ends shall not exceed 4 feet (1219 mm) in length. There shall be not less than two exits, and not more than one-half of the required means of egress shall require travel into a fabrication area. Doors from service corridors shall swing in the direction of egress travel and shall be self-closing.

[F] 415.8.4.5 Minimum width. The minimum clear width of a service corridor shall be 5 feet (1524 mm),

or 33 inches (838 mm) wider than the widest cart or truck used in the corridor, whichever is greater.

[F] 415.8.4.6 Emergency alarm system. Emergency alarm systems shall be provided in accordance with this section and Sections 414.7.1 and 414.7.2. The maximum allowable quantity per control area provisions shall not apply to emergency alarm systems required for HPM.

[F] 415.8.4.6.1 Service corridors. An emergency alarm system shall be provided in service corridors, with at least one alarm device in each service corridor.

[F] 415.8.4.6.2 Exit access corridors and exit enclosures. Emergency alarms for exit access corridors and exit enclosures shall comply with Section 414.7.2.

[F] 415.8.4.6.3 Liquid storage rooms, HPM rooms and gas rooms. Emergency alarms for liquid storage rooms, HPM rooms and gas rooms shall comply with Section 414.7.1.

[F] 415.8.4.6.4 Alarm-initiating devices. An approved emergency telephone system, local alarm manual pull stations, or other approved alarm-initiating devices are allowed to be used as emergency alarm-initiating devices.

[F] 415.8.4.6.5 Alarm signals. Activation of the emergency alarm system shall sound a local alarm and transmit a signal to the emergency control station.

[F] 415.8.5 Storage of hazardous production materials.

[F] 415.8.5.1 General. Storage of HPM in fabrication areas shall be within approved or listed storage cabinets or gas cabinets or within a workstation. The storage of HPM in quantities greater than those listed in Section 1804.2 of the *Fire Code of New York State* shall be in liquid storage rooms, HPM rooms or gas rooms as appropriate for the materials stored. The storage of other hazardous materials shall be in accordance with other applicable provisions of this code and the *Fire Code of New York State*.

[F] 415.8.5.2 Construction.

[F] 415.8.5.2.1 HPM rooms and gas rooms. HPM rooms and gas rooms shall be separated from other areas by not less than a 2-hour fire barrier where the area is 300 square feet (27.9 m²) or more and not less than a 1-hour fire barrier where the area is less than 300 square feet (27.9 m²).

[F] 415.8.5.2.2 Liquid storage rooms. Liquid storage rooms shall be constructed in accordance with the following requirements:

1. Rooms in excess of 500 square feet (46.5 m²) shall have at least one exterior door approved for fire department access.

2. Rooms shall be separated from other areas by fire barriers having a fire-resistance rating of not less than 1-hour for rooms up to 150

square feet (13.9 m²) in area and not less than 2 hours where the room is more than 150 square feet (13.9 m²) in area.

3. Shelving, racks and wainscoting in such areas shall be of noncombustible construction or wood of not less than 1inch (25 mm) nominal thickness.

4. Rooms used for the storage of Class I flammable liquids shall not be located in a basement.

[F] 415.8.5.2.3 Floors. Except for surfacing, floors of HPM rooms and liquid storage rooms shall be of noncombustible liquid-tight construction. Raised grating over floors shall be of noncombustible materials.

[F] 415.8.5.3 Location. Where HPM rooms, liquid storage rooms and gas rooms are provided, they shall have at least one exterior wall and such wall shall be not less than 30 feet (9144 mm) from lot lines, including lot lines adjacent to public ways.

[F] 415.8.5.4 Explosion control. Explosion control shall be provided where required by Section 414.5.1.

[F] 415.8.5.5 Exits. Where two exits are required from HPM rooms, liquid storage rooms and gas rooms, one shall be directly to the outside of the building.

[F] 415.8.5.6 Doors. Doors in a fire barrier wall, including doors to corridors, shall be self-closing fire door assemblies having a fire-protection rating of not less than $^3/_4$ hour.

[F] 415.8.5.7 Ventilation. Mechanical exhaust ventilation shall be provided in liquid storage rooms, HPM rooms and gas rooms at the rate of not less than 1 cubic foot per minute per square foot (0.044 L/s/m²) of floor area or six air changes per hour, whichever is greater, for categories of material.

Exhaust ventilation for gas rooms shall be designed to operate at a negative pressure in relation to the surrounding areas and direct the exhaust ventilation to an exhaust system.

[F] 415.8.5.8 Emergency alarm system. An approved emergency alarm system shall be provided for HPM rooms, liquid storage rooms and gas rooms.

Emergency alarm-initiating devices shall be installed outside of each interior exit door of such rooms.

Activation of an emergency alarm-initiating device shall sound a local alarm and transmit a signal to the emergency control station.

An approved emergency telephone system, local alarm manual pull stations or other approved alarm-initiating devices are allowed to be used as emergency alarm-initiating devices.

[F] 415.8.6 Piping and tubing.

[F] 415.8.6.1 General. Hazardous production materials piping and tubing shall comply with this section and ASME B 31.3.

[F] 415.8.6.2 Supply piping and tubing.

[F] 415.8.6.2.1 HPM having a health-hazard ranking of 3 or 4. Systems supplying HPM liquids or gases having a health-hazard ranking of 3 or 4 shall be welded throughout, except for connections, to the systems that are within a ventilated enclosure if the material is a gas, or an approved method of drainage or containment is provided for the connections if the material is a liquid.

[F] 415.8.6.2.2 Location in service corridors. Hazardous production materials supply piping or tubing in service corridors shall be exposed to view.

[F] 415.8.6.2.3 Excess flow control. Where HPM gases or liquids are carried in pressurized piping above 15 pounds per square inch gauge (psig) (103.4 kPa), excess flow control shall be provided. Where the piping originates from within a liquid storage room, HPM room or gas room, the excess flow control shall be located within the liquid storage room, HPM room or gas room. Where the piping originates from a bulk source, the excess flow control shall be located as close to the bulk source as practical.

[F] 415.8.6.3 Installations in corridors and above other occupancies. The installation of HPM piping and tubing within the space defined by the walls of corridors and the floor or roof above, or in concealed spaces above other occupancies, shall be in accordance with Section 415.8.6.2 and the following conditions:

1. Automatic sprinklers shall be installed within the space unless the space is less than 6 inches (152 mm) in the least dimension.

2. Ventilation not less than six air changes per hour shall be provided. The space shall not be used to convey air from any other area.

3. Where the piping or tubing is used to transport HPM liquids, a receptor shall be installed below such piping or tubing. The receptor shall be designed to collect any discharge or leakage and drain it to an approved location. The 1-hour enclosure shall not be used as part of the receptor.

4. HPM supply piping and tubing and nonmetallic waste lines shall be separated from the corridor and from occupancies other than Group H-5 by fire barriers that have a fire-resistance rating of not less than 1 hour. Where gypsum wallboard is used, joints on the piping side of the enclosure are not required to be taped, provided the joints occur over framing members. Access openings into the enclosure shall be protected by approved fire protection-rated assemblies.

5. Readily accessible manual or automatic remotely activated fail-safe emergency shutoff valves shall be installed on piping and tubing other than waste lines at the following locations:

    5.1. At branch connections into the fabrication area.

5.2. At entries into corridors.

Exception: Transverse crossings of the corridors by supply piping that is enclosed within a ferrous pipe or tube for the width of the corridor need not comply with Items 1 through 5.

[F] 415.8.6.4 Identification. Piping, tubing and HPM waste lines shall be identified in accordance with ANSI A13.1 to indicate the material being transported.

[F] 415.8.7 Continuous gas detection systems. A continuous gas detection system shall be provided for HPM gases when the physiological warning threshold level of the gas is at a higher level than the accepted PEL for the gas and for flammable gases in accordance with this section.

[F] 415.8.7.1 Where required. A continuous gas-detection system shall be provided in the areas identified in Sections 415.8.7.1.1 through 415.8.7.1.4.

[F] 415.8.7.1.1 Fabrication areas. A continuous gas-detection system shall be provided in fabrication areas when gas is used in the fabrication area.

[F] 415.8.7.1.2 HPM rooms. A continuous gas-detection system shall be provided in HPM rooms when gas is used in the room.

[F] 415.8.7.1.3 Gas cabinets, exhausted enclosures and gas rooms. A continuous gas-detection system shall be provided in gas cabinets and exhausted enclosures. A continuous gas-detection system shall be provided in gas rooms when gases are not located in gas cabinets or exhausted enclosures.

[F] 415.8.7.1.4 Corridors. When gases are transported in piping placed within the space defined by the walls of a corridor and the floor or roof above the corridor, a continuous gas-detection system shall be provided where piping is located and in the corridor.

Exception: A continuous gas-detection system is not required for occasional transverse crossings of the corridors by supply piping that is enclosed in a ferrous pipe or tube for the width of the corridor.

[F] 415.8.7.2 Gas-detection system operation. The continuous gas-detection system shall be capable of monitoring the room, area or equipment in which the gas is located at or below the PEL or ceiling limit of the gas for which detection is provided. For flammable gases, the monitoring detection threshold level shall be vapor concentrations in excess of 20 percent of the lower explosive limit (LEL). Monitoring for highly toxic and toxic gases shall also comply with the requirements for such material in the *Fire Code of New York State.*

[F] 415.8.7.2.1 Alarms. The gas detection system shall initiate a local alarm and transmit a signal to the emergency control station when a short-term hazard condition is detected. The alarm shall be both visual and audible and shall provide warning both inside and outside the area where the gas is detected. The audible alarm shall be distinct from all other alarms.

[F] 415.8.7.2.2 Shutoff of gas supply. The gas detection system shall automatically close the shutoff valve at the source on gas supply piping and tubing related to the system being monitored for which gas is detected when a short-term hazard condition is detected. Automatic closure of shutoff valves shall comply with the following:

1. Where the gas-detection sampling point initiating the gas detection system alarm is within a gas cabinet or exhausted enclosure, the shutoff valve in the gas cabinet or exhausted enclosure for the specific gas detected shall automatically close.

2. Where the gas-detection sampling point initiating the gas detection system alarm is within a room and compressed gas containers are not in gas cabinets or an exhausted enclosure, the shutoff valves on all gas lines for the specific gas detected shall automatically close.

3. Where the gas-detection sampling point initiating the gas detection system alarm is within a piping distribution manifold enclosure, the shutoff valve supplying the manifold for the compressed gas container of the specific gas detected shall automatically close.

Exception: Where the gas-detection sampling point initiating the gas detection system alarm is at the use location or within a gas valve enclosure of a branch line downstream of a piping distribution manifold, the shutoff valve for the branch line located in the piping distribution manifold enclosure shall automatically close.

[F] 415.8.8 Manual fire alarm system. An approved manual fire alarm system shall be provided throughout buildings containing Group H-5. Activation of the alarm system shall initiate a local alarm and transmit a signal to the emergency control station. The fire alarm system shall be designed and installed in accordance with Section 907.

415.8.9 Emergency control station. An emergency control station shall be provided in accordance with Sections 415.8.9.1 through 415.8.9.3.

415.8.9.1 Location. The emergency control station shall be located on the premises at an approved location outside the fabrication area.

415.8.9.2 Staffing. Trained personnel shall continuously staff the emergency control station.

415.8.9.3 Signals. The emergency control station shall receive signals from emergency equipment and alarm and detection systems. Such emergency equipment and alarm and detection systems shall include, but not be limited to, the following where such equipment or systems are required to be provided either in this chapter or elsewhere in this code:

1. Automatic fire sprinkler system alarm and monitoring systems.

2. Manual fire alarm systems.

3. Emergency alarm systems.

4. Continuous gas-detection systems.

5. Smoke detection systems.

6. Emergency power system.

7. Automatic detection and alarm systems for pyrophoric liquids and Class 3 water-reactive liquids required in Section 1805.2.3.5 of the *Fire Code of New York State*.

8. Exhaust ventilation flow alarm devices for pyrophoric liquids and Class 3 water-reactive liquids cabinet exhaust ventilation systems required in Section 1805.2.3.5 of the *Fire Code of New York State*.

[F] 415.8.10 Emergency power system. An emergency power system shall be provided in Group H-5 occupancies where required in Section 415.8.10.1. The emergency power system shall be designed to supply power automatically to required electrical systems when the normal electrical supply system is interrupted.

[F] 415.8.10.1 Required electrical systems. Emergency power shall be provided for electrically operated equipment and connected control circuits for the following systems:

1. HPM exhaust ventilation systems.

2. HPM gas cabinet ventilation systems.

3. HPM exhausted enclosure ventilation systems.

4. HPM gas room ventilation systems.

5. HPM gas detection systems.

6. Emergency alarm systems.

7. Manual fire alarm systems.

8. Automatic sprinkler system monitoring and alarm systems.

9. Automatic alarm and detection systems for pyrophoric liquids and Class 3 water-reactive liquids required in Section 1805.2.3.5 of the *Fire Code of New York State*.

10. Flow alarm switches for pyrophoric liquids and Class 3 water-reactive liquids cabinet exhaust ventilation systems required in Section 1805.2.3.5 of the *Fire Code of New York State*.

11. Electrically operated systems required elsewhere in this code or in the *Fire Code of New York State* applicable to the use, storage or handling of HPM.

[F] 415.8.10.2 Exhaust ventilation systems. Exhaust ventilation systems are allowed to be designed to operate at not less than one-half the normal fan speed on the emergency power system where it is demonstrated that the level of exhaust will maintain a safe atmosphere.

[F] 415.8.11 Automatic sprinkler system protection in exhaust ducts for HPM.

[F] 415.8.11.1 Exhaust ducts for HPM. An approved automatic sprinkler system shall be provided in exhaust ducts conveying gases, vapors, fumes, mists or dusts generated from HPM in accordance with this section and the *Mechanical Code of New York State*.

[F] 415.8.11.2 Metallic and noncombustible nonmetallic exhaust ducts. An approved automatic sprinkler system shall be provided in metallic and noncombustible nonmetallic exhaust ducts when all of the following conditions apply:

1. Where the largest cross-sectional diameter is equal to or greater than 10 inches (254 mm).

2. The ducts are within the building.

3. The ducts are conveying flammable gases, vapors or fumes.

[F] 415.8.11.3 Combustible nonmetallic exhaust ducts. Automatic sprinkler system protection shall be provided in combustible nonmetallic exhaust ducts where the largest cross-sectional diameter of the duct is equal to or greater than 10 inches (254 mm).

Exceptions:

1. Ducts listed or approved for applications without automatic fire sprinkler system protection.

2. Ducts not more than 12 feet (3658 mm) in length installed below ceiling level.

[F] 415.8.11.4 Automatic sprinkler locations. Sprinkler systems shall be installed at 12-foot (3658 mm) intervals in horizontal ducts and at changes in direction. In vertical ducts, sprinklers shall be installed at the top and at alternate floor levels.

SECTION 416
APPLICATION OF FLAMMABLE FINISHES

[F] 416.1 General. The provisions of this section shall apply to the construction, installation and use of buildings and structures, or parts thereof, for the spraying of flammable paints, varnishes and lacquers or other flammable materials or mixtures or compounds used for painting, varnishing, staining or similar purposes. Such construction and equipment shall comply with the *Fire Code of New York State*.

[F] 416.2 Spray rooms. Spray rooms shall be enclosed with fire barriers with not less than a 1-hour fire-resistance rating. Floors shall be waterproofed and drained in an approved manner.

[F] 416.2.1 Surfaces. The interior surfaces of spray rooms shall be smooth and shall be so constructed to permit the free passage of exhaust air from all parts of the interior and to facilitate washing and cleaning, and shall be so designed to confine residues within the room. Aluminum shall not be used.

[F] 416.3 Spraying spaces. Spraying spaces shall be ventilated with an exhaust system to prevent the accumulation of flammable mist or vapors in accordance with the *Mechanical Code of New York State*. Where such spaces are not separately enclosed, noncombustible spray curtains shall be provided to restrict the spread of flammable vapors.

[F] 416.3.1 Surfaces. The interior surfaces of spraying spaces shall be smooth and continuous without edges; shall be so constructed to permit the free passage of exhaust air from all parts of the interior and to facilitate washing and cleaning; and shall be so designed to confine residues within the spraying space. Aluminum shall not be used.

[F] 416.4 Fire protection. An automatic fire-extinguishing system shall be provided in all spray, dip and immersing spaces and storage rooms and shall be installed in accordance with Chapter 9.

SECTION 417
DRYING ROOMS

[F] 417.1 General. A drying room or dry kiln installed within a building shall be constructed entirely of approved noncombustible materials or assemblies of such materials regulated by the approved rules or as required in the general and specific sections of Chapter 4 for special occupancies and where applicable to the general requirements of Chapter 28.

[F] 417.2 Piping clearance. Overhead heating pipes shall have a clearance of not less than 2 inches (51 mm) from combustible contents in the dryer.

[F] 417.3 Insulation. Where the operating temperature of the dryer is 175°F (79°C) or more, metal enclosures shall be insulated from adjacent combustible materials by not less than 12 inches (305 mm) of airspace, or the metal walls shall be lined with $^1/_4$-inch (6.35 mm) insulating mill board or other approved equivalent insulation.

[F] 417.4 Fire protection. Drying rooms designed for high-hazard materials and processes, including special occupancies as provided for in Chapter 4, shall be protected by an approved automatic fire-extinguishing system complying with the provisions of Chapter 9.

SECTION 418
ORGANIC COATINGS

[F] 418.1 Building features. Manufacturing of organic coatings shall be done only in buildings that do not have pits or basements.

[F] 418.2 Location. Organic coating manufacturing operations and operations incidental to or connected therewith shall not be located in buildings having other occupancies.

[F] 418.3 Process mills. Mills operating with close clearances and that process flammable and heat-sensitive materials, such as nitrocellulose, shall be located in a detached building or noncombustible structure.

[F] 418.4 Tank storage. Storage areas for flammable and combustible liquid tanks inside of structures shall be located at or above grade and shall be separated from the processing area by not less than 2-hour fire barriers.

[F] 418.5 Nitrocellulose storage. Nitrocellulose storage shall be located on a detached pad or in a separate structure or a room enclosed with no less than 2-hour fire barriers.

[F] 418.6 Finished products. Storage rooms for finished products that are flammable or combustible liquids shall be separated from the processing area by fire barriers having a fire-resistance rating of at least 2 hours, and openings in the walls shall be protected with approved opening protectives.

SECTION 419
GROUP I-1, R-1, R-2, R-3

419.1 General. Occupancies in Groups I-1, R-1, R-2 and R-3 shall comply with the provisions of this section and other applicable provisions of this code.

419.2 Separation walls. Walls separating dwelling units in the same building and walls separating sleeping units in the same building shall comply with Section 708.

419.3 Horizontal separation. Floor/ceiling assemblies separating dwelling units in the same buildings and floor/ceiling assemblies separating sleeping units in the same building shall be constructed in accordance with Section 711.

SECTION 420
HYDROGEN CUTOFF ROOMS

[F] 420.1 General. When required by the *Fire Code of New York State*, hydrogen cutoff rooms shall be designed and constructed in accordance with this section.

[F] 420.2 Definitions. The following words and terms shall, for the purposes of this chapter and as used elsewhere in this code, have the meanings shown herein.

[F] GASEOUS HYDROGEN SYSTEM. An assembly of piping, devices and apparatus designed to generate, store, contain, distribute or transport a nontoxic, gaseous hydrogen-containing mixture having at least 95-percent hydrogen gas by volume and not more than 1-percent oxygen by volume. Gaseous hydrogen systems consist of items such as compressed gas containers, reactors and appurtenances, including pressure regulators, pressure relief devices, manifolds, pumps, compressors and interconnecting piping and tubing and controls.

[F] HYDROGEN CUTOFF ROOM. A room or space that is intended exclusively to house a gaseous hydrogen system.

[F] 420.3 Location. Hydrogen cut-off rooms shall not be located below grade.

[F] 420.4 Design and construction. Hydrogen cutoff rooms shall be classified with respect to occupancy in accordance with Section 302.1 and separated from other areas of the building by not less than 1-hour fire barriers or as required by Section 508.2 or 508.3 as applicable.

[F] 420.4.1 Opening protectives. Doors within such fire barrier walls, including doors to corridors, shall be self-closing in accordance with Section 715. Interior door openings shall be electronically interlocked to prevent operation of the hydrogen system when doors are opened or ajar or the room shall be provided with a mechanical exhaust ventilation system designed in accordance with Section 420.4.1.1.

[F] 420.4.1.1 Ventilation alternative. When an exhaust system is used in lieu of the interlock system required by Section 420.4, exhaust ventilation systems shall operate continuously and shall be designed to operate at a negative pressure in relation to the surrounding area. The average velocity of ventilation at the face of the door opening with the door in the fully open position shall not be less than 60 feet per minute (0.3048 m/s) with a minimum of 45 feet per minute (0.2287 m/s) at any point in the door opening.

[F] 420.4.2 Windows. Operable windows in interior walls shall not be permitted. Fixed windows shall be permitted when in accordance with Section 715.

[F] 420.5 Ventilation. Cutoff rooms shall be provided with mechanical ventilation in accordance with the applicable provisions for repair garages in Chapter 5 of the *Mechanical Code of New York State*.

[F] 420.6 Gas detection system. Hydrogen cutoff rooms shall be provided with an approved flammable gas-detection system in accordance with Sections 420.6.1 through 420.6.3.

[F] 420.6.1 System design. The flammable gas-detection system shall be listed for use with hydrogen and any other flammable gases used in the room. The gas detection system shall be designed to activate when the level of flammable gas exceeds 25 percent of the lower flammability limit (LFL) for the gas or mixtures present at their anticipated temperature and pressure.

[F] 420.6.2 Operation. Activation of the gas detection system shall result in all of the following:

1. Initiation of distinct audible and visual alarm signals both inside and outside of the cutoff room.

2. Activation of the mechanical ventilation system.

[F] 420.6.3 Failure of the gas detection system. Failure of the gas detection system shall result in activation of the mechanical ventilation system, cessation of hydrogen generation and the sounding of a trouble signal in an approved location.

[F] 420.7 Explosion control. Explosion control shall be provided in accordance with Chapter 9 of the *Fire Code of New York State*.

[F] 420.8 Standby power. Mechanical ventilation and gas detection systems shall be connected to a standby power system in accordance with Chapter 27.

CHAPTER 5

GENERAL BUILDING HEIGHTS AND AREAS

SECTION 501
GENERAL

501.1 Scope. The provisions of this chapter control the height and area of structures hereafter erected and additions to existing structures.

[F] 501.2 Address numbers. Buildings shall have approved address numbers, building numbers or approved building identification placed in a position that is plainly legible and visible from the street or road fronting the property. These numbers shall contrast with their background. Address numbers shall be Arabic numerals or alphabetical letters. Numbers shall be a minimum of 4 inches (102 mm) high with a minimum stroke width of 0.5 inch (12.7 mm).

501.3 Fire apparatus access roads. Fire apparatus access roads shall be provided in accordance with Section 503 of the *Fire Code of New York State.*

501.4 Required water supply. A water supply capable of supplying the required fire flow for fire protection shall be provided to premises upon which facilities, buildings or portions of buildings are hereafter constructed or moved into or within the jurisdiction in accordance with Section 508 of the *Fire Code of New York State.*

SECTION 502
DEFINITIONS

502.1 Definitions. The following words and terms shall, for the purposes of this chapter and as used elsewhere in this code, have the meanings shown herein.

AREA, BUILDING. The area included within surrounding exterior walls (or exterior walls and fire walls) exclusive of vent shafts and courts. Areas of the building not provided with surrounding walls shall be included in the building area if such areas are included within the horizontal projection of the roof or floor above.

BASEMENT. That portion of a building that is partly or completely below grade plane (see "Story above grade plane" in Section 202). A basement shall be considered as a story above grade plane where the finished surface of the floor above the basement is:

1. More than 6 feet (1829 mm) above grade plane; or

2. More than 12 feet (3658 mm) above the finished ground level at any point.

EQUIPMENT PLATFORM. An unoccupied, elevated platform used exclusively for mechanical systems or industrial process equipment, including the associated elevated walkways, stairs and ladders necessary to access the platform (see Section 505.5).

GRADE PLANE. A reference plane representing the average of finished ground level adjoining the building at exterior walls. Where the finished ground level slopes away from the exterior walls, the reference plane shall be established by the lowest points within the area between the building and the lot line or, where the lot line is more than 6 feet (1829 mm) from the building, between the building and a point 6 feet (1829 mm) from the building.

HEIGHT, BUILDING. The vertical distance from grade plane to the average height of the highest roof surface.

HEIGHT, STORY. The vertical distance from top to top of two successive finished floor surfaces; and, for the topmost story, from the top of the floor finish to the top of the ceiling joists or, where there is not a ceiling, to the top of the roof rafters.

MEZZANINE. An intermediate level or levels between the floor and ceiling of any story and in accordance with Section 505.

SECTION 503
GENERAL HEIGHT AND AREA LIMITATIONS

503.1 General. The height and area for buildings of different construction types shall be governed by the intended use of the building and shall not exceed the limits in Table 503 except as modified hereafter. Each part of a building included within the exterior walls or the exterior walls and fire walls where provided shall be permitted to be a separate building.

503.1.1 Special industrial occupancies. Buildings and structures designed to house special industrial processes that require large areas and unusual heights to accommodate craneways or special machinery and equipment, including, among others, rolling mills; structural metal fabrication shops and foundries; or the production and distribution of electric, gas or steam power, shall be exempt from the height and area limitations of Table 503.

503.1.2 Buildings on same lot. Two or more buildings on the same lot shall be regulated as separate buildings or shall be considered as portions of one building if the height of each building and the aggregate area of buildings are within the limitations of Table 503 as modified by Sections 504 and 506. The provisions of this code applicable to the aggregate building shall be applicable to each building.

503.1.3 Type I construction. Buildings of Type I construction permitted to be of unlimited tabular heights and areas are not subject to the special requirements that allow unlimited area buildings in Section 507 or unlimited height in Sections 503.1.1 and 504.3 or increased height and areas for other types of construction.

TABLE 503
ALLOWABLE HEIGHT AND BUILDING AREAS[a]
Height limitations shown as stories and feet above grade plane.
Area limitations as determined by the definition of 'Area, building,' per story

		TYPE OF CONSTRUCTION								
		TYPE I		TYPE II		TYPE III		TYPE IV	TYPE V	
		A	B	A	B	A	B	HT	A	B
GROUP	HGT(feet) HGT(S)	UL	160	65	55	65	55	65	50	40
A-1	S	UL	5	3	2	3	2	3	2	1
	A	UL	UL	15,500	8,500	14,000	8,500	15,000	11,500	5,500
A-2	S	UL	11	3	2	3	2	3	2	1
	A	UL	UL	15,500	9,500	14,000	9,500	15,000	11,500	6,000
A-3	S	UL	11	3	2	3	2	3	2	1
	A	UL	UL	15,500	9,500	14,000	9,500	15,000	11,500	6,000
A-4	S	UL	11	3	2	3	2	3	2	1
	A	UL	UL	15,500	9,500	14,000	9,500	15,000	11,500	6,000
A-5	S	UL	UL	UL	UL	UL	UL	UL	UL	UL
	A	UL	UL	UL	UL	UL	UL	UL	UL	UL
B	S	UL	11	5	4	5	4	5	3	2
	A	UL	UL	37,500	23,000	28,500	19,000	36,000	18,000	9,000
E	S	UL	5	3	2	3	2	3	1	1
	A	UL	UL	26,500	14,500	23,500	14,500	25,500	18,500	9,500
F-1	S	UL	11	4	2	3	2	4	2	1
	A	UL	UL	25,000	15,500	19,000	12,000	33,500	14,000	8,500
F-2	S	UL	11	5	3	4	3	5	3	2
	A	UL	UL	37,500	23,000	28,500	18,000	50,500	21,000	13,000
H-1	S	1	1	1	1	1	1	1	1	NP
	A	21,000	16,500	11,000	7,000	9,500	7,000	10,500	7,500	NP
H-2[d]	S	UL	3	2	1	2	1	2	1	1
	A	21,000	16,500	11,000	7,000	9,500	7,000	10,500	7,500	3,000
H-3[d]	S	UL	6	4	2	4	2	4	2	1
	A	UL	60,000	26,500	14,000	17,500	13,000	25,500	10,000	5,000
H-4	S	UL	7	5	3	5	3	5	3	2
	A	UL	UL	37,500	17,500	28,500	17,500	36,000	18,000	6,500
H-5	S	4	4	3	3	3	3	3	3	2
	A	UL	UL	37,500	23,000	28,500	19,000	36,000	18,000	9,000
I-1	S	UL	9	4	3	4	3	4	3	2
	A	UL	55,000	19,000	10,000	16,500	10,000	18,000	10,500	4,500
I-2	S	UL	4	2	1	1	NP	1	1	NP
	A	UL	UL	15,000	11,000	12,000	NP	12,000	9,500	NP
I-3	S	UL	4	2	1	2	1	2	2	1
	A	UL	UL	15,000	10,000	10,500	7,500	12,000	7,500	5,000
I-4	S	UL	5	3	2	3	2	3	1	1
	A	UL	60,500	26,500	13,000	23,500	13,000	25,500	18,500	9,000
M	S	UL	11	4	4	4	4	4	3	1
	A	UL	UL	21,500	12,500	18,500	12,500	20,500	14,000	9,000
R-1	S	UL	11	4	4	4	4	4	3	2
	A	UL	UL	24,000	16,000	24,000	16,000	20,500	12,000	7,000
R-2	S	UL	11	4	4	4	4	4	3	2
	A	UL	UL	24,000	16,000	24,000	16,000	20,500	12,000	7,000
R-3	S	UL	11	4	4	4	4	4	3	3
	A	UL	UL	UL	UL	UL	UL	UL	UL	UL
R-4	S	UL	11	4	4	4	4	4	3	2
	A	UL	UL	24,000	16,000	24,000	16,000	20,500	12,000	7,000
S-1	S	UL	11	4	3	3	3	4	3	1
	A	UL	48,000	26,000	17,500	26,000	17,500	25,500	14,000	9,000
S-2[b, c]	S	UL	11	5	4	4	4	5	4	2
	A	UL	79,000	39,000	26,000	39,000	26,000	38,500	21,000	13,500
U[c]	S	UL	5	4	2	3	2	4	2	1
	A	UL	35,500	19,000	8,500	14,000	8,500	18,000	9,000	5,500

For SI: 1 foot = 304.8 mm, 1 square foot = 0.0929m2.

UL = Unlimited, NP = Not permitted.

a. See the following sections for general exceptions to Table 503:
　1. Section 504.2, Allowable height increase due to automatic sprinkler system installation.
　2. Section 506.2, Allowable area increase due to street frontage.
　3. Section 506.3, Allowable area increase due to automatic sprinkler system installation.
　4. Section 507, Unlimited area buildings.
b. For open parking structures, see Section 406.3.
c. For private garages, see Section 406.1.
d. See Section 415.5 for limitations.

SECTION 504
HEIGHT

504.1 General. The height permitted by Table 503 shall be increased in accordance with this section.

Exception: The height of one-story aircraft hangars, aircraft paint hangars and buildings used for the manufacturing of aircraft shall not be limited if the building is provided with an automatic fire-extinguishing system in accordance with Chapter 9 and is entirely surrounded by public ways or yards not less in width than one and one-half times the height of the building.

504.2 Automatic sprinkler system increase. Where a building is equipped throughout with an approved automatic sprinkler system in accordance with Section 903.3.1.1, the value specified in Table 503 for maximum height is increased by 20 feet (6096 mm) and the maximum number of stories is increased by one. These increases are permitted in addition to the area increase in accordance with Sections 506.2 and 506.3. For Group R buildings equipped throughout with an approved automatic sprinkler system in accordance with Section 903.3.1.2, the value specified in Table 503 for maximum height is increased by 20 feet (6096 mm) and the maximum number of stories is increased by one, but shall not exceed 60 feet (18 288 mm) or four stories, respectively.

Exception:

1. The height increase shall not apply to portions of a building with a fire area which includes an occupancy Group I-2 in a building of Type IIB, III, IV or V construction.

2. The height increase shall not apply to portions of a building with a fire area which includes an occupancy in Group H-1, H-2, H-3 or H-5.

3. Where fire-resistance ratings have been reduced in accordance with footnote e of Table 601, the height increase shall not apply.

504.3 Roof structures. Towers, spires, steeples and other roof structures shall be constructed of materials consistent with the required type of construction of the building except where other construction is permitted by Section 1509.2.1. Such structures shall not be used for habitation or storage. The structures shall be unlimited in height if of noncombustible materials and shall not extend more than 20 feet (6096 mm) above the allowable height if of combustible materials (see Chapter 15 for additional requirements).

SECTION 505
MEZZANINES

505.1 General. A mezzanine or mezzanines in compliance with Section 505 shall be considered a portion of the story below. Such mezzanines shall not contribute to either the building area or number of stories as regulated by Section 503.1. The area of the mezzanine shall be included in determining the fire area defined in Section 702. The clear height above and below the mezzanine floor construction shall not be less than 7 feet (2134 mm).

505.2 Area limitation. The aggregate area of a mezzanine or mezzanines within a room shall not exceed one-third of the floor area of that room or space in which they are located. The enclosed portion of a room shall not be included in a determination of the floor area of the room in which the mezzanine is located. In determining the allowable mezzanine area, the area of the mezzanine shall not be included in the floor area of the room.

Exceptions:

1. The aggregate area of mezzanines in buildings and structures of Type I or II construction for special industrial occupancies in accordance with Section 503.1.1 shall not exceed two-thirds of the area of the room.

2. The aggregate area of mezzanines in buildings and structures of Type I or II construction shall not exceed one-half of the area of the room in buildings and structures equipped throughout with an approved automatic sprinkler system in accordance with Section 903.3.1.1 and an approved emergency voice/alarm communication system in accordance with Section 907.2.12.2.

505.3 Egress. Each occupant of a mezzanine shall have access to at least two independent means of egress where the common path of egress travel exceeds the limitations of Section 1014.3. Where a stairway provides a means of exit access from a mezzanine, the maximum travel distance includes the distance traveled on the stairway measured in the plane of the tread nosing. Accessible means of egress shall be provided in accordance with Section 1007.

Exception: A single means of egress shall be permitted in accordance with Section 1015.1.

505.4 Openness. A mezzanine shall be open and unobstructed to the room in which such mezzanine is located except for walls not more than 42 inches (1067 mm) high, columns and posts.

Exceptions:

1. Mezzanines or portions thereof are not required to be open to the room in which the mezzanines are located, provided that the occupant load of the aggregate area of the enclosed space does not exceed 10.

2. A mezzanine having two or more means of egress is not required to be open to the room in which the mezzanine is located if at least one of the means of egress provides direct access to an exit from the mezzanine level.

3. Mezzanines or portions thereof are not required to be open to the room in which the mezzanines are located, provided that the aggregate floor area of the enclosed space does not exceed 10 percent of the mezzanine area.

4. In industrial facilities, mezzanines used for control equipment are permitted to be glazed on all sides.

5. In other than Groups H and I occupancies no more than two stories in height above grade plane and

equipped throughout with an automatic sprinkler system in accordance with Section 903.3.1.1, a mezzanine having two or more means of egress shall not be required to be open to the room in which the mezzanine is located.

505.5 Equipment platforms. Equipment platforms in buildings shall not be considered as a portion of the floor below. Such equipment platforms shall not contribute to either the building area or the number of stories as regulated by Section 503.1. The area of the equipment platform shall not be included in determining the fire area. Equipment platforms shall not be a part of any mezzanine and such platforms and the walkways, stairs and ladders providing access to an equipment platform shall not serve as a part of the means of egress from the building.

505.5.1 Area limitations. The aggregate area of all equipment platforms within a room shall not exceed two-thirds of the area of the room in which they are located. Where an equipment platform is located in the same room as a mezzanine, the area of the mezzanine shall be determined by Section 505.2 and the combined aggregate area of the equipment platforms and mezzanines shall not exceed two-thirds of the room in which they are located.

[F] 505.5.2 Fire suppression. Where located in a building that is required to be protected by an automatic sprinkler system, equipment platforms shall be fully protected by sprinklers above and below the platform, where required by the standards referenced in Section 903.3.

505.5.3 Guards. Equipment platforms shall have guards where required by Section 1013.1.

SECTION 506
AREA MODIFICATIONS

506.1 General. The areas limited by Table 503 shall be permitted to be increased due to frontage (I_f) and automatic sprinkler system protection (I_s) in accordance with the following:

$$A_a = \{A_t + [A_t \times I_f] + [A_t \times I_s]\} \qquad \textbf{(Equation 5-1)}$$

where:

A_a = Allowable area per story (square feet).

A_t = Tabular area per story in accordance with Table 503 (square feet).

I_f = Area increase factor due to frontage as calculated in accordance with Section 506.2.

I_s = Area increase factor due to sprinkler protection as calculated in accordance with Section 506.3.

506.1.1 Basements. A single basement that is not a story above grade plane need not be included in the total allowable area, provided such basement does not exceed the area permitted for a building with no more than one story above grade plane.

506.2 Frontage increase. Every building shall adjoin or have access to a public way to receive an area increase for frontage. Where a building has more than 25 percent of its perimeter on a public way or open space having a minimum width of 20 feet (6096 mm), the frontage increase shall be determined in accordance with the following:

$$I_f = [F/P - 0.25](W/30) \qquad \textbf{(Equation 5-2)}$$

where:

I_f = Area increase due to frontage.

F = Building perimeter that fronts on a public way or open space having 20 feet (6096 mm) open minimum width (feet).

P = Perimeter of entire building (feet).

W = Width of public way or open space (feet) in accordance with Section 506.2.1.

506.2.1 Width limits. "W" must be at least 20 feet (6096 mm). Where the value of W varies along the perimeter of the building, the calculation performed in accordance with Equation 5-2 shall be based on the weighted average of each portion of exterior wall and open space where the value of W is greater than or equal to 20 feet (6096 mm). Where W exceeds 30 feet (9144 mm), a value of 30 feet (9144 mm) shall be used in calculating the weighted average, regardless of the actual width of the open space.

Exception: The quantity of W divided by 30 shall be permitted to be a maximum of 2 when the building meets all requirements of Section 507 except for compliance with the 60-foot (18 288 mm) public way or yard requirement, as applicable.

506.2.2 Open space limits. Such open space shall be either on the same lot or dedicated for public use and shall be accessed from a street or approved fire lane.

506.3 Automatic sprinkler system increase. Where a building is equipped throughout with an approved automatic sprinkler system in accordance with Section 903.3.1.1, the area limitation in Table 503 is permitted to be increased by an additional 200 percent ($I_s = 2$) for buildings with more than one story above grade plane and an additional 300 percent ($I_s = 3$) for buildings with no more than one story above grade plane. These increases are permitted in addition to the height and story increases in accordance with Section 504.2.

Exception: The area limitation increases shall not be permitted for the following conditions:

1. The automatic sprinkler system increase shall not apply to buildings with an occupancy in Use Group H-1.

2. The automatic sprinkler system increase shall not apply to the floor area of an occupancy in Use Group H-2 or H-3. For mixed-use buildings containing such occupancies, the allowable area shall be calculated in accordance with Section 508.3.3.2, with the sprinkler increase applicable only to the portions of the building not classified as Use Group H-2 or H-3.

3. Where fire-resistance ratings have been reduced in accordance with footnote e of Table 601, the area increase shall not apply.

506.4 Area determination. The maximum area of a building with more than one story above grade plane shall be determined by multiplying the allowable area of the first story (A_a), as determined in Section 506.1, by the number of stories above grade plane as listed below:

1. For buildings with two stories above grade plane, multiply by 2;

2. For buildings with three or more stories above grade plane, multiply by 3; and

3. No story shall exceed the allowable area per story (A_a), as determined in Section 506.1, for the occupancies on that story.

Exceptions:

1. Unlimited area buildings in accordance with Section 507.

2. The maximum area of a building equipped throughout with an automatic sprinkler system in accordance with Section 903.3.1.2 shall be determined by multiplying the allowable area per story (A_a), as determined in Section 506.1, by the number of stories above grade plane.

506.4.1 Mixed occupancies. In buildings with mixed occupancies, the allowable area per story (A_a) shall be based on the most restrictive provisions for each occupancy when the mixed occupancies are treated according to Section 508.3.2. When the occupancies are treated according to Section 508.3.3 as separated occupancies, the maximum total building area shall be such that the sum of the ratios for each such area on all floors as calculated according to Section 508.3.3.2 shall not exceed 2 for two-story buildings and 3 for buildings three stories or higher.

SECTION 507
UNLIMITED AREA BUILDINGS

507.1 General. The area of buildings of the occupancies and configurations specified herein shall not be limited.

507.2 Nonsprinklered, one story. The area of a one-story, Group F-2 or S-2 building shall not be limited when the building is surrounded and adjoined by public ways or yards not less than 60 feet (18 288 mm) in width.

507.3 Sprinklered, one story. The area of a one-story, Group B, F, M or S building or a one-story Group A-4 building, of other than Type V construction, shall not be limited when the building is provided with an automatic sprinkler system throughout in accordance with Section 903.3.1.1 and is surrounded and adjoined by public ways or yards not less than 60 feet (18 288 mm) in width.

Exceptions:

1. Buildings and structures of Type I and II construction for rack storage facilities that do not have access by the public shall not be limited in height, provided that such buildings conform to the requirements of Sections 507.2 and 903.3.1.1 and NFPA 230.

2. The automatic sprinkler system shall not be required in areas occupied for indoor participant sports, such as tennis, skating, swimming and equestrian activities in occupancies in Group A-4, provided that:

   2.1. Exit doors directly to the outside are provided for occupants of the participant sports areas; and

   2.2. The building is equipped with a fire alarm system with manual fire alarm boxes installed in accordance with Section 907.

3. Group A-1 and A-2 occupancies of other than Type V construction shall be permitted, provided:

   3.1. All assembly occupancies are separated from other spaces as required for separated uses in Section 508.3.3.4 with no reduction allowed in the fire-resistance rating of the separation based upon the installation of an automatic sprinkler system;

   3.2. Each Group A occupancy shall not exceed the maximum allowable area permitted in Section 503.1; and

   3.3. All required exits shall discharge directly to the exterior.

507.4 Two story. The area of a two-story, Group B, F, M or S building shall not be limited when the building is equipped throughout with an automatic sprinkler system in accordance with Section 903.3.1.1, and is surrounded and adjoined by public ways or yards not less than 60 feet (18 288 mm) in width.

507.5 Reduced open space. The permanent open space of 60 feet (18 288 mm) required in Sections 507.2, 507.3, 507.4, 507.6 and 507.10 shall be permitted to be reduced to not less than 40 feet (12 192 mm), provided the following requirements are met:

1. The reduced open space shall not be allowed for more than 75 percent of the perimeter of the building.

2. The exterior wall facing the reduced open space shall have a minimum fire-resistance rating of 3 hours.

3. Openings in the exterior wall facing the reduced open space shall have opening protectives with a minimum fire protection rating of 3 hours.

507.6 Group A-3 buildings. The area of a one-story, Group A-3 building used as a place of religious worship, community hall, dance hall, exhibition hall, gymnasium, lecture hall, indoor swimming pool or tennis court of Type II construction shall not be limited when all of the following criteria are met:

1. The building shall not have a stage other than a platform.

2. The building shall be equipped throughout with an automatic sprinkler system in accordance with Section 903.3.1.1.

3. The assembly floor shall be located at or within 21 inches (533 mm) of street or grade level and all exits are provided with ramps complying with Section 1010.1 to the street or grade level.

4. The building shall be surrounded and adjoined by public ways or yards not less than 60 feet (18 288 mm) in width.

507.7 Group H occupancies. Group H-2, H-3 and H-4 occupancies shall be permitted in unlimited area buildings containing Group F and S occupancies, in accordance with Sections 507.3 and 507.4 and the limitations of this section. The aggregate floor area of the Group H occupancies located at the perimeter of the unlimited area building shall not exceed 10 percent of the area of the building nor the area limitations for the Group H occupancies as specified in Table 503 as modified by Section 506.2, based upon the percentage of the perimeter of each Group H fire area that fronts on a street or other unoccupied space. The aggregate floor area of Group H occupancies not located at the perimeter of the building shall not exceed 25 percent of the area limitations for the Group H occupancies as specified in Table 503. Group H fire areas shall be separated from the rest of the unlimited area building and from each other in accordance with Table 508.3.3 For two-story unlimited area buildings, the Group H fire areas shall not be located above the first story unless permitted by the allowable height in stories and feet as set forth in Table 503 based on the type of construction of the unlimited area building.

507.8 Aircraft paint hangar. The area of a one-story, Group H-2 aircraft paint hangar shall not be limited where such aircraft paint hangar complies with the provisions of Section 412.4 and is entirely surrounded by public ways or yards not less in width than one and one-half times the height of the building.

507.9 Group E buildings. The area of a one-story Group E building of Type II, IIIA or IV construction shall not be limited when the following criteria are met:

1. Each classroom shall have not less than two means of egress, with one of the means of egress being a direct exit to the outside of the building complying with Section 1018.

2. The building is equipped throughout with an automatic sprinkler system in accordance with Section 903.3.1.1.

3. The building is surrounded and adjoined by public ways or yards not less than 60 feet (18 288 mm) in width.

507.10 Motion picture theaters. In buildings of Type II construction, the area of a one-story motion picture theater shall not be limited when the building is provided with an automatic sprinkler system throughout in accordance with Section 903.3.1.1 and is surrounded and adjoined by public ways or yards not less than 60 feet (18 288 mm) in width.

507.11 Covered mall buildings and anchor stores. The area of covered mall buildings and anchor stores not exceeding three stories in height that comply with Section 402.6 shall not be limited.

SECTION 508
MIXED USE AND OCCUPANCY

508.1 General. Where a building or portion thereof contains two or more occupancies or uses, the building or portion

thereof shall comply with the applicable provisions of this section.

508.2 Incidental uses. Incidental use areas shall comply with the provisions of this section.

Exception: Incidental use areas within and serving a dwelling unit are not required to comply with this section.

508.2.1 Occupancy classification. An incidental use area shall be classified in accordance with the occupancy of that portion of the building in which it is located or the building shall be classified as a mixed occupancy and shall comply with Section 508.3.

508.2.2 Separation. Incidental use areas shall be separated or protected, or both, in accordance with Table 508.2.

508.2.2.1 Construction. Where Table 508.2 requires a fire-resistance-rated separation, the incidental use area shall be separated from the remainder of the building by a fire barrier constructed in accordance with Section 706 or a horizontal assembly constructed in accordance with Section 711, or both. Where Table 508.2 permits an automatic fire-extinguishing system without a fire barrier, the incidental use area shall be separated from the remainder of the building by construction capable of resisting the passage of smoke. The partitions shall extend from the floor to the underside of the fire-resistance-rated floor/ceiling assembly or fire-resistance-rated roof/ceiling assembly above or to the underside of the floor or roof sheathing, or sub deck above. Doors shall be self- or automatic closing upon detection of smoke in accordance with Section 715.4.7.3. Doors shall not have air transfer openings and shall not be undercut in excess of the clearance permitted in accordance with NFPA 80.

508.2.3 Protection. Where an automatic fire-extinguishing system or an automatic sprinkler system is provided in accordance with Table 508.2, only the incidental use areas need be equipped with such a system.

508.3 Mixed occupancies. Each portion of a building shall be individually classified in accordance with Section 302.1.

Where a building contains more than one occupancy group, the building or portion thereof shall comply with Sections 508.3.1, 508.3.2, 508.3.3 or a combination of these sections.

Exceptions:

1. Occupancies separated in accordance with Section 509.

2. Where required by Table 415.3.2, areas of Group H-1, H-2 or H-3 occupancies shall be located in a separate and detached building or structure.

508.3.1 Accessory occupancies. Accessory occupancies are those occupancies subsidiary to the main occupancy of the building or portion thereof. Aggregate accessory occupancies shall not occupy more than 10 percent of the area of the story in which they are located and shall not exceed the tabular values in Table 503, without height and area increases in accordance with Sections 504 and 506 for such accessory occupancies.

Exceptions:

1. Accessory assembly areas having a floor area less than 750 square feet (69.7 m²) are not considered separate occupancies.

2. Assembly areas that are accessory to Group E occupancies are not considered separate occupancies except when applying the assembly occupancy requirements of Chapter 11.

3. Accessory religious educational rooms and religious auditoriums with occupant loads of less than 100 are not considered separate occupancies.

508.3.1.1 Occupancy classification. Accessory occupancies shall be individually classified in accordance with Section 302.1. Code requirements shall apply to each portion of the building based on the occupancy classification of that accessory space, except that the most restrictive applicable provisions of Section 403 and Chapter 9 shall apply to the entire building or portion thereof.

508.3.1.2 Allowable area and height. The allowable area and height of the building shall be based on the allowable area and height for the main occupancy in accordance with Section 503.1. The height of any accessory occupancy shall not exceed the tabular values in Table 503, without height and area increases in accordance with Sections 504 and 506 for such accessory occupancies.

508.3.1.3 Separation. No separation is required between accessory occupancies or the main occupancy.

> **Exception:** Group H-2, H-3, H-4 or H-5 occupancies shall be separated from all other occupancies in accordance with Section 508.3.3.

508.3.2 Nonseparated occupancies. Buildings or portions of buildings that comply with the provisions of this section shall qualify as nonseparated occupancies.

508.3.2.1 Occupancy classification. Nonseparated occupancies shall be individually classified in accordance with Section 302.1. Code requirements shall apply to each portion of the building based on the occupancy classification of that space except that the most restrictive applicable provisions of Section 403 and Chapter 9 shall apply to the entire building or portion thereof.

508.3.2.2 Allowable area and height. The allowable area and height of the building or portion thereof shall be based on the most restrictive allowances for the occupancy groups under consideration for the type of construction of the building in accordance with Section 503.1.

508.3.2.3 Separation. No separation is required between occupancies.

TABLE 508.2
INCIDENTAL USE AREAS

ROOM OR AREA	SEPARATION AND/OR PROTECTION
Furnace room where any piece of equipment is over 400,000 Btu per hour input	1 hour or provide automatic fire-extinguishing system
Rooms with boilers where the largest piece of equipment is over 15 psi and 10 horsepower	1 hour or provide automatic fire-extinguishing system
Refrigerant machinery rooms	1 hour or provide automatic sprinkler system
Parking garage (Section 406.2)	2 hours; or 1 hour and provide automatic fire-extinguishing system
Hydrogen cut-off rooms, not classified as Group H	1-hour in Group B, F, M, S and U occupancies. 2-hour in Group A, E, I and R occupancies.
Incinerator rooms	2 hours and automatic sprinkler system
Paint shops, not classified as Group H, located in occupancies other than Group F	2 hours; or 1 hour and provide automatic fire-extinguishing system
Laboratories and vocational shops, not classified as Group H, located in Group E or I-2 occupancies	1 hour or provide automatic fire-extinguishing system
Laundry rooms over 100 square feet	1 hour or provide automatic fire-extinguishing system
Storage rooms over 100 square feet[b]	1 hour or provide automatic fire-extinguishing system
Group I-3 cells equipped with padded surfaces	1 hour
Group I-2 waste and linen collection rooms	1 hour
Waste and linen collection rooms over 100 square feet	1 hour or provide automatic fire-extinguishing system
Stationary storage battery systems having a liquid capacity of more than 100 gallons used for facility standby power, emergency power or uninterrupted power supplies	1-hour in Group B, F, M, S and U occupancies. 2-hour in Group A, E, I and R occupancies.

For SI: 1 square foot = 0.0929 m², 1 pound per square inch = 6.9 kPa, 1 British thermal unit per hour = 0.293 watts, 1 horsepower = 746 watts, 1 gallon = 3.785 L.

a. Storage areas larger than the main occupancy shall be regulated as a mixed occupancy.

> **Exception:** Group H-2, H-3, H-4 or H-5 occupancies shall be separated from all other occupancies in accordance with Section 508.3.3.

508.3.3 Separated occupancies. Buildings or portions of buildings that comply with the provisions of this section shall qualify as separated occupancies.

508.3.3.1 Occupancy classification. Separated occupancies shall be individually classified in accordance with Section 302.1. Each fire area shall comply with this code based on the occupancy classification of that portion of the building.

508.3.3.2 Allowable area. In each story, the building area shall be such that the sum of the ratios of the actual floor area of each occupancy divided by the allowable area of each occupancy shall not exceed one. The sum of the ratios applies to every mixed use on the story even when Table 508.3.3 does not require a fire-resistance rating between the proposed uses.

Exception: The allowable area of any individual fire area may comply with 508.3.2 as a non-separated mixed use.

508.3.3.3 Allowable height. Each occupancy shall comply with the height limitations based on the type of construction of the building in accordance with Section 503.1. The height, in both feet and stories, of each fire area shall be measured from grade plane. This measurement shall include the height, in both feet and stories, of intervening fire areas.

Exception: Special provisions permitted by Section 509.

508.3.3.4 Separation. Individual occupancies shall be separated from adjacent occupancies in accordance with Table 508.3.3

508.3.3.4.1 Construction. Required separations shall be fire barriers constructed in accordance with Section 706 or horizontal assemblies constructed in accordance with Section 711, or both, so as to completely separate adjacent occupancies.

SECTION 509
SPECIAL PROVISIONS

509.1 General. The provisions in this section shall permit the use of special conditions that are exempt from, or modify, the specific requirements of this chapter regarding the allowable heights and areas of buildings based on the occupancy classification and type of construction, provided the special condition complies with the provisions specified in this section for such condition and other applicable requirements of this code.

509.2 Group S-2 enclosed or open parking garage with Group A, B, M, R or S above. A basement and/or the first story above grade plane of a building shall be considered as a separate and distinct building for the purpose of determining area limitations, continuity of fire walls, limitation of number of stories and type of construction when all of the following conditions are met:

1. The basement and/or the first story above grade plane is of Type IA construction and is separated from the building above with a horizontal assembly having a minimum 3-hour fire-resistance rating.

2. Shaft, stairway, ramp or escalator enclosures through the horizontal assembly shall have not less than a 2-hour fire-resistance rating with opening protectives in accordance with Table 715.4.

Exception: Where the enclosure walls below the horizontal assembly have not less than a 3-hour fire-resistance rating with opening protectives in accordance with Table 715.4, the enclosure walls extending above

TABLE 508.3.3
REQUIRED SEPARATION OF OCCUPANCIES (HOURS)

OCCUPANCY	A^e, E^e		I		R^d		B^b		F-2, S-2^{c,d},U^d		M^b		F-1, S-1		H-1		H-2		H-3, H-4, H-5	
	S	NS	S	NS	S	NS	S	NS	S	NS	S	NS	S	NS	S	NS	S	NS	S	NS
A^e, E^e	N	N	1	2	1	2	1	2	N	1	1	2	1	2	NP	NP	3	4	2	3^a
I	-	-	N	N	1	NP	1	2	1	2	1	2	1	2	NP	NP	3	NP	2	NP
R^d	-	-	-	-	N	N	1	2	1	2	1	2	1	2	NP	NP	3	NP	2	NP
B^b	-	-	-	-	-	-	N	N	1	2	1	2	1	2	NP	NP	2	3	1	2^a
F-2, S-2^{c,d}, U^d	-	-	-	-	-	-	-	-	N	N	1	2	1	2	NP	NP	3	4	2	3^a
M^b	-	-	-	-	-	-	-	-	-	-	N	N	1	2	NP	NP	2	3	1	2^a
F-1, S-1	-	-	-	-	-	-	-	-	-	-	-	-	N	N	NP	NP	2	3	1	2^a
H-1	-	-	-	-	-	-	-	-	-	-	-	-	-	-	N	NP	NP	NP	NP	NP
H-2	-	-	-	-	-	-	-	-	-	-	-	-	-	-	-	-	N	NP	1	NP
H-3, H-4, H-5	-	-	-	-	-	-	-	-	-	-	-	-	-	-	-	-	-	-	N	NP

For SI: 1 square foot = 0.0929 m^2.

S = Buildings equipped throughout with an automatic sprinkler system installed in accordance with Section 903.3.1.1

NS = Buildings not equipped throughout with an automatic sprinkler system installed in accordance with Section 903.3.1.1.

N = No separation requirement.

NP = Not permitted.

a. For Group H-5 occupancies, see Section 903.2.4.2
b. Occupancy separation need not be provided for storage areas within Groups B and M if the:
   1. Area is less than 10 percent of the floor area;
   2. Area is equipped with an automatic fire-extinguishing system and is less than 3,000 square feet; or
   3. Area is less than 1,000 square feet.
c. Areas used only for private or pleasure vehicles shall be allowed to reduce separation by 1 hour.
d. See Section 406.1.4.

the horizontal assembly shall be permitted to have a 1-hour fire-resistance rating, provided:

1. The building above the horizontal assembly is not required to be of Type I construction;

2. The enclosure connects less than four stories; and

3. The enclosure opening protectives above the horizontal assembly have a minimum 1-hour fire protection rating.

3. The building above the horizontal assembly shall be permitted to have multiple Group A uses, each with an occupant load of less than 300, or Group B, M, R or S uses.

4. The building below the horizontal assembly is a Group S-2 enclosed or open parking garage, used for the parking and storage of private motor vehicles.

Exceptions:

1. Entry lobbies, mechanical rooms and similar uses incidental to the operation of the building shall be permitted.

2. Multiple Group A uses, each with an occupant load of less than 300, or Group B or M uses shall be permitted, in addition to those uses incidental to the operation of the building (including storage areas), provided that the entire structure below the horizontal assembly is protected throughout by an approved automatic sprinkler system.

5. The maximum building height in feet shall not exceed the limits set forth in Section 503 for the building having the smaller allowable height as measured from the grade plane.

509.3 Group S-2 enclosed parking garage with Group S-2 open parking garage above. A Group S-2 enclosed parking garage located in the basement or first story below a Group S-2 open parking garage shall be classified as a separate and distinct building for the purpose of determining the type of construction when the following conditions are met:

1. The allowable area of the structure shall be such that the sum of the ratios of the actual area divided by the allowable area for each separate occupancy shall not exceed 1.0.

2. The Group S-2 enclosed parking garage is of Type I or II construction and is at least equal to the fire-resistance requirements of the Group S-2 open parking garage.

3. The height and the number of the floors above the basement shall be limited as specified in Table 406.3.5.

4. The floor assembly separating the Group S-2 enclosed parking garage and Group S-2 open parking garage shall be protected as required for the floor assembly of the Group S-2 enclosed parking garage. Openings between the Group S-2 enclosed parking garage and Group S-2 open parking garage, except exit openings, shall not be required to be protected.

5. The Group S-2 enclosed parking garage is used exclusively for the parking or storage of private motor vehicles, but shall be permitted to contain an office, waiting room and toilet room having a total area of not more than 1,000 square feet (93 m²), and mechanical equipment rooms incidental to the operation of the building.

509.4 Parking beneath Group R. Where a maximum one-story above grade plane Group S-2 parking garage, enclosed or open, or combination thereof, of Type I construction or open of Type IV construction, with grade entrance, is provided under a building of Group R, the number of stories to be used in determining the minimum type of construction shall be measured from the floor above such a parking area. The floor assembly between the parking garage and the Group R above shall comply with the type of construction required for the parking garage and shall also provide a fire-resistance rating not less than the mixed occupancy separation required in Section 508.3.3.

509.5 Group R-2 buildings of Type IIIA construction. The height limitation for buildings of Type IIIA construction in Group R-2 shall be increased to six stories and 75 feet (22 860 mm) where the first-floor construction above the basement has a fire-resistance rating of not less than 3 hours and the floor area is subdivided by 2-hour fire-resistance-rated fire walls into areas of not more than 3,000 square feet (279 m²).

509.6 Group R-2 buildings of Type IIA construction. The height limitation for buildings of Type IIA construction in Group R-2 shall be increased to nine stories and 100 feet (30 480 mm) where the building is separated by not less than 50 feet (15 240 mm) from any other building on the lot and from lot lines, the exits are segregated in an area enclosed by a 2-hour fire-resistance-rated fire wall and the first-floor construction has a fire-resistance rating of not less than $1^1/_2$ hours.

509.7 Open parking garage beneath Groups A, I, B, M and R. Open parking garages constructed under Groups A, I, B, M and R shall not exceed the height and area limitations permitted under Section 406.3. The height and area of the portion of the building above the open parking garage shall not exceed the limitations in Section 503 for the upper occupancy. The height, in both feet and stories, of the portion of the building above the open parking garage shall be measured from grade plane and shall include both the open parking garage and the portion of the building above the parking garage.

509.7.1 Fire separation. Fire barriers constructed in accordance with Section 706 or horizontal assemblies constructed in accordance with Section 711 between the parking occupancy and the upper occupancy shall correspond to the required fire-resistance rating prescribed in Table 508.3.3 for the uses involved. The type of construction shall apply to each occupancy individually, except that structural members, including main bracing within the open parking structure, which is necessary to support the upper occupancy, shall be protected with the more restrictive fire-resistance-rated assemblies of the groups involved as shown in Table 601. Means of egress for the upper occupancy shall conform to Chapter 10 and shall be separated from the parking occupancy by fire barriers having at least a 2-hour fire-resistance rating as required by

Section 706 with self-closing doors complying with Section 715 or horizontal assemblies having at least a 2-hour fire-resistance rating as required by Section 711, with self-closing doors complying with Section 715. Means of egress from the open parking garage shall comply with Section 406.3.

509.8 Group B or M with Group S-2 open parking garage above. Group B or M uses located in the basement or first story below a Group S-2 open parking garage shall be classified as a separate and distinct building for the purpose of determining the type of construction when all of the following conditions are met:

1. The basement or first story shall be Type I or II construction, but not less than the type of construction required for the open parking garage above. The height and area of the basement or first story shall not exceed the limitations in Section 503 for the Group B or M uses.

2. The height and area of the open parking garage shall not exceed the limitations permitted under Section 406.3. The height, in both feet and stories, of the open parking garage shall be measured from grade plane and include both the open parking garage and the basement or first story.

3. Fire separation assemblies between the open parking garage and the basement or first story use group shall correspond to the required fire-resistance rating prescribed by Table 508.3.3

4. Exits serving the open parking garage shall discharge directly to a street or public way and shall be separated from the basement or first story use group by not less than 2-hour fire barriers constructed in accordance with Section 706 or 2-hour horizontal assemblies constructed in accordance with Section 711, or both, with opening protectives in accordance with Table 715.4.

CHAPTER 6

TYPES OF CONSTRUCTION

SECTION 601
GENERAL

601.1 Scope. The provisions of this chapter shall control the classification of buildings as to type of construction.

SECTION 602
CONSTRUCTION CLASSIFICATION

602.1 General. Buildings and structures erected or to be erected, altered or extended in height or area shall be classified in one of the five construction types defined in Sections 602.2 through 602.5. The building elements shall have a fire-resistance rating not less than that specified in Table 601 and exterior walls shall have a fire-resistance rating not less than that specified in Table 602.

602.1.1 Minimum requirements. A building or portion thereof shall not be required to conform to the details of a type of construction higher than that type, which meets the minimum requirements based on occupancy even though certain features of such a building actually conform to a higher type of construction.

602.2 Types I and II. Type I and II construction are those types of construction in which the building elements listed in Table 601 are of noncombustible materials, except as permitted in Section 603 and elsewhere in this code.

602.3 Type III. Type III construction is that type of construction in which the exterior walls are of noncombustible materials and the interior building elements are of any material permitted by this code. Fire-retardant-treated wood framing complying with Section 2303.2 shall be permitted within exterior wall assemblies of a 2-hour rating or less.

602.4 Type IV. Type IV construction (Heavy Timber, HT) is that type of construction in which the exterior walls are of noncombustible materials and the interior building elements are of solid or laminated wood without concealed spaces. The details of Type IV construction shall comply with the provisions of this section. Fire-retardant-treated wood framing complying with Section 2303.2 shall be permitted within exterior wall assemblies with a 2-hour rating or less. Minimum solid sawn nominal dimensions are required for structures built using Type IV construction (HT). For glued-laminated members the equivalent net finished width and depths corresponding to the minimum nominal width and depths of solid sawn lumber are required as specified in Table 602.4.

602.4.1 Columns. Wood columns shall be sawn or glued laminated and shall not be less than 8 inches (203 mm), nominal, in any dimension where supporting floor loads and not less than 6 inches (152 mm) nominal in width and not less than 8 inches (203 mm) nominal in depth where supporting roof and ceiling loads only. Columns shall be continuous or superimposed and connected in an approved manner.

602.4.2 Floor framing. Wood beams and girders shall be of sawn or glued-laminated timber and shall be not less than 6 inches (152 mm) nominal in width and not less than 10 inches (254 mm) nominal in depth. Framed sawn or glued-laminated timber arches, which spring from the floor line and support floor loads, shall be not less than 8 inches (203 mm) nominal in any dimension. Framed timber trusses supporting floor loads shall have members of not less than 8 inches (203 mm) nominal in any dimension.

602.4.3 Roof framing. Wood-frame or glued-laminated arches for roof construction, which spring from the floor line or from grade and do not support floor loads, shall have members not less than 6 inches (152 mm) nominal in width and have not less than 8 inches (203 mm) nominal in depth for the lower half of the height and not less than 6 inches (152 mm) nominal in depth for the upper half. Framed or glued- laminated arches for roof construction that spring from the top of walls or wall abutments, framed timber trusses and other roof framing, which do not support floor loads, shall have members not less than 4 inches (102 mm) nominal in width and not less than 6 inches (152 mm) nominal in depth. Spaced members shall be permitted to be composed of two or more pieces not less than 3 inches (76 mm) nominal in thickness where blocked solidly throughout their intervening spaces or where spaces are tightly closed by a continuous wood cover plate of not less than 2 inches (51 mm) nominal in thickness secured to the underside of the members. Splice plates shall be not less than 3 inches (76 mm) nominal in thickness. Where protected by approved automatic sprinklers under the roof deck, framing members shall be not less than 3 inches (76 mm) nominal in width.

602.4.4 Floors. Floors shall be without concealed spaces. Wood floors shall be of sawn or glued-laminated planks, splined or tongue-and-groove, of not less than 3 inches (76 mm) nominal in thickness covered with 1-inch (25 mm) nominal dimension tongue-and-groove flooring, laid crosswise or diagonally, or 0.5-inch (12.7 mm) particleboard or planks not less than 4 inches (102 mm) nominal in width set on edge close together and well spiked and covered with 1-inch (25 mm) nominal dimension flooring or $^{15}/_{32}$-inch (12 mm) wood structural panel or 0.5-inch (12.7 mm) particleboard. The lumber shall be laid so that no continuous line of joints will occur except at points of support. Floors shall not extend closer than 0.5 inch (12.7 mm) to walls. Such 0.5-inch (12.7 mm) space shall be covered by a molding fastened to the wall and so arranged that it will not obstruct the swelling or shrinkage movements of the floor. Corbeling of masonry walls under the floor shall be permitted to be used in place of molding.

TABLE 601
FIRE-RESISTANCE RATING REQUIREMENTS FOR BUILDING ELEMENTS (hours)

BUILDING ELEMENT	TYPE I A	TYPE I B	TYPE II A[e]	TYPE II B	TYPE III A[e]	TYPE III B	TYPE IV HT	TYPE V A[e]	TYPE V B
Structural frame[a]	3[b]	2[b]	1	0	1	0	HT	1	0
Bearing walls									
Exterior[g]	3	2	1	0	2	2	2	1	0
Interior	3[b]	2[b]	1	0	1	0	1/HT	1	0
Nonbearing walls and partitions Exterior	See Table 602								
Nonbearing walls and partitions Interior[f]	0	0	0	0	0	0	See Section 602.4.6	0	0
Floor construction Including supporting beams and joists	2	2	1	0	1	0	HT	1	0
Roof construction Including supporting beams and joists	$1^1/_2$[c]	1[c, d]	1[c, d]	0[d]	1[c, d]	0[c, d]	HT	1[c, d]	0

For SI: 1 foot = 304.8 mm.

a. The structural frame shall be considered to be the columns and the girders, beams, trusses and spandrels having direct connections to the columns and bracing members designed to carry gravity loads. The members of floor or roof panels which have no connection to the columns shall be considered secondary members and not a part of the structural frame.

b. Roof supports: Fire-resistance ratings of structural frame and bearing walls are permitted to be reduced by 1 hour where supporting a roof only.

c. Except in Group F-1, H, M and S-1 occupancies, fire protection of structural members shall not be required, including protection of roof framing and decking where every part of the roof construction is 20 feet or more above any floor immediately below. Fire-retardant-treated wood members shall be allowed to be used for such unprotected members.

d. In all occupancies, heavy timber shall be allowed where a 1-hour or less fire-resistance rating is required.

e. An approved automatic sprinkler system in accordance with Section 903.3.1.1 shall be allowed to be substituted for 1-hour fire-resistance-rated construction, provided such system is not otherwise required by other provisions of the code or used for an allowable area increase in accordance with Section 506.3 or an allowable height increase in accordance with Section 504.2. The 1-hour substitution for the fire resistance of exterior walls shall not be permitted.

f. Not less than the fire-resistance rating required by other sections of this code.

g. Not less than the fire-resistance rating based on fire separation distance (see Table 602).

TABLE 602
FIRE-RESISTANCE RATING REQUIREMENTS FOR EXTERIOR WALLS BASED ON FIRE SEPARATION DISTANCE[a, e]

FIRE SEPARATION DISTANCE = X (feet)	TYPE OF CONSTRUCTION	OCCUPANCY GROUP H	OCCUPANCY GROUP F-1, M, S-1	OCCUPANCY GROUP A, B, E, F-2, I, R, S-2, U[b]
X<5[c]	All	3	2	1
5≤X<10	IA	3	2	1
	Others	2	1	1
10≤X<30	IA, IB	2	1	1[d]
	IIB, VB	1	0	0
	Others	1	1	1[d]
X≥30	All	0	0	0

For SI: 1 foot = 304.8 mm.

a. Load-bearing exterior walls shall also comply with the fire-resistance rating requirements of Table 601.

b. For special requirements for Group U occupancies see Section 406.1.2

c. See Section 705.1.1 for party walls.

d. Open parking garages complying with Section 406 shall not be required to have a fire-resistance rating.

e. The fire-resistance rating of an exterior wall is determined based upon the fire separation distance of the exterior wall and the story in which the wall is located.

TABLE 602.4
WOOD MEMBER SIZE

MINIMUM NOMINAL SOLID SAWN SIZE Width, inch	MINIMUM NOMINAL SOLID SAWN SIZE Depth, inch	MINIMUM GLUED-LAMINATED NET SIZE Width, inch	MINIMUM GLUED-LAMINATED NET SIZE Depth, inch
8	8	$6^3/_4$	$8^1/_4$
6	10	5	$10^1/_2$
6	8	5	$8^1/_4$
6	6	5	6
4	6	3	$6^7/_8$

For SI: 1 inch = 25.4 mm

602.4.5 Roofs. Roofs shall be without concealed spaces and wood roof decks shall be sawn or glued laminated, splined or tongue-and-groove plank, not less than 2 inches (51 mm) nominal in thickness, $1^1/_8$-inch-thick (32 mm) wood structural panel (exterior glue), or of planks not less than 3 inches (76 mm) nominal in width, set on edge close together and laid as required for floors. Other types of decking shall be permitted to be used if providing equivalent fire resistance and structural properties.

602.4.6 Partitions. Partitions shall be of solid wood construction formed by not less than two layers of 1-inch (25 mm) matched boards or laminated construction 4 inches (102 mm) thick, or of 1-hour fire-resistance-rated construction.

602.4.7 Exterior structural members. Where a horizontal separation of 20 feet (6096 mm) or more is provided, wood columns and arches conforming to heavy timber sizes shall be permitted to be used externally.

602.5 Type V. Type V construction is that type of construction in which the structural elements, exterior walls and interior walls are of any materials permitted by this code.

SECTION 603
COMBUSTIBLE MATERIAL IN TYPE I AND II CONSTRUCTION

603.1 Allowable materials. Combustible materials shall be permitted in buildings of Type I or Type II construction in the following applications and in accordance with Sections 603.1.1 through 603.1.3:

1. Fire-retardant-treated wood shall be permitted in:

   1.1. Nonbearing partitions where the required fire-resistance rating is 2 hours or less.

   1.2. Nonbearing exterior walls where no fire rating is required.

   1.3. Roof construction, including girders, trusses, framing and decking.

   Exception: In buildings of Type I construction exceeding two stories in height, fire-retardant-treated wood is not permitted in roof construction when the vertical distance from the upper floor to the roof is less than 20 feet (6096 mm).

2. Thermal and acoustical insulation, other than foam plastics, having a flame spread index of not more than 25.

   Exceptions:

   1. Insulation placed between two layers of noncombustible materials without an intervening airspace shall be allowed to have a flame spread index of not more than 100.

   2. Insulation installed between a finished floor and solid decking without intervening airspace shall be allowed to have a flame spread index of not more than 200.

3. Foam plastics in accordance with Chapter 26.

4. Roof coverings that have an A, B or C classification.

5. Interior floor finish and interior finish, trim and millwork such as doors, door frames, window sashes and frames.

6. Where not installed over 15 feet (4572 mm) above grade, show windows, nailing or furring strips and wooden bulkheads below show windows, including their frames, aprons and show cases.

7. Finished flooring applied directly to the floor slab or to wood sleepers that are fireblocked in accordance with Section 717.2.7.

8. Partitions dividing portions of stores, offices or similar places occupied by one tenant only and that do not establish a corridor serving an occupant load of 30 or more shall be permitted to be constructed of fire-retardant-treated wood, 1-hour fire-resistance-rated construction or of wood panels or similar light construction up to 6 feet (1829 mm) in height.

9. Stages and platforms constructed in accordance with Sections 410.3 and 410.4, respectively.

10. Combustible exterior wall coverings, balconies and similar projections and bay or oriel windows in accordance with Chapter 14.

11. Blocking such as for handrails, millwork, cabinets and window and door frames.

12. Light-transmitting plastics as permitted by Chapter 26.

13. Mastics and caulking materials applied to provide flexible seals between components of exterior wall construction.

14. Exterior plastic veneer installed in accordance with Section 2605.2.

15. Nailing or furring strips as permitted by Section 803.4.

16. Heavy timber as permitted by Note d to Table 601 and Sections 602.4.7 and 1406.3.

17. Aggregates, component materials and admixtures as permitted by Section 703.2.2.

18. Sprayed fire-resistant materials and intumescent and mastic fire-resistant coatings, determined on the basis of fire-resistance tests in accordance with Section 703.2 and installed in accordance with Section 1704.10 and 1704.11, respectively.

19. Materials used to protect penetrations in fire-resistance-rated assemblies in accordance with Section 712.

20. Materials used to protect joints in fire-resistance-rated assemblies in accordance with Section 713.

21. Materials allowed in the concealed spaces of buildings of Type I and II construction in accordance with Section 717.5.

22. Materials exposed within plenums complying with Section 602 of the *Mechanical Code of New York State*.

603.1.1 Ducts. The use of nonmetallic ducts shall be permitted when installed in accordance with the limitations of the *Mechanical Code of New York State.*

603.1.2 Piping. The use of combustible piping materials shall be permitted when installed in accordance with the limitations of the *Mechanical Code of New York State* and the *Plumbing Code of New York State.*

603.1.3 Electrical. The use of electrical wiring methods with combustible insulation, tubing, raceways and related components shall be permitted when installed in accordance with the limitations of NFPA 70.

CHAPTER 7

FIRE-RESISTANCE-RATED CONSTRUCTION

SECTION 701
GENERAL

701.1 Scope. The provisions of this chapter shall govern the materials and assemblies used for structural fire resistance and fire-resistance-rated construction separation of adjacent spaces to safeguard against the spread of fire and smoke within a building and the spread of fire to or from buildings.

SECTION 702
DEFINITIONS

702.1 Definitions. The following words and terms shall, for the purposes of this chapter, and as used elsewhere in this code, have the meanings shown herein.

ANNULAR SPACE. The opening around the penetrating item.

CEILING RADIATION DAMPER. A listed device installed in a ceiling membrane of a fire-resistance-rated floor/ceiling or roof/ceiling assembly to limit automatically the radiative heat transfer through an air inlet/outlet opening.

COMBINATION FIRE/SMOKE DAMPER. A listed device installed in ducts and air transfer openings designed to close automatically upon the detection of heat and resist the passage of flame and smoke. The device is installed to operate automatically, controlled by a smoke detection system, and where required, is capable of being positioned from a fire command center.

DAMPER. See "Ceiling radiation damper," "Combination fire/smoke damper," "Fire damper" and "Smoke damper."

DRAFTSTOP. A material, device or construction installed to restrict the movement of air within open spaces of concealed areas of building components such as crawl spaces, floor/ceiling assemblies, roof/ceiling assemblies and attics.

F RATING. The time period that the through-penetration firestop system limits the spread of fire through the penetration when tested in accordance with ASTM E 814.

FIRE AREA. The aggregate floor area enclosed and bounded by fire walls, fire barriers, exterior walls or fire-resistance-rated horizontal assemblies of a building.

FIRE BARRIER. A fire-resistance-rated wall assembly of materials designed to restrict the spread of fire in which continuity is maintained.

FIRE DAMPER. A listed device installed in ducts and air transfer openings designed to close automatically upon detection of heat and resist the passage of flame. Fire dampers are classified for use in either static systems that will automatically shut down in the event of a fire, or in dynamic systems that continue to operate during a fire. A dynamic fire damper is tested and rated for closure under elevated temperature airflow.

FIRE DOOR. The door component of a fire door assembly.

FIRE DOOR ASSEMBLY. Any combination of a fire door, frame, hardware, and other accessories that together provide a specific degree of fire protection to the opening.

FIRE PARTITION. A vertical assembly of materials designed to restrict the spread of fire in which openings are protected.

FIRE PROTECTION RATING. The period of time that an opening protective assembly will maintain the ability to confine a fire as determined by tests prescribed in Section 715. Ratings are stated in hours or minutes.

FIRE RESISTANCE. That property of materials or their assemblies that prevents or retards the passage of excessive heat, hot gases or flames under conditions of use.

FIRE-RESISTANCE RATING. The period of time a building element, component or assembly maintains the ability to confine a fire, continues to perform a given structural function, or both, as determined by the tests, or the methods based on tests, prescribed in Section 703.

FIRE-RESISTANT JOINT SYSTEM. An assemblage of specific materials or products that are designed, tested, and fire-resistance rated in accordance with either ASTM E 1966 or UL 2079 to resist for a prescribed period of time the passage of fire through joints made in or between fire-resistance-rated assemblies.

FIRE SEPARATION DISTANCE. The distance measured from the building face to one of the following:

1. The closest interior lot line;

2. To the centerline of a street, an alley or public way; or

3. To an imaginary line between two buildings on the property.

The distance shall be measured at right angles from the face of the wall.

FIRE WALL. A fire-resistance-rated wall having protected openings, which restricts the spread of fire and extends continuously from the foundation to or through the roof, with sufficient structural stability under fire conditions to allow collapse of construction on either side without collapse of the wall.

FIRE WINDOW ASSEMBLY. A window constructed and glazed to give protection against the passage of fire.

FIREBLOCKING. Building materials installed to resist the free passage of flame to other areas of the building through concealed spaces.

FLOOR FIRE DOOR ASSEMBLY. A combination of a fire door, a frame, hardware and other accessories installed in a horizontal plane, which together provide a specific degree of fire protection to a through-opening in a fire-resistance-rated floor (see Section 711.8).

HORIZONTAL ASSEMBLY. A fire-resistance-rated floor or roof assembly of materials designed to restrict the spread of fire in which continuity is maintained.

JOINT. The linear opening in or between adjacent fire-resistance-rated assemblies that is designed to allow independent movement of the building in any plane caused by thermal, seismic, wind or any other loading.

MEMBRANE PENETRATION. An opening made through one side (wall, floor or ceiling membrane) of an assembly.

MEMBRANE-PENETRATION FIRESTOP. A material, device or construction installed to resist for a prescribed time period the passage of flame and heat through openings in a protective membrane in order to accommodate cables, cable trays, conduit, tubing, pipes or similar items.

MINERAL FIBER. Insulation composed principally of fibers manufactured from rock, slag or glass, with or without binders.

MINERAL WOOL. Synthetic vitreous fiber insulation made by melting predominately igneous rock or furnace slag, and other inorganic materials, and then physically forming the melt into fibers.

PENETRATION FIRESTOP. A through-penetration firestop or a membrane-penetration firestop.

SELF-CLOSING. As applied to a fire door or other opening, means equipped with an approved device that will ensure closing after having been opened.

SHAFT. An enclosed space extending through one or more stories of a building, connecting vertical openings in successive floors, or floors and roof.

SHAFT ENCLOSURE. The walls or construction forming the boundaries of a shaft.

SMOKE BARRIER. A continuous membrane, either vertical or horizontal, such as a wall, floor, or ceiling assembly, that is designed and constructed to restrict the movement of smoke.

SMOKE COMPARTMENT. A space within a building enclosed by smoke barriers on all sides, including the top and bottom.

SMOKE DAMPER. A listed device installed in ducts and air transfer openings designed to resist the passage of smoke. The device is installed to operate automatically, controlled by a smoke detection system, and where required, is capable of being positioned from a fire command center.

SPLICE. The result of a factory and/or field method of joining or connecting two or more lengths of a fire-resistant joint system into a continuous entity.

T RATING. The time period that the penetration firestop system, including the penetrating item, limits the maximum temperature rise to 325°F (163°C) above its initial temperature through the penetration on the nonfire side when tested in accordance with ASTM E 814.

THROUGH PENETRATION. An opening that passes through an entire assembly.

THROUGH-PENETRATION FIRESTOP SYSTEM. An assemblage of specific materials or products that are designed, tested and fire-resistance rated to resist for a prescribed period of time the spread of fire through penetrations. The F and T rating criteria for penetration firestop systems shall be in accordance with ASTM E 814. See definitions of "F rating" and "T rating."

SECTION 703
FIRE-RESISTANCE RATINGS AND FIRE TESTS

703.1 Scope. Materials prescribed herein for fire resistance shall conform to the requirements of this chapter.

703.2 Fire-resistance ratings. The fire-resistance rating of building elements shall be determined in accordance with the test procedures set forth in ASTM E 119 or in accordance with Section 703.3. Where materials, systems or devices that have not been tested as part of a fire-resistance-rated assembly are incorporated into the assembly, sufficient data shall be made available to the code enforcement official to show that the required fire-resistance rating is not reduced. Materials and methods of construction used to protect joints and penetrations in fire-resistance-rated building elements shall not reduce the required fire-resistance rating.

> **Exception:** In determining the fire-resistance rating of exterior bearing walls, compliance with the ASTM E 119 criteria for unexposed surface temperature rise and ignition of cotton waste due to passage of flame or gases is required only for a period of time corresponding to the required fire-resistance rating of an exterior nonbearing wall with the same fire separation distance, and in a building of the same group. When the fire-resistance rating determined in accordance with this exception exceeds the fire-resistance rating determined in accordance with ASTM E 119, the fire exposure time period, water pressure, and application duration criteria for the hose stream test of ASTM E 119 shall be based upon the fire-resistance rating determined in accordance with this exception.

703.2.1 Nonsymmetrical wall construction. Interior walls and partitions of nonsymmetrical construction shall be tested with both faces exposed to the furnace, and the assigned fire-resistance rating shall be the shortest duration obtained from the two tests conducted in compliance with ASTM E 119. When evidence is furnished to show that the wall was tested with the least fire-resistant side exposed to the furnace, subject to acceptance of the code enforcement official, the wall need not be subjected to tests from the opposite side (see Section 704.5 for exterior walls).

703.2.2 Combustible components. Combustible aggregates are permitted in gypsum and portland cement concrete mixtures approved for fire-resistance-rated construction. Any approved component material or admixture is permitted in assemblies if the resulting tested assembly meets the fire-resistance test requirements of this code.

703.2.3 Restrained classification. Fire-resistance-rated assemblies tested under ASTM E 119 shall not be considered to be restrained unless evidence satisfactory to the code enforcement official is furnished by the registered design professional showing that the construction qualifies for a restrained classification in accordance with ASTM E 119. Restrained construction shall be identified on the plans.

703.3 Alternative methods for determining fire resistance. The application of any of the alternative methods listed in this section shall be based on the fire exposure and acceptance criteria specified in ASTM E 119. The required fire resistance of a building element shall be permitted to be established by any of the following methods or procedures:

1. Fire-resistance designs documented in approved sources.

2. Prescriptive designs of fire-resistance-rated building elements as prescribed in Section 720.

3. Calculations in accordance with Section 721.

4. Engineering analysis based on a comparison of building element designs having fire-resistance ratings as determined by the test procedures set forth in ASTM E 119.

5. Alternative protection methods as allowed by Section 103.3

703.4 Noncombustibility tests. The tests indicated in Sections 703.4.1 and 703.4.2 shall serve as criteria for acceptance of building materials as set forth in Sections 602.2, 602.3 and 602.4 in Type I, II, III and IV construction. The term "noncombustible" does not apply to the flame spread characteristics of interior finish or trim materials. A material shall not be classified as a noncombustible building construction material if it is subject to an increase in combustibility or flame spread beyond the limitations herein established through the effects of age, moisture or other atmospheric conditions.

703.4.1 Elementary materials. Materials required to be noncombustible shall be tested in accordance with ASTM E 136.

703.4.2 Composite materials. Materials having a structural base of noncombustible material as determined in accordance with Section 703.4.1 with a surfacing not more than 0.125 inch (3.18 mm) thick that has a flame spread index not greater than 50 when tested in accordance with ASTM E 84 shall be acceptable as noncombustible materials.

SECTION 704
EXTERIOR WALLS

704.1 General. Exterior walls shall comply with this section.

704.2 Projections. Cornices, eave overhangs, exterior balconies and similar projections extending beyond the floor area shall conform to the requirements of this section and Section 1406. Exterior egress balconies and exterior exit stairways shall also comply with Sections 1014.5 and 1023.1, respectively. Projections shall not extend beyond the distance determined by the following two methods, whichever results in the lesser projection:

1. A point one-third the distance to the lot line from an assumed vertical plane located where protected openings are required in accordance with Section 704.8.

2. More than 12 inches (305 mm) into areas where openings are prohibited.

704.2.1 Type I and II construction. Projections from walls of Type I or II construction shall be of noncombustible materials or combustible materials as allowed by Sections 1406.3 and 1406.4.

704.2.2 Type III, IV or V construction. Projections from walls of Type III, IV or V construction shall be of any approved material.

704.2.3 Combustible projections. Combustible projections located where openings are not permitted or where protection of openings is required shall be of at least 1-hour fire-resistance-rated construction, Type IV construction, fire-retardant-treated wood or as required by Section 1406.3.

Exception: Type V construction shall be allowed for R-3 occupancies.

704.3 Buildings on the same lot. For the purposes of determining the required wall and opening protection and roof-covering requirements, buildings on the same lot shall be assumed to have an imaginary line between them.

Where a new building is to be erected on the same lot as an existing building, the location of the assumed imaginary line with relation to the existing building shall be such that the exterior wall and opening protection of the existing building meet the criteria as set forth in Sections 704.5 and 704.8.

Exception: Two or more buildings on the same lot shall either be regulated as separate buildings or shall be considered as portions of one building if the aggregate area of such buildings is within the limits specified in Chapter 5 for a single building. Where the buildings contain different occupancy groups or are of different types of construction, the area shall be that allowed for the most restrictive occupancy or construction.

704.4 Materials. Exterior walls shall be of materials permitted by the building type of construction.

704.5 Fire-resistance ratings. Exterior walls shall be fire-resistance rated in accordance with Tables 601 and 602. The fire-resistance rating of exterior walls with a fire separation distance of greater than 5 feet (1524 mm) shall be rated for exposure to fire from the inside. The fire-resistance rating of exterior walls with a fire separation distance of 5 feet (1524 mm) or less shall be rated for exposure to fire from both sides.

704.6 Structural stability. The wall shall extend to the height required by Section 704.11 and shall have sufficient structural stability such that it will remain in place for the duration of time indicated by the required fire-resistance rating.

704.7 Unexposed surface temperature. Where protected openings are not limited by Section 704.8, the limitation on the rise of temperature on the unexposed surface of exterior walls as required by ASTM E 119 shall not apply. Where protected openings are limited by Section 704.8, the limitation on the rise of temperature on the unexposed surface of exterior walls as required by ASTM E 119 shall not apply provided that a correction is made for radiation from the unexposed exterior wall surface in accordance with the following formula:

$$A_e = A + (A_t \times F_{eo}) \qquad \text{(Equation 7-1)}$$

where:

A_e = Equivalent area of protected openings.

A = Actual area of protected openings.

A_f = Area of exterior wall surface in the story under consideration exclusive of openings, on which the temperature limitations of ASTM E 119 for walls are exceeded.

F_{eo} = An "equivalent opening factor" derived from Figure 704.7 based on the average temperature of the unexposed wall surface and the fire-resistance rating of the wall.

For SI: °C = [(°F) - 32] / 1.8.

FIGURE 704.7
EQUIVALENT OPENING FACTOR

704.8 Allowable area of openings. The maximum area of unprotected or protected openings permitted in an exterior wall in any story shall not exceed the values set forth in Table 704.8. Where both unprotected and protected openings are located in the exterior wall in any story, the total area of the openings shall comply with the following formula:

$$\left(\frac{A}{a} + \frac{A_u}{a_u}\right) \leq 1.0 \qquad \text{(Equation 7-2)}$$

where:

A = Actual area of protected openings, or the equivalent area of protected openings, A_e (see Section 704.7).

a = Allowable area of protected openings.

A_u = Actual area of unprotected openings.

a_u = Allowable area of unprotected openings.

704.8.1 Automatic sprinkler system. In buildings equipped throughout with an automatic sprinkler system in accordance with Section 903.3.1.1, the maximum allowable area of unprotected openings in occupancies other than Groups H-1, H-2 and H-3 shall be the same as the tabulated limitations for protected openings.

704.8.2 First story. In occupancies other than Group H, unlimited unprotected openings are permitted in the exterior walls of the first story above grade facing a street that have a fire separation distance of greater than 15 feet (4572 mm) or facing an unoccupied space. The unoccupied space shall be on the same lot or dedicated for public use, shall not be less than 30 feet (9144 mm) in width and shall have access from a street by a posted fire lane in accordance with the *Fire Code of New York State*.

704.9 Vertical separation of openings. Openings in exterior walls in adjacent stories shall be separated vertically to protect against fire spread on the exterior of the buildings where the openings are within 5 feet (1524 mm) of each other horizontally and the opening in the lower story is not a protected opening with a fire protection rating of not less than $^3/_4$ hour. Such openings shall be separated vertically at least 3 feet (914 mm) by spandrel girders, exterior walls or other similar assemblies that have a fire-resistance rating of at least 1 hour or by flame barriers that extend horizontally at least 30 inches (762 mm) beyond the exterior wall. Flame barriers shall also have a fire-resistance rating of at least 1 hour. The unexposed surface temperature limitations specified in ASTM E 119 shall not apply to the flame barriers or vertical separation unless otherwise required by the provisions of this code.

Exceptions:

1. This section shall not apply to buildings that are three stories or less in height.

2. This section shall not apply to buildings equipped throughout with an automatic sprinkler system in accordance with Section 903.3.1.1 or 903.3.1.2.

3. Open parking garages.

704.10 Vertical exposure. For buildings on the same lot, opening protectives having a fire-protection rating of not less than $^3/_4$ hour shall be provided in every opening that is less than 15 feet (4572 mm) vertically above the roof of an adjoining building or adjacent structure that is within a horizontal fire separation distance of 15 feet (4572 mm) of the wall in which the opening is located.

Exception: Opening protectives are not required where the roof construction has a fire-resistance rating of not less than 1 hour for a minimum distance of 10 feet (3048 mm) from the adjoining building, and the entire length and span of the supporting elements for the fire-resistance-rated roof assembly has a fire-resistance rating of not less than 1 hour.

TABLE 704.8
MAXIMUM AREA OF EXTERIOR WALL OPENINGS[a]

CLASSIFICATION OF OPENING	FIRE SEPARATION DISTANCE (feet)							
	0 to 3[f,j]	Greater than 3 to 5[c,g]	Greater than 5 to 10[c,e,g,h]	Greater than 10 to 15[d,e,g]	Greater than 15 to 20[d,g]	Greater than 20 to 25[d,g]	Greater than 25 to 30[d,g]	Greater than 30
Unprotected	Not Permitted	Not Permitted[c]	10%[i]	15%[i]	25%[i]	45%[i]	70%[i]	No Limit[b]
Protected	Not Permitted	15%	25%	45%	75%	No Limit[b]	No Limit[b]	No Limit[b]

For SI: 1 foot = 304.8 mm.

a. Values given are percentage of the area of the exterior wall.

b. Not used.

c. For occupancies in Group R-3, the maximum percentage of unprotected and protected exterior wall openings shall be 25 percent.

d. The area of openings in an open parking structure with a fire separation distance of greater than 10 feet shall not be limited.

e. For occupancies in Group H-2 or H-3, unprotected openings shall not be permitted for openings with a fire separation distance of 15 feet or less.

f. For requirements for fire walls for buildings with differing roof heights, see Section 705.6.1.

g. The area of unprotected and protected openings is not limited for occupancies in Group R-3, with a fire separation distance greater than 5 feet.

h. For special requirements for Group U occupancies, see Section 406.1.2.

i. Buildings whose exterior bearing wall, exterior nonbearing wall and exterior structural frame are not required to be fire-resistance rated by Table 601 or 602 shall be permitted to have unlimited unprotected openings.

j. Includes accessory buildings to Group R-3.

704.11 Parapets. Parapets shall be provided on exterior walls of buildings.

Exceptions: A parapet need not be provided on an exterior wall where any of the following conditions exist:

1. The wall is not required to be fire-resistance rated in accordance with Table 602 because of fire separation distance.

2. The building has an area of not more than 1,000 square feet (93 m²) on any floor.

3. Walls that terminate at roofs of not less than 2-hour fire-resistance-rated construction or where the roof, including the deck and supporting construction, is constructed entirely of noncombustible materials.

4. One-hour fire-resistance-rated exterior walls that terminate at the underside of the roof sheathing, deck or slab, provided:

    4.1. Where the roof/ceiling framing elements are parallel to the walls, such framing and elements supporting such framing shall not be of less than 1-hour fire-resistance-rated construction for a width of 4 feet (1220 mm) for Groups R and U and 10 feet (3048 mm) for other occupancies, measured from the interior side of the wall.

    4.2. Where roof/ceiling framing elements are not parallel to the wall, the entire span of such framing and elements supporting such framing shall not be of less than 1-hour fire-resistance-rated construction.

    4.3. Openings in the roof shall not be located within 5 feet (1524 mm) of the 1-hour fire-resistance-rated exterior wall for Groups R and U and 10 feet (3048 mm) for other occupancies, measured from the interior side of the wall.

    4.4. The entire building shall be provided with not less than a Class B roof covering.

5. In Groups R-2 and R-3 where the entire building is provided with a Class C roof covering, the exterior wall shall be permitted to terminate at the underside of the roof sheathing or deck in Type III, IV and V construction, provided:

    5.1. The roof sheathing or deck is constructed of approved noncombustible materials or of fire-retardant-treated wood for a distance of 4 feet (1220 mm); or

    5.2. The roof is protected with 0.625-inch (16 mm) Type X gypsum board directly beneath the underside of the roof sheathing or deck, supported by a minimum of nominal 2-inch (51 mm) ledgers attached to the sides of the roof framing members for a minimum distance of 4 feet (1220 mm).

6. Where the wall is permitted to have at least 25 percent of the exterior wall areas containing unprotected openings based on fire separation distance as determined in accordance with Section 704.8.

704.11.1 Parapet construction. Parapets shall have the same fire-resistance rating as that required for the supporting wall, and on any side adjacent to a roof surface, shall have noncombustible faces for the uppermost 18 inches (457 mm), including counterflashing and coping materials. The height of the parapet shall not be less than 30 inches (762 mm) above the point where the roof surface and the wall intersect. Where the roof slopes toward a parapet at a slope greater than two units vertical in 12 units horizontal (16.7-percent slope), the parapet shall extend to the same height as any portion of the roof within a fire separation distance where protection of wall openings is required, but in no case shall the height be less than 30 inches (762 mm).

704.12 Opening protection. Windows in exterior walls required to have protected openings in accordance with other sections of this code or determined to be protected in accordance with Section 704.3 or 704.8 shall comply with Section 715.5. Other openings required to be protected with fire door or shutter assemblies in accordance with other sections of this code or determined to be protected in accordance with Section 704.3 or 704.8 shall comply with Section 715.4.

Exception: Opening protectives are not required where the building is protected throughout by an automatic sprinkler system and the exterior openings are protected by an approved water curtain using automatic sprinklers approved for that use. The sprinklers and the water curtain shall be installed in accordance with Section 903.3.1.1 and shall have an automatic water supply and fire department connection.

704.12.1 Unprotected openings. Where protected openings are not required by Section 704, windows and doors shall be constructed of any approved materials. Glazing shall conform to the requirements of Chapters 24 and 26.

704.13 Joints. Joints made in or between exterior walls required by this section to have a fire-resistance rating shall comply with Section 713.

Exception: Joints in exterior walls that are permitted to have unprotected openings.

704.13.1 Voids. The void created at the intersection of a floor/ceiling assembly and an exterior curtain wall assembly shall be protected in accordance with Section 713.4.

704.14 Ducts and air transfer openings. Penetrations by air ducts and air transfer openings in fire-resistance-rated exterior walls required to have protected openings shall comply with Section 716.

Exception: Foundation vents installed in accordance with this code are permitted.

SECTION 705
FIRE WALLS

705.1 General. Each portion of a building separated by one or more fire walls that comply with the provisions of this section shall be considered a separate building. The extent and location of such fire walls shall provide a complete separation. Where a fire wall also separates occupancies that are required to be separated by a fire barrier wall, the most restrictive requirements of each separation shall apply.

705.1.1 Party walls. Any wall located on a lot line between adjacent buildings, which is used or adapted for joint service between the two buildings, shall be constructed as a fire wall in accordance with Section 705. Party walls shall be constructed without openings and shall create separate buildings.

705.2 Structural stability. Fire walls shall have sufficient structural stability under fire conditions to allow collapse of construction on either side without collapse of the wall for the duration of time indicated by the required fire-resistance rating.

705.3 Materials. Fire walls shall be of any approved noncombustible materials.

Exception: Buildings of Type V construction.

705.4 Fire-resistance rating. Fire walls shall have a fire-resistance rating of not less than that required by Table 705.4.

TABLE 705.4
FIRE WALL FIRE-RESISTANCE RATINGS

GROUP	FIRE-RESISTANCE RATING (hours)
A, B, E, H-4, I, R-1, R-2, U	3[a]
F-1, H-3[b], H-5, M, S-1	3
H-1, H-2	4[b]
F-2, S-2, R-3, R-4	2

a. Walls shall be not less than 2-hour fire-resistance rated where separating buildings of Type II or V construction.

b. For Group H-1, H-2 or H-3 buildings, also see Sections 415.4 and 415.5.

705.5 Horizontal continuity. Fire walls shall be continuous from exterior wall to exterior wall and shall extend at least 18 inches (457 mm) beyond the exterior surface of exterior walls.

Exceptions:

1. Fire walls shall be permitted to terminate at the interior surface of combustible exterior sheathing or siding provided the exterior wall has a fire-resistance rating of at least 1 hour for a horizontal distance of at least 4 feet (1220 mm) on both sides of the fire wall. Openings within such exterior walls shall be protected by opening protectives having a fire protection rating of not less than $^3/_4$ hour.

2. Fire walls shall be permitted to terminate at the interior surface of noncombustible exterior sheathing, exterior siding or other noncombustible exterior finishes provided the sheathing, siding, or other exterior noncombustible finish extends a horizontal distance of at least 4 feet (1220 mm) on both sides of the fire wall.

3. Fire walls shall be permitted to terminate at the interior surface of noncombustible exterior sheathing where the building on each side of the fire wall is protected by an automatic sprinkler system installed in accordance with Section 903.3.1.1 or 903.3.1.2.

705.5.1 Exterior walls. Where the fire wall intersects the exterior walls, the fire-resistance rating for the exterior walls on both sides of the fire wall shall have a 1-hour fire-resistance rating with $^3/_4$-hour opening protection where opening protection is required. The fire-resistance rating of the exterior wall shall extend a minimum of 4 feet (1220 mm) on each side of the intersection of the fire wall to exterior wall. Exterior wall intersections at fire walls that form an angle equal to or greater than 180 degrees (3.14 rad) do not need exterior wall protection.

705.5.2 Horizontal projecting elements. Fire walls shall extend to the outer edge of horizontal projecting elements such as balconies, roof overhangs, canopies, marquees and similar projections that are within 4 feet (1220 mm) of the fire wall.

Exceptions:

1. Horizontal projecting elements without concealed spaces, provided the exterior wall behind and below the projecting element has not less

than 1-hour fire-resistance-rated construction for a distance not less than the depth of the projecting element on both sides of the fire wall. Openings within such exterior walls shall be protected by opening protectives having a fire protection rating of not less than $^3/_4$ hour.

2. Noncombustible horizontal projecting elements with concealed spaces, provided a minimum 1-hour fire-resistance-rated wall extends through the concealed space. The projecting element shall be separated from the building by a minimum of 1-hour fire-resistance-rated construction for a distance on each side of the fire wall equal to the depth of the projecting element. The wall is not required to extend under the projecting element where the building exterior wall is not less than 1-hour fire-resistance rated for a distance on each side of the fire wall equal to the depth of the projecting element. Openings within such exterior walls shall be protected by opening protectives having a fire protection rating of not less than $^3/_4$ hour.

3. For combustible horizontal projecting elements with concealed spaces, the fire wall need only extend through the concealed space to the outer edges of the projecting elements. The exterior wall behind and below the projecting element shall be of not less than 1-hour fire-resistance-rated construction for a distance not less than the depth of the projecting elements on both sides of the fire wall. Openings within such exterior walls shall be protected by opening protectives having a fire-protection rating of not less than $^3/_4$ hour.

705.6 Vertical continuity. Fire walls shall extend from the foundation to a termination point at least 30 inches (762 mm) above both adjacent roofs.

Exceptions:

1. Stepped buildings in accordance with Section 705.6.1.

2. Two-hour fire-resistance-rated walls shall be permitted to terminate at the underside of the roof sheathing, deck or slab provided:

    2.1. The lower roof assembly within 4 feet (1220 mm) of the wall has not less than a 1-hour fire-resistance rating and the entire length and span of supporting elements for the rated roof assembly has a fire-resistance rating of not less than 1 hour.

    2.2. Openings in the roof shall not be located within 4 feet (1220 mm) of the fire wall.

    2.3. Each building shall be provided with not less than a Class B roof covering.

3. Walls shall be permitted to terminate at the underside of noncombustible roof sheathing, deck, or slabs where both buildings are provided with not less than a Class B roof covering. Openings in the

roof shall not be located within 4 feet (1220 mm) of the fire wall.

4. In buildings of Type III, IV and V construction, walls shall be permitted to terminate at the underside of combustible roof sheathing or decks provided:

    4.1. There are no openings in the roof within 4 feet (1220 mm) of the fire wall,

    4.2. The roof is covered with a minimum Class B roof covering, and

    4.3. The roof sheathing or deck is constructed of fire-retardant-treated wood for a distance of 4 feet (1220 mm) on both sides of the wall or the roof is protected with $^5/_8$ inch (15.9 mm) Type X gypsum board directly beneath the underside of the roof sheathing or deck, supported by a minimum of 2-inch (51 mm) nominal ledgers attached to the sides of the roof framing members for a minimum distance of 4 feet (1220 mm) on both sides of the fire wall.

5. Buildings located above a parking garage designed in accordance with Section 509.2 shall be permitted to have the fire walls for the buildings located above the parking garage extend from the horizontal separation between the parking garage and the buildings.

705.6.1 Stepped buildings. Where a fire wall serves as an exterior wall for a building and separates buildings having different roof levels, such wall shall terminate at a point not less than 30 inches (762 mm) above the lower roof level, provided the exterior wall for a height of 15 feet (4572 mm) above the lower roof is not less than 1-hour fire-resistance-rated construction from both sides with openings protected by fire assemblies having a fire protection rating of not less than $^3/_4$ hour.

Exception: Where the fire wall terminates at the underside of the roof sheathing, deck or slab of the lower roof, provided:

1. The lower roof assembly within 10 feet (3048 mm) of the wall has not less than a 1-hour fire-resistance rating and the entire length and span of supporting elements for the rated roof assembly has a fire-resistance rating of not less than 1 hour.

2. Openings in the lower roof shall not be located within 10 feet (3048 mm) of the fire wall.

705.7 Combustible framing in fire walls. Adjacent combustible members entering into a concrete or masonry fire wall from opposite sides shall not have less than a 4-inch (102 mm) distance between embedded ends. Where combustible members frame into hollow walls or walls of hollow units, hollow spaces shall be solidly filled for the full thickness of the wall and for a distance not less than 4 inches (102 mm) above, below and between the structural members, with noncombustible materials approved for fireblocking.

705.8 Openings. Each opening through a fire wall shall be protected in accordance with Section 715.4 and shall not exceed 120 square feet (11 m^2). The aggregate width of openings at any floor level shall not exceed 25 percent of the length of the wall.

Exceptions:

1. Openings are not permitted in party walls constructed in accordance with Section 705.1.1.

2. Openings shall not be limited to 120 square feet (11 m²) where both buildings are equipped throughout with an automatic sprinkler system installed in accordance with Section 903.3.1.1.

705.9 Penetrations. Penetrations of fire walls shall comply with Section 712.

705.10 Joints. Joints made in or between fire walls shall comply with Section 713.

705.11 Ducts and air transfer openings. Ducts and air transfer openings shall not penetrate fire walls.

Exception: Penetrations by ducts and air transfer openings of fire walls that are not on a lot line shall be allowed provided the penetrations comply with Sections 712 and 716. The size and aggregate width of all openings shall not exceed the limitations of Section 705.8.

SECTION 706
FIRE BARRIERS

706.1 General. Fire barriers installed as required elsewhere in this code or the *Fire Code of New York State* shall comply with this section.

706.2 Materials. Fire barriers shall be of materials permitted by the building type of construction.

706.2.1 Fire-resistance-rated glazing. Fire-resistance-rated glazing, when tested in accordance with ASTM E 119 and complying with the requirements of Section 706, shall be permitted. Fire-resistance-rated glazing shall bear a label or other identification showing the name of the manufacturer, the test standard and the identifier "W-XXX," where the "XXX" is the fire-resistance rating in minutes. Such label or identification shall be issued by an approved agency and shall be permanently affixed to the glazing.

706.3 Fire-resistance rating. The fire-resistance rating of fire barriers shall comply with this section.

706.3.1 Shaft enclosures. The fire-resistance rating of the fire barrier separating building areas from a shaft shall comply with Section 707.4.

706.3.2 Exit enclosures. The fire-resistance rating of the fire barrier separating building areas from an exit shall comply with Section 1020.1.

706.3.3 Exit passageway. The fire-resistance rating of the separation between building areas and an exit passageway shall comply with Section 1021.1.

706.3.4 Horizontal exit. The fire-resistance rating of the separation between building areas connected by a horizontal exit shall comply with Section 1022.1.

706.3.5 Atriums. The fire-resistance rating of the fire barrier separating atriums shall comply with Section 404.5.

706.3.6 Incidental use areas. The fire barrier separating incidental use areas shall have a fire-resistance rating of not less than that indicated in Table 508.2.

706.3.7 Control areas. Fire barriers separating control areas shall have a fire-resistance rating of not less than that required in Section 414.2.4.

706.3.8 Separation of mixed occupancies. Where the provisions of Section 508.3.3 are applicable, the fire barrier separating mixed occupancies shall have a fire-resistance rating of not less than that indicated in Section 508.3.3 based on the occupancies being separated.

706.3.9 Fire areas. The fire barrier or horizontal assembly, or both, separating a single occupancy into different fire areas shall have a fire-resistance rating of not less than that indicated in Table 706.3.9. The fire barriers or horizontal assemblies, or both, separating fire areas of mixed occupancies shall have a fire-resistance rating of not less than the highest value indicated in Table 706.3.9 for the occupancies under consideration.

TABLE 706.3.9
FIRE-RESISTANCE RATING REQUIREMENTS FOR FIRE BARRIER ASSEMBLIES BETWEEN FIRE AREAS

OCCUPANCY GROUP	FIRE-RESISTANCE RATING (hours)
H-1, H-2	4
F-1, H-3, S-1	3
A, B, E, F-2, H-4, H-5, I, M, R, S-2	2
U	1

706.4 Exterior walls. Where exterior walls serve as a part of a required fire-resistance-rated shaft or exit enclosure or separation, such walls shall comply with the requirements of Section 704 for exterior walls and the fire-resistance-rated enclosure requirements shall not apply.

Exception: Exterior walls required to be fire-resistance rated in accordance with Section 1014.5.1 for exterior egress balconies, Section 1020.1.4 for exit enclosures and Section 1023.6 for exterior exit ramps and stairways.

706.5 Continuity. Fire barriers shall extend from the top of the floor/ceiling assembly below to the underside of the floor or roof slab or deck above and shall be securely attached thereto. Such fire barriers shall be continuous through concealed spaces, such as the space above a suspended ceiling. The supporting construction for fire barrier walls shall be protected to afford the required fire-resistance rating of the fire barrier supported, except for 1-hour fire-resistance-rated incidental use area separations as required by Table 508.2 in buildings of Type IIB, IIIB and VB construction. Hollow vertical spaces within a fire barrier shall be fireblocked in accordance with Section 717.2 at every floor level.

Exceptions:

1. The maximum required fire-resistance rating for assemblies supporting fire barriers separating tank storage as provided for in Section 415.6.2.1 shall be 2 hours, but not less than required by Table 601 for the building construction type.

2. Shaft enclosures shall be permitted to terminate at a top enclosure complying with Section 707.12.

706.7 Openings. Openings in a fire barrier wall shall be protected in accordance with Section 715. Openings shall be limited to a maximum aggregate width of 25 percent of the length of the wall, and the maximum area of any single opening shall not exceed 156 square feet (15 m²). Openings in exit enclosures and exit passageways shall also comply with Sections 1020.1.1 and 1021.4, respectively.

Exceptions:

1. Openings shall not be limited to 156 square feet (15 m²) where adjoining fire areas are equipped throughout with an automatic sprinkler system in accordance with Section 903.3.1.1.

2. Fire doors serving an exit enclosure.

3. Openings shall not be limited to 156 square feet (15 m²) or an aggregate width of 25 percent of the length of the wall where the opening protective assembly has been tested in accordance with ASTM E 119 and has a minimum fire-resistance rating not less than the fire-resistance rating of the wall.

4. Fire windows permitted in atrium separation walls shall not be limited to a maximum aggregate width of 25 percent of length of the wall.

706.8 Penetrations. Penetrations of fire barriers shall comply with Section 712.

706.8.1 Prohibited penetrations. Penetrations into an exit enclosure or an exit passageway shall be allowed only when permitted by Section 1020.1.2 or 1021.5, respectively.

706.9 Joints. Joints made in or between fire barriers shall comply with Section 713.

706.10 Ducts and air transfer openings. Penetrations in a fire barrier by ducts and air transfer openings shall comply with Section 716.

SECTION 707
SHAFT ENCLOSURES

707.1 General. The provisions of this section shall apply to vertical shafts where such shafts are required to protect openings and penetrations through floor/ceiling and roof/ceiling assemblies. Shaft enclosures shall be constructed as fire barriers in accordance with Section 706 or horizontal assemblies in accordance with Section 711, or both.

707.2 Shaft enclosure required. Openings through a floor/ceiling assembly shall be protected by a shaft enclosure complying with this Section.

Exceptions:

1. A shaft enclosure is not required for openings totally within an individual residential dwelling unit and connecting four stories or less.

2. A shaft enclosure is not required in a building equipped throughout with an automatic sprinkler system in accordance with Section 903.3.1.1 for an escalator opening or stairway that is not a portion of the means of egress protected according to Item 2.1 or 2.2:

   2.1. Where the area of the floor opening between stories does not exceed twice the horizontal projected area of the escalator or stairway and the opening is protected by a draft curtain and closely spaced sprinklers in accordance with NFPA 13. In other than Groups B and M, this application is limited to openings that do not connect more than four stories.

   2.2. Where the opening is protected by approved power-operated automatic shutters at every penetrated floor. The shutters shall be of noncombustible construction and have a fire-resistance rating of not less than 1.5 hours. The shutter shall be so constructed as to close immediately upon the actuation of a smoke detector installed in accordance with Section 907.11 and shall completely shut off the well opening. Escalators shall cease operation when the shutter begins to close. The shutter shall operate at a speed of not more than 30 feet per minute (152.4 mm/s) and shall be equipped with a sensitive leading edge to arrest its progress where in contact with any obstacle, and to continue its progress on release therefrom.

3. A shaft enclosure is not required for penetrations by pipe, tube, conduit, wire, cable and vents protected in accordance with Section 712.4.

4. A shaft enclosure is not required for penetrations by ducts protected in accordance with Section 712.4. Grease ducts shall be protected in accordance with the *Mechanical Code of New York State.*

5. In other than Group H occupancies, a shaft enclosure is not required for floor openings complying with the provisions for atriums in Section 404.

6. A shaft enclosure is not required for approved masonry chimneys where annular space protection is provided at each floor level in accordance with Section 717.2.5.

7. In other than Groups I-2 and I-3, a shaft enclosure is not required for a floor opening or an air transfer opening that complies with the following:

   7.1. Does not connect more than two stories.

   7.2. Is not part of the required means of egress system, except as permitted in Section 1020.1.

   7.3. Is not concealed within the building construction.

   7.4. Is not open to a corridor in Group I and R occupancies.

   7.5. Is not open to a corridor on nonsprinklered floors in any occupancy.

   7.6. Is separated from floor openings and air transfer openings serving other floors by construction conforming to required shaft enclosures.

  7.7. Is limited to the same smoke compartment.

8. A shaft enclosure is not required for automobile ramps in open and enclosed parking garages constructed in accordance with Sections 406.3 and 406.4, respectively.

9. A shaft enclosure is not required for floor openings between a mezzanine and the floor below.

10. A shaft enclosure is not required for joints protected by a fire-resistant joint system in accordance with Section 713.

11. A shaft enclosure shall not be required for floor openings created by unenclosed stairs or ramps in accordance with Exception 8 or 9 in Section 1020.1.

12. Floor openings protected by floor fire doors in accordance with Section 711.8.

13. Where permitted by other sections of this code.

707.3 Materials. The shaft enclosure shall be of materials permitted by the building type of construction.

707.4 Fire-resistance rating. Shaft enclosures shall have a fire-resistance rating of not less than 2 hours where connecting four stories or more, and not less than 1 hour where connecting less than four stories. The number of stories connected by the shaft enclosure shall include any basements but not any mezzanines. Shaft enclosures shall have a fire-resistance rating not less than the floor assembly penetrated, but need not exceed 2 hours.

707.5 Continuity. Shaft enclosures shall be constructed as fire barriers in accordance with Section 706 or horizontal assemblies constructed in accordance with Section 711, or both, and shall have continuity in accordance with Section 706.5 for fire barriers or Section 711.4 for horizontal assemblies as applicable.

707.6 Exterior walls. Where exterior walls serve as a part of a required shaft enclosure, such walls shall comply with the requirements of Section 704 for exterior walls and the fire-resistance-rated enclosure requirements shall not apply.

  Exception: Exterior walls required to be fire-resistance rated in accordance with Section 1014.5.1 for exterior egress balconies, Section 1020.1.4 for exit enclosures and Section 1023.6 for exterior exit ramps and stairways.

707.7 Openings. Openings in a shaft enclosure shall be protected in accordance with Section 715 as required for fire barriers. Doors shall be self- or automatic closing by smoke detection in accordance with Section 715.4.7.3.

  707.7.1 Prohibited openings. Openings other than those necessary for the purpose of the shaft shall not be permitted in shaft enclosures.

707.8 Penetrations. Penetrations in a shaft enclosure shall be protected in accordance with Section 712 as required for fire barriers.

707.8.1 Prohibited penetrations. Penetrations other than those necessary for the purpose of the shaft shall not be permitted in shaft enclosures.

707.9 Joints. Joints in a shaft enclosure shall comply with Section 713.

707.10 Ducts and air transfer openings. Penetrations of a shaft enclosure by ducts and air transfer openings shall comply with Section 716.

707.11 Enclosure at the bottom. Shafts that do not extend to the bottom of the building or structure shall:

1. Be enclosed at the lowest level with construction of the same fire-resistance rating as the lowest floor through which the shaft passes, but not less than the rating required for the shaft enclosure;

2. Terminate in a room having a use related to the purpose of the shaft. The room shall be separated from the remainder of the building by a fire barrier having a fire-resistance rating and opening protectives at least equal to the protection required for the shaft enclosure; or

3. Be protected by approved fire dampers installed in accordance with their listing at the lowest floor level within the shaft enclosure.

Exceptions:

1. The fire-resistance-rated room separation is not required, provided there are no openings in or penetrations of the shaft enclosure to the interior of the building except at the bottom. The bottom of the shaft shall be closed off around the penetrating items with materials permitted by Section 717.3.1 for draftstopping, or the room shall be provided with an approved automatic fire suppression system.

2. A shaft enclosure containing a refuse chute or laundry chute shall not be used for any other purpose and shall terminate in a room protected in accordance with Section 707.13.4.

3. The fire-resistance-rated room separation and the protection at the bottom of the shaft are not required, provided there are no combustibles in the shaft and there are no openings or other penetrations through the shaft enclosure to the interior of the building.

707.12 Enclosure at the top. A shaft enclosure that does not extend to the underside of the roof sheathing, deck or slab of the building shall be enclosed at the top with construction of the same fire-resistance rating as the topmost floor penetrated by the shaft, but not less than the fire-resistance rating required for the shaft enclosure.

707.13 Refuse and laundry chutes. Refuse and laundry chutes, access and termination rooms and incinerator rooms shall meet the requirements of Sections 707.13.1 through 707.13.6.

  Exception: Chutes serving and contained within a single dwelling unit.

707.13.1 Refuse and laundry chute enclosures. A shaft enclosure containing a refuse or laundry chute shall not be used for any other purpose and shall be enclosed in accordance with Section 707.4. Openings into the shaft, including those from access rooms and termination rooms, shall be protected in accordance with this section and Section 715. Openings into chutes shall not be located in corridors. Doors shall be self- or automatic closing upon the actuation of a smoke detector in accordance with Section 715.4.7.3, except that heat-activated closing devices shall be permitted between the shaft and the termination room.

707.13.2 Materials. A shaft enclosure containing a refuse or laundry chute shall be constructed of materials as permitted by the building type of construction.

707.13.3 Refuse and laundry chute access rooms. Access openings for refuse and laundry chutes shall be located in rooms or compartments enclosed by a fire barrier that has a fire-resistance rating of not less than 1 hour. Openings into the access rooms shall be protected by opening protectives having a fire protection rating of not less than $^3/_4$ hour. Doors shall be self- or automatic closing upon the detection of smoke in accordance with Section 715.4.7.3.

707.13.4 Termination room. Refuse and laundry chutes shall discharge into an enclosed room separated from the remainder of the building by a fire barrier that has a fire-resistance rating of not less than 1 hour. Openings into the termination room shall be protected by opening protectives having a fire protection rating of not less than $^3/_4$ hour. Doors shall be self- or automatic closing upon the detection of smoke in accordance with Section 715.4.7.3. Refuse chutes shall not terminate in an incinerator room. Refuse and laundry rooms that are not provided with chutes need only comply with Table 508.2.

707.13.5 Incinerator room. Incinerator rooms shall comply with Table 508.2.

707.13.6 Automatic sprinkler system. An approved automatic sprinkler system shall be installed in accordance with Section 903.2.10.2.

707.14 Elevator, dumbwaiter and other hoistways. Elevator, dumbwaiter and other hoistway enclosures shall be constructed in accordance with Section 707 and Chapter 30.

707.14.1 Elevator lobby. An enclosed elevator lobby shall be provided at each floor where an elevator shaft enclosure connects more than three stories. The lobby shall separate the elevator shaft enclosure doors from each floor by fire partitions equal to the fire-resistance rating of the corridor and the required opening protection. Elevator lobbies shall have at least one means of egress complying with Chapter 10 and other provisions within this code.

Exceptions:

1. Enclosed elevator lobbies are not required at the street floor, provided the entire street floor is equipped with an automatic sprinkler system in accordance with Section 903.3.1.1.

2. Elevators not required to be located in a shaft in accordance with Section 707.2 are not required to have enclosed elevator lobbies.

3. Where additional doors are provided at the hoistway opening in accordance with Section 3002.6. Such doors shall be tested in accordance with UL 1784 without an artificial bottom seal.

4. Enclosed elevator lobbies are not required where the building is protected by an automatic sprinkler system installed in accordance with Section 903.3.1.1 or 903.3.1.2. This exception shall not apply to the following:

   4.1. Group I-2 occupancies with elevator shaft enclosures that connect stories used by patients for sleeping, treatment, or with an occupant load of 50 or more persons;

   4.2. Group I-3; and

   4.3. High-rise buildings.

5. Smoke partitions shall be permitted in lieu of fire partitions to separate the elevator lobby at each floor where the building is equipped throughout with an automatic sprinkler system installed in accordance with Section 903.3.1.1 or 903.3.1.2.

6. Enclosed elevator lobbies are not required where the elevator hoistway is pressurized in accordance with Section 707.14.2.

707.14.2 Enclosed elevator lobby pressurization alternative. Where elevator hoistway pressurization is provided in lieu of required enclosed elevator lobbies, the pressurization system shall comply with this section.

707.14.2.1 Pressurization requirements. Elevator hoistways shall be pressurized to maintain a minimum positive pressure of 0.04 inches of water column and a maximum positive pressure of 0.06 inches of water column with respect to adjacent occupied space on all floors. This pressure shall be measured at the midpoint of each hoistway door, with all ground floor level hoistway doors open and all other hoistway doors closed. The supply air intake shall be from an outside, uncontaminated source located a minimum distance of 20 feet (6096 mm) from any air exhaust system or outlet.

707.14.2.2 Ducts for system. Any duct system that is part of the pressurization system shall be protected with the same fire-resistance rating as required for the elevator shaft enclosure.

707.14.2.3 Fan system. The fan system provided for the pressurization system shall be as required by this section.

707.14.2.3.1 Fire resistance. When located within the building, the fan system that provides the pressurization shall be protected with the same fire-resistance rating required for the elevator shaft enclosure.

707.14.2.3.2 Smoke detection. The fan system shall be equipped with a smoke detector that will automatically shut down the fan system when smoke is detected within the system.

707.14.2.3.3 Separate systems. A separate fan system shall be used for each bank of elevators.

707.14.2.3.4 Fan capacity. The supply fan shall either be adjustable with a capacity of at least 1,000 cfm (.4719 m^3/s) per door, or that specified by a registered design professional to meet the requirements of a designed pressurization system.

707.14.2.4 Standby power. The pressurization system shall be provided with standby power from the same source as other required emergency systems for the building.

707.14.2.5 Activation of pressurization system. The elevator pressurization system shall be activated upon activation of the building fire alarm system or upon activation of the elevator lobby smoke detectors.

SECTION 708
FIRE PARTITIONS

708.1 General. The following wall assemblies shall comply with this section:

1. Walls separating dwelling units in the same building.

2. Walls separating sleeping units in occupancies in Group R-1 hotel, R-2 and I-1 occupancies.

3. Walls separating tenant spaces in covered mall buildings as required by Section 402.7.2.

4. Corridor walls as required by Section 1017.1.

5. Elevator lobby separation as required by Section 707.14.1.

6. Residential aircraft hangars.

708.2 Materials. The walls shall be of materials permitted by the building type of construction.

708.3 Fire-resistance rating. Fire partitions shall have a fire-resistance rating of not less than 1 hour.

Exceptions:

1. Corridor walls as permitted by Table 1017.1.

2. Dwelling and sleeping unit separations in buildings of Type IIB, IIIB and VB construction shall have fire-resistance ratings of not less than $^1/_2$ hour in buildings equipped throughout with an automatic sprinkler system in accordance with Section 903.3.1.1.

708.4 Continuity. Fire partitions shall extend from the top of the foundation or floor/ceiling assembly below to the underside of the floor or roof sheathing, slab or deck above or to the fire-resistance-rated floor/ceiling or roof/ceiling assembly above, and shall be securely attached thereto. If the partitions are not continuous to the sheathing, deck or slab, and where constructed of combustible construction, the space between the ceiling and the sheathing, deck or slab above shall be fire-blocked or draftstopped in accordance with Sections 717.2 and 717.3 at the partition line. The supporting construction shall be protected to afford the required fire-resistance rating

of the wall supported, except for tenant and sleeping unit separation walls and corridor walls in buildings of Types IIB, IIIB and VB construction.

Exceptions:

1. The wall need not be extended into the crawl space below where the floor above the crawl space has a minimum 1-hour fire-resistance rating.

2. Where the room-side fire-resistance-rated membrane of the corridor is carried through to the underside of the floor or roof sheathing, deck or slab of a fire-resistance-rated floor or roof above, the ceiling of the corridor shall be permitted to be protected by the use of ceiling materials as required for a 1-hour fire-resistance-rated floor or roof system.

3. Where the corridor ceiling is constructed as required for the corridor walls, the walls shall be permitted to terminate at the upper membrane of such ceiling assembly.

4. The fire partition separating tenant spaces in a mall, complying with Section 402.7.2, are not required to extend beyond the underside of a ceiling that is not part of a fire-resistance-rated assembly. A wall is not required in attic or ceiling spaces above tenant separation walls.

5. Fireblocking or draftstopping is not required at the partition line in Group R-2 buildings that do not exceed four stories in height, provided the attic space is subdivided by draftstopping into areas not exceeding 3,000 square feet (279 m^2) or above every two dwelling units, whichever is smaller.

6. Fireblocking or draftstopping is not required at the partition line in buildings equipped with an automatic sprinkler system installed throughout in accordance with Section 903.3.1.1 or 903.3.1.2, provided that automatic sprinklers are installed in combustible floor/ceiling and roof/ceiling spaces.

708.5 Exterior walls. Where exterior walls serve as a part of a required fire-resistance-rated separation, such walls shall comply with the requirements of Section 704 for exterior walls, and the fire-resistance-rated separation requirements shall not apply.

Exception: Exterior walls required to be fire-resistance rated in accordance with Section 1014.5.1 for exterior egress balconies, Section 1020.1.4 for exit enclosures and Section 1023.6 for exterior exit ramps and stairways.

708.6 Openings. Openings in a fire partition shall be protected in accordance with Section 715.

708.7 Penetrations. Penetrations of fire partitions shall comply with Section 712.

708.8 Joints. Joints made in or between fire partitions shall comply with Section 713.

708.9 Ducts and air transfer openings. Penetrations in a fire partition by ducts and air transfer openings shall comply with Section 716.

SECTION 709
SMOKE BARRIERS

709.1 General. Smoke barriers shall comply with this section.

709.2 Materials. Smoke barriers shall be of materials permitted by the building type of construction.

709.3 Fire-resistance rating. A 1-hour fire-resistance rating is required for smoke barriers.

> **Exception:** Smoke barriers constructed of minimum 0.10-inch-thick (2.5 mm) steel in Group I-3 buildings.

709.4 Continuity. Smoke barriers shall form an effective membrane continuous from outside wall to outside wall and from the top of the foundation or floor/ceiling assembly below to the underside of the floor or roof sheathing, deck or slab above, including continuity through concealed spaces, such as those found above suspended ceilings, and interstitial structural and mechanical spaces. The supporting construction shall be protected to afford the required fire-resistance rating of the wall or floor supported in buildings of other than Type IIB, IIIB or VB construction.

> **Exception:** Smoke-barrier walls are not required in interstitial spaces where such spaces are designed and constructed with ceilings that provide resistance to the passage of fire and smoke equivalent to that provided by the smoke-barrier walls.

709.5 Openings. Openings in a smoke barrier shall be protected in accordance with Section 715.

> **Exception:** In Group I-2, where doors are installed across corridors, a pair of opposite-swinging doors without a center mullion shall be installed having vision panels with fire-protection-rated glazing materials in fire-protection-rated frames, the area of which shall not exceed that tested. The doors shall be close fitting within operational tolerances, and shall not have undercuts, louvers or grilles. The doors shall have head and jamb stops, astragals or rabbets at meeting edges and shall be automatic closing by smoke detection in accordance with Section 715.4.7.3. Positive-latching devices are not required.

709.6 Penetrations. Penetrations of smoke barriers shall comply with Section 712.

709.7 Joints. Joints made in or between smoke barriers shall comply with Section 713.

709.8 Ducts and air transfer openings. Penetrations in a smoke barrier by ducts and air transfer openings shall comply with Section 716.

SECTION 710
SMOKE PARTITIONS

710.1 General. Smoke partitions installed as required elsewhere in the code shall comply with this section.

710.2 Materials. The walls shall be of materials permitted by the building type of construction.

710.3 Fire-resistance rating. Unless required elsewhere in the code, smoke partitions are not required to have a fire-resistance rating.

710.4 Continuity. Smoke partitions shall extend from the top of the foundation or floor below to the underside of the floor or roof sheathing, deck or slab above or to the underside of the ceiling above where the ceiling membrane is constructed to limit the transfer of smoke.

710.5 Openings. Windows shall be sealed to resist the free passage of smoke or be automatic-closing upon detection of smoke. Doors in smoke partitions shall comply with this section.

> **710.5.1 Louvers.** Doors in smoke partitions shall not include louvers.

> **710.5.2 Smoke and draft control doors.** Where required elsewhere in the code, doors in smoke partitions shall be tested in accordance with UL 1784 with an artificial bottom seal installed across the full width of the bottom of the door assembly during the test. The air leakage rate of the door assembly shall not exceed 3 cubic feet per minute per square foot $[ft^3/(min \cdot ft^2)](0.015424 \text{ m}^3/ s \cdot m^2)$ of door opening at 0.10 inch (24.9Pa) of water for both the ambient temperature test and the elevated temperature exposure test.

> **710.5.3 Self- or automatic-closing doors.** Where required elsewhere in the code, doors in smoke partitions shall be self- or automatic closing by smoke detection in accordance with Section 715.4.7.3.

710.6 Penetrations and joints. The space around penetrating items and in joints shall be filled with an approved material to limit the free passage of smoke.

710.7 Ducts and air transfer openings. The space around a duct penetrating a smoke partition shall be filled with an approved material to limit the free passage of smoke. Air transfer openings in smoke partitions shall be provided with a smoke damper complying with Section 716.3.2.

> **Exception:** Where the installation of a smoke damper will interfere with the operation of a required smoke control system in accordance with Section 909, approved alternative protection shall be utilized.

SECTION 711
HORIZONTAL ASSEMBLIES

711.1 General. Floor and roof assemblies required to have a fire-resistance rating shall comply with this section.

711.2 Materials. The floor and roof assemblies shall be of materials permitted by the building type of construction.

711.3 Fire-resistance rating. The fire-resistance rating of floor and roof assemblies shall not be less than that required by the building type of construction. Where the floor assembly separates mixed occupancies, the assembly shall have a fire-resistance rating of not less than that required by Section 508.3.3 based on the occupancies being separated. Where the floor assembly separates a single occupancy into different fire areas, the assembly shall have a fire-resistance rating of not less than that required by Section 706.3.9. Floor assemblies separating dwelling units in the same building or sleeping units in occupancies in Group R-1, hotel occupancies, R-

2 and I-1 shall be a minimum of 1-hour fire-resistance-rated construction.

Exception: Dwelling unit and sleeping unit separations in buildings of Type IIB, IIIB, and VB construction shall have fire-resistance ratings of not less than $^1/_2$ hour in buildings equipped throughout with an automatic sprinkler system in accordance with Section 903.3.1.1.

711.3.1 Ceiling panels. Where the weight of lay-in ceiling panels, used as part of fire-resistance-rated floor/ceiling or roof/ceiling assemblies, is not adequate to resist an upward force of 1 lb/ft.^{2} (48 Pa), wire or other approved devices shall be installed above the panels to prevent vertical displacement under such upward force.

711.3.2 Access doors. Access doors shall be permitted in ceilings of fire-resistance-rated floor/ceiling and roof/ceiling assemblies provided such doors are tested in accordance with ASTM E 119 as horizontal assemblies and labeled by an approved agency for such purpose.

711.3.3 Unusable space. In 1-hour fire-resistance-rated floor construction, the ceiling membrane is not required to be installed over unusable crawl spaces. In 1-hour fire-resistance-rated roof construction, the floor membrane is not required to be installed where unusable attic space occurs above.

711.4 Continuity. Assemblies shall be continuous without openings, penetrations or joints except as permitted by this section and Sections 707.2, 712.4, 713 and 1020.1. Skylights and other penetrations through a fire-resistance-rated roof deck or slab are permitted to be unprotected, provided that the structural integrity of the fire-resistance-rated roof construction is maintained. Unprotected skylights shall not be permitted in roof construction required to be fire-resistance rated in accordance with Section 704.10. The supporting construction shall be protected to afford the required fire-resistance rating of the horizontal assembly supported.

711.5 Penetrations. Penetrations of fire-resistance-rated horizontal assemblies shall comply with Section 712.

711.6 Joints. Joints made in or between fire-resistance-rated horizontal assemblies shall comply with Section 713. The void created at the intersection of a floor/ceiling assembly and an exterior curtain wall assembly shall be protected in accordance with Section 713.4.

711.7 Ducts and air transfer openings. Penetrations in horizontal assemblies by ducts and air transfer openings shall comply with Sections 716.

711.8 Floor fire door assemblies. Floor fire door assemblies used to protect openings in fire-resistance-rated floors shall be tested in accordance with NFPA 288, and shall achieve a fire-resistance rating not less than the assembly being penetrated. Floor fire door assemblies shall be labeled by an approved agency. The label shall be permanently affixed and shall specify the manufacturer, the test standard and the fire-resistance rating.

SECTION 712
PENETRATIONS

712.1 Scope. The provisions of this section shall govern the materials and methods of construction used to protect through penetrations and membrane penetrations of horizontal assemblies and fire-resistance-rated wall assemblies.

712.2 Installation details. Where sleeves are used, they shall be securely fastened to the assembly penetrated. The space between the item contained in the sleeve and the sleeve itself and any space between the sleeve and the assembly penetrated shall be protected in accordance with this section. Insulation and coverings on or in the penetrating item shall not penetrate the assembly unless the specific material used has been tested as part of the assembly in accordance with this section.

712.3 Fire-resistance-rated walls. Penetrations into or through fire walls, fire-barrier walls, smoke-barrier walls and fire partitions shall comply with Sections 712.3.1 through 712.3.4.

712.3.1 Through penetrations. Through penetrations of fire-resistance-rated walls shall comply with Section 712.3.1.1 or 712.3.1.2.

Exception: Where the penetrating items are steel, ferrous or copper pipes, tubes or conduits, the annular space between the penetrating item and the fire-resistance-rated wall is permitted to be protected as follows:

1. In concrete or masonry walls where the penetrating item is a maximum 6-inch (152 mm) nominal diameter and the area of the opening through the wall does not exceed 144 square inches (0.0929 m^2), concrete, grout or mortar is permitted where it is installed the full thickness of the wall or the thickness required to maintain the fire-resistance rating; or

2. The material used to fill the annular space shall prevent the passage of flame and hot gases sufficient to ignite cotton waste when subjected to ASTM E 119 time-temperature fire conditions under a minimum positive pressure differential of 0.01 inch (2.49 Pa) of water at the location of the penetration for the time period equivalent to the fire-resistance rating of the construction penetrated.

712.3.1.1 Fire-resistance-rated assemblies. Penetrations shall be installed as tested in an approved fire-resistance-rated assembly.

712.3.1.2 Through-penetration firestop system. Through penetrations shall be protected by an approved penetration firestop system installed as tested in accordance with ASTM E 814 or UL 1479, with a minimum positive pressure differential of 0.01 inch (2.49 Pa) of water and shall have an F rating of not less than the required fire-resistance rating of the wall penetrated.

712.3.2 Membrane penetrations. Membrane penetrations shall comply with Section 712.3.1. Where walls or partitions are required to have a fire-resistance rating, recessed fixtures shall be installed such that the required fire resistance will not be reduced.

Exceptions:

1. Membrane penetrations of maximum two-hour fire-resistance-rated walls and partitions by steel electrical boxes that do not exceed 16 square inches (0.0103 m²) in area, provided the aggregate area of the openings through the membrane does not exceed 100 square inches (0.0645 m²) in any 100 square feet (9.29 m²) of wall area. The annular space between the wall membrane and the box shall not exceed $^1/_8$ inch (3.1 mm). Such boxes on opposite sides of the wall or partition shall be separated by one of the following:

    1.1. By a horizontal distance of not less than 24 inches (610 mm);

    1.2. By a horizontal distance of not less than the depth of the wall cavity where the wall cavity is filled with cellulose loose-fill, rockwool or slag mineral wool insulation;

    1.3. By solid fireblocking in accordance with Section 717.2.1;

    1.4. By protecting both outlet boxes with listed putty pads; or

    1.5. By other listed materials and methods.

2. Membrane penetrations by listed electrical boxes of any material, provided such boxes have been tested for use in fire-resistance-rated assemblies and are installed in accordance with the instructions included in the listing. The annular space between the wall membrane and the box shall not exceed $^1/_8$ inch (3.1 mm) unless listed otherwise. Such boxes on opposite sides of the wall or partition shall be separated as follows:

    2.1. By a horizontal distance of not less than 24 inches (610 mm);

    2.2. By solid fireblocking in accordance with Section 717.2.1;

    2.3. By protecting both boxes with listed putty pads; or

    2.4. By other listed materials and methods.

3. The annular space created by the penetration of a fire sprinkler, provided it is covered by a metal escutcheon plate.

712.3.3 Ducts and air transfer openings. Penetrations of fire-resistance-rated walls by ducts that are not protected with dampers shall comply with Sections 712.2 through 712.3.1. Ducts and air transfer openings that are protected with dampers shall comply with Section 716.

712.3.4 Dissimilar materials. Noncombustible penetrating items shall not connect to combustible items beyond the point of firestopping unless it can be demonstrated that the fire-resistance integrity of the wall is maintained.

712.4 Horizontal assemblies. Penetrations of a floor, floor/ceiling assembly or the ceiling membrane of a roof/ceiling assembly shall be protected in accordance with Section 707.

712.4.1 Fire-resistance rated assemblies. Penetrations of the fire-resistance rated floor, floor/ceiling assembly or the ceiling membrane of a roof/ceiling assembly shall comply with Sections 712.4.1.1 through 712.4.1.4

712.4.1.1 Through penetrations. Through penetrations of fire-resistance-rated horizontal assemblies shall comply with Section 712.4.1.1.1 or 712.4.1.1.2.

Exceptions:

1. Penetrations by steel, ferrous or copper conduits, pipes, tubes or vents or concrete or masonry items through a single fire-resistance-rated floor assembly where the annular space is protected with materials that prevent the passage of flame and hot gases sufficient to ignite cotton waste when subjected to ASTM E 119 time-temperature fire conditions under a minimum positive pressure differential of 0.01 inch (2.49 Pa) of water at the location of the penetration for the time period equivalent to the fire-resistance rating of the construction penetrated. Penetrating items with a maximum 6-inch (152 mm) nominal diameter shall not be limited to the penetration of a single fire-resistance-rated floor assembly, provided the aggregate area of the openings through the assembly does not exceed 144 square inches (92 900 mm²) in any 100 square feet (9.3 m²) of floor area.

2. Penetrations in a single concrete floor by steel, ferrous or copper conduits, pipes, tubes or vents with a maximum 6-inch (152 mm) nominal diameter, provided the concrete, grout or mortar is installed the full thickness of the floor or the thickness required to maintain the fire-resistance rating. The penetrating items shall not be limited to the penetration of a single concrete floor, provided the area of the opening through each floor does not exceed 144 square inches (92 900 mm²).

3. Penetrations by listed electrical boxes of any material, provided such boxes have been tested for use in fire-resistance-rated assemblies and installed in accordance with the instructions included in the listing.

712.4.1.1.1 Installation. Through penetrations shall be installed as tested in the approved fire-resistance-rated assembly.

712.4.1.1.2 Through-penetration firestop system. Through penetrations shall be protected by an approved through-penetration firestop system installed and tested in accordance with ASTM E 814 or UL 1479, with a minimum positive pressure differential of 0.01 inch of water (2.49 Pa). The system shall have an F-rating and a T-rating of not less than 1 hour but not less than the required rating of the floor penetrated.

> **Exception:** Floor penetrations contained and located within the cavity of a wall do not require a T- rating.

712.4.1.2 Membrane penetrations. Penetrations of membranes that are part of a fire-resistance-rated horizontal assembly shall comply with Section 712.4.1.1.1 or 712.4.1.1.2. Where floor/ceiling assemblies are required to have a minimum 1-hour fire-resistance rating, recessed fixtures shall be installed such that the required fire resistance will not be reduced.

Exceptions:

1. Membrane penetrations by steel, ferrous or copper conduits, pipes, tubes or vents, or concrete or masonry items where the annular space is protected either in accordance with Section 712.4.1.1 or to prevent the free passage of flame and the products of combustion. The aggregate area of the openings through the membrane shall not exceed 100 square inches (64 500 mm²) in any 100 square feet (9.3 m²) of ceiling area in assemblies tested without penetrations.

2. Ceiling membrane penetrations of maximum 2-hour fire-resistance-rated horizontal assemblies by steel electrical boxes that do not exceed 16 square inches (10 323 mm²) in area, provided the aggregate area of such penetrations does not exceed 100 square inches (44 500 mm²) in any 100 square feet (9.29 m²) of ceiling area, and the annular space between the ceiling membrane and the box does not exceed ¹/₈ inch (3.12 mm).

3. Membrane penetrations by listed electrical boxes of any material, provided such boxes have been tested for use in fire-resistance-rated assemblies and are installed in accordance with the instructions included in the listing. The annular space between the ceiling membrane and the box shall not exceed ¹/₈ inch (3.1 mm) unless listed otherwise.

4. The annular space created by the penetration of a fire sprinkler, provided it is covered by a metal eschutcheon plate.

712.4.1.3 Ducts and air transfer openings. Penetrations of horizontal assemblies by ducts and air transfer openings shall comply with Section 716.

712.4.1.4 Dissimilar materials. Noncombustible penetrating items shall not connect to combustible materials beyond the point of firestopping unless it can be demonstrated that the fire-resistance integrity of the horizontal assembly is maintained.

712.4.2 Nonfire-resistance-rated assemblies. Penetrations of horizontal assemblies without a required fire-resistance rating shall meet the requirements of Section 707 or shall comply with Section 712.4.2.1 or 712.4.2.2.

712.4.2.1 Noncombustible penetrating items. Noncombustible penetrating items that connect not more than three stories are permitted, provided that the annular space is filled with an approved noncombustible material to resist the free passage of flame and the products of combustion.

712.4.2.2 Penetrating items. Penetrating items that connect not more than two stories are permitted, provided that the annular space is filled with an approved material to resist the free passage of flame and the products of combustion.

712.5 Penetrations in smoke barriers. Penetrations in smoke barriers shall be tested in accordance with the requirements of UL 1479 for air leakage. The air leakage rate of the penetration assembly shall not exceed 5.0 cfm per square foot (0.025 m³ / s • m²) of penetration opening at 0.30 inch (7.47 Pa) of water for both the ambient temperature and elevated temperature tests.

SECTION 713
FIRE-RESISTANT JOINT SYSTEMS

713.1 General. Joints installed in or between fire-resistance-rated walls, floor or floor/ceiling assemblies and roofs or roof/ceiling assemblies shall be protected by an approved fire-resistant joint system designed to resist the passage of fire for a time period not less than the required fire-resistance rating of the wall, floor or roof in or between which it is installed. Fire-resistant joint systems shall be tested in accordance with Section 713.3. The void created at the intersection of a floor/ceiling assembly and an exterior curtain wall assembly shall be protected in accordance with Section 713.4.

> **Exception:** Fire-resistant joint systems shall not be required for joints in all of the following locations:
>
> 1. Floors within a single dwelling unit.
>
> 2. Floors where the joint is protected by a shaft enclosure in accordance with Section 707.
>
> 3. Floors within atriums where the space adjacent to the atrium is included in the volume of the atrium for smoke control purposes.
>
> 4. Floors within malls.
>
> 5. Floors within open parking structures.
>
> 6. Mezzanine floors.
>
> 7. Walls that are permitted to have unprotected openings.
>
> 8. Roofs where openings are permitted.
>
> 9. Control joints not exceeding a maximum width of 0.625 inch (15.9 mm) and tested in accordance with ASTM E 119.

713.2 Installation. Fire-resistant joint systems shall be securely installed in or on the joint for its entire length so as not to dislodge, loosen or otherwise impair its ability to accommodate expected building movements and to resist the passage of fire and hot gases.

713.3 Fire test criteria. Fire-resistant joint systems shall be tested in accordance with the requirements of either ASTM E 1966 or UL 2079. Nonsymmetrical wall joint systems shall be tested with both faces exposed to the furnace, and the assigned fire-resistance rating shall be the shortest duration obtained from the two tests. When evidence is furnished to show that the wall was tested with the least fire-resistant side exposed to the furnace, subject to acceptance of the building official, the wall need not be subjected to tests from the opposite side.

> **Exception:** For exterior walls with a horizontal fire separation distance greater than 5 feet (1524 mm), the joint system shall be required to be tested for interior fire exposure only.

713.4 Exterior curtain wall/floor intersection. Where fire resistance-rated floor or floor/ceiling assemblies are required, voids created at the intersection of the exterior curtain wall assemblies and such floor assemblies shall be sealed with an approved material or system to prevent the interior spread of fire. Such material or systems shall be securely installed and capable of preventing the passage of flame and hot gases sufficient to ignite cotton waste where subjected either to ASTM E 119 time-temperature fire conditions under a minimum positive pressure differential of 0.01 inch (0.254 mm) of water column (2.5 Pa) or installed as tested in accordance with ASTM E 2307 for the time period at least equal to the fire-resistance rating of the floor assembly. Height and fire-resistance requirements for curtain wall spandrels shall comply with Section 704.9.

713.5 Spandrel wall. Height and fire-resistance requirements for curtain wall spandrels shall comply with Section 704.9. Where Section 704.9 does not require a fire-resistance-rated spandrel wall, the requirements of Section 713.4 shall still apply to the intersection between the spandrel wall and the floor.

713.6 Fire-resistant joint systems in smoke barriers. Fire-resistant joint systems in smoke barriers shall be tested in accordance with the requirements of UL 2079 for air leakage. The air leakage rate of the joint shall not exceed 5 cfm per lineal foot (0.00775 m³/slm) of joint at 0.30 inch (7.47 Pa) of water for both the ambient temperature and elevated temperature tests.

SECTION 714
FIRE-RESISTANCE RATING OF STRUCTURAL MEMBERS

714.1 Requirements. The fire-resistance rating of structural members and assemblies shall comply with the requirements for the type of construction and shall not be less than the rating required for the fire-resistance-rated assemblies supported.

> **Exception:** Fire barriers, fire partitions and smoke barriers as provided in Sections 706.5, 708.4 and 709.4, respectively.

714.2 Protection of structural members. Protection of columns, girders, trusses, beams, lintels or other structural members that are required to have a fire-resistance rating shall comply with this section.

714.2.1 Individual protection. Columns, girders, trusses, beams, lintels or other structural members that are required to have a fire-resistance rating and that support more than two floors or one floor and roof, or support a load-bearing wall or a nonload-bearing wall more than two stories high, shall be individually protected on all sides for the full length with materials having the required fire-resistance rating. Other structural members required to have a fire-resistance rating shall be protected by individual encasement, by a membrane or ceiling protection as specified in Section 711, or by a combination of both. Columns shall also comply with Section 714.2.2.

714.2.1.1 Membrane protection. King studs and boundary elements that are integral elements in load-bearing walls of light-framed construction shall be permitted to have required fire-resistance ratings provided by the membrane protection provided for the load-bearing wall.

714.2.2 Column protection above ceilings. Where columns require a fire-resistance rating, the entire column, including its connections to beams or girders, shall be protected. Where the column extends through a ceiling, fire resistance of the column shall be continuous from the top of the foundation or floor/ceiling assembly below through the ceiling space to the top of the column.

714.2.3 Truss protection. The required thickness and construction of fire-resistance-rated assemblies enclosing trusses shall be based on the results of full-scale tests or combinations of tests on truss components or on approved calculations based on such tests that satisfactorily demonstrate that the assembly has the required fire resistance.

714.2.4 Attachments to structural members. The edges of lugs, brackets, rivets and bolt heads attached to structural members shall be permitted to extend to within 1 inch (25 mm) of the surface of the fire protection.

714.2.5 Reinforcing. Thickness of protection for concrete or masonry reinforcement shall be measured to the outside of the reinforcement except that stirrups and spiral reinforcement ties are permitted to project not more than 0.5-inch (12.7 mm) into the protection.

714.3 Embedments and enclosures. Pipes, wires, conduits, ducts or other service facilities shall not be embedded in the required fire protective covering of a structural member that is required to be individually encased.

714.4 Impact protection. Where the fire protective covering of a structural member is subject to impact damage from moving vehicles, the handling of merchandise or other activity, the fire protective covering shall be protected by corner guards or by a substantial jacket of metal or other noncombustible material to a height adequate to provide full protection, but not less than 5 feet (1524 mm) from the finished floor.

714.5 Exterior structural members. Load-bearing structural members located within the exterior walls or on the outside of a building or structure shall be provided with the highest fire-resistance rating as determined in accordance with the following:

1. As required by Table 601 for the type of building element based on the type of construction of the building;

2. As required by Table 601 for exterior bearing walls based on the type of construction; and

3. As required by Table 602 for exterior walls based on the fire separation distance.

714.6 Bottom flange protection. Fire protection is not required at the bottom flange of lintels, shelf angles and plates, spanning not more than 6 feet (1829 mm) whether part of the structural frame or not, and from the bottom flange of lintels, shelf angles and plates not part of the structural frame, regardless of span.

714.7 Seismic isolation systems. Fire-resistance ratings for the isolation system shall meet the fire-resistance rating required for the columns, walls or other structural elements in which the isolation system is installed in accordance with Table 601.

Isolation systems required to have a fire-resistance rating shall be protected with approved materials or construction assemblies designed to provide the same degree of fire resistance as the structural element in which it is installed when tested in accordance with ASTM E 119 (see Section 703.2).

Such isolation system protection applied to isolator units shall be capable of retarding the transfer of heat to the isolator unit in such a manner that the required gravity load-carrying capacity of the isolator unit will not be impaired after exposure to the standard time-temperature curve fire test prescribed in ASTM E 119 for a duration not less than that required for the fire-resistance rating of the structure element in which it is installed.

Such isolation system protection applied to isolator units shall be suitably designed and securely installed so as not to dislodge, loosen, sustain damage or otherwise impair its ability to accommodate the seismic movements for which the isolator unit is designed and to maintain its integrity for the purpose of providing the required fire-resistance protection.

SECTION 715
OPENING PROTECTIVES

715.1 General. Opening protectives required by other sections of this code shall comply with the provisions of this section.

715.2 Fire-resistance-rated glazing. Labeled fire-resistance-rated glazing tested as part of a fire-resistance-rated wall assembly in accordance with ASTM E 119 shall not be required to comply with this section.

715.3 Alternative methods for determining fire protection ratings. The application of any of the alternative methods listed in this section shall be based on the fire exposure and acceptance criteria specified in NFPA 252 or NFPA 257. The required fire resistance of an opening protective shall be permitted to be established by any of the following methods or procedures:

1. Designs documented in approved sources.

2. Calculations performed in an approved manner.

3. Engineering analysis based on a comparison of opening protective designs having fire-protection ratings as determined by the test procedures set forth in NFPA 252 or NFPA 257.

4. Alternative protection methods as allowed by Section 103.3.

715.4 Fire door and shutter assemblies. Approved fire door and fire shutter assemblies shall be constructed of any mate-

TABLE 715.4
FIRE DOOR AND FIRE SHUTTER FIRE PROTECTION RATINGS

TYPE OF ASSEMBLY	REQUIRED ASSEMBLY RATING (hours)	MINIMUM FIRE DOOR AND FIRE SHUTTER ASSEMBLY RATING (hours)
Fire walls and fire barriers having a required fire-resistance rating greater than 1 hour	4 3 2 $1^1/_2$	3 3^a $1^1/_2$ $1^1/_2$
Fire barriers having a required fire-resistance rating of 1 hour: Shaft, exit enclosure and exit passageway walls Other fire barriers	1 1	1 $^3/_4$
Fire partitions: Corridor walls Other fire partitions	1 0.5 1 0.5	$^1/_3$ b $^1/_3$ b $^3/_4$ $^1/_3$
Exterior walls	3 2 1	$1^1/_2$ $1^1/_2$ $^3/_4$
Smoke barriers	1	$^1/_3$ b

a. Two doors, each with a fire protection rating of $1^1/_2$ hours, installed on opposite sides of the same opening in a fire wall, shall be deemed equivalent in fire protection rating to one 3-hour fire door.
b. For testing requirements, see Section 715.4.3.

rial or assembly of component materials that conforms to the test requirements of Section 715.4.1, 715.4.2 or 715.4.3 and the fire-protection rating indicated in Table 715.4. Fire door assemblies and shutters shall be installed in accordance with the provisions of this section and NFPA 80.

Exceptions:

1. Labeled protective assemblies that conform to the requirements of this section or UL 10A, UL 14B and UL 14C for tin-clad fire door assemblies.

2. Floor fire door assemblies in accordance with Section 711.8.

715.4.1 Side-hinged or pivoted swinging doors. Side-hinged and pivoted swinging doors shall be tested in accordance with NFPA 252 or UL 10C. After 5 minutes into the NFPA 252 test, the neutral pressure level in the furnace shall be established at 40 inches (1016 mm) or less above the sill.

715.4.2 Other types of doors. Other types of doors, including swinging elevator doors, shall be tested in accordance with NFPA 252 or UL 10B. The pressure in the furnace shall be maintained as nearly equal to the atmospheric pressure as possible. Once established, the pressure shall be maintained during the entire test period.

715.4.3 Door assemblies in corridors and smoke barriers. Fire door assemblies required to have a minimum fire protection rating of 20 minutes where located in corridor walls or smoke-barrier walls having a fire-resistance rating in accordance with Table 715.4 shall be tested in accordance with NFPA 252 or UL 10C without the hose stream test.

Exceptions:

1. Viewports that require a hole not larger than 1 inch (25 mm) in diameter through the door, have at least a 0.25-inch-thick (6.4 mm) glass disc and the holder is of metal that will not melt out where subject to temperatures of 1,700°F (927°C).

2. Corridor door assemblies in occupancies of Group I-2 shall be in accordance with Section 407.3.1.

3. Unprotected openings shall be permitted for corridors in multitheater complexes where each motion picture auditorium has at least one-half of its required exit or exit access doorways opening directly to the exterior or into an exit passageway.

715.4.3.1 Smoke and draft control. Fire door assemblies shall also meet the requirements for a smoke and draft control door assembly tested in accordance with UL 1784. Louvers shall be prohibited. Installation of smoke doors shall be in accordance with NFPA 105.

715.4.3.2 Glazing in door assemblies. In a 20-minute fire door assembly, the glazing material in the door itself shall have a minimum fire-protection rating of 20 minutes and shall be exempt from the hose stream test. Glazing material in any other part of the door assembly, including transom lites and sidelites, shall be tested in

accordance with NFPA 257, including the hose stream test, in accordance with Section 715.5.

715.4.4 Doors in exit enclosures and exit passageways. Fire door assemblies in exit enclosures and exit passageways shall have a maximum transmitted temperature end point of not more than 450°F (250° C) above ambient at the end of 30 minutes of standard fire test exposure.

Exception: The maximum transmitted temperature rise is not limited in buildings equipped throughout with an automatic sprinkler system installed in accordance with Section 903.3.1.1 or 903.3.1.2.

715.4.4.1 Glazing in doors. Fire-protection-rated glazing in excess of 100 square inches (0.065 m²) shall be permitted in fire door assemblies when tested in accordance with NFPA 252 as components of the door assemblies and not as glass lights, and shall have a maximum transmitted temperature rise of 450°F (250°C) in accordance with Section 715.4.4.

Exception: The maximum transmitted temperature end point is not required in buildings equipped throughout with an automatic sprinkler system installed in accordance with Section 903.3.1.1 or 903.3.1.2.

715.4.5 Labeled protective assemblies. Fire door assemblies shall be labeled by an approved agency. The labels shall comply with NFPA 80, and shall be permanently affixed to the door or frame.

715.4.5.1 Fire door labeling requirements. Fire doors shall be labeled showing the name of the manufacturer, the name of the third-party inspection agency, the fire protection rating and, where required for fire doors in exit enclosures and exit passageways by Section 715.4.4, the maximum transmitted temperature end point. Smoke and draft control doors complying with UL 1784 shall be labeled as such. Labels shall be approved and permanently affixed. The label shall be applied at the factory or location where fabrication and assembly are performed.

715.4.5.2 Oversized doors. Oversized fire doors shall bear an oversized fire door label by an approved agency or shall be provided with a certificate of inspection furnished by an approved testing agency. When a certificate of inspection is furnished by an approved testing agency, the certificate shall state that the door conforms to the requirements of design, materials and construction, but has not been subjected to the fire test.

715.4.5.3 Smoke and draft control door labeling requirements. Smoke and draft control doors complying with UL 1784 shall be labeled in accordance with Section 715.4.5.1 and shall show the letter "S" on the fire rating label of the door. This marking shall indicate that the door and frame assembly are in compliance when listed or labeled gasketing is also installed.

715.4.5.4 Fire door frame labeling requirements. Fire door frames shall be labeled showing the names of the manufacturer and the third-party inspection agency.

715.4.6 Glazing material. Fire-protection-rated glazing conforming to the opening protection requirements in Section 715.4 shall be permitted in fire door assemblies.

715.4.6.1 Size limitations. Wired glass used in fire doors shall comply with Table 715.5.3. Other fire-protection-rated glazing shall comply with the size limitations of NFPA 80.

Exceptions:

1. Fire-protection-rated glazing in fire doors located in fire walls shall be prohibited except that where serving as a horizontal exit, a self-closing swinging door shall be permitted to have a vision panel of not more than 100 square inches (0.065 m²) without a dimension exceeding 10 inches (254 mm).

2. Fire-protection-rated glazing shall not be installed in fire doors having a $1^1/_2$-hour fire protection rating intended for installation in fire barriers, unless the glazing is not more than 100 square inches (0.065 m²) in area.

715.4.6.2 Exit and elevator protectives. Approved fire-protection-rated glazing used in fire door assemblies in elevator and exit enclosures shall be so located as to furnish clear vision of the passageway or approach to the elevator, ramp or stairway.

715.4.6.3 Labeling. Fire-protection-rated glazing shall bear a label or other identification showing the name of the manufacturer, the test standard and information required in Section 715.5.8.1 that shall be issued by an approved agency and shall be permanently affixed to the glazing.

715.4.6.3.1 Identification. For fire-protection-rated glazing, the label shall bear the following four-part identification: "D - H or NH - T or NT - XXX." "D" indicates that the glazing shall be used in fire door assemblies and that the glazing meets the fire resistance requirements of the test standard. "H" shall indicate that the glazing meets the hose stream requirements of the test standard. "NH" shall indicate that the glazing does not meet the hose stream requirements of the test. "T" shall indicate that the glazing meets the temperature requirements of Section 715.4.4.1. "NT" shall indicate that the glazing does not meet the temperature requirements of Section 715.4.4.1. The placeholder "XXX" shall specify the fire-protection-rating period, in minutes.

715.4.6.4 Safety glazing. Fire-protection-rated glazing installed in fire doors or fire window assemblies in areas subject to human impact in hazardous locations shall comply with Chapter 24.

715.4.7 Door closing. Fire doors shall be self- or automatic closing in accordance with this section.

Exceptions:

1. Fire doors located in common walls separating sleeping units in Group R-1 shall be permitted without automatic- or self-closing devices.

2. The elevator car doors and the associated hoistway enclosure doors at the floor level designated for recall in accordance with Section 3003.2 shall be permitted to remain open during Phase I emergency recall operation.

715.4.7.1 Latch required. Unless otherwise specifically permitted, single fire doors and both leaves of pairs of side-hinged swinging fire doors shall be provided with an active latch bolt that will secure the door when it is closed.

715.4.7.2 Automatic-closing fire door assemblies. Automatic-closing fire door assemblies shall be self-closing in accordance with NFPA 80.

715.4.7.3 Smoke-activated doors. Automatic-closing doors installed in the following locations shall be automatic closing by the actuation of smoke detectors installed in accordance with Section 907.10 or by loss of power to the smoke detector or hold-open device. Doors that are automatic closing by smoke detection shall not have more than a 10-second delay before the door starts to close after the smoke detector is actuated:

1. Doors installed across a corridor.

2. Doors that protect openings in exits or corridors required to be of fire-resistance-rated construction.

3. Doors that protect openings in walls that are capable of resisting the passage of smoke in accordance with Section 508.2.2.1.

4. Doors installed in smoke barriers in accordance with Section 709.5.

5. Doors installed in fire partitions in accordance with Section 708.6.

6. Doors installed in a fire wall in accordance with Section 705.8.

7. Doors installed in shaft enclosures in accordance with Section 707.7.

8. Doors installed in refuse and laundry chutes and access and termination rooms in accordance with Section 707.13.

9. Doors installed in the walls for compartmentation of underground buildings in accordance with Section 405.4.2.

10. Doors installed in the elevator lobby walls of underground buildings in accordance with Section 405.4.3.

11. Doors installed in smoke partitions in accordance with Section 710.5.3.

715.4.7.4 Doors in pedestrian ways. Vertical sliding or vertical rolling steel fire doors in openings through which pedestrians travel shall be heat activated or activated by smoke detectors with alarm verification.

715.4.8 Swinging fire shutters. Where fire shutters of the swinging type are installed in exterior openings, not less than one row in every three vertical rows shall be arranged to be readily opened from the outside, and shall be identified by distinguishing marks or letters not less than 6 inches (152 mm) high.

715.4.9 Rolling fire shutters. Where fire shutters of the rolling type are installed, such shutters shall include approved automatic-closing devices.

715.5 Fire-protection-rated glazing. Glazing in fire window assemblies shall be fire-protection rated in accordance with this section and Table 715.5. Glazing in fire door assemblies shall comply with Section 715.4.6. Fire-protection-rated glazing shall be tested in accordance with and shall meet the acceptance criteria of NFPA 257. Fire-protection-rated glazing shall also comply with NFPA 80. Openings in nonfire-resistance-rated exterior wall assemblies that require protection in accordance with Section 704.3, 704.8, 704.9 or 704.10 shall have a fire-protection rating of not less than $^3/_4$ hour.

Exceptions:

1. Wired glass in accordance with Section 715.5.3.

2. Fire-protection-rated glazing in 0.5-hour fire-resistance-rated partitions is permitted to have an 0.33-hour fire-protection rating.

TABLE 715.5
FIRE WINDOW ASSEMBLY FIRE PROTECTION RATINGS

TYPE OF ASSEMBLY	REQUIRED ASSEMBLY RATING (hours)	MINIMUM FIRE WINDOW ASSEMBLY RATING (hours)
Interior walls:		
Fire walls	All	NP[a]
Fire barriers	>1	NP[a]
Smoke barriers and	1	$^3/_4$
fire partitions	1	$^3/_4$
Exterior walls	>1	$1^1/_2$
	1	$^3/_4$
Party wall	All	NP

NP = Not Permitted.

a. Not permitted except as specified in Section 715.2.

715.5.1 Testing under positive pressure. NFPA 257 shall evaluate fire-protection-rated glazing under positive pressure. Within the first 10 minutes of a test, the pressure in the furnace shall be adjusted so at least two-thirds of the test specimen is above the neutral pressure plane, and the neutral pressure plane shall be maintained at that height for the balance of the test.

715.5.2 Nonsymmetrical glazing systems. Nonsymmetrical fire-protection-rated glazing systems in fire partitions, fire barriers or in exterior walls with a fire separation distance of 5 feet (1524 mm) or less pursuant to Section 704 shall be tested with both faces exposed to the furnace, and the assigned fire protection rating shall be the shortest duration obtained from the two tests conducted in compliance with NFPA 257.

715.5.3 Wired glass. Steel window frame assemblies of 0.125-inch (3.2 mm) minimum solid section or of not less than nominal 0.048-inch-thick (1.2 mm) formed sheet steel members fabricated by pressing, mitering, riveting, interlocking or welding and having provision for glazing with $^1/_4$-inch (6.4 mm) wired glass where securely

installed in the building construction and glazed with $^1/_4$-inch (6.4 mm) labeled wired glass shall be deemed to meet the requirements for a $^3/_4$-hour fire window assembly. Wired glass panels shall conform to the size limitations set forth in Table 715.5.3.

TABLE 715.5.3
LIMITING SIZES OF WIRED GLASS PANELS

OPENING FIRE PROTECTION RATING	MAXIMUM AREA (square inches)	MAXIMUM HEIGHT (inches)	MAXIMUM WIDTH (inches)
3 hours	0	0	0
$1^1/_2$-hour doors in exterior walls	0	0	0
1 and $1^1/_2$ hours	100	33	10
$^3/_4$ hour	1,296	54	54
20 minutes	Not Limited	Not Limited	Not Limited
Fire window assemblies	1,296	54	54

For SI: 1 inch = 25.4 mm, 1 square inch = 645.2 mm^2.

715.5.4 Nonwired glass. Glazing other than wired glass in fire window assemblies shall be fire-protection-rated glazing installed in accordance with and complying with the size limitations set forth in NFPA 80.

715.5.5 Installation. Fire-protection-rated glazing shall be in the fixed position or be automatic-closing and shall be installed in approved frames.

715.5.6 Window mullions. Metal mullions that exceed a nominal height of 12 feet (3658 mm) shall be protected with materials to afford the same fire-resistance rating as required for the wall construction in which the protective is located.

715.5.7 Interior fire window assemblies. Fire-protection-rated glazing used in fire window assemblies located in fire partitions and fire barriers shall be limited to use in assemblies with a maximum fire-resistance rating of 1 hour in accordance with this section.

715.5.7.1 Where permitted. Fire-protection-rated glazing shall be limited to fire partitions designed in accordance with Section 708 and fire barriers utilized in the applications set forth in Sections 706.3.6 and 706.3.8 where the fire-resistance rating does not exceed 1 hour.

715.5.7.2 Size limitations. The total area of windows shall not exceed 25 percent of the area of a common wall with any room.

715.5.8 Labeling requirements. Fire-protection-rated glazing shall bear a label or other identification showing the name of the manufacturer, the test standard and information required in Section 715.5.8.1 that shall be issued by an approved agency and shall be permanently affixed to the glazing.

715.5.8.1 Identification. For fire-protection-rated glazing, the label shall bear the following two-part identification: "OH - XXX." "OH" indicates that the glazing meets both the fire-resistance and the hose-stream requirements of NFPA 257 and is permitted to be used in openings. "XXX" represents the fire-protection rating period, in minutes, that was tested.

SECTION 716
DUCTS AND AIR TRANSFER OPENINGS

716.1 General. The provisions of this section shall govern the protection of duct penetrations and air transfer openings in assemblies required to be protected.

716.1.1 Ducts without dampers. Ducts that penetrate fire-resistance-rated assemblies and are not required by this section to have dampers shall comply with the requirements of Section 712.

716.2 Installation. Fire dampers, smoke dampers, combination fire/smoke dampers and ceiling radiation dampers located within air distribution and smoke control systems shall be installed in accordance with the requirements of this section, the manufacturer's installation instructions and the dampers' listing.

716.2.1 Smoke control system. Where the installation of a fire damper will interfere with the operation of a required smoke control system in accordance with Section 909, approved alternative protection shall be utilized.

716.2.2 Hazardous exhaust ducts. Fire dampers for hazardous exhaust duct systems shall comply with the *Mechanical Code of New York State*.

716.3 Damper testing and ratings. Dampers shall be listed and bear the label of an approved testing agency indicating compliance with the standards in this section. Fire dampers shall comply with the requirements of UL 555. Only fire dampers labeled for use in dynamic systems shall be installed in heating, ventilation and air-conditioning systems designed to operate with fans on during a fire. Smoke dampers shall comply with the requirements of UL 555S. Combination fire/smoke dampers shall comply with the requirements of both UL 555 and UL 555S. Ceiling radiation dampers shall comply with the requirements of UL 555C.

716.3.1 Fire protection rating. Fire dampers shall have the minimum fire protection rating specified in Table 716.3.1 for the type of penetration.

TABLE 716.3.1
FIRE DAMPER RATING

TYPE OF PENETRATION	MINIMUM DAMPER RATING(hours)
Less than 3-hour fire-resistance-rated assemblies	1.5
3-hour or greater fire-resistance-rated assemblies	3

716.3.1.1 Fire damper actuating device. The fire damper actuating device shall meet one of the following requirements:

1. The operating temperature shall be approximately 50°F (10°C) above the normal temperature within the duct system, but not less than 160°F (71°C).

2. The operating temperature shall be not more than 286°F (141°C) where located in a smoke control system complying with Section 909.

3. Where a combination fire/smoke damper is located in a smoke control system complying with Section 909, the operating temperature rating shall be approximately 50°F (10°C) above the maximum smoke control system designed operating temperature, or a maximum temperature of 350°F (177°C). The temperature shall not exceed the UL 555S degradation test temperature rating for a combination fire/smoke damper.

716.3.2 Smoke damper ratings. Smoke damper leakage ratings shall not be less than Class II. Elevated temperature ratings shall not be less than 250°F (121°C).

716.3.2.1 Smoke damper actuation methods. The smoke damper shall close upon actuation of a listed smoke detector or detectors installed in accordance with Section 907.10 and one of the following methods, as applicable:

1. Where a damper is installed within a duct, a smoke detector shall be installed in the duct within 5 feet (1524 mm) of the damper with no air outlets or inlets between the detector and the damper. The detector shall be listed for the air velocity, temperature and humidity anticipated at the point where it is installed. Other than in mechanical smoke control systems, dampers shall be closed upon fan shutdown where local smoke detectors require a minimum velocity to operate.

2. Where a damper is installed above smoke barrier doors in a smoke barrier, a spot-type detector listed for releasing service shall be installed on either side of the smoke barrier door opening.

3. Where a damper is installed within an unducted opening in a wall, a spot-type detector listed for releasing service shall be installed within 5 feet (1524 mm) horizontally of the damper.

4. Where a damper is installed in a corridor wall or ceiling, the damper shall be permitted to be controlled by a smoke detection system installed in the corridor.

5. Where a total-coverage smoke detector system is provided within areas served by a heating, ventilation and air-conditioning (HVAC) system, dampers shall be permitted to be controlled by the smoke detection system.

716.4 Access and identification. Fire and smoke dampers shall be provided with an approved means of access, which is large enough to permit inspection and maintenance of the damper and its operating parts. The access shall not affect the integrity of fire-resistance-rated assemblies. The access openings shall not reduce the fire-resistance rating of the assembly. Access points shall be permanently identified on the exterior by a label having letters not less than 0.5 inch (12.7 mm) in height reading: FIRE/SMOKE DAMPER, SMOKE DAMPER or FIRE DAMPER. Access doors in ducts shall be tight fitting and suitable for the required duct construction.

716.5 Where required. Fire dampers, smoke dampers, combination fire/smoke dampers and ceiling radiation dampers shall be provided at the locations prescribed in Sections 716.5.1 through 716.5.5 and Section 716.6. Where an assembly is required to have both fire dampers and smoke dampers, combination fire/smoke dampers or a fire damper and a smoke damper shall be required.

716.5.1 Fire walls. Ducts and air transfer openings permitted in fire walls in accordance with Section 705.11 shall be protected with listed fire dampers installed in accordance with their listing.

716.5.2 Fire barriers. Ducts and air transfer openings of fire barriers shall be protected with approved fire dampers installed in accordance with their listing. Ducts and air transfer openings shall not penetrate exit enclosures and exit passageways except as permitted by Sections 1020.1.2 and 1021.5, respectively.

Exception: Fire dampers are not required at penetrations of fire barriers where any of the following apply:

1. Penetrations are tested in accordance with ASTM E 119 as part of the fire-resistance rated assembly.

2. Ducts are used as part of an approved smoke control system in accordance with Section 909 and where the use of a fire damper would interfere with the operation of a smoke control system.

3. Such walls are penetrated by ducted HVAC systems, have a required fire-resistance rating of 1 hour or less, are in areas of other than Group H and are in buildings equipped throughout with an automatic sprinkler system in accordance with Section 903.3.1.1 or 903.3.1.2. For the purposes of this exception, a ducted HVAC system shall be a duct system for conveying supply, return or exhaust air as part of the structure's HVAC system. Such a duct system shall be constructed of sheet steel not less than 26 gage thickness and shall be continuous from the air-handling appliance or equipment to the air outlet and inlet terminals.

716.5.3 Shaft enclosures. Shaft enclosures that are permitted to be penetrated by ducts and air transfer openings shall be protected with approved fire and smoke dampers installed in accordance with their listing.

Exceptions:

1. Fire dampers are not required at penetrations of shafts where:

   1.1. Steel exhaust subducts are extended at least 22 inches (559 mm) vertically in exhaust shafts, provided there is a continuous airflow upward to the outside; or

   1.2. Penetrations are tested in accordance with ASTM E 119 as part of the rated assembly; or

   1.3. Ducts are used as part of an approved smoke control system designed and installed in accordance with Section 909 and where the fire damper will interfere with the operation of the smoke control system; or

   1.4. The penetrations are in parking garage exhaust or supply shafts that are separated from other building shafts by not less than 2-hour fire-resistance-rated construction.

2. In Group B and R occupancies, equipped throughout with an automatic sprinkler system in accordance with Section 903.3.1.1, smoke dampers are not required at penetrations of shafts where:

   2.1. Kitchen, clothes dryer, bathroom and toilet room exhaust openings are installed with steel exhaust subducts, having a wall thickness of at least 0.019 inch (0.48 mm); and

   2.2. That extend at least 22 inches (559 mm) vertically; and

   2.3. An exhaust fan is installed at the upper terminus of the shaft that is, powered continuously in accordance with the provisions of Section 909.11, so as to maintain a continuous upward airflow to the outside.

3. Smoke dampers are not required at penetration of exhaust or supply shafts in parking garages that are separated from other building shafts by not less than 2-hour fire-resistance-rated construction.

4. Smoke dampers are not required at penetrations of shafts where ducts are used as part of an approved mechanical smoke control system designed in accordance with Section 909 and where the smoke damper will interfere with the operation of the smoke control system.

5. In Group R occupancies, fire dampers and smoke dampers are not required at penetrations of individual bathroom/toilet room exhaust, domestic clothes dryer exhaust and domestic kitchen exhaust systems with steel exhaust subducts which extend at least 22 inches (559 mm) vertically in exhaust shafts, provided there is a continuous air flow upward to the outside.

6. Fire dampers, smoke dampers, combination fire/smoke dampers and any similar device that will obstruct the exhaust flow shall be prohibited in laboratory exhaust systems.

7. Fire dampers, smoke dampers, combination fire/smoke dampers and any similar device that will

obstruct the exhaust flow shall be prohibited in clothes dryer exhaust systems.

8. Fire dampers and smoke dampers and any similar device that will obstruct the exhaust flow shall be prohibited in commercial kitchen exhaust systems.

716.5.4 Fire partitions. Ducts and air transfer openings that penetrate fire partitions shall be protected with listed fire dampers installed in accordance with their listing.

Exceptions: In occupancies other than Group H, fire dampers are not required where any of the following apply:

1. The partitions are tenant separation or corridor walls in buildings equipped throughout with an automatic sprinkler system in accordance with Section 903.3.1.1 or 903.3.1.2 and the duct is protected as a through penetration in accordance with Section 712.

2. Tenant partitions in covered mall buildings where the walls are not required by provisions elsewhere in the code to extend to the underside of the floor or roof deck above.

3. The duct system is constructed of approved materials in accordance with the *Mechanical Code of New York State* and the duct penetrating the wall complies with all of the following requirements:

    3.1. The duct shall not exceed 100 square inches (0.06 m²).

    3.2. The duct shall be constructed of steel a minimum of 0.0217 inch (0.55 mm) in thickness.

    3.3. The duct shall not have openings that communicate the corridor with adjacent spaces or rooms.

    3.4. The duct shall be installed above a ceiling.

    3.5. The duct shall not terminate at a wall register in the fire-resistance-rated wall.

    3.6. A minimum 12-inch-long (305 mm) by 0.060-inch-thick (1.52 mm) steel sleeve shall be centered in each duct opening. The sleeve shall be secured to both sides of the wall and all four sides of the sleeve with minimum 1¹⁄₂-inch by 1¹⁄₂-inch by 0.060-inch (38 mm by 38 mm by 1.52 mm) steel retaining angles. The retaining angles shall be secured to the sleeve and the wall with No. 10 (M5) screws. The annular space between the steel sleeve and the wall opening shall be filled with mineral wool batting on all sides.

716.5.4.1 Corridors. A listed smoke damper designed to resist the passage of smoke shall be provided at each point a duct or air transfer opening penetrates a corridor

enclosure required to have smoke and draft control doors in accordance with Section 715.4.3.

Exceptions:

1. Smoke dampers are not required where the building is equipped throughout with an approved smoke control system in accordance with Section 909, and smoke dampers are not necessary for the operation and control of the system.

2. Smoke dampers are not required in corridor penetrations where the duct is constructed of steel not less than 0.019 inch (0.48 mm) in thickness and there are no openings serving the corridor.

716.5.5 Smoke barriers. A listed smoke damper designed to resist the passage of smoke shall be provided at each point a duct or air transfer opening penetrates a smoke barrier. Smoke dampers and smoke damper actuation methods shall comply with Section 716.3.2.1.

Exception: Smoke dampers are not required where the openings in ducts are limited to a single smoke compartment and the ducts are constructed of steel.

716.6 Horizontal assemblies. Penetrations by ducts and air transfer openings of a floor, floor/ceiling assembly or the ceiling membrane of a roof/ceiling assembly shall be protected by a shaft enclosure that complies with Section 707 or shall comply with Sections 716.6.1 through 716.6.3.

716.6.1 Through penetrations. In occupancies other than Groups I-2 and I-3, a duct constructed of approved materials in accordance with the *Mechanical Code of New York State* that penetrates a fire-resistance-rated floor/ceiling assembly that connects not more than two stories is permitted without shaft enclosure protection, provided a listed fire damper is installed at the floor line or the duct is protected in accordance with Section 712.4. For air transfer openings, see Exception 7 to Section 707.2.

Exception: A duct is permitted to penetrate three floors or less without a fire damper at each floor, provided it meets all of the following requirements:

1. The duct shall be contained and located within the cavity of a wall and shall be constructed of steel not less than 0.019 inch (0.48 mm) (26 gage) in thickness.

2. The duct shall open into only one dwelling or sleeping unit and the duct system shall be continuous from the unit to the exterior of the building.

3. The duct shall not exceed 4-inch (102 mm) nominal diameter and the total area of such ducts shall not exceed 100 square inches (0.065 m²) in any 100 square feet (9.3 m²) of floor area.

4. The annular space around the duct is protected with materials that prevent the passage of flame and hot gases sufficient to ignite cotton waste where subjected to ASTM E 119 time-tempera-

ture conditions under a minimum positive pressure differential of 0.01 inch (2.49 Pa) of water at the location of the penetration for the time period equivalent to the fire-resistance rating of the construction penetrated.

5. Grille openings located in a ceiling of a fire-resistance-rated floor/ceiling or roof/ceiling assembly shall be protected with a listed ceiling radiation damper installed in accordance with Section 716.6.2.1.

716.6.2 Membrane penetrations. Ducts and air transfer openings constructed of approved materials in accordance with the *Mechanical Code of New York State* that penetrate the ceiling membrane of a fire-resistance-rated floor/ceiling or roof/ceiling assembly shall be protected with one of the following:

1. A shaft enclosure in accordance with Section 707.

2. A listed ceiling radiation damper installed at the ceiling line where a duct penetrates the ceiling of a fire-resistance-rated floor/ceiling or roof/ceiling assembly.

3. A listed ceiling radiation damper installed at the ceiling line where a diffuser with no duct attached penetrates the ceiling of a fire-resistance-rated floor/ceiling or roof/ceiling assembly.

716.6.2.1 Ceiling radiation dampers. Ceiling radiation dampers shall be tested in accordance with UL 555C and installed in accordance with the manufacturer's installation instructions and listing. Ceiling radiation dampers are not required where either of the following applies:

1. Tests in accordance with ASTM E 119 have shown that ceiling radiation dampers are not necessary in order to maintain the fire-resistance rating of the assembly.

2. Where exhaust duct penetrations are protected in accordance with Section 712.4.1.2, are located within the cavity of a wall and do not pass through another dwelling unit or tenant space.

716.6.3 Nonfire-resistance-rated floor assemblies. Duct systems constructed of approved materials in accordance with the *Mechanical Code of New York State* that penetrate nonfire-resistance-rated floor assemblies shall be protected by any of the following methods:

1. A shaft enclosure in accordance with Section 707.

2. The duct connects not more than two stories, the annular space around the penetrating duct is protected with an approved noncombustible material that resists the free passage of flame and the products of combustion.

3. The duct connects not more than three stories, the annular space around the penetrating duct is protected with an approved noncombustible material that resists the free passage of flame and the prod-

ucts of combustion and a fire damper is installed at each floor line.

Exception: Fire dampers are not required in ducts within individual residential dwelling units.

716.7 Flexible ducts and air connectors. Flexible ducts and air connectors shall not pass through any fire-resistance-rated assembly. Flexible air connectors shall not pass through any wall, floor or ceiling.

SECTION 717
CONCEALED SPACES

717.1 General. Fireblocking and draftstopping shall be installed in combustible concealed locations in accordance with this section. Fireblocking shall comply with Section 717.2. Draftstopping in floor/ceiling spaces and attic spaces shall comply with Sections 717.3 and 717.4, respectively. The permitted use of combustible materials in concealed spaces of buildings of Type I or II construction shall be limited to the applications indicated in Section 717.5.

717.2 Fireblocking. In combustible construction, fireblocking shall be installed to cut off concealed draft openings (both vertical and horizontal) and shall form an effective barrier between floors, between a top story and a roof or attic space. Fireblocking shall be installed in the locations specified in Sections 717.2.2 through 717.2.7.

717.2.1 Fireblocking materials. Fireblocking shall consist of 2-inch (51 mm) nominal lumber or two thicknesses of 1-inch (25 mm) nominal lumber with broken lap joints or one thickness of 0.719-inch (18.3 mm) wood structural panel with joints backed by 0.719-inch (18.3 mm) wood structural panel or one thickness of 0.75-inch (19 mm) particleboard with joints backed by 0.75-inch (19 mm) particleboard. Gypsum board, cement fiber board, batts or blankets of mineral wool, glass fiber or other approved materials installed in such a manner as to be securely retained in place shall be permitted as an acceptable fireblock. Batts or blankets of mineral or glass fiber or other approved nonrigid materials shall be permitted for compliance with the 10-foot (3048 mm) horizontal fireblocking in walls constructed using parallel rows of studs or staggered studs. Loose-fill insulation material shall not be used as a fireblock unless specifically tested in the form and manner intended for use to demonstrate its ability to remain in place and to retard the spread of fire and hot gases. The integrity of fireblocks shall be maintained.

717.2.1.1 Double stud walls. Batts or blankets of mineral or glass fiber or other approved nonrigid materials shall be allowed as fireblocking in walls constructed using parallel rows of studs or staggered studs.

717.2.2 Concealed wall spaces. Fireblocking shall be provided in concealed spaces of stud walls and partitions, including furred spaces, and parallel rows of studs or staggered studs, as follows:

1. Vertically at the ceiling and floor levels.

2. Horizontally at intervals not exceeding 10 feet (3048 mm).

717.2.3 Connections between horizontal and vertical spaces. Fireblocking shall be provided at interconnections between concealed vertical stud wall or partition spaces and concealed horizontal spaces created by an assembly of floor joists or trusses, and between concealed vertical and horizontal spaces such as occur at soffits, drop ceilings, cove ceilings and similar locations.

717.2.4 Stairways. Fireblocking shall be provided in concealed spaces between stair stringers at the top and bottom of the run. Enclosed spaces under stairs shall also comply with Section 1009.5.3.

717.2.5 Ceiling and floor openings. Where annular space protection is provided in accordance with Exception 6 of Section 707.2, Exception 1 of Section 712.4.1.2, or Section 712.4.2, fireblocking shall be installed at openings around vents, pipes, ducts, chimneys and fireplaces at ceiling and floor levels, with an approved material to resist the free passage of flame and the products of combustion. Factory-built chimneys and fireplaces shall be fireblocked in accordance with UL 103 and UL 127.

717.2.6 Architectural trim. Fireblocking shall be installed within concealed spaces of exterior wall finish and other exterior architectural elements where permitted to be of combustible construction as specified in Section 1406 or where erected with combustible frames, at maximum intervals of 20 feet (6096 mm), so that there will be no open space exceeding 100 square feet (9.3 m³). Where wood furring strips are used, they shall be of approved wood of natural decay resistance or preservative-treated wood. If noncontinuous, such elements shall have closed ends, with at least 4 inches (102 mm) of separation between sections.

Exceptions:

1. Fireblocking of cornices is not required in single-family dwellings. Fireblocking of cornices of a two-family dwelling is required only at the line of dwelling unit separation.

2. Fireblocking shall not be required where installed on noncombustible framing and the face of the exterior wall finish exposed to the concealed space is covered by one of the following materials:

   2.1. Aluminum having a minimum thickness of 0.019 inch (0.5 mm).

   2.2. Corrosion-resistant steel having a base metal thickness not less than 0.016 inch (0.4 mm) at any point.

   2.3. Other approved noncombustible materials.

717.2.7 Concealed sleeper spaces. Where wood sleepers are used for laying wood flooring on masonry or concrete fire-resistance-rated floors, the space between the floor slab and the underside of the wood flooring shall be filled with an approved material to resist the free passage of flame and products of combustion or fireblocked in such a

manner that there will be no open spaces under the flooring that will exceed 100 square feet (9.3 m²) in area and such space shall be filled solidly under permanent partitions so that there is no communication under the flooring between adjoining rooms.

Exceptions:

1. Fireblocking is not required for slab-on-grade floors in gymnasiums.

2. Fireblocking is required only at the juncture of each alternate lane and at the ends of each lane in a bowling facility.

717.3 Draftstopping in floors. In combustible construction, draftstopping shall be installed to subdivide floor/ceiling assemblies in the locations prescribed in Sections 717.3.2 through 717.3.3.

717.3.1 Draftstopping materials. Draftstopping materials shall not be less than 0.5-inch (12.7 mm) gypsum board, 0.375-inch (9.5 mm) wood structural panel, 0.375-inch (9.5 mm) particleboard, 1-inch (25-mm) nominal lumber, cement fiberboard, batts or blankets of mineral wool or glass fiber, or other approved materials adequately supported. The integrity of draftstops shall be maintained.

717.3.2 Groups R-1, R-2, R-3 and R-4. Draftstopping shall be provided in floor/ceiling spaces in Group R-1 buildings, in Group R-2 buildings with three or more dwelling units, in Group R-3 buildings with two dwelling units and in Group R-4 buildings. Draftstopping shall be located above and in line with the dwelling unit and sleeping unit separations.

Exceptions:

1. Draftstopping is not required in buildings equipped throughout with an automatic sprinkler system in accordance with Section 903.3.1.1.

2. Draftstopping is not required in buildings equipped throughout with an automatic sprinkler system in accordance with Section 903.3.1.2, provided that automatic sprinklers are also installed in the combustible concealed spaces.

717.3.3 Other groups. In other groups, draftstopping shall be installed so that horizontal floor areas do not exceed 1,000 square feet (93 m²).

Exception: Draftstopping is not required in buildings equipped throughout with an automatic sprinkler system in accordance with Section 903.3.1.1.

717.4 Draftstopping in attics. In combustible construction, draftstopping shall be installed to subdivide attic spaces and concealed roof spaces in the locations prescribed in Sections 717.4.2 and 717.4.3. Ventilation of concealed roof spaces shall be maintained in accordance with Section 1203.2.

717.4.1 Draftstopping materials. Materials utilized for draftstopping of attic spaces shall comply with Section 717.3.1.

717.4.1.1 Openings. Openings in the partitions shall be protected by self-closing doors with automatic latches constructed as required for the partitions.

717.4.2 Groups R-1 and R-2. Draftstopping shall be provided in attics, mansards, overhangs or other concealed roof spaces of Group R-2 buildings with three or more dwelling units and in all Group R-1 buildings. Draftstopping shall be installed above, and in line with, sleeping unit and dwelling unit separation walls that do not extend to the underside of the roof sheathing above.

Exceptions:

1. Where corridor walls provide a sleeping unit or dwelling unit separation, draftstopping shall only be required above one of the corridor walls.

2. Draftstopping is not required in buildings equipped throughout with an automatic sprinkler system in accordance with Section 903.3.1.1.

3. In occupancies in Group R-2 that do not exceed four stories in height, the attic space shall be subdivided by draftstops into areas not exceeding 3,000 square feet (279 m^2) or above every two dwelling units, whichever is smaller.

4. Draftstopping is not required in buildings equipped throughout with an automatic sprinkler system in accordance with Section 903.3.1.2, provided that automatic sprinklers are also installed in the combustible concealed spaces.

717.4.3 Other groups. Draftstopping shall be installed in attics and concealed roof spaces, such that any horizontal area does not exceed 3,000 square feet (279 m^2).

Exception: Draftstopping is not required in buildings equipped throughout with an automatic sprinkler system in accordance with Section 903.3.1.1.

717.5 Combustible materials in concealed spaces in Type I or II construction. Combustible materials shall not be permitted in concealed spaces of buildings of Type I or II construction.

Exceptions:

1. Combustible materials in accordance with Section 603.

2. Combustible materials exposed within plenums complying with Section 602 of the *Mechanical Code of New York State.*

3. Class A interior finish materials classified in accordance with Section 803.

4. Combustible piping within partitions or shaft enclosures installed in accordance with the provisions of this code.

5. Combustible piping within concealed ceiling spaces installed in accordance with the *Mechanical Code of New York State* and the *Plumbing Code of New York State.*

6. Combustible insulation and covering on pipe and tubing, installed in concealed spaces other than plenums, complying with Section 719.7.

SECTION 718
FIRE-RESISTANCE REQUIREMENTS FOR PLASTER

718.1 Thickness of plaster. The minimum thickness of gypsum plaster or portland cement plaster used in a fire-resistance-rated system shall be determined by the prescribed fire tests. The plaster thickness shall be measured from the face of the lath where applied to gypsum lath or metal lath.

718.2 Plaster equivalents. For fire-resistance purposes, 0.5 inch (12.7 mm) of unsanded gypsum plaster shall be deemed equivalent to 0.75 inch (19.1 mm) of one-to-three gypsum sand plaster or 1 inch (25 mm) of portland cement sand plaster.

718.3 Noncombustible furring. In buildings of Type I and II construction, plaster shall be applied directly on concrete or masonry or on approved noncombustible plastering base and furring.

718.4 Double reinforcement. Plaster protection more than 1 inch (25 mm) in thickness shall be reinforced with an additional layer of approved lath embedded at least 0.75 inch (19.1 mm) from the outer surface and fixed securely in place.

Exception: Solid plaster partitions or where otherwise determined by fire tests.

718.5 Plaster alternatives for concrete. In reinforced concrete construction, gypsum plaster or portland cement plaster is permitted to be substituted for 0.5 inch (12.7 mm) of the required poured concrete protection, except that a minimum thickness of 0.375 inch (9.5 mm) of poured concrete shall be provided in reinforced concrete floors and 1 inch (25 mm) in reinforced concrete columns in addition to the plaster finish. The concrete base shall be prepared in accordance with Section 2510.7.

SECTION 719
THERMAL- AND SOUND-INSULATING MATERIALS

719.1 General. Insulating materials, including facings such as vapor retarders and vapor-permeable membranes, similar coverings, and all layers of single and multilayer reflective foil insulations, shall comply with the requirements of this section. Where a flame spread index or a smoke-developed index is specified in this section, such index shall be determined in accordance with ASTM E 84. Any material that is subject to an increase in flame spread index or smoke-developed index beyond the limits herein established through the effects of age, moisture, or other atmospheric conditions shall not be permitted.

Exceptions:

1. Fiberboard insulation shall comply with Chapter 23.

2. Foam plastic insulation shall comply with Chapter 26.

3. Duct and pipe insulation and duct and pipe coverings and linings in plenums shall comply with the *Mechanical Code of New York State.*

719.2 Concealed installation. Insulating materials, where concealed as installed in buildings of any type of construction, shall have a flame spread index of not more than 25 and a smoke-developed index of not more than 450.

Exception: Cellulose loose-fill insulation that is not spray applied, complying with the requirements of Section 719.6, shall only be required to meet the smoke-developed index of not more than 450.

719.2.1 Facings. Where such materials are installed in concealed spaces in buildings of Type III, IV or V construction, the flame spread and smoke-developed limitations do not apply to facings, coverings, and layers of reflective foil insulation that are installed behind and in substantial contact with the unexposed surface of the ceiling, wall or floor finish.

719.3 Exposed installation. Insulating materials, where exposed as installed in buildings of any type of construction, shall have a flame spread index of not more than 25 and a smoke-developed index of not more than 450.

Exception: Cellulose loose-fill insulation that is not spray applied complying with the requirements of Section 719.6 shall only be required to meet the smoke-developed index of not more than 450.

719.3.1 Attic floors. Exposed insulation materials installed on attic floors shall have a critical radiant flux of not less than 0.12 watt per square centimeter when tested in accordance with ASTM E 970.

719.4 Loose-fill insulation. Loose-fill insulation materials that cannot be mounted in the ASTM E 84 apparatus without a screen or artificial supports shall comply with the flame spread and smoke-developed limits of Sections 719.2 and 719.3 when tested in accordance with CAN/ULC S102.2.

Exception: Cellulose loose-fill insulation shall not be required to comply with the flame spread index requirement of CAN/ULC S102.2, provided such insulation complies with the requirements of Section 719.6.

719.5 Roof insulation. The use of combustible roof insulation not complying with Sections 719.2 and 719.3 shall be permitted in any type of construction provided it is covered with approved roof coverings directly applied thereto.

719.6 Cellulose loose-fill insulation. Cellulose loose-fill insulation shall comply with CPSC 16 CFR, Part 1209 and CPSC 16 CFR, Part 1404. Each package of such insulating material shall be clearly labeled in accordance with CPSC 16 CFR, Part 1209 and CPSC 16 CFR, Part 1404.

719.7 Insulation and covering on pipe and tubing. Insulation and covering on pipe and tubing shall have a flame spread index of not more than 25 and a smoke-developed index of not more than 450.

Exception: Insulation and covering on pipe and tubing installed in plenums shall comply with the *Mechanical Code of New York State.*

TABLE 720.1(1)
MINIMUM PROTECTION OF STRUCTURAL PARTS BASED ON TIME PERIODS FOR VARIOUS NONCOMBUSTIBLE INSULATING MATERIALS[m]

STRUCTURAL PARTS TO BE PROTECTED	ITEM NUMBER	INSULATING MATERIAL USED	MINIMUM THICKNESS OF INSULATING MATERIAL FOR THE FOLLOWING FIRE-RESISTANCE PERIODS (inches)			
			4 hour	3 hour	2 hour	1 hour
1. Steel columns and all of primary trusses	1-1.1	Carbonate, lightweight and sand-lightweight aggregate concrete, members 6" × 6" or greater (not including sandstone, granite and siliceous gravel).[a]	$2^1/_2$	2	$1^1/_2$	1
	1-1.2	Carbonate, lightweight and sand-lightweight aggregate concrete, members 8" × 8" or greater (not including sandstone, granite and siliceous gravel).[a]	2	$1^1/_2$	1	1
	1-1.3	Carbonate, lightweight and sand-lightweight aggregate concrete, members 12" × 12" or greater (not including sandstone, granite and siliceous gravel).[a]	$1^1/_2$	1	1	1
	1-1.4	Siliceous aggregate concrete and concrete excluded in Item 1-1.1, members 6" × 6" or greater.[a]	3	2	$1^1/_2$	1
	1-1.5	Siliceous aggregate concrete and concrete excluded in Item 1-1.1, members 8" × 8" or greater.[a]	$2^1/_2$	2	1	1
	1-1.6	Siliceous aggregate concrete and concrete excluded in Item 1-1.1, members 12" × 12" or greater.[a]	2	1	1	1
	1-.2.1	Clay or shale brick with brick and mortar fill.[a]	$3^3/_4$	-	-	$2^1/_4$
	1-3.1	4" hollow clay tile in two 2" layers; $^1/_2$" mortar between tile and column; $^3/_8$" metal mesh 0.046" wire diameter in horizontal joints; tile fill.[a]	4	-	-	-
	1-3.2	2" hollow clay tile; $^3/_4$" mortar between tile and column; $^3/_8$" metal mesh 0.046" wire diameter in horizontal joints; limestone concrete fill;[a] plastered with $^3/_4$" gypsum plaster.	3	-	-	-
	1-3.3	2" hollow clay tile with outside wire ties 0.08" diameter at each course of tile or $^3/_8$" metal mesh 0.046" diameter wire in horizontal joints; limestone or trap-rock concrete fill[a] extending 1" outside column on all sides.	-	-	3	-
	1-3.4	2" hollow clay tile with outside wire ties 0.08" diameter at each course of tile with or without concrete fill; $^3/_4$" mortar between tile and column.	-	-	-	2
	1-4.1	Cement plaster over metal lath wire tied to $^3/_4$" cold-rolled vertical channels with 0.049" (No. 18 B.W. gage) wire ties spaced 3" to 6" on center. Plaster mixed1:$2^1/_2$ by volume, cement to sand.	-	-	$2^1/_2$[b]	$^7/_8$
	1-5.1	Vermiculite concrete, 1:4 mix by volume over paperbacked wire fabric lath wrapped directly around column with additional 2" × 2" 0.065"/0.065" (No. 16/16 B.W. gage) wire fabric placed $^3/_4$" from outer concrete surface. Wire fabric tied with 0.049" (No. 18 B.W. gage) wire spaced 6" on center for inner layer and 2" on center for outer layer.	2	-	-	-
	1-6.1	Perlite or vermiculite gypsum plaster over metal lath wrapped around column and furred $1^1/_4$" from column flanges. Sheets lapped at ends and tied at 6" intervals with 0.049" (No. 18 B.W. gage) tie wire. Plaster pushed through to flanges.	$1^1/_2$	1	-	-
	1-6.2	Perlite or vermiculite gypsum plaster over self-furring metal lath wrapped directly around column, lapped 1" and tied at 6" intervals with 0.049" (No. 18 B.W. gage) wire.	$1^3/_4$	$1^3/_8$	1	-
	1-6.3	Perlite or vermiculite gypsum plaster on metal lath applied to $^3/_4$" cold-rolled channels spaced 24" apart vertically and wrapped flatwise around column.	$1^1/_2$	-	-	-
	1-6.4	Perlite or vermiculite gypsum plaster over two layers of $^1/_2$" plain full-length gypsum lath applied tight to column flanges. Lath wrapped with 1" hexagonal mesh of No. 20 gage wire and tied with doubled 0.035" diameter (No. 18 B.W. gage) wire ties spaced 23" on center. For three-coat work, the plaster mix for the second coat shall not exceed 100 pounds of gypsum to $2^1/_2$ cubic feet of aggregate for the 3-hour system.	$2^1/_2$	2	-	-

(continued)

TABLE 720.1(1)—continued
MINIMUM PROTECTION OF STRUCTURAL PARTS BASED ON TIME PERIODS FOR VARIOUS NONCOMBUSTIBLE INSULATING MATERIALS[m]

STRUCTURAL PARTS TO BE PROTECTED	ITEM NUMBER	INSULATING MATERIAL USED	MINIMUM THICKNESS OF INSULATING MATERIAL FOR THE FOLLOWING FIRE-RESISTANCE PERIODS (inches)			
			4 hour	3 hour	2 hour	1 hour
1. Steel columns and all of primary trusses (continued)	1-6.5	Perlite or vermiculate gypsum plaster over one layer of $1/2$" plain full-length gypsum lath applied tight to column flanges. Lath tied with doubled 0.049" (No. 18 B.W. gage) wire ties spaced 23" on center and scratch coat wrapped with 1" hexagonal mesh 0.035" (No. 20 B.W. gage) wire fabric. For three-coat work, the plaster mix for the second coat shall not exceed 100 pounds of gypsum to $2^1/_2$ cubic feet of aggregate.	—	2	—	—
	1-7.1	Multiple layers of $1/2$" gypsum wallboard[c] adhesively[d] secured to column flanges and successive layers. Wallboard applied without horizontal joints. Corner edges of each layer staggered. Wallboard layer below outer layer secured to column with doubled 0.049" (No. 18 B.W. gage) steel wire ties spaced 15" on center. Exposed corners taped and treated.	—	—	2	1
	1-7.2	Three layers of $5/_8$" Type X gypsum wallboard[c]. First and second layer held in place by $1/_8$" diameter by $1^3/_8$"long ring shank nails with $5/_{16}$" diameter heads spaced 24" on center at corners. Middle layer also secured with metal straps at mid-height and 18" from each end, and by metal corner bead at each corner held by the metal straps. Third layer attached to corner bead with 1" long gypsum wallboard screws spaced 12" on center.	—	—	$1^7/_8$	—
	1-7.3	Three layers of $5/_8$" Type X gypsum wallboard,[c] each layer screw attached to $1^5/_8$" steel studs 0.018" thick (No. 25 carbon sheet steel gage) at each corner of column. Middle layer also secured with 0.049" (No. 18 B.W.gage) double-strand steel wire ties, 24" on center. Screws are No. 6 by 1" spaced 24" on center for inner layer, No. 6 by $1^5/_8$" spaced 12" on center for middle layer and No. 8 by $2^1/_4$" spaced 12" on center for outer layer.	—	$1^7/_8$	—	—
	1-8.1	Wood-fibered gypsum plaster mixed 1:1 by weight gypsum-to-sand aggregate applied over metal lath. Lath lapped 1" and tied 6" on center at all end, edges and spacers with 0.049" (No. 18 B.W. gage) steel tie wires. Lath applied over $1/2$" spacers made of $3/_4$" furring channel with 2" legs bent around each corner. Spacers located 1" from top and bottom of member and a maximum of 40" on center and wire tied with a single strand of 0.049" (No. 18 B.W. gage) steel tie wires. Corner bead tied to the lath at 6" on center along each corner to provide plaster thickness.	—	—	$1^5/_8$	—
	1-9.1	Minimum W8 x 35 wide flange steel column (w/d ≥ 0.75) with each web cavity filled even with the flange tip with normal weight carbonate or siliceous aggregate concrete (3,000 psi minimum compressive strength with 145 pcf ± 3 pcf unit weight). Reinforce the concrete in each web cavity with a minimum No. 4 deformed reinforcing bar installed vertically and centered in the cavity, and secured to the column web with a minimum No. 2 horizontal deformed reinforcing bar welded to the web every 18" on center vertically. As an alternative to the No. 4 rebar, $3/_4$" diameter by 3" long headed studs, spaced at 12" on center vertically, shall be welded on each side of the web midway between the column flanges.	—	—	—	See Note n
2. Webs or flanges of steel beams and girders	2-1.1	Carbonate, lightweight and sand-lightweight aggregate concrete (not including sandstone, granite and siliceous gravel) with 3" or finer metal mesh placed 1" from the finished surface anchored to the top flange and providing not less than 0.025 square inch of steel area per foot in each direction.	2	$1^1/_2$	1	1
	2-1.2	Siliceous aggregate concrete and concrete excluded in Item 2-1.1 with 3" or finer metal mesh placed 1" from the finished surface anchored to the top flange and providing not less than 0.025 square inch of steel area per foot in each direction.	$2^1/_2$	2	$1^1/_2$	1
	2-2.1	Cement plaster on metal lath attached to $3/_4$" cold-rolled channels with 0.04" (No. 18 B.W. gage) wire ties spaced 3" to 6" on center. Plaster mixed 1:2 $1/2$ by volume, cement to sand.	—	—	$2^1/_2$[b]	$7/_8$
	2-3.1	Vermiculite gypsum plaster on a metal lath cage, wire tied to 0.165" diameter (No. 8 B.W. gage) steel wire hangers wrapped around beam and spaced 16" on center. Metal lath ties spaced approximately 5" on center at cage sides and bottom.	—	$7/_8$	—	—

(continued)

TABLE 720.1(1)—continued
MINIMUM PROTECTION OF STRUCTURAL PARTS BASED ON TIME PERIODS FOR VARIOUS NONCOMBUSTIBLE INSULATING MATERIALS[m]

STRUCTURAL PARTS TO BE PROTECTED	ITEM NUMBER	INSULATING MATERIAL USED	MINIMUM THICKNESS OF INSULATING MATERIAL FOR THE FOLLOWING FIRE-RESISTANCE PERIODS (inches)			
			4 hour	3 hour	2 hour	1 hour
2. Webs or flanges of steelbeams and girders (continued)	2-4.1	Two layers of $^5/_8$" Type X gypsum wallboard[c] are attached to U-shaped brackets spaced 24" on center. 0.018" thick (No. 25 carbon sheet steel gage) $1^5/_8$" deep by 1" galvanized steel runner channels are first installed parallel to and on each side of the top beam flange to provide a $^1/_2$" clearance to the flange. The channel runners are attached to steel deck or concrete floor construction with approved fasteners spaced 12" on center. U-shaped brackets are formed from members identical to the channel runners. At the bent portion of the U-shaped bracket, the flanges of the channel are cut out so that $1^5/_8$" deep corner channels can be inserted without attachment parallel to each side of the lower flange. As an alternate, 0.021"thick (No. 24 carbon sheet steel gage) 1"× 2" runner and corner angles may be used in lieu of channels, and the web cutouts in the U-shaped brackets may be omitted. Each angle is attached to the bracket with $^1/_2$"-long No. 8 self-drilling screws. The vertical legs of the U-shaped bracket are attached to the runners with one $^1/_2$" long No. 8 self-drilling screw. The completed steel framing provides a $2^1/_8$" and $1^1/_2$" space between the inner layer of wallboard and the sides and bottom of the steel beam, respectively. The inner layer of wallboard is attached to the top runners and bottom corner channels or corner angles with $1^1/_4$"-long No. 6 self-drilling screws spaced 16" on center.The outer layer of wallboard is applied with $1^3/_4$"-long No. 6 self-drilling screws spaced 8" on center. The bottom corners are reinforced with metal corner beads.	—	—	$1^1/_4$	—
	2-4.2	Three layers of $^5/_8$" Type X gypsum wallboard[c] attached to a steel suspension system as described immediately above utilizing the 0.018" thick (No. 25 carbon sheet steel gage) 1" × 2" lower corner angles. The framing is located so that a $2^1/_8$" and 2" space is provided between the inner layer of wallboard and the sides and bottom of the beam, respectively. The first two layers of wallboard are attached as described immediately above. A layer of 0.035" thick (No. 20 B.W. gage) 1" hexagonal galvanized wire mesh is applied under the soffit of the middle layer and up the sides approximately 2". The mesh is held in position with the No. 6 $1^5/_8$"-long screws installed in the vertical leg of the bottom corner angles. The outer layer of wallboard is attached with No. 6 $2^1/_4$"-long screws spaced 8" on center. One screw is also installed at the mid-depth of the bracket in each layer. Bottom corners are finished as described above.	—	$1^7/_8$	—	—
3. Bonded pretensioned reinforcement in prestressed concrete[e]	3-1.1	Carbonate, lightweight, sand-lightweight and siliceous[f] aggregate concrete Beams or girders	4^g	3^g	$2^1/_2$	$1^1/_2$
		Solid slabs[h]	—	2	$1^1/_2$	1
4. Bonded or unbonded post-tensioned tendons in prestressed concrete[e, i]	4-1.1	Carbonate, lightweight, sand-lightweight and siliceous[f] aggregate concrete Unrestrained members: Solid slabs[h]	—	2	$1^1/_2$	—
		Beams and girders[j]				
		8" wide		$4^1/_2$	$2^1/_2$	$1^3/_4$
		greater than 12" wide	3	$2^1/_2$	2	$1^1/_2$
	4-1.2	Carbonate, lightweight, sand-lightweight and siliceous aggregate Restrained members:[k] Solid slabs[h]	$1^1/_4$	1	$^3/_4$	—
		Beams and girders[j]				
		8" wide	$2^1/_2$	2	$1^3/_4$	—
		greater than 12" wide	2	$1^3/_4$	$1^1/_2$	—

(continued)

TABLE 720.1(1)—continued
MINIMUM PROTECTION OF STRUCTURAL PARTS BASED ON TIME PERIODS FOR VARIOUS NONCOMBUSTIBLE INSULATING MATERIALS[m]

STRUCTURAL PARTS TO BE PROTECTED	ITEM NUMBER	INSULATING MATERIAL USED	MINIMUM THICKNESS OF INSULATING MATERIAL FOR THE FOLLOWING FIRE-RESISTANCE PERIODS (inches)			
			4 hour	3 hour	2 hour	1 hour
5. Reinforcing steel in reinforced concrete columns, beams girders and trusses	5-1.1	Carbonate, lightweight and sand-lightweight aggregate concrete, members 12" or larger, square or round. (Size limit does not apply to beams and girders monolithic with floors.)	$1^1/_2$	$1^1/_2$	$1^1/_2$	$1^1/_2$
		Siliceous aggregate concrete, members 12" or larger, square or round. (Size limit does not apply to beams and girders monolithic with floors.)	2	$1^1/_2$	$1^1/_2$	$1^1/_2$
6. Reinforcing steel in reinforced concrete joists[l]	6-1.1	Carbonate, lightweight and sand-lightweight aggregate concrete.	$1^1/_4$	$1^1/_4$	1	¾
	6-1.2	Siliceous aggregate concrete.	$1^3/_4$	$1^1/_2$	1	$^3/_4$
7. Reinforcing and tie rods in floor and roof slabs[l]	7-1.1	Carbonate, lightweight and sand-lightweight aggregate concrete.	1	1	¾	¾
	7-1.2	Siliceous aggregate concrete.	$1^1/_4$	1	1	$^3/_4$

For SI: 1 inch = 25.4 mm, 1 square inch = 645.2 mm^2, 1 cubic foot = 0.0283 m^3.

a. Reentrant parts of protected members to be filled solidly.

b. Two layers of equal thickness with a $^3/_4$-inch airspace between.

c. For all of the construction with gypsum wallboard described in Table 720.1(1), gypsum base for veneer plaster of the same size, thickness and core type shall be permitted to be substituted for gypsum wallboard, provided attachment is identical to that specified for the wallboard and the joints on the face layer are reinforced, and the entire surface is covered with a minimum of $^1/_{16}$-inch gypsum veneer plaster.

d. An approved adhesive qualified under ASTM E 119.

e. Where lightweight or sand-lightweight concrete having an oven-dry weight of 110 pounds per cubic foot or less is used, the tabulated minimum cover shall be permitted to be reduced 25 percent, except that in no case shall the cover be less than $^3/_4$ inch in slabs or $1^1/_2$ inches in beams or girders.

f. For solid slabs of siliceous aggregate concrete, increase tendon cover 20 percent.

g. Adequate provisions against spalling shall be provided by U-shaped or hooped stirrups spaced not to exceed the depth of the member with a clear cover of 1 inch.

h. Prestressed slabs shall have a thickness not less than that required in Table 720.1(3) for the respective fire resistance time period.

i. Fire coverage and end anchorages shall be as follows: Cover to the prestressing steel at the anchor shall be $^1/_2$ inch greater than that required away from the anchor. Minimum cover to steel-bearing plate shall be 1 inch in beams and $^3/_4$ inch in slabs.

j. For beam widths between 8 inches and 12 inches, cover thickness shall be permitted to be determined by interpolation.

k. Interior spans of continuous slabs, beams and girders shall be permitted to be considered restrained.

l. For use with concrete slabs having a comparable fire endurance where members are framed into the structure in such a manner as to provide equivalent performance to that of monolithic concrete construction.

m. Generic fire-resistance ratings (those not designated as PROPRIETARY* in the listing) in GA 600 shall be accepted as if herein listed.

n. No additional insulating material is required on the exposed outside face of the column flange to achieve a 1-hour fire-resistance rating.

TABLE 720.1(2)
RATED FIRE-RESISTANCE PERIODS FOR VARIOUS WALLS AND PARTITIONS [a,o,p]

MATERIAL	ITEM NUMBER	CONSTRUCTION	MINIMUM FINISHED THICKNESS FACE-TO-FACE[b] (inches)			
			4 hour	3 hour	2 hour	1 hour
1. Brick of clay or shale	1-1.1	Solid brick of clay or shale[c]	6	4.9	3.8	2.7
	1-1.2	Hollow brick, not filled.	5.0	4.3	3.4	2.3
	1-1.3	Hollow brick unit wall, grout or filled with perlite vermiculite or expanded shale aggregate.	6.6	5.5	4.4	3.0
	1-2.1	4" nominal thick units at least 75 percent solid backed with a hat-shaped metal furring channel $^3/_4$" thick formed from 0.021" sheet metal attached to the brick wall on 24" centers with approved fasteners, and $^1/_2$" Type X gypsum wallboard attached to the metal furring strips with 1"-long Type S screws spaced 8" on center.	—	—	5[d]	—
2. Combination of clay brick and load-bearing hollow clay tile	2-1.1	4" solid brick and 4" tile (at least 40 percent solid).	—	8	—	—
	2-1.2	4" solid brick and 8" tile (at least 40 percent solid).	12	—	—	—
3. Concrete masonry units	3-1.1[f, g]	Expanded slag or pumice.	4.7	4.0	3.2	2.1
	3-1.2[f, g]	Expanded clay, shale or slate.	5.1	4.4	3.6	2.6
	3-1.3[f]	Limestone, cinders or air-cooled slag.	5.9	5.0	4.0	2.7
	3-1.4[f, g]	Calcareous or siliceous gravel.	6.2	5.3	4.2	2.8
4. Solid concrete[h, i]	4-1.1	Siliceous aggregate concrete.	7.0	6.2	5.0	3.5
		Carbonate aggregate concrete.	6.6	5.7	4.6	3.2
		Sand-lightweight concrete.	5.4	4.6	3.8	2.7
		Lightweight concrete.	5.1	4.4	3.6	2.5
5. Glazed or unglazed facing tile, nonload-bearing	5-1.1	One 2" unit cored 15 percent maximum and one 4" unit cored 25 percent maximum with $^3/_4$" mortar-filled collar joint. Unit positions reversed in alternate courses.	—	$6^3/_8$	—	—
	5-1.2	One 2" unit cored 15 percent maximum and one 4" unit cored 40 percent maximum with $^3/_4$" mortar-filled collar joint. Unit positions side with $^3/_4$" gypsum plaster. Two wythes tied together every fourth course with No. 22 gage corrugated metal ties.	—	$6^3/_4$	—	—
	5-1.3	One unit with three cells in wall thickness, cored 29 percent maximum.	—	—	6	—
	5-1.4	One 2" unit cored 22 percent maximum and one 4" unit cored 41 percent maximum with $^1/_4$" mortar-filled collar joint. Two wythes tied together every third course with 0.030" (No. 22 galvanized sheet steel gage) corrugated metal ties.	—	—	6	—
	5-1.5	One 4" unit cored 25 percent maximum with $^3/_4$" gypsum plaster on one side.	—	—	$4^3/_4$	—
	5-1.6	One 4" unit with two cells in wall thickness, cored 22 percent maximum.	—	—	—	4
	5-1.7	One 4" unit cored 30 percent maximum with $^3/_4$" vermiculite gypsum plaster on one side.	—	—	$4^1/_2$	—
	5-1.8	One 4" unit cored 39 percent maximum with $^3/_4$" gypsum plaster on one side.	—	—	—	$4^1/_2$

(continued)

TABLE 720.1(2)—continued
RATED FIRE-RESISTANCE PERIODS FOR VARIOUS WALLS AND PARTITIONS [a,o,p]

MATERIAL	ITEM NUMBER	CONSTRUCTION	MINIMUM FINISHED THICKNESS FACE-TO-FACE[b] (inches)			
			4 hour	3 hour	2 hour	1 hour
6. Solid gypsum plaster	6-1.1	$^3/_4$" by 0.055" (No. 16 carbon sheet steel gage) vertical cold-rolled channels, 16" on center with 2.6-pound flat metal lath applied to one face and tied with 0.049"(No. 18 B.W. Gage) wire at 6" spacing. Gypsum plaster each side mixed 1:2 by weight, gypsum to sand aggregate.	—	—	—	2[d]
	6-1.2	$^3/_4$" by 0.05" (No. 16 carbon sheet steel gage) cold-rolled channels 16" on center with metal lath applied to one face and tied with 0.049"(No. 18 B.W. gage) wire at 6" spacing. Perlite or vermiculite gypsum plaster each side. For three-coat work, the plaster mix for the second coat shall not exceed 100 pounds of gypsum to $2^1/_2$ cubic feet of aggregate for the 1-hour system.	—	—	$2^1/_2$[d]	2[d]
	6-1.3	$^3/_4$" by 0.055" (No. 16 carbon sheet steel gage) vertical cold-rolled channels, 16" on center with$^3/_8$" gypsum lath applied to one face and attached with sheet metal clips. Gypsum plaster each side mixed 1:2 by weight, gypsum to sand aggregate.	—	—	—	2[d]
	6-2.1	Studless with $^1/_2$" full-length plain gypsum lath and gypsum plaster each side. Plaster mixed 1:1 for scratch coat and 1:2 for brown coat, by weight, gypsum to sand aggregate.	—	—	—	2[d]
	6-2.2	Studless with $^1/_2$" full-length plain gypsum lath and perlite or vermiculite gypsum plaster each side.	—	—	$2^1/_2$[d]	2[d]
	6-2.3	Studless partition with $^3/_8$" rib metal lath installed vertically adjacent edges tied 6" on center with No. 18 gage wire ties, gypsum plaster each side mixed 1:2 by weight, gypsum to sand aggregate.	—	—	—	2[d]
7. Solid perlite and portland cement	7-1.1	Perlite mixed in the ratio of 3 cubic feet to 100 pounds of portland cement and machine applied to stud side of $1^1/_2$" mesh by 0.058-inch (No. 17 B.W. gage) paper-backed woven wire fabric lath wire-tied to 4"-deep steel trussed wire[j] studs 16" on center. Wire ties of 0.049" (No. 18 B.W. gage) galvanized steel wire 6" on center vertically.	—	—	$3^1/_8$[d]	—
8. Solid neat wood fibered gypsum plaster	8-1.1	$^3/_4$" by 0.055-inch (No. 16 carbon sheet steel gage) cold-rolled channels, 12" on center with 2.5-pound flat metal lath applied to one face and tied with 0.049" (No. 18 B.W. gage) wire at 6" spacing. Neat gypsum plaster applied each side.	—	—	2[d]	—
9. Solid wallboard partition	9-1.1	One full-length layer $^1/_2$" Type X gypsum wallboard[e] laminated to each side of 1" full-length V-edge gypsum coreboard with approved laminating compound. Vertical joints of face layer and coreboard staggered at least 3".	—	—	2[d]	—
10. Hollow (studless) gypsum wallboard partition	10-1.1	One full-length layer of $^5/_8$" Type X gypsum wallboard[e] attached to both sides of wood or metal top and bottom runners laminated to each side of 1"× 6" full-length gypsum coreboard ribs spaced 2" on center with approved laminating compound. Ribs centered at vertical joints of face plies and joints staggered 24" in opposing faces. Ribs may be recessed 6" from the top and bottom.	—	—	—	$2^1/_4$[d]
	10-1.2	1" regular gypsum V-edge full-length backing board attached to both sides of wood or metal top and bottom runners with nails or $1^5/_8$" drywall screws at 24" on center. Minimum width of rumors $1^5/_8$". Face layer of $^1/_2$" regular full-length gypsum wallboard laminated to outer faces of backing board with approved laminating compound.	—	—	$4^5/_8$[d]	—

(continued)

TABLE 720.1(2)—continued
RATED FIRE-RESISTANCE PERIODS FOR VARIOUS WALLS AND PARTITIONS [a,o,p]

MATERIAL	ITEM NUMBER	CONSTRUCTION	MINIMUM FINISHED THICKNESS FACE-TO-FACE[b] (inches)			
			4 hour	3 hour	2 hour	1 hour
11. Noncombustible studs-interior partition with plaster each side	11-1.1	$3^1/_4$" × 0.044" (No. 18 carbon sheet steel gage) steel studs spaced 24" on center. $^5/_8$" gypsum plaster on metal lath each side mixed 1:2 by weight, gypsum to sand aggregate.	—	—	—	$4^3/_4$[d]
	11-1.2	$3^3/_8$" × 0.055" (No. 16 carbon sheet steel gage) approved nailable[k] studs spaced 24" on center. $^5/_8$" neat gypsum wood-fibered plaster each side over $^3/_8$" rib metal lath nailed to studs with 6d common nails, 8" on center. Nails driven $1^1/_4$" and bent over.	—	—	$5^5/_8$	—
	11-1.3	4" × 0.044" (No. 18 carbon sheet steel gage) channel-shaped steel studs at 16" on center. On each side approved resilient clips pressed onto stud flange at 16" vertical spacing, $^1/_4$" pencil rods snapped into or wire tied onto outer loop of clips, metal lath wire-tied to pencil rods at 6" intervals, 1" perlite gypsum plaster, each side.	—	$7^5/_8$[d]	—	—
	11-1.4	$2^1/_2$" × 0.044" (No. 18 carbon sheet steel gage) steel studs spaced 16" on center. Wood fibered gypsum plaster mixed 1:1 by weight gypsum to sand aggregate applied on $^3/_4$-pound metal lath wire tied to studs, each side. $^3/_4$" plaster applied over each face, including finish coat.	—	—	$4^1/_4$[d]	—
12. Wood studs interior partition with plaster each side	12-1.1[l,m]	2" × 4" wood studs 16" on center with $^5/_8$" gypsum plaster on metal lath. Lath attached by 4d common nails bent over or No. 14 gage by $1^1/_4$" by $^3/_4$" crown width staples spaced 6" on center. Plaster mixed $1:1^1/_2$ for scratch coat and 1:3 for brown coat, by weight, gypsum to sand aggregate.	—	—	—	$5^1/_8$
	12-1.2[l]	2" × 4" wood studs 16" on center with metal lath and $^7/_8$" neat wood-fibered gypsum plaster each side. Lath attached by 6d common nails, 7" on center. Nails driven $1^1/_4$" and bent over.	—	—	$5^1/_2$[d]	—
	12-1.3[l]	2" × 4" wood studs 16" on center with $^3/_8$"perforated or plain gypsum lath and $^1/_2$" gypsum plaster each side. Lath nailed with $1^1/_8$" by No. 13 gage by $^{19}/_{64}$" head plasterboard blued nails, 4" on center. Plaster mixed 1:2 by weight, gypsum to sand aggregate.	—	—	—	$5^1/_4$
	12-1.4[l]	2" × 4" wood studs 16" on center with $^3/_8$" Type X gypsum lath and $^1/_2$" gypsum plaster each side. Lath nailed with $1^1/_8$" by No. 13 gage by $^{19}/_{64}$" head plasterboard blued nails, 5" on center. Plaster mixed 1:2 by weight, gypsum to sand aggregate.	—	—	—	$5^1/_4$
13. Noncombustible studs-interior partition with gypsum wallboard each side	13-1.1	0.018" (No. 25 carbon sheet steel gage) channel-shaped studs 24" on center with one full-length layer of $^5/_8$" Type X gypsum wallboard[e] applied vertically attached with 1" long No. 6 drywall screws to each stud. Screws are 8" on center around the perimeter and 12" on center on the intermediate stud. The wallboard may be applied horizontally when attached to $3^5/_8$" studs and the horizontal joints are staggered with those on the opposite side. Screws for the horizontal application shall be 8" on center at vertical edges and 12" on center at intermediate studs.	—	—	—	$2^7/_8$[d]
	13-1.2	0.018" (No. 25 carbon sheet steel gage) channel-shaped studs 25" on center with two full-length layers of $^1/_2$" Type X gypsum wallboard[e] applied vertically each side. First layer attached with 1"-long, No. 6 drywall screws, 8" on center around the perimeter and 12" on center on the intermediate stud. Second layer applied with vertical joints offset one stud space from first layer using $1^5/_8$" long, No. 6 drywall screws spaced 9" on center along vertical joints, 12" on center at intermediate studs and 24" on center along top and bottom runners.	—	—	$3^5/_8$[d]	—
	13-1.3	0.055" (No. 16 carbon sheet steel gage) approved nailable metal studs[e] 24" on center with full-length $^5/_8$" Type X gypsum wallboard[e] applied vertically and nailed 7" on center with 6d cement-coated common nails. Approved metal fastener grips used with nails at vertical butt joints along studs.	—	—	—	$4^7/_8$

(continued)

TABLE 720.1(2)—continued
RATED FIRE-RESISTANCE PERIODS FOR VARIOUS WALLS AND PARTITIONS [a,o,p]

MATERIAL	ITEM NUMBER	CONSTRUCTION	MINIMUM FINISHED THICKNESS FACE-TO-FACE[b] (inches)			
			4 hour	3 hour	2 hour	1 hour
14. Wood studs-interior partition with gypsum wallboard each side	14-1.1[h,m]	2" × 4" wood studs 16" on center with two layers of $3/8$" regular gypsum wallboard[e] each side, 4d cooler[n] or wallboard[n] nails at 8" on center first layer, 5d cooler[n] or wallboard[n] nails at 8" on center second layer with laminating compound between layers, joints staggered. First layer applied full length vertically, second layer applied horizontally or vertically	—	—	—	5
	14-1.2[l,m]	2" × 4" wood studs 16" on center with two layers $1/2$" regular gypsum wallboard[e] applied vertically or horizontally each side[k], joints staggered. Nail base layer with 5d cooler[n] or wallboard[n] nails at 8" on center face layer with 8d cooler[n] or wallboard[n] nails at 8" on center.	—	—	—	$5^1/_2$
	14-1.3[l,m]	2" × 4" wood studs 24" on center with $5/8$" Type X gypsum wallboard[e] applied vertically or horizontally nailed with 6d cooler[n] or wallboard[n] nails at 7" on center with end joints on nailing members. Stagger joints each side.	—	—	—	$4^3/_4$
	14-1.4[l]	2" × 4" fire-retardant-treated wood studs spaced 24" on center with one layer of $5/8$" Type X gypsum wallboard[e] applied with face paper grain (long dimension) parallel to studs. Wallboard attached with 6d cooler[n] or wallboard[n] nails at 7" on center.	—	—	—	$4^3/_4$[d]
	14-1.5[l,m]	2" × 4" wood studs 16" on center with two layers $5/8$" Type X gypsum wallboard[e] each side. Base layers applied vertically and nailed with 6d cooler[n] or wallboard[n] nails at 9" on center. Face layer applied vertically or horizontally and nailed with 8d cooler[n] or wallboard[n] nails at 7" on center. For nail-adhesive application, base layers are nailed 6" on center. Face layers applied with coating of approved wallboard adhesive and nailed 12" on center.	—	—	6	—
	14-1.6[l]	2" × 3" fire-retardant-treated wood studs spaced 24" on center with one layer of $5/8$" Type X gypsum wallboard[e] applied with face paper grain (long dimension) at right angles to studs. Wallboard attached with 6d cement-coated box nails spaced 7" on center.	—	—	—	$3^5/_8$[d]
15. Exterior or interior walls	15-1.1[l,m]	Exterior surface with $3/4$" drop siding over $1/2$" gypsum sheathing on 2" × 4" wood studs at 16" on center, interior surface treatment as required for 1-hour-rated exterior or interior 2" × 4" wood stud partitions. Gypsum sheathing nailed with $1^3/_4$" by No. 11 gage by $7/_16$" head galvanized nails at 8" on center. Siding nailed with 7d galvanized smooth box nails.	—	—	—	Varies
	15-1.2[l,m]	2" × 4" wood studs 16" on center with metal lath and $3/4$" cement plaster on each side. Lath attached with 6d common nails 7" on center driven to 1" minimum penetration and bent over. Plaster mix 1:4 for scratch coat and 1:5 for brown coat, by volume, cement to sand.	—	—	—	$5^3/_8$
	15-1.3[l,m]	2" × 4" wood studs 16" on center with $7/8$" cement plaster (measured from the face of studs) on the exterior surface with interior surface treatment as required for interior wood stud partitions in this table. Plaster mix 1:4 for scratch coat and 1:5 for brown coat, by volume, cement to sand.	—	—	—	Varies
	15-1.4	$3^5/_8$" No. 16 gage noncombustible studs 16" on center with $7/8$" cement plaster (measured from the face of the studs) on the exterior surface with interior surface treatment as required for interior, nonbearing, noncombustible stud partitions in this table. Plaster mix 1:4 for scratch coat and 1:5 for brown coat, by volume, cement to sand.	—	—	—	Varies[d]

(continued)

TABLE 720.1(2)—continued
RATED FIRE-RESISTANCE PERIODS FOR VARIOUS WALLS AND PARTITIONS [a,o,p]

MATERIAL	ITEM NUMBER	CONSTRUCTION	MINIMUM FINISHED THICKNESS FACE-TO-FACE[b] (inches)			
			4 hour	3 hour	2 hour	1 hour
15. Exterior or interior walls (continued)	15-1.5[m]	$2^1/_4" \times 3^3/_4"$ clay face brick with cored holes over $^1/_2"$ gypsum sheathing on exterior surface of $2" \times 4"$ wood studs at 16" on center and two layers $^5/_8"$ Type X gypsum wallboard[e] on interior surface. Sheathing placed horizontally or vertically with vertical joints over studs nailed 6" on center with $1^3/_4" \times$ No. 11 gage by $^7/_{16}"$ head galvanized nails. Inner layer of wallboard placed horizontally or vertically and nailed 8" on center with 6d cooler[n] or wallboard[n] nails. Outer layer of wallboard placed horizontally or vertically and nailed 8" on center with 8d cooler[n] or wallboard[n] nails. All joints staggered with vertical joints over studs. Outer layer joints taped and finished with compound. Nail heads covered with joint compound. 0.035 inch (No. 20 galvanized sheet gage) corrugated galvanized steel wall ties $^3/_4"$ by $6^5/_8"$ attached to each stud with two 8d cooler[n] or wallboard[n] nails every sixth course of bricks.	—	—	10	—
	15-1.6[l,m]	$2" \times 6"$ fire-retardant-treated wood studs 16" on center. Interior face has two layers of $^5/_8"$ Type X gypsum with the base layer placed vertically and attached with 6d box nails 12" on center. The face layer is placed horizontally and attached with 8d box nails 8" on center at joints and 12" on center elsewhere. The exterior face has a base layer of $^5/_8"$ Type X gypsum sheathing placed vertically with 6d box nails 8" on center at joints and 12" on center elsewhere. An approved building paper is next applied, followed by self-furred exterior lath attached with $2^1/_2"$, No. 12 gage galvanized roofing nails with a $^3/_8"$ diameter head and spaced 6" on center along each stud. Cement plaster consisting of a $^1/_2"$ brown coat is then applied. The scratch coat is mixed in the proportion of 1:3 by weight, cement to sand with 10 pounds of hydrated lime and 3 pounds of approved additives or admixtures per sack of cement. The brown coat is mixed in the proportion of 1:4 by weight, cement to sand with the same amounts of hydrated lime and approved additives or admixtures used in the scratch coat.	—	—	$8^1/_4$	—
	15-1.7[l,m]	$2" \times 6"$ wood studs 16" on center. The exterior face has a layer of $^5/_8"$ Type X gypsum sheathing placed vertically with 6d box nails 8" on center at joints and 12" on center elsewhere. An approved building paper is next applied, followed by 1" by No. 18 gage self-furred exterior lath attached with 8d by $2^1/_2"$ long galvanized roofing nails spaced 6" on center along each stud. Cement plaster consisting of a $^1/_2"$ scratch coat, a bonding agent and a $^1/_2"$ brown coat and a finish coat is then applied. The scratch coat is mixed in the proportion of 1:3 by weight, cement to sand with 10 pounds of hydrated lime and 3 pounds of approved additives or admixtures per sack of cement. The brown coat is mixed in the proportion of 1:4 by weight, cement to sand with the same amounts of hydrated lime and approved additives or admixtures used in the scratch coat. The interior is covered with $^3/_8"$ gypsum lath with 1" hexagonal mesh of 0.035 inch (No. 20 B.W. gage) woven wire lath furred out $^5/_{16}"$ and 1" perlite or vermiculite gypsum plaster. Lath nailed with $1^1/_8"$ by No. 13 gage by $^{19}/_{64}"$ head plasterboard glued nails spaced 5" on center. Mesh attached by $1^3/_4"$ by No. 12 gage by $^3/_8"$ head nails with $^3/_8"$ furrings, spaced 8" on center. The plaster mix shall not exceed 100 pounds of gypsum to $2^1/_2$ cubic feet of aggregate.	—	—	$8^3/_8$	—
	15-1.8[l,m]	$2" \times 6"$ wood studs 16" on center. The exterior face has a layer of $^5/_8"$ Type X gypsum sheathing placed vertically with 6d box nails 8" on center at joints and 12" on center elsewhere. An approved building paper is next applied, followed by $1^1/_2"$ by No. 17 gage self-furred exterior lath attached with 8d by $2^1/_2"$ long galvanized roofing nails spaced 6" on center along each stud. Cement plaster consisting of a $^1/_2"$ scratch coat, and a $^1/_2"$ brown coat is then applied. The plaster may be placed by machine. The scratch coat is mixed in the proportion of 1:4 by weight, plastic cement to sand. The brown coat is mixed in the proportion of 1:5 by weight, plastic cement to sand. The interior is covered with $^3/_8"$ gypsum lath with 1" hexagonal mesh of No. 20 gage woven wire lath furred out $^5/_{16}"$ and 1" perlite or vermiculite gypsum plaster. Lath nailed with $1^1/_8"$ by No. 13 gage by $^{19}/_{64}"$ head plasterboard glued nails spaced 5" on center. Mesh attached by $1^3/_4"$ by No. 12 gage by $^3/_8"$ head nails with $^3/_8"$ furrings, spaced 8" on center. The plaster mix shall not exceed 100 pounds of gypsum to $2^1/_2$ cubic feet of aggregate.	—	—	$8^3/_8$	—

(continued)

TABLE 720.1(2)—continued
RATED FIRE-RESISTANCE PERIODS FOR VARIOUS WALLS AND PARTITIONS [a,o,p]

MATERIAL	ITEM NUMBER	CONSTRUCTION	MINIMUM FINISHED THICKNESS FACE-TO-FACE[b] (inches)			
			4 hour	3 hour	2 hour	1 hour
15. Exterior or interior walls (continued)	15-1.9	4" No. 18 gage, nonload-bearing metal studs, 16" on center, with 1" portland cement lime plaster [measured from the back side of the $^3/_4$-pound expanded metal lath] on the exterior surface. Interior surface to be covered with 1" of gypsum plaster on $^3/_4$-pound expanded metal lath proportioned by weight-1:2 for scratch coat, 1:3 for brown, gypsum to sand. Lath on one side of the partition fastened to $^1/_4$"diameter pencil rods supported by No. 20 gage metal clips, located 16" on center vertically, on each stud. 3" thick mineral fiber insulating batts friction fitted between the studs.	—	—	$6^1/_2$[d]	—
	15-1.10	Steel studs 0.060" thick, 4" deep or 6" at 16" or 24" centers, with $^1/_2$" Glass Fiber Reinforced Concrete (GFRC) on the exterior surface. GFRC is attached with flex anchors at 24" on center, with 5" leg welded to studs with two $^1/_2$"-long flare-bevel welds, and 4" foot attached to the GFRC skin with $^5/_8$" thick GFRC bonding pads that extend $2^1/_2$" beyond the flex anchor foot on both sides. Interior surface to have two layers of $^1/_2$" Type X gypsum wallboard.[e] The first layer of wallboard to be attached with 1"-long Type S buglehead screws spaced 24" on center and the second layer is attached with $1^5/_8$"-long Type S screws spaced at 12" on center. Cavity is to be filled with 5" of 4 pcf (nominal) mineral fiber batts. GFRC has $1^1/_2$" returns packed with mineral fiber and caulked on the exterior.	—	—	$6^1/_2$	—
	15-1.11	Steel studs 0.060" thick, 4" deep or 6" at 16" or 24" centers, respectively, with $^1/_2$" Glass Fiber Reinforced Concrete (GFRC) on the exterior surface. GFRC is attached with flex anchors at 24" on center, with 5" leg welded to studs with two $^1/_2$"-long flare-bevel welds, and 4" foot attached to the GFRC skin with $^5/_8$"-thick GFRC bonding pads that extend $2^1/_2$" beyond the flex anchor foot on both sides. Interior surface to have one layer of $^5/_8$" Type X gypsum wallboard[e], attached with $1^1/_4$"-long Type S buglehead screws spaced 12" on center. Cavity is to be filled with 5" of 4 pcf (nominal) mineral fiber batts. GFRC has $1^1/_2$" returns packed with mineral fiber and caulked on the exterior.	—	—	—	$6^1/_8$
	15-1.12[q]	2" × 6" wood studs at 16" with double top plates, single bottom plate; interior and exterior sides covered with $^5/_8$" Type X gypsum wallboard, 4' wide, applied horizontally or vertically with vertical joints over studs, and fastened with $2^1/_4$" Type S drywall screws, spaced 12" on center.	—	—	—	$6^3/_4$
	15-1.13[q]	2" × 6" wood studs at 16" with double top plates, single bottom plate; interior and exterior sides covered with $^5/_8$" Type X gypsum wallboard, 4' wide, applied vertically with all joints over framing or blocking and fastened with $2^1/_4$" Type S drywall screws, spaced 12" on center. R-19 fiberglass insulation installed in stud cavity.	—	—	—	$6^3/_4$
	15-1.14[q]	2"× 6" wood studs at 16" with double top plates, single bottom plate; interior and exterior sides covered with $^5/_8$" Type X gypsum wallboard, 4' wide, applied horizontally or vertically with vertical joints over studs, and fastened with $2^1/_4$" Type S drywall screws, spaced 7" on center.	—	—	—	$6^3/_4$
	15-1.15[q]	2"× 4" wood studs at 16" with double top plates, single bottom plate; interior and exterior sides covered with $^5/_8$" Type X gypsum wallboard and sheathing, respectively, 4' wide, applied horizontally or vertically with vertical joints over studs, and fastened with $2^1/_4$" Type S drywall screws, spaced 12" on center. Cavity to be filled with $3^1/_2$" mineral wool insulation.	—	—	—	$4^3/_4$
	15-1.16[q]	2"× 6" wood studs at 16" with double top plates, single bottom plate; interior sides covered with $^5/_8$" Type X gypsum wallboard, 4' wide, applied horizontally unblocked, and fastened with $2^1/_4$" Type S drywall screws, spaced 12" on center, wallboard joints covered with paper tape and joint compound, fastener heads covered with joint compound. Exterior covered with $^3/_8$" wood structural panels applied vertically, horizontal joints blocked and fastened with 6d common nails (bright)—12" on center in the field, 6" on center panel edges. Cavity to be filled with $3^1/_2$" mineral wool insulation. Rating established for exposure from interior side only.	—	—	—	$4^1/_2$

(continued)

TABLE 720.1(2)—continued
RATED FIRE-RESISTANCE PERIODS FOR VARIOUS WALLS AND PARTITIONS [a,o,p]

MATERIAL	ITEM NUMBER	CONSTRUCTION	MINIMUM FINISHED THICKNESS FACE-TO-FACE[b] (inches)			
			4 hour	3 hour	2 hour	1 hour
16. Exterior walls rated for fire resistance from the inside only in accordance with Section 704.5.	16-1.1[q]	2" × 4" wood studs at 16" centers with double top plates, single bottom plate; interior side covered with $^5/_8$" Type X gypsum wallboard, 4' wide, applied horizontally unblocked, and fastened with $2^1/_4$" Type S drywall screws, spaced 12" on center, wallboard joints covered with paper tape and joint compound, fastener heads covered with joint compound. Exterior covered with $^3/_8$" wood structural panels (oriented strand board), applied vertically, horizontal joints blocked and fastened with 6d common nails (bright) - 12" on center in the field, and 6" on center panel edges. Cavity to be filled with $3^1/_2$" mineral wool insulation. Rating established for exposure from interior side only.	—	—	—	$4^1/_2$
	16-1.2[q]	2" × 6" (51mm x 152 mm) wood studs at 16" centers with double top plates, single bottom plate; interior side covered with $^5/_8$" Type X gypsum wallboard, 4' wide, applied horizontally or vertically with vertical joints over studs and fastened with $2^1/_4$" Type S drywall screws, spaced 12" on center, wallboard joints covered with paper tape and joint compound, fastener heads covered with joint compound, exterior side covered with $^7/_{16}$" wood structural panels (oriented strand board) fastened with 6d common nails (bright) spaced 12" on center in the field and 6" on center along the panel edges. Cavity to be filled with $5^1/_2$" mineral wool insulation. Rating established from the gypsum-covered side only.	—	—	—	$6^9/_{16}$
	16-1.3	2" × 6" wood studs at 16" centers with double top plates, single bottom plates; interior side covered with $^5/_8$" Type X gypsum wallboard, 4' wide, applied vertically with all joints over framing or blocking and fastened with $2^1/_4$" Type S drywall screws spaced 7" on center. Joints to be covered with tape and joint compound. Exterior covered with $^3/_8$" wood structural panels (oriented strand board), applied vertically with edges over framing or blocking and fastened with 6d common nails (bright) at 12" on center in the field and 6" on center on panel edges. R-19 fiberglass insulation installed in stud cavity.	—	—	—	$6^1/_2$

For SI:1 inch = 25.4 mm, 1 square inch = 645.2 mm^2, 1 cubic foot = 0.0283 m^3.

a. Staples with equivalent holding power and penetration shall be permitted to be used as alternate fasteners to nails for attachment to wood framing.

b. Thickness shown for brick and clay tile is nominal thicknesses unless plastered, in which case thicknesses are net. Thickness shown for concrete masonry and clay masonry is equivalent thickness defined in Section 721.3.1 for concrete masonry and Section 721.4.1.1 for clay masonry. Where all cells are solid grouted or filled with silicone-treated perlite loose-fill insulation; vermiculite loose-fill insulation; or expanded clay, shale or slate lightweight aggregate, the equivalent thickness shall be the thickness of the block or brick using specified dimensions as defined in Chapter 21. Equivalent thickness may also include the thickness of applied plaster and lath or gypsum wallboard, where specified.

c. For units in which the net cross-sectional area of cored brick in any plane parallel to the surface containing the cores is at least 75 percent of the gross cross-sectional area measured in the same plane.

d. Shall be used for nonbearing purposes only.

e. For all of the construction with gypsum wallboard described in this table, gypsum base for veneer plaster of the same size, thickness and core type shall be permitted to be substituted for gypsum wallboard, provided attachment is identical to that specified for the wallboard, and the joints on the face layer are reinforced and the entire surface is covered with a minimum of $^1/_{16}$-inch gypsum veneer plaster.

f. The fire-resistance time period for concrete masonry units meeting the equivalent thicknesses required for a 2-hour fire-resistance rating in Item 3, and having a thickness of not less than $7^5/_8$ inches is 4 hours when cores which are not grouted are filled with silicone-treated perlite loose-fill insulation; vermiculite loose-fill insulation; or expanded clay, shale or slate lightweight aggregate, sand or slag having a maximum particle size of $^3/_8$ inch.

g. The fire-resistance rating of concrete masonry units composed of a combination of aggregate types or where plaster is applied directly to the concrete masonry shall be determined in accordance with ACI 216.1/TMS 0216. Lightweight aggregates shall have a maximum combined density of 65 pounds per cubic foot.

h. See also Note b. The equivalent thickness shall be permitted to include the thickness of cement plaster or 1.5 times the thickness of gypsum plaster applied in accordance with the requirements of Chapter 25.

i. Concrete walls shall be reinforced with horizontal and vertical temperature reinforcement as required by Chapter 19.

j. Studs are welded truss wire studs with 0.18 inch (No. 7 B.W. gage) flange wire and 0.18 inch (No. 7 B.W. gage) truss wires.

k. Nailable metal studs consist of two channel studs spot welded back to back with a crimped web forming a nailing groove.

l. Wood structural panels shall be permitted to be installed between the fire protection and the wood studs on either the interior or exterior side of the wood frame assemblies in this table, provided the length of the fasteners used to attach the fire protection is increased by an amount at least equal to the thickness of the wood structural panel.

m. The design stress of studs shall be reduced to 78 percent of allowable F'_c with the maximum not greater than 78 percent of the calculated stress with studs having a slenderness ratio l_e/d of 33.

n. For properties of cooler or wallboard nails, see ASTM C 514, ASTM C 547 or ASTM F 1667.

o. Generic fire-resistance ratings (those not designated as PROPRIETARY* in the listing) in the GA 600 shall be accepted as if herein listed.

p. NCMA TEK 5-8A shall be permitted for the design of fire walls.

q. The design stress of studs shall be equal to a maximum of 100 percent of the allowable F'_c calculated in accordance with Section 2306.

TABLE 720.1(3)
MINIMUM PROTECTION FOR FLOOR AND ROOF SYSTEMS[a,q]

FLOOR OR ROOF CONSTRUCTION	ITEM NUMBER	CEILING CONSTRUCTION	THICKNESS OF FLOOR OR ROOF SLAB (inches)				MINIMUM THICKNESS OF CEILING (inches)			
			4 hour	3 hour	2 hour	1 hour	4 hour	3 hour	2 hour	1 hour
1. Siliceous aggregate concrete	1-1.1	Slab (no ceiling required). Minimum cover over nonprestressed reinforcement shall not be less than $^3/_4$"[b].	7.0	6.2	5.0	3.5	—	—	—	—
2. Carbonate aggregate concrete	2-1.1		6.6	5.7	4.6	3.2	—	—	—	—
3. Sand-light weight concrete	3-1.1		5.4	4.6	3.8	2.7	—	—	—	—
4. Lightweight concrete	4-1.1		5.1	4.4	3.6	2.5	—	—	—	—
5. Reinforced concrete	5-1.1	Slab with suspended ceiling of vermiculite gypsum plaster over metal lath attached to $^3/_4$" cold-rolled channels spaced 12" on center. Ceiling located 6" minimum below joists.	3	2	—	—	1	$^3/_4$	—	—
	5-2.1	$^3/_8$" Type X gypsum wallboard[c] attached to 0.018 inch (No. 25 carbon sheet steel gage) by $^7/_8$" deep by $2^5/_8$" hat-shaped galvanized steel channels with 1"-long No. 6 screws. The channels are spaced 24" on center, span 35" and are supported along their length at 35" intervals by 0.033"(No. 21 galvanized sheet gage) galvanized steel flat strap hangers having formed edges that engage the lips of the channel. The strap hangers are attached to the side of the concrete joists with $^5/_{32}$" by $1^1/_4$" long power-driven fasteners. The wallboard is installed with the long dimension perpendicular to the channels. All end joints occur on channels and supplementary channels are installed parallel to the main channels, 12" each side, at end joint occurrences. The finished ceiling is located approximately 12" below the soffit of the floor slab.	—	—	$2^1/_2$	—	—	—	$^5/_8$	—
6. Steel joists constructed with a poured reinforced concrete slab on metal lath forms or steel form units[d, e]	6-1.1	Gypsum plaster on metal lath attached to the bottom cord with single No. 16 gage or doubled No. 18 gage wire ties spaced 6" on center. Plaster mixed 1:2 for scratch coat, 1:3 for brown coat, by weight, gypsum-to-sand aggregate for 2-hour system. For 3-hour system plaster is neat.	—	—	$2^1/_2$	$2^1/_4$	—	—	$^3/_4$	$^5/_8$
	6-2.1	Vermiculite gypsum plaster on metal lath attached to the bottom chord with single No.16 gage or doubled 0.049-inch (No. 18 B.W. gage) wire ties 6" on center.	—	2	—	—	—	$^5/_8$	—	—
	6-3.1	Cement plaster over metal lath attached to the bottom chord of joists with single No. 16 gage or doubled 0.049" (No. 18 B.W. gage) wire ties spaced 6" on center. Plaster mixed 1:2 for scratch coat, 1:3 for brown coat for 1-hour system and 1:1 for scratch coat, $1:1^1/_2$ for brown coat for 2-hour system, by weight, cement to sand.	—	—	—	2	—	—	—	$^5/_8$[f]
	6-4.1	Ceiling of $^5/_8$" Type X wallboard[c] attached to $^7/_8$" deep by $2^5/_8$" by 0.021 inch (No. 25 carbon sheet steel gage) hat-shaped furring channels 12" on center with 1" long No. 6 wallboard screws at 8" on center. Channels wire tied to bottom chord of joists with doubled 0.049 inch (No. 18 B.W. gage) wire or suspended below joists on wire hangers.[g]	—	—	$2^1/_2$	—	—	—	$^5/_8$	—
	6-5.1	Wood-fibered gypsum plaster mixed 1:1 by weight gypsum to sand aggregate applied over metal lath. Lath tied 6" on center to $^3/_4$" channels spaced $13^1/_2$" on center. Channels secured to joists at each intersection with two strands of 0.049 inch (No. 18 B.W. gage) galvanized wire.	—	—	$2^1/_2$	—	—	—	$^3/_4$	—

(continued)

TABLE 720.1(3)—continued
MINIMUM PROTECTION FOR FLOOR AND ROOF SYSTEMS[a,q]

FLOOR OR ROOF CONSTRUCTION	ITEM NUMBER	CEILING CONSTRUCTION	THICKNESS OF FLOOR OR ROOF SLAB (inches)				MINIMUM THICKNESS OF CEILING (inches)			
			4 hour	3 hour	2 hour	1 hour	4 hour	3 hour	2 hour	1 hour
7. Reinforced concrete slabs and joists with hollow clay tile fillers laid end to end in rows $2\frac{1}{2}$" or more apart; reinforcement placed between rows and concrete cast around and over tile.	7-1.1	$\frac{5}{8}$" gypsum plaster on bottom of floor or roof construction.	—	—	8^h	—	—	—	$\frac{5}{8}$	—
	7-1.2	None	—	—	—	$5\frac{1}{2}^i$	—	—	—	—
8. Steel joists constructed with a reinforced concrete slab on top poured on a $\frac{1}{2}$" deep steel deck.[e]	8-1.1	Vermiculite gypsum plaster on metal lath attached to $\frac{3}{4}$" cold-rolled channels with 0.049" (No. 18 B.W. gage) wire ties spaced 6" on center.	$2\frac{1}{2}^j$	—	—	—	$\frac{3}{4}$	—	—	—
9. 3" deep cellular steel deck with concrete slab on top. Slab thickness measured to top.	9-1.1	Suspended ceiling of vermiculite gypsum plaster base coat and vermiculite acoustical plaster on metal lath attached at 6" intervals to $\frac{3}{4}$" cold-rolled channels spaced 12" on center and secured to $1\frac{1}{2}$" cold-rolled channels spaced 36" on center with 0.065" (No. 16 B.W. gage) wire. $1\frac{1}{2}$" channels supported by No. 8 gage wire hangers at 36" on center. Beams within envelope and with a $2\frac{1}{2}$" airspace between beam soffit and lath have a 4-hour rating.	$2\frac{1}{2}$	—	—	—	$1\frac{1}{8}^k$	—	—	—
10. $1\frac{1}{2}$"-deep steel roof deck on steel framing. Insulation board, 30 pcf density, composed of wood fibers with cement binders of thickness shown bonded to deck with unified asphalt adhesive. Covered with a Class A or B roof covering.	10-1.1	Ceiling of gypsum plaster on metal lath. Lath attached to $\frac{3}{4}$" furring channels with 0.049" (No. 18 B.W. gage) wire ties spaced 6" on center. $\frac{3}{4}$" channel saddle tied to 2" channels with doubled 0.065" (No. 16 B.W. gage) wire ties. 2" channels spaced 36" on center suspended 2" below steel framing and saddle-tied with 0.165" (No. 8 B.W. gage) wire. Plaster mixed 1:2 by weight, gypsum-to-sand aggregate.	—	—	$1\frac{7}{8}$	1	—	—	$\frac{3}{4}^l$	$\frac{3}{4}^l$

(continued)

TABLE 720.1(3)—continued
MINIMUM PROTECTION FOR FLOOR AND ROOF SYSTEMS[a,q]

FLOOR OR ROOF CONSTRUCTION	ITEM NUMBER	CEILING CONSTRUCTION	THICKNESS OF FLOOR OR ROOF SLAB (inches)				MINIMUM THICKNESS OF CEILING (inches)			
			4 hour	3 hour	2 hour	1 hour	4 hour	3 hour	2 hour	1 hour
11. $1^1/_2$"-deep steel roof deck on steel-framing wood fiber insulation board, 17.5 pcf density on top applied over a 15-lb asphalt-saturated felt .Class A or B roof covering.	11-1.1	Ceiling of gypsum plaster on metal lath. Lath attached to $^3/_4$" furring channels with 0.049" (No. 18 B.W. gage) wire ties spaced 6" on center. $^3/_4$" channels saddle tied to 2" channels with doubled 0.065" (No. 16 B.W. gage) wire ties. 2" channels spaced 36" on center suspended 2" below steel framing and saddle tied with 0.165" (No. 8 B.W. gage) wire. Plaster mixed 1:2 for scratch coat and 1:3 for brown coat, by weight, gypsum-to-sand aggregate for 1-hour system. For 2-hour system, plaster mix is 1:2 by weight, gypsum-to-sand aggregate.	—	—	$1^1/_2$	1	—	—	$^7/_8$[g]	$^3/_4$[1]
12. $1^1/_2$" deep steel roof deck on steel-framing insulation of rigid board consisting of expanded perlite and fibers impregnated with integral asphalt waterproofing; density 9 to 12 pcf secured to metal roof deck by $^1/_2$" wide ribbons of waterproof, cold-process liquid adhesive spaced 6" apart. Steel joist or light steel construction with metal roof deck, insulation, and Class A or B built-up roof covering.[e]	12-1.1	Gypsum-vermiculite plaster on metal lath wire tied at 6" intervals to $^3/_4$" furring channels spaced 12" on center and wire tied to 2" runner channels spaced 32" on center. Runners wire tied to bottom chord of steel joists.	—	—	1	—	—	—	$^7/_8$	—
13. Double wood floor over wood joists spaced 16" on center.[m,n]	13-1.1	Gypsum plaster over $^3/_8$" Type X gypsum lath. Lath initially applied with not less than four $1^1/_8$" by No. 13 gage by $^{19}/_{64}$" head plasterboard blued nails per bearing. Continuous stripping over lath along all joist lines. Stripping consists of 3" wide strips of metal lath attached by $1^1/_2$" by No. 11 gage by $^1/_2$" head roofing nails spaced 6" on center. Alternate stripping consists of 3" wide 0.049" diameter wire stripping weighing 1 pound per square yard and attached by No.16 gage by $1^1/_2$" by $^3/_4$" crown width staples, spaced 4" on center. Where alternate stripping is used, the lath nailing may consist of two nails at each end and one nail at each intermediate bearing. Plaster mixed 1:2 by weight, gypsum-to-sand aggregate.	—	—	—	—	—	—	—	$^7/_8$

(continued)

TABLE 720.1(3)—continued
MINIMUM PROTECTION FOR FLOOR AND ROOF SYSTEMS[a,q]

FLOOR OR ROOF CONSTRUCTION	ITEM NUMBER	CEILING CONSTRUCTION	THICKNESS OF FLOOR OR ROOF SLAB (inches)				MINIMUM THICKNESS OF CEILING (inches)			
			4 hour	3 hour	2 hour	1 hour	4 hour	3 hour	2 hour	1 hour
13. Double wood floor over wood joists spaced 16" on center.[m,n]	13-1.2	Cement or gypsum plaster on metal lath. Lath fastened by $1^1/_2$" by No. 11 gage by $^7/_{16}$" head barbed shank roofing nails spaced 5" on center. Plaster mixed 1:2 for scratch coat and 1:3 for brown coat, by weight, cement to sand aggregate.	—	—	—	—	—	—	—	$^5/_8$
	13-1.3	Perlite or vermiculite gypsum plaster on metal lath secured to joists with $1^1/_2$" by No. 11 gage by $^7/_{16}$" head barbed shank roofing nails spaced 5" on center.	—	—	—	—	—	—	—	$^5/_8$
	13-1.4	$^1/_2$" Type X gypsum wallboard[c] nailed to joists with 5d cooler or wallboard nails at 6" on center. End joints of wallboard centered on joists.	—	—	—	—	—	—	—	$^1/_2$
14. Plywood stressed skin panels consisting of $^5/_8$"-thick interior C-D (exterior glue) top stressed skin on 2" × 6" nominal (minimum) stringers. Adjacent panel edges joined with 8d common wire nails spaced 6" on center. Stringers spaced 12" maximum on center.	14-1.1	$^1/_2$"-thick wood fiberboard weighing 15 to 18 pounds per cubic foot installed with long dimension parallel to stringers or $^3/_8$" C-D (exterior glue) plywood glued and/or nailed to stringers. Nailing to be with 5d cooler[o] or wallboard[o] nails at 12" on center. Second layer of $^1/_2$" Type X gypsum wallboard[c] applied with long dimension perpendicular to joists and attached with 8d cooler[o] or wallboard[o] nails at 6" on center at end joints and 8" on center elsewhere. Wallboard joints staggered with respect to fiberboard joints.	—	—	—	—	—	—	—	1
15. Vermiculite concrete slab proportioned 1:4 (portland cement to vermiculite aggregate) on a $1^1/_2$"-deep steel deck supported on individually protected steel framing. Maximum span of deck 6'-10" where deck is less than 0.019 inch (No. 26 carbon steel sheet gage) or greater. Slab reinforced with 4" × 8" 0.109/0.083" (No.$^{12}/_{14}$ B.W. gage) welded wire mesh.	15-1.1	None	—	—	—	3[j]	—	—	—	—
16. Perlite concrete slab proportioned 1:6 (portland cement to perlite aggregate) on a $1^1/_4$"-deep steel deck supported on individually protected steel framing. Slab reinforced with 4" × 8" 0.109/0.083" (No.$^{12}/_{14}$ B.W. gage) welded wire mesh.	16-1.1	None	—	—	—	$3^1/_2$[j]	—	—	—	—

(continued)

TABLE 720.1(3)—continued
MINIMUM PROTECTION FOR FLOOR AND ROOF SYSTEMS[a,q]

FLOOR OR ROOF CONSTRUCTION	ITEM NUMBER	CEILING CONSTRUCTION	THICKNESS OF FLOOR OR ROOF SLAB (inches)				MINIMUM THICKNESS OF CEILING (inches)			
			4 hour	3 hour	2 hour	1 hour	4 hour	3 hour	2 hour	1 hour
17. Perlite concrete slab proportioned 1:6 (portland cement to perlite aggregate) on a $^9/_{16}$"-deep steel deck supported by steel joists 4' on center. Class A or B roof covering on top.	17-1.1	Perlite gypsum plaster on metal lath wire tied to $^3/_4$" furring channels attached with 0.065" (No. 16 B.W. gage) wire ties to lower chord of joists.	—	2^p	2^p	—	—	$^7/_8$	$^3/_4$	—
18. Perlite concrete slab proportioned 1:6 (portland cement to perlite aggregate) on $1^1/_4$"-deep steel deck supported on individually protected steel framing. Maximum span of deck 6'-10" where deck is less than 0.019" (No. 26 carbon sheet steel gage) and 8'-0" where deck is 0.019" (No. 26 carbon sheet steel gage) or greater. Slab reinforced with 0.042" (No. 19 B.W. gage) hexagonal wire mesh. Class A or B roof covering on top.	18-1.1	None	—	$2^1/_4{}^p$	$2^1/_4{}^p$	—	—	—	—	—
19. Floor and beam construction consisting of 3"-deep cellular steel floor unit mounted on steel members with 1:4 (proportion of portland cement to perlite aggregate) perlite-concrete floor slab on top.	19-1.1	Suspended envelope ceiling of perlite gypsum plaster on metal lath attached to $^3/_4$"cold-rolled channels, secured to $1^1/_2$" cold-rolled channels spaced 42" on center supported by 0.203 inch (No. 6 B.W. gage) wire 36" on center. Beams in envelope with 3" minimum airspace between beam soffit and lath have a 4-hour rating.	2^p	—	—	—	1^l	—	—	—
20. Perlite concrete proportioned 1:6 (portland cement to perlite aggregate) poured to $^1/_8$" thickness above top of corrugations of $1^5/_{16}$"-deep galvanized steel deck maximum span 8'-0" for 0.024"(No. 24 galvanized sheet gage) or 6' 0" for 0.019" (No. 26 galvanized sheet gage) with deck supported by individually protected steel framing. Approved polystyrene foam plastic insulation board having a flame spread not exceeding 75 (1" to 4" thickness) with vent holes that approximate 3 percent of the board surface area placed on top of perlite slurry. A 2' by 4' insulation board contains six $2^3/_4$" diameter holes. Board covered with $2^1/_4$" minimum perlite concrete slab.	20-1.1	None	—	—	Varies	—	—	—	—	—
20. Slab reinforced with mesh consisting of 0.042" (No. 19 B.W. gage) galvanized steel wire twisted together to form 2" hexagons with straight 0.065" (No. 16 B.W. gage) galvanized steel wire woven into mesh and spaced 3". Alternate slab reinforcement shall be permitted to consist of 4" × 8", 0.109/0.238" (No. 12/4 B.W. gage), or 2" × 2", 0.083/0.083" (No. 14/14 B.W. gage) welded wire fabric. Class A or B roof covering on top.	20-1.1	None	—	—	Varies	—	—	—	—	—

(continued)

TABLE 720.1(3)—continued
MINIMUM PROTECTION FOR FLOOR AND ROOF SYSTEMS[a,q]

FLOOR OR ROOF CONSTRUCTION	ITEM NUMBER	CEILING CONSTRUCTION	THICKNESS OF FLOOR OR ROOF SLAB (inches)				MINIMUM THICKNESS OF CEILING (inches)			
			4 hour	3 hour	2 hour	1 hour	4 hour	3 hour	2 hour	1 hour
21. Wood joists, wood I-joist floor trusses and flat or pitched roof trusses spaced a maximum 24" o.c. with $^1/_2$" wood structural panels with exterior glue applied at right angles to top of joist or top chord of trusses with 8d nails. The wood structural panel thickness shall not be less than nominal $^1/_2$" nor less than required by Chapter 23.	21-1.1	Base layer $^5/_8$" Type X gypsum wallboard applied at right angles to joist or truss 24" o.c. with $1^1/_4$" Type S or Type W drywall screws 24" o.c. Face layer $^5/_8$" Type X gypsum wallboard or veneer base applied at right angles to joist or truss through base layer with $1^7/_8$" Type S or Type W drywall screws 12" o.c. at joints and intermediate joist or truss. Face layer Type G drywall screws placed 2" back on either side of face layer end joints, 12" o.c.	—	—	—	Varies	—	—	—	$1^1/_4$
22. Steel joists, floor trusses and flat or pitched roof trusses spaced a maximum 24" o.c. with $^1/_2$" wood structural panels with exterior glue applied at right angles to top of joist or top chord of trusses with No. 8 screws. The wood structural panel thickness shall not be less than nominal $^1/_2$" nor less than required by Chapter 23.	22-1.1	Base layer $^5/_8$" Type X gypsum board applied at right angles to steel framing 24" on center with 1" Type S drywall screws spaced 24" on center. Face layer $^5/_8$" Type X gypsum board applied at right angles to steel framing attached through base layer with $1^5/_8$" Type S drywall screws 12" on center at end joints and intermediate joints and $1^1/_2$" Type G drywall screws 12 inches on center placed 2" back on either side of face layer end joints. Joints of the face layer are offset 24" from the joints of the base layer.	—	—	—	Varies	—	—	—	$1^1/_4$
23. Wood I-joist (minimum joist depth $9^1/_4$" with a minimum flange depth of $1^5/_{16}$" and a minimum flange cross-sectional area of 2.3 square inches) at 24" o.c. spacing with 1 × 4 (nominal) wood furring strip spacer applied parallel to and covering the bottom of the bottom flange of each member, tacked in place. 2" mineral wool insulation, 3.5 pcf (nominal) installed adjacent to the bottom flange of the I-joist and supported by the 1 × 4 furring strip spacer.	23-1.1	$^1/_2$" deep single leg resilient channel 16" on center (channels doubled at wallboard end joints), placed perpendicular to the furring strip and joist and attached to each joist by $1^7/_8$" Type S drywall screws. $^5/_8$" Type C gypsum wallboard applied perpendicular to the channel with end joints staggered at least 4' and fastened with $1^1/_8$" Type S drywall screws spaced 7" on center. Wallboard joints to be taped and covered with joint compound.	—	—	—	Varies	—	—	—	—

(continued)

TABLE 720.1(3)—continued
MINIMUM PROTECTION FOR FLOOR AND ROOF SYSTEMS[a,q]

FLOOR OR ROOF CONSTRUCTION	ITEM NUMBER	CEILING CONSTRUCTION	THICKNESS OF FLOOR OR ROOF SLAB (inches)				MINIMUM THICKNESS OF CEILING (inches)			
			4 hour	3 hour	2 hour	1 hour	4 hour	3 hour	2 hour	1 hour
24. Wood I-joist (minimum joist depth $9^1/_4$" with a minimum flange depth of $^{15}/_{16}$" and a minimum flange cross sectional area of 2.3 square inches) at 24" o.c. spacing with 1 × 4 (nominal) wood furring strip spacer applied parallel to and covering the bottom of the bottom flange of each member, tacked in place. 2" mineral wool insulation, 3.5 pcf (nominal) installed adjacent to the bottom flange of the I-joist and supported by the 1 × 4 furring strip spacer.	24-1.1	$^1/_2$" deep single-leg resilient channel 16" o.c. (channels double at wallboard end joints), placed perpendicular to the furring strip and joist and attached to each joist by $1^7/_8$" Type S drywall screws. $^5/_8$" Type C gypsum wallboard applied perpendicular to the channel with end joints staggered at least 4' and fastened with $1^1/_8$" Type S drywall screws spaced 7" o.c. Wallboard jints to be taped and covered with joint compound.	—	—	Variies	—	—	$3^3/_8$	—
25. Wood I-joist (minimum I-joist depth $9^1/_4$" with a minimum flange depth of $1^1/_2$" and a minimum flange cross-sectional area of 5.25 square inches; minimum web thickness of $^3/_8$") @ 24" o.c., $1^1/_2$" mineral fiber insulation (2.5 pcf - nominal) resting on hat-shaped channels.	25-1.1	Minimum 0.026" thick hat-shaped channel 16" o.c. (channels doubled at wallboard end joints), placed perpendicular to the joist and attached to each joist by $1^5/_8$" Type S drywall screws. $^5/_8$" Type C gypsum wallboard applied perpendicular to the channel with end joints staggered and fastened with $1^1/_8$" Type S drywall screws spaced 12" o.c. in the field and 8" o.c. at the wallboard ends. Wallboard joints to be taped and covered with joint compound.	—	—	—	Varies	—	—	—	Varies
26. Wood I-joist (minimum I-joist depth $9^1/_4$" with a minimum flange depth of $1^1/_2$" and a minimum flange cross-sectional area of 5.25 square inches; minimum web thickness of $^7/_{16}$") @ 24" o.c., $1^1/_2$"mineral fiber insulation (2.5 pcf - nominal) resting on resilient channels.	26-1.1	Minimum 0.019" thick resilient channel 16" o.c. (channels doubled at wallboard end joints), placed perpendicular to the joist and attached to each joist by $1^5/_8$" Type S drywall screws. $^5/_8$" Type C gypsum wallboard applied perpendicular to the channel with end joints staggered and fastened with 1" Type S drywall screws spaced 12" o.c. in the field and 8" o.c. at the wallboard ends. Wallboard joints to be taped and covered with joint compound.	—	—	—	Varies	—	—	—	Varies
27. Wood I-joist (minimum I-joist depth $9^1/_4$" with a minimum flange thickness of $1^1/_2$" and a minimum flange cross-sectional area of 2.25 square inches; minimum web thickness of $^3/_8$") @ 24" o.c.	27-1.1	Two layers of $^1/_2$" Type X gypsum wallboard applied with the long dimension perpendicular to the I-joists with end joints staggered. The base layer is fastened with $1^5/_8$" Type S drywall screws spaced 12" o.c. and the face layer is fastened with 2" Type S drywall screws spaced 12" o.c. in the field and 8" o.c. on the edges. Face layer end joints shall not occur on the same I-joist as base layer end joints and edge joints shall be offset 24" from base layer joints. Face layer to also be attached to base layer with $1^1/_2$" Type G drywall screws spaced 8" o.c. placed 6" from face layer end joints. Face layer wallboard joints to be taped and covered with joint compound.	—	—	—	Varies	—	—	—	Varies

(continued)

TABLE 720.1(3)—continued
MINIMUM PROTECTION FOR FLOOR AND ROOF SYSTEMS[a,q]

FLOOR OR ROOF CONSTRUCTION	ITEM NUMBER	CEILING CONSTRUCTION	THICKNESS OF FLOOR OR ROOF SLAB (inches)				MINIMUM THICKNESS OF CEILING (inches)			
			4 hour	3 hour	2 hour	1 hour	4 hour	3 hour	2 hour	1 hour
28. Wood I-joist (minimum I-joist depth 9$^1/_2$" with a minimum flange depth of 1$^5/_{16}$" and a minimum flange cross-sectional area of 1.95 square inches; minimum web thickness of $^3/_8$") @ 24" o.c.	28-1.1	Minimum 0.019" thick resilient channel 16" o.c. (channels doubled at wallboard end joints), placed perpendicular to the joist and attached to each joist by 1$^5/_8$" Type S drywall screws. Two layers of $^1/_2$" Type X gypsum wallboard applied with the long dimension perpendicular to the I-joists with end joints staggered. The base layer is fastened with 1$^1/_4$" Type S drywall screws spaced 12" o.c. and the face layer is fastened with 1$^5/_8$" Type S drywall screws spaced 12" o.c. Face layer end joints shall not occur on the same I-Joist as base layer end joints and edge joints shall be offset 24" from base layer joints. Face layer to also be attached to base layer with 1$^1/_2$" Type G drywall screws spaced 8" o.c. placed 6" from face layer end joints. Face layer wallboard joints to be taped and covered with joint compound.	—	—	—	Varies	—	—	—	Varies
29. Wood I-joist (minimum I-joist depth 9$^1/_4$" with a minimum flange depth of 1$^1/_2$" and a minimum flange cross-sectional area of 2.25 square inches; minimum web thickness of $^3/_8$") @ 24" o.c., with hat-shaped channels supporting the middle and face layers of gypsum wallboard. Unfaced fiberglass insulation is installed between the I-joists supported on the upper surface of the flange by stay wires spaced 12" o.c.	29-1.1	Base layer of $^5/_8$" Type C gypsum wallboard attached directly to I-joists with 1$^5/_8$" Type S drywall screws spaced 12" o.c. with ends staggered. Minimum 0.0179" thick resilient channel 16" o.c. (channels doubled at wallboard end joints), placed perpendicular to the joist and attached to each joist by 1$^5/_8$" Type S drywall screws after the base layer of gypsum wall board has been applied. The middle and face layers of $^5/_8$" Type C gypsum wallboard applied perpendicular to the channel with end joints staggered. The middle layer is fastened with 1" Type S drywall screws spaced 12" o.c. The face layer is applied parallel to the middle layer but with the edge joints offset 24" from those of the middle layer and fastened with 1$^5/_8$" Type S drywall screws 8" o.c. The joints shall be taped and covered with joint compound.	—	—	—	Varies	—	—	—	Varies

(continued)

TABLE 720.1(3)—continued
MINIMUM PROTECTION FOR FLOOR AND ROOF SYSTEMS[a,q]

FLOOR OR ROOF CONSTRUCTION	ITEM NUMBER	CEILING CONSTRUCTION	THICKNESS OF FLOOR OR ROOF SLAB (inches)				MINIMUM THICKNESS OF CEILING (inches)			
			4 hour	3 hour	2 hour	1 hour	4 hour	3 hour	2 hour	1 hour
30. Channel-shaped 18 gauge steel joists (minimum depth 8") spaced a maximum 24" o.c. supporting tongue-and-groove wood structural panels (nominal minimum $^3/_4$" thick) applied perpendicular to framing members. Structural panels attached with $1^5/_8$" Type S-12 screws spaced 12" o.c.	30-1.1	Base layer $^5/_8$" Type X gypsum board applied perpendicular to bottom of framing members with $1^1/_8$" Type S-12 screws spaced 12" o.c. Second layer $^5/_8$" Type X gypsum board attached perpendicular to framing members with $1^5/_8$" Type S-12 screws spaced 12" o.c. Second layer joints offset 24" from base layer. Third layer $^5/_8$" Type X gypsum board attached perpendicular to framing members with $2^3/_8$" Type S-12 screws spaced 12" o.c. Third layer joints offset 12" from second layer joints. Hat-shaped rigid furring channels applied at right angles to framing members over third layer with two $2^3/_8$" Type S-12 screws at each framing member. Face layer $^5/_8$" Type X gypsum board applied at right angles to furring channels with $1^1/_8$" Type S screws spaced 12" o.c.	—	—	Varies	—	—	—	$3^3/_8$	—

For SI: 1 inch = 25.4 mm, 1 foot = 304.8 mm, 1 pound = 0.454 kg, 1 cubic foot = 0.0283 m^3, 1 pound per square inch = 6.895 kPa, 1 pound per lineal foot = 1.4882 kg/m.

a. Staples with equivalent holding power and penetration shall be permitted to be used as alternate fasteners to nails for attachment to wood framing.

b. When the slab is in an unrestrained condition, minimum reinforcement cover shall not be less than $1^5/_8$ inches for 4-hour (siliceous aggregate only); $1^1/_4$ inches for 4- and 3-hour; 1 inch for 2-hour (siliceous aggregate only); and $^3/_4$ inch for all other restrained and unrestrained conditions.

c. For all of the construction with gypsum wallboard described in this table, gypsum base for veneer plaster of the same size, thickness and core type shall be permitted to be substituted for gypsum wallboard, provided attachment is identical to that specified for the wallboard, and the joints on the face layer are reinforced and the entire surface is covered with a minimum of $^1/_{16}$-inch gypsum veneer plaster.

d. Slab thickness over steel joists measured at the joists for metal lath form and at the top of the form for steel form units.

e. (a) The maximum allowable stress level for H-Series joists shall not exceed 22,000 psi.
(b) The allowable stress for K-Series joists shall not exceed 26,000 psi, the nominal depth of such joist shall not be less than 10 inches and the nominal joist weight shall not be less than 5 pounds per lineal foot.

f. Cement plaster with 15 pounds of hydrated lime and 3 pounds of approved additives or admixtures per bag of cement.

g. Gypsum wallboard ceilings attached to steel framing shall be permitted to be suspended with $1^1/_2$-inch cold-formed carrying channels spaced 48 inches on center, which are suspended with No. 8 SWG galvanized wire hangers spaced 48 inches on center. Cross-furring channels are tied to the carrying channels with No. 18 SWG galvanized wire hangers spaced 48 inches on center. Cross-furring channels are tied to the carrying channels with No. 18 SWG galvanized wire (double strand) and spaced as required for direct attachment to the framing. This alternative is also applicable to those steel framing assemblies recognized under Note q.

h. Six-inch hollow clay tile with 2-inch concrete slab above.

i. Four-inch hollow clay tile with $1^1/_2$-inch concrete slab above.

j. Thickness measured to bottom of steel form units.

k. Five-eighths inch of vermiculite gypsum plaster plus $^1/_2$ inch of approved vermiculite acoustical plastic.

l. Furring channels spaced 12 inches on center.

m. Double wood floor shall be permitted to be either of the following:
(a) Subfloor of 1-inch nominal boarding, a layer of asbestos paper weighing not less than 14 pounds per 100 square feet and a layer of 1-inch nominal tongue and-groove finished flooring; or
(b) Subfloor of 1-inch nominal tongue-and-groove boarding or $^{15}/_{32}$-inch wood structural panels with exterior glue and a layer of 1-inch nominal tongue-and-groove finished flooring or $^{19}/_{32}$-inch wood structural panel finish flooring or a layer of Type I Grade M-1 particleboard not less than $^5/_8$-inch thick.

n. The ceiling shall be permitted to be omitted over unusable space, and flooring shall be permitted to be omitted where unusable space occurs above.

o. For properties of cooler or wallboard nails, see ASTM C 514, ASTM C 547 or ASTM F 1667.

p. Thickness measured on top of steel deck unit.

q. Generic fire-resistance ratings (those not designated as PROPRIETARY* in the listing) in the GA 600 shall be accepted as if herein listed.

SECTION 720
PRESCRIPTIVE FIRE RESISTANCE

720.1 General. The provisions of this section contain prescriptive details of fire-resistance-rated building elements. The materials of construction listed in Tables 720.1(1), 720.1(2), and 720.1(3) shall be assumed to have the fire-resistance ratings prescribed therein. Where materials that change the capacity for heat dissipation are incorporated into a fire-resistance-rated assembly, fire test results or other substantiating data shall be made available to the building official to show that the required fire-resistance-rating time period is not reduced.

720.1.1 Thickness of protective coverings. The thickness of fire-resistant materials required for protection of structural members shall be not less than set forth in Table 720.1(1), except as modified in this section. The figures shown shall be the net thickness of the protecting materials and shall not include any hollow space in back of the protection.

720.1.2 Unit masonry protection. Where required, metal ties shall be embedded in bed joints of unit masonry for protection of steel columns. Such ties shall be as set forth in Table 720.1(1) or be equivalent thereto.

720.1.3 Reinforcement for cast-in-place concrete column protection. Cast-in-place concrete protection for steel columns shall be reinforced at the edges of such members with wire ties of not less than 0.18 inch (4.6 mm) in diameter wound spirally around the columns on a pitch of not more than 8 inches (203 mm) or by equivalent reinforcement.

720.1.4 Plaster application. The finish coat is not required for plaster protective coatings where they comply with the design mix and thickness requirements of Tables 720.1(1), 720.1(2) and 720.1(3).

720.1.5 Bonded prestressed concrete tendons. For members having a single tendon or more than one tendon installed with equal concrete cover measured from the nearest surface, the cover shall not be less than that set forth in Table 720.1(1). For members having multiple tendons installed with variable concrete cover, the average tendon cover shall not be less than that set forth in Table 720.1(1), provided:

1. The clearance from each tendon to the nearest exposed surface is used to determine the average cover.

2. In no case can the clear cover for individual tendons be less than one-half of that set forth in Table 720.1(1). A minimum cover of 0.75 inch (19.1 mm) for slabs and 1 inch (25 mm) for beams is required for any aggregate concrete.

3. For the purpose of establishing a fire-resistance rating, tendons having a clear covering less than that set forth in Table 720.1(1) shall not contribute more than 50 percent of the required ultimate moment capacity for members less than 350 square inches (0.226 m^2) in cross-sectional area and 65 percent for larger members. For structural design purposes, however, tendons having a reduced cover are assumed to be fully effective.

SECTION 721
CALCULATED FIRE RESISTANCE

721.1 General. The provisions of this section contain procedures by which the fire resistance of specific materials or combinations of materials is established by calculations. These procedures apply only to the information contained in this section and shall not be otherwise used. The calculated fire resistance of concrete, concrete masonry, and clay masonry assemblies shall be permitted in accordance with ACI 216.1/TMS 0216. The calculated fire resistance of steel assemblies shall be permitted in accordance with Chapter 5 of ASCE 29.

721.1.1 Definitions. The following words and terms shall, for the purposes of this chapter and as used elsewhere in this code, have the meanings shown herein.

CERAMIC FIBER BLANKET. A mineral wool insulation material made of alumina-silica fibers and weighing 4 to 10 pounds per cubic foot (pcf) (64 to 160 kg/m^3).

CONCRETE, CARBONATE AGGREGATE. Concrete made with aggregates consisting mainly of calcium or magnesium carbonate, such as limestone or dolomite, and containing 40 percent or less quartz, chert, or flint.

CONCRETE, CELLULAR. A lightweight insulating concrete made by mixing a preformed foam with portland cement slurry and having a dry unit weight of approximately 30 pcf (480 kg/m^3).

CONCRETE, LIGHTWEIGHT AGGREGATE. Concrete made with aggregates of expanded clay, shale, slag or slate or sintered fly ash or any natural lightweight aggregate meeting ASTM C 330 and possessing equivalent fire-resistance properties and weighing 85 to 115 pcf (1360 to 1840 kg/m^3).

CONCRETE, PERLITE. A lightweight insulating concrete having a dry unit weight of approximately 30 pcf (480 kg/m^3) made with perlite concrete aggregate. Perlite aggregate is produced from a volcanic rock which, when heated, expands to form a glass-like material of cellular structure.

CONCRETE, SAND-LIGHTWEIGHT. Concrete made with a combination of expanded clay, shale, slag, slate, sintered fly ash, or any natural lightweight aggregate meeting ASTM C 330 and possessing equivalent fire-resistance properties and natural sand. Its unit weight is generally between 105 and 120 pcf (1680 and 1920 kg/m^3).

CONCRETE, SILICEOUS AGGREGATE. Concrete made with normal-weight aggregates consisting mainly of silica or compounds other than calcium or magnesium carbonate, which contains more than 40-percent quartz, chert, or flint.

CONCRETE, VERMICULITE. A lightweight insulating concrete made with vermiculite concrete aggregate which is laminated micaceous material produced by expanding the ore at high temperatures. When added to a portland cement slurry the resulting concrete has a dry unit weight of approximately 30 pcf (480 kg/m³).

GLASS FIBERBOARD. Fibrous glass roof insulation consisting of inorganic glass fibers formed into rigid boards using a binder. The board has a top surface faced with asphalt and kraft reinforced with glass fiber.

MINERAL BOARD. A rigid felted thermal insulation board consisting of either felted mineral fiber or cellular beads of expanded aggregate formed into flat rectangular units.

721.2 Concrete assemblies. The provisions of this section contain procedures by which the fire-resistance ratings of concrete assemblies are established by calculations.

721.2.1 Concrete walls. Cast-in-place and precast concrete walls shall comply with Section 721.2.1.1. Multi-wythe concrete walls shall comply with Section 721.2.1.2. Joints between precast panels shall comply with Section 721.2.1.3. Concrete walls with gypsum wallboard or plaster finish shall comply with Section 721.2.1.4.

721.2.1.1 Cast-in-place or precast walls. The minimum equivalent thicknesses of cast-in-place or precast concrete walls for fire-resistance ratings of 1 hour to 4 hours are shown in Table 721.2.1.1. For solid walls with flat vertical surfaces, the equivalent thickness is the same as the actual thickness. The values in Table 721.2.1.1 apply to plain, reinforced or prestressed concrete walls.

TABLE 721.2.1.1
MINIMUM EQUIVALENT THICKNESS OF CAST-IN-PLACE OR PRECAST CONCRETE WALLS, LOAD-BEARING OR NONLOAD-BEARING

CONCRETE TYPE	MINIMUM SLAB THICKNESS (inches) FOR FIRE-RESISTANCE RATING OF				
	1-hour	1¹/₂-hour	2-hour	3-hour	4-hour
Siliceous	3.5	4.3	5.0	6.2	7.0
Carbonate	3.2	4.0	4.6	5.7	6.6
Sand-Lightweight	2.7	3.3	3.8	4.6	5.4
Lightweight	2.5	3.1	3.6	4.4	5.1

For SI: 1 inch = 25.4 mm.

721.2.1.1.1 Hollow-core precast wall panels. For hollow-core precast concrete wall panels in which the cores are of constant cross section throughout the length, calculation of the equivalent thickness by dividing the net cross-sectional area (the gross cross section minus the area of the cores) of the panel by its width shall be permitted.

721.2.1.1.2 Core spaces filled. Where all of the core spaces of hollow-core wall panels are filled with loose-fill material, such as expanded shale, clay, or slag, or vermiculite or perlite, the fire-resistance rating of the wall is the same as that of a solid wall of the same concrete type and of the same overall thickness.

721.2.1.1.3 Tapered cross sections. The thickness of panels with tapered cross sections shall be that determined at a distance 2t or 6 inches (152 mm),

whichever is less, from the point of minimum thickness, where t is the minimum thickness.

721.2.1.1.4 Ribbed or undulating surfaces. The equivalent thickness of panels with ribbed or undulating surfaces shall be determined by one of the following expressions:

For $s \geq 4t$, the thickness to be used shall be t

For $s \leq 2t$, the thickness to be used shall be t_e

For $4t > s > 2t$, the thickness to be used shall be

$$t + \left(\frac{4_t}{s} - 1\right)(t_e - t) \qquad \text{(Equation 7-3)}$$

where:

s = Spacing of ribs or undulations.

t = Minimum thickness.

t_e = Equivalent thickness of the panel calculated as the net cross-sectional area of the panel divided by the width, in which the maximum thickness used in the calculation shall not exceed $2t$.

721.2.1.2 Multiwythe walls. For walls that consist of two wythes of different types of concrete, the fire-resistance ratings shall be permitted to be determined from Figure 721.2.1.2.

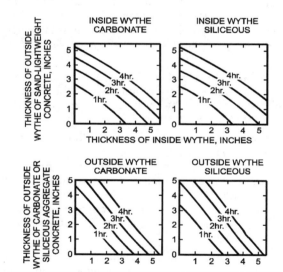

FIGURE 721.2.1.2
FIRE-RESISTANCE RATINGS OF TWO-WYTHE CONCRETE WALLS

For SI: 1 inch = 25.4 mm.

TABLE 721.2.1.2(2)
FIRE-RESISTANCE RATINGS BASED ON $R^{0.59}$

R^a, MINUTES	$R^{0.59}$
60	11.20
120	16.85
180	21.41
240	25.37

a. Based on Equation 7-4.

721.2.1.2.1 Two or more wythes. The fire-resistance rating for wall panels consisting of two or more wythes shall be permitted to be determined by the formula:

$$R = (R_1^{0.59} + R_2^{0.59} + \ldots + R_n^{0.59})^{1.7} \qquad \textbf{(Equation 7-4)}$$

where:

R = The fire endurance of the assembly, minutes.

R_1, R_2, and R_n = The fire endurances of the individual wythes, minutes. Values of $R_n^{0.59}$ for use in Equation 7-4 are given in Table 721.2.1.2(1). Calculated fire-resistance ratings are shown in Table 721.2.1.2(2).

721.2.1.2.2 Foam plastic insulation. The fire-resistance ratings of precast concrete wall panels consisting of a layer of foam plastic insulation sandwiched between two wythes of concrete shall be permitted to be determined by use of Equation 7-4. Foam plastic insulation with a total thickness of less than 1 inch (25 mm) shall be disregarded. The R_n value for thickness of foam plastic insulation of 1 inch (25 mm) or greater, for use in the calculation, is 5 minutes; therefore $R_n^{0.59} = 2.5$.

721.2.1.3 Joints between precast wall panels. Joints between precast concrete wall panels which are not insulated as required by this section shall be considered as openings in walls. Uninsulated joints shall be included in determining the percentage of openings permitted by Table 704.8. Where openings are not permitted or are required by this code to be protected, the provisions of this section shall be used to determine the amount of joint insulation required. Insulated joints shall not be considered openings for purposes of determining compliance with the allowable percentage of openings in Table 704.8.

721.2.1.3.1 Ceramic fiber joint protection. Figure 721.2.1.3.1 shows thicknesses of ceramic fiber blankets to be used to insulate joints between precast concrete wall panels for various panel thicknesses and for joint widths of $^3/_8$ inch (9.5 mm) and 1 inch (25 mm) for fire-resistance ratings of 1 hour to 4 hours. For joint widths between $^3/_8$ inch (9.5 mm) and 1 inch (25 mm), the thickness of ceramic fiber blanket is allowed to be determined by direct

interpolation. Other tested and labeled materials are acceptable in place of ceramic fiber blankets.

For SI: 1 inch = 25.4 mm.

**FIGURE 721.2.1.3.1
CERAMIC FIBER JOINT PROTECTION**

721.2.1.4 Walls with gypsum wallboard or plaster finishes. The fire-resistance rating of cast-in-place or precast concrete walls with finishes of gypsum wallboard or plaster applied to one or both sides shall be permitted to be calculated in accordance with the provisions of this section.

721.2.1.4.1 Nonfire-exposed side. Where the finish of gypsum wallboard or plaster is applied to the side of the wall not exposed to fire, the contribution of the finish to the total fire-resistance rating shall be determined as follows: The thickness of the finish shall first be corrected by multiplying the actual thickness of the finish by the applicable factor determined from Table 721.2.1.4(1) based on the type of aggregate in the concrete. The corrected thickness of finish shall then be added to the actual or equivalent thickness of concrete and fire-resistance rating of the concrete and finish determined from Table 721.2.1.1, Figure 721.2.1.2 or Table 721.2.1.2(1).

**TABLE 721.2.1.2(1)
VALUES OF $R_n^{0.59}$ FOR USE IN EQUATION 7-4**

TYPE OF MATERIAL	THICKNESS OF MATERIAL (inches)										
	$1^1/_2$	2	$2^1/_2$	3	$3^1/_2$	4	$4^1/_2$	5	$5^1/_2$	6	$6^1/_2$	7
Siliceous aggregate concrete	5.3	6.5	8.1	9.5	11.3	13.0	14.9	16.9	18.8	20.7	22.8	25.1
Carbonate aggregate concrete	5.5	7.1	8.9	10.4	12.0	14.0	16.2	18.1	20.3	21.9	24.7	27.2[c]
Sand-lightweight concrete	6.5	8.2	10.5	12.8	15.5	18.1	20.7	23.3	26.0[c]	Note c	Note c	Note c
Lightweight concrete	6.6	8.8	11.2	13.7	16.5	19.1	21.9	24.7	27.8[c]	Note c	Note c	Note c
Insulating concrete[a]	9.3	13.3	16.6	18.3	23.1	26.5[c]	Note c	Note c	Note c	Note c	Note c	Note c
Airspace[b]	-	-	-	-	-	-	-	-	-	-	-	-

For SI: 1 inch = 25.4 mm, 1 pound per cubic foot = 16.02 kg/m³.

a. Dry unit weight of 35 pcf or less and consisting of cellular, perlite or vermiculite concrete.

b. The $R_n^{0.59}$ value for one $^1/_2$" to 3 $^1/_2$" airspace is 3.3. The $R_n^{0.59}$ value for two $^1/_2$" to 3 $^1/_2$" airspaces is 6.7.

c. The fire-resistance rating for this thickness exceeds 4 hours.

721.2.1.4.2 Fire-exposed side. Where gypsum wallboard or plaster is applied to the fire-exposed side of the wall, the contribution of the finish to the total fire-resistance rating shall be determined as follows: The time assigned to the finish as established by Table 721.2.1.4(2) shall be added to the fire-resistance rating determined from Table 721.2.1.1 or Figure 721.2.1.2, or Table 721.2.1.2(1) for the concrete alone, or to the rating determined in Section 721.2.1.4.1 for the concrete and finish on the nonfire-exposed side.

721.2.1.4.3 Nonsymmetrical assemblies. For a wall having no finish on one side or different types or thicknesses of finish on each side, the calculation procedures of Sections 721.2.1.4.1 and 721.2.1.4.2 shall be performed twice, assuming either side of the wall to be the fire-exposed side. The fire-restance rating of the wall shall not exceed the lower of the two values.

Exception: For an exterior wall with more than 5 feet (1524 mm) of horizontal separation, the fire shall be assumed to occur on the interior side only.

TABLE 721.2.1.4(1)
MULTIPLYING FACTOR FOR FINISHES ON NONFIRE-EXPOSED SIDE OF WALL

TYPE OF FINISH APPLIED TO MASONRY WALL	TYPE OF AGGREGATE USED IN CONCRETE OR CONCRETE MASONRY			
	Concrete: siliceous or carbonate Masonry: siliceous or calcareous gravel	Concrete: sand lightweight concrete Masonry: limestone, cinders or unexpanded slag	Concrete: lightweight concrete Masonry: expanded shale, clay or slate	Concrete: pumice, or expanded slag
Portland cement-sand plaster	1.00	0.75[a]	0.75[a]	0.50[a]
Gypsum-sand plaster or gypsum wallboard	1.25	1.00	1.00	1.00
Gypsum-vermiculite or perlite plaster	1.75	1.50	1.50	1.25

For SI: 1 inch = 25.4 mm.

a. For portland cement-sand plaster $^5/_8$ inch or less in thickness and applied directly to the masonry on the nonfire-exposed side of the wall, the multiplying factor shall be 1.00.

TABLE 721.2.1.4(2)
TIME ASSIGNED TO FINISH MATERIALS ON FIRE-EXPOSED SIDE OF WALL

FINISH DESCRIPTION	TIME (minute)
Gypsum wallboard	
$^3/_8$ inch	10
$^1/_2$ inch	15
$^5/_8$ inch	20
2 layers of $^3/_8$ inch	25
1 layer $^3/_8$ inch, 1 layer $^1/_2$ inch	35
2 layers $^1/_2$ inch	40
Type X gypsum wallboard	
$^1/_2$ inch	25
$^5/_8$ inch	40
Portland cement-sand plaster applied directly to concrete masonry	See Note a
Portland cement-sand plaster on metal lath	
$^3/_4$ inch	20
$^7/_8$ inch	25
1 inch	30
Gypsum sand plaster on $^3/_8$-inch gypsum lath	
$^1/_2$ inch	35
$^5/_8$ inch	40
$^3/_4$ inch	50
Gypsum sand plaster on metal lath	
$^3/_4$ inch	50
$^7/_8$ inch	60
1 inch	80

For SI: 1 inch = 25.4 mm.

a. The actual thickness of portland cement-sand plaster, provided it is $^5/_8$ inch or less in thickness, shall be permitted to be included in determining the equivalent thickness of the masonry for use in Table 721.3.2.

TABLE 721.2.2.1
MINIMUM SLAB THICKNESS (inches)

CONCRETE TYPE	FIRE-RESISTANCE RATING (hour)				
	1	1$\frac{1}{2}$	2	3	4
Siliceous	3.5	4.3	5.0	6.2	7.0
Carbonate	3.2	4.0	4.6	5.7	6.6
Sand-lightweight	2.7	3.3	3.8	4.6	5.4
Lightweight	2.5	3.1	3.6	4.4	5.1

For SI: 1 inch = 25.4 mm.

721.2.1.4.4 Minimum concrete fire-resistance rating. Where finishes applied to one or both sides of a concrete wall contribute to the fire-resistance rating, the concrete alone shall provide not less than one-half of the total required fire-resistance rating. Additionally, the contribution to the fire resistance of the finish on the nonfire-exposed side of a load-bearing wall shall not exceed one-half the contribution of the concrete alone.

721.2.1.4.5 Concrete finishes. Finishes on concrete walls that are assumed to contribute to the total fire-resistance rating of the wall shall comply with the installation requirements of Section 721.3.2.5.

721.2.2 Concrete floor and roof slabs. Reinforced and prestressed floors and roofs shall comply with Section 721.2.2.1. Multicourse floors and roofs shall comply with Sections 721.2.2.2 and 721.2.2.3, respectively.

721.2.2.1 Reinforced and prestressed floors and roofs. The minimum thicknesses of reinforced and prestressed concrete floor or roof slabs for fire-resistance ratings of 1 hour to 4 hours are shown in Table 721.2.2.1.

721.2.2.1.1 Hollow-core prestressed slabs. For hollow-core prestressed concrete slabs in which the cores are of constant cross section throughout the length, the equivalent thickness shall be permitted to be obtained by dividing the net cross-sectional area of the slab including grout in the joints, by its width.

721.2.2.1.2 Slabs with sloping soffits. The thickness of slabs with sloping soffits (see Figure 721.2.2.1.2) shall be determined at a distance 2t or 6 inches (152 mm), whichever is less, from the point of minimum thickness, where t is the minimum thickness.

For SI: 1 inch = 25.4 mm.

FIGURE 721.2.2.1.2
DETERMINATION OF SLAB THICKNESS FOR SLOPING SOFFITS

721.2.2.1.3 Slabs with ribbed soffits. The thickness of slabs with ribbed or undulating soffits (see Figure 721.2.2.1.3) shall be determined by one of the following expressions, whichever is applicable:

For $s > 4t$, the thickness to be used shall be t

For $s \le 2t$, the thickness to be used shall be t_e

For $4t > s > 2t$, the thickness to be used shall be

$$t + \left(\frac{4t}{s} - 1\right)(t_e - t) \qquad \textbf{(Equation 7-5)}$$

where:

s = Spacing of ribs or undulations.

t = Minimum thickness.

t_e = Equivalent thickness of the slab calculated as the net area of the slab divided by the width, in which the maximum thickness used in the calculation shall not exceed 2t.

NEGLECT SHADED AREA IN CALCULATION OF EQUIVALENT THICKNESS

For SI: 1 inch = 25.4 mm.

FIGURE 721.2.2.1.3
SLABS WITH RIBBED OR UNDULATING SOFFITS

721.2.2.2 Multicourse floors. The fire-resistance ratings of floors that consist of a base slab of concrete with a topping (overlay) of a different type of concrete shall comply with Figure 721.2.2.2.

721.2.2.3 Multicourse roofs. The fire-resistance ratings of roofs which consist of a base slab of concrete with a topping (overlay) of an insulating concrete or with an insulating board and built-up roofing shall comply with Figures 721.2.2.3(1) and 721.2.2.3(2).

721.2.2.3.1 Heat transfer. For the transfer of heat, three-ply built-up roofing contributes 10 minutes to the fire-resistance rating. The fire-resistance rating for concrete assemblies such as those shown in Figure 721.2.2.3(1) shall be increased by 10 minutes. This increase is not applicable to those shown in Figure 721.2.2.3(2).

721.2.2.4 Joints in precast slabs. Joints between adjacent precast concrete slabs need not be considered in calculating the slab thickness provided that a concrete topping at least 1 inch (25 mm) thick is used. Where no concrete topping is used, joints must be grouted to a depth of at least one-third the slab thickness at the joint, but not less than 1 inch (25 mm), or the joints must be made fire resistant by other approved methods.

For SI: 1 inch = 25.4 mm.

FIGURE 721.2.2.2
FIRE-RESISTANCE RATINGS FOR TWO-COURSE CONCRETE FLOORS

For SI: 1 inch = 25.4 mm.

FIGURE 721.2.2.3(1)
FIRE-RESISTANCE RATINGS FOR CONCRETE ROOF ASSEMBLIES

For SI: 1 inch = 25.4 mm.

FIGURE 721.2.2.3(2)
FIRE-RESISTANCE RATINGS FOR CONCRETE

721.2.3 Concrete cover over reinforcement. The minimum thickness of concrete cover over reinforcement in concrete slabs, reinforced beams and prestressed beams shall comply with this section.

721.2.3.1 Slab cover. The minimum thickness of concrete cover to the positive moment reinforcement shall comply with Table 721.2.3(1) for reinforced concrete and Table 721.2.3(2) for prestressed concrete. These tables are applicable for solid or hollow-core one-way or two-way slabs with flat undersurfaces. These tables are applicable to slabs that are either cast in place or precast. For precast prestressed concrete not covered elsewhere, the procedures contained in PCI MNL 124 shall be acceptable.

721.2.3.2 Reinforced beam cover. The minimum thickness of concrete cover to the positive moment reinforcement (bottom steel) for reinforced concrete beams is shown in Table 721.2.3(3) for fire-resistance ratings of 1 hour to 4 hours.

721.2.3.3 Prestressed beam cover. The minimum thickness of concrete cover to the positive moment pre-stressing tendons (bottom steel) for restrained and unre-strained prestressed concrete beams and stemmed units shall comply with the values shown in Tables 721.2.3(4) and 721.2.3(5) for fire-resistance ratings of

1 hour to 4 hours. Values in Table 721.2.3(4) apply to beams 8 inches (203 mm) or greater in width. Values in Table 721.2.3(5) apply to beams or stems of any width, provided the cross-section area is not less than 40 square inches (25 806 mm^2). In case of differences between the values determined from Table 721.2.3(4) or 721.2.3(5), it is permitted to use the smaller value. The concrete cover shall be calculated in accordance with Section 721.2.3.3.1. The minimum concrete cover for nonprestressed reinforcement in prestressed concrete beams shall comply with Section 721.2.3.2.

721.2.3.3.1 Calculating concrete cover. The concrete cover for an individual tendon is the minimum thickness of concrete between the surface of the tendon and the fire-exposed surface of the beam, except that for ungrouted ducts, the assumed cover thickness is the minimum thickness of concrete between the surface of the duct and the fire-exposed surface of the beam. For beams in which two or more tendons are used, the cover is assumed to be the average of the minimum cover of the individual tendons. For corner tendons (tendons equal distance from the bottom and side), the minimum cover used in the calculation shall be one-half the actual value. For stemmed members with two or more prestressing tendons located along the vertical centerline of the stem, the average cover shall be the distance from the bottom of the member to the centroid of the tendons. The actual cover for any individual tendon shall not be less than one-half the smaller value shown in Tables 721.2.3(4) and 721.2.3(5), or 1 inch (25 mm), whichever is greater.

721.2.4 Concrete columns. Concrete columns shall comply with this section.

TABLE 721.2.3(1)
COVER THICKNESS FOR REINFORCED CONCRETE FLOOR OR ROOF SLABS (inches)

CONCRETE AGGREGATE TYPE	FIRE-RESISTANCE RATING (hours)									
	Restrained					Unrestrained				
	1	$1^1/_2$	2	3	4	1	$1^1/_2$	2	3	4
Siliceous	$^3/_4$	$^3/_4$	$^3/_4$	$^3/_4$	$^3/_4$	$^3/_4$	$^3/_4$	1	$1^1/_4$	$1^5/_8$
Carbonate	$^3/_4$	$^3/_4$	$^3/_4$	$^3/_4$	$^3/_4$	$^3/_4$	$^3/_4$	$^3/_4$	$1^1/_4$	$1^1/_4$
Sand-lightweight or lightweight	$^3/_4$	$^3/_4$	$^3/_4$	$^3/_4$	$^3/_4$	$^3/_4$	$^3/_4$	$^3/_4$	$1^1/_4$	$1^1/_4$

For SI: 1 inch = 25.4 mm.

TABLE 721.2.3(2)
COVER THICKNESS FOR PRESTRESSED CONCRETE FLOOR OR ROOF SLABS (inches)

CONCRETE AGGREGATE TYPE	FIRE-RESISTANCE RATING (hours)									
	Restrained					Unrestrained				
	1	$1^1/_2$	2	3	4	1	$1^1/_2$	2	3	4
Siliceous	$^3/_4$	$^3/_4$	$^3/_4$	$^3/_4$	$^3/_4$	$1^1/_8$	$1^1/_2$	$1^3/_4$	$2^3/_8$	$2^3/_4$
Carbonate	$^3/_4$	$^3/_4$	$^3/_4$	$^3/_4$	$^3/_4$	1	$1^3/_8$	$1^5/_8$	$2^1/_8$	$2^1/_4$
Sand-lightweight or lightweight	$^3/_4$	$^3/_4$	$^3/_4$	$^3/_4$	$^3/_4$	1	$1^3/_8$	$1^1/_2$	2	$2^1/_4$

For SI: 1 inch = 25.4 mm.

TABLE 721.2.3(3)
MINIMUM COVER FOR MAIN REINFORCING BARS OF REINFORCED CONCRETE BEAMS[c] (APPLICABLE TO ALL TYPES OF STRUCTURAL CONCRETE)

RESTRAINED OR UNRESTRAINED[a]	BEAM WIDTH[b] (inches)	FIRE-RESISTANCE RATING (hours)				
		1	$1^1/_2$	2	3	4
Restrained	5	$^3/_4$	$^3/_4$	$^3/_4$	1[a]	$1^1/_4$[a]
	7	$^3/_4$	$^3/_4$	$^3/_4$	$^3/_4$	$^3/_4$
	≥10	$^3/_4$	$^3/_4$	$^3/_4$	$^3/_4$	$^3/_4$
Unrestrained	5	$^3/_4$	1	$1^1/_4$	-	-
	7	$^3/_4$	$^3/_4$	$^3/_4$	$1^3/_4$	3
	≥10	$^3/_4$	$^3/_4$	$^3/_4$	1	$1^3/_4$

For SI:1 inch = 25.4 mm, 1 foot = 304.8 mm.

a. Tabulated values for restrained assemblies apply to beams spaced more than 4 feet on center. For restrained beams spaced 4 feet or less on center, minimum cover of $^3/_4$ inch is adequate for ratings of 4 hours or less.

b. For beam widths between the tabulated values, the minimum cover thickness can be determined by direct interpolation.

c. The cover for an individual reinforcing bar is the minimum thickness of concrete between the surface of the bar and the fire-exposed surface of the beam. For beams in which several bars are used, the cover for corner bars used in the calculation shall be reduced to one-half of the actual value. The cover for an individual bar must be not less than one-half of the value given in Table 721.2.3(3) nor less than $^3/_4$ inch.

721.2.4.1 Minimum size. The minimum overall dimensions of reinforced concrete columns for fire-resistance ratings of 1 hour to 4 hours shall comply with Table 721.2.4.

TABLE 721.2.4
MINIMUM DIMENSION OF CONCRETE COLUMNS (inches)

TYPES OF CONCRETE	FIRE-RESISTANCE RATING (hours)				
	1	$1^1/_2$	2[a]	3[a]	4[b]
Siliceous	8	9	10	12	14
Carbonate	8	9	10	11	12
Sand-lightweight	8	$8^1/_2$	9	$10^1/_2$	12

For SI: 1 inch = 25 mm.

a. The minimum dimension is permitted to be reduced to 8 inches for rectangular columns with two parallel sides at least 36 inches in length.

b. The minimum dimension is permitted to be reduced to 10 inches for rectangular columns with two parallel sides at least 36 inches in length.

721.2.4.2 Minimum cover for R/C columns. The minimum thickness of concrete cover to the main longitudinal reinforcement in columns, regardless of the type of aggregate used in the concrete, shall not be less than 1 inch (25 mm) times the number of hours of required fire resistance or 2 inches (51 mm), whichever is less.

721.2.4.3 Columns built into walls. The minimum dimensions of Table 721.2.4 do not apply to a reinforced concrete column that is built into a concrete or masonry wall provided all of the following are met:

1. The fire-resistance rating for the wall is equal to or greater than the required rating of the column;

2. The main longitudinal reinforcing in the column has cover not less than that required by Section 721.2.4.2; and

3. Openings in the wall are protected in accordance with Table 715.4.

Where openings in the wall are not protected as required by Section 715.4, the minimum dimension of columns required to have a fire-resistance rating of 3 hours or less shall be 8 inches (203 mm), and 10 inches (254 mm) for columns required to have a fire-resistance rating of 4 hours, regardless of the type of aggregate used in the concrete.

721.2.4.4 Precast cover units for steel columns. See Section 721.5.1.4.

TABLE 721.2.3(4)
MINIMUM COVER FOR PRESTRESSED CONCRETE BEAMS 8 INCHES OR GREATER IN WIDTH

RESTRAINED OR UNRESTRAINED[a]	CONCRETE AGGREGATE TYPE	BEAM WIDTH[b] (inches)	FIRE-RESISTANCE RATING (hours)				
			1	$1^1/_2$	2	3	4
Restrained	Carbonate or siliceous	8	$1^1/_2$	$1^1/_2$	$1^1/_2$	$1^3/_4$[a]	$2^1/_2$[a]
	Carbonate or siliceous	≥12	$1^1/_2$	$1^1/_2$	$1^1/_2$	$1^1/_2$	$1^7/_8$[a]
	Sand lightweight	8	$1^1/_2$	$1^1/_2$	$1^1/_2$	$1^1/_2$	2[a]
	Sand lightweight	≥12	$1^1/_2$	$1^1/_2$	$1^1/_2$	$1^1/_2$	$1^5/_8$[a]
Unrestrained	Carbonate or siliceous	8	$1^1/_2$	$1^3/_4$	$2^1/_2$	5[c]	-
	Carbonate or siliceous	≥12	$1^1/_2$	$1^1/_2$	$1^7/_8$[a]	$2^1/_2$	3
	Sand lightweight	8	$1^1/_2$	$1^1/_2$	2	$3^1/_4$	-
	Sand lightweight	≥12	$1^1/_2$	$1^1/_2$	$1^5/_8$	2	$2^1/_2$

For SI: 1 inch = 25.4 mm, 1 foot = 304.8 mm.

a. Tabulated values for restrained assemblies apply to beams spaced more than 4 feet on center. For restrained beams spaced 4 feet or less on center, minimum cover of $^3/_4$ inch is adequate for 4-hour ratings or less.

b. For beam widths between 8 inches and 12 inches, minimum cover thickness can be determined by direct interpolation.

c. Not practical for 8-inch-wide beam but shown for purposes of interpolation.

TABLE 721.2.3(5)
MINIMUM COVER FOR PRESTRESSED CONCRETE BEAMS OF ALL WIDTHS

RESTRAINED OR UNRESTRAINED[a]	CONCRETE AGGREGATE TYPE	BEAM AREA[b] A (square inches)	FIRE-RESISTANCE RATING (hours)				
			1	$1^1/_2$	2	3	4
Restrained	All	40 ≤ A ≤ 150	$1^1/_2$	$1^1/_2$	2	$2^1/_2$	-
	Carbonate or siliceous	150 <A ≤ 300	$1^1/_2$	$1^1/_2$	$1^1/_2$	$1^3/_4$	$2^1/_2$
		300 <A	$1^1/_2$	$1^1/_2$	$1^1/_2$	$1^1/_2$	2
	Sand lightweight	150 <A	$1^1/_2$	$1^1/_2$	$1^1/_2$	$1^1/_2$	2
Unrestrained	All	40 ≤A ≤ 150	2	$2^1/_2$	-	-	-
	Carbonate or siliceous	150 <A ≤ 300	$1^1/_2$	$1^3/_4$	$2^1/_2$	-	-
		300 < A	$1^1/_2$	$1^1/_2$	2	3[c]	4[c]
	Sand lightweight	150 < A	$1^1/_2$	$1^1/_2$	2	3[c]	4[c]

For SI: 1 inch = 25.4 mm, 1 foot = 304.8 mm.

a. Tabulated values for restrained assemblies apply to beams spaced more than 4 feet on center. For restrained beams spaced 4 feet or less on center, minimum cover of $^3/_4$ inch is adequate for 4-hour ratings or less.

b. The cross-sectional area of a stem is permitted to include a portion of the area in the flange, provided the width of the flange used in the calculation does not exceed three times the average width of the stem.

c. U-shaped or hooped stirrups spaced not to exceed the depth of the member and having a minimum cover of 1 inch shall be provided.

721.3 Concrete masonry. The provisions of this section contain procedures by which the fire-resistance ratings of concrete masonry are established by calculations.

721.3.1 Equivalent thickness. The equivalent thickness of concrete masonry construction shall be determined in accordance with the provisions of this section.

721.3.1.1 Concrete masonry unit plus finishes. The equivalent thickness of concrete masonry assemblies, T_{ea}, shall be computed as the sum of the equivalent thickness of the concrete masonry unit, T_e, as determined by Section 721.3.1.2, 721.3.1.3, or 721.3.1.4, plus the equivalent thickness of finishes, T_{ef}, determined in accordance with Section 721.3.2:

$$T_{ea} = T_e + T_{ef} \qquad \text{(Equation 7-6)}$$

$T_e = V_n/LH$ = Equivalent thickness of concrete masonry unit (inch) (mm).

where:

V_n = Net volume of masonry unit (inch^3) (mm^3).

L = Specified length of masonry unit (inch) (mm).

H = Specified height of masonry unit (inch) (mm).

721.3.1.2 Ungrouted or partially grouted construction. T_e shall be the value obtained for the concrete masonry unit determined in accordance with ASTM C 140.

721.3.1.3 Solid grouted construction. The equivalent thickness, T_e, of solid grouted concrete masonry units is the actual thickness of the unit.

721.3.1.4 Airspaces and cells filled with loose-fill material. The equivalent thickness of completely filled hollow concrete masonry is the actual thickness of the unit when loose-fill materials are: sand, pea gravel, crushed stone, or slag that meet ASTM C 33 requirements; pumice, scoria, expanded shale, expanded clay, expanded slate, expanded slag, expanded fly ash, or cinders that comply with ASTM C 331; or perlite or vermiculite meeting the requirements of ASTM C 549 and ASTM C 516, respectively.

721.3.2 Concrete masonry walls. The fire-resistance rating of walls and partitions constructed of concrete masonry units shall be determined from Table 721.3.2.

The rating shall be based on the equivalent thickness of the masonry and type of aggregate used.

721.3.2.1 Finish on nonfire-exposed side. Where plaster or gypsum wallboard is applied to the side of the wall not exposed to fire, the contribution of the finish to the total fire-resistance rating shall be determined as follows: The thickness of gypsum wallboard or plaster shall be corrected by multiplying the actual thickness of the finish by applicable factor determined from Table 721.2.1.4(1). This corrected thickness of finish shall be added to the equivalent thickness of masonry and the fire-resistance rating of the masonry and finish determined from Table 721.3.2.

721.3.2.2 Finish on fire-exposed side. Where plaster or gypsum wallboard is applied to the fire-exposed side of the wall, the contribution of the finish to the total fire-resistance rating shall be determined as follows: The time assigned to the finish as established by Table 721.2.1.4(2) shall be added to the fire-resistance rating determined in Section 721.3.2 for the masonry alone, or in Section 721.3.2.1 for the masonry and finish on the nonfire-exposed side.

721.3.2.3 Nonsymmetrical assemblies. For a wall having no finish on one side or having different types or thicknesses of finish on each side, the calculation procedures of this section shall be performed twice, assuming either side of the wall to be the fire-exposed side. The fire-resistance rating of the wall shall not exceed the lower of the two values calculated.

Exception: For exterior walls with more than 5 feet (1524 mm) of horizontal separation, the fire shall be assumed to occur on the interior side only.

721.3.2.4 Minimum concrete masonry fire-resistance rating. Where the finish applied to a concrete masonry wall contributes to its fire-resistance rating, the masonry alone shall provide not less than one-half the total required fire-resistance rating.

721.3.2.5 Attachment of finishes. Installation of finishes shall be as follows:

1. Gypsum wallboard and gypsum lath applied to concrete masonry or concrete walls shall be secured to wood or steel furring members spaced not more than 16 inches (406 mm) on center (o.c.).

TABLE 721.3.2
MINIMUM EQUIVALENT THICKNESS (inches) OF BEARING OR NONBEARING CONCRETE MASONRY WALLS[a,b,c,d]

| TYPE OF AGGREGATE | FIRE-RESISTANCE RATING (hours) | | | | | | | | | | | | | | |
	1/2	3/4	1	1 1/4	1 1/2	1 3/4	2	2 1/4	2 1/2	2 3/4	3	3 1/4	3 1/2	3 3/4	4
Pumice or expanded slag	1.5	1.9	2.1	2.5	2.7	3.0	3.2	3.4	3.6	3.8	4.0	4.2	4.4	4.5	4.7
Expanded shale, clay or slate	1.8	2.2	2.6	2.9	3.3	3.4	3.6	3.8	4.0	4.2	4.4	4.6	4.8	4.9	5.1
Limestone, cinders or unexpanded slag	1.9	2.3	2.7	3.1	3.4	3.7	4.0	4.3	4.5	4.8	5.0	5.2	5.5	5.7	5.9
Calcareous or siliceous gravel	2.0	2.4	2.8	3.2	3.6	3.9	4.2	4.5	4.8	5.0	5.3	5.5	5.8	6.0	6.2

For SI: 1 inch = 25.4 mm.

a. Values between those shown in the table can be determined by direct interpolation.

b. Where combustible members are framed into the wall, the thickness of solid material between the end of each member and the opposite face of the wall, or between members set in from opposite sides, shall be not less than 93 percent of the thickness shown in the table.

c. Requirements of ASTM C 55, ASTM C 73 or ASTM C 90 shall apply.

d. Minimum required equivalent thickness corresponding to the hourly fire-resistance rating for units with a combination of aggregate shall be determined by linear interpolation based on the percent by volume of each aggregate used in manufacture.

2. Gypsum wallboard shall be installed with the long dimension parallel to the furring members and shall have all joints finished.

3. Other aspects of the installation of finishes shall comply with the applicable provisions of Chapters 7 and 25.

721.3.3 Multiwythe masonry walls. The fire-resistance rating of wall assemblies constructed of multiple wythes of masonry materials shall be permitted to be based on the fire-resistance rating period of each wythe and the continuous airspace between each wythe in accordance with the following formula:

$$R_A = (R_1^{0.59} + R_2^{0.59} + ... + R_n^{0.59} + A_1 + A_2 + ... + A_n)^{1.7}$$

(Equation 7-7)

where:

R_A = Fire-resistance rating of the assembly (hours).

$R_1, R_2, ..., R_n$ = Fire-resistance rating of wythes for 1, 2, n (hours), respectively.

$A_1, A_2, ..., A_n$ = 0.30, factor for each continuous airspace for 1, 2, ...n, respectively, having a depth of $1/2$ inch (12.7 mm) or more between wythes.

721.3.4 Concrete masonry lintels. Fire-resistance ratings for concrete masonry lintels shall be determined based upon the nominal thickness of the lintel and the minimum thickness of concrete masonry or concrete, or any combination thereof, covering the main reinforcing bars, as determined according to Table 721.3.4, or by approved alternate methods.

TABLE 721.3.4
MINIMUM COVER OF LONGITUDINAL REINFORCEMENT IN FIRE-RESISTANCE-RATED REINFORCED CONCRETE MASONRY LINTELS (inches)

NOMINAL WIDTH OF LINTEL (inches)	FIRE-RESISTANCE RATING (hours)			
	1	2	3	4
6	$1^1/_2$	2	-	-
8	$1^1/_2$	$1^1/_2$	$1^3/_4$	3
10 or greater	$1^1/_2$	$1^1/_2$	$1^1/_2$	$1^3/_4$

For SI: 1 inch = 25.4 mm.

721.3.5 Concrete masonry columns. The fire-resistance rating of concrete masonry columns shall be determined based upon the least plan dimension of the column in accordance with Table 721.3.5 or by approved alternate methods.

TABLE 721.3.5
MINIMUM DIMENSION OF CONCRETE MASONRY COLUMNS (inches)

FIRE-RESISTANCE RATING (hours)			
1	2	3	4
8 inches	10 inches	12 inches	14 inches

For SI:1 inch = 25.4 mm.

721.4 Clay brick and tile masonry. The provisions of this section contain procedures by which the fire-resistance ratings of clay brick and tile masonry are established by calculations.

721.4.1 Masonry walls. The fire-resistance rating of masonry walls shall be based upon the equivalent thickness as calculated in accordance with this section. The calculation shall take into account finishes applied to the wall and airspaces between wythes in multiwythe construction.

721.4.1.1 Equivalent thickness. The fire-resistance ratings of walls or partitions constructed of solid or hollow clay masonry units shall be determined from Table 721.4.1(1) or 721.4.1(2). The equivalent thickness of the clay masonry unit shall be determined by Equation 7-8 when using Table 721.4.1(1). The fire-resistance rating determined from Table 721.4.1(1) shall be permitted to be used in the calculated fire-resistance rating procedure in Section 721.4.2.

$$T_e = V_n/LH$$

(Equation 7-8)

where:

T_e = The equivalent thickness of the clay masonry unit (inches).

V_n = The net volume of the clay masonry unit (inch^3).

L = The specified length of the clay masonry unit (inches).

H = The specified height of the clay masonry unit (inches).

TABLE 721.4.1(1)
FIRE-RESISTANCE PERIODS OF CLAY MASONRY WALLS

MATERIAL TYPE	MINIMUM REQUIRED EQUIVALENT THICKNESS FOR FIRE RESISTANCE[a,b,c](inches)			
	1 hour	2 hour	3 hour	4 hour
Solid brick of clay or shale[d]	2.7	3.8	4.9	6.0
Hollow brick or tile of clay or shale, unfilled	2.3	3.4	4.3	5.0
Hollow brick or tile of clay or shale, grouted or filled with materials specified in Section 721.4.1.1.3	3.0	4.4	5.5	6.6

For SI: 1 inch = 25.4 mm.

a. Equivalent thickness as determined from Section 721.4.1.1.

b. Calculated fire resistance between the hourly increments listed shall be determined by linear interpolation.

c. Where combustible members are framed in the wall, the thickness of solid material between the end of each member and the opposite face of the wall, or between members set in from opposite sides, shall be not less than 93 percent of the thickness shown.

d. For units in which the net cross-sectional area of cored brick in any plane parallel to the surface containing the cores is at least 75 percent of the gross cross-sectional area measured in the same plane.

TABLE 721.4.1(2)
FIRE-RESISTANCE RATINGS FOR BEARING STEEL FRAME BRICK VENEER WALLS OR PARTITIONS

WALL OR PARTITION ASSEMBLY	PLASTER SIDE EXPOSED (hours)	BRICK FACED SIDE EXPOSED (hours)
Outside facing of steel studs: $1/2$" wood fiberboard sheathing next to studs, $3/4$"airspace formed with $3/4$" × $1^5/8$" wood strips placed over the fiberboard and secured to the studs;metal or wire lath nailed to such strips, $3^3/4$" brick veneer held in place by filling $3/4$" airspace between the brick and lath with mortar. Inside facing of studs: $3/4$" unsanded gypsum plaster on metal or wire lath attached to $5/16$" wood strips secured to edges of the studs.	1.5	4
Outside facing of steel studs: 1" insulation board sheathing attached to studs, 1" airspace, and $3^3/4$"brick veneer attached to steel frame with metal ties every 5th course. Inside facing of studs: $7/8$" sanded gypsum plaster (1:2 mix) applied on metal or wire lath attached directly to the studs.	1.5	4
Same as above except use $7/8$" vermiculite-gypsum plaster or 1" sanded gypsum plaster (1:2 mix) applied to metal or wire.	2	4
Outside facing of steel studs: $1/2$" gypsum sheathing board, attached to studs, and $3^3/4$"brick veneer attached to steel frame with metal ties every 5th course. Inside facing of studs: $1/2$" sanded gypsum plaster (1:2 mix) applied to $1/2$" perforated gypsum lath securely attached to studs and having strips of metal lath 3 inches wide applied to all horizontal joints of gypsum lath.	2	4

For SI: 1 inch = 25.4 mm.

TABLE 721.4.1(3)
VALUES OF $R_n^{0.59}$

$R_n^{0.59}$	R(hours)
1	1.0
2	1.50
3	1.91
4	2.27

TABLE 721.4.1(4)
COEFFICIENTS FOR PLASTER, pl [a]

THICKNESS OF PLASTER (inch)	ONE SIDE	TWO SIDE
$1/2$	0.3	0.6
$5/8$	0.37	0.75
$3/4$	0.45	0.90

For SI: 1 inch = 25.4 mm.

a. Values listed in table are for 1:3 sanded gypsum plaster.

TABLE 721.4.1(5)
REINFORCED MASONRY LINTELS

NOMINAL LINTEL WIDTH (inches)	MINIMUM LONGITUDINAL REINFORCEMENT COVER FOR FIRE RESISTANCE (inch)			
	1 hour	2 hour	3 hour	4 hour
6	$1^1/2$	2	NP	NP
8	$1^1/2$	$1^1/2$	$1^3/4$	3
10 or more	$1^1/2$	$1^1/2$	$1^1/2$	$1^3/4$

For SI: 1 inch = 25.4 mm.
NP = Not permitted.

TABLE 721.4.1(6)
REINFORCED CLAY MASONRY COLUMNS

COLUMN SIZE	FIRE-RESISTANCE RATING (hour)			
	1	2	3	4
Minimum column dimension (inches)	8	10	12	14

For SI: 1 inch = 25.4 mm.

721.4.1.1.1 Hollow clay units. The equivalent thickness, T_e, shall be the value obtained for hollow clay units as determined in accordance with ASTM C 67.

721.4.1.1.2 Solid grouted clay units. The equivalent thickness of solid grouted clay masonry units shall be taken as the actual thickness of the units.

721.4.1.1.3 Units with filled cores. The equivalent thickness of the hollow clay masonry units is the actual thickness of the unit when completely filled with loose-fill materials of: sand, pea gravel, crushed stone, or slag that meet ASTM C 33 requirements; pumice, scoria, expanded shale, expanded clay, expanded slate, expanded slag, expanded fly ash, or cinders in compliance with ASTM C 331; or perlite or vermiculite meeting the requirements of ASTM C 549 and ASTM C 516, respectively.

721.4.1.2 Plaster finishes. Where plaster is applied to the wall, the total fire-resistance rating shall be determined by the formula:

$$R = (R_n^{0.59} + pl)^{1.7} \qquad \textbf{(Equation 7-9)}$$

where:

R = The fire-resistance rating of the assembly (hours).

R_n = The fire-resistance rating of the individual wall (hours).

pl = Coefficient for thickness of plaster.

Values for $R_n^{0.59}$ for use in Equation 7-9 are given in Table 721.4.1(3). Coefficients for thickness of plaster shall be selected from Table 721.4.1(4) based on the actual thickness of plaster applied to the wall or partition and whether one or two sides of the wall are plastered.

721.4.1.3 Multiwythe walls with airspace. Where a continuous airspace separates multiple wythes of the wall or partition, the total fire-resistance rating shall be determined by the formula:

$$R = (R_1^{0.59} + R_2^{0.59} + ... + R_n^{0.59} + as)^{1.7}$$

(Equation 7-10)

where:

R = The fire-resistance rating of the assembly (hours).

R_1, R_2 and R_n = The fire-resistance rating of the individual wythes (hours).

as = Coefficient for continuous airspace.

Values for $R_n^{0.59}$ for use in Equation 7-10 are given in Table 721.4.1(3). The coefficient for each continuous airspace of $^1/_2$ inch to $3^1/_2$ inches (12.7 to 89 mm) separating two individual wythes shall be 0.3.

721.4.1.4 Nonsymmetrical assemblies. For a wall having no finish on one side or having different types or thicknesses of finish on each side, the calculation procedures of this section shall be performed twice, assuming either side to be the fire-exposed side of the wall. The fire resistance of the wall shall not exceed the lower of the two values determined.

> **Exception:** For exterior walls with more than 5 feet (1524 mm) of horizontal separation, the fire shall be assumed to occur on the interior side only.

721.4.2 Multiwythe walls. The fire-resistance rating for walls or partitions consisting of two or more dissimilar wythes shall be permitted to be determined by the formula:

$$R = (R_1^{0.59} + R_2^{0.59} + ... + R_n^{0.59})^{1.7}$$

(Equation 7-11)

where:

R = The fire-resistance rating of the assembly (hours).

R_1, R_2 and R_n = The fire-resistance rating of the individual wythes (hours).

Values for $R_n^{0.59}$ for use in Equation 7-11 are given in Table 721.4.1(3).

721.4.2.1 Multiwythe walls of different material. For walls that consist of two or more wythes of different materials (concrete or concrete masonry units) in combination with clay masonry units, the fire-resistance rating of the different materials shall be permitted to be determined from Table 721.2.1.1 for concrete; Table 721.3.2 for concrete masonry units or Table 721.4.1(1) or 721.4.1(2) for clay and tile masonry units.

721.4.3 Reinforced clay masonry lintels. Fire-resistance ratings for clay masonry lintels shall be determined based on the nominal width of the lintel and the minimum covering for the longitudinal reinforcement in accordance with Table 721.4.1(5).

721.4.4 Reinforced clay masonry columns. The fire-resistance ratings shall be determined based on the last plan dimension of the column in accordance with Table 721.4.1(6). The minimum cover for longitudinal reinforcement shall be 2 inches (51 mm).

721.5 Steel assemblies. The provisions of this section contain procedures by which the fire-resistance ratings of steel assemblies are established by calculations.

721.5.1 Structural steel columns. The fire-resistance ratings of steel columns shall be based on the size of the element and the type of protection provided in accordance with this section.

721.5.1.1 General. These procedures establish a basis for determining the fire resistance of column assemblies as a function of the thickness of fire-resistant material and, the weight, W, and heated perimeter, D, of steel columns. As used in these sections, W is the average weight of a structural steel column in pounds per linear foot. The heated perimeter, D, is the inside perimeter of the fire-resistant material in inches as illustrated in Figure 721.5.1(1).

$D=4b_f + 2d - 2t_w$ $D=2(a+d)$ $D=2(b_f + d)$

FIGURE 721.5.1(1)
DETERMINATION OF THE HEATED PERIMETER OF
STRUCTURAL STEEL COLUMNS

721.5.1.1.1 Nonload-bearing protection. The application of these procedures shall be limited to column assemblies in which the fire-resistant material is not designed to carry any of the load acting on the column.

721.5.1.1.2 Embedments. In the absence of substantiating fire-endurance test results, ducts, conduit, piping, and similar mechanical, electrical, and plumbing installations shall not be embedded in any required fire-resistant materials.

721.5.1.1.3 Weight-to-perimeter ratio. Table 721.5.1(1) contains weight-to-heated-perimeter ratios (W/D) for both contour and box fire-resistant profiles, for the wide flange shapes most often used as columns. For different fire-resistant protection profiles or column cross sections, the weight-to-heated-perimeter ratios (W/D) shall be determined in accordance with the definitions given in this section.

TABLE 721.5.1(1)
_W/D_ RATIOS FOR STEEL COLUMNS

STRUCTURAL SHAPE	CONTOUR PROFILE	BOX PROFILE	STRUCTURAL SHAPE	CONTOUR PROFILE	BOX PROFILE
W14 × 233	2.49	3.65	W10 × 112	1.78	2.57
× 211	2.28	3.35	× 100	1.61	2.33
× 193	2.10	3.09	× 88	1.43	2.08
× 176	1.93	2.85	× 77	1.26	1.85
× 159	1.75	2.60	× 68	1.13	1.66
× 145	1.61	2.39	× 60	1.00	1.48
× 132	1.52	2.25	× 54	0.91	1.34
× 120	1.39	2.06	× 49	0.83	1.23
× 109	1.27	1.88	× 45	0.87	1.24
× 99	1.16	1.72	× 39	0.76	1.09
× 90	1.06	1.58	× 33	0.65	0.93
× 82	1.20	1.68			
× 74	1.09	1.53	W8 × 67	1.34	1.94
× 68	1.01	1.41	× 58	1.18	1.71
× 61	0.91	1.28	× 48	0.99S	1.44
× 53	0.89	1.21	× 40	0.83	1.23
× 48	0.81	1.10	× 35	0.73	1.08
× 43	0.73	0.99	× 31	0.65	0.97
			× 28	0.67	0.96
W12 × 190	2.46	3.51	× 24	0.58	0.83
× 170	2.22	3.20	× 21	0.57	0.77
× 152	2.01	2.90	× 18	0.49	0.67
× 136	1.82	2.63			
× 120	1.62	2.36	W6 × 25	0.69	1.00
× 106	1.44	2.11	× 20	0.56	0.82
× 96	1.32	1.93	× 16	0.57	0.78
× 87	1.20	1.76	× 15	0.42	0.63
× 79	1.10	1.61	× 12	0.43	0.60
× 72	1.00	1.48	× 9	0.33	0.46
× 65	0.91	1.35			
× 58	0.91	1.31	W5 × 19	0.64	0.93
× 53	0.84	1.20	× 16	0.54	0.80
× 50	0.89	1.23			
× 45	0.81	1.12	W4 × 13	0.54	0.79
× 40	0.72	1.00			

For SI: 1 pound per linear foot per inch = 0.059 kg/m/mm.

TABLE 721.5.1(2)
PROPERTIES OF CONCRETE

PROPERTY	NORMAL-WEIGHT CONCRETE	STRUCTURAL LIGHTWEIGHT CONCRETE
Thermal conductivity (k_c)	0.95 Btu/hr ft °F	0.35 Btu/hr ft °F
Specific heat (c_c)	0.20 Btu/lb °F	0.20 Btu/lb °F
Density (P_c)	145 lb/ft^3	110 lb/ft^3
Equilibrium (free) moisture content (m) by volume	4%	5%

For SI: 1 inch = 25.4 mm, 1 foot = 304.8 mm, 1 lb/ft^3 = 16.0185 kg/m^3, Btu/hr ft °F = 1.731 W/(m • K).

TABLE 721.5.1(3)
THERMAL CONDUCTIVITY OF CONCRETE OR CLAY MASONRY UNITS

DENSITY (d_m) OF UNITS (lb/ft^3)	THERMAL CONDUCTIVITY (K) OF UNITS (Btu/hr ft °F)
Concrete Masonry Units	
80	0.207
85	0.228
90	0.252
95	0.278
100	0.308
105	0.340
110	0.376
115	0.416
120	0.459
125	0.508
130	0.561
135	0.620
140	0.685
145	0.758
150	0.837
Clay Masonry Units	
120	1.25
130	2.25

For SI: 1 pound per cubic foot = 16.0185 kg/m^3, Btu per hour foot °F = 1.731 W/(m K).

TABLE 721.5.1(4)
WEIGHT-TO-HEATED-PERIMETER RATIOS (*W/D*) FOR TYPICAL WIDE FLANGE BEAM AND GIRDER SHAPES

STRUCTURAL SHAPE	CONTOUR PROFILE	BOX PROFILE	STRUCTURAL SHAPE	CONTOUR PROFILE	BOX PROFILE
W36 × 300	2.47	3.33	× 68	0.92	1.21
× 280	2.31	3.12	× 62	0.92	1.14
× 260	2.16	2.92	× 55	0.82	1.02
× 245	2.04	2.76			
× 230	1.92	2.61	W21 × 147	1.83	2.60
× 210	1.94	2.45	× 132	1.66	2.35
× 194	1.80	2.28	× 122	1.54	2.19
× 182	1.69	2.15	× 111	1.41	2.01
× 170	1.59	2.01	× 101	1.29	1.84
× 160	1.50	1.90	× 93	1.38	1.80
× 150	1.41	1.79	× 83	1.24	1.62
× 135	1.28	1.63	× 73	1.10	1.44
			× 68	1.03	1.35
W33 × 241	2.11	2.86	× 62	0.94	1.23
× 221	1.94	2.64	× 57	0.93	1.17
× 201	1.78	2.42	× 50	0.83	1.04
× 152	1.51	1.94	× 44	0.73	0.92
× 141	1.41	1.80			
× 130	1.31	1.67	W18 × 119	1.69	2.42
× 118	1.19	1.53	× 106	1.52	2.18
			× 97	1.39	2.01
W30 × 211	2.00	2.74	× 86	1.24	1.80
× 191	1.82	2.50	× 76	1.11	1.60
× 173	1.66	2.28	× 71	1.21	1.59
× 132	1.45	1.85	× 65	1.11	1.47
× 124	1.37	1.75	× 60	1.03	1.36
× 116	1.28	1.65	× 55	0.95	1.26
× 108	1.20	1.54	× 50	0.87	1.15
× 99	1.10	1.42	× 46	0.86	1.09
			× 40	0.75	0.96
W27 × 178	1.85	2.55	× 35	0.66	0.85
× 161	1.68	2.33			
× 146	1.53	2.12	W16 × 100	1.56	2.25
× 114	1.36	1.76	× 89	1.40	2.03
× 102	1.23	1.59	× 77	1.22	1.78
× 94	1.13	1.47	× 67	1.07	1.56
× 84	1.02	1.33	× 57	1.07	1.43
			× 50	0.94	1.26
			× 45	0.85	1.15
W24 × 162	1.85	2.57	× 40	0.76	1.03
× 146	1.68	2.34	× 36	0.69	0.93
× 131	1.52	2.12	× 31	0.65	0.83
× 117	1.36	1.91	× 26	0.55	0.70
× 104	1.22	1.71			
× 94	1.26	1.63	W14 × 132	1.83	3.00
× 84	1.13	1.47	× 120	1.67	2.75
× 76	1.03	1.34	× 109	1.53	2.52

(continued)

TABLE 721.5.1(4)—continued
WEIGHT-TO-HEATED-PERIMETER RATIOS (*W/D*) FOR TYPICAL WIDE FLANGE BEAM AND GIRDER SHAPES

STRUCTURAL SHAPE	CONTOUR PROFILE	BOX PROFILE	STRUCTURAL SHAPE	CONTOUR PROFILE	BOX PROFILE
× 99	1.39	2.31	× 30	0.79	1.12
× 90	1.27	2.11	× 26	0.69	0.98
× 82	1.41	2.12	× 22	0.59	0.84
× 74	1.28	1.93	× 19	0.59	0.78
× 68	1.19	1.78	× 17	0.54	0.70
× 61	1.07	1.61	× 15	0.48	0.63
× 53	1.03	1.48	× 12	0.38	0.51
× 48	0.94	1.35			
× 43	0.85	1.22	W8 × 67	1.61	2.55
× 38	0.79	1.09	× 58	1.41	2.26
× 34	0.71	0.98	× 48	1.18	1.91
× 30	0.63	0.87	× 40	1.00	1.63
× 26	0.61	0.79	× 35	0.88	1.44
× 22	0.52	0.68	× 31	0.79	1.29
			× 28	0.80	1.24
W12 × 87	1.44	2.34	× 24	0.69	1.07
× 79	1.32	2.14	× 21	0.66	0.96
× 72	1.20	1.97	× 18	0.57	0.84
× 65	1.09	1.79	× 15	0.54	0.74
× 58	1.08	1.69	× 13	0.47	0.65
× 53	0.99	1.55	× 10	0.37	0.51
× 50	1.04	1.54			
× 45	0.95	1.40	W6 × 25	0.82	1.33
× 40	0.85	1.25	× 20	0.67	1.09
× 35	0.79	1.11	× 16	0.66	0.96
× 30	0.69	0.96	× 15	0.51	0.83
× 26	0.60	0.84	× 12	0.51	0.75
× 22	0.61	0.77	× 9	0.39	0.57
× 19	0.53	0.67			
× 16	0.45	0.57	W5 × 19	0.76	1.24
× 14	0.40	0.50	× 16	0.65	1.07
W10 × 112	2.14	3.38	W4 × 13	0.65	1.05
× 100	1.93	3.07			
× 88	1.70	2.75			
× 77	1.52	2.45			
× 68	1.35	2.20			
× 60	1.20	1.97			
× 54	1.09	1.79			
× 49	0.99	1.64			
× 45	1.03	1.59			
× 39	0.94	1.40			
× 33	0.77	1.20			

For SI: Pounds per linear foot per inch = 0.059 kg/m/mm.

TABLE 721.5.1(5)
FIRE RESISTANCE OF CONCRETE MASONRY PROTECTED STEEL COLUMNS

COLUMN SIZE	CONCRETE MASONRY DENSITY POUNDS PER CUBIC FOOT	MINIMUM REQUIRED EQUIVALENT THICKNESS FOR FIRE-RESISTANCE RATING OF CONCRETE MASONRY PROTECTION ASSEMBLY, T_e(inches)				COLUMN SIZE	CONCRETE MASONRY DENSITY POUNDS PER CUBIC FOOT	MINIMUM REQUIRED EQUIVALENT THICKNESS FOR FIRE-RESISTANCE RATING OF CONCRETE MASONRY PROTECTION ASSEMBLY, T_e(inches)			
		1-hour	2-hour	3-hour	4-hour			1-hour	2-hour	3-hour	4-hour
W14 × 82	80	0.74	1.61	2.36	3.04	W10 × 68	80	0.72	1.58	2.33	3.01
	100	0.89	1.85	2.67	3.40		100	0.87	1.83	2.65	3.38
	110	0.96	1.97	2.81	3.57		110	0.94	1.95	2.79	3.55
	120	1.03	2.08	2.95	3.73		120	1.01	2.06	2.94	3.72
W14 × 68	80	0.83	1.70	2.45	3.13	W10 × 54	80	0.88	1.76	2.53	3.21
	100	0.99	1.95	2.76	3.49		100	1.04	2.01	2.83	3.57
	110	1.06	2.06	2.91	3.66		110	1.11	2.12	2.98	3.73
	120	1.14	2.18	3.05	3.82		120	1.19	2.24	3.12	3.90
W14 × 53	80	0.91	1.81	2.58	3.27	W10 × 45	80	0.92	1.83	2.60	3.30
	100	1.07	2.05	2.88	3.62		100	1.08	2.07	2.90	3.64
	110	1.15	2.17	3.02	3.78		110	1.16	2.18	3.04	3.80
	120	1.22	2.28	3.16	3.94		120	1.23	2.29	3.18	3.96
W14 × 43	80	1.01	1.93	2.71	3.41	W10 × 33	80	1.06	2.00	2.79	3.49
	100	1.17	2.17	3.00	3.74		100	1.22	2.23	3.07	3.81
	110	1.25	2.28	3.14	3.90		110	1.30	2.34	3.20	3.96
	120	1.32	2.38	3.27	4.05		120	1.37	2.44	3.33	4.12
W12 × 72	80	0.81	1.66	2.41	3.09	W8 × 40	80	0.94	1.85	2.63	3.33
	100	0.91	1.88	2.70	3.43		100	1.10	2.10	2.93	3.67
	110	0.99	1.99	2.84	3.60		110	1.18	2.21	3.07	3.83
	120	1.06	2.10	2.98	3.76		120	1.25	2.32	3.20	3.99
W12 × 58	80	0.88	1.76	2.52	3.21	W8 × 31	80	1.06	2.00	2.78	3.49
	100	1.04	2.01	2.83	3.56		100	1.22	2.23	3.07	3.81
	110	1.11	2.12	2.97	3.73		110	1.29	2.33	3.20	3.97
	120	1.19	2.23	3.11	3.89		120	1.36	2.44	3.33	4.12
W12 × 50	80	0.91	1.81	2.58	3.27	W8 × 24	80	1.14	2.09	2.89	3.59
	100	1.07	2.05	2.88	3.62		100	1.29	2.31	3.16	3.90
	110	1.15	2.17	3.02	3.78		110	1.36	2.42	3.28	4.05
	120	1.22	2.28	3.16	3.94		120	1.43	2.52	3.41	4.20
W12 × 40	80	1.01	1.94	2.72	3.41	W8 × 18	110	1.22	2.20	3.01	3.72
	100	1.17	2.17	3.01	3.75		100	1.36	2.40	3.25	4.01
	110	1.25	2.28	3.14	3.90		110	1.42	2.50	3.37	4.14
	120	1.32	2.39	3.27	4.06		120	1.48	2.59	3.49	4.28

(continued)

TABLE 721.5.1(5)—continued
FIRE RESISTANCE OF CONCRETE MASONRY PROTECTED STEEL COLUMNS

NOMINAL TUBE SIZE (inches)	CONCRETE MASONRY DENSITY, POUNDS PER CUBIC FOOT	MINIMUM REQUIRED EQUIVALENT THICKNESS FOR FIRE-RESISTANCE RATING OF CONCRETE MASONRY PROTECTION ASSEMBLY, T_e (inches)				NOMINAL PIPE SIZE (inches)	CONCRETE MASONRY DENSITY, POUNDS PER CUBIC FOOT	MINIMUM REQUIRED EQUIVALENT THICKNESS FOR FIRE-RESISTANCE RATING OF CONCRETE MASONRY PROTECTION ASSEMBLY, T_e (inches)			
		1-hour	2-hour	3-hour	4-hour			1-hour	2-hour	3-hour	4-hour
4 × 4 × 1/2 wall thickness	80	0.93	1.90	2.71	3.43	4 double extra strong 0.674 wall thickness	80	0.80	1.75	2.56	3.28
	100	1.08	2.13	2.99	3.76		100	0.95	1.99	2.85	3.62
	110	1.16	2.24	3.13	3.91		110	1.02	2.10	2.99	3.78
	120	1.22	2.34	3.26	4.06		120	1.09	2.20	3.12	3.93
4 × 4 × 3/8 wall thickness	80	1.05	2.03	2.84	3.57	4 extra strong 0.337 wall thickness	80	1.12	2.11	2.93	3.65
	100	1.20	2.25	3.11	3.88		100	1.26	2.32	3.19	3.95
	110	1.27	2.35	3.24	4.02		110	1.33	2.42	3.31	4.09
	120	1.34	2.45	3.37	4.17		120	1.40	2.52	3.43	4.23
4 × 4 × 1/4 wall thickness	80	1.21	2.20	3.01	3.73	4 standard 0.237 wall thickness	80	1.26	2.25	3.07	3.79
	100	1.35	2.40	3.26	4.02		100	1.40	2.45	3.31	4.07
	110	1.41	2.50	3.38	4.16		110	1.46	2.55	3.43	4.21
	120	1.48	2.59	3.50	4.30		120	1.53	2.64	3.54	4.34
6 × 6 × 1/2 wall thickness	80	0.82	1.75	2.54	3.25	5 double extra strong 0.750 wall thickness	80	0.70	1.61	2.40	3.12
	100	0.98	1.99	2.84	3.59		100	0.85	1.86	2.71	3.47
	110	1.05	2.10	2.98	3.75		110	0.91	1.97	2.85	3.63
	120	1.12	2.21	3.11	3.91		120	0.98	2.02	2.99	3.79
6 × 6 × 3/8 wall thickness	80	0.96	1.91	2.71	3.42	5 extra strong 0.375 wall thickness	80	1.04	2.01	2.83	3.54
	100	1.12	2.14	3.00	3.75		100	1.19	2.23	3.09	3.85
	110	1.19	2.25	3.13	3.90		110	1.26	2.34	3.22	4.00
	120	1.26	2.35	3.26	4.05		120	1.32	2.44	3.34	4.14
6 × 6 × 1/4 wall thickness	80	1.14	2.11	2.92	3.63	5 standard 0.258 wall thickness	80	1.20	2.19	3.00	3.72
	100	1.29	2.32	3.18	3.93		100	1.34	2.39	3.25	4.00
	110	1.36	2.43	3.30	4.08		110	1.41	2.49	3.37	4.14
	120	1.42	2.52	3.43	4.22		120	1.47	2.58	3.49	4.28
8 × 8 × 1/2 wall thickness	80	0.77	1.66	2.44	3.13	6 double extra strong 0.864 wall thickness	80	0.59	1.46	2.23	2.92
	100	0.92	1.91	2.75	3.49		100	0.73	1.71	2.54	3.29
	110	1.00	2.02	2.89	3.66		110	0.80	1.82	2.69	3.47
	120	1.07	2.14	3.03	3.82		120	0.86	1.93	2.83	3.63
8 × 8 × 3/8 wall thickness	80	0.91	1.84	2.63	3.33	6 extra strong 0.432 wall thickness	80	0.94	1.90	2.70	3.42
	100	1.07	2.08	2.92	3.67		100	1.10	2.13	2.98	3.74
	110	1.14	2.19	3.06	3.83		110	1.17	2.23	3.11	3.89
	120	1.21	2.29	3.19	3.98		120	1.24	2.34	3.24	4.04
8 × 8 × 1/4 wall thickness	80	1.10	2.06	2.86	3.57	6 standard 0.280 wall thickness	80	1.14	2.12	2.93	3.64
	100	1.25	2.28	3.13	3.87		100	1.29	2.33	3.19	3.94
	110	1.32	2.38	3.25	4.02		110	1.36	2.43	3.31	4.08
	120	1.39	2.48	3.38	4.17		120	1.42	2.53	3.43	4.22

For SI: 1 inch = 25.4 mm, 1 pound per cubic feet = 16.02 kg/m³.

Note: Tabulated values assume 1-inch air gap between masonry and steel section.

TABLE 721.5.1(6)
FIRE RESISTANCE OF CLAY MASONRY PROTECTED STEEL COLUMNS

COLUMN SIZE	CLAY MASONRY DENSITY, POUNDS PER CUBIC FOOT	MINIMUM REQUIRED EQUIVALENT THICKNESS FOR FIRE-RESISTANCE RATING OF CLAY MASONRY PROTECTION ASSEMBLY, T_e(inches)				COLUMN SIZE	CLAY MASONRY DENSITY, POUNDS PER CUBIC FOOT	MINIMUM REQUIRED EQUIVALENT THICKNESS FOR FIRE-RESISTANCE RATING OF CLAY MASONRY PROTECTION ASSEMBLY, T_e(inches)			
		1-hour	2-hour	3-hour	4-hour			1-hour	2-hour	3-hour	4-hour
W14 × 82	120	1.23	2.42	3.41	4.29	W10 × 68	120	1.27	2.46	3.26	4.35
	130	1.40	2.70	3.78	4.74		130	1.44	2.75	3.83	4.80
W14 × 68	120	1.34	2.54	3.54	4.43	W10 × 54	120	1.40	2.61	3.62	4.51
	130	1.51	2.82	3.91	4.87		130	1.58	2.89	3.98	4.95
W14 × 53	120	1.43	2.65	3.65	4.54	W10 × 45	120	1.44	2.66	3.67	4.57
	130	1.61	2.93	4.02	4.98		130	1.62	2.95	4.04	5.01
W14 × 43	120	1.54	2.76	3.77	4.66	W10 × 33	120	1.59	2.82	3.84	4.73
	130	1.72	3.04	4.13	5.09		130	1.77	3.10	4.20	5.13
W12 × 72	120	1.32	2.52	3.51	4.40	W8 × 40	120	1.47	2.70	3.71	4.61
	130	1.50	2.80	3.88	4.84		130	1.65	2.98	4.08	5.04
W12 × 58	120	1.40	2.61	3.61	4.50	W8 × 31	120	1.59	2.82	3.84	4.73
	130	1.57	2.89	3.98	4.94		130	1.77	3.10	4.20	5.17
W12 × 50	120	1.43	2.65	3.66	4.55	W8 × 24	120	1.66	2.90	3.92	4.82
	130	1.61	2.93	4.02	4.99		130	1.84	3.18	4.28	5.25
W12 × 40	120	1.54	2.77	3.78	4.67	W8 × 18	120	1.75	3.00	4.01	4.91
	130	1.72	3.05	4.14	5.10		130	1.93	3.27	4.37	5.34

STEEL TUBING						STEEL PIPE					
NOMINAL TUBE SIZE (inches)	CLAY MASONRY DENSITY, POUNDS PER CUBIC FOOT	MINIMUM REQUIRED EQUIVALENT THICKNESS FOR FIRE-RESISTANCE RATING OF CLAY MASONRY PROTECTION ASSEMBLY, T_e(inches)				NOMINAL PIPE SIZE (inches)	CLAY MASONRY DENSITY, POUNDS PER CUBIC FOOT	MINIMUM REQUIRED EQUIVALENT THICKNESS FOR FIRE-RESISTANCE RATING OF CLAY MASONRY PROTECTION ASSEMBLY, T_e(inches)			
		1-hour	2-hour	3-hour	4-hour			1-hour	2-hour	3-hour	4-hour
4 × 4 × $^1/_2$ wall thickness	120	1.44	2.72	3.76	4.68	4 double extra strong 0.674 wall	120	1.26	2.55	3.60	4.52
	130	1.62	3.00	4.12	5.11		130	1.42	2.82	3.96	4.95
4 × 4 × $^3/_8$ wall thickness	120	1.56	2.84	3.88	4.78	4 extra strong 0.337 wall thickness	120	1.60	2.89	3.92	4.83
	130	1.74	3.12	4.23	5.21		130	1.77	3.16	4.28	5.25
4 × 4 × $^1/_4$ wall thickness	120	1.72	2.99	4.02	4.92	4 standard 0.237 wall thickness	120	1.74	3.02	4.05	4.95
	130	1.89	3.26	4.37	5.34		130	1.92	3.29	4.40	5.37
6 × 6 × $^1/_2$ wall thickness	120	1.33	2.58	3.62	4.52	5 double extra strong 0.750 wall	120	1.17	2.44	3.48	4.40
	130	1.50	2.86	3.98	4.96		130	1.33	2.72	3.84	4.83
6 × 6 × $^3/_8$ wall thickness	120	1.48	2.74	3.76	4.67	5 extra strong 0.375 wall thickness	120	1.55	2.82	3.85	4.76
	130	1.65	3.01	4.13	5.10		130	1.72	3.09	4.21	5.18
6 × 6 × $^1/_4$ wall thickness	120	1.66	2.91	3.94	4.84	5 standard 0.258 wall thickness	120	1.71	2.97	4.00	4.90
	130	1.83	3.19	4.30	5.27		130	1.88	3.24	4.35	5.32

(continued)

TABLE 721.5.1(6)—continued
FIRE RESISTANCE OF CLAY MASONRY PROTECTED STEEL COLUMNS

STEEL TUBING						STEEL PIPE					
NOMINAL TUBE SIZE (inches)	CLAY MASONRY DENSITY, POUNDS PER CUBIC FOOT	MINIMUM REQUIRED EQUIVALENT THICKNESS FOR FIRE-RESISTANCE RATING OF CLAY MASONRY PROTECTION ASSEMBLY, T_e (inches)				NOMINAL PIPE SIZE (inches)	CLAY MASONRY DENSITY, POUNDS PER CUBIC FOOT	MINIMUM REQUIRED EQUIVALENT THICKNESS FOR FIRE-RESISTANCE RATING OF CLAY MASONRY PROTECTION ASSEMBLY, T_e (inches)			
		1-hour	2-hour	3-hour	4-hour			1-hour	2-hour	3-hour	4-hour
8 × 8 × $^1/_2$ wall thickness	120	1.27	2.50	3.52	4.42	6 double extra strong 0.864 wall thickness	120	1.04	2.28	3.32	4.23
	130	1.44	2.78	3.89	4.86		130	1.19	2.60	3.68	4.67
8 × 8 × $^3/_8$ wall thickness	120	1.43	2.67	3.69	4.59	6 extra strong 0.432 wall thickness	120	1.45	2.71	3.75	4.65
	130	1.60	2.95	4.05	5.02		130	1.62	2.99	4.10	5.08
8 × 8 × $^1/_4$ wall thickness	120	1.62	2.87	3.89	4.78	6 standard 0.280 wall thickness	120	1.65	2.91	3.94	4.84
	130	1.79	3.14	4.24	5.21		130	1.82	3.19	4.30	5.27

TABLE 721.5.1(7)
MINIMUM COVER (inch) FOR STEEL COLUMNS ENCASED IN NORMAL-WEIGHT CONCRETE[a] [FIGURE 721.5.1(6)(c)]

STRUCTURAL SHAPE	FIRE-RESISTANCE RATING (hours)				
	1	1½	2	3	4
W14 × 233				1½	2
× 176			1		
× 132		1			2½
× 90	1			2	
× 61					
× 48		1½	1½	2½	3
× 43		1½			
W12 × 152		1	1		2½
× 96				2	
× 65	1				
× 50		1½	1½	2½	3
× 40		1½			
W10 × 88	1			2	
× 49			1½		3
× 45		1½			
× 39	1			2½	
× 33			2		3½
W8 × 67		1	1½		3
× 58					
× 48				2½	
× 31	1	1½			3½
× 21			2		
× 18				3	4
W6 × 25		1½	2		3½
× 20				3	
× 16	1	2			4
× 15	1½		2½		
× 9				3½	

For SI: 1 inch = 25.4 mm.

a. The tabulated thicknesses are based upon the assumed properties of normal-weight concrete given in Table 721.5.1(2).

TABLE 721.5.1(8)
MINIMUM COVER (inch) FOR STEEL COLUMNS ENCASED IN STRUCTURAL LIGHTWEIGHT CONCRETE[a] [FIGURE 721.5.1(6)(c)]

STRUCTURAL SHAPE	FIRE-RESISTANCE RATING (HOURS)				
	1	1½	2	3	4
W14 × 233				1	1½
× 193					
× 74	1	1	1	1½	2
× 61					2½
× 43		1½	2		
W12 × 65				1½	2
× 53	1	1	1		2½
× 40		1½		2	
W10 × 112				1½	2
× 88	1		1		2½
× 60		1		2	
× 33		1½			
W8 × 35	1			2	2½
× 28		1			3
× 24		1½	1½	2½	
× 18		1½			

For SI: 1 inch = 25.4 mm.

a. The tabulated thicknesses are based upon the assumed properties of structural lightweight concrete given in Table 721.5.1(2).

TABLE 721.5.1(9)
MINIMUM COVER (inch) FOR STEEL COLUMNS IN NORMAL-WEIGHT PRECAST COVERS[a] [FIGURE 721.5.1(6)(a)]

STRUCTURAL SHAPE	FIRE-RESISTANCE RATING (hours)				
	1	1½	2	3	4
W14 × 233	1½	1½	1½	2½	3
× 211	1½	1½	1½	2½	3½
× 176	1½	1½	2	3	3½
× 145	1½	1½	2	3	3½
× 109	1½	1½	2	3	3½
× 99	1½	2	2	3	4
× 61	2	2	2½	3½	4
× 43	2	2	2½	3½	4½
W12 × 190	1½	1½	1½	2½	3½
× 152	1½	1½	1½	2½	3½
× 120	1½	1½	2	3	4
× 96	1½	1½	2	3	4
× 87	1½	1½	2	3	4
× 58	1½	2	2	3	4
× 40	2	2	2½	3½	4½
W10 × 112	1½	1½	2	3	3½
× 88	1½	1½	2	3	4
× 77	1½	1½	2	3	4
× 54	2	2	2½	3½	4½
× 33	2	2	2½	3½	4½
W8 × 67	1½	1½	2	3	4
× 58	1½	1½	2	3	4
× 48	1½	2	2½	3½	4
× 28	1½	2	2½	3½	4
× 21	2	2½	3	4	4½
× 18	2	2½	3	4	4½
W6 × 25	1½	2	2½	3½	4½
× 20	1½	2	2½	3½	4½
× 16	1½	2	3	4	4½
× 12	2	2½	3	4	5
× 9	2	2½	3	4	5

For SI: 1 inch = 25.4 mm.

a. The tabulated thicknesses are based upon the assumed properties of normal-weight concrete given in Table 721.5.1(2).

TABLE 721.5.1(10)
MINIMUM COVER (inch) FOR STEEL COLUMNS IN STRUCTURAL LIGHTWEIGHT PRECAST COVERS[a] [FIGURE 721.5.1(6)(a)]

STRUCTURAL SHAPE	FIRE-RESISTANCE RATING (hours)				
	1	1½	2	3	4
W14 × 233	1½	1½	1½	2	2½
× 176	1½	1½	1½	2	3
× 145	1½	1½	1½	2	3
× 132	1½	1½	1½	2	3
× 109	1½	1½	1½	2	3
× 99	1½	1½	2	2½	3½
× 68	1½	1½	2	2½	3½
× 43	1½	1½	2	3	3½
W12 × 190	1½	1½	1½	2	2½
× 152	1½	1½	1½	2	3
× 136	1½	1½	1½	2½	3
× 106	1½	1½	1½	2½	3
× 96	1½	1½	1½	2½	3½
× 87	1½	1½	1½	2½	3½
× 65	1½	1½	2	3	3½
× 40	1½	1½	2	3	3½
W10 × 112	1½	1½	1½	2	2
× 100	1½	1½	1½	2	3
× 88	1½	1½	1½	2½	3
× 77	1½	1½	1½	2½	3
× 60	1½	1½	1½	2½	3½
× 39	1½	1½	2	3	3½
× 33	1½	1½	2	3	3½
W8 × 67	1½	1½	1½	2½	3
× 48	1½	1½	2	3	3½
× 35	1½	2	2	3	3½
× 28	1½	2	2½	3	4
× 18	1½	2	2½	3	4
W6 × 25	1½	2	2	3	3½
× 15	1½	2	2½	3	4
× 9	1½	2	2½	3½	4

For SI: 1 inch = 25.4 mm.

a. The tabulated thicknesses are based upon the assumed properties of structural lightweight concrete given in Table 721.5.1(2).

721.5.1.2 Gypsum wallboard protection. The fire resistance of structural steel columns with weight- to-heated-perimeter ratios (*W/D*) less than or equal to 3.65 and which are protected with Type X gypsum wallboard shall be permitted to be determined from the following expression:

$$(R = 130)\left[\frac{h(W/D)}{2}\right]^{0.75}$$ **(Equation 7-12)**

where:

R = Fire resistance (minutes).

h = Total thickness of gypsum wallboard (inches).

D = Heated perimeter of the structural steel column (inches).

W' = Total weight of the structural steel column and gypsum wallboard protection (pounds per linear foot).

$W' = W + 50hD/144$.

721.5.1.2.1 Attachment. The gypsum wallboard shall be supported as illustrated in either Figure 721.5.1(2) for fire-resistance ratings of 4 hours or less, or Figure 721.5.1(3) for fire-resistance ratings of 3 hours or less.

721.5.1.2.2 Gypsum wallboard equivalent to concrete. The determination of the fire resistance of structural steel columns from Figure 721.5.1(4) is permitted for various thicknesses of gypsum wallboard as a function of the weight-to-heated-perimeter ratio (*W/D*) of the column. For structural steel columns with weight-to-heated-perimeter ratios (*W/D*) greater than 3.65, the thickness of gypsum wallboard required for specified fire-resistance ratings shall be the same as the thickness determined for a *W*14 x 233 wide flange shape.

721.5.1.3 Spray-applied fire-resistant materials. The fire resistance of wide-flange structural steel columns protected with spray-applied fire-resistant materials, as illustrated in Figure 721.5.1(5), shall be permitted to be determined from the following expression:

$$R = [C_1(W/D) + C_2]h$$ **(Equation 7-13)**

where:

R = Fire resistance (minutes).

h = Thickness of spray-applied fire-resistant material (inches).

D = Heated perimeter of the structural steel column (inches).

C_1 and C_2 = Material-dependent constants.

W = Weight of structural steel columns (pounds per linear foot).

The fire resistance of structural steel columns protected with intumescent or mastic fire-resistant coatings shall be determined on the basis of fire-resistance tests in accordance with Section 703.2.

CORNER JOINT DETAILS (A)

FIGURE 721.5.1(2)
GYPSUM WALLBOARD PROTECTED STRUCTURAL STEEL COLUMNS WITH SHEET STEEL COLUMN COVERS

For SI: 1 inch = 25.4 mm, 1 foot = 305 mm.

1. Structural steel column, either wide flange or tubular shapes.

2. Type X gypsum wallboard in accordance with ASTM C 36. For single-layer applications, the wallboard shall be applied vertically with no horizontal joints. For multiple-layer applications, horizontal joints are permitted at a minimum spacing of 8 feet, provided that the joints in successive layers are staggered at least 12 inches. The total required thickness of wallboard shall be determined on the basis of the specified fire-resistance rating and the weight-to-heated-perimeter ratio (*W/D*) of the column. For fire-resistance ratings of 2 hours or less, one of the required layers of gypsum wallboard may be applied to the exterior of the sheet steel column covers with 1-inch- long Type S screws spaced 1 inch from the wallboard edge and 8 inches on center. For such installations, 0.0149-inch minimum thickness galvanized steel corner beads with $1^1/_2$-inch legs shall be attached to the wallboard with Type S screws spaced 12 inches on center.

3. For fire-resistance ratings of 3 hours or less, the column covers shall be fabricated from 0.0239-inch minimum thickness galvanized or stainless steel. For 4-hour fire-resistance ratings, the column covers shall be fabricated from 0.0239-inch minimum thickness stainless steel. The column covers shall be erected with the Snap Lock or Pittsburgh joint details.

For fire-resistance ratings of 2 hours or less, column covers fabricated from 0.0269-inch minimum thickness galvanized or stainless steel shall be permitted to be erected with lap joints. The lap joints shall be permitted to be located anywhere around the perimeter of the column cover. The lap joints shall be secured with $1/_2$-inch-long No. 8 sheet metal screws spaced 12 inches on center.

The column covers shall be provided with a minimum expansion clearance of $1/_8$ inch per linear foot between the ends of the cover and any restraining construction.

FIGURE 721.5.1(3)
GYPSUM WALLBOARD PROTECTED STRUCTURAL STEEL COLUMNS WITH STEEL STUD/SCREW ATTACHMENT SYSTEM

For SI: 1 inch = 25.4 mm, 1 foot = -305 mm.

1. Structural steel column, either wide flange or tubular shapes.

2. $1^5/_8$-inch deep studs fabricated from 0.0179-inch minimum thickness galvanized steel with $1^5/_{16}$ or $1^7/_{16}$-inch legs. The length of the steel studs shall be $^1/_2$ inch less than the height of the assembly.

3. Type X gypsum wallboard in accordance with ASTM C 36. For single-layer applications, the wallboard shall be applied vertically with no horizontal joints. For multiple-layer applications, horizontal joints are permitted at a minimum spacing of 8 feet, provided that the joints in successive layers are staggered at least 12 inches. The total required thickness of wallboard shall be determined on the basis of the specified fire-resistance rating and the weight-to-heated-perimeter ratio (*W/D*) of the column.

4. Galvanized 0.0149-inch minimum thickness steel corner beads with $1^1/_2$-inch legs attached to the wallboard with 1-inch-long Type S screws spaced 12 inches on center.

5. No. 18 SWG steel tie wires spaced 24 inches on center.

6. Sheet metal angles with 2-inch legs fabricated from 0.0221-inch minimum thickness galvanized steel.

7. Type S screws, 1 inch long, shall be used for attaching the first layer of wallboard to the steel studs and the third layer to the sheet metal angles at 24 inches on center. Type S screws $1^3/_4$-inch long shall be used for attaching the second layer of wallboard to the steel studs and the fourth layer to the sheet metal angles at 12 inches on center. Type S screws $2^1/_4$ inches long shall be used for attaching the third layer of wallboard to the steel studs at 12 inches on center.

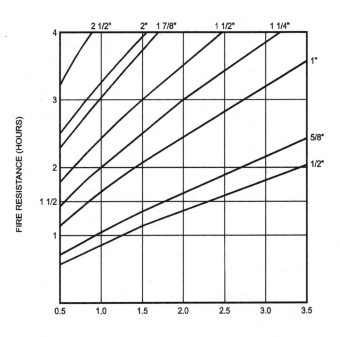

For SI: 1 inch = 25.4 mm, 1 pound per linear foot/inch = 0.059 kg/m/mm.

FIGURE 721.5.1(4)
FIRE RESISTANCE OF STRUCTURAL STEEL COLUMNS PROTECTED WITH VARIOUS THICKNESSES OF TYPE X GYPSUM WALLBOARD

(a).The *W/D* ratios for typical wide flange columns are listed in Table 721.5.1(1). For other column shapes, the *W/D* ratios shall be determined in accordance with Section 720.5.1.1.

FIGURE 721.5.1(5)
WIDE FLANGE STRUCTURAL STEEL COLUMNS WITH SPRAY-APPLIED FIRE-RESISTANT MATERIALS

721.5.1.3.1 Material-dependent constants. The material-dependent constants, C_1 and C_2, shall be determined for specific fire-resistant materials on the basis of standard fire endurance tests in accordance with Section 703.2. Unless evidence is submitted to the building official substantiating a broader application, this expression shall be limited to determining the fire resistance of structural steel columns with weight-to-heated-perimeter ratios (W/D) between the largest and smallest columns for which standard fire-resistance test results are available.

721.5.1.3.2 Spray-applied identification. Spray-applied fire-resistant materials shall be identified by density and thickness required for a given fire-resistance rating.

721.5.1.4 Concrete-protected columns. The fire resistance of structural steel columns protected with concrete, as illustrated in Figure 721.5.1(6) (a) and (b), shall be permitted to be determined from the following expression:

$$R = R_o(1 + 0.03_m) \qquad \textbf{(Equation 7-14)}$$

where:

$$R_o = 10\,(W/D)^{0.7} + 17\,(h^{1.6}/k_c^{0.2}) \times (1 + 26 \\ (H/p_c c_c h\,(L + h))^{0.8})$$

As used in these expressions:

R = Fire endurance at equilibrium moisture conditions (minutes).

R_o = Fire endurance at zero moisture content (minutes).

m = Equilibrium moisture content of the concrete by volume (percent).

W = Average weight of the steel column (pounds per linear foot).

FIGURE 721.5.1(6)
CONCRETE PROTECTED STRUCTURAL STEEL COLUMNS[a,b]

a. When the inside perimeter of the concrete protection is not square, L shall be taken as the average of L_1 and L_2. When the thickness of concrete cover is not constant, h shall be taken as the average of h_1 and h_2.

b. Joints shall be protected with a minimum 1 inch thickness of ceramic fiber blanket but in no case less than one-half the thickness of the column cover (see Section 720.2.1.3).

D = Heated perimeter of the steel column (inches).

h = Thickness of the concrete cover (inches).

k_c = Ambient temperature thermal conductivity of the concrete (Btu/hr ft °F).

H = Ambient temperature thermal capacity of the steel column = 0.11W (Btu/ ft °F).

p_c = Concrete density (pounds per cubic foot).

c_c = Ambient temperature specific heat of concrete (Btu/lb °F).

L = Interior dimension of one side of a square concrete box protection (inches).

721.5.1.4.1 Reentrant space filled. For wide-flange steel columns completely encased in concrete with all reentrant spaces filled [Figure 721.5.1(6)(c)], the thermal capacity of the concrete within the reentrant spaces shall be permitted to be added to the thermal capacity of the steel column, as follows:

$$H = 0.11W + (p_c/c_c)(b_f d - A_s) \qquad \textbf{(Equation 7-15)}$$

where:

b_f = Flange width of the steel column (inches).

d = Depth of the steel column (inches).

A_s = Cross-sectional area of the steel column (square inches).

721.5.1.4.2 Concrete properties unknown. If specific data on the properties of concrete are not available, the values given in Table 721.5.1(2) are permitted.

721.5.1.4.3 Minimum concrete cover. For structural steel column encased in concrete with all reentrant spaces filled, Figure 721.5.1(6)(c) and Tables 721.5.1(7) and 721.5.1(8) indicate the thickness of concrete cover required for various fire-resistance ratings for typical wide-flange sections. The thicknesses of concrete indicated in these tables also apply to structural steel columns larger than those listed.

721.5.1.4.4 Minimum precast concrete cover. For structural steel columns protected with precast concrete column covers as shown in Figure 721.5.1(6)(a), Tables 721.5.1(9) and 721.5.1(10) indicate the thickness of the column covers required for various fire-resistance ratings for typical wide-flange shapes. The thicknesses of concrete given in these tables also apply to structural steel columns larger than those listed.

721.5.1.4.5 Masonry protection. The fire resistance of structural steel columns protected with concrete masonry units or clay masonry units as illustrated in Figure 721.5.1(7), shall be permitted to be determined from the following expression:

$$R = 0.17 \, (W/D)^{0.7} + [0.285 \, (T_e^{1.6}/K^{0.2})]$$
$$[1.0 + 42.7\{(A_s/d_mT_e)/(0.25p + T_e)\}^{0.8}]$$

(Equation 7-16)

where:

R = Fire-resistance rating of column assembly (hours).

W = Average weight of steel column (pounds per foot).

D = Heated perimeter of steel column (inches) [see Figure 721.5.1(7)].

T_e = Equivalent thickness of concrete or clay masonry unit (inches) (see Table 721.3.2 Note a or Section 721.4.1).

K = Thermal conductivity of concrete or clay masonry unit (Btu/hr ft °F) [see Table 721.5.1(3)].

A_s = Cross-sectional area of steel column (square inches).

d_m = Density of the concrete or clay masonry unit (pounds per cubic foot).

W SHAPE COLUMN STEEL PIPE COLUMN STRUCTURAL TUBE COLUMN

For SI:1 inch = 25.4 mm.

FIGURE 721.5.1(7)
CONCRETE OR CLAY MASONRY PROTECTED STRUCTURAL STEEL COLUMNS

d = Depth of a wide flange column, outside diameter of pipe column, or outside dimension of structural tubing column (inches).

t_{web} = Thickness of web of wide flange column (inches).

w = Width of flange of wide flange column (inches).

p = Inner perimeter of concrete or clay masonry protection (inches) [see Figure 721.5.1(7)].

721.5.1.4.6 Equivalent concrete masonry thickness. For structural steel columns protected with concrete masonry, Table 721.5.1(5) gives the equivalent thickness of concrete masonry required for various fire-resistance ratings for typical column shapes. For structural steel columns protected with clay masonry, Table 721.5.1(6) gives the equivalent thickness of concrete masonry required for various fire-resistance ratings for typical column shapes.

721.5.2 Structural steel beams and girders. The fire-resistance ratings of steel beams and girders shall be based upon the size of the element and the type of protection provided in accordance with this section.

721.5.2.1 Determination of fire resistance. These procedures establish a basis for determining resistance of structural steel beams and girders which differ in size from that specified in approved fire-resistance-rated assemblies as a function of the thickness of fire-resistant material and the weight (W) and heated perimeter (D) of the beam or girder. As used in these sections, W is the average weight of a structural steel member in pounds per linear foot (plf). The heated perimeter, D, is the inside perimeter of the fire-resistant material in inches as illustrated in Figure 721.5.2.

FIGURE 721.5.2
DETERMINATION OF THE HEATED PERIMETER OF STRUCTURAL STEEL BEAMS AND GIRDERS

721.5.2.1.1 Weight-to-heated perimeter. The weight-to-heated-perimeter ratios (W/D), for both contour and box fire-resistant protection profiles, for the wide flange shapes most often used as beams or girders are given in Table 721.5.1(4). For different shapes, the weight-to-heated-perimeter ratios (W/D) shall be determined in accordance with the definitions given in this section.

721.5.2.1.2 Beam and girder substitutions. Except as provided for in Section 721.5.2.2, structural steel beams in approved fire-resistance-rated assemblies shall be considered the minimum permissible size. Other beam or girder shapes shall be permitted to be substituted provided that the weight-to-heated-perimeter ratio (W/D) of the substitute beam is equal to or greater than that of the beam specified in the approved assembly.

721.5.2.2 Spray-applied fire-resistant materials. The provisions in this section apply to structural steel beams and girders protected with spray-applied fire-resistant materials. Larger or smaller beam and girder shapes shall be permitted to be substituted for beams specified in approved unrestrained or restrained fire-resistance-rated assemblies, provided the thickness of the fire-resistant material is adjusted in accordance with the following expression:

$$h_2 = h_1[(W_1/D_1) + 0.60]/[(W_2/D_2) + 0.60]$$

(Equation 7-17)

where:

h = Thickness of spray-applied fire-resistant material in inches.

W = Weight of the structural steel beam or girder in pounds per linear foot.

D = Heated perimeter of the structural steel beam in inches.

Subscript 1 refers to the beam and fire-resistant material thickness in the approved assembly.

Subscript 2 refers to the substitute beam or girder and the required thickness of fire-resistant material.

The fire resistance of structural steel beams and girders protected with intumescent or mastic fire-resistant coatings shall be determined on the basis of fire-resistance tests in accordance with Section 703.2.

721.5.2.2.1 Minimum thickness. The use of Equation 7-17 is subject to the following conditions:

1. The weight-to-heated-perimeter ratio for the substitute beam or girder (W_2/D_2) shall not be less than 0.37.

2. The thickness of fire protection materials calculated for the substitute beam or girder (T_1) shall not be less than $^3/_8$ inch (9.5 mm).

3. The unrestrained or restrained beam rating shall not be less than 1 hour.

4. When used to adjust the material thickness for a restrained beam, the use of this procedure is limited to steel sections classified as compact in accordance with the AISC *Specification for Structural Steel Buildings*, (AISC 360-05).

721.5.2.3 Structural steel trusses. The fire resistance of structural steel trusses protected with fire-resistant materials spray-applied to each of the individual truss elements shall be permitted to be determined in accordance with this section. The thickness of the fire-resistant material shall be determined in accordance with Section 721.5.1.3. The weight-to-heated-perimeter ratio (W/D) of truss elements that can be simultaneously exposed to fire on all sides shall be determined on the same basis as columns, as specified in Section 721.5.1.1. The weight-to-heated-perimeter ratio (W/D) of truss elements that directly support floor or roof construction shall be determined on the same basis as beams and girders, as specified in Section 721.5.2.1.

The fire resistance of structural steel trusses protected with intumescent or mastic fire-resistant coatings shall be determined on the basis of fire-resistance tests in accordance with Section 703.2.

721.6 Wood assemblies. The provisions of this section contain procedures by which the fire-resistance ratings of wood assemblies are established by calculations.

721.6.1 General. This section contains procedures for calculating the fire-resistance ratings of walls, floor/ceiling and roof/ceiling assemblies based in part on the standard method of testing referenced in Section 703.2.

721.6.1.1 Maximum fire-resistance rating. Fire-resistance ratings calculated using the procedures in this section shall be used only for 1-hour rated assemblies.

721.6.1.2 Dissimilar membranes. Where dissimilar membranes are used on a wall assembly, the calculation shall be made from the least fire-resistant (weaker) side.

721.6.2 Walls, floors and roofs. These procedures apply to both load-bearing and nonload-bearing assemblies.

721.6.2.1 Fire-resistance rating of wood frame assemblies. The fire-resistance rating of a wood frame assembly is equal to the sum of the time assigned to the membrane on the fire-exposed side, the time assigned to the framing members and the time assigned for additional contribution by other protective measures such as insulation. The membrane on the unexposed side shall not be included in determining the fire resistance of the assembly.

721.6.2.2 Time assigned to membranes. Table 721.6.2(1) indicates the time assigned to membranes on the fire-exposed side.

TABLE 721.6.2(1)
TIME ASSIGNED TO WALLBOARD MEMBRANES[a,b,c,d]

DESCRIPTION OF FINISH	TIME[e] (minutes)
$^3/_8$-inch wood structural panel bonded with exterior glue	5
$^{15}/_{32}$-inch wood structural panel bonded with exterior glue	10
$^{19}/_{32}$-inch wood structural panel bonded with exterior glue	15
$^3/_8$-inch gypsum wallboard	10
$^1/_2$-inch gypsum wallboard	15
$^5/_8$-inch gypsum wallboard	30
$^1/_2$-inch Type X gypsum wallboard	25
$^5/_8$-inch Type X gypsum wallboard	40
Double $^3/_8$-inch gypsum wallboard	25
$^1/_2$- + $^3/_8$-inch gypsum wallboard	35
Double $^1/_2$-inch gypsum wallboard	40

For SI: 1 inch = 25.4 mm.

a. These values apply only when membranes are installed on framing members which are spaced 16 inches o.c.

b. Gypsum wallboard installed over framing or furring shall be installed so that all edges are supported, except $^5/_8$-inch Type X gypsum wallboard shall be permitted to be installed horizontally with the horizontal joints staggered 24 inches each side and unsupported but finished.

c. On wood frame floor/ceiling or roof/ceiling assemblies, gypsum board shall be installed with the long dimension perpendicular to framing members and shall have all joints finished.

d. The membrane on the unexposed side shall not be included in determining the fire resistance of the assembly. When dissimilar membranes are used on a wall assembly, the calculation shall be made from the least fire-resistant (weaker) side.

e. The time assigned is not a finished rating.

721.6.2.3 Exterior walls. For an exterior wall having more than 5 feet (1524 mm) of horizontal separation, the wall is assigned a rating dependent on the interior membrane and the framing as described in Tables 721.6.2(1) and 721.6.2(2). The membrane on the outside of the nonfire-exposed side of exterior walls having more than 5 feet (1524 mm) of horizontal separation may consist of sheathing, sheathing paper, and siding as described in Table 721.6.2(3).

721.6.2.4 Floors and roofs. In the case of a floor or roof, the standard test provides only for testing for fire exposure from below. Except as noted in Section 703.3, Item 5, floor or roof assemblies of wood framing shall have an upper membrane consisting of a subfloor and finished floor conforming to Table 721.6.2(4) or any other membrane that has a contribution to fire resistance of at least 15 minutes in Table 721.6.2(1).

721.6.2.5 Additional protection. Table 721.6.2(5) indicates the time increments to be added to the fire resistance where glass fiber, rockwool, slag mineral wool, or cellulose insulation is incorporated in the assembly.

721.6.2.6 Fastening. Fastening of wood frame assemblies and the fastening of membranes to the wood framing members shall be done in accordance with Chapter 23.

TABLE 721.6.2(2)
TIME ASSIGNED FOR CONTRIBUTION OF WOOD FRAME [a,b,c]

DESCRIPTION	TIME ASSIGNED TO FRAME (minutes)
Wood studs 16 inches o.c.	20
Wood floor and roof joists 16 inches o.c.	10

For SI: 1 inch = 25.4 mm.

a. This table does not apply to studs or joists spaced more than 16 inches o.c.
b. All studs shall be nominal 2 × 4 and all joists shall have a nominal thickness of at least 2 inches.
c. Allowable spans for joists shall be determined in accordance with Sections 2308.8, 2308.10.2 and 2308.10.3.

TABLE 721.6.2(3)
MEMBRANE[a] ON EXTERIOR FACE OF WOOD STUD WALLS

SHEATHING	PAPER	EXTERIOR FINISH
$5/8$-inch T & G lumber $5/16$-inch exterior glue wood structural panel $1/2$-inch gypsum wallboard $5/8$-inch gypsum wallboard $1/2$-inch fiberboard	Sheathing paper	Lumber siding Wood shingles and shakes $1/4$-inch wood structural panels-exterior type $1/4$-inch hardboard Metal siding Stucco on metal lath Masonry veneer
None	—	$3/8$-inch exterior-grade wood structural panels

For SI: 1 pound/cubic foot = 16.0185 kg/m^2.

a. Any combination of sheathing, paper and exterior finish is permitted.

TABLE 721.6.2(4)
FLOORING OR ROOFING OVER WOOD FRAMING[a]

ASSEMBLY	STRUCTURAL MEMBERS	SUBFLOOR OR ROOF DECK	FINISHED FLOORING OR ROOFING
Floor	Wood	$15/32$-inch wood structural panels or $11/16$-inch T & G softwood	Hardwood or softwood flooring on building paper resilient flooring, parquet floor felted-synthetic fiber floor coverings, carpeting, or ceramic tile on $3/8$-inch-thick panel-type underlay. Ceramic tile on $1 1/4$-inch mortar bed
Roof	Wood	$15/32$-inch wood structural panels or $11/16$-inch T & G softwood	Finished roofing material with or without insulation

For SI: 1 inch = 25.4 mm.

a. This table applies only to wood joist construction. It is not applicable to wood truss construction.

TABLE 721.6.2(5)
TIME ASSIGNED FOR ADDITIONAL PROTECTION

DESCRIPTION OF ADDITIONAL PROTECTION	FIRE RESISTANCE (minutes)
Add to the fire-resistance rating of wood stud walls if the spaces between the studs are completely filled with glass fiber mineral wool batts weighing not less than 2 pounds per cubic foot (0.6 pound per square foot of wall surface) or rockwool or slag material wool batts weighing not less than 3.3 pounds per cubic foot (1 pound per square foot of wall surface), or cellulose insulation having a nominal density not less than 2.6 pounds per cubic foot.	15

For SI: 1 pound/cubic foot = 16.0185 kg/m^3.

721.6.3 Design of fire-resistant exposed wood members. The fire-resistance rating, in minutes, of timber beams and columns with a minimum nominal dimension of 6 inches (152 mm) is equal to:

Beams: $2.54Zb$ $[4 -2(b/d)]$ for beams which may be exposed to fire on four sides. **(Equation 7-18)**

$2.54Zb$ $[4 -(b/d)]$ for beams which may be exposed to fire on three sides. **(Equation 7-19)**

FIGURE 721.6.3(1)
LOAD FIGURE

K_e =The effective length factor as noted in
l =The unsupported length of columns (inches).

Columns: $2.54Zd$ $[3 -(d/b)]$ for columns which may be exposed to fire on four sides **(Equation 7-20)**

$2.54Zd$ $[3 -(d/2b)]$ for columns which may be exposed to fire on three sides. **(Equation 7-21)**

where:

b = The breadth (width) of a beam or larger side of acolumn before exposure to fire (inches).

d = The depth of a beam or smaller side of a column before exposure to fire (inches).

Z = Load factor, based on Figure 721.6.3(1).

721.6.3.1 Equation 7-21. Equation 7-21 applies only where the unexposed face represents the smaller side of the column. If a column is recessed into a wall, its full dimension shall be used for the purpose of these calculations.

721.6.3.2 Allowable loads. Allowable loads on beams and columns are determined using design values given in AF&PA NDS.

721.6.3.3 Fastener protection. Where minimum 1-hour fire resistance is required, connectors and fasteners shall be protected from fire exposure by $1^1/_2$ inches (38 mm) of wood, or other approved covering or coating for a 1-hour rating. Typical details for commonly used fasteners and connectors are shown in AITC Technical Note 7.

721.6.3.4 Minimum size. Wood members are limited to dimensions of 6 inches (152 mm) nominal or greater. Glued-laminated timber beams utilize standard laminating combinations except that a core lamination is removed. The tension zone is moved inward and the equivalent of an extra nominal 2-inch-thick (51 mm) outer tension lamination is added.

BUCKLING MODES						
THEORETICAL K_e VALUE	0.5	0.7	1.0	1.0	2.0	2.0
RECOMMENDED DESIGN K_e WHEN IDEAL CONDITIONS APPROXIMATED	0.65	0.80	1.2	1.0	2.10	2.4
END CONDITION CODE	ROTATION FIXED, TRANSLATION FIXED					
	ROTATION FREE, TRANSLATION FIXED					
	ROTATION FIXED, TRANSLATION FREE					
	ROTATION FREE, TRANSLATION FREE					

FIGURE 721.6.3(2)
EFFECTIVE LENGTH FACTORS

CHAPTER 8

INTERIOR FINISHES

SECTION 801
GENERAL

801.1 Scope. Provisions of this chapter shall govern the use of materials used as interior finishes, trim and decorative materials.

801.1.1 Interior finishes. These provisions shall limit the allowable flame spread and smoke development based on location and occupancy classification.

Exceptions:

1. Materials having a thickness less than 0.036 inch (0.9 mm) applied directly to the surface of walls or ceilings.

2. Exposed portions of structural members complying with the requirements for buildings of Type IV construction in Section 602.4 shall not be subject to interior finish requirements.

801.1.2 Decorative materials and trim. Decorative materials and trim shall be restricted by combustibility and the flame propagation performance criteria of NFPA 701, in accordance with Section 806.

801.1.3 Applicability. For buildings in flood hazard areas as established in Section 1612.3, interior finishes, trim and decorative materials below the design flood elevation shall be flood-damage-resistant materials.

801.2 Application. Combustible materials shall be permitted to be used as finish for walls, ceilings, floors and other interior surfaces of buildings.

801.2.1 Windows. Show windows in the exterior walls of the first story above grade shall be permitted to be of wood or of unprotected metal framing.

801.2.2 Foam plastics. Foam plastics shall not be used as interior finish or trim except as provided in Section 2603.9 or 2604. This section shall apply both to exposed foam plastics and to foam plastics used in conjunction with a textile or vinyl facing or cover.

SECTION 802
DEFINITIONS

802.1 General. The following words and terms shall, for the purposes of this chapter and as used elsewhere in this code, have the meanings shown herein.

EXPANDED VINYL WALL COVERING. Wall covering consisting of a woven textile backing, an expanded vinyl base coat layer and a nonexpanded vinyl skin coat. The expanded base coat layer is a homogeneous vinyl layer that contains a blowing agent. During processing, the blowing agent decomposes, causing this layer to expand by forming closed cells. The total thickness of the wall covering is approximately 0.055 inch to 0.070 inch (1.4 mm to 1.78 mm).

FLAME SPREAD. The propagation of flame over a surface.

FLAME SPREAD INDEX. A comparative measure, expressed as a dimensionless number, derived from visual measurements of the spread of flame versus time for a material tested in accordance with ASTM E 84.

INTERIOR FINISH. Interior finish includes interior wall and ceiling finish and interior floor finish.

INTERIOR FLOOR FINISH. The exposed floor surfaces of buildings including coverings applied over a finished floor or stair, including risers.

INTERIOR WALL AND CEILING FINISH. The exposed interior surfaces of buildings, including but not limited to: fixed or movable walls and partitions; toilet room privacy partitions; columns; ceilings; and interior wainscoting, paneling or other finish applied structurally or for decoration, acoustical correction, surface insulation, structural fire resistance or similar purposes, but not including trim.

SMOKE-DEVELOPED INDEX. A comparative measure, expressed as a dimensionless number, derived from measurements of smoke obscuration versus time for a material tested in accordance with ASTM E 84.

TRIM. Picture molds, chair rails, baseboards, handrails, door and window frames and similar decorative or protective materials used in fixed applications.

SECTION 803
WALL AND CEILING FINISHES

803.1 General. Interior wall and ceiling finishes shall be classified in accordance with ASTM E 84. Such interior finish materials shall be grouped in the following classes in accordance with their flame spread and smoke-developed indexes..

Class A: Flame spread 0-25; smoke-developed 0-450.

Class B: Flame spread 26-75; smoke-developed 0-450.

Class C: Flame spread 76-200; smoke-developed 0-450.

Exception: Materials, other than textiles, tested in accordance with Section 803.2.

803.2 Interior wall or ceiling finishes other than textiles. Interior wall or ceiling finishes, other than textiles, shall be permitted to be tested in accordance with NFPA 286. Finishes tested in accordance with NFPA 286 shall comply with Section 803.2.1.

803.2.1 Acceptance criteria. During the 40 kW exposure, the interior finish shall comply with Item 1. During the 160 kW exposure, the interior finish shall comply with Item 2. During the entire test, the interior finish shall comply with Items 3 and 4.

1. During the 40kW exposure, flames shall not spread to the ceiling.

2. During the 160 kW exposure, the interior finish shall comply with the following:

2.1. Flame shall not spread to the outer extremity of the sample on any wall or ceiling.

2.2. Flashover, as defined in NFPA 286, shall not occur.

3. The peak rate of heat release throughout the NFPA 286 test shall not exceed 800 kW.

4. The total smoke released throughout the NFPA 286 test shall not exceed 1,000 m².

803.3 Stability. Interior finish materials regulated by this chapter shall be applied or otherwise fastened in such a manner that such materials will not readily become detached where subjected to room temperatures of 200°F (93°C) for not less than 30 minutes.

803.4 Application. Where these materials are applied on walls, ceilings or structural elements required to have a fire-resistance rating or to be of noncombustible construction, they shall comply with the provisions of this section.

803.4.1 Direct attachment and furred construction. Where walls and ceilings are required by any provision in this code to be of fire-resistance-rated or noncombustible construction, the interior finish material shall be applied directly against such construction or to furring strips not exceeding 1.75 inches (44 mm) applied directly against such surfaces. The intervening spaces between such furring strips shall be filled with inorganic or Class A material or shall be fireblocked at a maximum of 8 feet (2438 mm) in any direction in accordance with Section 717.

803.4.2 Set-out construction. Where walls and ceilings are required to be of fire-resistance-rated or noncombustible construction and walls are set out or ceilings are dropped distances greater than specified in Section 803.4.1, Class A finish materials shall be used except where interior finish materials are protected on both sides by an automatic sprinkler system or attached to noncombustible backing or furring strips installed as specified in Section 803.4.1. The hangers and assembly members of such dropped ceilings that are below the main ceiling line shall be of noncombustible materials, except that in Type III and V construction, fire-retardant-treated wood shall be permitted. The construction of each set-out wall shall be of fire-resistance-rated construction as required elsewhere in this code.

803.4.3 Heavy timber construction. Wall and ceiling finishes of all classes as permitted in this chapter that are installed directly against the wood decking or planking of Type IV construction or to wood furring strips applied directly to the wood decking or planking shall be fireblocked as specified in Section 803.4.1.

803.4.4 Materials. An interior wall or ceiling finish that is not more than 0.25 inch (6.4 mm) thick shall be applied directly against a noncombustible backing.

Exceptions:

1. Class A materials.

2. Materials where the qualifying tests were made with the material suspended or furred out from the noncombustible backing.

803.5 Interior finish requirements based on group. Interior wall and ceiling finish shall have a flame spread index not greater than that specified in Table 803.5 for the group and location designated. Interior wall and ceiling finish materials, other than textiles, tested in accordance with NFPA 286 and meeting the acceptance criteria of Section 803.2.1, shall be permitted to be used where a Class A classification in accordance with ASTM E 84 is required.

803.6 Textiles. Where used as interior wall or ceiling finish materials, textiles, including materials having woven or nonwoven, napped, tufted, looped or similar surface and carpet and similar textile materials, shall comply with the requirements of Section 803.6.1, 803.6.2 or 803.6.3.

803.6.1 Surface burning characteristic test. Textile wall and ceiling coverings shall have a Class A flame spread index in accordance with ASTM E 84 and be protected by automatic sprinklers installed in accordance with Section 903.3.1.1 or 903.3.1.2.

803.6.2 Room corner test, textiles. Textile wall coverings shall meet the criteria of Section 803.6.2.1 when tested in the manner intended for use in accordance with the Method B protocol of NFPA 265 using the product-mounting system, including adhesive.

803.6.2.1 Method B test protocol. During the 40 kW exposure, the interior finish shall comply with Item 1. During the 150 kW exposure, the interior finish shall comply with Item 2. During the entire test, the interior finish shall comply with Item 3.

1. During the 40 kW exposure, flames shall not spread to the ceiling.

2. During the 150 kW exposure, the interior finish shall comply with the following:

2.1. Flame shall not spread to the outer extremities of the samples on the 8-foot by 12-foot (203 mm by 305 mm) walls.

2.2. Flashover, as described in NFPA 265, shall not occur.

3. The total smoke released throughout the NFPA 265 test shall not exceed 1000 m².

803.6.3 Room corner test, ceiling and wall finish. Textile wall and ceiling coverings shall meet the criteria of Section 803.2.1 when tested in the manner intended for use in accordance with NFPA 286 using the product-mounting system, including adhesive.

803.7 Expanded vinyl wall coverings. Expanded vinyl wall coverings shall comply with the requirements for textile wall and ceiling materials and their use shall comply with Section 803.6.

Exception: Expanded vinyl wall or ceiling coverings complying with Section 803.2 shall not be required to comply with Section 803.1 or 803.6.

TABLE 803.5
INTERIOR WALL AND CEILING FINISH REQUIREMENTS BY OCCUPANCY[k]

GROUP	SPRINKLERED[l]			NONSPRINKLERED		
	Exit enclosures and exit passageways[a,b]	Corridors	Rooms and enclosed spaces[c]	Exit enclosures and exit passageways[a,b]	Corridors	Rooms and enclosed spaces[c]
A-1 & A-2	B	B	C	A	A[d]	B[e]
A-3[f], A-4, A-5	B	B	C	A	A[d]	C
B, E, M, R-1, R-4	B	C	C	A	B	C
F	C	C	C	B	C	C
H	B	B	C[g]	A	A	B
I-1	B	C	C	A	B	B
I-2	B	B	B[h, i]	A	A	B
I-3	A	A[j]	C	A	A	B
I-4	B	B	B[h, i]	A	A	B
R-2	C	C	C	B	B	C
R-3	C	C	C	C	C	C
S	C	C	C	B	B	C
U	No restrictions			No restrictions		

For SI: 1 inch = 25.4 mm, 1 square foot = 0.0929 m^2.

a. Class C interior finish materials shall be permitted for wainscotting or paneling of not more than 1,000 square feet of applied surface area in the grade lobby where applied directly to a noncombustible base or over furring strips applied to a noncombustible base and fireblocked as required by Section 803.4.1.

b. In exit enclosures of buildings less than three stories in height of other than Group I-3, Class B interior finish for nonsprinklered buildings and Class C interior finish for sprinklered buildings shall be permitted.

c. Requirements for rooms and enclosed spaces shall be based upon spaces enclosed by partitions. Where a fire-resistance rating is required for structural elements, the enclosing partitions shall extend from the floor to the ceiling. Partitions that do not comply with this shall be considered enclosing spaces and the rooms or spaces on both sides shall be considered one. In determining the applicable requirements for rooms and enclosed spaces, the specific occupancy thereof shall be the governing factor regardless of the group classification of the building or structure.

d. Lobby areas in Group A-1, A-2 and A-3 occupancies shall not be less than Class B materials.

e. Class C interior finish materials shall be permitted in places of assembly with an occupant load of 300 persons or less.

f. For places of religious worship, wood used for ornamental purposes, trusses, paneling or chancel furnishing shall be permitted.

g. Class B material is required where the building exceeds two stories.

h. Class C interior finish materials shall be permitted in administrative spaces.

i. Class C interior finish materials shall be permitted in rooms with a capacity of four persons or less.

j. Class B materials shall be permitted as wainscotting extending not more than 48 inches above the finished floor in corridors.

k Finish materials as provided for in other sections of this code

l. Applies when the exit enclosures, exit passageways, corridors or rooms and enclosed spaces are protected by a sprinkler system installed in accordance with Section 903.3.1.1 or 903.3.1.2.

803.8 Insulation. Thermal and acoustical insulation shall comply with Section 719.

803.9 Acoustical ceiling systems. The quality, design, fabrication and erection of metal suspension systems for acoustical tile and lay-in panel ceilings in buildings or structures shall conform with generally accepted engineering practice, the provisions of this chapter and other applicable requirements of this code.

803.9.1 Materials and installation. Acoustical materials complying with the interior finish requirements of Section 803 shall be installed in accordance with the manufacturer's recommendations and applicable provisions for applying interior finish.

803.9.1.1 Suspended acoustical ceilings. Suspended acoustical ceiling systems shall be installed in accordance with the provisions of ASTM C 635 and ASTM C 636.

803.9.1.2 Fire-resistance-rated construction. Acoustical ceiling systems that are part of fire-resistance-rated construction shall be installed in the same manner used in the assembly tested and shall comply with the provisions of Chapter 7.

SECTION 804
INTERIOR FLOOR FINISH

804.1 General. Interior floor finish and floor covering materials shall comply with Section 804.2 through 804.4.1.

Exception: Floor finishes and coverings of a traditional type, such as wood, vinyl, linoleum or terrazzo, and resilient floor covering materials that are not comprised of fibers.

804.2 Classification. Interior floor finish and floor covering materials required by Section 804.4.1 to be of Class I or II materials shall be classified in accordance with NFPA 253. The classification referred to herein corresponds to the classifications determined by NFPA 253 as follows: Class I, 0.45 watts/cm^2 or greater; Class II, 0.22 watts/cm^2 or greater.

804.3 Testing and identification. Interior floor finish and floor covering materials shall be tested by an approved agency in accordance with NFPA 253 and identified by a hang tag or other suitable method so as to identify the manufacturer or supplier and style, and shall indicate the interior floor finish or floor covering classification according to Section 804.2. Carpet-type floor coverings shall be tested as proposed for use, including underlayment. Test reports confirming the information provided in the manufacturer's product identification shall be furnished to the code enforcement official upon request.

804.4 Interior floor finish requirements. In all occupancies, interior floor finish and floor covering materials in exit enclosures, exit passageways, corridors and rooms or spaces not separated from corridors by full-height partitions extending from the floor to the underside of the ceiling shall withstand a minimum critical radiant flux as specified in Section 804.4.1.

804.4.1 Minimum critical radiant flux. Interior floor finish and floor covering materials in exit enclosures, exit passageways and corridors shall not be less than Class I in Groups I-2 and I-3 and not less than Class II in Groups A, B, E, H, I-4, M, R-1, R-2 and S. In all areas, floor covering materials shall comply with the DOC FF-1 "pill test" (CPSC 16 CFR, Part 1630).

Exception: Where a building is equipped throughout with an automatic sprinkler system in accordance with Section 903.3.1.1 or 903.3.1.2, Class II materials are permitted in any area where Class I materials are required, and materials complying with the DOC FF-1 "pill test" (CPSC 16 CFR, Part 1630) are permitted in any area where Class II materials are required.

SECTION 805
COMBUSTIBLE MATERIALS IN TYPE I AND II CONSTRUCTION

805.1 Application. Combustible materials installed on or embedded in floors of buildings of Type I or II construction shall comply with Sections 805.1.1 through 805.1.3.

Exception: Stages and platforms constructed in accordance with Sections 410.3 and 410.4, respectively.

805.1.1 Subfloor construction. Floor sleepers, bucks and nailing blocks shall not be constructed of combustible materials, unless the space between the fire-resistance-rated floor construction and the flooring is either solidly filled with approved noncombustible materials or fireblocked in accordance with Section 717, and provided that such open spaces shall not extend under or through permanent partitions or walls.

805.1.2 Wood finish flooring. Wood finish flooring is permitted to be attached directly to the embedded or fireblocked wood sleepers and shall be permitted where cemented directly to the top surface of approved fire-resistance-rated floor construction or directly to a wood subfloor attached to sleepers as provided for in Section 805.1.1.

805.1.3 Insulating boards. Combustible insulating boards not more than $1/2$ inch (12.7 mm) thick and covered with approved finish flooring are permitted where attached directly to a noncombustible floor assembly or to wood

subflooring attached to sleepers as provided for in Section 805.1.1.

SECTION 806
DECORATIVE MATERIALS AND TRIM [F]

[F] 806.1 General requirements. In occupancies in Groups A, E, I and R-1 and dormitories in Group R-2, curtains, draperies, hangings and other decorative materials suspended from walls or ceilings shall meet the flame propagation performance criteria of NFPA 701 in accordance with Section 806.2 or be noncombustible.

In Groups I-1 and I-2, combustible decorative materials shall meet the flame propagation criteria of NFPA 701 unless the decorative materials, including, but not limited to, photographs and paintings, are of such limited quantities that a hazard of fire development or spread is not present. In Group I-3, combustible decorative materials are prohibited.

Fixed or movable walls and partitions, paneling, wall pads and crash pads applied structurally or for decoration, acoustical correction, surface insulation or other purposes shall be considered interior finish if they cover 10 percent or more of the wall or of the ceiling area, and shall not be considered decorative materials or furnishings.

In Group B and M occupancies, fabric partitions suspended from the ceiling and not supported by the floor shall meet the flame propagation performance criteria in accordance with Section 806.2 and NFPA 701 or shall be noncombustible.

[F] 806.1.1 Noncombustible materials. The permissible amount of noncombustible decorative material shall not be limited.

[F] 806.1.2 Combustible decorative materials. The permissible amount of decorative materials meeting the flame propagation performance criteria of NFPA 701 shall not exceed 10 percent of the aggregate area of walls and ceilings

Exceptions:

1. In auditoriums in Group A, the permissible amount of decorative material meeting the flame propagation performance criteria of NFPA 701 shall not exceed 50 percent of the aggregate area of walls and ceiling where the building is equipped throughout with an automatic sprinkler system in accordance with Section 903.3.1.1 and where the material is installed in accordance with Section 803.4.

2. The amount of fabric partitions suspended from the ceiling and not supported by the floor in Group B and M occupancies shall not be limited.

[F] 806.2 Acceptance criteria and reports. Where required by Section 806.1, decorative materials shall be tested by an approved agency and meet the flame propagation performance criteria of NFPA 701 or such materials shall be noncombustible. Reports of test results shall be prepared in accordance with NFPA 701 and furnished to the code enforcement official upon request.

[F] 806.3 Foam plastic. Foam plastic used as trim in any occupancy shall comply with Section 2604.2.

[F] 806.4 Pyroxylin plastic. Imitation leather or other material consisting of or coated with a pyroxylin or similarly hazardous base shall not be used in Group A occupancies.

[F] 806.5 Interior trim. Material, other than foam plastic used as interior trim shall have a minimum Class C flame spread and smoke-developed index when tested in accordance with ASTM E 84, as described in Section 803.1. Combustible trim, excluding handrails and guardrails, shall not exceed 10 percent of the aggregate wall or ceiling area in which it is located.

CHAPTER 9

FIRE PROTECTION SYSTEMS

SECTION 901
GENERAL

901.1 Scope. The provisions of this chapter shall specify where fire protection systems are required and shall apply to the design, installation and operation of fire protection systems.

901.2 Fire protection systems. Fire protection systems shall be installed, repaired, operated and maintained in accordance with this code and the *Fire Code of New York State*.

Any fire protection system for which an exception or reduction to the provisions of this code has been granted shall be considered to be a required system.

> **Exception:** Any fire protection system or portion thereof not required by this code shall be permitted to be installed for partial or complete protection provided that such system meets the requirements of this code.

901.3 Modifications. No person shall remove or modify any fire protection system installed or maintained under the provisions of this code or the *Fire Code of New York State* without approval by the code enforcement official.

901.4 Threads. Threads provided for fire department connections to sprinkler systems, standpipes, yard hydrants or any other fire hose connection shall be compatible with the connections used by the local fire department.

901.5 Acceptance tests. Fire protection systems shall be tested in accordance with the requirements of this code and the *Fire Code of New York State*. When required, the tests shall be conducted in the presence of the code enforcement official. Tests required by this code, the *Fire Code of New York State* and the standards listed in this code shall be conducted at the expense of the owner or the owner's representative. It shall be unlawful to occupy portions of a structure until the required fire protection systems within that portion of the structure have been tested and approved.

901.6 Supervisory service. Where required, fire protection systems shall be monitored by an approved supervising station in accordance with NFPA 72.

> **901.6.1 Automatic sprinkler systems.** Automatic sprinkler systems shall be monitored by an approved supervising station.
>
> **Exceptions:**
> 1. A supervising station is not required for automatic sprinkler systems protecting one- and two-family dwellings.
> 2. Limited area systems serving fewer than 20 sprinklers.
>
> **901.6.2 Fire alarm systems.** Fire alarm systems required by the provisions of Section 907.2 of this code and Section 907.2 of the *Fire Code of New York State* shall be monitored by an approved supervising station in accordance with Section 907.14.
>
> **Exceptions:**
> 1. Single- and multiple-station smoke alarms required by Section 907.2.10.
> 2. Smoke detectors in Group I-3 occupancies.
> 3. Supervisory service is not required for automatic sprinkler systems in one- and two-family dwellings.
>
> **901.6.3 Group H.** Manual fire alarm, automatic fire-extinguishing and emergency alarm systems in Group H occupancies shall be monitored by an approved supervising station.
>
> **Exception:** When approved by the code enforcement official, on-site monitoring at a constantly attended location shall be permitted provided that notifications to the fire department will be equal to those provided by an approved supervising station.

901.7 Fire areas. Where buildings, or portions thereof, are divided into fire areas so as not to exceed the limits established for requiring a fire protection system in accordance with this chapter, such fire areas shall be separated by fire barriers having a fire-resistance rating of not less than that determined in accordance with Section 706.3.9.

SECTION 902
DEFINITIONS

902.1 Definitions. The following words and terms shall, for the purposes of this chapter, and as used elsewhere in this code, have the meanings shown herein.

[F] ALARM NOTIFICATION APPLIANCE. A fire alarm system component such as a bell, horn, speaker, light or text display that provides audible, tactile or visible outputs, or any combination thereof.

[F] ALARM SIGNAL. A signal indicating an emergency requiring immediate action, such as a signal indicative of fire.

[F] ALARM VERIFICATION FEATURE. A feature of automatic fire detection and alarm systems to reduce unwanted alarms wherein smoke detectors report alarm conditions for a minimum period of time, or confirm alarm conditions within a given time period, after being automatically reset, in order to be accepted as a valid alarm-initiation signal.

[F] ANNUNCIATOR. A unit containing one or more indicator lamps, alphanumeric displays or other equivalent means in which each indication provides status information about a circuit, condition or location.

[F] AUDIBLE ALARM NOTIFICATION APPLIANCE. A notification appliance that alerts by the sense of hearing.

[F] AUTOMATIC. As applied to fire protection devices, is a device or system providing an emergency function without the necessity for human intervention and activated as a result of a predetermined temperature rise, rate of temperature rise or combustion products.

[F] AUTOMATIC FIRE-EXTINGUISHING SYSTEM. An approved system of devices and equipment which automatically detects a fire and discharges an approved fire-extinguishing agent onto or in the area of a fire.

[F] AUTOMATIC SPRINKLER SYSTEM. A sprinkler system, for fire protection purposes, is an integrated system of underground and overhead piping designed in accordance with fire protection engineering standards. The system includes a suitable water supply. The portion of the system above the ground is a network of specially sized or hydraulically designed piping installed in a structure or area, generally overhead, and to which automatic sprinklers are connected in a systematic pattern. The system is usually activated by heat from a fire and discharges water over the fire area.

[F] AVERAGE AMBIENT SOUND LEVEL. The root mean square, A-weighted sound pressure level measured over a 24-hour period.

CARBON DIOXIDE EXTINGUISHING SYSTEM. A system supplying carbon dioxide (CO_2) from a pressurized vessel through fixed pipes and nozzles. The system includes a manual- or automatic-actuating mechanism.

[F] CEILING LIMIT. The maximum concentration of an air-borne contaminant to which one may be exposed, as published in DOL 29 CFR Part 1910.1000.

[F] CLEAN AGENT. Electrically nonconducting, volatile or gaseous fire extinguishant that does not leave a residue upon evaporation.

[F] CONSTANTLY ATTENDED LOCATION. A designated location at a facility staffed by trained personnel on a continuous basis where alarm or supervisory signals are monitored and facilities are provided for notification of the fire department or other emergency services.

[F] DELUGE SYSTEM. A sprinkler system employing open sprinklers attached to a piping system connected to a water supply through a valve that is opened by the operation of a detection system installed in the same areas as the sprinklers. When this valve opens, water flows into the piping system and discharges from all sprinklers attached thereto.

[F] DETECTOR, HEAT. A fire detector that senses heat produced by burning substances. Heat is the energy produced by combustion that causes substances to rise in temperature.

[F] DRY-CHEMICAL EXTINGUISHING AGENT. A powder composed of small particles, usually of sodium bicarbonate, potassium bicarbonate, urea-potassium-based bicarbonate, potassium chloride or monoammonium phosphate, with added particulate material supplemented by special treatment to provide resistance to packing, resistance to moisture absorption (caking) and the proper flow capabilities.

[F] EMERGENCY ALARM SYSTEM. A system to provide indication and warning of emergency situations involving hazardous materials.

[F] EMERGENCY VOICE/ALARM COMMUNICATIONS. Dedicated manual or automatic facilities for originating and distributing voice instructions, as well as alert and evacuation signals pertaining to a fire emergency, to the occupants of a building.

[F] FIRE ALARM BOX, MANUAL. See "Manual Fire Alarm Box."

[F] FIRE ALARM CONTROL UNIT. A system component that receives inputs from automatic and manual fire alarm devices and is capable of supplying power to detection devices and transponder(s) or off-premises transmitter(s). The control unit is capable of providing a transfer of power to the notification appliances and transfer of condition to relays or devices.

[F] FIRE ALARM SIGNAL. A signal initiated by a fire alarm-initiating device such as a manual fire alarm box, automatic fire detector, water flow switch, or other device whose activation is indicative of the presence of a fire or fire signature.

[F] FIRE ALARM SYSTEM. A system or portion of a combination system consisting of components and circuits arranged to monitor and annunciate the status of fire alarm or supervisory signal-initiating devices and to initiate the appropriate response to those signals.

[F] FIRE COMMAND CENTER. The principal attended or unattended location where the status of detection, alarm communications and control systems is displayed, and from which the system(s) can be manually controlled.

[F] FIRE DETECTOR, AUTOMATIC. A device designed to detect the presence of a fire signature and to initiate action.

[F] FIRE PROTECTION SYSTEM. Approved devices, equipment and systems or combinations of systems used to detect a fire, activate an alarm, extinguish or control a fire, control or manage smoke and products of a fire or any combination thereof.

[F] FIRE SAFETY FUNCTIONS. Building and fire control functions that are intended to increase the level of life safety for occupants or to control the spread of harmful effects of fire.

[F] FOAM-EXTINGUISHING SYSTEM. A special system discharging a foam made from concentrates, either mechanically or chemically, over the area to be protected.

[F] HALOGENATED EXTINGUISHING SYSTEM. A fire-extinguishing system using one or more atoms of an element from the halogen chemical series: fluorine, chlorine, bromine and iodine.

[F] INITIATING DEVICE. A system component that originates transmission of a change-of-state condition, such as in a smoke detector, manual fire alarm box or supervisory switch.

LISTED. Equipment, materials or services included in a list published by an organization acceptable to the building official and concerned with evaluation of products or services that maintains periodic inspection of production of listed equipment or materials or periodic evaluation of services and whose listing states either that the equipment, material or service meets identified standards or has been tested and found suitable for a specified purpose.

[F] MANUAL FIRE ALARM BOX. A manually operated device used to initiate an alarm signal.

[F] MULTIPLE-STATION ALARM DEVICE. Two or more single-station alarm devices that are capable of interconnection such that actuation of one causes all integral or separate audible alarms to operate. It also can consist of one single-station alarm device having connections to other detectors or to a manual fire alarm box.

[F] MULTIPLE-STATION SMOKE ALARM. Two or more single-station alarm devices that are capable of interconnection such that actuation of one causes all integral or separate audible alarms to operate.

[F] NUISANCE ALARM. An alarm caused by mechanical failure, malfunction, improper installation or lack of proper maintenance, or an alarm activated by a cause that cannot be determined.

[F] RECORD DRAWINGS. Drawings ("as builts") that document the location of all devices, appliances, wiring sequences, wiring methods and connections of the components of a fire alarm system as installed.

[F] SINGLE-STATION SMOKE ALARM. An assembly incorporating the detector, the control equipment and the alarm-sounding device in one unit, operated from a power supply either in the unit or obtained at the point of installation.

[F] SMOKE ALARM. A single- or multiple-station alarm responsive to smoke and not connected to a system.

[F] SMOKE DETECTOR. A listed device that senses visible or invisible particles of combustion.

SMOKEPROOF ENCLOSURE. An exit stairway designed and constructed so that the movement of the products of combustion produced by a fire occurring in any part of the building into the enclosure is limited.

[F] STANDPIPE SYSTEM, CLASSES OF. Standpipe classes are as follows:

Class I system. A system providing 2$^1/_2$-inch (64 mm) hose connections to supply water for use by fire departments and those trained in handling heavy fire streams.

Class II system. A system providing 1$^1/_2$-inch (38 mm) hose stations to supply water for use primarily by the building occupants or by the fire department during initial response.

Class III system. A system providing 1$^1/_2$-inch (38 mm) hose stations to supply water for use by building occupants and 2.5-inch (64 mm) hose connections to supply a larger volume of water for use by fire departments and those trained in handling heavy fire streams.

[F] STANDPIPE, TYPES OF. Standpipe types are as follows:

Automatic dry. A dry standpipe system, normally filled with pressurized air, that is arranged through the use of a device, such as dry pipe valve, to admit water into the system piping automatically upon the opening of a hose valve. The water supply for an automatic dry standpipe system shall be capable of supplying the system demand.

Automatic wet. A wet standpipe system that has a water supply that is capable of supplying the system demand automatically.

Manual dry. A dry standpipe system that does not have a permanent water supply attached to the system. Manual dry standpipe systems require water from a fire department pumper to be pumped into the system through the fire department connection in order to supply the system demand.

Manual wet. A wet standpipe system connected to a water supply for the purpose of maintaining water within the system but does not have a water supply capable of delivering the system demand attached to the system. Manual-wet standpipe systems require water from a fire department pumper (or the like) to be pumped into the system in order to supply the system demand.

Semiautomatic dry. A dry standpipe system that is arranged through the use of a device, such as a deluge valve, to admit water into the system piping upon activation of a remote control device located at a hose connection. A remote control activation device shall be provided at each hose connection. The water supply for a semiautomatic dry standpipe system shall be capable of supplying the system demand.

[F] SUPERVISING STATION. A facility that receives signals and at which personnel are in attendance at all times to respond to these signals.

[F] SUPERVISORY SERVICE. The service required to monitor performance of guard tours and the operative condition of fixed suppression systems or other systems for the protection of life and property.

[F] SUPERVISORY SIGNAL. A signal indicating the need of action in connection with the supervision of guard tours, the fire suppression systems or equipment or the maintenance features of related systems.

[F] SUPERVISORY SIGNAL-INITIATING DEVICE. An initiating device, such as a valve supervisory switch, water-level indicator or low-air pressure switch on a dry-pipe sprinkler system, whose change of state signals an off-normal condition and its restoration to normal of a fire protection or life safety system, or a need for action in connection with guard tours, fire suppression systems or equipment or maintenance features of related systems.

[F] TIRES, BULK STORAGE OF. Storage of tires where the area available for storage exceeds 20,000 cubic feet (566 m^3).

[F] TROUBLE SIGNAL. A signal initiated by the fire alarm system or device indicative of a fault in a monitored circuit or component.

[F] VISIBLE ALARM NOTIFICATION APPLIANCE. A notification appliance that alerts by the sense of sight.

[F] WET-CHEMICAL EXTINGUISHING AGENT. A solution of water and potassium-carbonate-based chemical, potassium-acetate-based chemical or a combination thereof, forming an extinguishing agent.

[F] WIRELESS PROTECTION SYSTEM. A system or a part of a system that can transmit and receive signals without the aid of wire.

[F] ZONE. A defined area within the protected premises. A zone can define an area from which a signal can be received, an area to which a signal can be sent or an area in which a form of control can be executed.

SECTION 903
AUTOMATIC SPRINKLER SYSTEMS

[F] 903.1 General. Automatic sprinkler systems shall comply with this section.

[F] 903.1.1 Alternative protection. Alternative automatic fire-extinguishing systems complying with Section 904 shall be permitted in lieu of automatic sprinkler protection where recognized by the applicable standard and approved by the code enforcement official.

[F] 903.2 Where required. Approved automatic sprinkler systems in new buildings and structures shall be provided in the locations described in this section.

Exception: Spaces or areas in telecommunications buildings used exclusively for telecommunications equipment, associated electrical power distribution equipment, batteries and standby engines, provided those spaces or areas are equipped throughout with an automatic fire alarm system and are separated from the remainder of the building by fire barriers consisting of not less than 1-hour fire-resistance-rated walls and 2-hour fire-resistance-rated floor/ceiling assemblies.

[F] 903.2.1 Group A. An automatic sprinkler system shall be provided throughout buildings and portions thereof used as Group A occupancies as provided in this section. For Group A-1, A-2, A-3 and A-4 occupancies, the automatic sprinkler system shall be provided throughout the floor area where the Group A-1, A-2, A-3 or A-4 occupancy is located, and in all floors between the Group A occupancy and the level of exit discharge. For Group A-5 occupancies, the automatic sprinkler system shall be provided in the spaces indicated in Section 903.2.1.5.

903.2.1.1 Group A-1. An automatic sprinkler system shall be provided for Group A-1 occupancies where one of the following conditions exists:

1. The fire area exceeds 12,000 square feet (1115 m^2);

2. The fire area has an occupant load of 100 or more;

3. The fire area is located on a floor other than the level of exit discharge; or

4. The fire area contains a multitheater complex.

903.2.1.2 Group A-2. An automatic sprinkler system shall be provided for Group A-2 occupancies where one of the following conditions exists:

1. The fire area exceeds 5,000 square feet (465 m^2);

2. The fire area has an occupant load of 100 or more; or

3. The fire area is located on a floor other than the level of exit discharge.

903.2.1.3 Group A-3. An automatic sprinkler system shall be provided for Group A-3 occupancies where one of the following conditions exists:

1. The fire area exceeds 12,000 square feet (1115 m^2);

2. The fire area has an occupant load of 100 or more; or

3. The fire area is located on a floor other than the level of exit discharge.

Exception: Areas used exclusively as participant sports areas where the main floor area is located at the same level as the level of exit discharge of the main entrance and exit.

903.2.1.4 Group A-4. An automatic sprinkler system shall be provided for Group A-4 occupancies where one of the following conditions exists:

1. The fire area exceeds 12,000 square feet (1115 m^2);

2. The fire area has an occupant load of 100 or more;or

3. The fire area is located on a floor other than the level of exit discharge.

Exception: Areas used exclusively as participant sports areas where the main floor area is located at the same level as the level of exit discharge of the main entrance and exit.

[F] 903.2.1.5 Group A-5. An automatic sprinkler system shall be provided for Group A-5 occupancies in the following areas: concession stands, retail areas, press boxes and other accessory use areas in excess of 1,000 square feet (93 m^2).

[F] 903.2.2 Group E. An automatic sprinkler system shall be provided for Group E occupancies as follows:

1. Throughout all Group E fire areas greater than 20,000 square feet (1858 m^2) in area.

2. Throughout every portion of educational buildings below the level of exit discharge.

Exception: An automatic sprinkler system is not required in any fire area or area below the level of exit discharge where every classroom throughout the building has at least one exterior exit door at ground level.

[F] 903.2.3 Group F-1. An automatic sprinkler system shall be provided throughout all buildings containing a Group F-1 occupancy where one of the following conditions exists:

1. Where a Group F-1 fire area exceeds 12,000 square feet (1115 m²);

2. Where a Group F-1 fire area is located more than three stories above grade plane; or

3. Where the combined area of all Group F-1 fire areas on all floors, including any mezzanines, exceeds 24,000 square feet (2230 m²).

[F] 903.2.3.1 Woodworking operations. An automatic sprinkler system shall be provided throughout all Group F-1 occupancy fire areas that contain woodworking operations in excess of 2,500 square feet (232 m²) in area which generate finely divided combustible waste or which use finely divided combustible materials.

[F] 903.2.4 Group H. Automatic sprinkler systems shall be provided in high-hazard occupancies as required in Sections 903.2.4.1 through 903.2.4.3.

[F] 903.2.4.1 General. An automatic sprinkler system shall be installed in Group H occupancies.

[F] 903.2.4.2 Group H-5. An automatic sprinkler system shall be installed throughout buildings containing Group H-5 occupancies. The design of the sprinkler system shall not be less than that required by this code for the occupancy hazard classifications in accordance with Table 903.2.4.2. Where the design area of the sprinkler system consists of a corridor protected by one row of sprinklers, the maximum number of sprinklers required to be calculated is 13.

[F] TABLE 903.2.4.2
GROUP H-5 SPRINKLER DESIGN CRITERIA

LOCATION	OCCUPANCY HAZARD CLASSIFICATION
Fabrication areas	Ordinary Hazard Group 2
Service corridors	Ordinary Hazard Group 2
Storage rooms without dispensing	Ordinary Hazard Group 2
Storage rooms with dispensing	Extra Hazard Group 2
Corridors	Ordinary Hazard Group 2

[F] 903.2.4.3 Pyroxylin plastics. An automatic sprinkler system shall be provided in buildings, or portions thereof, where cellulose nitrate film or pyroxylin plastics are manufactured, stored or handled in quantities exceeding 100 pounds (45 kg).

[F] 903.2.5 Group I. An automatic sprinkler system shall be provided throughout buildings with a Group I fire area.

Exception: An automatic sprinkler system installed in accordance with Section 903.3.1.2 or 903.3.1.3 shall be allowed in Group I-1 facilities.

[F] 903.2.6 Group M. An automatic sprinkler system shall be provided throughout buildings containing a Group M occupancy where one of the following conditions exists:

1. Where a Group M fire area exceeds 12,000 square feet (1115 m²);

2. Where a Group M fire area is located more than three stories above grade plane; or

3. Where the combined area of all Group M fire areas on all floors, including any mezzanines, exceeds 24,000 square feet (2230 m²).

[F] 903.2.6.1 High-piled storage. An automatic sprinkler system shall be provided in accordance with the *Fire Code of New York State* in all buildings of Group M where storage of merchandise is in high-piled or rack storage arrays.

[F] 903.2.7 Group R. An automatic sprinkler system installed in accordance with Section 903.3 shall be provided throughout all buildings with a Group R fire area.

[F] 903.2.8 Group S-1. An automatic sprinkler system shall be provided throughout all buildings containing a Group S-1 occupancy where one of the following conditions exists:

1. A Group S-1 fire area exceeds 12,000 square feet (1115 m²);

2. A Group S-1 fire area is located more than three stories above grade plane; or

3. The combined area of all Group S-1 fire areas on all floors, including any mezzanines, exceeds 24,000 square feet (2230 m²).

4. An automatic sprinkler system shall be provided throughout buildings used for storage of commercial trucks or buses where the fire area exceeds 5000 square feet (464 m²).

[F] 903.2.8.1 Repair garages. An automatic sprinkler system shall be provided throughout all buildings used as repair garages in accordance with Section 406, as shown:

1. Buildings two or more stories in height, including basements, with a fire area containing a repair garage exceeding 10,000 square feet (929 m²).

2. One-story buildings with a fire area containing a repair garage exceeding 12,000 square feet (1115 m²).

3. Buildings with a repair garage servicing vehicles parked in the basement.

[F] 903.2.8.2 Bulk storage of tires. Buildings and structures where the area for the storage of tires exceeds 20,000 cubic feet (566 m³) shall be equipped throughout with an automatic sprinkler system in accordance with Section 903.3.1.1.

[F] 903.2.9 Group S-2. An automatic sprinkler system shall be provided throughout buildings classified as enclosed parking garages in accordance with Section 406.4 or where located beneath other groups.

Exception: Enclosed parking garages located beneath Group R-3 occupancies.

[F] 903.2.9.1 Commercial parking garages. An automatic sprinkler system shall be provided throughout buildings used for storage of commercial trucks or buses where the fire area exceeds 5,000 square feet (464 m²).

[F] 903.2.10 Windowless stories in all occupancies. An automatic sprinkler system shall be installed in the locations set forth in Sections 903.2.10.1 through 903.2.10.1.3.

Exception: Group R-3 and Group U.

903.2.10.1 Stories and basements without openings. An automatic sprinkler system shall be installed in every story or basement of all buildings where the floor area exceeds 1,500 square feet (139.4 m²) and where there is not provided at least one of the following types of exterior wall openings:

1. Openings below grade that lead directly to ground level by an exterior stairway complying with Section 1009 or an outside ramp complying with Section 1010. Openings shall be located in each 50 linear feet (15 240 mm), or fraction thereof, of exterior wall in the story on at least one side.

2. Openings entirely above the adjoining ground level totaling at least 20 square feet (1.86 m²) in each 50 linear feet (15 240 mm), or fraction thereof, of exterior wall in the story on at least one side.

[F] 903.2.10.1.1 Opening dimensions and access. Openings shall have a minimum dimension of not less than 30 inches (762 mm). Such openings shall be accessible to the fire department from the exterior and shall not be obstructed in a manner that fire fighting or rescue cannot be accomplished from the exterior.

[F] 903.2.10.1.2 Openings on one side only. Where openings in a story are provided on only one side and the opposite wall of such story is more than 75 feet (22 860 mm) from such openings, the story shall be equipped throughout with an approved automatic sprinkler system, or openings as specified above shall be provided on at least two sides of the story.

[F] 903.2.10.1.3 Basements. Where any portion of a basement is located more than 75 feet (22 860 mm) from openings required by Section 903.2.10.1, the basement shall be equipped throughout with an approved automatic sprinkler system.

[F] 903.2.10.2 Rubbish and linen chutes. An automatic sprinkler system shall be installed at the top of rubbish and linen chutes and in their terminal rooms. Chutes extending through three or more floors shall have additional sprinkler heads installed within such chutes at alternate floors. Chute sprinklers shall be accessible for servicing.

[F] 903.2.10.3 Buildings 30 feet or more in height. An automatic sprinkler system shall be installed throughout buildings with a floor level having an occu-

pant load of 30 or more that is located 30 feet (16 764 mm) or more above the lowest level of fire department vehicle access.

Exceptions:

1. Airport control towers.

2. Open parking structures.

3. Occupancies in Group F-2.

[F] 903.2.11 During construction. Automatic sprinkler systems required during construction, alteration and demolition operations shall be provided in accordance with the *Fire Code of New York State*.

[F] 903.2.12 Other hazards. Automatic sprinkler protection shall be provided for the hazards indicated in Sections 903.2.12.1 and 903.2.12.2.

903.2.12.1 Ducts conveying hazardous exhausts. Where required by the *Mechanical Code of New York State*, automatic sprinklers shall be provided in ducts conveying hazardous exhaust, or flammable or combustible materials.

Exception: Ducts where the largest cross-sectional diameter of the duct is less than 10 inches (254 mm).

903.2.12.2 Commercial cooking operations. An automatic sprinkler system shall be installed in commercial kitchen exhaust hood and duct system where an automatic sprinkler system is used to comply with Section 904.

[F] 903.2.13 Other required suppression systems. In addition to the requirements of Section 903.2, the provisions indicated in Table 903.2.13 also require the installation of a suppression system for certain buildings and areas.

[F] TABLE 903.2.13
ADDITIONAL REQUIRED SUPPRESSION SYSTEMS

SECTION	SUBJECT
402.8	Covered malls
403.2, 403.3	High-rise buildings
404.3	Atriums
405.3	Underground structures
407.5	Group I-2
410.6	Stages
411.4	Special amusement buildings
412.2.5, 412.2.6	Aircraft hangars
415.6.2.4	Group H-2
416.4	Flammable finishes
417.4	Drying rooms
507	Unlimited area buildings
508.2	Incidental use areas
1025.6.2.3	Smoke-protected assembly seating
IFC	Sprinkler system requirements as set forth in Section 903.2.13 of the *Fire Code of New York State*

[F] 903.3 Installation requirements. Automatic sprinkler systems shall be designed and installed in accordance with Sections 903.3.1 through 903.3.7.

903.3.1 Standards. Sprinkler systems shall be designed and installed in accordance with Sections 903.3.1.1, 903.3.1.2 or 903.3.1.3.

[F] 903.3.1.1 NFPA 13 sprinkler systems. Where the provisions of this code require that a building or portion thereof be equipped throughout with an automatic sprinkler system in accordance with this section, sprinklers shall be installed throughout in accordance with NFPA 13 except as provided in Section 903.3.1.1.1.

[F] 903.3.1.1.1 Exempt locations. Automatic sprinklers shall not be required in the following rooms or areas where such rooms or areas are protected with an approved automatic fire detection system, in accordance with Section 907.2, that will respond to visible or invisible particles of combustion. Sprinklers shall not be omitted from any room merely because it is damp, of fire-resistance-rated construction or contains electrical equipment.

1. Any room where the application of water, or flame and water, constitutes a serious life or fire hazard.

2. Any room or space where sprinklers are considered undesirable because of the nature of the contents, when approved by the code enforcement official.

3. Generator and transformer rooms separated from the remainder of the building by walls and floor/ceiling or roof/ceiling assemblies having a fire-resistance rating of not less than 2 hours.

4. In rooms or areas that are of noncombustible construction with wholly noncombustible contents.

[F] 903.3.1.2 NFPA 13R sprinkler systems. Where allowed in buildings of Group R, up to and including four stories in height, automatic sprinkler systems shall be installed throughout in accordance with NFPA 13R.

[F] 903.3.1.2.1 Balconies and decks. Sprinkler protection shall be provided for exterior balconies, decks and ground floor patios of dwelling units where the building is of Type V construction. Sidewall sprinklers that are used to protect such areas shall be permitted to be located such that their deflectors are within 1 inch (25 mm) to 6 inches (152 mm) below the structural members and a maximum distance of 14 inches (356 mm) below the deck of the exterior balconies and decks that are constructed of open wood joist construction.

[F] 903.3.1.3 NFPA 13D sprinkler systems. Where allowed, automatic sprinkler systems installed in one- and two-family dwellings shall be installed throughout in accordance with NFPA 13D.

[F] 903.3.2 Quick-response and residential sprinklers. Where automatic sprinkler systems are required by this code, quick-response or residential automatic sprinklers shall be installed in the following areas in accordance with Section 903.3.1 and their listings:

1. Throughout all spaces within a smoke compartment containing patient sleeping units in Group I-2 in accordance with this code.

2. Dwelling units, and sleeping units in Group R and I-1 occupancies.

3. Light-hazard occupancies as defined in NFPA 13.

[F] 903.3.3 Obstructed locations. Automatic sprinklers shall be installed with due regard to obstructions that will delay activation or obstruct the water distribution pattern. Automatic sprinklers shall be installed in or under covered kiosks, displays, booths, concession stands, or equipment that exceeds 4 feet (1219 mm) in width. Not less than a 3-foot (914 mm) clearance shall be maintained between automatic sprinklers and the top of piles of combustible fibers.

Exception: Kitchen equipment under exhaust hoods protected with a fire-extinguishing system in accordance with Section 904.

[F] 903.3.4 Actuation. Automatic sprinkler systems shall be automatically actuated unless specifically provided for in this code.

[F] 903.3.5 Water supplies. Water supplies for automatic sprinkler systems shall comply with this section and the standards referenced in Section 903.3.1. The potable water supply shall be protected against backflow in accordance with the requirements of this section and the *Plumbing Code of New York State.*

[F] 903.3.5.1 Domestic services. Where the domestic service provides the water supply for the automatic sprinkler system, the supply shall be in accordance with this section.

[F] 903.3.5.1.1 Limited area sprinkler systems. Limited area sprinkler systems serving fewer than 20 sprinklers on any single connection are permitted to be connected to the domestic service where a wet automatic standpipe is not available. Limited area sprinkler systems connected to domestic water supplies shall comply with each of the following requirements:

1. Valves shall not be installed between the domestic water riser control valve and the sprinklers.

Exception: An approved indicating control valve supervised in the open position in accordance with Section 903.4.

2. The domestic service shall be capable of supplying the simultaneous domestic demand and the sprinkler demand required to be hydraulically calculated by NFPA 13, NFPA 13R or NFPA 13D.

[F] 903.3.5.1.2 Residential combination services. A single combination water supply shall be allowed provided that the domestic demand is added to the sprinkler demand as required by NFPA 13R.

[F] 903.3.5.2 Secondary water supply. A secondary on-site water supply equal to the hydraulically calculated sprinkler demand, including the hose stream requirement, shall be provided for high-rise buildings in Seismic Design Category C, D, E or F as determined by this code. The secondary water supply shall have a duration of not less than 30 minutes as determined by the occupancy hazard classification in accordance with NFPA 13.

Exception: Existing buildings.

903.3.6 Hose threads. Fire hose threads and fittings used in connection with automatic sprinkler systems shall be as prescribed by the code enforcement official.

903.3.7 Fire department connections. The location of fire department connections shall be approved by the code enforcement official.

[F] 903.4 Sprinkler system monitoring and alarms. All valves controlling the water supply for automatic sprinkler systems, pumps, tanks, water levels and temperatures, critical air pressures and water-flow switches on all sprinkler systems shall be electrically supervised.

Exceptions:

1. Automatic sprinkler systems protecting one- and two-family dwellings.

2. Limited area systems serving fewer than 20 sprinklers.

3. Automatic sprinkler systems installed in accordance with NFPA 13R where a common supply main is used to supply both domestic water and the automatic sprinkler systems and a separate shutoff valve for the automatic sprinkler system is not provided.

4. Jockey pump control valves that are sealed or locked in the open position.

5. Control valves to commercial kitchen hoods, paint spray booths or dip tanks that are sealed or locked in the open position.

6. Valves controlling the fuel supply to fire pump engines that are sealed or locked in the open position.

7. Trim valves to pressure switches in dry, preaction and deluge sprinkler systems that are sealed or locked in the open position.

903.4.1 Signals. Alarm, supervisory and trouble signals shall be distinctly different and shall be automatically transmitted to an approved central station, remote supervising station or proprietary supervising station as defined in NFPA 72 or, when approved by the code enforcement official, shall sound an audible signal at a constantly attended location.

Exceptions:

1. Underground key or hub valves in roadway boxes provided by the municipality or public utility are not required to be monitored.

2. Backflow prevention device test valves located in limited area sprinkler system supply piping shall be locked in the open position. In occupancies required to be equipped with a fire alarm system, the backflow preventer valves shall be electrically supervised by a tamper switch installed in accordance with NFPA 72 and separately annunciated.

[F] 903.4.2 Alarms. Approved audible devices shall be connected to every automatic sprinkler system. Such sprinkler water-flow alarm devices shall be activated by water flow equivalent to the flow of a single sprinkler of the smallest orifice size installed in the system. Alarm devices shall be provided on the exterior of the building in an approved location. Where a fire alarm system is installed, actuation of the automatic sprinkler system shall actuate the building fire alarm system.

[F] 903.4.3 Floor control valves. Approved supervised indicating control valves shall be provided at the point of connection to the riser on each floor in high-rise buildings.

[F] 903.5 Testing and maintenance. Sprinkler systems shall be tested and maintained in accordance with the *Fire Code of New York State*.

SECTION 904
ALTERNATIVE AUTOMATIC FIRE-EXTINGUISHING SYSTEMS

[F] 904.1 General. Automatic fire-extinguishing systems, other than automatic sprinkler systems, shall be designed, installed, inspected, tested and maintained in accordance with the provisions of this section and the applicable referenced standards.

[F] 904.2 Where required. Automatic fire-extinguishing systems installed as an alternative to the required automatic sprinkler systems of Section 903 shall be approved by the code enforcement official. Automatic fire-extinguishing systems shall not be considered alternatives for the purposes of exceptions or reductions allowed by other requirements of this code.

[F] 904.2.1 Commercial hood and duct systems. Each required commercial kitchen exhaust hood and duct system required by the *Fire Code of New York State* or the *Mechanical Code of New York State* to have a Type I hood shall be protected with an approved automatic fire-extinguishing system installed in accordance with this code.

[F] 904.3 Installation. Automatic fire-extinguishing systems shall be installed in accordance with this section.

[F] 904.3.1 Electrical wiring. Electrical wiring shall be in accordance with the NFPA 70.

[F] 904.3.2 Actuation. Automatic fire-extinguishing systems shall be automatically actuated and provided with a manual means of actuation in accordance with Section 904.11.1.

[F] 904.3.3 System interlocking. Automatic equipment interlocks with fuel shutoffs, ventilation controls, door closers, window shutters, conveyor openings, smoke and heat vents and other features necessary for proper operation of the fire-extinguishing system shall be provided as required by the design and installation standard utilized for the hazard.

[F] 904.3.4 Alarms and warning signs. Where alarms are required to indicate the operation of automatic fire-extinguishing systems, distinctive audible and visible alarms and warning signs shall be provided to warn of pending agent discharge. Where exposure to automatic-extinguishing agents poses a hazard to persons and a delay is required to ensure the evacuation of occupants before agent discharge, a separate warning signal shall be provided to alert occupants once agent discharge has begun. Audible signals shall be in accordance with Section 907.9.2.

[F] 904.3.5 Monitoring. Where a building fire alarm system is installed, automatic fire-extinguishing systems shall be monitored by the building fire alarm system in accordance with NFPA 72.

[F] 904.4 Inspection and testing. Automatic fire-extinguishing systems shall be inspected and tested in accordance with the provisions of this section prior to acceptance.

[F] 904.4.1 Inspection. Prior to conducting final acceptance tests, the following items shall be inspected:

1. Hazard specification for consistency with design hazard.

2. Type, location and spacing of automatic- and manual-initiating devices.

3. Size, placement and position of nozzles or discharge orifices.

4. Location and identification of audible and visible alarm devices.

5. Identification of devices with proper designations.

6. Operating instructions.

[F] 904.4.2 Alarm testing. Notification appliances, connections to fire alarm systems and connections to approved supervising stations shall be tested in accordance with this section and Section 907 to verify proper operation.

[F] 904.4.2.1 Audible and visible signals. The audibility and visibility of notification appliances signaling agent discharge or system operation, where required, shall be verified.

[F] 904.4.3 Monitor testing. Connections to protected premises and supervising station fire alarm systems shall be tested to verify proper identification and retransmission of alarms from automatic fire-extinguishing systems.

[F] 904.5 Wet-chemical systems. Wet-chemical extinguishing systems shall be installed, maintained, periodically inspected and tested in accordance with NFPA 17A and their listing.

[F] 904.6 Dry-chemical systems. Dry-chemical extinguishing systems shall be installed, maintained, periodically inspected and tested in accordance with NFPA 17 and their listing.

904.7 Foam systems. Foam-extinguishing systems shall be installed, maintained, periodically inspected and tested in accordance with NFPA 11 and their listing.

[F] 904.8 Carbon dioxide systems. Carbon dioxide extinguishing systems shall be installed, maintained, periodically inspected and tested in accordance with NFPA 12 and their listing.

[F] 904.9 Halon systems. Halogenated extinguishing systems shall be installed, maintained, periodically inspected and tested in accordance with NFPA 12A and their listing.

[F] 904.10 Clean-agent systems. Clean-agent fire-extinguishing systems shall be installed, maintained, periodically inspected and tested in accordance with NFPA 2001 and their listing.

[F] 904.11 Commercial cooking systems. The automatic fire-extinguishing system for commercial cooking systems shall be of a type recognized for protection of commercial cooking equipment and exhaust systems of the type and arrangement protected. Preengineered automatic dry- and wet-chemical extinguishing systems shall be tested in accordance with UL 300 and listed and labeled for the intended application. Other types of automatic fire-extinguishing systems shall be listed and labeled for specific use as protection for commercial cooking operations. The system shall be installed in accordance with this code, its listing and the manufacturer's installation instructions. Automatic fire-extinguishing systems of the following types shall be installed in accordance with the referenced standard indicated, as follows:

1. Carbon dioxide extinguishing systems, NFPA 12.

2. Automatic sprinkler systems, NFPA 13.

3. Foam-water sprinkler system or foam-water spray systems, NFPA 16.

4. Dry-chemical extinguishing systems, NFPA 17.

5. Wet-chemical extinguishing systems, NFPA 17A.

Exception: Factory-built commercial cooking recirculating systems that are tested in accordance with UL 710B and listed, labeled and installed in accordance with Section 304.1 of the *Mechanical Code of New York State.*

904.11.1 Manual system operation. A manual actuation device shall be located at or near a means of egress from the cooking area a minimum of 10 feet (3048 mm) and a maximum of 20 feet (6096 mm) from the kitchen exhaust system. The manual actuation device shall be installed not more than 48 inches (1200 mm) nor less than 42 inches (1067 mm) above the floor and shall clearly identify the hazard protected. The manual actuation shall require a maximum force of 40 pounds (178 N) and a maximum movement of 14 inches (356 mm) to actuate the fire suppression system.

> **Exception:** Automatic sprinkler systems shall not be required to be equipped with manual actuation means.

904.11.2 System interconnection. The actuation of the fire extinguishing system shall automatically shut down the fuel or electrical power supply to the cooking equipment. The fuel and electrical supply reset shall be manual.

904.11.3 Carbon dioxide systems. When carbon dioxide systems are used, there shall be a nozzle at the top of the ventilating duct. Additional nozzles that are symmetrically arranged to give uniform distribution shall be installed within vertical ducts exceeding 20 feet (6096 mm) and horizontal ducts exceeding 50 feet (15 240 mm). Dampers shall be installed at either the top or the bottom of the duct and shall be arranged to operate automatically upon activation of the fire-extinguishing system. When the damper is installed at the top of the duct, the top nozzle shall be immediately below the damper. Automatic carbon dioxide fire-extinguishing systems shall be sufficiently sized to protect against all hazards venting through a common duct simultaneously.

> **[F] 904.11.3.1 Ventilation system.** Commercial-type cooking equipment protected by an automatic carbon dioxide-extinguishing system shall be arranged to shut off the ventilation system upon activation.

[F] 904.11.4 Special provisions for automatic sprinkler systems. Automatic sprinkler systems protecting commercial-type cooking equipment shall be supplied from a separate, readily accessible, indicating-type control valve that is identified.

> **904.11.4.1 Listed sprinklers.** Sprinklers used for the protection of fryers shall be tested in accordance with UL 199E, listed for that application and installed in accordance with their listing.

904.12 Water-mist systems. Water-mist systems shall conform with the provisions of NFPA 750 for design, installation, inspection, testing and maintenance. All devices and appurtenances shall be listed and installed in conformance with the terms of the listing.

SECTION 905
STANDPIPE SYSTEMS

[F] 905.1 General. Standpipe systems shall be provided in new buildings and structures in accordance with this section. Fire hose threads used in connection with standpipe systems shall be approved and shall be compatible with fire department hose threads. The location of fire department hose connections shall be approved. In buildings used for high-piled combustible storage, fire protection shall be in accordance with the *Fire Code of New York State*.

[F] 905.2 Installation standard. Standpipe systems shall be installed in accordance with this section and NFPA 14.

[F] 905.3 Required installations. Standpipe systems shall be installed where required by Sections 905.3.1 through 905.3.7 and in the locations indicated in Sections 905.4, 905.5 and 905.6. Standpipe systems are allowed to be combined with automatic sprinkler systems.

> **Exception:** Standpipe systems are not required in Group R-3 occupancies.

905.3.1 Building height. Class III standpipe systems shall be installed throughout buildings where the floor level of the highest story is located more than 30 feet (9144 mm) above the lowest level of the fire department vehicle access, or where the floor level of the lowest story is located more than 30 feet (9144 mm) below the highest level of fire department vehicle access.

> **Exceptions:**
>
> 1. Class I standpipes are allowed in buildings equipped throughout with an automatic sprinkler system in accordance with Section 903.3.1.1 or 903.3.1.2.
>
> 2. Class I manual standpipes are allowed in open parking garages where the highest floor is located not more than 150 feet (45 720 mm) above the lowest level of fire department vehicle access.
>
> 3. Class I manual dry standpipes are allowed in open parking garages that are subject to freezing temperatures, provided that the hose connections are located as required for Class II standpipes in accordance with Section 905.5.
>
> 4. Class I standpipes are allowed in basements equipped throughout with an automatic sprinkler system.
>
> 5. In determining the lowest level of fire department vehicle access, it shall not be required to consider:
>
>   5.1. Recessed loading docks for four vehicles or less, and
>
>   5.2. Conditions where topography makes access from the fire department vehicle to the building impractical or impossible.

[F] 905.3.2 Group A. Class I automatic wet standpipes shall be provided in nonsprinklered Group A buildings having an occupant load exceeding 1,000 persons.

> **Exceptions:**
>
> 1. Open-air-seating spaces without enclosed spaces.
>
> 2. Class I automatic dry and semiautomatic dry standpipes or manual wet standpipes are allowed in buildings where the highest floor surface used for human occupancy is 75 feet (22 860 mm) or less above the lowest level of fire department vehicle access.

905.3.3 Covered mall buildings. A covered mall building shall be equipped throughout with a standpipe system where required by Section 905.3.1. Covered mall buildings not required to be equipped with a standpipe system by Section 905.3.1 shall be equipped with Class I hose connections connected to a sprinkler system. Hose connections shall be provided at each of the following locations:

1. Within the mall at the entrance to each exit passageway or corridor.

2. At each floor-level landing within enclosed stairways opening directly on the mall.

3. At exterior public entrances to the mall.

905.3.3.1 System design. The installation of Class I hose connections, when required by Section 905.3.3, shall be sized to deliver 250 gallons per minute (946 L/min) at 100 pounds per square inch (689.4 kPa) from the two most hydraulically remote outlets without sprinkler demand and the single most hydraulically remote outlet with sprinkler demand. This shall be achieved with a maximum supply pressure at the fire department connection of not more than 175 pounds per square inch (1206.6 kPa).

905.3.4 Stages. Stages greater than 1,000 square feet in area (93 m²) shall be equipped with a Class III wet standpipe system with $1^1/_2$-inch and $2^1/_2$-inch (38 mm and 64 mm) hose connections on each side of the stage.

Exception: Where the building or area is equipped throughout with an automatic sprinkler system, a $1^1/_2$ inch (38 mm) hose connection shall be installed in accordance with NFPA 13 or in accordance with NFPA 14 for Class II or III standpipes.

905.3.4.1 Hose and cabinet. The $1^1/_2$-inch (38 mm) hose connections shall be equipped with sufficient lengths of $1^1/_2$-inch (38 mm) hose to provide fire protection for the stage area. Hose connections shall be equipped with an approved adjustable fog nozzle and be mounted in a cabinet or on a rack.

[F] 905.3.5 Underground buildings. Underground buildings shall be equipped throughout with a Class I automatic wet or manual wet standpipe system.

[F] 905.3.6 Helistops and heliports. Buildings with a helistop or heliport that are equipped with a standpipe shall extend the standpipe to the roof level on which the helistop or heliport is located in accordance with Section 1107.5 of the *Fire Code of New York State.*

905.3.7 Marinas and boatyards. Marinas and boatyards shall be equipped throughout with standpipe systems in accordance with NFPA 303.

905.4 Location of Class I standpipe hose connections. Class I standpipe hose connections shall be provided in all of the following locations:

1. In every required stairway, a hose connection shall be provided for each floor level above or below grade. Hose connections shall be located at an intermediate floor level landing between floors, unless otherwise approved by the code enforcement official. Nonrequired enclosed stairways are not required to have

hose connections. Stairways without hose connections shall have a sign on the door to the stairway stating "No standpipe connections in stairway."

2. On each side of the wall adjacent to the exit opening of a horizontal exit.

Exception: Where floor areas adjacent to a horizontal exit are reachable from exit stairway hose connections by a 30-foot (9144 mm) hose stream from a nozzle attached to 100 feet (30480 mm) of hose, a hose connection shall not be required at the horizontal exit.

3. In every exit passageway at the entrance from the exit passageway to other areas of a building.

4. In covered mall buildings, adjacent to each exterior public entrance to the mall and adjacent to each entrance from an exit passageway or exit corridor to the mall.

5. Where the roof has a slope less than four units vertical in 12 units horizontal (33.3-percent slope), each standpipe shall be provided with a hose connection located either on the roof or at the highest landing of a stairway with stair access to the roof. An additional hose connection shall be provided at the top of the most hydraulically remote standpipe for testing purposes.

6. Where the most remote portion of a nonsprinklered floor or story is more than 150 feet (45 720 mm) from a hose connection or the most remote portion of a sprinklered floor or story is more than 200 feet (60 960 mm) from a hose connection, the code enforcement official is authorized to require that additional hose connections be provided in approved locations.

[F] 905.4.1 Protection. Risers and laterals of Class I standpipe systems not located within an enclosed stairway or pressurized enclosure shall be protected by a degree of fire resistance equal to that required for vertical enclosures in the building in which they are located.

Exception: In buildings equipped throughout with an approved automatic sprinkler system, laterals that are not located within an enclosed stairway or pressurized enclosure are not required to be enclosed within fire-resistance-rated construction.

[F] 905.4.2 Interconnection. In buildings where more than one standpipe is provided, the standpipes shall be interconnected in accordance with NFPA 14.

905.5 Location of Class II standpipe hose connections. Class II standpipe hose connections shall be accessible and shall be located so that all portions of the building are within 30 feet (9144 mm) of a nozzle attached to 100 feet (30 480 mm) of hose.

[F] 905.5.1 Groups A-1 and A-2. In Group A-1 and A-2 occupancies with occupant loads of more than 1,000, hose connections shall be located on each side of any stage, on each side of the rear of the auditorium, on each side of the balcony and on each tier of dressing rooms.

[F] 905.5.2 Protection. Fire-resistance-rated protection of risers and laterals of Class II standpipe systems is not required.

905.5.3 Class II system 1-inch hose. A minimum 1-inch (25 mm) hose shall be allowed to be used for hose stations in light-hazard occupancies where investigated and listed for this service and where approved by the code enforcement official.

[F] 905.6 Location of Class III standpipe hose connections. Class III standpipe systems shall have hose connections located as required for Class I standpipes in Section 905.4 and shall have Class II hose connections as required in Section 905.5.

[F] 905.6.1 Protection. Risers and laterals of Class III standpipe systems shall be protected as required for Class I systems in accordance with Section 905.4.1.

[F] 905.6.2 Interconnection. In buildings where more than one Class III standpipe is provided, the standpipes shall be interconnected at the bottom.

[F] 905.7 Cabinets. Cabinets containing fire-fighting equipment such as standpipes, fire hoses, fire extinguishers or fire department valves shall not be blocked from use or obscured from view.

[F] 905.7.1 Cabinet equipment identification. Cabinets shall be identified in an approved manner by a permanently attached sign with letters not less than 2 inches (51 mm) high in a color that contrasts with the background color, indicating the equipment contained therein.

Exceptions:

1. Doors not large enough to accommodate a written sign shall be marked with a permanently attached pictogram of the equipment contained therein.

2. Doors that have either an approved visual identification clear glass panel or a complete glass door panel are not required to be marked.

[F] 905.7.2 Locking cabinet doors. Cabinets shall be unlocked.

Exceptions:

1. Visual identification panels of glass or other approved transparent frangible material that is easily broken and allows access.

2. Approved locking arrangements.

3. Group I-3.

[F] 905.8 Dry standpipes. Dry standpipes shall not be installed.

Exception: Where subject to freezing and in accordance with NFPA 14.

[F] 905.9 Valve supervision. Valves controlling water supplies shall be supervised in the open position so that a change in the normal position of the valve will generate a supervisory signal at the supervising station required by Section 903.4. Where a fire alarm system is provided, a signal shall also be transmitted to the control unit.

Exceptions:

1. Valves to underground key or hub valves in roadway boxes provided by the municipality or public utility do not require supervision.

2. Valves locked in the normal position and inspected as provided in this code in buildings not equipped with a fire alarm system.

[F] 905.10 During construction. Standpipe systems required during construction and demolition operations shall be provided in accordance with Section 3311.

SECTION 906
PORTABLE FIRE EXTINGUISHERS

[F] 906.1 General. Portable fire extinguishers shall be provided in occupancies and locations as required by the *Fire Code of New York State.*

SECTION 907
FIRE ALARM AND DETECTION SYSTEMS

[F] 907.1 General. This section covers the application, installation, performance and maintenance of fire alarm systems and their components.

[F] 907.1.1 Construction documents. Construction documents for fire alarm systems shall be submitted for review and approval prior to system installation. Construction documents shall include, but not be limited to, all of the following:

1. A floor plan which indicates the use of all rooms.

2. Locations of alarm-initiating and notification appliances.

3. Alarm control and trouble signaling equipment.

4. Annunciation.

5. Power connection.

6. Battery calculations.

7. Conductor type and sizes.

8. Voltage drop calculations.

9. Manufacturers, model numbers and listing information for equipment, devices and materials.

10. Details of ceiling height and construction.

11. The interface of fire safety control functions.

[F] 907.1.2 Equipment. Systems and their components shall be listed and approved for the purpose for which they are installed.

907.2 Where required-new buildings and structures. An approved manual fire alarm system, automatic fire detection system or automatic heat detection system installed in accordance with the provisions of this code and NFPA 72 shall be provided in new buildings and structures in accordance with Sections 907.2.1 through 907.2.23 and provide occupant notification in accordance with Section 907.9, unless other requirements are provided by another section of this code. Where automatic sprinkler protection installed in accordance with Section 903.3.1.1 or 903.3.1.2 is provided and connected to the building fire alarm system, automatic heat detection required by this section shall not be required.

The automatic fire detectors shall be smoke detectors. Where ambient conditions prohibit installation of automatic smoke detection, other automatic fire detection shall be allowed.

907.2.1 Group A. A manual fire alarm system and automatic fire detection system shall be installed in Group A occupancies. Portions of Group E occupancies occupied for assembly purposes shall be provided with a fire alarm system as required for the Group E occupancy.

[F] 907.2.1.1 System initiation in Group A occupancies with an occupant load of 1,000 or more. Activation of the fire alarm in Group A occupancies with an occupant load of 1,000 or more shall initiate a signal using an emergency voice/alarm communications system in accordance with NFPA 72.

Exception: Where approved, the prerecorded announcement is allowed to be manually deactivated for a period of time, not to exceed 3 minutes, for the sole purpose of allowing a live voice announcement from an approved, constantly attended location.

[F] 907.2.1.2 Emergency power. Emergency voice/alarm communications systems shall be provided with an approved emergency power source.

[F] 907.2.2 Group B. A manual fire alarm system shall be installed in Group B occupancies having an occupant load of 500 or more persons or more than 100 persons above or below the lowest level of exit discharge.

907.2.2.1 Fire detection. Areas of Group B buildings that are not protected by an automatic sprinkler system and that have an occupant load of more than 100 persons shall be provided with automatic fire detection or automatic heat detection installed in accordance with NFPA 72.

907.2.3 Group E. A manual fire alarm system shall be installed in Group E occupancies. When automatic sprinkler systems or smoke detectors are installed, such systems or detectors shall be connected to the building fire alarm system.

Exceptions:

1. Group E occupancies with an occupant load of less than 50.

2. Manual fire alarm boxes are not required in Group E occupancies where all all the following apply:

   2.1. Interior corridors are protected by smoke detectors with alarm verification.

   2.2. Auditoriums, cafeterias, gymnasiums and the like are protected by heat detectors or other approved detection devices.

   2.3. Shops and laboratories involving dusts or vapors are protected by heat detectors or other approved detection devices.

   2.4. Off-premises monitoring is provided.

   2.5. The capability to activate the evacuation signal from a central point is provided.

   2.6. In buildings where normally occupied spaces are provided with a two-way communication system between such spaces and a constantly attended receiving station from where a general evacuation alarm can be sounded, except in locations specifically designated by the code enforcement official.

907.2.4 Group F. A manual fire alarm system shall be installed in Group F occupancies that have an occupant load of 100 or more.

[F] 907.2.5 Group H. A manual fire alarm system shall be installed in Group H-5 occupancies and in occupancies used for the manufacture of organic coatings. An automatic fire detection system shall be installed for highly toxic gases, organic peroxides and oxidizers in accordance with Chapters 37, 39 and 40, respectively, of the *Fire Code of New York State.*

907.2.6 Group I. A manual fire alarm system shall be installed in Group I occupancies. An automatic fire detection system shall be provided in accordance with Sections 907.2.6.1 and 907.2.6.2.

Exception: Manual fire alarm boxes in resident or patient sleeping areas of Group I-1 and I-2 occupancies shall not be required at exits if located at all nurses' control stations or other constantly attended staff locations, provided such stations are visible and continuously accessible and that travel distances required in Section 907.3.1 are not exceeded.

907.2.6.1 Group I-1. Corridors, habitable spaces other than sleeping units and kitchens, and waiting areas that are open to corridors shall be equipped with an automatic smoke detection system.

Exceptions:

1. Smoke detection in habitable spaces is not required where the facility is equipped throughout with an automatic sprinkler system.

2. Smoke detection is not required for exterior balconies.

907.2.6.2 Group I-2. Corridors in nursing homes (both intermediate care and skilled nursing facilities), detoxification facilities and spaces permitted to be open to the corridors by Section 407.2 of the *Building Code of New York State* shall be equipped with an automatic fire detection system. Hospitals shall be equipped with smoke detection as required in *Section 407.2 of the Building Code of New York State*.

Exceptions:

1. Corridor smoke detection is not required in smoke compartments that contain patient sleeping units where patient sleeping units are provided with smoke detectors that comply with UL 268. Such detectors shall provide a visual display on the corridor side of each patient sleeping unit and an audible and visual alarm at the nursing station attending each unit.

2. Corridor smoke detection is not required in smoke compartments that contain patient sleeping units where patient sleeping unit doors are equipped with automatic door-closing devices with integral smoke detectors on the unit sides installed in accordance with their listing, provided that the integral detectors perform the required alerting function.

907.2.6.3 Group I-3. Group I-3 occupancies shall be equipped with a manual fire alarm system and automatic fire detection system installed for alerting staff.

[F] 907.2.6.3.1 System initiation. Actuation of an automatic fire-extinguishing system, a manual fire alarm box or a fire detector shall initiate an approved fire alarm signal which automatically notifies staff. Presignal systems shall not be used.

[F] 907.2.6.3.2 Manual fire alarm boxes. Manual fire alarm boxes are not required to be located in accordance with Section 907.3 where the fire alarm boxes are provided at staff-attended locations having direct supervision over areas where manual fire alarm boxes have been omitted.

Manual fire alarm boxes shall be permitted to be locked in areas occupied by detainees, provided that staff members are present within the subject area and have keys readily available to operate the manual fire alarm boxes.

907.2.6.3.3 Smoke detectors. An approved automatic fire detection system shall be installed throughout resident housing areas, including sleeping units and contiguous day rooms, group activity spaces and other common spaces normally accessible to residents.

Exceptions:

1. Other approved smoke detection arrangements providing equivalent protection including, but not limited to, placing detectors in exhaust ducts from cells or behind protective guards listed for the purpose are allowed when necessary to prevent damage or tampering.

2. Sleeping units in Use Conditions 2 and 3.

3. Smoke detectors are not required in sleeping units with four or fewer occupants in smoke compartments that are equipped throughout with an approved automatic sprinkler system.

[F] 907.2.7 Group M. A manual fire alarm system shall be installed in Group M occupancies having an occupant load of 500 or more persons or more than 100 persons above or below the lowest level of exit discharge. The initiation of a signal from a manual fire alarm box shall initiate alarm notification appliances as required by Section 907.9.

Exceptions:

1. Covered mall buildings complying with Section 402.

2. Manual fire alarm boxes are not required where the building is equipped throughout with an automatic sprinkler system and the alarm notification appliances will automatically activate upon sprinkler water flow.

907.2.7.1 Occupant notification. During times that the building is occupied, the initiation of a signal from a manual fire alarm box or from a water flow switch shall not be required to activate the alarm notification appliances when an alarm signal is activated at a constantly attended location from which evacuation instructions shall be initiated over an emergency voice/alarm communication system installed in accordance with Section 907.2.12.2.

The emergency voice/alarm communication system shall be allowed to be used for other announcements provided the manual fire alarm use takes precedence over any other use.

907.2.7.2 Fire detection. Areas of Group M buildings that are not protected by an automatic sprinkler system and that have an occupant load of more than 100 persons shall be provided with automatic smoke detection or automatic heat detection installed in accordance with NFPA 72.

907.2.8 Group R-1. Fire alarm systems shall be installed in Group R-1 occupancies as required in Sections 907.2.8.1 through 907.2.8.3.

[F] 907.2.8.1 Manual fire alarm system. A manual fire alarm system shall be installed in Group R-1 occupancies.

Exception: A manual fire alarm system is not required in buildings not more than two stories in height where all individual sleeping units and contiguous attic and crawl spaces are separated from each other and public or common areas by at least 1-hour fire partitions and each individual sleeping unit has an exit directly to a public way, exit court or yard.

907.2.8.2 Automatic fire detection system. An automatic fire detection system shall be installed throughout all interior corridors serving sleeping units.

Exception: An automatic fire detection system is not required in buildings that do not have interior corridors serving sleeping units and where each sleeping unit has a means of egress door opening directly to an exterior exit access that leads directly to an exit.

[F] 907.2.8.3 Smoke alarms. Smoke alarms shall be installed as required by Section 907.2.10. In buildings that are not equipped throughout with an automatic sprinkler system installed in accordance with Section 903.3.1.1 or 903.3.1.2, the smoke alarms in sleeping units shall be connected to an emergency electrical system and shall be annunciated by sleeping unit at a constantly attended location from which the fire alarm system is capable of being manually activated.

[F] 907.2.9 Group R-2. A manual fire alarm system shall be installed in Group R-2 occupancies where:

1. Any dwelling unit or sleeping unit is located three or more stories above the lowest level of exit discharge;

2. Any dwelling unit or sleeping unit is located more than one story below the highest level of exit discharge of exits serving the dwelling unit or sleeping unit; or

3. The building contains more than 16 dwelling units or sleeping units.

Exceptions:

1. A fire alarm system is not required in buildings not more than two stories in height where all dwelling units or sleeping units and contiguous attic and crawl spaces are separated from each other and public or common areas by at least 1-hour fire partitions and each dwelling unit or sleeping unit has an exit directly to a public way, exit court or yard.

2. A fire alarm system is not required in buildings that do not have interior corridors serving dwelling units and are protected by an approved automatic sprinkler system installed in accordance with Section 903.3.1.1 or 903.3.1.2, provided that dwelling units either have a means of egress door opening directly to an exterior exit access that leads directly to the exits or are served by open-ended corridors designed in accordance with Section 1023.6, Exception 4.

907.2.9.1 Student housing. An approved automatic fire detection system shall be installed in all Group R-2 occupancies used as dormitories, fraternities, sororities and similar student housing in accordance with this section.

907.2.9.1.1 Common and utility spaces. Automatic fire detection shall be provided in common and utility spaces outside of dwelling and sleeping units including but not limited to recreation rooms, lounges, dining rooms, laundry rooms, mechanical equipment rooms and storage rooms.

907.2.9.1.2 Exits and corridors. Automatic fire detection shall be required in corridors and exits.

907.2.9.1.3 Dwelling units and sleeping units. Automatic fire detection shall be installed in dwelling units and sleeping units. The automatic fire detectors shall be installed to send a supervisory signal upon activation of one fire detector. For sleeping units or dwelling units that are equipped with more than one fire detector, a fire alarm signal shall be sent upon activation of two or more fire detectors within a sleeping unit or dwelling unit.

907.2.9.1.3.1 Notification. Notification devices shall be provided in dwelling units and sleeping units meeting the audible requirements of this code and NFPA 72. The notification appliances in dwelling units and sleeping units shall activate when an initiation device activates within the dwelling unit or sleeping unit or when the building fire alarm system is activated.

Exception: In high-rise buildings, the building fire alarm shall activate in accordance with Section 907.2.12.2.

[F] 907.2.10 Single- and multiple-station smoke alarms. Listed single- and multiple-station smoke alarms complying with UL 217 shall be installed in accordance with the provisions of this code and the household fire-warning equipment provisions of NFPA 72.

[F] 907.2.10.1 Where required. Single- or multiple-station smoke alarms shall be installed in the locations described in Sections 907.2.10.1.1 through 907.2.10.1.3.

[F] 907.2.10.1.1 Group R-1. Single- or multiple-station smoke alarms shall be installed in all of the following locations in Group R-1:

1. In sleeping areas.

2. In every room in the path of the means of egress from the sleeping area to the door leading from the sleeping unit.

3. In each story within the sleeping unit, including basements. For sleeping units with split levels and without an intervening door between the adjacent levels, a smoke alarm installed on the upper level shall suffice for the adjacent lower level provided that the lower level is less than one full story below the upper level.

[F] 907.2.10.1.2 Groups R-2, R-3, R-4 and I-1. Single- or multiple-station smoke alarms shall be installed and maintained in Groups R-2, R-3, R-4 and I-1, regardless of occupant load at all of the following locations:

1. On the ceiling or wall outside of each separate sleeping area in the immediate vicinity of bedrooms.

2. In each room used for sleeping purposes.

3. In each story within a dwelling unit, including basements but not including crawl spaces and uninhabitable attics. In dwellings or dwelling units with split levels and without an intervening door between the adjacent levels, a smoke alarm installed on the upper level shall suffice for the adjacent lower level provided that the lower level is less than one full story below the upper level.

Exception: Group R-2 occupancies used as dormitories, fraternities, sororities and similar student housing meeting the requirements of 907.2.9.1.3.

907.2.10.1.3 Group I-1. Single- or multiple-station smoke alarms shall be installed and maintained in sleeping areas in Group I-1 occupancies.

Exception: Single- or multiple-station smoke alarms shall not be required where the building is equipped throughout with an automatic fire detection system in accordance with Section 907.2.6.

[F] 907.2.10.2 Power source. In new construction, required smoke alarms shall receive their primary power from the building wiring where such wiring is served from a commercial source and shall be equipped with a battery backup. Smoke alarms shall emit a signal when the batteries are low. Wiring shall be permanent and without a disconnecting switch other than as required for overcurrent protection.

Exception: Smoke alarms are not required to be equipped with battery backup in Group R-1 where they are connected to an emergency electrical system.

907.2.10.3 Interconnection. Where more than one smoke alarm is required to be installed within an individual dwelling unit or sleeping unit in Group R-2, R-3 or R-4, or within an individual sleeping unit in Group R-1, the smoke alarms shall be interconnected in such a manner that the activation of one alarm will activate all of the alarms in the individual unit. The alarm shall be clearly audible in all bedrooms over background noise levels with all intervening doors closed.

[F] 907.2.10.4 Acceptance testing. When the installation of the alarm devices is complete, each detector and interconnecting wiring for multiple-station alarm devices shall be tested in accordance with the household fire warning equipment provisions of NFPA 72.

[F] 907.2.11 Special amusement buildings. An approved automatic smoke detection system shall be provided in

special amusement buildings in accordance with this section.

Exception: In areas where ambient conditions will cause a smoke detection system to alarm, an approved alternative type of automatic detector shall be installed.

[F] 907.2.11.1 Alarm. Activation of any single smoke detector, the automatic sprinkler system or any other automatic fire detection device shall immediately sound an alarm at the building at a constantly attended location from which emergency action can be initiated, including the capability of manual initiation of requirements in Section 907.2.11.2.

[F] 907.2.11.2 System response. The activation of two or more smoke detectors, a single smoke detector with alarm verification, the automatic sprinkler system or other approved fire detection device shall automatically:

1. Cause illumination of the means of egress with light of not less than 1 foot-candle (11 lux) at the walking surface level;

2. Stop any conflicting or confusing sounds and visual distractions; and

3. Activate an approved directional exit marking that will become apparent in an emergency.

Such system response shall also include activation of a prerecorded message, clearly audible throughout the special amusement building, instructing patrons to proceed to the nearest exit. Alarm signals used in conjunction with the prerecorded message shall produce a sound which is distinctive from other sounds used during normal operation.

The wiring to the auxiliary devices and equipment used to accomplish the above fire safety functions shall be monitored for integrity in accordance with NFPA 72.

[F] 907.2.11.3 Emergency voice/alarm communication system. An emergency voice/alarm communication system, which is also allowed to serve as a public address system, shall be installed in accordance with NFPA 72, and shall be audible throughout the entire special amusement building.

[F] 907.2.12 High-rise buildings. Buildings with a floor used for human occupancy located more than 75 feet (22 860 mm) above the lowest level of fire department vehicle access shall be provided with an automatic fire alarm system and an emergency voice/alarm communication system in accordance with Section 907.2.12.2.

Exceptions:

1. Airport traffic control towers in accordance with Sections 412 and 907.2.22.

2. Open parking garages in accordance with Section 406.3.

3. Buildings with an occupancy in Group A-5.

4. Low-hazard special occupancies in accordance with Section 503.1.1.

5. Buildings with an occupancy in Group H-1, H-2 or H-3 in accordance with Section 415.

[F] 907.2.12.1 Automatic fire detection. Smoke detectors shall be provided in accordance with this section. Smoke detectors shall be connected to an automatic fire alarm system. The activation of any detector required by this section shall operate the emergency voice/alarm communication system. Smoke detectors shall be located as follows:

1. In each mechanical equipment, electrical, transformer, telephone equipment or similar room which is not provided with sprinkler protection, elevator machine rooms and in elevator lobbies.

2. In the main return air and exhaust air plenum of each air-conditioning system having a capacity greater than 2,000 cubic feet per minute (cfm) (0.94 m^3/s). Such detectors shall be located in a serviceable area downstream of the last duct inlet.

3. At each connection to a vertical duct or riser serving two or more stories from a return air duct or plenum of an air-conditioning system. In Group R-1 and R-2 occupancies a listed smoke detector is allowed to be used in each return air riser carrying not more than 5,000 cfm (2.4 m^3/s) and serving not more than 10 air inlet openings.

[F] 907.2.12.2 Emergency voice/alarm communication system. The operation of any automatic fire detector, sprinkler water-flow device or manual fire alarm box shall automatically sound an alert tone followed by voice instructions giving approved information and directions for a general or staged evacuation on a minimum of the alarming floor, the floor above and the floor below in accordance with the building's fire safety and evacuation plans required by Section 404 of the *Fire Code of New York State*. Speakers shall be provided throughout the building by paging zones. As a minimum, paging zones shall be provided as follows:

1. Elevator groups.

2. Exit stairways.

3. Each floor.

4. Areas of refuge as defined in Section 1002.1.

Exception: In Group I-1 and I-2 occupancies, the alarm shall sound in a constantly attended area and a general occupant notification shall be broadcast over the overhead page.

[F] 907.2.12.2.1 Manual override. A manual override for emergency voice communication shall be provided on a selective and all-call basis for all paging zones.

[F] 907.2.12.2.2 Live voice messages. The emergency voice/alarm communication system shall also have the capability to broadcast live voice messages through paging zones on a selective and all-call basis.

[F] 907.2.12.2.3 Standard. The emergency voice/alarm communication system shall be designed and installed in accordance with NFPA 72.

907.2.12.3 Fire department communication system. An approved two-way, fire department communication system designed and installed in accordance with NFPA 72 shall be provided for fire department use. It shall operate between a fire command center complying with Section 911 and elevators, elevator lobbies, emergency and standby power rooms, fire pump rooms, areas of refuge and inside enclosed exit stairways. The fire department communication device shall be provided at each floor level within the enclosed stairway.

Exception: Fire department radio systems where approved by the fire department.

[F] 907.2.13 Atriums connecting more than two stories. A fire alarm system shall be installed in occupancies with an atrium that connects more than two stories. The system shall be activated in accordance with Section 907.6. Such occupancies in Group A, E or M shall be provided with an emergency voice/alarm communication system complying with the requirements of Section 907.2.12.2.

[F] 907.2.14 High-piled combustible storage areas. An automatic fire detection system shall be installed throughout high-piled combustible storage areas where required by the *Fire Code of New York State*.

[F] 907.2.15 Delayed egress locks. Where delayed egress locks are installed on means of egress doors in accordance with Section 1008.1.8.6, an automatic smoke or heat detection system shall be installed as required by that section.

[F] 907.2.16 Aerosol storage uses. Aerosol storage rooms and general-purpose warehouses containing aerosols shall be provided with an approved manual fire alarm system where required by the *Fire Code of New York State*.

[F] 907.2.17 Lumber, wood structural panel and veneer mills. Lumber, wood structural panel and veneer mills shall be provided with a manual fire alarm system.

[F] 907.2.18 Underground buildings with smoke exhaust system. Where a smoke exhaust system is installed in an underground building in accordance with this code, automatic fire detectors shall be provided in accordance with this section.

[F] 907.2.18.1 Smoke detectors. A minimum of one smoke detector listed for the intended purpose shall be installed in the following areas:

1. Mechanical equipment, electrical, transformer, telephone equipment, elevator machine or similar rooms.

2. Elevator lobbies.

3. The main return and exhaust air plenum of each air-conditioning system serving more than one story and located in a serviceable area downstream of the last duct inlet.

4. Each connection to a vertical duct or riser serving two or more floors from return air ducts or plenums of heating, ventilating and air-conditioning systems, except that in Group R occupancies, a listed smoke detector is allowed to be used in each return air riser carrying not more than 5,000 cfm (2.4 m³/s) and serving not more than 10 air inlet openings.

[F] 907.2.18.2 Alarm required. Activation of the smoke exhaust system shall activate an audible alarm at a constantly attended location.

[F] 907.2.19 Underground buildings. Where the lowest level of a structure is more than 60 feet (18 288 mm) below the lowest level of exit discharge, the structure shall be equipped throughout with a manual fire alarm system, including an emergency voice/alarm communication system installed in accordance with Section 907.2.12.2.

907.2.19.1 Public address system. Where a fire alarm system is not required by Section 907.2, a public address system shall be provided which shall be capable of transmitting voice communications to the highest level of exit discharge serving the underground portions of the structure and all levels below.

[F] 907.2.20 Covered mall buildings. Covered mall buildings exceeding 50,000 square feet (4645 m²) in total floor area shall be provided with an emergency voice/alarm communication system. An emergency voice/alarm communication system serving a mall, required or otherwise, shall be accessible to the fire department. The system shall be provided in accordance with Section 907.2.12.2.

907.2.21 Residential aircraft hangars. A minimum of one listed smoke alarm shall be installed within a residential aircraft hangar as defined in Section 412.3.1 and shall be interconnected into the residential smoke alarm or other sounding device to provide an alarm which will be audible in all sleeping areas of the dwelling.

[F] 907.2.22 Airport traffic control towers. An automatic fire detection system shall be provided in airport traffic control towers.

907.2.23 Battery rooms. An approved automatic smoke detection system shall be installed in areas containing stationary storage battery systems having a liquid capacity of more than 50 gallons (189 L). The detection system shall be supervised by an approved central, proprietary or remote station service or a local alarm which will sound an audible signal at a constantly attended location.

[F] 907.3 Manual fire alarm boxes. Manual fire alarm boxes shall be installed in accordance with Sections 907.3.1 through 907.3.5.

[F] 907.3.1 Location. Manual fire alarm boxes shall be located not more than 5 feet (1524 mm) from the entrance to each exit. Additional manual fire alarm boxes shall be located so that travel distance to the nearest box does not exceed 200 feet (60 960 mm).

Exception: In buildings protected by an automatic sprinkler system in accordance with 903.3.1.1 or 903.3.1.2, the travel distance to the nearest box shall not apply.

[F] 907.3.2 Height. The height of the manual fire alarm boxes shall be a minimum of 42 inches (1067 mm) and a maximum of 48 inches (1219 mm), measured vertically, from the floor level to the activating handle or lever of the box.

[F] 907.3.3 Color. Manual fire alarm boxes shall be red in color.

[F] 907.3.4 Signs. Where fire alarm systems are not monitored by a supervising station, an approved permanent sign shall be installed adjacent to each manual fire alarm box that reads: WHEN ALARM SOUNDS-CALL FIRE DEPARTMENT.

Exception: Where the manufacturer has permanently provided this information on the manual fire alarm box.

[F] 907.3.5 Protective covers. The code enforcement official is authorized to require the installation of listed manual fire alarm box protective covers to prevent malicious false alarms or to provide the manual fire alarm box with protection from physical damage. The protective cover shall be transparent or red in color with a transparent face to permit visibility of the manual fire alarm box. Each cover shall include proper operating instructions. A protective cover that emits a local alarm signal shall not be installed unless approved.

907.4 Power supply. The primary and secondary power supply for the fire alarm system shall be provided in accordance with NFPA 72.

[F] 907.5 Wiring. Wiring shall comply with the requirements of NFPA 70 and NFPA 72. Wireless protection systems utilizing radio-frequency transmitting devices shall comply with the special requirements for supervision of low-power wireless systems in NFPA 72.

[F] 907.6 Activation. Where an alarm notification system is required by another section of this code, it shall be activated by:

1. A required automatic fire alarm system.

2. Sprinkler water-flow devices.

3. Required manual fire alarm boxes.

[F] 907.7 Presignal system. Presignal systems shall not be installed unless approved by the code enforcement official and the fire department. Where a presignal system is installed, 24-hour personnel supervision shall be provided at a location approved by the fire department, in order that the alarm signal can be actuated in the event of fire or other emergency.

[F] 907.8 Zones. Each floor shall be zoned separately and a zone shall not exceed 22,500 square feet (2090 m²). The length of any zone shall not exceed 300 feet (91 440 mm) in any direction.

Exception: Automatic sprinkler system zones shall not exceed the area permitted by NFPA 13.

[F] 907.8.1 Zoning indicator panel. A zoning indicator panel and the associated controls shall be provided in an approved location. The visual zone indication shall lock in until the system is reset and shall not be canceled by the operation of an audible alarm-silencing switch.

[F] 907.8.2 High-rise buildings. In buildings with a floor used for human occupancy that is located more than 75 feet (22 860 mm) above the lowest level of fire department vehicle access, a separate zone by floor shall be provided for all of the following types of alarm-initiating devices where provided:

1. Smoke detectors.

2. Sprinkler water-flow devices.

3. Manual fire alarm boxes.

4. Other approved types of automatic fire detection devices or suppression systems.

[F] 907.9 Alarm notification appliances. Alarm notification appliances shall be provided and shall be listed for their purpose.

[F] 907.9.1 Visible alarms. Visible alarm notification appliances shall be provided in accordance with Sections 907.9.1.1 through 907.9.1.4.

Exceptions:

1. Visible alarm notification appliances are not required in alterations, except where an existing fire alarm system is upgraded or replaced, or a new fire alarm system is installed.

2. Visible alarm notification appliances shall not be required in exits as defined in Section 1002.1.

[F] 907.9.1.1 Public and common areas. Visible alarm notification appliances shall be provided in public areas and common areas.

[F] 907.9.1.2 Employee work areas. Where employee work areas have audible alarm coverage, the notification appliance circuits serving the employee work areas shall be initially designed with a minimum of 20 percent spare capacity to account for the potential of adding visible notification appliances in the future to accommodate hearing impaired employees.

[F] 907.9.1.3 Groups I-1 and R-1. Group I-1 and R-1 sleeping units in accordance with Table 907.9.1.3 shall be provided with a visible alarm notification appliance, activated by both the in-room smoke alarm and the building fire alarm system.

907.9.1.4 Group R-2. In Group R-2 occupancies required by Section 907 to have a fire alarm system, all dwelling units and sleeping units shall be provided with the capability to support visible alarm notification appliances in accordance with ICC/ANSI A117.1.

[F] 907.9.2 Audible alarms. Audible alarm notification appliances shall be provided and shall sound a distinctive sound that is not to be used for any purpose other than that of a fire alarm. The audible alarm notification appliances shall provide a sound pressure level of 15 decibels (dBA) above the average ambient sound level or 5 dBA above the maximum sound level having a duration of at least 60 seconds, whichever is greater, in every occupied space within

[F] TABLE 907.9.1.3
VISIBLE AND AUDIBLE ALARMS

NUMBER OF SLEEPING UNITS	SLEEPING UNITS WITH VISIBLE AND AUDIBLE ALARMS
6 to 25	2
26 to 50	4
51 to 75	7
76 to 100	9
101 to 150	12
151 to 200	14
201 to 300	17
301 to 400	20
401 to 500	22
501 to 1,000	5% of total
1,001 and over	50 plus 3 for each 100 over 1,000

the building. The minimum sound pressure levels shall be: 70 dBA in occupancies in Groups R and I-1; 90 dBA in mechanical equipment rooms and 60 dBA in other occupancies. The maximum sound pressure level for audible alarm notification appliances shall be 120 dBA at the minimum hearing distance from the audible appliance. Where the average ambient noise is greater than 105 dBA, visible alarm notification appliances shall be provided in accordance with NFPA 72 and audible alarm notification appliances shall not be required.

Exception: Visible alarm notification appliances shall be allowed in lieu of audible alarm notification appliances in critical-care areas of Group I-2 occupancies.

[F] 907.10 Fire safety functions. Automatic fire detectors utilized for the purpose of performing fire safety functions shall be connected to the building's fire alarm control panel where a fire alarm system is required by Section 907.2. Detectors shall, upon actuation, perform the intended function and activate the alarm notification appliances or a visible and audible supervisory signal at a constantly attended location. In buildings not required to be equipped with a fire alarm system, the automatic fire detector shall be powered by normal electrical service and, upon actuation, perform the intended function. The detectors shall be located in accordance with NFPA 72.

[F] 907.11 Duct smoke detectors. Duct smoke detectors shall be connected to the building's fire alarm control panel when a fire alarm system is provided. Activation of a duct smoke detector shall initiate a visible and audible supervisory signal at a constantly attended location. Duct smoke detectors shall not be used as a substitute for required open-area detection.

Exceptions:

1. The supervisory signal at a constantly attended location is not required where duct smoke detectors activate the building's alarm notification appliances.

2. In occupancies not required to be equipped with a fire alarm system, actuation of a smoke detector

shall activate a visible and audible signal in an approved location. Smoke detector trouble conditions shall activate a visible or audible signal in an approved location and shall be identified as air duct detector trouble.

[F] 907.12 Access. Access shall be provided to each detector for periodic inspection, maintenance and testing.

[F] 907.13 Fire-extinguishing systems. Automatic fire-extinguishing systems shall be connected to the building fire alarm system where a fire alarm system is required by another section of this code or is otherwise installed.

[F] 907.14 Monitoring. Fire alarm systems required by this chapter or the *Fire Code of New York State* shall be monitored by an approved supervising station in accordance with NFPA 72.

> **Exception:** Supervisory service is not required for:
>
> 1. Single- and multiple-station smoke alarms required by Section 907.2.10.
>
> 2. Smoke detectors in Group I-3 occupancies.
>
> 3. Automatic sprinkler systems in one- and two-family dwellings.

[F] 907.15 Automatic telephone-dialing devices. Automatic telephone-dialing devices used to transmit an emergency alarm shall not be connected to any fire department telephone number unless approved by the fire chief.

[F] 907.16 Acceptance tests. Upon completion of the installation of the fire alarm system, alarm notification appliances and circuits, alarm-initiating devices and circuits, supervisory-signal initiating devices and circuits, signaling line circuits, and primary and secondary power supplies shall be tested in accordance with NFPA 72.

[F] 907.17 Record of completion. A record of completion in accordance with NFPA 72 verifying that the system has been installed in accordance with the approved plans and specifications shall be provided.

[F] 907.18 Instructions. Operating, testing and maintenance instructions, and record drawings ("as builts") and equipment specifications shall be provided at an approved location.

[F] 907.19 Inspection, testing and maintenance. The maintenance and testing schedules and procedures for fire alarm and fire detection systems shall be in accordance with the *Fire Code of New York State.*

SECTION 908
EMERGENCY ALARM SYSTEMS

[F] 908.1 Group H occupancies. Emergency alarms for the detection and notification of an emergency condition in Group H occupancies shall be provided in accordance with Section 414.7.

[F] 908.2 Group H-5 occupancy. Emergency alarms for notification of an emergency condition in an HPM facility shall be provided as required in Section 415.8.4.6. A continuous gas-detection system shall be provided for HPM gases in accordance with Section 415.8.7.

[F] 908.3 Highly toxic and toxic materials. A gas detection system shall be provided to detect the presence of gas at or below the permissible exposure limit (PEL) or ceiling limit of the gas for which detection is provided. The system shall be capable of monitoring the discharge from the treatment system at or below one-half the immediately dangerous to life and health (IDLH) limit.

> **Exception:** A gas-detection system is not required for toxic gases when the physiological warning threshold level for the gas is at a level below the accepted PEL for the gas.

[F] 908.3.1 Alarms. The gas detection system shall initiate a local alarm and transmit a signal to a constantly attended control station when a short-term hazard condition is detected. The alarm shall be both visible and audible and shall provide warning both inside and outside the area where gas is detected. The audible alarm shall be distinct from all other alarms.

> **Exception:** Signal transmission to a constantly attended control station is not required when not more than one cylinder of highly toxic or toxic gas is stored.

[F] 908.3.2 Shutoff of gas supply. The gas detection system shall automatically close the shutoff valve at the source on gas supply piping and tubing related to the system being monitored for whichever gas is detected.

> **Exception:** Automatic shutdown is not required for reactors utilized for the production of highly toxic or toxic compressed gases where such reactors are:
>
> 1. Operated at pressures less than 15 pounds per square inch gauge (psig) (103.4 kPa).
>
> 2. Constantly attended.
>
> 3. Provided with readily accessible emergency shutoff valves.

[F] 908.3.3 Valve closure. The automatic closure of shutoff valves shall be in accordance with the following:

1. When the gas-detection sampling point initiating the gas detection system alarm is within a gas cabinet or exhausted enclosure, the shutoff valve in the gas cabinet or exhausted enclosure for the specific gas detected shall automatically close.

2. Where the gas-detection sampling point initiating the gas detection system alarm is within a gas room and compressed gas containers are not in gas cabinets or exhausted enclosures, the shutoff valves on all gas lines for the specific gas detected shall automatically close.

3. Where the gas-detection sampling point initiating the gas detection system alarm is within a piping distribution manifold enclosure, the shutoff valve for the compressed container of specific gas detected supplying the manifold shall automatically close.

> **Exception:** When the gas-detection sampling point initiating the gas-detection system alarm is at a use location or within a gas valve enclosure of a branch line downstream of a piping distribution manifold, the shut-

off valve in the gas valve enclosure for the branch line located in the piping distribution manifold enclosure shall automatically close.

[F] 908.4 Ozone gas-generator rooms. Ozone gas-generator rooms shall be equipped with a continuous gas-detection system that will shut off the generator and sound a local alarm when concentrations above the PEL occur.

[F] 908.5 Repair garages. A flammable-gas detection system shall be provided in repair garages for vehicles fueled by nonodorized gases in accordance with Section 406.6.6.

[F] 908.6 Refrigerant detector. Machinery rooms shall contain a refrigerant detector with an audible and visual alarm. The detector, or a sampling tube that draws air to the detector, shall be located in an area where refrigerant from a leak will concentrate. The alarm shall be actuated at a value not greater than the corresponding TLV-TWA values for the refrigerant classification indicated in the *Mechanical Code of New York State*. Detectors and alarms shall be placed in approved locations.

SECTION 909
SMOKE CONTROL SYSTEMS

[F] 909.1 Scope and purpose. This section applies to mechanical or passive smoke control systems when they are required by other provisions of this code. The purpose of this section is to establish minimum requirements for the design, installation and acceptance testing of smoke control systems that are intended to provide a tenable environment for the evacuation or relocation of occupants. These provisions are not intended for the preservation of contents, the timely restoration of operations or for assistance in fire suppression or overhaul activities. Smoke control systems regulated by this section serve a different purpose than the smoke- and heat-venting provisions found in Section 910. Mechanical smoke control systems shall not be considered exhaust systems under Chapter 5 of the *Mechanical Code of New York State*.

909.1.1 Definitions. The following definitions are added for the purposes of this section only.

PRESSURIZATION. The creation and maintenance of pressure levels in zones of a building, including elevator shafts and stairwells, that are higher than the pressure level at the smoke source, such pressure levels being produced by positive pressures of a supply of uncontaminated air, by exhausting air and smoke at the smoke source, or by a combination of these methods.

SMOKE. Airborne solid and liquid particulates and gases evolve when a material undergoes pyrolysis or combustion, including the quantity of air that is entrained or otherwise mixed into the mass.

SMOKE BARRIER. A continuous membrane, either vertical or horizontal, such as a wall, floor or ceiling assembly, that is designed and constructed to restrict the movement of smoke.

SMOKE-CONTROL MODE. A predefined operational configuration of a system or device for the purpose of smoke control.

SMOKE-CONTROL SYSTEM, MECHANICAL. An engineered system that uses mechanical fans to produce pressure differences across smoke barriers or to establish air flows to limit and direct smoke movement.

SMOKE-CONTROL SYSTEM, PASSIVE. A system of smoke barriers arranged to limit the migration of smoke.

SMOKE-CONTROL ZONE. A space within a building enclosed by smoke barriers.

SMOKE DAMPER. A device that meets the requirements of approved recognized standards and that is designed to resist the passage of air or smoke. A combination fire and smoke damper shall meet the requirements of approved recognized standards.

SMOKE-EXHAUST SYSTEM. A mechanical or gravity system intended to move smoke from the smoke zone to the exterior of the building, including smoke removal, purging and venting systems, as well as the function of exhaust fans used to reduce the pressure in a smoke zone.

STACK EFFECT. The vertical airflow within buildings caused by temperature differences.

TENABLE ENVIRONMENT. An environment in which the quantity and location of smoke is limited or otherwise restricted to allow for ready evacuation through the space.

ZONED SMOKE CONTROL. A smoke-control system using pressure differences between adjacent smoke-control zones.

[F] 909.2 General design requirements. Buildings, structures or parts thereof required by this code to have a smoke control system or systems shall have such systems designed in accordance with the applicable requirements of Section 909 and the generally accepted and well-established principles of engineering relevant to the design. The construction documents shall include sufficient information and detail to adequately describe the elements of the design necessary for the proper implementation of the smoke control systems. These documents shall be accompanied by sufficient information and analysis to demonstrate compliance with these provisions.

[F] 909.3 Special inspection and test requirements. In addition to the ordinary inspection and test requirements which buildings, structures and parts thereof are required to undergo, smoke control systems subject to the provisions of Section 909 shall undergo special inspections and tests sufficient to verify the proper commissioning of the smoke control design in its final installed condition. The design submission accompanying the construction documents shall clearly detail procedures and methods to be used and the items subject to such inspections and tests. Such commissioning shall be in accordance with generally accepted engineering practice and, where possible, based on published standards for the particular testing involved. The special inspections and tests required by this section shall be conducted under the same terms in Section 1704.

[F] 909.4 Analysis. A rational analysis supporting the types of smoke control systems to be employed, their methods of operation, the systems supporting them and the methods of construction to be utilized shall accompany the submitted construction documents and shall include, but not be limited to, the items indicated in Sections 909.4.1 through 909.4.6.

[F] 909.4.1 Stack effect. The system shall be designed such that the maximum probable normal or reverse stack effect will not adversely interfere with the system's capabilities. In determining the maximum probable stack effect, altitude, elevation, weather history and interior temperatures shall be used.

[F] 909.4.2 Temperature effect of fire. Buoyancy and expansion caused by the design fire in accordance with Section 909.9 shall be analyzed. The system shall be designed such that these effects do not adversely interfere with the system's capabilities.

[F] 909.4.3 Wind effect. The design shall consider the adverse effects of wind. Such consideration shall be consistent with the wind-loading provisions of Chapter 16.

[F] 909.4.4 HVAC systems. The design shall consider the effects of the heating, ventilating and air-conditioning (HVAC) systems on both smoke and fire transport. The analysis shall include all permutations of systems status. The design shall consider the effects of the fire on the HVAC systems.

[F] 909.4.5 Climate. The design shall consider the effects of low temperatures on systems, property and occupants. Air inlets and exhausts shall be located so as to prevent snow or ice blockage.

909.4.6 Duration of operation. All portions of active or passive smoke control systems shall be capable of continued operation after detection of the fire event for a period of not less than either 20 minutes or 1.5 times the calculated egress time, whichever is less.

[F] 909.5 Smoke barrier construction. Smoke barriers shall comply with Section 709, and shall be constructed and sealed to limit leakage areas exclusive of protected openings. The maximum allowable leakage area shall be the aggregate area calculated using the following leakage area ratios:

1. Walls: $A/A_w = 0.00100$
2. Exit enclosures: $A/A_w = 0.00035$
3. All other shafts: $A/A_w = 0.00150$
4. Floors and roofs: $A/A_F = 0.00050$

where:

A = Total leakage area, square feet (m²).

A_F = Unit floor or roof area of barrier, square feet (m²).

A_w = Unit wall area of barrier, square feet (m²).

The leakage area ratios shown do not include openings due to doors, operable windows or similar gaps. These shall be included in calculating the total leakage area.

[F] 909.5.1 Leakage area. The total leakage area of the barrier is the product of the smoke barrier gross area multiplied by the allowable leakage area ratio, plus the area of other openings such as gaps and operable windows. Compliance shall be determined by achieving the minimum air pressure difference across the barrier with the system in the smoke control mode for mechanical smoke control

systems. Passive smoke control systems tested using other approved means such as door fan testing shall be as approved by the code enforcement official.

[F] 909.5.2 Opening protection. Openings in smoke barriers shall be protected by automatic-closing devices actuated by the required controls for the mechanical smoke control system. Door openings shall be protected by fire door assemblies complying with Section 715.4.3.

Exceptions:

1. Passive smoke control systems with automatic-closing devices actuated by spot-type smoke detectors listed for releasing service installed in accordance with Section 907.10.

2. Fixed openings between smoke zones that are protected utilizing the airflow method.

3. In Group I-2, where such doors are installed across corridors, a pair of opposite-swinging doors without a center mullion shall be installed having vision panels with fire protection-rated glazing materials in fire protection-rated frames, the area of which shall not exceed that tested. The doors shall be close-fitting within operational tolerances and shall not have undercuts, louvers or grilles. The doors shall have head and jamb stops, astragals or rabbets at meeting edges and shall be automatic-closing by smoke detection in accordance with Section 715.4.7.3. Positive-latching devices are not required.

4. Group I-3.

5. Openings between smoke zones with clear ceiling heights of 14 feet (4267 mm) or greater and bank-down capacity of greater than 20 minutes as determined by the design fire size.

[F] 909.5.2.1 Ducts and air transfer openings. Ducts and air transfer openings are required to be protected with a minimum Class II, 250°F (121°C) smoke damper complying with Section 716.

[F] 909.6 Pressurization method. The primary mechanical means of controlling smoke shall be by pressure differences across smoke barriers. Maintenance of a tenable environment is not required in the smoke control zone of fire origin.

[F] 909.6.1 Minimum pressure difference. The minimum pressure difference across a smoke barrier shall be 0.05-inch water gage (0.0124 kPa) in fully sprinklered buildings.

In buildings permitted to be other than fully sprinklered, the smoke control system shall be designed to achieve pressure differences at least two times the maximum calculated pressure difference produced by the design fire.

[F] 909.6.2 Maximum pressure difference. The maximum air pressure difference across a smoke barrier shall be determined by required door-opening or closing forces. The actual force required to open exit doors when the system is in the smoke control mode shall be in accordance with Section 1008.1.2. Opening and closing forces for other doors shall be determined by standard engineering methods for the resolution of forces and reactions. The calculated force to set a side-hinged, swinging door in motion shall be determined by:

$$F = F_{dc} + K(WA\Delta P)/2(W - d) \quad \textbf{(Equation 9-1)}$$

where:

A = Door area, square feet (m²).

d = Distance from door handle to latch edge of door, feet (m).

F = Total door opening force, pounds (N).

F_{dc} = Force required to overcome closing device, pounds (N).

K = Coefficient 5.2 (1.0).

W = Door width, feet (m).

ΔP = Design pressure difference, inches of water (Pa).

[F] 909.7 Airflow design method. When approved by the code enforcement official, smoke migration through openings fixed in a permanently open position, which are located between smoke control zones by the use of the airflow method, shall be permitted. The design airflow shall be in accordance with this section. Airflow shall be directed to limit smoke migration from the fire zone. The geometry of openings shall be considered to prevent flow reversal from turbulent effects.

[F] 909.7.1 Velocity. The minimum average velocity through a fixed opening shall not be less than:

$$v = 217.2\,[h\,(T_f - T_o)/(T_f + 460)]^{1/2} \quad \textbf{(Equation 9-2)}$$

For SI:$v = 119.9\,[h\,(T_f - T_o)/T_f]^{1/2}$

where:

h = Height of opening, feet (m).

T_f = Temperature of smoke, °F (K).

T_o = Temperature of ambient air, °F (K).

v = Air velocity, feet per minute (m/minute).

[F] 909.7.2 Prohibited conditions. This method shall not be employed where either the quantity of air or the velocity of the airflow will adversely affect other portions of the smoke control system, unduly intensify the fire, disrupt plume dynamics or interfere with exiting. In no case shall airflow toward the fire exceed 200 feet per minute (1.02 m/s). Where the formula in Section 909.7.1 requires airflow to exceed this limit, the airflow method shall not be used.

909.8 Exhaust method. When approved by the code enforcement official, mechanical smoke control for large enclosed volumes, such as in atriums or malls, shall be permitted to utilize the exhaust method. Smoke control systems using the exhaust method shall be designed in accordance with NFPA 92B.

909.8.1 Smoke layer. The height of the lowest horizontal surface of the accumulating smoke layer shall be maintained at least 6 feet (1829 mm) above any walking surface that forms a portion of a required egress system within the smoke zone.

[F] 909.9 Design fire. The design fire shall be based on a rational analysis performed by the registered design professional and approved by the code enforcement official. The design fire shall be based on the analysis in accordance with Section 909.4 and this section.

[F] 909.9.1 Factors considered. The engineering analysis shall include the characteristics of the fuel, fuel load, effects included by the fire and whether the fire is likely to be steady or unsteady.

909.9.2 Separation distance. Determination of the design fire shall include consideration of the type of fuel, fuel spacing and configuration.

[F] 909.9.3 Heat-release assumptions. The analysis shall make use of best available data from approved sources and shall not be based on excessively stringent limitations of combustible material.

[F] 909.9.4 Sprinkler effectiveness assumptions. A documented engineering analysis shall be provided for conditions that assume fire growth is halted at the time of sprinkler activation.

[F] 909.10 Equipment. Equipment including, but not limited to, fans, ducts, automatic dampers and balance dampers, shall be suitable for its intended use, suitable for the probable exposure temperatures that the rational analysis indicates and as approved by the code enforcement official.

[F] 909.10.1 Exhaust fans. Components of exhaust fans shall be rated and certified by the manufacturer for the probable temperature rise to which the components will be exposed. This temperature rise shall be computed by:

$$T_s = (Q_c/mc) + (T_a) \quad \textbf{(Equation 9-3)}$$

where:

c = Specific heat of smoke at smoke layer temperature, Btu/lb°F (kJ/kg · K).

m = Exhaust rate, pounds per second (kg/s).

Q_c = Convective heat output of fire, Btu/s (kW).

T_a = Ambient temperature, °F (K).

T_s = Smoke temperature, °F (K).

> **Exception:** Reduced T_s as calculated based on the assurance of adequate dilution air.

[F] 909.10.2 Ducts. Duct materials and joints shall be capable of withstanding the probable temperatures and pressures to which they are exposed as determined in accordance with Section 909.10.1. Ducts shall be constructed and supported in accordance with the *Mechanical Code of New York State*. Ducts shall be leak tested to 1.5 times the maximum design pressure in accordance with nationally accepted practices. Measured leakage shall not exceed 5 percent of design flow. Results of such testing shall be a part of the documentation procedure. Ducts shall be supported directly from fire-resistance-rated structural elements of the building by substantial, noncombustible supports.

> **Exception:** Flexible connections (for the purpose of vibration isolation) complying with the *Mechanical*

Code of New York State, that are constructed of approved fire-resistance-rated materials.

[F] 909.10.3 Equipment, inlets and outlets. Equipment shall be located so as to not expose uninvolved portions of the building to an additional fire hazard. Outside air inlets shall be located so as to minimize the potential for introducing smoke or flame into the building. Exhaust outlets shall be so located as to minimize reintroduction of smoke into the building and to limit exposure of the building or adjacent buildings to an additional fire hazard.

[F] 909.10.4 Automatic dampers. Automatic dampers, regardless of the purpose for which they are installed within the smoke control system, shall be listed and conform to the requirements of approved, recognized standards.

[F] 909.10.5 Fans. In addition to other requirements, belt-driven fans shall have 1.5 times the number of belts required for the design duty, with the minimum number of belts being two. Fans shall be selected for stable performance based on normal temperature and, where applicable, elevated temperature. Calculations and manufacturer's fan curves shall be part of the documentation procedures. Fans shall be supported and restrained by noncombustible devices in accordance with the requirements of Chapter 16. Motors driving fans shall not be operated beyond their nameplate horsepower (kilowatts), as determined from measurement of actual current draw, and shall have a minimum service factor of 1.15.

[F] 909.11 Power systems. The smoke control system shall be supplied with two sources of power. Primary power shall be from the normal building power system. Secondary power shall be from an approved standby source complying with NFPA 70. The standby power source and its transfer switches shall be in a separate room from the normal power transformers and switch gear and shall be enclosed in a room constructed of not less than 1-hour fire barriers ventilated directly to and from the exterior. Power distribution from the two sources shall be by independent routes. Transfer to full standby power shall be automatic and within 60 seconds of failure of the primary power. The systems shall comply with this code or NFPA 70.

[F] 909.11.1 Power sources and power surges. Elements of the smoke management system relying on volatile memories or the like shall be supplied with uninterruptable power sources of sufficient duration to span a 15-minute primary power interruption. Elements of the smoke management system susceptible to power surges shall be suitably protected by conditioners, suppressors or other approved means.

[F] 909.12 Detection and control systems. Fire detection systems providing control input or output signals to mechanical smoke control systems or elements thereof shall comply with the requirements of Section 907. Such systems shall be equipped with a control unit complying with UL 864 and listed as smoke control equipment.

Control systems for mechanical smoke control systems shall include provisions for verification. Verification shall include positive confirmation of actuation, testing, manual override, the presence of power downstream of all disconnects and, through a preprogrammed weekly test sequence, report abnormal conditions audibly, visually and by printed report.

[F] 909.12.1 Wiring. In addition to meeting requirements of NFPA 70, all wiring, regardless of voltage, shall be fully enclosed within continuous raceways.

[F] 909.12.2 Activation. Smoke control systems shall be activated in accordance with this section.

[F] 909.12.2.1 Pressurization, airflow or exhaust method. Mechanical smoke control systems using the pressurization, airflow or exhaust method shall have completely automatic control.

[F] 909.12.2.2 Passive method. Passive smoke control systems actuated by approved spot-type detectors listed for releasing service shall be permitted.

[F] 909.12.3 Automatic control. Where completely automatic control is required or used, the automatic-control sequences shall be initiated from an appropriately zoned automatic sprinkler system complying with Section 903.3.1.1, manual controls that are readily accessible to the fire department and any smoke detectors required by engineering analysis.

[F] 909.13 Control air tubing. Control air tubing shall be of sufficient size to meet the required response times. Tubing shall be flushed clean and dry prior to final connections and shall be adequately supported and protected from damage. Tubing passing through concrete or masonry shall be sleeved and protected from abrasion and electrolytic action.

[F] 909.13.1 Materials. Control air tubing shall be hard drawn copper, Type L, ACR in accordance with ASTM B 42, ASTM B 43, ASTM B 68, ASTM B 88, ASTM B 251 and ASTM B 280. Fittings shall be wrought copper or brass, solder type, in accordance with ASME B 16.18 or ASME B 16.22. Changes in direction shall be made with appropriate tool bends. Brass compression-type fittings shall be used at final connection to devices; other joints shall be brazed using a BCuP5 brazing alloy with solidus above 1,100°F (593°C) and liquids below 1,500°F (816°C). Brazing flux shall be used on copper-to-brass joints only.

Exception: Nonmetallic tubing used within control panels and at the final connection to devices, provided that all of the following conditions are met:

1. Tubing shall be listed by an approved agency for flame and smoke characteristics.

2. Tubing and connected devices shall be completely enclosed within galvanized or paint-grade steel enclosure of not less than 0.030 inch (0.76 mm) (No. 22 galvanized sheet gage) thickness. Entry to the enclosure shall be by copper tubing with a protective grommet of neoprene or teflon or by suitable brass compression to male-barbed adapter.

3. Tubing shall be identified by appropriately documented coding.

4. Tubing shall be neatly tied and supported within enclosure. Tubing bridging cabinet and door or moveable device shall be of sufficient length to avoid tension and excessive stress. Tubing shall be protected against abrasion. Tubing serving devices on doors shall be fastened along hinges.

[F] 909.13.2 Isolation from other functions. Control tubing serving other than smoke control functions shall be isolated by automatic isolation valves or shall be an independent system.

[F] 909.13.3 Testing. Control air tubing shall be tested at three times the operating pressure for not less than 30 minutes without any noticeable loss in gauge pressure prior to final connection to devices.

[F] 909.14 Marking and identification. The detection and control systems shall be clearly marked at all junctions, accesses and terminations.

[F] 909.15 Control diagrams. Identical control diagrams showing all devices in the system and identifying their location and function shall be maintained current and kept on file with the code enforcement official, the fire department and in the fire command center in a format and manner approved by the fire chief.

909.16 Fire-fighter's smoke control panel. A fire-fighter's smoke control panel for fire department emergency response purposes only shall be provided and shall include manual control or override of automatic control for mechanical smoke control systems. The panel shall be located in a fire command center complying with Section 911 in high-rise buildings or buildings with smoke-protected assembly seating. In all other buildings, the fire-fighter's smoke control panel shall be installed in an approved location adjacent to the fire alarm control panel. The fire-fighter's smoke control panel shall comply with Sections 909.16.1 through 909.16.3.

[F] 909.16.1 Smoke control systems. Fans within the building shall be shown on the fire-fighter's control panel. A clear indication of the direction of airflow and the relationship of components shall be displayed. Status indicators shall be provided for all smoke control equipment, annunciated by fan and zone, and by pilot-lamp-type indicators as follows:

1. Fans, dampers and other operating equipment in their normal status-WHITE.

2. Fans, dampers and other operating equipment in their off or closed status-RED.

3. Fans, dampers and other operating equipment in their on or open status-GREEN.

4. Fans, dampers and other operating equipment in a fault status-YELLOW/AMBER.

[F] 909.16.2 Smoke control panel. The fire-fighter's control panel shall provide control capability over the complete smoke-control system equipment within the building as follows:

1. ON-AUTO-OFF control over each individual piece of operating smoke control equipment that can also be controlled from other sources within the building. This includes stairway pressurization fans; smoke exhaust fans; supply, return and exhaust fans; elevator shaft fans and other operating equipment used or intended for smoke control purposes.

2. OPEN-AUTO-CLOSE control over individual dampers relating to smoke control and that are also controlled from other sources within the building.

3. ON-OFF or OPEN-CLOSE control over smoke control and other critical equipment associated with a fire or smoke emergency and that can only be controlled from the fire-fighter's control panel.

Exceptions:

1. Complex systems, where approved, where the controls and indicators are combined to control and indicate all elements of a single smoke zone as a unit.

2. Complex systems, where approved, where the control is accomplished by computer interface using approved, plain English commands.

[F] 909.16.3 Control action and priorities. The fire-fighter's control panel actions shall be as follows:

1. ON-OFF and OPEN-CLOSE control actions shall have the highest priority of any control point within the building. Once issued from the fire-fighter's control panel, no automatic or manual control from any other control point within the building shall contradict the control action. Where automatic means are provided to interrupt normal, nonemergency equipment operation or produce a specific result to safeguard the building or equipment (i.e., duct freezestats, duct smoke detectors, high-temperature cutouts, temperature-actuated linkage and similar devices), such means shall be capable of being overridden by the fire-fighter's control panel. The last control action as indicated by each fire-fighter's control panel switch position shall prevail. In no case shall control actions require the smoke control system to assume more than one configuration at any one time.

Exception: Power disconnects required by NFPA 70.

2. Only the AUTO position of each three-position fire-fighter's control panel switch shall allow automatic or manual control action from other control points within the building. The AUTO position shall be the NORMAL, nonemergency, building control position. Where a fire-fighter's control panel is in the AUTO position, the actual status of the device (on, off, open, closed) shall continue to be indicated by the status indicator described above. When directed by an automatic signal to assume an emergency condition, the NORMAL position shall become the emergency condition for that device or group of devices within the zone. In no case shall control actions require the smoke control system to assume more than one configuration at any one time.

[F] 909.17 System response time. Smoke-control system activation shall be initiated immediately after receipt of an appropriate automatic or manual activation command. Smoke control systems shall activate individual components (such as dampers and fans) in the sequence necessary to prevent physical damage to the fans, dampers, ducts and other equipment. For purposes of smoke control, the fire-fighter's control panel response time shall be the same for automatic or manual smoke control action initiated from any other building control point. The total response time, including that necessary for detection, shutdown of operating equipment and smoke control system startup, shall allow for full operational mode to be achieved before the conditions in the space exceed the design smoke condition. The system response time for each component and their sequential relationships shall be detailed in the required rational analysis and verification of their installed condition reported in the required final report.

[F] 909.18 Acceptance testing. Devices, equipment, components and sequences shall be individually tested. These tests, in addition to those required by other provisions of this code, shall consist of determination of function, sequence and, where applicable, capacity of their installed condition.

[F] 909.18.1 Detection devices. Smoke or fire detectors that are a part of a smoke control system shall be tested in accordance with Chapter 9 in their installed condition. When applicable, this testing shall include verification of airflow in both minimum and maximum conditions.

[F] 909.18.2 Ducts. Ducts that are part of a smoke control system shall be traversed using generally accepted practices to determine actual air quantities.

[F] 909.18.3 Dampers. Dampers shall be tested for function in their installed condition.

[F] 909.18.4 Inlets and outlets. Inlets and outlets shall be read using generally accepted practices to determine air quantities.

[F] 909.18.5 Fans. Fans shall be examined for correct rotation. Measurements of voltage, amperage, revolutions per minute (rpm) and belt tension shall be made.

[F] 909.18.6 Smoke barriers. Measurements using inclined manometers or other approved calibrated measuring devices shall be made of the pressure differences across smoke barriers. Such measurements shall be conducted for each possible smoke control condition.

[F] 909.18.7 Controls. Each smoke zone, equipped with an automatic-initiation device, shall be put into operation by the actuation of one such device. Each additional device within the zone shall be verified to cause the same sequence without requiring the operation of fan motors in order to prevent damage. Control sequences shall be verified throughout the system, including verification of override from the fire-fighter's control panel and simulation of standby power conditions.

[F] 909.18.8 Special inspections for smoke control. Smoke control systems shall be tested by a special inspector.

[F] 909.18.8.1 Scope of testing. Special inspections shall be conducted in accordance with the following:

1. During erection of ductwork and prior to concealment for the purposes of leakage testing and recording of device location.

2. Prior to occupancy and after sufficient completion for the purposes of pressure-difference testing, flow measurements, and detection and control verification.

[F] 909.18.8.2 Qualifications. Special inspection agencies for smoke control shall have expertise in fire protection engineering, mechanical engineering and certification as air balancers.

[F] 909.18.8.3 Reports. A complete report of testing shall be prepared by the special inspector or special inspection agency. The report shall include identification of all devices by manufacturer, nameplate data, design values, measured values and identification tag or mark. The report shall be reviewed by the responsible registered design professional and, when satisfied that the design intent has been achieved, the responsible registered design professional shall seal, sign and date the report.

[F] 909.18.8.3.1 Report filing. A copy of the final report shall be filed with the code enforcement official and an identical copy shall be maintained in an approved location at the building.

[F] 909.18.9 Identification and documentation. Charts, drawings and other documents identifying and locating each component of the smoke control system, and describing its proper function and maintenance requirements, shall be maintained on file at the building as an attachment to the report required by Section 909.18.8.3. Devices shall have an approved identifying tag or mark on them consistent with the other required documentation and shall be dated indicating the last time they were successfully tested and by whom.

[F] 909.19 System acceptance. Buildings, or portions thereof, required by this code to comply with this section shall not be issued a certificate of occupancy until such time that the code enforcement official determines that the provisions of this section have been fully complied with and that the fire department has received satisfactory instruction on the operation, both automatic and manual, of the system.

Exception: In buildings of phased construction, a temporary certificate of occupancy, as approved by the code enforcement official, shall be allowed provided that those portions of the building to be occupied meet the requirements of this section and that the remainder does not pose a significant hazard to the safety of the proposed occupants or adjacent buildings.

909.20 Smokeproof enclosures. Where required by Section 1020.1.7, a smokeproof enclosure shall be constructed in accordance with this section. A smokeproof enclosure shall consist of an enclosed interior exit stairway that conforms to Section 1020.1 and an open exterior balcony or ventilated vestibule meeting the requirements of this section. Where access to the roof is required by the *Fire Code of New York State*, such access shall be from the smokeproof enclosure where a smokeproof enclosure is required.

909.20.1 Access. Access to the stair shall be by way of a vestibule or an open exterior balcony. The minimum dimension of the vestibule shall not be less than the required width of the corridor leading to the vestibule but shall not have a width of less than 44 inches (1118 mm) and shall not have a length of less than 72 inches (1829 mm) in the direction of egress travel.

909.20.2 Construction. The smokeproof enclosure shall be separated from the remainder of the building by not less than a 2-hour fire barrier without openings other than the required means of egress doors. The vestibule shall be separated from the stairway by not less than a 2-hour fire barrier. The open exterior balcony shall be constructed in accordance with the fire-resistance-rating requirements for floor construction.

909.20.2.1 Door closers. Doors in a smokeproof enclosure shall be self- or automatic closing by actuation of a smoke detector installed at the floor-side entrance to the smokeproof enclosure. The actuation of the smoke detector on any door shall activate the closing devices on all doors in the smokeproof enclosure at all levels. Smoke detectors shall be installed in accordance with Section 907.10.

909.20.3 Natural ventilation alternative. The provisions of Sections 909.20.3.1 through 909.20.3.3 shall apply to ventilation of smokeproof enclosures by natural means.

909.20.3.1 Balcony doors. Where access to the stairway is by way of an open exterior balcony, the door assembly into the enclosure shall be a fire door assembly in accordance with Section 715.4.

909.20.3.2 Vestibule doors. Where access to the stairway is by way of a vestibule, the door assembly into the vestibule shall be a fire door complying with Section 715.4. The door assembly from the vestibule to the stairway shall have not less than a 20-minute fire protection rating complying with Section 715.4.

909.20.3.3 Vestibule ventilation. Each vestibule shall have a minimum net area of 16 square feet (1.5 m²) of opening in a wall facing an outer court, yard or public way that is at least 20 feet (6096 mm) in width.

909.20.4 Mechanical ventilation alternative. The provisions of Sections 909.20.4.1 through 909.20.4.4 shall apply to ventilation of smokeproof enclosures by mechanical means.

909.20.4.1 Vestibule doors. The door assembly from the building into the vestibule shall be a fire door assembly complying with Section 715.4.3. The door assembly from the vestibule to the stairway shall not have less than a 20-minute fire protection rating and meet the requirements for a smoke door assembly in accordance with Section 715.4.3. The door shall be installed in accordance with NFPA 105.

909.20.4.2 Vestibule ventilation. The vestibule shall be supplied with not less than one air change per min-

ute and the exhaust shall not be less than 150 percent of supply. Supply air shall enter and exhaust air shall discharge from the vestibule through separate, tightly constructed ducts used only for that purpose. Supply air shall enter the vestibule within 6 inches (152 mm) of the floor level. The top of the exhaust register shall be located at the top of the smoke trap but not more than 6 inches (152 mm) down from the top of the trap, and shall be entirely within the smoke trap area. Doors in the open position shall not obstruct duct openings. Duct openings with controlling dampers are permitted where necessary to meet the design requirements, but dampers are not otherwise required.

909.20.4.2.1 Engineered ventilation system. Where a specially engineered system is used, the system shall exhaust a quantity of air equal to not less than 90 air changes per hour from any vestibule in the emergency operation mode and shall be sized to handle three vestibules simultaneously. Smoke detectors shall be located at the floor-side entrance to each vestibule and shall activate the system for the affected vestibule. Smoke detectors shall be installed in accordance with Section 907.10.

909.20.4.3 Smoke trap. The vestibule ceiling shall be at least 20 inches (508 mm) higher than the door opening into the vestibule to serve as a smoke and heat trap and to provide an upward-moving air column. The height shall not be decreased unless approved and justified by design and test.

909.20.4.4 Stair shaft air movement system. The stair shaft shall be provided with a dampered relief opening and supplied with sufficient air to maintain a minimum positive pressure of 0.10 inch of water (25 Pa) in the shaft relative to the vestibule with all doors closed.

909.20.5 Stair pressurization alternative. Where the building is equipped throughout with an automatic sprinkler system in accordance with Section 903.3.1.1, the vestibule is not required, provided that interior exit stairways are pressurized to a minimum of 0.15 inch of water (37 Pa) and a maximum of 0.35 inch of water (87 Pa) in the shaft relative to the building measured with all stairway doors closed under maximum anticipated stack pressures.

909.20.6 Ventilating equipment. The activation of ventilating equipment required by the alternatives in Sections 909.20.4 and 909.20.5 shall be by smoke detectors installed at each floor level at an approved location at the entrance to the smokeproof enclosure. When the closing device for the stair shaft and vestibule doors is activated by smoke detection or power failure, the mechanical equipment shall activate and operate at the required performance levels. Smoke detectors shall be installed in accordance with Section 907.10.

909.20.6.1 Ventilation systems. Smokeproof enclosure ventilation systems shall be independent of other building ventilation systems. The equipment and ductwork shall comply with one of the following:

1. Equipment and ductwork shall be located exterior to the building and directly connected to the

smokeproof enclosure or connected to the smokeproof enclosure by ductwork enclosed by 2-hour fire barriers.

2. Equipment and ductwork shall be located within the smokeproof enclosure with intake or exhaust directly from and to the outside or through ductwork enclosed by 2-hour fire barriers.

3. Equipment and ductwork shall be located within the building if separated from the remainder of the building, including other mechanical equipment, by 2-hour fire barriers.

909.20.6.2 Standby power. Mechanical vestibule and stair shaft ventilation systems and automatic fire detection systems shall be powered by an approved standby power system conforming to Section 403.10.1 and Chapter 27.

909.20.6.3 Acceptance and testing. Before the mechanical equipment is approved, the system shall be tested in the presence of the building official to confirm that the system is operating in compliance with these requirements.

SECTION 910
SMOKE AND HEAT VENTS

[F] 910.1 General. Where required by this code or otherwise installed, smoke and heat vents, or mechanical smoke exhaust systems, and draft curtains shall conform to the requirements of this section.

Exceptions:

1. Frozen food warehouses used solely for storage of Class I and II commodities where protected by an approved automatic sprinkler system.

2. Where areas of buildings are equipped with early suppression fast-response (ESFR) sprinklers, automatic smoke and heat vents shall not be required within these areas.

[F] 910.2 Where required. Smoke and heat vents shall be installed in the roofs of one-story buildings or portions thereof occupied for the uses set forth in Sections 910.2.1 through 910.2.3.

[F] 910.2.1 Group F-1 or S-1. Buildings and portions thereof used as a Group F-1 or S-1 occupancy having more than 50,000 square feet (4645 m²) in undivided area.

Exception: Group S-1 aircraft repair hangars.

[F] 910.2.2 High-piled combustible storage. Buildings and portions thereof containing high-piled combustible stock or rack storage in any occupancy group when required by Section 2306.7 of the *Fire Code of New York State*.

[F] 910.2.3 Exit access travel distance increase. Buildings and portions thereof used as a Group F-1 or S-1 occupancy where the maximum exit access travel distance is increased in accordance with Section 1016.2.

[F] 910.3 Design and installation. The design and installation of smoke and heat vents and draft curtains shall be as specified in Sections 910.3.1 through 910.3.5.2 and Table 910.3.

[F] 910.3.1 Design. Smoke and heat vents shall be listed and labeled to indicate compliance with UL 793.

[F] 910.3.2 Vent operation. Smoke and heat vents shall be capable of being operated by approved automatic and manual means. Automatic operation of smoke and heat vents shall conform to the provisions of Sections 910.3.2.1 through 910.3.2.3.

[F] 910.3.2.1 Gravity-operated drop-out vents. Automatic smoke and heat vents containing heat-sensitive glazing designed to shrink and drop out of the vent opening when exposed to fire shall fully open within 5 minutes after the vent cavity is exposed to a simulated fire, represented by a time-temperature gradient that reaches an air temperature of 500°F (260°C) within 5 minutes.

[F] 910.3.2.2 Sprinklered buildings. Where installed in buildings provided with an approved automatic sprinkler system, smoke and heat vents shall be designed to operate automatically.

[F] 910.3.2.3 Nonsprinklered buildings. Where installed in buildings not provided with an approved automatic sprinkler system, smoke and heat vents shall operate automatically by actuation of a heat-responsive device rated at between 100°F (38°C) and 220°F (104°C) above ambient.

Exception: Gravity-operated drop-out vents complying with Section 910.3.2.1

[F] 910.3.3 Vent dimensions. The effective venting area shall not be less than 16 square feet (1.5 m²) with no dimension less than 4 feet (1219 mm), excluding ribs or gutters having a total width not exceeding 6 inches (152 mm).

[F] 910.3.4 Vent locations. Smoke and heat vents shall be located 20 feet (6096 mm) or more from adjacent lot lines and fire walls and 10 feet (3048 mm) or more from fire barrier walls. Vents shall be uniformly located within the roof area above high-piled storage areas, with consideration given to roof pitch, draft curtain location, sprinkler location and structural members.

[F] 910.3.5 Draft curtains. Where required by Table 910.3, draft curtains shall be provided in accordance with this section.

Exception: Where areas of buildings are equipped with ESFR sprinklers, draft curtains shall not be provided within these areas. Draft curtains shall only be provided at the separation between the ESFR sprinklers and the conventional sprinklers.

[F] 910.3.5.1 Construction. Draft curtains shall be constructed of sheet metal, lath and plaster, gypsum board or other approved materials which provide equivalent performance to resist the passage of smoke. Joints and connections shall be smoke tight.

[F] TABLE 910.3
REQUIREMENTS FOR DRAFT CURTAINS AND SMOKE AND HEAT VENTS[a]

OCCUPANCY GROUP AND COMMODITY CLASSIFICATION	DESIGNATED STORAGE HEIGHT (feet)	MINIMUM DRAFT CURTAIN DEPTH (feet)	MAXIMUM AREA FORMED BY DRAFT CURTAINS (square feet)	VENT-AREA-TO-FLOOR-AREA RATIO[c]	MAXIMUM SPACING OF VENT CENTERS (feet)	MAXIMUM DISTANCE TO VENTS FROM WALL OR DRAFT CURTAINS[b] (feet)
Group F-1and S-1	≤ 20	$0.2 \times H^d$ but ≥ 4	50,000	1:100	120	60
High-piled Storage (see Section 910.2.2) I-IV (Option 1)	≥ 20	6	10,000	1:100	100	60
	$> 20 \leq 40$	6	8,000	1:75	100	55
High-piled Storage (see Section 910.2.2) I-IV (Option 2)	≤ 20	4	3,000	1:75	100	55
	$> 20 \leq 40$	4	3,000	1:50	100	50
High-piled Storage (see Section 910.2.2) High hazard (Option 1)	≤ 20	6	6,000	1:50	100	50
	$> 20 \leq 30$	6	6,000	1:40	90	45
High-piled Storage (see Section 910.2.2) High hazard (Option 2)	≤ 20	4	4,000	1:50	100	50
	$> 20 \leq 30$	4	2,000	1:30	75	40

For SI: 1 foot = 304.8 mm, 1 square foot = 0.0929 m^2.

a. Requirements for rack storage heights in excess of those indicated shall be in accordance with Chapter 23 of the *Fire Code* of New York State solid-piled storage heights in excess of those indicated, an approved engineered design shall be used.

b. The distance specified is the maximum distance from any vent in a particular draft curtained area to walls or draft curtains which form the perimeter of the draft curtained area.

c. Where draft curtains are not required, the vent-area-to-floor-area ratio shall be calculated based on a minimum draft curtain depth of 6 feet (Option 1).

d. "H" is the height of the vent, in feet, above the floor.

[F] 910.3.5.2 Location and depth. The location and minimum depth of draft curtains shall be in accordance with Table 910.3.

[F] 910.4 Mechanical smoke exhaust. Where approved by the code enforcement official, engineered mechanical smoke exhaust shall be an acceptable alternate to smoke and heat vents.

[F] 910.4.1 Location. Exhaust fans shall be uniformly spaced within each draft-curtained area and the maximum distance between fans shall not be greater than 100 feet (30 480 mm).

[F] 910.4.2 Size. Fans shall have a maximum individual capacity of 30,000 cfm (14.2 m^3/s). The aggregate capacity of smoke exhaust fans shall be determined by the equation:

$$C = A \times 300 \qquad \text{(Equation 9-4)}$$

where:

C = Capacity of mechanical ventilation required, in cubic feet per minute (m^3/s).

A = Area of roof vents provided in square feet (m^2) in accordance with Table 910.3.

[F] 910.4.3 Operation. Mechanical smoke exhaust fans shall be automatically activated by the automatic sprinkler system or by heat detectors having operating characteristics equivalent to those described in Section 910.3.2. Indi-

vidual manual controls of each fan unit shall also be provided.

[F] 910.4.4 Wiring and control. Wiring for operation and control of smoke exhaust fans shall be connected ahead of the main disconnect and protected against exposure to temperatures in excess of 1,000°F (538°C) for a period of not less than 15 minutes. Controls shall be located so as to be immediately accessible to the fire service from the exterior of the building and protected against interior fire exposure by fire barriers having a fire-resistance rating not less than 1 hour.

[F] 910.4.5 Supply air. Supply air for exhaust fans shall be provided at or near the floor level and shall be sized to provide a minimum of 50 percent of required exhaust. Openings for supply air shall be uniformly distributed around the periphery of the area served.

[F] 910.4.6 Interlocks. In combination comfort air-handling/smoke removal systems or independent comfort air-handling systems, fans shall be controlled to shut down in accordance with the approved smoke control sequence.

SECTION 911
FIRE COMMAND CENTER

[F] 911.1 Features. Where required by other sections of this code, a fire command center for fire department operations shall be provided. The location and accessibility of the fire command center shall be approved by the fire department. The fire command center shall be separated from the remainder of the building by not less than a 1-hour fire barrier constructed in accordance with Section 706 or horizontal assembly constructed in accordance with Section 711, or both. The room shall be a minimum of 96 square feet (9 m^2) with a minimum dimension of 8 feet (2438 mm). A layout of the fire command center and all features required by the section to be contained therein shall be submitted for approval prior to installation. The fire command center shall comply with NFPA 72 and shall contain the following features:

1. The emergency voice/alarm communication system unit.

2. The fire department communications unit.

3. Fire detection and alarm system annunciator unit.

4. Annunciator unit visually indicating the location of the elevators and whether they are operational.

5. Status indicators and controls for air-handling systems.

6. The fire-fighter's control panel required by Section 909.16 for smoke control systems installed in the building.

7. Controls for unlocking stairway doors simultaneously.

8. Sprinkler valve and water-flow detector display panels.

9. Emergency and standby power status indicators.

10. A telephone for fire department use with controlled access to the public telephone system.

11. Fire pump status indicators.

12. Schematic building plans indicating the typical floor plan and detailing the building core, means of egress, fire protection systems, fire-fighting equipment and fire department access.

13. Worktable.

14. Generator supervision devices, manual start and transfer features.

15. Public address system, where specifically required by other sections of this code.

SECTION 912
FIRE DEPARTMENT CONNECTIONS

[F] **912.1 Installation.** Fire department connections shall be installed in accordance with the NFPA standard applicable to the system design and shall comply with Sections 912.2 through 912.5.

[F] **912.2 Location.** With respect to hydrants, driveways, buildings and landscaping, fire department connections shall be so located that fire apparatus and hose connected to supply the system will not obstruct access to the buildings for other fire apparatus. The location of fire department connections shall be approved.

[F] **912.2.1 Visible location.** Fire department connections shall be located on the street side of buildings, fully visible and recognizable from the street or nearest point of fire department vehicle access or as otherwise approved by the code enforcement official.

[F] **912.2.2 Existing buildings.** On existing buildings, wherever the fire department connection is not visible to approaching fire apparatus, the fire department connection shall be indicated by an approved sign mounted on the street front or on the side of the building. Such sign shall have the letters "FDC" at least 6 inches (152 mm) high and words in letters at least 2 inches (51 mm) high or an arrow to indicate the location. All such signs shall be subject to the approval of the code enforcement official.

[F] **912.3 Access.** Immediate access to fire department connections shall be maintained at all times and without obstruction by fences, bushes, trees, walls or any other object for a minimum of 3 feet (914 mm).

[F] **912.3.1 Locking fire department connection caps.** The code enforcement official is authorized to require locking caps on fire department connections for water-based fire protection systems where the responding fire department carries appropriate key wrenches for removal.

[F] **912.4 Signs.** A metal sign with raised letters at least 1 inch (25 mm) in size shall be mounted on all fire department connections serving automatic sprinklers, standpipes or fire pump connections. Such signs shall read: AUTOMATIC SPRINKLERS, STANDPIPES or TEST CONNECTION, or a combination thereof as applicable.

[P] **912.5 Backflow protection.** The potable water supply to automatic sprinkler and standpipe systems shall be protected against backflow as required by the *Plumbing Code of New York State*.

CHAPTER 10
MEANS OF EGRESS

SECTION 1001
ADMINISTRATION

1001.1 General. Buildings or portions thereof shall be provided with a means of egress system as required by this chapter. The provisions of this chapter shall control the design, construction and arrangement of means of egress components required to provide an approved means of egress from structures and portions thereof.

1001.2 Minimum requirements. It shall be unlawful to alter a building or structure in a manner that will reduce the number of exits or the capacity of the means of egress to less than required by this code.

[F] 1001.3 Maintenance. Means of egress shall be maintained in accordance with the *Fire Code of New York State*.

SECTION 1002
DEFINITIONS

1002.1 Definitions. The following words and terms shall, for the purposes of this chapter and as used elsewhere in this code, have the meanings shown herein.

ACCESSIBLE MEANS OF EGRESS. A continuous and unobstructed way of egress travel from any accessible point in a building or facility to a public way.

AISLE. An exit access component that defines and provides a path of egress travel.

AISLE ACCESSWAY. That portion of an exit access that leads to an aisle.

ALTERNATING TREAD DEVICE. A device that has a series of steps between 50 and 70 degrees (0.87 and 1.22 rad) from horizontal, usually attached to a center support rail in an alternating manner so that the user does not have both feet on the same level at the same time.

AREA OF REFUGE. An area where persons unable to use stairways can remain temporarily to await instructions or assistance during emergency evacuation.

BLEACHERS. Tiered seating facilities.

COMMON PATH OF EGRESS TRAVEL. That portion of exit access which the occupants are required to traverse before two separate and distinct paths of egress travel to two exits are available. Paths that merge are common paths of travel. Common paths of egress travel shall be included within the permitted travel distance.

CORRIDOR. An enclosed exit access component that defines and provides a path of egress travel to an exit.

DOOR, BALANCED. A door equipped with double-pivoted hardware so designed as to cause a semi-counterbalanced swing action when opening.

EGRESS COURT. A court or yard which provides access to a public way for one or more exits.

EMERGENCY ESCAPE AND RESCUE OPENING. An operable window, door or other similar device that provides for a means of escape and access for rescue in the event of an emergency.

EXIT. That portion of a means of egress system which is separated from other interior spaces of a building or structure by fire-resistance-rated construction and opening protectives as required to provide a protected path of egress travel between the exit access and the exit discharge. Exits include exterior exit doors at ground level, exit enclosures, exit passageways, exterior exit stairs, exterior exit ramps and horizontal exits.

EXIT, HORIZONTAL. A path of egress travel from one building to an area in another building on approximately the same level, or a path of egress travel through or around a wall or partition to an area on approximately the same level in the same building, which affords safety from fire and smoke from the area of incidence and areas communicating therewith.

EXIT ACCESS. That portion of a means of egress system that leads from any occupied portion of a building or structure to an exit.

EXIT DISCHARGE. That portion of a means of egress system between the termination of an exit and a public way.

EXIT DISCHARGE, LEVEL OF. The horizontal plane located at the point at which an exit terminates and an exit discharge begins.

EXIT ENCLOSURE. An exit component that is separated from other interior spaces of a building or structure by fire-resistance-rated construction and opening protectives, and provides for a protected path of egress travel in a vertical or horizontal direction to the exit discharge or the public way.

EXIT PASSAGEWAY. An exit component that is separated from all other interior spaces of a building or structure by fire-resistance-rated construction and opening protectives, and provides for a protected path of egress travel in a horizontal direction to the exit discharge or the public way.

FIRE EXIT HARDWARE. Panic hardware that is listed for use on fire door assemblies.

FLOOR AREA, GROSS. The floor area within the inside perimeter of the exterior walls of the building under consideration, exclusive of vent shafts and courts, without deduction for corridors, stairways, closets, the thickness of interior walls, columns or other features. The floor area of a building, or portion thereof, not provided with surrounding exterior walls shall be the usable area under the horizontal projection of the roof or floor above. The gross floor area shall not include shafts with no openings or interior courts.

FLOOR AREA, NET. The actual occupied area not including unoccupied accessory areas such as corridors, stairways, toilet rooms, mechanical rooms and closets.

FOLDING AND TELESCOPIC SEATING. Tiered seating facilities having an overall shape and size that are capable of being reduced for purposes of moving or storing.

GRANDSTAND. Tiered seating facilities.

GUARD. A building component or a system of building components located at or near the open sides of elevated walking surfaces that minimizes the possibility of a fall from the walking surface to a lower level.

HANDRAIL. A horizontal or sloping rail intended for grasping by the hand for guidance or support.

MEANS OF EGRESS. A continuous and unobstructed path of vertical and horizontal egress travel from any occupied portion of a building or structure to a public way. A means of egress consists of three separate and distinct parts: the exit access, the exit and the exit discharge.

MERCHANDISE PAD. A merchandise pad is an area for display of merchandise surrounded by aisles, permanent fixtures or walls. Merchandise pads contain elements such as nonfixed and moveable fixtures, cases, racks, counters and partitions not over 5 feet 9 inches in height from which customers browse or shop.

NOSING. The leading edge of treads of stairs and of landings at the top of stairway flights.

OCCUPANT LOAD. The number of persons for which the means of egress of a building or portion thereof is designed.

PANIC HARDWARE. A door-latching assembly incorporating a device that releases the latch upon the application of a force in the direction of egress travel.

PUBLIC WAY. A street, alley or other parcel of land open to the outside air leading to a street, that has been deeded,

dedicated or otherwise permanently appropriated to the public for public use and which has a clear width and height of not less than 10 feet (3048 mm).

RAMP. A walking surface that has a running slope steeper than one unit vertical in 20 units horizontal (5-percent slope).

SCISSOR STAIR. Two interlocking stairways providing two separate paths of egress located within one stairwell enclosure.

SMOKE-PROTECTED ASSEMBLY SEATING. Seating served by means of egress that is not subject to smoke accumulation within or under a structure.

STAIR. A change in elevation, consisting of one or more risers.

STAIRWAY. One or more flights of stairs, either exterior or interior, with the necessary landings and platforms connecting them, to form a continuous and uninterrupted passage from one level to another.

STAIRWAY, EXTERIOR. A stairway that is open on at least one side, except for required structural columns, beams, handrails and guards. The adjoining open areas shall be either yards, courts or public ways. The other sides of the exterior stairway need not be open.

STAIRWAY, INTERIOR. A stairway not meeting the definition of an exterior stairway.

STAIRWAY, SPIRAL. A stairway having a closed circular form in its plan view with uniform section-shaped treads attached to and radiating from a minimum-diameter supporting column.

WINDER. A tread with nonparallel edges.

SECTION 1003
GENERAL MEANS OF EGRESS

1003.1 Applicability. The general requirements specified in Sections 1003 through 1013 shall apply to all three elements of the means of egress system, in addition to those specific requirements for the exit access, the exit and the exit discharge detailed elsewhere in this chapter.

1003.2 Ceiling height. The means of egress shall have a ceiling height of not less than 7 feet 6 inches (2286 mm).

Exceptions:

1. Sloped ceilings in accordance with Section 1208.2.

2. Ceilings of dwelling units and sleeping units within residential occupancies in accordance with Section 1208.2.

3. Allowable projections in accordance with Section 1003.3.

4. Stair headroom in accordance with Section 1009.2.

5. Door height in accordance with Section 1008.1.1.

1003.3 Protruding objects. Protruding objects shall comply with the requirements of Sections 1003.3.1 through 1003.3.4.

1003.3.1 Headroom. Protruding objects are permitted to extend below the minimum ceiling height required by Section 1003.2 provided a minimum headroom of 80 inches (2032 mm) shall be provided for any walking surface, including walks, corridors, aisles and passageways. Not more than 50 percent of the ceiling area of a means of egress shall be reduced in height by protruding objects.

Exception: Door closers and stops shall not reduce headroom to less than 78 inches (1981 mm).

A barrier shall be provided where the vertical clearance is less than 80 inches (2032 mm) high. The leading edge of such a barrier shall be located 27 inches (686 mm) maximum above the floor.

1003.3.2 Free-standing objects. A free-standing object mounted on a post or pylon shall not overhang that post or pylon more than 4 inches (102 mm) where the lowest point of the leading edge is more than 27 inches (686 mm) and less than 80 inches (2032 mm) above the walking surface. Where a sign or other obstruction is mounted between posts or pylons and the clear distance between the posts or pylons is greater than 12 inches (305 mm), the lowest edge of such sign or obstruction shall be 27 inches (685 mm) maximum or 80 inches (2030 mm) minimum above the finished floor or ground.

Exception: This requirement shall not apply to sloping portions of handrails serving stairs and ramps.

1003.3.3 Horizontal projections. Structural elements, fixtures or furnishings shall not project horizontally from either side more than 4 inches (102 mm) over any walking surface between the heights of 27 inches (686 mm) and 80 inches (2032 mm) above the walking surface.

Exception: Handrails serving stairs and ramps are permitted to protrude 4.5 inches (114 mm) from the wall.

1003.3.4 Clear width. Protruding objects shall not reduce the minimum clear width of accessible routes as required in Section 1104.

1003.4 Floor surface. Walking surfaces of the means of egress shall have a slip-resistant surface and be securely attached.

1003.5 Elevation change. Where changes in elevation of less than 12 inches (305 mm) exist in the means of egress, sloped surfaces shall be used. Where the slope is greater than one unit vertical in 20 units horizontal (5-percent slope), ramps complying with Section 1010 shall be used. Where the difference in elevation is 6 inches (152 mm) or less, the ramp shall be equipped with either handrails or floor finish materials that contrast with adjacent floor finish materials.

Exceptions:

1. A single step with a maximum riser height of 7 inches (178 mm) is permitted for buildings with occupancies in Groups F, H, R-2 and R-3 and Groups S and U at exterior doors not required to be accessible by Chapter 11.

2. A stair with a single riser or with two risers and a tread is permitted at locations not required to be accessible by Chapter 11, provided that the risers and treads comply with Section 1009.3, the minimum depth of the tread is 13 inches (330 mm) and at least one handrail complying with Section 1012 is provided within 30 inches (762 mm) of the centerline of the normal path of egress travel on the stair.

3. A step is permitted in aisles serving seating that has a difference in elevation less than 12 inches (305 mm) at locations not required to be accessible by Chapter 11, provided that the risers and treads comply with Section 1025.11 and the aisle is provided with a handrail complying with Section 1025.13.

Any change in elevation in a corridor serving nonambulatory persons in a Group I-2 occupancy shall be by means of a ramp or sloped walkway.

1003.6 Means of egress continuity. The path of egress travel along a means of egress shall not be interrupted by any building element other than a means of egress component as specified in this chapter. Obstructions shall not be placed in the required width of a means of egress except projections permitted by this chapter. The required capacity of a means of egress system shall not be diminished along the path of egress travel.

1003.7 Elevators, escalators and moving walks. Elevators, escalators and moving walks shall not be used as a component of a required means of egress from any other part of the building.

Exception: Elevators used as an accessible means of egress in accordance with Section 1007.4.

SECTION 1004
OCCUPANT LOAD

1004.1 Design occupant load. In determining means of egress requirements, the number of occupants for whom means of egress facilities shall be provided shall be determined in accordance with this section. Where occupants from accessory areas egress through a primary space, the calculated occupant load for the primary space shall include the total occupant load of the primary space plus the number of occupants egressing through it from the accessory area.

1004.1.1 Areas without fixed seating. The number of occupants shall be computed at the rate of one occupant per unit of area as prescribed in Table 1004.1.1. For areas without fixed seating, the occupant load shall not be less than that number determined by dividing the floor area under consideration by the occupant per unit of area factor assigned to the occupancy as set forth in Table 1004.1.1. Where an intended use is not listed in Table 1004.1.1, the code enforcement official shall establish a use based on a listed use that most nearly resembles the intended use.

TABLE 1004.1.1
MAXIMUM FLOOR AREA ALLOWANCES PER OCCUPANT

FUNCTION OF SPACE	FLOOR AREA IN SQ. FT. PER OCCUPANT
Accessory storage areas, mechanical equipment room	300 gross
Agricultural building	300 gross
Aircraft hangars	500 gross
Airport terminal Baggage claim Baggage handling Concourse Waiting areas	 20 gross 300 gross 100 gross 15 gross
Assembly Gaming floors (keno, slots, etc.)	 11 gross
Assembly with fixed seats	See Section 1004.7
Assembly without fixed seats Concentrated (chairs only—not fixed) Standing space Unconcentrated (tables and chairs)	 7 net 5 net 15 net
Bowling centers, allow 5 persons for each lane including 15 feet of runway, and for additional areas	7 net
Business areas	100 gross
Courtrooms—other than fixed seating areas	40 net
Day care	35 net
Dormitories	50 gross
Educational Classroom area Shops and other vocational room areas	 20 net 50 net
Exercise rooms	50 gross
H-5 Fabrication and manufacturing areas	200 gross
Industrial areas	100 gross
Institutional areas Inpatient treatment areas Outpatient areas Sleeping areas	 240 gross 100 gross 120 gross
Kitchens, commercial	200 gross
Library Reading rooms Stack area	 50 net 100 gross
Locker rooms	50 gross
Mercantile Areas on other floors Basement and grade floor areas Storage, stock, shipping areas	 60 gross 30 gross 300 gross
Parking garages	200 gross
Residential	200 gross
Skating rinks, swimming pools Rink and pool Decks	 50 gross 15 gross
Stages and platforms	15 net
Warehouses	500 gross

For SI: 1 square foot = 0.0929 m^2.

1004.2 Increased occupant load. The occupant load permitted in any building, or portion thereof, is permitted to be increased from that number established for the occupancies in Table 1004.1.1, provided that all other requirements of the code are also met based on such modified number and the occupant load does not exceed one occupant per 7 square feet (0.65 m^2) of occupiable floor space. Where required by the code enforcement official, an approved aisle, seating or fixed equipment diagram substantiating any increase in occupant load shall be submitted. Where required by the code enforcement official, such diagram shall be posted.

1004.3 Posting of occupant load. Every room or space that is an assembly occupancy shall have the occupant load of the room or space posted in a conspicuous place, near the main exit or exit access doorway from the room or space. Posted signs shall be of an approved legible permanent design and shall be maintained by the owner or authorized agent.

1004.4 Exiting from multiple levels. Where exits serve more than one floor, only the occupant load of each floor considered individually shall be used in computing the required capacity of the exits at that floor, provided that the exit capacity shall not decrease in the direction of egress travel.

1004.5 Egress convergence. Where means of egress from floors above and below converge at an intermediate level, the capacity of the means of egress from the point of convergence shall not be less than the sum of the two floors.

1004.6 Mezzanine levels. The occupant load of a mezzanine level with egress onto a room or area below shall be added to that room or area's occupant load, and the capacity of the exits shall be designed for the total occupant load thus established.

1004.7 Fixed seating. For areas having fixed seats and aisles, the occupant load shall be determined by the number of fixed seats installed therein. The occupant load for areas in which fixed seating is not installed, such as waiting spaces and wheelchair spaces, shall be determined in accordance with Section 1004.1.1 and added to the number of fixed seats.

For areas having fixed seating without dividing arms, the occupant load shall not be less than the number of seats based on one person for each 18 inches (457 mm) of seating length.

The occupant load of seating booths shall be based on one person for each 24 inches (610 mm) of booth seat length measured at the backrest of the seating booth.

1004.8 Outdoor areas. Yards, patios, courts and similar outdoor areas accessible to and usable by the building occupants shall be provided with means of egress as required by this chapter. The occupant load of such outdoor areas shall be assigned by the code enforcement official in accordance with the anticipated use. Where outdoor areas are to be used by persons in addition to the occupants of the building, and the path of egress travel from the outdoor areas passes through the building, means of egress requirements for the building shall be based on the sum of the occupant loads of the building plus the outdoor areas.

Exceptions:

1. Outdoor areas used exclusively for service of the building need only have one means of egress.

2. Both outdoor areas associated with Group R-3 and individual dwelling units of Group R-2.

TABLE 1005.1
EGRESS WIDTH PER OCCUPANT SERVED

OCCUPANCY	WITHOUT SPRINKLER SYSTEM		WITH SPRINKLER SYSTEM[a]	
	Stairways (inches per occupant)	Other egress components (inches per occupant)	Stairways (inches per occupant)	Other egress components (inches per occupant)
Occupancies other than those listed below	0.3	0.2	0.2	0.15
Hazardous: H-1, H-2, H-3 and H-4	0.7	0.4	0.3	0.2
Institutional: I-2	NA	NA	0.3	0.2

For SI: 1 inch = 25.4 mm. NA = Not applicable.

a. Buildings equipped throughout with an automatic sprinkler system in accordance with Section 903.3.1.1 or 903.3.1.2.

1004.9 Multiple occupancies. Where a building contains two or more occupancies, the means of egress requirements shall apply to each portion of the building based on the occupancy of that space. Where two or more occupancies utilize portions of the same means of egress system, those egress components shall meet the more stringent requirements of all occupancies that are served.

SECTION 1005
EGRESS WIDTH

1005.1 Minimum required egress width. The means of egress width shall not be less than required by this section. The total width of means of egress in inches (mm) shall not be less than the total occupant load served by the means of egress multiplied by the factors in Table 1005.1 and not less than specified elsewhere in this code. Multiple means of egress shall be sized such that the loss of any one means of egress shall not reduce the available capacity to less than 50 percent of the required capacity. The maximum capacity required from any story of a building shall be maintained to the termination of the means of egress.

Exception: Means of egress complying with Section 1025.

1005.2 Door encroachment. Doors opening into the path of egress travel shall not reduce the required width to less than one-half during the course of the swing. When fully open, the door shall not project more than 7 inches (178 mm) into the required width.

Exception: The restrictions on a door swing shall not apply to doors within individual dwelling units and sleeping units of Group R-2 and dwelling units of Group R-3.

SECTION 1006
MEANS OF EGRESS ILLUMINATION

1006.1 Illumination required. The means of egress, including the exit discharge, shall be illuminated at all times the building space served by the means of egress is occupied.

Exceptions:

1. Occupancies in Group U.

2. Aisle accessways in Group A.

3. Dwelling units and sleeping units in Groups R-1, R-2 and R-3.

4. Sleeping units of Group I occupancies.

1006.2 Illumination level. The means of egress illumination level shall not be less than 1 foot-candle (11 lux) at the walking surface level.

Exception: For auditoriums, theaters, concert or opera halls and similar assembly occupancies, the illumination at the walking surface level is permitted to be reduced during performances to not less than 0.2 foot-candle (2.15 lux), provided that the required illumination is automatically restored upon activation of a premises' fire alarm system where such system is provided.

1006.3 Illumination emergency power. The power supply for means of egress illumination shall normally be provided by the premises' electrical supply.

In the event of power supply failure, an emergency electrical system shall automatically illuminate the following areas:

1. Aisles and unenclosed egress stairways in rooms and spaces that require two or more means of egress.

2. Corridors, exit enclosures and exit passageways in buildings required to have two or more exits.

3. Exterior egress components at other than the level of exit discharge until exit discharge is accomplished for buildings required to have two or more exits.

4. Interior exit discharge elements, as permitted in Section 1024.1, in buildings required to have two or more exits.

5. Exterior landings, as required by Section 1008.1.5, for exit discharge doorways in buildings required to have two or more exits.

6. Public utilization toilet rooms in occupancy groups A, B, E, F and M, with two or more water closets or one water closet and one or more urinals installed as required in Chapter 29 of this code and the *Plumbing Code of New York State*.

The emergency power system shall provide power for a duration of not less than 90 minutes and shall consist of storage batteries, unit equipment or an on-site generator. The installation of the emergency power system shall be in accordance with Section 2702.

1006.4 Performance of system. Emergency lighting facilities shall be arranged to provide initial illumination that is at least an average of 1 foot-candle (11 lux) and a minimum at any point of 0.1 foot-candle (1 lux) measured along the path of egress at floor level. Illumination levels shall be permitted to decline to 0.6 foot-candle (6 lux) average and a minimum at any point of 0.06 foot-candle (0.6 lux) at the end of the emergency lighting time duration. A maximum-to-minimum illumination uniformity ratio of 40 to 1 shall not be exceeded.

SECTION 1007
ACCESSIBLE MEANS OF EGRESS

1007.1 Accessible means of egress required. Accessible means of egress shall comply with this section. Accessible spaces shall be provided with not less than one accessible means of egress. Where more than one means of egress is required by Section 1015.1 or 1019.1 from any accessible space, each accessible portion of the space shall be served by not less than two accessible means of egress.

Exceptions:

1. One accessible means of egress is required from an accessible mezzanine level in accordance with Section 1007.3, 1007.4 or 1007.5.

2. In assembly spaces with sloped floors, one accessible means of egress is required from a space where the common path of travel of the accessible route for access to the wheelchair spaces meets the requirements in Section 1025.8.

1007.2 Continuity and components. Each required accessible means of egress shall be continuous to a public way and shall consist of one or more of the following components:

1. Accessible routes complying with Section 1104.

2. Stairways within vertical exit enclosures complying with Sections 1007.3 and 1020.

3. Exterior exit stairways complying with Sections 1007.3 and 1023.

4. Elevators complying with Section 1007.4.

5. Platform lifts complying with Section 1007.5.

6. Horizontal exits complying with Section 1022.

7. Ramps complying with Section 1010.

8. Areas of refuge complying with Section 1007.6.

Exceptions:

1. Where the exit discharge is not accessible, an exterior area for assisted rescue must be provided in accordance with Section 1007.8.

2. Where the exit stairway is open to the exterior, the accessible means of egress shall include either an area of refuge in accordance with Section 1007.6 or an exterior area for assisted rescue in accordance with Section 1007.8.

1007.2.1 Elevators required. In buildings where a required accessible floor is four or more stories above or below a level of exit discharge, at least one required accessible means of egress shall be an elevator complying with Section 1007.4.

Exceptions:

1. In buildings equipped throughout with an automatic sprinkler system installed in accordance with Section 903.3.1.1 or 903.3.1.2, the elevator shall not be required on floors provided with a horizontal exit and located at or above the level of exit discharge.

2. In buildings equipped throughout with an automatic sprinkler system installed in accordance with Section 903.3.1.1 or 903.3.1.2, the elevator shall not be required on floors provided with a ramp conforming to the provisions of Section 1010.

1007.3 Exit stairways. In order to be considered part of an accessible means of egress, an exit stairway shall have a clear width of 48 inches (1219 mm) minimum between handrails and shall either incorporate an area of refuge within an enlarged floor-level landing or shall be accessed from either an area of refuge complying with Section 1007.6 or a horizontal exit.

Exceptions:

1. Unenclosed exit stairways as permitted by Section 1020.1 are permitted to be considered part of an accessible means of egress.

2. The area of refuge is not required at unenclosed exit stairways as permitted by Section 1020.1 in buildings or facilities that are equipped throughout with an automatic sprinkler system installed in accordance with Section 903.3.1.1.

3. The clear width of 48 inches (1219 mm) between handrails is not required at exit stairways in buildings or facilities equipped throughout with an automatic sprinkler system installed in accordance with Section 903.3.1.1 or 903.3.1.2.

4. The clear width of 48 inches (1219 mm) between handrails is not required for exit stairways accessed from a horizontal exit.

5. Areas of refuge are not required at exit stairways serving open parking garages.

1007.4 Elevators. In order to be considered part of an accessible means of egress, an elevator shall comply with the emergency operation and signaling device requirements of Section 2.27 of ASME A17.1. Standby power shall be provided in accordance with Sections 2702 and 3003. The elevator shall be accessed from either an area of refuge complying with Section 1007.6 or a horizontal exit.

Exception: Elevators are not required to be accessed from an area of refuge or horizontal exit in open parking garages.

1007.5 Platform lifts. Platform (wheelchair) lifts shall not serve as part of an accessible means of egress, except where allowed as part of a required accessible route in Section 1109.7, Items 1 through 9. Standby power shall be provided in accordance with Section 2702.2.6 for platform lifts permitted to serve as part of a means of egress.

1007.5.1 Openness. Platform lifts on an accessible means of egress shall not be installed in a fully enclosed hoistway.

1007.6 Areas of refuge. Every required area of refuge shall be accessible from the space it serves by an accessible means of egress. The maximum travel distance from any accessible space to an area of refuge shall not exceed the travel distance permitted for the occupancy in accordance with Section

1016.1. Every required area of refuge shall have direct access to an enclosed stairway complying with Sections 1007.3 and 1020.1 or an elevator complying with Section 1007.4. Where an elevator lobby is used as an area of refuge, the shaft and lobby shall comply with Section 1020.1.7 for smokeproof enclosures except where the elevators are in an area of refuge formed by a horizontal exit or smoke barrier.

1007.6.1 Size. Each area of refuge shall be sized to accommodate one wheelchair space of 30 inches by 48 inches (762 mm by 1219 mm) for each 200 occupants or portion thereof, based on the occupant load of the area of refuge and areas served by the area of refuge. Such wheelchair spaces shall not reduce the required means of egress width. Access to any of the required wheelchair spaces in an area of refuge shall not be obstructed by more than one adjoining wheelchair space.

1007.6.2 Separation. Each area of refuge shall be separated from the remainder of the story by a smoke barrier complying with Section 709 or a horizontal exit complying with Section 1022. Each area of refuge shall be designed to minimize the intrusion of smoke.

Exception: Areas of refuge located within a vertical exit enclosure.

1007.6.3 Two-way communication. Areas of refuge shall be provided with a two-way communication system between the area of refuge and a central control point. If the central control point is not constantly attended, the area of refuge shall also have controlled access to a public telephone system. Location of the central control point shall be approved by the fire department. The two-way communication system shall include both audible and visible signals.

1007.6.4 Instructions. In areas of refuge that have a two-way emergency communications system, instructions on the use of the area under emergency conditions shall be posted adjoining the communications system. The instructions shall include all of the following:

1. Directions to find other means of egress.

2. Persons able to use the exit stairway do so as soon as possible, unless they are assisting others.

3. Information on planned availability of assistance in the use of stairs or supervised operation of elevators and how to summon such assistance.

4. Directions for use of the emergency communications system.

1007.6.5 Identification. Each door providing access to an area of refuge from an adjacent floor area shall be identified by a sign complying with ICC/ANSI A117.1, stating: AREA OF REFUGE, and including the International Symbol of Accessibility. Where exit sign illumination is required by Section 1011.2, the area of refuge sign shall be illuminated. Additionally, tactile signage complying with ICC A117.1 shall be located at each door to an area of refuge.

1007.7 Signage. At exits and elevators serving a required accessible space but not providing an approved accessible means of egress, signage shall be installed indicating the location of accessible means of egress.

1007.8 Exterior area for assisted rescue. The exterior area for assisted rescue must be open to the outside air and meet the requirements of Section 1007.6.1. Separation walls shall comply with the requirements of Section 704 for exterior walls. Where walls or openings are between the area for assisted rescue and the interior of the building, the building exterior walls within 10 feet (3048 mm) horizontally of a nonrated wall or unprotected opening shall have a fire-resistance rating of not less than 1 hour. Openings within such exterior walls shall be protected by opening protectives having a fire protection rating of not less than $^{3}/_{4}$ hour. This construction shall extend vertically from the ground to a point 10 feet (3048 mm) above the floor level of the area for assisted rescue or to the roof line, whichever is lower.

1007.8.1 Openness. The exterior area for assisted rescue shall be at least 50 percent open, and the open area above the guards shall be so distributed as to minimize the accumulation of smoke or toxic gases.

1007.8.2 Exterior exit stairway. Exterior exit stairways that are part of the means of egress for the exterior area for assisted rescue shall provide a clear width of 48 inches (1219 mm) between handrails.

1007.8.3 Identification. Exterior areas for assisted rescue shall have identification as required for area of refuge that complies with Section 1007.6.5.

SECTION 1008
DOORS, GATES AND TURNSTILES

1008.1 Doors. Means of egress doors shall meet the requirements of this section. Doors serving a means of egress system shall meet the requirements of this section and Section 1018.2. Doors provided for egress purposes in numbers greater than required by this code shall meet the requirements of this section.

Means of egress doors shall be readily distinguishable from the adjacent construction and finishes such that the doors are easily recognizable as doors. Mirrors or similar reflecting materials shall not be used on means of egress doors. Means of egress doors shall not be concealed by curtains, drapes, decorations or similar materials.

1008.1.1 Size of doors. The minimum width of each door opening shall be sufficient for the occupant load thereof and shall provide a clear width of not less than 32 inches (813 mm). Clear openings of doorways with swinging doors shall be measured between the face of the door and the stop, with the door open 90 degrees (1.57 rad). Where this section requires a minimum clear width of 32 inches (813 mm) and a door opening includes two door leaves without a mullion, one leaf shall provide a clear opening width of 32 inches (813 mm). The maximum width of a swinging door leaf shall be 48 inches (1219 mm) nominal. Means of egress doors in a Group I-2 occupancy used for the movement of beds shall provide a clear width not less than 41.5 inches (1054 mm). The height of doors shall not be less than 80 inches (2032 mm).

Exceptions:

1. The minimum and maximum width shall not apply to door openings that are not part of the required means of egress in Group R-2 and R-3 occupancies.

2. Door openings to resident sleeping units in Group I-3 occupancies shall have a clear width of not less than 28 inches (711 mm).

3. Door openings to storage closets less than 10 square feet (0.93 m²) in area shall not be limited by the minimum width.

4. Width of door leafs in revolving doors that comply with Section 1008.1.3.1 shall not be limited.

5. Door openings within a dwelling unit or sleeping unit shall not be less than 78 inches (1981 mm) in height.

6. Exterior door openings in dwelling units and sleeping units, other than the required exit door, shall not be less than 76 inches (1930 mm) in height.

7. In other than Group R-1 occupancies, the minimum widths shall not apply to interior egress doors within a dwelling unit or sleeping unit that is not required to be an Accessible unit, Type A unit or Type B unit.

8. Door openings required to be accessible within Type B units shall have a minimum clear width of 32 inches (813 mm).

1008.1.1.1 Projections into clear width. There shall not be projections into the required clear width lower than 34 inches (864 mm) above the floor or ground. Projections into the clear opening width between 34 inches (864 mm) and 80 inches (2032 mm) above the floor or ground shall not exceed 4 inches (102 mm).

1008.1.2 Door swing. Egress doors shall be side-hinged swinging.

Exceptions:

1. Private garages, office areas, factory and storage areas with an occupant load of 10 or less.

2. Group I-3 occupancies used as a place of detention.

3. Critical or intensive care patient rooms within suites of health care facilities.

4. Doors within or serving a single dwelling unit in Groups R-2 and R-3.

5. In other than Group H occupancies, revolving doors complying with Section 1008.1.3.1.

6. In other than Group H occupancies, horizontal sliding doors complying with Section 1008.1.3.3 are permitted in a means of egress.

7. Power-operated doors in accordance with Section 1008.1.3.2.

8. Doors serving a bathroom within an individual sleeping unit in Group R-1.

Doors shall swing in the direction of egress travel where serving an occupant load of 50 or more persons or a Group H occupancy.

The opening force for interior side-swinging doors without closers shall not exceed a 5-pound (22 N) force. For other side-swinging, sliding and folding doors, the door latch shall release when subjected to a 15-pound (67 N) force. The door shall be set in motion when subjected to a 30-pound (133 N) force. The door shall swing to a full-open position when subjected to a 15-pound (67 N) force. Forces shall be applied to the latch side.

1008.1.3 Special doors. Special doors and security grilles shall comply with the requirements of Sections 1008.1.3.1 through 1008.1.3.5.

1008.1.3.1 Revolving doors. Revolving doors shall comply with the following:

1. Each revolving door shall be capable of collapsing into a bookfold position with parallel egress paths providing an aggregate width of 36 inches (914 mm).

2. A revolving door shall not be located within 10 feet (3048 mm) of the foot of or top of stairs or escalators. A dispersal area shall be provided between the stairs or escalators and the revolving doors.

3. The revolutions per minute (rpm) for a revolving door shall not exceed those shown in Table 1008.1.3.1.

4. Each revolving door shall have a side-hinged swinging door which complies with Section 1008.1 in the same wall and within 10 feet (3048 mm) of the revolving door.

TABLE 1008.1.3.1
REVOLVING DOOR SPEEDS

INSIDE DIAMETER (feet-inches)	POWER-DRIVEN-TYPE SPEED CONTROL (rpm)	MANUAL-TYPE SPEED CONTROL (rpm)
6-6	11	12
7-0	10	11
7-6	9	11
8-0	9	10
8-6	8	9
9-0	8	9
9-6	7	8
10-0	7	8

For SI: 1 inch = 25.4 mm, 1 foot = 304.8 mm

1008.1.3.1.1 Egress component. A revolving door used as a component of a means of egress shall comply with Section 1008.1.3.1 and the following three conditions:

1. Revolving doors shall not be given credit for more than 50 percent of the required egress capacity.

2. Each revolving door shall be credited with no more than a 50-person capacity.

3. Each revolving door shall be capable of being collapsed when a force of not more than 130 pounds (572 N) is applied within 3 inches (76 mm) of the outer edge of a wing.

1008.1.3.1.2 Other than egress component. A revolving door used as other than a component of a means of egress shall comply with Section 1008.1.3.1. The collapsing force of a revolving door not used as a component of a means of egress shall not be more than 180 pounds (801 N).

Exception: A collapsing force in excess of 180 pounds (801 N) is permitted if the collapsing force is reduced to not more than 130 pounds (572 N) when at least one of the following conditions is satisfied:

1. There is a power failure or power is removed to the device holding the door wings in position.

2. There is an actuation of the automatic sprinkler system where such system is provided.

3. There is an actuation of a smoke detection system which is installed in accordance with Section 907 to provide coverage in areas within the building which are within 75 feet (22 860 mm) of the revolving doors.

4. There is an actuation of a manual control switch, in an approved location and clearly defined, which reduces the holding force to below the 130-pound (572 N) force level.

1008.1.3.2 Power-operated doors. Where means of egress doors are operated by power, such as doors with a photoelectric-actuated mechanism to open the door upon the approach of a person, or doors with power-assisted manual operation, the design shall be such that in the event of power failure, the door is capable of being opened manually to permit means of egress travel or closed where necessary to safeguard means of egress. The forces required to open these doors manually shall not exceed those specified in Section 1008.1.2, except that the force to set the door in motion shall not exceed 50 pounds (220 N). The door shall be capable of swinging from any position to the full width of the opening in which such door is installed when a force is applied to the door on the side from which egress is made. Full-power-operated doors shall comply with BHMA A156.10. Power-assisted and low-energy doors shall comply with BHMA A156.19.

Exceptions:

1. Occupancies in Group I-3.

2. Horizontal sliding doors complying with Section 1008.1.3.3.

3. For a biparting door in the emergency breakout mode, a door leaf located within a multiple-leaf opening shall be exempt from the minimum 32-inch (813 mm) single-leaf requirement of Section 1008.1.1, provided a minimum 32-inch (813 mm) clear opening is provided when the two biparting leaves meeting in the center are broken out.

1008.1.3.3 Horizontal sliding doors. In other than Group H occupancies, horizontal sliding doors permitted to be a component of a means of egress in accordance with Exception 6 to Section 1008.1.2 shall comply with all of the following criteria:

1. The doors shall be power operated and shall be capable of being operated manually in the event of power failure.

2. The doors shall be openable by a simple method from both sides without special knowledge or effort.

3. The force required to operate the door shall not exceed 30 pounds (133 N) to set the door in motion and 15 pounds (67 N) to close the door or open it to the minimum required width.

4. The door shall be openable with a force not to exceed 15 pounds (67 N) when a force of 250 pounds (1100 N) is applied perpendicular to the door adjacent to the operating device.

5. The door assembly shall comply with the applicable fire protection rating and, where rated, shall be self-closing or automatic closing by smoke detection in accordance with Section 715.4.7.3, shall be installed in accordance with NFPA 80 and shall comply with Section 715.

6. The door assembly shall have an integrated standby power supply.

7. The door assembly power supply shall be electrically supervised.

8. The door shall open to the minimum required width within 10 seconds after activation of the operating device.

1008.1.3.4 Access-controlled egress doors. The entrance doors in a means of egress in buildings with an occupancy in Group A, B, E, M, R-1 or R-2 and entrance doors to tenant spaces in occupancies in Groups A, B, E, M, R-1 and R-2 are permitted to be equipped with an approved entrance and egress access control system which shall be installed in accordance with all of the following criteria:

1. A sensor shall be provided on the egress side arranged to detect an occupant approaching the doors. The doors shall be arranged to unlock by a signal from or loss of power to the sensor.

2. Loss of power to that part of the access control system which locks the doors shall automatically unlock the doors.

3. The doors shall be arranged to unlock from a manual unlocking device located 40 inches to 48 inches (1016 mm to 1219 mm) vertically above the floor and within 5 feet (1524 mm) of the secured doors. Ready access shall be provided to the manual unlocking device and the device shall be clearly identified by a sign that reads "PUSH TO EXIT." When operated, the manual unlocking device shall result in direct interruption of power to the lock-independent of the access control system electronics-and the doors shall remain unlocked for a minimum of 30 seconds.

4. Activation of the building fire alarm system, if provided, shall automatically unlock the doors, and the doors shall remain unlocked until the fire alarm system has been reset.

5. Activation of the building automatic sprinkler or fire detection system, if provided, shall automatically unlock the doors. The doors shall remain unlocked until the fire alarm system has been reset.

6. Entrance doors in buildings with an occupancy in Group A, B, E or M shall not be secured from the egress side during periods that the building is open to the general public.

1008.1.3.5 Security grilles. In Groups B, F, M and S, horizontal sliding or vertical security grilles are permitted at the main exit and shall be openable from the inside without the use of a key or special knowledge or effort during periods that the space is occupied. The grilles shall remain secured in the full-open position during the period of occupancy by the general public. Where two or more means of egress are required, not more than one-half of the exits or exit access doorways shall be equipped with horizontal sliding or vertical security grilles.

1008.1.4 Floor elevation. There shall be a floor or landing on each side of a door. Such floor or landing shall be at the same elevation on each side of the door. Landings shall be level except for exterior landings, which are permitted to have a slope not to exceed 0.25 unit vertical in 12 units horizontal (2-percent slope).

Exceptions:

1. Doors serving individual dwelling units in Groups R-2 and R-3 where the following apply:

   1.1. A door is permitted to open at the top step of an interior flight of stairs, provided the door does not swing over the top step.

   1.2. Screen doors and storm doors are permitted to swing over stairs or landings.

2. Exterior doors as provided for in Section 1003.5, Exception 1, and Section 1018.2, which are not on an accessible route.

3. In Group R-3 occupancies not required to be Accessible units, Type A units or Type B units, the landing at an exterior doorway shall not be more than 7.75 inches (197 mm) below the top of the threshold, provided the door, other than an exterior storm or screen door, does not swing over the landing.

4. Variations in elevation due to differences in finish materials, but not more than 0.5 inch (12.7 mm).

5. Exterior decks, patios or balconies that are part of Type B dwelling units, have impervious surfaces and that are not more than 4 inches (102 mm) below the finished floor level of the adjacent interior space of the dwelling unit.

1008.1.5 Landings at doors. Landings shall have a width not less than the width of the stairway or the door, whichever is greater. Doors in the fully open position shall not reduce a required dimension by more than 7 inches (178 mm). When a landing serves an occupant load of 50 or more, doors in any position shall not reduce the landing to less than one-half its required width. Landings shall have a length measured in the direction of travel of not less than 44 inches (1118 mm).

Exception: Landing length in the direction of travel in Groups R-3 and U and within individual units of Group R-2 need not exceed 36 inches (914 mm).

1008.1.6 Thresholds. Thresholds at doorways shall not exceed 0.75 inch (19.1 mm) in height for sliding doors serving dwelling units or 0.5 inch (12.7 mm) for other doors. Raised thresholds and floor level changes greater than 0.25 inch (6.4 mm) at doorways shall be beveled with a slope not greater than one unit vertical in two units horizontal (50-percent slope).

Exception: The threshold height shall be limited to 7.75 inches (197 mm) where the occupancy is Group R-2 or R-3; the door is an exterior door that is not a component of the required means of egress; the door, other than an exterior storm or screen door does not swing over the landing or step; and the doorway is not on an accessible route as required by Chapter 11 and is not part of an Accessible unit, Type A unit or Type B unit.

1008.1.7 Door arrangement. Space between two doors in a series shall be 48 inches (1219 mm) minimum plus the width of a door swinging into the space. Doors in a series shall swing either in the same direction or away from the space between the doors.

Exceptions:

1. The minimum distance between horizontal sliding power-operated doors in a series shall be 48 inches (1219 mm).

2. Storm and screen doors serving individual dwelling units in Groups R-2 and R-3 need not be spaced 48 inches (1219 mm) from the other door.

3. Doors within individual dwelling units in Groups R-2 and R-3 other than within Type A dwelling units.

1008.1.8 Door operations. Except as specifically permitted by this section egress doors shall be readily openable from the egress side without the use of a key or special knowledge or effort.

1008.1.8.1 Hardware. Door handles, pulls, latches, locks and other operating devices on doors required to be accessible by Chapter 11 shall not require tight grasping, tight pinching or twisting of the wrist to operate.

1008.1.8.2 Hardware height. Door handles, pulls, latches, locks and other operating devices shall be installed 34 inches (864 mm) minimum and 48 inches (1219 mm) maximum above the finished floor. Locks used only for security purposes and not used for normal operation are permitted at any height.

Exception: Access doors or gates in barrier walls and fences protecting pools, spas and hot tubs shall be permitted to have operable parts of the release of latch on self-latching devices at 54 inches (1370 mm) maximum above the finished floor or ground, provided the self-latching devices are not also self-locking devices operated by means of a key, electronic opener or integral combination lock.

1008.1.8.3 Locks and latches. Locks and latches shall be permitted to prevent operation of doors where any of the following exists:

1. Places of detention or restraint.

2. In buildings in occupancy Group A having an occupant load of 300 or less, Groups B, F, M and S, and in places of religious worship, the main exterior door or doors are permitted to be equipped with key-operated locking devices from the egress side provided:

    2.1. The locking device is readily distinguishable as locked,

    2.2. A readily visible durable sign is posted on the egress side on or adjacent to the door stating: THIS DOOR TO REMAIN UNLOCKED WHEN BUILDING IS OCCUPIED. The sign shall be in letters 1 inch (25 mm) high on a contrasting background,

    2.3. The use of the key-operated locking device is revokable by the code enforcement official for due cause.

3. Where egress doors are used in pairs, approved automatic flush bolts shall be permitted to be used, provided that the door leaf having the automatic flush bolts has no doorknob or surface-mounted hardware.

4. Doors from individual dwelling or sleeping units of Group R occupancies having an occupant load of 10 or less are permitted to be equipped with a

night latch, dead bolt or security chain, provided such devices are openable from the inside without the use of a key or tool.

1008.1.8.4 Bolt locks. Manually operated flush bolts or surface bolts are not permitted.

Exceptions:

1. On doors not required for egress in individual dwelling units or sleeping units.

2. Where a pair of doors serves a storage or equipment room, manually operated edge- or surface-mounted bolts are permitted on the inactive leaf.

1008.1.8.5 Unlatching. The unlatching of any door or leaf shall not require more than one operation.

Exceptions:

1. Places of detention or restraint.

2. Where manually operated bolt locks are permitted by Section 1008.1.8.4.

3. Doors with automatic flush bolts as permitted by Section 1008.1.8.3, Exception 3.

4. Doors from individual dwelling units and sleeping units of Group R occupancies as permitted by Section 1008.1.8.3, Exception 4.

1008.1.8.6 Delayed egress locks. Approved, listed, delayed egress locks shall be permitted to be installed on doors serving any occupancy except Group A, E and H occupancies in buildings that are equipped throughout with an automatic sprinkler system in accordance with Section 903.3.1.1 or an approved automatic smoke or heat detection system installed in accordance with Section 907, provided that the doors unlock in accordance with Items 1 through 6 below. A building occupant shall not be required to pass through more than one door equipped with a delayed egress lock before entering an exit.

1. The doors unlock upon actuation of the automatic sprinkler system or automatic fire detection system.

2. The doors unlock upon loss of power controlling the lock or lock mechanism.

3. The door locks shall have the capability of being unlocked by a signal from the fire command center.

4. The initiation of an irreversible process which will release the latch in not more than 15 seconds when a force of not more than 15 pounds (67 N) is applied for 1 second to the release device. Initiation of the irreversible process shall activate an audible signal in the vicinity of the door. Once the door lock has been released by the application of force to the releasing device, relocking shall be by manual means only.

    Exception: Where approved, a delay of not more than 30 seconds is permitted.

5. A sign shall be provided on the door located above and within 12 inches (305 mm) of the release device reading: PUSH UNTIL ALARM SOUNDS. DOOR CAN BE OPENED IN 15 [30] SECONDS.

6. Emergency lighting shall be provided at the door.

1008.1.8.7 Stairway doors. Interior stairway means of egress doors shall be openable from both sides without the use of a key or special knowledge or effort.

Exceptions:

1. Stairway discharge doors shall be openable from the egress side and shall only be locked from the opposite side.

2. This section shall not apply to doors arranged in accordance with Section 403.12.

3. In stairways serving not more than four stories, doors are permitted to be locked from the side opposite the egress side, provided they are openable from the egress side and capable of being unlocked simultaneously without unlatching upon a signal from the fire command center, if present, or a signal by emergency personnel from a single location inside the main entrance to the building.

1008.1.9 Panic and fire exit hardware. Where panic and fire exit hardware is installed, it shall comply with the following:

1. The actuating portion of the releasing device shall extend at least one-half of the door leaf width.

2. The maximum unlatching force shall not exceed 15 pounds (67 N).

Each door in a means of egress from a Group A or E occupancy having an occupant load of 50 or more and any Group H occupancy shall not be provided with a latch or lock unless it is panic hardware or fire exit hardware.

Exception: A main exit of a Group A occupancy in compliance with Section 1008.1.8.3, Item 2.

Electrical rooms with equipment rated 1,200 amperes or more and over 6 feet (1829 mm) wide that contain overcurrent devices, switching devices or control devices with exit access doors must be equipped with panic hardware and doors must swing in the direction of egress.

If balanced doors are used and panic hardware is required, the panic hardware shall be the push-pad type and the pad shall not extend more then one-half the width of the door measured from the latch side.

1008.2 Gates. Gates serving the means of egress system shall comply with the requirements of this section. Gates used as a component in a means of egress shall conform to the applicable requirements for doors.

Exception: Horizontal sliding or swinging gates exceeding the 4-foot (1219 mm) maximum leaf width limitation are permitted in fences and walls surrounding a stadium.

1008.2.1 Stadiums. Panic hardware is not required on gates surrounding stadiums where such gates are under constant immediate supervision while the public is present, and where safe dispersal areas based on 3 square feet (0.28 m^2) per occupant are located between the fence and enclosed space. Such required safe dispersal areas shall not be located less than 50 feet (15 240 mm) from the enclosed space. See Section 1024.6 for means of egress from safe dispersal areas.

1008.3 Turnstiles. Turnstiles or similar devices that restrict travel to one direction shall not be placed so as to obstruct any required means of egress.

Exception: Each turnstile or similar device shall be credited with no more than a 50-person capacity where all of the following provisions are met:

1. Each device shall turn free in the direction of egress travel when primary power is lost, and upon the manual release by an employee in the area.

2. Such devices are not given credit for more than 50 percent of the required egress capacity.

3. Each device is not more than 39 inches (991 mm) high.

4. Each device has at least 16.5 inches (419 mm) clear width at and below a height of 39 inches (991 mm) and at least 22 inches (559 mm) clear width at heights above 39 inches (991 mm).

Where located as part of an accessible route, turnstiles shall have at least 36 inches (914 mm) clear at and below a height of 34 inches (864 mm), at least 32 inches (813 mm) clear width between 34 inches (864 mm) and 80 inches (2032 mm) and shall consist of a mechanism other than a revolving device.

1008.3.1 High turnstile. Turnstiles more than 39 inches (991 mm) high shall meet the requirements for revolving doors.

1008.3.2 Additional door. Where serving an occupant load greater than 300, each turnstile that is not portable shall have a side-hinged swinging door which conforms to Section 1008.1 within 50 feet (15 240 mm).

SECTION 1009
STAIRWAYS

1009.1 Stairway width. The width of stairways shall be determined as specified in Section 1005.1, but such width shall not be less than 44 inches (1118 mm). See Section 1007.3 for accessible means of egress stairways.

Exceptions:

1. Stairways serving an occupant load of less than 50 shall have a width of not less than 36 inches (914 mm).

2. Spiral stairways as provided for in Section 1009.8.

3. Aisle stairs complying with Section 1025.

4. Where an incline platform lift or stairway chairlift is installed on stairways serving occupancies in Group

R-3, or within dwelling units in occupancies in Group R-2, a clear passage width not less than 20 inches (508 mm) shall be provided. If the seat and platform can be folded when not in use, the distance shall be measured from the folded position.

1009.2 Headroom. Stairways shall have a minimum headroom clearance of 80 inches (2032 mm) measured vertically from a line connecting the edge of the nosings. Such headroom shall be continuous above the stairway to the point where the line intersects the landing below, one tread depth beyond the bottom riser. The minimum clearance shall be maintained the full width of the stairway and landing.

Exception: Spiral stairways complying with Section 1009.8 are permitted a 78-inch (1981 mm) headroom clearance.

1009.3 Stair treads and risers. Stair riser heights shall be 7 inches (178 mm) maximum and 4 inches (102 mm) minimum. Stair tread depths shall be 11 inches (279 mm) minimum. The riser height shall be measured vertically between the leading edges of adjacent treads. The tread depth shall be measured horizontally between the vertical planes of the foremost projection of adjacent treads and at a right angle to the tread's leading edge. Winder treads shall have a minimum tread depth of 11 inches (279 mm) measured at a right angle to the tread's leading edge at a point 12 inches (305 mm) from the side where the treads are narrower and a minimum tread depth of 10 inches (254 mm).

Exceptions:

1. Alternating tread devices in accordance with Section 1009.9.

2. Spiral stairways in accordance with Section 1009.8.

3. Aisle stairs in assembly seating areas where the stair pitch or slope is set, for sightline reasons, by the slope of the adjacent seating area in accordance with Section 1025.11.2.

4. In Group R-3 occupancies; within dwelling units in Group R-2 occupancies; and in Group U occupancies that are accessory to a Group R-3 occupancy or accessory to individual dwelling units in Group R-2 occupancies; the maximum riser height shall be 7.75 inches (197 mm); the minimum tread depth shall be 10 inches (254 mm); the minimum winder tread depth at the walk line shall be 10 inches (254 mm); and the minimum winder tread depth shall be 6 inches (152 mm). A nosing not less than 0.75 inch (19.1 mm) but not more than 1.25 inches (32 mm) shall be provided on stairways with solid risers where the tread depth is less than 11 inches (279 mm).

5. See the *Existing Building Code of New York State* for the replacement of existing stairways.

1009.3.1 Winder treads. Winder treads are not permitted in means of egress stairways except within a dwelling unit.

Exceptions:

1. Curved stairways in accordance with Section 1009.7.

2. Spiral stairways in accordance with Section 1009.8.

1009.3.2 Dimensional uniformity. Stair treads and risers shall be of uniform size and shape. The tolerance between the largest and smallest riser height or between the largest and smallest tread depth shall not exceed 0.375 inch (9.5 mm) in any flight of stairs. The greatest winder tread depth at the 12-inch (305 mm) walk line within any flight of stairs shall not exceed the smallest by more than 0.375 inch (9.5 mm) measured at a right angle to the tread's leading edge.

Exceptions:

1. Nonuniform riser dimensions of aisle stairs complying with Section 1025.11.2.

2. Consistently shaped winders, complying with Section 1009.3, differing from rectangular treads in the same stairway flight.

Where the bottom or top riser adjoins a sloping public way, walkway or driveway having an established grade and serving as a landing, the bottom or top riser is permitted to be reduced along the slope to less than 4 inches (102 mm) in height, with the variation in height of the bottom or top riser not to exceed one unit vertical in 12 units horizontal (8-percent slope) of stairway width. The nosings or leading edges of treads at such nonuniform height risers shall have a distinctive marking stripe, different from any other nosing marking provided on the stair flight. The distinctive marking stripe shall be visible in descent of the stair and shall have a slip-resistant surface. Marking stripes shall have a width of at least 1 inch (25 mm) but not more than 2 inches (51 mm).

1009.3.3 Profile. The radius of curvature at the leading edge of the tread shall be not greater than 0.5 inch (12.7 mm). Beveling of nosings shall not exceed 0.5 inch (12.7 mm). Risers shall be solid and vertical or sloped from the underside of the leading edge of the tread above at an angle not more than 30 degrees (0.52 rad) from the vertical. The leading edge (nosings) of treads shall project not more than 1.25 inches (32 mm) beyond the tread below and all projections of the leading edges shall be of uniform size, including the leading edge of the floor at the top of a flight.

Exceptions:

1. Solid risers are not required for stairways that are not required to comply with Section 1007.3, provided that the opening between treads does not

permit the passage of a sphere with a diameter of 4 inches (102 mm).

2. Solid risers are not required for occupancies in Group I-3.

1009.4 Stairway landings. There shall be a floor or landing at the top and bottom of each stairway. The width of landings shall not be less than the width of stairways they serve. Every landing shall have a minimum dimension measured in the direction of travel equal to the width of the stairway. Such dimension need not exceed 48 inches (1219 mm) where the stairway has a straight run.

Exceptions:

1. Aisle stairs complying with Section 1025.

2. Doors opening onto a landing shall not reduce the landing to less than one-half the required width. When fully open, the door shall not project more than 7 inches (178 mm) into a landing.

1009.5 Stairway construction. All stairways shall be built of materials consistent with the types permitted for the type of construction of the building, except that wood handrails shall be permitted for all types of construction.

1009.5.1 Stairway walking surface. The walking surface of treads and landings of a stairway shall not be sloped steeper than one unit vertical in 48 units horizontal (2-percent slope) in any direction. Stairway treads and landings shall have a solid surface. Finish floor surfaces shall be securely attached.

Exception: In Group F, H and S occupancies, other than areas of parking structures accessible to the public, openings in treads and landings shall not be prohibited provided a sphere with a diameter of 1.125 inches (29 mm) cannot pass through the opening.

1009.5.2 Outdoor conditions. Outdoor stairways and outdoor approaches to stairways shall be designed so that water will not accumulate on walking surfaces.

1009.5.3 Enclosures under stairways. The walls and soffits within enclosed usable spaces under enclosed and unenclosed stairways shall be protected by 1-hour fire-resistance-rated construction or the fire-resistance rating of the stairway enclosure, whichever is greater. Access to the enclosed space shall not be directly from within the stair enclosure.

Exception: Spaces under stairways serving and contained within a single residential dwelling unit in Group R-2 or R-3 shall be permitted to be protected on the enclosed side with 0.5-inch (12.7 mm) gypsum board.

There shall be no enclosed usable space under exterior exit stairways unless the space is completely enclosed in 1-hour fire-resistance-rated construction. The open space under exterior stairways shall not be used for any purpose.

1009.6 Vertical rise. A flight of stairs shall not have a vertical rise greater than 12 feet (3658 mm) between floor levels or landings.

Exception: Aisle stairs complying with Section 1025.

1009.7 Curved stairways. Curved stairways with winder treads shall have treads and risers in accordance with Section 1009.3 and the smallest radius shall not be less than twice the required width of the stairway.

Exception: The radius restriction shall not apply to curved stairways for occupancies in Group R-3 and within individual dwelling units in occupancies in Group R-2.

1009.8 Spiral stairways. Spiral stairways are permitted to be used as a component in the means of egress only within dwelling units or from a space not more than 250 square feet (23 m²) in area and serving not more than five occupants, or from galleries, catwalks and gridirons in accordance with Section 1015.6.

A spiral stairway shall have a 7.5 inch (191 mm) minimum clear tread depth at a point 12 inches (305 mm) from the narrow edge. The risers shall be sufficient to provide a headroom of 78 inches (1981 mm) minimum, but riser height shall not be more than 9.5 inches (241 mm). The minimum stairway width shall be 26 inches (660 mm).

1009.9 Alternating tread devices. Alternating tread devices are limited to an element of a means of egress in buildings of Groups F, H and S from a mezzanine not more than 250 square feet (23 m²) in area and which serves not more than five occupants; in buildings of Group I-3 from a guard tower, observation station or control room not more than 250 square feet (23 m²) in area and for access to unoccupied roofs.

1009.9.1 Handrails of alternating tread devices. Handrails shall be provided on both sides of alternating tread devices and shall comply with Section 1012.

1009.9.2 Treads of alternating tread devices. Alternating tread devices shall have a minimum projected tread of 5 inches (127 mm), a minimum tread depth of 8.5 inches (216 mm), a minimum tread width of 7 inches (178 mm) and a maximum riser height of 9.5 inches (241 mm). The initial tread of the device shall begin at the same elevation as the platform, landing or floor surface.

Exception: Alternating tread devices used as an element of a means of egress in buildings from a mezzanine area not more than 250 square feet (23 m²) in area which serves not more than five occupants shall have a minimum projected tread of 8.5 inches (216 mm) with a minimum tread depth of 10.5 inches (267 mm). The rise to the next alternating tread surface should not be more than 8 inches (203 mm).

1009.10 Handrails. Stairways shall have handrails on each side and shall comply with Section 1012. Where glass is used to provide the handrail, the handrail shall also comply with Section 2407.

Exceptions:

1. Aisle stairs complying with Section 1025 provided with a center handrail need not have additional handrails.

2. Stairways within dwelling units, spiral stairways and aisle stairs serving seating only on one side are permitted to have a handrail on one side only.

3. Decks, patios and walkways that have a single change in elevation where the landing depth on each side of the change of elevation is greater than what is required for a landing do not require handrails.

4. In Group R-3 occupancies, a change in elevation consisting of a single riser at an entrance or egress door does not require handrails.

5. Changes in room elevations of only one riser within dwelling units and sleeping units in Group R-2 and R-3 occupancies do not require handrails.

1009.11 Stairway to roof. In buildings located four or more stories in height above grade plane, one stairway shall extend to the roof surface, unless the roof has a slope steeper than four units vertical in 12 units horizontal (33-percent slope). In buildings without an occupied roof, access to the roof from the top story shall be permitted to be by an alternating tread device.

1009.11.1 Roof access. Where a stairway is provided to a roof, access to the roof shall be provided through a penthouse complying with Section 1509.2.

Exception: In buildings without an occupied roof, access to the roof shall be permitted to be a roof hatch or trap door not less than 16 square feet (1.5 m^2) in area and having a minimum dimension of 2 feet (610 mm).

1009.11.2 Protection at roof hatch openings. Where the roof hatch opening providing the required access is located within 10 feet (3049 mm) of the roof edge, such roof access or roof edge shall be protected by guards installed in accordance with the provisions of Section 1013.

SECTION 1010
RAMPS

1010.1 Scope. The provisions of this section shall apply to ramps used as a component of a means of egress.

Exceptions:

1. Other than ramps that are part of the accessible routes providing access in accordance with Sections 1108.2 through 1108.2.3 and 1108.2.5, ramped aisles within assembly rooms or spaces shall conform with the provisions in Section 1025.11.

2. Curb ramps shall comply with ICC/ANSI A117.1.

3. Vehicle ramps in parking garages for pedestrian exit access shall not be required to comply with Sections 1010.3 through 1010.9 when they are not an accessible route serving accessible parking spaces, other required accessible elements or part of an accessible means of egress.

1010.2 Slope. Ramps used as part of a means of egress shall have a running slope not steeper than one unit vertical in 12 units horizontal (8-percent slope). The slope of other pedestrian ramps shall not be steeper than one unit vertical in eight units horizontal (12.5-percent slope).

Exception: An aisle ramp slope in occupancies of Group A shall comply with Section 1025.11.

1010.3 Cross slope. The slope measured perpendicular to the direction of travel of a ramp shall not be steeper than one unit vertical in 48 units horizontal (2-percent slope).

1010.4 Vertical rise. The rise for any ramp run shall be 30 inches (762 mm) maximum.

1010.5 Minimum dimensions. The minimum dimensions of means of egress ramps shall comply with Sections 1010.5.1 through 1010.5.3.

1010.5.1 Width. The minimum width of a means of egress ramp shall not be less than that required for corridors by Section 1017.2. The clear width of a ramp and the clear width between handrails, if provided, shall be 36 inches (914 mm) minimum.

1010.5.2 Headroom. The minimum headroom in all parts of the means of egress ramp shall not be less than 80 inches (2032 mm).

1010.5.3 Restrictions. Means of egress ramps shall not reduce in width in the direction of egress travel. Projections into the required ramp and landing width are prohibited. Doors opening onto a landing shall not reduce the clear width to less than 42 inches (1067 mm).

1010.6 Landings. Ramps shall have landings at the bottom and top of each ramp, points of turning, entrance, exits and at doors. Landings shall comply with Sections 1010.6.1 through 1010.6.5.

1010.6.1 Slope. Landings shall have a slope not steeper than one unit vertical in 48 units horizontal (2-percent slope) in any direction. Changes in level are not permitted.

1010.6.2 Width. The landing shall be at least as wide as the widest ramp run adjoining the landing.

1010.6.3 Length. The landing length shall be 60 inches (1525 mm) minimum.

Exceptions:

1. Landings in nonaccessible Group R-2 and R-3 individual dwelling units are permitted to be 36 inches (914 mm) minimum.

2. Where the ramp is not a part of an accessible route, the length of the landing shall not be required to be more than 48 inches (1220 mm) in the direction of travel.

1010.6.4 Change in direction. Where changes in direction of travel occur at landings provided between ramp runs, the landing shall be 60 inches by 60 inches (1524 mm by 1524 mm) minimum.

Exception: Landings in nonaccessible Group R-2 and R-3 individual dwelling units are permitted to be 36 inches by 36 inches (914 mm by 914 mm) minimum.

1010.6.5 Doorways. Where doorways are located adjacent to a ramp landing, maneuvering clearances required by ICC/ANSI A117.1 are permitted to overlap the required landing area.

1010.7 Ramp construction. All ramps shall be built of materials consistent with the types permitted for the type of construction of the building, except that wood handrails shall be permitted for all types of construction. Ramps used as an exit shall conform to the applicable requirements of Sections 1020.1 through 1020.1.3 for exit enclosures.

1010.7.1 Ramp surface. The surface of ramps shall be of slip-resistant materials that are securely attached.

1010.7.2 Outdoor conditions. Outdoor ramps and outdoor approaches to ramps shall be designed so that water will not accumulate on walking surfaces.

1010.8 Handrails. Ramps with a rise greater than 6 inches (152 mm) shall have handrails on both sides. Handrails shall comply with Section 1012.

1010.9 Edge protection. Edge protection complying with Sections 1010.9.1 or 1010.9.2 shall be provided on each side of ramp runs and at each side of ramp landings.

Exceptions:

1. Edge protection is not required on ramps that are not required to have handrails, provided they have flared sides that comply with the ICC/ANSI A117.1 curb ramp provisions.

2. Edge protection is not required on the sides of ramp landings serving an adjoining ramp run or stairway.

3. Edge protection is not required on the sides of ramp landings having a vertical dropoff of not more than 0.5 inch (12.7 mm) within 10 inches (254 mm) horizontally of the required landing area.

1010.9.1 Curb, rail, wall or barrier. A curb, rail, wall or barrier shall be provided that prevents the passage of a 4-inch-diameter (102 mm) sphere, where any portion of the sphere is within 4 inches (102 mm) of the floor or ground surface.

1010.9.2 Extended floor or ground surface. The floor or ground surface of the ramp run or landing shall extend 12 inches (305 mm) minimum beyond the inside face of a handrail complying with Section 1012.

1010.10 Guards. Guards shall be provided where required by Section 1013 and shall be constructed in accordance with Section 1013.

SECTION 1011
EXIT SIGNS

1011.1 Where required. Exits and exit access doors shall be marked by an approved exit sign readily visible from any direction of egress travel. Access to exits shall be marked by readily visible exit signs in cases where the exit or the path of egress travel is not immediately visible to the occupants. Exit sign placement shall be such that no point in a corridor is more than 100 feet (30 480 mm) or the listed viewing distance for the sign, whichever is less, from the nearest visible exit sign.

Exceptions:

1. Exit signs are not required in rooms or areas that require only one exit or exit access.

2. Main exterior exit doors or gates that are obviously and clearly identifiable as exits need not have exit

signs where approved by the code enforcement official.

3. Exit signs are not required in occupancies in Group U and individual sleeping units or dwelling units in Group R-1, R-2 or R-3.

4. Exit signs are not required in sleeping areas in occupancies in Group I-3.

5. In occupancies in Groups A-4 and A-5, exit signs are not required on the seating side of vomitories or openings into seating areas where exit signs are provided in the concourse that are readily apparent from the vomitories. Egress lighting is provided to identify each vomitory or opening within the seating area in an emergency.

1011.2 Illumination. Exit signs shall be internally or externally illuminated.

Exception: Tactile signs required by Section 1011.3 need not be provided with illumination.

1011.3 Tactile exit signs. A tactile sign stating EXIT and complying with ICC/ANSI A117.1 shall be provided adjacent to each door to an egress stairway, an exit passageway and the exit discharge.

1011.4 Internally illuminated exit signs. Internally illuminated exit signs shall be listed and labeled and shall be installed in accordance with the manufacturer's instructions and Section 2702. Exit signs shall be illuminated at all times.

1011.5 Externally illuminated exit signs. Externally illuminated exit signs shall comply with Sections 1011.5.1 through 1011.5.3.

1011.5.1 Graphics. Every exit sign and directional exit sign shall have plainly legible letters not less than 6 inches (152 mm) high with the principal strokes of the letters not less than 0.75 inch (19.1 mm) wide. The word "EXIT" shall have letters having a width not less than 2 inches (51 mm) wide, except the letter "I," and the minimum spacing between letters shall not be less than 0.375 inch (9.5 mm). Signs larger than the minimum established in this section shall have letter widths, strokes and spacing in proportion to their height.

The word "EXIT" shall be in high contrast with the background and shall be clearly discernible when the means of exit sign illumination is or is not energized. If a chevron directional indicator is provided as part of the exit sign, the construction shall be such that the direction of the chevron directional indicator cannot be readily changed.

1011.5.2 Exit sign illumination. The face of an exit sign illuminated from an external source shall have an intensity of not less than 5 foot-candles (54 lux).

1011.5.3 Power source. Exit signs shall be illuminated at all times. To ensure continued illumination for a duration of not less than 90 minutes in case of primary power loss, the sign illumination means shall be connected to an emergency power system provided from storage batteries, unit equipment or an on-site generator. The installation of the emergency power system shall be in accordance with Section 2702.

Exception: Approved exit sign illumination means that provide continuous illumination independent of external power sources for a duration of not less than 90 minutes, in case of primary power loss, are not required to be connected to an emergency electrical system.

SECTION 1012
HANDRAILS

1012.1 Where required. Handrails for stairways and ramps shall be adequate in strength and attachment in accordance with Section 1607.7. Handrails required for stairways by Section 1009.10 shall comply with Sections 1012.2 through 1012.8. Handrails required for ramps by Section 1010.8 shall comply with Sections 1012.2 through 1012.7.

1012.2 Height. Handrail height, measured above stair tread nosings, or finish surface of ramp slope shall be uniform, not less than 34 inches (864 mm) and not more than 38 inches (965 mm).

1012.3 Handrail graspability. Handrails with a circular cross-section shall have an outside diameter of at least 1.25 inches (32 mm) and not greater than 2 inches (51 mm) or shall provide equivalent graspability. If the handrail is not circular, it shall have a perimeter dimension of at least 4 inches (102 mm) and not greater than 6.25 inches (160 mm) with a maximum cross-section dimension of 2.25 inches (57 mm). Edges shall have a minimum radius of 0.01 inch (0.25 mm).

1012.4 Continuity. Handrail-gripping surfaces shall be continuous, without interruption by newel posts or other obstructions.

Exceptions:

1. Handrails within dwelling units are permitted to be interrupted by a newel post at a stair or ramp landing.

2. Within a dwelling unit, the use of a volute, turnout or starting easing is allowed on the lowest tread.

3. Handrail brackets or balusters attached to the bottom surface of the handrail that do not project horizontally beyond the sides of the handrail within 1.5 inches (38 mm) of the bottom of the handrail shall not be considered obstructions. For each 0.5 inch (12.7 mm) of additional handrail perimeter dimension above 4 inches (102 mm), the vertical clearance dimension of 1.5 inches (38 mm) shall be permitted to be reduced by 0.125 inch (3 mm).

1012.5 Handrail extensions. Handrails shall return to a wall, guard or the walking surface or shall be continuous to the handrail of an adjacent stair flight or ramp run. At stairways where handrails are not continuous between flights, the handrails shall extend horizontally at least 12 inches (305 mm) beyond the top riser and continue to slope for the depth of one tread beyond the bottom riser. At ramps where handrails are not continuous between runs, the handrails shall extend hori-zontally above the landing 12 inches (305 mm) minimum beyond the top and bottom of ramp runs.

Exceptions:

1. Handrails within a dwelling unit that is not required to be accessible need extend only from the top riser to the bottom riser.

2. Aisle handrails in Group A occupancies in accordance with Section 1025.13.

1012.6 Clearance. Clear space between a handrail and a wall or other surface shall be a minimum of 1.5 inches (38 mm). A handrail and a wall or other surface adjacent to the handrail shall be free of any sharp or abrasive elements.

1012.7 Projections. On ramps, the clear width between handrails shall be 36 inches (914 mm) minimum. Projections into the required width of stairways and ramps at each handrail shall not exceed 4.5 inches (114 mm) at or below the handrail height. Projections into the required width shall not be limited above the minimum headroom height required in Section 1009.2.

1012.8 Intermediate handrails. Stairways shall have intermediate handrails located in such a manner so that all portions of the stairway width required for egress capacity are within 30 inches (762 mm) of a handrail. On monumental stairs, handrails shall be located along the most direct path of egress travel.

SECTION 1013
GUARDS

1013.1 Where required. Guards shall be located along open-sided walking surfaces, mezzanines, industrial equipment platforms, stairways, ramps and landings that are located more than 30 inches (762 mm) above the floor or grade below. Guards shall be adequate in strength and attachment in accordance with Section 1607.7. Where glass is used to provide a guard or as a portion of the guard system, the guard shall also comply with Section 2407. Guards shall also be located along glazed sides of stairways, ramps and landings that are located more than 30 inches (762 mm) above the floor or grade below where the glazing provided does not meet the strength and attachment requirements in Section 1607.7.

Exception: Guards are not required for the following locations:

1. On the loading side of loading docks or piers.

2. On the audience side of stages and raised platforms, including steps leading up to the stage and raised platforms.

3. On raised stage and platform floor areas, such as runways, ramps and side stages used for entertainment or presentations.

4. At vertical openings in the performance area of stages and platforms.

5. At elevated walking surfaces appurtenant to stages and platforms for access to and utilization of special lighting or equipment.

6. Along vehicle service pits not accessible to the public.

7. In assembly seating where guards in accordance with Section 1025.14 are permitted and provided.

1013.2 Height. Guards shall form a protective barrier not less than 42 inches (1067 mm) high, measured vertically above the leading edge of the tread, adjacent walking surface or adjacent seatboard.

Exceptions:

1. For occupancies in Group R-3, and within individual dwelling units in occupancies in Group R-2, guards whose top rail also serves as a handrail shall have a height not less than 34 inches (864 mm) and not more than 38 inches (965 mm) measured vertically from the leading edge of the stair tread nosing.

2. The height in assembly seating areas shall be in accordance with Section 1025.14.

1013.3 Opening limitations. Open guards shall have balusters or ornamental patterns such that a 4-inch-diameter (102 mm) sphere cannot pass through any opening up to a height of 34 inches (864 mm). From a height of 34 inches (864 mm) to 42 inches (1067 mm) above the adjacent walking surfaces, a sphere 8 inches (203 mm) in diameter shall not pass.

Exceptions:

1. The triangular openings formed by the riser, tread and bottom rail at the open side of a stairway shall be of a maximum size such that a sphere of 6 inches (152 mm) in diameter cannot pass through the opening.

2. At elevated walking surfaces for access to and use of electrical, mechanical or plumbing systems or equipment, guards shall have balusters or be of solid materials such that a sphere with a diameter of 21 inches (533 mm) cannot pass through any opening.

3. In areas that are not open to the public within occupancies in Group I-3, F, H or S, balusters, horizontal intermediate rails or other construction shall not permit a sphere with a diameter of 21 inches (533 mm) to pass through any opening.

4. In assembly seating areas, guards at the end of aisles where they terminate at a fascia of boxes, balconies and galleries shall have balusters or ornamental patterns such that a 4-inch-diameter (102 mm) sphere cannot pass through any opening up to a height of 26 inches (660 mm). From a height of 26 inches (660 mm) to 42 inches (1067 mm) above the adjacent walking surfaces, a sphere 8 inches (203 mm) in diameter shall not pass.

5. Within individual dwelling units and sleeping units in Group R-2 and R-3 occupancies, openings for required guards on the sides of stair treads shall not allow a sphere of 4.375 inches (111 mm) to pass through.

1013.4 Screen porches. Porches and decks which are enclosed with insect screening shall be provided with guards where the walking surface is located more than 30 inches (762 mm) above the floor or grade below.

1013.5 Mechanical equipment. Guards shall be provided where appliances, equipment, fans, roof hatch openings or other components that require service are located within 10 feet (3048 mm) of a roof edge or open side of a walking surface and such edge or open side is located more than 30 inches (762 mm) above the floor, roof or grade below. The guard shall be constructed so as to prevent the passage of a 21-inch-diameter (533 mm) sphere. The guard shall extend not less than 30 inches (762 mm) beyond each end of such appliance, equipment, fan or component.

1013.6 Roof access. Guards shall be provided where the roof hatch opening is located within 10 feet (3048 mm) of a roof edge or open side of a walking surface and such edge or open side is located more than 30 inches (762 mm) above the floor, roof or grade below. The guard shall be constructed so as to prevent the passage of a 21-inch-diameter (533 mm) sphere.

SECTION 1014
EXIT ACCESS

1014.1 General. The exit access arrangement shall comply with Sections 1014 through 1017 and the applicable provisions of Sections 1003 through 1013.

1014.2 Egress through intervening spaces. Egress through intervening spaces shall comply with this section.

1. Egress from a room or space shall not pass through adjoining or intervening rooms or areas, except where such adjoining rooms or areas are accessory to the area served, are not a high-hazard occupancy and provide a discernible path of egress travel to an exit.

    Exception: Means of egress are not prohibited through adjoining or intervening rooms or spaces in a Group H, S or F occupancy when the adjoining or intervening rooms or spaces are the same or a lesser hazard occupancy group.

2. An exit access shall not pass through a room that can be locked to prevent egress.

3. Means of egress from dwelling units or sleeping areas shall not lead through other sleeping areas, toilet rooms or bathrooms.

4. Egress shall not pass through kitchens, storage rooms, closets or spaces used for similar purposes.

    Exception: Means of egress are not prohibited through a kitchen serving adjoining rooms constituting part of the same dwelling unit or sleeping unit.

1014.2.1 Multiple tenants. Where more than one tenant occupies any one floor of a building or structure, each tenant space, dwelling unit and sleeping unit shall be provided with access to the required exits without passing through adjacent tenant spaces, dwelling units and sleeping units.

Exception: Means of egress shall not be prohibited through adjoining tenant space where such rooms or spaces occupy less than 10 percent of the area of the larger tenant space through which they pass; are designed to routinely and primarily be accessed from the larger tenant space allowing egress; are the same or similar occupancy group; a discernable path of egress travel to an exit is provided; and the means of egress into the adjoining space is not subject to locking from the egress side. A required means of egress serving the larger tenant space shall not pass through the smaller tenant space or spaces.

1014.2.2 Group I-2. Habitable rooms or suites in Group I-2 occupancies shall have an exit access door leading directly to a corridor.

Exceptions:

1. Rooms with exit doors opening directly to the outside at ground level.

2. Patient sleeping rooms are permitted to have one intervening room if the intervening room is not used as an exit access for more than eight patient beds.

3. Special nursing suites are permitted to have one intervening room where the arrangement allows for direct and constant visual supervision by nursing personnel.

4. For rooms other than patient sleeping rooms located within a suite, exit access travel from within the suite shall be permitted through one intervening room where the travel distance to the exit access door is not greater than 100 feet (30 480 mm).

5. For rooms other than patient sleeping rooms located within a suite, exit access travel from within the suite shall be permitted through two intervening rooms where the travel distance to the exit access door is not greater than 50 feet (15 240 mm).

Suites of sleeping rooms shall not exceed 5,000 square feet (465 m^2). Suites of rooms other than patient sleeping rooms shall not exceed 10,000 square feet (929 m^2). Any patient sleeping room, or any suite that includes patient sleeping rooms, of more than 1,000 square feet (93 m^2) shall have at least two exit access doors remotely located from each other. Any room or suite of rooms other than patient sleeping rooms of more than 2,500 square feet (232 m^2) shall have at least two access doors remotely located from each other. The travel distance between any point in a Group I-2 occupancy and an exit access door in the room shall not exceed 50 feet (15 240 mm). The travel distance between any point in a suite of sleeping rooms and an exit access door of that suite shall not exceed 100 feet (30 480 mm).

1014.3 Common path of egress travel. In occupancies other than Groups H-1, H-2 and H-3, the common path of egress travel shall not exceed 75 feet (22 860 mm). In Group H-1, H-2 and H-3 occupancies, the common path of egress travel shall not exceed 25 feet (7620 mm). For common path of egress travel in Group A occupancies having fixed seating, see Section 1025.8.

Exceptions:

1. The length of a common path of egress travel in Group B, F and S occupancies shall not be more than 100 feet (30 480 mm), provided that the building is equipped throughout with an automatic sprinkler system installed in accordance with Section 903.3.1.1.

2. Where a tenant space in Group B, S and U occupancies has an occupant load of not more than 30, the length of a common path of egress travel shall not be more than 100 feet (30 480 mm).

3. The length of a common path of egress travel in a Group I-3 occupancy shall not be more than 100 feet (30 480 mm).

4. The length of a common path of egress travel in a Group R-2 occupancy shall not be more than 125 feet (38 100 mm), provided that the building is protected throughout with an approved automatic sprinkler system in accordance with Section 903.3.1.1.

1014.4 Aisles. Aisles serving as a portion of the exit access in the means of egress system shall comply with the requirements of this section. Aisles shall be provided from all occupied portions of the exit access which contain seats, tables, furnishings, displays and similar fixtures or equipment. Aisles serving assembly areas, other than seating at tables, shall comply with Section 1025. Aisles serving reviewing stands, grandstands and bleachers shall also comply with Section 1025.

The required width of aisles shall be unobstructed.

Exception: Doors, when fully opened, and handrails shall not reduce the required width by more than 7 inches (178 mm). Doors in any position shall not reduce the required width by more than one-half. Other nonstructural projections such as trim and similar decorative features are permitted to project into the required width 1.5 inches (38 mm) from each side.

1014.4.1 Aisles in Groups B and M. In Group B and M occupancies, the minimum clear aisle width shall be determined by Section 1005.1 for the occupant load served, but shall not be less than 36 inches (914 mm).

Exception: Nonpublic aisles serving less than 50 people and not required to be accessible by Chapter 11 need not exceed 28 inches (711 mm) in width.

1014.4.2 Aisle accessways in Group M. An aisle accessway shall be provided on at least one side of each element within the merchandise pad. The minimum clear width for an aisle accessway not required to be accessible shall be 30 inches (762 mm). The required clear width of the aisle accessway shall be measured perpendicular to the elements and merchandise within the merchandise pad. The 30-inch (762 mm) minimum clear width shall be maintained to provide a path to an adjacent aisle or aisle accessway. The common path of travel shall not exceed 30 feet (9144 mm) from any point in the merchandise pad.

> **Exception:** For areas serving not more than 50 occupants, the common path of travel shall not exceed 75 feet (22 880 mm).

1014.4.3 Seating at tables. Where seating is located at a table or counter and is adjacent to an aisle or aisle accessway, the measurement of required clear width of the aisle or aisle accessway shall be made to a line 19 inches (483 mm) away from and parallel to the edge of the table or counter. The 19-inch (483 mm) distance shall be measured perpendicular to the side of the table or counter. In the case of other side boundaries for aisle or aisle accessways, the clear width shall be measured to walls, edges of seating and tread edges, except that handrail projections are permitted.

> **Exception:** Where tables or counters are served by fixed seats, the width of the aisle accessway shall be measured from the back of the seat.

1014.4.3.1 Aisle accessway for tables and seating. Aisle accessways serving arrangements of seating at tables or counters shall have sufficient clear width to conform to the capacity requirements of Section 1005.1 but shall not have less than the appropriate minimum clear width specified in Section 1014.4.3.2.

1014.4.3.2 Table and seating accessway width. Aisle accessways shall provide a minimum of 12 inches (305 mm) of width plus 0.5 inch (12.7 mm) of width for each additional 1 foot (305 mm), or fraction thereof, beyond 12 feet (3658 mm) of aisle accessway length measured from the center of the seat farthest from an aisle.

> **Exception:** Portions of an aisle accessway having a length not exceeding 6 feet (1829 mm) and used by a total of not more than four persons.

1014.4.3.3 Table and seating aisle accessway length. The length of travel along the aisle accessway shall not exceed 30 feet (9144 mm) from any seat to the point where a person has a choice of two or more paths of egress travel to separate exits.

1014.5 Egress balconies. Balconies used for egress purposes shall conform to the same requirements as corridors for width, headroom, dead ends and projections.

1014.5.1 Wall separation. Exterior egress balconies shall be separated from the interior of the building by walls and opening protectives as required for corridors.

> **Exception:** Separation is not required where the exterior egress balcony is served by at least two stairs and a dead-end travel condition does not require travel past an unprotected opening to reach a stair.

1014.5.2 Openness. The long side of an egress balcony shall be at least 50 percent open, and the open area above the guards shall be so distributed as to minimize the accumulation of smoke or toxic gases.

SECTION 1015
EXIT AND EXIT ACCESS DOORWAYS

1015.1 Exit or exit access doorways required. Two exits or exit access doorways from any space shall be provided where one of the following conditions exists:

1. The occupant load of the space exceeds the values in Table 1015.1.
2. The common path of egress travel exceeds the limitations of Section 1014.3.
3. Where required by Sections 1015.3, 1015.4 and 1015.5.

> **Exception:** Group I-2 occupancies shall comply with Section 1014.2.2.

TABLE 1015.1
SPACES WITH ONE MEANS OF EGRESS

OCCUPANCY	MAXIMUM OCCUPANT LOAD
A, B,E[a], F, M, U	49
H-1, H-2, H-3	3
H-4, H-5, I-1, I-3, I-4, R	10
S	29

a. Day care maximum occupant load is 10.

1015.1.1 Three or more exits. Access to three or more exits shall be provided from a floor area where required by Section 1019.1.

1015.2 Exit or exit access doorway arrangement. Required exits shall be located in a manner that makes their availability obvious. Exits shall be unobstructed at all times. Exit and exit access doorways shall be arranged in accordance with Sections 1015.2.1 and 1015.2.2.

1015.2.1 Two exits or exit access doorways. Where two exits or exit access doorways are required from any portion of the exit access, the exit doors or exit access doorways shall be placed a distance apart equal to not less than one-half of the length of the maximum overall diagonal dimension of the building or area to be served measured in a straight line between exit doors or exit access doorways. Interlocking or scissor stairs shall be counted as one exit stairway.

> **Exceptions:**
>
> 1. Where exit enclosures are provided as a portion of the required exit and are interconnected by a 1-hour fire-resistance-rated corridor conforming to the requirements of Section 1017, the required exit separation shall be measured along the shortest direct line of travel within the corridor.
>
> 2. Where a building is equipped throughout with an automatic sprinkler system in accordance with Section 903.3.1.1 or 903.3.1.2, the separation distance of the exit doors or exit access doorways shall not be less than one-third of the length of the maximum overall diagonal dimension of the area served.

1015.2.2 Three or more exits or exit access doorways. Where access to three or more exits is required, at least two exit doors or exit access doorways shall be arranged in accordance with the provisions of Section 1015.2.1.

1015.3 Boiler, incinerator and furnace rooms. Two exit access doorways are required in boiler, incinerator and furnace rooms where the area is over 500 square feet (46 m²) and any fuel-fired equipment exceeds 400,000 British thermal units (Btu) (422 000 KJ) input capacity. Where two exit access doorways are required, one is permitted to be a fixed ladder or an alternating tread device. Exit access doorways shall be separated by a horizontal distance equal to one-half the length of the maximum overall diagonal dimension of the room.

1015.4 Refrigeration machinery rooms. Machinery rooms larger than 1,000 square feet (93 m²) shall have not less than two exits or exit access doors. Where two exit access doorways are required, one such doorway is permitted to be served by a fixed ladder or an alternating tread device. Exit access doorways shall be separated by a horizontal distance equal to one-half the maximum horizontal dimension of room.

All portions of machinery rooms shall be within 150 feet (45 720 mm) of an exit or exit access doorway. An increase in travel distance is permitted in accordance with Section 1016.1.

Doors shall swing in the direction of egress travel, regardless of the occupant load served. Doors shall be tight fitting and self-closing.

1015.5 Refrigerated rooms or spaces. Rooms or spaces having a floor area of 1,000 square feet (93 m²) or more, containing a refrigerant evaporator and maintained at a temperature below 68°F (20°C), shall have access to not less than two exits or exit access doors.

Travel distance shall be determined as specified in Section 1016.1, but all portions of a refrigerated room or space shall be within 150 feet (45 720 mm) of an exit or exit access door where such rooms are not protected by an approved automatic sprinkler system. Egress is allowed through adjoining refrigerated rooms or spaces.

Exception: Where using refrigerants in quantities limited to the amounts based on the volume set forth in the *Mechanical Code of New York State.*

1015.6 Stage means of egress. Where two means of egress are required, based on the stage size or occupant load, one means of egress shall be provided on each side of the stage.

1015.6.1 Gallery, gridiron and catwalk means of egress. The means of egress from lighting and access cat-

walks, galleries and gridirons shall meet the requirements for occupancies in Group F-2.

Exceptions:

1. A minimum width of 22 inches (559 mm) is permitted for lighting and access catwalks.

2. Spiral stairs are permitted in the means of egress.

3. Stairways required by this subsection need not be enclosed.

4. Stairways with a minimum width of 22 inches (559 mm), ladders, or spiral stairs are permitted in the means of egress.

5. A second means of egress is not required from these areas where a means of escape to a floor or to a roof is provided. Ladders, alternating tread devices or spiral stairs are permitted in the means of escape.

6. Ladders are permitted in the means of egress.

SECTION 1016
EXIT ACCESS TRAVEL DISTANCE

1016.1 Travel distance limitations. Exits shall be so located on each story such that the maximum length of exit access travel, measured from the most remote point within a story to the entrance to an exit along the natural and unobstructed path of egress travel, shall not exceed the distances given in Table 1016.1.

Where the path of exit access includes unenclosed stairways or ramps within the exit access or includes unenclosed exit ramps or stairways as permitted in Section 1020.1, the distance of travel on such means of egress components shall also be included in the travel distance measurement. The measurement along stairways shall be made on a plane parallel and tangent to the stair tread nosings in the center of the stairway.

Exceptions:

1. Travel distance in open parking garages is permitted to be measured to the closest riser of open stairs.

2. In outdoor facilities with open exit access components and open exterior stairs or ramps, travel distance is permitted to be measured to the closest riser of a stair or the closest slope of the ramp.

3. Where an exit stair is permitted to be unenclosed in accordance with Exception 8 or 9 of Section 1020.1, the travel distance shall be measured from the most remote point within a building to an exit discharge.

TABLE 1016.1
EXIT ACCESS TRAVEL DISTANCE[a]

OCCUPANCY	WITHOUT SPRINKLER SYSTEM (feet)	WITH SPRINKLER SYSTEM (feet)
A, E, F-1, I-1, M, R, S-1	200	250[b]
B	200	300[c]
F-2, S-2, U	300	400[c]
H-1	Not Permitted	75[c]
H-2	Not Permitted	100[c]
H-3	Not Permitted	150[c]
H-4	Not Permitted	175[c]
H-5	Not Permitted	200[c]
I-2, I-3, I-4	150	200[c]

For SI: 1 foot = 304.8 mm.

a. See the following sections for modifications to exit access travel distance requirements:

Section 402: for the distance limitation in malls.

Section 404: for the distance limitation through an atrium space.

Section 1016.2: for increased limitations in Groups F-1 and S-1.

Section 1025.7: for increased limitation in assembly seating.

Section 1025.7: for increased limitation for assembly open-air seating.

Section 1019.2: for buildings with one exit.

Chapter 31: for the limitation in temporary structures.

b. Buildings equipped throughout with an automatic sprinkler system in accordance with Section 903.3.1.1 or 903.3.1.2. See Section 903 for occupancies where automatic sprinkler systems in accordance with Section 903.3.1.2 are permitted.

c. Buildings equipped throughout with an automatic sprinkler system in accordance with Section 903.3.1.1.

1016.2 Roof vent increase. In buildings that are one story in height, equipped with automatic heat and smoke roof vents complying with Section 910 and equipped throughout with an automatic sprinkler system in accordance with Section 903.3.1.1, the maximum exit access travel distance shall be 400 feet (122 m) for occupancies in Group F-1 or S-1.

1016.3 Exterior egress balcony increase. Travel distances specified in Section 1016.1 shall be increased up to an additional 100 feet (30 480 mm) provided the last portion of the exit access leading to the exit occurs on an exterior egress balcony constructed in accordance with Section 1014.5. The length of such balcony shall not be less than the amount of the increase taken.

SECTION 1017
CORRIDORS

1017.1 Construction. Corridors shall be fire-resistance rated in accordance with Table 1017.1. The corridor walls required to be fire-resistance rated shall comply with Section 708 for fire partitions.

Exceptions:

1. A fire-resistance rating is not required for corridors in an occupancy in Group E where each room that is used for instruction has at least one door directly to the exterior and rooms for assembly purposes have at least one-half of the required means of egress doors opening directly to the exterior. Exterior doors

specified in this exception are required to be at ground level.

2. A fire-resistance rating is not required for corridors contained within a dwelling or sleeping unit in an occupancy in Group R.

3. A fire-resistance rating is not required for corridors in open parking garages.

4. A fire-resistance rating is not required for corridors in an occupancy in Group B which is a space requiring only a single means of egress complying with Section 1015.1.

TABLE 1017.1
CORRIDOR FIRE-RESISTANCE RATING

OCCUPANCY	OCCUPANT LOAD SERVED BY CORRIDOR	REQUIRED FIRE-RESISTANCE RATING (hours)	
		Without sprinkler system	With sprinkler system[c]
H-1, H-2, H-3	All	Not Permitted	1
H-4, H-5	Greater than 30	Not Permitted	1
A, B, E, F, M, S, U	Greater than 30	1	0
R	Greater than 10	Not Permitted	0.5
I-2[a], I-4	All	Not Permitted	0
I-1, I-3	All	Not Permitted	1[b]

a. For requirements for occupancies in Group I-2, see Section 407.3.

b. For a reduction in the fire-resistance rating for occupancies in Group I-3, see Section 408.7.

c. Buildings equipped throughout with an automatic sprinkler system in accordance with Section 903.3.1.1 or 903.3.1.2 where allowed.

1017.2 Corridor width. The minimum corridor width shall be as determined in Section 1005.1, but not less than 44 inches (1118 mm).

Exceptions:

1. Twenty-four inches (610 mm)—For access to and utilization of electrical, mechanical or plumbing systems or equipment.

2. Thirty-six inches (914 mm)—With a required occupant capacity of less than 50.

3. Thirty-six inches (914 mm)—Within a dwelling unit.

4. Seventy-two inches (1829 mm)—In Group E with a corridor having a required capacity of 100 or more.

5. Seventy-two inches (1829 mm)—In corridors serving surgical Group I, health care centers for ambulatory patients receiving outpatient medical care, which causes the patient to be not capable of self-preservation.

6. Ninety-six inches (2438 mm)—In Group I-2 in areas where required for bed movement.

1017.3 Dead ends. Where more than one exit or exit access doorway is required, the exit access shall be arranged such that there are no dead ends in corridors more than 20 feet (6096 mm) in length.

Exceptions:

1. In occupancies in Group I-3 of Occupancy Condition 2, 3 or 4 (see Section 308.4), the dead end in a corridor shall not exceed 50 feet (15 240 mm).

2. In occupancies in Groups B and F where the building is equipped throughout with an automatic sprinkler system in accordance with Section 903.3.1.1, the length of dead-end corridors shall not exceed 50 feet (15 240 mm).

3. A dead-end corridor shall not be limited in length where the length of the dead-end corridor is less than 2.5 times the least width of the dead-end corridor.

1017.4 Air movement in corridors. Corridors shall not serve as supply, return, exhaust, relief or ventilation air ducts.

Exceptions:

1. Use of a corridor as a source of makeup air for exhaust systems in rooms that open directly onto such corridors, including toilet rooms, bathrooms, dressing rooms, smoking lounges and janitor closets, shall be permitted, provided that each such corridor is directly supplied with outdoor air at a rate greater than the rate of makeup air taken from the corridor.

2. Where located within a dwelling unit, the use of corridors for conveying return air shall not be prohibited.

3. Where located within tenant spaces of 1,000 square feet (93 m²) or less in area, utilization of corridors for conveying return air is permitted.

1017.4.1 Corridor ceiling. Use of the space between the corridor ceiling and the floor or roof structure above as a return air plenum is permitted for one or more of the following conditions:

1. The corridor is not required to be of fire-resistance-rated construction;

2. The corridor is separated from the plenum by fire-resistance-rated construction;

3. The air-handling system serving the corridor is shut down upon activation of the air-handling unit smoke detectors required by the *Mechanical Code of New York State.*

4. The air-handling system serving the corridor is shut down upon detection of sprinkler waterflow where the building is equipped throughout with an automatic sprinkler system; or

5. The space between the corridor ceiling and the floor or roof structure above the corridor is used as a component of an approved engineered smoke control system.

1017.5 Corridor continuity. Fire-resistance-rated corridors shall be continuous from the point of entry to an exit, and shall not be interrupted by intervening rooms.

Exception: Foyers, lobbies or reception rooms constructed as required for corridors shall not be construed as intervening rooms.

SECTION 1018
EXITS

1018.1 General. Exits shall comply with Sections 1018 through 1023 and the applicable requirements of Sections 1003 through 1013. An exit shall not be used for any purpose that interferes with its function as a means of egress. Once a given level of exit protection is achieved, such level of protection shall not be reduced until arrival at the exit discharge.

1018.2 Exterior exit doors. Buildings or structures used for human occupancy shall have at least one exterior door that meets the requirements of Section 1008.1.1.

1018.2.1 Detailed requirements. Exterior exit doors shall comply with the applicable requirements of Section 1008.1.

1018.2.2 Arrangement. Exterior exit doors shall lead directly to the exit discharge or the public way.

SECTION 1019
NUMBER OF EXITS AND CONTINUITY

1019.1 Minimum number of exits. All rooms and spaces within each story shall be provided with and have access to the minimum number of approved independent exits required by Table 1019.1 based on the occupant load of the story, except as modified in Section 1015.1 or 1019.2. For the purposes of this chapter, occupied roofs shall be provided with exits as required for stories. The required number of exits from any story, basement or individual space shall be maintained until arrival at grade or the public way.

1019.1.1 Parking structures. Parking structures shall not have less than two exits from each parking tier, except that only one exit is required where vehicles are mechanically parked. Vehicle ramps shall not be considered as required exits unless pedestrian facilities are provided.

TABLE 1019.1
MINIMUM NUMBER OF EXITS FOR OCCUPANT LOAD

OCCUPANT LOAD (persons per story)	MINIMUM NUMBER OF EXITS (per story)
1-500	2
501-1,000	3
More than 1,000	4

1019.1.2 Helistops. The means of egress from helistops shall comply with the provisions of this chapter, provided that landing areas located on buildings or structures shall have two or more exits. For landing platforms or roof areas less than 60 feet (18 288 mm) long, or less than 2,000 square feet (186 m²) in area, the second means of egress is permitted to be a fire escape or ladder leading to the floor below.

1019.2 Buildings with one exit. Only one exit shall be required in buildings as described below:

1. Buildings described in Table 1019.2, provided that the building has not more than one level below the first story above grade plane.

2. Buildings of Group R-3 occupancy.

3. Single-level buildings with the occupied space at the level of exit discharge provided that the story or space complies with Section 1015.1 as a space with one means of egress.

TABLE 1019.2
BUILDINGS WITH ONE EXIT

OCCUPANCY	MAXIMUM HEIGHT OF BUILDING ABOVE GRADE PLANE	MAXIMUM OCCUPANTS (OR DWELLING UNITS) PER FLOOR AND TRAVEL DISTANCE
A, B^d, E^e, F, M, U	1 Story	49 occupants and 75 feet travel distance
H-2, H-3	1 Story	3 occupants and 25 feet travel distance
H-4, H-5, I, R	1 Story	10 occupants and 75 feet travel distance
S^a	1 Story	29 occupants and 100 feet travel distance
B^b, F, M, S^a	2 Stories	30 occupants and 75 feet travel distance
R-2	2 Stories^c	4 dwelling units and 50 feet travel distance

For SI: 1 foot = 304.8 mm.

a. For the required number of exits for open parking structures, see Section 1019.1.1.

b. For the required number of exits for air traffic control towers, see Section 412.1.

c. Buildings classified as Group R-2 equipped throughout with an automatic sprinkler system in accordance with Section 903.3.1.1 or 903.3.1.2 and provided with emergency escape and rescue openings in accordance with Section 1026 shall have a maximum height of three stories above grade plane.

d. Buildings equipped throughout with an automatic sprinkler system in accordance with Section 903.3.1.1 with an occupancy in Group B shall have a maximum travel distance of 100 feet.

e. Day care maximum occupant load is 10.

1019.3 Exit continuity. Exits shall be continuous from the point of entry into the exit to the exit discharge.

1019.4 Exit door arrangement. Exit door arrangement shall meet the requirements of Sections 1015.2 through 1015.2.2.

SECTION 1020
VERTICAL EXIT ENCLOSURES

1020.1 Enclosures required. Interior exit stairways and interior exit ramps shall be enclosed with fire barriers constructed in accordance with Section 706 or horizontal assemblies constructed in accordance with Section 711, or both. Exit enclosures shall have a fire-resistance rating of not less than 2 hours where connecting four stories or more and not less than

1 hour where connecting less than four stories. The number of stories connected by the exit enclosure shall include any basements but not any mezzanines. An exit enclosure shall not be used for any purpose other than means of egress.

Exceptions:

1. In all occupancies, other than Group H and I occupancies, a stairway is not required to be enclosed when the stairway serves an occupant load of less than 10 and the stairway complies with either Item 1.1 or 1.2. In all cases, the maximum number of connecting open stories shall not exceed two.

    1.1. The stairway is open to not more than one story above the story at the level of exit discharge; or

    1.2. The stairway is open to not more than one story below the story at the level of exit discharge.

2. Exits in buildings of Group A-5 where all portions of the means of egress are essentially open to the outside need not be enclosed.

3. Stairways serving and contained within a single residential dwelling unit or sleeping unit in Group R-1, R-2 or R-3 occupancies are not required to be enclosed.

4. Stairways that are not a required means of egress element are not required to be enclosed where such stairways comply with Section 707.2.

5. Stairways in open parking structures that serve only the parking structure are not required to be enclosed.

6. Stairways in Group I-3 occupancies, as provided for in Section 408.3.6, are not required to be enclosed.

7. Means of egress stairways as required by Section 410.5.3 are not required to be enclosed.

8. In other than Group H and I occupancies, a maximum of 50 percent of egress stairways serving one adjacent floor are not required to be enclosed, provided at least two means of egress are provided from both floors served by the unenclosed stairways. Any two such interconnected floors shall not be open to other floors. Unenclosed exit stairways shall be remotely located as required in Section 1015.2.

9. In other than Group H and I occupancies, interior egress stairways serving only the first and second stories of a building equipped throughout with an automatic sprinkler system in accordance with Section 903.3.1.1 are not required to be enclosed, provided at least two means of egress are provided from both floors served by the unenclosed stairways. Such interconnected stories shall not be open to other stories. Unenclosed exit stairways shall be remotely located as required in Section 1015.2.

1020.1.1 Openings and penetrations. Exit enclosure opening protectives shall be in accordance with the requirements of Section 715.

Except as permitted in Section 402.4.6, openings in exit enclosures other than unprotected exterior openings shall be limited to those necessary for exit access to the enclosure from normally occupied spaces and for egress from the enclosure.

Where interior exit enclosures are extended to the exterior of a building by an exit passageway, the door assembly from the exit enclosure to the exit passageway shall be protected by a fire door assembly conforming to the requirements in Section 715.4. Fire door assemblies in exit enclosures shall comply with Section 715.4.4.

Elevators shall not open into an exit enclosure.

1020.1.2 Penetrations. Penetrations into and openings through an exit enclosure are prohibited except for required exit doors, equipment and ductwork necessary for independent pressurization, sprinkler piping, standpipes, electrical raceway for fire department communication systems and electrical raceway serving the exit enclosure and terminating at a steel box not exceeding 16 square inches (0.010 m^2). Such penetrations shall be protected in accordance with Section 712. There shall be no penetrations or communication openings, whether protected or not, between adjacent exit enclosures.

1020.1.3 Ventilation. Equipment and ductwork for exit enclosure ventilation as permitted by Section 1020.1.2 shall comply with one of the following items:

1. Such equipment and ductwork shall be located exterior to the building and shall be directly connected to the exit enclosure by ductwork enclosed in construction as required for shafts.

2. Where such equipment and ductwork is located within the exit enclosure, the intake air shall be taken directly from the outdoors and the exhaust air shall be discharged directly to the outdoors, or such air shall be conveyed through ducts enclosed in construction as required for shafts.

3. Where located within the building, such equipment and ductwork shall be separated from the remainder of the building, including other mechanical equipment, with construction as required for shafts.

In each case, openings into the fire-resistance-rated construction shall be limited to those needed for maintenance and operation and shall be protected by opening protectives in accordance with Section 715 for shaft enclosures.

Exit enclosure ventilation systems shall be independent of other building ventilation systems.

1020.1.4 Exit enclosure exterior walls. Exterior walls of an exit enclosure shall comply with the requirements of Section 704 for exterior walls. Where nonrated walls or unprotected openings enclose the exterior of the stairway and the walls or openings are exposed by other parts of the building at an angle of less than 180 degrees (3.14 rad), the building exterior walls within 10 feet (3048 mm) horizontally of a nonrated wall or unprotected opening shall have a fire-resistance rating of not less than 1 hour. Openings within such exterior walls shall be protected by opening protectives having a fire protection rating of not less than $^3/_4$ hour. This construction shall extend vertically from the ground to a point 10 feet (3048 mm) above the

topmost landing of the stairway or to the roof line, whichever is lower.

1020.1.5 Discharge identification barrier. A stairway in an exit enclosure shall not continue below the level of exit discharge unless an approved barrier is provided at the level of exit discharge to prevent persons from unintentionally continuing into levels below. Directional exit signs shall be provided as specified in Section 1011.

1020.1.6 Stairway floor number signs. A sign shall be provided at each floor landing in interior exit enclosures connecting more than three stories designating the floor level, the terminus of the top and bottom of the stair enclosure and the identification of the stair. The signage shall also state the story of, and the direction to the exit discharge and the availability of roof access from the stairway for the fire department. The sign shall be located 5 feet (1524 mm) above the floor landing in a position that is readily visible when the doors are in the open and closed positions.

1020.1.7 Smokeproof enclosures. In buildings required to comply with Section 403 or 405, each of the exits of a building that serves stories where the floor surface is located more than 75 feet (22 860 mm) above the lowest level of fire department vehicle access or more than 30 feet (9144 mm) below the level of exit discharge serving such floor levels shall be a smokeproof enclosure or pressurized stairway in accordance with Section 909.20.

1020.1.7.1 Enclosure exit. A smokeproof enclosure or pressurized stairway shall exit into a public way or into an exit passageway, yard or open space having direct access to a public way. The exit passageway shall be without other openings and shall be separated from the remainder of the building by 2-hour fire-resistance-rated construction.

Exceptions:

1. Openings in the exit passageway serving a smokeproof enclosure are permitted where the exit passageway is protected and pressurized in the same manner as the smokeproof enclosure, and openings are protected as required for access from other floors.

2. Openings in the exit passageway serving a pressurized stairway are permitted where the exit passageway is protected and pressurized in the same manner as the pressurized stairway.

3. A smokeproof enclosure or pressurized stairway shall be permitted to egress through areas on the level of discharge or vestibules as permitted by Section 1024.

1020.1.7.2 Enclosure access. Access to the stairway within a smokeproof enclosure shall be by way of a vestibule or an open exterior balcony.

Exception: Access is not required by way of a vestibule or exterior balcony for stairways using the pressurization alternative complying with Section 909.20.5.

SECTION 1021
EXIT PASSAGEWAYS

1021.1 Exit passageway. Exit passageways serving as an exit component in a means of egress system shall comply with the requirements of this section. An exit passageway shall not be used for any purpose other than as a means of egress.

1021.2 Width. The width of exit passageways shall be determined as specified in Section 1005.1 but such width shall not be less than 44 inches (1118 mm), except that exit passageways serving an occupant load of less than 50 shall not be less than 36 inches (914 mm) in width.

The required width of exit passageways shall be unobstructed.

Exception: Doors, when fully opened, and handrails, shall not reduce the required width by more than 7 inches (178 mm). Doors in any position shall not reduce the required width by more than one-half. Other nonstructural projections such as trim and similar decorative features are permitted to project into the required width 1.5 inches (38 mm) on each side.

1021.3 Construction. Exit passageway enclosures shall have walls, floors and ceilings of not less than 1-hour fire-resistance rating, and not less than that required for any connecting exit enclosure. Exit passageways shall be constructed as fire barriers in accordance with Section 706.

1021.4 Openings and penetrations. Exit passageway opening protectives shall be in accordance with the requirements of Section 715.

Except as permitted in Section 402.4.6, openings in exit passageways other than unexposed exterior openings shall be limited to those necessary for exit access to the exit passageway from normally occupied spaces and for egress from the exit passageway.

Where interior exit enclosures are extended to the exterior of a building by an exit passageway, the door assembly from the exit enclosure to the exit passageway shall be protected by a fire door conforming to the requirements in Section 715.4. Fire door assemblies in exit passageways shall comply with Section 715.4.4.

Elevators shall not open into an exit passageway.

1021.5 Penetrations. Penetrations into and openings through an exit passageway are prohibited except for required exit doors, equipment and ductwork necessary for independent pressurization, sprinkler piping, standpipes, electrical raceway for fire department communication and electrical raceway serving the exit passageway and terminating at a steel box not exceeding 16 square inches (0.010 m²). Such penetrations shall be protected in accordance with Section 712. There shall be no penetrations or communicating openings, whether protected or not, between adjacent exit passageways.

SECTION 1022
HORIZONTAL EXITS

1022.1 Horizontal exits. Horizontal exits serving as an exit in a means of egress system shall comply with the require-

ments of this section. A horizontal exit shall not serve as the only exit from a portion of a building, and where two or more exits are required, not more than one-half of the total number of exits or total exit width shall be horizontal exits.

Exceptions:

1. Horizontal exits are permitted to comprise two-thirds of the required exits from any building or floor area for occupancies in Group I-2.

2. Horizontal exits are permitted to comprise 100 percent of the exits required for occupancies in Group I-3. At least 6 square feet (0.6 m²) of accessible space per occupant shall be provided on each side of the horizontal exit for the total number of people in adjoining compartments.

Every fire compartment for which credit is allowed in connection with a horizontal exit shall not be required to have a stairway or door leading directly outside, provided the adjoining fire compartments have stairways or doors leading directly outside and are so arranged that egress shall not require the occupants to return through the compartment from which egress originates.

The area into which a horizontal exit leads shall be provided with exits adequate to meet the occupant requirements of this chapter, but not including the added occupant capacity imposed by persons entering it through horizontal exits from another area. At least one of its exits shall lead directly to the exterior or to an exit enclosure.

1022.2 Separation. The separation between buildings or refuge areas connected by a horizontal exit shall be provided by a fire wall complying with Section 705 or a fire barrier complying with Section 706 and having a fire-resistance rating of not less than 2 hours. Opening protectives in horizontal exit walls shall also comply with Section 715. The horizontal exit separation shall extend vertically through all levels of the building unless floor assemblies have a fire-resistence rating of not less than 2 hours with no unprotected openings.

Exception: A fire-resistance rating is not required at horizontal exits between a building area and an above-grade pedestrian walkway constructed in accordance with Section 3104, provided that the distance between connected buildings is more than 20 feet (6096 mm).

Horizontal exit walls constructed as fire barriers shall be continuous from exterior wall to exterior wall so as to divide completely the floor served by the horizontal exit.

1022.3 Opening protectives. Fire doors in horizontal exits shall be self-closing or automatic-closing when activated by a smoke detector in accordance with Section 715.4.7.3. Doors, where located in a cross-corridor condition, shall be automatic-closing by activation of a smoke detector installed in accordance with Section 715.4.7.3.

1022.4 Capacity of refuge area. The refuge area of a horizontal exit shall be a space occupied by the same tenant or a public area and each such refuge area shall be adequate to accommodate the original occupant load of the refuge area plus the occupant load anticipated from the adjoining compartment. The anticipated occupant load from the adjoining compartment shall be based on the capacity of the horizontal exit doors entering the refuge area. The capacity of the refuge area shall be computed based on a net floor area allowance of 3 square feet (0.2787 m^2) for each occupant to be accommodated therein.

Exception: The net floor area allowable per occupant shall be as follows for the indicated occupancies:

1. Six square feet (0.6 m^2) per occupant for occupancies in Group I-3.

2. Fifteen square feet (1.4 m^2) per occupant for ambulatory occupancies in Group I-2.

3. Thirty square feet (2.8 m^2) per occupant for nonambulatory occupancies in Group I-2.

SECTION 1023
EXTERIOR EXIT RAMPS AND STAIRWAYS

1023.1 Exterior exit ramps and stairways. Exterior exit ramps and stairways serving as an element of a required means of egress shall comply with this section.

Exception: Exterior exit ramps and stairways for outdoor stadiums complying with Section 1020.1, Exception 2.

1023.2 Use in a means of egress. Exterior exit ramps and stairways shall not be used as an element of a required means of egress for Group I-2 occupancies. For occupancies in other than Group I-2, exterior exit ramps and stairways shall be permitted as an element of a required means of egress for buildings not exceeding six stories above grade plane or having occupied floors more than 75 feet (22 860 mm) above the lowest level of fire department vehicle access.

1023.3 Open side. Exterior exit ramps and stairways serving as an element of a required means of egress shall be open on at least one side. An open side shall have a minimum of 35 square feet (3.3 m^2) of aggregate open area adjacent to each floor level and the level of each intermediate landing. The required open area shall be located not less than 42 inches (1067 mm) above the adjacent floor or landing level.

1023.4 Side yards. The open areas adjoining exterior exit ramps or stairways shall be either yards, courts or public ways; the remaining sides are permitted to be enclosed by the exterior walls of the building.

1023.5 Location. Exterior exit ramps and stairways shall be located in accordance with Section 1024.3.

1023.6 Exterior ramps and stairway protection. Exterior exit ramps and stairways shall be separated from the interior of the building as required in Section 1020.1. Openings shall be limited to those necessary for egress from normally occupied spaces.

Exceptions:

1. Separation from the interior of the building is not required for occupancies, other than those in Group R-1 or R-2, in buildings that are no more than two stories above grade plane where the level of exit discharge is the first story above grade plane.

2. Separation from the interior of the building is not required where the exterior ramp or stairway is served by an exterior ramp and/or balcony that connects two remote exterior stairways or other approved exits with a perimeter that is not less than 50 percent open. To be considered open, the opening shall be a minimum of 50 percent of the height of the enclosing wall, with the top of the openings no less than 7 feet (2134 mm) above the top of the balcony.

3. Separation from the interior of the building is not required for an exterior ramp or stairway located in a building or structure that is permitted to have unenclosed interior stairways in accordance with Section 1020.1.

4. Separation from the interior of the building is not required for exterior ramps or stairways connected to open-ended corridors, provided that Items 4.1 through 4.4 are met:

    4.1. The building, including corridors and ramps and/or stairs, shall be equipped throughout with an automatic sprinkler system in accordance with Section 903.3.1.1 or 903.3.1.2.

    4.2. The open-ended corridors comply with Section 1017.

    4.3. The open-ended corridors are connected on each end to an exterior exit ramp or stairway complying with Section 1023.

    4.4. At any location in an open-ended corridor where a change of direction exceeding 45 degrees (0.79 rad) occurs, a clear opening of not less than 35 square feet (3.3 m^2) or an exterior ramp or stairway shall be provided. Where clear openings are provided, they shall be located so as to minimize the accumulation of smoke or toxic gases.

SECTION 1024
EXIT DISCHARGE

1024.1 General. Exits shall discharge directly to the exterior of the building. The exit discharge shall be at grade or shall provide direct access to grade. The exit discharge shall not reenter a building.

Exceptions:

1. A maximum of 50 percent of the number and capacity of the exit enclosures is permitted to egress through areas on the level of discharge provided all of the following are met:

    1.1. Such exit enclosures egress to a free and unobstructed way to the exterior of the building, which way is readily visible and identifiable from the point of termination of the exit enclosure.

    1.2. The entire area of the level of discharge is separated from areas below by construction conforming to the fire-resistance rating for the exit enclosure.

1.3. The egress path from the exit enclosure on the level of discharge is protected throughout by an approved automatic sprinkler system. All portions of the level of discharge with access to the egress path shall either be protected throughout with an automatic sprinkler system installed in accordance with Section 903.3.1.1 or 903.3.1.2, or separated from the egress path in accordance with the requirements for the enclosure of exits.

2. A maximum of 50 percent of the number and capacity of the exit enclosures is permitted to egress through a vestibule provided all of the following are met:

2.1. The entire area of the vestibule is separated from areas below by construction conforming to the fire-resistance rating for the exit enclosure.

2.2. The depth from the exterior of the building is not greater than 10 feet (3048 mm) and the length is not greater than 30 feet (9144 mm).

2.3. The area is separated from the remainder of the level of exit discharge by construction providing protection at least the equivalent of approved wired glass in steel frames.

2.4. The area is used only for means of egress and exits directly to the outside.

3. Stairways in open parking garages complying with Section 1020.1, Exception 5, are permitted to egress through the open parking garage at the level of exit discharge.

1024.2 Exit discharge capacity. The capacity of the exit discharge shall be not less than the required discharge capacity of the exits being served.

1024.3 Exit discharge location. Exterior balconies, stairways and ramps shall be located at least 10 feet (3048 mm) from adjacent lot lines and from other buildings on the same lot unless the adjacent building exterior walls and openings are protected in accordance with Section 704 based on fire separation distance.

1024.4 Exit discharge components. Exit discharge components shall be sufficiently open to the exterior so as to minimize the accumulation of smoke and toxic gases.

1024.5 Egress courts. Egress courts serving as a portion of the exit discharge in the means of egress system shall comply with the requirements of Section 1024.

1024.5.1 Width. The width of egress courts shall be determined as specified in Section 1005.1, but such width shall not be less than 44 inches (1118 mm), except as specified herein. Egress courts serving Group R-3 and U occupancies shall not be less than 36 inches (914 mm) in width.

The required width of egress courts shall be unobstructed to a height of 7 feet (2134 mm).

Exception: Doors, when fully opened, and handrails shall not reduce the required width by more than 7 inches (178 mm). Doors in any position shall not reduce the required width by more than one-half. Other nonstructural projections such as trim and similar decorative features are permitted to project into the required width 1.5 inches (38 mm) from each side.

Where an egress court exceeds the minimum required width and the width of such egress court is then reduced along the path of exit travel, the reduction in width shall be gradual. The transition in width shall be affected by a guard not less than 36 inches (914 mm) in height and shall not create an angle of more than 30 degrees (0.52 rad) with respect to the axis of the egress court along the path of egress travel. In no case shall the width of the egress court be less than the required minimum.

1024.5.2 Construction and openings. Where an egress court serving a building or portion thereof is less than 10 feet (3048 mm) in width, the egress court walls shall have not less than 1-hour fire-resistance-rated construction for a distance of 10 feet (3048 mm) above the floor of the court. Openings within such walls shall be protected by opening protectives having a fire protection rating of not less than $^{3}/_{4}$ hour.

Exceptions:

1. Egress courts serving an occupant load of less than 10.

2. Egress courts serving Group R-3.

1024.6 Access to a public way. The exit discharge shall provide a direct and unobstructed access to a public way.

Exception: Where access to a public way cannot be provided, a safe dispersal area shall be provided where all of the following are met:

1. The area shall be of a size to accommodate at least 5 square feet (0.28 m^2) for each person.

2. The area shall be located on the same property, away from the building requiring egress a minimum distance equal to at least 150 percent of the height of the building but no less than 50 feet (15 240 mm).

3. The area shall be permanently maintained and identified as a safe dispersal area.

4. The area shall be provided with a safe and unobstructed path of travel from the building.

5. The area shall be provided with a two-way voice communication system connecting the safe dispersal area to the main entrance. If a fire command center is provided, voice communication shall connect the safe dispersal area with both the main entrance and fire command center.

SECTION 1025
ASSEMBLY

1025.1 General. Occupancies in Group A shall comply with this section.

1025.1.1 Bleachers. Bleachers, grandstands, and folding and telescopic seating shall comply with ICC 300.

1025.2 Assembly main exit. Group A occupancies that have an occupant load of greater than 300 shall be provided with a main exit. The main exit shall be of sufficient width to accommodate not less than one-half of the occupant load, but such width shall not be less than the total required width of all means of egress leading to the exit. Where the building is classified as a Group A occupancy, the main exit shall front on at least one street or an unoccupied space of not less than 10 feet (3048 mm) in width that adjoins a street or public way.

> **Exception:** In assembly occupancies where there is no well-defined main exit or where multiple main exits are provided, exits shall be permitted to be distributed around the perimeter of the building provided that the total width of egress is not less than 100 percent of the required width.

1025.3 Assembly other exits. In addition to having access to a main exit, each level in a Group A occupancy having an occupant load greater than 300 shall be provided with additional means of egress that shall provide an egress capacity for at least one-half of the total occupant load served by that level and comply with Section 1015.2. The minimum number of exits provided, consisting of the main exit and other exits, shall be at least 3 exits for an occupant load of 350–700 persons and at least 4 exits for an occupant load of more than 700 persons.

> **Exception:** In assembly occupancies where there is no well-defined main exit or where multiple main exits are provided, exits shall be permitted to be distributed around the perimeter of the building, provided that the total width of egress is not less than 100 percent of the required width.

1025.4 Foyers and lobbies. In Group A-1 occupancies, where persons are admitted to the building at times when seats are not available and are allowed to wait in a lobby or similar space, such use of lobby or similar space shall not encroach upon the required clear width of the means of egress. Such waiting areas shall be separated from the required means of egress by substantial permanent partitions or by fixed rigid railings not less than 42 inches (1067 mm) high. Such foyer, if not directly connected to a public street by all the main entrances or exits, shall have a straight and unobstructed corridor or path of travel to every such main entrance or exit.

1025.5 Interior balcony and gallery means of egress. For balconies or galleries having a seating capacity of 50 or more located in Group A occupancies, at least two means of egress shall be provided, with one from each side of every balcony or gallery and at least one leading directly to an exit.

1025.5.1 Enclosure of balcony openings. Interior stairways and other vertical openings shall be enclosed in an exit enclosure as provided in Section 1020.1, except that stairways are permitted to be open between the balcony and the main assembly floor in occupancies such as theaters, places of religious worship and auditoriums. At least one accessible means of egress is required from a balcony or gallery level containing accessible seating locations in accordance with Section 1007.3 or 1007.4.

1025.6 Width of means of egress for assembly. The clear width of aisles and other means of egress shall comply with Section 1025.6.1 where smoke-protected seating is not provided and with Section 1025.6.2 or 1025.6.3 where smoke-protected seating is provided. The clear width shall be measured to walls, edges of seating and tread edges except for permitted projections.

1025.6.1 Without smoke protection. The clear width of the means of egress shall provide sufficient capacity in accordance with all of the following, as applicable:

1. At least 0.3 inch (7.6 mm) of width for each occupant served shall be provided on stairs having riser heights 7 inches (178 mm) or less and tread depths 11 inches (279 mm) or greater, measured horizontally between tread nosings.

2. At least 0.005 inch (0.127 mm) of additional stair width for each occupant shall be provided for each 0.10 inch (2.5 mm) of riser height above 7 inches (178 mm).

3. Where egress requires stair descent, at least 0.075 inch (1.9 mm) of additional width for each occupant shall be provided on those portions of stair width having no handrail within a horizontal distance of 30 inches (762 mm).

4. Ramped means of egress, where slopes are steeper than one unit vertical in 12 units horizontal (8-percent slope), shall have at least 0.22 inch (5.6 mm) of clear width for each occupant served. Level or ramped means of egress, where slopes are not steeper than one unit vertical in 12 units horizontal (8-percent slope), shall have at least 0.20 inch (5.1 mm) of clear width for each occupant served.

1025.6.2 Smoke-protected seating. The clear width of the means of egress for smoke-protected assembly seating shall not be less than the occupant load served by the egress element multiplied by the appropriate factor in Table 1025.6.2. The total number of seats specified shall be those within the space exposed to the same smoke-protected environment. Interpolation is permitted between the specific values shown. A life safety evaluation, complying with NFPA 101, shall be done for a facility utilizing the reduced width requirements of Table 1025.6.2 for smoke-protected assembly seating.

> **Exception:** For an outdoor smoke-protected assembly with an occupant load not greater than 18,000, the clear width shall be determined using the factors in Section 1025.6.3.

1025.6.2.1 Smoke control. Means of egress serving a smoke-protected assembly seating area shall be provided with a smoke control system complying with Section 909 or natural ventilation designed to maintain the smoke level at least 6 feet (1829 mm) above the floor of the means of egress.

1025.6.2.2 Roof height. A smoke-protected assembly seating area with a roof shall have the lowest portion of the roof deck not less than 15 feet (4572 mm) above the highest aisle or aisle accessway.

> **Exception:** A roof canopy in an outdoor stadium shall be permitted to be less than 15 feet (4572 mm)

TABLE 1025.6.2
WIDTH OF AISLES FOR SMOKE-PROTECTED ASSEMBLY

TOTAL NUMBER OF SEATS IN THE SMOKE- PROTECTED ASSEMBLY OCCUPANCY	INCHES OF CLEAR WIDTH PER SEAT SERVED			
	Stairs and aisle steps with handrails within 30 inches	Stairs and aisle steps without handrails within 30 inches	Passageways, doorways and ramps not steeper than 1 in 10 in slope	Ramps steeper than 1 in 10 in slope
Equal to or less than 5,000	0.200	0.250	0.150	0.165
10,000	0.130	0.163	0.100	0.110
15,000	0.096	0.120	0.070	0.077
20,000	0.076	0.095	0.056	0.062
Equal to or greater than 25,000	0.060	0.075	0.044	0.048

For SI: 1 inch = 25.4 mm.

above the highest aisle or aisle accessway provided that there are no objects less than 80 inches (2032 mm) above the highest aisle or aisle accessway.

1025.6.2.3 Automatic sprinklers. Enclosed areas with walls and ceilings in buildings or structures containing smoke-protected assembly seating shall be protected with an approved automatic sprinkler system in accordance with Section 903.3.1.1.

Exceptions:

1. The floor area used for contests, performances or entertainment provided the roof construction is more than 50 feet (15 240 mm) above the floor level and the use is restricted to low fire hazard uses.

2. Press boxes and storage facilities less than 1,000 square feet (93 m^2) in area.

3. Outdoor seating facilities where seating and the means of egress in the seating area are essentially open to the outside.

1025.6.3 Width of means of egress for outdoor smoke-protected assembly. The clear width in inches (mm) of aisles and other means of egress shall be not less than the total occupant load served by the egress element multiplied by 0.08 (2.0 mm) where egress is by aisles and stairs and multiplied by 0.06 (1.52 mm) where egress is by ramps, corridors, tunnels or vomitories.

Exception: The clear width in inches (mm) of aisles and other means of egress shall be permitted to comply with Section 1025.6.2 for the number of seats in the outdoor smoke-protected assembly where Section 1025.6.2 permits less width.

1025.7 Travel distance. Exits and aisles shall be so located that the travel distance to an exit door shall not be greater than 200 feet (60 960 mm) measured along the line of travel in nonsprinklered buildings. Travel distance shall not be more than 250 feet (76 200 mm) in sprinklered buildings. Where aisles are provided for seating, the distance shall be measured along the aisles and aisle accessway without travel over or on the seats.

Exceptions:

1. Smoke-protected assembly seating: The travel distance from each seat to the nearest entrance to a vomitory or concourse shall not exceed 200 feet (60 960 mm). The travel distance from the entrance to the vomitory or concourse to a stair, ramp or walk on the exterior of the building shall not exceed 200 feet (60 960 mm).

2. Open-air seating: The travel distance from each seat to the building exterior shall not exceed 400 feet (122 m). The travel distance shall not be limited in facilities of Type I or II construction.

1025.8 Common path of travel. The common path of egress travel shall not exceed 30 feet (9144 mm) from any seat to a point where an occupant has a choice of two paths of egress travel to two exits.

Exceptions:

1. For areas serving less than 50 occupants, the common path of egress travel shall not exceed 75 feet (22 860 mm).

2. For smoke-protected assembly seating, the common path of egress travel shall not exceed 50 feet (15 240 mm).

1025.8.1 Path through adjacent row. Where one of the two paths of travel is across the aisle through a row of seats to another aisle, there shall be not more than 24 seats between the two aisles, and the minimum clear width between rows for the row between the two aisles shall be 12 inches (305 mm) plus 0.6 inch (15.2 mm) for each additional seat above seven in the row between aisles.

Exception: For smoke-protected assembly seating there shall not be more than 40 seats between the two aisles and the minimum clear width shall be 12 inches (305 mm) plus 0.3 inch (7.6 mm) for each additional seat.

1025.9 Assembly aisles are required. Every occupied portion of any occupancy in Group A that contains seats, tables, displays, similar fixtures or equipment shall be provided with aisles leading to exits or exit access doorways in accordance with this section. Aisle accessways for tables and seating shall comply with Section 1014.4.3.

1025.9.1 Minimum aisle width. The minimum clear width for aisles shall be as shown:

1. Forty-eight inches (1219 mm) for aisle stairs having seating on each side.

   Exception: Thirty-six inches (914 mm) where the aisle serves less than 50 seats.

2. Thirty-six inches (914 mm) for aisle stairs having seating on only one side.

3. Twenty-three inches (584 mm) between an aisle stair handrail or guard and seating where the aisle is subdivided by a handrail.

4. Forty-two inches (1067 mm) for level or ramped aisles having seating on both sides.

Exceptions:

1. Thirty-six inches (914 mm) where the aisle serves less that 50 seats.

2. Thirty inches (762 mm) where the aisle does not serve more than 14 seats.

5. Thirty-six inches (914 mm) for level or ramped aisles having seating on only one side.

Exceptions:

1. Thirty inches (762 mm) where the aisle does not serve more than 14 seats.

2. Twenty-three inches (584 mm) between an aisle stair handrail and seating where an aisle does not serve more than five rows on one side.

1025.9.2 Aisle width. The aisle width shall provide sufficient egress capacity for the number of persons accommodated by the catchment area served by the aisle. The catchment area served by an aisle is that portion of the total space that is served by that section of the aisle. In establishing catchment areas, the assumption shall be made that there is a balanced use of all means of egress, with the number of persons in proportion to egress capacity.

1025.9.3 Converging aisles. Where aisles converge to form a single path of egress travel, the required egress capacity of that path shall not be less than the combined required capacity of the converging aisles.

1025.9.4 Uniform width. Those portions of aisles, where egress is possible in either of two directions, shall be uniform in required width.

1025.9.5 Assembly aisle termination. Each end of an aisle shall terminate at cross aisle, foyer, doorway, vomitory or concourse having access to an exit.

Exceptions:

1. Dead-end aisles shall not be greater than 20 feet (6096 mm) in length.

2. Dead-end aisles longer than 20 feet (6096 mm) are permitted where seats beyond the 20-foot (6096 mm) dead-end aisle are no more than 24 seats from another aisle, measured along a row of seats having a minimum clear width of 12 inches (305 mm) plus 0.6 inch (15.2 mm) for each additional seat above seven in the row.

3. For smoke-protected assembly seating, the dead-end aisle length of vertical aisles shall not exceed a distance of 21 rows.

4. For smoke-protected assembly seating, a longer dead-end aisle is permitted where seats beyond the 21-row dead-end aisle are not more than 40 seats from another aisle, measured along a row of seats having an aisle accessway with a minimum clear width of 12 inches (305 mm) plus 0.3 inch (7.6 mm) for each additional seat above seven in the row.

1025.9.6 Assembly aisle obstructions. There shall be no obstructions in the required width of aisles except for handrails as provided in Section 1025.13.

1025.10 Clear width of aisle accessways serving seating. Where seating rows have 14 or fewer seats, the minimum clear aisle accessway width shall not be less than 12 inches (305 mm) measured as the clear horizontal distance from the back of the row ahead and the nearest projection of the row behind. Where chairs have automatic or self-rising seats, the measurement shall be made with seats in the raised position. Where any chair in the row does not have an automatic or self-rising seat, the measurements shall be made with the seat in the down position. For seats with folding tablet arms, row spacing shall be determined with the tablet arm down.

1025.10.1 Dual access. For rows of seating served by aisles or doorways at both ends, there shall not be more than 100 seats per row. The minimum clear width of 12 inches (305 mm) between rows shall be increased by 0.3 inch (7.6 mm) for every additional seat beyond 14 seats, but the minimum clear width is not required to exceed 22 inches (559 mm).

Exception: For smoke-protected assembly seating, the row length limits for a 12-inch-wide (305 mm) aisle accessway, beyond which the aisle accessway minimum clear width shall be increased, are in Table 1025.10.1.

TABLE 1025.10.1
SMOKE-PROTECTED ASSEMBLY AISLE ACCESSWAYS

TOTAL NUMBER OF SEATS IN THE SMOKE-PROTECTED ASSEMBLY OCCUPANCY	MAXIMUM NUMBER OF SEATS PER ROW PERMITTED TO HAVE A MINIMUM 12-INCH CLEAR WIDTH AISLE ACCESSWAY	
	Aisle or doorway at both ends of row	Aisle or doorway at one end of row only
Less than 4,000	14	7
4,000	15	7
7,000	16	8
10,000	17	8
13,000	18	9
16,000	19	9
19,000	20	10
22,000 and greater	21	11

For SI: 1 inch = 25.4 mm.

1025.10.2 Single access. For rows of seating served by an aisle or doorway at only one end of the row, the minimum clear width of 12 inches (305 mm) between rows shall be increased by 0.6 inch (15.2 mm) for every additional seat beyond seven seats, but the minimum clear width is not required to exceed 22 inches (559 mm).

Exception: For smoke-protected assembly seating, the row length limits for a 12-inch-wide (305 mm) aisle accessway, beyond which the aisle accessway minimum clear width shall be increased, are in Table 1025.10.1.

1025.11 Assembly aisle walking surfaces. Aisles with a slope not exceeding one unit vertical in eight units horizontal (12.5-percent slope) shall consist of a ramp having a slip-resistant walking surface. Aisles with a slope exceeding one unit vertical in eight units horizontal (12.5-percent slope) shall consist of a series of risers and treads that extends across the full width of aisles and complies with Sections 1025.11.1 through 1025.11.3.

1025.11.1 Treads. Tread depths shall be a minimum of 11 inches (279 mm) and shall have dimensional uniformity.

Exception: The tolerance between adjacent treads shall not exceed 0.188 inch (4.8 mm).

1025.11.2 Risers. Where the gradient of aisle stairs is to be the same as the gradient of adjoining seating areas, the riser height shall not be less than 4 inches (102 mm) nor more than 8 inches (203 mm) and shall be uniform within each flight.

Exceptions:

1. Riser height nonuniformity shall be limited to the extent necessitated by changes in the gradient of the adjoining seating area to maintain adequate sightlines. Where nonuniformities exceed 0.188 inch (4.8 mm) between adjacent risers, the exact location of such nonuniformities shall be indicated with a distinctive marking stripe on each tread at the nosing or leading edge adjacent to the nonuniform risers. Such stripe shall be a minimum of 1 inch (25 mm), and a maximum of 2 inches (51 mm), wide. The edge marking stripe shall be distinctively different from the contrasting marking stripe.

2. Riser heights not exceeding 9 inches (229 mm) shall be permitted where they are necessitated by the slope of the adjacent seating areas to maintain sightlines.

1025.11.3 Tread contrasting marking stripe. A contrasting marking stripe shall be provided on each tread at the nosing or leading edge such that the location of each tread is readily apparent when viewed in descent. Such stripe shall be a minimum of 1 inch (25 mm), and a maximum of 2 inches (51 mm), wide.

Exception: The contrasting marking stripe is permitted to be omitted where tread surfaces are such that the location of each tread is readily apparent when viewed in descent.

1025.12 Seat stability. In places of assembly, the seats shall be securely fastened to the floor.

Exceptions:

1. In places of assembly or portions thereof without ramped or tiered floors for seating and with 200 or fewer seats, the seats shall not be required to be fastened to the floor.

2. In places of assembly or portions thereof with seating at tables and without ramped or tiered floors for seating, the seats shall not be required to be fastened to the floor.

3. In places of assembly or portions thereof without ramped or tiered floors for seating and with greater than 200 seats, the seats shall be fastened together in groups of not less than three or the seats shall be securely fastened to the floor.

4. In places of assembly where flexibility of the seating arrangement is an integral part of the design and function of the space and seating is on tiered levels, a maximum of 200 seats shall not be required to be fastened to the floor. Plans showing seating, tiers and aisles shall be submitted for approval.

5. Groups of seats within a place of assembly separated from other seating by railings, guards, partial height walls or similar barriers with level floors and having no more than 14 seats per group shall not be required to be fastened to the floor.

6. Seats intended for musicians or other performers and separated by railings, guards, partial height walls or similar barriers shall not be required to be fastened to the floor.

1025.13 Handrails. Ramped aisles having a slope exceeding one unit vertical in 15 units horizontal (6.7-percent slope) and aisle stairs shall be provided with handrails located either at the side or within the aisle width.

Exceptions:

1. Handrails are not required for ramped aisles having a gradient no greater than one unit vertical in eight units horizontal (12.5-percent slope) and seating on both sides.

2. Handrails are not required if, at the side of the aisle, there is a guard that complies with the graspability requirements of handrails.

1025.13.1 Discontinuous handrails. Where there is seating on both sides of the aisle, the handrails shall be discontinuous with gaps or breaks at intervals not exceeding five rows to facilitate access to seating and to permit crossing from one side of the aisle to the other. These gaps or breaks shall have a clear width of at least 22 inches (559 mm) and not greater than 36 inches (914 mm), measured horizontally, and the handrail shall have rounded terminations or bends.

1025.13.2 Intermediate handrails. Where handrails are provided in the middle of aisle stairs, there shall be an additional intermediate handrail located approximately 12 inches (305 mm) below the main handrail.

1025.14 Assembly guards. Assembly guards shall comply with Sections 1025.14.1 through 1025.14.3.

1025.14.1 Cross aisles. Cross aisles located more than 30 inches (762 mm) above the floor or grade below shall have guards in accordance with Section 1013.

Where an elevation change of 30 inches (762 mm) or less occurs between a cross aisle and the adjacent floor or grade below, guards not less than 26 inches (660 mm) above the aisle floor shall be provided.

Exception: Where the backs of seats on the front of the cross aisle project 24 inches (610 mm) or more above the adjacent floor of the aisle, a guard need not be provided.

1025.14.2 Sightline-constrained guard heights. Unless subject to the requirements of Section 1025.14.3, a fascia or railing system in accordance with the guard requirements of Section 1013 and having a minimum height of 26 inches (660 mm) shall be provided where the floor or footboard elevation is more than 30 inches (762 mm) above the floor or grade below and the fascia or railing would otherwise interfere with the sightlines of immediately adjacent seating. At bleachers, a guard must be provided where the floor or footboard elevation is more than 24 inches (610 mm) above the floor or grade below and the fascia or railing would otherwise interfere with the sightlines of the immediately adjacent seating.

1025.14.3 Guards at the end of aisles. A fascia or railing system complying with the guard requirements of Section 1013 shall be provided for the full width of the aisle where the foot of the aisle is more than 30 inches (762 mm) above the floor or grade below. The fascia or railing shall be a minimum of 36 inches (914 mm) high and shall provide a minimum 42 inches (1067 mm) measured diagonally between the top of the rail and the nosing of the nearest tread.

1025.15 Bench seating. Where bench seating is used, the number of persons shall be based on one person for each 18 inches (457 mm) of length of the bench.

SECTION 1026
EMERGENCY ESCAPE AND RESCUE

1026.1 General. In addition to the means of egress required by this chapter, provisions shall be made for emergency escape and rescue in Group R and I-1 occupancies. Basements and sleeping rooms below the fourth story above grade plane shall have at least one exterior emergency escape and rescue opening in accordance with this section. Where basements contain one or more sleeping rooms, emergency egress and rescue openings shall be required in each sleeping room, but shall not be required in adjoining areas of the basement. Such openings shall open directly into a public way or to a yard or court that opens to a public way.

Exceptions:

1. In other than Group R-3 occupancies, buildings equipped throughout with an approved automatic sprinkler system in accordance with Section 903.3.1.1 or 903.3.1.2.

2. In other than Group R-3 occupancies, sleeping rooms provided with a door to a fire-resistance-rated corridor having access to two remote exits in opposite directions.

3. The emergency escape and rescue opening is permitted to open onto a balcony within an atrium in accordance with the requirements of Section 404, provided the balcony provides access to an exit and the dwelling unit or sleeping unit has a means of egress that is not open to the atrium.

4. Basements with a ceiling height of less than 80 inches (2032 mm) shall not be required to have emergency escape and rescue windows.

5. High-rise buildings in accordance with Section 403.

6. Emergency escape and rescue openings are not required from basements or sleeping rooms that have an exit door or exit access door that opens directly into a public way or to a yard, court or exterior exit balcony that opens to a public way.

7. Basements without habitable spaces and having no more than 200 square feet (18.6 m^2) in floor area shall not be required to have emergency escape windows.

1026.2 Minimum size. Emergency escape and rescue openings shall have a minimum net clear opening of 5.7 square feet (0.53 m^2).

Exception: The minimum net clear opening for emergency escape and rescue grade-floor openings shall be 5 square feet (0.46 m^2).

1026.2.1 Minimum dimensions. The minimum net clear opening height dimension shall be 24 inches (610 mm). The minimum net clear opening width dimension shall be 20 inches (508 mm). The net clear opening dimensions shall be the result of normal operation of the opening.

1026.3 Maximum height from floor. Emergency escape and rescue openings shall have the bottom of the clear opening not greater than 44 inches (1118 mm) measured from the floor.

1026.4 Operational constraints. Emergency escape and rescue openings shall be operational from the inside of the room without the use of keys or tools. Bars, grilles, grates or similar devices are permitted to be placed over emergency escape and rescue openings provided the minimum net clear opening size complies with Section 1026.2 and such devices shall be releasable or removable from the inside without the use of a key, tool or force greater than that which is required for normal operation of the escape and rescue opening. Where such bars, grilles, grates or similar devices are installed in existing buildings, smoke alarms shall be installed in accordance with Section 907.2.10 regardless of the valuation of the alteration.

1026.5 Window wells. An emergency escape and rescue opening with a finished sill height below the adjacent ground level shall be provided with a window well in accordance with Sections 1026.5.1 and 1026.5.2.

1026.5.1 Minimum size. The minimum horizontal area of the window well shall be 9 square feet (0.84 m^2), with a minimum dimension of 36 inches (914 mm). The area of the window well shall allow the emergency escape and rescue opening to be fully opened.

1026.5.2 Ladders or steps. Window wells with a vertical depth of more than 44 inches (1118 mm) shall be equipped with an approved permanently affixed ladder or steps. Ladders or rungs shall have an inside width of at least 12 inches (305 mm), shall project at least 3 inches (76 mm) from the wall and shall be spaced not more than 18 inches (457 mm) on center (o.c.) vertically for the full height of the window well. The ladder or steps shall not encroach into the required dimensions of the window well by more than 6 inches (152 mm). The ladder or steps shall not be obstructed by the emergency escape and rescue opening. Ladders or steps required by this section are exempt from the stairway requirements of Section 1009.

CHAPTER 11

ACCESSIBILITY

SECTION 1101
GENERAL

1101.1 Scope. The provisions of this chapter shall control the design and construction of facilities for accessibility to physically disabled persons.

1101.2 Design. Buildings and facilities shall be designed and constructed to be accessible in accordance with this code and ICC/ANSI A117.1.

SECTION 1102
DEFINITIONS

1102.1 Definitions. The following words and terms shall, for the purposes of this chapter and as used elsewhere in the code, have the following meanings:

ACCESSIBLE. A site, building, facility or portion thereof that complies with this chapter.

ACCESSIBLE ROUTE. A continuous, unobstructed path that complies with this chapter.

ACCESSIBLE UNIT. A dwelling unit or sleeping unit that complies with this code and the provisions for Accessible units in ICC/ANSI A117.1.

CIRCULATION PATH. An exterior or interior way of passage from one place to another for pedestrians.

COMMON USE. Interior or exterior circulation paths, rooms, spaces or elements that are not for public use and are made available for the shared use of two or more people.

DETECTABLE WARNING. A standardized surface feature built in or applied to walking surfaces or other elements to warn visually impaired persons of hazards on a circulation path.

DWELLING UNIT OR SLEEPING UNIT, MULTISTORY. See definition for "Multistory unit."

DWELLING UNIT OR SLEEPING UNIT, TYPE A. See definition for "Type A unit."

DWELLING UNIT OR SLEEPING UNIT, TYPE B. See definition for "Type B unit."

EMPLOYEE WORK AREA. All or any portion of a space used only by employees and only for work. Corridors, toilet rooms, kitchenettes and break rooms are not employee work areas.

FACILITY. All or any portion of buildings, structures, site improvements, elements and pedestrian or vehicular routes located on a site.

INTENDED TO BE OCCUPIED AS A RESIDENCE. This refers to a dwelling unit or sleeping unit that can or will be used all or part of the time as the occupant's place of abode.

MULTILEVEL ASSEMBLY SEATING. Seating that is arranged in distinct levels where each level is comprised of either multiple rows, or a single row of box seats accessed from a separate level.

MULTISTORY UNIT. A dwelling unit or sleeping unit with habitable space located on more than one story.

PUBLIC ENTRANCE. An entrance that is not a service entrance or a restricted entrance.

PUBLIC-USE AREAS. Interior or exterior rooms or spaces that are made available to the general public.

RESTRICTED ENTRANCE. An entrance that is made available for common use on a controlled basis, but not public use, and that is not a service entrance.

SELF-SERVICE STORAGE FACILITY. Real property designed and used for the purpose of renting or leasing individual storage spaces to customers for the purpose of storing and removing personal property on a self-service basis.

SERVICE ENTRANCE. An entrance intended primarily for delivery of goods or services.

SITE. A parcel of land bounded by a lot line or a designated portion of a public right-of-way.

TYPE A UNIT. A dwelling unit or sleeping unit designed and constructed for accessibility in accordance with this code and the provisions for Type A units in ICC/ANSI A117.1.

TYPE B UNIT. A dwelling unit or sleeping unit designed and constructed for accessibility in accordance with this code and the provisions for Type B units in ICC/ANSI A117.1, consistent with the design and construction requirements of the federal Fair Housing Act.

WHEELCHAIR SPACE. A space for a single wheelchair and its occupant.

SECTION 1103
SCOPING REQUIREMENTS

1103.1 Where required. Sites, buildings, structures, facilities, elements and spaces, temporary or permanent, shall be accessible to persons with physical disabilities.

1103.2 General exceptions. Sites, buildings, structures, facilities, elements and spaces shall be exempt from this chapter to the extent specified in this section.

1103.2.1 Specific requirements. Accessibility is not required in buildings and facilities, or portions thereof, to the extent permitted by Sections 1104 through 1110.

1103.2.2 Existing buildings. Existing buildings shall comply with the *Existing Building Code of New York State.*

1103.2.3 Employee work areas. Spaces and elements within employee work areas shall only be required to comply with Sections 907.9.1.2, 1007 and 1104.3.1 and shall be designed and constructed so that individuals with disabilities can approach, enter and exit the work area. Work areas, or portions of work areas, that are less than 150 square feet (14 m²) in area and elevated 7 inches (178 mm) or more above the ground or finish floor where the elevation is essential to the function of the space shall be exempt from all requirements.

1103.2.4 Detached dwellings. Detached one- and two-family dwellings and accessory structures, and their associated sites and facilities, are not required to be accessible.

1103.2.5 Utility buildings. Occupancies in Group U are exempt from the requirements of this chapter other than the following:

1. In agricultural buildings, access is required to paved work areas and areas open to the general public.

2. Private garages or carports that contain required accessible parking.

1103.2.6 Construction sites. Structures, sites and equipment directly associated with the actual processes of construction including, but not limited to, scaffolding, bridging, materials hoists, materials storage or construction trailers are not required to be accessible.

1103.2.7 Raised areas. Raised areas used primarily for purposes of security, life safety or fire safety including, but not limited to, observation galleries, prison guard towers, fire towers or lifeguard stands are not required to be accessible or to be served by an accessible route.

1103.2.8 Limited access spaces. Nonoccupiable spaces accessed only by ladders, catwalks, crawl spaces, freight elevators or very narrow passageways are not required to be accessible.

1103.2.9 Equipment spaces. Spaces frequented only by personnel for maintenance, repair or monitoring of equipment are not required to be accessible. Such spaces include, but are not limited to, elevator pits, elevator penthouses, mechanical, electrical or communications equipment rooms, piping or equipment catwalks, water or sewage treatment pump rooms and stations, electric substations and transformer vaults, and highway and tunnel utility facilities.

1103.2.10 Single-occupant structures. Single-occupant structures accessed only by passageways below grade or elevated above grade including, but not limited to, toll booths that are accessed only by underground tunnels, are not required to be accessible.

1103.2.11 Residential Group R-1. Buildings of Group R-1 containing not more than five sleeping units for rent or hire that are also occupied as the residence of the proprietor are not required to be accessible.

1103.2.12 Day care facilities. Where a day care facility (Groups A-3, E, I-4 and R-3) is part of a dwelling unit, only the portion of the structure utilized for the day care facility is required to be accessible.

1103.2.13 Detention and correctional facilities. In detention and correctional facilities, common use areas that are used only by inmates or detainees and security personnel, and that do not serve holding cells or housing cells required to be accessible, are not required to be accessible or to be served by an accessible route.

1103.2.14 Fuel-dispensing systems. The operable parts on fuel-dispensing devices shall comply with ICC/ANSI A117.1, Section 308.2.1 or 308.3.1.

1103.2.15 Walk-in coolers and freezers. Walk-in coolers and freezers intended for employee use only are not required to be accessible.

SECTION 1104
ACCESSIBLE ROUTE

1104.1 Site arrival points. Accessible routes within the site shall be provided from public transportation stops; accessible parking; accessible passenger loading zones; and public streets or sidewalks to the accessible building entrance served.

Exception: Other than in buildings or facilities containing or serving Type B units, an accessible route shall not be required between site arrival points and the building or facility entrance if the only means of access between them is a vehicular way not providing for pedestrian access.

1104.2 Within a site. At least one accessible route shall connect accessible buildings, accessible facilities, accessible elements and accessible spaces that are on the same site.

Exception: An accessible route is not required between accessible buildings, accessible facilities, accessible elements and accessible spaces that have, as the only means of access between them, a vehicular way not providing for pedestrian access.

1104.3 Connected spaces. When a building or portion of a building is required to be accessible, an accessible route shall be provided to each portion of the building, to accessible building entrances connecting accessible pedestrian walkways and the public way.

Exception: In assembly areas with fixed seating required to be accessible, an accessible route shall not be required to serve fixed seating where wheelchair spaces or designated aisle seats required to be on an accessible route are not provided.

1104.3.1 Employee work areas. Common use circulation paths within employee work areas shall be accessible routes.

Exceptions:

1. Common use circulation paths, located within employee work areas that are less than 300 square feet (27.9 m²) in size and defined by permanently installed partitions, counters, casework or furnishings, shall not be required to be accessible routes.

2. Common use circulation paths, located within employee work areas, that are an integral component of equipment, shall not be required to be accessible routes.

3. Common use circulation paths, located within exterior employee work areas that are fully exposed to the weather, shall not be required to be accessible routes.

1104.3.2 Press boxes. Press boxes in assembly areas shall be on an accessible route.

Exceptions:

1. An accessible route shall not be required to press boxes in bleachers that have points of entry at only one level, provided that the aggregate area of all press boxes is 500 square feet (46 m²) maximum.

2. An accessible route shall not be required to freestanding press boxes that are elevated above grade 12 feet (3660 mm) minimum provided that the aggregate area of all press boxes is 500 square feet (46 m²) maximum.

1104.4 Multilevel buildings and facilities. At least one accessible route shall connect each accessible level, including mezzanines, in multilevel buildings and facilities.

Exceptions:

1. An accessible route is not required to stories and mezzanines above and below accessible levels that have an aggregate area of not more than 3,000 square feet (278.7 m²). This exception shall not apply to:

    1.1. Multiple tenant facilities of Group M occupancies containing five or more tenant spaces;

    1.2. Levels containing offices of health care providers (Group B or I); or

    1.3. Passenger transportation facilities and airports (Group A-3 or B).

2. In Group A, I, R and S occupancies, levels that do not contain accessible elements or other spaces required by Section 1107 or 1108 are not required to be served by an accessible route from an accessible level.

3. In air traffic control towers, an accessible route is not required to serve the cab and the floor immediately below the cab.

4. Where a two-story building or facility has one story with an occupant load of five or fewer persons that does not contain public use space, that story shall not be required to be connected by an accessible route to the story above or below.

1104.5 Location. Accessible routes shall coincide with or be located in the same area as a general circulation path. Where the circulation path is interior, the accessible route shall also be interior. Where only one accessible route is provided, the accessible route shall not pass through kitchens, storage rooms, restrooms, closets or similar spaces.

Exceptions:

1. Accessible routes from parking garages contained within and serving Type B dwelling units are not required to be interior.

2. A single accessible route is permitted to pass through a kitchen or storage room in an Accessible, Type A or Type B dwelling unit.

1104.6 Security barriers. Security barriers including, but not limited to, security bollards and security check points shall not obstruct a required accessible route or accessible means of egress.

Exception: Where security barriers incorporate elements that cannot comply with these requirements, such as certain metal detectors, fluoroscopes or other similar devices, the accessible route shall be permitted to be provided adjacent to security screening devices. The accessible route shall permit persons with disabilities passing around security barriers to maintain visual contact with their personal items to the same extent provided others passing through the security barrier.

SECTION 1105
ACCESSIBLE ENTRANCES

1105.1 Public entrances. In addition to accessible entrances required by Sections 1105.1.1 through 1105.1.6, at least 60 percent of all public entrances shall be accessible.

Exceptions:

1. An accessible entrance is not required to areas not required to be accessible.

2. Loading and service entrances that are not the only entrance to a tenant space.

1105.1.1 Parking garage entrances. Where provided, direct access for pedestrians from parking structures to buildings or facility entrances shall be accessible.

1105.1.2 Entrances from tunnels or elevated walkways. Where direct access is provided for pedestrians from a pedestrian tunnel or elevated walkway to a building or facility, at least one entrance to the building or facility from each tunnel or walkway shall be accessible.

1105.1.3 Restricted entrances. Where restricted entrances are provided to a building or facility, at least one restricted entrance to the building or facility shall be accessible.

1105.1.4 Entrances for inmates or detainees. Where entrances used only by inmates or detainees and security personnel are provided at judicial facilities, detention facilities or correctional facilities, at least one such entrance shall be accessible.

1105.1.5 Service entrances. If a service entrance is the only entrance to a building or a tenant space in a facility, that entrance shall be accessible.

1105.1.6 Tenant spaces, dwelling units and sleeping units. At least one accessible entrance shall be provided to each tenant, dwelling unit and sleeping unit in a facility.

Exceptions:

1. An accessible entrance is not required to tenants that are not required to be accessible.

2. An accessible entrance is not required to dwelling units and sleeping units that are not required to be Accessible units, Type A units or Type B units.

SECTION 1106
PARKING AND PASSENGER LOADING FACILITIES

1106.1 Required. Where parking is provided, accessible parking spaces shall be provided in compliance with Table 1106.1, except as required by Sections 1106.2 through 1106.4. Where more than one parking facility is provided on a site, the number of parking spaces required to be accessible shall be calculated separately for each parking facility.

Exception: This section does not apply to parking spaces used exclusively for buses, trucks, other delivery vehicles, law enforcement vehicles or vehicular impound and motor pools where lots accessed by the public are provided with an accessible passenger loading zone.

1106.1.1 Access aisles. Accessible parking spaces shall be in conformance with ICC/ANSI A117.1 except that spaces shall be provided with access aisles at least 8 feet (2440 mm) in width.

TABLE 1106.1
ACCESSIBLE PARKING SPACES

TOTAL PARKING SPACES PROVIDED	REQUIRED MINIMUM NUMBER OF ACCESSIBLE SPACES
1 to 25	1
26 to 50	2
51 to 75	3
76 to 100	4
101 to 150	5
151 to 200	6
201 to 300	7
301 to 400	8
401 to 500	9
501 to 1,000	2% of total
1,001 and over	20, plus one for each 100, or fraction thereof, over 1,000

1106.2 Groups R-2 and R-3. Two percent, but not less than one, of each type of parking space provided for occupancies in Groups R-2 and R-3, which are required to have Accessible, Type A or Type B dwelling or sleeping units, shall be accessible. Where parking is provided within or beneath a building, accessible parking spaces shall also be provided within or beneath the building.

1106.3 Hospital outpatient facilities. Ten percent of patient and visitor parking spaces provided to serve hospital outpatient facilities shall be accessible.

1106.4 Rehabilitation facilities and outpatient physical therapy facilities. Twenty percent, but not less than one, of the portion of patient and visitor parking spaces serving rehabilitation facilities and outpatient physical therapy facilities shall be accessible.

1106.5 Signage. Each accessible parking space shall be provided with signage displaying the international symbol of accessibility. Each access aisle shall be provided with signage reading "NO PARKING ANYTIME". Signs shall be permanently installed at a clear height of between 60 inches (1525 mm) and 84 inches (2185 mm) above grade and shall not interfere with an accessible route from an access aisle.

1106.6 Location. Accessible parking spaces shall be located on the shortest accessible route of travel from adjacent parking to an accessible building entrance. In parking facilities that do not serve a particular building, accessible parking spaces shall be located on the shortest route to an accessible pedestrian entrance to the parking facility. Where buildings have multiple accessible entrances with adjacent parking, accessible parking spaces shall be dispersed and located near the accessible entrances.

Exceptions:

1. In multilevel parking structures, for every eight or fraction of eight accessible spaces, at least one shall be in a location having a minimum vertical clearance of 98 inches (2490 mm) maintained along the vehicular route connecting the space with a designated entrance and exit. Such spaces are permitted on one level.

2. Accessible parking spaces shall be permitted to be located in different parking facilities if substantially equivalent or greater accessibility is provided in terms of distance from an accessible entrance or entrances, parking fee and user convenience.

1106.7 Passenger loading zones. Passenger loading zones shall be designed and constructed in accordance with ICC/ANSI A117.1.

1106.7.1 Continuous loading zones. Where passenger loading zones are provided, one passenger loading zone in every continuous 100 linear feet (30.4 m) maximum of loading zone space shall be accessible.

1106.7.2 Medical facilities. A passenger loading zone shall be provided at an accessible entrance to licensed medical and long-term care facilities where people receive physical or medical treatment or care and where the period of stay exceeds 24 hours.

1106.7.3 Valet parking. A passenger loading zone shall be provided at valet parking services.

SECTION 1107
DWELLING UNITS AND SLEEPING UNITS

1107.1 General. In addition to the other requirements of this chapter, occupancies having dwelling units or sleeping units shall be provided with accessible features in accordance with this section.

1107.2 Design. Dwelling units and sleeping units that are required to be Accessible units or Type B units shall comply with this code and the applicable portions of Chapter 10 of ICC/ANSI A117.1. Dwelling units in Groups R-2 and R-3 shall also comply with Sections 1107.2.1 and 1107.2.2. Units required to be Type B units are permitted to be designed and constructed as Accessible units or as Type A units.

1107.2.1 Type B unit doors. Clear width and maneuvering clearances required by Sections 404.2.2 and 404.2.3 of ICC/ANSI A117 shall be provided at the primary entrance door to the dwelling or sleeping unit and at all other doors within the dwelling or sleeping unit meant for human passage.

Exception: Maneuvering clearances shall not be required at doors of a room containing only a lavatory and a water closet, provided the room does not contain the only lavatory or water closet on the accessible level of the unit.

1107.2.2 Type B unit toilet and bathing facilities. At least one toilet and bathing facility in the dwelling or sleeping unit shall be constructed in accordance with the toilet and bathing facilities requirements of Section 1003.11 of ICC/ANSI A117.1 (Type A Unit Toilet and Bathing Facilities). All remaining toilet and bathing facilities in such units shall be constructed in accordance with toilet and bathing facilities requirements of Section 1004.11 of ICC/ANSI A117.1 (Type B Unit Toilet and Bathing Facilities).

1107.3 Accessible spaces. Rooms and spaces available to the general public or available for use by residents and serving Accessible units, Type A units or Type B units shall be accessible. Accessible spaces shall include toilet and bathing rooms, kitchen, living and dining areas and any exterior spaces, including patios, terraces and balconies.

Exception: Recreational facilities in accordance with Section 1109.14.

1107.4 Accessible route. At least one accessible route shall connect accessible building or facility entrances with the primary entrance of each Accessible unit, Type A unit and Type B unit within the building or facility and with those exterior and interior spaces and facilities that serve the units.

Exceptions:

1. If due to circumstances outside the control of the owner, either the slope of the finished ground level between accessible facilities and buildings exceeds one unit vertical in 12 units horizontal (1:12), or where physical barriers or legal restrictions prevent the installation of an accessible route, a vehicular route with parking that complies with Section 1106 at each public or common use facility or building is permitted in place of the accessible route.

2. Exterior decks, patios or balconies that are part of Type B units and have impervious surfaces, and that are not more than 4 inches (102 mm) below the finished floor level of the adjacent interior space of the unit.

1107.5 Group I. Accessible units and Type B units shall be provided in Group I occupancies in accordance with Sections 1107.5.1 through 1107.5.5.

1107.5.1 Group I-1. Accessible units and Type B units shall be provided in Group I-1 occupancies in accordance with Sections 1107.5.1.1 and 1107.5.1.2.

1107.5.1.1 Accessible units. At least 4 percent, but not less than one, of the dwelling units and sleeping units shall be Accessible units.

1107.5.1.2 Type B units. In structures with four or more dwelling or sleeping units intended to be occupied as a residence, every dwelling and sleeping unit intended to be occupied as a residence shall be a Type B unit.

Exception: The number of Type B units is permitted to be reduced in accordance with Section 1107.7.

1107.5.2 Group I-2 nursing homes. Accessible units and Type B units shall be provided in nursing homes of Group I-2 occupancies in accordance with Sections 1107.5.2.1 and 1107.5.2.2.

1107.5.2.1 Accessible units. At least 50 percent but not less than one of each type of the dwelling and sleeping units shall be Accessible units.

1107.5.2.2 Type B units. In structures with four or more dwelling or sleeping units intended to be occupied as a residence, every dwelling and sleeping unit intended to be occupied as a residence shall be a Type B unit.

Exception: The number of Type B units is permitted to be reduced in accordance with Section 1107.7.

1107.5.3 Group I-2 hospitals. Accessible units and Type B units shall be provided in General-purpose hospitals, psychiatric facilities, detoxification facilities and residential care/assisted living facilities of Group I-2 occupancies in accordance with Sections 1107.5.3.1 and 1107.5.3.2.

1107.5.3.1 Accessible units. At least 10 percent, but not less than one, of the dwelling units and sleeping units shall be Accessible units.

1107.5.3.2 Type B units. In structures with four or more dwelling or sleeping units intended to be occupied as a residence, every dwelling and sleeping unit intended to be occupied as a residence shall be a Type B unit.

Exception: The number of Type B units is permitted to be reduced in accordance with Section 1107.7.

1107.5.4 Group I-2 rehabilitation facilities. In hospitals and rehabilitation facilities of Group I-2 occupancies which specialize in treating conditions that affect mobility, or units within either which specialize in treating conditions that affect mobility, 100 percent of the dwelling units and sleeping units shall be Accessible units.

1107.5.5 Group I-3. Accessible units shall be provided in Group I-3 occupancies in accordance with with Sections 1107.5.5.1 through 1107.5.5.3.

1107.5.5.1 Group I-3 sleeping units. In Group I-3 occupancies, at least 2 percent, but not less than one, of the dwelling units and sleeping units shall be Accessible units.

1107.5.5.2 Special holding cells and special housing cells or rooms. In addition to the Accessible units required by Section 1107.5.5.1, where special holding cells or special housing cells or rooms are provided, at least one serving each purpose shall be an Accessible unit. Cells or rooms subject to this requirement include, but are not limited to, those used for purposes of orientation, protective custody, administrative or disciplinary detention or segregation, detoxification and medical isolation.

> **Exception:** Cells or rooms specially designed without protrusions and that are used solely for purposes of suicide prevention shall not be required to include grab bars.

1107.5.5.3 Medical care facilities. Patient sleeping units or cells required to be Accessible units in medical care facilities shall be provided in addition to any medical isolation cells required to comply with Section 1107.5.5.2.

1107.6 Group R. Accessible units, Type A units and Type B units shall be provided in Group R occupancies in accordance with Sections 1107.6.1 through 1107.6.4.

1107.6.1 Group R-1. Accessible units and Type B units shall be provided in Group R-1 occupancies in accordance with Sections 1107.6.1.1 and 1107.6.1.2.

1107.6.1.1 Accessible units. In Group R-1 occupancies, Accessible dwelling units and sleeping units shall be provided in accordance with Table 1107.6.1.1. All facilities on a site shall be considered to determine the total number of Accessible units. Accessible units shall be dispersed among the various classes of units. Roll-in showers provided in Accessible units shall include a permanently mounted folding shower seat.

1107.6.1.2 Type B units. In structures with four or more dwelling or sleeping units intended to be occupied as a residence, every dwelling and sleeping unit intended to be occupied as a residence shall be a Type B unit.

> **Exception:** The number of Type B units is permitted to be reduced in accordance with Section 1107.7.

1107.6.2 Group R-2. Accessible units and Type B units shall be provided in Group R-2 occupancies in accordance with Sections 1107.6.2.1 and 1107.6.2.2.

1107.6.2.1 Apartment houses, monasteries and convents. Type B units shall be provided in apartment houses, monasteries and convents in accordance with Sections 1107.6.2.1.1.

1107.6.2.1.1 Type B units. Where there are four or more dwelling units or sleeping units intended to be occupied as a residence in a single structure, every dwelling unit and sleeping unit intended to be occupied as a residence shall be a Type B unit.

> **Exception:** The number of Type B units is permitted to be reduced in accordance with Section 1107.7

1107.6.2.2 Group R-2 other than apartment houses, monasteries and convents. In Group R-2 occupancies, other than apartment houses, monasteries and convents, Accessible units and Type B units shall be provided in accordance with Sections 1107.6.2.2.1 and 1107.6.2.2.2.

1107.6.2.2.1 Accessible units. Accessible dwelling units and sleeping units shall be provided in accordance with Table 1107.6.1.1.

TABLE 1107.6.1.1
ACCESSIBLE DWELLING AND SLEEPING UNITS

TOTAL NUMBER OF UNITS PROVIDED	MINIMUM REQUIRED NUMBER OF ACCESSIBLE UNITS WITHOUT ROLL-IN SHOWERS	MINIMUM REQUIRED NUMBER OF ACCESSIBLE UNITS ASSOCIATED WITH ROLL-IN SHOWERS	TOTAL NUMBER OF REQUIRED ACCESSIBLE UNITS
1 to 25	1	0	1
26 to 50	2	0	2
51 to 75	3	1	4
76 to 100	4	1	5
101 to 150	5	2	7
151 to 200	6	2	8
201 to 300	7	3	10
301 to 400	8	4	12
401 to 500	9	4	13
501 to 1,000	2% of total	1% of total	3% of total
Over 1,001	20, plus 1 for each 100, or fraction thereof, over 1,000	10 plus 1 for each 100, or fraction thereof, over 1,000	30 plus 2 for each 100, or fraction thereof, over 1,000

1107.6.2.2.2 Type B units. Where there are four or more dwelling units or sleeping units intended to be occupied as a residence in a single structure, every dwelling unit and every sleeping unit intended to be occupied as a residence shall be a Type B unit.

Exceptions:

1. The number of Type B units is permitted to be reduced in accordance with Section 1107.7.

2. Compliance with Sections 1107.2.1 and 1107.2.2 is not required.

1107.6.3 Group R-3. In Group R-3 occupancies where there are four or more dwelling units or sleeping units intended to be occupied as a residence in a single structure, every dwelling and sleeping unit intended to be occupied as a residence shall be a Type B unit.

Exception: The number of Type B units is permitted to be reduced in accordance with Section 1107.7.

1107.6.4 Group R-4. Accessible units and Type B units shall be provided in Group R-4 occupancies in accordance with Sections 1107.6.4.1 and 1107.6.4.2.

1107.6.4.1 Accessible units. At least one of the dwelling or sleeping units shall be an Accessible unit.

1107.6.4.2 Type B units. In structures with four or more dwelling or sleeping units intended to be occupied as a residence, every dwelling and sleeping unit intended to be occupied as a residence shall be a Type B unit.

Exception: The number of Type B units is permitted to be reduced in accordance with Section 1107.7.

1107.7 General exceptions. Where specifically permitted by Section 1107.5 or 1107.6, the required number of Type A and Type B units is permitted to be reduced in accordance with Sections 1107.7.1 through 1107.7.5.

1107.7.1 Structures without elevator service. Where no elevator service is provided in a structure, only the dwelling and sleeping units that are located on stories indicated in Sections 1107.7.1.1 and 1107.7.1.2 are required to be Type B units.

1107.7.1.1 One story with Type B units required. At least one story containing dwelling units or sleeping units intended to be occupied as a residence shall be provided with an accessible entrance from the exterior of the structure and all units intended to be occupied as a residence on that story shall be Type B units.

1107.7.1.2 Additional stories with Type B units. On all other stories that have a building entrance in proximity to arrival points intended to serve units on that story, as indicated in Items 1 and 2, all dwelling units and sleeping units intended to be occupied as a residence served by that entrance on that story shall be Type B units.

1. Where the slopes of the undisturbed site measured between the planned entrance and all

vehicular or pedestrian arrival points within 50 feet (15 240 mm) of the planned entrance are 10 percent or less, and

2. Where the slopes of the planned finished grade measured between the entrance and all vehicular or pedestrian arrival points within 50 feet (15 240 mm) of the planned entrance are 10 percent or less.

Where no such arrival points are within 50 feet (15 240 mm) of the entrance, the closest arrival point shall be used unless that arrival point serves the story required by Section 1107.7.1.1.

1107.7.1.3 Additional stories with entrance through fire walls. Where an entrance is provided to a story of a building from an accessory story of an adjacent building by an opening in a fire wall, all dwelling and sleeping units intended to be occupied as a residence on that story shall be Type B units, provided that the planned finish floor elevation within 5 feet (1524 mm) of each side of the door does not include a change in level in excess of 12 inches (305 mm).

Exception: This provision shall not apply to existing buildings unless specifically required in the *Existing Building Code of New York State.*

1107.7.1.4 Additional stories with entrances from bridges or elevated walkways. Where an entrance is provided to a story of a building from an accessible story of an adjacent building by a bridge or elevated walkway, all dwelling and sleeping units intended to be occupied as a residence on that story shall be Type B units, provided the slope between the planned finish floor elevation at the building entrance and the planned finish floor elevation at the bridge or elevated walkway connection to the adjacent building is 10 percent or less.

Exception: This provision shall not apply to existing buildings unless specifically required in the *Existing Building Code of New York State.*

1107.7.2 Multistory units. A multistory dwelling or sleeping unit which is not provided with elevator service is not required to be a Type B unit. Where a multistory unit is provided with external elevator service to only one floor, the floor provided with elevator service shall be the primary entry to the unit, shall comply with the requirements for a Type B unit and a toilet facility shall be provided on that floor.

1107.7.3 Elevator service to the lowest story with units. Where elevator service in the building provides an accessible route only to the lowest story containing dwelling or sleeping units intended to be occupied as a residence, only the units on that story which are intended to be occupied as a residence are required to be Type B units.

1107.7.4 Site impracticality. On a site with multiple non-elevator buildings, the number of units required by Section 1107.7.1 to be Type B units is permitted to be reduced to a percentage which is equal to the percentage of the entire site having grades, prior to development, which are less than 10 percent, provided that all of the following conditions are met:

1. Not less than 20 percent of the units required by Section 1107.7.1 on the site are Type B units;

2. Units required by Section 1107.7.1, where the slope between the building entrance serving the units on that story and a pedestrian or vehicular arrival point is no greater than 8.33 percent, are Type B units;

3. Units required by Section 1107.7.1, where an elevated walkway is planned between a building entrance serving the units on that story and a pedestrian or vehicular arrival point and the slope between them is 10 percent or less are Type B units; and

4. Units served by an elevator in accordance with Section 1107.7.3 are Type B units.

1107.7.5 Design flood elevation. The required number of Type A and Type B units shall not apply to a site where the required elevation of the lowest floor or the lowest horizontal structural building members of nonelevator buildings are at or above the design flood elevation resulting in:

1. A difference in elevation between the minimum required floor elevation at the primary entrances and vehicular and pedestrian arrival points within 50 feet (15 240 mm) exceeding 30 inches (762 mm); and

2. A slope exceeding 10 percent between the minimum required floor elevation at the primary entrances and vehicular and pedestrian arrival points within 50 feet (15 240 mm).

Where no such arrival points are within 50 feet (15240 mm) of the primary entrances, the closest arrival points shall be used.

SECTION 1108
SPECIAL OCCUPANCIES

1108.1 General. In addition to the other requirements of this chapter, the requirements of Sections 1108.2 through 1108.4 shall apply to specific occupancies.

1108.2 Assembly area seating. Assembly areas with fixed seating shall comply with Sections 1108.2.1 through 1108.2.7. Dining areas shall comply with Section 1108.2.8. In addition, lawn seating shall comply with Section 1108.2.5.

1108.2.1 Services. Services and facilities provided in areas not required to be accessible shall be provided on an accessible level and shall be accessible.

1108.2.2 Wheelchair spaces. In theaters, bleachers, grandstands, stadiums, arenas and other fixed seating assembly areas, accessible wheelchair spaces complying with ICC/ANSI A117.1 shall be provided in accordance with Sections 1108.2.2.1 through 1108.2.2.4.

1108.2.2.1 General seating. Wheelchair spaces shall be provided in accordance with Table 1108.2.2.1.

1108.2.2.2 Luxury boxes, club boxes and suites. In each luxury box, club box, and suite within arenas, stadiums and grandstands, wheelchair spaces shall be provided in accordance with Table 1108.2.2.1.

1108.2.2.3 Other boxes. In boxes other than those required to comply with Section 1108.2.2.2, the total number of wheelchair spaces provided shall be determined in accordance with Table 1108.2.2.1. Wheelchair spaces shall be located in not less than 20 percent of all boxes provided.

TABLE 1108.2.2.1
ACCESSIBLE WHEELCHAIR SPACES

CAPACITY OF SEATING IN ASSEMBLY AREAS	MINIMUM REQUIRED NUMBER OF WHEELCHAIR SPACES
4 to 25	1
26 to 50	2
51 to 100	4
101 to 300	5
301 to 500	6
501 to 5,000	6, plus 1 for each 150, or fraction thereof, between 501 through 5,000
5,001 and over	36 plus 1 for each 200, or fraction thereof, over 5,000

1108.2.2.4 Team or player seating. At least one wheelchair space shall be provided in team or player seating areas serving areas of sport activity.

Exception: Wheelchair spaces shall not be required in team or player seating areas serving bowling lanes that are not required to be located on an accessible route per Section 1109.14.4.1.

1108.2.3 Dispersion of wheelchair spaces in multilevel assembly seating areas. In multilevel assembly seating areas, wheelchair spaces shall be provided on the main floor level and on one of each two additional floor or mezzanine levels. Wheelchair spaces shall be provided in each luxury box, club box and suite within assembly facilities.

Exceptions:

1. In multilevel assembly spaces utilized for worship services where the second floor or mezzanine level contains 25 percent or less of the total seating capacity, wheelchair spaces shall be permitted to all be located on the main level.

2. In multilevel assembly seating where the second floor or mezzanine level provides 25 percent or less of the total seating capacity and 300 or fewer seats, all wheelchair spaces shall be permitted to be located on the main level.

3. Wheelchair spaces in team or player seating serving areas of sport activity are not required to be dispersed.

1108.2.4 Designated aisle seats. At least 5 percent, but not less than one, of the total number of aisle seats provided shall be designated aisle seats.

Exception: Designated aisle seats are not required in team or player seating serving areas of sport activity.

1108.2.5 Lawn seating. Lawn seating areas and exterior overflow seating areas, where fixed seats are not provided, shall connect to an accessible route.

1108.2.6 Assistive listening systems. Each assembly area where audible communications are integral to the use of the space shall have an assistive listening system. The assistive listening system shall comply with Appendix L, Assistive Listening Systems Performance Standards.

Exception: Other than in courtrooms, an assistive listening system is not required where there is no audio amplification system.

1108.2.6.1 Receivers. Receivers shall be provided for assistive listening systems in accordance with Table 1108.2.6.1.

Exceptions:

1. Where a building contains more than one assembly area, the total number of required receivers shall be permitted to be calculated according to the total number of seats in the assembly areas in the building, provided that all receivers are usable with all systems and if assembly areas required to provide assistive listening are under one management.

2. Where all seats in an assembly area are served by an induction loop assistive listening system, the minimum number of receivers required by Table 1108.2.6.1 to be hearing-aid compatible shall not be required.

TABLE 1108.2.6.1
RECEIVERS FOR ASSISTIVE LISTENING SYSTEMS

CAPACITY OF SEATING IN ASSEMBLY AREAS	MINIMUM REQUIRED NUMBER OF RECEIVERS	MINIMUM NUMBER OF RECEIVERS TO BE HEARING-AID COMPATIBLE
50 or less	2	2
51 to 200	2, plus 1 per 25 seats over 50 seats*	2
201 to 500	2, plus 1 per 25 seats over 50 seats.*	1 per 4 receivers*
501 to 1,000	20, plus 1 per 33 seats over 500 seats*	1 per 4 receivers*
1,001 to 2,000	35, plus 1 per 50 seats over 1,000 seats*	1 per 4 receivers*
Over 2,000	55, plus 1 per 100 seats over 2,000 seats*	1 per 4 receivers*

NOTE: * = or fraction thereof

1108.2.6.2 Public address systems. Where stadiums, arenas and grandstands provide audible public announcements, they shall also provide equivalent text information regarding events and facilities in compliance with Sections 1108.2.6.2.1 and 1108.2.6.2.2.

1108.2.6.2.1 Prerecorded text messages. Where electronic signs are provided and have the capability to display prerecorded text messages containing information that is the same, or substan-

tiequivalent, to information that is provided audibly, signs shall display text that is equivalent to audible announcements.

Exception: Announcements that cannot be prerecorded in advance of the event shall not be required to be displayed.

1108.2.6.2.2 Real-time messages. Where electronic signs are provided and have the capability to display real-time messages containing information that is the same, or substantially equivalent, to information that is provided audibly, signs shall display text that is equivalent to audible announcements.

1108.2.7 Performance areas. An accessible route shall directly connect the performance area to the assembly seating area where a circulation path directly connects a performance area to an assembly seating area. An accessible route shall be provided from performance areas to ancillary areas or facilities used by performers.

1108.2.8 Dining areas. In dining areas, the total floor area allotted for seating and tables shall be accessible.

Exceptions:

1. In buildings or facilities not required to provide an accessible route between levels, an accessible route to a mezzanine seating area is not required, provided that the mezzanine contains less than 25 percent of the total area and the same services are provided in the accessible area.

2. In sports facilities, tiered dining areas providing seating required to be accessible shall be required to have accessible routes serving at least 25 percent of the dining area, provided that accessible routes serve accessible seating and where each tier is provided with the same services.

1108.2.8.1 Dining surfaces. Where dining surfaces for the consumption of food or drink are provided, at least 5 percent, but not less than one, of the seating and standing spaces at the dining surfaces shall be accessible and be distributed throughout the facility.

1108.3 Self-service storage facilities. Self-service storage facilities shall provide accessible individual self-storage spaces in accordance with Table 1108.3.

TABLE 1108.3
ACCESSIBLE SELF-SERVICE STORAGE FACILITIES

TOTAL SPACES IN FACILITY	MINIMUM NUMBER OF REQUIRED ACCESSIBLE SPACES
1 to 200	5%, but not less than 1
Over 200	10, plus 2% of total number of units over 200

1108.3.1 Dispersion. Accessible individual self-service storage spaces shall be dispersed throughout the various classes of spaces provided. Where more classes of spaces are provided than the number of required accessible spaces, the number of accessible spaces shall not be required to exceed that required by Table 1108.3. Accessible spaces are permitted to be dispersed in a single building of a multibuilding facility.

1108.4 Judicial facilities. Judicial facilities shall comply with Sections 1108.4.1 through 1108.4.3.

1108.4.1 Courtrooms. Each courtroom shall be accessible.

1108.4.2 Holding cells. Central holding cells and court-floor holding cells shall comply with Sections 1108.4.2.1 and 1108.4.2.2.

1108.4.2.1 Central holding cells. Where separate central holding cells are provided for adult males, juvenile males, adult females or juvenile females, one of each type shall be accessible. Where central holding cells are provided and are not separated by age or sex, at least one accessible cell shall be provided.

1108.4.2.2 Court-floor holding cells. Where separate court-floor holding cells are provided for adult males, juvenile males, adult females or juvenile females, each courtroom shall be served by one accessible cell of each type. Where court-floor holding cells are provided and are not separated by age or sex, courtrooms shall be served by at least one accessible cell. Accessible cells shall be permitted to serve more than one courtroom.

1108.4.3 Visiting areas. Visiting areas shall comply with Sections 1108.4.3.1 and 1108.4.3.2.

1108.4.3.1 Cubicles and counters. At least 5 percent but no fewer than one of the cubicles shall be accessible on both the visitor and detainee sides. Where counters are provided, at least one shall be accessible on both the visitor and detainee sides.

Exception: This requirement shall not apply to the detainee side of cubicles or counters at noncontact visiting areas not serving accessible unit holding cells.

1108.4.3.2 Partitions. Where solid partitions or security glazing separate visitors from detainees, at least one of each type of cubicle or counter partition shall be accessible.

SECTION 1109
OTHER FEATURES AND FACILITIES

1109.1 General. Accessible building features and facilities shall be provided in accordance with Sections 1109.2 through 1109.14.

Exception: Type A and Type B dwelling and sleeping units shall comply with ICC/ANSI A117.1.

1109.2 Toilet and bathing facilities. Toilet rooms and bathing facilities shall be accessible. Where a floor level is not required to be connected by an accessible route, the only toilet rooms or bathing facilities provided within the facility shall not be located on the inaccessible floor. At least one of each type of fixture, element, control or dispenser in each accessible toilet room and bathing facility shall be accessible.

Exceptions:

1. In toilet rooms or bathing facilities accessed only through a private office, not for common or public use and intended for use by a single occupant, any of the following alternatives are allowed:

   1.1. Doors are permitted to swing into the clear floor space, provided the door swing can be reversed to meet the requirements in ICC/ANSI A117.1;

   1.2 The height requirements for the water closet in ICC/ANSI A117.1 are not applicable;

   1.3. Grab bars are not required to be installed in a toilet room, provided that reinforcement has been installed in the walls and located so as to permit the installation of such grab bars; and

   1.4. The requirement for height, knee and toe clearance shall not apply to a lavatory.

2. This section is not applicable to toilet and bathing facilities that serve dwelling units or sleeping units that are not required to be accessible by Section 1107.

3. Where multiple single-user toilet rooms or bathing facilities are clustered at a single location, at least 50 percent but not less than one room for each use at each cluster shall be accessible.

4. Where no more than one urinal is provided in a toilet room or bathing facility, the urinal is not required to be accessible.

5. Toilet rooms that are part of critical care or intensive care patient sleeping rooms are not required to be accessible.

1109.2.1 Unisex toilet and bathing rooms. In assembly and mercantile occupancies, an accessible unisex toilet room shall be provided where an aggregate of six or more male and female water closets is required. In buildings of mixed occupancy, only those water closets required for the assembly or mercantile occupancy shall be used to determine the unisex toilet room requirement. In recreational facilities where separate-sex bathing rooms are provided, an accessible unisex bathing room shall be provided. Fixtures located within unisex toilet and bathing rooms shall be included in determining the number of fixtures provided in an occupancy.

Exception: Where each separate-sex bathing room has only one shower or bathtub fixture, a unisex bathing room is not required.

1109.2.1.1 Standard. Unisex toilet and bathing rooms shall comply with Sections 1109.2.1.2 through 1109.2.1.7 and ICC/ANSI A117.1.

1109.2.1.2 Unisex toilet rooms. Unisex toilet rooms shall include only one water closet and only one lavatory. A unisex bathing room in accordance with Section 1109.2.1.3 shall be considered a unisex toilet room.

Exception: A urinal is permitted to be provided in addition to the water closet in a unisex toilet room.

1109.2.1.3 Unisex bathing rooms. Unisex bathing rooms shall include only one shower or bathtub fixture. Unisex bathing rooms shall also include one water closet and one lavatory. Where storage facilities are provided for separate-sex bathing rooms, accessible storage facilities shall be provided for unisex bathing rooms.

1109.2.1.4 Location. Unisex toilet and bathing rooms shall be located on an accessible route. Unisex toilet rooms shall be located not more than one story above or below separate-sex toilet rooms. The accessible route from any separate-sex toilet room to a unisex toilet room shall not exceed 500 feet (152 m).

1109.2.1.5 Prohibited location. In passenger transportation facilities and airports, the accessible route from separate-sex toilet rooms to a unisex toilet room shall not pass through security checkpoints.

1109.2.1.6 Clear floor space. Where doors swing into a unisex toilet or bathing room, a clear floor space not less than 30 inches by 48 inches (762 mm by 1219 mm) shall be provided, within the room, beyond the area of the door swing.

1109.2.1.7 Privacy. Doors to unisex toilet and bathing rooms shall be securable from within the room.

1109.2.2 Water closet compartment. Where water closet compartments are provided in a toilet room or bathing facility, at least one wheelchair-accessible compartment shall be provided. Where the combined total water closet compartments and urinals provided in a toilet room or bathing facility is six or more, at least one ambulatory-accessible water closet compartment shall be provided in addition to the wheelchair-accessible compartment. Wheelchair-accessible and ambulatory-accessible compartments shall comply with ICC/ANSI A117.1.

1109.3 Sinks. Where sinks are provided, at least 5 percent but not less than one provided in accessible spaces shall comply with ICC/ANSI A117.1.

➡ **Exception:** Mop or service sinks are not required to be accessible.

1109.4 Kitchens and kitchenettes. Where kitchens and kitchenettes are provided in accessible spaces or rooms, they shall be accessible in accordance with ICC/ANSI A117.1.

1109.5 Drinking fountains. Where drinking fountains are provided on an exterior site, on a floor or within a secured area, the drinking fountains shall be provided in accordance with Sections 1109.5.1 and 1109.5.2.

1109.5.1 Minimum number. No fewer than two drinking fountains shall be provided. One drinking fountain shall comply with the requirements for people who use a wheelchair and one drinking fountain shall comply with the requirements for standing persons.

Exception: A single drinking fountain that complies with the requirements for people who use a wheelchair and standing persons shall be permitted to be substituted for two separate drinking fountains.

1109.5.2 More than the minimum number. Where more than the minimum number of drinking fountains specified in Section 1109.5.1 are provided, 50 percent of the total number of drinking fountains provided shall comply with

the requirements for persons who use a wheelchair and 50 percent of the total number of drinking fountains provided shall comply with the requirements for standing persons.

Exception: Where 50 percent of the drinking fountains yields a fraction, 50 percent shall be permitted to be rounded up or down, provided that the total number of drinking fountains complying with this section equals 100 percent of the drinking fountains.

1109.6 Elevators. Passenger elevators on an accessible route shall be accessible and comply with Section 3001.3.

1109.7 Lifts. Platform (wheelchair) lifts are permitted to be a part of a required accessible route in new construction where indicated in Items 1 through 10. Platform (wheelchair) lifts shall be installed in accordance with ASME A18.1.

1. An accessible route to a performing area and speaker platforms in Group A occupancies.

2. An accessible route to wheelchair spaces required to comply with the wheelchair space dispersion requirements of Sections 1108.2.2 through 1108.2.5.

3. An accessible route to spaces that are not open to the general public with an occupant load of not more than five.

4. An accessible route within a dwelling or sleeping unit.

5. An accessible route to wheelchair seating spaces located in outdoor dining terraces in Group A-5 occupancies where the means of egress from the dining terraces to a public way are open to the outdoors.

6. An accessible route to jury boxes and witness stands; raised courtroom stations including judges' benches, clerks' stations, bailiffs' stations, deputy clerks' stations and court reporters' stations; and to depressed areas such as the well of the court.

7. An accessible route to load and unload areas serving amusement rides.

8. An accessible route to play components or soft contained play structures.

9. An accessible route to team or player seating areas serving areas of sport activity.

10. An accessible route where existing exterior site constraints make use of a ramp or elevator infeasible.

1109.8 Storage. Where fixed or built-in storage elements such as cabinets, shelves, medicine cabinets, closets and drawers are provided in required accessible spaces, at least one of each type shall contain storage space complying with ICC/ANSI A117.1.

1109.8.1 Lockers. Where lockers are provided in accessible spaces, at least five percent, but not less than one, of each type shall be accessible.

1109.8.2 Shelving and display units. Self-service shelves and display units shall be located on an accessible route. Such shelving and display units shall not be required to comply with reach-range provisions.

1109.8.3 Coat hooks and shelves. Where coat hooks and shelves are provided in toilet rooms or toilet compartments or in dressing, fitting or locker rooms, at least one of each type shall be accessible and shall be provided in accessible toilet rooms without toilet compartments, accessible toilet compartments and accessible dressing, fitting and locker rooms.

1109.9 Detectable warnings. Passenger transit platform edges bordering a drop-off and not protected by platform screens or guards shall have a detectable warning.

Exception: Detectable warnings are not required at bus stops.

1109.10 Assembly area seating. Assembly areas with fixed seating shall comply with Section 1108.2 for accessible seating and assistive listening devices.

1109.11 Seating at tables, counters and work surfaces. Where seating or standing space at fixed or built-in tables, counters or work surfaces is provided in accessible spaces, at least 5 percent of the seating and standing spaces, but not less than one, shall be accessible. In Group I-3 occupancy visiting areas at least 5 percent, but not less than one, cubicle or counter shall be accessible on both the visitor and detainee sides.

Exceptions:

1. Check-writing surfaces at check-out aisles not required to comply with Section 1109.12.2 are not required to be accessible.

2. In Group I-3 occupancies, the counter or cubicle on the detainee side is not required to be accessible at noncontact visiting areas or in areas not serving accessible holding cells or sleeping units.

1109.11.1 Dispersion. Accessible fixed or built-in seating at tables, counters or work surfaces shall be distributed throughout the space or facility containing such elements.

1109.12 Service facilities. Service facilities shall provide for accessible features in accordance with Sections 1109.12.1 through 1109.12.5.

1109.12.1 Dressing, fitting and locker rooms. Where dressing rooms, fitting rooms or locker rooms are provided, at least 5 percent, but not less than one, of each type of use in each cluster provided shall be accessible.

1109.12.2 Check-out aisles. Where check-out aisles are provided, accessible check-out aisles shall be provided in accordance with Table 1109.12.2. Where check-out aisles serve different functions, at least one accessible check-out aisle shall be provided for each function. Where checkout aisles serve different functions, accessible check-out aisles shall be provided in accordance with Table 1109.12.2 for each function. Where check-out aisles are dispersed throughout the building or facility, accessible check-out

TABLE 1109.12.2
ACCESSIBLE CHECK-OUT AISLES

TOTAL CHECK-OUT AISLES OF EACH FUNCTION	MINIMUM NUMBER OF ACCESSIBLE CHECK-OUT AISLES OF EACH FUNCTION
1 to 4	1
5 to 8	2
9 to 15	3
Over 15	3, plus 20% of additional aisles

aisles shall also be dispersed. Traffic control devices, security devices and turnstiles located in accessible check-out aisles or lanes shall be accessible.

1109.12.3 Point of sale and service counters. Where counters are provided for sales or distribution of goods or services, at least one of each type provided shall be accessible. Where such counters are dispersed throughout the building or facility, accessible counters shall also be dispersed.

1109.12.4 Food service lines. Food service lines shall be accessible. Where self-service shelves are provided, at least 50 percent, but not less than one, of each type provided shall be accessible.

1109.12.5 Queue and waiting lines. Queue and waiting lines servicing accessible counters or check-out aisles shall be accessible.

1109.13 Controls, operating mechanisms and hardware. Controls, operating mechanisms and hardware intended for operation by the occupant, including switches that control lighting and ventilation and electrical convenience outlets, in accessible spaces, along accessible routes or as parts of accessible elements shall be accessible.

Exceptions:

1. Operable parts that are intended for use only by service or maintenance personnel shall not be required to be accessible.

2. Electrical or communication receptacles serving a dedicated use shall not be required to be accessible.

3. Where two or more outlets are provided in a kitchen above a length of counter top that is uninterrupted by a sink or appliance, one outlet shall not be required to be accessible.

4. Floor electrical receptacles shall not be required to be accessible.

5. HVAC diffusers shall not be required to be accessible.

6. Except for light switches, where redundant controls are provided for a single element, one control in each space shall not be required to be accessible.

7. Access doors or gates in barrier walls and fences protecting pools, spas and hot tubs shall be permitted to have operable parts of the release of latch on self-latching devices at 54 inches (1370 mm) maximum and 48 inches minimum above the finished floor or ground, provided the self-latching devices are not also self-locking devices, operated by means of a key, electronic opener, or integral combination lock.

1109.13.1 Operable window. Where operable windows are provided in rooms that are required to be accessible in accordance with Sections 1107.5.1.1, 1107.5.2.1, 1107.5.3.1, 1107.5.4, 1107.6.1.1, 1107.6.2.2.1 and 1107.6.4.1, at least one window in each room shall be accessible and each required operable window shall be accessible.

Exception: Accessible windows are not required in bathrooms or kitchens.

1109.14 Recreational and sports facilities. Recreational and sports facilities shall be provided with accessible features in accordance with Sections 1109.14.1 through 1109.14.4.

1109.14.1 Facilities serving a single building. In Group R-2 and R-3 occupancies where recreational facilities are provided serving a single building containing Type A units or Type B units, 25 percent, but not less than one, of each type of recreational facility shall be accessible. Every recreational facility of each type on a site shall be considered to determine the total number of each type that is required to be accessible.

1109.14.2 Facilities serving multiple buildings. In Group R-2 and R-3 occupancies on a single site where multiple buildings containing Type A units or Type B units are served by recreational facilities, 25 percent, but not less than one, of each type of recreational facility serving each building shall be accessible. The total number of each type of recreational facility that is required to be accessible shall be determined by considering every recreational facility of each type serving each building on the site.

1109.14.3 Other occupancies. All recreational and sports facilities not falling within the purview of Section 1109.14.1 or 1109.14.2 shall be accessible.

1109.14.4 Recreational and sports facilities exceptions. Recreational and sports facilities required to be accessible shall be exempt from this chapter to the extent specified in this section.

1109.14.4.1 Bowling lanes. An accessible route shall be provided to at least 5 percent, but no less than one, of each type of bowling lane.

1109.14.4.2 Court sports. In court sports, at least one accessible route shall directly connect both sides of the court.

1109.14.4.3 Raised boxing or wrestling rings. Raised boxing or wrestling rings are not required to be accessible.

1109.14.4.4 Raised refereeing, judging and scoring areas. Raised structures used solely for refereeing, judging or scoring a sport are not required to be accessible.

1109.14.4.5 Raised diving boards and diving platforms. Raised diving boards and diving platforms are not required to be accessible.

SECTION 1110
SIGNAGE

1110.1 Signs. Required accessible elements shall be identified by the International Symbol of Accessibility at the following locations:

1. Accessible parking spaces required by Section 1106.1 except where the total number of parking spaces provided is four or less.

2. Accessible passenger loading zones.

3. Accessible areas of refuge required by Section 1007.6.

4. Accessible rooms where multiple single-user toilet or bathing rooms are clustered at a single location.

5. Accessible entrances where not all entrances are accessible.

6. Accessible check-out aisles where not all aisles are accessible. The sign, where provided, shall be above the check-out aisle in the same location as the check-out aisle number or type of check-out identification.

7. Unisex toilet and bathing rooms.

8. Accessible dressing, fitting and locker rooms where not all such rooms are accessible.

1110.2 Directional signage. Directional signage indicating the route to the nearest like accessible element shall be provided at the following locations. These directional signs shall include the International Symbol of Accessibility:

1. Inaccessible building entrances.

2. Inaccessible public toilets and bathing facilities.

3. Elevators not serving an accessible route.

4. At each separate-sex toilet and bathing room indicating the location of the nearest unisex toilet or bathing room where provided in accordance with Section 1109.2.1.

5. At exits and elevators serving a required accessible space, but not providing an approved accessible means of egress, signage shall be provided in accordance with Section 1007.7.

1110.3 Other signs. Signage indicating special accessibility provisions shall be provided as shown:

1. Each assembly area required to comply with Section 1108.2.6 shall provide a sign notifying patrons of the availability of assistive listening systems.

   Exception: Where ticket offices or windows are provided, signs are not required at each assembly area provided that signs are displayed at each ticket office or window informing patrons of the availability of assistive listening systems.

2. At each door to an egress stairway, exit passageway and exit discharge, signage shall be provided in accordance with Section 1011.3.

3. At areas of refuge, signage shall be provided in accordance with Sections 1007.6.3 through 1007.6.5.

4. At areas for assisted rescue, signage shall be provided in accordance with Section 1007.8.3.

CHAPTER 12

INTERIOR ENVIRONMENT

SECTION 1201
GENERAL

1201.1 Scope. The provisions of this chapter shall govern ventilation, temperature control, lighting, yards and courts, sound transmission, room dimensions, surrounding materials and rodent proofing associated with the interior spaces of buildings.

SECTION 1202
DEFINITIONS

1202.1 General. The following words and terms shall, for the purposes of this chapter and as used elsewhere in this code, have the meanings shown herein.

SUNROOM ADDITION. A one-story addition added to an existing building with a glazing area in excess of 40 percent of the gross area of the structure's exterior walls and roof.

THERMAL ISOLATION. A separation of conditioned spaces, between a sunroom addition and a dwelling unit, consisting of existing or new wall(s), doors and/or windows.

SECTION 1203
VENTILATION

1203.1 General. Buildings shall be provided with natural ventilation in accordance with Section 1203.4, or mechanical ventilation in accordance with the *Mechanical Code of New York State* .

1203.2 Attic spaces. Enclosed attics and enclosed rafter spaces formed where ceilings are applied directly to the underside of roof framing members shall have cross ventilation for each separate space by ventilating openings protected against the entrance of rain and snow. Blocking and bridging shall be arranged so as not to interfere with the movement of air. A minimum of 1 inch (25 mm) of airspace shall be provided between the insulation and the roof sheathing. The net free ventilating area shall not be less than $1/150$ of the area of the space ventilated, with 50 percent of the required ventilating area provided by ventilators located in the upper portion of the space to be ventilated at least 3 feet (914 mm) above eave or cornice vents with the balance of the required ventilation provided by eave or cornice vents.

> **Exception:** The minimum required net free ventilating area shall be $1/300$ of the area of the space ventilated, provided a vapor retarder having a transmission rate not exceeding 1 perm in accordance with ASTM E 96 is installed on the warm side of the attic insulation and provided 50 percent of the required ventilating area provided by ventilators located in the upper portion of the space to be ventilated at least 3 feet (914 mm) above eave or cornice vents, with the balance of the required ventilation provided by eave or cornice vents.

1203.2.1 Openings into attic. Exterior openings into the attic space of any building intended for human occupancy shall be covered with corrosion-resistant wire cloth screening, hardware cloth, perforated vinyl or similar material that will prevent the entry of birds, squirrels, rodents, snakes and other similar creatures. The openings therein shall be a minimum of $1/8$ inch (3.2 mm) and shall not exceed $1/4$ inch (6.4 mm). Where combustion air is obtained from an attic area, it shall be in accordance with Chapter 7 of the *Mechanical Code of New York State*.

1203.3 Under-floor ventilation. The space between the bottom of the floor joists and the earth under any building except spaces occupied by a basement shall be provided with ventilation openings through foundation walls or exterior walls. Such openings shall be placed so as to provide cross ventilation of the under-floor space.

1203.3.1 Openings for under-floor ventilation. The minimum net area of ventilation openings shall not be less than 1 square foot for each 150 square feet (0.67 m² for each 100 m²) of crawl-space area. Ventilation openings shall be covered for their height and width with any of the following materials, provided that the least dimension of the covering shall not exceed $1/4$ inch (6 mm):

1. Perforated sheet metal plates not less than 0.070 inch (1.8 mm) thick.

2. Expanded sheet metal plates not less than 0.047 inch (1.2 mm) thick.

3. Cast-iron grilles or gratings.

4. Extruded load-bearing vents.

5. Hardware cloth of 0.035 inch (0.89 mm) wire or heavier.

6. Corrosion-resistant wire mesh, with the least dimension not exceeding $1/8$ inch (3.2 mm).

1203.3.2 Exceptions. The following are exceptions to Sections 1203.3 and 1203.3.1:

1. Where warranted by climatic conditions, ventilation openings to the outdoors are not required if ventilation openings to the interior are provided.

2. The total area of ventilation openings is permitted to be reduced to $1/1,500$ of the under-floor area where the ground surface is treated with an approved vapor retarder material and the required openings are placed so as to provide cross ventilation of the space. The installation of operable louvers shall not be prohibited.

3. Ventilation openings are not required where continuously operated mechanical ventilation is provided at a rate of 1.0 cubic foot per minute (cfm) for each 50 square feet (1.02 L/s for each 10 m²) of crawl-

space floor area and the ground surface is covered with an approved vapor retarder.

4. Ventilation openings are not required when the ground surface is covered with an approved vapor retarder, the perimeter walls are insulated and the space is conditioned in accordance with the *Energy Conservation Code of New York State*.

5. For buildings in flood hazard areas as established in Section 1612.3, the openings for under-floor ventilation shall be deemed as meeting the flood opening requirements of ASCE 24 provided that the ventilation openings are designed and installed in accordance with ASCE 24.

1203.4 Natural ventilation. Natural ventilation of an occupied space shall be through windows, doors, louvers or other openings to the outdoors. The operating mechanism for such openings shall be provided with ready access so that the openings are readily controllable by the building occupants.

1203.4.1 Ventilation area required. The minimum openable area to the outdoors shall be 4 percent of the floor area being ventilated.

1203.4.1.1 Adjoining spaces. Where rooms and spaces without openings to the outdoors are ventilated through an adjoining room, the opening to the adjoining room shall be unobstructed and shall have an area of not less than 8 percent of the floor area of the interior room or space, but not less than 25 square feet (2.3 m²). The minimum openable area to the outdoors shall be based on the total floor area being ventilated.

Exception: Exterior openings required for ventilation shall be permitted to open into a thermally isolated sunroom addition or patio cover provided that the openable area between the sunroom addition or patio cover and the interior room shall have an area of not less than 8 percent of the floor area of the interior room or space, but not less than 20 square feet (1.86 m²). The minimum openable area to the outdoors shall be based on the total floor area being ventilated.

1203.4.1.2 Openings below grade. Where openings below grade provide required natural ventilation, the outside horizontal clear space measured perpendicular to the opening shall be one and one-half times the depth of the opening. The depth of the opening shall be measured from the average adjoining ground level to the bottom of the opening.

1203.4.2 Contaminants exhausted. Contaminant sources in naturally ventilated spaces shall be removed in accordance with the *Mechanical Code of New York State* and the *Fire Code of New York State*.

1203.4.2.1 Bathrooms. Rooms containing bathtubs, showers, spas and similar bathing fixtures shall be mechanically ventilated in accordance with the *Mechanical Code of New York State*.

1203.4.3 Openings on yards or courts. Where natural ventilation is to be provided by openings onto yards or courts, such yards or courts shall comply with Section 1206.

1203.5 Other ventilation and exhaust systems. Ventilation and exhaust systems for occupancies and operations involving flammable or combustible hazards or other contaminant sources as covered in the *Mechanical Code of New York State* or the *Fire Code of New York State* shall be provided as required by both codes.

SECTION 1204
TEMPERATURE CONTROL

1204.1 Equipment and systems. Interior spaces intended for human occupancy shall be provided with active or passive space-heating systems capable of maintaining a minimum indoor temperature of 68°F (20°C) at a point 3 feet (914 mm) above the floor on the design heating day.

Exception: Interior spaces where the primary purpose is not associated with human comfort.

SECTION 1205
LIGHTING

1205.1 General. Every space intended for human occupancy shall be provided with natural light by means of exterior glazed openings in accordance with Section 1205.2 or shall be provided with artificial light in accordance with Section 1205.3. Exterior glazed openings shall open directly onto a public way or onto a yard or court in accordance with Section 1206.

1205.2 Natural light. The minimum net glazed area shall not be less than 8 percent of the floor area of the room served.

1205.2.1 Adjoining spaces. For the purpose of natural lighting, any room is permitted to be considered as a portion of an adjoining room where one-half of the area of the common wall is open and unobstructed and provides an opening of not less than one-tenth of the floor area of the interior room or 25 square feet (2.32 m²), whichever is greater.

Exception: Openings required for natural light shall be permitted to open into a thermally isolated sunroom addition or patio cover where the common wall provides a glazed area of not less than one-tenth of the floor area of the interior room or 20 square feet (1.86 m²), whichever is greater.

1205.2.2 Exterior openings. Exterior openings required by Section 1205.2 for natural light shall open directly onto a public way, yard or court, as set forth in Section 1206.

Exceptions:

1. Required exterior openings are permitted to open into a roofed porch where the porch:

   1.1. Abuts a public way, yard or court.

   1.2. Has a ceiling height of not less than 7 feet (2134 mm).

   1.3. Has a longer side at least 65 percent open and unobstructed.

2. Skylights are not required to open directly onto a public way, yard or court.

1205.3 Artificial light. Artificial light shall be provided that is adequate to provide an average illumination of 10 foot-candles (107 lux) over the area of the room at a height of 30 inches (762 mm) above the floor level.

1205.4 Stairway illumination. Stairways within dwelling units and exterior stairways serving a dwelling unit shall have an illumination level on tread runs of not less than 1 foot-candle (11 lux). Stairs in other occupancies shall be governed by Chapter 10.

1205.4.1 Controls. The control for activation of the required stairway lighting shall be in accordance with the NFPA 70.

1205.5 Emergency egress lighting. The means of egress shall be illuminated in accordance with Section 1006.1.

SECTION 1206
YARDS OR COURTS

1206.1 General. This section shall apply to yards and courts adjacent to exterior openings that provide natural light or ventilation. Such yards and courts shall be on the same property as the building.

1206.2 Yards. Yards shall not be less than 3 feet (914 mm) in width for one- and two-story buildings. For buildings more than two stories in height, the minimum width of the yard shall be increased at the rate of 1 foot (305 mm) for each additional story. For buildings exceeding 14 stories in height, the required width of the yard shall be computed on the basis of 14 stories.

1206.3 Courts. Courts shall not be less than 3 feet (914 mm) in width. Courts having windows opening on opposite sides shall not be less than 6 feet (1829 mm) in width. Courts shall not be less than 10 feet (3048 mm) in length unless bounded on one end by a public way or yard. For buildings more than two stories in height, the court shall be increased 1 foot (305 mm) in width and 2 feet (310 mm) in length for each additional story. For buildings exceeding 14 stories in height, the required dimensions shall be computed on the basis of 14 stories.

1206.3.1 Court access. Access shall be provided to the bottom of courts for cleaning purposes.

1206.3.2 Air intake. Courts more than two stories in height shall be provided with a horizontal air intake at the bottom not less than 10 square feet (0.93 m²) in area and leading to the exterior of the building unless abutting a yard or public way.

1206.3.3 Court drainage. The bottom of every court shall be properly graded and drained to a public sewer or other approved disposal system complying with the *Plumbing Code of New York State*.

SECTION 1207
SOUND TRANSMISSION

1207.1 Scope. This section shall apply to common interior walls, partitions and floor/ceiling assemblies between adjacent dwelling units or between dwelling units and adjacent public areas such as halls, corridors, stairs or service areas.

1207.2 Air-borne sound. Walls, partitions and floor/ceiling assemblies separating dwelling units from each other or from public or service areas shall have a sound transmission class (STC) of not less than 50 (45 if field tested) for air-borne noise when tested in accordance with ASTM E 90. Penetrations or openings in construction assemblies for piping; electrical devices; recessed cabinets; bathtubs; soffits; or heating, ventilating or exhaust ducts shall be sealed, lined, insulated or otherwise treated to maintain the required ratings. This requirement shall not apply to dwelling unit entrance doors; however, such doors shall be tight fitting to the frame and sill.

1207.3 Structure-borne sound. Floor/ceiling assemblies between dwelling units or between a dwelling unit and a public or service area within the structure shall have an impact insulation class (IIC) rating of not less than 50 (45 if field tested) when tested in accordance with ASTM E 492.

SECTION 1208
INTERIOR SPACE DIMENSIONS

1208.1 Minimum room widths. Habitable spaces, other than a kitchen, shall not be less than 7 feet (2134 mm) in any plan dimension. Kitchens shall have a clear passageway of not less than 3 feet (914 mm) between counter fronts and appliances or counter fronts and walls.

1208.2 Minimum ceiling heights. Occupiable spaces, habitable spaces and corridors shall have a ceiling height of not less than 7 feet 6 inches (2286 mm). Bathrooms, toilet rooms, kitchens, storage rooms and laundry rooms shall be permitted to have a ceiling height of not less than 7 feet (2134 mm).

Exceptions:

1. In one- and two-family dwellings, beams or girders spaced not less than 4 feet (1219 mm) on center and projecting not more than 6 inches (152 mm) below the required ceiling height.

2. If any room in a building has a sloped ceiling, the prescribed ceiling height for the room is required in one-half the area thereof. Any portion of the room measuring less than 5 feet (1524 mm) from the finished floor to the ceiling shall not be included in any computation of the minimum area thereof.

3. Mezzanines constructed in accordance with Section 505.1.

4. Basement rooms in one- and two-family dwellings, other than habitable space, may have a ceiling height of not less than 6 feet 8 inches (2033 mm) with not less than 6 feet 4 inches (1932 mm) of clear height under beams, girders, ducts and similar obstructions.

5. Habitable space in basements of one- and two-family dwellings may have a ceiling height of not less than 7 feet (2134 mm) with not less than 6 feet 8

inches (2033 mm) of clear height under beams, girders or other similar obstructions.

1208.2.1 Furred ceiling. Any room with a furred ceiling shall be required to have the minimum ceiling height in two-thirds of the area thereof, but in no case shall the height of the furred ceiling be less than 7 feet (2134 mm).

1208.3 Room area. Every dwelling unit shall have at least one room that shall have not less than 120 square feet (13.9 m^2) of net floor area. Other habitable rooms shall have a net floor area of not less than 70 square feet (6.5 m^2).

> **Exception:** Every kitchen in a one- and two-family dwelling shall have not less than 50 square feet (4.64 m^2) of gross floor area.

1208.4 Efficiency dwelling units. An efficiency living unit shall conform to the requirements of the code except as modified herein:

1. The unit shall have a living room of not less than 220 square feet (20.4 m^2) of floor area. An additional 100 square feet (9.3 m^2) of floor area shall be provided for each occupant of such unit in excess of two.

2. The unit shall be provided with a separate closet.

3. The unit shall be provided with a kitchen sink, cooking appliance and refrigeration facilities, each having a clear working space of not less than 30 inches (762 mm) in front. Light and ventilation conforming to this code shall be provided.

4. The unit shall be provided with a separate bathroom containing a water closet, lavatory and bathtub or shower.

SECTION 1209
ACCESS TO UNOCCUPIED SPACES

1209.1 Crawl spaces. Crawl spaces shall be provided with a minimum of one access opening not less than 18 inches by 24 inches (457 mm by 610 mm).

1209.2 Attic spaces. An opening not less than 20 inches by 30 inches (559 mm by 762 mm) shall be provided to any attic area having a clear height of over 30 inches (762 mm). A 30-inch (762 mm) minimum clear headroom in the attic space shall be provided at or above the access opening.

1209.3 Mechanical appliances. Access to mechanical appliances installed in under-floor areas, in attic spaces and on roofs or elevated structures shall be in accordance with the *Mechanical Code of New York State*.

SECTION 1210
SURROUNDING MATERIALS

1210.1 Floors. In other than dwelling units, toilet and bathing room floors shall have a smooth, hard, nonabsorbent surface that extends upward onto the walls at least 6 inches (152 mm).

1210.2 Walls. Walls within 2 feet (610 mm) of urinals and water closets shall have a smooth, hard, nonabsorbent surface, to a height of 4 feet (1219 mm) above the floor, and except for structural elements, the materials used in such walls shall be of a type that is not adversely affected by moisture.

> **Exceptions:**
>
> 1. Dwelling units and sleeping units.
>
> 2. Toilet rooms that are not accessible to the public and which have not more than one water closet.

Accessories such as grab bars, towel bars, paper dispensers and soap dishes, provided on or within walls, shall be installed and sealed to protect structural elements from moisture.

1210.3 Showers. Shower compartments and walls above bathtubs with installed shower heads shall be finished with a smooth, nonabsorbent surface to a height not less than 70 inches (1778 mm) above the drain inlet.

1210.4 Waterproof joints. Built-in tubs with showers shall have waterproof joints between the tub and adjacent wall.

1210.5 Toilet rooms. Toilet rooms shall not open directly into a room used for the preparation of food for service to the public.

CHAPTER 13

ENERGY EFFICIENCY

SECTION 1301
GENERAL

1301.1 Scope. This chapter governs the design and construction of buildings for energy efficiency.

1301.1.1 Criteria. Buildings shall be designed and constructed in accordance with the *Energy Conservation Construction Code of New York State*.

CHAPTER 14

EXTERIOR WALLS

SECTION 1401
GENERAL

1401.1 Scope. The provisions of this chapter shall establish the minimum requirements for exterior walls; exterior wall coverings; exterior wall openings; exterior windows and doors; architectural trim; balconies and similar projections; and bay and oriel windows.

SECTION 1402
DEFINITIONS

1402.1 General. The following words and terms shall, for the purposes of this chapter and as used elsewhere in this code, have the meanings shown herein.

ADHERED MASONRY VENEER. Veneer secured and supported through the adhesion of an approved bonding material applied to an approved backing.

ANCHORED MASONRY VENEER. Veneer secured with approved mechanical fasteners to an approved backing.

BACKING. The wall or surface to which the veneer is secured.

EXTERIOR WALL. A wall, bearing or nonbearing, that is used as an enclosing wall for a building, other than a fire wall, and that has a slope of 60 degrees (1.05 rad) or greater with the horizontal plane.

EXTERIOR WALL COVERING. A material or assembly of materials applied on the exterior side of exterior walls for the purpose of providing a weather-resisting barrier, insulation or for aesthetics, including but not limited to, veneers, siding, exterior insulation and finish systems, architectural trim and embellishments such as cornices, soffits, facias, gutters and leaders.

EXTERIOR WALL ENVELOPE. A system or assembly of exterior wall components, including exterior wall finish materials, that provides protection of the building structural members, including framing and sheathing materials, and conditioned interior space, from the detrimental effects of the exterior environment.

FIBER CEMENT SIDING. A manufactured, fiber-reinforcing product made with an inorganic hydraulic or calcium silicate binder formed by chemical reaction and reinforced with organic or inorganic nonasbestos fibers, or both. Additives that enhance manufacturing or product performance are permitted. Fiber cement siding products have either smooth or textured faces and are intended for exterior wall and related applications.

METAL COMPOSITE MATERIAL (MCM). A factory-manufactured panel consisting of metal skins bonded to both faces of a plastic core.

METAL COMPOSITE MATERIAL (MCM) SYSTEM. An exterior wall finish system fabricated using MCM in a specific assembly including joints, seams, attachments, substrate, framing and other details as appropriate to a particular design.

VENEER. A facing attached to a wall for the purpose of providing ornamentation, protection or insulation, but not counted as adding strength to the wall.

VINYL SIDING. A shaped material, made principally from rigid polyvinyl chloride (PVC), that is used as an exterior wall covering.

WATER-RESISTIVE BARRIER. A material behind an exterior wall covering that is intended to resist liquid water that has penetrated behind the exterior covering from futher intruding into the exterior wall assembly.

SECTION 1403
PERFORMANCE REQUIREMENTS

1403.1 General. The provisions of this section shall apply to exterior walls, wall coverings and components thereof.

1403.2 Weather protection. Exterior walls shall provide the building with a weather-resistant exterior wall envelope. The exterior wall envelope shall include flashing, as described in Section 1405.3. The exterior wall envelope shall be designed and constructed in such a manner as to prevent the accumulation of water within the wall assembly by providing a water-resistive barrier behind the exterior veneer, as described in Section 1404.2, and a means for draining water that enters the assembly to the exterior. Protection against condensation in the exterior wall assembly shall be provided in accordance with Section 1403.7 and the *Energy Conservation Code of New York State.*

Exceptions:

1. A weather-resistant exterior wall envelope shall not be required over concrete or masonry walls designed in accordance with Chapters 19 and 21, respectively.

2. Compliance with the requirements for a means of drainage, and the requirements of Sections 1404.2 and 1405.3, shall not be required for an exterior wall envelope that has been demonstrated through testing to resist wind-driven rain, including joints, penetrations and intersections with dissimilar materials, in accordance with ASTM E 331 under the following conditions:

   2.1. Exterior wall envelope test assemblies shall include at least one opening, one control joint, one wall/eave interface and one wall sill. All tested openings and penetrations shall be representative of the intended end-use configuration.

2.2. Exterior wall envelope test assemblies shall be at least 4 feet by 8 feet (1219 mm by 2438 mm) in size.

2.3. Exterior wall envelope assemblies shall be tested at a minimum differential pressure of 6.24 pounds per square foot (psf) (0.297 kN/m²).

2.4. Exterior wall envelope assemblies shall be subjected to a minimum test exposure duration of 2 hours.

The exterior wall envelope design shall be considered to resist wind-driven rain where the results of testing indicate that water did not penetrate control joints in the exterior wall envelope, joints at the perimeter of openings or intersections of terminations with dissimilar materials.

1403.3 Structural. Exterior walls, and the associated openings, shall be designed and constructed to resist safely the superimposed loads required by Chapter 16.

1403.4 Fire resistance. Exterior walls shall be fire-resistance rated as required by other sections of this code with opening protection as required by Chapter 7.

1403.5 Flood resistance. For buildings in flood hazard areas as established in Section 1612.3, exterior walls extending below the design flood elevation shall be resistant to water damage. Wood shall be pressure-preservative treated in accordance with AWPA U1 for the species, product and end use using a preservative listed in Section 4 of AWPA U1 or decay-resistant heartwood of redwood, black locust or cedar.

1403.6 Flood resistance for high-velocity wave action areas. For buildings in flood hazard areas subject to high-velocity wave action as established in Section 1612.3, electrical, mechanical and plumbing system components shall not be mounted on or penetrate through exterior walls that are designed to break away under flood loads.

1403.7 Condensation protection. Class I or II vapor retarders are required on the interior side of frame walls in Zones 5 & 6 as defined in the *Energy Conservation Construction Code of New York State.*

Exceptions:

1. Basement walls.

2. Below grade portion of any wall.

3. Construction where moisture or its freezing will not damage the materials.

1403.7.1 Class III vapor retarders. Class III vapor retarders shall be permitted where any one of the conditions in Table 1403.7.1 is met.

1403.7.2 Material vapor retarder class. The vapor retarder class shall be based on the manufacturer's certified testing or a tested assembly. The following shall be deemed to meet the class specified:

Class I: Sheet polyethylene, unperforated aluminum foil.

Class II: Kraft-faced fiberglass batts.

Class III: Latex or enamel paint.

1403.7.3 Minimum clear air spaces and vented openings for vented cladding. For the purposes of this section, vented cladding shall include the following minimum clear air spaces. Other openings with the equivalent vent area shall be permitted.

1. Vinyl lap or horizontal aluminum siding applied over a weather resistive barrier as specified in this chapter.

2. Brick veneer with a clear airspace as specified in this chapter.

3. Other approved vented claddings.

SECTION 1404
MATERIALS

1404.1 General. Materials used for the construction of exterior walls shall comply with the provisions of this section. Materials not prescribed herein shall be permitted, provided that any such alternative has been approved.

1404.2 Water-resistive barrier. A minimum of one layer of No.15 asphalt felt, complying with ASTM D 226 for Type 1 felt or other approved materials, shall be attached to the studs or sheathing, with flashing as described in Section 1405.3, in such a manner as to provide a continuous water-resistive barrier behind the exterior wall veneer.

1404.3 Wood. Exterior walls of wood construction shall be designed and constructed in accordance with Chapter 23.

1404.3.1 Basic hardboard. Basic hardboard shall conform to the requirements of AHA A135.4.

TABLE 1403.3.1
CLASS III VAPOR RETARDERS

ZONE	CLASS III VAPOR RETARDERS PERMITTED FOR:[1]
5	Vented cladding over OSB Vented cladding over Plywood Vented cladding over Fiberboard Vented cladding over Gypsum Insulated sheathing with R-value ≥ R5 over 2 × 4 wall Insulated sheathing with R-value ≥ R7.5 over 2 × 6 wall
6	Vented cladding over Fiberboard Vented cladding over Gypsum Insulated sheathing with R-value ≥ R7.5 over 2 × 4 wall Insulated sheathing with R-value ≥ R11.25 over 2 × 6 wall

1. Spray foam with a minimum density of 2 lbs/ft3 applied to the interior cavity side of OSB, plywood, fiberboard, insulating sheathing or gypsum is deemed to meet the insulating sheathing requirement where the spray foam R-value meets or exceeds the specified insulating sheathing R-value.

1404.3.2 Hardboard siding. Hardboard siding shall conform to the requirements of AHA A135.6 and, where used structurally, shall be so identified by the label of an approved agency.

1404.4 Masonry. Exterior walls of masonry construction shall be designed and constructed in accordance with this section and Chapter 21. Masonry units, mortar and metal accessories used in anchored and adhered veneer shall meet the physical requirements of Chapter 21. The backing of anchored and adhered veneer shall be of concrete, masonry, steel framing or wood framing.

1404.5 Metal. Exterior walls of formed steel construction, structural steel or lightweight metal alloys shall be designed in accordance with Chapters 22 and 20, respectively.

1404.5.1 Aluminum siding. Aluminum siding shall conform to the requirements of AAMA 1402.

1404.5.2 Cold-rolled copper. Copper shall conform to the requirements of ASTM B 370.

1404.5.3 Lead-coated copper. Lead-coated copper shall conform to the requirements of ASTM B 101.

1404.6 Concrete. Exterior walls of concrete construction shall be designed and constructed in accordance with Chapter 19.

1404.7 Glass-unit masonry. Exterior walls of glass-unit masonry shall be designed and constructed in accordance with Chapter 21.

1404.8 Plastics. Plastic panel, apron or spandrel walls as defined in this code shall not be limited in thickness, provided that such plastics and their assemblies conform to the requirements of Chapter 26 and are constructed of approved weather-resistant materials of adequate strength to resist the wind loads for cladding specified in Chapter 16.

1404.9 Vinyl siding. Vinyl siding shall be certified and labeled as conforming to the requirements of ASTM D 3679 by an approved quality control agency.

1404.10 Fiber cement siding. Fiber cement siding shall conform to the requirements of ASTM C 1186 and shall be so identified on labeling listing an approved quality control agency.

SECTION 1405
INSTALLATION OF WALL COVERINGS

1405.1 General. Exterior wall coverings shall be designed and constructed in accordance with the applicable provisions of this section.

1405.2 Weather protection. Exterior walls shall provide weather protection for the building. The materials of the minimum nominal thickness specified in Table 1405.2 shall be acceptable as approved weather coverings.

1405.3 Flashing. Flashing shall be installed in such a manner so as to prevent moisture from entering the wall or to redirect it to the exterior. Flashing shall be installed at the perimeters of exterior door and window assemblies, penetrations and terminations of exterior wall assemblies, exterior wall intersections with roofs, chimneys, porches, decks, balconies and

similar projections and at built-in gutters and similar locations where moisture could enter the wall. Flashing with projecting flanges shall be installed on both sides and the ends of copings, under sills and continuously above projecting trim.

TABLE 1405.2
MINIMUM THICKNESS OF WEATHER COVERINGS

COVERING TYPE	MINIMUM THICKNESS (inches)
Adhered masonry veneer	0.25
Aluminum siding	0.019
Anchored masonry veneer	2.625
Asbestos-cement boards	0.125
Asbestos shingles	0.156
Cold-rolled copper[d]	0.0216 nominal
Copper shingles[d]	0.0162 nominal
Exterior plywood (with sheathing)	0.313
Exterior plywood (without sheathing)	See Section 2304.6
Fiber cement lap siding	0.25[c]
Fiber cement panel siding	0.25[c]
Fiberboard siding	0.5
Glass-fiber reinforced concrete panels	0.375
Hardboard siding[c]	0.25
High-yield copper[d]	0.0162 nominal
Lead-coated copper[d]	0.0216 nominal
Lead-coated high-yield copper	0.0162 nominal
Marble slabs	1
Particleboard (with sheathing)	See Section 2304.6
Particleboard (without sheathing)	See Section 2304.6
Precast stone facing	0.625
Steel (approved corrosion resistant)	0.0149
Stone (cast artificial)	1.5
Stone (natural)	2
Structural glass	0.344
Stucco or exterior portland cement plaster	
Three-coat work over:	
Metal plaster base	0.875[b]
Unit masonry	0.625[b]
Cast-in-place or precast concrete	0.625[b]
Two-coat work over:	
Unit masonry	0.5[b]
Cast-in-place or precast concrete	0.375[b]
Terra cotta (anchored)	1
Terra cotta (adhered)	0.25
Vinyl siding	0.035
Wood shingles	0.375
Wood siding (without sheathing)[a]	0.5

For SI: 1 inch = 25.4 mm.

a. Wood siding of thicknesses less than 0.5 inch shall be placed over sheathing that conforms to Section 2304.6.

b. Exclusive of texture.

c. As measured at the bottom of decorative grooves.

d. 16 ounces per square foot for cold-rolled copper and lead-coated copper, 12 ounces per square foot for copper shingles, high-yield copper and lead-coated high-yield coppe.

1405.3.1 Exterior wall pockets. In exterior walls of buildings or structures, wall pockets or crevices in which moisture can accumulate shall be avoided or protected with caps or drips, or other approved means shall be provided to prevent water damage.

1405.3.2 Masonry. Flashing and weepholes shall be located in the first course of masonry above finished ground level above the foundation wall or slab, and other points of support, including structural floors, shelf angles and lintels where anchored veneers are designed in accordance with Section 1405.5.

1405.4 Wood veneers. Wood veneers on exterior walls of buildings of Type I, II, III and IV construction shall be not less than 1 inch (25 mm) nominal thickness, 0.438-inch (11.1 mm) exterior hardboard siding or 0.375-inch (9.5 mm) exterior-type wood structural panels or particleboard and shall conform to the following:

1. The veneer shall not exceed three stories in height, measured from the grade plane. Where fire-retardant-treated wood is used, the height shall not exceed four stories.

2. The veneer is attached to or furred from a noncombustible backing that is fire-resistance rated as required by other provisions of this code.

3. Where open or spaced wood veneers (without concealed spaces) are used, they shall not project more than 24 inches (610 mm) from the building wall.

1405.5 Anchored masonry veneer. Anchored masonry veneer shall comply with the provisions of Sections 1405.5, 1405.6, 1405.7 and 1405.8 and Sections 6.1 and 6.2 of ACI 530/ASCE 5/TMS 402.

1405.5.1 Tolerances. Anchored masonry veneers in accordance with Chapter 14 are not required to meet the tolerances in Article 3.3 G1 of ACI 530.1/ASCE 6/TMS 602.

1405.5.2 Seismic requirements. Anchored masonry veneer located in Seismic Design Category C, E or F shall conform to the requirements of Section 6.2.2.10 of ACI530/ASCE5/TMS 402. Anchored masonry veneer located in Seismic Design Category D shall conform to the requirements for Seismic Design Category E or F.

1405.6 Stone veneer. Stone veneer units not exceeding 10 inches (254 mm) in thickness shall be anchored directly to masonry, concrete or to stud construction by one of the following methods:

1. With concrete or masonry backing, anchor ties shall be not less than 0.1055-inch (2.68 mm) corrosion-resistant wire, or approved equal, formed beyond the base of the backing. The legs of the loops shall be not less than 6 inches (152 mm) in length bent at right angles and laid in the mortar joint, and spaced so that the eyes or loops are 12 inches (305 mm) maximum on center (o.c.) in both directions. There shall be provided not less than a 0.1055-inch (2.68 mm) corrosion-resistant wire tie, or approved equal, threaded through the exposed loops for every 2 square feet (0.2 m²) of stone veneer. This tie shall be a loop having legs not less than 15 inches (381

mm) in length bent so that it will lie in the stone veneer mortar joint. The last 2 inches (51 mm) of each wire leg shall have a right-angle bend. One-inch (25 mm) minimum thickness of cement grout shall be placed between the backing and the stone veneer.

2. With stud backing, a 2-inch by 2-inch (51 by 51 mm) 0.0625-inch (1.59 mm) corrosion-resistant wire mesh with two layers of water-resistive barrier in accordance with Section 1404.2 shall be applied directly to wood studs spaced a maximum of 16 inches (406 mm) o.c. On studs, the mesh shall be attached with 2-inch-long (51 mm) corrosion-resistant steel wire furring nails at 4 inches (102 mm) o.c. providing a minimum 1.125-inch (29 mm) penetration into each stud and with 8d common nails at 8 inches (203 mm) o.c. into top and bottom plates or with equivalent wire ties. There shall be not less than a 0.1055-inch (2.68 mm) corrosion-resistant wire, or approved equal, looped through the mesh for every 2 square feet (0.2 m²) of stone veneer. This tie shall be a loop having legs not less than 15 inches (381 mm) in length, so bent that it will lie in the stone veneer mortar joint. The last 2 inches (51 mm) of each wire leg shall have a right-angle bend. One-inch (25 mm) minimum thickness of cement grout shall be placed between the backing and the stone veneer.

1405.7 Slab-type veneer. Slab-type veneer units not exceeding 2 inches (51 mm) in thickness shall be anchored directly to masonry, concrete or stud construction. For veneer units of marble, travertine, granite or other stone units of slab form ties of corrosion-resistant dowels in drilled holes shall be located in the middle third of the edge of the units, spaced a maximum of 24 inches (610 m) apart around the periphery of each unit with not less than four ties per veneer unit. Units shall not exceed 20 square feet (1.9 m²) in area. If the dowels are not tight fitting, the holes shall be drilled not more than 0.063 inch (1.6 mm) larger in diameter than the dowel, with the hole countersunk to a diameter and depth equal to twice the diameter of the dowel in order to provide a tight-fitting key of cement mortar at the dowel locations when the mortar in the joint has set. Veneer ties shall be corrosion-resistant metal capable of resisting, in tension or compression, a force equal to two times the weight of the attached veneer. If made of sheet metal, veneer ties shall be not smaller in area than 0.0336 by 1 inch (0.853 by 25 mm) or, if made of wire, not smaller in diameter than 0.1483-inch (3.76 mm) wire.

1405.8 Terra cotta. Anchored terra cotta or ceramic units not less than 1.625 inches (41 mm) thick shall be anchored directly to masonry, concrete or stud construction. Tied terra cotta or ceramic veneer units shall be not less than 1.625 inches (41 mm) thick with projecting dovetail webs on the back surface spaced approximately 8 inches (203 mm) o.c. The facing shall be tied to the backing wall with corrosion-resistant metal anchors of not less than No. 8 gage wire installed at the top of each piece in horizontal bed joints not less than 12 inches (305 mm) nor more than 18 inches (457 mm) o.c.; these anchors shall be secured to 0.25-inch (6.4 mm) corrosion-resistant pencil rods that pass through the vertical aligned loop anchors in the backing wall. The veneer ties shall have sufficient strength to support the full weight of the veneer in tension. The facing shall be set with not less than a 2-inch (51 mm) space from the backing wall and the space shall be filled solidly with portland cement grout and pea gravel. Immediately prior to setting, the backing wall and the facing shall be drenched with clean water and shall be distinctly damp when the grout is poured.

1405.9 Adhered masonry veneer. Adhered masonry veneer shall comply with the applicable requirements in Section 1405.9.1 and Sections 6.1 and 6.3 of ACI 530/ASCE 5/TMS 402.

> **1405.9.1 Interior adhered masonry veneers.** Interior adhered masonry veneers shall have a maximum weight of 20 psf (0.958 kg/m²) and shall be installed in accordance with Section 1405.9. Where the interior adhered masonry veneer is supported by wood construction, the supporting members shall be designed to limit deflection to $^1/_{600}$ of the span of the supporting members.

1405.10 Metal veneers. Veneers of metal shall be fabricated from approved corrosion-resistant materials or shall be protected front and back with porcelain enamel, or otherwise be treated to render the metal resistant to corrosion. Such veneers shall not be less than 0.0149-inch (0.378 mm) nominal thickness sheet steel mounted on wood or metal furring strips or approved sheathing on the wood construction.

> **1405.10.1 Attachment.** Exterior metal veneer shall be securely attached to the supporting masonry or framing members with corrosion-resistant fastenings, metal ties or by other approved devices or methods. The spacing of the fastenings or ties shall not exceed 24 inches (610 mm) either vertically or horizontally, but where units exceed 4 square feet (0.4 m²) in area there shall be not less than four attachments per unit. The metal attachments shall have a cross-sectional area not less than provided by W 1.7 wire. Such attachments and their supports shall be capable of resisting a horizontal force in accordance with the wind loads specified in Section 1609, but in no case less than 20 psf (0.958 kg/m²).

> **1405.10.2 Weather protection.** Metal supports for exterior metal veneer shall be protected by painting, galvanizing or by other equivalent coating or treatment. Wood studs, furring strips or other wood supports for exterior metal veneer shall be approved pressure-treated wood or protected as required in Section 1403.2. Joints and edges exposed to the weather shall be caulked with approved durable waterproofing material or by other approved means to prevent penetration of moisture.

> **1405.10.3 Backup.** Masonry backup shall not be required for metal veneer except as is necessary to meet the fire-resistance requirements of this code.

> **1405.10.4 Grounding.** Grounding of metal veneers on buildings shall comply with the requirements of Chapter 27 of the *Building Code of New York State*.

1405.11 Glass veneer. The area of a single section of thin exterior structural glass veneer shall not exceed 10 square feet (0.93 m²) where it is not more than 15 feet (4572 mm) above the level of the sidewalk or grade level directly below,

and shall not exceed 6 square feet (0.56 m²) where it is more than 15 feet (4572 mm) above that level.

> **1405.11.1 Length and height.** The length or height of any section of thin exterior structural glass veneer shall not exceed 48 inches (1219 mm).

> **1405.11.2 Thickness.** The thickness of thin exterior structural glass veneer shall be not less than 0.344 inch (8.7 mm).

> **1405.11.3 Application.** Thin exterior structural glass veneer shall be set only after backing is thoroughly dry and after application of an approved bond coat uniformly over the entire surface of the backing so as to effectively seal the surface. Glass shall be set in place with an approved mastic cement in sufficient quantity so that at least 50 percent of the area of each glass unit is directly bonded to the backing by mastic not less than 0.25 inch (6.4 mm) thick and not more than 0.625 inch (15.9 mm) thick. The bond coat and mastic shall be evaluated for compatibility and shall bond firmly together.

> **1405.11.4 Installation at sidewalk level.** Where glass extends to a sidewalk surface, each section shall rest in an approved metal molding, and be set at least 0.25 inch (6.4 mm) above the highest point of the sidewalk. The space between the molding and the sidewalk shall be thoroughly caulked and made water tight.

>> **1405.11.4.1 Installation above sidewalk level.** Where thin exterior structural glass veneer is installed above the level of the top of a bulkhead facing, or at a level more than 36 inches (914 mm) above the sidewalk level, the mastic cement binding shall be supplemented with approved nonferrous metal shelf angles located in the horizontal joints in every course. Such shelf angles shall be not less than 0.0478-inch (1.2 mm) thick and not less than 2 inches (51 mm) long and shall be spaced at approved intervals, with not less than two angles for each glass unit. Shelf angles shall be secured to the wall or backing with expansion bolts, toggle bolts or by other approved methods.

> **1405.11.5 Joints.** Unless otherwise specifically approved by the code enforcement official, abutting edges of thin exterior structural glass veneer shall be ground square. Mitered joints shall not be used except where specifically approved for wide angles. Joints shall be uniformly buttered with an approved jointing compound and horizontal joints shall be held to not less than 0.063 inch (1.6 mm) by an approved nonrigid substance or device. Where thin exterior structural glass veneer abuts nonresilient material at sides or top, expansion joints not less than 0.25 inch (6.4 mm) wide shall be provided.

> **1405.11.6 Mechanical fastenings.** Thin exterior structural glass veneer installed above the level of the heads of show windows and veneer installed more than 12 feet (3658 mm) above sidewalk level shall, in addition to the mastic cement and shelf angles, be held in place by the use of fastenings at each vertical or horizontal edge, or at the four corners of each glass unit. Fastenings shall be secured to the wall or backing with expansion bolts, toggle bolts or by other methods. Fastenings shall be so designed as to

hold the glass veneer in a vertical plane independent of the mastic cement. Shelf angles providing both support and fastenings shall be permitted.

1405.11.7 Flashing. Exposed edges of thin exterior structural glass veneer shall be flashed with overlapping corrosion-resistant metal flashing and caulked with a waterproof compound in a manner to effectively prevent the entrance of moisture between the glass veneer and the backing.

1405.12 Exterior windows and doors. Windows and doors installed in exterior walls shall conform to the testing and performance requirements of Section 1714.5.

1405.12.1 Installation. Windows and doors shall be installed in accordance with approved manufacturer's instructions. Fastener size and spacing shall be provided in such instructions and shall be calculated based on maximum loads and spacing used in the tests.

1405.13 Vinyl siding. Vinyl siding conforming to the requirements of this section and complying with ASTM D 3679 shall be permitted on exterior walls of buildings of Type V construction located in areas where the basic wind speed specified in Chapter 16 does not exceed 100 miles per hour (45 m/s) and the building height is less than or equal to 40 feet (12 192 mm) in Exposure C. Where construction is located in areas where the basic wind speed exceeds 100 miles per hour (45 m/s), or building heights are in excess of 40 feet (12 192 mm), tests or calculations indicating compliance with Chapter 16 shall be submitted. Vinyl siding shall be secured to the building so as to provide weather protection for the exterior walls of the building.

1405.13.1 Application. The siding shall be applied over sheathing or materials listed in Section 2304.6. Siding shall be applied to conform with the water-resistive barrier requirements in Section 1403. Siding and accessories shall be installed in accordance with approved manufacturer's instructions. Unless otherwise specified in the approved manufacturer's instructions, nails used to fasten the siding and accessories shall have a minimum 0.313-inch (7.9 mm) head diameter and 0.125-inch (3.18 mm) shank diameter. The nails shall be corrosion resistant and shall be long enough to penetrate the studs or nailing strip at least 0.75 inch (19 mm). Where the siding is installed horizontally, the fastener spacing shall not exceed 16 inches (406 mm) horizontally and 12 inches (305 mm) vertically. Where the siding is installed vertically, the fastener spacing shall not exceed 12 inches (305 mm) horizontally and 12 inches (305 mm) vertically.

1405.14 Cement plaster. Cement plaster applied to exterior walls shall conform to the requirements specified in Chapter 25.

1405.15 Fiber cement siding. Fiber cement siding complying with Section 1404.10 shall be permitted on exterior walls of Type I, II, III, IV and V construction for wind pressure resistance or wind speed exposures as indicated in the manufacturer's compliance report and approved installation instructions. Where specified, the siding shall be installed over sheathing or materials listed in Section 2304.6 and shall be installed to conform to the water-resistive barrier requirements in Section 1403. Siding and accessories shall be installed in accordance with approved manufacturer's instructions. Unless otherwise specified in the approved manufacturer's instructions, nails used to fasten the siding to wood studs shall be corrosion-resistant round head smooth shank and shall be long enough to penetrate the studs at least 1 inch (25 mm). For metal framing, all-weather screws shall be used and shall penetrate the metal framing at least three full threads.

1405.16 Fastening. Weather boarding and wall coverings shall be securely fastened with aluminum, copper, zinc, zinc-coated or other approved corrosion-resistant fasteners in accordance with the nailing schedule in Table 2304.9.1 or the approved manufacturer's installation instructions. Shingles and other weather coverings shall be attached with appropriate standard-shingle nails to furring strips securely nailed to studs, or with approved mechanically bonding nails, except where sheathing is of wood not less than 1-inch (25 mm) nominal thickness or of wood structural panels as specified in Table 2308.9.3(3).

1405.17 Fiber cement siding.

1405.17.1 Panel siding. Panels shall be installed with the long dimension parallel to framing. Vertical joints shall occur over framing members and shall be sealed with caulking or covered with battens. Horizontal joints shall be flashed with Z-flashing and blocked with solid wood framing.

1405.17.2 1405.17.2 Horizontal lap siding. Lap siding shall be lapped a minimum of $1^1/_4$ inches (32 mm) and shall have the ends sealed with caulking, covered with an H-section joint cover or located over a strip of flashing. Lap siding courses shall be permitted to be installed with the fastener heads exposed or concealed, according to approved manufacturers' instructions.

SECTION 1406
COMBUSTIBLE MATERIALS ON THE EXTERIOR SIDE OF EXTERIOR WALLS

1406.1 General. Section 1406 shall apply to exterior wall coverings; balconies and similar projections; and bay and oriel windows constructed of combustible materials.

1406.2 Combustible exterior wall coverings. Combustible exterior wall coverings shall comply with this section.

Exception: Plastics complying with Chapter 26.

1406.2.1 Ignition resistance. Combustible exterior wall coverings shall be tested in accordance with NFPA 268.

Exceptions:

1. Wood or wood-based products.

2. Other combustible materials covered with an exterior covering other than vinyl sidings listed in Table 1405.2.

3. Aluminum having a minimum thickness of 0.019 inch (0.48 mm).

4. Exterior wall coverings on exterior walls of Type V construction.

1406.2.1.1 Fire separation 5 feet or less. Where installed on exterior walls having a fire separation distance of 5 feet (1524 mm) or less, combustible exterior wall coverings shall not exhibit sustained flaming as defined in NFPA 268.

1406.2.1.2 Fire separation greater than 5 feet. For fire separation distances greater than 5 feet (1524 mm), an assembly shall be permitted that has been exposed to a reduced level of incident radiant heat flux in accordance with the NFPA 268 test method without exhibiting sustained flaming. The minimum fire separation distance required for the assembly shall be determined from Table 1406.2.1.2 based on the maximum tolerable level of incident radiant heat flux that does not cause sustained flaming of the assembly.

1406.2.2 Architectural trim. In buildings of Type I, II, III and IV construction that do not exceed three stories or 40 feet (12 192 mm) in height above grade plane, exterior wall coverings shall be permitted to be constructed of wood where permitted by Section 1405.4 or other equivalent combustible material. Combustible exterior wall coverings, other than fire-retardant-treated wood complying with Section 2303.2 for exterior installation, shall not exceed 10 percent of an exterior wall surface area where the fire separation distance is 5 feet (1524 mm) or less. Architectural trim that exceeds 40 feet (12 192 mm) in height above grade plane shall be constructed of approved noncombustible materials and shall be secured to the wall with metal or other approved noncombustible brackets.

1406.2.3 Location. Where combustible exterior wall covering is located along the top of exterior walls, such trim shall be completely backed up by the exterior wall and shall not extend over or above the top of exterior walls.

1406.2.4 Fireblocking. Where the combustible exterior wall covering is furred from the wall and forms a solid surface, the distance between the back of the covering and the wall shall not exceed 1.625 inches (41 mm) and the space thereby created shall be fireblocked in accordance with Section 717.

1406.3 Balconies and similar projections. Balconies and similar projections of combustible construction other than fire-retardant-treated wood shall be fire-resistance rated in accordance with Table 601 for floor construction or shall be of Type IV construction in accordance with Section 602.4. The aggregate length shall not exceed 50 percent of the building's perimeter on each floor.

Exceptions:

1. On buildings of Type I and II construction, three stories or less in height, fire-retardant-treated wood shall be permitted for balconies, porches, decks and exterior stairways not used as required exits.

2. Untreated wood is permitted for pickets and rails or similar guardrail devices that are limited to 42 inches (1067 mm) in height.

3. Balconies and similar projections on buildings of Type III, IV and V construction shall be permitted to be of Type V construction, and shall not be required to have a fire-resistance rating where sprinkler protection is extended to these areas.

4. Where sprinkler protection is extended to the balcony areas, the aggregate length of the balcony on each floor shall not be limited.

1406.4 Bay windows and oriel windows. Bay and oriel windows shall conform to the type of construction required for the building to which they are attached.

Exception: Fire-retardant-treated wood shall be permitted on buildings three stories or less of Type I, II, III and IV construction.

SECTION 1407
METAL COMPOSITE MATERIALS (MCM)

1407.1 General. The provisions of this section shall govern the materials, construction and quality of metal composite materials (MCM) for use as exterior wall coverings in addition to other applicable requirements of Chapters 14 and 16.

TABLE 1406.2.1.2
MINIMUM FIRE SEPARATION FOR COMBUSTIBLE VENEERS

FIRE SEPARATION DISTANCE (feet)	TOLERABLE LEVEL INCIDENT RADIANT HEAT ENERGY (kW/m²)	FIRE SEPARATION DISTANCE (feet)	TOLERABLE LEVEL INCIDENT RADIANT HEAT ENERGY (kW/m²)
5	12.5	16	5.9
6	11.8	17	5.5
7	11.0	18	5.2
8	10.3	19	4.9
9	9.6	20	4.6
10	8.9	21	4.4
11	8.3	22	4.1
12	7.7	23	3.9
13	7.2	24	3.7
14	6.7	25	3.5
15	6.3		

For SI: 1 foot = 304.8 mm, 1 Btu/H^2 ×°F = 0.0057 kW/m^2 × K.

1407.1.1 Plastic core. The plastic core of the MCM shall not contain foam plastic insulation as defined in Section 2602.1.

1407.2 Exterior wall finish. MCM used as exterior wall finish or as elements of balconies and similar projections and bay and oriel windows to provide cladding or weather resistance shall comply with Sections 1407.4 through 1407.13.

1407.3 Architectural trim and embellishments. MCM used as architectural trim or embellishments shall comply with Sections 1407.7 through 1407.13.

1407.4 Structural design. MCM systems shall be designed and constructed to resist wind loads as required by Chapter 16 for components and cladding.

1407.5 Approval. Results of approved tests or an engineering analysis shall be submitted to the code enforcement official to verify compliance with the requirements of Chapter 16 for wind loads.

1407.6 Weather resistance. MCM systems shall comply with Section 1403 and shall be designed and constructed to resist wind and rain in accordance with this section and the manufacturer's installation instructions.

1407.7 Durability. MCM systems shall be constructed of approved materials that maintain the performance characteristics required in Section 1407 for the duration of use.

1407.8 Fire-resistance rating. Where MCM systems are used on exterior walls required to have a fire-resistance rating in accordance with Section 704, evidence shall be submitted to the code enforcement official that the required fire-resistance rating is maintained.

1407.9 Surface-burning characteristics. Unless otherwise specified, MCM shall have a flame spread index of 75 or less and a smoke-developed index of 450 or less when tested as an assembly in the maximum thickness intended for use in accordance with ASTM E 84.

1407.10 Type I, II, III and IV construction. Where installed on buildings of Type I, II, III and IV construction, MCM systems shall comply with Sections 1407.10.1 through 1407.10.4, or 1407.11.

1407.10.1 Surface-burning characteristics. MCM shall have a flame spread index of not more than 25 and a smoke-developed index of not more than 450 when tested as an assembly in the maximum thickness intended for use in accordance with ASTM E 84.

1407.10.2 Thermal barriers. MCM shall be separated from the interior of a building by an approved thermal barrier consisting of 0.5-inch (12.7 mm) gypsum wallboard or equivalent thermal barrier material that will limit the average temperature rise of the unexposed surface to not more than 250°F (121°C) after 15 minutes of fire exposure in accordance with the standard time-temperature curve of ASTM E 119. The thermal barrier shall be installed in such a manner that it will remain in place for not less than 15 minutes based on a test conducted in accordance with UL 1715.

1407.10.3 Thermal barrier not required. The thermal barrier specified for MCM in Section 1407.10.2 is not required where:

1. The MCM system is specifically approved based on tests conducted in accordance with UL 1040 or UL 1715. Such testing shall be performed with the MCM in the maximum thickness intended for use. The MCM system shall include seams, joints and other typical details used in the installation and shall be tested in the manner intended for use.

2. The MCM is used as elements of balconies and similar projections, architectural trim or embellishments.

1407.10.4 Full-scale tests. The MCM exterior wall assembly shall be tested in accordance with, and comply with, the acceptance criteria of NFPA 285. Such testing shall be performed on the MCM system with the MCM in the maximum thickness intended for use.

1407.11 Alternate conditions. MCM and MCM systems shall not be required to comply with Sections 1407.10.1 through 1407.10.4 provided such systems comply with Section 1407.11.1 or 1407.11.2.

1407.11.1 Installations up to 40 feet in height. MCM shall not be installed more than 40 feet (12 190 mm) in height above the grade plane where installed in accordance with Sections 1407.11.1.1 and 1407.11.1.2.

1407.11.1.1 Fire separation distance of 5 feet or less. Where the fire separation distance is 5 feet (1524 mm) or less, the area of MCM shall not exceed 10 percent of the exterior wall surface.

1407.11.1.2 Fire separation distance greater than 5 feet. Where the fire separation distance is greater than 5 feet (1524 mm), there shall be no limit on the area of exterior wall surface coverage using MCM.

1407.11.2 Installations up to 50 feet in height. MCM shall not be installed more than 50 feet (15 240 mm) in height above the grade plane where installed in accordance with Sections 1407.11.2.1 and 1407.11.2.2.

1407.11.2.1 Self-ignition temperature. MCM shall have a self-ignition temperature of 650°F (343°C) or greater when tested in accordance with ASTM D 1929.

1407.11.2.2 Limitations. Sections of MCM shall not exceed 300 square feet (27.9 m^2) in area and shall be separated by a minimum of 4 feet (1219 mm) vertically.

1407.12 Type V construction. MCM shall be permitted to be installed on buildings of Type V construction.

1407.13 Labeling. MCM shall be labeled in accordance with Section 1703.5.

CHAPTER 15

ROOF ASSEMBLIES AND ROOFTOP STRUCTURES

SECTION 1501
GENERAL

1501.1 Scope. The provisions of this chapter shall govern the design, materials, construction and quality of roof assemblies, and rooftop structures.

SECTION 1502
DEFINITIONS

1502.1 General. The following words and terms shall, for the purposes of this chapter and as used elsewhere in this code, have the meanings shown herein.

BUILT-UP ROOF COVERING. Two or more layers of felt cemented together and surfaced with a cap sheet, mineral aggregate, smooth coating or similar surfacing material.

INTERLAYMENT. A layer of felt or nonbituminous saturated felt not less than 18 inches (457 mm) wide, shingled between each course of a wood-shake roof covering.

MECHANICAL EQUIPMENT SCREEN. A partially enclosed rooftop structure used to aesthetically conceal heating, ventilating and air conditioning (HVAC) electrical or mechanical equipment from view.

METAL ROOF PANEL. An interlocking metal sheet having a minimum installed weather exposure of 3 square feet (0.279 m^2) per sheet.

METAL ROOF SHINGLE. An interlocking metal sheet having an installed weather exposure less than 3 square feet (0.279 m^2) per sheet.

MODIFIED BITUMEN ROOF COVERING. One or more layers of polymer-modified asphalt sheets. The sheet materials shall be fully adhered or mechanically attached to the substrate or held in place with an approved ballast layer.

PENTHOUSE. An enclosed, unoccupied structure above the roof of a building, other than a tank, tower, spire, dome cupola or bulkhead, occupying not more than one-third of the roof area.

POSITIVE ROOF DRAINAGE. The drainage condition in which consideration has been made for all loading deflections of the roof deck, and additional slope has been provided to ensure drainage of the roof within 48 hours of precipitation.

REROOFING. The process of recovering or replacing an existing roof covering. See "Roof recover" and "Roof replacement."

ROOF ASSEMBLY. A system designed to provide weather protection and resistance to design loads. The system consists of a roof covering and roof deck or a single component serving as both the roof covering and the roof deck. A roof assembly includes the roof deck, vapor retarder, substrate or thermal barrier, insulation, vapor retarder and roof covering.

ROOF COVERING. The covering applied to the roof deck for weather resistance, fire classification or appearance.

ROOF COVERING SYSTEM. See "Roof assembly."

ROOF DECK. The flat or sloped surface not including its supporting members or vertical supports.

ROOF RECOVER. The process of installing an additional roof covering over a prepared existing roof covering without removing the existing roof covering.

ROOF REPAIR. Reconstruction or renewal of any part of an existing roof for the purposes of its maintenance.

ROOF REPLACEMENT. The process of removing the existing roof covering, repairing any damaged substrate and installing a new roof covering.

ROOF VENTILATION. The natural or mechanical process of supplying conditioned or unconditioned air to, or removing such air from, attics, cathedral ceilings or other enclosed spaces over which a roof assembly is installed.

ROOFTOP STRUCTURE. An enclosed structure on or above the roof of any part of a building.

SCUPPER. An opening in a wall or parapet that allows water to drain from a roof.

SINGLE-PLY MEMBRANE. A roofing membrane that is field applied using one layer of membrane material (either homogeneous or composite) rather than multiple layers.

UNDERLAYMENT. One or more layers of felt, sheathing paper, nonbituminous saturated felt or other approved material over which a steep-slope roof covering is applied.

SECTION 1503
WEATHER PROTECTION

1503.1 General. Roof decks shall be covered with approved roof coverings secured to the building or structure in accordance with the provisions of this chapter. Roof coverings shall be designed, installed and maintained in accordance with this code and the approved manufacturer's instructions such that the roof covering shall serve to protect the building or structure.

1503.2 Flashing. Flashing shall be installed in such a manner so as to prevent moisture entering the wall and roof through joints in copings, through moisture-permeable materials and at intersections with parapet walls and other penetrations through the roof plane.

1503.2.1 Locations. Flashing shall be installed at wall and roof intersections, at gutters, wherever there is a change in roof slope or direction and around roof openings. Where flashing is of metal, the metal shall be corrosion resistant with a thickness of not less than 0.019 inch (0.483 mm) (No. 26 galvanized sheet).

1503.3 Coping. Parapet walls shall be properly coped with noncombustible, weatherproof materials of a width no less than the thickness of the parapet wall.

[P] 1503.4 Roof drainage. Design and installation of roof drainage systems shall comply with the *Plumbing Code of New York State.*

1503.4.1 Gutters. Gutters and leaders placed on the outside of buildings, other than Group R-3, private garages and buildings of Type V construction, shall be of noncombustible material or a minimum of Schedule 40 plastic pipe.

1503.5 Roof ventilation. Intake and exhaust vents shall be provided in accordance with Section 1203.2 and the manufacturer's installation instructions.

SECTION 1504
PERFORMANCE REQUIREMENTS

1504.1 Wind resistance of roofs. Roof decks and roof coverings shall be designed for wind loads in accordance with Chapter 16 and Sections 1504.2, 1504.3 and 1504.4.

1504.1.1 Wind resistance of asphalt shingles. Asphalt shingles shall be installed in accordance with Section 1507.2.7. For roofs located where the basic wind speed in accordance with Figure 1609 is 110 mph or greater, asphalt shingles shall be tested in accordance with ASTM D 3161, Class F. As an alternative, load and wind resistance of asphalt shingle roof coverings shall be determined in accordance with Section 1609.5.2.

1504.2 Wind resistance of clay and concrete tile. Clay and concrete tile roof coverings shall be connected to the roof deck in accordance with Chapter 16.

1504.2.1 Alternative test method. Testing the acceptability of special fastening methods using the methodology in this section is permitted. The wind-induced uplift force on the shingle shall be determined using the method in UL 2390. The resistance of the shingle to the uplift force shall be determined using ASTM D 6381. Shingles passing this test shall be considered suitable for roofs located where the basic wind speed per Figure 1609 is as given in Table 1504.2.1.

Classification requires that the resistance of the shingle to wind uplift, measured using the method in ASTM D 6381, exceed the calculated load imposed by wind in the applicable zone as determined using UL 2390.

Classification by this method applies to buildings less than 60 feet (18 288 mm) high and with Wind Exposures B and C only in an Occupancy Category of I or II. Wrappers of shingle bundles that have been qualified using this alternative method shall be labeled with the tested wind classification and reference UL 2390/ASTM D 6381.

1504.3 Wind resistance of nonballasted roofs. Roof coverings installed on roofs in accordance with Section 1507 that are mechanically attached or adhered to the roof deck shall be designed to resist the design wind load pressures for cladding in Chapter 16.

TABLE 1504.2.1
ROOF COVERING CLASSIFICATION USING ALTERNATIVE METHOD

MAXIMUM BASIC WIND SPEED (mph)	ASTM D 6381 CLASSIFICATION
90	Class D
120	Class G
150	Class H

For SI: 1 mile per hour = 0.447m/s.

1504.3.1 Other roof systems. Roof systems with built-up, modified bitumen, fully adhered or mechanically attached single-ply through fastened metal panel roof systems, and other types of membrane roof coverings shall also be tested in accordance with FM 4450, FM 4470, UL 580 or UL 1897.

1504.3.2 Metal panel roof systems. Metal panel roof systems through fastened or standing seam shall be tested in accordance with UL 580 or ASTM E 1592.

Exception: Metal roofs constructed of cold-formed steel, where the roof deck acts as the roof covering and provides both weather protection and support for structural loads, shall be permitted to be designed and tested in accordance with the applicable referenced structural design standard in Section 2209.1.

1504.4 Ballasted low-slope roof systems. Ballasted low-slope (roof slope < 2:12) single-ply roof system coverings installed in accordance with Section 1507 shall be designed in accordance with Section 1504.8 and ANSI/SPRI RP-4.

1504.5 Edge securement for low-slope roofs. Low-slope membrane roof system metal edge securement, except gutters, shall be designed and installed for wind loads in accordance with Chapter 16 and tested for resistance in accordance with ANSI/SPRI ES-1, except the basic wind speed shall be determined from Figure 1609.

1504.6 Physical properties. Roof coverings installed on low-slope roofs (roof slope < 2:12) in accordance with Section 1507 shall demonstrate physical integrity over the working life of the roof based upon 2,000 hours of exposure to accelerated weathering tests conducted in accordance with ASTM G 152, ASTM G 155 or ASTM G 154. Those roof coverings that are subject to cyclical flexural response due to wind loads shall not demonstrate any significant loss of tensile strength for unreinforced membranes or breaking strength for reinforced membranes when tested as herein required.

1504.7 Impact resistance. Roof coverings installed on low-slope roofs (roof slope < 2:12) in accordance with Section 1507 shall resist impact damage based on the results of tests conducted in accordance with ASTM D 3746, ASTM D 4272, CGSB 37-GP-52M or the "Resistance to Foot Traffic Test" in Section 5.5 of FM 4470.

1504.8 Gravel and stone. Gravel or stone shall not be used on the roof of a building located in a hurricane-prone region as defined in Section 1609.2, or on any other building with a mean roof height exceeding that permitted by Table 1504.8 based on the exposure category and basic wind speed at the building site.

**TABLE 1504.8
MAXIMUM ALLOWABLE MEAN ROOF HEIGHT PERMITTED FOR
BUILDINGS WITH GRAVEL OR STONE ON THE ROOF IN AREAS
OUTSIDE A HURRICANE-PRONE REGION**

BASIC WIND SPEED FROMFIGURE1609 (mph)[b]	MAXIMUM MEAN ROOF HEIGHT (ft)[a,c]		
	Exposure category		
	B	C	D
85	170	60	30
90	110	35	15
95	75	20	NP
100	55	15	NP
105	40	NP	NP
110	30	NP	NP
115	20	NP	NP
120	15	NP	NP
Greater than 120	NP	NP	NP

For SI: 1 foot = 304.8 mm; 1 mile per hour = 0.447 m/s.

a. Mean roof height in accordance with Section 1609.2.

b. For intermediate values of basic wind speed, the height associated with the next higher value of wind speed shall be used, or direct interpolation is permitted.

c. NP = gravel and stone not permitted for any roof height.

SECTION 1505
FIRE CLASSIFICATION

1505.1 General. Roof assemblies shall be divided into the classes defined below. Class A, B and C roof assemblies and roof coverings required to be listed by this section shall be tested in accordance with ASTM E 108 or UL 790. In addition, fire-retardant-treated wood roof coverings shall be tested in accordance with ASTM D 2898. The minimum roof coverings installed on buildings shall comply with Table 1505.1 based on the type of construction of the building.

Exception: Skylights and sloped glazing that comply with Chapter 24 or Section 2610.

**TABLE 1505.1[a, b]
MINIMUM ROOF COVERING CLASSIFICATION FOR TYPES OF
CONSTRUCTION**

IA	IB	IIA	IIB	IIIA	IIIB	IV	VA	VB
B	B	B	C[b]	B	C[b]	B	B	C[b]

For SI: 1 foot = 304.8 mm, 1 square foot = 0.0929 m².

a. Nonclassified roof coverings shall be permitted on buildings of Group R-3 and Group U occupancies, where there is a minimum fire-separation distance of 6 feet measured from the leading edge of the roof.

b. Buildings that are not more than two stories in height and having not more than 6,000 square feet of projected roof area and where there is a minimum 10-foot fire-separation distance from the leading edge of the roof to a lot line on all sides of the building, except for street fronts or public ways, shall be permitted to have roofs of No. 1 cedar or redwood shakes and No. 1 shingles.

1505.2 Class A roof assemblies. Class A roof assemblies are those that are effective against severe fire test exposure. Class A roof assemblies and roof coverings shall be listed and identified as Class A by an approved testing agency. Class A roof assemblies shall be permitted for use in buildings or structures of all types of construction.

Exception: Class A roof assemblies include those with coverings of brick, masonry, slate, clay or concrete roof tile, exposed concrete roof deck, ferrous or copper shingles or sheets.

1505.3 Class B roof assemblies. Class B roof assemblies are those that are effective against moderate fire-test exposure. Class B roof assemblies and roof coverings shall be listed and identified as Class B by an approved testing agency.

Exception: Class B roof assemblies include those with coverings of metal sheets and shingles.

1505.4 Class C roof assemblies. Class C roof assemblies are those that are effective against light fire-test exposure. Class C roof assemblies and roof coverings shall be listed and identified as Class C by an approved testing agency.

1505.5 Nonclassified roofing. Nonclassified roofing is approved material that is not listed as a Class A, B or C roof covering.

1505.6 Fire-retardant-treated wood shingles and shakes. Fire-retardant-treated wood shakes and shingles shall be treated by impregnation with chemicals by the full-cell vacuum-pressure process, in accordance with AWPA C1. Each bundle shall be marked to identify the manufactured unit and the manufacturer, and shall also be labeled to identify the classification of the material in accordance with the testing required in Section 1505.1, the treating company and the quality control agency.

1505.7 Special purpose roofs. Special purpose wood shingle or wood shake roofing shall conform with the grading and application requirements of Section 1507.8 or 1507.9. In addition, an underlayment of 0.625-inch (15.9 mm) Type X water-resistant gypsum backing board or gypsum sheathing shall be placed under minimum nominal 0.5-inch-thick (12.7 mm) wood structural panel solid sheathing or 1-inch (25 mm) nominal spaced sheathing.

SECTION 1506
MATERIALS

1506.1 Scope. The requirements set forth in this section shall apply to the application of roof-covering materials specified herein. Roof coverings shall be applied in accordance with this chapter and the manufacturer's installation instructions. Installation of roof coverings shall comply with the applicable provisions of Section 1507.

1506.2 Compatibility of materials. Roofs and roof coverings shall be of materials that are compatible with each other and with the building or structure to which the materials are applied.

1506.3 Material specifications and physical characteristics. Roof-covering materials shall conform to the applicable standards listed in this chapter. In the absence of applicable standards or where materials are of questionable suitability, testing by an approved agency shall be required by the code enforcement official to determine the character, quality and limitations of application of the materials.

1506.4 Product identification. Roof-covering materials shall be delivered in packages bearing the manufacturer's identifying marks and approved testing agency labels required in accordance with Section 1505. Bulk shipments of materials shall be accompanied with the same information issued in the form of a certificate or on a bill of lading by the manufacturer.

SECTION 1507
REQUIREMENTS FOR ROOF COVERINGS

1507.1 Scope. Roof coverings shall be applied in accordance with the applicable provisions of this section and the manufacturer's installation instructions.

➡ **1507.2 Asphalt shingles.** The installation of asphalt shingles shall comply with the provisions of this section.

1507.2.1 Deck requirements. Asphalt shingles shall be fastened to solidly sheathed decks.

1507.2.2 Slope. Asphalt shingles shall only be used on roof slopes of two units vertical in 12 units horizontal (17-percent slope) or greater. For roof slopes from two units vertical in 12 units horizontal (17-percent slope) up to four units vertical in 12 units horizontal (33-percent slope), double underlayment application is required in accordance with Section 1507.2.8.

1507.2.3 Underlayment. Unless otherwise noted, required underlayment shall conform to ASTM D 226, Type I, ASTM D 4869, Type I, or ASTM D 6757.

1507.2.4 Self-adhering polymer modified bitumen sheet. Self-adhering polymer modified bitumen sheet shall comply with ASTM D 1970.

1507.2.5 Asphalt shingles. Asphalt shingles shall have self-seal strips or be interlocking and comply with ASTM D 225 or ASTM D 3462. Asphalt shingle packaging shall bear labeling indicating compliance with ASTM D 3161 or a listing by an approved testing agency in accordance with the requirements of Section 1609.5.2.

1507.2.6 Fasteners. Fasteners for asphalt shingles shall be galvanized, stainless steel, aluminum or copper roofing nails, minimum 12 gage [0.105 inch (2.67 mm)] shank with a minimum 0.375 inch-diameter (9.5 mm) head, of a length to penetrate through the roofing materials and a minimum of 0.75 inch (19.1 mm) into the roof sheathing. Where the roof sheathing is less than 0.75 inch (19.1 mm) thick, the nails shall penetrate through the sheathing. Fasteners shall comply with ASTM F 1667.

1507.2.7 Attachment. Asphalt shingles shall have the minimum number of fasteners required by the manufacturer and Section 1504.1. Asphalt shingles shall be secured to the roof with not less than four fasteners per strip shingle or two fasteners per individual shingle. Where the roof slope exceeds 20 units vertical in 12 units horizontal (166-percent slope), asphalt shingles shall be installed in accordance with the manufacturer's printed installation instructions for steep-slope roof applications.

1507.2.8 Underlayment application. For roof slopes from two units vertical in 12 units horizontal (17-percent slope) and up to four units vertical in 12 units horizontal (33-percent slope), underlayment shall be two layers applied in the following manner. Apply a minimum 19-inch-wide (483 mm) strip of underlayment felt parallel

with and starting at the eaves, fastened sufficiently to hold in place. Starting at the eave, apply 36-inch-wide (914 mm) sheets of underlayment overlapping successive sheets 19 inches (483 mm), by fastened sufficiently to hold in place. Distortions in the underlayment shall not interfere with the ability of the shingles to seal. For roof slopes of four units vertical in 12 units horizontal (33-percent slope) or greater, underlayment shall be one layer applied in the following manner. Underlayment shall be applied shingle fashion, parallel to and starting from the eave and lapped 2 inches (51 mm), fastened sufficiently to hold in place. Distortions in the underlayment shall not interfere with the ability of the shingles to seal.

1507.2.8.1 High wind attachment. Underlayment applied in areas subject to high winds (greater than 110 mph in accordance with Figure 1609) shall be applied with corrosion- resistant fasteners in accordance with the manufacturer's instructions. Fasteners are to be applied along the overlap at a maximum spacing of 36 inches (914 mm) on center.

1507.2.8.2 Ice dam membrane. In areas where there has been a history of ice forming along the eaves causing a backup of water, a membrane that consists of at least two layers of underlayment cemented together or of a self-adhering polymer modified bitumen sheet shall be used in lieu of normal underlayment and extend from the eave's edge to a point at least 24 inches (610 mm) inside the exterior wall line of the building.

> **Exception:** Detached accessory structures that contain no conditioned floor area.

1507.2.9 Flashings. Flashing for asphalt shingles shall comply with this section. Flashing shall be applied in accordance with this section and the asphalt shingle manufacturer's printed instructions.

1507.2.9.1 Base and cap flashing. Base and cap flashing shall be installed in accordance with the manufacturer's instructions. Base flashing shall be of either corrosion-resistant metal of minimum nominal 0.019-inch (0.483 mm) thickness or mineral-surfaced roll roofing weighing a minimum of 77 pounds per 100 square feet (3.76 kg/m²). Cap flashing shall be corrosion-resistant metal of minimum nominal 0.019-inch (0.483 mm) thickness.

1507.2.9.2 Valleys. Valley linings shall be installed in accordance with the manufacturer's instructions before applying shingles. Valley linings of the following types shall be permitted:

1. For open valleys (valley lining exposed) lined with metal, the valley lining shall be at least 16 inches (406 mm) wide and of any of the corrosion-resistant metals in Table 1507.2.9.2.

2. For open valleys, valley lining of two plies of mineral-surfaced roll roofing complying with ASTM D 3909 or ASTM D 6380 shall be permitted. The bottom layer shall be 18 inches (457 mm) and the top layer a minimum of 36 inches (914 mm) wide.

3. For closed valleys (valleys covered with shingles), valley lining of one ply of smooth roll roofing complying with ASTM D 6380, Class S Type III, Class M Type II or ASTM D 3909 and at least 36 inches (914 mm) wide or types as described in Items 1 and 2 above shall be permitted. Specialty underlayment shall comply with ASTM D 1970.

1507.2.9.3 Drip edge. Provide drip edge at eaves and gables of shingle roofs. Overlap to be a minimum of 2 inches (51 mm). Eave drip edges shall extend 0.25 inch (6.4 mm) below sheathing and extend back on the roof a minimum of 2 inches (51 mm). Drip edge shall be mechanically fastened a maximum of 12 inches (305 mm) o.c.

1507.2.9.4 Crickets and saddles. A cricket or saddle shall be installed on the ridge side of any chimney or penetration greater than 30 inches (762 mm) wide as measured perpendicular to the slope. Cricket or saddle coverings shall be sheet metal or of the same material as the roof covering.

1507.3 Clay and concrete tile. The installation of clay and concrete tile shall comply with the provisions of this section.

1507.3.1 Deck requirements. Concrete and clay tile shall be installed only over solid sheathing or spaced structural sheathing boards.

1507.3.2 Deck slope. Clay and concrete roof tile shall be installed on roof slopes of $2^1/_2$ units vertical in 12 units horizontal (21-percent slope) or greater. For roof slopes from $2^1/_2$ units vertical in 12 units horizontal (21-percent slope) to four units vertical in 12 units horizontal (33-percent slope), double underlayment application is required in accordance with Section 1507.3.3.

1507.3.3 Underlayment. Unless otherwise noted, required underlayment shall conform to: ASTM D 226, Type II; ASTM D 2626 or ASTM D 6380, Class M mineral-surfaced roll roofing.

1507.3.3.1 Low-slope roofs. For roof slopes from $2^1/_2$ units vertical in 12 units horizontal (21-percent slope), up to four units vertical in 12 units horizontal (33-percent slope), underlayment shall be a minimum of two layers applied as follows:

1. Starting at the eave, a 19-inch (483 mm) strip of underlayment shall be applied parallel with the eave and fastened sufficiently in place.

2. Starting at the eave, 36-inch-wide (914 mm) strips of underlayment felt shall be applied overlapping successive sheets 19 inches (483 mm) and fastened sufficiently in place.

1507.3.3.2 High-slope roofs. For roof slopes of four units vertical in 12 units horizontal (33-percent slope) or greater, underlayment shall be a minimum of one layer of underlayment felt applied shingle fashion, parallel to, and starting from the eaves and lapped 2 inches (51 mm), fastened only as necessary to hold in place.

1507.3.4 Clay tile. Clay roof tile shall comply with ASTM C 1167.

1507.3.5 Concrete tile. Concrete roof tile shall comply with ASTM C 1492.

1507.3.6 Fasteners. Tile fasteners shall be corrosion resistant and not less than 11 gage, $^5/_{16}$-inch (8.0 mm) head, and of sufficient length to penetrate the deck a minimum of 0.75 inch (19.1 mm) or through the thickness of the deck, whichever is less. Attaching wire for clay or concrete tile shall not be smaller than 0.083 inch (2.1 mm). Perimeter fastening areas include three tile courses but not less than 36 inches (914 mm) from either side of hips or ridges and edges of eaves and gable rakes.

1507.3.7 Attachment. Clay and concrete roof tiles shall be fastened in accordance with Table 1507.3.7.

1507.3.8 Application. Tile shall be applied according to the manufacturer's installation instructions, based on the following:

1. Climatic conditions.

TABLE 1507.2.9.2
VALLEY LINING MATERIAL

MATERIAL	MINIMUM THICKNESS	GAGE	WEIGHT
Aluminum	0.024 in.	-	-
Cold-rolled copper	0.0216 in.	-	ASTM B 370, 16 oz. per square ft.
Copper	-	-	16 oz
Galvanized steel	0.0179 in.	26 (zinc-coated G90)	-
High-yield copper	0.0162 in.	-	ASTM B 370, 12 oz. per square ft.
Lead	-	-	2.5 pounds
Lead-coated copper	0.0216 in.	-	ASTM B 101, 16 oz. per square ft.
Lead-coated high-yield copper	0.0162 in.	-	ASTM B 101, 12 oz. per square ft.
Painted terne	-	-	20 pounds
Stainless steel	-	28	-
Zinc alloy	0.027 in.	-	-

For SI: 1 inch = 25.4 mm, 1 pound = 0.454 kg, 1 ounce = 28.35 g.

TABLE 1507.3.7
CLAY AND CONCRETE TILE ATTACHMENT[a, b, c]

GENERAL—CLAY OR CONCRETE ROOF TILE			
Maximum basic wind speed (mph)	Mean roof height (feet)	Roof slope up to<3:12	Roof slope 3:12 and over
85	0-60	One fastener per tile. Flat tile without vertical laps, two fasteners per tile.	Two fasteners per tile. Only one fastener on slopes of 7:12 and less for tiles with installed weight exceeding 7.5 lbs./sq. ft. having a width no greater than 16 inches.
100	0-40		
100	> 40-60	The head of all tiles shall be nailed. The nose of all eave tiles shall be fastened with approved clips. All rake tiles shall be nailed with two nails. The nose of all ridge, hip and rake tiles shall be set in a bead of roofer's mastic.	
110	0-60	The fastening system shall resist the wind forces in Section 1609.5.2.	
120	0-60	The fastening system shall resist the wind forces in Section 1609.5.2.	
130	0-60	The fastening system shall resist the wind forces in Section 1609.5.2.	
All	> 60	The fastening system shall resist the wind forces in Section 1609.5.2.	

INTERLOCKING CLAY OR CONCRETE ROOF TILE WITH PROJECTING ANCHOR LUGS[d, e] (Installations on spaced/solid sheathing with battens or spaced sheathing)				
Maximum basic wind speed (mph)	Mean roof height (feet)	Roof slope up to<5:12	Roof slope 5:12<12:12	Roof slope 12:12 and over
85	0-60	Fasteners are not required. Tiles with installed weight less than 9 lbs./sq. ft. require a minimum of one fastener per tile.	One fastener per tile every other row. All perimeter tiles require one fastener. Tiles with installed weight less than 9 lbs./sq. ft. require a minimum of one fastener per tile.	One fastener required for every tile. Tiles with installed weight less than 9 lbs./sq. ft. require a minimum of one fastener per tile.
100	0-40			
100	> 40-60	The head of all tiles shall be nailed. The nose of all eave tiles shall be fastened with approved clips. All rake tiles shall be nailed with two nails The nose of all ridge, hip and rake tiles shall be set in a bead of roofers's mastic.		
110	0-60	The fastening system shall resist the wind forces in Section 1609.5.2.		
120	0-60	The fastening system shall resist the wind forces in Section 1609.5.2.		
130	0-60	The fastening system shall resist the wind forces in Section 1609.5.2.		
All	> 60	The fastening system shall resist the wind forces in Section 1609.5.2.		

INTERLOCKING CLAY OR CONCRETE ROOF TILE WITH PROJECTING ANCHOR LUGS (Installations on solid sheathing without battens)		
Maximum basic wind speed (mph)	Mean roof height (feet)	All roof slopes
85	0-60	One fastener per tile.
100	0-40	One fastener per tile.
100	> 40-60	The head of all tiles shall be nailed. The nose of all eave tiles shall be fastened with approved clips. All rake tiles shall be nailed with two nails The nose of all ridge, hip and rake tiles shall be set in a bead of roofer's mastic.
110	0-60	The fastening system shall resist the wind forces in Section 1609.5.2.
120	0-60	The fastening system shall resist the wind forces in Section 1609.5.2.
130	0-60	The fastening system shall resist the wind forces in Section 1609.5.2.
All	> 60	The fastening system shall resist the wind forces in Section 1609.5.2.

For SI: 1 inch = 25.4 mm, 1 foot = 304.8 mm, 1 mile per hour = 0.447 m/s, 1 pound per square foot = 4.882 kg/m^2.

a. Minimum fastener size. Corrosion-resistant nails not less than No. 11 gage with $5/16$-inch head. Fasteners shall be long enough to penetrate into the sheathing 0.75 inch or through the thickness of the sheathing, whichever is less. Attaching wire for clay and concrete tile shall not be smaller than 0.083 inch.

b. Snow areas. A minimum of two fasteners per tile are required or battens and one fastener.

c. Roof slopes greater than 24:12. The nose of all tiles shall be securely fastened.

d. Horizontal battens. Battens shall be not less than 1inch by 2 inch nominal. Provisions shall be made for drainage by a minimum of $1/8$-inch riser at each nail or by 4-foot-long battens with at least a 0.5-inch separation between battens. Horizontal battens are required for slopes over 7:12.

e. Perimeter fastening areas include three tile courses but not less than 36 inches from either side of hips or ridges and edges of eaves and gable rakes.

2. Roof slope.

3. Underlayment system.

4. Type of tile being installed.

1507.3.9 Flashing. At the juncture of the roof vertical surfaces, flashing and counterflashing shall be provided in accordance with the manufacturer's installation instructions, and where of metal, shall not be less than 0.019-inch (0.48 mm) (No. 26 galvanized sheet gage) corrosion-resistant metal. The valley flashing shall extend at least 11 inches (279 mm) from the centerline each way and have a splash diverter rib not less than 1 inch (25 mm) high at the flow line formed as part of the flashing. Sections of flashing shall have an end lap of not less than 4 inches (102 mm). For roof slopes of three units vertical in 12 units horizontal (25-percent slope) and over, the valley flashing shall have a 36-inch-wide (914 mm) underlayment of either one layer of Type I underlayment running the full length of the valley, or a self-adhering polymer-modified bitumen sheet complying with ASTM D 1970, in addition to other required underlayment. In areas where the average daily temperature in January is 25°F (-4°C) or less or where there is a possibility of ice forming along the eaves causing a backup of water, the metal valley flashing underlayment shall be solid cemented to the roofing underlayment for slopes under seven units vertical in 12 units horizontal (58-percent slope) or self-adhering polymer-modified bitumen sheet shall be installed.

1507.4 Metal roof panels. The installation of metal roof panels shall comply with the provisions of this section.

1507.4.1 Deck requirements. Metal roof panel roof coverings shall be applied to a solid or closely fitted deck, except where the roof covering is specifically designed to be applied to spaced supports.

1507.4.2 Deck slope. Minimum slopes for metal roof panels shall comply with the following:

1. The minimum slope for lapped, nonsoldered seam metal roofs without applied lap sealant shall be three units vertical in 12 units horizontal (25-percent slope).

2. The minimum slope for lapped, nonsoldered seam metal roofs with applied lap sealant shall be one-half unit vertical in 12 units horizontal (4-percent slope). Lap sealants shall be applied in accordance with the approved manufacturer's installation instructions.

3. The minimum slope for standing seam of roof systems shall be one-quarter unit vertical in 12 units horizontal (2-percent slope).

1507.4.3 Material standards. Metal-sheet roof covering systems that incorporate supporting structural members shall be designed in accordance with Chapter 22. Metal-sheet roof coverings installed over structural decking shall comply with Table 1507.4.3.(1). The materials used for metal-sheet roof coverings shall be naturally corrosion resistant or provided with corrosion resistance in accordance with the standards and minimum thicknesses shown in Table 1507.4.3(2).

TABLE 1507.4.3(1)
METAL ROOF COVERINGS

ROOF COVERING TYPE	STANDARD APPLICATION RATE/THICKNESS
Aluminum	ASTM B 209, 0.024 inch minimum thickness for roll-formed panels and 0.019 inch minimum thickness for press-formed shingles.
Aluminum-zinc alloy coated steel	ASTM A 792 AZ 50
Cold-rolled copper	ASTM B 370 minimum 16 oz./sq. ft. and 12 oz./sq. ft. high yield copper for metal-sheet roof covering systems: 12 oz./sq. ft. for preformed metal shingle systems.
Copper	16 oz./sq. ft. for metal-sheet roof-covering systems; 12 oz./sq. ft. for preformed metal shingle systems.
Galvanized steel	ASTM A 653 G-90 zinc-coated[a].
Hard lead	2 lbs./sq. ft.
Lead-coated copper	ASTM B 101
Prepainted steel	ASTM A 755
Soft lead	3 lbs./sq. ft.
Stainless steel	ASTM A 240, 300 Series Alloys
Steel	ASTM A 924
Terne and terne-coated stainless	Terne coating of 40 lbs. per double base box, field painted where applicable in accordance with manufacturer's installation instructions.
Zinc	0.027 inch minimum thickness; 99.995% electrolytic high grade zinc with alloy additives of copper (0.08% - 0.20%), titanium (0.07% - 0.12%) and aluminum (0.015%).

For SI: 1 ounce per square foot = 0.0026 kg/m^2, 1 pound per square foot = 4.882 kg/m^2, 1 inch = 25.4 mm, 1 pound = 0.454 kg.

a. For Group U buildings, the minimum coating thickness for ASTM A 653 galvanized steel roofing shall be G-60.

TABLE 1507.4.3(2)
MINIMUM CORROSION RESISTANCE

55% Aluminum-Zinc Alloy Coated Steel	ASTM A 792 AZ 50
5% Aluminum Alloy-coated steel	ASTM A875 GF60
Aluminum-coated steel	ASTM A463 T2 65
Galvanized Steel	ASTM A 653 G-90
Prepainted Steel	ASTM A 755[a]

a. Paint systems in accordance with ASTM A 755 shall be applied over steel products with corrosion resistant coatings complying with ASTM A 792, ASTM A 875, ASTM A 463, or ASTM A 653.

1507.4.4 Attachment. Metal roof panels shall be secured to the supports in accordance with the approved manufacturer's fasteners. In the absence of manufacturer recommendations, the following fasteners shall be used:

1. Galvanized fasteners shall be used for steel roofs.

2. 300 series stainless-steel fasteners shall be used for copper roofs.

3. Stainless-steel fasteners are acceptable for all types of metal roofs.

1507.5 Metal roof shingles. The installation of metal roof shingles shall comply with the provisions of this section.

1507.5.1 Deck requirements. Metal roof shingles shall be applied to a solid or closely fitted deck, except where the roof covering is specifically designed to be applied to spaced sheathing.

1507.5.2 Deck slope. Metal roof shingles shall not be installed on roof slopes below three units vertical in 12 units horizontal (25-percent slope).

1507.5.3 Underlayment. Underlayment shall comply with ASTM D 226, Type I or ASTM D 4869. In areas where there has been a history of ice forming along the eaves causing a backup of water, an ice barrier that consists of at least two layers of underlayment cemented together or of a self-adhering polymer-modified bitumen sheet shall be used in lieu of normal underlayment and extend from the eave's edge to a point at least 24 inches (610 mm) inside the exterior wall line of the building.

Exception: Detached accessory structures that contain no conditioned floor area.

1507.5.4 Material standards. Metal roof shingle roof coverings shall comply with Table 1507.4.3(1). The materials used for metal-roof shingle roof coverings shall be naturally corrosion resistant or provided with corrosion resistance in accordance with the standards and minimum thicknesses specified in the standards listed in Table 1507.4.3(2).

1507.5.5 Attachment. Metal roof shingles shall be secured to the roof in accordance with the approved manufacturer's installation instructions.

1507.5.6 Flashing. Roof valley flashing shall be of corrosion-resistant metal of the same material as the roof covering or shall comply with the standards in Table 1507.4.3(1). The valley flashing shall extend at least 8 inches (203 mm) from the centerline each way and shall have a splash diverter rib not less than 0.75 inch (19.1 mm) high at the flow line formed as part of the flashing. Sections of flashing shall have an end lap of not less than 4 inches (102 mm). In areas where the average daily temperature in January is 25°F (-4°C) or less or where there is a possibility of ice forming along the eaves causing a backup of water, the metal valley flashing shall have a 36-inch-wide (914 mm) underlayment directly under it consisting of either one layer of underlayment running the full length of the valley or a self-adhering polymer-modified bitumen sheet complying with ASTM D 1970, in addition to underlayment required for metal roof shingles. The metal valley flashing underlayment shall be solidly cemented to the roofing underlayment for roof slopes under seven units vertical in 12 units horizontal (58-percent slope) or self-adhering polymer-modified bitumen sheet shall be installed.

1507.6 Mineral-surfaced roll roofing. The installation of mineral-surfaced roll roofing shall comply with this section.

1507.6.1 Deck requirements. Mineral-surfaced roll roofing shall be fastened to solidly sheathed roofs.

1507.6.2 Deck slope. Mineral-surfaced roll roofing shall not be applied on roof slopes below one unit vertical in 12 units horizontal (8-percent slope).

1507.6.3 Underlayment. Underlayment shall comply with ASTM D 226, Type I or ASTM D 4869. In areas where there has been a history of ice forming along the eaves causing a backup of water, an ice barrier that consists of at least two layers of underlayment cemented together or of a self-adhering polymer-modified bitumen sheet shall be used in lieu of normal underlayment and extend from the eave's edge to a point at least 24 inches (610 mm) inside the exterior wall line of the building.

Exception: Detached accessory structures that contain no conditioned floor area.

1507.6.4 Material standards. Mineral-surfaced roll roofing shall conform to ASTM D 3909 or ASTM D 6380.

1507.7 Slate shingles. The installation of slate shingles shall comply with the provisions of this section.

1507.7.1 Deck requirements. Slate shingles shall be fastened to solidly sheathed roofs.

1507.7.2 Deck slope. Slate shingles shall only be used on slopes of four units vertical in 12 units horizontal (4:12) or greater.

1507.7.3 Underlayment. Underlayment shall comply with ASTM D 226, Type I or ASTM D 4869. In areas where the average daily temperature in January is 25°F (-4°C) or less or where there is a possibility of ice forming along the eaves causing a backup of water, an ice barrier that consists of at least two layers of underlayment cemented together or of a self-adhering polymer-modified bitumen sheet shall extend from the eave's edge to a point at least 24 inches (610 mm) inside the exterior wall line of the building.

Exception: Detached accessory structures that contain no conditioned floor area.

1507.7.4 Material standards. Slate shingles shall comply with ASTM C 406.

1507.7.5 Application. Minimum headlap for slate shingles shall be in accordance with Table 1507.7.5. Slate shingles shall be secured to the roof with two fasteners per slate.

1507.7.6 Flashing. Flashing and counterflashing shall be made with sheet metal. Valley flashing shall be a minimum of 15 inches (381 mm) wide. Valley and flashing metal shall be a minimum uncoated thickness of 0.0179-

TABLE 1507.7.5
SLATE SHINGLE HEADLAP

SLOPE	HEADLAP (inches)
4:12 < slope < 8:12	4
8:12 < slope < 20:12	3
slope ≥ 20:12	2

For SI: 1 inch = 25.4 mm.

inch (0.455 mm) zinc-coated G90. Chimneys, stucco or brick walls shall have a minimum of two plies of felt for a cap flashing consisting of a 4-inch-wide (102 mm) strip of felt set in plastic cement and extending 1 inch (25 mm) above the first felt and a top coating of plastic cement. The felt shall extend over the base flashing 2 inches (51 mm).

1507.8 Wood shingles. The installation of wood shingles shall comply with the provisions of this section and Table 1507.8.

1507.8.1 Deck requirements. Wood shingles shall be installed on solid or spaced sheathing. Where spaced sheathing is used, sheathing boards shall not be less than 1-inch by 4-inch (25 mm by 102 mm) nominal dimensions and shall be spaced on centers equal to the weather exposure to coincide with the placement of fasteners.

1507.8.1.1 Solid sheathing required. Solid sheathing is required in areas where the average daily temperature in January is 25°F (-4°C) or less or where there is a possibility of ice forming along the eaves causing a backup of water.

1507.8.2 Deck slope. Wood shingles shall be installed on slopes of three units vertical in 12 units horizontal (25-percent slope) or greater.

1507.8.3 Underlayment. Underlayment shall comply with ASTM D 226, Type I or ASTM D 4869. In areas where there has been a history of ice forming along the eaves causing a backup of water, an ice barrier that consists of at least two layers of underlayment cemented together or of a self-adhering polymer-modified bitumen sheet shall be used in lieu of normal underlayment and extend from the eave's edge to a point at least 24 inches (610 mm) inside the exterior wall line of the building.

Exception: Detached accessory structures that contain no conditioned floor area.

1507.8.4 Material standards. Wood shingles shall be of naturally durable wood and comply with the requirements of Table 1507.8.4.

1507.8.5 Attachment. Fasteners for wood shingles shall be corrosion resistant with a minimum penetration of 0.75 inch (19.1 mm) into the sheathing. For sheathing less than 0.5 inch (12.7 mm) in thickness, the fasteners shall extend through the sheathing. Each shingle shall be attached with a minimum of two fasteners.

1507.8.6 Application. Wood shingles shall be laid with a side lap not less than 1.5 inches (38 mm) between joints in adjacent courses, and not be in direct alignment in alternate courses. Spacing between shingles shall be 0.25 to 0.375 inches (6.4 to 9.5 mm). Weather exposure for wood shingles shall not exceed that set in Table 1507.8.6.

1507.8.7 Flashing. At the juncture of the roof and vertical surfaces, flashing and counterflashing shall be provided in accordance with the manufacturer's installation instructions, and where of metal, shall not be less than 0.019-inch

(0.48 mm) (No. 26 galvanized sheet gage) corrosion-resistant metal. The valley flashing shall extend at least 11 inches (279 mm) from the centerline each way and have a splash diverter rib not less than 1 inch (25 mm) high at the flow line formed as part of the flashing. Sections of flashing shall have an end lap of not less than 4 inches (102 mm). For roof slopes of three units vertical in 12 units horizontal (25-percent slope) and over, the valley flashing shall have a 36-inch-wide (914 mm) underlayment of either one layer of Type I underlayment running the full length of the valley or a self-adhering polymer-modified bitumen sheet complying with ASTM D 1970, in addition to other required underlayment. In areas where the average daily temperature in January is 25°F (-4°C) or less or where there is a possibility of ice forming along the eaves causing a backup of water, the metal valley flashing underlayment shall be solidly cemented to the roofing underlayment for slopes under seven units vertical in 12 units horizontal (58-percent slope) or self-adhering polymer-modified bitumen sheet shall be installed.

1507.9 Wood shakes. The installation of wood shakes shall comply with the provisions of this section and Table 1507.8.

1507.9.1 Deck requirements. Wood shakes shall only be used on solid or spaced sheathing. Where spaced sheathing is used, sheathing boards shall not be less than 1-inch by 4-inch (25 mm by 102 mm) nominal dimensions and shall be spaced on centers equal to the weather exposure to coincide with the placement of fasteners. Where 1-inch by 4-inch (25 mm by 102 mm) spaced sheathing is installed at 10 inches (254 mm) o.c., additional 1-inch by 4-inch (25 mm by 102 mm) boards shall be installed between the sheathing boards.

1507.9.1.1 Solid sheathing required. Solid sheathing is required in areas where the average daily temperature in January is 25°F (-4°C) or less or where there is a possibility of ice forming along the eaves causing a backup of water.

1507.9.2 Deck slope. Wood shakes shall only be used on slopes of four units vertical in 12 units horizontal (33-percent slope) or greater.

1507.9.3 Underlayment. Underlayment shall comply with ASTM D 226, Type I or ASTM D 4869. In areas where there has been a history of ice forming along the eaves causing a backup of water, an ice barrier that consists of at least two layers of underlayment cemented together or of a self-adhering polymer-modified bitumen sheet shall be used in lieu of normal underlayment and extend from the eave's edge to a point at least 24 inches (610 mm) inside the exterior wall line of the building.

Exception: Detached accessory structures that contain no conditioned floor area.

1507.9.4 Interlayment. Interlayment shall comply with ASTM D 226, Type I.

TABLE 1507.8
WOOD SHINGLE AND SHAKE INSTALLATION

ROOF ITEM	WOOD SHINGLES	WOOD SHAKES
1. Roof slope	Wood shingles shall be installed on slopes of three units vertical in 12 units horizontal (3:12) or greater.	Wood shakes shall be installed on slopes of four units vertical in 12 units horizontal (4:12) or greater.
2. Deck requirement	—	—
Temperate climate	Shingles shall be applied to roofs with solid or spaced sheathing. Where spaced sheathing is used, sheathing boards shall not be less than 1″ × 4″ nominal dimensions and shall be spaced on center equal to the weather exposure to coincide with the placement of fasteners.	Shakes shall be applied to roofs with solid or spaced sheathing. Where spaced sheathing is used, sheathing boards shall not be less than 1″ × 4″ nominal dimensions and shall be spaced on center equal to the weather exposure to coincide with the placement of fasteners. When 1″ × 4″ spaced sheathing is installed at 10 inches, boards must be installed between the sheathing boards.
In areas where the average daily temperature in January is 25°F or less or where there is a possibility of ice forming along the eaves causing a backup of water.	Solid sheathing required.	Solid sheathing is required.
3. Interlayment	No requirements.	Interlayment shall comply with ASTM D 226, Type 1.
4. Underlayment	—	—
Temperate climate	Underlayment shall comply with ASTM D 226, Type 1.	Underlayment shall comply with ASTM D 226, Type 1.
In areas where there is a possibility of ice forming along the eaves causing a backup of water.	An ice shield that consists of at least two layers of underlayment cemented together or of a self-adhering polymer-modified bitumen sheet shall extend from the eave's edge to a point at least 24 inches inside the exterior wall line of the building.	An ice shield that consists of at least two layers of underlayment cemented together or of a self-adhering polymer-modified bitumen sheet shall extend from the eave's edge to a point at least 24 inches inside the exterior wall line of the building.
5. Application	—	—
Attachment	Fasteners for wood shingles shall be corrosion resistant with a minimum penetration of 0.75 inch into the sheathing. For sheathing less than 0.5 inch thick, the fasteners shall extend through the sheathing.	Fasteners for wood shakes shall be corrosion resistant with a minimum penetration of 0.75 inch into the sheathing. For sheathing less than 0.5 inch thick, the fasteners shall extend through the sheathing.
No. of fasteners	Two per shingle.	Two per shake.
Exposure	Weather exposures shall not exceed those set forth in Table 1507.8.6	Weather exposures shall not exceed those set forth in Table 1507.9.7
Method	Shingles shall be laid with a side lap of not less than 1.5 inches between joints in courses, and no two joints in any three adjacent courses shall be in direct alignment. Spacing between shingles shall be 0.25 to 0.375 inch.	Shakes shall be laid with a side lap of not less than 1.5 inches between joints in adjacent courses. Spacing between shakes shall not be less than 0.375 inch or more than 0.625 inch for shakes and tapersawn shakes of naturally durable wood and shall be 0.25 to 0.375 inch for preservative taper sawn shakes.
Flashing	In accordance with Section 1507.8.7.	In accordance with Section 1507.9.8.

For SI: 1 inch = 25.4 mm, °C = [(°F) - 32]/1.8.

TABLE 1507.8.4
WOOD SHINGLE MATERIAL REQUIREMENTS

MATERIAL	APPLICABLE MINIMUM GRADES	GRADING RULES
Wood shingles of naturally durable wood	1, 2 or 3	CSSB

CSSB = Cedar Shake and Shingle Bureau

TABLE 1507.8.6 WOOD
SHINGLE WEATHER EXPOSURE AND ROOF SLOPE

ROOFING MATERIAL	LENGTH (inches)	GRADE	EXPOSURE (inches)	
			3:12 pitch to < 4:12	4:12 pitch or steeper
Shingles of naturally durable wood	16	No. 1	3.75	5
		No. 2	3.5	4
		No. 3	3	3.5
	18	No. 1	4.25	5.5
		No. 2	4	4.5
		No. 3	3.5	4
	24	No. 1	5.75	7.5
		No. 2	5.5	6.5
		No. 3	5	5.5

For SI: 1 inch = 25.4 mm.

TABLE 1507.9.5
WOOD SHAKE MATERIAL REQUIREMENTS

MATERIAL	MINIMUM GRADES	APPLICABLE GRADING RULES
Wood shakes of naturally durable wood	1	CSSB
Taper sawn shakes of naturally durable wood	1 or 2	CSSB
Preservative-treated shakes and shingles of naturally durable wood	1	CSSB
Fire-retardant-treated shakes and shingles of naturally durable wood	1	CSSB
Preservative-treated taper sawn shakes of Southern pine treated in accordance with AWPA U1 (Commodity Specification A, Use Category 3B andSection5.6)	1 or 2	TFS

CSSB = Cedar Shake and Shingle Bureau.

TFS = Forest Products Laboratory of the Texas Forest Services.

1507.9.5 Material standards. Wood shakes shall comply with the requirements of Table 1507.9.5.

1507.9.6 Attachment. Fasteners for wood shakes shall be corrosion resistant with a minimum penetration of 0.75 inch (19.1 mm) into the sheathing. For sheathing less than 0.5 inch (12.7 mm) in thickness, the fasteners shall extend through the sheathing. Each shake shall be attached with a minimum of two fasteners.

1507.9.7 Application. Wood shakes shall be laid with a side lap not less than 1.5 inches (38 mm) between joints in adjacent courses. Spacing between shakes in the same course shall be 0.375 to 0.625 inches (9.5 to 15.9 mm) for shakes and taper sawn shakes of naturally durable wood and shall be 0.25 to 0.375 inch (6.4 to 9.5 mm) for preservative taper sawn shakes. Weather exposure for wood

TABLE 1507.9.7
WOOD SHAKE WEATHER EXPOSURE AND ROOF SLOPE

ROOFING MATERIAL	LENGTH (inches)	GRADE	EXPOSURE (inches) 4:12 PITCH OR STEEPER
Shakes of naturally durable wood	18	No. 1	7.5
	24	No. 1	10[a]
Preservative-treated taper sawn shakes of Southern yellow pine	18	No. 1	7.5
	24	No. 1	10
	18	No. 2	5.5
	24	No. 2	7.5
Taper sawn shakes of naturally durable wood	18	No. 1	7.5
	24	No. 1	10
	18	No. 2	5.5
	24	No. 2	7.5

For SI: 1 inch = 25.4 mm.

a. For 24-inch by 0.375-inch handsplit shakes, the maximum exposure is 7.5 inches.

shakes shall not exceed those set in Table 1507.9.7.

1507.9.8 Flashing. At the juncture of the roof and vertical surfaces, flashing and counterflashing shall be provided in accordance with the manufacturer's installation instruc-

tions, and where of metal, shall not be less than 0.019-inch (0.48 mm) (No. 26 galvanized sheet gage) corrosion-resistant metal. The valley flashing shall extend at least 11 inches (279 mm) from the centerline each way and have a splash diverter rib not less than 1 inch (25 mm) high at the flow line formed as part of the flashing. Sections of flashing shall have an end lap of not less than 4 inches (102 mm). For roof slopes of three units vertical in 12 units horizontal (25-percent slope) and over, the valley flashing shall have a 36-inch-wide (914 mm) underlayment of either one layer of Type I underlayment running the full length of the valley or a self-adhering polymer-modified bitumen sheet complying with ASTM D 1970, in addition to other required underlayment. In areas where the average daily temperature in January is 25°F (-4°C) or less or where there is a possibility of ice forming along the eaves causing a backup of water, the metal valley flashing underlayment shall be solidly cemented to the roofing underlayment for slopes under seven units vertical in 12 units horizontal (58-percent slope) or self-adhering polymer-modified bitumen sheet shall be installed.

1507.10 Built-up roofs. The installation of built-up roofs shall comply with the provisions of this section.

TABLE 1507.10.2
BUILT-UP ROOFING MATERIAL STANDARDS

MATERIAL STANDARD	STANDARD
Acrylic coatings used in roofing	ASTM D 6083
Aggregate surfacing	ASTM D 1863
Asphalt adhesive used in roofing	ASTM D 3747
Asphalt cements used in roofing	ASTM D 3019; D 2822; D 4586
Asphalt-coated glass fiber base sheet	ASTM D 4601
Asphalt coatings used in roofing	ASTM D1227; D 2823; D 4479
Asphalt glass felt	ASTM D 2178
Asphalt primer used in roofing	ASTM D 41
Asphalt-saturated and asphalt-coated organic felt base sheet	ASTM D 2626
Asphalt-saturated organic felt (perforated)	ASTM D 226
Asphalt used in roofing	ASTM D 312
Coal-tar cements used in roofing	ASTM D 4022; D 5643
Coal-tar saturated organic felt	ASTM D 227
Coal-tar pitch used in roofing	ASTM D 450; Type I or II
Coal-tar primer used in roofing, dampproofing and waterproofing	ASTM D 43
Glass mat, coal tar	ASTM D 4990
Glass mat, venting type	ASTM D 4897
Mineral-surfaced inorganic cap sheet	ASTM D 3909
Thermoplastic fabrics used in roofing	ASTM D 5665, D 5726

1507.10.1 Slope. Built-up roofs shall have a design slope of a minimum of one-fourth unit vertical in 12 units horizontal (2-percent slope) for drainage, except for coal-tar built-up roofs that shall have a design slope of a minimum one-eighth unit vertical in 12 units horizontal (1-percent slope).

1507.10.2 Material standards. Built-up roof covering materials shall comply with the standards in Table 1507.10.2.

1507.11 Modified bitumen roofing. The installation of modified bitumen roofing shall comply with the provisions of this section.

1507.11.1 Slope. Modified bitumen membrane roofs shall have a design slope of a minimum of one-fourth unit vertical in 12 units horizontal (2-percent slope) for drainage.

1507.11.2 Material standards. Modified bitumen roof coverings shall comply with CGSB 37-GP-56M, ASTM D 6162, ASTM D 6163, ASTM D 6164, ASTM D 6222, ASTM D 6223 or ASTM D 6298.

1507.12 Thermoset single-ply roofing. The installation of thermoset single-ply roofing shall comply with the provisions of this section.

1507.12.1 Slope. Thermoset single-ply membrane roofs shall have a design slope of a minimum of one-fourth unit vertical in 12 units horizontal (2-percent slope) for drainage.

1507.12.2 Material standards. Thermoset single-ply roof coverings shall comply with ASTM D 4637, ASTM D 5019 or CGSB 37-GP-52M.

1507.13 Thermoplastic single-ply roofing. The installation of thermoplastic single-ply roofing shall comply with the provisions of this section.

1507.13.1 Slope. Thermoplastic single-ply membrane roofs shall have a design slope of a minimum of one-fourth unit vertical in 12 units horizontal (2-percent slope).

1507.13.2 Material standards. Thermoplastic single-ply roof coverings shall comply with ASTM D 4434, ASTM D 6754, ASTM D 6878 or CGSB CAN/CGSB 37-54.

1507.14 Sprayed polyurethane foam roofing. The installation of sprayed polyurethane foam roofing shall comply with the provisions of this section.

1507.14.1 Slope. Sprayed polyurethane foam roofs shall have a design slope of a minimum of one-fourth unit vertical in 12 units horizontal (2-percent slope) for drainage.

1507.14.2 Material standards. Spray-applied polyurethane foam insulation shall comply with ASTM C 1029.

1507.14.3 Application. Foamed-in-place roof insulation shall be installed in accordance with the manufacturer's instructions. A liquid-applied protective coating that complies with Section 1507.15 shall be applied no less than 2 hours nor more than 72 hours following the application of the foam.

1507.14.4 Foam plastics. Foam plastic materials and installation shall comply with Chapter 26.

1507.15 Liquid-applied coatings. The installation of liquid-applied coatings shall comply with the provisions of this section.

1507.15.1 Slope. Liquid-applied roofs shall have a design slope of a minimum of one-fourth unit vertical in 12 units horizontal (2-percent slope).

1507.15.2 Material standards. Liquid-applied roof coatings shall comply with ASTM C 836, ASTM C 957, ASTM D 1227 or ASTM D 3468, ASTM D 6083 or ASTM D 6694.

SECTION 1508
ROOF INSULATION

1508.1 General. The use of above-deck thermal insulation shall be permitted provided such insulation is covered with an approved roof covering and passes the tests of FM 4450 or UL 1256 when tested as an assembly.

Exceptions:

1. Foam plastic roof insulation shall conform to the material and installation requirements of Chapter 26.

2. Where a concrete roof deck is used and the above-deck thermal insulation is covered with an approved roof covering.

1508.1.1 Cellulosic fiberboard. Cellulosic fiberboard roof insulation shall conform to the material and installation requirements of Chapter 23.

1508.2 Material standards. Above-deck thermal insulation board shall comply with the standards in Table 1508.2.

TABLE 1508.2
MATERIAL STANDARDS FOR ROOF INSULATION

Cellular glass board	ASTM C 552
Composite boards	ASTM C 1289, Type III, IV, V or VI
Expanded polystyrene	ASTM C 578
Extruded polystyrene board	ASTM C 578
Perlite board	ASTM C 728
Polyisocyanurate board	ASTM C 1289, Type I or Type II
Wood fiberboard	ASTM C 208

SECTION 1509
ROOFTOP STRUCTURES

1509.1 General. The provisions of this section shall govern the construction of rooftop structures.

1509.2 Penthouses. A penthouse or other projection above the roof in structures of other than Type I construction shall not exceed 28 feet (8534 mm) above the roof where used as an enclosure for tanks or for elevators that run to the roof and in all other cases shall not extend more than 18 feet (5486 mm) above the roof. The aggregate area of penthouses and other rooftop structures shall not exceed one-third the area of the supporting roof. A penthouse, bulkhead or any other similar projection above the roof shall not be used for purposes other than shelter of mechanical equipment or shelter of vertical shaft openings in the roof. Provisions such as louvers, louver blades or flashing shall be made to protect the mechanical equipment and the building interior from the elements. Penthouses or bulkheads used for purposes other than permitted by this section shall conform to the requirements of this code for an additional story. The restrictions of this section shall not prohibit the placing of wood flagpoles or similar structures on the roof of any building.

1509.2.1 Type of construction. Penthouses shall be constructed with walls, floors and roof as required for the building.

Exceptions:

1. On buildings of Type I and II construction, the exterior walls and roofs of penthouses with a fire separation distance of more than 5 feet (1524 mm) and less than 20 feet (6096 mm) shall be of at least 1-hour fire-resistance-rated noncombustible construction. Walls and roofs with a fire separation distance of 20 feet (6096 mm) or greater shall be of noncombustible construction. Interior framing and walls shall be of noncombustible construction.

2. On buildings of Type III, IV and V construction, the exterior walls of penthouses with a fire separation distance of more than 5 feet (1524 mm) and less than 20 feet (6096 mm) shall be at least 1-hour fire-resistance-rated construction. Walls with a fire separation distance of 20 feet (6096 mm) or greater from a common property line shall be of Type IV or noncombustible construction. Roofs shall be constructed of materials and fire-resistance rated as required in Table 601. Interior framing and walls shall be Type IV or noncombustible construction.

3. Unprotected noncombustible enclosures housing only mechanical equipment and located with a minimum fire separation distance of 20 feet (6096 mm) shall be permitted.

4. On one-story buildings, combustible unroofed mechanical equipment screens, fences or similar enclosures are permitted where located with a fire separation distance of at least 20 feet (6096 mm) from adjacent property lines and where not exceeding 4 feet (1219 mm) in height above the roof surface.

5. Dormers shall be of the same type of construction as the roof on which they are placed, or of the exterior walls of the building.

1509.3 Tanks. Tanks having a capacity of more than 500 gallons (2 m^3) placed in or on a building shall be supported on masonry, reinforced concrete, steel or Type IV construction provided that, where such supports are located in the building above the lowest story, the support shall be fire-resistance rated as required for Type IA construction.

1509.3.1 Valve. Such tanks shall have in the bottom or on the side near the bottom, a pipe or outlet, fitted with a suitable quick opening valve for discharging the contents in an emergency through an adequate drain.

1509.3.2 Location. Such tanks shall not be placed over or near a line of stairs or an elevator shaft, unless there is a solid roof or floor underneath the tank.

1509.3.3 Tank cover. Unenclosed roof tanks shall have covers sloping toward the outer edges.

1509.4 Cooling towers. Cooling towers in excess of 250 square feet (23.2 m^2) in base area or in excess of 15 feet (4572 mm) high where located on building roofs more than 50 feet (15 240 mm) high shall be of noncombustible construction. Cooling towers shall not exceed one-third of the supporting roof area.

Exception: Drip boards and the enclosing construction of wood not less than 1 inch (25 mm) nominal thickness, provided the wood is covered on the exterior of the tower with noncombustible material.

1509.5 Towers, spires, domes and cupolas. Any tower, spire, dome or cupola shall be of a type of construction not less in fire-resistance rating than required for the building to which it is attached, except that any such tower, spire, dome or cupola that exceeds 85 feet (25 908 mm) in height above grade plane, exceeds 200 square feet (18.6 m^2) in horizontal area or is used for any purpose other than a belfry or an architectural embellishment shall be constructed of and supported on Type I or II construction.

1509.5.1 Noncombustible construction required. Any tower, spire, dome or cupola that exceeds 60 feet (18 288) in height above the highest point at which it comes in contact with the roof, or that exceeds 200 square feet (18.6 m^2) in area at any horizontal section, or which is intended to be used for any purpose other than a belfry or architectural embellishment, shall be entirely constructed of and supported by noncombustible materials. Such structures shall be separated from the building below by construction having a fire-resistance rating of not less than 1.5 hours with openings protected with a minimum 1.5-hour fire-protection rating. Structures, except aerial supports 12 feet (3658 mm) high or less, flagpoles, water tanks and cooling towers, placed above the roof of any building more than 50 feet (15 240 mm) in height, shall be of noncombustible material and shall be supported by construction of noncombustible material.

1509.5.2 Towers and spires. Towers and spires where enclosed shall have exterior walls as required for the building to which they are attached. The roof covering of spires shall be of a class of roof covering as required for the main roof of the rest of the structure.

SECTION 1510
REROOFING

1510.1 General. Materials and methods of application used for recovering or replacing an existing roof covering shall comply with the requirements of the *Existing Building Code of New York State.*

CHAPTER 16

STRUCTURAL DESIGN

SECTION 1601
GENERAL

1601.1 Scope. The provisions of this chapter shall govern the structural design of buildings, structures and portions thereof regulated by this code.

SECTION 1602
DEFINITIONS AND NOTATIONS

1602.1 Definitions. The following words and terms shall, for the purposes of this chapter, have the meanings shown herein.

ALLOWABLE STRESS DESIGN. A method of proportioning structural members, such that elastically computed stresses produced in the members by nominal loads do not exceed specified allowable stresses (also called "working stress design").

BALCONY, EXTERIOR. An exterior floor projecting from and supported by a structure without additional independent supports.

DEAD LOADS. The weight of materials of construction incorporated into the building, including but not limited to walls, floors, roofs, ceilings, stairways, built-in partitions, finishes, cladding and other similarly incorporated architectural and structural items, and the weight of fixed service equipment, such as cranes, plumbing stacks and risers, electrical feeders, heating, ventilating and air-conditioning systems and fire sprinkler systems.

DECK. An exterior floor supported on at least two opposing sides by an adjacent structure, and/or posts, piers or other independent supports.

DESIGN STRENGTH. The product of the nominal strength and a resistance factor (or strength reduction factor).

DIAPHRAGM. A horizontal or sloped system acting to transmit lateral forces to the vertical-resisting elements. When the term "diaphragm" is used, it shall include horizontal bracing systems.

Diaphragm, blocked. In light-frame construction, a diaphragm in which all sheathing edges not occurring on a framing member are supported on and fastened to blocking.

Diaphragm boundary. In light-frame construction, a location where shear is transferred into or out of the diaphragm sheathing. Transfer is either to a boundary element or to another force-resisting element.

Diaphragm chord. A diaphragm boundary element perpendicular to the applied load that is assumed to take axial stresses due to the diaphragm moment.

Diaphragm flexible. A diaphragm is flexible for the purpose of distribution of story shear and torsional moment where so indicated in Section 12.3.1 of ASCE 7, as modified in Section 1613.6.1.

Diaphragm, rigid. A diaphragm is rigid for the purpose of distribution of story shear and torsional moment when the lateral deformation of the diaphragm is less than or equal to two times the average story drift.

DURATION OF LOAD. The period of continuous application of a given load, or the aggregate of periods of intermittent applications of the same load.

ESSENTIAL FACILITIES. Buildings and other structures that are intended to remain operational in the event of extreme environmental loading from flood, wind, snow or earthquakes.

FABRIC PARTITIONS. A partition consisting of a finished surface made of fabric, without a continuous rigid backing, that is directly attached to a framing system in which the vertical framing members are spaced greater than 4 feet (1219 mm) on center.

FACTORED LOAD. The product of a nominal load and a load factor.

GUARD. See Section 1002.1.

IMPACT LOAD. The load resulting from moving machinery, elevators, craneways, vehicles and other similar forces and kinetic loads, pressure and possible surcharge from fixed or moving loads.

LIMIT STATE. A condition beyond which a structure or member becomes unfit for service and is judged to be no longer useful for its intended function (serviceability limit state) or to be unsafe (strength limit state).

LIVE LOADS. Those loads produced by the use and occupancy of the building or other structure and do not include construction or environmental loads such as wind load, snow load, rain load, earthquake load, flood load or dead load.

LIVE LOADS (ROOF). Those loads produced (1) during maintenance by workers, equipment and materials; and (2) during the life of the structure by movable objects such as planters and by people.

LOAD AND RESISTANCE FACTOR DESIGN (LRFD). A method of proportioning structural members and their connections using load and resistance factors such that no applicable limit state is reached when the structure is subjected to appropriate load combinations. The term "LRFD" is used in the design of steel and wood structures.

LOAD EFFECTS. Forces and deformations produced in structural members by the applied loads.

LOAD FACTOR. A factor that accounts for deviations of the actual load from the nominal load, for uncertainties in the analysis that transforms the load into a load effect, and for the probability that more than one extreme load will occur simultaneously.

LOADS. Forces or other actions that result from the weight of building materials, occupants and their possessions, environmental effects, differential movement and restrained dimensional changes. Permanent loads are those loads in which variations over time are rare or of small magnitude, such as dead loads. All other loads are variable loads (see also "Nominal loads").

NOMINAL LOADS. The magnitudes of the loads specified in this chapter (dead, live, soil, wind, snow, rain, flood and earthquake).

OCCUPANCY CATEGORY. A category used to determine structural requirements based on occupancy.

OTHER STRUCTURES. Structures, other than buildings, for which loads are specified in this chapter.

PANEL (PART OF A STRUCTURE). The section of a floor, wall or roof comprised between the supporting frame of two adjacent rows of columns and girders or column bands of floor or roof construction.

RESISTANCE FACTOR. A factor that accounts for deviations of the actual strength from the nominal strength and the manner and consequences of failure (also called "strength reduction factor").

STRENGTH, NOMINAL. The capacity of a structure or member to resist the effects of loads, as determined by computations using specified material strengths and dimensions and equations derived from accepted principles of structural mechanics or by field tests or laboratory tests of scaled models, allowing for modeling effects and differences between laboratory and field conditions.

STRENGTH, REQUIRED. Strength of a member, cross section or connection required to resist factored loads or related internal moments and forces in such combinations as stipulated by these provisions.

STRENGTH DESIGN. A method of proportioning structural members such that the computed forces produced in the members by factored loads do not exceed the member design strength [also called "load and resistance factor design" (LRFD)]. The term "strength design" is used in the design of concrete and masonry structural elements.

VEHICLE BARRIER SYSTEM. A system of building components near open sides of a garage floor or ramp or building walls that act as restraints for vehicles.

NOTATIONS.

D = Dead load.

E = Combined effect of horizontal and vertical earthquake induced forces as defined in Section 12.4.2 of ASCE 7.

E_m = Maximum seismic load effect of horizontal and vertical seismic forces as set forth in Section 12.4.3 of ASCE 7.

F = Load due to fluids with well-defined pressures and maximum heights.

F_a = Flood load.

H = Load due to lateral earth pressures, ground water pressure or pressure of bulk materials.

L = Live load, except roof live load, including any permitted live load reduction.

L_r = Roof live load including any permitted live load reduction.

R = Rain load.

S = Snow load.

T = Self-straining force arising from contraction or expansion resulting from temperature change, shrinkage, moisture change, creep in component materials, movement due to differential settlement or combinations thereof.

W = Load due to wind pressure.

SECTION 1603
CONSTRUCTION DOCUMENTS

1603.1 General. Construction documents shall show the size, section and relative locations of structural members with floor levels, column centers and offsets dimensioned. The design loads and other information pertinent to the structural design required by Sections 1603.1.1 through 1603.1.8 shall be indicated on the construction documents.

Exception: Construction documents for buildings constructed in accordance with the conventional light-frame construction provisions of Section 2308 shall indicate the following structural design information:

1. Floor and roof live loads.

2. Ground snow load, P_g.

3. Basic wind speed (3-second gust), miles per hour (mph) (km/hr) and wind exposure.

4. Seismic design category and site class.

5. Flood design data, if located in flood hazard areas established in Section 1612.3.

1603.1.1 Floor live load. The uniformly distributed, concentrated and impact floor live load used in the design shall be indicated for floor areas. Use of live load reduction in accordance with Section 1607.9 shall be indicated for each type of live load used in the design.

1603.1.2 Roof live load. The roof live load used in the design shall be indicated for roof areas (Section 1607.11).

1603.1.3 Roof snow load. The ground snow load, P_g, shall be indicated. In areas where the ground snow load, P_g, exceeds 10 pounds per square foot (psf) (0.479 kN/m^2), the following additional information shall also be provided, regardless of whether snow loads govern the design of the roof:

1. Flat-roof snow load, P_f.

2. Snow exposure factor, C_e.

3. Snow load importance factor, I.

4. Thermal factor, C_t.

1603.1.4 Wind design data. The following information related to wind loads shall be shown, regardless of whether wind loads govern the design of the lateral-force-resisting system of the building:

1. Basic wind speed (3-second gust), miles per hour (km/hr).

2. Wind importance factor, I, and occupancy category.

3. Wind exposure, if more than one wind exposure is utilized, the wind exposure and applicable wind direction shall be indicated.

4. The applicable internal pressure coefficient.

5. Components and cladding. The design wind pressures in terms of psf (kN/m^2) to be used for the design of exterior component and cladding materials not specifically designed by the registered design professional.

1603.1.5 Earthquake design data. The following information related to seismic loads shall be shown, regardless of whether seismic loads govern the design of the lateral-force-resisting system of the building:

1. Seismic importance factor, I, and occupancy category.

2. Mapped spectral response accelerations, S_S and S_1.

3. Site class.

4. Spectral response coefficients, S_{DS} and S_{D1}.

5. Seismic design category.

6. Basic seismic-force-resisting system(s).

7. Design base shear.

8. Seismic response coefficient(s), C_S.

9. Response modification factor(s), R.

10. Analysis procedure used.

1603.1.6 Flood design data. For buildings located in whole or in part in flood hazard areas as established in Section 1612.3, the documentation pertaining to design, if required in Section 1612.5, shall be included and the following information, referenced to the datum on the community's Flood Insurance Rate Map (FIRM), shall be shown, regardless of whether flood loads govern the design of the building:

1. In flood hazard areas not subject to high-velocity wave action, the elevation of the proposed lowest floor, including the basement.

2. In flood hazard areas not subject to high-velocity wave action, the elevation to which any nonresidential building will be dry floodproofed.

3. In flood hazard areas subject to high-velocity wave action, the proposed elevation of the bottom of the lowest horizontal structural member of the lowest floor, including the basement.

1603.1.7 Special loads. Special loads that are applicable to the design of the building, structure or portions thereof shall be indicated along with the specified section of this code that addresses the special loading condition.

1603.1.8 Systems and components requiring special inspections for seismic resistance. Construction documents or specifications shall be prepared for those systems and components requiring special inspection for seismic resistance as specified in Section 1707.1 by the registered design professional responsible for their design and shall be submitted for approval in accordance with Section 106.1. Reference to seismic standards in lieu of detailed drawings is acceptable.

1603.2 Restrictions on loading. It shall be unlawful to place, or cause or permit to be placed, on any floor or roof of a building, structure or portion thereof, a load greater than is permitted by these requirements.

1603.3 Live loads posted. Where the live loads for which each floor or portion thereof of a commercial or industrial building is or has been designed to exceed 50 psf (2.40 kN/m^2), such design live loads shall be conspicuously posted by the owner in that part of each story in which they apply, using durable signs. It shall be unlawful to remove or deface such notices.

1603.4 Occupancy permits for changed loads. Occupancy permits for buildings hereafter erected shall not be issued until the floor load signs, required by Section 1603.3, have been installed.

SECTION 1604
GENERAL DESIGN REQUIREMENTS

1604.1 General. Building, structures and parts thereof shall be designed and constructed in accordance with strength design, load and resistance factor design, allowable stress design, empirical design or conventional construction methods, as permitted by the applicable material chapters.

1604.2 Strength. Buildings and other structures, and parts thereof, shall be designed and constructed to support safely the factored loads in load combinations defined in this code without exceeding the appropriate strength limit states for the materials of construction. Alternatively, buildings and other structures, and parts thereof, shall be designed and constructed to support safely the nominal loads in load combinations defined in this code without exceeding the appropriate specified allowable stresses for the materials of construction.

Loads and forces for occupancies or uses not covered in this chapter shall be subject to the approval of the code enforcement official.

1604.3 Serviceability. Structural systems and members thereof shall be designed to have adequate stiffness to limit deflections and lateral drift. See Section 12.12.1 of ASCE 7 for drift limits applicable to earthquake loading.

1604.3.1 Deflections. The deflections of structural members shall not exceed the more restrictive of the limitations of Sections 1604.3.2 through 1604.3.5 or that permitted by Table 1604.3.

1604.3.2 Reinforced concrete. The deflection of reinforced concrete structural members shall not exceed that permitted by ACI 318.

TABLE 1604.3
DEFLECTION LIMITS[a, b, c, h, i]

CONSTRUCTION	L	S or W[f]	D+L[d,g]
Roof members:[e]			
Supporting plaster ceiling	*l*/360	*l*/360	*l*/240
Supporting nonplaster ceiling	*l*/240	*l*/240	*l*/180
Not supporting ceiling	*l*/180	*l*/180	*l*/120
Floor members	*l*/360	-	*l*/240
Exterior walls and interior partitions:			
With brittle finishes	-	*l*/240	-
With flexible finishes	-	*l*/120	-
Farm buildings	-	-	*l*/180
Greenhouses	-	-	*l*/120

For SI: 1 foot = 304.8 mm.

a. For structural roofing and siding made of formed metal sheets, the total load deflection shall not exceed *l*/60. For secondary roof structural members supporting formed metal roofing, the live load deflection shall not exceed *l*/150. For secondary wall members supporting formed metal siding, the design wind load deflection shall not exceed *l*/90. For roofs, this exception only applies when the metal sheets have no roof covering.

b. Interior partitions not exceeding 6 feet in height and flexible, folding and portable partitions are not governed by the provisions of this section. The deflection criterion for interior partitions is based on the horizontal load defined in Section 1607.13.

c. See Section 2403 for glass supports.

d. For wood structural members having a moisture content of less than 16 percent at time of installation and used under dry conditions, the deflection resulting from $L + 0.5D$ is permitted to be substituted for the deflection resulting from $L + D$.

e. The above deflections do not ensure against ponding. Roofs that do not have sufficient slope or camber to assure adequate drainage shall be investigated for ponding. See Section 1611 for rain and ponding requirements and Section 1503.4 for roof drainage requirements.

f. The wind load is permitted to be taken as 0.7 times the "component and cladding" loads for the purpose of determining deflection limits herein.

g. For steel structural members, the dead load shall be taken as zero.

h. For aluminum structural members or aluminum panels used in skylights and sloped glazing framing, roofs or walls of sunroom additions or patio covers, not supporting edge of glass or aluminum sandwich panels, the total load deflection shall not exceed $^1/_{60}$. For aluminum sandwich panels used in roofs or walls of sunroom additions or patio covers, the total load deflection shall not exceed $^1/_{120}$.

i. For cantilever members, *l* shall be taken as twice the length of the cantilever.

1604.3.3 Steel. The deflection of steel structural members shall not exceed that permitted by AISC 360, AISI-NAS, AISI-General, AISI-Truss, ASCE 3, ASCE 8, SJI JG-1.1, SJI K-1.1 or SJI LH/DLH-1.1, as applicable.

1604.3.4 Masonry. The deflection of masonry structural members shall not exceed that permitted by ACI 530/ASCE 5/TMS 402.

1604.3.5 Aluminum. The deflection of aluminum structural members shall not exceed that permitted by AA ADM1.

1604.3.6 Limits. Deflection of structural members over span, *l*, shall not exceed that permitted by Table 1604.3.

1604.4 Analysis. Load effects on structural members and their connections shall be determined by methods of structural analysis that take into account equilibrium, general sta-

bility, geometric compatibility and both short- and long-term material properties.

Members that tend to accumulate residual deformations under repeated service loads shall have included in their analysis the added eccentricities expected to occur during their service life.

Any system or method of construction to be used shall be based on a rational analysis in accordance with well-established principles of mechanics. Such analysis shall result in a system that provides a complete load path capable of transferring loads from their point of origin to the load-resisting elements.

The total lateral force shall be distributed to the various vertical elements of the lateral-force-resisting system in proportion to their rigidities, considering the rigidity of the horizontal bracing system or diaphragm. Rigid elements assumed not to be a part of the lateral-force-resisting system are permitted to be incorporated into buildings provided their effect on the action of the system is considered and provided for in the design. Except where diaphragms are flexible, or are permitted to be analyzed as flexible, provisions shall be made for the increased forces induced on resisting elements of the structural system resulting from torsion due to eccentricity between the center of application of the lateral forces and the center of rigidity of the lateral-force-resisting system.

Every structure shall be designed to resist the overturning effects caused by the lateral forces specified in this chapter. See Section 1609 for wind loads, Section 1610 for lateral soil loads and Section 1613 for earthquake loads.

1604.5 Occupancy category. Buildings shall be assigned an occupancy category in accordance with Table 1604.5.

1604.5.1 Multiple occupancies. Where a structure is occupied by two or more occupancies not included in the same occupancy category, the structure shall be assigned the classification of the highest occupancy category corresponding to the various occupancies. Where structures have two or more portions that are structurally separated, each portion shall be separately classified. Where a separated portion of a structure provides required access to, required egress from or shares life safety components with another portion having a higher occupancy category, both portions shall be assigned to the higher occupancy category.

1604.6 In-situ load tests. The code enforcement official is authorized to require an engineering analysis or a load test, or both, of any construction whenever there is reason to question the safety of the construction for the intended occupancy. Engineering analysis and load tests shall be conducted in accordance with Section 1713.

1604.7 Preconstruction load tests. Materials and methods of construction that are not capable of being designed by approved engineering analysis or that do not comply with the applicable material design standards listed in Chapter 35, or alternative test procedures in accordance with Section 1711, shall be load tested in accordance with Section 1714.

TABLE 1604.5
OCCUPANCY CATEGORY OF BUILDINGS AND OTHER STRUCTURES

OCCUPANCY CATEGORY	NATURE OF OCCUPANCY
I	Buildings and other structures that represent a low hazard to human life in the event of failure, including but not limited to: • Agricultural facilities. • Certain temporary facilities. • Minor storage facilities.
II	Buildings and other structures except those listed in Occupancy Categories I, III and IV
III	Buildings and other structures that represent a substantial hazard to human life in the event of failure, including but not limited to: • Covered structures whose primary occupancy is public assembly with an occupant load greater than 300. • Buildings and other structures with elementary school, secondary school or day care facilities with an occupant load greater than 250. • Buildings and other structures with an occupant load greater than 500 for colleges or adult education facilities. • Health care facilities with an occupant load of 50 or more resident patients, but not having surgery or emergency treatment facilities. • Jails and detention facilities. • Any other occupancy with an occupant load greater than 5,000. • Power-generating stations, water treatment for potable water, waste water treatment facilities and other public utility facilities not included in Occupancy Category IV. • Buildings and other structures not included in Occupancy Category IV containing sufficient quantities of toxic or explosive substances to be dangerous to the public if released.
IV	Buildings and other structures designated as essential facilities, including but not limited to: • Hospitals and other health care facilities having surgery or emergency treatment facilities. • Fire, rescue and police stations and emergency vehicle garages. • Designated earthquake, hurricane or other emergency shelters. • Designated emergency preparedness, communication, and operation centers and other facilities required for emergency response. • Power-generating stations and other public utility facilities required as emergency backup facilities for Occupancy Category IV structures. • Structures containing highly toxic materials as defined by Section 307 where the quantity of the material exceeds the maximum allowable quantities of Table 307.1.(2). • Aviation control towers, air traffic control centers and emergency aircraft hangars. • Buildings and other structures having critical national defense functions. • Water treatment facilities required to maintain water pressure for fire suppression.

1604.8 Anchorage.

1604.8.1 General. Anchorage of the roof to walls and columns, and of walls and columns to foundations, shall be provided to resist the uplift and sliding forces that result from the application of the prescribed loads.

1604.8.2 Concrete and masonry walls. Concrete and masonry walls shall be anchored to floors, roofs and other structural elements that provide lateral support for the wall. Such anchorage shall provide a positive direct connection capable of resisting the horizontal forces specified in this chapter but not less than a minimum strength design horizontal force of 280 plf (4.10 kN/m) of wall, substituted for "*E*" in the load combinations of Section 1605.2 or 1605.3. Walls shall be designed to resist bending between anchors where the anchor spacing exceeds 4 feet (1219 mm). Required anchors in masonry walls of hollow units or cavity walls shall be embedded in a reinforced grouted structural element of the wall. See Sections 1609 for wind design requirements and see Section 1613 for earthquake design requirements.

1604.8.3 Decks. Where supported by attachment to an exterior wall, decks shall be positively anchored to the primary structure and designed for both vertical and lateral loads as applicable. Such attachment shall not be accomplished by the use of toenails or nails subject to withdrawal. Where positive connection to the primary building structure cannot be verified during inspection, decks shall be self-supporting. For decks with cantilevered framing members, connections to exterior walls or other framing members shall be designed and constructed to resist uplift resulting from the full live load specified in Table 1607.1 acting on the cantilevered portion of the deck.

1604.9 Counteracting structural actions. Structural members, systems, components and cladding shall be designed to resist forces due to earthquake and wind, with consideration of overturning, sliding, and uplift. Continuous load paths shall be provided for transmitting these forces to the foundation. Where sliding is used to isolate the elements, the effects of friction between sliding elements shall be included as a force.

1604.10 Wind and seismic detailing. Lateral-force-resisting systems shall meet seismic detailing requirements and limitations prescribed in this code and ASCE 7, excluding Chapter 14 and Appendix 11A, even when wind code prescribed load effects are greater than seismic load effects.

SECTION 1605
LOAD COMBINATIONS

1605.1 General. Buildings and other structures and portions thereof shall be designed to resist the load combinations specified in Section 1605.2 or 1605.3 and Chapters 18 through 23, and the special seismic load combinations of Section 1605.4 where required by Section 12.3.3.3 or 12.10.2.1 of ASCE 7. Applicable loads shall be considered, including both earthquake and wind, in accordance with the specified load combinations. Each load combination shall also be investigated with one or more of the variable loads set to zero.

1605.2 Load combinations using strength design or load and resistance factor design.

1605.2.1 Basic load combinations. Where strength design or load and resistance factor design is used, structures and portions thereof shall resist the most critical effects from the following combinations of factored loads:

$1.4(D + F)$ **(Equation 16-1)**

$1.2(D + F + T) + 1.6(L + H) + 0.5 (L_r \text{ or } S \text{ or } R)$ **(Equation 16-2)**

$1.2D + 1.6(L_r \text{ or } S \text{ or } R) + (f_1 L \text{ or } 0.8W)$ **(Equation 16-3)**

$1.2D + 1.6W + f_1 L + 0.5(L_r \text{ or } S \text{ or } R)$ **(Equation 16-4)**

$1.2D + 1.0E + f_1 L + f_2 S$ **(Equation 16-5)**

$0.9D + 1.6W + 1.6H$ **(Equation 16-6)**

$0.9D + 1.0E + 1.6H$ **(Equation 16-7)**

f_1 = 1 for floors in places of public assembly, for live loads in excess of 100 pounds per square foot (4.79 kN/m^2), and for parking garage live load, and

  = 0.5 for other live loads.

f_2 = 0.7 for roof configurations (such as saw tooth) that do not shed snow off the structure, and

  = 0.2 for other roof configurations.

Exception: Where other factored load combinations are specifically required by the provisions of this code, such combinations shall take precedence.

1605.2.2 Other loads. Where F_a is to be considered in the design, the load combinations of Section 2.3.3 of ASCE 7 shall be used.

1605.3 Load combinations using allowable stress design.

1605.3.1 Basic load combinations. Where allowable stress design (working stress design), as permitted by this code, is used, structures and portions thereof shall resist the most critical effects resulting from the following combinations of loads:

$D + F$ **(Equation 16-8)**

$D + H + F + L + T$ **(Equation 16-9)**

$D + H + F + (L_r \text{ or } S \text{ or } R)$ **(Equation 16-10)**

$D + H + F + 0.75(L + T) + 0.75 (L_r \text{ or } S \text{ or } R)$ **(Equation 16-11)**

$D + H + F + (W \text{ or } 0.7E)$ **(Equation 16-12)**

$D + H + F + 0.75(W \text{ or } 0.7E) + 0.75L + 0.75 (L_r \text{ or } S \text{ or } R)$ **(Equation 16-13)**

$0.6D + W + H$ **(Equation 16-14)**

$0.6D + 0.7E + H$ **(Equation 16-15)**

Exceptions:

1. Crane hook loads need not be combined with roof live load or with more than three-fourths of the snow load or one-half of the wind load.

2. Flat roof snow loads of 30 psf (1.44 kN/m^2) or less need not be combined with seismic loads. Where flat roof snow loads exceed 30 psf (1.44 kN/m^2), 20 percent shall be combined with seismic loads.

1605.3.1.1 Stress increases. Increases in allowable stresses specified in the appropriate material chapter or the referenced standards shall not be used with the load combinations of Section 1605.3.1, except that a duration of load increase shall be permitted in accordance with Chapter 23.

1605.3.1.2 Other loads. Where F_a is to be considered in design, the load combinations of Section 2.4.2 of ASCE 7 shall be used.

1605.3.2 Alternative basic load combinations. In lieu of the basic load combinations specified in Section 1605.3.1, structures and portions thereof shall be permitted to be designed for the most critical effects resulting from the following combinations. When using these alternative basic load combinations that include wind or seismic loads, allowable stresses are permitted to be increased or load combinations reduced where permitted by the material chapter of this code or the referenced standards. For load combinations that include the counteracting effects of dead and wind loads, only two-thirds of the minimum dead load likely to be in place during a design wind event shall be used. Where wind loads are calculated in accordance with Chapter 6 of ASCE 7, the coefficient ω in the following equations shall be taken as 1.3. For other wind loads, ω shall be taken as 1. When using these alternative load combinations to evaluate sliding, overturning and soil bearing at the soil-structure interface, the reduction of foundation overturning from Section 12.13.4 in ASCE 7 shall not be used. When using these alternative basic load combinations for proportioning foundations for loadings, which include seismic loads, the vertical seismic load effect, E_v, in Equation 12.4-4 of ASCE 7 is permitted to be taken equal to zero.

$D + L + (L_r \text{ or } S \text{ or } R)$ **(Equation 16-16)**

$D + L + (\omega W)$ **(Equation 16-17)**

$D + L + \omega W + S/2$ **(Equation 16-18)**

$D + L + S + \omega W/2$ **(Equation 16-19)**

$D + L + S + E/1.4$ **(Equation 16-20)**

$0.9D + E/1.4$ **(Equation 16-21)**

Exceptions:

1. Crane hook loads need not be combined with roof live loads or with more than three-fourths of the snow load or one-half of the wind load.

2. Flat roof snow loads of 30 psf (1.44 kN/m²) or less need not be combined with seismic loads. Where flat roof snow loads exceed 30 psf (1.44 kN/m²), 20 percent shall be combined with seismic loads.

1605.3.2.1 Other loads. Where *F*, *H* or *T* are to be considered in the design, each applicable load shall be added to the combinations specified in Section 1605.3.2.

1605.4 Special seismic load combinations. For both allowable stress design and strength design methods where specifically required by Section 1605.1 or by Chapters 18 through 23, elements and components shall be designed to resist the forces calculated using Equation 16-22 when the effects of the seismic ground motion are additive to gravity forces and those calculated using Equation 16-23 when the effects of the seismic ground motion counteract gravity forces.

$$1.2D + f_1 L + E_m \qquad \text{(Equation 16-22)}$$
$$0.9D + E_m \qquad \text{(Equation 16-23)}$$

where:

E_m = The maximum effect of horizontal and vertical forces as set forth in Section 12.4.3 of ASCE 7.

f_1 = 1 for floors in places of public assembly, for live loads in excess of 100 psf (4.79 kN/m²) and for parking garage live load, or

= 0.5 for other live loads.

1605.5 Heliports and helistops. Heliport and helistop landing areas shall be designed for the following loads, combined in accordance with Section 1605:

1. Dead load, *D*, plus the gross weight of the helicopter, D_h, plus snow load, *S*.

2. Dead load, *D*, plus two single concentrated impact loads, *L*, approximately 8 feet (2438 mm) apart applied anywhere on the landing area (representing the helicopter's two main landing gear, whether skid type or wheeled type), having a magnitude of 0.75 times the gross weight of the helicopter. Both loads acting together total one-and one half times the gross weight of the helicopter.

3. Dead load, *D*, plus a uniform live load, *L*, of 100 psf (4.79 kN/m²).

   Exception: Landing areas designed for helicopters with gross weights not exceeding 3,000 pounds (13.34 kN) in accordance with Items 1 and 2 shall be permitted to be designed using a 40 psf (1.92 kN/m²) uniform live load in Item 3, provided the landing area is identified with a 3,000 pound (13.34 kN) weight limitation. This 40 psf (1.92 kN/m²) uniform live load shall not be reduced. The landing area weight limitation shall be indicated by the numeral "3" (kips) located in the bottom right corner of the landing area as viewed from the primary approach path. The landing area weight limitation shall be a minimum of 5 feet (1524 mm) in height.

SECTION 1606
DEAD LOADS

1606.1 General. Dead loads are those loads defined in Section 1602.1. Dead loads shall be considered permanent loads.

1606.2 Design dead load. For purposes of design, the actual weights of materials of construction and fixed service equipment shall be used. In the absence of definite information, values used shall be subject to the approval of the code enforcement official.

SECTION 1607
LIVE LOADS

1607.1 General. Live loads are those loads defined in Section 1602.1.

1607.2 Loads not specified. For occupancies or uses not designated in Table 1607.1, the live load shall be determined in accordance with a method approved by the code enforcement official.

1607.3 Uniform live loads. The live loads used in the design of buildings and other structures shall be the maximum loads expected by the intended use or occupancy but shall in no case be less than the minimum uniformly distributed unit loads required by Table 1607.1.

1607.4 Concentrated loads. Floors and other similar surfaces shall be designed to support the uniformly distributed live loads prescribed in Section 1607.3 or the concentrated load, in pounds (kilonewtons), given in Table 1607.1, whichever produces the greater load effects. Unless otherwise specified, the indicated concentration shall be assumed to be uniformly distributed over an area 2.5 feet by 2.5 feet [6.25 square feet (0.58 m²)] and shall be located so as to produce the maximum load effects in the structural members.

1607.5 Partition loads. In office buildings and in other buildings where partition locations are subject to change, provisions for partition weight shall be made, whether or not partitions are shown on the construction documents, unless the specified live load exceeds 80 psf (3.83 kN/m²). The partition load shall not be less than a uniformly distributed live load of 15 psf (0.74 kN/m²).

1607.6 Truck and bus garages. Minimum live loads for garages having trucks or buses shall be as specified in Table 1607.6, but shall not be less than 50 psf (2.40 kN/m²), unless other loads are specifically justified and approved by the code enforcement official. Actual loads shall be used where they are greater than the loads specified in the table.

1607.6.1 Truck and bus garage live load application. The concentrated load and uniform load shall be uniformly distributed over a 10-foot (3048 mm) width on a line normal to the centerline of the lane placed within a 12-foot-wide (3658 mm) lane. The loads shall be placed within their individual lanes so as to produce the maximum stress in each structural member. Single spans shall be designed for the uniform load in Table 1607.6 and one simultaneous concentrated load positioned to produce the maximum effect. Multiple spans shall be designed for the uniform load in Table 1607.6 on the spans and two simultaneous concentrated loads in two spans positioned to produce the maximum negative moment effect. Multiple span design loads, for other effects, shall be the same as for single spans.

TABLE 1607.6
UNIFORM AND CONCENTRATED LOADS

LOADING CLASS[a]	UNIFORM LOAD (pounds/linear foot of lane)	CONCENTRATED LOAD (pounds)[b]	
		For moment design	For shear design
H20-44 and HS20-44	640	18,000	26,000
H15-44 and HS15-44	480	13,500	19,500

For SI: 1 pound per linear foot = 0.01459 kN/m, 1 pound = 0.004448 kN, 1 ton = 8.90 kN.

a. An H loading class designates a two-axle truck with a semitrailer. An HS loading class designates a tractor truck with a semitrailer. The numbers following the letter classification indicate the gross weight in tons of the standard truck and the year the loadings were instituted.

b. See Section 1607.6.1 for the loading of multiple spans.

1607.7 Loads on handrails, guards, grab bars and vehicle barriers. Handrails, guards, grab bars as designed in ICC/ANSI A117.1 and vehicle barriers shall be designed and constructed to the structural loading conditions set forth in this section.

1607.7.1 Handrails and guards. Handrail assemblies and guards shall be designed to resist a load of 50 plf (0.73 kN/m) applied in any direction at the top and to transfer this load through the supports to the structure. Glass handrail assemblies and guards shall also comply with Section 2407.

Exceptions:

1. For one- and two-family dwellings, only the single concentrated load required by Section 1607.7.1.1 shall be applied.

2. In Group I-3, F, H and S occupancies, for areas that are not accessible to the general public and that have an occupant load less than 50, the minimum load shall be 20 pounds per foot (0.29 kN/m).

1607.7.1.1 Concentrated load. Handrail assemblies and guards shall be able to resist a single concentrated load of 200 pounds (0.89 kN), applied in any direction at any point along the top, and have attachment devices and supporting structure to transfer this loading to appropriate structural elements of the building. This load need not be assumed to act concurrently with the loads specified in the preceding paragraph.

1607.7.1.2 Components. Intermediate rails (all those except the handrail), balusters and panel fillers shall be designed to withstand a horizontally applied normal load of 50 pounds (0.22 kN) on an area equal to 1 square foot (0.093m²), including openings and space between rails. Reactions due to this loading are not required to be superimposed with those of Section 1607.7.1 or 1607.7.1.1.

TABLE 1607.1
MINIMUM UNIFORMLY DISTRIBUTED LIVE LOADS AND MINIMUM CONCENTRATED LIVE LOADS[g]

OCCUPANCY OR USE	UNIFORM (psf)	CONCENTRATED (lbs.)
1. Apartments (see residential)	-	-
2. Access floor systems		
Office use	50	2,000
Computer use	100	2,000
3. Armories and drill rooms	150	-
4. Assembly areas and theaters	-	-
Fixed seats (fastened to floor)	60	-
Follow spot, projections and control rooms	50	-
Lobbies	100	-
Movable seats	100	
Stages and platforms	125	
5. Balconies	100	-
On one- and two-family residences only, and not exceeding 100 sq ft	60	
6. Bowling alleys	75	-
7. Catwalks	40	300
8. Dance halls and ballrooms	100	-
9. Decks	Same as occupancy served[h]	-
10. Dining rooms and restaurants	100	-
11. Dwellings (see residential)	-	-
12. Cornices	60	-
13. Corridors, except as otherwise indicated	100	-
14. Elevator machine room grating (on area of 4 in²)	-	300
15. Finish light floor plate construction (on area of 1 in²)	-	200
16. Fire escapes	100	-
On single-family dwellings only	40	-
17. Garages (passenger vehicles only)	40	Note a
Trucks and buses	See Section 1607.6	
18. Grandstands (see stadium and arena bleachers)	-	-
19. Gymnasiums, main floors and balconies	100	-
20. Handrails, guards and grab bars	See Section 1607.7	
21. Hospitals		
Corridors above first floor	80	1,000
Operating rooms, laboratories	60	1,000
Patient rooms	40	1,000
22. Hotels (see residential)	-	-
23. Libraries	-	-
Corridors above first floor	80	1,000
Reading rooms	60	1,000
Stack rooms	150[b]	1,000

continued

TABLE 1607.1—continued
MINIMUM UNIFORMLY DISTRIBUTED LIVE LOADS AND
MINIMUM CONCENTRATED LIVE LOADS[g]

OCCUPANCY OR USE	UNIFORM (psf)	CONCENTRATED (lbs.)
24. Manufacturing		
Heavy	250	3,000
Light	125	2,000
25. Marquees	75	-
26. Office buildings		
Corridors above first floor	80	2,000
File and computer rooms shall be designed for heavier loads based on anticipated occupancy	-	-
Lobbies and first-floor corridors	100	2,000
Offices	50	2,000
27. Penal institutions		
Cell blocks	40	-
Corridors	100	
28. Residential		
One- and two-family dwellings		
Uninhabitable attics without storage[i]	10	
Uninhabitable attics with limited storage[i, j, k]	20	
Habitable attics and sleeping areas	30	
All other areas except balconies and decks	40	-
Hotels and multiple-family dwellings		
Private rooms and corridors serving them	40	
Public rooms and corridors serving them	100	
29. Reviewing stands, grandstands and bleachers	Note c	
30. Roofs		
All roof surfaces subject to maintenance workers		300
Awnings and canopies		
Fabric construction supported by a lightweight rigid skeleton structure	5 nonreduceable	
All other construction	20	
Ordinary flat, pitched, and curved roofs	20	
Primary roof members, exposed to a work floor		
Single panel point of lower chord of roof trusses or any point along primary structural members supporting roofs:		
Over manufacturing, storage warehouses, and repair garages		2,000
All other occupancies		300
Roofs used for other special purposes	Note l	Note l
Roofs used for promenade purposes	60	
Roofs used for roof gardens or assembly purposes	100	

continued

TABLE 1607.1—continued
MINIMUM UNIFORMLY DISTRIBUTED LIVE LOADS AND
MINIMUM CONCENTRATED LIVE LOADS[g]

OCCUPANCY OR USE	UNIFORM (psf)	CONCENTRATED (lbs.)
31. Schools		
Classrooms	40	1,000
Corridors above first floor	80	1,000
First-floor corridors	100	1,000
32. Scuttles, skylight ribs and accessible ceilings	-	200
33. Sidewalks, vehicular driveways and yards, subject to trucking	250[d]	8,000[e]
34. Skating rinks	100	
35. Stadiums and arenas		
Bleachers	100[c]	-
Fixed seats (fastened to floor)	60[c]	
36. Stairs and exits		
One- and two-family dwellings	40	Note f
All other	100	
37. Storage warehouses (shall be designed for heavier loads if required for anticipated storage)		
Heavy	250	
Light	125	
38. Stores		
Retail		
First floor	100	1,000
Upper floors	75	1,000
Wholesale, all floors	125	1,000
39. Vehicle barriers	See Section 1607.7.3	
40. Walkways and elevated platforms (other than exitways)	60	-
41. Yards and terraces, pedestrians	100	-

For SI: 1 inch = 25.4 mm, 1 square inch = 645.16 mm^2, 1 square foot = 0.0929 m^2, 1 pound per square foot = 0.0479 kN/m^2, 1 pound = 0.004448 kN, 1 pound per cubic foot = 16 kg/m^3

a. Floors in garages or portions of buildings used for the storage of motor vehicles shall be designed for the uniformly distributed live loads of Table 1607.1 or the following concentrated loads: (1) for garages restricted to vehicles accommodating not more than nine passengers, 3,000 pounds acting on an area of 4.5 inches by 4.5 inches; (2) for mechanical parking structures without slab or deck which are used for storing passenger vehicles only, 2,250 pounds per wheel.

b. The loading applies to stack room floors that support nonmobile, double-faced library bookstacks, subject to the following limitations:
  1. The nominal bookstack unit height shall not exceed 90 inches;
  2. The nominal shelf depth shall not exceed 12 inches for each face; and
  3. Parallel rows of double-faced bookstacks shall be separated by aisles not less than 36 inches wide.

c. Design in accordance with the ICC 300.

d. Other uniform loads in accordance with an approved method which contains provisions for truck loadings shall also be considered where appropriate.

(continued)

TABLE 1607.1—continued
MINIMUM UNIFORMLY DISTRIBUTED LIVE LOADS AND
MINIMUM CONCENTRATED LIVE LOADS[g]

e. The concentrated wheel load shall be applied on an area of 20 square inches.

f. Minimum concentrated load on stair treads (on area of 4 square inches) is 300 pounds.

g. Where snow loads occur that are in excess of the design conditions, the structure shall be designed to support the loads due to the increased loads caused by drift buildup or a greater snow design determined by the code enforcement official (see Section 1608). For special-purpose roofs, see Section 1607.11.2.2.

h. See Section 1604.8.3 for decks attached to exterior walls.

i. Attics without storage are those where the maximum clear height between the joist and rafter is less than 42 inches, or where there are not two or more adjacent trusses with the same web configuration capable of containing a rectangle 42 inches high by 2 feet wide, or greater, located within the plane of the truss. For attics without storage, this live load need not be assumed to act concurrently with any other live load requirements.

j. For attics with limited storage and constructed with trusses, this live load need only be applied to those portions of the bottom chord where there are two or more adjacent trusses with the same web configuration capable of containing a rectangle 42 inches high by 2 feet wide or greater, located within the plane of the truss. The rectangle shall fit between the top of the bottom chord and the bottom of any other truss member, provided that each of the following criteria is met:

  i. The attic area is accessible by a pull-down stairway or framed opening in accordance with Section 1209.2, and

  ii. The truss shall have a bottom chord pitch less than 2:12.

  iii. Bottom chords of trusses shall be designed for the greater of actual imposed dead load or 10 psf, uniformly distributed over the entire span.

k. Attic spaces served by a fixed stair shall be designed to support the minimum live load specified for habitable attics and sleeping rooms.

l. Roofs used for other special purposes shall be designed for appropriate loads as approved by the code enforcement official.

1607.7.1.3 Stress increase. Where handrails and guards are designed in accordance with the provisions for allowable stress design (working stress design) exclusively for the loads specified in Section 1607.7.1, the allowable stress for the members and their attachments are permitted to be increased by one-third.

1607.7.2 Grab bars, shower seats and dressing room bench seats. Grab bars, shower seats and dressing room bench seat systems shall be designed to resist a single concentrated load of 250 pounds (1.11 kN) applied in any direction at any point.

1607.7.3 Vehicle barriers. Vehicle barrier systems for passenger cars shall be designed to resist a single load of 6,000 pounds (26.70 kN) applied horizontally in any direction to the barrier system and shall have anchorage or attachment capable of transmitting this load to the structure. For design of the system, the load shall be assumed to act at a minimum height of 1 foot, 6 inches (457 mm) above the floor or ramp surface on an area not to exceed 1 square foot (305 mm²), and is not required to be assumed to act concurrently with any handraolil or guard loadings specified in the preceding paragraphs of Section 1607.7.1. Garages accommodating trucks and buses shall be designed in accordance with an approved method that contains provision for traffic railings.

1607.8 Impact loads. The live loads specified in Section 1607.3 include allowance for impact conditions. Provisions shall be made in the structural design for uses and loads that involve unusual vibration and impact forces.

1607.8.1 Elevators. Elevator loads shall be increased by 100 percent for impact and the structural supports shall be designed within the limits of deflection prescribed by ASME A17.1.

1607.8.2 Machinery. For the purpose of design, the weight of machinery and moving loads shall be increased as follows to allow for impact: (1) elevator machinery, 100 percent; (2) light machinery, shaft- or motor-driven, 20 percent; (3) reciprocating machinery or power-driven units, 50 percent; (4) hangers for floors or balconies, 33 percent. Percentages shall be increased where specified by the manufacturer.

1607.9 Reduction in live loads. Except for roof uniform live loads, all other minimum uniformly distributed live loads, L_o, in Table 1607.1 are permitted to be reduced in accordance with Section 1607.9.1 or 1607.9.2.

1607.9.1 General. Subject to the limitations of Sections 1607.9.1.1 through 1607.9.1.4, members for which a value of $K_{LL}A_T$ is 400 square feet (37.16 m²) or more are permitted to be designed for a reduced live load in accordance with the following equation:

$$L = L_o\left(0.25 + \frac{15}{\sqrt{K_{LL}A_T}}\right)$$

For SI: $L = L_o\left(0.25 + \frac{457}{\sqrt{K_{LL}A_T}}\right)$

(Equation 16-24)

where:

L = Reduced design live load per square foot (meter) of area supported by the member.

L_o = Unreduced design live load per square foot (meter) of area supported by the member (see Table 1607.1).

K_{LL} = Live load element factor (see Table 1607.9.1).

A_T = Tributary area, in square feet (square meters). L shall not be less than $0.50L_o$ for members supporting one floor and L shall not be less than $0.40L_o$ for members supporting two or more floors.

1607.9.1.1 Heavy live loads. Live loads that exceed 100 psf (4.79 kN/m²) shall not be reduced.

Exceptions:

1. The live loads for members supporting two or more floors are permitted to be reduced by a maximum of 20 percent, but the live load shall not be less than L as calculated in Section 1607.9.1.

2. For uses other than storage, where approved, additional live load reductions shall be permitted where shown by the registered design professional that a rational approach has been used and that such reductions are warranted.

1607.9.1.2 Passenger vehicle garages. The live loads shall not be reduced in passenger vehicle garages

TABLE 1607.9.1
LIVE LOAD ELEMENT FACTOR, K_{LL}

ELEMENT	K_{LL}
Interior columns	4
Exterior columns without cantilever slabs	4
Edge columns with cantilever slabs	3
Corner columns with cantilever slabs	2
Edge beams without cantilever slabs	2
Interior beams	2
All other members not identified above including: Edge beams with cantilever slabs Cantilever beams Two-way slabs Members without provisions for continuous shear transfer normal to their span	1

except the live loads for members supporting two or more floors are permitted to be reduced by a maximum of 20 percent, but the live load shall not be less than L as calculated in Section 1607.9.1.

1607.9.1.3 Special occupancies. Live loads of 100 psf (4.79 kN/m^2) or less shall not be reduced in public assembly occupancies.

1607.9.1.4 Special structural elements. Live loads shall not be reduced for one-way slabs except as permitted in Section 1607.9.1.1. Live loads of 100 psf (4.79 kN/m^2) or less shall not be reduced for roof members except as specified in Section 1607.11.2.

1607.9.2 Alternate floor live load reduction. As an alternative to Section 1607.9.1, floor live loads are permitted to be reduced in accordance with the following provisions. Such reductions shall apply to slab systems, beams, girders, columns, piers, walls and foundations.

1. A reduction shall not be permitted in Group A occupancies.

2. A reduction shall not be permitted where the live load exceeds 100 psf (4.79 kN/m^2) except that the design live load for members supporting two or more floors is permitted to be reduced by 20 percent.

3. A reduction shall not be permitted in passenger vehicle parking garages except that the live loads for members supporting two or more floors are permitted to be reduced by a maximum of 20 percent.

4. For live loads not exceeding 100 psf (4.79 kN/m^2), the design live load for any structural member supporting 150 square feet (13.94 m^2) or more is permitted to be reduced in accordance with the following equation:

$$R = 0.08 (A - 150) \qquad \textbf{(Equation 16-25)}$$

For SI: $R = 0.861 (A - 13.94)$

Such reduction shall not exceed the smallest of:

1. 40 percent for horizontal members;
2. 60 percent for vertical members; or
3. R as determined by the following equation.

$$R = 23.1 (1 + D/L_o) \qquad \textbf{(Equation 16-26)}$$

where:

A = Area of floor supported by the member, square feet (m^2).

D = Dead load per square foot (m^2) of area supported.

L_o = Unreduced live load per square foot (m^2) of area supported.

R = Reduction in percent.

1607.10 Distribution of floor loads. Where uniform floor live loads are involved in the design of structural members arranged so as to create continuity, the minimum applied loads shall be the full dead loads on all spans in combination with the floor live loads on spans selected to produce the greatest effect at each location under consideration. It shall be permitted to reduce floor live loads in accordance with Section 1607.9.

1607.11 Roof loads. The structural supports of roofs and marquees shall be designed to resist wind and, where applicable, snow and earthquake loads, in addition to the dead load of construction and the appropriate live loads as prescribed in this section, or as set forth in Table 1607.1. The live loads acting on a sloping surface shall be assumed to act vertically on the horizontal projection of that surface.

1607.11.1 Distribution of roof loads. Where uniform roof live loads are reduced to less than 20 psf (0.96 kN/m^2) in accordance with Section 1607.11.2.1 and are involved in the design of structural members arranged so as to create continuity, the minimum applied loads shall be the full dead loads on all spans in combination with the roof live loads on adjacent spans or on alternate spans, whichever produces the greatest effect. See Section 1607.11.2 for minimum roof live loads and Section 7.5 of ASCE 7 for partial snow loading.

1607.11.2 Reduction in roof live loads. The minimum uniformly distributed roof live loads, L_o, in Table 1607.1 are permitted to be reduced according to the following provisions.

1607.11.2.1 Flat, pitched and curved roofs. Ordinary flat, pitched and curved roofs are permitted to be designed for a reduced roof live load as specified in the following equation or other controlling combinations of loads in Section 1605, whichever produces the greater load. In structures where special scaffolding is used as a work surface for workers and materials during maintenance and repair operations, a lower roof load than specified in the following equation shall not be used unless approved by the code enforcement official. Greenhouses shall be designed for a minimum roof live load of 12 psf (0.58 kN/m^2).

$$L_r = L_o R_1 R_2 \qquad \textbf{(Equation 16-27)}$$

where: $12 \leq L_r \leq 20$

For SI: $L_r = L_o R_1 R_2$

where: $0.58 \leq L_r \leq 0.96$

L_r = Reduced live load per square foot (m^2) of horizontal projection in pounds per square foot (kN/m^2).

The reduction factors R_1 and R_2 shall be determined as follows:

$R_1 = 1$ for $A_t \leq 200$ square feet (18.58 m²)

(Equation 16-28)

$R_1 = 1.2 - 0.001A_t$ for 200 square feet $< A_t < 600$ square feet **(Equation 16-29)**

For SI:$1.2 - 0.011A_t$ for 18.58 square meters $< A_t < 55.74$ square meters

$R_1 = 0.6$ for $A_t > 600$ square feet (55.74 m²)

(Equation 16-30)

where:

A_t = Tributary area (span length multiplied by effective width) in square feet (m²) supported by any structural member, and

$R_2 = 1$ for $F \leq 4$ **(Equation 16-31)**

$R_2 = 1.2 - 0.05 F$ for $4 < F < 12$ **(Equation 16-32)**

$R_2 = 0.6$ for $F > 12$ **(Equation 16-33)**

where:

F = For a sloped roof, the number of inches of rise per foot (for SI: $F = 0.12 \times$ slope, with slope expressed as a percentage), or for an arch or dome, the rise-to-span ratio multiplied by 32.

1607.11.2.2 Special-purpose roofs. Roofs used for promenade purposes, roof gardens, assembly purposes or other special purposes shall be designed for a minimum live load as required in Table 1607.1. Such roof live loads are permitted to be reduced in accordance with 1607.9.

1607.11.2.3 Landscaped roofs. Where roofs are to be landscaped, the uniform design live load in the landscaped area shall be 20 psf (0.958 kN/m²). The weight of the landscaping materials shall be considered as dead load and shall be computed on the basis of saturation of the soil.

1607.11.2.4 Awnings and canopies. Awnings and canopies shall be designed for uniform live loads as required in Table 1607.1 as well as for snow loads and wind loads as specified in Sections 1608 and 1609.

1607.12 Crane loads. The crane live load shall be the rated capacity of the crane. Design loads for the runway beams, including connections and support brackets, of moving bridge cranes and monorail cranes shall include the maximum wheel loads of the crane and the vertical impact, lateral and longitudinal forces induced by the moving crane.

1607.12.1 Maximum wheel load. The maximum wheel loads shall be the wheel loads produced by the weight of the bridge, as applicable, plus the sum of the rated capacity and the weight of the trolley with the trolley positioned on its runway at the location where the resulting load effect is maximum.

1607.12.2 Vertical impact force. The maximum wheel loads of the crane shall be increased by the percentages shown below to determine the induced vertical impact or vibration force:

Monorail cranes (powered)................................25 percent

Cab-operated or remotely operated bridge cranes (powered) ....25 percent

Pendant-operated bridge cranes (powered) ....10 percent

Bridge cranes or monorail cranes with hand-geared bridge, trolley and hoist ....0 percent

1607.12.3 Lateral force. The lateral force on crane runway beams with electrically powered trolleys shall be calculated as 20 percent of the sum of the rated capacity of the crane and the weight of the hoist and trolley. The lateral force shall be assumed to act horizontally at the traction surface of a runway beam, in either direction perpendicular to the beam, and shall be distributed according to the lateral stiffness of the runway beam and supporting structure.

1607.12.4 Longitudinal force. The longitudinal force on crane runway beams, except for bridge cranes with hand-geared bridges, shall be calculated as 10 percent of the maximum wheel loads of the crane. The longitudinal force shall be assumed to act horizontally at the traction surface of a runway beam, in either direction parallel to the beam.

1607.13 Interior walls and partitions. Interior walls and partitions that exceed 6 feet (1829 mm) in height, including their finish materials, shall have adequate strength to resist the loads to which they are subjected but not less than a horizontal load of 5 psf (0.240 kN/m²).

Exception: Fabric partitions complying with Section 1607.13.1 shall not be required to resist the minimum horizontal load of 5 psf (0.24 kN/m²).

1607.13.1 Fabric partitions. Fabric partitions that exceed 6 feet (1829 mm) in height, including their finish materials, shall have adequate strength to resist the following load conditions:

1. A horizontal distributed load of 5 psf (0.24 kN/m²) applied to the partition framing. The total area used to determine the distributed load shall be the area of the fabric face between the framing members to which the fabric is attached. The total distributed load shall be uniformly applied to such framing members in proportion to the length of each member.

2. A concentrated load of 40 pounds (0.176 kN) applied to an 8-inch diameter (203 mm) area [50.3 square inches (32 452 mm²)] of the fabric face at a height of 54 inches (1372 mm) above the floor.

SECTION 1608
SNOW LOADS

1608.1 General. Design snow loads shall be determined in accordance with Chapter 7 of ASCE 7, but the design roof load shall not be less than that determined by Section 1607.

1608.2 Ground snow loads. The ground snow loads to be used in determining the design snow loads for roofs shall be determined in accordance with ASCE 7 or Figure 1608.2. When using Figure 1608.2 for sites at elevations above 1,000 feet (304 m), the ground snow load shall be increased from the mapped value by 2 psf (0.095 kN/m²) for every 100 feet (30 480 mm) above 1,000 feet (304 m). Site-specific case studies may be made in lieu of snow loads in Figure 1608.2 or ASCE 7. Ground snow load determination for site-specific case studies shall be approved and shall be based on an extreme value statistical analysis of data available in the vicinity of the site using a value with a 2-percent annual probability of being exceeded (50-year mean recurrence interval).

SECTION 1609
WIND LOADS

1609.1 Applications. Buildings, structures and parts thereof shall be designed to withstand the minimum wind loads prescribed herein. Decreases in wind loads shall not be made for the effect of shielding by other structures.

1609.1.1 Determination of wind loads. Wind loads on every building or structure shall be determined in accordance with Chapter 6 of ASCE 7. The type of opening protection required, the basic wind speed and the exposure category for a site is permitted to be determined in accordance with Section 1609 or ASCE 7. Wind shall be assumed to come from any horizontal direction and wind

pressures shall be assumed to act normal to the surface considered.

Exceptions:

1. Subject to the limitations of Section 1609.1.1.1, the provisions of SBCCI SSTD 10 shall be permitted for applicable Group R-2 and R-3 buildings.

2. Subject to the limitations of Section 1609.1.1.1, residential structures using the provisions of the AF&PA WFCM.

3. Designs using NAAMM FP 1001.

4. Designs using TIA/EIA-222 for antenna-supporting structures and antennas.

1609.1.1.1 Applicability. The provisions of SSTD 10 are applicable only to buildings located within Exposure B or C as defined in Section 1609.4. The provisions of SBCCI SSTD 10 and the AF&PA WFCM shall not apply to buildings sited on the upper half of an isolated hill, ridge or escarpment meeting the following conditions:

1. The hill, ridge or escarpment is 60 feet (18 288 mm) or higher if located in Exposure B or 30 feet (9144 mm) or higher if located in Exposure C;

For Si: 1 foot = 304.8 mm, 1 pound per square foot = 0.0479 kN/m².

FIGURE 1608.2
GROUND SNOW LOADS, *pg*, FOR NEW YORK STATE (psf) GROUND SNOW LOADS AT ELEVATIONS ABOVE 1000 FEET SHALL BE INCREASED BY 2 PSF FOR EVERY 100 FEET ABOVE ELEVATION 1000 FEET

2. The maximum average slope of the hill exceeds 10 percent; and

3. The hill, ridge or escarpment is unobstructed upwind by other such topographic features for a distance from the high point of 50 times the height of the hill or 1 mile (1.61 km), whichever is greater.

1609.1.2 Protection of openings. In wind-borne debris regions, glazing in buildings shall be impact-resistant or protected with an impact-resistant covering meeting the requirements of an approved impact-resisting standard or ASTM E 1996 and ASTM E 1886 referenced therein as follows:

1. Glazed openings located within 30 feet (9144 mm) of grade shall meet the requirements of the Large Missile Test of ASTM E 1996.

2. Glazed openings located more than 30 feet (9144 mm) above grade shall meet the provisions of the Small Missile Test of ASTM E 1996.

Exceptions:

1. Wood structural panels with a minimum thickness of $^7/_{16}$ inch (11.1 mm) and maximum panel span of 8 feet (2438 mm) shall be permitted for opening protection in one- and two-story buildings. Panels shall be precut so that they shall be attached to the framing surrounding the opening containing the product with the glazed opening. Panels shall be secured with the attachment hardware provided. Attachments shall be designed to resist the components and cladding loads determined in accordance with the provisions of ASCE 7. Attachment in accordance with Table 1609.1.2 is permitted for buildings with a mean roof height of 33 feet (10 058 mm) or less where wind speeds do not exceed 130 mph (57.2 m/s).

2. Glazing in Occupancy Category I and II buildings as defined in Section 1604.5, shall be permitted to be unprotected. Where glazing is unprotected, it shall be assumed to be an opening, and the building shall be evaluated to determine if the openings are of sufficient area to constitute an open or partially enclosed building as defined by ASCE 7. Open and partially enclosed buildings shall be designed in accordance with the applicable provisions of ASCE 7.

3. Glazing in Occupancy Category III or IV buildings located over 60 feet (18 288 mm) above the ground and over 30 feet (9144 mm) above aggregate surface roofs located within 1,500 feet (458 m) of the building shall be permitted to be unprotected.

1609.1.2.1 Louvers. Louvers protecting intake and exhaust ventilation ducts not assumed to be open that are located within 30 feet (9144 mm) of grade shall meet requirements of an approved impact-resisting standard or the Large Missile Test of ASTM E 1996.

TABLE 1609.1.2
WIND-BORNE DEBRIS PROTECTION FASTENING SCHEDULE FOR WOOD STRUCTURAL PANELS[a,b,c,d]

FASTENER TYPE	FASTENER SPACING (inches)		
	Panel Span ≤ 4 feet	4 feet < Panel Span ≤ 6 feet	6 feet < Panel Span ≤ 8 feet
No. 6 screws	16	12	9
No. 8 screws	16	16	12

For SI: 1 inch = 25.4 mm, 1 foot = 304.8 mm, 1 pound = 4.4 N, 1 mile per hour = 0.44 m/s.

a. This table is based on a maximum wind speed (3-second gust) of 130 mph and mean roof height of 33 feet or less.

b. Fasteners shall be installed at opposing ends of the wood structural panel. Fasteners shall be located a minimum of 1 inch from the edge of the panel.

c. Fasteners shall be long enough to penetrate through the exterior wall covering a minimum of 1.75 inches into wood wall framing; a minimum of 1.25 inches into concrete block or concrete; or into steel framing by at least three threads. Fasteners shall be located a minimum of 2.5 inches from the edge of concrete block or concrete.

d. Where screws are attached to masonry or masonry/stucco, they shall be attached utilizing vibration-resistant anchors having a minimum withdrawal capacity of 490 pounds.

1609.2 Definitions. The following words and terms shall, for the purposes of Section 1609, have the meanings shown herein.

HURRICANE-PRONE REGIONS. Areas vulnerable to hurricanes defined as:

1. The U. S. Atlantic Ocean and Gulf of Mexico coasts where the basic wind speed is greater than 90 mph (40 m/s) and

2. Hawaii, Puerto Rico, Guam, Virgin Islands and American Samoa.

WIND-BORNE DEBRIS REGION. Portions of hurricane-prone regions that are within 1 mile (1.61 km) of the coastal mean high water line where the basic wind speed is 110 mph (48 m/s) or greater; or portions of hurricane-prone regions where the basic wind speed is 120 mph (53 m/s) or greater; or Hawaii.

1609.3 Basic wind speed. The basic wind speed, in mph, for the determination of the wind loads shall be determined by Figure 1609. Basic wind speed for the special wind regions indicated, near mountainous terrain and near gorges shall be in accordance with local jurisdiction requirements. Basic wind speeds determined by the local jurisdiction shall be in accordance with Section 6.5.4 of ASCE 7.

In nonhurricane-prone regions, when the basic wind speed is estimated from regional climatic data, the basic wind speed shall be not less than the wind speed associated with an annual probability of 0.02 (50-year mean recurrence interval), and the estimate shall be adjusted for equivalence to a 3-second gust wind speed at 33 feet (10 m) above ground in Exposure Category C. The data analysis shall be performed in accordance with Section 6.5.4.2 of ASCE 7.

1609.3.1 Wind speed conversion. When required, the 3-second gust basic wind speeds of Figure 1609 shall be converted to fastest-mile wind speeds, V_{fm}, using Table 1609.3.1 or Equation 16-34.

$$V_{fm} = \frac{(V_{3s} - 10.5)}{1.05}$$

(Equation 16-34)

where:

V_{3S} = 3-second gust basic wind speed from Figure 1609.

TABLE 1609.3.1
EQUIVALENT BASIC WIND SPEEDS[a,b,c]

V_{3S}	85	90	100	105	110	120	125	130	140	145	150	160	170
V_{fm}	71	76	85	90	95	104	109	114	123	128	133	142	152

For SI: 1 mile per hour = 0.44 m/s.

a. Linear interpolation is permitted.

b. V_{3S} is the 3-second gust wind speed (mph).

c. V_{fm} is the fastest mile wind speed (mph).

1609.4 Exposure category. For each wind direction considered, an exposure category that adequately reflects the characteristics of ground surface irregularities shall be determined for the site at which the building or structure is to be constructed. Account shall be taken of variations in ground surface roughness that arise from natural topography and vegetation as well as from constructed features.

1609.4.1 Wind directions and sectors. For each selected wind direction at which the wind loads are to be evaluated, the exposure of the building or structure shall be determined for the two upwind sectors extending 45 degrees (0.79 rad) either side of the selected wind direction. The exposures in these two sectors shall be determined in accordance with Sections 1609.4.2 and 1609.4.3 and the exposure resulting in the highest wind loads shall be used to represent winds from that direction.

1609.4.2 Surface roughness categories. A ground surface roughness within each 45-degree (0.79 rad) sector shall be determined for a distance upwind of the site as defined in Section 1609.4.3 from the categories defined below, for the purpose of assigning an exposure category as defined in Section 1609.4.3.

Surface Roughness B. Urban and suburban areas, wooded areas or other terrain with numerous closely spaced obstructions having the size of single-family dwellings or larger.

Special Wind Region

Notes:
1. Values are nominal design 3-second gust wind speeds in miles per hour (m/s) at 33 ft (10 m) above ground for Exposure C category.
2. Linear interpolation between wind contours is permitted.
3. Islands and coastal areas outside the last contour shall use the last wind speed contour of the coastal area.
4. Mountainous terrain, gorges, ocean promontories, and special wind regions shall be examined for unusual wind conditions.

FIGURE 1609
BASIC WIND SPEED (3-SECOND GUST) MID AND NORTHERN ATLANTIC HURRICANE COASTLINE

Surface Roughness C. Open terrain with scattered obstructions having heights generally less than 30 feet (9144 mm). This category includes flat open country, grasslands, and all water surfaces in hurricane-prone regions.

Surface Roughness D. Flat, unobstructed areas and water surfaces outside hurricane-prone regions. This category includes smooth mud flats, salt flats and unbroken ice.

1609.4.3 Exposure categories. An exposure category shall be determined in accordance with the following:

Exposure B. Exposure B shall apply where the ground surface roughness condition, as defined by Surface Roughness B, prevails in the upwind direction for a distance of at least 2,600 feet (792 m) or 20 times the height of the building, whichever is greater.

Exception: For buildings whose mean roof height is less than or equal to 30 feet (9144 mm), the upwind distance is permitted to be reduced to 1,500 feet (457 m).

Exposure C. Exposure C shall apply for all cases where Exposures B or D do not apply.

Exposure D. Exposure D shall apply where the ground surface roughness, as defined by Surface Roughness D, prevails in the upwind direction for a distance of at least 5,000 feet (1524 m) or 20 times the height of the building, whichever is greater. Exposure D shall extend inland from the shoreline for a distance of 600 feet (183 m) or 20 times the height of the building, whichever is greater.

1609.5 Roof systems.

1609.5.1 Roof deck. The roof deck shall be designed to withstand the wind pressures determined in accordance with ASCE 7.

1609.5.2 Roof coverings. Roof coverings shall comply with Section 1609.5.1.

Exception: Rigid tile roof coverings that are air permeable and installed over a roof deck complying with Section 1609.5.1 are permitted to be designed in accordance with Section 1609.5.3.

Asphalt shingles installed over a roof deck complying with Section 1609.5.1 shall be tested to determine the resistance of the sealant to uplift forces using ASTM D 6381.

Asphalt shingles installed over a roof deck complying with Section 1609.5.1 are permitted to be designed using UL 2390 to determine appropriate uplift and force coefficients applied to the shingle.

1609.5.3 Rigid tile. Wind loads on rigid tile roof coverings shall be determined in accordance with the following equation:

$$M_a = q_h C_L b L L_a [1.0 - GC_p] \qquad \textbf{(Equation 16-35)}$$

For SI: $\left(M_a = \dfrac{q_h C_L b L L_a [1.0 - GC_p]}{1,000} \right)$

where:

b = Exposed width, feet (mm) of the roof tile.

C_L = Lift coefficient. The lift coefficient for concrete and clay tile shall be 0.2 or shall be determined by test in accordance with Section 1715.2.

GC_p = Roof pressure coefficient for each applicable roof zone determined from Chapter 6 of ASCE 7. Roof coefficients shall not be adjusted for internal pressure.

L = Length, feet (mm) of the roof tile.

L_a = Moment arm, feet (mm) from the axis of rotation to the point of uplift on the roof tile. The point of uplift shall be taken at 0.76L from the head of the tile and the middle of the exposed width. For roof tiles with nails or screws (with or without a tail clip), the axis of rotation shall be taken as the head of the tile for direct deck application or as the top edge of the batten for battened applications. For roof tiles fastened only by a nail or screw along the side of the tile, the axis of rotation shall be determined by testing. For roof tiles installed with battens and fastened only by a clip near the tail of the tile, the moment arm shall be determined about the top edge of the batten with consideration given for the point of rotation of the tiles based on straight bond or broken bond and the tile profile.

M_a = Aerodynamic uplift moment, feet-pounds (N-mm) acting to raise the tail of the tile.

q_h = Wind velocity pressure, psf (kN/m²) determined from Section 6.5.10 of ASCE 7.

Concrete and clay roof tiles complying with the following limitations shall be designed to withstand the aerodynamic uplift moment as determined by this section.

1. The roof tiles shall be either loose laid on battens, mechanically fastened, mortar set or adhesive set.

2. The roof tiles shall be installed on solid sheathing which has been designed as components and cladding.

3. An underlayment shall be installed in accordance with Chapter 15.

4. The tile shall be single lapped interlocking with a minimum head lap of not less than 2 inches (51 mm).

5. The length of the tile shall be between 1.0 and 1.75 feet (305 mm and 533 mm).

6. The exposed width of the tile shall be between 0.67 and 1.25 feet (204 mm and 381 mm).

7. The maximum thickness of the tail of the tile shall not exceed 1.3 inches (33 mm).

8. Roof tiles using mortar set or adhesive set systems shall have at least two-thirds of the tile's area free of mortar or adhesive contact.

SECTION 1610
SOIL LATERAL LOADS

1610.1 General. Basement, foundation and retaining walls shall be designed to resist lateral soil loads. Soil loads specified in Table 1610.1 shall be used as the minimum design lateral soil loads unless specified otherwise in a soil investigation report approved by the code enforcement official. Basement walls and other walls in which horizontal movement is restricted at the top shall be designed for at-rest pressure. Retaining walls free to move and rotate at the top are permitted to be designed for active pressure. Design lateral pressure from surcharge loads shall be added to the lateral earth pressure load. Design lateral pressure shall be increased if soils with expansion potential are present at the site.

> **Exception:** Basement walls extending not more than 8 feet (2438 mm) below grade and supporting flexible floor systems shall be permitted to be designed for active pressure.

SECTION 1611
RAIN LOADS

1611.1 Design rain loads. Each portion of a roof shall be designed to sustain the load of rainwater that will accumulate on it if the primary drainage system for that portion is blocked plus the uniform load caused by water that rises above the inlet of the secondary drainage system at its design flow.

$$R = 5.2 \, (d_s + d_h) \qquad \textbf{(Equation 16-36)}$$

For SI: $R = 0.0098 \, (d_s + d_h)$

where:

d_h = Additional depth of water on the undeflected roof above the inlet of secondary drainage system at its design flow (i.e., the hydraulic head), in inches (mm).

d_s = Depth of water on the undeflected roof up to the inlet of secondary drainage system when the primary drainage system is blocked (i.e., the static head), in inches (mm).

R = Rain load on the undeflected roof, in psf (kN/m²). When the phrase "undeflected roof" is used, deflections from loads (including dead loads) shall not be considered when determining the amount of rain on the roof.

1611.2 Ponding instability. For roofs with a slope less than $^1/_4$ inch per foot [1.19 degrees (0.0208 rad)], the design calculations shall include verification of adequate stiffness to preclude progressive deflection in accordance with Section 8.4 of ASCE 7.

1611.3 Controlled drainage. Roofs equipped with hardware to control the rate of drainage shall be equipped with a secondary drainage system at a higher elevation that limits accumulation of water on the roof above that elevation. Such roofs shall be designed to sustain the load of rainwater that will accumulate on them to the elevation of the secondary drainage system plus the uniform load caused by water that rises above the inlet of the secondary drainage system at its design flow determined from Section 1611.1. Such roofs shall also be checked for ponding instability in accordance with Section 1611.2.

TABLE 1610.1
SOIL LATERAL LOAD

DESCRIPTION OF BACKFILL MATERIAL[c]	UNIFIED SOIL CLASSIFICATION	DESIGN LATERAL SOIL LOAD[a] (pound per square foot per foot of depth)	
		Active pressure	At-rest pressure
Well-graded, clean gravels; gravel-sand mixes	GW	30	60
Poorly graded clean gravels; gravel-sand mixes	GP	30	60
Silty gravels, poorly graded gravel-sand mixes	GM	40	60
Clayey gravels, poorly graded gravel-and-clay mixes	GC	45	60
Well-graded, clean sands; gravelly sand mixes	SW	30	60
Poorly graded clean sands; sand-gravel mixes	SP	30	60
Silty sands, poorly graded sand-silt mixes	SM	45	60
Sand-silt clay mix with plastic fines	SM-SC	45	100
Clayey sands, poorly graded sand-clay mixes	SC	60	100
Inorganic silts and clayey silts	ML	45	100
Mixture of inorganic silt and clay	ML-CL	60	100
Inorganic clays of low to medium plasticity	CL	60	100
Organic silts and silt clays, low plasticity	OL	Note b	Note b
Inorganic clayey silts, elastic silts	MH	Note b	Note b
Inorganic clays of high plasticity	CH	Note b	Note b
Organic clays and silty clays	OH	Note b	Note b

For SI: 1 pound per square foot per foot of depth = 0.157 kPa/m, 1 foot = 304.8 mm.

a. Design lateral soil loads are given for moist conditions for the specified soils at their optimum densities. Actual field conditions shall govern. Submerged or saturated soil pressures shall include the weight of the buoyant soil plus the hydrostatic loads.

b. Unsuitable as backfill material.

c. The definition and classification of soil materials shall be in accordance with ASTM D 2487.

SECTION 1612
FLOOD LOADS

1612.1 General. Within flood hazard areas as established in Section 1612.3, all new construction of buildings, structures and portions of buildings and structures, including substantial improvement and restoration of substantial damage to buildings and structures, shall be designed and constructed to resist the effects of flood hazards and flood loads. For buildings that are located in more than one flood hazard area, the provisions associated with the most restrictive flood hazard area shall apply.

1612.2 Definitions. The following words and terms shall, for the purposes of this section, have the meanings shown herein.

BASE FLOOD. The flood having a 1-percent chance of being equaled or exceeded in any given year.

BASE FLOOD ELEVATION. The elevation of the base flood, including wave height, relative to the National Geodetic Vertical Datum (NGVD), North American Vertical Datum (NAVD) or other datum specified on the Flood Insurance Rate Map (FIRM).

BASEMENT. The portion of a building having its floor subgrade (below ground level) on all sides.

DESIGN FLOOD. The flood associated with the greater of the following two areas:

1. Area with a flood plain subject to a 1-percent or greater chance of flooding in any year; or

2. Area designated as a flood hazard area on a community's flood hazard map, or otherwise legally designated.

DESIGN FLOOD ELEVATION. The elevation of the "design flood," including wave height, relative to the datum specified on the community's legally designated flood hazard map. In areas designated as Zone AO, the design flood elevation shall be the elevation of the highest existing grade of the building's perimeter plus the depth number (in feet) specified on the flood hazard map. In areas designated as Zone AO where a depth number is not specified on the map, the depth number shall be taken as being equal to 2 feet (610 mm).

DRY FLOODPROOFING. A combination of design modifications that results in a building or structure, including the attendant utility and sanitary facilities, being water tight with walls substantially impermeable to the passage of water and with structural components having the capacity to resist loads as identified in ASCE 7.

EXISTING CONSTRUCTION. Any buildings and structures for which the "start of construction" commenced before the effective date of the community's first flood plain management code, ordinance or standard. "Existing construction" is also referred to as "existing structures."

EXISTING STRUCTURE. See "Existing construction."

FLOOD or FLOODING. A general and temporary condition of partial or complete inundation of normally dry land from:

1. The overflow of inland or tidal waters.

2. The unusual and rapid accumulation or runoff of surface waters from any source.

FLOOD DAMAGE-RESISTANT MATERIALS. Any construction material capable of withstanding direct and prolonged contact with floodwaters without sustaining any damage that requires more than cosmetic repair.

FLOOD HAZARD AREA. The greater of the following two areas:

1. The area within a flood plain subject to a 1-percent or greater chance of flooding in any year.

2. The area designated as a flood hazard area on a community's flood hazard map, or otherwise legally designated.

FLOOD HAZARD AREA SUBJECT TO HIGH VELOCITY WAVE ACTION. Area within the flood hazard area that is subject to high velocity wave action, and shown on a Flood Insurance Rate Map (FIRM) or other flood hazard map as Zone V, VO, VE or V1-30.

FLOOD INSURANCE RATE MAP (FIRM). An official map of a community on which the Federal Emergency Management Agency (FEMA) has delineated both the special flood hazard areas and the risk premium zones applicable to the community.

FLOOD INSURANCE STUDY. The official report provided by the Federal Emergency Management Agency containing the Flood Insurance Rate Map (FIRM), the Flood Boundary and Floodway Map (FBFM), the water surface elevation of the base flood and supporting technical data.

FLOODWAY. The channel of the river, creek or other watercourse and the adjacent land areas that must be reserved in order to discharge the base flood without cumulatively increasing the water surface elevation more than a designated height.

LOWEST FLOOR. The floor of the lowest enclosed area, including basement, but excluding any unfinished or flood-resistant enclosure, usable solely for vehicle parking, building access or limited storage provided that such enclosure is not built so as to render the structure in violation of this section.

SPECIAL FLOOD HAZARD AREA. The land area subject to flood hazards and shown on a Flood Insurance Rate Map or other flood hazard map as Zone A, AE, A1-30, A99, AR, AO, AH, V, VO, VE or V1-30.

START OF CONSTRUCTION. The date of permit issuance for new construction and substantial improvements to existing structures, provided the actual start of construction, repair, reconstruction, rehabilitation, addition, placement or other improvement is within 180 days after the date of issuance. The actual start of construction means the first placement of permanent construction of a building (including a manufactured home) on a site, such as the pouring of a slab or footings, installation of pilings or construction of columns.

Permanent construction does not include land preparation (such as clearing, excavation, grading or filling), the installation of streets or walkways, excavation for a basement, footings, piers or foundations, the erection of temporary forms or the installation of accessory buildings such as garages or sheds not occupied as dwelling units or not part of the main building. For a substantial improvement, the actual "start of construction" means the first alteration of any wall, ceiling, floor or other structural part of a building, whether or not that alteration affects the external dimensions of the building.

SUBSTANTIAL DAMAGE. Damage of any origin sustained by a structure whereby the cost of restoring the structure to its before-damaged condition would equal or exceed 50 percent of the market value of the structure before the damage occurred.

SUBSTANTIAL IMPROVEMENT. Any repair, reconstruction, rehabilitation, addition or improvement of a building or structure, the cost of which equals or exceeds 50 percent of the market value of the structure before the improvement or repair is started. If the structure has sustained substantial damage, any repairs are considered substantial improvement regardless of the actual repair work performed. The term does not, however, include either:

1. Any project for improvement of a building required to correct existing health, sanitary or safety code violations identified by the code enforcement official and that are the minimum necessary to assure safe living conditions.

2. Any alteration of a historic structure provided that the alteration will not preclude the structure's continued designation as a historic structure.

1612.3 Establishment of flood hazard areas. To establish flood hazard areas, the governing body shall adopt a flood hazard map and supporting data. The flood hazard map shall include, at a minimum, areas of special flood hazard as identified by the Federal Emergency Management Agency in the applicable flood insurance study for the region, as amended or revised with the accompanying Flood Insurance Rate Map (FIRM) and Flood Boundary and Floodway Map (FBFM) and related supporting data along with any revisions thereto. The adopted flood hazard map and supporting data are hereby adopted by reference and declared to be part of this section.

1612.4 Design and construction. The design and construction of buildings and structures located in flood hazard areas, including flood hazard areas subject to high velocity wave action, shall be in accordance with ASCE 24.

1612.5 Flood hazard documentation. The following documentation shall be prepared and sealed by a registered design professional and submitted to the code enforcement official:

1. For construction in flood hazard areas not subject to high-velocity wave action:

   1.1. The elevation of the lowest floor, including the basement, as required by the lowest floor elevation inspection in Section 109.3.3.

   1.2. For fully enclosed areas below the design flood elevation where provisions to allow for the automatic entry and exit of floodwaters do not meet the minimum requirements in Section 2.6.2.1 of ASCE 24, construction documents shall include a statement that the design will provide for equalization of hydrostatic flood forces in accordance with Section 2.6.2.2 of ASCE 24.

   1.3. For dry floodproofed nonresidential buildings, construction documents shall include a statement that the dry floodproofing is designed in accordance with ASCE 24.

2. For construction in flood hazard areas subject to high-velocity wave action:

   2.1. The elevation of the bottom of the lowest horizontal structural member as required by the lowest floor elevation inspection in Section 109.3.3.

   2.2. Construction documents shall include a statement that the building is designed in accordance with ASCE 24, including that the pile or column foundation and building or structure to be attached thereto is designed to be anchored to resist flotation, collapse and lateral movement due to the effects of wind and flood loads acting simultaneously on all building components, and other load requirements of Chapter 16.

   2.3. For breakaway walls designed to resist a nominal load of less than 10 psf (0.48 kN/m^2) or more than 20 psf (0.96 kN/m^2), construction documents shall include a statement that the breakaway wall is designed in accordance with ASCE 24.

SECTION 1613
EARTHQUAKE LOADS

1613.1 Scope. Every structure, and portion thereof, including nonstructural components that are permanently attached to structures and their supports and attachments, shall be designed and constructed to resist the effects of earthquake motions in accordance with ASCE 7, excluding Chapter 14 and Appendix 11A. The seismic design category for a structure is permitted to be determined in accordance with Section 1613 or ASCE 7.

Exceptions:

1. Detached one- and two-family dwellings, assigned to Seismic Design Category A, B or C, or located where the mapped short-period spectral response acceleration, S_S, is less than 0.4 g.

2. The seismic-force-resisting system of wood-frame buildings that conform to the provisions of Section 2308 are not required to be analyzed as specified in this section.

3. Agricultural storage structures intended only for incidental human occupancy.

4. Structures that require special consideration of their response characteristics and environment that are not addressed by this code or ASCE 7 and for which other regulations provide seismic criteria, such as vehicular bridges, electrical transmission towers, hydraulic structures, buried utility lines and their appurtenances and nuclear reactors.

FIGURE 1613.5(1) MAXIMUM CONSIDERED EARTHQUAKE GROUND MOTION FOR NEW YORK STATE OF 0.2 SEC SPECTRAL RESPONSE ACCELERATION (5% OF CRITICAL DAMPING), SITE CLASS B

NOTE: Contours are % g. This map is based on the 2008 USGS map representing a 2% probability of exceedance within a 50 year period.

FIGURE 1613.5(2) MAXIMUM CONSIDERED EARTHQUAKE GROUND MOTION FOR NEW YORK STATE OF 1 SEC SPECTRAL RESPONSE ACCELERATION (5% OF CRITICAL DAMPING), SITE CLASS B

NOTE: Contours are % g. This map is based on the 2008 USGS map representing a 2% probability of exceedance within a 50 year period.

TABLE 1613.5.2
SITE CLASS DEFINITIONS

SITE CLASS	SOIL PROFILE NAME	AVERAGE PROPERTIES IN TOP 100 feet, SEE SECTION 1613.5.5		
		Soil shear wave velocity, $\overline{v}_s$, (ft/s)	Standard penetration resistance, $\overline{N}$	Soil undrained shear strength, $\overline{s}_u$, (psf)
A	Hard rock	$\overline{v}_s > 5,000$	N/A	N/A
B	Rock	$2,500 < \overline{v}_s \le 5,000$	N/A	N/A
C	Very dense soil and soft rock	$1,200 < \overline{v}_s \le 2,500$	$\overline{N} > 50$	$\overline{s}_u \ge 2,000$
D	Stiff soil profile	$600 \le \overline{v}_s \le 1,200$	$15 \le \overline{N} \le 50$	$1,000 ? \overline{s}_u \le 2,000$
E	Soft soil profile	$\overline{v}_s < 600$	$\overline{N} < 15$	$\overline{s}_u < 1,000$
E	-	Any profile with more than 10 feet of soil having the following characteristics: 1. Plasticity index $PI > 20$, 2. Moisture content $w \ge 40\%$, and 3. Undrained shear strength $\overline{s}_u < 500$ psf		
F	-	Any profile containing soils having one or more of the following characteristics: 1. Soils vulnerable to potential failure or collapse under seismic loading such as liquefiable soils, quick and highly sensitive clays, collapsible weakly cemented soils. 2. Peats and/or highly organic clays ($H > 10$ feet of peat and/or highly organic clay where H= thickness of soil) 3. Very high plasticity clays ($H > 25$ feet with plasticity index $PI > 75$) 4. Very thick soft/medium stiff clays ($H > 120$ feet)		

For SI: 1 foot = 304.8 mm, 1 square foot = 0.0929 m², 1 pound per square foot = 0.0479 kPa. N/A = Not applicable

1613.2 Definitions. The following words and terms shall, for the purposes of this section, have the meanings shown herein.

DESIGN EARTHQUAKE GROUND MOTION. The earthquake ground motion that buildings and structures are specifically proportioned to resist in Section 1613.

MAXIMUM CONSIDERED EARTHQUAKE GROUND MOTION. The most severe earthquake effects considered by this code.

MECHANICAL SYSTEMS. For the purposes of determining seismic loads in ASCE 7, mechanical systems shall include plumbing systems as specified therein.

ORTHOGONAL. To be in two horizontal directions, at 90 degrees (1.57 rad) to each other.

SEISMIC DESIGN CATEGORY. A classification assigned to a structure based on its occupancy category and the severity of the design earthquake ground motion at the site.

SEISMIC-FORCE-RESISTING SYSTEM. That part of the structural system that has been considered in the design to provide the required resistance to the prescribed seismic forces.

SITE CLASS. A classification assigned to a site based on the types of soils present and their engineering properties as defined in Section 1613.5.2.

SITE COEFFICIENTS. The values of F_a and F_v indicated in Tables 1613.5.3(1) and 1613.5.3(2), respectively.

1613.3 Existing buildings. Additions, alterations, modification, or change of occupancy of existing buildings shall be in accordance with the *Existing Building Code of New York State*.

1613.4 Special inspections. Where required by Section 1705.3, the statement of special inspections shall include the special inspections required by Section 1705.3.1.

1613.5 Seismic ground motion values. Seismic ground motion values shall be determined in accordance with this section.

1613.5.1 Mapped acceleration parameters. The parameters S_s and S_1 shall be determined from the 0.2 and 1-second spectral response accelerations shown on Figures 1613.5(1) and 1613.5(2). Where S_1 is less than or equal to 0.04 and S_s is less than or equal to 0.15, the structure is permitted to be assigned to Seismic Design Category A.

1613.5.2 Site class definitions. Based on the site soil properties, the site shall be classified as either Site Class A, B, C, D, E or F in accordance with Table 1613.5.2. When the soil properties are not known in sufficient detail to determine the site class, Site Class D shall be used unless the code enforcement official or geotechnical data determines that Site Class E or F soil is likely to be present at the site.

1613.5.3 Site coefficients and adjusted maximum considered earthquake spectral response acceleration parameters. The maximum considered earthquake spectral response acceleration for short periods, S_{MS}, and at 1-second period, S_{M1}, adjusted for site class effects shall be determined by Equations 16-37 and 16-38, respectively:

$$S_{MS} = F_a S_s \qquad \text{(Equation 16-37)}$$
$$S_{M1} = F_v S_1 \qquad \text{(Equation 16-38)}$$

where:

F_a = Site coefficient defined in Table 1613.5.3(1).

F_v = Site coefficient defined in Table 1613.5.3(2).

S_S = The mapped spectral accelerations for short periods as determined in Section 1613.5.1.

S_1 = The mapped spectral accelerations for a 1-second period as determined in Section 1613.5.1.

TABLE 1613.5.3(1)
VALUES OF SITE COEFFICIENT $F_a{}^a$

SITE CLASS	MAPPED SPECTRAL RESPONSE ACCELERATION AT SHORT PERIOD				
	$S_s \leq 0.25$	$S_s = 0.50$	$S_s = 0.75$	$S_s = 1.00$	$S_s \geq 1.25$
A	0.8	0.8	0.8	0.8	0.8
B	1.0	1.0	1.0	1.0	1.0
C	1.2	1.2	1.1	1.0	1.0
D	1.6	1.4	1.2	1.1	1.0
E	2.5	1.7	1.2	0.9	0.9
F	Note b	Note b	Note b	Note b	Note b

a. Use straight-line interpolation for intermediate values of mapped spectral response acceleration at short period, S_s.
b. Values shall be determined in accordance with Section 11.4.7 of ASCE 7.

TABLE 1613.5.3(2)
VALUES OF SITE COEFFICIENT $F_v{}^a$

SITE CLASS	MAPPED SPECTRAL RESPONSE ACCELERATION AT 1-SECOND PERIOD				
	$S_1 \leq 0.1$	$S_1 = 0.2$	$S_1 = 0.3$	$S_1 = 0.4$	$S_1 \geq 0.5$
A	0.8	0.8	0.8	0.8	0.8
B	1.0	1.0	1.0	1.0	1.0
C	1.7	1.6	1.5	1.4	1.3
D	2.4	2.0	1.8	1.6	1.5
E	3.5	3.2	2.8	2.4	2.4
F	Note b	Note b	Note b	Note b	Note b

a. Use straight-line interpolation for intermediate values of mapped spectral response acceleration at 1-second period, S_1.
b. Values shall be determined in accordance with Section 11.4.7 of ASCE 7.

1613.5.4 Design spectral response acceleration parameters. Five-percent damped design spectral response acceleration at short periods, S_{DS}, and at 1-second period, S_{D1}, shall be determined from Equations 16-39 and 16-40, respectively:

$$S_{DS} = \frac{2}{3} S_{MS}$$ **(Equations 16-39)**

$$S_{D1} = \frac{2}{3} S_{M1}$$ **(Equations 16-40)**

where:

S_{MS} = The maximum considered earthquake spectral response accelerations for short period as determined in Section 1613.5.3.

S_{M1} = The maximum considered earthquake spectral response accelerations for 1-second period as determined in Section 1613.5.3.

1613.5.5 Site classification for seismic design. Site classification for Site Class C, D or E shall be determined from Table 1613.5.5.

The notations presented below apply to the upper 100 feet (30 480 mm) of the site profile. Profiles containing distinctly different soil and/or rock layers shall be subdivided into those layers designated by a number that ranges from 1 to n at the bottom where there is a total of n distinct layers in the upper 100 feet (30 480 mm). The symbol i then refers to any one of the layers between 1 and n.

where:

v_{si} = The shear wave velocity in feet per second (m/s).

d_i = The thickness of any layer between 0 and 100 feet (30 480 mm).

where:

$$\bar{v}_s = \frac{\sum\limits_{i=1}^{n} d_i}{\sum\limits_{i=1}^{n} \dfrac{d_i}{v_{si}}}$$ **(Equation 16-41)**

$$\sum\limits_{i=1}^{n} di = 100 \text{ feet (30 480 mm)}$$

N_i is the Standard Penetration Resistance (ASTM D 1586) not to exceed 100 blows/foot (305 mm) as directly measured in the field without corrections. When refusal is met for a rock layer, N_i shall be taken as 100 blows/foot (305 mm).

$$\bar{N} = \frac{\sum\limits_{i=1}^{n} d_i}{\sum\limits_{i=1}^{n} \dfrac{d_i}{N_i}}$$ **(Equation 16-42)**

where N_i and d_i in Equation 16-42 are for cohesionless soil, cohesive soil and rock layers.

$$\bar{N}_{ch} = \frac{d_s}{\sum\limits_{i=1}^{m} \dfrac{d_i}{N_i}}$$ **(Equation 16-43)**

where:

$$\sum\limits_{i=1}^{m} d_i = d_s$$

Use d_i and N_i for cohesionless soil layers only in Equation 16-43.

d_s = The total thickness of cohesionless soil layers in the top 100 feet (30 480 mm).

m = The number of cohesionless soil layers in the top 100 feet (30 480 mm).

s_{ui} = The undrained shear strength in psf (kPa), not to exceed 5,000 psf (240 kPa), ASTM D 2166 or D 2850.

$$\bar{s}_u = \frac{d_c}{\displaystyle\sum_{i=1}^{k} \frac{d_i}{s_{ui}}}$$ (Equation 16-44)

where:

$$\sum_{i=1}^{k} d_i = d_c$$

d_c = The total thickness of cohesive soil layers in the top 100 feet (30 480 mm).

k = The number of cohesive soil layers in the top 100 feet (30 480 mm).

PI = The plasticity index, ASTM D 4318.

w = The moisture content in percent, ASTM D 2216.

Where a site does not qualify under the criteria for Site Class F and there is a total thickness of soft clay greater than 10 feet (3048 mm) where a soft clay layer is defined by: $s_u < 500$ psf (24 kPa), $w \geq 40$ percent, and PI > 20, it shall be classified as Site Class E.

The shear wave velocity for rock, Site Class B, shall be either measured on site or estimated by a geotechnical engineer or engineering geologist/seismologist for competent rock with moderate fracturing and weathering. Softer and more highly fractured and weathered rock shall either be measured on site for shear wave velocity or classified as Site Class C.

The hard rock category, Site Class A, shall be supported by shear wave velocity measurements either on site or on profiles of the same rock type in the same formation with an equal or greater degree of weathering and fracturing. Where hard rock conditions are known to be continuous to a depth of 100 feet (30 480 mm), surficial shear wave velocity measurements are permitted to be extrapolated to assess $\bar{v}_s$.

The rock categories, Site Classes A and B, shall not be used if there is more than 10 feet (3048 mm) of soil between the rock surface and the bottom of the spread footing or mat foundation.

TABLE 1613.5.5
SITE CLASSIFICATION[a]

SITE CLASS	$\bar{v}_s$	$\bar{N}$ or $\bar{N}_{ch}$	$\bar{s}_u$
E	< 600 ft/s	< 15	< 1,000 psf
D	600 to 1,200 ft/s	15 to 50	1,000 to 2,000 psf
C	1,200 to 2,500 ft/s	> 50	> 2,000

For SI: 1 foot per second = 304.8 mm per second, 1 pound per square foot = 0.0479 kN/m².

a. If the $\bar{s}_u$ method is used and the $\bar{N}_{ch}$ and $\bar{s}_u$ criteria differ, select the category ith the softer soils (for example, use Site Class E instead of D).

1613.5.5.1 Steps for classifying a site.

1. Check for the four categories of Site Class F requiring site-specific evaluation. If the site corresponds to any of these categories, classify the site as Site Class F and conduct a site-specific evaluation.

2. Check for the existence of a total thickness of soft clay > 10 feet (3048 mm) where a soft clay layer is defined by: $\bar{s}_u < 500$ psf (24 kPa), $w \geq 40$ percent and $PI > 20$. If these criteria are satisfied, classify the site as Site Class E.

3. Categorize the site using one of the following three methods with $\bar{v}_s$, $\bar{N}$, and $\bar{s}_u$ and computed in all cases as specified.

   3.1. $\bar{v}_s$, for the top 100 feet (30 480 mm) ($\bar{v}_s$ method).

   3.2. $\bar{N}$ for the top 100 feet (30 480 mm) ($\bar{N}$ method).

   3.3. $\bar{N}_{ch}$ for cohesionless soil layers ($PI < 20$) in the top 100 feet (30 480 mm) and average, $\bar{s}_u$ for cohesive soil layers ($PI > 20$) in the top 100 feet (30 480 mm) ($\bar{s}_u$ method).

1613.5.6 Determination of seismic design category. Occupancy Category I, II or III structures located where the mapped spectral response acceleration parameter at 1-second period, S_1, is greater than or equal to 0.75 shall be assigned to Seismic Design Category E. Occupancy Category IV structures located where the mapped spectral response acceleration parameter at 1-second period, S_1, is greater than or equal to 0.75 shall be assigned to Seismic Design Category F. All other structures shall be assigned to a seismic design category based on their occupancy category and the design spectral response acceleration coefficients, S_{DS} and S_{D1}, determined in accordance with Section 1613.5.4 or the site-specific procedures of ASCE 7. Each building and structure shall be assigned to the more severe seismic design category in accordance with Table 1613.5.6(1) or 1613.5.6(2), irrespective of the fundamental period of vibration of the structure, T.

TABLE 1613.5.6(1)
SEISMIC DESIGN CATEGORY BASED ON SHORT-PERIOD RESPONSE ACCELERATIONS

VALUE OF S_{DS}	OCCUPANCY CATEGORY		
	I or II	III	IV
$S_{DS} < 0.167g$	A	A	A
$0.167g \leq S_{DS} < 0.33g$	B	B	C
$0.33g \leq S_{DS} < 0.50g$	C	C	D
$0.50g \leq S_{DS}$	D	D	D

TABLE 1613.5.6(2)
SEISMIC DESIGN CATEGORY BASED ON 1-SECOND PERIOD RESPONSE ACCELERATION

VALUE OF S_{D1}	OCCUPANCY CATEGORY		
	I or II	III	IV
$S_{D1} < 0.067g$	A	A	A
$0.067g \leq S_{D1} < 0.133g$	B	B	C
$0.133g \leq S_{D1} < 0.20g$	C	C	D
$0.20g \leq S_{D1}$	D	D	D

1613.5.6.1 Alternative seismic design category determination. Where S_1 is less than 0.75, the seismic design category is permitted to be determined from Table 1613.5.6(1) alone when all of the following apply:

1. In each of the two orthogonal directions, the approximate fundamental period of the structure, T_a, in each of the two orthogonal directions determined in accordance with Section 12.8.2.1 of ASCE 7, is less than 0.8 T_s determined in accordance with Section 11.4.5 of ASCE 7.

2. In each of the two orthogonal directions, the fundamental period of the structure used to calculate the story drift is less than T_s.

3. Equation 12.8-2 of ASCE 7 is used to determine the seismic response coefficient, C_s.

4. The diaphragms are rigid as defined in Section 12.3.1 in ASCE 7 or for diaphragms that are flexible, the distance between vertical elements of the seismic-force-resisting system does not exceed 40 feet (12 192 mm).

1613.5.6.2 Simplified design procedure. Where the alternate simplified design procedure of ASCE 7 is used, the seismic design category shall be determined in accordance with ASCE 7.

1613.6 Alternatives to ASCE 7. The provisions of Section 1613.6 shall be permitted as alternatives to the relevant provisions of ASCE 7.

1613.6.1 Assumption of flexible diaphragm. Add the following text at the end of Section 12.3.1.1 of ASCE 7:

Diaphragms constructed of wood structural panels or untopped steel decking shall also be permitted to be idealized as flexible, provided all of the following conditions are met:

1. Toppings of concrete or similar materials are not placed over wood structural panel diaphragms except for nonstructural toppings no greater than $1^1/_2$ inches (38 mm) thick.

2. Each line of vertical elements of the lateral-force-resisting system complies with the allowable story drift of Table 12.12-1.

3. Vertical elements of the lateral-force-resisting system are light-framed walls sheathed with wood structural panels rated for shear resistance or steel sheets.

4. Portions of wood structural panel diaphragms that cantilever beyond the vertical elements of the lateral-force-resisting system are designed in accordance with Section 2305.2.5 of the *Building Code of New York State*.

1613.6.2 Additional seismic-force-resisting systems for seismically isolated structures. Add the following exception to the end of Section 17.5.4.2 of ASCE 7:

Exception: For isolated structures designed in accordance with this standard, the Structural System Limitations and the Building Height Limitations in Table 12.2-1 for ordinary steel concentrically braced frames (OCBFs) as defined in Chapter 11 and ordinary moment frames (OMFs) as defined in Chapter 11 are permitted to be taken as 160 feet (48 768 mm) for struc-

tures assigned to Seismic Design Category D, E or F, provided that the following conditions are satisfied:

1. The value of R_I as defined in Chapter 17 is taken as 1.

2. For OMFs and OCBFs, design is in accordance with AISC 341.

CHAPTER 17

STRUCTURAL TESTS AND SPECIAL INSPECTIONS

SECTION 1701
GENERAL

1701.1 Scope. The provisions of this chapter shall govern the quality, workmanship and requirements for materials covered. Materials of construction and tests shall conform to the applicable standards listed in this code.

1701.2 New materials. New building materials, equipment, appliances, systems or methods of construction not provided for in this code, and any material of questioned suitability proposed for use in the construction of a building or structure, shall be subjected to the tests prescribed in this chapter and in the approved rules to determine character, quality and limitations of use.

1701.3 Used materials. The use of second-hand materials that meet the minimum requirements of this code for new materials shall be permitted.

SECTION 1702
DEFINITIONS

1702.1 General. The following words and terms shall, for the purposes of this chapter and as used elsewhere in this code, have the meanings shown herein.

APPROVED AGENCY. An established and recognized agency regularly engaged in conducting tests or furnishing inspection services, when such agency has been approved.

APPROVED FABRICATOR. An established and qualified person, firm or corporation approved by the code enforcement official pursuant to Chapter 17 of this code.

CERTIFICATE OF COMPLIANCE. A certificate stating that materials and products meet specified standards or that work was done in compliance with approved construction documents.

DESIGNATED SEISMIC SYSTEM. Those architectural, electrical and mechanical systems and their components that require design in accordance with Chapter 13 of ASCE 7 and for which the component importance factor, I_p, is greater than 1 in accordance with Section 13.1.3 of ASCE 7.

FABRICATED ITEM. Structural, load-bearing or lateral load-resisting assemblies consisting of materials assembled prior to installation in a building or structure or subjected to operations such as heat treatment, thermal cutting, cold working or reforming after manufacture and prior to installation in a building or structure. Materials produced in accordance with standard specifications referenced by this code, such as rolled structural steel shapes, steel-reinforcing bars, masonry units and wood structural panels shall not be considered "fabricated items."

INSPECTION CERTIFICATE. An identification applied on a product by an approved agency containing the name of the manufacturer, the function and performance characteris-

tics, and the name and identification of an approved agency that indicates that the product or material has been inspected and evaluated by an approved agency (see Section 1703.5 and "Label," "Manufacturer's designation" and "Mark").

LABEL. An identification applied on a product by the manufacturer that contains the name of the manufacturer, the function and performance characteristics of the product or material, and the name and identification of an approved agency and that indicates that the representative sample of the product or material has been tested and evaluated by an approved agency (see Section 1703.5 and "Inspection certificate," "Manufacturer's designation" and "Mark").

MAIN WIND-FORCE-RESISTING SYSTEM. An assemblage of structural elements assigned to provide support and stability for the overall structure. The system generally receives wind loading from more than one surface.

MANUFACTURER'S DESIGNATION. An identification applied on a product by the manufacturer indicating that a product or material complies with a specified standard or set of rules (see also "Inspection certificate," "Label" and "Mark").

MARK. An identification applied on a product by the manufacturer indicating the name of the manufacturer and the function of a product or material (see also "Inspection certificate," "Label" and "Manufacturer's designation").

SPECIAL INSPECTION. Inspection as herein required of the materials, installation, fabrication, erection or placement of components and connections requiring special expertise to ensure compliance with approved construction documents and referenced standards (see Section 1704).

SPECIAL INSPECTION, CONTINUOUS. The full-time observation of work requiring special inspection by an approved special inspector who is present in the area where the work is being performed.

SPECIAL INSPECTION, PERIODIC. The part-time or intermittent observation of work requiring special inspection by an approved special inspector who is present in the area where the work has been or is being performed and at the completion of the work.

SPRAYED FIRE-RESISTANT MATERIALS. Cementitious or fibrous materials that are spray applied to provide fire-resistant protection of the substrates.

STRUCTURAL OBSERVATION. The visual observation of the structural system by a registered design professional for general conformance to the approved construction documents at significant construction stages and at completion of the structural system. Structural observation does not include or waive the responsibility for the inspection required by Section 109, 1704 or other sections of this code.

SECTION 1703
APPROVALS

1703.1 Approved agency. An approved agency shall provide all information as necessary for the code enforcement official to determine that the agency meets the applicable requirements.

1703.1.1 Independent. An approved agency shall be objective and competent. The agency shall also disclose possible conflicts of interest so that objectivity can be confirmed.

1703.1.2 Equipment. An approved agency shall have adequate equipment to perform required tests. The equipment shall be periodically calibrated.

1703.1.3 Personnel. An approved agency shall employ experienced personnel educated in conducting, supervising and evaluating tests and/or inspections.

1703.2 Written approval. Any material, appliance, equipment, system or method of construction meeting the requirements of this code shall be approved in writing after satisfactory completion of the required tests and submission of required test reports.

1703.3 Approved record. For any material, appliance, equipment, system or method of construction that has been approved, a record of such approval, including the conditions and limitations of the approval, shall be kept on file in the code enforcement official's office and shall be open to public inspection at appropriate times.

1703.4 Performance. Specific information consisting of test reports conducted by an approved testing agency in accordance with standards referenced in Chapter 35, or other such information as necessary, shall be provided for the code enforcement official to determine that the material meets the applicable code requirements.

1703.4.1 Research and investigation. Sufficient technical data shall be submitted to the code enforcement official to substantiate the proposed use of any material or assembly. If it is determined that the evidence submitted is satisfactory proof of performance for the use intended, the code enforcement official shall approve the use of the material or assembly subject to the requirements of this code. The costs, reports and investigations required under these provisions shall be paid by the permit applicant.

1703.4.2 Research reports. Supporting data, where necessary to assist in the approval of materials or assemblies not specifically provided for in this code, shall consist of valid research reports from approved sources.

1703.5 Labeling. Where materials or assemblies are required by this code to be labeled, such materials and assemblies shall be labeled by an approved agency in accordance with Section 1703. Products and materials required to be labeled shall be labeled in accordance with the procedures set forth in Sections 1703.5.1 through 1703.5.3.

1703.5.1 Testing. An approved agency shall test a representative sample of the product or material being labeled to the relevant standard or standards. The approved agency shall maintain a record of the tests performed. The record shall provide sufficient detail to verify compliance with the test standard.

1703.5.2 Inspection and identification. The approved agency shall periodically perform an inspection, which shall be in-plant if necessary, of the product or material that is to be labeled. The inspection shall verify that the labeled product or material is representative of the product or material tested.

1703.5.3 Label information. The label shall contain the manufacturer's or distributor's identification, model number, serial number or definitive information describing the product or material's performance characteristics and approved agency's identification.

1703.6 Heretofore approved materials. The use of any material already fabricated or of any construction already erected, which conformed to requirements or approvals heretofore in effect, shall be permitted to continue, if not detrimental to life, health or safety to the public.

1703.7 Evaluation and follow-up inspection services. Where structural components or other items regulated by this code are not visible for inspection after completion of a prefabricated assembly, the permit applicant shall submit a report of each prefabricated assembly. The report shall indicate the complete details of the assembly, including a description of the assembly and its components, the basis upon which the assembly is being evaluated, test results and similar information and other data as necessary for the code enforcement official to determine conformance to this code. Such a report shall be approved by the code enforcement official.

1703.7.1 Follow-up inspection. The permit applicant shall provide for special inspections of fabricated items in accordance with Section 1704.2.

1703.7.2 Test and inspection records. Copies of necessary test and inspection records shall be filed with the code enforcement official.

SECTION 1704
SPECIAL INSPECTIONS

1704.1 General. Where application is made for construction as described in this section, the owner or the registered design professional in responsible charge acting as the owner's agent shall employ one or more special inspectors to provide inspections during construction on the types of work listed under Section 1704. The special inspector shall be a qualified person who shall demonstrate competence, to the satisfaction of the code enforcement official, for inspection of the particular type of construction or operation requiring special inspection. The qualifications outlined in Table 1704.1 identify the minimum qualifications of the special inspector. The special inspector shall provide written documentation to the code enforcement official demonstrating their competence and relevant experience or training. Experience or training shall be considered relevant when the documented experience or training is related in complexity to the same type of special inspection activities for projects of similar complexity and material qualities.

Exceptions:

1. Special inspections are not required for work of a minor nature or as warranted by conditions in the jurisdiction as approved by the code enforcement official.

2. Special inspections are not required for building components unless the design involves the practice of professional engineering or architecture as defined by applicable state statutes and regulations governing the professional registration and certification of engineers or architects.

3. Unless otherwise required by the code enforcement official, special inspections are not required for occupancies in Group R-3 as applicable in Section 101.2 and occupancies in Group U that are accessory to a residential occupancy including, but not limited to, those listed in Section 312.1.

4. The code enforcement official can approve alternate qualifications for special inspectors.

1704.1.1 Statement of special inspections. The permit applicant shall submit a statement of special inspections prepared by the registered design professional in responsible charge as a condition for permit issuance. This statement shall be in accordance with Section 1705.

Exceptions:

1. A statement of special inspections is not required for structures designed and constructed in accordance with the conventional construction provisions of Section 2308.

2. The statement of special inspections is permitted to be prepared by a qualified person approved by the code enforcement official for construction not designed by a registered design professional.

1704.1.2 Report requirement. Special inspectors shall keep records of inspections. The special inspector shall furnish inspection reports to the code enforcement official, and to the registered design professional in responsible charge. Reports shall indicate that work inspected was done in conformance to approved construction documents. Discrepancies shall be brought to the immediate attention of the contractor for correction. If the discrepancies are not corrected, the discrepancies shall be brought to the attention of the code enforcement official and to the registered design professional in responsible charge prior to the completion of that phase of the work. A final report documenting required special inspections and correction of any discrepancies noted in the inspections shall be submitted at a point in time agreed upon by the permit applicant and the code enforcement official prior to the start of work.

1704.2 Inspection of fabricators. Where fabrication of structural load-bearing members and assemblies is being performed on the premises of a fabricator's shop, special inspection of the fabricated items shall be required by this section and as required elsewhere in this code.

1704.2.1 Fabrication and implementation procedures. The special inspector shall verify that the fabricator maintains detailed fabrication and quality control procedures that provide a basis for inspection control of the workmanship and the fabricator's ability to conform to approved construction documents and referenced standards. The special inspector shall review the procedures for completeness and adequacy relative to the code requirements for the fabricator's scope of work.

Exception: Special inspections as required by Section 1704.2 shall not be required where the fabricator is approved in accordance with Section 1704.2.2.

1704.2.2 Fabricator approval. Special inspections required by this code are not required where the work is done on the premises of a fabricator registered and approved to perform such work without special inspection. Approval shall be based upon review of the fabricator's written procedural and quality control manuals and periodic auditing of fabrication practices by an approved special inspection agency. At completion of fabrication, the approved fabricator shall submit a certificate of compliance to the code enforcement official stating that the work was performed in accordance with the approved construction documents.

1704.3 Steel construction. The special inspections for steel elements of buildings and structures shall be as required by Section 1704.3 and Table 1704.3.

Exceptions:

1. Special inspection of the steel fabrication process shall not be required where the fabricator does not perform any welding, thermal cutting or heating operation of any kind as part of the fabrication process. In such cases, the fabricator shall be required to submit a detailed procedure for material control that demonstrates the fabricator's ability to maintain suitable records and procedures such that, at any time during the fabrication process, the material specification, grade and mill test reports for the main stress-carrying elements are capable of being determined.

2. The special inspector need not be continuously present during welding of the following items, provided the materials, welding procedures and qualifications of welders are verified prior to the start of the work; periodic inspections are made of the work in progress; and a visual inspection of all welds is made prior to completion or prior to shipment of shop welding.

   2.1. Single-pass fillet welds not exceeding $^5/_{16}$ inch (7.9 mm) in size.

   2.2. Floor and roof deck welding.

   2.3. Welded studs when used for structural diaphragm.

   2.4. Welded sheet steel for cold-formed steel framing members such as studs and joists.

   2.5. Welding of stairs and railing systems.

TABLE 1704.1
MINIMUM QUALIFICATIONS FOR SPECIAL INSPECTORS

CATEGORY	CODE REFERENCES	MINIMUM QUALIFICATIONS
Reinforced Concrete	1704.4	1. Current ICC Reinforced Concrete Special Inspector or ACI Concrete Construction Inspector. 2. Concrete field testing can be by an ACI Concrete Field Testing Technician with Grade 1 certification. 3. Engineer-in-Training (EIT) with relevant experience. 4. New York State Licensed Professional Engineer (P.E.) with relevant experience.
Prestressed Concrete	Table 1704.4	Pretension Tendons 1. Current ICC Reinforced Concrete certification and ICC prestressed concrete certification and ACI Concrete Field Testing Technician with Grade 1 certification plus one year relevant experience. 2. EIT with relevant experience. 3. P.E. with relevant experience. Post-tension Tendons 1. Current Post-Tensioning Institute (PTI) certification. 2. EIT with relevant experience. 3. P.E. with relevant experience.
Welding	1704.3; Table 1704.3, Item 5; Table 1704.4, Item 2; 1707.2; 2208	1. Current AWS Certified Welding Inspector. 2. Current ICC Structural Steel and Welding certificate plus one year of relevant experience. 3. Current Level II certification from the American Society for Nondestructive Testing (NDT). 4. Current NDT Level III provided previously certified as NDT level II.
High-strength Bolting & Steel Frame Inspection	1704.3.3; Table 1704.3	1. Current ICC Structural Steel and Welding certification and one year of relevant experience. 2. EIT with relevant experience. 3. P.E. with relevant experience.
Masonry	1704.5; Table 1704.5.1; Table 1704.5.3	1. Current ICC Structural Masonry certification and one year of relevant experience. 2. EIT with relevant experience. 3. P.E. with relevant experience.
Sprayed Fire-Resistant Materials	1704.11	1. Current ICC Spray-Applied Fire Proofing certification and one year of relevant experience. 2. EIT with relevant experience. 3. P.E. with relevant experience
Excavation and Filling; Verification of Soils; Piling & Drilled Piers; Modular Retaining Walls	1704.7; 704.8; 1704.9; 704.13	1. Current Level II certification in geotechnical engineering technology/construction from the National Institute for Certification in Engineering Technologies (NICET). 2. EIT with relevant experience. 3. P.E. with relevant experience
Inspection of Fabricators	1704.2	1. Precast: Current ICC Reinforced Concrete certification plus one year relevant experience. 2. Bar Joist: see welding requirements. 3. Metal Building: see welding requirements. 4. Structural Steel: see welding requirements.
Exterior and Interior Architectural Wall Panels	1704.10	1. P.E. with relevant experience. 2. EIT with relevant experience. 3. See the masonry requirements for the SI of masonry veneers subject to BCNYS Section 1704.10.
Exterior Insulation and Finish System	1704.12	1. Registered Design Professional (RDP) with relevant experience. 2. EIT with relevant experience.
Smoke Control	1704.14	1. See the requirements in BCNYS Section 1704.14.2 2. 2. The RDP responsible for design.
Seismic Resistance	1707; 1708	1. See the applicable categories in this table.

TABLE 1704.3
REQUIRED VERIFICATION AND INSPECTION OF STEEL CONSTRUCTION

VERIFICATION AND INSPECTION	CONTINUOUS	PERIODIC	REFERENCED STANDARD[a]	REFERENCE
1. Material verification of high-strength bolts, nuts and washers:				
a. Identification markings to conform to ASTM standards specified in the approved construction documents.	-	X	Applicable ASTM material specifications; AISC 360, Section A3.3	-
b. Manufacturer's certificate of compliance required.	-	X	-	-
2. Inspection of high-strength bolting:				
a. Bearing-type connections.	-	X	AISC 360, Section M2.5	1704.3.3
b. Slip-critical connections.	X	X		
3. Material verification of structural steel:				
a. Identification markings to conform to ASTM standards specified in the approved construction documents.	-	-	ASTM A 6 or ASTM A 568	1708.4
b. Manufacturers' certified mill test reports.	-	-	ASTM A 6 or ASTM A 568	
4. Material verification of weld filler materials:				
a. Identification markings to conform to AWS specification in the approved construction documents.	-	-	AISC 360, Section A3.5	-
b. Manufacturer's certificate of compliance required.	-	-	-	-
5. Inspection of welding:				
a. Structural steel:	-	-		
1) Complete and partial penetration groove welds.	X	-	AWS D1.1	1704.3.1
2) Multipass fillet welds.	X	-		
3) Single-pass fillet welds > $^5/_{16}$"	X	-		
4) Single-pass fillet welds ≤ $^5/_{16}$"	-	X		
5) Floor and roof deck welds.	-	X	AWS D1.3	-
b. Reinforcing steel:	-	-		
1) Verification of weldability of reinforcing steel other than ASTM A 706.	-	X	AWS D1.4 ACI 318: 3.5.2	-
2) Reinforcing steel-resisting flexural and axial forces in intermediate and special moment frames, and boundary elements of special reinforced concrete shear walls and shear reinforcement.	X	-		
3) Shear reinforcement.	X	-		
4) Other reinforcing steel.	-	X		
6. Inspection of steel frame joint details for compliance with approved construction documents:		X	-	1704.3.2
a. Details such as bracing and stiffening.	-	-		
b. Member locations.	-	-		
c. Application of joint details at each connection.	-			

For SI: 1 inch = 25.4 mm.

a. Where applicable, see also Section 1707.1, Special inspection for seismic resistance.

1704.3.1 Welding. Welding inspection shall be in compliance with AWS D1.1. The basis for welding inspector qualification shall be AWS D1.1.

1704.3.2 Details. The special inspector shall perform an inspection of the steel frame to verify compliance with the details shown on the approved construction documents, such as bracing, stiffening, member locations and proper application of joint details at each connection.

1704.3.3 High-strength bolts. Installation of high-strength bolts shall be periodically inspected in accordance with AISC specifications.

1704.3.3.1 General. While the work is in progress, the special inspector shall determine that the requirements for bolts, nuts, washers and paint; bolted parts and installation and tightening in such standards are met. For bolts requiring pretensioning, the special inspector shall observe the preinstallation testing and calibration procedures when such procedures are required by the installation method or by project plans or specifications; determine that all plies of connected materials have been drawn together and properly snugged and monitor the installation of bolts to verify that the selected procedure for installation is properly used to tighten bolts. For joints required to be tightened only to the snug-tight condition, the special inspector need only verify that the connected materials have been drawn together and properly snugged.

1704.3.3.2 Periodic monitoring. Monitoring of bolt installation for pretensioning is permitted to be performed on a periodic basis when using the turn-of-nut method with matchmarking techniques, the direct tension indicator method or the alternate design fastener (twist-off bolt) method. Joints designated as snug tight need be inspected only on a periodic basis.

1704.3.3.3 Continuous monitoring. Monitoring of bolt installation for pretensioning using the calibrated wrench method or the turn-of-nut method without matchmarking shall be performed on a continuous basis.

1704.4 Concrete construction. The special inspections and verifications for concrete construction shall be as required by this section and Table 1704.4.

Exception: Special inspections shall not be required for:

1. Isolated spread concrete footings of buildings three stories or less in height that are fully supported on earth or rock.

2. Continuous concrete footings supporting walls of buildings three stories or less in height that are fully supported on earth or rock where:

   2.1. The footings support walls of light-frame construction;

   2.2. The footings are designed in accordance with Table 1805.4.2; or

   2.3. The structural design of the footing is based on a specified compressive strength, f'_c, no greater than 2,500 pounds per square inch (psi) (17.2

MPa), regardless of the compressive strength specified in the construction documents or used in the footing construction.

3. Nonstructural concrete slabs supported directly on the ground, including prestressed slabs on grade, where the effective prestress in the concrete is less than 150 psi (1.03 MPa).

4. Concrete foundation walls constructed in accordance with Table 1805.5(5).

5. Concrete patios, driveways and sidewalks, on grade.

1704.4.1 Materials. In the absence of sufficient data or documentation providing evidence of conformance to quality standards for materials in Chapter 3 of ACI 318, the code enforcement official shall require testing of materials in accordance with the appropriate standards and criteria for the material in Chapter 3 of ACI 318. Weldability of reinforcement, except that which conforms to ASTM A 706, shall be determined in accordance with the requirements of Section 3.5.2 of ACI 318.

1704.5 Masonry construction. Masonry construction shall be inspected and evaluated in accordance with the requirements of Sections 1704.5.1 through 1704.5.3, depending on the classification of the building or structure or nature of the occupancy, as defined by this code.

Exception: Special inspections shall not be required for:

1. Empirically designed masonry, glass unit masonry or masonry veneer designed by Section 2109, 2110 or Chapter 14, respectively, or by Chapter 5, 7 or 6 of ACI 530/ASCE 5/TMS 402, respectively, when they are part of structures classified as Occupancy Category I, II or III in accordance with Section 1604.5.

2. Masonry foundation walls constructed in accordance with Table 1805.5(1), 1805.5(2), 1805.5(3) or 1805.5(4).

3. Masonry fireplaces, masonry heaters or masonry chimneys installed or constructed in accordance with Section 2111, 2112 or 2113, respectively.

1704.5.1 Empirically designed masonry, glass unit masonry and masonry veneer in Occupancy Category IV. The minimum special inspection program for empirically designed masonry, glass unit masonry or masonry veneer designed by Section 2109, 2110 or Chapter 14, respectively, or by Chapter 5, 7 or 6 of ACI 530/ASCE 5/TMS 402, respectively, in structures classified as Occupancy Category IV, in accordance with Section 1604.5, shall comply with Table 1704.5.1.

1704.5.2 Engineered masonry in Occupancy Category I, II or III. The minimum special inspection program for masonry designed by Section 2107 or 2108 or by chapters other than Chapters 5, 6 or 7 of ACI 530/ASCE 5/TMS 402 in structures classified as Occupancy Category I, II or III, in accordance with Section 1604.5, shall comply with Table 1704.5.1.

TABLE 1704.4
REQUIRED VERIFICATION AND INSPECTION OF CONCRETE CONSTRUCTION

VERIFICATION AND INSPECTION	CONTINUOUS	PERIODIC	REFERENCED STANDARD[a]	REFERENCE
1. Inspection of reinforcing steel, including prestressing tendons, and placement.	-	X	ACI 318: 3.5, 7.1-7.7	1913.4
2. Inspection of reinforcing steel welding in accordance with Table 1704.3, Item 5b.	-	-	AWS D1.4 ACI 318: 3.5.2	-
3. Inspect bolts to be installed in concrete prior to and during placement of concrete where allowable loads have been increased.	X	-	-	1911.5
4. Verifying use of required design mix.	-	X	ACI 318: Ch. 4, 5.2-5.4	1904.2.2, 1913.2, 1913.3
5. At the time fresh concrete is sampled to fabricate specimens for strength tests, perform slump and air content tests, and determine the temperature of the concrete.	X	-	ASTM C 172 ASTM C 31 ACI 318: 5.6, 5.8	1913.10
6. Inspection of concrete and shotcrete placement for proper application techniques.	X	-	ACI 318: 5.9, 5.10	1913.6, 1913.7, 1913.8
7. Inspection for maintenance of specified curing temperature and techniques.	-	X	ACI 318: 5.11-5.13	1913.9
8. Inspection of prestressed concrete: a. Application of prestressing forces. b. Grouting of bonded prestressing tendons in the seismic-force-resisting system.	X X	-	ACI 318: 18.20 ACI 318: 18.18.4	-
9. Erection of precast concrete members.	-	X	ACI 318: Ch. 16	-
10. Verification of in-situ concrete strength, prior to stressing of tendons in posttensioned concrete and prior to removal of shores and forms from beams and structural slabs.	-	X	ACI 318: 6.2	-
11. Inspect formwork for shape, location and dimensions of the concrete member being formed.	-	X	ACI 318: 6.1.1	-

For SI: 1 inch = 25.4 mm.

a. Where applicable, see also Section 1707.1, Special inspection for seismic resistance.

1704.5.3 Engineered masonry in Occupancy Category IV. The minimum special inspection program for masonry designed by Section 2107 or 2108 or by chapters other than Chapters 5, 6 or 7 of ACI 530/ASCE 5/TMS 402 in structures classified as Occupancy Category IV, in accordance with Section 1604.5, shall comply with Table 1704.5.3.

1704.6 Wood construction. Special inspections of the fabrication process of prefabricated wood structural elements and assemblies shall be in accordance with Section 1704.2. Special inspections of site-built assemblies shall be in accordance with this section.

1704.6.1 High-load diaphragms. High-load diaphragms designed in accordance with Table 2306.3.2 shall be installed with special inspections as indicated in Section 1704.1. The special inspector shall inspect the wood structural panel sheathing to ascertain whether it is of the grade and thickness shown on the approved building plans. Additionally, the special inspector must verify the nominal size of framing members at adjoining panel edges, the nail or staple diameter and length, the number of fastener lines and that the spacing between fasteners in each line and at edge margins agrees with the approved building plans.

1704.7 Soils. Special inspections for existing site soil conditions, fill placement and load-bearing requirements shall be as required by this section and Table 1704.7. The approved soils report, required by Section 1802.2, and the documents prepared by the registered design professional in responsible charge shall be used to determine compliance. During fill placement, the special inspector shall determine that proper materials and procedures are used in accordance with the provisions of the approved soils report, as specified in Section 1803.5.

> **Exception:** Special inspection is not required during placement of controlled fill having a total depth of 12 inches (305 mm) or less.

1704.8 Pile foundations. Special inspections shall be performed during installation and testing of pile foundations as required by Table 1704.8. The approved soils report, required by Section 1802.2, and the documents prepared by the registered design professional in responsible charge shall be used to determine compliance.

1704.9 Pier foundations. Special inspections shall be performed during installation and testing of pier foundations as required by Table 1704.9. The approved soils report, required by Section 1802.2, and the documents prepared by the registered design professional in responsible charge shall be used to determine compliance.

TABLE 1704.5.1
LEVEL 1 SPECIAL INSPECTION

INSPECTION TASK	FREQUENCY OF INSPECTION		REFERENCE FOR CRITERIA		
	Continuous during task listed	Periodically during task listed	IBC section	ACI 530/ASCE 5/TMS 402[a]	ACI 530.1/ASCE 6/TMS 602[a]
1. As masonry construction begins, the following shall be verified to ensure compliance:					
a. Proportions of site-prepared mortar.	-	X	-	-	Art. 2.6A
b. Construction of mortar joints.		X	-	-	Art. 3.3B
c. Location of reinforcement, connectors, prestressing tendons and anchorages.		X	-	-	Art. 3.4, 3.6A
d. Prestressing technique.	-	X	-	-	Art. 3.6B
e. Grade and size of prestressing tendons and anchorages.	-	X	-	-	Art. 2.4B, 2.4H
2. The inspection program shall verify:					
a. Size and location of structural elements.	-	X	-	-	Art. 3.3G
b. Type, size and location of anchors, including other details of anchorage of masonry to structural members, frames or other construction.	-	X	-	Sec. 1.2.2(e), 2.1.4, 3.1.6	-
c. Specified size, grade and type of reinforcement.	-	X	-	Sec. 1.13	Art. 2.4, 3.4
d. Welding of reinforcing bars.	X	-	-	Sec. 2.1.10.7.2, 3.3.3.4(b)	-
e. Protection of masonry during cold weather (temperature below 40°F) or hot weather (temperature above 90°F).	-	X	Sec. 2104.3, 2104.4	-	Art. 1.8C, 1.8D
f. Application and measurement of prestressing force.	-	X	-	-	Art. 3.6B
3. Prior to grouting, the following shall be verified to ensure compliance:					
a. Grout space is clean.	-	X	-	-	Art. 3.2D
b. Placement of reinforcement and connectors and prestressing tendons and anchorages.		X	-	Sec. 1.13	Art. 3.4
c. Proportions of site-prepared grout and prestressing grout for bonded tendons.		X		-	Art. 2.6B
d. Construction of mortar joints.		X		-	Art. 3.3B
4. Grout placement shall be verified to ensure compliance with code and construction document provisions.	X	-	-	-	Art 3.5
a. Grouting of prestressing bonded tendons.	X	-	-	-	Art. 3.6C
5. Preparation of any required grout specimens, mortar specimens and/or prisms shall be observed.	X	-	Sec. 2105.2.2, 2105.3	-	Art. 1.4
6. Compliance with required inspection provisions of the construction documents and the approved submittals shall be verified.	-	X	-	-	Art. 1.5

For SI: °C = (°F - 32)/1.8.

a. The specific standards referenced are those listed in Chapter 35.

TABLE 1704.5.3
LEVEL 2 SPECIAL INSPECTION

INSPECTION TASK	FREQUENCY OF INSPECTION		REFERENCE FOR CRITERIA		
	Continuous during task listed	Periodically during task listed	IBC section	ACI 530/ ASCE 5/ TMS 402[a]	ACI 530.1/ ASCE 6/ TMS 602[a]
1. From the beginning of masonry construction, the following shall be verified to ensure compliance:					
a. Proportions of site-prepared mortar, grout and prestressing grout for bonded tendons.	-	X	-	-	Art. 2.6A
b. Placement of masonry units and construction of mortar joints.	-	X	-	-	Art. 3.3B
c. Placement of reinforcement, connectors and prestressing tendons and anchorages.	-	X	-	Sec. 1.13	Art. 3.4, 3.6A
d. Grout space prior to grouting.	X	-	-	-	Art. 3.2D
e. Placement of grout.	X	-	-	-	Art. 3.5
f. Placement of prestressing grout.	X	-	-	-	Art. 3.6C
2. The inspection program shall verify:					
a. Size and location of structural elements.	-	X	-	-	Art. 3.3G
b. Type, size and location of anchors, including other details of anchorage of masonry to structural members, frames or other construction.	X	-	-	Sec. 1.2.2(e), 2.1.4, 3.1.6	-
c. Specified size, grade and type of reinforcement.	-	X	-	Sec. 1.13	Art. 2.4, 3.4
d. Welding of reinforcing bars.	X	-	-	Sec. 2.1.10.7.2, 3.3.3.4(b)	-
e. Protection of masonry during cold weather (temperature below 40°F) or hot weather (temperature above 90°F).	-	X	Sec. 2104.3, 2104.4	-	Art. 1.8C, 1.8D
f. Application and measurement of prestressing force.	X	-	-	-	Art. 3.6B
3. Preparation of any required grout specimens, mortar specimens and/or prisms shall be observed.	X	-	Sec. 2105.2.2, 2105.3	-	Art. 1.4
4. Compliance with required inspection provisions of the construction documents and the approved submittals shall be verified.	-	X	-	-	Art. 1.5

For SI: °C = (°F - 32)/1.8.

a. The specific standards referenced are those listed in Chapter 35.

TABLE 1704.7
REQUIRED VERIFICATION AND INSPECTION OF SOILS

VERIFICATION AND INSPECTION TASK	CONTINUOUS DURING TASK LISTED	PERIODICALLY DURING TASK LISTED
1. Verify materials below footings are adequate to achieve the design bearing capacity.	-	X
2. Verify excavations are extended to proper depth and have reached proper material.	-	X
3. Perform classification and testing of controlled fill materials.	-	X
4. Verify use of proper materials, densities and lift thicknesses during placement and compaction of controlled fill.	X	-
5. Prior to placement of controlled fill, observe subgrade and verify that site has been prepared properly.	-	X

TABLE 1704.8
REQUIRED VERIFICATION AND INSPECTION OF PILE FOUNDATIONS

VERIFICATION AND INSPECTION TASK	CONTINUOUS DURING TASK LISTED	PERIODICALLY DURING TASK LISTED
1. Verify pile materials, sizes and lengths comply with the requirements.	X	-
2. Determine capacities of test piles and conduct additional load tests, as required.	X	-
3. Observe driving operations and maintain complete and accurate records for each pile.	X	-
4. Verify placement locations and plumbness, confirm type and size of hammer, record number of blows per foot of penetration, determine required penetrations to achieve design capacity, record tip and butt elevations and document any pile damage.	X	-
5. For steel piles, perform additional inspections in accordance with Section 1704.3.	-	-
6. For concrete piles and concrete-filled piles, perform additional inspections in accordance with Section 1704.4.	-	-
7. For specialty piles, perform additional inspections as determined by the registered design professional in responsible charge.	-	-
8. For augered uncased piles and caisson piles, perform inspections in accordance with Section 1704.9.	-	-

TABLE 1704.9
REQUIRED VERIFICATION AND INSPECTION OF PIER FOUNDATIONS

VERIFICATION AND INSPECTION TASK	CONTINUOUS DURING TASK LISTED	PERIODICALLY DURING TASK LISTED
1. Observe drilling operations and maintain complete and accurate records for each pier.	X	-
2. Verify placement locations and plumbness, confirm pier diameters, bell diameters (if applicable), lengths, embedment into bedrock (if applicable) and adequate end bearing strata capacity.	X	-
3. For concrete piers, perform additional inspections in accordance with Section 1704.4.	-	-
4. For masonry piers, perform additional inspections in accordance with Section 1704.5.	-	-

1704.10 Sprayed fire-resistant materials. Special inspections for sprayed fire-resistant materials applied to structural elements and decks shall be in accordance with Sections 1704.10.1 through 1704.10.5. Special inspections shall be based on the fire-resistance design as designated in the approved construction documents.

1704.10.1 Structural member surface conditions. The surfaces shall be prepared in accordance with the approved fire-resistance design and the approved manufacturer's written instructions. The prepared surface of structural members to be sprayed shall be inspected before the application of the sprayed fire-resistant material.

1704.10.2 Application. The substrate shall have a minimum ambient temperature before and after application as specified in the approved manufacturer's written instructions. The area for application shall be ventilated during and after application as required by the approved manufacturer's written instructions.

1704.10.3 Thickness. The average thickness of the sprayed fire-resistant materials applied to structural elements shall not be less than the thickness required by the approved fire-resistant design. Individually measured thickness, which exceeds the thickness specified in a design by $^1/_4$ inch (6.4 mm) or more, shall be recorded as the thickness specified in the design plus $^1/_4$ inch (6.4 mm). For design thicknesses 1 inch (25 mm) or greater, the minimum allowable individual thickness shall be the design thickness minus $^1/_4$ inch (6.4 mm). For design thicknesses less than 1 inch (25 mm), the minimum allowable individual thickness shall be the design thickness minus 25 percent. Thickness shall be determined in accordance with ASTM E 605. Samples of the sprayed fire-resistant materials shall be selected in accordance with Sections 1704.10.3.1 and 1704.10.3.2.

1704.10.3.1 Floor, roof and wall assemblies. The thickness of the sprayed fire-resistant material applied to floor, roof and wall assemblies shall be determined in accordance with ASTM E 605 by taking the average of not less than four measurements for each 1,000 square feet (93 m²) of the sprayed area on each floor or part thereof.

1704.10.3.2 Structural framing members. The thickness of the sprayed fire-resistant material applied to structural members shall be determined in accordance with ASTM E 605. Thickness testing shall be performed on not less than 25 percent of the structural members on each floor.

1704.10.4 Density. The density of the sprayed fire-resistant material shall not be less than the density specified in the approved fire-resistant design. Density of the sprayed fire-resistant material shall be determined in accordance with ASTM E 605.

1704.10.5 Bond strength. The cohesive/adhesive bond strength of the cured sprayed fire-resistant material applied to structural elements shall not be less than 150 pounds per square foot (psf) (7.18 kN/m²). The cohesive/adhesive bond strength shall be determined in accordance with the field test specified in ASTM E 736 by testing in-place samples of the sprayed fire-resistant material selected in accordance with Sections 1704.10.5.1 and 1704.10.5.2.

1704.10.5.1 Floor, roof and wall assemblies. The test samples for determining the cohesive/adhesive bond strength of the sprayed fire-resistant materials shall be selected from each floor, roof and wall assembly at the rate of not less than one sample for every 10,000 square feet (929 m²) or part thereof of the sprayed area in each story.

1704.10.5.2 Structural framing members. The test samples for determining the cohesive/adhesive bond strength of the sprayed fire-resistant materials shall be selected from beams, girders, joists, trusses and columns at the rate of not less than one sample for each type of structural framing member for each 10,000 square feet (929 m²) of floor area or part thereof in each story.

1704.11 Mastic and intumescent fire-resistant coatings. Special inspections for mastic and intumescent fire-resistant coatings applied to structural elements and decks shall be in accordance with AWCI 12-B. Special inspections shall be based on the fire-resistance design as designated in the approved construction documents.

1704.12 Exterior insulation and finish systems (EIFS). Special inspections shall be required for all EIFS applications.

Exceptions:

1. Special inspections shall not be required for EIFS applications installed over a water-resistive barrier with a means of draining moisture to the exterior.

2. Special inspections shall not be required for EIFS applications installed over masonry or concrete walls.

1704.13 Special cases. Special inspections shall be required for proposed work that is, in the opinion of the code enforcement official, unusual in its nature, such as, but not limited to, the following examples:

1. Construction materials and systems that are alternatives to materials and systems prescribed by this code.

2. Unusual design applications of materials described in this code.

3. Materials and systems required to be installed in accordance with additional manufacturer's instructions that

prescribe requirements not contained in this code or in standards referenced by this code.

[F] 1704.14 Special inspection for smoke control. Smoke control systems shall be tested by a special inspector.

[F] 1704.14.1 Testing scope. The test scope shall be as follows:

1. During erection of ductwork and prior to concealment for the purposes of leakage testing and recording of device location.

2. Prior to occupancy and after sufficient completion for the purposes of pressure difference testing, flow measurements and detection and control verification.

[F] 1704.14.2 Qualifications. Special inspection agencies for smoke control shall have expertise in fire protection engineering, mechanical engineering and certification as air balancers.

SECTION 1705
STATEMENT OF SPECIAL INSPECTIONS

1705.1 General. Where special inspection or testing is required by Section 1704, 1707 or 1708, the registered design professional in responsible charge shall prepare a statement of special inspections in accordance with Section 1705 for submittal by the permit applicant (see Section 1704.1.1).

1705.2 Content of statement of special inspections. The statement of special inspections shall identify the following:

1. The materials, systems, components and work required to have special inspection or testing by the code enforcement official or by the registered design professional responsible for each portion of the work.

2. The type and extent of each special inspection.

3. The type and extent of each test.

4. Additional requirements for special inspection or testing for seismic or wind resistance as specified in Section 1705.3, 1705.4, 1707 or 1708.

5. For each type of special inspection, identification as to whether it will be continuous special inspection or periodic special inspection.

1705.3 Seismic resistance. The statement of special inspections shall include seismic requirements for the following cases:

1. The seismic-force-resisting systems in structures assigned to Seismic Design Category C, D, E or F in accordance with Section 1613.

2. Designated seismic systems in structures assigned to Seismic Design Category D, E or F.

3. The following additional systems and components in structures assigned to Seismic Design Category C:

   3.1. Heating, ventilating and air-conditioning (HVAC) ductwork containing hazardous materials and anchorage of such ductwork.

3.2. Piping systems and mechanical units containing flammable, combustible or highly toxic materials.

3.3. Anchorage of electrical equipment used for emergency or standby power systems.

4. The following additional systems and components in structures assigned to Seismic Design Category D:

4.1. Systems required for Seismic Design Category C.

4.2. Exterior wall panels and their anchorage.

4.3. Suspended ceiling systems and their anchorage.

4.4. Access floors and their anchorage.

4.5. Steel storage racks and their anchorage, where the importance factor is equal to 1.5 in accordance with Section 15.5.3 of ASCE 7.

5. The following additional systems and components in structures assigned to Seismic Design Category E or F:

5.1. Systems required for Seismic Design Categories C and D.

5.2. Electrical equipment.

Exception: Seismic requirements are permitted to be excluded from the statement of special inspections for structures designed and constructed in accordance with the following:

1. The structure consists of light-frame construction; the design spectral response acceleration at short periods, S_{DS}, as determined in Section 1613.5.4, does not exceed 0.5g; and the height of the structure does not exceed 35 feet (10 668 mm) above grade plane; or

2. The structure is constructed using a reinforced masonry structural system or reinforced concrete structural system; the design spectral response acceleration at short periods, S_{DS}, as determined in Section 1613.5.4, does not exceed 0.5g; and the height of the structure does not exceed 25 feet (7620 mm) above grade plane; or

3. Detached one- or two-family dwellings not exceeding two stories in height, provided the structure does not have any of the following plan or vertical irregularities in accordance with Section 12.3.2 of ASCE 7:

3.1. Torsional irregularity.

3.2. Nonparallel systems.

3.3. Stiffness irregularity-extreme soft story and soft story.

3.4. Discontinuity in capacity-weak story.

1705.3.1 Seismic requirements in the statement of special inspections. When Section 1705.3 specifies that seismic requirements be included, the statement of special inspections shall identify the following:

1. The designated seismic systems and seismic-force-resisting systems that are subject to special inspections in accordance with Section 1705.3.

2. The additional special inspections and testing to be provided as required by Sections 1707 and 1708 and other applicable sections of this code, including the applicable standards referenced by this code.

1705.4 Wind resistance. The statement of special inspections shall include wind requirements for structures constructed in the following areas:

1. In wind Exposure Category B, where the 3-second-gust basic wind speed is 120 miles per hour (mph) (52.8 m/s) or greater.

2. In wind Exposure Category C or D, where the 3-second-gust basic wind speed is 110 mph (49 m/s) or greater.

1705.4.1 Wind requirements in the statement of special inspections. When Section 1705.4 specifies that wind requirements be included, the statement of special inspections shall identify the main windforce-resisting systems and wind-resisting components subject to special inspections as specified in Section 1705.4.2.

1705.4.2 Detailed requirements. The statement of special inspections shall include at least the following systems and components:

1. Roof cladding and roof framing connections.

2. Wall connections to roof and floor diaphragms and framing.

3. Roof and floor diaphragm systems, including collectors, drag struts and boundary elements.

4. Vertical windforce-resisting systems, including braced frames, moment frames and shear walls.

5. Windforce-resisting system connections to the foundation.

6. Fabrication and installation of systems or components required to meet the impact-resistance requirements of Section 1609.1.2.

Exception: Fabrication of manufactured systems or components that have a label indicating compliance with the wind-load and impact-resistance requirements of this code.

SECTION 1706
CONTRACTOR RESPONSIBILITY

1706.1 Contractor responsibility. Each contractor responsible for the construction of a main wind- or seismic-force-resisting system, designated seismic system or a wind- or seismic-resisting component listed in the statement of special inspections shall submit a written statement of responsibility to the code enforcement official and the owner prior to the commencement of work on the system or component. The contractor's statement of responsibility shall contain the following:

1. Acknowledgment of awareness of the special requirements contained in the statement of special inspections;

2. Acknowledgment that control will be exercised to obtain conformance with the construction documents approved by the code enforcement official;

3. Procedures for exercising control within the contractor's organization, the method and frequency of reporting and the distribution of the reports; and

4. Identification and qualifications of the person(s) exercising such control and their position(s) in the organization.

SECTION 1707
SPECIAL INSPECTIONS FOR SEISMIC RESISTANCE

1707.1 Special inspections for seismic resistance. Special inspections itemized in Sections 1707.2 through 1707.10, unless exempted by the exceptions of Section 1704.1, are required for the following:

1. The seismic-force-resisting systems in structures assigned to Seismic Design Category C, D, E or F, as determined in Section 1613.

2. Designated seismic systems in structures assigned to Seismic Design Category D, E or F.

3. Architectural, mechanical and electrical components in structures assigned to Seismic Design Category C, D, E or F that are required in Sections 1707.7 and 1707.8.

1707.2 Structural steel. Continuous special inspection is required for structural welding in accordance with AISC 341.

Exceptions:

1. Single-pass fillet welds not exceeding $^5/_{16}$ inch (7.9 mm) in size.

2. Floor and roof deck welding.

1707.3 Structural wood. Continuous special inspection is required during field gluing operations of elements of the seismic-force-resisting system. Periodic special inspection is required for nailing, bolting, anchoring and other fastening of components within the seismic-force-resisting system, including wood shear walls, wood diaphragms, drag struts, braces, shear panels and hold-downs.

Exception: Special inspection is not required for wood shear walls, shear panels and diaphragms, including nailing, bolting, anchoring and other fastening to other components of the seismic-force-resisting system, where the fastener spacing of the sheathing is more than 4 inches (102 mm) on center (o.c.).

1707.4 Cold-formed steel framing. Periodic special inspections is required during welding operations of elements of the seismic-force-resisting system. Periodic special inspection is required for screw attachment, bolting, anchoring and other fastening of components within the seismic-force-resisting system, including struts, braces, and hold-downs.

1707.5 Pier foundations. Special inspection is required for pier foundations for buildings assigned to Seismic Design Category C, D, E or F in accordance with Section 1613. Periodic special inspection is required during placement of reinforcement and continuous special inspection is required during placement of the concrete.

1707.6 Storage racks and access floors. Periodic special inspection is required during the anchorage of access floors and storage racks 8 feet (2438 mm) or greater in height in structures assigned to Seismic Design Category D, E or F.

1707.7 Architectural components. Periodic special inspection is required during the erection and fastening of exterior cladding, interior and exterior nonbearing walls and interior and exterior veneer in structures assigned to Seismic Design Category D, E or F.

Exceptions:

1. Special inspection is not required for architectural components in structures 30 feet (9144 mm) or less in height.

2. Special inspection is not required for cladding and veneer weighing 5 psf (24.5 N/m²) or less.

3. Special inspection is not required for interior nonbearing walls weighing 15 psf (73.5 N/m²) or less.

1707.8 Mechanical and electrical components. Special inspection for mechanical and electrical equipment shall be as follows:

1. Periodic special inspection is required during the anchorage of electrical equipment for emergency or standby power systems in structures assigned to Seismic Design Category C, D, E or F;

2. Periodic special inspection is required during the installation of anchorage of other electrical equipment in structures assigned to Seismic Design Category E or F;

3. Periodic special inspection is required during installation of piping systems intended to carry flammable, combustible or highly toxic contents and their associated mechanical units in structures assigned to Seismic Design Category C, D, E or F;

4. Periodic special inspection is required during the installation of HVAC ductwork that will contain hazardous materials in structures assigned to Seismic Design Category C, D, E or F; and

5. Periodic special inspection is required during the installation of vibration isolation systems in structures assigned to Seismic Design Category C, D, E or F where the construction documents require a nominal clearance of 0.25 inches (6.4 mm) or less between the equipment support frame and restraint.

1707.9 Designated seismic system verifications. The special inspector shall examine designated seismic systems requiring seismic qualification in accordance with Section 1708.5 and verify that the label, anchorage or mounting conforms to the certificate of compliance.

1707.10 Seismic isolation system. Periodic special inspection is required during the fabrication and installation of isolator units and energy dissipation devices that are part of the seismic isolation system.

SECTION 1708
STRUCTURAL TESTING FOR SEISMIC RESISTANCE

1708.1 Masonry. Testing and verification of masonry materials and assemblies prior to construction shall comply with the requirements of Sections 1708.1.1 through 1708.1.4, depending on the classification of the building or structure or nature of the occupancy, as defined by this code.

1708.1.1 Empirically designed masonry and glass unit masonry in Occupancy Category I, II or III. For masonry designed by Section 2109 or 2110 or by Chapter 5 or 7 of ACI 530/ASCE 5/TMS 402 in structures classified as Occupancy Category I, II or III, in accordance with Section 1604.5, certificates of compliance used in masonry construction shall be verified prior to construction.

1708.1.2 Empirically designed masonry and glass unit masonry in Occupancy Category IV. The minimum testing and verification prior to construction for masonry designed by Section 2109 or 2110 or by Chapter 5 or 7 of ACI 530/ASCE 5/TMS 402 in structures classified as Occupancy Category IV, in accordance with Section 1604.5, shall comply with the requirements of Table 1708.1.2.

TABLE 1708.1.2
LEVEL 1 QUALITY ASSURANCE

MINIMUM TESTS AND SUBMITTALS
Certificates of compliance used in masonry construction.
Verification of f'_m and f'_{AAC} prior to construction, except where specifically exempted by this code.

1708.1.3 Engineered masonry in Occupancy Category I, II or III. The minimum testing and verification prior to construction for masonry designed by Section 2107 or 2108 or by chapters other than Chapter 5, 6 or 7 of ACI 530/ASCE 5/TMS 402 in structures classified as Occupancy Category I, II or III, in accordance with Section 1604.5, shall comply with Table 1708.1.2.

1708.1.4 Engineered masonry in Occupancy Category IV. The minimum testing and verification prior to construction for masonry designed by Section 2107 or 2108 or by chapters other than Chapter 5, 6 or 7 of ACI 530/ASCE 5/TMS 402 in structures classified as Occupancy Category IV, in accordance with Section 1604.5, shall comply with Table 1708.1.4.

TABLE 1708.1.4
LEVEL 2 QUALITY ASSURANCE

MINIMUM TESTS AND SUBMITTALS
Certificates of compliance used in masonry construction.
Verification of f'_m and f'_{AAC} prior to construction and every 5,000 square feet during construction.
Verification of proportions of materials in mortar and grout as delivered to the site.

For SI: 1 square foot = 0.0929 m^2.

1708.2 Testing for seismic resistance. The tests specified in Sections 1708.3 through 1708.6 are required for the following:

1. The seismic-force-resisting systems in structures assigned to Seismic Design Category C, D, E or F, as determined in Section 1613.

2. Designated seismic systems in structures assigned to Seismic Design Category D, E or F.

3. Architectural, mechanical and electrical components in structures assigned to Seismic Design Category C, D, E or F that are required in Section 1708.5.

1708.3 Reinforcing and prestressing steel. Certified mill test reports shall be provided for each shipment of reinforcing steel used to resist flexural, shear and axial forces in reinforced concrete intermediate frames, special moment frames and boundary elements of special reinforced concrete or reinforced masonry shear walls. Where ASTM A 615 reinforcing steel is used to resist earthquake-induced flexural and axial forces in special moment frames and in wall boundary elements of shear walls in structures assigned to Seismic Design Category D, E or F, as determined in Section 1613, the testing requirements of ACI 318 shall be met. Where ASTM A 615 reinforcing steel is to be welded, chemical tests shall be performed to determine weldability in accordance with Section 3.5.2 of ACI 318.

1708.4 Structural steel. The testing contained in the quality assurance plan shall be as required by AISC 341 and the additional requirements herein. The acceptance criteria for nondestructive testing shall be as required in AWS D1.1 as specified by the registered design professional.

Base metal thicker than 1.5 inches (38 mm), where subject to through-thickness weld shrinkage strains, shall be ultrasonically tested for discontinuities behind and adjacent to such welds after joint completion. Any material discontinuities shall be accepted or rejected on the basis of ASTM A 435 or ASTM A 898 (Level 1 criteria) and criteria as established by the registered design professional(s) in responsible charge and the construction documents.

1708.5 Seismic qualification of mechanical and electrical equipment. The registered design professional in responsible charge shall state the applicable seismic qualification requirements for designated seismic systems on the construction documents. Each manufacturer of designated seismic system components shall test or analyze the component and its mounting system or anchorage and submit a certificate of compliance for review and acceptance by the registered design professional in responsible charge of the design of the designated seismic system and for approval by the code enforcement official. Qualification shall be by an actual test on a shake table, by three-dimensional shock tests, by an analytical method using dynamic characteristics and forces, by the use of experience data (i.e., historical data demonstrating acceptable seismic performance) or by a more rigorous analysis providing for equivalent safety.

1708.6 Seismically isolated structures. For required system tests, see Section 17.8 of ASCE 7.

SECTION 1709
STRUCTURAL OBSERVATIONS

1709.1 General. Where required by the provisions of Section 1709.2 or 1709.3 the owner shall employ a registered design professional to perform structural observations as defined in Section 1702.

At the conclusion of the work included in the permit, the structural observer shall submit to the code enforcement official a written statement that the site visits have been made and identify any reported deficiencies that, to the best of the structural observer's knowledge, have not been resolved.

1709.2 Structural observations for seismic resistance. Structural observations shall be provided for those structures included in Seismic Design Category D, E or F, as determined in Section 1613, where one or more of the following conditions exist:

1. The structure is classified as Occupancy Category III or IV in accordance with Section 1604.5.

2. The height of the structure is greater than 75 feet (22 860 mm) above the base.

3. The structure is assigned to Seismic Design Category E, is classified as Occupancy Category I or II in accordance with Section 1604.5 and is greater than two stories in height.

4. When so designated by the registered design professional in responsible charge of the design.

5. When such observation is specifically required by the code enforcement official.

1709.3 Structural observations for wind requirements. Structural observations shall be provided for those structures sited where the basic wind speed exceeds 110 mph (49 m/s), determined from Figure 1609, where one or more of the following conditions exist:

1. The structure is classified as Occupancy Category III or IV in accordance with Table 1604.5.

2. The building height is greater than 75 feet (22 860 mm).

3. When so designated by the registered design professional in responsible charge of the design.

4. When such observation is specifically required by the code enforcement official.

SECTION 1710
DESIGN STRENGTHS OF MATERIALS

1710.1 Conformance to standards. The design strengths and permissible stresses of any structural material that are identified by a manufacturer's designation as to manufacture and grade by mill tests, or the strength and stress grade is otherwise confirmed to the satisfaction of the code enforcement official, shall conform to the specifications and methods of design of accepted engineering practice or the approved rules in the absence of applicable standards.

1710.2 New materials. For materials that are not specifically provided for in this code, the design strengths and permissible stresses shall be established by tests as provided for in Section 1711.

SECTION 1711
ALTERNATIVE TEST PROCEDURE

1711.1 General. In the absence of approved rules or other approved standards, the code enforcement official shall make, or cause to be made, the necessary tests and investigations; or the code enforcement official shall accept duly authenticated reports from approved agencies in respect to the quality and manner of use of new materials or assemblies as provided for in Section 104.11. The cost of all tests and other investigations required under the provisions of this code shall be borne by the permit applicant.

SECTION 1712
TEST SAFE LOAD

1712.1 Where required. Where proposed construction is not capable of being designed by approved engineering analysis, or where proposed construction design method does not comply with the applicable material design standard, the system of construction or the structural unit and the connections shall be subjected to the tests prescribed in Section 1714. The code enforcement official shall accept certified reports of such tests conducted by an approved testing agency, provided that such tests meet the requirements of this code and approved procedures.

SECTION 1713
IN-SITU LOAD TESTS

1713.1 General. Whenever there is a reasonable doubt as to the stability or load-bearing capacity of a completed building, structure or portion thereof for the expected loads, an engineering assessment shall be required. The engineering assessment shall involve either a structural analysis or an in-situ load test, or both. The structural analysis shall be based on actual material properties and other as-built conditions that affect stability or load-bearing capacity, and shall be conducted in accordance with the applicable design standard. If the structural assessment determines that the load-bearing capacity is less than that required by the code, load tests shall be conducted in accordance with Section 1713.2. If the building, structure or portion thereof is found to have inadequate stability or load-bearing capacity for the expected loads, modifications to ensure structural adequacy or the removal of the inadequate construction shall be required.

1713.2 Test standards. Structural components and assemblies shall be tested in accordance with the appropriate material standards listed in Chapter 35. In the absence of a standard that contains an applicable load test procedure, the test procedure shall be developed by a registered design professional and approved. The test procedure shall simulate loads and conditions of application that the completed structure or portion thereof will be subjected to in normal use.

1713.3 In-situ load tests. In-situ load tests shall be conducted in accordance with Section 1713.3.1 or 1713.3.2 and shall be supervised by a registered design professional. The test shall simulate the applicable loading conditions specified in Chapter 16 as necessary to address the concerns regarding structural stability of the building, structure or portion thereof.

1713.3.1 Load test procedure specified. Where a standard listed in Chapter 35 contains an applicable load test procedure and acceptance criteria, the test procedure and acceptance criteria in the standard shall apply. In the absence of specific load factors or acceptance criteria, the load factors and acceptance criteria in Section 1713.3.2 shall apply.

1713.3.2 Load test procedure not specified. In the absence of applicable load test procedures contained within a standard referenced by this code or acceptance criteria for a specific material or method of construction, such existing structure shall be subjected to a test procedure developed by a registered design professional that simulates applicable loading and deformation conditions. For components that are not a part of the seismic-load-resisting system, the test load shall be equal to two times the unfactored design loads. The test load shall be left in place for a period of 24 hours. The structure shall be considered to have successfully met the test requirements where the following criteria are satisfied:

1. Under the design load, the deflection shall not exceed the limitations specified in Section 1604.3.

2. Within 24 hours after removal of the test load, the structure shall have recovered not less than 75 percent of the maximum deflection.

3. During and immediately after the test, the structure shall not show evidence of failure.

SECTION 1714
PRECONSTRUCTION LOAD TESTS

1714.1 General. In evaluating the physical properties of materials and methods of construction that are not capable of being designed by approved engineering analysis or do not comply with applicable material design standards listed in Chapter 35, the structural adequacy shall be predetermined based on the load test criteria established in this section.

1714.2 Load test procedures specified. Where specific load test procedures, load factors and acceptance criteria are included in the applicable design standards listed in Chapter 35, such test procedures, load factors and acceptance criteria shall apply. In the absence of specific test procedures, load factors or acceptance criteria, the corresponding provisions in Section 1714.3 shall apply.

1714.3 Load test procedures not specified. Where load test procedures are not specified in the applicable design standards listed in Chapter 35, the load-bearing and deformation capacity of structural components and assemblies shall be determined on the basis of a test procedure developed by a registered design professional that simulates applicable loading and deformation conditions. For components and assemblies that are not a part of the seismic-load-resisting system, the test shall be as specified in Section 1714.3.1. Load tests

shall simulate the applicable loading conditions specified in Chapter 16.

1714.3.1 Test procedure. The test assembly shall be subjected to an increasing superimposed load equal to not less than two times the superimposed design load. The test load shall be left in place for a period of 24 hours. The tested assembly shall be considered to have successfully met the test requirements if the assembly recovers not less than 75 percent of the maximum deflection within 24 hours after the removal of the test load. The test assembly shall then be reloaded and subjected to an increasing superimposed load until either structural failure occurs or the superimposed load is equal to two and one-half times the load at which the deflection limitations specified in Section 1714.3.2 were reached, or the load is equal to two and one-half times the superimposed design load. In the case of structural components and assemblies for which deflection limitations are not specified in Section 1714.3.2, the test specimen shall be subjected to an increasing superimposed load until structural failure occurs or the load is equal to two and one-half times the desired superimposed design load. The allowable superimposed design load shall be taken as the lesser of:

1. The load at the deflection limitation given in Section 1714.3.2.

2. The failure load divided by 2.5.

3. The maximum load applied divided by 2.5.

1714.3.2 Deflection. The deflection of structural members under the design load shall not exceed the limitations in Section 1604.3.

1714.4 Wall and partition assemblies. Load-bearing wall and partition assemblies shall sustain the test load both with and without window framing. The test load shall include all design load components. Wall and partition assemblies shall be tested both with and without door and window framing.

1714.5 Exterior window and door assemblies. The design pressure rating of exterior windows and doors in buildings shall be determined in accordance with Section 1714.5.1 or 1714.5.2.

Exception: Structural wind load design pressures for window units smaller than the size tested in accordance with Section 1714.5.1 or 1714.5.2 shall be permitted to be higher than the design value of the tested unit provided such higher pressures are determined by accepted engineering analysis. All components of the small unit shall be the same as the tested unit. Where such calculated design pressures are used, they shall be validated by an additional test of the window unit having the highest allowable design pressure.

1714.5.1 Exterior windows and doors. Exterior windows and sliding doors shall be tested and labeled as conforming to AAMA/WDMA/CSA101/I.S.2/A440. The label shall state the name of the manufacturer, the approved labeling agency and the product designation as specified in AAMA/ WDMA/CSA101/I.S.2/A440. Exterior side-hinged doors shall be tested and labeled as conforming to AAMA/WDMA/CSA101/I.S.2/A440 or comply with Section 1714.5.2. Products tested and labeled as conforming to AAMA/WDMA/CSA 101/I.S.2/A440 shall not be subject to the requirements of Sections 2403.2 and 2403.3.

1714.5.2 Exterior windows and door assemblies not provided for in Section 1714.5.1. Exterior window and door assemblies shall be tested in accordance with ASTM E 330. Exterior window and door assemblies containing glass shall comply with Section 2403. The design pressure for testing shall be calculated in accordance with Chapter 16. Each assembly shall be tested for 10 seconds at a load equal to 1.5 times the design pressure.

1714.6 Test specimens. Test specimens and construction shall be representative of the materials, workmanship and details normally used in practice. The properties of the materials used to construct the test assembly shall be determined on the basis of tests on samples taken from the load assembly or on representative samples of the materials used to construct the load test assembly. Required tests shall be conducted or witnessed by an approved agency.

SECTION 1715
MATERIAL AND TEST STANDARDS

1715.1 Test standards for joist hangers and connectors.

1715.1.1 Test standards for joist hangers. The vertical load-bearing capacity, torsional moment capacity and deflection characteristics of joist hangers shall be determined in accordance with ASTM D 1761 using lumber having a specific gravity of 0.49 or greater, but not greater than 0.55, as determined in accordance with AF&PA NDS for the joist and hangers.

> **Exception:** The joist length shall not be required to exceed 24 inches (610 mm).

1715.1.2 Vertical load capacity for joist hangers. The vertical load capacity for the joist hanger shall be determined by testing a minimum of three joist hanger assemblies as specified in ASTM D 1761. If the ultimate vertical load for any one of the tests varies more than 20 percent from the average ultimate vertical load, at least three additional tests shall be conducted. The allowable vertical load of the joist hanger shall be the lowest value determined from the following:

1. The lowest ultimate vertical load for a single hanger from any test divided by three (where three tests are conducted and each ultimate vertical load does not vary more than 20 percent from the average ultimate vertical load).

2. The average ultimate vertical load for a single hanger from all tests divided by three (where six or more tests are conducted).

3. The average from all tests of the vertical loads that produce a vertical movement of the joist with respect to the header of 0.125 inch (3.2 mm).

4. The sum of the allowable design loads for nails or other fasteners utilized to secure the joist hanger to the wood members and allowable bearing loads that contribute to the capacity of the hanger.

5. The allowable design load for the wood members forming the connection.

1715.1.3 Torsional moment capacity for joist hangers. The torsional moment capacity for the joist hanger shall be determined by testing at least three joist hanger assemblies as specified in ASTM D 1761. The allowable torsional moment of the joist hanger shall be the average torsional moment at which the lateral movement of the top or bottom of the joist with respect to the original position of the joist is 0.125 inch (3.2 mm).

1715.1.4 Design value modifications for joist hangers. Allowable design values for joist hangers that are determined by Item 4 or 5 in Section 1715.1.2 shall be permitted to be modified by the appropriate duration of loading factors as specified in AF&PA NDS but shall not exceed the direct loads as determined by Item 1, 2 or 3 in Section 1715.1.2. Allowable design values determined by Item 1, 2 or 3 in Section 1715.1.2 shall not be modified by duration of loading factors.

1715.2 Concrete and clay roof tiles.

1715.2.1 Overturning resistance. Concrete and clay roof tiles shall be tested to determine their resistance to overturning due to wind in accordance with SBCCI SSTD 11 and Chapter 15.

1715.2.2 Wind tunnel testing. When roof tiles do not satisfy the limitations in Chapter 16 for rigid tile, a wind tunnel test shall be used to determine the wind characteristics of the concrete or clay tile roof covering in accordance with SBCCI SSTD 11 and Chapter 15.

CHAPTER 18

SOILS AND FOUNDATIONS

SECTION 1801
GENERAL

1801.1 Scope. The provisions of this chapter shall apply to building and foundation systems in those areas not subject to scour or water pressure by wind and wave action. Buildings and foundations subject to such scour or water pressure loads shall be designed in accordance with Chapter 16.

1801.2 Design. Allowable bearing pressures, allowable stresses and design formulas provided in this chapter shall be used with the allowable stress design load combinations specified in Section 1605.3. The quality and design of materials used structurally in excavations, footings and foundations shall conform to the requirements specified in Chapters 16, 19, 21, 22 and 23 of this code. Excavations and fills shall also comply with Chapter 33.

1801.2.1 Foundation design for seismic overturning. Where the foundation is proportioned using the load combinations of Section 1605.2, and the computation of the seismic overturning moment is by the equivalent lateral-force method or the modal analysis method, the proportioning shall be in accordance with Section 12.13.4 of ASCE 7.

SECTION 1802
FOUNDATION AND SOILS INVESTIGATIONS

1802.1 General. Foundation and soils investigations shall be conducted in conformance with Sections 1802.2 through 1802.6. Where required by the code enforcement official, the classification and investigation of the soil shall be made by a registered design professional.

1802.2 Where required. The owner or applicant shall submit a foundation and soils investigation to the code enforcement official where required in Sections 1802.2.1 through 1802.2.7.

Exception: The code enforcement official need not require a foundation or soils investigation where satisfactory data from adjacent areas is available that demonstrates an investigation is not necessary for any of the conditions in Sections 1802.2.1 through 1802.2.6.

1802.2.1 Questionable soil. Where the classification, strength or compressibility of the soil are in doubt or where a load-bearing value superior to that specified in this code is claimed, the code enforcement official shall require that the necessary investigation be made. Such investigation shall comply with the provisions of Sections 1802.4 through 1802.6.

1802.2.2 Expansive soils. In areas likely to have expansive soil, the code enforcement official shall require soil tests to determine where such soils do exist.

1802.2.3 Ground-water table. A subsurface soil investigation shall be performed to determine whether the existing ground-water table is above or within 5 feet (1524 mm) below the elevation of the lowest floor level where such floor is located below the finished ground level adjacent to the foundation.

Exception: A subsurface soil investigation shall not be required where waterproofing is provided in accordance with Section 1807.

1802.2.4 Pile and pier foundations. Pile and pier foundations shall be designed and installed on the basis of a foundation investigation and report as specified in Sections 1802.4 through 1802.6 and Section 1808.2.2.

1802.2.5 Rock strata. Where subsurface explorations at the project site indicate variations or doubtful characteristics in the structure of the rock upon which foundations are to be constructed, a sufficient number of borings shall be made to a depth of not less than 10 feet (3048 mm) below the level of the foundations to provide assurance of the soundness of the foundation bed and its load-bearing capacity.

1802.2.6 Seismic Design Category C. Where a structure is determined to be in Seismic Design Category C in accordance with Section 1613, an investigation shall be conducted and shall include an evaluation of the following potential hazards resulting from earthquake motions: slope instability, liquefaction and surface rupture due to faulting or lateral spreading.

1802.2.7 Seismic Design Category D, E or F. Where the structure is determined to be in Seismic Design Category D, E or F, in accordance with Section 1613, the soils investigation requirements for Seismic Design Category C, given in Section 1802.2.6, shall be met, in addition to the following. The investigation shall include:

1. A determination of lateral pressures on basement and retaining walls due to earthquake motions.

2. An assessment of potential consequences of any liquefaction and soil strength loss, including estimation of differential settlement, lateral movement or reduction in foundation soil-bearing capacity, and shall address mitigation measures. Such measures shall be given consideration in the design of the structure and can include but are not limited to ground stabilization, selection of appropriate foundation type and depths, selection of appropriate structural systems to accommodate anticipated displacements or any combination of these measures. The potential for liquefaction and soil strength loss shall be evaluated for site peak ground acceleration magnitudes and source characteristics consistent

with the design earthquake ground motions. Peak ground acceleration shall be determined from a site-specific study taking into account soil amplification effects, as specified in Chapter 21 of ASCE 7.

Exception: A site-specific study need not be performed, provided that peak ground acceleration equal to $S_{DS}/2.5$ is used, where S_{DS} is determined in accordance with Section 21.2.1 of ASCE 7.

1802.3 Soil classification. Where required, soils shall be classified in accordance with Section 1802.3.1 or 1802.3.2.

1802.3.1 General. For the purposes of this chapter, the definition and classification of soil materials for use in Table 1804.2 shall be in accordance with ASTM D 2487.

1802.3.2 Expansive soils. Soils meeting all four of the following provisions shall be considered expansive, except that tests to show compliance with Items 1, 2 and 3 shall not be required if the test prescribed in Item 4 is conducted:

1. Plasticity index (PI) of 15 or greater, determined in accordance with ASTM D 4318.

2. More than 10 percent of the soil particles pass a No. 200 sieve (75 μm), determined in accordance with ASTM D 422.

3. More than 10 percent of the soil particles are less than 5 micrometers in size, determined in accordance with ASTM D 422.

4. Expansion index greater than 20, determined in accordance with ASTM D 4829.

1802.4 Investigation. Soil classification shall be based on observation and any necessary tests of the materials disclosed by borings, test pits or other subsurface exploration made in appropriate locations. Additional studies shall be made as necessary to evaluate slope stability, soil strength, position and adequacy of load-bearing soils, the effect of moisture variation on soil-bearing capacity, compressibility, liquefaction and expansiveness.

1802.4.1 Exploratory boring. The scope of the soil investigation including the number and types of borings or soundings, the equipment used to drill and sample, the in-situ testing equipment and the laboratory testing program shall be determined by a registered design professional.

1802.5 Soil boring and sampling. The soil boring and sampling procedure and apparatus shall be in accordance with generally accepted engineering practice. The registered design professional shall have a fully qualified representative on the site during all boring and sampling operations.

1802.6 Reports. The soil classification and design load-bearing capacity shall be shown on the construction document. Where required by the code enforcement official, a written report of the investigation shall be submitted that includes, but need not be limited to, the following information:

1. A plot showing the location of test borings and/or excavations.

2. A complete record of the soil samples.

3. A record of the soil profile.

4. Elevation of the water table, if encountered.

5. Recommendations for foundation type and design criteria, including but not limited to: bearing capacity of natural or compacted soil; provisions to mitigate the effects of expansive soils; mitigation of the effects of liquefaction, differential settlement and varying soil strength; and the effects of adjacent loads.

6. Expected total and differential settlement.

7. Pile and pier foundation information in accordance with Section 1808.2.2.

8. Special design and construction provisions for footings or foundations founded on expansive soils, as necessary.

9. Compacted fill material properties and testing in accordance with Section 1803.5.

SECTION 1803
EXCAVATION, GRADING AND FILL

1803.1 Excavations near footings or foundations. Excavations for any purpose shall not remove lateral support from any footing or foundation without first underpinning or protecting the footing or foundation against settlement or lateral translation.

1803.2 Placement of backfill. The excavation outside the foundation shall be backfilled with soil that is free of organic material, construction debris, cobbles and boulders or a controlled low-strength material (CLSM). The backfill shall be placed in lifts and compacted, in a manner that does not damage the foundation or the waterproofing or dampproofing material.

Exception: Controlled low-strength material need not be compacted.

1803.3 Site grading. The ground immediately adjacent to the foundation shall be sloped away from the building at a slope of not less than one unit vertical in 20 units horizontal (5-percent slope) for a minimum distance of 10 feet (3048 mm) measured perpendicular to the face of the wall. If physical obstructions or lot lines prohibit 10 feet (3048 mm) of horizontal distance, a 5-percent slope shall be provided to an approved alternative method of diverting water away from the foundation. Swales used for this purpose shall be sloped a minimum of 2 percent where located within 10 feet (3048 mm) of the building foundation. Impervious surfaces within 10 feet (3048 mm) of the building foundation shall be sloped a minimum of 2 percent away from the building.

Exception: Where climatic or soil conditions warrant, the slope of the ground away from the building foundation is permitted to be reduced to not less than one unit vertical in 48 units horizontal (2-percent slope).

The procedure used to establish the final ground level adjacent to the foundation shall account for additional settlement of the backfill.

1803.4 Grading and fill in flood hazard areas. In flood hazard areas established in Section 1612.3, grading and/or fill shall not be approved:

1. Unless such fill is placed, compacted and sloped to minimize shifting, slumping and erosion during the rise and fall of flood water and, as applicable, wave action.

2. In floodways, unless it has been demonstrated through hydrologic and hydraulic analyses performed by a registered design professional in accordance with standard engineering practice that the proposed grading or fill, or both, will not result in any increase in flood levels during the occurrence of the design flood.

3. In flood hazard areas subject to high-velocity wave action, unless such fill is conducted and/or placed to avoid diversion of water and waves toward any building or structure.

4. Where design flood elevations are specified but floodways have not been designated, unless it has been demonstrated that the cumulative effect of the proposed flood hazard area encroachment, when combined with all other existing and anticipated flood hazard area encroachment, will not increase the design flood elevation more than 1 foot (305 mm) at any point.

1803.5 Compacted fill material. Where footings will bear on compacted fill material, the compacted fill shall comply with the provisions of an approved report, which shall contain the following:

1. Specifications for the preparation of the site prior to placement of compacted fill material.

2. Specifications for material to be used as compacted fill.

3. Test method to be used to determine the maximum dry density and optimum moisture content of the material to be used as compacted fill.

4. Maximum allowable thickness of each lift of compacted fill material.

5. Field test method for determining the in-place dry density of the compacted fill.

6. Minimum acceptable in-place dry density expressed as a percentage of the maximum dry density determined in accordance with Item 3.

7. Number and frequency of field tests required to determine compliance with Item 6.

Exception: Compacted fill material less than 12 inches (305 mm) in depth need not comply with an approved report, provided it has been compacted to a minimum of 90 percent Modified Proctor in accordance with ASTM D 1557. The compaction shall be verified by a qualified inspector approved by the code enforcement official.

1803.6 Controlled low-strength material (CLSM). Where footings will bear on controlled low-strength material (CLSM), the CLSM shall comply with the provisions of an approved report, which shall contain the following:

1. Specifications for the preparation of the site prior to placement of the CLSM.

2. Specifications for the CLSM.

3. Laboratory or field test method(s) to be used to determine the compressive strength or bearing capacity of the CLSM.

4. Test methods for determining the acceptance of the CLSM in the field.

5. Number and frequency of field tests required to determine compliance with Item 4.

SECTION 1804
ALLOWABLE LOAD-BEARING VALUES OF SOILS

1804.1 Design. The presumptive load-bearing values provided in Table 1804.2 shall be used with the allowable stress design load combinations specified in Section 1605.3.

1804.2 Presumptive load-bearing values. The maximum allowable foundation pressure, lateral pressure or lateral sliding-resistance values for supporting soils near the surface shall not exceed the values specified in Table 1804.2 unless data to substantiate the use of a higher value are submitted and approved.

Presumptive load-bearing values shall apply to materials with similar physical characteristics and dispositions.

Mud, organic silt, organic clays, peat or unprepared fill shall not be assumed to have a presumptive load-bearing capacity unless data to substantiate the use of such a value are submitted.

Exception: A presumptive load-bearing capacity is permitted to be used where the code enforcement official deems the load-bearing capacity of mud, organic silt or unprepared fill is adequate for the support of lightweight and temporary structures.

1804.3 Lateral sliding resistance. The resistance of structural walls to lateral sliding shall be calculated by combining the values derived from the lateral bearing and the lateral sliding resistance shown in Table 1804.2 unless data to substantiate the use of higher values are submitted for approval.

For clay, sandy clay, silty clay and clayey silt, in no case shall the lateral sliding resistance exceed one-half the dead load.

1804.3.1 Increases in allowable lateral sliding resistance. The resistance values derived from the table are permitted to be increased by the tabular value for each additional foot (305 mm) of depth to a maximum of 15 times the tabular value.

Isolated poles for uses such as flagpoles or signs and poles used to support buildings that are not adversely affected by a 0.5 inch (12.7 mm) motion at the ground surface due to short-term lateral loads are permitted to be designed using lateral-bearing values equal to two times the tabular values.

TABLE 1804.2
ALLOWABLE FOUNDATION AND LATERAL PRESSURE

CLASS OF MATERIALS	ALLOWABLE FOUNDATION PRESSURE (psf)[d]	LATERAL BEARING (psf/f below natural grade)[d]	LATERAL SLIDING	
			Coefficient of friction[a]	Resistance (psf)[b]
1. Crystalline bedrock	12,000	1,200	0.70	-
2. Sedimentary and foliated rock	4,000	400	0.35	-
3. Sandy gravel and/or gravel (GW and GP)	3,000	200	0.35	-
4. Sand, silty sand, clayey sand, silty gravel and clayey gravel (SW, SP, SM, SC, GM and GC)	2,000	150	0.25	-
5. Clay, sandy clay, silty clay, clayey silt, silt and sandy silt (CL, ML, MH and CH)	1,500[c]	100	-	130

For SI: 1 pound per square foot = 0.0479 kPa, 1 pound per square foot per foot = 0.157 kPa/m.

a. Coefficient to be multiplied by the dead load.

b. Lateral sliding resistance value to be multiplied by the contact area, as limited by Section 1804.3.

c. Where the code enforcement official determines that in-place soils with an allowable bearing capacity of less than 1,500 psf are likely to be present at the site, the allowable bearing capacity shall be determined by a soils investigation.

d. An increase of one-third is permitted when using the alternate load combinations in Section 1605.3.2 that include wind or earthquake loads.

SECTION 1805
FOOTINGS AND FOUNDATIONS

1805.1 General. Footings and foundations shall be designed and constructed in accordance with Sections 1805.1 through 1805.9. Footings and foundations shall be built on undisturbed soil, compacted fill material or CLSM. Compacted fill material shall be placed in accordance with Section 1803.5. CLSM shall be placed in accordance with Section 1803.6.

The top surface of footings shall be level. The bottom surface of footings is permitted to have a slope not exceeding one unit vertical in 10 units horizontal (10-percent slope). Footings shall be stepped where it is necessary to change the elevation of the top surface of the footing or where the surface of the ground slopes more than one unit vertical in 10 units horizontal (10-percent slope).

1805.2 Depth of footings. The minimum depth of footings below the undisturbed ground surface shall be 12 inches (305 mm). Where applicable, the depth of footings shall also conform to Sections 1805.2.1 through 1805.2.3.

1805.2.1 Frost protection. Except where otherwise protected from frost, foundation walls, piers and other permanent supports of buildings and structures shall be protected by one or more of the following methods:

1. Extending below the frost line of the locality;

2. Constructing in accordance with ASCE 32; or

3. Erecting on solid rock.

Exception: Free-standing buildings meeting all of the following conditions shall not be required to be protected:

1. Classified in Occupancy Category I, in accordance with Section1604.5;

2. Area of 600 square feet (56 m²) or less for light-frame construction or 400 square feet (37 m²) or less for other than light-frame construction; and

3. Eave height of 10 feet (3048 mm) or less.

Footings shall not bear on frozen soil unless such frozen condition is of a permanent character.

1805.2.2 Isolated footings. Footings on granular soil shall be so located that the line drawn between the lower edges of adjoining footings shall not have a slope steeper than 30 degrees (0.52 rad) with the horizontal, unless the material supporting the higher footing is braced or retained or otherwise laterally supported in an approved manner or a greater slope has been properly established by engineering analysis.

1805.2.3 Shifting or moving soils. Where it is known that the shallow subsoils are of a shifting or moving character, footings shall be carried to a sufficient depth to ensure stability.

1805.3 Footings on or adjacent to slopes. The placement of buildings and structures on or adjacent to slopes steeper than one unit vertical in three units horizontal (33.3-percent slope) shall conform to Sections 1805.3.1 through 1805.3.5.

1805.3.1 Building clearance from ascending slopes. In general, buildings below slopes shall be set a sufficient distance from the slope to provide protection from slope drainage, erosion and shallow failures. Except as provided for in Section 1805.3.5 and Figure 1805.3.1, the following criteria will be assumed to provide this protection. Where the existing slope is steeper than one unit vertical in one unit horizontal (100-percent slope), the toe of the slope shall be assumed to be at the intersection of a horizontal plane drawn from the top of the foundation and a plane drawn tangent to the slope at an angle of 45 degrees (0.79 rad) to the horizontal. Where a retaining wall is constructed at the toe of the slope, the height of the slope shall be measured from the top of the wall to the top of the slope.

1805.3.2 Footing setback from descending slope surface. Footings on or adjacent to slope surfaces shall be founded in firm material with an embedment and set back from the slope surface sufficient to provide vertical and lateral support for the footing without detrimental settlement. Except as provided for in Section 1805.3.5 and Figure 1805.3.1, the following setback is deemed adequate to meet the criteria. Where the slope is steeper than 1 unit vertical in 1 unit horizontal (100-percent slope), the

For SI: 1 foot = 304.8 mm.

FIGURE 1805.3.1
FOUNDATION CLEARANCES FROM SLOPES

required setback shall be measured from an imaginary plane 45 degrees (0.79 rad) to the horizontal, projected upward from the toe of the slope.

1805.3.3 Pools. The setback between pools regulated by this code and slopes shall be equal to one-half the building footing setback distance required by this section. That portion of the pool wall within a horizontal distance of 7 feet (2134 mm) from the top of the slope shall be capable of supporting the water in the pool without soil support.

1805.3.4 Foundation elevation. On graded sites, the top of any exterior foundation shall extend above the elevation of the street gutter at point of discharge or the inlet of an approved drainage device a minimum of 12 inches (305 mm) plus 2 percent. Alternate elevations are permitted subject to the approval of the code enforcement official, provided it can be demonstrated that required drainage to the point of discharge and away from the structure is provided at all locations on the site.

1805.3.5 Alternate setback and clearance. Alternate setbacks and clearances are permitted, subject to the approval of the code enforcement official. The code enforcement official is permitted to require an investigation and recommendation of a registered design professional to demonstrate that the intent of this section has been satisfied. Such an investigation shall include consideration of material, height of slope, slope gradient, load intensity and erosion characteristics of slope material.

1805.4 Footings. Footings shall be designed and constructed in accordance with Sections 1805.4.1 through 1805.4.6.

1805.4.1 Design. Footings shall be so designed that the allowable bearing capacity of the soil is not exceeded, and that differential settlement is minimized. The minimum width of footings shall be 12 inches (305 mm).

Footings in areas with expansive soils shall be designed in accordance with the provisions of Section 1805.8.

1805.4.1.1 Design loads. Footings shall be designed for the most unfavorable effects due to the combinations of loads specified in Section 1605.2 or 1605.3. The dead load is permitted to include the weight of foundations, footings and overlying fill. Reduced live loads, as specified in Sections 1607.9 and 1607.11, are permitted to be used in the design of footings.

1805.4.1.2 Vibratory loads. Where machinery operations or other vibrations are transmitted through the foundation, consideration shall be given in the footing design to prevent detrimental disturbances of the soil.

1805.4.2 Concrete footings. The design, materials and construction of concrete footings shall comply with Sections 1805.4.2.1 through 1805.4.2.6 and the provisions of Chapter 19.

Exception: Where a specific design is not provided, concrete footings supporting walls of light-frame construction are permitted to be designed in accordance with Table 1805.4.2.

1805.4.2.1 Concrete strength. Concrete in footings shall have a specified compressive strength (f'_c) of not less than 2,500 pounds per square inch (psi) (17 237 kPa) at 28 days.

1805.4.2.2 Footing seismic ties. Where a structure is assigned to Seismic Design Category D, E or F in accordance with Section 1613, individual spread footings founded on soil defined in Section 1613.5.2 as Site Class E or F shall be interconnected by ties. Ties shall be capable of carrying, in tension or compression, a force equal to the product of the larger footing load times the seismic coefficient, S_{DS}, divided by 10 unless it is demonstrated that equivalent restraint is provided by reinforced concrete beams within slabs on grade or reinforced concrete slabs on grade.

TABLE 1805.4.2
FOOTINGS SUPPORTING WALLS OF LIGHT-FRAME CONSTRUCTION[a, b, c, d, e]

NUMBER OF FLOORS SUPPORTED BY THE FOOTING[f]	WIDTH OF FOOTING (inches)	THICKNESS OF FOOTING (inches)
1	12	6
2	15	6
3	18	8[g]

For SI: 1 inch = 25.4 mm, 1 foot = 304.8 mm.

a. Depth of footings shall be in accordance with Section 1805.2.

b. The ground under the floor is permitted to be excavated to the elevation of the top of the footing.

c. Interior-stud-bearing walls are permitted to be supported by isolated footings. The footing width and length shall be twice the width shown in this table, and footings shall be spaced not more than 6 feet on center.

d. See Section 1908 for additional requirements for footings of structures assigned to Seismic Design Category C, D, E or F.

e. For thickness of foundation walls, see Section 1805.5.

f. Footings are permitted to support a roof in addition to the stipulated number of floors. Footings supporting roof only shall be as required for supporting one floor.

g. Plain concrete footings for Group R-3 occupancies are permitted to be 6 inches thick.

1805.4.2.3 Plain concrete footings. The edge thickness of plain concrete footings supporting walls of other than light-frame construction shall not be less than 8 inches (203 mm) where placed on soil.

> **Exception:** For plain concrete footings supporting Group R-3 occupancies, the edge thickness is permitted to be 6 inches (152 mm), provided that the footing does not extend beyond a distance greater than the thickness of the footing on either side of the supported wall.

1805.4.2.4 Placement of concrete. Concrete footings shall not be placed through water unless a tremie or other method approved by the code enforcement official is used. Where placed under or in the presence of water, the concrete shall be deposited by approved means to ensure minimum segregation of the mix and negligible turbulence of the water.

1805.4.2.5 Protection of concrete. Concrete footings shall be protected from freezing during depositing and for a period of not less than five days thereafter. Water shall not be allowed to flow through the deposited concrete.

1805.4.2.6 Forming of concrete. Concrete footings are permitted to be cast against the earth where, in the opinion of the code enforcement official, soil conditions do not require forming. Where forming is required, it shall be in accordance with Chapter 6 of ACI 318.

1805.4.3 Masonry-unit footings. The design, materials and construction of masonry-unit footings shall comply with Sections 1805.4.3.1 and 1805.4.3.2, and the provisions of Chapter 21.

> **Exception:** Where a specific design is not provided, masonry-unit footings supporting walls of light-frame construction are permitted to be designed in accordance with Table 1805.4.2.

1805.4.3.1 Dimensions. Masonry-unit footings shall be laid in Type M or S mortar complying with Section 2103.8 and the depth shall not be less than twice the projection beyond the wall, pier or column. The width shall not be less than 8 inches (203 mm) wider than the wall supported thereon.

1805.4.3.2 Offsets. The maximum offset of each course in brick foundation walls stepped up from the footings shall be 1.5 inches (38 mm) where laid in single courses, and 3 inches (76 mm) where laid in double courses.

1805.4.4 Steel grillage footings. Grillage footings of structural steel shapes shall be separated with approved steel spacers and be entirely encased in concrete with at least 6 inches (152 mm) on the bottom and at least 4 inches (102 mm) at all other points. The spaces between the shapes shall be completely filled with concrete or cement grout.

1805.4.5 Timber footings. Timber footings are permitted for buildings of Type V construction and as otherwise approved by the code enforcement official. Such footings shall be treated in accordance with AWPA U1 (Commodity Specification A, Use Category 4B). Treated timbers are not required where placed entirely below permanent water level or where used as capping for wood piles that project above the water level over submerged or marsh lands. The compressive stresses perpendicular to the grain in untreated timber footings supported upon treated piles shall not exceed 70 percent of the allowable stresses for the species and grade of timber as specified in the AF&PA NDS.

1805.4.6 Wood foundations. Wood foundation systems shall be designed and installed in accordance with AF&PA PWF. Lumber and plywood shall be treated in accordance with AWPA U1 (Commodity Specification A, Use Category 4B and Section 5.2) and shall be identified in accordance with Section 2303.1.8.1.

1805.5 Foundation walls. Concrete and masonry foundation walls shall be designed in accordance with Chapter 19 or 21, respectively. Foundation walls that are laterally supported at the top and bottom and within the parameters of Tables 1805.5(1) through 1805.5(5) are permitted to be designed and constructed in accordance with Sections 1805.5.1 through 1805.5.5.

1805.5.1 Foundation wall thickness. The minimum thickness of concrete and masonry foundation walls shall comply with Sections 1805.5.1.1 through 1805.5.1.3.

1805.5.1.1 Thickness at top of foundation wall. The thickness of foundation walls shall not be less than the thickness of the wall supported, except that foundation walls of at least 8-inch (203 mm) nominal width are permitted to support brick-veneered frame walls and 10-inch-wide (254 mm) cavity walls provided the requirements of Section 1805.5.1.2 are met. Corbeling of masonry shall be in accordance with Section 2104.2.

Where an 8-inch (203 mm) wall is corbeled, the top corbel shall not extend higher than the bottom of the floor framing and shall be a full course of headers at least 6 inches (152 mm) in length or the top course bed joint shall be tied to the vertical wall projection. The tie shall be W2.8 (4.8 mm) and spaced at a maximum horizontal distance of 36 inches (914 mm); the hollow space behind the corbelled masonry shall be filled with mortar or grout.

1805.5.1.2 Thickness based on soil loads, unbalanced backfill height and wall height. The thickness of foundation walls shall comply with the requirements of Table 1805.5(5) for concrete walls, Table 1805.5(1) for plain masonry walls or Table 1805.5(2), 1805.5(3) or 1805.5(4) for masonry walls with reinforcement. When using the tables, masonry shall be laid in running bond and the mortar shall be Type M or S.

Unbalanced backfill height is the difference in height between the exterior finish ground level and the lower of the top of the concrete footing that supports the foundation wall or the interior finish ground level. Where an interior concrete slab on grade is provided and is in contact with the interior surface of the foundation wall, the unbalanced backfill height is permitted to be measured from the exterior finish ground level to the top of the interior concrete slab.

1805.5.1.3 Rubble stone. Foundation walls of rough or random rubble stone shall not be less than 16 inches (406 mm) thick. Rubble stone shall not be used for foundations for structures in Seismic Design Category C, D, E or F.

1805.5.2 Foundation wall materials. Concrete foundation walls constructed in accordance with Table 1805.5(5) shall comply with Section 1805.5.2.1. Masonry foundation walls constructed in accordance with Table 1805.5(1), 1805.5(2), 1805.5(3) or 1805.5(4) shall comply with Section 1805.5.2.2.

TABLE 1805.5(1)
PLAIN MASONRY FOUNDATION WALLS[a, b, c]

MAXIMUM WALL HEIGHT (feet)	MAXIMUMUN BALANCED BACKFILL HEIGHT[e] (feet)	MINIMUM NOMINAL WALL THICKNESS (inches)		
		Soil classes and lateral soil load[a] (psf per foot below natural grade)		
		GW, GP, SW and SP soils 30	GM, GC, SM, SM-SC and ML soils 45	SC, ML-CL and Inorganic CL soils 60
7	4 (or less)	8	8	8
	5	8	10	10
	6	10	12	10 (solid[c])
	7	12	10 (solid[c])	10 (solid[c])
8	4 (or less)	8	8	8
	5	8	10	12
	6	10	12	12 (solid[c])
	7	12	12 (solid[c])	Note d
	8	10 (solid[c])	12 (solid[c])	Note d
9	4 (or less)	8	8	8
	5	8	10	12
	6	12	12	12 (solid[c])
	7	12 (solid[c])	12 (solid[c])	Note d
	8	12 (solid[c])	Note d	Note d
	9	Note d	Note d	Note d

For SI: 1 inch = 25.4 mm, 1 foot = 304.8 mm, 1 pound per square foot per foot = 0.157 kPa/m.

a. For design lateral soil loads, see Section 1610. Soil classes are in accordance with the Unified Soil Classification System and design lateral soil loads are for moist soil conditions without hydrostatic pressure.

b. Provisions for this table are based on construction requirements specified in Section 1805.5.2.2.

c. Solid grouted hollow units or solid masonry units.

d. A design in compliance with Chapter 21 or reinforcement in accordance with Table 1805.5(2) is required.

e. For height of unbalanced backfill, see Section 1805.5.1.2.

TABLE 1805.5(2)
8-INCH MASONRY FOUNDATION WALLS WITH REINFORCEMENT WHERE d ≥ 5 INCHES[a, b, c]

MAXIMUM WALL HEIGHT (feet-inches)	MAXIMUM UNBALANCED BACKFILL HEIGHT[d] (feet-inches)	VERTICAL REINFORCEMENT		
		Soil classes and lateral soil load[a](psf per foot below natural grade)		
		GW, GP, SW and SP soils 30	GM, GC, SM, SM-SC and ML soils 45	SC, ML-CL and Inorganic CL soils 60
7-4	4-0 (or less)	#4 at 48" o.c.	#4 at 48" o.c.	#4 at 48" o.c.
	5-0	#4 at 48" o.c.	#4 at 48" o.c.	#4 at 48" o.c.
	6-0	#4 at 48" o.c.	#5 at 48" o.c.	#5 at 48" o.c.
	7-4	#5 at 48" o.c.	#6 at 48" o.c.	#7 at 48" o.c.
8-0	4-0 (or less)	#4 at 48" o.c.	#4 at 48" o.c.	#4 at 48" o.c.
	5-0	#4 at 48" o.c.	#4 at 48" o.c.	#4 at 48" o.c.
	6-0	#4 at 48" o.c.	#5 at 48" o.c.	#5 at 48" o.c.
	7-0	#5 at 48" o.c.	#6 at 48" o.c.	#7 at 48" o.c.
	8-0	#5 at 48" o.c.	#6 at 48" o.c.	#7 at 48" o.c.
8-8	4-0 (or less)	#4 at 48" o.c.	#4 at 48" o.c.	#4 at 48" o.c.
	5-0	#4 at 48" o.c.	#4 at 48" o.c.	#5 at 48" o.c.
	6-0	#4 at 48" o.c.	#5 at 48" o.c.	#6 at 48" o.c.
	7-0	#5 at 48" o.c.	#6 at 48" o.c.	#7 at 48" o.c.
	8-8	#6 at 48" o.c.	#7 at 48" o.c.	#8 at 48" o.c.
9-4	4-0 (or less)	#4 at 48" o.c.	#4 at 48" o.c.	#4 at 48" o.c.
	5-0	#4 at 48" o.c.	#4 at 48" o.c.	#5 at 48" o.c.
	6-0	#4 at 48" o.c.	#5 at 48" o.c.	#6 at 48v o.c.
	7-0	#5 at 48" o.c.	#6 at 48" o.c.	#7 at 48" o.c.
	8-0	#6 at 48" o.c.	#7 at 48" o.c.	#8 at 48" o.c.
	9-4	#7 at 48" o.c.	#8 at 48" o.c.	#9 at 48" o.c.
10-0	4-0 (or less)	#4 at 48" o.c.	#4 at 48" o.c.	#4 at 48" o.c.
	5-0	#4 at 48" o.c.	#4 at 48" o.c.	#5 at 48" o.c.
	6-0	#4 at 48" o.c.	#5 at 48" o.c.	#6 at 48" o.c.
	7-0	#5 at 48" o.c.	#6 at 48" o.c.	#7 at 48" o.c.
	8-0	#6 at 48" o.c.	#7 at 48" o.c.	#8 at 48" o.c.
	9-0	#7 at 48" o.c.	#8 at 48" o.c.	#9 at 48" o.c.
	10-0	#7 at 48" o.c.	#9 at 48" o.c.	#9 at 48" o.c.

For SI: 1 inch = 25.4 mm, 1 foot = 304.8 mm, 1 pound per square foot per foot = 0.157 kPa/m.

a. For design lateral soil loads, see Section 1610. Soil classes are in accordance with the Unified Soil Classification System and design lateral soil loads are for moist soil conditions without hydrostatic pressure.

b. Provisions for this table are based on construction requirements specified in Section 1805.5.2.2.

c. For alternative reinforcement, see Section 1805.5.3.

d. For height of unbalanced backfill, see Section 1805.5.1.2.

TABLE 1805.5(3)
10-INCH MASONRY FOUNDATION WALLS WITH REINFORCEMENT WHERE d $\geq$ 6.75 INCHES[a, b, c]

MAXIMUM WALL HEIGHT (feet-inches)	MAXIMUM UNBALANCED BACKFILL HEIGHT[d](feet-inches)	VERTICAL REINFORCEMENT		
		Soil classes and lateral soil load[a](psf per foot below natural grade)		
		GW, GP, SW and SP soils 30	GM, GC, SM, SM-SC and ML soils 45	SC, ML-CL and Inorganic CL soils 60
7-4	4-0 (or less)	#4 at 56" o.c.	#4 at 56" o.c.	#4 at 56" o.c.
	5-0	#4 at 56" o.c.	#4 at 56" o.c.	#4 at 56" o.c.
	6-0	#4 at 56" o.c.	#4 at 56" o.c.	#5 at 56" o.c.
	7-4	#4 at 56" o.c.	#5 at 56" o.c.	#6 at 56" o.c.
8-0	4-0 (or less)	#4 at 56" o.c.	#4 at 56" o.c.	#4 at 56" o.c.
	5-0	#4 at 56" o.c.	#4 at 56" o.c.	#4 at 56" o.c.
	6-0	#4 at 56" o.c.	#4 at 56" o.c.	#5 at 56" o.c.
	7-0	#4 at 56" o.c.	#5 at 56" o.c.	#6 at 56" o.c.
	8-0	#5 at 56" o.c.	#6 at 56" o.c.	#7 at 56" o.c.
8-8	4-0 (or less)	#4 at 56" o.c.	#4 at 56" o.c.	#4 at 56" o.c.
	5-0	#4 at 56" o.c.	#4 at 56" o.c.	#4 at 56" o.c.
	6-0	#4 at 56" o.c.	#4 at 56" o.c.	#5 at 56" o.c.
	7-0	#4 at 56" o.c.	#5 at 56" o.c.	#6 at 56" o.c.
	8-8	#5 at 56" o.c.	#7 at 56" o.c.	#8 at 56" o.c.
9-4	4-0 (or less)	#4 at 56" o.c.	#4 at 56" o.c.	#4 at 56" o.c.
	5-0	#4 at 56" o.c.	#4 at 56" o.c.	#4 at 56" o.c.
	6-0	#4 at 56" o.c.	#5 at 56" o.c.	#5 at 56" o.c.
	7-0	#4 at 56" o.c.	#5 at 56" o.c.	#6 at 56" o.c.
	8-0	#5 at 56" o.c.	#6 at 56" o.c.	#7 at 56" o.c.
	9-4	#6 at 56" o.c.	#7 at 56" o.c.	#8 at 56" o.c.
10-0	4-0 (or less)	#4 at 56" o.c.	#4 at 56" o.c.	#4 at 56" o.c.
	5-0	#4 at 56" o.c.	#4 at 56"o.c.	#4 at 56" o.c.
	6-0	#4 at 56" o.c.	#5 at 56" o.c.	#5 at 56"o.c.
	7-0	#5 at 56" o.c.	#6 at 56" o.c.	#7 at 56" o.c.
	8-0	#5 at 56" o.c.	#7 at 56" o.c.	#8 at 56" o.c.
	9-0	#6 at 56" o.c.	#7 at 56" o.c.	#9 at 56" o.c.
	10-0	#7 at 56" o.c.	#8 at 56" o.c.	#9 at 56" o.c.

For SI: 1 inch = 25.4 mm, 1 foot = 304.8 mm, 1 pound per square foot per foot = 0.157 kPa/m.

a. For design lateral soil loads, see Section 1610. Soil classes are in accordance with the Unified Soil Classification System and design lateral soil loads are for moist soil conditions without hydrostatic pressure.

b. Provisions for this table are based on construction requirements specified in Section 1805.5.2.2.

c. For alternative reinforcement, see Section 1805.5.3.

d. For height of unbalanced fill, see Section 1805.5.1.2.

TABLE 1805.5(4)
12-INCH MASONRY FOUNDATION WALLS WITH REINFORCEMENT WHERE d ≥ 8.75 INCHES[a, b, c]

MAXIMUM WALL HEIGHT (feet-inches)	MAXIMUM UNBALANCED BACKFILL HEIGHT[d] (feet-inches)	VERTICAL REINFORCEMENT		
		Soil classes and lateral soil load[a] (psf per foot below natural grade)		
		GW, GP, SW and SP soils 30	GM, GC, SM, SM-SC and ML soils 45	SC, ML-CL and Inorganic CL soils 60
7-4	4-0 (or less)	#4 at 72" o.c.	#4 at 72" o.c.	#4 at 72" o.c.
	5-0	#4 at 72" o.c.	#4 at 72" o.c.	#4 at 72" o.c.
	6-0	#4 at 72" o.c.	#4 at 72" o.c.	#5 at 72" o.c.
	7-4	#4 at 72" o.c.	#5 at 72" o.c.	#6 at 72" o.c.
8-0	4-0 (or less)	#4 at 72" o.c.	#4 at 72" o.c.	#4 at 72" o.c.
	5-0	#4 at 72" o.c.	#4 at 72" o.c.	#4 at 72" o.c.
	6-0	#4 at 72" o.c.	#4 at 72" o.c.	#5 at 72" o.c.
	7-0	#4 at 72" o.c.	#5 at 72" o.c.	#6 at 72" o.c.
	8-0	#5 at 72" o.c.	#6 at 72" o.c.	#7 at 72" o.c.
8-8	4-0 (or less)	#4 at 72" o.c.	#4 at 72" o.c.	#4 at 72" o.c.
	5-0	#4 at 72" o.c.	#4 at 72" o.c.	#4 at 72" o.c.
	6-0	#4 at 72" o.c.	#4 at 72" o.c.	#5 at 72" o.c.
	7-0	#4 at 72" o.c.	#5 at 72" o.c.	#6 at 72" o.c.
	8-8	#5 at 72" o.c.	#7 at 72" o.c.	#8 at 72" o.c.
9-4	4-0 (or less)	#4 at 72" o.c.	#4 at 72" o.c.	#4 at 72" o.c.
	5-0	#4 at 72" o.c.	#4 at 72" o.c.	#4 at 72" o.c.
	6-0	#4 at 72" o.c.	#5 at 72" o.c.	#5 at 72" o.c.
	7-0	#4 at 72" o.c.	#5 at 72" o.c.	#6 at 72" o.c.
	8-0	#5 at 72" o.c.	#6 at 72" o.c.	#7 at 72" o.c.
	9-4	#6 at 72" o.c.	#7 at 72" o.c.	#8 at 72" o.c.
10-0	4-0 (or less)	#4 at 72" o.c.	#4 at 72" o.c.	#4 at 72" o.c.
	5-0	#4 at 72" o.c.	#4 at 72" o.c.	#4 at 72" o.c.
	6-0	#4 at 72" o.c.	#5 at 72" o.c.	#5 at 72" o.c.
	7-0	#4 at 72" o.c.	#6 at 72" o.c.	#6 at 72" o.c.
	8-0	#5 at 72" o.c.	#6 at 72" o.c.	#7 at 72" o.c.
	9-0	#6 at 72" o.c.	#7 at 72" o.c.	#8 at 72" o.c.
	10-0	#7 at 72" o.c.	#8 at 72" o.c.	#9 at 72" o.c.

For SI: 1 inch = 25.4 mm, 1 foot = 304.8 mm, 1 pound per square foot per foot = 0.157 kPa/m.

a. For design lateral soil loads, see Section 1610. Soil classes are in accordance with the Unified Soil Classification System and design lateral soil loads are for moist soil conditions without hydrostatic pressure.

b. Provisions for this table are based on construction requirements specified in Section 1805.5.2.2.

c. For alternative reinforcement, see Section 1805.5.3.

d. For height of unbalanced backfill, see Section 1805.5.1.2.

TABLE 1805.5(5)
CONCRETE FOUNDATION WALLS[b, c]

MAXIMUM WALL HEIGHT (feet)	MAXIMUM UNBALANCED BACKFILL HEIGHT[e] (feet)	VERTICAL REINFORCEMENT AND SPACING (inches)								
		Design lateral soil load[a] (psf per foot of depth)								
		30			45			60		
		Minimum wall thickness (inches)								
		7.5	9.5	11.5	7.5	9.5	11.5	7.5	9.5	11.5
5	4	PC	PC	PC	PC	PC	PC	PC	PC	PC
	5	PC	PC	PC	PC	PC	PC	PC	PC	PC
6	4	PC	PC	PC	PC	PC	PC	PC	PC	PC
	5	PC	PC	PC	PC	PC	PC	PC	PC	PC
	6	PC	PC	PC	PC	PC	PC	PC	PC	PC
7	4	PC	PC	PC	PC	PC	PC	PC	PC	PC
	5	PC	PC	PC	PC	PC	PC	PC	PC	PC
	6	PC	PC	PC	PC	PC	PC	#5 at 48"	PC	PC
	7	PC	PC	PC	#5 at 46"	PC	PC	#6 at 48"	PC	PC
8	4	PC	PC	PC	PC	PC	PC	PC	PC	PC
	5	PC	PC	PC	PC	PC	PC	PC	PC	PC
	6	PC	PC	PC	PC	PC	PC	#5 at 43"	PC	PC
	7	PC	PC	PC	#5 at 41"	PC	PC	#6 at 43"	PC	PC
	8	#5 at 47"	PC	PC	#6 at 43"	PC	PC	#6 at 32"	#6 at 44"	PC
9	4	PC	PC	PC	PC	PC	PC	PC	PC	PC
	5	PC	PC	PC	PC	PC	PC	PC	PC	PC
	6	PC	PC	PC	PC	PC	PC	#5 at 39"	PC	PC
	7	PC	PC	PC	#5 at 37"	PC	PC	#6 at 38"	#5 at 37"	PC
	8	#5 at 41"	PC	PC	#6 at 38"	#5 at 37"	PC	#7 at 39"	#6 at 39"	#4 at 48"
	9[d]	#6 at 46"	PC	PC	#7 at 41"	#6 at 41"	PC	#7 at 31"	#7 at 41"	#6 at 39"
10	4	PC	PC	PC	PC	PC	PC	PC	PC	PC
	5	PC	PC	PC	PC	PC	PC	PC	PC	PC
	6	PC	PC	PC	PC	PC	PC	#5 at 37"	PC	PC
	7	PC	PC	PC	#6 at 48"	PC	PC	#6 at 35"	#6 at 48"	PC
	8	#5 at 38"	PC	PC	#7 at 47"	#6 at 47"	PC	#7 at 35"	#7 at 48"	#6 at 45"
	9[d]	#6 at 41"	#4 at 48"	PC	#7 at 37"	#7 at 48"	#4 at 48"	#6 at 22"	#7 at 37"	#7 at 47"
	10[d]	#7 at 45"	#6 at 45"	PC	#7 at 31"	#7 at 40"	#6 at 38"	#6 at 22"	#7 at 30"	#7 at 38"

For SI: 1 inch = 25.4 mm, 1 foot = 304.8 mm, 1 pound per square foot = 0.157 kPa/m.

a. For design lateral soil loads for different classes of soil, see Section 1610.

b. Provisions for this table are based on construction requirements specified in Section 1805.5.2.1.

c. "PC" means plain concrete.

d. Where design lateral soil loads from Table 1610.1 are used, the requirements for 30 and 45 psf per foot of depth are not applicable. See Section 1610.

e. For height of unbalanced backfill, see Section 1805.5.1.2.

1805.5.2.1 Concrete foundation walls. Concrete foundation walls shall comply with the following:

1. The size and spacing of vertical reinforcement shown in Table 1805.5(5) is based on the use of reinforcement with a minimum yield strength of 60,000 psi (414 MPa). Vertical reinforcement with a minimum yield strength of 40,000 psi (276 MPa) or 50,000 psi (345 MPa) is permitted, provided the same size bar is used and the spacing shown in the table is reduced by multiplying the spacing by 0.67 or 0.83, respectively.

2. Vertical reinforcement, when required, shall be placed nearest the inside face of the wall a distance, d, from the outside face (soil side) of the wall. The distance, d, is equal to the wall thickness, t, minus 1.25 inches (32 mm) plus one-half the bar diameter, d_b [$d = t - (1.25 + d_b/2)$]. The reinforcement shall be placed within a tolerance of $\pm \, ^3/_8$ inch (9.5 mm) where d is less than or equal to 8 inches (203 mm) or $\pm \, ^1/_2$ inch (2.7 mm) where d is greater than 8 inches (203 mm).

3. In lieu of the reinforcement shown in Table 1805.5(5), smaller reinforcing bar sizes with

closer spacings that provide an equivalent cross-sectional area of reinforcement per unit length of wall are permitted.

4. Concrete cover for reinforcement measured from the inside face of the wall shall not be less than $3/_4$ inch (19.1 mm). Concrete cover for reinforcement measured from the outside face of the wall shall not be less than 1.5 inches (38 mm) for No. 5 bars and smaller and not less than 2 inches (51 mm) for larger bars.

5. Concrete shall have a specified compressive strength, f'_c, of not less than 2,500 psi (17.2 MPa) at 28 days.

6. The unfactored axial load per linear foot of wall shall not exceed 1.2 tf'_c, where t is the specified wall thickness in inches.

1805.5.2.2 Masonry foundation walls. Masonry foundation walls shall comply with the following:

1. Vertical reinforcement shall have a minimum yield strength of 60,000 psi (414 MPa).

2. The specified location of the reinforcement shall equal or exceed the effective depth distance, d, noted in Tables 1805.5(2), 1805.5(3) and 1805.5(4) and shall be measured from the face of the exterior (soil) side of the wall to the center of the vertical reinforcement. The reinforcement shall be placed within the tolerances specified in ACI 530.1/ASCE 6/TMS 402, Article 3.4 B7 of the specified location.

3. Grout shall comply with Section 2103.12.

4. Concrete masonry units shall comply with ASTM C 90.

5. Clay masonry units shall comply with ASTM C 652 for hollow brick, except compliance with ASTM C 62 or ASTM C 216 is permitted when solid masonry units are installed in accordance with Table 1805.5(1) for plain masonry.

6. Masonry units shall be installed with Type M or S mortar in accordance with Section 2103.8.

7. The unfactored axial load per linear foot of wall shall not exceed 1.2 tf'_m where t is the specified well thickness in inches and f'_m is the specified compressive strength of masonry in pounds per square inch.

1805.5.3 Alternative foundation wall reinforcement. In lieu of the reinforcement provisions for masonry foundation walls in Table 1805.5(2), 1805.5(3) or 1805.5(4), alternative reinforcing bar sizes and spacings having an equivalent cross-sectional area of reinforcement per linear foot (mm) of wall are permitted to be used, provided the spacing of reinforcement does not exceed 72 inches (1829 mm) and reinforcing bar sizes do not exceed No. 11.

1805.5.4 Hollow masonry walls. At least 4 inches (102 mm) of solid masonry shall be provided at girder supports at the top of hollow masonry unit foundation walls.

1805.5.5 Seismic requirements. Tables 1805.5(1) through 1805.5(5) shall be subject to the following limitations in Sections 1805.5.5.1 and 1805.5.5.2 based on the seismic design category assigned to the structure as defined in Section 1613.

1805.5.5.1 Seismic requirements for concrete foundation walls. Concrete foundation walls designed using Table 1805.5(5) shall be subject to the following limitations:

1. Seismic Design Categories A and B. No additional seismic requirements, except provide not less than two No. 5 bars around window and door openings. Such bars shall extend at least 24 inches (610 mm) beyond the corners of the openings.

2. Seismic Design Categories C, D, E and F. Tables shall not be used except as allowed for plain concrete members in Section 1908.1.15.

1805.5.5.2 Seismic requirements for masonry foundation walls. Masonry foundation walls designed using Tables 1805.5(1) through 1805.5(4) shall be subject to the following limitations:

1. Seismic Design Categories A and B. No additional seismic requirements.

2. Seismic Design Category C. A design using Tables 1805.5(1) through 1805.5(4) is subject to the seismic requirements of Section 2106.4.

3. Seismic Design Category D. A design using Tables 1805.2(2) through 1805.5(4) is subject to the seismic requirements of Section 2106.5.

4. Seismic Design Categories E and F. A design using Tables 1805.2(2) through 1805.5(4) is subject to the seismic requirements of Section 2106.6.

1805.5.6 Foundation wall drainage. Foundation walls shall be designed to support the weight of the full hydrostatic pressure of undrained backfill unless a drainage system is installed in accordance with Sections 1807.4.2 and 1807.4.3.

1805.5.7 Pier and curtain wall foundations. Except in Seismic Design Categories D, E and F, pier and curtain wall foundations are permitted to be used to support light-frame construction not more than two stories in height, provided the following requirements are met:

1. All load-bearing walls shall be placed on continuous concrete footings bonded integrally with the exterior wall footings.

2. The minimum actual thickness of a load-bearing masonry wall shall not be less than 4 inches (102 mm) nominal or 3.625 inches (92 mm) actual thickness, and shall be bonded integrally with piers spaced 6 feet (1829 mm) on center (o.c.).

3. Piers shall be constructed in accordance with Chapter 21 and the following:

3.1. The unsupported height of the masonry piers shall not exceed 10 times their least dimension.

3.2. Where structural clay tile or hollow concrete masonry units are used for piers supporting beams and girders, the cellular spaces shall be filled solidly with concrete or Type M or S mortar.

Exception: Unfilled hollow piers are permitted where the unsupported height of the pier is not more than four times its least dimension.

3.3. Hollow piers shall be capped with 4 inches (102 mm) of solid masonry or concrete or the cavities of the top course shall be filled with concrete or grout.

4. The maximum height of a 4-inch (102 mm) load-bearing masonry foundation wall supporting wood frame walls and floors shall not be more than 4 feet (1219 mm) in height.

5. The unbalanced fill for 4-inch (102 mm) foundation walls shall not exceed 24 inches (610 mm) for solid masonry, nor 12 inches (305 mm) for hollow masonry.

1805.6 Foundation plate or sill bolting. Wood foundation plates or sills shall be bolted or strapped to the foundation or foundation wall as provided in Chapter 23.

1805.7 Designs employing lateral bearing. Designs to resist both axial and lateral loads employing posts or poles as columns embedded in earth or embedded in concrete footings in the earth shall conform to the requirements of Sections 1805.7.1 through 1805.7.3.

1805.7.1 Limitations. The design procedures outlined in this section are subject to the following limitations:

1. The frictional resistance for structural walls and slabs on silts and clays shall be limited to one-half of the normal force imposed on the soil by the weight of the footing or slab.

2. Posts embedded in earth shall not be used to provide lateral support for structural or nonstructural materials such as plaster, masonry or concrete unless bracing is provided that develops the limited deflection required.

Wood poles shall be treated in accordance with AWPA U1 for sawn timber posts (Commodity Specification A, Use Category 4B) and for round timber posts (Commodity Specification B, Use Category 4B).

1805.7.2 Design criteria. The depth to resist lateral loads shall be determined by the design criteria established in Sections 1805.7.2.1 through 1805.7.2.3, or by other methods approved by the code enforcement official.

1805.7.2.1 Nonconstrained. The following formula shall be used in determining the depth of embedment required to resist lateral loads where no constraint is provided at the ground surface, such as rigid floor or rigid ground surface pavement, and where no lateral constraint is provided above the ground surface, such as a structural diaphragm.

$$d = 0.5A\{1 + [1 + (4.36h/A)]^{1/2}\} \qquad \textbf{Equation 18-1)}$$

where:

A = $2.34P/S_1\,b$.

b = Diameter of round post or footing or diagonal dimension of square post or footing, feet (m).

d = Depth of embedment in earth in feet (m) but not over 12 feet (3658 mm) for purpose of computing lateral pressure.

h = Distance in feet (m) from ground surface to point of application of "P."

P = Applied lateral force in pounds (kN).

S_1 = Allowable lateral soil-bearing pressure as set forth in Section 1804.3 based on a depth of one-third the depth of embedment in pounds per square foot (psf) (kPa).

1805.7.2.2 Constrained. The following formula shall be used to determine the depth of embedment required to resist lateral loads where constraint is provided at the ground surface, such as a rigid floor or pavement.

$$d^2 = 4.25(Ph/S_3\,b) \qquad \textbf{(Equation 18-2)}$$

or alternatively

$$d^2 = 4.25\,(M_g/S_3\,b) \qquad \textbf{(Equation 18-3)}$$

where:

M_g = Moment in the post at grade, in foot-pounds (kN-m).

S_3 = Allowable lateral soil-bearing pressure as set forth in Section 1804.3 based on a depth equal to the depth of embedment in pounds per square foot (kPa).

1805.7.2.3 Vertical load. The resistance to vertical loads shall be determined by the allowable soil-bearing pressure set forth in Table 1804.2.

1805.7.3 Backfill. The backfill in the annular space around columns not embedded in poured footings shall be by one of the following methods:

1. Backfill shall be of concrete with an ultimate strength of 2,000 psi (13.8 MPa) at 28 days. The hole shall not be less than 4 inches (102 mm) larger than the diameter of the column at its bottom or 4 inches (102 mm) larger than the diagonal dimension of a square or rectangular column.

2. Backfill shall be of clean sand. The sand shall be thoroughly compacted by tamping in layers not more than 8 inches (203 mm) in depth.

3. Backfill shall be of controlled low-strength material (CLSM).

1805.8 Design for expansive soils. Footings or foundations for buildings and structures founded on expansive soils shall be designed in accordance with Section 1805.8.1 or 1805.8.2.

Footing or foundation design need not comply with Section 1805.8.1 or 1805.8.2 where the soil is removed in accordance with Section 1805.8.3, nor where the code enforcement official approves stabilization of the soil in accordance with Section 1805.8.4.

1805.8.1 Foundations. Footings or foundations placed on or within the active zone of expansive soils shall be designed to resist differential volume changes and to prevent structural damage to the supported structure. Deflection and racking of the supported structure shall be limited to that which will not interfere with the usability and serviceability of the structure.

Foundations placed below where volume change occurs or below expansive soil shall comply with the following provisions:

1. Foundations extending into or penetrating expansive soils shall be designed to prevent uplift of the supported structure.

2. Foundations penetrating expansive soils shall be designed to resist forces exerted on the foundation due to soil volume changes or shall be isolated from the expansive soil.

1805.8.2 Slab-on-ground foundations. Moments, shears and deflections for use in designing slab-on-ground, mat or raft foundations on expansive soils shall be determined in accordance with *WRI/CRSI Design of Slab-on-Ground Foundations* or *PTI Standard Requirements for Analysis of Shallow Concrete Foundations on Expansive Soils.* Using the moments, shears and deflections determined above, nonprestressed slabs-on-ground, mat or raft foundations on expansive soils shall be designed in accordance with *WRI/CRSI Design of Slab-on-Ground Foundations* and post-tensioned slab-on-ground, mat or raft foundations on expansive soils shall be designed in accordance with *PTI Standard Requirements for Design of Shallow Post-Tensioned Concrete Foundations on Expansive Soils.* It shall be permitted to analyze and design such slabs by other methods that account for soil-structure interaction, the deformed shape of the soil support, the plate or stiffened plate action of the slab as well as both center lift and edge lift conditions. Such alternative methods shall be rational and the basis for all aspects and parameters of the method shall be available for peer review.

1805.8.3 Removal of expansive soil. Where expansive soil is removed in lieu of designing footings or foundations in accordance with Section 1805.8.1 or 1805.8.2, the soil shall be removed to a depth sufficient to ensure a constant moisture content in the remaining soil. Fill material shall not contain expansive soils and shall comply with Section 1803.5 or 1803.6.

Exception: Expansive soil need not be removed to the depth of constant moisture, provided the confining pressure in the expansive soil created by the fill and supported structure exceeds the swell pressure.

1805.8.4 Stabilization. Where the active zone of expansive soils is stabilized in lieu of designing footings or foundations in accordance with Section 1805.8.1 or 1805.8.2, the soil shall be stabilized by chemical, dewatering, presaturation or equivalent techniques.

1805.9 Seismic requirements. See Section 1908 for additional requirements for footings and foundations of structures assigned to Seismic Design Category C, D, E or F.

For structures assigned to Seismic Design Category D, E or F, provisions of ACI 318, Sections 21.10.1 to 21.10.3, shall apply when not in conflict with the provisions of Section 1805. Concrete shall have a specified compressive strength of not less than 3,000 psi (20.68 MPa) at 28 days.

Exceptions:

1. Group R or U occupancies of light-framed construction and two stories or less in height are permitted to use concrete with a specified compressive strength of not less than 2,500 psi (17.2 MPa) at 28 days.

2. Detached one- and two-family dwellings of light-frame construction and two stories or less in height are not required to comply with the provisions of ACI 318, Sections 21.10.1 to 21.10.3.

SECTION 1806
RETAINING WALLS

1806.1 General. Retaining walls shall be designed to ensure stability against overturning, sliding, excessive foundation pressure and water uplift. Retaining walls shall be designed for a safety factor of 1.5 against lateral sliding and overturning.

SECTION 1807
DAMPPROOFING AND WATERPROOFING

1807.1 Where required. Walls or portions thereof that retain earth and enclose interior spaces and floors below grade shall be waterproofed and dampproofed in accordance with this section, with the exception of those spaces containing groups other than residential and institutional where such omission is not detrimental to the building or occupancy.

Ventilation for crawl spaces shall comply with Section 1203.4.

1807.1.1 Story above grade plane. Where a basement is considered a story above grade plane and the finished ground level adjacent to the basement wall is below the basement floor elevation for 25 percent or more of the perimeter, the floor and walls shall be dampproofed in accordance with Section 1807.2 and a foundation drain shall be installed in accordance with Section 1807.4.2. The foundation drain shall be installed around the portion of the perimeter where the basement floor is below ground level. The provisions of Sections 1802.2.3, 1807.3 and 1807.4.1 shall not apply in this case.

1807.1.2 Under-floor space. The finished ground level of an under-floor space such as a crawl space shall not be located below the bottom of the footings. Where there is evidence that the ground-water table rises to within 6 inches (152 mm) of the ground level at the outside building perimeter, or that the surface water does not readily drain from the building site, the ground level of the under-floor space shall be as high as the outside finished ground level, unless an approved drainage system is provided. The provisions of Sections 1802.2.3, 1807.2, 1807.3 and 1807.4 shall not apply in this case.

1807.1.2.1 Flood hazard areas. For buildings and structures in flood hazard areas as established in Section 1612.3, the finished ground level of an under-floor space such as a crawl space shall be equal to or higher than the outside finished ground level.

> **Exception:** Under-floor spaces of Group R-3 buildings that meet the requirements of FEMA/FIA-TB-11.

1807.1.3 Ground-water control. Where the ground-water table is lowered and maintained at an elevation not less than 6 inches (152 mm) below the bottom of the lowest floor, the floor and walls shall be dampproofed in accordance with Section 1807.2. The design of the system to lower the ground-water table shall be based on accepted principles of engineering that shall consider, but not necessarily be limited to, permeability of the soil, rate at which water enters the drainage system, rated capacity of pumps, head against which pumps are to operate and the rated capacity of the disposal area of the system.

1807.2 Dampproofing required. Where hydrostatic pressure will not occur as determined by Section 1802.2.3, floors and walls for other than wood foundation systems shall be dampproofed in accordance with this section. Wood foundation systems shall be constructed in accordance with AF&PA PWF.

1807.2.1 Floors. Dampproofing materials for floors shall be installed between the floor and the base course required by Section 1807.4.1, except where a separate floor is provided above a concrete slab.

Where installed beneath the slab, dampproofing shall consist of not less than 6-mil (0.006 inch; 0.152 mm) polyethylene with joints lapped not less than 6 inches (152 mm), or other approved methods or materials. Where permitted to be installed on top of the slab, dampproofing shall consist of mopped-on bitumen, not less than 4-mil (0.004 inch; 0.102 mm) polyethylene, or other approved methods or materials. Joints in the membrane shall be lapped and sealed in accordance with the manufacturer's installation instructions.

1807.2.2 Walls. Dampproofing materials for walls shall be installed on the exterior surface of the wall, and shall extend from the top of the footing to above ground level.

Dampproofing shall consist of a bituminous material, 3 pounds per square yard (16 N/m^2) of acrylic modified cement, 0.125 inch (3.2 mm) coat of surface-bonding mortar complying with ASTM C 887, any of the materials permitted for waterproofing by Section 1807.3.2 or other approved methods or materials.

1807.2.2.1 Surface preparation of walls. Prior to application of dampproofing materials on concrete walls, holes and recesses resulting from the removal of form ties shall be sealed with a bituminous material or other approved methods or materials. Unit masonry walls shall be parged on the exterior surface below ground level with not less than 0.375 inch (9.5 mm) of portland cement mortar. The parging shall be coved at the footing.

> **Exception:** Parging of unit masonry walls is not required where a material is approved for direct application to the masonry.

1807.3 Waterproofing required. Where the ground-water investigation required by Section 1802.2.3 indicates that a hydrostatic pressure condition exists, and the design does not include a ground-water control system as described in Section 1807.1.3, walls and floors shall be waterproofed in accordance with this section.

1807.3.1 Floors. Floors required to be waterproofed shall be of concrete and designed and constructed to withstand the hydrostatic pressures to which the floors will be subjected.

Waterproofing shall be accomplished by placing a membrane of rubberized asphalt, butyl rubber, fully adhered/fully bonded HDPE or polyolefin composite membrane or not less than 6-mil [0.006 inch (0.152 mm)] polyvinyl chloride with joints lapped not less than 6 inches (152 mm) or other approved materials under the slab. Joints in the membrane shall be lapped and sealed in accordance with the manufacturer's installation instructions.

1807.3.2 Walls. Walls required to be waterproofed shall be of concrete or masonry and shall be designed and constructed to withstand the hydrostatic pressures and other lateral loads to which the walls will be subjected.

Waterproofing shall be applied from the bottom of the wall to not less than 12 inches (305 mm) above the maximum elevation of the ground-water table. The remainder of the wall shall be dampproofed in accordance with Section 1807.2.2. Waterproofing shall consist of two-ply hot-mopped felts, not less than 6-mil (0.006 inch; 0.152 mm) polyvinyl chloride, 40-mil (0.040 inch; 1.02 mm) polymer-modified asphalt, 6-mil (0.006 inch; 0.152 mm) polyethylene or other approved methods or materials capable of bridging nonstructural cracks. Joints in the membrane shall be lapped and sealed in accordance with the manufacturer's installation instructions.

1807.3.2.1 Surface preparation of walls. Prior to the application of waterproofing materials on concrete or masonry walls, the walls shall be prepared in accordance with Section 1807.2.2.1.

1807.3.3 Joints and penetrations. Joints in walls and floors, joints between the wall and floor and penetrations of the wall and floor shall be made water-tight utilizing approved methods and materials.

1807.4 Subsoil drainage system. Where a hydrostatic pressure condition does not exist, dampproofing shall be provided and a base shall be installed under the floor and a drain installed around the foundation perimeter. A subsoil drainage system designed and constructed in accordance with Section 1807.1.3 shall be deemed adequate for lowering the ground-water table.

1807.4.1 Floor base course. Floors of basements, except as provided for in Section 1807.1.1, shall be placed over a floor base course not less than 4 inches (102 mm) in thickness that consists of gravel or crushed stone containing not more than 10 percent of material that passes through a No. 4 (4.75 mm) sieve.

Exception: Where a site is located in well-drained gravel or sand/gravel mixture soils, a floor base course is not required.

1807.4.2 Foundation drain. A drain shall be placed around the perimeter of a foundation that consists of gravel or crushed stone containing not more than 10-percent material that passes through a No. 4 (4.75 mm) sieve. The drain shall extend a minimum of 12 inches (305 mm) beyond the outside edge of the footing. The thickness shall be such that the bottom of the drain is not higher than the bottom of the base under the floor, and that the top of the drain is not less than 6 inches (152 mm) above the top of the footing. The top of the drain shall be covered with an approved filter membrane material. Where a drain tile or perforated pipe is used, the invert of the pipe or tile shall not be higher than the floor elevation. The top of joints or the top of perforations shall be protected with an approved filter membrane material. The pipe or tile shall be placed on not less than 2 inches (51 mm) of gravel or crushed stone complying with Section 1807.4.1, and shall be covered with not less than 6 inches (152 mm) of the same material.

1807.4.3 Drainage discharge. The floor base and foundation perimeter drain shall discharge by gravity or mechanical means into an approved drainage system that complies with the *Plumbing Code of New York State*.

Exception: Where a site is located in well-drained gravel or sand/gravel mixture soils, a dedicated drainage system is not required.

SECTION 1808
PIER AND PILE FOUNDATIONS

1808.1 Definitions. The following words and terms shall, for the purposes of this section, have the meanings shown herein.

FLEXURAL LENGTH. Flexural length is the length of the pile from the first point of zero lateral deflection to the underside of the pile cap or grade beam.

MICROPILES. Micropiles are 12-inch-diameter (305 mm) or less bored, grouted-in-place piles incorporating steel pipe (casing) and/or steel reinforcement.

PIER FOUNDATIONS. Pier foundations consist of isolated masonry or cast-in-place concrete structural elements extending into firm materials. Piers are relatively short in comparison to their width, with lengths less than or equal to 12 times the least horizontal dimension of the pier. Piers derive their load-carrying capacity through skin friction, through end bearing, or a combination of both.

Belled piers. Belled piers are cast-in-place concrete piers constructed with a base that is larger than the diameter of the remainder of the pier. The belled base is designed to increase the load-bearing area of the pier in end bearing.

PILE FOUNDATIONS. Pile foundations consist of concrete, wood or steel structural elements either driven into the ground or cast in place. Piles are relatively slender in comparison to their length, with lengths exceeding 12 times the least horizontal dimension. Piles derive their load-carrying capacity through skin friction, end bearing or a combination of both.

Augered uncased piles. Augered uncased piles are constructed by depositing concrete into an uncased augered hole, either during or after the withdrawal of the auger.

Caisson piles. Caisson piles are cast-in-place concrete piles extending into bedrock. The upper portion of a caisson pile consists of a cased pile that extends to the bedrock. The lower portion of the caisson pile consists of an uncased socket drilled into the bedrock.

Concrete-filled steel pipe and tube piles. Concrete-filled steel pipe and tube piles are constructed by driving a steel pipe or tube section into the soil and filling the pipe or tube section with concrete. The steel pipe or tube section is left in place during and after the deposition of the concrete.

Driven uncased piles. Driven uncased piles are constructed by driving a steel shell into the soil to shore an unexcavated hole that is later filled with concrete. The steel casing is lifted out of the hole during the deposition of the concrete.

Enlarged base piles. Enlarged base piles are cast-in-place concrete piles constructed with a base that is larger than the diameter of the remainder of the pile. The enlarged base is designed to increase the load-bearing area of the pile in end bearing.

Steel-cased piles. Steel-cased piles are constructed by driving a steel shell into the soil to shore an unexcavated hole. The steel casing is left permanently in place and filled with concrete.

Timber piles. Timber piles are round, tapered timbers with the small (tip) end embedded into the soil.

1808.2 Piers and piles-general requirements.

1808.2.1 Design. Piles are permitted to be designed in accordance with provisions for piers in Section 1808 and Sections 1812.3 through 1812.10 where either of the following conditions exists, subject to the approval of the code enforcement official:

1. Group R-3 and U occupancies not exceeding two stories of light-frame construction, or

2. Where the surrounding foundation materials furnish adequate lateral support for the pile.

1808.2.2 General. Pier and pile foundations shall be designed and installed on the basis of a foundation investigation as defined in Section 1802, unless sufficient data upon which to base the design and installation is available.

The investigation and report provisions of Section 1802 shall be expanded to include, but not be limited to, the following:

1. Recommended pier or pile types and installed capacities.

2. Recommended center-to-center spacing of piers or piles.

3. Driving criteria.

4. Installation procedures.

5. Field inspection and reporting procedures (to include procedures for verification of the installed bearing capacity where required).

6. Pier or pile load test requirements.

7. Durability of pier or pile materials.

8. Designation of bearing stratum or strata.

9. Reductions for group action, where necessary.

1808.2.3 Special types of piles. The use of types of piles not specifically mentioned herein is permitted, subject to the approval of the code enforcement official, upon the submission of acceptable test data, calculations and other information relating to the structural properties and load capacity of such piles. The allowable stresses shall not in any case exceed the limitations specified herein.

1808.2.4 Pile caps. Pile caps shall be of reinforced concrete, and shall include all elements to which piles are connected, including grade beams and mats. The soil immediately below the pile cap shall not be considered as carrying any vertical load. The tops of piles shall be embedded not less than 3 inches (76 mm) into pile caps and the caps shall extend at least 4 inches (102 mm) beyond the edges of piles. The tops of piles shall be cut back to sound material before capping.

1808.2.5 Stability. Piers or piles shall be braced to provide lateral stability in all directions. Three or more piles connected by a rigid cap shall be considered braced, provided that the piles are located in radial directions from the centroid of the group not less than 60 degrees (1 rad) apart. A two-pile group in a rigid cap shall be considered to be braced along the axis connecting the two piles. Methods used to brace piers or piles shall be subject to the approval of the code enforcement official.

Piles supporting walls shall be driven alternately in lines spaced at least 1 foot (305 mm) apart and located symmetrically under the center of gravity of the wall load carried, unless effective measures are taken to provide for eccentricity and lateral forces, or the wall piles are adequately braced to provide for lateral stability. A single row of piles without lateral bracing is permitted for one- and two-family dwellings and lightweight construction not exceeding two stories or 35 feet (10 668 mm) in height, provided the centers of the piles are located within the width of the foundation wall.

1808.2.6 Structural integrity. Piers or piles shall be installed in such a manner and sequence as to prevent distortion or damage that may adversely affect the structural integrity of piles being installed or already in place.

1808.2.7 Splices. Splices shall be constructed so as to provide and maintain true alignment and position of the component parts of the pier or pile during installation and subsequent thereto and shall be of adequate strength to transmit the vertical and lateral loads and moments occur-

ring at the location of the splice during driving and under service loading. Splices shall develop not less than 50 percent of the least capacity of the pier or pile in bending. In addition, splices occurring in the upper 10 feet (3048 mm) of the embedded portion of the pier or pile shall be capable of resisting at allowable working stresses the moment and shear that would result from an assumed eccentricity of the pier or pile load of 3 inches (76 mm), or the pier or pile shall be braced in accordance with Section 1808.2.5 to other piers or piles that do not have splices in the upper 10 feet (3048 mm) of embedment.

1808.2.8 Allowable pier or pile loads.

1808.2.8.1 Determination of allowable loads. The allowable axial and lateral loads on piers or piles shall be determined by an approved formula, load tests or method of analysis.

1808.2.8.2 Driving criteria. The allowable compressive load on any pile where determined by the application of an approved driving formula shall not exceed 40 tons (356 kN). For allowable loads above 40 tons (356 kN), the wave equation method of analysis shall be used to estimate pile driveability of both driving stresses and net displacement per blow at the ultimate load. Allowable loads shall be verified by load tests in accordance with Section 1808.2.8.3. The formula or wave equation load shall be determined for gravity-drop or power-actuated hammers and the hammer energy used shall be the maximum consistent with the size, strength and weight of the driven piles. The use of a follower is permitted only with the approval of the code enforcement official. The introduction of fresh hammer cushion or pile cushion material just prior to final penetration is not permitted.

1808.2.8.3 Load tests. Where design compressive loads per pier or pile are greater than those permitted by Section 1808.2.10 or where the design load for any pier or pile foundation is in doubt, control test piers or piles shall be tested in accordance with ASTM D 1143 or ASTM D 4945. At least one pier or pile shall be test loaded in each area of uniform subsoil conditions. Where required by the code enforcement official, additional piers or piles shall be load tested where necessary to establish the safe design capacity. The resulting allowable loads shall not be more than one-half of the ultimate axial load capacity of the test pier or pile as assessed by one of the published methods listed in Section 1808.2.8.3.1 with consideration for the test type, duration and subsoil. The ultimate axial load capacity shall be determined by a registered design professional with consideration given to tolerable total and differential settlements at design load in accordance with Section 1808.2.12. In subsequent installation of the balance of foundation piles, all piles shall be deemed to have a supporting capacity equal to the control pile where such piles are of the same type, size and relative length as the test pile; are installed using the same or comparable methods and equipment as the test pile; are installed in similar subsoil conditions as the test pile; and, for driven piles, where the rate of penetration (e.g., net displacement per blow) of such piles is equal to or less than that of the test pile driven with the same hammer through a comparable driving distance.

1808.2.8.3.1 Load test evaluation. It shall be permitted to evaluate pile load tests with any of the following methods:

1. Davisson Offset Limit.

2. Brinch-Hansen 90% Criterion.

3. Butler-Hoy Criterion.

4. Other methods approved by the code enforcement official.

1808.2.8.4 Allowable frictional resistance. The assumed frictional resistance developed by any pier or uncased cast-in-place pile shall not exceed one-sixth of the bearing value of the soil material at minimum depth as set forth in Table 1804.2, up to a maximum of 500 psf (24 kPa), unless a greater value is allowed by the code enforcement official after a soil investigation, as specified in Section 1802, is submitted or a greater value is substantiated by a load test in accordance with Section 1808.2.8.3. Frictional resistance and bearing resistance shall not be assumed to act simultaneously unless recommended by a soil investigation as specified in Section 1802.

1808.2.8.5 Uplift capacity. Where required by the design, the uplift capacity of a single pier or pile shall be determined by an approved method of analysis based on a minimum factor of safety of three or by load tests conducted in accordance with ASTM D 3689. The maximum allowable uplift load shall not exceed the ultimate load capacity as determined in Section 1808.2.8.3 divided by a factor of safety of two. For pile groups subjected to uplift, the allowable working uplift load for the group shall be the lesser of:

1. The proposed individual pile uplift working load times the number of piles in the group.

2. Two-thirds of the effective weight of the pile group and the soil contained within a block defined by the perimeter of the group and the length of the pile.

1808.2.8.6 Load-bearing capacity. Piers, individual piles and groups of piles shall develop ultimate load capacities of at least twice the design working loads in the designated load-bearing layers. Analysis shall show that no soil layer underlying the designated load-bearing layers causes the load-bearing capacity safety factor to be less than two.

1808.2.8.7 Bent piers or piles. The load-bearing capacity of piers or piles discovered to have a sharp or sweeping bend shall be determined by an approved method of analysis or by load testing a representative pier or pile.

1808.2.8.8 Overloads on piers or piles. The maximum compressive load on any pier or pile due to mislocation shall not exceed 110 percent of the allowable design load.

1808.2.9 Lateral support.

1808.2.9.1 General. Any soil other than fluid soil shall be deemed to afford sufficient lateral support to the pier or pile to prevent buckling and to permit the design of the pier or pile in accordance with accepted engineering practice and the applicable provisions of this code.

1808.2.9.2 Unbraced piles. Piles standing unbraced in air, water or in fluid soils shall be designed as columns in accordance with the provisions of this code. Such piles driven into firm ground can be considered fixed and laterally supported at 5 feet (1524 mm) below the ground surface and in soft material at 10 feet (3048 mm) below the ground surface unless otherwise prescribed by the code enforcement official after a foundation investigation by an approved agency.

1808.2.9.3 Allowable lateral load. Where required by the design, the lateral load capacity of a pier, a single pile or a pile group shall be determined by an approved method of analysis or by lateral load tests to at least twice the proposed design working load. The resulting allowable load shall not be more than one-half of that test load that produces a gross lateral movement of 1 inch (25 mm) at the ground surface.

1808.2.10 Use of higher allowable pier or pile stresses. Allowable stresses greater than those specified for piers or for each pile type in Sections 1809 and 1810 are permitted where supporting data justifying such higher stresses is filed with the code enforcement official. Such substantiating data shall include:

1. A soils investigation in accordance with Section 1802.

2. Pier or pile load tests in accordance with Section 1808.2.8.3, regardless of the load supported by the pier or pile.

The design and installation of the pier or pile foundation shall be under the direct supervision of a registered design professional knowledgeable in the field of soil mechanics and pier or pile foundations who shall certify to the code enforcement official that the piers or piles as installed satisfy the design criteria.

1808.2.11 Piles in subsiding areas. Where piles are installed through subsiding fills or other subsiding strata and derive support from underlying firmer materials, consideration shall be given to the downward frictional forces that may be imposed on the piles by the subsiding upper strata.

Where the influence of subsiding fills is considered as imposing loads on the pile, the allowable stresses specified in this chapter are permitted to be increased where satisfactory substantiating data are submitted.

1808.2.12 Settlement analysis. The settlement of piers, individual piles or groups of piles shall be estimated based on approved methods of analysis. The predicted settlement shall cause neither harmful distortion of, nor instability in, the structure, nor cause any stresses to exceed allowable values.

1808.2.13 Preexcavation. The use of jetting, augering or other methods of preexcavation shall be subject to the approval of the code enforcement official. Where permitted, preexcavation shall be carried out in the same manner as used for piers or piles subject to load tests and in such a manner that will not impair the carrying capacity of the piers or piles already in place or damage adjacent structures. Pile tips shall be driven below the preexcavated depth until the required resistance or penetration is obtained.

1808.2.14 Installation sequence. Piles shall be installed in such sequence as to avoid compacting the surrounding soil to the extent that other piles cannot be installed properly, and to prevent ground movements that are capable of damaging adjacent structures.

1808.2.15 Use of vibratory drivers. Vibratory drivers shall only be used to install piles where the pile load capacity is verified by load tests in accordance with Section 1808.2.8.3. The installation of production piles shall be controlled according to power consumption, rate of penetration or other approved means that ensure pile capacities equal or exceed those of the test piles.

1808.2.16 Pile driveability. Pile cross sections shall be of sufficient size and strength to withstand driving stresses without damage to the pile, and to provide sufficient stiffness to transmit the required driving forces.

1808.2.17 Protection of pile materials. Where boring records or site conditions indicate possible deleterious action on pier or pile materials because of soil constituents, changing water levels or other factors, the pier or pile materials shall be adequately protected by materials, methods or processes approved by the code enforcement official. Protective materials shall be applied to the piles so as not to be rendered ineffective by driving. The effectiveness of such protective measures for the particular purpose shall have been thoroughly established by satisfactory service records or other evidence.

1808.2.18 Use of existing piers or piles. Piers or piles left in place where a structure has been demolished shall not be used for the support of new construction unless satisfactory evidence is submitted to the code enforcement official, which indicates that the piers or piles are sound and meet the requirements of this code. Such piers or piles shall be load tested or redriven to verify their capacities. The design load applied to such piers or piles shall be the lowest allowable load as determined by tests or redriving data.

1808.2.19 Heaved piles. Piles that have heaved during the driving of adjacent piles shall be redriven as necessary to develop the required capacity and penetration, or the capacity of the pile shall be verified by load tests in accordance with Section 1808.2.8.3.

1808.2.20 Identification. Pier or pile materials shall be identified for conformity to the specified grade with this identity maintained continuously from the point of manufacture to the point of installation or shall be tested by an approved agency to determine conformity to the specified grade. The approved agency shall furnish an affidavit of compliance to the code enforcement official.

1808.2.21 Pier or pile location plan. A plan showing the location and designation of piers or piles by an identification system shall be filed with the code enforcement official prior to installation of such piers or piles. Detailed records for piers or individual piles shall bear an identification corresponding to that shown on the plan.

1808.2.22 Special inspection. Special inspections in accordance with Sections 1704.8 and 1704.9 shall be provided for piles and piers, respectively.

1808.2.23 Seismic design of piers or piles.

1808.2.23.1 Seismic Design Category C. Where a structure is assigned to Seismic Design Category C in accordance with Section 1613, the following shall apply. Individual pile caps, piers or piles shall be interconnected by ties. Ties shall be capable of carrying, in tension and compression, a force equal to the product of the larger pile cap or column load times the seismic coefficient, S_{DS}, divided by 10 unless it can be demonstrated that equivalent restraint is provided by reinforced concrete beams within slabs on grade, reinforced concrete slabs on grade, confinement by competent rock, hard cohesive soils or very dense granular soils.

Exception: Piers supporting foundation walls, isolated interior posts detailed so the pier is not subject to lateral loads, lightly loaded exterior decks and patios of Group R-3 and U occupancies not exceeding two stories of light-frame construction, are not subject to interconnection if it can be shown the soils are of adequate stiffness, subject to the approval of the code enforcement official.

1808.2.23.1.1 Connection to pile cap. Concrete piles and concrete-filled steel pipe piles shall be connected to the pile cap by embedding the pile reinforcement or field-placed dowels anchored in the concrete pile in the pile cap for a distance equal to the development length. For deformed bars, the development length is the full development length for compression or tension, in the case of uplift, without reduction in length for excess area. Alternative measures for laterally confining concrete and maintaining toughness and ductile-like behavior at the top of the pile will be permitted provided the design is such that any hinging occurs in the confined region.

Ends of hoops, spirals and ties shall be terminated with seismic hooks, as defined in Section 21.1 of ACI 318, turned into the confined concrete core. The minimum transverse steel ratio for confinement shall not be less than one-half of that required for columns.

For resistance to uplift forces, anchorage of steel pipe (round HSS sections), concrete-filled steel pipe or H-piles to the pile cap shall be made by means other than concrete bond to the bare steel section.

Exception: Anchorage of concrete-filled steel pipe piles is permitted to be accomplished using deformed bars developed into the concrete portion of the pile.

Splices of pile segments shall develop the full strength of the pile, but the splice need not develop the nominal strength of the pile in tension, shear and bending when it has been designed to resist axial and shear forces and moments from the load combinations of Section 1605.4.

1808.2.23.1.2 Design details. Pier or pile moments, shears and lateral deflections used for design shall be established considering the nonlinear interaction of the shaft and soil, as recommended by a registered design professional. Where the ratio of the depth of embedment of the pile-to-pile diameter or width is less than or equal to six, the pile may be assumed to be rigid.

Pile group effects from soil on lateral pile nominal strength shall be included where pile center-to-center spacing in the direction of lateral force is less than eight pile diameters. Pile group effects on vertical nominal strength shall be included where pile center-to-center spacing is less than three pile diameters. The pile uplift soil nominal strength shall be taken as the pile uplift strength as limited by the frictional force developed between the soil and the pile.

Where a minimum length for reinforcement or the extent of closely spaced confinement reinforcement is specified at the top of the pier or pile, provisions shall be made so that those specified lengths or extents are maintained after pier or pile cutoff.

1808.2.23.2 Seismic Design Category D, E or F. Where a structure is assigned to Seismic Design Category D, E or F in accordance with Section 1613, the requirements for Seismic Design Category C given in Section 1808.2.23.1 shall be met, in addition to the following. Provisions of ACI 318, Section 21.10.4, shall apply when not in conflict with the provisions of Sections 1808 through 1812. Concrete shall have a specified compressive strength of not less than 3,000 psi (20.68 MPa) at 28 days.

Exceptions:

1. Group R or U occupancies of light-framed construction and two stories or less in height are permitted to use concrete with a specified compressive strength of not less than 2,500 psi (17.2 MPa) at 28 days.

2. Detached one- and two-family dwellings of light-frame construction and two stories or less in height are not required to comply with the provisions of ACI 318, Section 21.10.4.

3. Section 21.10.4.4(a) of ACI 318 need not apply to concrete piles.

1808.2.23.2.1 Design details for piers, piles and grade beams. Piers or piles shall be designed and constructed to withstand maximum imposed curvatures from earthquake ground motions and structure response. Curvatures shall include free-field soil strains modified for soil-pile-structure interaction coupled with pier or pile deformations induced by lateral pier or pile resistance to structure seismic forces. Concrete piers or piles on Site Class E or F sites, as determined in Section 1613.5.2, shall be designed and detailed in accordance with Sections 21.4.4.1, 21.4.4.2 and 21.4.4.3 of ACI 318 within seven pile diameters of the pile cap and the interfaces of soft to medium stiff clay or liquefiable strata. For precast prestressed concrete piles, detailing provisions as given in Sections 1809.2.3.2.1 and 1809.2.3.2.2 shall apply. Grade beams shall be designed as beams in accordance with ACI 318, Chapter 21. When grade beams have the capacity to resist the forces from the load combinations in Section 1605.4, they need not conform to ACI 318, Chapter 21.

1808.2.23.2.2 Connection to pile cap. For piles required to resist uplift forces or provide rotational restraint, design of anchorage of piles into the pile cap shall be provided considering the combined effect of axial forces due to uplift and bending moments due to fixity to the pile cap. Anchorage shall develop a minimum of 25 percent of the strength of the pile in tension. Anchorage into the pile cap shall be capable of developing the following:

1. In the case of uplift, the lesser of the nominal tensile strength of the longitudinal reinforcement in a concrete pile, or the nominal tensile strength of a steel pile, or the pile uplift soil nominal strength factored by 1.3 or the axial tension force resulting from the load combinations of Section 1605.4.

2. In the case of rotational restraint, the lesser of the axial and shear forces, and moments resulting from the load combinations of Section 1605.4 or development of the full axial, bending and shear nominal strength of the pile.

1808.2.23.2.3 Flexural strength. Where the vertical lateral-force-resisting elements are columns, the grade beam or pile cap flexural strengths shall exceed the column flexural strength.

The connection between batter piles and grade beams or pile caps shall be designed to resist the nominal strength of the pile acting as a short column. Batter piles and their connection shall be capable of resisting forces and moments from the load combinations of Section 1605.4.

SECTION 1809
DRIVEN PILE FOUNDATIONS

1809.1 Timber piles. Timber piles shall be designed in accordance with the AFPA NDS.

1809.1.1 Materials. Round timber piles shall conform to ASTM D 25. Sawn timber piles shall conform to DOC PS-20.

1809.1.2 Preservative treatment. Timber piles used to support permanent structures shall be treated in accordance with this section unless it is established that the tops of the untreated timber piles will be below the lowest ground-water level assumed to exist during the life of the structure. Preservative and minimum final retention shall be in accordance with AWPA U1 (Commodity Specification E, Use Category 4C) for round timber piles and AWPA U1 (Commodity Specification A, Use Category 4B) for sawn timber piles. Preservative-treated timber piles shall be subject to a quality control program administered by an approved agency. Pile cutoffs shall be treated in accordance with AWPA M4.

1809.1.3 Defective piles. Any substantial sudden increase in rate of penetration of a timber pile shall be investigated for possible damage. If the sudden increase in rate of penetration cannot be correlated to soil strata, the pile shall be removed for inspection or rejected.

1809.1.4 Allowable stresses. The allowable stresses shall be in accordance with the AF&PA NDS.

1809.2 Precast concrete piles.

1809.2.1 General. The materials, reinforcement and installation of precast concrete piles shall conform to Sections 1809.2.1.1 through 1809.2.1.4.

1809.2.1.1 Design and manufacture. Piles shall be designed and manufactured in accordance with accepted engineering practice to resist all stresses induced by handling, driving and service loads.

1809.2.1.2 Minimum dimension. The minimum lateral dimension shall be 8 inches (203 mm). Corners of square piles shall be chamfered.

1809.2.1.3 Reinforcement. Longitudinal steel shall be arranged in a symmetrical pattern and be laterally tied with steel ties or wire spiral spaced not more than 4 inches (102 mm) apart, center to center, for a distance of 2 feet (610 mm) from the ends of the pile; and not more than 6 inches (152 mm) elsewhere except that at the ends of each pile, the first five ties or spirals shall be spaced 1 inch (25 mm) center to center. The gage of ties and spirals shall be as follows:

For piles having a diameter of 16 inches (406 mm) or less, wire shall not be smaller than 0.22 inch (5.6 mm) (No. 5 gage).

For piles having a diameter of more than 16 inches (406 mm) and less than 20 inches (508 mm), wire shall not be smaller than 0.238 inch (6 mm) (No. 4 gage).

For piles having a diameter of 20 inches (508 mm) and larger, wire shall not be smaller than 0.25 inch (6.4 mm) round or 0.259 inch (6.6 mm) (No. 3 gage).

1809.2.1.4 Installation. Piles shall be handled and driven so as not to cause injury or overstressing, which affects durability or strength.

1809.2.2 Precast nonprestressed piles. Precast nonprestressed concrete piles shall conform to Sections 1809.2.2.1 through 1809.2.2.5.

1809.2.2.1 Materials. Concrete shall have a 28-day specified compressive strength ($f?_c$) of not less than 3,000 psi (20.68 MPa).

1809.2.2.2 Minimum reinforcement. The minimum amount of longitudinal reinforcement shall be 0.8 percent of the concrete section and shall consist of at least four bars.

1809.2.2.2.1 Seismic reinforcement in Seismic Design Category C. Where a structure is assigned to Seismic Design Category C in accordance with Section 1613, the following shall apply. Longitudinal reinforcement with a minimum steel ratio of 0.01 shall be provided throughout the length of precast concrete piles. Within three pile diameters of the bottom of the pile cap, the longitudinal reinforcement shall be confined with closed ties or spirals of a minimum $^3/_8$ inch (9.5 mm) diameter. Ties or spirals shall be provided at a maximum spacing of eight times the diameter of the smallest longitudinal bar, not to exceed 6 inches (152 mm). Throughout the remainder of the pile, the closed ties or spirals shall have a maximum spacing of 16 times the smallest longitudinal bar diameter not to exceed 8 inches (203 mm).

1809.2.2.2.2 Seismic reinforcement in Seismic Design Category D, E or F. Where a structure is assigned to Seismic Design Category D, E or F in accordance with Section 1613, the requirements for Seismic Design Category C in Section 1809.2.2.2.1 shall apply except as modified by this section. Transverse confinement reinforcement consisting of closed ties or equivalent spirals shall be provided in accordance with Sections 21.4.4.1, 21.4.4.2 and 21.4.4.3 of ACI 318 within three pile diameters of the bottom of the pile cap. For other than Site Class E or F, or liquefiable sites and where spirals are used as the transverse reinforcement, a volumetric ratio of spiral reinforcement of not less than one-half that required by Section 21.4.4.1(a) of ACI 318 shall be permitted.

1809.2.2.3 Allowable stresses. The allowable compressive stress in the concrete shall not exceed 33 percent of the 28-day specified compressive strength (f'_c) applied to the gross cross-sectional area of the pile. The allowable compressive stress in the reinforcing steel shall not exceed 40 percent of the yield strength of the steel (f_y) or a maximum of 30,000 psi (207 MPa). The allowable tensile stress in the reinforcing steel shall not exceed 50 percent of the yield strength of the steel (f_y) or a maximum of 24,000 psi (165 MPa).

1809.2.2.4 Installation. A precast concrete pile shall not be driven before the concrete has attained a compressive strength of at least 75 percent of the 28-day specified compressive strength (f'_c), but not less than the strength sufficient to withstand handling and driving forces.

1809.2.2.5 Concrete cover. Reinforcement for piles that are not manufactured under plant conditions shall have a concrete cover of not less than 2 inches (51 mm).

Reinforcement for piles manufactured under plant control conditions shall have a concrete cover of not less than 1.25 inches (32 mm) for No. 5 bars and smaller, and not less than 1.5 inches (38 mm) for No. 6 through No. 11 bars except that longitudinal bars spaced less than 1.5 inches (38 mm) clear distance apart shall be considered bundled bars for which the minimum concrete cover shall be equal to that for the equivalent diameter of the bundled bars.

Reinforcement for piles exposed to seawater shall have a concrete cover of not less than 3 inches (76 mm).

1809.2.3 Precast prestressed piles. Precast prestressed concrete piles shall conform to the requirements of Sections 1809.2.3.1 through 1809.2.3.5.

1809.2.3.1 Materials. Prestressing steel shall conform to ASTM A 416. Concrete shall have a 28-day specified compressive strength (f'_c) of not less than 5,000 psi (34.48 MPa).

1809.2.3.2 Design. Precast prestressed piles shall be designed to resist stresses induced by handling and driving as well as by loads. The effective prestress in the pile shall not be less than 400 psi (2.76 MPa) for piles up to 30 feet (9144 mm) in length, 550 psi (3.79 MPa) for piles up to 50 feet (15 240 mm) in length and 700 psi (4.83 MPa) for piles greater than 50 feet (15 240 mm) in length.

Effective prestress shall be based on an assumed loss of 30,000 psi (207 MPa) in the prestressing steel. The tensile stress in the prestressing steel shall not exceed the values specified in ACI 318.

1809.2.3.2.1 Design in Seismic Design Category C. Where a structure is assigned to Seismic Design Category C in accordance with Section 1613, the following shall apply. The minimum volumetric ratio of spiral reinforcement shall not be less than 0.007 or the amount required by the following formula for the upper 20 feet (6096 mm) of the pile.

$$\rho_s = 0.12 f'_c / f_{yh} \qquad \textbf{(Equation 18-4)}$$

where:

f'_c = Specified compressive strength of concrete, psi (MPa).

f_{yh} = Yield strength of spiral reinforcement ≤ 85,000 psi (586 MPa).

ρ_s = Spiral reinforcement index (vol. spiral/vol. core).

At least one-half the volumetric ratio required by Equation 18-4 shall be provided below the upper 20 feet (6096 mm) of the pile.

The pile cap connection by means of dowels as indicated in Section 1808.2.23.1 is permitted. Pile cap connection by means of developing pile reinforcing strand is permitted provided that the pile reinforcing strand results in a ductile connection.

1809.2.3.2.2 Design in Seismic Design Category D, E or F. Where a structure is assigned to Seismic Design Category D, E or F in accordance with Section 1613, the requirements for Seismic Design Category C in Section 1809.2.3.2.1 shall be met, in addition to the following:

1. Requirements in ACI 318, Chapter 21, need not apply, unless specifically referenced.

2. Where the total pile length in the soil is 35 feet (10 668 mm) or less, the lateral transverse reinforcement in the ductile region shall occur through the length of the pile. Where the pile length exceeds 35 feet (10 668 mm), the ductile pile region shall be taken as the greater of 35 feet (10 668 mm) or the distance from the underside of the pile cap to the point of zero curvature plus three times the least pile dimension.

3. In the ductile region, the center-to-center spacing of the spirals or hoop reinforcement shall not exceed one-fifth of the least pile dimension, six times the diameter of the longtitudinal strand, or 8 inches (203 mm), whichever is smaller.

4. Circular spiral reinforcement shall be spliced by lapping one full turn and bending the end of the spiral to a 90-degree hook or by use of a mechanical or welded splice complying with Sec. 12.14.3 of ACI 318.

5. Where the transverse reinforcement consists of circular spirals, the volumetric ratio of spiral transverse reinforcement in the ductile region shall comply with the following:

$$\rho_s = 0.25(f'_c / f_{yh})(A_g / A_{ch} - 1.0)[0.5 + 1.4P/(f'_c A_g)] \qquad \textbf{(Equation 18-5)}$$

but not less than:

$$\rho_s = 0.12(f'_c / f_{yh})[0.5 + 1.4P/(f'_c A_g)]$$

$$\textbf{(Equation 18-6)}$$

and need not exceed:

$$\rho_s = 0.021 \qquad \textbf{(Equation 18-7)}$$

where:

A_g = Pile cross-sectional area, square inches (mm^2).

A_{ch} = Core area defined by spiral outside diameter, square inches (mm^2).

f'_c = Specified compressive strength of concrete, psi (MPa).

f_{yh} = Yield strength of spiral reinforcement? 85,000 psi (586 MPa).

P = Axial load on pile, pounds (kN), as determined from Equations 16-5 and 16-6.

ρ_s = Volumetric ratio (vol. spiral/ vol. core).

This required amount of spiral reinforcement is permitted to be obtained by providing an inner and outer spiral.

6. When transverse reinforcement consists of rectangular hoops and cross ties, the total cross-sectional area of lateral transverse reinforcement in the ductile region with spacings, and perpendicular to dimension, h_c, shall conform to:

$$A_{sh} = 0.3sh_c\,(f'_c/f_{yh})(A_g/A_{ch} - 1.0)[0.5 + 1.4P/(f'_c A_g)] \quad \textbf{(Equation 18-8)}$$

but not less than:

$$A_{sh} = 0.12sh_c\,(f'_c/f_{yh})[0.5 + 1.4P/(f'_c A_g) \quad \textbf{(Equation 18-9)}$$

where:

f_{yh} = $\le$ 70,000 psi (483 MPa).

h_c = Cross-sectional dimension of pile core measured center to center of hoop reinforcement, inch (mm).

s = Spacing of transverse reinforcement measured along length of pile, inch (mm).

A_{sh} = Cross-sectional area of tranverse reinforcement, square inches (mm²).

f'_c = Specified compressive strength of concrete, psi (MPa).

The hoops and cross ties shall be equivalent to deformed bars not less than No. 3 in size. Rectangular hoop ends shall terminate at a corner with seismic hooks.

Outside of the length of the pile requiring transverse confinement reinforcing, the spiral or hoop reinforcing with a volumetric ratio not less than one-half of that required for transverse confinement reinforcing shall be provided.

1809.2.3.3 Allowable stresses. The allowable design compressive stress, f_c, in concrete shall be determined as follows:

$$f_c = 0.33 f'_c - 0.27 f_{pc} \quad \textbf{(Equation 18-10)}$$

where:

f'_c = The 28-day specified compressive strength of the concrete.

f_{pc} = The effective prestress stress on the gross section.

1809.2.3.4 Installation. A prestressed pile shall not be driven before the concrete has attained a compressive strength of at least 75 percent of the 28-day specified compressive strength (f'_c), but not less than the strength sufficient to withstand handling and driving forces.

1809.2.3.5 Concrete cover. Prestressing steel and pile reinforcement shall have a concrete cover of not less than 1^1/$_4$ inches (32 mm) for square piles of 12 inches (305 mm) or smaller size and 1^1/$_2$ inches (38 mm) for larger piles, except that for piles exposed to seawater, the minimum protective concrete cover shall not be less than 2^1/$_2$ inches (64 mm).

1809.3 Structural steel piles. Structural steel piles shall conform to the requirements of Sections 1809.3.1 through 1809.3.4.

1809.3.1 Materials. Structural steel piles, steel pipe and fully welded steel piles fabricated from plates shall conform to ASTM A 36, ASTM A 252, ASTM A 283, ASTM A 572, ASTM A 588, ASTM A 690, ASTM A 913 or ASTM A 992.

1809.3.2 Allowable stresses. The allowable axial stresses shall not exceed 35 percent of the minimum specified yield strength (F_y).

Exception: Where justified in accordance with Section 1808.2.10, the allowable axial stress is permitted to be increased above 0.35F_y, but shall not exceed 0.5F_y.

1809.3.3 Dimensions of H-piles. Sections of H-piles shall comply with the following:

1. The flange projections shall not exceed 14 times the minimum thickness of metal in either the flange or the web and the flange widths shall not be less than 80 percent of the depth of the section.

2. The nominal depth in the direction of the web shall not be less than 8 inches (203 mm).

3. Flanges and web shall have a minimum nominal thickness of ^{3}/$_8$ inch (9.5 mm).

1809.3.4 Dimensions of steel pipe piles. Steel pipe piles driven open ended shall have a nominal outside diameter of not less than 8 inches (203 mm). The pipe shall have a minimum cross section of 0.34 square inch (219 mm²) to resist each 1,000 foot-pounds (1356 N-m) of pile hammer energy, or shall have the equivalent strength for steels having a yield strength greater than 35,000 psi (241 Mpa) or the wave equation analysis shall be permitted to be used to assess compression stresses induced by driving to evaluate if the pile section is appropriate for the selected hammer. Where pipe wall thickness less than 0.179 inch (4.6 mm) is driven open ended, a suitable cutting shoe shall be provided.

SECTION 1810
CAST-IN-PLACE CONCRETE PILE FOUNDATIONS

1810.1 General. The materials, reinforcement and installation of cast-in-place concrete piles shall conform to Sections 1810.1.1 through 1810.1.3.

1810.1.1 Materials. Concrete shall have a 28-day specified compressive strength (f'_c) of not less than 2,500 psi (17.24 MPa). Where concrete is placed through a funnel hopper at the top of the pile, the concrete mix shall be designed and proportioned so as to produce a cohesive workable mix having a slump of not less than 4 inches (102 mm) and not more than 6 inches (152 mm). Where concrete is to be pumped, the mix design including slump shall be adjusted to produce a pumpable concrete.

1810.1.2 Reinforcement. Except for steel dowels embedded 5 feet (1524 mm) or less in the pile and as provided in Section 1810.3.4, reinforcement where required shall be assembled and tied together and shall be placed in the pile as a unit before the reinforced portion of the pile is filled with concrete except in augered uncased cast-in-place piles. Tied reinforcement in augered uncased cast-in-place piles shall be placed after piles are concreted, while the concrete is still in a semifluid state.

1810.1.2.1 Reinforcement in Seismic Design Category C. Where a structure is assigned to Seismic Design Category C in accordance with Section 1613, the following shall apply. A minimum longitudinal reinforcement ratio of 0.0025 shall be provided for uncased cast-in-place concrete drilled or augered piles, piers or caissons in the top one-third of the pile length, a minimum length of 10 feet (3048 mm) below the ground or that required by analysis, whichever length is greatest. The minimum reinforcement ratio, but no less than that ratio required by rational analysis, shall be continued throughout the flexural length of the pile. There shall be a minimum of four longitudinal bars with closed ties (or equivalent spirals) of a minimum $^3/_8$ inch (9 mm) diameter provided at 16-longitudinal-bar diameter maximum spacing. Transverse confinement reinforcement with a maximum spacing of 6 inches (152 mm) or 8-longitudinal-bar diameters, whichever is less, shall be provided within a distance equal to three times the least pile dimension of the bottom of the pile cap.

1810.1.2.2 Reinforcement in Seismic Design Category D, E or F. Where a structure is assigned to Seismic Design Category D, E or F in accordance with Section 1613, the requirements for Seismic Design Category C given above shall be met, in addition to the following. A minimum longitudinal reinforcement ratio of 0.005 shall be provided for uncased cast-in-place drilled or augered concrete piles, piers or caissons in the top one-half of the pile length a minimum length of 10 feet (3048 mm) below ground or throughout the flexural length of the pile, whichever length is greatest. The flexural length shall be taken as the length of the pile to a point where the concrete section cracking moment strength multiplied by 0.4 exceeds the required moment strength at that point. There shall be a minimum of four longitudinal bars with transverse confinement reinforcement provided in the pile in accordance with Sections 21.4.4.1, 21.4.4.2 and 21.4.4.3 of ACI 318 within three times the least pile dimension of the bottom of the pile cap. A transverse spiral reinforcement ratio of not less than one-half of that required in Section 21.4.4.1(a) of ACI 318 for other than Class E, F or liquefiable sites is permitted. Tie spacing throughout the remainder of the concrete section shall neither exceed 12-longitudinal-bar diameters, one-half the least dimension of the section, nor 12 inches (305 mm). Ties shall be a minimum of No. 3 bars for piles with a least dimension up to 20 inches (508 mm), and No. 4 bars for larger piles.

1810.1.3 Concrete placement. Concrete shall be placed in such a manner as to ensure the exclusion of any foreign matter and to secure a full-sized shaft. Concrete shall not be placed through water except where a tremie or other approved method is used. When depositing concrete from the top of the pile, the concrete shall not be chuted directly into the pile but shall be poured in a rapid and continuous operation through a funnel hopper centered at the top of the pile.

1810.2 Enlarged base piles. Enlarged base piles shall conform to the requirements of Sections 1810.2.1 through 1810.2.5.

1810.2.1 Materials. The maximum size for coarse aggregate for concrete shall be $^3/_4$ inch (19.1 mm). Concrete to be compacted shall have a zero slump.

1810.2.2 Allowable stresses. The maximum allowable design compressive stress for concrete not placed in a permanent steel casing shall be 25 percent of the 28-day specified compressive strength (f'_c). Where the concrete is place in a permanent steel casing, the maximum allowable concrete stress shall be 33 percent of the 28-day specified compressive strength (f'_c).

1810.2.3 Installation. Enlarged bases formed either by compacting concrete or driving a precast base shall be formed in or driven into granular soils. Piles shall be constructed in the same manner as successful prototype test piles driven for the project. Pile shafts extending through peat or other organic soil shall be encased in a permanent steel casing. Where a cased shaft is used, the shaft shall be adequately reinforced to resist column action or the annular space around the pile shaft shall be filled sufficiently to reestablish lateral support by the soil. Where pile heave occurs, the pile shall be replaced unless it is demonstrated that the pile is undamaged and capable of carrying twice its design load.

1810.2.4 Load-bearing capacity. Pile load-bearing capacity shall be verified by load tests in accordance with Section 1808.2.8.3.

1810.2.5 Concrete cover. The minimum concrete cover shall be $2^1/_2$ inches (64 mm) for uncased shafts and 1 inch (25 mm) for cased shafts.

1810.3 Drilled or augered uncased piles. Drilled or augered uncased piles shall conform to Sections 1810.3.1 through 1810.3.5.

1810.3.1 Allowable stresses. The allowable design stress in the concrete of drilled or augered uncased piles shall not exceed 33 percent of the 28-day specified compressive strength (f'_c). The allowable compressive stress of reinforcement shall not exceed 40 percent of the yield strength of the steel or 25,500 psi (175.8 MPa).

1810.3.2 Dimensions. The pile length shall not exceed 30 times the average diameter. The minimum diameter shall be 12 inches (305 mm).

> **Exception:** The length of the pile is permitted to exceed 30 times the diameter, provided that the design and installation of the pile foundation are under the direct supervision of a registered design professional knowledgeable in the field of soil mechanics and pile foundations. The registered design professional shall certify to the code enforcement official that the piles were installed in compliance with the approved construction documents.

1810.3.3 Installation. Where pile shafts are formed through unstable soils and concrete is placed in an open-drilled hole, a steel liner shall be inserted in the hole prior to placing the concrete. Where the steel liner is withdrawn during concreting, the level of concrete shall be maintained above the bottom of the liner at a sufficient height to offset any hydrostatic or lateral soil pressure.

Where concrete is placed by pumping through a hollow-stem auger, the auger shall be permitted to rotate in a clockwise direction during withdrawal. The auger shall be withdrawn in continuous increments. Concreting pumping pressures shall be measured and maintained high enough at all times to offset hydrostatic and lateral earth pressures. Concrete volumes shall be measured to ensure that the volume of concrete placed in each pile is equal to or greater than the theoretical volume of the hole created by the auger. Where the installation process of any pile is interrupted or a loss of concreting pressure occurs, the pile shall be redrilled to 5 feet (1524 mm) below the elevation of the tip of the auger when the installation was interrupted or concrete pressure was lost and reformed. Augered cast-in-place piles shall not be installed within six pile diameters center to center of a pile filled with concrete less than 12 hours old, unless approved by the code enforcement official. If the concrete level in any completed pile drops due to installation of an adjacent pile, the pile shall be replaced.

1810.3.4 Reinforcement. For piles installed with a hollow-stem auger where full-length longitudinal steel reinforcement is placed without lateral ties, the reinforcement shall be placed through the hollow stem of the auger prior to filling the pile with concrete. All pile reinforcement shall have a concrete cover of not less than 2.5 inches (64 mm).

> **Exception:** Where physical constraints do not allow the placement of the longitudinal reinforcement prior to filling the pile with concrete or where partial-length longitudinal reinforcement is placed without lateral ties, the reinforcement is allowed to be placed after the piles are completely concreted but while concrete is still in a semifluid state.

1810.3.5 Reinforcement in Seismic Design Category C, D, E or F. Where a structure is assigned to Seismic Design Category C, D, E or F in accordance with Section 1613, the corresponding requirements of Sections 1810.1.2.1 and 1810.1.2.2 shall be met.

1810.4 Driven uncased piles. Driven uncased piles shall conform to Sections 1810.4.1 through 1810.4.4.

1810.4.1 Allowable stresses. The allowable design stress in the concrete shall not exceed 25 percent of the 28-day specified compressive strength (f'_c) applied to a cross-sectional area not greater than the inside area of the drive casing or mandrel.

1810.4.2 Dimensions. The pile length shall not exceed 30 times the average diameter. The minimum diameter shall be 12 inches (305 mm).

> **Exception:** The length of the pile is permitted to exceed 30 times the diameter, provided that the design and installation of the pile foundation is under the direct supervision of a registered design professional knowledgeable in the field of soil mechanics and pile foundations. The registered design professional shall certify to the code enforcement official that the piles were installed in compliance with the approved design.

1810.4.3 Installation. Piles shall not be driven within six pile diameters center to center in granular soils or within one-half the pile length in cohesive soils of a pile filled with concrete less than 48 hours old unless approved by the code enforcement official. If the concrete surface in any completed pile rises or drops, the pile shall be replaced. Piles shall not be installed in soils that could cause pile heave.

1810.4.4 Concrete cover. Pile reinforcement shall have a concrete cover of not less than 2.5 inches (64 mm), measured from the inside face of the drive casing or mandrel.

1810.5 Steel-cased piles. Steel-cased piles shall comply with the requirements of Sections 1810.5.1 through 1810.5.4.

1810.5.1 Materials. Pile shells or casings shall be of steel and shall be sufficiently strong to resist collapse and sufficiently water tight to exclude any foreign materials during the placing of concrete. Steel shells shall have a sealed tip with a diameter of not less than 8 inches (203 mm).

1810.5.2 Allowable stresses. The allowable design compressive stress in the concrete shall not exceed 33 percent of the 28-day specified compressive strength (f'_c). The allowable concrete compressive stress shall be 0.40 (f'_c) for that portion of the pile meeting the conditions specified in Sections 1810.5.2.1 through 1810.5.2.4.

1810.5.2.1 Shell thickness. The thickness of the steel shell shall not be less than manufacturer's standard gage No. 14 gage (0.068 inch) (1.75 mm) minimum.

1810.5.2.2 Shell type. The shell shall be seamless or provided with seams of strength equal to the basic material and be of a configuration that will provide confinement to the cast-in-place concrete.

1810.5.2.3 Strength. The ratio of steel yield strength (f_y) to 28-day specified compressive strength (f'_c) shall not be less than six.

1810.5.2.4 Diameter. The nominal pile diameter shall not be greater than 16 inches (406 mm).

1810.5.3 Installation. Steel shells shall be mandrel driven their full length in contact with the surrounding soil.

The steel shells shall be driven in such order and with such spacing as to ensure against distortion of or injury to piles already in place. A pile shall not be driven within four and one-half average pile diameters of a pile filled with concrete less than 24 hours old unless approved by the code enforcement official. Concrete shall not be placed in steel shells within heave range of driving.

1810.5.4 Reinforcement. Reinforcement shall not be placed within 1 inch (25 mm) of the steel shell. Reinforcing shall be required for unsupported pile lengths or where the pile is designed to resist uplift or unbalanced lateral loads.

1810.5.4.1 Seismic reinforcement. Where a structure is assigned to Seismic Design Category C, D, E or F in accordance with Section 1613, the reinforcement requirements for drilled or augered uncased piles in Section 1810.3.5 shall be met.

> **Exception:** A spiral-welded metal casing of a thickness no less than the manufacturer's standard gage No. 14 gage [0.068 inch (1.7 mm)] is permitted to provide concrete confinement in lieu of the closed ties or equivalent spirals required in an uncased concrete pile. Where used as such, the metal casing shall be protected against possible deleterious action due to soil constituents, changing water levels or other factors indicated by boring records of site conditions.

1810.6 Concrete-filled steel pipe and tube piles. Concrete-filled steel pipe and tube piles shall conform to the requirements of Sections 1810.6.1 through 1810.6.5.

1810.6.1 Materials. Steel pipe and tube sections used for piles shall conform to ASTM A 252 or ASTM A 283. Concrete shall conform to Section 1810.1.1. The maximum coarse aggregate size shall be $^3/_4$ inch (19.1 mm).

1810.6.2 Allowable stresses. The allowable design compressive stress in the concrete shall not exceed 33 percent of the 28-day specified compressive strength (f'_c). The allowable design compressive stress in the steel shall not exceed 35 percent of the minimum specified yield strength of the steel (F_y), provided F_y shall not be assumed greater than 36,000 psi (248 MPa) for computational purposes.

> **Exception:** Where justified in accordance with Section 1808.2.10, the allowable stresses are permitted to be increased to 0.50 F_y.

1810.6.3 Minimum dimensions. Piles shall have a nominal outside diameter of not less than 8 inches (203 mm) and a minimum wall thickness in accordance with Section 1809.3.4. For mandrel-driven pipe piles, the minimum wall thickness shall be $^1/_{10}$ inch (2.5 mm).

1810.6.4 Reinforcement. Reinforcement steel shall conform to Section 1810.1.2. Reinforcement shall not be placed within 1 inch (25 mm) of the steel casing.

1810.6.4.1 Seismic reinforcement. Where a structure is assigned to Seismic Design Category C, D, E or F in accordance with Section 1613, the following shall apply. Minimum reinforcement no less than 0.01 times the cross-sectional area of the pile concrete shall be provided in the top of the pile with a length equal to two times the required cap embedment anchorage into the pile cap, but not less than the tension development length of the reinforcement. The wall thickness of the steel pipe shall not be less than $^3/_{16}$ inch (5 mm).

1810.6.5 Placing concrete. The placement of concrete shall conform to Section 1810.1.3, but is permitted to be chuted directly into smooth-sided pipes and tubes without a centering funnel hopper.

1810.7 Caisson piles. Caisson piles shall conform to the requirements of Sections 1810.7.1 through 1810.7.6.

1810.7.1 Construction. Caisson piles shall consist of a shaft section of concrete-filled pipe extending to bedrock with an uncased socket drilled into the bedrock and filled with concrete. The caisson pile shall have a full-length structural steel core or a stub core installed in the rock socket and extending into the pipe portion a distance equal to the socket depth.

1810.7.2 Materials. Pipe and steel cores shall conform to the material requirements in Section 1809.3. Pipes shall have a minimum wall thickness of $^3/_8$ inch (9.5 mm) and shall be fitted with a suitable steel-driving shoe welded to the bottom of the pipe. Concrete shall have a 28-day specified compressive strength (f'_c) of not less than 4,000 psi (27.58 MPa). The concrete mix shall be designed and proportioned so as to produce a cohesive workable mix with a slump of 4 inches to 6 inches (102 mm to 152 mm).

1810.7.3 Design. The depth of the rock socket shall be sufficient to develop the full load-bearing capacity of the caisson pile with a minimum safety factor of two, but the depth shall not be less than the outside diameter of the pipe. The design of the rock socket is permitted to be predicated on the sum of the allowable load-bearing pressure on the bottom of the socket plus bond along the sides of the socket. The minimum outside diameter of the caisson pile shall be 18 inches (457 mm), and the diameter of the rock socket shall be approximately equal to the inside diameter of the pile.

1810.7.4 Structural core. The gross cross-sectional area of the structural steel core shall not exceed 25 percent of the gross area of the caisson. The minimum clearance between the structural core and the pipe shall be 2 inches (51 mm). Where cores are to be spliced, the ends shall be milled or ground to provide full contact and shall be full-depth welded.

1810.7.5 Allowable stresses. The allowable design compressive stresses shall not exceed the following: concrete, $0.33 f'_c$; steel pipe, $0.35 F_y$ and structural steel core, $0.50 F_y$.

1810.7.6 Installation. The rock socket and pile shall be thoroughly cleaned of foreign materials before filling with concrete. Steel cores shall be bedded in cement grout at the base of the rock socket. Concrete shall not be placed through water except where a tremie or other approved method is used.

1810.8 Micropiles. Micropiles shall conform to the requirements of Sections 1810.8.1 through 1810.8.5.

1810.8.1 Construction. Micropiles shall consist of a grouted section reinforced with steel pipe or steel reinforcing. Micropiles shall develop their load-carrying capacity through a bond zone in soil, bedrock or a combination of soil and bedrock. The full length of the micropile shall contain either a steel pipe or steel reinforcement.

1810.8.2 Materials. Grout shall have a 28-day specified compressive strength (f'_c) of not less than 4,000 psi (27.58 MPa). The grout mix shall be designed and proportioned so as to produce a pumpable mixture. Reinforcement steel shall be deformed bars in accordance with ASTM A 615 Grade 60 or 75 or ASTM A 722 Grade 150.

Pipe/casing shall have a minimum wall thickness of $^3/_{16}$ inch (4.8 mm) and as required to meet Section 1808.2.7. Pipe/casing shall meet the tensile requirements of ASTM A 252 Grade 3, except the minimum yield strength shall be as used in the design submittal [typically 50,000 psi to 80,000 psi (345 MPa to 552 MPa)] and minimum elongation shall be 15 percent.

1810.8.3 Allowable stresses. The allowable design compressive stress on grout shall not exceed $0.33 f'_c$. The allowable design compressive stress on steel pipe and steel reinforcement shall not exceed the lesser of 0.4 F_y, or 32,000 psi (220 MPa). The allowable design tensile stress for steel reinforcement shall not exceed 0.60 F_y. The allowable design tensile stress for the cement grout shall be zero.

1810.8.4 Reinforcement. For piles or portions of piles grouted inside a temporary or permanent casing or inside a hole drilled into bedrock or a hole drilled with grout, the steel pipe or steel reinforcement shall be designed to carry at least 40 percent of the design compression load. Piles or portions of piles grouted in an open hole in soil without temporary or permanent casing and without suitable means of verifying the hole diameter during grouting shall be designed to carry the entire compression load in the reinforcing steel. Where a steel pipe is used for reinforcement, the portion of the cement grout enclosed within the pipe is permitted to be included at the allowable stress of the grout.

1810.8.4.1 Seismic reinforcement. Where a structure is assigned to Seismic Design Category C, a permanent steel casing shall be provided from the top of the pile down 120 percent times the flexural length. The flexural length shall be determined in accordance with Section 1808.1. Where a structure is assigned to Seismic Design Category D, E or F, the pile shall be considered as an alternative system. In accordance with Section 104.11, the alternative pile system design, supporting documentation and test data shall be submitted to the code enforcement official for review and approval.

1810.8.5 Installation. The pile shall be permitted to be formed in a hole advanced by rotary or percussive drilling methods, with or without casing. The pile shall be grouted with a fluid cement grout. The grout shall be pumped through a tremie pipe extending to the bottom of the pile until grout of suitable quality returns at the top of the pile. The following requirements apply to specific installation methods:

1. For piles grouted inside a temporary casing, the reinforcing steel shall be inserted prior to withdrawal of the casing. The casing shall be withdrawn in a controlled manner with the grout level maintained at the top of the pile to ensure that the grout completely fills the drill hole. During withdrawal of the casing, the grout level inside the casing shall be monitored to check that the flow of grout inside the casing is not obstructed.

2. For a pile or portion of a pile grouted in an open drill hole in soil without temporary casing, the minimum design diameter of the drill hole shall be verified by a suitable device during grouting.

3. For piles designed for end bearing, a suitable means shall be employed to verify that the bearing surface is properly cleaned prior to grouting.

4. Subsequent piles shall not be drilled near piles that have been grouted until the grout has had sufficient time to harden.

5. Piles shall be grouted as soon as possible after drilling is completed.

6. For piles designed with casing full length, the casing must be pulled back to the top of the bond zone and reinserted or some other suitable means shall be employed to verify grout coverage outside the casing.

SECTION 1811
COMPOSITE PILES

1811.1 General. Composite piles shall conform to the requirements of Sections 1811.2 through 1811.5.

1811.2 Design. Composite piles consisting of two or more approved pile types shall be designed to meet the conditions of installation.

1811.3 Limitation of load. The maximum allowable load shall be limited by the capacity of the weakest section incorporated in the pile.

1811.4 Splices. Splices between concrete and steel or wood sections shall be designed to prevent separation both before and after the concrete portion has set, and to ensure the alignment and transmission of the total pile load. Splices shall be designed to resist uplift caused by upheaval during driving of adjacent piles, and shall develop the full compressive strength and not less than 50 percent of the tension and bending strength of the weaker section.

1811.5 Seismic reinforcement. Where a structure is assigned to Seismic Design Category C, D, E or F in accordance with Section 1613, the following shall apply. Where concrete and steel are used as part of the pile assembly, the concrete reinforcement shall comply with that given in Sections 1810.1.2.1 and 1810.1.2.2 or the steel section shall comply with Section 1810.6.4.1.

SECTION 1812
PIER FOUNDATIONS

1812.1 General. Isolated and multiple piers used as foundations shall conform to the requirements of Sections 1812.2 through 1812.10, as well as the applicable provisions of Section 1808.2.

1812.2 Lateral dimensions and height. The minimum dimension of isolated piers used as foundations shall be 2 feet (610 mm), and the height shall not exceed 12 times the least horizontal dimension.

1812.3 Materials. Concrete shall have a 28-day specified compressive strength (f'_c) of not less than 2,500 psi (17.24 MPa). Where concrete is placed through a funnel hopper at the top of the pier, the concrete mix shall be designed and proportioned so as to produce a cohesive workable mix having a slump of not less than 4 inches (102 mm) and not more than 6 inches (152 mm). Where concrete is to be pumped, the mix design including slump shall be adjusted to produce a pumpable concrete.

1812.4 Reinforcement. Except for steel dowels embedded 5 feet (1524 mm) or less in the pier, reinforcement where required shall be assembled and tied together and shall be placed in the pier hole as a unit before the reinforced portion of the pier is filled with concrete.

Exception: Reinforcement is permitted to be wet set and the $2^1/_2$-inch (64 mm) concrete cover requirement be reduced to 2 inches (51 mm) for Group R-3 and U occupancies not exceeding two stories of light-frame construction, provided the construction method can be demonstrated to the satisfaction of the code enforcement official.

Reinforcement shall conform to the requirements of Sections 1810.1.2.1 and 1810.1.2.2.

Exceptions:

1. Isolated piers supporting posts of Group R-3 and U occupancies not exceeding two stories of light-frame construction are permitted to be reinforced as required by rational analysis but not less than a minimum of one No. 4 bar, without ties or spirals, when detailed so the pier is not subject to lateral loads and the soil is determined to be of adequate stiffness.

2. Isolated piers supporting posts and bracing from decks and patios appurtenant to Group R-3 and U occupancies not exceeding two stories of light-frame construction are permitted to be reinforced as required by rational analysis but not less than one No. 4 bar, without ties or spirals, when the lateral load, E, to the top of the pier does not exceed 200 pounds (890 N) and the soil is determined to be of adequate stiffness.

3. Piers supporting the concrete foundation wall of Group R-3 and U occupancies not exceeding two stories of light-frame construction are permitted to be reinforced as required by rational analysis but not less than two No. 4 bars, without ties or spirals, when it can be shown the concrete pier will not rupture when designed for the maximum seismic load, E_m, and the soil is determined to be of adequate stiffness.

4. Closed ties or spirals where required by Section 1810.1.2.2 are permitted to be limited to the top 3 feet (914 mm) of the piers 10 feet (3048 mm) or less in depth supporting Group R-3 and U occupancies of Seismic Design Category D, not exceeding two stories of light-frame construction.

1812.5 Concrete placement. Concrete shall be placed in such a manner as to ensure the exclusion of any foreign matter and to secure a full-sized shaft. Concrete shall not be placed through water except where a tremie or other approved method is used. When depositing concrete from the top of the pier, the concrete shall not be chuted directly into the pier but shall be poured in a rapid and continuous operation through a funnel hopper centered at the top of the pier.

1812.6 Belled bottoms. Where pier foundations are belled at the bottom, the edge thickness of the bell shall not be less than that required for the edge of footings. Where the sides of the bell slope at an angle less than 60 degrees (1 rad) from the horizontal, the effects of vertical shear shall be considered.

1812.7 Masonry. Where the unsupported height of foundation piers exceeds six times the least dimension, the allowable working stress on piers of unit masonry shall be reduced in accordance with ACI 530/ASCE 5/TMS 402.

1812.8 Concrete. Where adequate lateral support is not provided, and the unsupported height to least lateral dimension does not exceed three, piers of plain concrete shall be designed and constructed as pilasters in accordance with ACI 318. Where the unsupported height to least lateral dimension exceeds three, piers shall be constructed of reinforced concrete, and shall conform to the requirements for columns in ACI 318.

Exception: Where adequate lateral support is furnished by the surrounding materials as defined in Section 1808.2.9, piers are permitted to be constructed of plain or reinforced concrete. The requirements of ACI 318 for bearing on concrete shall apply.

1812.9 Steel shell. Where concrete piers are entirely encased with a circular steel shell, and the area of the shell steel is considered reinforcing steel, the steel shall be protected under the conditions specified in Section 1808.2.17. Horizontal joints in the shell shall be spliced to comply with Section 1808.2.7.

1812.10 Dewatering. Where piers are carried to depths below water level, the piers shall be constructed by a method that will provide accurate preparation and inspection of the bottom, and the depositing or construction of sound concrete or other masonry in the dry.

CHAPTER 19

CONCRETE

Italics are used for text within Sections 1903 through 1908 of this code to indicate provisions that differ from ACI 318.

SECTION 1901
GENERAL

1901.1 Scope. The provisions of this chapter shall govern the materials, quality control, design and construction of concrete used in structures.

1901.2 Plain and reinforced concrete. Structural concrete shall be designed and constructed in accordance with the requirements of this chapter and ACI 318 as amended in Section 1908 of this code. Except for the provisions of Sections 1904 and 1910, the design and construction of slabs on grade shall not be governed by this chapter unless they transmit vertical loads or lateral forces from other parts of the structure to the soil.

1901.3 Source and applicability. The format and subject matter of Sections 1902 through 1907 of this chapter are patterned after, and in general conformity with, the provisions for structural concrete in ACI 318.

1901.4 Construction documents. The construction documents for structural concrete construction shall include:

1. The specified compressive strength of concrete at the stated ages or stages of construction for which each concrete element is designed.

2. The specified strength or grade of reinforcement.

3. The size and location of structural elements, reinforcement, and anchors.

4. Provision for dimensional changes resulting from creep, shrinkage and temperature.

5. The magnitude and location of prestressing forces.

6. Anchorage length of reinforcement and location and length of lap splices.

7. Type and location of mechanical and welded splices of reinforcement.

8. Details and location of contraction or isolation joints specified for plain concrete.

9. Minimum concrete compressive strength at time of posttensioning.

10. Stressing sequence for posttensioning tendons.

11. For structures assigned to Seismic Design Category D, E or F, a statement if slab on grade is designed as a structural diaphragm (see Section 21.10.3.4 of ACI 318).

1901.5 Special inspection. The special inspection of concrete elements of buildings and structures and concreting operations shall be as required by Chapter 17.

SECTION 1902
DEFINITIONS

1902.1 General. The words and terms defined in ACI 318 shall, for the purposes of this chapter and as used elsewhere in this code for concrete construction, have the meanings shown in ACI 318.

SECTION 1903
SPECIFICATIONS FOR TESTS AND MATERIALS

1903.1 General. Materials used to produce concrete, concrete itself and testing thereof shall comply with the applicable standards listed in ACI 318. *Where required, special inspections and tests shall be in accordance with Chapter 17.*

1903.2 Glass fiber reinforced concrete. *Glass fiber reinforced concrete (GFRC) and the materials used in such concrete shall be in accordance with the PCI MNL 128 standard.*

SECTION 1904
DURABILITY REQUIREMENTS

1904.1 Water-cementitious materials ratio. Where maximum water-cementitious materials ratios are specified in ACI 318, they shall be calculated in accordance with ACI 318, Section 4.1.

1904.2 Freezing and thawing exposures. Concrete that will be exposed to freezing and thawing, deicing chemicals or other exposure conditions as defined below shall comply with Sections 1904.2.1 through 1904.2.3.

1904.2.1 Air entrainment. Concrete exposed to freezing and thawing or deicing chemicals shall be air entrained in accordance with ACI 318, Section 4.2.1:

1904.2.2 Concrete properties. Concrete that will be subject to the following exposures shall conform to the corresponding maximum water-cementitious materials ratios and minimum specified concrete compressive strength requirements of ACI 318, Section 4.2.2:

1. Concrete intended to have low permeability where exposed to water;

2. Concrete exposed to freezing and thawing in a moist condition or deicer chemicals; or

3. Concrete with reinforcement where the concrete is exposed to chlorides from deicing chemicals, salt, salt water, brackish water, seawater or spray from these sources.

Exception: For occupancies and appurtenances thereto in Group R occupancies that are in buildings less than four stories in height, normal-weight aggregate concrete shall comply with the requirements of Table 1904.2.2 based on the weathering classification (freezing and thawing) determined from Figure 1904.2.2.

TABLE 1904.2.2
MINIMUM SPECIFIED COMPRESSIVE STRENGTH (f'_c)

TYPE OR LOCATION OF CONCRETE CONSTRUCTION	MINIMUM SPECIFIED COMPRESSIVE STRENGTH (f'_c at 28 days, psi)		
	Negligible exposure	Moderate exposure	Severe exposure
Basement walls[c] and foundations not exposed to the weather	2,500	2,500	2,500[a]
Basement slabs and interior slabs on grade, except garage floor slabs	2,500	2,500	2,500[a]
Basement walls[c], foundation walls, exterior walls and other vertical concrete surfaces exposed to the weather	2,500	3,000[b]	3,000[b]
Driveways, curbs, walks, patios, porches, carport slabs, steps and other flatwork exposed to the weather, and garage floor slabs	2,500	3,000[b, d]	3,500[b, d]

For SI: 1 pound per square inch = 0.00689 MPa.

a. Concrete in these locations that can be subjected to freezing and thawing during construction shall be of air-entrained concrete in accordance with Section 1904.2.1.

b. Concrete shall be air entrained in accordance with Section 1904.2.1.

c. Structural plain concrete basement walls are exempt from the requirements for exposure conditions of Section 1904.2.2 (see Section 1909.6.1).

d. For garage floor slabs where a steel trowel finish is used, the total air content required by Section 1904.2.1 is permitted to be reduced to not less than 3 percent, provided the minimum specified compressive strength of the concrete is increased to 4,000 psi.

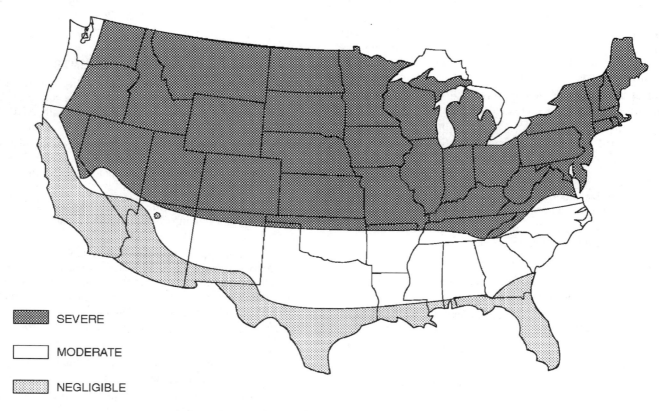

SEVERE

MODERATE

NEGLIGIBLE

FIGURE 1904.2.2
WEATHERING PROBABILITY MAP FOR CONCRETE[a, b, c]

a. Lines defining areas are approximate only. Local areas can be more or less severe than indicated by the region classification.

b. A "severe" classification is where weather conditions encourage or require the use of deicing chemicals or where there is potential for a continuous presence of moisture during frequent cycles of freezing and thawing. A "moderate" classification is where weather conditions occasionally expose concrete in the presence of moisture to freezing and thawing, but where deicing chemicals are not generally used. A "negligible" classification is where weather conditions rarely expose concrete in the presence of moisture to freezing and thawing.

c. Alaska and Hawaii are classified as severe and negligible, respectively.

In addition, concrete exposed to deicing chemicals shall conform to the limitations of Section 1904.2.3.

1904.2.3 Deicing chemicals. For concrete exposed to deicing chemicals, the maximum weight of fly ash, other pozzolans, silica fume or slag that is included in the concrete shall not exceed the percentages of the total weight of cementitious materials permitted by ACI 318, Section 4.2.3.

1904.3 Sulfate exposures. Concrete that will be exposed to sulfate-containing solutions or soils shall comply with the maximum water-cementitious materials ratios, minimum specified compressive strength and be made with the appropriate type of cement in accordance with the provisions of ACI 318, Section 4.3.

1904.4 Corrosion protection of reinforcement. Reinforcement in concrete shall be protected from corrosion and exposure to chlorides in accordance with ACI 318, Section 4.4.

SECTION 1905
CONCRETE QUALITY, MIXING AND PLACING

1905.1 General. The required strength and durability of concrete shall be determined by compliance with the proportioning, testing, mixing and placing provisions of Sections 1905.1.1 through 1905.13.

1905.1.1 Strength. Concrete shall be proportioned to provide an average compressive strength as prescribed in Section 1905.3 and shall satisfy the durability criteria of Section 1904. Concrete shall be produced to minimize the frequency of strengths below f'_c as prescribed in Section 1905.6.3. *For concrete designed and constructed in accordance with this chapter, f'_c shall not be less than 2,500 psi (17.22 MPa).* No maximum specified compressive strength shall apply unless restricted by a specific provision of this code or ACI 318.

1905.2 Selection of concrete proportions. Concrete proportions shall be determined in accordance with the provisions of ACI 318, Section 5.2.

1905.3 Proportioning on the basis of field experience and/or trial mixtures. Concrete proportioning determined on the basis of field experience and/or trial mixtures shall be done in accordance with ACI 318, Section 5.3.

1905.4 Proportioning without field experience or trial mixtures. Concrete proportioning determined without field experience or trial mixtures shall be done in accordance with ACI 318, Section 5.4.

1905.5 Average strength reduction. As data become available during construction, it is permissible to reduce the amount by which the average compressive strength (f'_c) is required to exceed the specified value of f'_c in accordance with ACI 318, Section 5.5.

1905.6 Evaluation and acceptance of concrete. The criteria for evaluation and acceptance of concrete shall be as specified in Sections 1905.6.2 through 1905.6.5.

1905.6.1 Qualified technicians. Concrete shall be tested in accordance with the requirements in Sections 1905.6.2 through 1905.6.5. Qualified field testing technicians shall perform tests on fresh concrete at the job site, prepare specimens required for curing under field conditions, prepare specimens required for testing in the laboratory and record the temperature of the fresh concrete when preparing specimens for strength tests. Qualified laboratory technicians shall perform all required laboratory tests.

1905.6.2 Frequency of testing. The frequency of conducting strength tests of concrete and the minimum number of tests shall be as specified in ACI 318, Section 5.6.2.

Exception: When the total volume of a given class of concrete is less than 50 cubic yards (38 m³), strength tests are not required when evidence of satisfactory strength is submitted to and approved by the code enforcement official.

1905.6.3 Strength test specimens. Specimens prepared for acceptance testing of concrete in accordance with Section 1905.6.2 and strength test acceptance criteria shall comply with the provisions of ACI 318, Section 5.6.3.

1905.6.4 Field-cured specimens. Where required by the code enforcement official to determine adequacy of curing and protection of concrete in the structure, specimens shall be prepared, cured, tested and test results evaluated for acceptance in accordance with ACI 318, Section 5.6.4.

1905.6.5 Low-strength test results. Where any strength test (see ACI 318, Section 5.6.2.4) falls below the specified value of f'_c, the provisions of ACI 318, Section 5.6.5, shall apply.

1905.7 Preparation of equipment and place of deposit. Prior to concrete being placed, the space to receive the concrete and the equipment used to deposit it shall comply with ACI 318, Section 5.7.

1905.8 Mixing. Mixing of concrete shall be performed in accordance with ACI 318, Section 5.8.

1905.9 Conveying. The method and equipment for conveying concrete to the place of deposit shall comply with ACI 318, Section 5.9.

1905.10 Depositing. The depositing of concrete shall comply with the provisions of ACI 318, Section 5.10.

1905.11 Curing. The length of time, temperature and moisture conditions for curing of concrete shall be in accordance with ACI 318, Section 5.11.

1905.12 Cold weather requirements. Concrete to be placed during freezing or near-freezing weather shall comply with the requirements of ACI 318, Section 5.12.

1905.13 Hot weather requirements. Concrete to be placed during hot weather shall comply with the requirements of ACI 318, Section 5.13.

SECTION 1906
FORMWORK, EMBEDDED PIPES AND
CONSTRUCTION JOINTS

1906.1 Formwork. The design, fabrication and erection of forms shall comply with ACI 318, Section 6.1.

1906.2 Removal of forms, shores and reshores. The removal of forms and shores, including from slabs and beams (except where cast on the ground), and the installation of reshores shall comply with ACI 318, Section 6.2.

1906.3 Conduits and pipes embedded in concrete. Conduits, pipes and sleeves of any material not harmful to concrete and within the limitations of ACI 318, Section 6.3, are permitted to be embedded in concrete with approval of the registered design professional.

1906.4 Construction joints. Construction joints, including their location, shall comply with the provisions of ACI 318, Section 6.4.

SECTION 1907
DETAILS OF REINFORCEMENT

1907.1 Hooks. Standard hooks on reinforcing bars used in concrete construction shall comply with ACI 318, Section 7.1.

1907.2 Minimum bend diameters. Minimum reinforcement bend diameters utilized in concrete construction shall comply with ACI 318, Section 7.2.

1907.3 Bending. The bending of reinforcement shall comply with ACI 318, Section 7.3.

1907.4 Surface conditions of reinforcement. The surface conditions of reinforcement shall comply with the provisions of ACI 318, Section 7.4.

1907.5 Placing reinforcement. The placement of reinforcement, including tolerances on depth and cover, shall comply with the provisions of ACI 318, Section 7.5. Reinforcement shall be accurately placed and adequately supported before concrete is placed.

1907.6 Spacing limits for reinforcement. The clear distance between reinforcing bars, bundled bars, tendons and ducts shall comply with ACI 318, Section 7.6.

1907.7 Concrete protection for reinforcement. The minimum concrete cover for reinforcement shall comply with Sections 1907.7.1 through 1907.7.7.

1907.7.1 Cast-in-place concrete (nonprestressed). Minimum concrete cover shall be provided for reinforcement in nonprestressed, cast-in-place concrete construction in accordance with ACI 318, Section 7.7.1.

1907.7.2 Cast-in-place concrete (prestressed). The minimum concrete cover for prestressed and nonprestressed reinforcement, ducts and end fittings in cast-in-place prestressed concrete shall comply with ACI 318, Section 7.7.2.

1907.7.3 Precast concrete (manufactured under plant control conditions). The minimum concrete cover for prestressed and nonprestressed reinforcement, ducts and end fittings in precast concrete manufactured under plant control conditions shall comply with ACI 318, Section 7.7.3.

1907.7.4 Bundled bars. The minimum concrete cover for bundled bars shall comply with ACI 318, Section 7.7.4.

1907.7.5 Corrosive environments. In corrosive environments or other severe exposure conditions, prestressed and nonprestressed reinforcement shall be provided with additional protection in accordance with ACI 318, Section 7.7.5.

1907.7.6 Future extensions. Exposed reinforcement, inserts and plates intended for bonding with future extensions shall be protected from corrosion.

1907.7.7 Fire protection. When this code requires a thickness of cover for fire protection greater than the minimum concrete cover specified in Section 1907.7, such greater thickness shall be used.

1907.8 Special reinforcement details for columns. Offset bent longitudinal bars in columns and load transfer in structural steel cores of composite compression members shall comply with the provisions of ACI 318, Section 7.8.

1907.9 Connections. Connections between concrete framing members shall comply with the provisions of ACI 318, Section 7.9.

1907.10 Lateral reinforcement for compression members. Lateral reinforcement for concrete compression members shall comply with the provisions of ACI 318, Section 7.10.

1907.11 Lateral reinforcement for flexural members. Lateral reinforcement for compression reinforcement in concrete flexural members shall comply with the provisions of ACI 318, Section 7.11.

1907.12 Shrinkage and temperature reinforcement. Reinforcement for shrinkage and temperature stresses in concrete members shall comply with the provisions of ACI 318, Section 7.12.

1907.13 Requirements for structural integrity. The detailing of reinforcement and connections between concrete members shall comply with the provisions of ACI 318, Section 7.13, to improve structural integrity.

SECTION 1908
MODIFICATIONS TO ACI 318

1908.1 General. The text of ACI 318 shall be modified as indicated in Sections 1908.1.1 through 1908.1.16.

1908.1.1 ACI 318, Section 10.5. Modify ACI 318, **Section 10.5, by adding new Section 10.5.5 to read as follows:**

10.5.5 - In structures assigned to Seismic Design Category B, beams in ordinary moment frames forming part of the seismic-force-resisting system shall have at least two main flexural reinforcing bars continuously top and bottom throughout the beam and continuous through or developed within exterior columns or boundary elements.

1908.1.2 ACI 318, Section 11.11. Modify ACI 318, Section 11.11, by changing its title to read as shown below and by adding new Section 11.11.3 to read as follows:

11.11- Special provisions for columns.

11.11.3 - In structures assigned to Seismic Design Category B, columns of ordinary moment frames having a clear height-to-maximum-plan-dimension ratio of five or less shall be designed for shear in accordance with 21.12.3.

1908.1.3 ACI 318, Section 21.1. Modify existing definitions and add the following definitions to ACI 318, Section 21.1.

DESIGN DISPLACEMENT. Total lateral displacement expected for the design-basis earthquake, *as specified by Section 12.8.6 of ASCE 7.*

DETAILED PLAIN CONCRETE STRUCTURAL WALL. A wall complying with the requirements of Chapter 22, including 22.6.7.

ORDINARY PRECAST STRUCTURAL WALL. A precast wall complying with the requirements of Chapters 1 through 18.

ORDINARY REINFORCED CONCRETE STRUCTURAL WALL. A *cast-in-place* wall complying with the requirements of Chapters 1 through 18.

ORDINARY STRUCTURAL PLAIN CONCRETE WALL. A wall complying with the requirements of Chapter 22, *excluding 22.6.7.*

WALL PIER. A wall segment with a horizontal length-to-thickness ratio of at least 2.5, but not exceeding 6, whose clear height is at least two times its horizontal length.

1908.1.4 ACI 318, Section 21.2.1. Modify ACI 318 Sections 21.2.1.2, 21.2.1.3 and 21.2.1.4, to read as follows:

21.2.1.2 - For structures assigned to Seismic Design Category A or B, provisions of Chapters 1 through 18 and 22 shall apply except as modified by the provisions of this chapter. Where the seismic design loads are computed using provisions for intermediate or special concrete systems, the requirements of Chapter 21 for intermediate or special systems, as applicable, shall be satisfied.

21.2.1.3 - For structures assigned to Seismic Design Category C, intermediate or special moment frames, intermediate precast structural walls *or ordinary or special reinforced concrete structural walls* shall be used to resist *seismic* forces induced by earthquake motions. Where the design seismic loads are computed using provisions for special concrete systems, the requirements of Chapter 21 for special systems, as applicable, shall be satisfied.

21.2.1.4 - For structures assigned to Seismic Design Category D, E or F, special moment frames, *special reinforced concrete structural walls,* diaphragms and trusses *and foundations* complying with 21.2 through 21.10 *or intermediate precast structural walls complying with* 21.13 shall be used to resist forces induced by earthquake motions. Members not proportioned to resist earthquake forces shall comply with 21.11.

1908.1.5 ACI 318, Section 21.2.5. Modify ACI 318, Section 21.2.5, by renumbering as Section 21.2.5.1 and adding new Section 21.2.5.2 to read as follows:

21.2.5 - Reinforcement in members resisting earthquake-induced forces.

21.2.5.1 - Except as permitted in 21.2.5.2, reinforcement resisting earthquake-induced flexural and axial forces in frame members and in structural wall boundary elements shall comply with ASTM A 706. ASTM A 615, Grades 40 and 60 reinforcement, shall be permitted in these members if (a) the actual yield strength based on mill tests does not exceed the specified yield, f_y, strength by more than 18,000 psi (124 MPa) [retests shall not exceed this value by more than an additional 3,000 psi (21 MPa)], and (b) the ratio of the actual tensile strength to the actual yield strength is not less than 1.25.

For computing shear strength, the value of f_{yt} for transverse reinforcement, including spiral reinforcement, shall not exceed 60,000 psi (414 MPa).

21.2.5.2 - Prestressing steel shall be permitted in flexural members of frames, provided the average prestress, f_{pc}, calculated for an area equal to the member's shortest cross-sectional dimension multiplied by the perpendicular dimension shall be the lesser of 700 psi (4.83 MPa) or $f'_c/6$ at locations of nonlinear action where prestressing steel is used in members of frames.

1908.1.6 ACI 318, Section 21.2. Modify ACI 318, Section 21.2, by adding new Section 21.2.9 to read as follows:

21.2.9 - Anchorages for unbonded post-tensioning tendons resisting earthquake induced forces in structures assigned to Seismic Design Category C, D, E or F shall withstand, without failure, 50 cycles of loading ranging between 40 and 85 percent of the specified tensile strength of the prestressing steel.

1908.1.7 ACI 318, Section 21.3. Modify ACI 318, Section 21.3, by adding new Section 21.3.2.5 to read as follows:

21.3.2.5 - Unless the special moment frame is qualified for use through structural testing as required by 21.6.3, for flexural members prestressing steel shall not provide more than one-quarter of the strength for either positive or negative moment at the critical section in a plastic hinge location and shall be anchored at or beyond the exterior face of a joint.

1908.1.8 ACI 318, Section 21.7. Modify ACI 318, Section 21.7, by adding new Section 21.7.10 to read as follows:

21.7.10 - Wall piers and wall segments.

21.7.10.1 - Wall piers not designed as a part of a special moment frame shall have transverse reinforcement designed to satisfy the requirements in 21.7.10.2.

Exceptions:

1. *Wall piers that satisfy 21.11.*

2. *Wall piers along a wall line within a story where other shear wall segments provide lateral support to the wall piers and such segments have a total stiffness of at least six times the sum of the stiffness of all the wall piers.*

21.7.10.2 - Transverse reinforcement with seismic hooks at both ends shall be designed to resist the shear forces determined from 21.4.5.1. Spacing of transverse reinforcement shall not exceed 6 inches (152 mm).

Transverse reinforcement shall be extended beyond the pier clear height for at least 12 inches (305 mm).

21.7.10.3 - Wall segments with a horizontal length-to-thickness ratio less than 2.5 shall be designed as columns.

1908.1.9 ACI 318, Section 21.8. Modify Section 21.8.1 to read as follows:

21.8.1 - Special structural walls constructed using precast concrete shall satisfy all the requirements of 21.7 for cast-in-place special structural walls in addition to Sections 21.13.2 *through 21.13.4.*

1908.1.10 ACI 318, Section 21.10.1.1. Modify ACI 318, Section 21.10.1.1, to read as follows:

21.10.1.1 - Foundations resisting earthquake-induced forces or transferring earthquake-induced forces between a structure and the ground shall comply with the requirements of Section 21.10 and other applicable provisions of ACI 318 *unless modified by Chapter 18 of the Building Code of New York State.*

1908.1.11 ACI 318, Section 21.11. Modify ACI 318, Section 21.11.2.2 to read as follows:

21.11.2.2 - Members with factored gravity axial forces exceeding $(A_g f'/10)$ shall satisfy 21.4.3, 21.4.4.1(c), 21.4.4.3 and 21.4.5. The maximum longitudinal spacing of ties shall be s_o for the full column height. Spacing, s_o, shall not exceed the smaller of six diameters of the smallest longitudinal bar enclosed and 6 inches (152 mm). *Lap splices of longitudinal reinforcement in such members need not satisfy 21.4.3.2 in structures where the seismic-force-resisting system does not include special moment frames.*

1908.1.12 ACI 318, Section 21.12.5. Modify ACI 318, Section 21.12.5, by adding new Section 21.12.5.6 to read as follows:

21.12.5.6 - Columns supporting reactions from discontinuous stiff members, such as walls, shall be designed for the special load combinations in Section 1605.4 of the Building Code of New York State and shall be provided with transverse reinforcement at the spacing, s_o, as defined in 21.12.5.2 over their full height beneath the level at which the discontinuity occurs. This transverse reinforcement shall be extended above and below the column as required in 21.4.4.5.

1908.1.13 ACI 318, Section 21.13. Modify ACI 318, Section 21.13, by renumbering Section 21.13.3 to become 21.13.4 and adding new Sections 21.13.3, 21.13.5 and 21.13.6 to read as follows:

21.13.3 - Except for Type 2 mechanical splices, connection elements that are designed to yield shall be capable of maintaining 80 percent of their design strength at the deformation induced by the design displacement.

21.13.4 - Elements of the connection that are not designed to yield shall develop at least 1.5 S_y.

21.13.5 - Wall piers not designed as part of a moment frame shall have transverse reinforcement designed to resist the shear forces determined from 21.12.3. Spacing of transverse reinforcement shall not exceed 8 inches (203 mm). Transverse reinforcement shall be extended beyond the pier clear height for at least 12 inches (305 mm).

Exceptions:

1. *Wall piers that satisfy 21.11.*

2. *Wall piers along a wall line within a story where other shear wall segments provide lateral support to the wall piers and such segments have a total stiffness of at least six times the sum of the stiffnesses of all the wall piers.*

21.13.6 - Wall segments with a horizontal length-to-thickness ratio less than 2.5 shall be designed as columns.

1908.1.14 ACI 318, Section 22.6. Modify ACI 318, Section 22.6, by adding new Section 22.6.7 to read:

22.6.7 - Detailed plain concrete structural walls.

22.6.7.1 - Detailed plain concrete structural walls are walls conforming to the requirements of ordinary structural plain concrete walls and 22.6.7.2.

22.6.7.2 - Reinforcement shall be provided as follows:

(a) *Vertical reinforcement of at least 0.20 square inch (129 mm²) in cross-sectional area shall be provided continuously from support to support at each corner, at each side of each opening and at the ends of walls. The continuous vertical bar required beside an opening is permitted to substitute for one of the two No. 5 bars required by 22.6.6.5.*

(b) *Horizontal reinforcement at least 0.20 square inch (129 mm²) in cross-sectional area shall be provided:*

1. *Continuously at structurally connected roof and floor levels and at the top of walls;*

2. *At the bottom of load-bearing walls or in the top of foundations where doweled to the wall; and*

3. *At a maximum spacing of 120 inches (3048 mm).*

Reinforcement at the top and bottom of openings, where used in determining the maximum spacing specified in Item 3 above, shall be continuous in the wall.

1908.1.15 ACI 318, Section 22.10. Delete ACI 318, Section 22.10, and replace with the following:

22.10 - Plain concrete in structures assigned to Seismic Design Category C, D, E or F.

22.10.1 - Structures assigned to Seismic Design Category C, D, E or F shall not have elements of structural plain concrete, except as follows:

(a) *Structural plain concrete basement, foundation or other walls below the base are permitted in detached one- and two-family dwellings three* stories or less in height constructed with stud-bearing walls. In dwellings assigned to Seismic Design Category D or E, the height of the wall shall not exceed 8 feet (2438 mm), the thickness shall not be less than $7^1/_2$ inches (190 mm), and the wall shall retain no more than 4 feet (1219 mm) of unbalanced fill. Walls shall have reinforcement in accordance with 22.6.6.5.

(b) Isolated footings of plain concrete supporting pedestals or columns are permitted, provided the projection of the footing beyond the face of the supported member does not exceed the footing thickness.

Exception: In detached one- and two-family dwellings three stories or less in height, the projection of the footing beyond the face of the supported member is permitted to exceed the footing thickness.

(c) Plain concrete footings supporting walls are permitted, provided the footings have at least two continuous longitudinal reinforcing bars. Bars shall not be smaller than No. 4 and shall have a total area of not less than 0.002 times the gross cross-sectional area of the footing. For footings that exceed 8 inches (203 mm) in thickness, a minimum of one bar shall be provided at the top and bottom of the footing. Continuity of reinforcement shall be provided at corners and intersections.

Exceptions:

1. In detached one- and two-family dwellings three stories or less in height and constructed with stud-bearing walls, plain concrete footings without longitudinal reinforcement supporting walls are permitted.

2. For foundation systems consisting of a plain concrete footing and a plain concrete stemwall, a minimum of one bar shall be provided at the top of the stemwall and at the bottom of the footing.

3. Where a slab on ground is cast monolithically with the footing, one No. 5 bar is permitted to be located at either the top of the slab or bottom of the footing.

1908.1.16 ACI 318, Section D.3.3. Modify ACI 318, Sections D.3.3.2 through D.3.3.5, to read as follows:

D.3.3.2 - In structures assigned to Seismic Design Category C, D, E or F, post-installed anchors for use under D.2.3 shall have passed the Simulated Seismic Tests of ACI 355.2.

D.3.3.3 - In structures assigned to Seismic Design Category C, D, E or F, the design strength of anchors shall be taken as $0.75\phi N_n$ and $0.75\phi V_n$, where ϕ is given in D.4.4 or D.4.5, and N_n and V_n are determined in accordance with D.4.1.

D.3.3.4 - In structures assigned to Seismic Design Category C, D, E or F, anchors shall be designed to be governed by tensile or shear strength of a ductile steel element, unless D.3.3.5 is satisfied.

D.3.3.5 - Instead of D.3.3.4, the attachment that the anchor is connecting to the structure shall be designed so that the attachment will undergo ductile yielding at a load level corresponding to anchor forces no greater than the design strength of anchors specified in D.3.3.3, or the minimum design strength of the anchors shall be at least 2.5 times the factored forces transmitted by the attachment.

SECTION 1909
STRUCTURAL PLAIN CONCRETE

1909.1 Scope. The design and construction of structural plain concrete, both cast-in-place and precast, shall comply with the minimum requirements of Section 1909 and ACI 318, Chapter 22, as modified in Section 1908.

1909.1.1 Special structures. For special structures, such as arches, underground utility structures, gravity walls and shielding walls, the provisions of this section shall govern where applicable.

1909.2 Limitations. The use of structural plain concrete shall be limited to:

1. Members that are continuously supported by soil, such as walls and footings, or by other structural members capable of providing continuous vertical support.

2. Members for which arch action provides compression under all conditions of loading.

3. Walls and pedestals.

The use of structural plain concrete columns and structural plain concrete footings on piles is not permitted. See Section 1908.1.15 for additional limitations on the use of structural plain concrete.

1909.3 Joints. Contraction or isolation joints shall be provided to divide structural plain concrete members into flexurally discontinuous elements in accordance with ACI 318, Section 22.3.

1909.4 Design. Structural plain concrete walls, footings and pedestals shall be designed for adequate strength in accordance with ACI 318, Sections 22.4 through 22.8.

Exception: For Group R-3 occupancies and buildings of other occupancies less than two stories in height of light-frame construction, the required edge thickness of ACI 318 is permitted to be reduced to 6 inches (152 mm), provided that the footing does not extend more than 4 inches (102 mm) on either side of the supported wall.

1909.5 Precast members. The design, fabrication, transportation and erection of precast, structural plain concrete elements shall be in accordance with ACI 318, Section 22.9.

1909.6 Walls. In addition to the requirements of this section, structural plain concrete walls shall comply with the applicable requirements of ACI 318, Chapter 22.

1909.6.1 Basement walls. The thickness of exterior basement walls and foundation walls shall be not less than $7^1/_2$ inches (191 mm). Structural plain concrete exterior basement walls shall be exempt from the requirements for special exposure conditions of Section 1904.2.2.

1909.6.2 Other walls. Except as provided for in Section 1909.6.1, the thickness of bearing walls shall be not less than $^1/_{24}$ the unsupported height or length, whichever is shorter, but not less than $5^1/_2$ inches (140 mm).

1909.6.3 Openings in walls. Not less than two No. 5 bars shall be provided around window and door openings. Such bars shall extend at least 24 inches (610 mm) beyond the corners of openings.

SECTION 1910
MINIMUM SLAB PROVISIONS

1910.1 General. The thickness of concrete floor slabs supported directly on the ground shall not be less than $3^1/_2$ inches (89 mm). A 6-mil (0.006 inch; 0.15 mm) polyethylene vapor retarder with joints lapped not less than 6 inches (152 mm) shall be placed between the base course or subgrade and the concrete floor slab, or other approved equivalent methods or materials shall be used to retard vapor transmission through the floor slab.

Exception: A vapor retarder is not required:

1. For detached structures accessory to occupancies in Group R-3, such as garages, utility buildings or other unheated facilities.

2. For unheated storage rooms having an area of less than 70 square feet (6.5 m²) and carports attached to occupancies in Group R-3.

3. For buildings of other occupancies where migration of moisture through the slab from below will not be detrimental to the intended occupancy of the building.

4. For driveways, walks, patios and other flatwork which will not be enclosed at a later date.

5. Where approved based on local site conditions.

SECTION 1911
ANCHORAGE TO CONCRETE—ALLOWABLE STRESS DESIGN

1911.1 Scope. The provisions of this section shall govern the allowable stress design of headed bolts and headed stud anchors cast in normal-weight concrete for purposes of transmitting structural loads from one connected element to the other. These provisions do not apply to anchors installed in hardened concrete or where load combinations include earthquake loads or effects. The bearing area of headed anchors shall be not less than one and one-half times the shank area. Where strength design is used, or where load combinations include earthquake loads or effects, the design strength of anchors shall be determined in accordance with Section 1912. Bolts shall conform to ASTM A 307 or an approved equivalent.

1911.2 Allowable service load. The allowable service load for headed anchors in shear or tension shall be as indicated in Table 1911.2. Where anchors are subject to combined shear and tension, the following relationship shall be satisfied:

$$(P_s/P_t)^{5/3} + (V_s/V_t)^{5/3} \leq 1 \qquad \textbf{(Equation 19-1)}$$

where:

P_s = Applied tension service load, pounds (N).

P_t = Allowable tension service load from Table 1911.2, pounds (N).

V_s = Applied shear service load, pounds (N).

V_t = Allowable shear service load from Table 1911.2, pounds (N).

1911.3 Required edge distance and spacing. The allowable service loads in tension and shear specified in Table 1911.2 are for the edge distance and spacing specified. The edge distance and spacing are permitted to be reduced to 50 percent of the values specified with an equal reduction in allowable service load. Where edge distance and spacing are reduced less than 50 percent, the allowable service load shall be determined by linear interpolation.

1911.4 Increase in allowable load. Increase of the values in Table 1911.2 by one-third is permitted where the provisions of Section 1605.3.2 permit an increase in allowable stress for wind loading.

1911.5 Increase for special inspection. Where special inspection is provided for the installation of anchors, a 100-percent increase in the allowable tension values of Table 1911.2 is permitted. No increase in shear value is permitted.

SECTION 1912
ANCHORAGE TO CONCRETE—STRENGTH DESIGN

1912.1 Scope. The provisions of this section shall govern the strength design of anchors installed in concrete for purposes of transmitting structural loads from one connected element to the other. Headed bolts, headed studs and hooked (J- or L-) bolts cast in concrete and expansion anchors and undercut anchors installed in hardened concrete shall be designed in accordance with Appendix D of ACI 318 as modified by Section 1908.1.16, provided they are within the scope of Appendix D.

Exception: Where the basic concrete breakout strength in tension of a single anchor, N_b, is determined in accordance with Equation (D-7), the concrete breakout strength requirements of Section D.4.2.2 shall be considered satisfied by the design procedures of Sections D.5.2 and D.6.2 for anchors exceeding 2 inches (51 mm) in diameter or 25 inches (635 mm) tensile embedment depth.

The strength design of anchors that are not within the scope of Appendix D of ACI 318, and as amended above, shall be in accordance with an approved procedure.

TABLE 1911.2
ALLOWABLE SERVICE LOAD ON EMBEDDED BOLTS (pounds)

BOLT DIAMETER (inches)	MINIMUM EMBEDMENT (inches)	EDGE DISTANCE (inches)	SPACING (inches)	MINIMUM CONCRETE STRENGTH (psi)					
				f'_c = 2,500		f'_c = 3,000		f'_c = 4,000	
				Tension	Shear	Tension	Shear	Tension	Shear
$^1/_4$	$2^1/_2$	$1^1/_2$	3	200	500	200	500	200	500
$^3/_8$	3	$2^1/_4$	$4^1/_2$	500	1,100	500	1,100	500	1,100
$^1/_2$	4	3	6	950	1,250	950	1,250	950	1,250
	4	5	6	1,450	1,600	1,500	1,650	1,550	1,750
$^5/_8$	$4^1/_2$	$3^3/_4$	$7^1/_2$	1,500	2,750	1,500	2,750	1,500	2,750
	$4^1/_2$	$6^1/_4$	$7^1/_2$	2,125	2,950	2,200	3,000	2,400	3,050
$^3/_4$	5	$4^1/_2$	9	2,250	3,250	2,250	3,560	2,250	3,560
	5	$7^1/_2$	9	2,825	4,275	2,950	4,300	3,200	4,400
$^7/_8$	6	$5^1/_4$	$10^1/_2$	2,550	3,700	2,550	4,050	2,550	4,050
1	7	6	12	3,050	4,125	3,250	4,500	3,650	5,300
$1^1/_8$	8	$6^3/_4$	$13^1/_2$	3,400	4,750	3,400	4,750	3,400	4,750
$1^1/_4$	9	$7^1/_2$	15	4,000	5,800	4,000	5,800	4,000	5,800

For SI: 1 inch = 25.4 mm, 1 pound per square inch = 0.00689 MPa, 1 pound = 4.45 N.

SECTION 1913
SHOTCRETE

1913.1 General. Shotcrete is mortar or concrete that is pneumatically projected at high velocity onto a surface. Except as specified in this section, shotcrete shall conform to the requirements of this chapter for plain or reinforced concrete.

1913.2 Proportions and materials. Shotcrete proportions shall be selected that allow suitable placement procedures using the delivery equipment selected and shall result in finished in-place hardened shotcrete meeting the strength requirements of this code.

1913.3 Aggregate. Coarse aggregate, if used, shall not exceed $^3/_4$ inch (19.1 mm).

1913.4 Reinforcement. Reinforcement used in shotcrete construction shall comply with the provisions of Sections 1913.4.1 through 1913.4.4.

1913.4.1 Size. The maximum size of reinforcement shall be No. 5 bars unless it is demonstrated by preconstruction tests that adequate encasement of larger bars will be achieved.

1913.4.2 Clearance. When No. 5 or smaller bars are used, there shall be a minimum clearance between parallel reinforcement bars of $2^1/_2$ inches (64 mm). When bars larger than No. 5 are permitted, there shall be a minimum clearance between parallel bars equal to six diameters of the bars used. When two curtains of steel are provided, the curtain nearer the nozzle shall have a minimum spacing equal to 12 bar diameters and the remaining curtain shall have a minimum spacing of six bar diameters.

> **Exception:** Subject to the approval of the code enforcement official, required clearances shall be reduced where it is demonstrated by preconstruction tests that adequate encasement of the bars used in the design will be achieved.

1913.4.3 Splices. Lap splices of reinforcing bars shall utilize the noncontact lap splice method with a minimum clearance of 2 inches (51 mm) between bars. The use of contact lap splices necessary for support of the reinforcing is permitted when approved by the code enforcement official, based on satisfactory preconstruction tests that show that adequate encasement of the bars will be achieved, and provided that the splice is oriented so that a plane through the center of the spliced bars is perpendicular to the surface of the shotcrete.

1913.4.4 Spirally tied columns. Shotcrete shall not be applied to spirally tied columns.

1913.5 Preconstruction tests. When required by the code enforcement official, a test panel shall be shot, cured, cored or sawn, examined and tested prior to commencement of the project. The sample panel shall be representative of the project and simulate job conditions as closely as possible. The panel thickness and reinforcing shall reproduce the thickest and most congested area specified in the structural design. It shall be shot at the same angle, using the same nozzleman and with the same concrete mix design that will be used on the project. The equipment used in preconstruction testing shall be the same equipment used in the work requiring such testing, unless substitute equipment is approved by the code enforcement official.

1913.6 Rebound. Any rebound or accumulated loose aggregate shall be removed from the surfaces to be covered prior to placing the initial or any succeeding layers of shotcrete. Rebound shall not be used as aggregate.

1913.7 Joints. Except where permitted herein, unfinished work shall not be allowed to stand for more than 30 minutes unless edges are sloped to a thin edge. For structural elements that will be under compression and for construction joints shown on the approved construction documents, square joints are permitted. Before placing additional material adjacent to previously applied work, sloping and square edges shall be cleaned and wetted.

1913.8 Damage. In-place shotcrete that exhibits sags, sloughs, segregation, honeycombing, sand pockets or other obvious defects shall be removed and replaced. Shotcrete above sags and sloughs shall be removed and replaced while still plastic.

1913.9 Curing. During the curing periods specified herein, shotcrete shall be maintained above 40°F (4°C) and in moist condition.

1913.9.1 Initial curing. Shotcrete shall be kept continuously moist for 24 hours after shotcreting is complete or shall be sealed with an approved curing compound.

1913.9.2 Final curing. Final curing shall continue for seven days after shotcreting, or for three days if high-early-strength cement is used, or until the specified strength is obtained. Final curing shall consist of the initial curing process or the shotcrete shall be covered with an approved moisture-retaining cover.

1913.9.3 Natural curing. Natural curing shall not be used in lieu of that specified in this section unless the relative humidity remains at or above 85 percent, and is authorized by the registered design professional and approved by the code enforcement official.

1913.10 Strength tests. Strength tests for shotcrete shall be made by an approved agency on specimens that are representative of the work and which have been water soaked for at least 24 hours prior to testing. When the maximum-size aggregate is larger than $^3/_8$ inch (9.5 mm), specimens shall consist of not less than three 3-inch-diameter (76 mm) cores or 3-inch (76 mm) cubes. When the maximum-size aggregate is $^3/_8$ inch (9.5 mm) or smaller, specimens shall consist of not less than 2-inch-diameter (51 mm) cores or 2-inch (51 mm) cubes.

1913.10.1 Sampling. Specimens shall be taken from the in-place work or from test panels, and shall be taken at least once each shift, but not less than one for each 50 cubic yards (38.2 m³) of shotcrete.

1913.10.2 Panel criteria. When the maximum-size aggregate is larger than $^3/_8$ inch (9.5 mm), the test panels shall have minimum dimensions of 18 inches by 18 inches (457 mm by 457 mm). When the maximum size aggregate is $^3/_8$ inch (9.5 mm) or smaller, the test panels shall have minimum dimensions of 12 inches by 12 inches (305 mm by 305 mm). Panels shall be shot in the same position as the work, during the course of the work and by the nozzlemen doing the work. The conditions under which the panels are cured shall be the same as the work.

1913.10.3 Acceptance criteria. The average compressive strength of three cores from the in-place work or a single test panel shall equal or exceed $0.85\,f'_c$ with no single core less than $0.75\,f'_c$. The average compressive strength of three cubes taken from the in-place work or a single test panel shall equal or exceed f'_c with no individual cube less than $0.88\,f'_c$. To check accuracy, locations represented by erratic core or cube strengths shall be retested.

SECTION 1914
REINFORCED GYPSUM CONCRETE

1914.1 General. Reinforced gypsum concrete shall comply with the requirements of ASTM C 317 and ASTM C 956.

1914.2 Minimum thickness. The minimum thickness of reinforced gypsum concrete shall be 2 inches (51 mm) except the minimum required thickness shall be reduced to $1^1/_2$ inches (38 mm), provided the following conditions are satisfied:

1. The overall thickness, including the formboard, is not less than 2 inches (51 mm).

2. The clear span of the gypsum concrete between supports does not exceed 33 inches (838 mm).

3. Diaphragm action is not required.

4. The design live load does not exceed 40 pounds per square foot (psf) (1915 Pa).

SECTION 1915
CONCRETE-FILLED PIPE COLUMNS

1915.1 General. Concrete-filled pipe columns shall be manufactured from standard, extra-strong or double-extra-strong steel pipe or tubing that is filled with concrete so placed and manipulated as to secure maximum density and to ensure complete filling of the pipe without voids.

1915.2 Design. The safe supporting capacity of concrete-filled pipe columns shall be computed in accordance with the approved rules or as determined by a test.

1915.3 Connections. Caps, base plates and connections shall be of approved types and shall be positively attached to the shell and anchored to the concrete core. Welding of brackets without mechanical anchorage shall be prohibited. Where the pipe is slotted to accommodate webs of brackets or other connections, the integrity of the shell shall be restored by welding to ensure hooping action of the composite section.

1915.4 Reinforcement. To increase the safe load-supporting capacity of concrete-filled pipe columns, the steel reinforcement shall be in the form of rods, structural shapes or pipe embedded in the concrete core with sufficient clearance to ensure the composite action of the section, but not nearer than 1 inch (25 mm) to the exterior steel shell. Structural shapes used as reinforcement shall be milled to ensure bearing on cap and base plates.

1915.5 Fire-resistance-rating protection. Pipe columns shall be of such size or so protected as to develop the required fire-resistance ratings specified in Table 601. Where an outer steel shell is used to enclose the fire-resistant covering, the shell shall not be included in the calculations for strength of the column section. The minimum diameter of pipe columns shall be 4 inches (102 mm) except that in structures of Type V construction not exceeding three stories or 40 feet (12 192 mm) in height, pipe columns used in the basement and as secondary steel members shall have a minimum diameter of 3 inches (76 mm).

1915.6 Approvals. Details of column connections and splices shall be shop fabricated by approved methods and shall be approved only after tests in accordance with the approved rules. Shop-fabricated concrete-filled pipe columns shall be inspected by the code enforcement official or by an approved representative of the manufacturer at the plant.

CHAPTER 20

ALUMINUM

SECTION 2001
GENERAL

2001.1 Scope. This chapter shall govern the quality, design, fabrication and erection of aluminum.

SECTION 2002
MATERIALS

2002.1 General. Aluminum used for structural purposes in buildings and structures shall comply with AA ASM 35 and AA ADM 1. The nominal loads shall be the minimum design loads required by Chapter 16.

CHAPTER 21

MASONRY

SECTION 2101
GENERAL

2101.1 Scope. This chapter shall govern the materials, design, construction and quality of masonry.

2101.2 Design methods. Masonry shall comply with the provisions of one of the following design methods in this chapter as well as the requirements of Sections 2101 through 2104. Masonry designed by the allowable stress design provisions of Section 2101.2.1, the strength design provisions of Section 2101.2.2 or the prestressed masonry provisions of Section 2101.2.3 shall comply with Section 2105.

2101.2.1 Allowable stress design. Masonry designed by the allowable stress design method shall comply with the provisions of Sections 2106 and 2107.

2101.2.2 Strength design. Masonry designed by the strength design method shall comply with the provisions of Sections 2106 and 2108, except that autoclaved aerated concrete (AAC) masonry shall comply with the provisions of Section 2106 and Chapter 1 and Appendix A of ACI 530/ASCE 5/TMS 402. AAC masonry shall not be used in the seismic-force-resisting system of structures classified as Seismic Design Category B, C, D, E or F.

2101.2.3 Prestressed masonry. Prestressed masonry shall be designed in accordance with Chapters 1 and 4 of ACI 530/ASCE 5/TMS 402 and Section 2106. Special inspection during construction shall be provided as set forth in Section 1704.5.

2101.2.4 Empirical design. Masonry designed by the empirical design method shall comply with the provisions of Sections 2106 and 2109 or Chapter 5 of ACI 530/ASCE 5/TMS 402.

2101.2.5 Glass unit masonry. Glass unit masonry shall comply with the provisions of Section 2110 or Chapter 7 of ACI 530/ASCE 5/TMS 402.

2101.2.6 Masonry veneer. Masonry veneer shall comply with the provisions of Chapter 14 or Chapter 6 of ACI 530/ASCE 5/TMS 402.

2101.3 Construction documents. The construction documents shall show all of the items required by this code including the following:

1. Specified size, grade, type and location of reinforcement, anchors and wall ties.

2. Reinforcing bars to be welded and welding procedure.

3. Size and location of structural elements.

4. Provisions for dimensional changes resulting from elastic deformation, creep, shrinkage, temperature and moisture.

2101.3.1 Fireplace drawings. The construction documents shall describe in sufficient detail the location, size and construction of masonry fireplaces. The thickness and characteristics of materials and the clearances from walls, partitions and ceilings shall be clearly indicated.

SECTION 2102
DEFINITIONS AND NOTATIONS

2102.1 General. The following words and terms shall, for the purposes of this chapter and as used elsewhere in this code, have the meanings shown herein.

AAC MASONRY. Masonry made of autoclaved aerated concrete (AAC) units, manufactured without internal reinforcement and bonded together using thin- or thick-bed mortar.

ADOBE CONSTRUCTION. Construction in which the exterior load-bearing and nonload-bearing walls and partitions are of unfired clay masonry units, and floors, roofs and interior framing are wholly or partly of wood or other approved materials.

    Adobe, stabilized. Unfired clay masonry units to which admixtures, such as emulsified asphalt, are added during the manufacturing process to limit the units' water absorption so as to increase their durability.

    Adobe, unstabilized. Unfired clay masonry units that do not meet the definition of "Adobe, stabilized."

ANCHOR. Metal rod, wire or strap that secures masonry to its structural support.

ARCHITECTURAL TERRA COTTA. Plain or ornamental hard-burned modified clay units, larger in size than brick, with glazed or unglazed ceramic finish.

AREA.

    Bedded. The area of the surface of a masonry unit that is in contact with mortar in the plane of the joint.

    Gross cross-sectional. The area delineated by the out-to-out specified dimensions of masonry in the plane under consideration.

    Net cross-sectional. The area of masonry units, grout and mortar crossed by the plane under consideration based on out-to-out specified dimensions.

AUTOCLAVED AERATED CONCRETE (AAC). Low-density cementitious product of calcium silicate hydrates, whose material specifications are defined in ASTM C 1386.

BED JOINT. The horizontal layer of mortar on which a masonry unit is laid.

BOND BEAM. A horizontal grouted element within masonry in which reinforcement is embedded.

BOND REINFORCING. The adhesion between steel reinforcement and mortar or grout.

BRICK.

Calcium silicate (sand lime brick). A masonry unit made of sand and lime.

Clay or shale. A masonry unit made of clay or shale, usually formed into a rectangular prism while in the plastic state and burned or fired in a kiln.

Concrete. A masonry unit having the approximate shape of a rectangular prism and composed of inert aggregate particles embedded in a hardened cementitious matrix.

BUTTRESS. A projecting part of a masonry wall built integrally therewith to provide lateral stability.

CAST STONE. A building stone manufactured from portland cement concrete precast and used as a trim, veneer or facing on or in buildings or structures.

CELL. A void space having a gross cross-sectional area greater than $1^1/_2$ square inches (967 mm^2).

CHIMNEY. A primarily vertical enclosure containing one or more passageways for conveying flue gases to the outside atmosphere.

CHIMNEY TYPES.

High-heat appliance type. An approved chimney for removing the products of combustion from fuel-burning, high-heat appliances producing combustion gases in excess of 2,000°F (1093°C) measured at the appliance flue outlet (see Section 2113.11.3).

Low-heat appliance type. An approved chimney for removing the products of combustion from fuel-burning, low-heat appliances producing combustion gases not in excess of 1,000°F (538°C) under normal operating conditions, but capable of producing combustion gases of 1,400°F (760°C) during intermittent forces firing for periods up to 1 hour. Temperatures shall be measured at the appliance flue outlet.

Masonry type. A field-constructed chimney of solid masonry units or stones.

Medium-heat appliance type. An approved chimney for removing the products of combustion from fuel-burning, medium-heat appliances producing combustion gases not exceeding 2,000°F (1093°C) measured at the appliance flue outlet (see Section 2113.11.2).

CLEANOUT. An opening to the bottom of a grout space of sufficient size and spacing to allow the removal of debris.

COLLAR JOINT. Vertical longitudinal joint between wythes of masonry or between masonry and backup construction that is permitted to be filled with mortar or grout.

COLUMN, MASONRY. An isolated vertical member whose horizontal dimension measured at right angles to its thickness does not exceed three times its thickness and whose height is at least four times its thickness.

COMPOSITE ACTION. Transfer of stress between components of a member designed so that in resisting loads, the combined components act together as a single member.

COMPOSITE MASONRY. Multiwythe masonry members acting with composite action.

COMPRESSIVE STRENGTH OF MASONRY. Maximum compressive force resisted per unit of net cross-sectional area of masonry, determined by the testing of masonry prisms or a function of individual masonry units, mortar and grout.

CONNECTOR. A mechanical device for securing two or more pieces, parts or members together, including anchors, wall ties and fasteners.

COVER. Distance between surface of reinforcing bar and edge of member.

DIAPHRAGM. A roof or floor system designed to transmit lateral forces to shear walls or other lateral-load-resisting elements.

DIMENSIONS.

Actual. The measured dimension of a masonry unit or element.

Nominal. The specified dimension plus an allowance for the joints with which the units are to be laid. Thickness is given first, followed by height and then length.

Specified. The dimensions specified for the manufacture or construction of masonry, masonry units, joints or any other component of a structure.

EFFECTIVE HEIGHT. For braced members, the effective height is the clear height between lateral supports and is used for calculating the slenderness ratio. The effective height for unbraced members is calculated in accordance with engineering mechanics.

FIREPLACE. A hearth and fire chamber or similar prepared place in which a fire may be made and which is built in conjunction with a chimney.

FIREPLACE THROAT. The opening between the top of the firebox and the smoke chamber.

FOUNDATION PIER. An isolated vertical foundation member whose horizontal dimension measured at right angles to its thickness does not exceed three times its thickness and whose height is equal to or less than four times its thickness.

GLASS UNIT MASONRY. Masonry composed of glass units bonded by mortar.

GROUTED MASONRY.

Grouted hollow-unit masonry. That form of grouted masonry construction in which certain designated cells of hollow units are continuously filled with grout.

Grouted multiwythe masonry. That form of grouted masonry construction in which the space between the wythes is solidly or periodically filled with grout.

HEAD JOINT. Vertical mortar joint placed between masonry units within the wythe at the time the masonry units are laid.

HEADER (Bonder). A masonry unit that connects two or more adjacent wythes of masonry.

HEIGHT, WALLS. The vertical distance from the foundation wall or other immediate support of such wall to the top of the wall.

MASONRY. A built-up construction or combination of building units or materials of clay, shale, concrete, glass, gypsum, stone or other approved units bonded together with or without mortar or grout or other accepted methods of joining.

> **Ashlar masonry.** Masonry composed of various-sized rectangular units having sawed, dressed or squared bed surfaces, properly bonded and laid in mortar.

> **Coursed ashlar.** Ashlar masonry laid in courses of stone of equal height for each course, although different courses shall be permitted to be of varying height.

> **Glass unit masonry.** Masonry composed of glass units bonded by mortar.

> **Plain masonry.** Masonry in which the tensile resistance of the masonry is taken into consideration and the effects of stresses in reinforcement are neglected.

> **Random ashlar.** Ashlar masonry laid in courses of stone set without continuous joints and laid up without drawn patterns. When composed of material cut into modular heights, discontinuous but aligned horizontal joints are discernible.

> **Reinforced masonry.** Masonry construction in which reinforcement acting in conjunction with the masonry is used to resist forces.

> **Solid masonry.** Masonry consisting of solid masonry units laid contiguously with the joints between the units filled with mortar.

> **Unreinforced (plain) masonry.** Masonry in which the tensile resistance of masonry is taken into consideration and the resistance of the reinforcing steel, if present, is neglected.

MASONRY UNIT. Brick, tile, stone, glass block or concrete block conforming to the requirements specified in Section 2103.

> **Clay.** A building unit larger in size than a brick, composed of burned clay, shale, fired clay or mixtures thereof.

> **Concrete.** A building unit or block larger in size than 12 inches by 4 inches by 4 inches (305 mm by 102 mm by 102 mm) made of cement and suitable aggregates.

> **Hollow.** A masonry unit whose net cross-sectional area in any plane parallel to the load-bearing surface is less than 75 percent of its gross cross-sectional area measured in the same plane.

> **Solid.** A masonry unit whose net cross-sectional area in every plane parallel to the load-bearing surface is 75 percent or more of its gross cross-sectional area measured in the same plane.

MEAN DAILY TEMPERATURE. The average daily temperature of temperature extremes predicted by a local weather bureau for the next 24 hours.

MORTAR. A plastic mixture of approved cementitious materials, fine aggregates and water used to bond masonry or other structural units.

MORTAR, SURFACE-BONDING. A mixture to bond concrete masonry units that contains hydraulic cement, glass fiber reinforcement with or without inorganic fillers or organic modifiers and water.

PLASTIC HINGE. The zone in a structural member in which the yield moment is anticipated to be exceeded under loading combinations that include earthquakes.

PRESTRESSED MASONRY. Masonry in which internal stresses have been introduced to counteract potential tensile stresses in masonry resulting from applied loads.

PRISM. An assemblage of masonry units and mortar with or without grout used as a test specimen for determining properties of the masonry.

RUBBLE MASONRY. Masonry composed of roughly shaped stones.

> **Coursed rubble.** Masonry composed of roughly shaped stones fitting approximately on level beds and well bonded.

> **Random rubble.** Masonry composed of roughly shaped stones laid without regularity of coursing but well bonded and fitted together to form well-divided joints.

> **Rough or ordinary rubble.** Masonry composed of unsquared field stones laid without regularity of coursing but well bonded.

RUNNING BOND. The placement of masonry units such that head joints in successive courses are horizontally offset at least one-quarter the unit length.

SHEAR WALL.

> **Detailed plain masonry shear wall.** A masonry shear wall designed to resist lateral forces neglecting stresses in reinforcement, and designed in accordance with Section 2106.1.1.

> **Intermediate prestressed masonry shear wall.** A prestressed masonry shear wall designed to resist lateral forces considering stresses in reinforcement, and designed in accordance with Section 2106.1.1.2.

> **Intermediate reinforced masonry shear wall.** A masonry shear wall designed to resist lateral forces considering stresses in reinforcement, and designed in accordance with Section 2106.1.1.

> **Ordinary plain masonry shear wall.** A masonry shear wall designed to resist lateral forces neglecting stresses in reinforcement, and designed in accordance with Section 2106.1.1.

> **Ordinary plain prestressed masonry shear wall.** A prestressed masonry shear wall designed to resist lateral forces considering stresses in reinforcement, and designed in accordance with Section 2106.1.1.1.

> **Ordinary reinforced masonry shear wall.** A masonry shear wall designed to resist lateral forces considering

stresses in reinforcement, and designed in accordance with Section 2106.1.1.

Special prestressed masonry shear wall. A prestressed masonry shear wall designed to resist lateral forces considering stresses in reinforcement and designed in accordance with Section 2106.1.1.3 except that only grouted, laterally restrained tendons are used.

Special reinforced masonry shear wall. A masonry shear wall designed to resist lateral forces considering stresses in reinforcement, and designed in accordance with Section 2106.1.1.

SHELL. The outer portion of a hollow masonry unit as placed in masonry.

SPECIFIED. Required by construction documents.

SPECIFIED COMPRESSIVE STRENGTH OF MASONRY, f'_m. Minimum compressive strength, expressed as force per unit of net cross-sectional area, required of the masonry used in construction by the construction documents, and upon which the project design is based. Whenever the quantity f'_m is under the radical sign, the square root of numerical value only is intended and the result has units of pounds per square inch (psi) (MPa).

STACK BOND. The placement of masonry units in a bond pattern is such that head joints in successive courses are vertically aligned. For the purpose of this code, requirements for stack bond shall apply to masonry laid in other than running bond.

STONE MASONRY. Masonry composed of field, quarried or cast stone units bonded by mortar.

Ashlar stone masonry. Stone masonry composed of rectangular units having sawed, dressed or squared bed surfaces and bonded by mortar.

Rubble stone masonry. Stone masonry composed of irregular-shaped units bonded by mortar.

STRENGTH.

Design strength. Nominal strength multiplied by a strength reduction factor.

Nominal strength. Strength of a member or cross section calculated in accordance with these provisions before application of any strength-reduction factors.

Required strength. Strength of a member or cross section required to resist factored loads.

THIN-BED MORTAR. Mortar for use in construction of AAC unit masonry with joints 0.06 inch (1.5 mm) or less.

TIE, LATERAL. Loop of reinforcing bar or wire enclosing longitudinal reinforcement.

TIE, WALL. A connector that connects wythes of masonry walls together.

TILE. A ceramic surface unit, usually relatively thin in relation to facial area, made from clay or a mixture of clay or other ceramic materials, called the body of the tile, having either a "glazed" or "unglazed" face and fired above red heat in the course of manufacture to a temperature sufficiently high enough to produce specific physical properties and characteristics.

TILE, STRUCTURAL CLAY. A hollow masonry unit composed of burned clay, shale, fire clay or mixture thereof, and having parallel cells.

WALL. A vertical element with a horizontal length-to-thickness ratio greater than three, used to enclose space.

Cavity wall. A wall built of masonry units or of concrete, or a combination of these materials, arranged to provide an airspace within the wall, and in which the inner and outer parts of the wall are tied together with metal ties.

Composite wall. A wall built of a combination of two or more masonry units bonded together, one forming the backup and the other forming the facing elements.

Dry-stacked, surface-bonded walls. A wall built of concrete masonry units where the units are stacked dry, without mortar on the bed or head joints, and where both sides of the wall are coated with a surface-bonding mortar.

Masonry-bonded hollow wall. A wall built of masonry units so arranged as to provide an airspace within the wall, and in which the facing and backing of the wall are bonded together with masonry units.

Parapet wall. The part of any wall entirely above the roof line.

WEB. An interior solid portion of a hollow masonry unit as placed in masonry.

WYTHE. Each continuous, vertical section of a wall, one masonry unit in thickness.

NOTATIONS.

A_n = Net cross-sectional area of masonry, square inches (mm²).

b = Effective width of rectangular member or width of flange for T and I sections, inches (mm).

d_b = Diameter of reinforcement, inches (mm).

F_s = Allowable tensile or compressive stress in reinforcement, psi (MPa).

f_r = Modulus of rupture, psi (MPa).

f_y = Specified yield stress of the reinforcement or the anchor bolt, psi (MPa).

f'_{AAC} = Specified compressive strength of AAC masonry, the minimum compressive strength for a class of AAC masonry as specified in ASTM C 1386, psi (MPa).

f'_m = Specified compressive strength of masonry at age of 28 days, psi (MPa).

f'_{mi} = Specified compressive strength of masonry at the time of prestress transfer, psi (MPa).

K = The lesser of the masonry cover, clear spacing between adjacent reinforcement, or five times d_b, inches (mm).

L_s = Distance between supports, inches (mm).

L_w = Length of wall, inches (mm).

l_d = Required development length or lap length of reinforcement, inches (mm).

l_{de} = Embedment length of reinforcement, inches (mm).

P_w = Weight of wall tributary to section under consideration, pounds (N).

t = Specified wall thickness dimension or the least lateral dimension of a column, inches (mm).

V_n = Nominal shear strength, pounds (N).

V_u = Required shear strength due to factored loads, pounds (N).

W = Wind load, or related internal moments in forces.

γ = Reinforcement size factor.

ρ_n = Ratio of distributed shear reinforcement on plane perpendicular to plane of A_{mv}.

ρ_{max} = Maximum reinforcement ratio.

Φ = Strength reduction factor.

SECTION 2103
MASONRY CONSTRUCTION MATERIALS

2103.1 Concrete masonry units. Concrete masonry units shall conform to the following standards: ASTM C 55 for concrete brick; ASTM C 73 for calcium silicate face brick; ASTM C 90 for load-bearing concrete masonry units or ASTM C 744 for prefaced concrete and calcium silicate masonry units.

2103.2 Clay or shale masonry units. Clay or shale masonry units shall conform to the following standards: ASTM C 34 for structural clay load-bearing wall tile; ASTM C 56 for structural clay nonload-bearing wall tile; ASTM C 62 for building brick (solid masonry units made from clay or shale); ASTM C 1088 for solid units of thin veneer brick; ASTM C 126 for ceramic-glazed structural clay facing tile, facing brick and solid masonry units; ASTM C 212 for structural clay facing tile; ASTM C 216 for facing brick (solid masonry units made from clay or shale); ASTM C 652 for hollow brick (hollow masonry units made from clay or shale); and ASTM C 1405 for glazed brick (single-fired solid brick units).

> **Exception:** Structural clay tile for nonstructural use in fireproofing of structural members and in wall furring shall not be required to meet the compressive strength specifications. The fire-resistance rating shall be determined in accordance with ASTM E 119 and shall comply with the requirements of Table 602.

2103.3 AAC masonry. AAC masonry units shall conform to ASTM C 1386 for the strength class specified.

2103.4 Stone masonry units. Stone masonry units shall conform to the following standards: ASTM C 503 for marble building stone (exterior); ASTM C 568 for limestone building stone; ASTM C 615 for granite building stone; ASTM C 616 for sandstone building stone; or ASTM C 629 for slate building stone.

2103.5 Ceramic tile. Ceramic tile shall be as defined in, and shall conform to the requirements of, ANSI A137.1.

2103.6 Glass unit masonry. Hollow glass units shall be partially evacuated and have a minimum average glass face thickness of $^3/_{16}$ inch (4.8 mm). Solid glass-block units shall be provided when required. The surfaces of units intended to be in contact with mortar shall be treated with a polyvinyl butyral coating or latex-based paint. Reclaimed units shall not be used.

2103.7 Second-hand units. Second-hand masonry units shall not be reused unless they conform to the requirements of new units. The units shall be of whole, sound materials and free from cracks and other defects that will interfere with proper laying or use. Old mortar shall be cleaned from the unit before reuse.

2103.8 Mortar. Mortar for use in masonry construction shall conform to ASTM C 270 and shall conform to the proportion specifications of Table 2103.8(1) or the property specifications of Table 2103.8(2). Type S or N mortar shall be used for glass unit masonry. The amount of water used in mortar for glass unit masonry shall be adjusted to account for the lack of absorption. Retempering of mortar for glass unit masonry shall not be permitted after initial set. Unused mortar shall be discarded within $2^1/_2$ hours after initial mixing, except that unused mortar for glass unit masonry shall be discarded within $1^1/_2$ hours after initial mixing.

2103.9 Surface-bonding mortar. Surface-bonding mortar shall comply with ASTM C 887. Surface bonding of concrete masonry units shall comply with ASTM C 946.

2103.10 Mortars for ceramic wall and floor tile. Portland cement mortars for installing ceramic wall and floor tile shall comply with ANSI A108.1A and ANSI A108.1B and be of the compositions indicated in Table 2103.10.

TABLE 2103.10
CERAMic TILE MORTAR COMPOSITIONS

LOCATION	MORTAR	COMPOSITION
Walls	Scratchcoat	1 cement; $^1/_5$ hydrated lime; 4 dry or 5 damp sand
Walls	Setting bed and leveling coat	1 cement; $^1/_2$ hydrated lime; 5 damp sand to 1 cement 1 hydrated lime, 7 damp sand
Floors	Setting bed	1 cement; $^1/_{10}$ hydrated lime; 5 dry or 6 damp sand; or 1 cement; 5 dry or 6 damp sand
Ceilings	Scratchcoat and sand bed	1 cement; $^1/_2$ hydrated lime; $2^1/_2$ dry sand or 3 damp sand

2103.10.1 Dry-set portland cement mortars. Premixed prepared portland cement mortars, which require only the addition of water and are used in the installation of ceramic tile, shall comply with ANSI A118.1. The shear bond strength for tile set in such mortar shall be as required in accordance with ANSI A118.1. Tile set in dry-set portland cement mortar shall be installed in accordance with ANSI A108.5.

2103.10.2 Latex-modified portland cement mortar. Latex-modified portland cement thin-set mortars in which latex is added to dry-set mortar as a replacement for all or part of the gauging water that are used for the installation of ceramic tile shall comply with ANSI A118.4. Tile set in

TABLE 2103.8(1)
MORTAR PROPORTIONS

MORTAR	TYPE	PROPORTIONS BY VOLUME (cementitious materials)							HYDRATED LIME^e OR LIME PUTTY	AGGREGATE MEASURED IN A DAMP, LOOSE CONDITION
		Portland cement^a or blended cement^b	Masonry cement^c			Mortar cement^d				
			M	S	N	M	S	N		
Cement-lime	M	1	-	-	-	-	-	-	$^1/_4$	Not less than $2^1/_4$ and not more than 3 times the sum of the separate volumes of cementitious materials
	S	1	-	-	-	-	-	-	over $^1/_4$ to $^1/_2$	
	N	1	-	-	-	-	-	-	over $^1/_2$ to $1^1/_4$	
	O	1	-	-	-	-	-	-	over $1^1/_4$ to $2^1/_2$	
Mortar cement	M	1	-	-	-	-	-	1	-	
	M	-	-	-	-	1	-	-	-	
	S	$^1/_2$	-	-	-	-	-	1	-	
	S	-	-	-	-	-	1	-	-	
	N	-	-	-	-	-	-	1	-	
	O	-	-	-	-	-	-	1	-	
Masonry cement	M	1	-	-	1	-	-	-	-	
	M	-	1	-	-	-	-	-	-	
	S	$^1/_2$	-	-	1	-	-	-	-	
	S	-	-	1	-	-	-	-	-	
	N	-	-	-	1	-	-	-	-	
	O	-	-	-	1	-	-	-	-	

a. Portland cement conforming to the requirements of ASTM C 150.
b. Blended cement conforming to the requirements of ASTM C 595.
c. Masonry cement conforming to the requirements of ASTM C 91.
d. Mortar cement conforming to the requirements of ASTM C 1329.
e. Hydrated lime conforming to the requirements of ASTM C 207.

TABLE 2103.8(2)
MORTAR PROPERTIES^a

MORTAR	TYPE	AVERAGE COMPRESSIVE^b STRENGTH AT 28 DAYS minimum (psi)	WATER RETENTION minimum (%)	AIR CONTENT maximum (%)
Cement-lime	M	2,500	75	12
	S	1,800	75	12
	N	750	75	14^c
	O	350	75	14^c
Mortar cement	M	2,500	75	12
	S	1,800	75	12
	N	750	75	14^c
	O	350	75	14^c
Masonry cement	M	2,500	75	18
	S	1,800	75	18
	N	750	75	20^d
	O	350	75	20^d

For SI: 1 inch = 25.4 mm, 1 pound per square inch = 6.895 kPa.

a. This aggregate ratio (measured in damp, loose condition) shall not be less than $2^1/_4$ and not more than 3 times the sum of the separate volumes of cementitious materials.
b. Average of three 2-inch cubes of laboratory-prepared mortar, in accordance with ASTM C 270.
c. When structural reinforcement is incorporated in cement-lime or mortar cement mortars, the maximum air content shall not exceed 12 percent.
d. When structural reinforcement is incorporated in masonry cement mortar, the maximum air content shall not exceed 18 percent.

latex-modified portland cement shall be installed in accordance with ANSI A108.5.

2103.10.3 Epoxy mortar. Ceramic tile set and grouted with chemical-resistant epoxy shall comply with ANSI A118.3. Tile set and grouted with epoxy shall be installed in accordance with ANSI A108.6.

2103.10.4 Furan mortar and grout. Chemical-resistant furan mortar and grout that are used to install ceramic tile shall comply with ANSI A118.5. Tile set and grouted with furan shall be installed in accordance with ANSI A108.8.

2103.10.5 Modified epoxy-emulsion mortar and grout. Modified epoxy-emulsion mortar and grout that are used to install ceramic tile shall comply with ANSI A118.8. Tile set and grouted with modified epoxy-emulsion mortar and grout shall be installed in accordance with ANSI A108.9.

2103.10.6 Organic adhesives. Water-resistant organic adhesives used for the installation of ceramic tile shall comply with ANSI A136.1. The shear bond strength after water immersion shall not be less than 40 psi (275 kPa) for Type I adhesive and not less than 20 psi (138 kPa) for

Type II adhesive when tested in accordance with ANSI A136.1. Tile set in organic adhesives shall be installed in accordance with ANSI A108.4.

2103.10.7 Portland cement grouts. Portland cement grouts used for the installation of ceramic tile shall comply with ANSI A118.6. Portland cement grouts for tile work shall be installed in accordance with ANSI A108.10.

2103.11 Mortar for AAC masonry. Thin-bed mortar for AAC masonry shall comply with Section 2103.11.1. Mortar for leveling courses of AAC masonry shall comply with Section 2103.11.2.

2103.11.1 Thin-bed mortar for AAC masonry. Thin-bed mortar for AAC masonry shall be specifically manufactured for use with AAC masonry. Testing to verify mortar properties shall be conducted by the thin-bed mortar manufacturer and confirmed by an independent testing agency:

1. The compressive strength of thin-bed mortar, as determined by ASTM C 109, shall meet or exceed the strength of the AAC masonry units.

2. The shear strength of thin-bed mortar shall meet or exceed the shear strength of the AAC masonry units for wall assemblages tested in accordance with ASTM E 519.

3. The flexural tensile strength of thin-bed mortar shall not be less than the modulus of rupture of the masonry units. Flexural strength shall be determined by testing in accordance with ASTM E 72 (transverse load test), ASTM E 518 Method A (flexural bond strength test) or ASTM C 1072 (flexural bond strength test).

   3.1. For conducting flexural strength tests in accordance with ASTM E 518, at least five test specimens shall be constructed as stack-bonded prisms at least 32 inches (810 mm) high. The type of mortar specified by the AAC unit manufacturer shall be used.

   3.2. For flexural strength tests in accordance with ASTM C 1072, test specimens shall be constructed as stack-bonded prisms comprised with at least three bed joints. A total of at least five joints shall be tested using the type of mortar specified by the AAC unit manufacturer.

4. The splitting tensile strength of AAC masonry assemblages composed of two AAC masonry units bonded with one thin-bed mortar joint shall be determined in accordance with ASTM C 1006 and shall equal or exceed $2.4 \sqrt{f'AAC}$

2103.11.2 Mortar for leveling courses of AAC masonry. Mortar used for the leveling courses of AAC masonry shall conform to Section 2103.8 and shall be Type M or S.

2103.12 Grout. Grout shall conform to Table 2103.12 or to ASTM C 476. When grout conforms to ASTM C 476, the grout shall be specified by proportion requirements or property requirements.

2103.13 Metal reinforcement and accessories. Metal reinforcement and accessories shall conform to Sections 2103.13.1 through 2103.13.8.

2103.13.1 Deformed reinforcing bars. Deformed reinforcing bars shall conform to one of the following standards: ASTM A 615 for deformed and plain billet-steel bars for concrete reinforcement; ASTM A 706 for low-alloy steel deformed bars for concrete reinforcement; ASTM A 767 for zinc-coated reinforcing steel bars; ASTM A 775 for epoxy-coated reinforcing steel bars; and ASTM A 996 for rail and axle steel-deformed bars for concrete reinforcement.

2103.13.2 Joint reinforcement. Joint reinforcement shall comply with ASTM A 951. The maximum spacing of crosswires in ladder-type joint reinforcement and point of connection of cross wires to longitudinal wires of truss-type reinforcement shall be 16 inches (400 mm).

2103.13.3 Deformed reinforcing wire. Deformed reinforcing wire shall conform to ASTM A 496.

2103.13.4 Wire fabric. Wire fabric shall conform to ASTM A 185 for plain steel-welded wire fabric for concrete reinforcement or ASTM A 497 for welded deformed steel wire fabric for concrete reinforcement.

2103.13.5 Anchors, ties and accessories. Anchors, ties and accessories shall conform to the following standards: ASTM A 36 for structural steel; ASTM A 82 for plain steel wire for concrete reinforcement; ASTM A 185 for plain steel-welded wire fabric for concrete reinforcement; ASTM A 240 for chromium and chromium-nickle stainless steel plate, sheet and strip; ASTM A 307 Grade A for anchor bolts; ASTM A 480 for flat rolled stainless and heat-resisting steel plate, sheet and strip; and ASTM A 1008 for cold-rolled carbon steel sheet.

TABLE 2103.12
GROUT PROPORTIONS BY VOLUME FOR MASONRY CONSTRUCTION

TYPE	PARTS BY VOLUME OF PORTLAND CEMENT OR BLENDED CEMENT	PARTS BY VOLUME OF HYDRATED LIME OR LIME PUTTY	AGGREGATE, MEASURED IN A DAMP, LOOSE CONDITION	
			Fine	Coarse
Fine grout	1	0-$\frac{1}{10}$	$2\frac{1}{4}$-3 times the sum of the volumes of the cementitious materials	-
Coarse grout	1	0-$\frac{1}{10}$	$2\frac{1}{4}$-3 times the sum of the volumes of the cementitious materials	1-2 times the sum of the volumes of the cementitious materials

2103.13.6 Prestressing tendons. Prestressing tendons shall conform to one of the following standards:

1. Wire	ASTM A 421
2. Low-relaxation wire	ASTM A 421
3. Strand	ASTM A 416
4. Low-relaxation strand	ASTM A 416
5. Bar	ASTM A 722

Exceptions:

1. Wire, strands and bars not specifically listed in ASTM A 421, ASTM A 416 or ASTM A 722 are permitted, provided they conform to the minimum requirements in ASTM A 421, ASTM A 416 or ASTM A 722 and are approved by the architect/engineer.

2. Bars and wires of less than 150 kips per square inch (ksi) (1034 MPa) tensile strength and conforming to ASTM A 82, ASTM A 510, ASTM A 615, ASTM A 996 or ASTM A 706 are permitted to be used as prestressed tendons, provided that:

    2.1. The stress relaxation properties have been assessed by tests according to ASTM E 328 for the maximum permissible stress in the tendon.

    2.2. Other nonstress-related requirements of ACI 530/ASCE 5/TMS 402, Chapter 4, addressing prestressing tendons are met.

2103.13.7 Corrosion protection. Corrosion protection for prestressing tendons shall comply with the requirements of ACI 530.1/ASCE 6/TMS 602, Article 2.4G. Corrosion protection for prestressing anchorages, couplers and end blocks shall comply with the requirements of ACI 530.1/ASCE 6/TMS 602, Article 2.4H. Corrosion protection for carbon steel accessories used in exterior wall construction or interior walls exposed to a mean relative humidity exceeding 75 percent shall comply with either Section 2103.13.7.2 or 2103.13.7.3. Corrosion protection for carbon steel accessories used in interior walls exposed to a mean relative humidity equal to or less than 75 percent shall comply with either Section 2103.13.7.1, 2103.13.7.2 or 2103.13.7.3.

2103.13.7.1 Mill galvanized. Mill galvanized coatings shall be applied as follows:

1. For joint reinforcement, wall ties, anchors and inserts, a minimum coating of 0.1 ounce per square foot (31 g/m^2) complying with the requirements of ASTM A 641 shall be applied.

2. For sheet metal ties and sheet metal anchors, a minimum coating complying with Coating Designation G-60 according to the requirements of ASTM A 653 shall be applied.

3. For anchor bolts, steel plates or bars not exposed to the earth, weather or a mean relative humidity exceeding 75 percent, a coating is not required.

2103.13.7.2 Hot-dipped galvanized. Hot-dipped galvanized coatings shall be applied after fabrication as follows:

1. For joint reinforcement, wall ties, anchors and inserts, a minimum coating of 1.5 ounces per square foot (458 g/m^2) complying with the requirements of ASTM A 153, Class B shall be applied.

2. For sheet metal ties and anchors, the requirements of ASTM A 153, Class B shall be met.

3. For steel plates and bars, the requirements of either ASTM A 123 or ASTM A 153, Class B shall be met.

2103.13.7.3 Epoxy coatings. Carbon steel accessories shall be epoxy coated as follows:

1. For joint reinforcement, the requirements of ASTM A 884, Class A, Type 1 having a minimum thickness of 7 mils (175 μm) shall be met.

2. For wire ties and anchors, the requirements of ASTM A 899, Class C having a minimum thickness of 20 mils (508 μm) shall be met.

3. For sheet metal ties and anchors, a minimum thickness of 20 mils (508 μm) per surface shall be provided or a minimum thickness in accordance with the manufacturer's specification shall be provided.

2103.13.8 Tests. Where unidentified reinforcement is approved for use, not less than three tension and three bending tests shall be made on representative specimens of the reinforcement from each shipment and grade of reinforcing steel proposed for use in the work.

SECTION 2104
CONSTRUCTION

2104.1 Masonry construction. Masonry construction shall comply with the requirements of Sections 2104.1.1 through 2104.5 and with ACI 530.1/ASCE 6/TMS 602.

2104.1.1 Tolerances. Masonry, except masonry veneer, shall be constructed within the tolerances specified in ACI 530.1/ASCE 6/TMS 602.

2104.1.2 Placing mortar and units. Placement of mortar and clay and concrete units shall comply with Sections 2104.1.2.1, 2104.1.2.2, 2104.1.2.3 and 2104.1.2.5. Placement of mortar and glass unit masonry shall comply with Sections 2104.1.2.4 and 2104.1.2.5. Placement of thin-bed mortar and AAC masonry shall comply with Section 2104.1.2.6.

2104.1.2.1 Bed and head joints. Unless otherwise required or indicated on the construction documents, head and bed joints shall be $^3/_8$ inch (9.5 mm) thick, except that the thickness of the bed joint of the starting course placed over foundations shall not be less than $^1/_4$ inch (6.4 mm) and not more than $^3/_4$ inch (19.1 mm).

2104.1.2.1.1 Open-end units. Open-end units with beveled ends shall be fully grouted. Head joints of open-end units with beveled ends need not be mortared. The beveled ends shall form a grout key that permits grouts within $^5/_8$ inch (15.9 mm) of the face of the unit. The units shall be tightly butted to prevent leakage of the grout.

2104.1.2.2 Hollow units. Hollow units shall be placed such that face shells of bed joints are fully mortared. Webs shall be fully mortared in all courses of piers, columns, pilasters, in the starting course on foundations where adjacent cells or cavities are to be grouted, and where otherwise required. Head joints shall be mortared a minimum distance from each face equal to the face shell thickness of the unit.

2104.1.2.3 Solid units. Unless otherwise required or indicated on the construction documents, solid units shall be placed in fully mortared bed and head joints. The ends of the units shall be completely buttered. Head joints shall not be filled by slushing with mortar. Head joints shall be constructed by shoving mortar tight against the adjoining unit. Bed joints shall not be furrowed deep enough to produce voids.

2104.1.2.4 Glass unit masonry. Glass units shall be placed so head and bed joints are filled solidly. Mortar shall not be furrowed.

Unless otherwise required, head and bed joints of glass unit masonry shall be $^1/_4$ inch (6.4 mm) thick, except that vertical joint thickness of radial panels shall not be less than $^1/_8$ inch (3.2 mm). The bed joint thickness tolerance shall be minus $^1/_{16}$ inch (1.6 mm) and plus $^1/_8$ inch (3.2 mm). The head joint thickness tolerance shall be plus or minus $^1/_8$ inch (3.2 mm).

2104.1.2.5 Placement in mortar. Units shall be placed while the mortar is soft and plastic. Any unit disturbed to the extent that the initial bond is broken after initial positioning shall be removed and relaid in fresh mortar.

2104.1.2.6 Thin-bed mortar and AAC masonry units. AAC masonry construction shall begin with a leveling course of masonry meeting the requirements of Section 2104.1.2. Subsequent courses of AAC masonry units shall be laid with thin-bed mortar using a special notched trowel manufactured for use with thin-bed mortar to spread the mortar so that it completely fills the bed joints. Unless otherwise specified, the head joints shall be similarly filled. Joints in AAC masonry shall be approximately $^1/_{16}$ inch (1.5 mm) and shall be formed by striking on the ends and tops of AAC masonry units with a rubber mallet. Minor adjustments in unit position shall be made while the mortar is still soft and plastic by tapping it into the proper position. Minor sanding of the exposed faces of AAC masonry shall be permitted to provide a smooth and plumb surface.

2104.1.2.7 Grouted masonry. Between grout pours, a horizontal construction joint shall be formed by stopping all wythes at the same elevation and with the grout stopping a minimum of $1^1/_2$ inches (38 mm) below a mortar joint, except at the top of the wall. Where bond beams occur, the grout pour shall be stopped a mini-

mum of $^1/_2$ inch (12.7 mm) below the top of the masonry.

2104.1.3 Installation of wall ties. The ends of wall ties shall be embedded in mortar joints. Wall tie ends shall engage outer face shells of hollow units by at least $^1/_2$ inch (12.7 mm). Wire wall ties shall be embedded at least $1^1/_2$ inches (38 mm) into the mortar bed of solid masonry units or solid-grouted hollow units. Wall ties shall not be bent after being embedded in grout or mortar.

2104.1.4 Chases and recesses. Chases and recesses shall be constructed as masonry units are laid. Masonry directly above chases or recesses wider than 12 inches (305 mm) shall be supported on lintels.

2104.1.5 Lintels. The design for lintels shall be in accordance with the masonry design provisions of either Section 2107 or 2108. Minimum length of end support shall be 4 inches (102 mm).

2104.1.6 Support on wood. Masonry shall not be supported on wood girders or other forms of wood construction except as permitted in Section 2304.12.

2104.1.7 Masonry protection. The top of unfinished masonry work shall be covered to protect the masonry from the weather.

2104.1.8 Weep holes. Weep holes provided in the outside wythe of masonry walls shall be at a maximum spacing of 33 inches (838 mm) on center (o.c.). Weep holes shall not be less than $^3/_{16}$ inch (4.8 mm) in diameter.

2104.2 Corbeled masonry. Except for corbels designed per Section 2107 or 2108, the following shall apply:

1. Corbels shall be constructed of solid masonry units.

2. The maximum corbeled projection beyond the face of the wall shall not exceed:

    2.1. One-half of the wall thickness for multiwythe walls bonded by mortar or grout and wall ties or masonry headers or

    2.2. One-half the wythe thickness for single wythe walls, masonry bonded hollow walls, multiwythe walls with open collar joints and veneer walls.

3. The maximum projection of one unit shall not exceed:

    3.1. One-half the nominal unit height of the unit or

    3.2. One-third the nominal thickness of the unit or wythe.

4. The back surface of the corbelled section shall remain within 1 inch (25 mm) of plane.

2104.2.1 Molded cornices. Unless structural support and anchorage are provided to resist the overturning moment, the center of gravity of projecting masonry or molded cornices shall lie within the middle one-third of the supporting wall. Terra cotta and metal cornices shall be provided with a structural frame of approved noncombustible material anchored in an approved manner.

2104.3 Cold weather construction. The cold weather construction provisions of ACI 530.1/ASCE 6/TMS 602, Article 1.8 C, or the following procedures shall be implemented when either the ambient temperature falls below 40°F (4°C) or the temperature of masonry units is below 40°F (4°C).

2104.3.1 Preparation.

1. Temperatures of masonry units shall not be less than 20°F (-7°C) when laid in the masonry. Masonry units containing frozen moisture, visible ice or snow on their surface shall not be laid.

2. Visible ice and snow shall be removed from the top surface of existing foundations and masonry to receive new construction. These surfaces shall be heated to above freezing, using methods that do not result in damage.

2104.3.2 Construction. The following requirements shall apply to work in progress and shall be based on ambient temperature.

2104.3.2.1 Construction requirements for temperatures between 40°F (4°C) and 32°F (0°C). The following construction requirements shall be met when the ambient temperature is between 40°F (4°C) and 32°F (0°C):

1. Glass unit masonry shall not be laid.

2. Water and aggregates used in mortar and grout shall not be heated above 140°F (60°C).

3. Mortar sand or mixing water shall be heated to produce mortar temperatures between 40°F (4°C) and 120°F (49°C) at the time of mixing. When water and aggregates for grout are below 32°F(0°C), they shall be heated.

2104.3.2.2 Construction requirements for temperatures between 32°F (0°C) and 25°F (-4°C). The requirements of Section 2104.3.2.1 and the following construction requirements shall be met when the ambient temperature is between 32°F (0°C) and 25°F (-4°C):

1. The mortar temperature shall be maintained above freezing until used in masonry.

2. Aggregates and mixing water for grout shall be heated to produce grout temperature between 70°F (21°C) and 120°F (49°C) at the time of mixing. Grout temperature shall be maintained above 70°F (21°C) at the time of grout placement.

3. Heat AAC masonry units to a minimum temperature of 40°F (4°C) before installing thin-bed mortar.

2104.3.2.3 Construction requirements for temperatures between 25°F (-4°C) and 20°F (-7°C). The requirements of Sections 2104.3.2.1 and 2104.3.2.2 and the following construction requirements shall be met when the ambient temperature is between 25°F (-4°C) and 20°F (-7°C):

1. Masonry surfaces under construction shall be heated to 40°F (4°C).

2. Wind breaks or enclosures shall be provided when the wind velocity exceeds 15 miles per hour (mph) (24 km/h).

3. Prior to grouting, masonry shall be heated to a minimum of 40°F (4°C).

2104.3.2.4 Construction requirements for temperatures below 20°F (-7°C). The requirements of Sections 2104.3.2.1, 2104.3.2.2 and 2104.3.2.3 and the following construction requirement shall be met when the ambient temperature is below 20°F (-7°C): Enclosures and auxiliary heat shall be provided to maintain air temperature within the enclosure to above 32°F (0°C).

2104.3.3 Protection. The requirements of this section and Sections 2104.3.3.1 through 2104.3.3.5 apply after the masonry is placed and shall be based on anticipated minimum daily temperature for grouted masonry and anticipated mean daily temperature for ungrouted masonry.

2104.3.3.1 Glass unit masonry. The temperature of glass unit masonry shall be maintained above 40°F (4°C) for 48 hours after construction.

2104.3.3.2 AAC masonry. The temperature of AAC masonry shall be maintained above 32°F (0°C) for the first 4 hours after thin-bed mortar application.

2104.3.3.3 Protection requirements for temperatures between 40°F (4°C) and 25°F (-4°C). When the temperature is between 40°F (4°C) and 25°F (-4°C), newly constructed masonry shall be covered with a weather-resistive membrane for 24 hours after being completed.

2104.3.3.4 Protection requirements for temperatures between 25°F (-4°C) and 20°F (-7°C). When the temperature is between 25°F (-4°C) and 20°F (-7°C), newly constructed masonry shall be completely covered with weather-resistive insulating blankets, or equal protection, for 24 hours after being completed. The time period shall be extended to 48 hours for grouted masonry, unless the only cement in the grout is Type III portland cement.

2104.3.3.5 Protection requirements for temperatures below 20°F (-7°C). When the temperature is below 20°F (-7°C), newly constructed masonry shall be maintained at a temperature above 32°F (0°C) for at least 24 hours after being completed by using heated enclosures, electric heating blankets, infrared lamps or other acceptable methods. The time period shall be extended to 48 hours for grouted masonry, unless the only cement in the grout is Type III portland cement.

2104.4 Hot weather construction. The hot weather construction provisions of ACI 530.1/ASCE 6/TMS 602, Article 1.8 D, or the following procedures shall be implemented when the temperature or the temperature and wind-velocity limits of this section are exceeded.

2104.4.1 Preparation. The following requirements shall be met prior to conducting masonry work.

2104.4.1.1 Temperature. When the ambient temperature exceeds 100°F (38°C), or exceeds 90°F (32°C) with a wind velocity greater than 8 mph (3.5 m/s):

1. Necessary conditions and equipment shall be provided to produce mortar having a temperature below 120°F (49°C).

2. Sand piles shall be maintained in a damp, loose condition.

2104.4.1.2 Special conditions. When the ambient temperature exceeds 115°F (46°C), or 105°F (40°C) with a wind velocity greater than 8 mph (3.5 m/s), the requirements of Section 2104.4.1.1 shall be implemented, and materials and mixing equipment shall be shaded from direct sunlight.

2104.4.2 Construction. The following requirements shall be met while masonry work is in progress.

2104.4.2.1 Temperature. When the ambient temperature exceeds 100°F (38°C), or exceeds 90°F (32°C) with a wind velocity greater than 8 mph (3.5 m/s):

1. The temperature of mortar and grout shall be maintained below 120°F (49°C).

2. Mixers, mortar transport containers and mortar boards shall be flushed with cool water before they come into contact with mortar ingredients or mortar.

3. Mortar consistency shall be maintained by retempering with cool water.

4. Mortar shall be used within 2 hours of initial mixing.

5. Thin-bed mortar shall be spread no more than 4 feet (1219 mm) ahead of AAC masonry units.

6. AAC masonry units shall be placed within one minute after spreading thin-bed mortar.

2104.4.2.2 Special conditions. When the ambient temperature exceeds 115°F (46°C), or exceeds 105°F (40°C) with a wind velocity greater than 8 mph (3.5 m/s), the requirements of Section 2104.4.2.1 shall be implemented and cool mixing water shall be used for mortar and grout. The use of ice shall be permitted in the mixing water prior to use. Ice shall not be permitted in the mixing water when added to the other mortar or grout materials.

2104.4.3 Protection. When the mean daily temperature exceeds 100°F (38°C) or exceeds 90°F (32°C) with a wind velocity greater than 8 mph (3.5 m/s), newly constructed masonry shall be fog sprayed until damp at least three times a day until the masonry is three days old.

2104.5 Wetting of brick. Brick (clay or shale) at the time of laying shall require wetting if the unit's initial rate of water absorption exceeds 30 grams per 30 square inches (19 355 mm^2) per minute or 0.035 ounce per square inch (1 g/645 mm^2) per minute, as determined by ASTM C 67.

SECTION 2105
QUALITY ASSURANCE

2105.1 General. A quality assurance program shall be used to ensure that the constructed masonry is in compliance with the construction documents.

The quality assurance program shall comply with the inspection and testing requirements of Chapter 17.

2105.2 Acceptance relative to strength requirements.

2105.2.1 Compliance with f'_m and f'_{AAC}. Compressive strength of masonry shall be considered satisfactory if the compressive strength of each masonry wythe and grouted collar joint equals or exceeds the value of f'_m for clay and concrete masonry and f'_{AAC} for AAC masonry. For partially grouted clay and concrete masonry, the compressive strength of both the grouted and ungrouted masonry shall equal or exceed the applicable f'_m. At the time of prestress, the compressive strength of the masonry shall equal or exceed f'_{mi}, which shall be less than or equal to f'_m.

2105.2.2 Determination of compressive strength. The compressive strength for each wythe shall be determined by the unit strength method or by the prism test method as specified herein.

2105.2.2.1 Unit strength method.

2105.2.2.1.1 Clay masonry. The compressive strength of masonry shall be determined based on the strength of the units and the type of mortar specified using Table 2105.2.2.1.1, provided:

1. Units conform to ASTM C 62, ASTM C 216 or ASTM C 652 and are sampled and tested in accordance with ASTM C 67.

2. Thickness of bed joints does not exceed $^5/_8$ inch (15.9 mm).

3. For grouted masonry, the grout meets one of the following requirements:

    3.1. Grout conforms to ASTM C 476.

    3.2. Minimum grout compressive strength equals or exceeds f'_m but not less than 2,000 psi (13.79 MPa). The compressive strength of grout shall be determined in accordance with ASTM C 1019.

TABLE 2105.2.2.1.1
COMPRESSIVE STRENGTH OF CLAY MASONRY

NET AREA COMPRESSIVE STRENGTH OF CLAY MASONRY UNITS (psi)		NET AREA COMPRESSIVE STRENGTH OF MASONRY (psi)
Type M or S mortar	Type N mortar	
1,700	2,100	1,000
3,350	4,150	1,500
4,950	6,200	2,000
6,600	8,250	2,500
8,250	10,300	3,000
9,900	-	3,500
13,200	-	4,000

For SI: 1 pound per square inch = 0.00689 MPa.

2105.2.2.1.2 Concrete masonry. The compressive strength of masonry shall be determined based on the strength of the unit and type of mortar specified using Table 2105.2.2.1.2, provided:

1. Units conform to ASTM C 55 or ASTM C 90 and are sampled and tested in accordance with ASTM C 140.

2. Thickness of bed joints does not exceed $^5/_8$ inch (15.9 mm).

3. For grouted masonry, the grout meets one of the following requirements:

    3.1. Grout conforms to ASTM C 476.

    3.2. Minimum grout compressive strength equals or exceeds f'_m but not less than 2,000 psi (13.79 MPa). The compressive strength of grout shall be determined in accordance with ASTM C 1019.

TABLE 2105.2.2.1.2
COMPRESSIVE STRENGTH OF CONCRETE MASONRY

NET AREA COMPRESSIVE STRENGTH OF CONCRETE MASONRY UNITS (psi)		NET AREA COMPRESSIVE STRENGTH OF MASONRY (psi)[a]
Type M or S mortar	Type N mortar	
1,250	1,300	1,000
1,900	2,150	1,500
2,800	3,050	2,000
3,750	4,050	2,500
4,800	5,250	3,000

For SI: 1 inch = 25.4 mm, 1 pound per square inch = 0.00689 MPa.
a. For units less than 4 inches in height, 85 percent of the values listed.

2105.2.2.1.3 AAC masonry. The compressive strength of AAC masonry shall be based on the strength of the AAC masonry unit only and the following shall be met:

1. Units conform to ASTM C 1386.

2. Thickness of bed joints does not exceed $^1/_8$ inch (3.2 mm).

3. For grouted masonry, the grout meets one of the following requirements:

    3.1. Grout conforms to ASTM C 476.

    3.2. Minimum grout compressive strength equals or exceeds f'_{AAC} but not less than 2,000 psi (13.79 MPa). The compressive strength of grout shall be determined in accordance with ASTM C 1019.

2105.2.2.2 Prism test method.

2105.2.2.2.1 General. The compressive strength of clay and concrete masonry shall be determined by the prism test method:

1. Where specified in the construction documents.

2. Where masonry does not meet the requirements for application of the unit strength method in Section 2105.2.2.1.

2105.2.2.2.2 Number of prisms per test. A prism test shall consist of three prisms constructed and tested in accordance with ASTM C 1314.

2105.3 Testing prisms from constructed masonry. When approved by the building official, acceptance of masonry that does not meet the requirements of Section 2105.2.2.1 or 2105.2.2.2 shall be permitted to be based on tests of prisms cut from the masonry construction in accordance with Sections 2105.3.1, 2105.3.2 and 2105.3.3.

2105.3.1 Prism sampling and removal. A set of three masonry prisms that are at least 28 days old shall be saw cut from the masonry for each 5,000 square feet (465 m²) of the wall area that is in question but not less than one set of three masonry prisms for the project. The length, width and height dimensions of the prisms shall comply with the requirements of ASTM C 1314. Transporting, preparation and testing of prisms shall be in accordance with ASTM C 1314.

2105.3.2 Compressive strength calculations. The compressive strength of prisms shall be the value calculated in accordance ASTM C 1314, except that the net cross-sectional area of the prism shall be based on the net mortar bedded area.

2105.3.3 Compliance. Compliance with the requirement for the specified compressive strength of masonry, f'_m, shall be considered satisfied provided the modified compressive strength equals or exceeds the specified f'_m. Additional testing of specimens cut from locations in question shall be permitted.

SECTION 2106
SEISMIC DESIGN

2106.1 Seismic design requirements for masonry. Masonry structures and components shall comply with the requirements in Section 1.14.2.2 and Section 1.14.3, 1.14.4, 1.14.5, 1.14.6 or 1.14.7 of ACI 530/ASCE 5/TMS 402 depending on the structure's seismic design category as determined in Section 1613. All masonry walls, unless isolated on three edges from in-plane motion of the basic structural systems, shall be considered to be part of the seismic-force-resisting system. In addition, the following requirements shall be met.

2106.1.1 Basic seismic-force-resisting system. Buildings relying on masonry shear walls as part of the basic seismic-force-resisting system shall comply with Section 1.14.2.2 of ACI 530/ASCE 5/TMS 402 or with Section 2106.1.1.1, 2106.1.1.2 or 2106.1.1.3.

2106.1.1.1 Ordinary plain prestressed masonry shear walls. Ordinary plain prestressed masonry shear walls shall comply with the requirements of Chapter 4 of ACI 530/ASCE 5/TMS 402.

2106.1.1.2 Intermediate prestressed masonry shear walls. Intermediate prestressed masonry shear walls shall comply with the requirements of Section 1.14.2.2.4 of ACI 530/ASCE 5/TMS 402 and shall be designed by Chapter 4, Section 4.4.3, of ACI 530/ASCE 5/TMS 402 for flexural strength and by Section 3.3.4.1.2 of ACI 530/ASCE 5/TMS 402 for shear strength. Sections 1.14.2.2.5, 3.3.3.5 and 3.3.4.3.2(c) of ACI 530/ASCE 5/TMS 402 shall be applicable for reinforcement. Flexural elements subjected to load reversals shall be symmetrically reinforced. The nominal moment strength at any section along a member shall not be less than one-fourth the maximum moment strength. The cross-sectional area of bonded tendons shall be considered to contribute to the minimum reinforcement in Section 1.14.2.2.4 of ACI 530/ASCE 5/TMS 402. Tendons shall be located in cells that are grouted the full height of the wall.

2106.1.1.3 Special prestressed masonry shear walls. Special prestressed masonry shear walls shall comply with the requirements of Section 1.14.2.2.5 of ACI 530/ASCE 5/TMS 402 and shall be designed by Chapter 4, Section 4.4.3, of ACI 530/ASCE 5/TMS 402 for flexural strength and by Section 3.3.4.1.2 of ACI 530/ASCE 5/TMS 402 for shear strength. Sections 1.14.2.2.5(a), 3.3.3.5 and 3.3.4.3.2(c) of ACI 530/ASCE 5/TMS 402 shall be applicable for reinforcement. Flexural elements subjected to load reversals shall be symmetrically reinforced. The nominal moment strength at any section along a member shall not be less than one-fourth the maximum moment strength. The cross-sectional area of bonded tendons shall be considered to contribute to the minimum reinforcement in Section 1.14.2.2.5 of ACI 530/ASCE 5/TMS 402.

2106.1.1.3.1 Prestressing tendons. Prestressing tendons shall consist of bars conforming to ASTM A 722.

2106.1.1.3.2 Grouting. All cells of the masonry wall shall be grouted.

2106.2 Anchorage of masonry walls. Masonry walls shall be anchored to the roof and floors that provide lateral support for the wall in accordance with Section 1604.8.2.

2106.3 Seismic Design Category B. Structures assigned to Seismic Design Category B shall conform to the requirements of Section 1.14.4 of ACI 530/ASCE 5/TMS 402 and to the additional requirements of this section.

2106.3.1 Masonry walls not part of the lateral-force-resisting system. Masonry partition walls, masonry screen walls and other masonry elements that are not designed to resist vertical or lateral loads, other than those induced by their own mass, shall be isolated from the structure so that the vertical and lateral forces are not imparted to these elements. Isolation joints and connectors between these elements and the structure shall be designed to accommodate the design story drift.

2106.4 Additional requirements for structures in Seismic Design Category C. Structures assigned to Seismic Design Category C shall conform to the requirements of Section 2106.3, Section 1.14.5 of ACI 530/ASCE 5/TMS 402 and the additional requirements of this section.

2106.4.1 Design of discontinuous members that are part of the lateral-force-resisting system. Columns and pilasters that are part of the lateral-force-resisting system and that support reactions from discontinuous stiff members such as walls shall be provided with transverse reinforcement spaced at no more than one-fourth of the least nominal dimension of the column or pilaster. The minimum transverse reinforcement ratio shall be 0.0015. Beams supporting reactions from discontinuous walls or frames shall be provided with transverse reinforcement spaced at no more than one-half of the nominal depth of the beam. The minimum transverse reinforcement ratio shall be 0.0015.

2106.5 Additional requirements for structures in Seismic Design Category D. Structures assigned to Seismic Design Category D shall conform to the requirements of Section 2106.4, Section 1.14.6 of ACI 530/ASCE 5/TMS 402 and the additional requirements of this section.

2106.5.1 Loads for shear walls designed by the working stress design method. When calculating in-plane shear or diagonal tension stresses by the working stress design method, shear walls that resist seismic forces shall be designed to resist 1.5 times the seismic forces required by Chapter 16. The 1.5 multiplier need not be applied to the overturning moment.

2106.5.2 Shear wall shear strength. For a shear wall whose nominal shear strength exceeds the shear corresponding to development of its nominal flexural strength, two shear regions exist.

For all cross sections within a region defined by the base of the shear wall and a plane at a distance L_w above the base of the shear wall, the nominal shear strength shall be determined by Equation 21-1.

$$V_n = A_n \rho_n f_y \qquad \text{(Equation 21-1)}$$

The required shear strength for this region shall be calculated at a distance $L_w/2$ above the base of the shear wall, but not to exceed one-half story height.

For the other region, the nominal shear strength of the shear wall shall be determined from Section 2108.

2106.6 Additional requirements for structures in Seismic Design Category E or F. Structures assigned to Seismic Design Category E or F shall conform to the requirements of Section 2106.5 and Section 1.14.7 of ACI 530/ASCE 5/TMS 402.

SECTION 2107
ALLOWABLE STRESS DESIGN

2107.1 General. The design of masonry structures using allowable stress design shall comply with Section 2106 and the requirements of Chapters 1 and 2 of ACI 530/ASCE 5/TMS 402 except as modified by Sections 2107.2 through 2107.8.

2107.2 ACI 530/ASCE 5/TMS 402, Section 2.1.2, load combinations. Delete Section 2.1.2.1.

2107.3 ACI 530/ASCE 5/TMS 402, Section 2.1.3, design strength. Delete Sections 2.1.3.4 through 2.1.3.4.3.

2107.4 ACI 530/ASCE 5/TMS 402, Section 2.1.6, columns. Add the following text to Section 2.1.6:

2.1.6.6 Light-frame construction. Masonry columns used only to support light-frame roofs of carports, porches, sheds or similar structures with a maximum area of 450 square feet (41.8 m²) assigned to Seismic Design Category A, B or C are permitted to be designed and constructed as follows:

1. Concrete masonry materials shall be in accordance with Section 2103.1 of the *Building Code of New York State.* Clay or shale masonry units shall be in accordance with Section 2103.2 of the *Building Code of New York State.*

2. The nominal cross-sectional dimension of columns shall not be less than 8 inches (203 mm).

3. Columns shall be reinforced with not less than one No. 4 bar centered in each cell of the column.

4. Columns shall be grouted solid.

5. Columns shall not exceed 12 feet (3658 mm) in height.

6. Roofs shall be anchored to the columns. Such anchorage shall be capable of resisting the design loads specified in Chapter 16 of the *Building Code of New York State.*

7. Where such columns are required to resist uplift loads, the columns shall be anchored to their footings with two No. 4 bars extending a minimum of 24 inches (610 mm) into the columns and bent horizontally a minimum of 15 inches (381 mm) in opposite directions into the footings. One of these bars is permitted to be the reinforcing bar specified in Item 3 above. The total weight of a column and its footing shall not be less than 1.5 times the design uplift load.

2107.5 ACI 530/ASCE 5/TMS 402, Section 2.1.10.7.1.1, lap splices. Modify Section 2.1.10.7.1.1 as follows:

2.1.10.7.1.1 The minimum length of lap splices for reinforcing bars in tension or compression, l_d, shall be

$$l_d = 0.002 d_b f_s \qquad \text{(Equation 21-2)}$$

For SI: $l_d = 0.29 d_b f_s$

but not less than 12 inches (305 mm). In no case shall the length of the lapped splice be less than 40 bar diameters.

where:

d_b = Diameter of reinforcement, inches (mm).

f_s = Computed stress in reinforcement due to design loads, psi (MPa).

In regions of moment where the design tensile stresses in the reinforcement are greater than 80 percent of the allowable steel tension stress, F_s, the lap length of splices shall be increased not less than 50 percent of the minimum required length. Other equivalent means of stress transfer to accomplish the same 50 percent increase shall be permitted.

Where epoxy coated bars are used, lap length shall be increased by 50 percent.

2107.6 ACI 530/ASCE 5/TMS 402, Section 2.1.10.7, splices of reinforcement. Modify **Section 2.1.10.7 as follows:**

2.1.10.7 Splices of reinforcement. Lap splices, welded splices or mechanical splices are permitted in accordance with the provisions of this section. All welding shall conform to AWS D1.4. Reinforcement larger than No. 9 (M #29) shall be spliced using mechanical connections in accordance with Section 2.1.10.7.3.

2107.7 ACI 530/ASCE 5/TMS 402, Section 2.3.6, maximum bar size. Add the following to Chapter 2:

2.3.6 Maximum bar size. The bar diameter shall not exceed one-eighth of the nominal wall thickness and shall not exceed one-quarter of the least dimension of the cell, course or collar joint in which it is placed.

2107.8 ACI 530/ASCE 5/TMS 402, Section 2.3.7, maximum reinforcement percentage. Add the following text to Chapter 2:

2.3.7 Maximum reinforcement percentage. Special reinforced masonry shear walls having a shear span ratio, M/Vd, equal to or greater than 1.0 and having an axial load, P, greater than $0.05 f'_m A_n$ that are subjected to in-plane forces shall have a maximum reinforcement ratio, ρ_{max}, not greater than that computed as follows:

$$\rho_{max} = \frac{n f'_m}{2 f y \left(n + \dfrac{f_y}{f'_m} \right)} \qquad \text{(Equation 21-3)}$$

The maximum reinforcement ratio does not apply in the out-of-plane direction.

SECTION 2108
STRENGTH DESIGN OF MASONRY

2108.1 General. The design of masonry structures using strength design shall comply with Section 2106 and the requirements of Chapters 1 and 3 of ACI 530/ASCE 5/TMS 402, except as modified by Sections 2108.2 through 2108.4.

Exception: AAC masonry shall comply with the requirements of Chapter 1 and Appendix A of ACI 530/ASCE 5/TMS 402.

2108.2 ACI 530/ASCE 5/TMS 402, Section 3.3.3.3 development. Add the following text to Section 3.3.3.3:

The required development length of reinforcement shall be determined by Equation (3-15), but shall not be less than 12 inches (305 mm) and need not be greater than 72 d_b.

2108.3 ACI 530/ASCE 5/TMS 402, Section 3.3.3.4, splices. Modify items (b) and (c) of Section 3.3.3.4 as follows:

3.3.3.4 (b). A welded splice shall have the bars butted and welded to develop at least 125 percent of the yield strength, f_y, of the bar in tension or compression, as required. Welded splices shall be of ASTM A 706 steel reinforcement. Welded splices shall not be permitted in plastic hinge zones of intermediate or special reinforced walls or special moment frames of masonry.

3.3.3.4 (c). Mechanical splices shall be classified as Type 1 or 2 according to Section 21.2.6.1 of ACI 318. Type 1 mechanical splices shall not be used within a plastic hinge zone or within a beam-column joint of intermediate or special reinforced masonry shear walls or special moment frames. Type 2 mechanical splices are permitted in any location within a member.

2108.4 ACI 530/ASCE 5/TMS 402, Section 3.3.3.5, maximum areas of flexural tensile reinforcement. Add the following text to Section 3.3.3.5:

3.3.3.5.5 For special prestressed masonry shear walls, strain in all prestressing steel shall be computed to be compatible with a strain in the extreme tension reinforcement equal to five times the strain associated with the reinforcement yield stress, f_y. The calculation of the maximum reinforcement shall consider forces in the prestressing steel that correspond to these calculated strains.

SECTION 2109
EMPIRICAL DESIGN OF MASONRY

2109.1 General. Empirically designed masonry shall conform to this chapter or Chapter 5 of ACI 530/ASCE 5/TMS 402.

2109.1.1 Limitations. The use of empirical design of masonry shall be limited as follows:

1. Empirical design shall not be used for buildings assigned to Seismic Design Category D, E or F as specified in Section 1613, nor for the design of the seismic-force-resisting system for buildings assigned to Seismic Design Category B or C.

2. Empirical design shall not be used for masonry elements that are part of the lateral-force-resisting system where the basic wind speed exceeds 110 mph (48 m/s).

3. Empirical design shall not be used for interior masonry elements that are not part of the lateral-force-resisting system in buildings other than enclosed buildings as defined in Chapter 6 of ASCE 7 in:

   3.1. Buildings over 180 feet (55 100 mm) in height.

   3.2. Buildings over 60 feet (18 400 mm) in height where the basic wind speed exceeds 90 mph (40 m/s).

   3.3. Buildings over 35 feet (10 700 mm) in height where the basic wind speed exceeds 100 mph (45 m/s).

   3.4. Where the basic wind speed exceeds 110 mph (48 m/s).

4. Empirical design shall not be used for exterior masonry elements that are not part of the lateral-force-resisting system and that are more than 35 feet (10 700 mm) above ground:

   4.1. Buildings over 180 feet (55 100 mm) in height.

   4.2. Buildings over 60 feet (18 400 mm) in height where the basic wind speed exceeds 90 mph (40 m/s).

   4.3. Buildings over 35 feet (10 700 mm) in height where the basic wind speed exceeds 100 mph (45 m/s).

5. Empirical design shall not be used for exterior masonry elements that are less than or equal to 35 feet (10 700 mm) above ground where the basic wind speed exceeds 110 mph (79 m/s).

6. Empirical design shall only be used when the resultant of gravity loads is within the center third of the wall thickness and within the central area bounded by lines at one-third of each cross-sectional dimension of foundation piers.

7. Empirical design shall not be used for AAC masonry.

In buildings that exceed one or more of the above limitations, masonry shall be designed in accordance with the engineered design provisions of Section 2107 or 2108 or the foundation wall provisions of Section 1805.5.

2109.2 Lateral stability.

2109.2.1 Shear walls. Where the structure depends upon masonry walls for lateral stability, shear walls shall be provided parallel to the direction of the lateral forces resisted.

2109.2.1.1 Cumulative length of shear walls. In each direction in which shear walls are required for lateral stability, shear walls shall be positioned in two separate planes. The minimum cumulative length of shear walls provided shall be 0.4 times the long dimension of the building. Cumulative length of shear walls shall not include openings or any element with a length that is less than one-half its height.

2109.2.1.2 Maximum diaphragm ratio. Masonry shear walls shall be spaced so that the length-to-width ratio of each diaphragm transferring lateral forces to the shear walls does not exceed the values given in Table 2109.2.1.2.

TABLE 2109.2.1.2
DIAPHRAGM LENGTH-TO-WIDTH RATIOS

FLOOR OR ROOF DIAPHRAGM CONSTRUCTION	MAXIMUM LENGTH-TO-WIDTH RATIO OF DIAPHRAGM PANEL
Cast-in-place concrete	5:1
Precast concrete	4:1
Metal deck with concrete fill	3:1
Metal deck with no fill	2:1
Wood	2:1

2109.2.2 Roofs. The roof construction shall be designed so as not to impart out-of-plane lateral thrust to the walls under roof gravity load.

2109.2.3 Surface-bonded walls. Dry-stacked, surface-bonded concrete masonry walls shall comply with the requirements of this code for masonry wall construction, except where otherwise noted in this section.

2109.2.3.1 Strength. Dry-stacked, surface-bonded concrete masonry walls shall be of adequate strength and proportions to support all superimposed loads without exceeding the allowable stresses listed in Table 2109.2.3.1. Allowable stresses not specified in Table 2109.2.3.1 shall comply with the requirements of ACI 530/ASCE 5/TMS 402.

TABLE 2109.2.3.1
ALLOWABLE STRESS GROSS CROSS-SECTIONAL AREA FOR DRY-STACKED, SURFACE-BONDED CONCRETE MASONRY WALLS

DESCRIPTION	MAXIMUM ALLOWABLE STRESS (psi)
Compression standard block	45
Flexural tension	
Horizontal span	30
Vertical span	18
Shear	10

For SI:1 pound per square inch = 0.006895 MPa.

2109.2.3.2 Construction. Construction of dry-stacked, surface-bonded masonry walls, including stacking and leveling of units, mixing and application of mortar and curing and protection shall comply with ASTM C 946.

2109.3 Compressive stress requirements.

2109.3.1 Calculations. Compressive stresses in masonry due to vertical dead plus live loads, excluding wind or seismic loads, shall be determined in accordance with Section 2109.3.2.1. Dead and live loads shall be in accordance with Chapter 16, with live load reductions as permitted in Section 1607.9.

2109.3.2 Allowable compressive stresses. The compressive stresses in masonry shall not exceed the values given in Table 2109.3.2. Stress shall be calculated based on specified rather than nominal dimensions.

2109.3.2.1 Calculated compressive stresses. Calculated compressive stresses for single wythe walls and for multiwythe composite masonry walls shall be determined by dividing the design load by the gross cross-sectional area of the member. The area of openings, chases or recesses in walls shall not be included in the gross cross-sectional area of the wall.

2109.3.2.2 Multiwythe walls. The allowable stress shall be as given in Table 2109.3.2 for the weakest combination of the units used in each wythe.

2109.4 Lateral support.

2109.4.1 Intervals. Masonry walls shall be laterally supported in either the horizontal or vertical direction at intervals not exceeding those given in Table 2109.4.1.

TABLE 2109.4.1
WALL LATERAL SUPPORT REQUIREMENTS

CONSTRUCTION	MAXIMUM WALL LENGTH TO THICKNESS OR WALL HEIGHT TO THICKNESS
Bearing walls	
Solid units or fully grouted	20
All others	18
Nonbearing walls	
Exterior	18
Interior	36

2109.4.2 Thickness. Except for cavity walls and cantilever walls, the thickness of a wall shall be its nominal thickness measured perpendicular to the face of the wall. For cavity walls, the thickness shall be determined as the sum of the nominal thicknesses of the individual wythes. For cantilever walls, except for parapets, the ratio of height-to-nominal thickness shall not exceed 6 for solid masonry or 4 for hollow masonry. For parapets, see Section 2109.5.4.

2109.4.3 Support elements. Lateral support shall be provided by cross walls, pilasters, buttresses or structural frame members when the limiting distance is taken horizontally, or by floors, roofs acting as diaphragms or structural frame members when the limiting distance is taken vertically.

2109.5 Thickness of masonry. Minimum thickness requirements shall be based on nominal dimensions of masonry.

2109.5.1 Thickness of walls. The thickness of masonry walls shall conform to the requirements of Section 2109.5.

2109.5.2 Minimum thickness.

2109.5.2.1 Bearing walls. The minimum thickness of masonry bearing walls more than one story high shall be 8 inches (203 mm). Bearing walls of one-story buildings shall not be less than 6 inches (152 mm) thick.

2109.5.2.2 Rubble stone walls. The minimum thickness of rough, random or coursed rubble stone walls shall be 16 inches (406 mm).

2109.5.2.3 Shear walls. The minimum thickness of masonry shear walls shall be 8 inches (203 mm).

2109.5.2.4 Foundation walls. The minimum thickness of foundation walls shall be 8 inches (203 mm) and as required by Section 2109.5.3.1.

2109.5.2.5 Foundation piers. The minimum thickness of foundation piers shall be 8 inches (203 mm).

2109.5.2.6 Parapet walls. The minimum thickness of parapet walls shall be 8 inches (203 mm) and as required by Section 2109.5.4.1.

2109.5.2.7 Change in thickness. Where walls of masonry of hollow units or masonry bonded hollow walls are decreased in thickness, a course or courses of solid masonry shall be interposed between the wall below and the thinner wall above, or special units or construction shall be used to transmit the loads from face shells or wythes above to those below.

TABLE 2109.3.2
ALLOWABLE COMPRESSIVE STRESSES FOR EMPIRICAL DESIGN OF MASONRY

CONSTRUCTION; COMPRESSIVE STRENGTH OF UNIT GROSS AREA (psi)	ALLOWABLE COMPRESSIVE STRESSES[a] GROSS CROSS-SECTIONAL AREA (psi)	
	Type M or S mortar	Type N mortar
Solid masonry of brick and other solid units of clay or shale; sand-lime or concrete brick:		
8,000 or greater	350	300
4,500	225	200
2,500	160	140
1,500	115	100
Grouted masonry, of clay or shale; sand-lime or concrete:		
4,500 or greater	225	200
2,500	160	140
1,500	115	100
Solid masonry of solid concrete masonry units:		
3,000 or greater	225	200
2,000	160	140
1,200	115	100
Masonry of hollow load-bearing units:		
2,000 or greater	140	120
1,500	115	100
1,000	75	70
700	60	55
Hollow walls (noncomposite masonry bonded)[b] Solid units:		
2,500 or greater	160	140
1,500	115	100
Hollow units	75	70
Stone ashlar masonry:		
Granite	720	640
Limestone or marble	450	400
Sandstone or cast stone	360	320
Rubble stone masonry Coursed, rough or random	120	100

For SI: 1 pound per square inch = 0.006895 MPa.

a. Linear interpolation for determining allowable stresses for masonry units having compressive strengths which are intermediate between those given in the table is permitted.

b. Where floor and roof loads are carried upon one wythe, the gross cross-sectional area is that of the wythe under load; if both wythes are loaded, the gross cross-sectional area is that of the wall minus the area of the cavity between the wythes. Walls bonded with metal ties shall be considered as noncomposite walls unless collar joints are filled with mortar or grout.

2109.5.3 Foundation walls. Foundation walls shall comply with the requirements of Section 2109.5.3.1 or 2109.5.3.2.

2109.5.3.1 Minimum thickness. Minimum thickness for foundation walls shall comply with the requirements of Table 2109.5.3.1. The provisions of Table 2109.5.3.1 are only applicable where the following conditions are met:

1. The foundation wall does not exceed 8 feet (2438 mm) in height between lateral supports;

2. The terrain surrounding foundation walls is graded to drain surface water away from foundation walls;

3. Backfill is drained to remove ground water away from foundation walls;

4. Lateral support is provided at the top of foundation walls prior to backfilling;

5. The length of foundation walls between perpendicular masonry walls or pilasters is a maximum of three times the basement wall height;

6. The backfill is granular and soil conditions in the area are nonexpansive; and

7. Masonry is laid in running bond using Type M or S mortar.

2109.5.3.2 Design requirements. Where the requirements of Section 2109.5.3.1 are not met, foundation walls shall be designed in accordance with Section 1805.5.

2109.5.4 Parapet walls.

2109.5.4.1 Minimum thickness. The minimum thickness of unreinforced masonry parapets shall meet Section 2109.5.2.6 and their height shall not exceed three times their thickness.

TABLE 2109.5.3.1
FOUNDATION WALL CONSTRUCTION

WALL CONSTRUCTION	NOMINAL WALL THICKNESS (inches)	MAXIMUM DEPTH OF UNBALANCED BACKFILL (feet)
Fully grouted masonry	8	7
	10	8
	12	8
Hollow unit masonry	8	5
	10	6
	12	7
Solid unit masonry	8	5
	10	7
	12	7

For SI: 1 inch = 25.4 mm, 1 foot = 304.8 mm.

2109.5.4.2 Additional provisions. Additional provisions for parapet walls are contained in Sections 1503.2 and 1503.3.

2109.6 Bond.

2109.6.1 General. The facing and backing of multiwythe masonry walls shall be bonded in accordance with Section 2109.6.2, 2109.6.3 or 2109.6.4.

2109.6.2 Bonding with masonry headers.

2109.6.2.1 Solid units. Where the facing and backing (adjacent wythes) of solid masonry construction are bonded by means of masonry headers, no less than 4 percent of the wall surface of each face shall be composed of headers extending not less than 3 inches (76 mm) into the backing. The distance between adjacent full-length headers shall not exceed 24 inches (610 mm) either vertically or horizontally. In walls in which a single header does not extend through the wall, headers from the opposite sides shall overlap at least 3 inches (76 mm), or headers from opposite sides shall be covered with another header course overlapping the header below at least 3 inches (76 mm).

2109.6.2.2 Hollow units. Where two or more hollow units are used to make up the thickness of a wall, the stretcher courses shall be bonded at vertical intervals not exceeding 34 inches (864 mm) by lapping at least 3 inches (76 mm) over the unit below, or by lapping at vertical intervals not exceeding 17 inches (432 mm) with units that are at least 50 percent greater in thickness than the units below.

2109.6.2.3 Masonry bonded hollow walls. In masonry bonded hollow walls, the facing and backing shall be bonded so that not less than 4 percent of the wall surface of each face is composed of masonry bonded units extending not less than 3 inches (76 mm) into the backing. The distance between adjacent bonders shall not exceed 24 inches (610 mm) either vertically or horizontally.

2109.6.3 Bonding with wall ties or joint reinforcement.

2109.6.3.1 Bonding with wall ties. Except as required by Section 2109.6.3.1.1, where the facing and backing (adjacent wythes) of masonry walls are bonded with wire size W2.8 (MW18) wall ties or metal wire of equivalent stiffness embedded in the horizontal mortar joints, there shall be at least one metal tie for each $4^1/_2$ square feet (0.42 m²) of wall area. The maximum vertical distance between ties shall not exceed 24 inches (610 mm), and the maximum horizontal distance shall not exceed 36 inches (914 mm). Rods or ties bent to rectangular shape shall be used with hollow masonry units laid with the cells vertical. In other walls, the ends of ties shall be bent to 90-degree (1.57 rad) angles to provide hooks no less than 2 inches (51 mm) long. Wall ties shall be without drips. Additional bonding ties shall be provided at all openings, spaced not more than 36 inches (914 mm) apart around the perimeter and within 12 inches (305 mm) of the opening.

2109.6.3.1.1 Bonding with adjustable wall ties. Where the facing and backing (adjacent wythes) of masonry are bonded with adjustable wall ties, there shall be at least one tie for each 1.77 square feet (0.164 m²) of wall area. Neither the vertical nor horizontal spacing of the adjustable wall ties shall exceed 16 inches (406 mm). The maximum vertical offset of bed joints from one wythe to the other shall be $1^1/_4$ inches (32 mm). The maximum clearance between connecting parts of the ties shall be $^1/_{16}$ inch (1.6 mm). When pintle legs are used, ties shall have at least two wire size W2.8 (MW18) legs.

2109.6.3.2 Bonding with prefabricated joint reinforcement. Where the facing and backing (adjacent wythes) of masonry are bonded with prefabricated joint reinforcement, there shall be at least one cross wire serving as a tie for each $2^2/_3$ square feet (0.25 m²) of wall area. The vertical spacing of the joint reinforcing shall not exceed 24 inches (610 mm). Cross wires on prefabricated joint reinforcement shall not be less than W1.7 (MW11) and shall be without drips. The longitudinal wires shall be embedded in the mortar.

2109.6.4 Bonding with natural or cast stone.

2109.6.4.1 Ashlar masonry. In ashlar masonry, bonder units, uniformly distributed, shall be provided to the extent of not less than 10 percent of the wall area. Such bonder units shall extend not less than 4 inches (102 mm) into the backing wall.

2109.6.4.2 Rubble stone masonry. Rubble stone masonry 24 inches (610 mm) or less in thickness shall have bonder units with a maximum spacing of 36 inches (914 mm) vertically and 36 inches (914 mm) horizontally, and if the masonry is of greater thickness than 24 inches (610 mm), shall have one bonder unit for each 6 square feet (0.56 m²) of wall surface on both sides.

2109.6.5 Masonry bonding pattern.

2109.6.5.1 Masonry laid in running bond. Each wythe of masonry shall be laid in running bond, head joints in successive courses shall be offset by not less than one-fourth the unit length or the masonry walls shall be reinforced longitudinally as required in Section 2109.6.5.2.

2109.6.5.2 Masonry laid in stack bond. Where unit masonry is laid with less head joint offset than in Section 2109.6.5.1, the minimum area of horizontal reinforcement placed in mortar bed joints or in bond beams spaced not more than 48 inches (1219 mm) apart, shall be 0.0003 times the vertical cross-sectional area of the wall.

2109.7 Anchorage.

2109.7.1 General. Masonry elements shall be anchored in accordance with Sections 2109.7.2 through 2109.7.4.

2109.7.2 Intersecting walls. Masonry walls depending upon one another for lateral support shall be anchored or bonded at locations where they meet or intersect by one of the methods indicated in Sections 2109.7.2.1 through 2109.7.2.5.

2109.7.2.1 Bonding pattern. Fifty percent of the units at the intersection shall be laid in an overlapping masonry bonding pattern, with alternate units having a bearing of not less than 3 inches (76 mm) on the unit below.

2109.7.2.2 Steel connectors. Walls shall be anchored by steel connectors having a minimum section of $^1/_4$ inch (6.4 mm) by $1^1/_2$ inches (38 mm), with ends bent up at least 2 inches (51 mm) or with cross pins to form anchorage. Such anchors shall be at least 24 inches (610 mm) long and the maximum spacing shall be 48 inches (1219 mm).

2109.7.2.3 Joint reinforcement. Walls shall be anchored by joint reinforcement spaced at a maximum distance of 8 inches (203 mm). Longitudinal wires of such reinforcement shall be at least wire size W1.7 (MW 11) and shall extend at least 30 inches (762 mm) in each direction at the intersection.

2109.7.2.4 Interior nonload-bearing walls. Interior nonload-bearing walls shall be anchored at their intersection, at vertical intervals of not more than 16 inches (406 mm) with joint reinforcement or $^1/_4$-inch (6.4 mm) mesh galvanized hardware cloth.

2109.7.2.5 Ties, joint reinforcement or anchors. Other metal ties, joint reinforcement or anchors, if used, shall be spaced to provide equivalent area of anchorage to that required by this section.

2109.7.3 Floor and roof anchorage. Floor and roof diaphragms providing lateral support to masonry shall comply with the live loads in Section 1607.3 and shall be connected to the masonry in accordance with Sections 2109.7.3.1 through 2109.7.3.3. Roof loading shall be determined in accordance with Chapter 16 and, when net uplift occurs, uplift shall be resisted entirely by an anchorage system designed in accordance with the provisions of Sections 2.1 and 2.3, Sections 3.1 and 3.3 or Chapter 4 of ACI 530/ASCE 5/TMS 402.

2109.7.3.1 Wood floor joists. Wood floor joists bearing on masonry walls shall be anchored to the wall at intervals not to exceed 72 inches (1829 mm) by metal strap anchors. Joists parallel to the wall shall be anchored with metal straps spaced not more than 72 inches (1829 mm) o.c. extending over or under and secured to at least three joists. Blocking shall be provided between joists at each strap anchor.

2109.7.3.2 Steel floor joists. Steel floor joists bearing on masonry walls shall be anchored to the wall with $^3/_8$-inch (9.5 mm) round bars, or their equivalent, spaced not more than 72 inches (1829 mm) o.c. Where joists are parallel to the wall, anchors shall be located at joist bridging.

2109.7.3.3 Roof diaphragms. Roof diaphragms shall be anchored to masonry walls with $^1/_2$-inch-diameter (12.7 mm) bolts, 72 inches (1829 mm) o.c. or their equivalent. Bolts shall extend and be embedded at least 15 inches (381 mm) into the masonry, or be hooked or welded to not less than 0.20 square inch (129 mm²) of bond beam reinforcement placed not less than 6 inches (152 mm) from the top of the wall.

2109.7.4 Walls adjoining structural framing. Where walls are dependent upon the structural frame for lateral support, they shall be anchored to the structural members with metal anchors or otherwise keyed to the structural members. Metal anchors shall consist of $^1/_2$-inch (12.7 mm) bolts spaced at 48 inches (1219 mm) o.c. embedded 4 inches (102 mm) into the masonry, or their equivalent area.

2109.8 Adobe construction. Adobe construction shall comply with this section and shall be subject to the requirements of this code for Type V construction.

2109.8.1 Unstabilized adobe.

2109.8.1.1 Compressive strength. Adobe units shall have an average compressive strength of 300 psi (2068 kPa) when tested in accordance with ASTM C 67. Five samples shall be tested and no individual unit is permitted to have a compressive strength of less than 250 psi (1724 kPa).

2109.8.1.2 Modulus of rupture. Adobe units shall have an average modulus of rupture of 50 psi (345 kPa) when tested in accordance with the following procedure. Five samples shall be tested and no individual unit shall have a modulus of rupture of less than 35 psi (241 kPa).

2109.8.1.2.1 Support conditions. A cured unit shall be simply supported by 2-inch-diameter (51 mm) cylindrical supports located 2 inches (51 mm) in from each end and extending the full width of the unit.

2109.8.1.2.2 Loading conditions. A 2-inch-diameter (51 mm) cylinder shall be placed at midspan parallel to the supports.

2109.8.1.2.3 Testing procedure. A vertical load shall be applied to the cylinder at the rate of 500 pounds per minute (37 N/s) until failure occurs.

2109.8.1.2.4 Modulus of rupture determination. The modulus of rupture shall be determined by the equation:

$$f_r = 3WL_s/2bt^2 \qquad \text{(Equation 21-4)}$$

where, for the purposes of this section only:

b = Width of the test specimen measured parallel to the loading cylinder, inches (mm).

f_r = Modulus of rupture, psi (MPa).

L_s = Distance between supports, inches (mm).

t = Thickness of the test specimen measured parallel to the direction of load, inches (mm).

W = The applied load at failure, pounds (N).

2109.8.1.3 Moisture content requirements. Adobe units shall have a moisture content not exceeding 4 percent by weight.

2109.8.1.4 Shrinkage cracks. Adobe units shall not contain more than three shrinkage cracks and any single shrinkage crack shall not exceed 3 inches (76 mm) in length or $1/_8$ inch (3.2 mm) in width.

2109.8.2 Stabilized adobe.

2109.8.2.1 Material requirements. Stabilized adobe shall comply with the material requirements of unstabilized adobe in addition to Sections 2109.8.2.1.1 and 2109.8.2.1.2.

2109.8.2.1.1 Soil requirements. Soil used for stabilized adobe units shall be chemically compatible with the stabilizing material.

2109.8.2.1.2 Absorption requirements. A 4-inch (102 mm) cube, cut from a stabilized adobe unit dried to a constant weight in a ventilated oven at 212°F to 239°F (100°C to 115°C), shall not absorb more than $2^1/_2$ percent moisture by weight when placed upon a constantly water-saturated, porous surface for seven days. A minimum of five specimens shall be tested and each specimen shall be cut from a separate unit.

2109.8.3 Allowable stress. The allowable compressive stress based on gross cross-sectional area of adobe shall not exceed 30 psi (207 kPa).

2109.8.3.1 Bolts. Bolt values shall not exceed those set forth in Table 2109.8.3.1.

TABLE 2109.8.3.1
ALLOWABLE SHEAR ON BOLTS IN ADOBE MASONRY

DIAMETER OF BOLTS (inches)	MINIMUM EMBEDMENT (inches)	SHEAR (pounds)
$1/_2$	-	-
$5/_8$	12	200
$3/_4$	15	300
$7/_8$	18	400
1	21	500
$1^1/_8$	24	600

For SI: 1 inch = 25.4 mm, 1 pound = 4.448 N.

2109.8.4 Construction.

2109.8.4.1 General.

2109.8.4.1.1 Height restrictions. Adobe construction shall be limited to buildings not exceeding one story, except that two-story construction is allowed when designed by a registered design professional.

2109.8.4.1.2 Mortar restrictions. Mortar for stabilized adobe units shall comply with Chapter 21 or adobe soil. Adobe soil used as mortar shall comply with material requirements for stabilized adobe. Mortar for unstabilized adobe shall be portland cement mortar.

2109.8.4.1.3 Mortar joints. Adobe units shall be laid with full head and bed joints and in full running bond.

2109.8.4.1.4 Parapet walls. Parapet walls constructed of adobe units shall be waterproofed.

2109.8.4.2 Wall thickness. The minimum thickness of exterior walls in one-story buildings shall be 10 inches (254 mm). The walls shall be laterally supported at intervals not exceeding 24 feet (7315 mm). The minimum thickness of interior load-bearing walls shall be 8 inches (203 mm). In no case shall the unsupported height of any wall constructed of adobe units exceed 10 times the thickness of such wall.

2109.8.4.3 Foundations.

2109.8.4.3.1 Foundation support. Walls and partitions constructed of adobe units shall be supported by foundations or footings that extend not less than 6 inches (152 mm) above adjacent ground surfaces and are constructed of solid masonry (excluding adobe) or concrete. Footings and foundations shall comply with Chapter 18.

2109.8.4.3.2 Lower course requirements. Stabilized adobe units shall be used in adobe walls for the first 4 inches (102 mm) above the finished first-floor elevation.

2109.8.4.4 Isolated piers or columns. Adobe units shall not be used for isolated piers or columns in a load-bearing capacity. Walls less than 24 inches (610 mm) in length shall be considered isolated piers or columns.

2109.8.4.5 Tie beams. Exterior walls and interior load-bearing walls constructed of adobe units shall have a continuous tie beam at the level of the floor or roof bearing and meeting the following requirements.

2109.8.4.5.1 Concrete tie beams. Concrete tie beams shall be a minimum depth of 6 inches (152 mm) and a minimum width of 10 inches (254 mm). Concrete tie beams shall be continuously reinforced with a minimum of two No. 4 reinforcing bars. The ultimate compressive strength of concrete shall be at least 2,500 psi (17.2 MPa) at 28 days.

2109.8.4.5.2 Wood tie beams. Wood tie beams shall be solid or built up of lumber having a minimum nominal thickness of 1 inch (25 mm), and shall have a minimum depth of 6 inches (152 mm) and a minimum width of 10 inches (254 mm). Joints in wood tie beams shall be spliced a minimum of 6 inches (152 mm). No splices shall be allowed within 12 inches (305 mm) of an opening. Wood used in tie beams shall be approved naturally decay-resistant or pressure-treated wood.

2109.8.4.6 Exterior finish. Exterior walls constructed of unstabilized adobe units shall have their exterior surface covered with a minimum of two coats of portland cement plaster having a minimum thickness of $^3/_4$ inch (19.1 mm) and conforming to ASTM C 926. Lathing shall comply with ASTM C 1063. Fasteners shall be spaced at 16 inches (406 mm) o.c. maximum. Exposed wood surfaces shall be treated with an approved wood preservative or other protective coating prior to lath application.

2109.8.4.7 Lintels. Lintels shall be considered structural members and shall be designed in accordance with the applicable provisions of Chapter 16.

SECTION 2110
GLASS UNIT MASONRY

2110.1 Scope. This section covers the empirical requirements for nonload-bearing glass unit masonry elements in exterior or interior walls.

2110.1.1 Limitations. Solid or hollow approved glass block shall not be used in fire walls, party walls, fire barriers or fire partitions, or for load-bearing construction. Such blocks shall be erected with mortar and reinforcement in metal channel-type frames, structural frames, masonry or concrete recesses, embedded panel anchors as provided for both exterior and interior walls or other approved joint materials. Wood strip framing shall not be used in walls required to have a fire-resistance rating by other provisions of this code.

Exceptions:

1. Glass-block assemblies having a fire protection rating of not less than $^3/_4$ hour shall be permitted as opening protectives in accordance with Section 715 in fire barriers and fire partitions that have a required fire-resistance rating of 1 hour or less and do not enclose exit stairways or exit passageways.

2. Glass-block assemblies as permitted in Section 404.5, Exception 2.

2110.2 Units. Hollow or solid glass-block units shall be standard or thin units.

2110.2.1 Standard units. The specified thickness of standard units shall be at least 3 $^7/_8$ inches (98 mm).

2110.2.2 Thin units. The specified thickness of thin units shall be $3^1/_8$ inches (79 mm) for hollow units or 3 inches (76 mm) for solid units.

2110.3 Panel size.

2110.3.1 Exterior standard-unit panels. The maximum area of each individual exterior standard-unit panel shall be 144 square feet (13.4 m²) when the design wind pressure is 20 psf (958 N/m²). The maximum panel dimension between structural supports shall be 25 feet (7620 mm) in width or 20 feet (6096 mm) in height. The panel areas are permitted to be adjusted in accordance with Figure 2110.3.1 for other wind pressures.

For SI: 1 square foot = 0.0929 m², 1 pound per square foot = 47.9 N/m².

FIGURE 2110.3.1
GLASS MASONRY DESIGN WIND LOAD RESISTANCE

2110.3.2 Exterior thin-unit panels. The maximum area of each individual exterior thin-unit panel shall be 85 square feet (7.9 m²). The maximum dimension between structural supports shall be 15 feet (4572 mm) in width or 10 feet (3048 mm) in height. Thin units shall not be used in applications where the design wind pressure exceeds 20 psf (958 N/m²).

2110.3.3 Interior panels. The maximum area of each individual standard-unit panel shall be 250 square feet (23.2 m²). The maximum area of each thin-unit panel shall be 150 square feet (13.9 m²). The maximum dimension between structural supports shall be 25 feet (7620 mm) in width or 20 feet (6096 mm) in height.

2110.3.4 Solid units. The maximum area of solid glass-block wall panels in both exterior and interior walls shall not be more than 100 square feet (9.3 m²).

2110.3.5 Curved panels. The width of curved panels shall conform to the requirements of Sections 2110.3.1, 2110.3.2 and 2110.3.3, except additional structural supports shall be provided at locations where a curved section joins a straight section, and at inflection points in multi-curved walls.

2110.4 Support.

2110.4.1 General requirements. Glass unit masonry panels shall be isolated so that in-plane loads are not imparted to the panel.

2110.4.2 Vertical. Maximum total deflection of structural members supporting glass unit masonry shall not exceed $^1/_{600}$.

2110.4.2.1 Support on wood construction. Glass unit masonry having an installed weight of 40 psf (195 kg/m²) or less and a maximum height of 12 feet (3658 mm) shall be permitted to be supported on wood construction.

2110.4.2.2 Expansion joint. A vertical expansion joint in glass unit masonry shall be provided to isolate the glass unit masonry supported by wood construction from that supported by other types of construction.

2110.4.3 Lateral. Glass unit masonry panels more than one unit wide or one unit high shall be laterally supported along their tops and sides. Lateral support shall be provided by panel anchors along the top and sides spaced not more than 16 inches (406 mm) o.c. or by channel-type restraints. Glass unit masonry panels shall be recessed at least 1 inch (25 mm) within channels and chases. Channel-type restraints shall be oversized to accommodate expansion material in the opening and packing and sealant between the framing restraints and the glass unit masonry perimeter units. Lateral supports for glass unit masonry panels shall be designed to resist applied loads, or a minimum of 200 pounds per lineal feet (plf) (2919 N/m) of panel, whichever is greater.

Exceptions:

1. Lateral support at the top of glass unit masonry panels that are no more than one unit wide shall not be required.

2. Lateral support at the sides of glass unit masonry panels that are no more than one unit high shall not be required.

2110.4.3.1 Single unit panels. Single unit glass unit masonry panels shall conform to the requirements of Section 2110.4.3, except lateral support shall not be provided by panel anchors.

2110.5 Expansion joints. Glass unit masonry panels shall be provided with expansion joints along the top and sides at structural supports. Expansion joints shall have sufficient thickness to accommodate displacements of the supporting structure, but shall not be less than $^3/_8$ inch (9.5 mm) in thickness. Expansion joints shall be entirely free of mortar or other debris and shall be filled with resilient material. The sills of glass-block panels shall be coated with approved water-based asphaltic emulsion, or other elastic waterproofing material, prior to laying the first mortar course.

2110.6 Mortar. Mortar for glass unit masonry shall comply with Section 2103.8.

2110.7 Reinforcement. Glass unit masonry panels shall have horizontal joint reinforcement spaced not more than 16 inches (406 mm) on center, located in the mortar bed joint, and extending the entire length of the panel but not across expansion joints. Longitudinal wires shall be lapped a minimum of 6 inches (152 mm) at splices. Joint reinforcement shall be placed in the bed joint immediately below and above openings in the panel. The reinforcement shall have not less than two parallel longitudinal wires of size W1.7 (MW11), and have welded cross wires of size W1.7 (MW11).

SECTION 2111
MASONRY FIREPLACES

2111.1 Definition. A masonry fireplace is a fireplace constructed of concrete or masonry. Masonry fireplaces shall be constructed in accordance with this section.

2111.2 Footings and foundations. Footings for masonry fireplaces and their chimneys shall be constructed of concrete or solid masonry at least 12 inches (305 mm) thick and shall extend at least 6 inches (153 mm) beyond the face of the fireplace or foundation wall on all sides. Footings shall be founded on natural undisturbed earth or engineered fill below frost depth. In areas not subjected to freezing, footings shall be at least 12 inches (305 mm) below finished grade.

2111.2.1 Ash dump cleanout. Cleanout openings, located within foundation walls below fireboxes, when provided, shall be equipped with ferrous metal or masonry doors and frames constructed to remain tightly closed, except when in use. Cleanouts shall be accessible and located so that ash removal will not create a hazard to combustible materials.

2111.3 Seismic reinforcing. Masonry or concrete fireplaces shall be constructed, anchored, supported and reinforced as required in this chapter. In Seismic Design Category D, masonry and concrete fireplaces shall be reinforced and anchored as detailed in Sections 2111.3.1, 2111.3.2, 2111.4 and 2111.4.1 for chimneys serving fireplaces. In Seismic Design Category A, B or C, reinforcement and seismic anchorage is not required. In Seismic Design Category E or F, masonry and concrete chimneys shall be reinforced in accordance with the requirements of Sections 2101 through 2108.

2111.3.1 Vertical reinforcing. For fireplaces with chimneys up to 40 inches (1016 mm) wide, four No. 4 continuous vertical bars, anchored in the foundation, shall be placed in the concrete between wythes of solid masonry or within the cells of hollow unit masonry and grouted in accordance with Section 2103.12. For fireplaces with chimneys greater than 40 inches (1016 mm) wide, two additional No. 4 vertical bars shall be provided for each additional 40 inches (1016 mm) in width or fraction thereof.

2111.3.2 Horizontal reinforcing. Vertical reinforcement shall be placed enclosed within $^1/_4$-inch (6.4 mm) ties or other reinforcing of equivalent net cross-sectional area, spaced not to exceed 18 inches (457 mm) on center in concrete; or placed in the bed joints of unit masonry at a minimum of every 18 inches (457 mm) of vertical height. Two such ties shall be provided at each bend in the vertical bars.

2111.4 Seismic anchorage. Masonry and concrete chimneys in Seismic Design Category D shall be anchored at each floor, ceiling or roof line more than 6 feet (1829 mm) above grade, except where constructed completely within the exterior walls. Anchorage shall conform to the following requirements.

2111.4.1 Anchorage. Two $^3/_{16}$-inch by 1-inch (4.8 mm by 25.4 mm) straps shall be embedded a minimum of 12 inches (305 mm) into the chimney. Straps shall be hooked around the outer bars and extend 6 inches (152 mm) beyond the bend. Each strap shall be fastened to a minimum of four floor joists with two $^1/_2$-inch (12.7 mm) bolts.

2111.5 Firebox walls. Masonry fireboxes shall be constructed of solid masonry units, hollow masonry units grouted solid, stone or concrete. When a lining of firebrick at least 2 inches (51 mm) in thickness or other approved lining is provided, the minimum thickness of back and sidewalls shall each be 8 inches (203 mm) of solid masonry, including the lining. The width of joints between firebricks shall not be greater than $^1/_4$ inch (6.4 mm). When no lining is provided, the total minimum thickness of back and sidewalls shall be 10 inches (254 mm) of solid masonry. Firebrick shall conform to ASTM C 27 or ASTM C 1261 and shall be laid with medium-duty refractory mortar conforming to ASTM C 199.

2111.5.1 Steel fireplace units. Steel fireplace units are permitted to be installed with solid masonry to form a masonry fireplace provided they are installed according to either the requirements of their listing or the requirements of this section. Steel fireplace units incorporating a steel firebox lining shall be constructed with steel not less than $^1/_4$ inch (6.4 mm) in thickness, and an air-circulating chamber which is ducted to the interior of the building. The firebox lining shall be encased with solid masonry to provide a total thickness at the back and sides of not less than 8 inches (203 mm), of which not less than 4 inches (102 mm) shall be of solid masonry or concrete. Circulat-

ing air ducts employed with steel fireplace units shall be constructed of metal or masonry.

2111.6 Firebox dimensions. The firebox of a concrete or masonry fireplace shall have a minimum depth of 20 inches (508 mm). The throat shall not be less than 8 inches (203 mm) above the fireplace opening. The throat opening shall not be less than 4 inches (102 mm) in depth. The cross-sectional area of the passageway above the firebox, including the throat, damper and smoke chamber, shall not be less than the cross-sectional area of the flue.

Exception: Rumford fireplaces shall be permitted provided that the depth of the fireplace is at least 12 inches (305 mm) and at least one-third of the width of the fireplace opening, and the throat is at least 12 inches (305 mm) above the lintel, and at least $^1/_{20}$ the cross-sectional area of the fireplace opening.

2111.7 Lintel and throat. Masonry over a fireplace opening shall be supported by a lintel of noncombustible material. The minimum required bearing length on each end of the fireplace opening shall be 4 inches (102 mm). The fireplace throat or damper shall be located a minimum of 8 inches (203 mm) above the top of the fireplace opening.

2111.7.1 Damper. Masonry fireplaces shall be equipped with a ferrous metal damper located at least 8 inches (203 mm) above the top of the fireplace opening. Dampers shall be installed in the fireplace or at the top of the flue venting the fireplace, and shall be operable from the room containing the fireplace. Damper controls shall be permitted to be located in the fireplace.

2111.8 Smoke chamber walls. Smoke chamber walls shall be constructed of solid masonry units, hollow masonry units grouted solid, stone or concrete. Corbeling of masonry units shall not leave unit cores exposed to the inside of the smoke chamber. The inside surface of corbeled masonry shall be parged smooth. Where no lining is provided, the total minimum thickness of front, back and sidewalls shall be 8 inches (203 mm) of solid masonry. When a lining of firebrick at least 2 inches (51 mm) thick, or a lining of vitrified clay at least $^5/_8$ inch (15.9 mm) thick, is provided, the total minimum thickness of front, back and sidewalls shall be 6 inches (152 mm) of solid masonry, including the lining. Firebrick shall conform to ASTM C 27 or ASTM C 1261 and shall be laid with refractory mortar conforming to ASTM C 199.

2111.8.1 Smoke chamber dimensions. The inside height of the smoke chamber from the fireplace throat to the beginning of the flue shall not be greater than the inside width of the fireplace opening. The inside surface of the smoke chamber shall not be inclined more than 45 degrees (0.76 rad) from vertical when prefabricated smoke chamber linings are used or when the smoke chamber walls are rolled or sloped rather than corbeled. When the inside surface of the smoke chamber is formed by corbeled masonry, the walls shall not be corbeled more than 30 degrees (0.52 rad) from vertical.

2111.9 Hearth and hearth extension. Masonry fireplace hearths and hearth extensions shall be constructed of concrete or masonry, supported by noncombustible materials, and reinforced to carry their own weight and all imposed loads.

No combustible material shall remain against the underside of hearths or hearth extensions after construction.

2111.9.1 Hearth thickness. The minimum thickness of fireplace hearths shall be 4 inches (102 mm).

2111.9.2 Hearth extension thickness. The minimum thickness of hearth extensions shall be 2 inches (51 mm).

Exception: When the bottom of the firebox opening is raised at least 8 inches (203 mm) above the top of the hearth extension, a hearth extension of not less than $^3/_8$-inch-thick (9.5 mm) brick, concrete, stone, tile or other approved noncombustible material is permitted.

2111.10 Hearth extension dimensions. Hearth extensions shall extend at least 16 inches (406 mm) in front of, and at least 8 inches (203 mm) beyond, each side of the fireplace opening. Where the fireplace opening is 6 square feet (0.557 m²) or larger, the hearth extension shall extend at least 20 inches (508 mm) in front of, and at least 12 inches (305 mm) beyond, each side of the fireplace opening.

2111.11 Fireplace clearance. Any portion of a masonry fireplace located in the interior of a building or within the exterior wall of a building shall have a clearance to combustibles of not less than 2 inches (51 mm) from the front faces and sides of masonry fireplaces and not less than 4 inches (102 mm) from the back faces of masonry fireplaces. The airspace shall not be filled, except to provide fireblocking in accordance with Section 2111.12.

Exceptions:

1. Masonry fireplaces listed and labeled for use in contact with combustibles in accordance with UL 127 and installed in accordance with the manufacturer's installation instructions are permitted to have combustible material in contact with their exterior surfaces.

2. When masonry fireplaces are constructed as part of masonry or concrete walls, combustible materials shall not be in contact with the masonry or concrete walls less than 12 inches (306 mm) from the inside surface of the nearest firebox lining.

3. Exposed combustible trim and the edges of sheathing materials, such as wood siding, flooring and drywall, are permitted to abut the masonry fireplace sidewalls and hearth extension, in accordance with Figure 2111.11, provided such combustible trim or sheathing is a minimum of 12 inches (306 mm) from the inside surface of the nearest firebox lining.

4. Exposed combustible mantels or trim is permitted to be placed directly on the masonry fireplace front surrounding the fireplace opening, provided such combustible materials shall not be placed within 6 inches (153 mm) of a fireplace opening. Combustible material directly above and within 12 inches (305 mm) of the fireplace opening shall not project more than $^1/_8$ inch (3.2 mm) for each 1-inch (25 mm) distance from such opening. Combustible materials located along the sides of the fireplace opening that project more than $1^1/_2$ inches (38 mm) from the face

of the fireplace shall have an additional clearance equal to the projection.

For SI: 1 inch = 25.4 mm

FIGURE 2111.11
ILLUSTRATION OF EXCEPTION TO FIREPLACE
CLEARANCE PROVISION

2111.12 Fireplace fireblocking. All spaces between fireplaces and floors and ceilings through which fireplaces pass shall be fireblocked with noncombustible material securely fastened in place. The fireblocking of spaces between wood joists, beams or headers shall be to a depth of 1 inch (25 mm) and shall only be placed on strips of metal or metal lath laid across the spaces between combustible material and the chimney.

2111.13 Exterior air. Factory-built or masonry fireplaces covered in this section shall be equipped with an exterior air supply to ensure proper fuel combustion unless the room is mechanically ventilated and controlled so that the indoor pressure is neutral or positive.

2111.13.1 Factory-built fireplaces. Exterior combustion air ducts for factory-built fireplaces shall be listed components of the fireplace, and installed according to the fireplace manufacturer's instructions.

2111.13.2 Masonry fireplaces. Listed combustion air ducts for masonry fireplaces shall be installed according to the terms of their listing and manufacturer's instructions.

2111.13.3 Exterior air intake. The exterior air intake shall be capable of providing all combustion air from the exterior of the dwelling. The exterior air intake shall not be located within the garage, attic, basement or crawl space of the dwelling nor shall the air intake be located at an elevation higher than the firebox. The exterior air intake shall be covered with a corrosion-resistant screen of $^1/_4$-inch (6.4 mm) mesh.

2111.13.4 Clearance. Unlisted combustion air ducts shall be installed with a minimum 1-inch (25 mm) clearance to combustibles for all parts of the duct within 5 feet (1524 mm) of the duct outlet.

2111.13.5 Passageway. The combustion air passageway shall be a minimum of 6 square inches (3870 mm²) and not more than 55 square inches (0.035 m²), except that combustion air systems for listed fireplaces or for fireplaces tested for emissions shall be constructed according to the fireplace manufacturer's instructions.

2111.13.6 Outlet. The exterior air outlet is permitted to be located in the back or sides of the firebox chamber or within 24 inches (610 mm) of the firebox opening on or near the floor. The outlet shall be closable and designed to prevent burning material from dropping into concealed combustible spaces.

SECTION 2112
MASONRY HEATERS

2112.1 Definition. A masonry heater is a heating appliance constructed of concrete or solid masonry, hereinafter referred to as "masonry," which is designed to absorb and store heat from a solid fuel fire built in the firebox by routing the exhaust gases through internal heat exchange channels in which the flow path downstream of the firebox may include flow in a horizontal or downward direction before entering the chimney and which delivers heat by radiation from the masonry surface of the heater.

2112.2 Installation. Masonry heaters shall be installed in accordance with this section and comply with one of the following:

1. Masonry heaters shall comply with the requirements of ASTM E 1602; or

2. Masonry heaters shall be listed and labeled in accordance with UL 1482 and installed in accordance with the manufacturer's installation instructions.

2112.3 Footings and foundation. The firebox floor of a masonry heater shall be a minimum thickness of 4 inches (102 mm) of noncombustible material and be supported on a noncombustible footing and foundation in accordance with Section 2113.2.

2112.4 Seismic reinforcing. In Seismic Design Category D, E and F, masonry heaters shall be anchored to the masonry foundation in accordance with Section 2113.3. Seismic reinforcing shall not be required within the body of a masonry heater with a height that is equal to or less than 3.5 times its body width and where the masonry chimney serving the heater is not supported by the body of the heater. Where the masonry chimney shares a common wall with the facing of the masonry heater, the chimney portion of the structure shall be reinforced in accordance with Section 2113.

2112.5 Masonry heater clearance. Combustible materials shall not be placed within 36 inches (765 mm) of the outside surface of a masonry heater in accordance with NFPA 211, Section 8-7 (clearances for solid fuel-burning appliances), and the required space between the heater and combustible material shall be fully vented to permit the free flow of air around all heater surfaces.

Exceptions:

1. When the masonry heater wall thickness is at least 8 inches (203 mm) thick of solid masonry and the wall thickness of the heat exchange channels is at least 5 inches (127 mm) thick of solid masonry, combustible materials shall not be placed within 4 inches (102 mm) of the outside surface of a masonry heater. A clearance of at least 8 inches (203 mm) shall be provided between the gas-tight capping slab of the heater and a combustible ceiling.

2. Masonry heaters listed and labeled in accordance with UL 1482 and installed in accordance with the manufacturer's instructions.

SECTION 2113
MASONRY CHIMNEYS

2113.1 Definition. A masonry chimney is a chimney constructed of concrete or masonry, hereinafter referred to as "masonry." Masonry chimneys shall be constructed, anchored, supported and reinforced as required in this chapter.

2113.2 Footings and foundations. Footings for masonry chimneys shall be constructed of concrete or solid masonry at least 12 inches (305 mm) thick and shall extend at least 6 inches (152 mm) beyond the face of the foundation or support wall on all sides. Footings shall be founded on natural undisturbed earth or engineered fill below frost depth. In areas not subjected to freezing, footings shall be at least 12 inches (305 mm) below finished grade.

2113.3 Seismic reinforcing. Masonry or concrete chimneys shall be constructed, anchored, supported and reinforced as required in this chapter. In Seismic Design Category D, masonry and concrete chimneys shall be reinforced and anchored as detailed in Sections 2113.3.1, 2113.3.2 and 2113.4. In Seismic Design Category A, B or C, reinforcement and seismic anchorage is not required. In Seismic Design Category E or F, masonry and concrete chimneys shall be reinforced in accordance with the requirements of Sections 2101 through 2108.

2113.3.1 Vertical reinforcing. For chimneys up to 40 inches (1016 mm) wide, four No. 4 continuous vertical bars anchored in the foundation shall be placed in the concrete between wythes of solid masonry or within the cells of hollow unit masonry and grouted in accordance with Section 2103.12. Grout shall be prevented from bonding with the flue liner so that the flue liner is free to move with thermal expansion. For chimneys greater than 40 inches (1016 mm) wide, two additional No. 4 vertical bars shall be provided for each additional 40 inches (1016 mm) in width or fraction thereof.

2113.3.2 Horizontal reinforcing. Vertical reinforcement shall be placed enclosed within $^1/_4$-inch (6.4 mm) ties, or other reinforcing of equivalent net cross-sectional area, spaced not to exceed 18 inches (457 mm) o.c. in concrete, or placed in the bed joints of unit masonry, at a minimum of every 18 inches (457 mm) of vertical height. Two such ties shall be provided at each bend in the vertical bars.

2113.4 Seismic anchorage. Masonry and concrete chimneys and foundations in Seismic Design Category D shall be anchored at each floor, ceiling or roof line more than 6 feet (1829 mm) above grade, except where constructed completely within the exterior walls. Anchorage shall conform to the following requirements.

2113.4.1 Anchorage. Two $^3/_{16}$-inch by 1-inch (4.8 mm by 25 mm) straps shall be embedded a minimum of 12 inches (305 mm) into the chimney. Straps shall be hooked around the outer bars and extend 6 inches (152 mm) beyond the bend. Each strap shall be fastened to a minimum of four floor joists with two $^1/_2$-inch (12.7 mm) bolts.

2113.5 Corbeling. Masonry chimneys shall not be corbeled more than half of the chimney's wall thickness from a wall or foundation, nor shall a chimney be corbeled from a wall or foundation that is less than 12 inches (305 mm) in thickness unless it projects equally on each side of the wall, except that on the second story of a two-story dwelling, corbeling of chimneys on the exterior of the enclosing walls is permitted to equal the wall thickness. The projection of a single course shall not exceed one-half the unit height or one-third of the unit bed depth, whichever is less.

2113.6 Changes in dimension. The chimney wall or chimney flue lining shall not change in size or shape within 6 inches (152 mm) above or below where the chimney passes through floor components, ceiling components or roof components.

2113.7 Offsets. Where a masonry chimney is constructed with a fireclay flue liner surrounded by one wythe of masonry, the maximum offset shall be such that the centerline of the flue above the offset does not extend beyond the center of the chimney wall below the offset. Where the chimney offset is supported by masonry below the offset in an approved manner, the maximum offset limitations shall not apply. Each individual corbeled masonry course of the offset shall not exceed the projection limitations specified in Section 2113.5.

2113.8 Additional load. Chimneys shall not support loads other than their own weight unless they are designed and constructed to support the additional load. Masonry chimneys are permitted to be constructed as part of the masonry walls or concrete walls of the building.

2113.9 Termination. Chimneys shall extend at least 2 feet (610 mm) higher than any portion of the building within 10 feet (3048 mm), but shall not be less than 3 feet (914 mm) above the highest point where the chimney passes through the roof.

2113.9.1 Spark arrestors. Where a spark arrestor is installed on a masonry chimney, the spark arrestor shall meet all of the following requirements:

1. The net free area of the arrestor shall not be less than four times the net free area of the outlet of the chimney flue it serves.

2. The arrestor screen shall have heat and corrosion resistance equivalent to 19-gage galvanized steel or 24-gage stainless steel.

3. Openings shall not permit the passage of spheres having a diameter greater than $^1/_2$ inch (13 mm) nor block the passage of spheres having a diameter less than $^3/_8$ inch (11 mm).

4. The spark arrestor shall be accessible for cleaning and the screen or chimney cap shall be removable to allow for cleaning of the chimney flue.

2113.10 Wall thickness. Masonry chimney walls shall be constructed of concrete, solid masonry units or hollow masonry units grouted solid with not less than 4 inches (102 mm) nominal thickness.

2113.10.1 Masonry veneer chimneys. Where masonry is used as veneer for a framed chimney, through flashing and weep holes shall be provided as required by Chapter 14.

2113.11 Flue lining (material). Masonry chimneys shall be lined. The lining material shall be appropriate for the type of appliance connected, according to the terms of the appliance listing and the manufacturer's instructions.

2113.11.1 Residential-type appliances (general). Flue lining systems shall comply with one of the following:

1. Clay flue lining complying with the requirements of ASTM C 315, or equivalent.

2. Listed chimney lining systems complying with UL 1777.

3. Factory-built chimneys or chimney units listed for installation within masonry chimneys.

4. Other approved materials that will resist corrosion, erosion, softening or cracking from flue gases and condensate at temperatures up to 1,800°F (982°C).

2113.11.1.1 Flue linings for specific appliances. Flue linings other than those covered in Section 2113.11.1 intended for use with specific appliances shall comply with Sections 2113.11.1.2 through 2113.11.1.4 and Sections 2113.11.2 and 2113.11.3.

2113.11.1.2 Gas appliances. Flue lining systems for gas appliances shall be in accordance with the *Fuel Gas Code of New York State*.

2113.11.1.3 Pellet fuel-burning appliances. Flue lining and vent systems for use in masonry chimneys with pellet fuel-burning appliances shall be limited to flue lining systems complying with Section 2113.11.1 and pellet vents listed for installation within masonry chimneys (see Section 2113.11.1.5 for marking).

2113.11.1.4 Oil-fired appliances approved for use with L-vent. Flue lining and vent systems for use in masonry chimneys with oil-fired appliances approved for use with Type L vent shall be limited to flue lining systems complying with Section 2113.11.1 and listed chimney liners complying with UL 641 (see Section 2113.11.1.5 for marking).

2113.11.1.5 Notice of usage. When a flue is relined with a material not complying with Section 2113.11.1, the chimney shall be plainly and permanently identified by a label attached to a wall, ceiling or other conspicuous location adjacent to where the connector enters the chimney. The label shall include the following message or equivalent language: "This chimney is for use only with (type or category of appliance) that burns (type of fuel). Do not connect other types of appliances."

2113.11.2 Concrete and masonry chimneys for medium-heat appliances.

2113.11.2.1 General. Concrete and masonry chimneys for medium-heat appliances shall comply with Sections 2113.1 through 2113.5.

2113.11.2.2 Construction. Chimneys for medium-heat appliances shall be constructed of solid masonry units or of concrete with walls a minimum of 8 inches (203 mm) thick, or with stone masonry a minimum of 12 inches (305 mm) thick.

2113.11.2.3 Lining. Concrete and masonry chimneys shall be lined with an approved medium-duty refractory brick a minimum of $4^1/_2$ inches (114 mm) thick laid on the $4^1/_2$-inch bed (114 mm) in an approved medium-duty refractory mortar. The lining shall start 2 feet (610 mm) or more below the lowest chimney connector entrance. Chimneys terminating 25 feet (7620 mm) or less above a chimney connector entrance shall be lined to the top.

2113.11.2.4 Multiple passageway. Concrete and masonry chimneys containing more than one passageway shall have the liners separated by a minimum 4-inch-thick (102 mm) concrete or solid masonry wall.

2113.11.2.5 Termination height. Concrete and masonry chimneys for medium-heat appliances shall extend a minimum of 10 feet (3048 mm) higher than any portion of any building within 25 feet (7620 mm).

2113.11.2.6 Clearance. A minimum clearance of 4 inches (102 mm) shall be provided between the exterior surfaces of a concrete or masonry chimney for medium-heat appliances and combustible material.

2113.11.3 Concrete and masonry chimneys for high-heat appliances.

2113.11.3.1 General. Concrete and masonry chimneys for high-heat appliances shall comply with Sections 2113.1 through 2113.5.

2113.11.3.2 Construction. Chimneys for high-heat appliances shall be constructed with double walls of solid masonry units or of concrete, each wall to be a minimum of 8 inches (203 mm) thick with a minimum airspace of 2 inches (51 mm) between the walls.

2113.11.3.3 Lining. The inside of the interior wall shall be lined with an approved high-duty refractory brick, a minimum of $4^1/_2$ inches (114 mm) thick laid on the $4^1/_2$-inch bed (114 mm) in an approved high-duty refractory mortar. The lining shall start at the base of the chimney and extend continuously to the top.

2113.11.3.4 Termination height. Concrete and masonry chimneys for high-heat appliances shall extend a minimum of 20 feet (6096 mm) higher than any portion of any building within 50 feet (15 240 mm).

2113.11.3.5 Clearance. Concrete and masonry chimneys for high-heat appliances shall have approved clearance from buildings and structures to prevent overheating combustible materials, permit inspection and maintenance operations on the chimney and prevent danger of burns to persons.

2113.12 Clay flue lining (installation). Clay flue liners shall be installed in accordance with ASTM C 1283 and extend from a point not less than 8 inches (203 mm) below the lowest inlet or, in the case of fireplaces, from the top of the smoke chamber to a point above the enclosing walls. The lining shall be carried up vertically, with a maximum slope no greater than 30 degrees (0.52 rad) from the vertical.

Clay flue liners shall be laid in medium-duty refractory mortar conforming to ASTM C 199 with tight mortar joints left smooth on the inside and installed to maintain an air space or insulation not to exceed the thickness of the flue liner separating the flue liners from the interior face of the chimney masonry walls. Flue lining shall be supported on all sides. Only enough mortar shall be placed to make the joint and hold the liners in position.

2113.13 Additional requirements.

2113.13.1 Listed materials. Listed materials used as flue linings shall be installed in accordance with the terms of their listings and the manufacturer's instructions.

2113.13.2 Space around lining. The space surrounding a chimney lining system or vent installed within a masonry chimney shall not be used to vent any other appliance.

Exception: This shall not prevent the installation of a separate flue lining in accordance with the manufacturer's instructions.

2113.14 Multiple flues. When two or more flues are located in the same chimney, masonry wythes shall be built between adjacent flue linings. The masonry wythes shall be at least 4 inches (102 mm) thick and bonded into the walls of the chimney.

Exception: When venting only one appliance, two flues are permitted to adjoin each other in the same chimney with only the flue lining separation between them. The joints of the adjacent flue linings shall be staggered at least 4 inches (102 mm).

2113.15 Flue area (appliance). Chimney flues shall not be smaller in area than the area of the connector from the appliance. Chimney flues connected to more than one appliance shall not be less than the area of the largest connector plus 50 percent of the areas of additional chimney connectors.

Exceptions:

1. Chimney flues serving oil-fired appliances sized in accordance with NFPA 31.

2. Chimney flues serving gas-fired appliances sized in accordance with the *Fuel Gas Code of New York State*.

2113.16 Flue area (masonry fireplace). Flue sizing for chimneys serving fireplaces shall be in accordance with Section 2113.16.1 or 2113.16.2.

2113.16.1 Minimum area. Round chimney flues shall have a minimum net cross-sectional area of at least $^1/_{12}$ of the fireplace opening. Square chimney flues shall have a minimum net cross-sectional area of at least $^1/_{10}$ of the fireplace opening. Rectangular chimney flues with an aspect ratio less than 2 to 1 shall have a minimum net cross-sectional area of at least $^{1}/_{10}$ of the fireplace opening. Rectangular chimney flues with an aspect ratio of 2 to 1 or more shall have a minimum net cross-sectional area of at least $^{1}/_{8}$ of the fireplace opening.

TABLE 2113.16(1)
NET CROSS-SECTIONAL AREA OF ROUND FLUE SIZES[a]

FLUE SIZE, INSIDE DIAMETER (inches)	CROSS-SECTIONAL AREA (square inches)
6	28
7	38
8	50
10	78
10 $^{3}/_{4}$	90
12	113
15	176
18	254

For SI: 1 inch = 25.4 mm, 1 square inch = 645.16 mm^2.
a. Flue sizes are based on ASTM C 315.

TABLE 2113.16(2)
NET CROSS-SECTIONAL AREA OF SQUARE AND RECTANGULAR FLUE SIZES

FLUE SIZE, OUTSIDE NOMINAL DIMENSIONS (inches)	CROSS-SECTIONAL AREA (square inches)
4.5 × 8.5	23
4.5 × 13	34
8 × 8	42
8.5 × 8.5	49
8 × 12	67
8.5 × 13	76
12 × 12	102
8.5 × 18	101
13 × 13	127
12 × 16	131
13 × 18	173
16 × 16	181
16 × 20	222
18 × 18	233
20 × 20	298
20 × 24	335
24 × 24	431

For SI: 1 inch = 25.4 mm, 1 square inch = 645.16 mm^2.

2113.16.2 Determination of minimum area. The minimum net cross-sectional area of the flue shall be determined in accordance with Figure 2113.16. A flue size providing at least the equivalent net cross-sectional area shall be used. Cross-sectional areas of clay flue linings are as provided in Tables 2113.16(1) and 2113.16(2) or as provided by the manufacturer or as measured in the field. The height of the chimney shall be measured from the firebox floor to the top of the chimney flue.

2113.17 Inlet. Inlets to masonry chimneys shall enter from the side. Inlets shall have a thimble of fireclay, rigid refractory material or metal that will prevent the connector from pulling out of the inlet or from extending beyond the wall of the liner.

2113.18 Masonry chimney cleanout openings. Cleanout openings shall be provided within 6 inches (152 mm) of the base of each flue within every masonry chimney. The upper edge of the cleanout shall be located at least 6 inches (152 mm) below the lowest chimney inlet opening. The height of the opening shall be at least 6 inches (152 mm). The cleanout shall be provided with a noncombustible cover.

> **Exception:** Chimney flues serving masonry fireplaces, where cleaning is possible through the fireplace opening.

2113.19 Chimney clearances. Any portion of a masonry chimney located in the interior of the building or within the exterior wall of the building shall have a minimum airspace clearance to combustibles of 2 inches (51 mm). Chimneys located entirely outside the exterior walls of the building, including chimneys that pass through the soffit or cornice, shall have a minimum airspace clearance of 1 inch (25 mm). The airspace shall not be filled, except to provide fireblocking in accordance with Section 2113.20.

> **Exceptions:**
>
> 1. Masonry chimneys equipped with a chimney lining system listed and labeled for use in chimneys in contact with combustibles in accordance with UL 1777, and installed in accordance with the manufacturer's instructions, are permitted to have combustible material in contact with their exterior surfaces.
>
> 2. Where masonry chimneys are constructed as part of masonry or concrete walls, combustible materials shall not be in contact with the masonry or concrete wall less than 12 inches (305 mm) from the inside surface of the nearest flue lining.
>
> 3. Exposed combustible trim and the edges of sheathing materials, such as wood siding, are permitted to abut the masonry chimney sidewalls, in accordance with Figure 2113.19, provided such combustible trim or sheathing is a minimum of 12 inches (305 mm) from the inside surface of the nearest flue lining. Combustible material and trim shall not overlap the corners of the chimney by more than 1 inch (25 mm).

2113.20 Chimney fireblocking. All spaces between chimneys and floors and ceilings through which chimneys pass shall be fireblocked with noncombustible material securely fastened in place. The fireblocking of spaces between wood joists, beams or headers shall be to a depth of 1 inch (25 mm) and shall only be placed on strips of metal or metal lath laid across the spaces between combustible material and the chimney.

For SI: 1 inch = 25.4 mm, 1 square inch = 645 mm².

FIGURE 2113.16
FLUE SIZES FOR MASONRY CHIMNEYS

For SI: 1 inch = 25.4 mm.

FIGURE 2113.19
ILLUSTRATION OF EXCEPTION THREE CHIMNEY CLEARANCE PROVISION

CHAPTER 22

STEEL

SECTION 2201
GENERAL

2201.1 Scope. The provisions of this chapter govern the quality, design, fabrication and erection of steel used structurally in buildings or structures.

SECTION 2202
DEFINITIONS

2202.1 Definitions. The following words and terms shall, for the purposes of this chapter and as used elsewhere in this code, have the meaning shown herein.

STEEL CONSTRUCTION, COLD-FORMED. That type of construction made up entirely or in part of steel structural members cold formed to shape from sheet or strip steel such as roof deck, floor and wall panels, studs, floor joists, roof joists and other structural elements.

STEEL JOIST. Any steel structural member of a building or structure made of hot-rolled or cold-formed solid or open-web sections, or riveted or welded bars, strip or sheet steel members, or slotted and expanded, or otherwise deformed rolled sections.

STEEL MEMBER, STRUCTURAL. Any steel structural member of a building or structure consisting of a rolled steel structural shape other than cold-formed steel, or steel joist members.

SECTION 2203
IDENTIFICATION AND PROTECTION OF STEEL FOR STRUCTURAL PURPOSES

2203.1 Identification. Steel furnished for structural load-carrying purposes shall be properly identified for conformity to the ordered grade in accordance with the specified ASTM standard or other specification and the provisions of this chapter. Steel that is not readily identifiable as to grade from marking and test records shall be tested to determine conformity to such standards.

2203.2 Protection. Painting of structural steel shall comply with the requirements contained in AISC 360. Individual structural members and assembled panels of cold-formed steel construction, except where fabricated of approved corrosion-resistant steel or of steel having a corrosion-resistant or other approved coating, shall be protected against corrosion with an approved coat of paint, enamel or other approved protection.

SECTION 2204
CONNECTIONS

2204.1 Welding. The details of design, workmanship and technique for welding, inspection of welding and qualification of welding operators shall conform to the requirements of the specifications listed in Sections 2205, 2206, 2207, 2209 and 2210. Special inspection of welding shall be provided where required by Section 1704.

2204.2 Bolting. The design, installation and inspection of bolts shall be in accordance with the requirements of the specifications listed in Sections 2205, 2206, 2209 and 2210. Special inspection of the installation of high-strength bolts shall be provided where required by Section 1704.

2204.2.1 Anchor rods. Anchor rods shall be set accurately to the pattern and dimensions called for on the plans. The protrusion of the threaded ends through the connected material shall be sufficient to fully engage the threads of the nuts, but shall not be greater than the length of the threads on the bolts.

SECTION 2205
STRUCTURAL STEEL

2205.1 General. The design, fabrication and erection of structural steel for buildings and structures shall be in accordance with AISC 360. Where required, the seismic design of steel structures shall be in accordance with the additional provisions of Section 2205.2.

2205.2 Seismic requirements for steel structures. The design of structural steel structures to resist seismic forces shall be in accordance with the provisions of Section 2205.2.1 or 2205.2.2 for the appropriate seismic design category.

2205.2.1 Seismic Design Category A, B or C. Structural steel structures assigned to Seismic Design Category A, B or C shall be of any construction permitted in Section 2205. An *R* factor as set forth in Section 12.2.1 of ASCE 7 for the appropriate steel system is permitted where the structure is designed and detailed in accordance with the provisions of AISC 341, Part I. Systems not detailed in accordance with the above shall use the *R* factor in Section 12.2.1 of ASCE 7 designated for "structural steel systems not specifically detailed for seismic resistance."

2205.2.2 Seismic Design Category D, E or F. Structural steel structures assigned to Seismic Design Category D, E or F shall be designed and detailed in accordance with AISC 341, Part I.

2205.3 Seismic requirements for composite construction. The design, construction and quality of composite steel and concrete components that resist seismic forces shall conform to the requirements of the AISC 360 and ACI 318. An *R* factor as set forth in Section 12.2.1 of ASCE 7 for the appropriate composite steel and concrete system is permitted where the structure is designed and detailed in accordance with the provisions of AISC 341, Part II. In Seismic Design Category B or above, the design of such systems shall conform to the requirements of AISC 341, Part II.

2205.3.1 Seismic Design Categories D, E and F. Composite structures are permitted in Seismic Design Categories D , E and F, subject to the limitations in Section 12.2.1 of ASCE 7, where substantiating evidence is provided to demonstrate that the proposed system will perform as intended by AISC 341, Part II. The substantiating evidence shall be subject to code enforcement official approval. Where composite elements or connections are required to sustain inelastic deformations, the substantiating evidence shall be based on cyclic testing.

SECTION 2206
STEEL JOISTS

2206.1 General. The design, manufacture and use of open web steel joists and joist girders shall be in accordance with one of the following Steel Joist Institute (SJI) specifications:

1. SJI K-1.1

2. SJI LH/DLH-1.1

3. SJI JG-1.1

Where required, the seismic design of buildings shall be in accordance with the additional provisions of Section 2205.2 or 2210.5.

2206.2 Design. The registered design professional shall indicate on the construction documents the steel joist and/or steel joist girder designations from the specifications listed in Section 2206.1 and shall indicate the requirements for joist and joist girder design, layout, end supports, anchorage, non-SJI standard bridging, bridging termination connections and bearing connection design to resist uplift and lateral loads. These documents shall indicate special requirements as follows:

1. Special loads including:

    1.1. Concentrated loads;

    1.2. Nonuniform loads;

    1.3. Net uplift loads;

    1.4. Axial loads;

    1.5. End moments; and

    1.6. Connection forces.

2. Special considerations including:

    2.1. Profiles for nonstandard joist and joist girder configurations (standard joist and joist girder configurations are as indicated in the SJI catalog);

    2.2. Oversized or other nonstandard web openings; and

    2.3. Extended ends.

3. Deflection criteria for live and total loads for non-SJI standard joists.

2206.3 Calculations. The steel joist and joist girder manufacturer shall design the steel joists and/or steel joist girders in accordance with the current SJI specifications and load tables to support the load requirements of Section 2206.2. The registered design professional may require submission of the steel joist and joist girder calculations as prepared by a registered design professional responsible for the product design.

If requested by the registered design professional, the steel joist manufacturer shall submit design calculations with a cover letter bearing the seal and signature of the joist manufacturer's registered design professional. In addition to standard calculations under this seal and signature, submittal of the following shall be included:

1. Non-SJI standard bridging details (e.g. for cantilevered conditions, net uplift, etc.).

2. Connection details for:

    2.1. Non-SJI standard connections (e.g. flush-framed or framed connections);

    2.2. Field splices; and

    2.3. Joist headers.

2206.4 Steel joist drawings. Steel joist placement plans shall be provided to show the steel joist products as specified on the construction documents and are to be utilized for field installation in accordance with specific project requirements as stated in Section 2206.2. Steel placement plans shall include, at a minimum, the following:

1. Listing of all applicable loads as stated in Section 2206.2 and used in the design of the steel joists and joist girders as specified in the construction documents.

2. Profiles for nonstandard joist and joist girder configurations (standard joist and joist girder configurations are as indicated in the SJI catalog).

3. Connection requirements for:

    3.1. Joist supports;

    3.2. Joist girder supports;

    3.3. Field splices; and

    3.4. Bridging attachments.

4. Deflection criteria for live and total loads for non-SJI standard joists.

5. Size, location and connections for all bridging.

6. Joist headers.

Steel joist placement plans do not require the seal and signature of the joist manufacturer's registered design professional.

2206.5 Certification. At completion of fabrication, the steel joist manufacturer shall submit a certificate of compliance in accordance with Section 1704.2.2 stating that work was performed in accordance with approved construction documents and with SJI standard specifications.

SECTION 2207
STEEL CABLE STRUCTURES

2207.1 General. The design, fabrication and erection including related connections, and protective coatings of steel cables for buildings shall be in accordance with ASCE 19.

2207.2 Seismic requirements for steel cable. The design strength of steel cables shall be determined by the provisions of ASCE 19 except as modified by these provisions.

1. A load factor of 1.1 shall be applied to the prestress force included in T_3 and T_4 as defined in Section 3.12.

2. In Section 3.2.1, Item (c) shall be replaced with "1.5 T_3," and Item (d) shall be replaced with "1.5 T_4"

SECTION 2208
STEEL STORAGE RACKS

2208.1 Storage racks. The design, testing and utilization of industrial steel storage racks shall be in accordance with the *RMI Specification for the Design, Testing and Utilization of Industrial Steel Storage Racks*. Racks in the scope of this specification include industrial pallet racks, movable shelf racks and stacker racks and does not apply to other types of racks, such as drive-in and drive-through racks, cantilever racks, portable racks or rack buildings. Where required, the seismic design of storage racks shall be in accordance with the provisions of Section 15.5.3 of ASCE 7.

SECTION 2209
COLD-FORMED STEEL

2209.1 General. The design of cold-formed carbon and low-alloy steel structural members shall be in accordance with AISI-NAS. The design of cold-formed stainless-steel structural members shall be in accordance with ASCE 8. Cold-formed steel light-framed construction shall comply with Section 2210.

2209.2 Composite slabs on steel decks. Composite slabs of concrete and steel deck shall be designed and constructed in accordance with ASCE 3.

SECTION 2210
COLD-FORMED STEEL LIGHT-FRAMED CONSTRUCTION

2210.1 General. The design, installation and construction of cold-formed carbon or low-alloy steel, structural and non-structural steel framing shall be in accordance with AISI-General and AISI-NAS.

2210.2 Headers. The design and installation of cold-formed steel box headers, back-to-back headers and single and double L-headers used in single-span conditions for load-carrying purposes shall be in accordance with AISI-Header, subject to the limitations therein.

2210.3 Trusses. The design, quality assurance, installation and testing of cold-formed steel trusses shall be in accordance with AISI-Truss, subject to the limitations therein.

2210.4 Wall stud design. The design and installation of cold-formed steel studs for structural and nonstructural walls shall be in accordance with AISI-WSD.

2210.5 Lateral design. The design of light-framed cold-formed steel walls and diaphragms to resist wind and seismic loads shall be in accordance with AISI-Lateral except as modified by Section 2210.5.1.

2210.5.1 Modification to AISI-Lateral, Section C3.3.4. Wood structural panel sheathing and fastening designed to transfer resultant forces across horizontal framing joints shall constitute an acceptable continuous load path as an alternative to the use of anchorage devices when calculated by principles of mechanics using values of fastener strength and sheathing shear resistance.

2210.6 Prescriptive framing. Detached one- and two-family dwellings and townhouses, up to two stories in height, shall be permitted to be constructed in accordance with AISI-PM, subject to the limitations therein.

CHAPTER 23

WOOD

SECTION 2301
GENERAL

2301.1 Scope. The provisions of this chapter shall govern the materials, design, construction and quality of wood members and their fasteners.

2301.2 General design requirements. The design of structural elements or systems, constructed partially or wholly of wood or wood-based products, shall be in accordance with one of the following methods:

1. Allowable stress design in accordance with Sections 2304, 2305 and 2306.

2. Load and resistance factor design in accordance with Sections 2304, 2305 and 2307.

3. Conventional light-frame construction in accordance with Sections 2304 and 2308.

   Exception: Buildings designed in accordance with the provisions of the AF&PA WFCM shall be deemed to meet the requirements of the provisions of Section 2308.

2301.3 Nominal sizes. For the purposes of this chapter, where dimensions of lumber are specified, they shall be deemed to be nominal dimensions unless specifically designated as actual dimensions (see Section 2304.2).

SECTION 2302
DEFINITIONS

2302.1 Definitions. The following words and terms shall, for the purposes of this chapter, have the meanings shown herein.

ACCREDITATION BODY. An approved, third-party organization that is independent of the grading and inspection agencies, and the lumber mills, and that initially accredits and subsequently monitors, on a continuing basis, the competency and performance of a grading or inspection agency related to carrying out specific tasks.

BRACED WALL LINE. A series of braced wall panels in a single story that meets the requirements of Section 2308.3 or 2308.12.4.

BRACED WALL PANEL. A section of wall braced in accordance with Section 2308.9.3 or 2308.12.4.

COLLECTOR. A horizontal diaphragm element parallel and in line with the applied force that collects and transfers diaphragm shear forces to the vertical elements of the lateral-force-resisting system and/or distributes forces within the diaphragm.

CONVENTIONAL LIGHT-FRAME WOOD CONSTRUCTION. A type of construction whose primary structural elements are formed by a system of repetitive wood-framing members. See Section 2308 for conventional light-frame wood construction provisions.

CRIPPLE WALL. A framed stud wall extending from the top of the foundation to the underside of floor framing for the lowest occupied floor level.

DIAPHRAGM, UNBLOCKED. A diaphragm that has edge nailing at supporting members only. Blocking between supporting structural members at panel edges is not included. Diaphragm panels are field nailed to supporting members.

DRAG STRUT. See "Collector."

FIBERBOARD. A fibrous, homogeneous panel made from lignocellulosic fibers (usually wood or cane) and having a density of less than 31 pounds per cubic foot (pcf) (497 kg/m³) but more than 10 pcf (160 kg/m³).

GLUED BUILT-UP MEMBER. A structural element, the section of which is composed of built-up lumber, wood structural panels or wood structural panels in combination with lumber, all parts bonded together with structural adhesives.

GRADE (LUMBER). The classification of lumber in regard to strength and utility in accordance with American Softwood Lumber Standard DOC PS 20 and the grading rules of an approved lumber rules-writing agency.

HARDBOARD. A fibrous-felted, homogeneous panel made from lignocellulosic fibers consolidated under heat and pressure in a hot press to a density not less than 31 pcf (497 kg/m³).

NAILING, BOUNDARY. A special nailing pattern required by design at the boundaries of diaphragms.

NAILING, EDGE. A special nailing pattern required by design at the edges of each panel within the assembly of a diaphragm or shear wall.

NAILING, FIELD. Nailing required between the sheathing panels and framing members at locations other than boundary nailing and edge nailing.

NATURALLY DURABLE WOOD. The heartwood of the following species with the exception that an occasional piece with corner sapwood is permitted if 90 percent or more of the width of each side on which it occurs is heartwood.

    Decay resistant. Redwood, cedar, black locust and black walnut.

    Termite resistant. Redwood and Eastern red cedar.

NOMINAL SIZE (LUMBER). The commercial size designation of width and depth, in standard sawn lumber and glued-laminated lumber grades; somewhat larger than the standard net size of dressed lumber, in accordance with DOC PS 20 for sawn lumber and with the AF&PA NDS for glued-laminated lumber.

PARTICLEBOARD. A generic term for a panel primarily composed of cellulosic materials (usually wood), generally in the form of discrete pieces or particles, as distinguished from fibers. The cellulosic material is combined with synthetic resin or other suitable bonding system by a process in which the interparticle bond is created by the bonding system under heat and pressure.

PREFABRICATED WOOD I-JOIST. Structural member manufactured using sawn or structural composite lumber flanges and wood structural panel webs bonded together with exterior exposure adhesives, which forms an "I" cross-sectional shape.

PRESERVATIVE-TREATED WOOD. Wood (including plywood) pressure treated with preservatives in accordance with Section 2303.1.8.

SHEAR WALL. A wall designed to resist lateral forces parallel to the plane of a wall.

Shear wall, perforated. A wood structural panel sheathed wall with openings, that has not been specifically designed and detailed for force transfer around openings.

Shear wall segment, perforated. A section of shear wall with full-height sheathing that meets the height-to-width ratio limits of Section 2305.3.4.

STRUCTURAL COMPOSITE LUMBER. Structural member manufactured using wood elements bonded together with exterior adhesives. Examples of structural composite lumber are:

Laminated veneer lumber (LVL). A composite of wood veneer sheet elements with wood fibers primarily oriented along the length of the member.

Parallel strand lumber (PSL). A composite of wood strand elements with wood fibers primarily oriented along the length of the member.

STRUCTURAL GLUED-LAMINATED TIMBER. An engineered, stress-rated product of a timber laminating plant, comprised of assemblies of specially selected and prepared wood laminations in which the grain of all laminations is approximately parallel longitudinally and the laminations are bonded with adhesives.

SUBDIAPHRAGM. A portion of a larger wood diaphragm designed to anchor and transfer local forces to primary diaphragm struts and the main diaphragm.

TIE-DOWN (HOLD-DOWN). A device used to resist uplift of the chords of shear walls.

TREATED WOOD. Wood impregnated under pressure with compounds that reduce its susceptibility to flame spread or to deterioration caused by fungi, insects or marine borers.

WOOD SHEAR PANEL. A wood floor, roof or wall component sheathed to act as a shear wall or diaphragm.

WOOD STRUCTURAL PANEL. A panel manufactured from veneers, wood strands or wafers or a combination of veneer and wood strands or wafers bonded together with waterproof synthetic resins or other suitable bonding systems. Examples of wood structural panels are:

Composite panels. A wood structural panel that is comprised of wood veneer and reconstituted wood-based material and bonded together with waterproof adhesive;

Oriented strand board (OSB). A mat-formed wood structural panel comprised of thin rectangular wood strands arranged in cross-aligned layers with surface layers normally arranged in the long panel direction and bonded with waterproof adhesive; or

Plywood. A wood structural panel comprised of plies of wood veneer arranged in cross-aligned layers. The plies are bonded with waterproof adhesive that cures on application of heat and pressure.

SECTION 2303
MINIMUM STANDARDS AND QUALITY

2303.1 General. Structural sawn lumber; end-jointed lumber; prefabricated wood I-joists; structural glued-laminated timber; wood structural panels, fiberboard sheathing (when used structurally); hardboard siding (when used structurally); particleboard; preservative-treated wood; structural log members; structural composite lumber; round timber poles and piles; fire-retardant-treated wood; hardwood plywood; wood trusses; joist hangers; nails; and staples shall conform to the applicable provisions of this section.

2303.1.1 Sawn lumber. Sawn lumber used for load-supporting purposes, including end-jointed or edge-glued lumber, machine stress-rated or machine-evaluated lumber, shall be identified by the grade mark of a lumber grading or inspection agency that has been approved by an accreditation body that complies with DOC PS 20 or equivalent. Grading practices and identification shall comply with rules published by an agency approved in accordance with the procedures of DOC PS 20 or equivalent procedures. In lieu of a grade mark on the material, a certificate of inspection as to species and grade issued by a lumber grading or inspection agency meeting the requirements of this section is permitted to be accepted for precut, remanufactured or rough-sawn lumber and for sizes larger than 3 inches (76 mm) nominal thickness.

Approved end-jointed lumber is permitted to be used interchangeably with solid-sawn members of the same species and grade.

Exception: In lieu of compliance with Section 2303.1.1, lumber used for load-supporting purposes, which is neither identified by a grade mark nor issued a certificate of inspection by a lumber grading or inspection agency, may be used under the following conditions when authorized by the authority having jurisdiction:

1. The producing mill shall sell or provide the lumber directly to the ultimate consumer or the consumer's contract builder for use in an approved structure.

2. The producing mill shall certify in writing to the consumer or contract builder on a form to be produced by the authority having jurisdiction that the quality and safe working stresses of such lumber are equal to or exceed No. 2 grade of the species in accordance with the conditions set

forth in DOC PS 20. Such certification shall be filed as part of the building permit application.

3. The use of such lumber shall be in accordance with Section 503 of the *Building Code of New York State,* limited to:

a. Buildings of residential Group R occupancy not exceeding three stories in height.

b. Buildings of assembly Group A, business Group B, educational Group E, factory industrial Group F, high-hazard Group H, institutional Group I, mercantile Group M, storage Group S and utility miscellaneous Group U occupancies not exceeding 10,000 square feet (929 m²) of cumulative floor area or 35 feet (10 668 mm) in height.

2303.1.2 Prefabricated wood I-joists. Structural capacities and design provisions for prefabricated wood I-joists shall be established and monitored in accordance with ASTM D 5055.

2303.1.3 Structural glued-laminated timber. Glued-laminated timbers shall be manufactured and identified as required in AITC A190.1 and ASTM D 3737.

2303.1.4 Wood structural panels. Wood structural panels, when used structurally (including those used for siding, roof and wall sheathing, subflooring, diaphragms and built-up members), shall conform to the requirements for their type in DOC PS 1 or PS 2. Each panel or member shall be identified for grade and glue type by the trademarks of an approved testing and grading agency. Wood structural panel components shall be designed and fabricated in accordance with the applicable standards listed in Section 2306.1 and identified by the trademarks of an approved testing and inspection agency indicating conformance with the applicable standard. In addition, wood structural panels when permanently exposed in outdoor applications shall be of exterior type, except that wood structural panel roof sheathing exposed to the outdoors on the underside is permitted to be interior type bonded with exterior glue, Exposure 1.

2303.1.5 Fiberboard. Fiberboard for its various uses shall conform to ASTM C 208. Fiberboard sheathing, when used structurally, shall be identified by an approved agency as conforming to ASTM C 208.

2303.1.5.1 Jointing. To ensure tight-fitting assemblies, edges shall be manufactured with square, shiplapped, beveled, tongue-and-groove or U-shaped joints.

2303.1.5.2 Roof insulation. Where used as roof insulation in all types of construction, fiberboard shall be protected with an approved roof covering.

2303.1.5.3 Wall insulation. Where installed and fireblocked to comply with Chapter 7, fiberboards are permitted as wall insulation in all types of construction. In fire walls and fire barriers, unless treated to comply with Section 803.1 for Class A materials, the boards shall be cemented directly to the concrete, masonry or other noncombustible base and shall be protected with an approved noncombustible veneer anchored to the base without intervening airspaces.

2303.1.5.3.1 Protection. Fiberboard wall insulation applied on the exterior of foundation walls shall be protected below ground level with a bituminous coating.

2303.1.6 Hardboard. Hardboard siding used structurally shall be identified by an approved agency conforming to AHA A135.6. Hardboard underlayment shall meet the strength requirements of $7/_{32}$-inch (5.6 mm) or $1/_4$-inch (6.4 mm) service class hardboard planed or sanded on one side to a uniform thickness of not less than 0.200 inch (5.1 mm). Prefinished hardboard paneling shall meet the requirements of AHA A135.5. Other basic hardboard products shall meet the requirements of AHA A135.4. Hardboard products shall be installed in accordance with manufacturer's recommendations.

2303.1.7 Particleboard. Particleboard shall conform to ANSI A208.1. Particleboard shall be identified by the grade mark or certificate of inspection issued by an approved agency. Particleboard shall not be utilized for applications other than indicated in this section unless the particleboard complies with the provisions of Section 2306.4.3.

2303.1.7.1 Floor underlayment. Particleboard floor underlayment shall conform to Type PBU of ANSI A208.1. Type PBU underlayment shall not be less than $1/_4$-inch (6.4 mm) thick and shall be installed in accordance with the instructions of the Composite Panel Association.

2303.1.8 Preservative-treated wood. Lumber, timber, plywood, piles and poles supporting permanent structures required by Section 2304.11 to be preservative treated shall conform to the requirements of the applicable AWPA Standard U1 and M4 for the species, product, preservative and end use. Preservatives shall be listed in Section 4 of AWPA U1. Lumber and plywood used in wood foundation systems shall conform to Chapter 18.

2303.1.8.1 Identification. Wood required by Section 2304.11 to be preservative treated shall bear the quality mark of an inspection agency that maintains continuing supervision, testing and inspection over the quality of the preservative-treated wood. Inspection agencies for preservative-treated wood shall be listed by an accreditation body that complies with the requirements of the American Lumber Standards Treated Wood Program, or equivalent. The quality mark shall be on a stamp or label affixed to the preservative-treated wood, and shall include the following information:

1. Identification of treating manufacturer.

2. Type of preservative used.

3. Minimum preservative retention (pcf).

4. End use for which the product is treated.

5. AWPA standard to which the product was treated.

6. Identity of the accredited inspection agency.

2303.1.8.2 Moisture content. Where preservative-treated wood is used in enclosed locations where drying in service cannot readily occur, such wood shall be at a moisture content of 19 percent or less before being covered with insulation, interior wall finish, floor covering or other materials.

2303.1.9 Structural composite lumber. Structural capacities for structural composite lumber shall be established and monitored in accordance with ASTM D 5456.

2303.1.10 Structural log members. Stress grading of structural log members of nonrectangular shape, as typically used in log buildings, shall be in accordance with ASTM D 3957. Such structural log members shall be identified by the grade mark of an approved lumber grading or inspection agency. In lieu of a grade mark on the material, a certificate of inspection as to species and grade issued by a lumber grading or inspection agency meeting the requirements of this section shall be permitted.

2303.1.11 Round timber poles and piles. Round timber poles and piles shall comply with ASTM D 3200 and ASTM D 25, respectively

2303.2 Fire-retardant-treated wood. Fire-retardant-treated wood is any wood product which, when impregnated with chemicals by a pressure process or other means during manufacture, shall have, when tested in accordance with ASTM E 84, a listed flame spread index of 25 or less and show no evidence of significant progressive combustion when the test is continued for an additional 20-minute period. In addition, the flame front shall not progress more than 10.5 feet (3200 mm) beyond the centerline of the burners at any time during the test.

2303.2.1 Labeling. Fire-retardant-treated lumber and wood structural panels shall be labeled. The label shall contain the following items:

1. The identification mark of an approved agency in accordance with Section 1703.5.

2. Identification of the treating manufacturer.

3. The name of the fire-retardant treatment.

4. The species of wood treated.

5. Flame spread and smoke-developed index.

6. Method of drying after treatment.

7. Conformance with appropriate standards in accordance with Sections 2303.2.2 through 2303.2.5.

8. For fire-retardant-treated wood exposed to weather, damp or wet locations, include the words "No increase in the listed classification when subjected to the Standard Rain Test" (ASTM D 2898).

2303.2.2 Strength adjustments. Design values for untreated lumber and wood structural panels, as specified in Section 2303.1, shall be adjusted for fire-retardant-treated wood. Adjustments to design values shall be based on an approved method of investigation that takes into consideration the effects of the anticipated temperature and humidity to which the fire-retardant-treated wood will

be subjected, the type of treatment and redrying procedures.

2303.2.2.1 Wood structural panels. The effect of treatment and the method of redrying after treatment, and exposure to high temperatures and high humidities on the flexure properties of fire-retardant-treated softwood plywood shall be determined in accordance with ASTM D 5516. The test data developed by ASTM D 5516 shall be used to develop adjustment factors, maximum loads and spans, or both, for untreated plywood design values in accordance with ASTM D 6305. Each manufacturer shall publish the allowable maximum loads and spans for service as floor and roof sheathing for its treatment.

2303.2.2.2 Lumber. For each species of wood that is treated, the effects of the treatment, the method of redrying after treatment and exposure to high temperatures and high humidities on the allowable design properties of fire-retardant-treated lumber shall be determined in accordance with ASTM D 5664. The test data developed by ASTM D 5664 shall be used to develop modification factors for use at or near room temperature and at elevated temperatures and humidity in accordance with ASTM D 6841. Each manufacturer shall publish the modification factors for service at temperatures of not less than 80°F (27°C) and for roof framing. The roof framing modification factors shall take into consideration the climatological location.

2303.2.3 Exposure to weather, damp or wet locations. Where fire-retardant-treated wood is exposed to weather, or damp or wet locations, it shall be identified as "Exterior" to indicate there is no increase in the listed flame spread index as defined in Section 2303.2 when subjected to ASTM D 2898.

2303.2.4 Interior applications. Interior fire-retardant-treated wood shall have moisture content of not over 28 percent when tested in accordance with ASTM D 3201 procedures at 92-percent relative humidity. Interior fire-retardant-treated wood shall be tested in accordance with Section 2303.2.2.1 or 2303.2.2.2. Interior fire-retardant-treated wood designated as Type A shall be tested in accordance with the provisions of this section.

2303.2.5 Moisture content. Fire-retardant-treated wood shall be dried to a moisture content of 19 percent or less for lumber and 15 percent or less for wood structural panels before use. For wood kiln dried after treatment (KDAT), the kiln temperatures shall not exceed those used in kiln drying the lumber and plywood submitted for the tests described in Section 2303.2.2.1 for plywood and 2303.2.2.2 for lumber.

2303.2.6 Type I and II construction applications. See Section 603.1 for limitations on the use of fire-retardant-treated wood in buildings of Type I or II construction.

2303.3 Hardwood and plywood. Hardwood and decorative plywood shall be manufactured and identified as required in HPVA HP-1.

2303.4 Trusses.

2303.4.1 Design. Wood trusses shall be designed in accordance with the provisions of this code and accepted engineering practice. Members are permitted to be joined by nails, glue, bolts, timber connectors, metal connector plates or other approved framing devices.

2303.4.1.1 Truss designer. The individual or organization responsible for the design of trusses.

2303.4.1.2 Truss design drawings. The written, graphic and pictorial **depiction** of each individual truss shall be provided to the code enforcement official and approved prior to installation. Truss design drawings shall also be provided with the shipment of trusses delivered to the job site. Truss design drawings shall include, at a minimum, the information specified below:

1. Slope or depth, span and spacing;
2. Location of joints;
3. Required bearing widths;
4. Design loads as applicable;
5. Top chord live load (including snow loads);
6. Top chord dead load;
7. Bottom chord live load;
8. Bottom chord dead load;
9. Concentrated loads and their points of application as applicable;
10. Controlling wind and earthquake loads as applicable;
11. Adjustments to lumber and metal connector plate design value for conditions of use;
12. Each reaction force and direction;
13. Metal connector plate type, size, thickness or gage, and the dimensioned location of each metal connector plate except where symmetrically located relative to the joint interface;
14. Lumber size, species and grade for each member;
15. Connection requirements for:
    15.1. Truss to truss;
    15.2. Truss ply to ply; and
    15.3. Field splices.
16. Calculated deflection ratio and maximum vertical and horizontal deflection for live and total load as applicable;
17. Maximum axial tensile and compression forces in the truss members; and
18. Required permanent individual truss member bracing and method per Section 2303.4.1.5, unless a specific truss member permanent bracing plan for the roof or floor structural system is provided by a registered design professional.

Where required by one of the following, each individual truss design drawing shall bear the seal and signature of the truss designer:

1. Registered design professional; or
2. code enforcement official; or
3. Statutes of the jurisdiction in which the project is to be constructed.

Exceptions:

1. When a cover sheet/truss index sheet combined into a single cover sheet is attached to the set of truss design drawings for the project, the single sheet/truss index sheet is the only document that needs to be signed and sealed within the truss submittal package.
2. When a cover sheet and a truss index sheet are separately provided and attached to the set of truss design drawings for the project, both the cover sheet and the truss index sheet are the only documents that need to be signed and sealed within the truss submittal package.

2303.4.1.3 Truss placement diagram. The truss manufacturer shall provide a truss placement diagram that identifies the proposed location for each individually designated truss and references the corresponding truss design drawing. The truss placement diagram shall be provided as part of the truss submittal package, and with the shipment of trusses delivered to the job site. Truss placement diagrams shall not be required to bear the seal or signature of the truss designer.

Exception: When the truss placement diagram is prepared under the direct supervision of a registered design professional, it is required to be signed and sealed.

2303.4.1.4 Truss submittal package. The truss submittal package shall consist of each individual truss design drawing, the truss placement diagram for the project, the truss member permanent bracing specification and, as applicable, the cover sheet/truss index sheet.

2303.4.1.5 Truss member permanent bracing. Where permanent bracing of truss members is required on the truss design drawings, it shall be accomplished by one of the following methods:

1. The trusses shall be designed so that the buckling of any individual truss member can be resisted internally by the structure (e.g. buckling member T-bracing, L-bracing, etc.) of the individual truss. The truss individual member buckling reinforcement shall be installed as shown on the truss design drawing or on supplemental truss member buckling reinforcement diagrams provided by the truss designer.
2. Permanent bracing shall be installed using standard industry bracing details that conform with

generally accepted engineering practice. Individual truss member continuous lateral bracing location(s) shall be shown on the truss design drawing.

2303.4.1.6 Anchorage. All transfer of loads and anchorage of each truss to the supporting structure is the responsibility of the registered design professional.

2303.4.1.7 Alterations to trusses. Truss members and components shall not be cut, notched, drilled, spliced or otherwise altered in any way without written concurrence and approval of a registered design professional. Alterations resulting in the addition of loads to any member (e.g., HVAC equipment, water heater) shall not be permitted without verification that the truss is capable of supporting such additional loading.

2303.4.2 Metal-plate-connected trusses. In addition to Sections 2303.4.1 through 2303.4.1.7, the design, manufacture and quality assurance of metal-plate-connected wood trusses shall be in accordance with TPI 1. Manufactured trusses shall comply with Section 1704.6 as applicable.

2303.5 Test standard for joist hangers and connectors. For the required test standards for joist hangers and connectors, see Section 1715.1.

2303.6 Nails and staples. Nails and staples shall conform to requirements of ASTM F 1667. Nails used for framing and sheathing connections shall have minimum average bending yield strengths as follows: 80 kips per square inch (ksi) (551 MPa) for shank diameters larger than 0.177 inch (4.50 mm) but not larger than 0.254 inch (6.45 mm), 90 ksi (620 MPa) for shank diameters larger than 0.142 inch (3.61 mm) but not larger than 0.177 inch (4.50 mm) and 100 ksi (689 MPa) for shank diameters of at least 0.099 inch (2.51 mm) but not larger than 0.142 inch (3.61 mm).

2303.7 Shrinkage. Consideration shall be given in design to the possible effect of cross-grain dimensional changes considered vertically which may occur in lumber fabricated in a green condition.

SECTION 2304
GENERAL CONSTRUCTION REQUIREMENTS

2304.1 General. The provisions of this section apply to design methods specified in Section 2301.2.

2304.2 Size of structural members. Computations to determine the required sizes of members shall be based on the net dimensions (actual sizes) and not nominal sizes.

2304.3 Wall framing. The framing of exterior and interior walls shall be in accordance with the provisions specified in Section 2308 unless a specific design is furnished.

2304.3.1 Bottom plates. Studs shall have full bearing on a 2-inch-thick (actual $1^1/_2$-inch, 38 mm) or larger plate or sill having a width at least equal to the width of the studs.

2304.3.2 Framing over openings. Headers, double joists, trusses or other approved assemblies that are of adequate size to transfer loads to the vertical members shall be provided over window and door openings in load-bearing walls and partitions.

2304.3.3 Shrinkage. Wood walls and bearing partitions shall not support more than two floors and a roof unless an analysis satisfactory to the code enforcement official shows that shrinkage of the wood framing will not have adverse effects on the structure or any plumbing, electrical or mechanical systems, or other equipment installed therein due to excessive shrinkage or differential movements caused by shrinkage. The analysis shall also show that the roof drainage system and the foregoing systems or equipment will not be adversely affected or, as an alternate, such systems shall be designed to accommodate the differential shrinkage or movements.

2304.4 Floor and roof framing. The framing of wood-joisted floors and wood framed roofs shall be in accordance with the provisions specified in Section 2308 unless a specific design is furnished.

2304.5 Framing around flues and chimneys. Combustible framing shall be a minimum of 2 inches (51 mm), but shall not be less than the distance specified in Sections 2111 and 2113 and the *Mechanical Code of New York State*, from flues, chimneys and fireplaces, and 6 inches (152 mm) away from flue openings.

2304.6 Wall sheathing. Except as provided for in Section 1405 for weatherboarding or where stucco construction that complies with Section 2510 is installed, enclosed buildings shall be sheathed with one of the materials of the nominal thickness specified in Table 2304.6 or any other approved material of equivalent strength or durability.

2304.6.1 Wood structural panel sheathing. Where wood structural panel sheathing is used as the exposed finish on the exterior of outside walls, it shall have an exterior exposure durability classification. Where wood structural panel sheathing is used on the exterior of outside walls but not as the exposed finish, it shall be of a type manufactured with exterior glue (Exposure 1 or Exterior). Where wood structural panel sheathing is used elsewhere, it shall be of a type manufactured with intermediate or exterior glue.

2304.6.2 Interior paneling. Softwood wood structural panels used for interior paneling shall conform with the provisions of Chapter 8 and shall be installed in accordance with Table 2304.9.1. Panels shall comply with DOC PS 1 or PS 2. Prefinished hardboard paneling shall meet the requirements of AHA A135.5. Hardwood plywood shall conform to HPVA HP-1.

2304.7 Floor and roof sheathing.

2304.7.1 Structural floor sheathing. Structural floor sheathing shall be designed in accordance with the general provisions of this code and the special provisions in this section.

Floor sheathing conforming to the provisions of Table 2304.7(1), 2304.7(2), 2304.7(3) or 2304.7(4) shall be deemed to meet the requirements of this section.

2304.7.2 Structural roof sheathing. Structural roof sheathing shall be designed in accordance with the general

TABLE 2304.6
MINIMUM THICKNESS OF WALL SHEATHING

SHEATHING TYPE	MINIMUM THICKNESS	MAXIMUM WALL STUD SPACING
Wood boards	$^5/_8$ inch	24 inches on center
Fiberboard	$^1/_2$ inch	16 inches on center
Wood structural panel	In accordance with Tables 2308.9.3(2) and 2308.9.3(3)	—
M-S "Exterior Glue" and M-2 "Exterior Glue" Particleboard	In accordance with Tables 2306.4.3 and 2308.9.3(4)	—
Gypsum sheathing	$^1/_2$ inch	16 inches on center
Gypsum wallboard	$^1/_2$ inch	24 inches on center
Reinforced cement mortar	1 inch	24 inches on center

For SI: 1 inch = 25.4 mm.

TABLE 2304.7(1)
ALLOWABLE SPANS FOR LUMBER FLOOR AND ROOF SHEATHING[a,b]

SPAN (inches)	MINIMUM NET THICKNESS (inches) OF LUMBER PLACED			
	Perpendicular to supports		Diagonally to supports	
	Surfaced dry[c]	Surfaced unseasoned	Surfaced dry[c]	Surfaced unseasoned
Floors				
24	$^3/_4$	$^{25}/_{32}$	$^3/_4$	$^{25}/_{32}$
16	$^5/_8$	$^{11}/_{16}$	$^5/_8$	$^{11}/_{16}$
Roofs				
24	$^5/_8$	$^{11}/_{16}$	$^3/_4$	$^{25}/_{32}$

For SI: 1 inch = 25.4 mm.

a. Installation details shall conform to Sections 2304.7.1 and 2304.7.2 for floor and roof sheathing, respectively.

b. Floor or roof sheathing conforming with this table shall be deemed to meet the design criteria of Section 2304.7.

c. Maximum 19-percent moisture content.

TABLE 2304.7(2)
SHEATHING LUMBER, MINIMUM GRADE REQUIREMENTS: BOARD GRADE

SOLID FLOOR OR ROOF SHEATHING	SPACED ROOF SHEATHING	GRADING RULES
Utility	Standard	NLGA, WCLIB, WWPA
4 common or utility	3 common or standard	NLGA, WCLIB, WWPA, NSLB or NELMA
No. 3	No. 2	SPIB
Merchantable	Construction common	RIS

provisions of this code and the special provisions in this section.

Roof sheathing conforming to the provisions of Table 2304.7(1), 2304.7(2), 2304.7(3) or 2304.7(5) shall be deemed to meet the requirements of this section. Wood structural panel roof sheathing shall be bonded by exterior glue.

2304.8 Lumber decking.

2304.8.1 General. Lumber decking shall be designed and installed in accordance with the general provisions of this code and the provisions of this section. Each piece shall be square-end trimmed. When random lengths are furnished, each piece shall be square-end trimmed across the face so that at least 90 percent of the pieces will be within 0.5 degrees (0.00873 rad) of square. The ends of the pieces shall be permitted to be beveled up to 2 degrees (0.0349 rad) from vertical with the exposed face of the piece slightly longer than the back of the piece. Tongue-and-groove decking shall be installed with the tongues up on sloped or pitched roofs with pattern faces down.

2304.8.2 Layup patterns. Lumber decking is permitted to be laid up following one of five standard patterns as defined in Sections 2304.8.2.1 through 2304.8.2.5. Other patterns are permitted to be used if justified by engineering analysis.

2304.8.2.1 Simple span pattern. All pieces shall be supported by two supports.

2304.8.2.2 Two-span continuous pattern. All pieces shall be supported by three supports, and all end joints shall occur in line on every other support. Supporting members shall be designed to accommodate the load redistribution caused by this pattern.

2304.8.2.3 Combination simple and two-span continuous pattern. Courses in end spans shall be alternating simple span and two span continuous. End joints are staggered in adjacent courses and occur only over supports.

TABLE 2304.7(3)
ALLOWABLE SPANS AND LOADS FOR WOOD STRUCTURAL PANEL SHEATHING AND SINGLE-FLOOR GRADES CONTINUOUS OVER TWO OR MORE SPANS WITH STRENGTH AXIS PERPENDICULAR TO SUPPORTS[a,b]

SHEATHING GRADES		ROOF[c]				FLOOR[d]
		Maximum span (inches)		Load[e](psf)		
Panel span rating roof/floor span	Panel thickness (inches)	With edge support[f]	Without edge support	Total load	Live load	Maximum span (inches)
12/0	$^5/_{16}$	12	12	40	30	0
16/0	$^5/_{16}$, $^3/_8$	16	16	40	30	0
20/0	$^5/_{16}$, $^3/_8$	20	20	40	30	0
24/0	$^3/_8$, $^7/_{16}$, $^1/_2$	24	20[g]	40	30	0
24/16	$^7/_{16}$, $^1/_2$	24	24	50	40	16
32/16	$^{15}/_{32}$, $^1/_2$, $^5/_8$	32	28	40	30	16[h]
40/20	$^{19}/_{32}$, $^5/_8$, $^3/_4$, $^7/_8$	40	32	40	30	20[h, i]
48/24	$^{23}/_{32}$, $^3/_4$, $^7/_8$	48	36	45	35	24
54/32	$^7/_8$, 1	54	40	45	35	32
60/32	$^7/_8$, $1^1/_8$	60	48	45	35	32
SINGLE FLOOR GRADES		ROOF[c]				FLOOR[d]
		Maximum span (inches)		Load[e](psf)		
Panel span rating	Panel thickness (inches)	With edge support[f]	Without edge support	Total load	Live load	Maximum span (inches)
16 o.c.	$^1/_2$, $^{19}/_{32}$, $^5/_8$	24	24	50	40	16[h]
20 o.c.	$^{19}/_{32}$, $^5/_8$, $^3/_4$	32	32	40	30	20[h,i]
24 o.c.	$^{23}/_{32}$, $^3/_4$	48	36	35	25	24
32 o.c.	$^7/_8$, 1	48	40	50	40	32
48 o.c.	$1^3/_{32}$, $1^1/_8$	60	48	50	40	48

For SI: 1 inch = 25.4 mm, 1 pound per square foot = 0.0479 kN/m².

a. Applies to panels 24 inches or wider.

b. Floor and roof sheathing conforming with this table shall be deemed to meet the design criteria of Section 2304.7.

c. Uniform load deflection limitations $^1/_{180}$ of span under live load plus dead load, $^1/_{240}$ under live load only.

d. Panel edges shall have approved tongue-and-groove joints or shall be supported with blocking unless $^1/_4$-inch minimum thickness underlayment or $1^1/_2$ inches of approved cellular or lightweight concrete is placed over the subfloor, or finish floor is $^3/_4$-inch wood strip. Allowable uniform load based on deflection of $^1/_{360}$ of span is 100 pounds per square foot except the span rating of 48 inches on center is based on a total load of 65 pounds per square foot.

e. Allowable load at maximum span.

f. Tongue-and-groove edges, panel edge clips (one midway between each support, except two equally spaced between supports 48 inches on center), lumber blocking or other. Only lumber blocking shall satisfy blocked diaphragm requirements.

g. For $^1/_2$-inch panel, maximum span shall be 24 inches.

h. Span is permitted to be 24 inches on center where $^3/_4$-inch wood strip flooring is installed at right angles to joist.

i. Span is permitted to be 24 inches on center for floors where $1^1/_2$ inches of cellular or lightweight concrete is applied over the panels.

TABLE 2304.7(4)
ALLOWABLE SPAN FOR WOOD STRUCTURAL PANEL COMBINATION SUBFLOOR-UNDERLAYMENT (SINGLE FLOOR)[a,b]
(Panels Continuous Over Two or More Spans and Strength Axis Perpendicular to Supports)

IDENTIFICATION	MAXIMUM SPACING OF JOISTS (inches)				
	16	20	24	32	48
Species group[c]	Thickness (inches)				
1	$^1/_2$	$^5/_8$	$^3/_4$	—	—
2, 3	$^5/_8$	$^3/_4$	$^7/_8$	—	—
4	$^3/_4$	$^7/_8$	1	—	—
Single floor span rating[d]	16 o.c.	20 o.c.	24 o.c.	32 o.c.	48 o.c.

For SI: 1 inch = 25.4 mm, 1 pound per square foot = 0.0479 kN/m².

a. Spans limited to value shown because of possible effects of concentrated loads. Allowable uniform loads based on deflection of $^1/_{360}$ of span is 100 pounds per square foot except allowable total uniform load for $1^1/_8$-inch wood structural panels over joists spaced 48 inches on center is 65 pounds per square foot. Panel edges shall have approved tongue-and-groove joints or shall be supported with blocking, unless $^1/_4$-inch minimum thickness underlayment or $1^1/_2$ inches of approved cellular or lightweight concrete is placed over the subfloor, or finish floor is $^3/_4$-inch wood strip.

b. Floor panels conforming with this table shall be deemed to meet the design criteria of Section 2304.7.

c. Applicable to all grades of sanded exterior-type plywood. See DOC PS 1 for plywood species groups.

d. Applicable to Underlayment grade, C-C (Plugged) plywood, and Single Floor grade wood structural panels.

TABLE 2304.7(5)
ALLOWABLE LOAD (PSF) FOR WOOD STRUCTURAL PANEL ROOF SHEATHING CONTINUOUS OVER TWO OR MORE SPANS AND STRENGTH AXIS PARALLEL TO SUPPORTS (Plywood Structural Panels Are Five-Ply, Five-Layer Unless Otherwise Noted)[a,b]

PANEL GRADE	THICKNESS (inch)	MAXIMUM SPAN (inches)	LOAD AT MAXIMUM SPAN (psf)	
			Live	Total
Structural I sheathing	$7/16$	24	20	30
	$15/32$	24	35[c]	45[c]
	$1/2$	24	40[c]	50[c]
	$19/32, 5/8$	24	70	80
	$23/32, 3/4$	24	90	100
Sheathing, other grades covered in DOC PS 1 or DOC PS 2	$7/16$	16	40	50
	$15/32$	24	20	25
	$1/2$	24	25	30
	$19/32$	24	40[c]	50[c]
	$5/8$	24	45[c]	55[c]
	$23/32, 3/4$	24	60[c]	65[c]

For SI: 1 inch = 25.4 mm, 1 pound per square foot = 0.0479 kN/m^2.

a. Roof sheathing conforming with this table shall be deemed to meet the design criteria of Section 2304.7.

b. Uniform load deflection limitations $1/180$ of span under live load plus dead load, $1/240$ under live load only. Edges shall be blocked with lumber or other approved type of edge supports.

c. For composite and four-ply plywood structural panel, load shall be reduced by 15 pounds per square foot.

2304.8.2.4 Cantilevered pieces intermixed pattern. The decking shall cover a minimum of three spans. Pieces in the starter course and every third course shall be simple span. Pieces in other courses shall be cantilevered over the supports with end joints at alternate quarter or third points of the spans, and each piece shall bear on at least one support.

2304.8.2.5 Controlled random pattern. The decking shall cover a minimum of three spans. End joints within 6 inches (152 mm) of being in line in either direction shall be separated by at least two intervening courses. In the end bays each piece shall bear on at least one support. Where an end joint occurs in an end bay, the next piece in the same course shall continue over the first inner support for at least 24 inches (610 mm). The details of the controlled random pattern shall be as described for each decking material in Section 2304.8.3.3, 2304.8.4.3 or 2304.8.5.3.

For cantilevered spans with the controlled random pattern, special considerations shall be made when the overhang exceeds 18 inches (457 mm), 24 inches (610 mm) or 36 inches (914 mm) for 2-inch (51 mm), 3-inch (76 mm) or 4-inch (102 mm) nominal thickness decking, respectively. The maximum cantilevered length for the controlled random pattern shall be 30 percent of the length of the first adjacent interior span. For cantilever overhangs within these limits, a structural fascia shall be fastened to each decking piece to maintain a continuous, straight roof line. There shall be no end joints in the cantilevered portion or within one-half of the first adjacent interior span.

2304.8.3 Mechanically laminated decking.

2304.8.3.1 General. Mechanically laminated decking consists of square-edged dimension lumber laminations

set on edge and nailed to the adjacent pieces and to the supports.

2304.8.3.2 Nailing. The length of nails connecting laminations shall not be less than two and one-half times the net thickness of each lamination. Where deck supports are 48 inches (1219 mm) on center (o.c.) or less, side nails shall be spaced not more than 30 inches (762 mm) o.c. alternately near top and bottom edges, and staggered one-third of the spacing in adjacent laminations. Where supports are spaced more than 48 inches (1219 mm) o.c., side nails shall be spaced not more than 18 inches (457 mm) o.c. alternately near top and bottom edges and staggered one-third of the spacing in adjacent laminations. Two side nails shall be used at each end of butt-jointed pieces.

Laminations shall be toenailed to supports with 20d or larger common nails. Where the supports are 48 inches (1219 mm) o.c. or less, alternate laminations shall be toenailed to alternate supports; where supports are spaced more than 48 inches (1219 mm) o.c., alternate laminations shall be toenailed to every support.

2304.8.3.3 Controlled random pattern. There shall be a minimum distance of 24 inches (610 mm) between end joints in adjacent courses. The pieces in the first and second courses shall bear on at least two supports with end joints in these two courses occurring on alternate supports. A maximum of seven intervening courses shall be permitted before this pattern is repeated.

2304.8.4 Two-inch sawn tongue-and-groove decking.

2304.8.4.1 General. Two-inch (51 mm) decking shall have a maximum moisture content of 15 percent. Decking shall be machined with a single tongue-and-groove pattern. Each deck piece shall be nailed to each support as required.

2304.8.4.2 Nailing. Each piece of decking shall be toe-nailed at each support with one 16d common nail through the tongue and face-nailed with one 16d common nail.

2304.8.4.3 Controlled random pattern. There shall be a minimum distance of 24 inches (610 mm) between end joints in adjacent courses. The pieces in the first and second courses shall bear on at least two supports with end joints in these two courses occurring on alternate supports. A maximum of seven intervening courses shall be permitted before this pattern is repeated.

2304.8.5 Three- and 4-inch sawn tongue-and-groove decking.

2304.8.5.1 General. Three-inch (76 mm) and 4-inch (102 mm) decking shall have a maximum moisture content of 19 percent. Decking shall be machined with a double tongue-and-groove pattern. Deck pieces shall be interconnected and fastened to the supports as required.

2304.8.5.2 Nailing. Each piece shall be toenailed at each support with one 40d common nail and face-nailed with one 60d common nail. Courses shall be spiked to each other with 8-inch (203 mm) spikes at intervals not to exceed 30 inches (762 mm) through predrilled edge holes penetrating to a depth of approximately 4 inches (102 mm) and with one spike at a distance not exceeding 10 inches (254 mm) from the end of each piece.

2304.8.5.3 Controlled random pattern. There shall be a minimum distance of 48 inches (1219 mm) between end joints in adjacent courses. Pieces not bearing over a support are permitted to occur in interior bays, provided the adjacent pieces in the same course continue over the support for at least 24 inches (610 mm). This condition shall not occur more than once in every six courses in each interior bay.

2304.9 Connections and fasteners.

2304.9.1 Fastener requirements. Connections for wood members shall be designed in accordance with the appropriate methodology in Section 2301.2. The number and size of fasteners connecting wood members shall not be less than that set forth in Table 2304.9.1.

2304.9.2 Sheathing fasteners. Sheathing nails or other approved sheathing connectors shall be driven so that their head or crown is flush with the surface of the sheathing.

2304.9.3 Joist hangers and framing anchors. Connections depending on joist hangers or framing anchors, ties and other mechanical fastenings not otherwise covered are permitted where approved. The vertical load-bearing capacity, torsional moment capacity and deflection characteristics of joist hangers shall be determined in accordance with Section 1715.1.

2304.9.4 Other fasteners. Clips, staples, glues and other approved methods of fastening are permitted where approved.

2304.9.5 Fasteners in preservative-treated and fire-retardant-treated wood. Fasteners for preservative-treated and fire-retardant-treated wood shall be of hot dipped zinc-coated galvanized steel, stainless steel, silicon bronze or copper. The coating weights for zinc-coated fasteners shall be in accordance with ASTM A 153.

> **Exception:** Fasteners other than nails, timber rivets, wood screws and lag screws shall be permitted to be of mechanically deposited zinc coated steel with coating weights in accordance with ASTM B 695, Class 55 minimum.

Fastenings for wood foundations shall be as required in AF&PA PWF.

2304.9.6 Load path. Where wall framing members are not continuous from foundation sill to roof, the members shall be secured to ensure a continuous load path. Where required, sheet metal clamps, ties or clips shall be formed of galvanized steel or other approved corrosion-resistant material not less than 0.040 inch (1.01 mm) nominal thickness. Wood structural panel sheathing and fastening designed to transfer resultant forces across horizontal framing joints shall constitute an acceptable continuous load path as an alternative to the use of anchorage devices when calculated by principles of mechanics using values of fastener strength and sheathing shear resistance.

2304.9.7 Framing requirements. Wood columns and posts shall be framed to provide full end bearing. Alternatively, column-and-post end connections shall be designed to resist the full compressive loads, neglecting end-bearing capacity. Column-and-post end connections shall be fastened to resist lateral and net induced uplift forces.

2304.10 Heavy timber construction.

2304.10.1 Columns. Columns shall be continuous or superimposed throughout all stories by means of reinforced concrete or metal caps with brackets, or shall be connected by properly designed steel or iron caps, with pintles and base plates, or by timber splice plates affixed to the columns by metal connectors housed within the contact faces, or by other approved methods.

2304.10.1.1 Column connections. Girders and beams shall be closely fitted around columns and adjoining ends shall be cross tied to each other, or intertied by caps or ties, to transfer horizontal loads across joints. Wood bolsters shall not be placed on tops of columns unless the columns support roof loads only.

2304.10.2 Floor framing. Approved wall plate boxes or hangers shall be provided where wood beams, girders or trusses rest on masonry or concrete walls. Where intermediate beams are used to support a floor, they shall rest on top of girders, or shall be supported by ledgers or blocks securely fastened to the sides of the girders, or they shall be supported by an approved metal hanger into which the ends of the beams shall be closely fitted.

TABLE 2304.9.1
FASTENING SCHEDULE

CONNECTION	FASTENING[a,m]	LOCATION
1. Joist to sill or girder	3 - 8d common ($2^1/_2$" × 0.131") 3 - 3" × 0.131" nails 3 - 3" 14 gage staples	toenail
2. Bridging to joist	2 - 8d common ($2^1/_2$" × 0.131") 2 - 3" × 0.131" nails 2 - 3" 14 gage staples	toenail each end
3. 1" × 6" subfloor or less to each joist	2 - 8d common ($2^1/_2$" × 0.131")	face nail
4. Wider than 1" × 6" subfloor to each joist	3 - 8d common ($2^1/_2$" × 0.131")	face nail
5. 2" subfloor to joist or girder	2 - 16d common ($3^1/_2$" × 0.162")	blind and face nail
6. Sole plate to joist or blocking	16d ($3^1/_2$" × 0.135") at 16" o.c. 3" × 0.131" nails at 8" o.c. 3" 14 gage staples at 12" o.c.	typical face nail
Sole plate to joist or blocking at braced wall panel	3- 16d ($3^1/_2$" × 0.135") at 16" o.c. 4 - 3" × 0.131" nails at 16" o.c. 4 - 3" 14 gage staples at 16" o.c.	braced wall panels
7. Top plate to stud	2 - 16d common ($3^1/_2$" × 0.162") 3 - 3" × 0.131" nails 3 - 3" 14 gage staples	end nail
8. Stud to sole plate	4 - 8d common ($2^1/_2$" × 0.131") 4 - 3" × 0.131" nails 3 - 3" 14 gage staples	toenail
	2 - 16d common ($3^1/_2$" × 0.162") 3 - 3" × 0.131" nails 3 - 3" 14 gage staples	end nail
9. Double studs	16d ($3^1/_2$" × 0.135") at 24" o.c. 3" × 0.131" nail at 8" o.c. 3" 14 gage staple at 8" o.c.	face nail
10. Double top plates	16d ($3^1/_2$" × 0.135") at 16" o.c. 3" × 0.131" nail at 12" o.c. 3" 14 gage staple at 12" o.c.	typical face nail
Double top plates	8-16d common ($3^1/_2$" × 0.162") 12-3" × 0.131" nails 12-3" 14 gage staples	lap splice
11. Blocking between joists or rafters to top plate	3 - 8d common ($2^1/_2$" × 0.131") 3 - 3" × 0.131" nails 3 - 3" 14 gage staples	toenail
12. Rim joist to top plate	8d ($2^1/_2$" × 0.131") at 6" o.c. 3" × 0.131″ nail at 6" o.c. 3" 14 gage staple at 6" o.c.	toenail
13. Top plates, laps and intersections	2 - 16d common ($3^1/_2$" × 0.162") 3 - 3" × 0.131" nails 3 -3" 14 gage staples	face nail
14. Continuous header, two pieces	16d common ($3^1/_2$″ × 0.162″)	16"o.c. along edge
15. Ceiling joists to plate	3 - 8d common ($2^1/_2$" × 0.131") 5 - 3" × 0.131" nails 5 - 3" 14 gage staples	toenail
16. Continuous header to stud	4 - 8d common ($2^1/_2$" × 0.131")	toenail

(continued)

TABLE 2304.9.1—continued
FASTENING SCHEDULE

CONNECTION	FASTENING[a,m]	LOCATION
17. Ceiling joists, laps over partitions (see Section 2308.10.4.1, Table 2308.10.4.1)	3 - 16d common ($3^1/_2$" × 0.162") minimum, Table 2308.10.4.1 4 - 3" × 0.131" nails 4 - 3" 14 gage staples	face nail
18. Ceiling joists to parallel rafters (see Section 2308.10.4.1, Table 2308.10.4.1)	3 - 16d common ($3^1/_2$" × 0.162") minimum, Table 2308.10.4.1 4 - 3" × 0.131" nails 4 - 3" 14 gage staples	face nail
19. Rafter to plate (see Section 2308.10.1, Table 2308.10.1)	3 - 8d common ($2^1/_2$" × 0.131") 3 - 3" × 0.131" nails 3 - 3" 14 gage staples	toenail
20. 1" diagonal brace to each stud and plate	2 - 8d common ($2^1/_2$" × 0.131") 2 - 3" × 0.131" nails 3 - 3" 14 gage staples	face nail
21. 1" × 8" sheathing to each bearing	3 - 8d common ($2^1/_2$" × 0.131")	face nail
22. Wider than 1" × 8" sheathing to each bearing	3 - 8d common ($2^1/_2$" × 0.131")	face nail
23. Built-up corner studs	16d common ($3^1/_2$" × 0.162") 3" × 0.131" nails 3" 14 gage staples	24" o.c. 16" o.c. 16" o.c.
24. Built-up girder and beams	20d common (4" × 0.192") 32" o.c. 3" × 0.131" nail at 24" o.c. 3" 14 gage staple at 24" o.c. 2 - 20d common (4" × 0.192") 3 - 3" × 0.131" nails 3 - 3" 14 gage staples	face nail at top and bottom staggered on opposite sides face nail at ends and at each splice
25. 2" planks	16d common ($3^1/_2$" × 0.162")	at each bearing
26. Collar tie to rafter	3 - 10d common (3" × 0.148") 4 - 3" × 0.131" nails 4 - 3" 14 gage staples	face nail
27. Jack rafter to hip	3 - 10d common (3" × 0.148") 4 - 3" × 0.131" nails 4 - 3" 14 gage staples 2 - 16d common ($3^1/_2$" × 0.162") 3 - 3" × 0.131? nails 3 - 3" 14 gage staples	toenail face nail
28. Roof rafter to 2-by ridge beam	2 - 16d common ($3^1/_2$" × 0.162") 3 - 3" × 0.131" nails 3 - 3" 14 gage staples 2-16d common ($3^1/_2$" × 0.162") 3 - 3" × 0.131" nails 3 - 3" 14 gage staples	toenail face nail

(continued)

TABLE 2304.9.1—continued
FASTENING SCHEDULE

CONNECTION	FASTENING[a,m]		LOCATION
29. Joist to band joist	3 - 16d common ($3^1/_2$" × 0.162") 4 - 3" × 0.131" nails 4 - 3" 14 gage staples		face nail
30. Ledger strip	3 - 16d common ($3^1/_2$" × 0.162") 4 - 3" × 0.13" nails 4 - 3" 14 gage staples		face nail
31. Wood structural panels and particleboard[b] Subfloor, roof and wall sheathing (to framing) Single Floor (combination subfloor-underlayment to framing)	$^1/_2$" and less $^{19}/_{32}$" to $^3/_4$" $^7/_8$" to 1" $1^1/_8$" to $1^1/_4$" $^3/_4$" and less $^7/_8$" to 1" $1^1/_8$" to $1^1/_4$"	6d[c,l] $2^3/_8$" × 0.113" nail[n] $1^3/_4$" 16 gage[o] 8d[d] or 6d[e] $2^3/_8$" × 0.113" nail[p] 2" 16 gage[p] 8d[c] 10d[d] or 8d[e] 6d[e] 8d[e] 10d[d] or 8d[e]	
32. Panel siding (to framing)	$^1/_2$" or less $^5/_8$"	6d[f] 8d[f]	
33. Fiberboard sheathing[g]	$^1/_2$" $^{25}/_{32}$"	No. 11 gage roofing nail[h] 6d common nail (2" × 0.113") No. 16 gage staple[i] No. 11 gage roofing nail[h] 8d common nail ($2^1/_2$" × 0.131") No. 16 gage staple[i]	
34. Interior paneling	$^1/_4$" $^3/_8$"	4d[j] 6d[k]	

For SI: 1 inch = 25.4 mm.

a. Common or box nails are permitted to be used except where otherwise stated.

b. Nails spaced at 6 inches on center at edges, 12 inches at intermediate supports except 6 inches at supports where spans are 48 inches or more. For nailing of wood structural panel and particleboard diaphragms and shear walls, refer to Section 2305. Nails for wall sheathing are permitted to be common, box or casing.

c. Common or deformed shank (6d - 2" × 0.113"; 8d - $2^1/_2$" × 0.131"; 10d - 3" × 0.148").

d. Common (6d - 2" × 0.113"; 8d - $2^1/_2$" × 0.131"; 10d - 3" × 0.148").

e. Deformed shank (6d - 2" × 0.113"; 8d - $2^1/_2$" × 0.131"; 10d - 3" × 0.148").

f. Corrosion-resistant siding (6d - $1^7/_8$" × 0.106"; 8d - $2^3/_8$" × 0.128") or casing (6d - 2" × 0.099"; 8d - $2^1/_2$" × 0.113") nail.

g. Fasteners spaced 3 inches on center at exterior edges and 6 inches on center at intermediate supports, when used as structural sheathing. Spacing shall be 6 inches on center on the edges and 12 inches on center at intermediate supports for nonstructural applications.

h. Corrosion-resistant roofing nails with $^7/_{16}$-inch-diameter head and $1^1/_2$-inch length for $^1/_2$-inch sheathing and $1^3/_4$-inch length for $^{25}/_{32}$-inch sheathing.

i. Corrosion-resistant staples with nominal $^7/_{16}$-inch crown and $1^1/_8$-inch length for $^1/_2$-inch sheathing and $1^1/_2$-inch length for $^{25}/_{32}$-inch sheathing. Panel supports at 16 inches (20 inches if strength axis in the long direction of the panel, unless otherwise marked).

j. Casing ($1^1/_2$" × 0.080") or finish ($1^1/_2$" × 0.072") nails spaced 6 inches on panel edges, 12 inches at intermediate supports.

k. Panel supports at 24 inches. Casing or finish nails spaced 6 inches on panel edges, 12 inches at intermediate supports.

l. For roof sheathing applications, 8d nails ($2^1/_2$" × 0.113") are the minimum required for wood structural panels.

m. Staples shall have a minimum crown width of $^7/_{16}$ inch.

n. For roof sheathing applications, fasteners spaced 4 inches on center at edges, 8 inches at intermediate supports.

o. Fasteners spaced 4 inches on center at edges, 8 inches at intermediate supports for subfloor and wall sheathing and 3 inches on center at edges, 6 inches at intermediate supports for roof sheathing.

p. Fasteners spaced 4 inches on center at edges, 8 inches at intermediate supports.

2304.10.3 Roof framing. Every roof girder and at least every alternate roof beam shall be anchored to its supporting member; and every monitor and every sawtooth construction shall be anchored to the main roof construction. Such anchors shall consist of steel or iron bolts of sufficient strength to resist vertical uplift of the roof.

2304.10.4 Floor decks. Floor decks and covering shall not extend closer than $^1/_2$ inch (12.7 mm) to walls. Such $^1/_2$-inch (12.7 mm) spaces shall be covered by a molding fastened to the wall either above or below the floor and arranged such that the molding will not obstruct the expansion or contraction movements of the floor. Corbeling of masonry walls under floors is permitted in place of such molding.

2304.10.5 Roof decks. Where supported by a wall, roof decks shall be anchored to walls to resist uplift forces determined in accordance with Chapter 16. Such anchors shall consist of steel or iron bolts of sufficient strength to resist vertical uplift of the roof.

2304.11 Protection against decay and termites.

2304.11.1 General. Where required by this section, protection from decay and termites shall be provided by the use of naturally durable or preservative-treated wood.

2304.11.2 Wood used above ground. Wood used above ground in the locations specified in Sections 2304.11.2.1 through 2304.11.2.7, 2304.11.3 and 2304.11.5 shall be naturally durable wood or preservative-treated wood using water-borne preservatives, in accordance with AWPA U1 (Commodity Specifications A or F) for above-ground use.

2304.11.2.1 Joists, girders and subfloor. Where wood joists or the bottom of a wood structural floor without joists are closer than 18 inches (457 mm), or wood girders are closer than 12 inches (305 mm) to the exposed ground in crawl spaces or unexcavated areas located within the perimeter of the building foundation, the floor assembly (including posts, girders, joists and subfloor) shall be of naturally durable or preservative-treated wood.

2304.11.2.2 Wood supported by exterior foundation walls. Wood framing members, including wood sheathing, that rest on exterior foundation walls and are less than 8 inches (203 mm) from exposed earth shall be of naturally durable or preservative-treated wood.

2304.11.2.3 Exterior walls below grade. Wood framing members and furring strips attached directly to the interior of exterior masonry or concrete walls below grade shall be of approved naturally durable or preservative-treated wood.

2304.11.2.4 Sleepers and sills. Sleepers and sills on a concrete or masonry slab that is in direct contact with earth shall be of naturally durable or preservative-treated wood.

2304.11.2.5 Girder ends. The ends of wood girders entering exterior masonry or concrete walls shall be provided with a $^1/_2$-inch (12.7 mm) air space on top, sides and end, unless naturally durable or preservative-treated wood is used.

2304.11.2.6 Wood siding. Clearance between wood siding and earth on the exterior of a building shall not be less than 6 inches (152 mm) except where siding, sheathing and wall framing are of naturally durable or preservative-treated wood.

2304.11.2.7 Posts or columns. Posts or columns supporting permanent structures and supported by a concrete or masonry slab or footing that is in direct contact with the earth shall be of naturally durable or preservative-treated wood.

Exceptions:

1. Posts or columns that are either exposed to the weather or located in basements, supported by concrete piers or metal pedestals projected at least 1 inch (25 mm) above the slab or deck and 6 inches (152 mm) above exposed earth, and are separated therefrom by an impervious moisture barrier.

2. Posts or columns in enclosed crawl spaces or unexcavated areas located within the periphery of the building, supported by a concrete pier or metal pedestal at a height greater than 8 inches (203 mm) from exposed ground, and are separated therefrom by an impervious moisture barrier.

2304.11.3 Laminated timbers. The portions of glued-laminated timbers that form the structural supports of a building or other structure and are exposed to weather and not fully protected from moisture by a roof, eave or similar covering shall be pressure treated with preservative or be manufactured from naturally durable or preservative-treated wood.

2304.11.4 Wood in contact with the ground or fresh water. Wood used in contact with the ground (exposed earth) in the locations specified in Sections 2304.11.4.1 and 2304.11.4.2 shall be naturally durable (species for both decay and termite resistance) or preservative treated using water-borne preservatives in accordance with AWPA U1 (Commodity Specifications A or F) for soil or fresh water use.

Exception: Untreated wood is permitted where such wood is continuously and entirely below the groundwater level or submerged in fresh water.

2304.11.4.1 Posts or columns. Posts and columns supporting permanent structures that are embedded in concrete that is in direct contact with the earth, embedded in concrete that is exposed to the weather or in direct contact with the earth shall be of preservative-treated wood.

2304.11.4.2 Wood structural members. Wood structural members that support moisture-permeable floors or roofs that are exposed to the weather, such as concrete or masonry slabs, shall be of naturally durable or preservative-treated wood unless separated from such floors or roofs by an impervious moisture barrier.

2304.11.5 Supporting member for permanent appurtenances. Naturally durable or preservative-treated wood shall be utilized for those portions of wood members that form the structural supports of buildings, balconies, porches or similar permanent building appurtenances where such members are exposed to the weather without adequate protection from a roof, eave, overhang or other covering to prevent moisture or water accumulation on the surface or at joints between members.

Exception: When a building is located in a geographical region where experience has demonstrated that climatic conditions preclude the need to use durable materials where the structure is exposed to the weather.

2304.11.6 Termite protection. In geographical areas where hazard of termite damage is known to be very heavy, wood floor framing shall be of naturally durable species (termite resistant) or preservative treated in accordance with AWPA U1 for the species, product preservative and end use or provided with approved methods of termite protection.

2304.11.7 Wood used in retaining walls and cribs. Wood installed in retaining or crib walls shall be preservative treated in accordance with AWPA U1 (Commodity Specifications A or F) for soil and fresh water use.

2304.11.8 Attic ventilation. For attic ventilation, see Section 1203.2.

2304.11.9 Under-floor ventilation (crawl space). For under-floor ventilation (crawl space), see Section 1203.3.

2304.12 Long-term loading. Wood members supporting concrete, masonry or similar materials shall be checked for the effects of long-term loading using the provisions of the AF&PA NDS. The total deflection, including the effects of long-term loading, shall be limited in accordance with Section 1604.3.1 for these supported materials.

Exception: Horizontal wood members supporting masonry or concrete nonstructural floor or roof surfacing not more than 4 inches (102 mm) thick need not be checked for long-term loading.

SECTION 2305
GENERAL DESIGN REQUIREMENTS FOR LATERAL-FORCE-RESISTING SYSTEMS

2305.1 General. Structures using wood shear walls and diaphragms to resist wind, seismic and other lateral loads shall be designed and constructed in accordance with the provisions of this section. Alternatively, compliance with the AF&PA SDPWS shall be permitted subject to the limitations therein and the limitations of this code.

2305.1.1 Shear resistance based on principles of mechanics. Shear resistance of diaphragms and shear walls are permitted to be calculated by principles of mechanics using values of fastener strength and sheathing shear resistance.

2305.1.2 Framing. Boundary elements shall be provided to transmit tension and compression forces. Perimeter members at openings shall be provided and shall be detailed to distribute the shearing stresses. Diaphragm and shear wall sheathing shall not be used to splice boundary

elements. Diaphragm chords and collectors shall be placed in, or tangent to, the plane of the diaphragm framing unless it can be demonstrated that the moments, shears and deformations, considering eccentricities resulting from other configurations can be tolerated without exceeding the adjusted resistance and drift limits.

2305.1.2.1 Framing members. Framing members shall be at least 2 inch (51 mm) nominal width. In general, adjoining panel edges shall bear and be attached to the framing members and butt along their centerlines. Nails shall be placed not less than $^3/_8$ inch (9.5 mm) from the panel edge, not more than 12 inches (305 mm) apart along intermediate supports, and 6 inches (152 mm) along panel edge bearings, and shall be firmly driven into the framing members.

2305.1.3 Openings in shear panels. Openings in shear panels that materially affect their strength shall be fully detailed on the plans, and shall have their edges adequately reinforced to transfer all shearing stresses.

2305.1.4 Shear panel connections. Positive connections and anchorages capable of resisting the design forces shall be provided between the shear panel and the attached components. In Seismic Design Category D, E or F, the capacity of toenail connections shall not be used when calculating lateral load resistance to transfer lateral earthquake forces in excess of 150 pounds per foot (2189 N/m) from diaphragms to shear walls, drag struts (collectors) or other elements, or from shear walls to other elements.

2305.1.5 Wood members resisting horizontal seismic forces contributed by masonry and concrete walls. Wood shear walls, diaphragms, horizontal trusses and other members shall not be used to resist horizontal seismic forces contributed by masonry or concrete walls in structures over one story in height.

Exceptions:

1. Wood floor and roof members are permitted to be used in horizontal trusses and diaphragms to resist horizontal seismic forces contributed by masonry or concrete walls, provided such forces do not result in torsional force distribution through the truss or diaphragm.

2. Wood structural panel sheathed shear walls are permitted to be used to provide resistance to seismic forces contributed by masonry or concrete walls in two-story structures of masonry or concrete walls, provided the following requirements are met:

   2.1. Story-to-story wall heights shall not exceed 12 feet (3658 mm).

   2.2. Diaphragms shall not be designed to transmit lateral forces by rotation and shall not cantilever past the outermost supporting shear wall.

   2.3. Combined deflections of diaphragms and shear walls shall not permit story drift of supported masonry or concrete walls to exceed the limit of Section 12.12.1 in ASCE 7.

    2.4. Wood structural panel sheathing in diaphragms shall have unsupported edges blocked. Wood structural panel sheathing for both stories of shear walls shall have unsupported edges blocked and, for the lower story, shall have a minimum thickness of $^{15}/_{32}$ inch (11.9 mm).

    2.5. There shall be no out-of-plane horizontal offsets between the first and second stories of wood structural panel shear walls.

2305.1.6 Wood members resisting seismic forces from nonstructural concrete or masonry. Wood members shall be permitted to resist horizontal seismic forces from nonstructural concrete, masonry veneer or concrete floors.

2305.2 Design of wood diaphragms.

2305.2.1 General. Wood diaphragms are permitted to be used to resist horizontal forces provided the deflection in the plane of the diaphragm, as determined by calculations, tests or analogies drawn therefrom, does not exceed the permissible deflection of attached distributing or resisting elements. Connections shall extend into the diaphragm a sufficient distance to develop the force transferred into the diaphragm.

2305.2.2 Deflection. Permissible deflection shall be that deflection up to which the diaphragm and any attached distributing or resisting element will maintain its structural integrity under design load conditions, such that the resisting element will continue to support design loads without danger to occupants of the structure. Calculations for diaphragm deflection shall account for the usual bending and shear components as well as any other factors, such as nail deformation, which will contribute to deflection.

The deflection (Δ) of a blocked wood structural panel diaphragm uniformly nailed throughout is permitted to be calculated by using the following equation. If not uniformly nailed, the constant 0.188 (For SI: $^1/_{1627}$) in the third term must be modified accordingly.

$$\Delta = \frac{5vL^3}{8EAb} + \frac{vL}{4Gt} + 0.188Le_n + \frac{\Sigma(\Delta_c X)}{2b} \qquad \textbf{(Equation 23-1)}$$

For SI:

$$\Delta = \frac{0052vL^3}{EAb} + \frac{vL}{4Gt} + \frac{Le_n}{1627} + \frac{\Sigma(\Delta_c X)}{2b}$$

where:

A = Area of chord cross section, in square inches (mm^2).

b = Diaphragm width, in feet (mm).

E = Elastic modulus of chords, in pounds per square inch (N/mm^2).

e_n = Nail or staple deformation, in inches (mm) [see Table 2305.2.2(1)].

Gt = Panel rigidity through the thickness, in pounds per inch (N/mm) of panel width or depth [see Table 2305.2.2(2)].

L = Diaphragm length, in feet (mm).

v = Maximum shear due to design loads in the direction under consideration, in pounds per linear foot (plf) (N/mm).

Δ = The calculated deflection, in inches (mm).

$\Sigma(\Delta_c X)$ = Sum of individual chord-splice slip values on both sides of the diaphragm, each multiplied by its distance to the nearest support.

TABLE 2305.2.2(1)
e_n VALUES (inches) FOR USE IN CALCULATING DIAPHRAGM DEFLECTION DUE TO FASTENER SLIP (Structural I)[a,d]

LOAD PER FASTENER[c] (pounds)	FASTENER DESIGNATIONS[b]			
	6d	8d	10d	14-Ga staple × 2 inches long
60	0.01	0.00	0.00	0.011
80	0.02	0.01	0.01	0.018
100	0.03	0.01	0.01	0.028
120	0.04	0.02	0.01	0.04
140	0.06	0.03	0.02	0.053
160	0.10	0.04	0.02	0.068
180	—	0.05	0.03	—
200	—	0.07	0.47	—
220	—	0.09	0.06	—
240	—	—	0.07	—

For SI: 1 inch = 25.4 mm, 1 foot = 304.8 mm, 1 pound = 4.448 N.

a. Increase e_n values 20 percent for plywood grades other than Structural I.

b. Nail values apply to common wire nails or staples identified.

c. Load per fastener = maximum shear per foot divided by the number of fasteners per foot at interior panel edges.

d. Decrease e_n values 50 percent for seasoned lumber (moisture content < 19 percent).

2305.2.3 Diaphragm aspect ratios. Size and shape of diaphragms shall be limited as set forth in Table 2305.2.3.

TABLE 2305.2.3
MAXIMUM DIAPHRAGM DIMENSION RATIOS HORIZONTAL AND SLOPED DIAPHRAGM

TYPE	MAXIMUM LENGTH - WIDTH RATIO
Wood structural panel, nailed all edges	4:1
Wood structural panel, blocking omitted at intermediate joints	3:1
Diagonal sheathing, single	3:1
Diagonal sheathing, double	4:1

2305.2.4 Construction. Wood diaphragms shall be constructed of wood structural panels manufactured with exterior glue and not less than 4 feet by 8 feet (1219 mm by 2438 mm), except at boundaries and changes in framing where minimum sheet dimension shall be 24 inches (610 mm) unless all edges of the undersized sheets are supported by and fastened to framing members or blocking.

TABLE 2305.2.2(2)
VALUES OF *Gt* FOR USE IN CALCULATING DEFLECTION OF WOOD STRUCTURAL PANEL SHEAR WALLS AND DIAPHRAGMS

PANEL TYPE	SPAN RATING	VALUES OF *Gt* (lb/in. panel depth or width)							
		OTHER				STRUCTURAL I			
		3-ply Plywood	4-ply Plywood	5-ply Plywood[a]	OSB	3-ply Plywood	4-ply Plywood	5-ply Plywood[a]	OSB
Sheathing	24/0	25,000	32,500	37,500	77,500	32,500	42,500	41,500	77,500
	24/16	27,000	35,000	40,500	83,500	35,000	45,500	44,500	83,500
	32/16	27,000	35,000	40,500	83,500	35,000	45,500	44,500	83,500
	40/20	28,500	37,000	43,000	88,500	37,000	48,000	47,500	88,500
	48/24	31,000	40,500	46,500	96,000	40,500	52,500	51,000	96,000
Single Floor	16 o.c.	27,000	35,000	40,500	83,500	35,000	45,500	44,500	83,500
	20 o.c.	28,000	36,500	42,000	87,000	36,500	47,500	46,000	87,000
	24 o.c.	30,000	39,000	45,000	93,000	39,000	50,500	49,500	93,000
	32 o.c.	36,000	47,000	54,000	110,000	47,000	61,000	59,500	110,000
	48 o.c.	50,500	65,500	76,000	155,000	65,500	85,000	83,500	155,000

	Thickness (in.)	OTHER			STRUCTURAL I		
		A-A, A-C	Marine	All Other Grades	A-A, A-C	Marine	All Other Grades
Sanded Plywood	$1/4$	24,000	31,000	24,000	31,000	31,000	31,000
	$11/32$	25,500	33,000	25,500	33,000	33,000	33,000
	$3/8$	26,000	34,000	26,000	34,000	34,000	34,000
	$15/32$	38,000	49,500	38,000	49,500	49,500	49,500
	$1/2$	38,500	50,000	38,500	50,000	50,000	50,000
	$19/32$	49,000	63,500	49,000	63,500	63,500	63,500
	$5/8$	49,500	64,500	49,500	64,500	64,500	64,500
	$23/32$	50,500	65,500	50,500	65,500	65,500	65,500
	$3/4$	51,000	66,500	51,000	66,500	66,500	66,500
	$7/8$	52,500	68,500	52,500	68,500	68,500	68,500
	1	73,500	95,500	73,500	95,500	95,500	95,500
	$1 1/8$	75,000	97,500	75,000	97,500	97,500	97,500

For SI: 1 inch = 25.4 mm, 1 pound/inch = 0.1751 N/mm.

a. Applies to plywood with five or more layers; for five-ply/three-layer plywood, use values for four ply.

Wood structural panel thickness for horizontal diaphragms shall not be less than the valves set forth in Tables 2304.7(3), 2304.7(4) and 2304.7(5) for corresponding joist spacing and loads.

2305.2.4.1 Seismic Design Category F. Structures assigned to Seismic Design Category F shall conform to the additional requirements of this section.

Wood structural panel sheathing used for diaphragms and shear walls that are part of the seismic-force-resisting system shall be applied directly to the framing members.

Exception: Wood structural panel sheathing in a diaphragm is permitted to be fastened over solid lumber planking or laminated decking, provided the panel joints and lumber planking or laminated decking joints do not coincide.

2305.2.5 Rigid diaphragms. Design of structures with rigid diaphragms shall conform to the structure configuration requirements of Section 12.3.2 of ASCE 7 and the horizontal shear distribution requirements of Section 12.8.4 of ASCE 7.

Open-front structures with rigid wood diaphragms resulting in torsional force distribution are permitted, provided the length, *l*, of the diaphragm normal to the open side does not exceed 25 feet (7620 mm), the diaphragm sheathing conforms to Section 2305.2.4 and the *l/w* ratio [as shown in Figure 2305.2.5(1)] is less than 1 for one-story structures or 0.67 for structures over one story in height.

Exception: Where calculations show that diaphragm deflections can be tolerated, the length, *l*, normal to the open end is permitted to be increased to a l/w ratio not greater than 1.5 where sheathed in compliance with Section 2305.2.4 or to 1 where sheathed in compliance with Section 2306.3.4 or 2306.3.5.

Rigid wood diaphragms are permitted to cantilever past the outermost supporting shearwall (or other vertical resisting element) a length, *l*, of not more than 25 feet (7620 mm) or two-thirds of the diaphragm width, *w*, whichever is smaller. Figure 2305.2.5(2) illustrates the dimensions of *l* and *w* for a cantilevered diaphragm.

Structures with rigid wood diaphragms having a torsional irregularity in accordance with Table 12.3-1, Item 1, of ASCE 7 shall meet the following requirements: the *l/w* ratio shall not exceed 1 for one-story structures or 0.67 for structures over one story in height, where *l* is the dimension parallel to the load direction for which the irregularity exists.

Exception: Where calculations demonstrate that the diaphragm deflections can be tolerated, the width is permitted to be increased and the *l/w* ratio is permitted to be increased to 1.5 where sheathed in compliance with Section 2305.2.4 or 1 where sheathed in compliance with Section 2306.3.4 or 2306.3.5.

FIGURE 2305.2.5(1)
DIAPHRAGM LENGTH AND WIDTH FOR PLAN VIEW OF OPEN-FRONT BUILDING

FIGURE 2305.2.5(2)
DIAPHRAGM LENGTH AND WIDTH FOR PLAN VIEW OF CANTILEVERED DIAPHRAGM

2305.3 Design of wood shear walls.

2305.3.1 General. Wood shear walls are permitted to resist horizontal forces in vertical distributing or resisting elements, provided the deflection in the plane of the shear wall, as determined by calculations, tests or analogies drawn therefrom, does not exceed the more restrictive of the permissible deflection of attached distributing or resisting elements or the drift limits of Section 12.12.1 of ASCE 7. Shear wall sheathing other than wood structural panels shall not be permitted in Seismic Design Category E or F (see Section 1613).

2305.3.2 Deflection. Permissible deflection shall be that deflection up to which the shear wall and any attached dis-

tributing or resisting element will maintain its structural integrity under design load conditions, i.e., continue to support design loads without danger to occupants of the structure.

The deflection (Δ) of a blocked wood structural panel shear wall uniformly fastened throughout is permitted to be calculated by the use of the following equation:

$$\Delta = \frac{8vh^3}{EAb} + \frac{vh}{Gt} + 0.75he_n + d_a\frac{h}{b} \qquad \textbf{(Equation 23-2)}$$

For SI: $\Delta = \frac{vh^3}{3EAb} + \frac{vh}{Gt} + \frac{he_n}{407.6} + da\frac{h}{b}$

where:

A = Area of boundary element cross section in square inches (mm²) (vertical member at shear wall boundary).

b = Wall width, in feet (mm).

d_a = Vertical elongation of overturning anchorage (including fastener slip, device elongation, anchor rod elongation, etc.) at the design shear load (*v*).

E = Elastic modulus of boundary element (vertical member at shear wall boundary), in pounds per square inch (N/mm²).

e_n = Nail or staple deformation, in inches (mm) [see Table 2305.2.2(1)].

Gt = Panel rigidity through the thickness, in pounds per inch (N/mm) of panel width or depth [see Table 2305.2.2(2)].

h = Wall height, in feet (mm).

v = Maximum shear due to design loads at the top of the wall, in pounds per linear foot (N/mm).

Δ = The calculated deflection, in inches (mm).

2305.3.3 Construction. Wood shear walls shall be constructed of wood structural panels manufactured with exterior glue and not less than 4 feet by 8 feet (1219 mm by 2438 mm), except at boundaries and at changes in framing. All edges of all panels shall be supported by and fastened to framing members or blocking. Wood structural panel thickness for shear walls shall not be less than set forth in Table 2304.6.1 for corresponding framing spacing and loads, except that $^{1}/_{4}$ inch (6.4 mm) is permitted to be used where perpendicular loads permit.

2305.3.4 Shear wall aspect ratios. Size and shape of shear walls, perforated shear wall segments within perforated shear walls and wall piers within shear walls that are designed for force transfer around openings shall be limited as set forth in Table 2305.3.4. The height, *h*, and the width, *w*, shall be determined in accordance with Sections 2305.3.5 through 2305.3.5.2 and 2305.3.6 through 2305.3.6.2, respectively.

TABLE 2305.3.4
MAXIMUM SHEAR WALL DIMENSION RATIOS

TYPE	MAXIMUM HEIGHT-WIDTH RATIO
Wood structural panels or particleboard, nailed edges	For other than seismic: $3^1/_2$:1 For seismic: 2:1[a]
Diagonal sheathing, single	2:1
Fiberboard	$1^1/_2$:1
Gypsum board, gypsum lath, cement plaster	$1^1/_2$:1[b]

a. For design to resist seismic forces, shear wall height-width ratios greater than 2:1, but not exceeding $3^1/_2$:1, are permitted provided the allowable shear values in Table 2306.4.1 are multiplied by $2w/h$.

b. Ratio shown is for unblocked construction. Height-to-width ratio is permitted to be 2:1 where the wall is installed as blocked construction in accordance with Section 2306.4.5.1.2.

2305.3.5 Shear wall height definition. The height of a shear wall, h, shall be defined as:

1. The maximum clear height from the top of the foundation to the bottom of the diaphragm framing above; or

2. The maximum clear height from the top of the diaphragm to the bottom of the diaphragm framing above [see Figure 2305.3.5(a)].

2305.3.5.1 Perforated shear wall segment height definition. The height of a perforated shear wall segment, h, shall be defined as specified in Section 2305.3.5 for shear walls.

2305.3.5.2 Force transfer shear wall pier height definition. The height, h, of a wall pier in a shear wall with openings designed for force transfer around openings shall be defined as the clear height of the pier at the side of an opening [see Figure 2305.3.5(b)].

2305.3.6 Shear wall width definition. The width of a shear wall, w, shall be defined as the sheathed dimension of the shear wall in the direction of application of force [see Figure 2305.3.5(a)].

2305.3.6.1 Perforated shear wall segment width definition. The width of a perforated shear wall segment, w, shall be defined as the width of full-height sheathing adjacent to openings in the perforated shear wall [see Figure 2305.3.5(a)].

2305.3.6.2 Force transfer shear wall pier width definition. The width, w, of a wall pier in a shear wall with openings designed for force transfer around openings shall be defined as the sheathed width of the pier at the side of an opening [see Figure 2305.3.5(b)].

2305.3.7 Overturning restraint. Where the dead load stabilizing moment in accordance with Chapter 16 allowable stress design load combinations is not sufficient to prevent uplift due to overturning moments on the wall, an anchoring device shall be provided. Anchoring devices shall maintain a continuous load path to the foundation. Wood structural panel sheathing and fastening designed to transfer resultant forces across horizontal framing joints shall constitute an acceptable continuous load path as an alternative to the use of anchorage devices when calculated by principles of mechanics using values of fastener strength and sheathing shear resistance.

(a) HEIGHT-TO-WIDTH RATIO FOR SHEAR WALLS AND PERFORATED SHEAR WALLS

(b) HEIGHT-TO-WIDTH RATIO WITH DESIGN FOR FORCE TRANSFER AROUND OPENINGS

FIGURE 2305.3.5
GENERAL DEFINITION OF SHEAR WALL HEIGHT, WIDTH AND HEIGHT-TO-WIDTH RATIO

2305.3.8 Shear walls with openings. The provisions of this section shall apply to the design of shear walls with openings. Where framing and connections around the openings are designed for force transfer around the openings, the provisions of Section 2305.3.8.1 shall apply. Where framing and connections around the openings are not designed for force transfer around the openings, the provisions of Section 2305.3.8.2 shall apply.

2305.3.8.1 Force transfer around openings. Where shear walls with openings are designed for force transfer around the openings, the limitations of Table 2305.3.4 shall apply to the overall shear wall, including openings, and to each wall pier at the side of an opening. Design for force transfer shall be based on a rational analysis. Detailing of boundary elements around the opening shall be provided in accordance with the provisions of this section[see Figure 2305.3.5(b)].

2305.3.8.2 Perforated shear walls. The provisions of Section 2305.3.8.2 shall be permitted to be used for the design of perforated shear walls. For the determination of the height and width of perforated shear wall segments, see Sections 2305.3.5.1 and 2305.3.6.1, respectively.

TABLE 2305.3.8.2
SHEAR RESISTANCE ADJUSTMENT FACTOR, C_o

WALL HEIGHT, H	MAXIMUM OPENING HEIGHT[a]				
	H/3	H/2	2H/3	5H/6	H
8' wall	2'- 8"	4'- 0"	5'- 4"	6'- 8"	8'- 0"
10' wall	3'- 4"	5'- 0"	6'- 8"	8'- 4"	10'- 0"
Percentage of full-height sheathing[b]	Shear resistance adjustment factor				
10%	1.00	0.69	0.53	0.43	0.36
20%	1.00	0.71	0.56	0.45	0.38
30%	1.00	0.74	0.59	0.49	0.42
40%	1.00	0.77	0.63	0.53	0.45
50%	1.00	0.80	0.67	0.57	0.50
60%	1.00	0.83	0.71	0.63	0.56
70%	1.00	0.87	0.77	0.69	0.63
80%	1.00	0.91	0.83	0.77	0.71
90%	1.00	0.95	0.91	0.87	0.83
100%	1.00	1.00	1.00	1.00	1.00

For SI: 1 inch = 25.4 mm, 1 foot = 304.8 mm.
a. See Section 2305.3.8.2.2, Item 2.
b. See Section 2305.3.8.2.2, Item 1.

2305.3.8.2.1 Limitations. The following limitations shall apply to the use of Section 2305.3.8.2:

1. A perforated shear wall segment shall be located at each end of a perforated shear wall. Openings shall be permitted to occur beyond the ends of the perforated shear wall, provided the width of such openings is not be included in the width of the perforated shear wall.

2. The allowable shear set forth in Table 2306.4.1 shall not exceed 490 plf (7150 N/m).

3. Where out-of-plane offsets occur, portions of the wall on each side of the offset shall be considered as separate perforated shear walls.

4. Collectors for shear transfer shall be provided through the full length of the perforated shear wall.

5. A perforated shear wall shall have uniform top of wall and bottom of wall elevations. Perforated shear walls not having uniform elevations shall be designed by other methods.

6. Perforated shear wall height, h, shall not exceed 20 feet (6096 mm).

2305.3.8.2.2 Perforated shear wall resistance. The resistance of a perforated shear wall shall be calculated in accordance with the following:

1. The percentage of full-height sheathing shall be calculated as the sum of the widths of perforated shear wall segments divided by the total width of the perforated shear wall, including openings.

2. The maximum opening height shall be taken as the maximum opening clear height. Where areas above and below an opening remain unsheathed, the height of the opening shall be defined as the height of the wall.

3. The unadjusted shear resistance shall be the allowable shear set forth in Table 2306.4.1 for height-to-width ratios of perforated shear wall segments that do not exceed 2:1 for seismic forces and $3^1/_2$:1 for other than seismic forces. For seismic forces, where the height-to-width ratio of any perforated shear wall segment used in the calculation of the sum of the widths of perforated shear wall segments, ΣL_i, is greater than 2:1 but does not exceed $3^1/_2$:1, the unadjusted shear resistance shall be multiplied by 2 w/h.

4. The adjusted shear resistance shall be calculated by multiplying the unadjusted shear resistance by the shear resistance adjustment factors of Table 2305.3.8.2. For intermediate percentages of full-height sheathing, the values in Table 2305.3.8.2 are permitted to be interpolated.

5. The perforated shear wall resistance shall be equal to the adjusted shear resistance times the sum of the widths of the perforated shear wall segments.

2305.3.8.2.3 Anchorage and load path. Design of perforated shear wall anchorage and load path shall conform to the requirements of Sections 2305.3.8.2.4 through 2305.3.8.2.8, or shall be calculated using principles of mechanics. Except as modified by these sections, wall framing, sheathing, sheathing attachment and fastener schedules shall conform to the requirements of Section 2305.2.4 and Table 2306.4.1.

2305.3.8.2.4 Uplift anchorage at perforated shear wall ends. Anchorage for uplift forces due to overturning shall be provided at each end of the perforated shear wall. The uplift anchorage shall conform to the requirements of Section 2305.3.7, except that for each story the minimum tension chord uplift force, *T*, shall be calculated in accordance with the following:

$$T = \frac{Vh}{C_o \Sigma L_i} \qquad \text{Equation 23-3)}$$

where:

T = Tension chord uplift force, pounds (N).

V = Shear force in perforated shear wall, pounds (N).

h = Perforated shear wall height, feet (mm).

C_o= Shear resistance adjustment factor from Table 2305.3.8.2.

ΣL_i= Sum of widths of perforated shear wall segments, feet (mm).

2305.3.8.2.5 Anchorage for in-plane shear. The unit shear force, *v*, transmitted into the top of a perforated shear wall, out of the base of the perforated shear wall at full height sheathing and into collectors connecting shear wall segments shall be calculated in accordance with the following:

$$v = \frac{V}{C_o \Sigma L_i} \qquad \textbf{(Equation 23-4)}$$

where:

v = Unit shear force, pounds per lineal feet (N/m).

V = Shear force in perforated shear wall, pounds (N).

C_o= Shear resistance adjustment factor from Table 2305.3.8.2.

ΣL_i= Sum of widths of perforated shear wall segments, feet (mm).

2305.3.8.2.6 Uplift anchorage between perforated shear wall ends. In addition to the requirements of Section 2305.3.8.2.4, perforated shear wall bottom plates at full-height sheathing shall be anchored for a uniform uplift force, *t*, equal to the unit shear force, *v*, determined in Section 2305.3.8.2.5.

2305.3.8.2.7 Compression chords. Each end of each perforated shear wall segment shall be designed for a compression chord force, *C*, equal to the tension chord uplift force, *T*, calculated in Section 2305.3.8.2.4.

2305.3.8.2.8 Load path. A load path to the foundation shall be provided for each uplift force, T and t, for each shear force, V and v, and for each compression chord force, C. Elements resisting

shear wall forces contributed by multiple stories shall be designed for the sum of forces contributed by each story. Wood structural panel sheathing and fastening designed to transfer resultant forces across horizontal framing joints shall constitute an acceptable continuous load path as an alternative to the use of anchorage devices when calculated by principles of mechanics using values of fastener strength and sheathing shear resistance.

2305.3.8.2.9 Deflection of shear walls with openings. The controlling deflection of a blocked shear wall with openings uniformly fastened throughout shall be taken as the maximum individual deflection of the shear wall segments calculated in accordance with Section 2305.3.2, divided by the appropriate shear resistance adjustment factors of Table 2305.3.8.2.

2305.3.9 Summing shear capacities. The shear values for shear panels of different capacities applied to the same side of the wall are not cumulative except as allowed in Table 2306.4.1.

The shear values for material of the same type and capacity applied to both faces of the same wall are cumulative. Where the material capacities are not equal, the allowable shear shall be either two times the smaller shear capacity or the capacity of the stronger side, whichever is greater.

Summing shear capacities of dissimilar materials applied to opposite faces or to the same wall line is not allowed.

Exception: For wind design, the allowable shear capacity of shear wall segments sheathed with a combination of wood structural panels and gypsum wallboard on opposite faces, fiberboard structural sheathing and gypsum wallboard on opposite faces or hardboard panel siding and gypsum wallboard on opposite faces shall equal the sum of the sheathing capacities of each face separately.

2305.3.10 Adhesives. Adhesive attachment of shear wall sheathing is not permitted as a substitute for mechanical fasteners, and shall not be used in shear wall strength calculations alone, or in combination with mechanical fasteners in Seismic Design Category D, E or F.

2305.3.11 Sill plate size and anchorage in Seismic Design Category D, E or F. Anchor bolts for shear walls shall include steel plate washers, a minimum of 0.229 inch by 3 inches by 3 inches (5.82 mm by 76 mm by 76 mm) in size, between the sill plate and nut. The hole in the plate washer is permitted to be diagonally slotted with a width of up to $^3/_{16}$ inch (4.76 mm) larger than the bolt diameter and a slot length not to exceed $1^3/_4$ inches (44 mm), provided a standard cut washer is placed between the plate washer and the nut. Sill plates resisting a design load greater than 490 plf (7154 N/m) using load and resistance factor design or 350 plf (5110 N/m) using allowable stress design shall not be less than a 3-inch (76 mm) nominal member. Where a single 3-inch (76 mm) nominal sill plate is used, 2-20d box end nails shall be substituted for 2-16d common end nails found in line 8 of Table 2304.9.1.

Exception: In shear walls where the design load is greater than 490 plf (7151 N/m) but less than 840 plf (12 264 N/m) using load and resistance factor design or greater than 350 plf (5110 N/m) but less than 600 plf (8760 N/m) using allowable stress design, the sill plate is permitted to be a 2-inch (51 mm) nominal member if the sill plate is anchored by two times the number of bolts required by design and 0.229-inch by 3-inch by 3-inch (5.82 mm by 76 mm by 76 mm) plate washers are used.

SECTION 2306
ALLOWABLE STRESS DESIGN

2306.1 Allowable stress design. The structural analysis and construction of wood elements in structures using allowable stress design shall be in accordance with the following applicable standards:

American Forest & Paper Association.

NDS National Design Specification for Wood Construction

American Institute of Timber Construction.

AITC 104 Typical Construction Details

AITC 110 Standard Appearance Grades for Structural Glued Laminated Timber

AITC 113 Standard for Dimensions of Structural Glued Laminated Timber

AITC 117 Standard Specifications for Structural Glued Laminated Timber of Softwood Species

AITC 119 Structural Standard Specifications for Glued Laminated Timber of Hardwood Species

AITC A190.1 Structural Glued Laminated Timber

AITC 200 Inspection Manual

American Society of Agricultural Engineers.

ASAE EP 484.2 Diaphragm Design of Metal-Clad, Post-Frame Rectangular Buildings

ASAE EP 486.1 Shallow Post Foundation Design

ASAE 559 Design Requirements and Bending Properties for Mechanically Laminated Columns

APA-The Engineered Wood Association.

Panel Design Specification

Plywood Design Specification Supplement 1 - Design & Fabrication of Plywood Curved Panel

Plywood Design Specification Supplement 2 - Design & Fabrication of Glued Plywood-Lumber Beams

Plywood Design Specification Supplement 3 - Design & Fabrication of Plywood Stressed-Skin Panels

Plywood Design Specification Supplement 4 - Design & Fabrication of Plywood Sandwich Panels

Plywood Design Specification Supplement 5 - Design & Fabrication of All-Plywood Beams

EWS T300 Glulam Connection Details

EWS S560 Field Notching and Drilling of Glued Laminated Timber Beams

EWS S475 Glued Laminated Beam Design Tables

EWS X450 Glulam in Residential Construction

EWS X440 Product and Application Guide: Glulam

EWS R540 Builders Tips: Proper Storage and Handling of Glulam Beams

Truss Plate Institute, Inc.

TPI 1 National Design Standard for Metal Plate Connected Wood Truss Construction

2306.1.1 Joists and rafters. The design of rafter spans is permitted to be in accordance with the *AF&PA Span Tables for Joists and Rafters.*

2306.1.2 Plank and beam flooring. The design of plank and beam flooring is permitted to be in accordance with the *AF&PA Wood Construction Data No. 4.*

2306.1.3 Treated wood stress adjustments. The allowable unit stresses for preservative-treated wood need no adjustment for treatment, but are subject to other adjustments.

The allowable unit stresses for fire-retardant-treated wood, including fastener values, shall be developed from an approved method of investigation that considers the effects of anticipated temperature and humidity to which the fire-retardant-treated wood will be subjected, the type of treatment and the redrying process. Other adjustments are applicable except that the impact load duration shall not apply.

2306.1.4 Lumber decking. The capacity of lumber decking arranged according to the patterns described in Section 2304.8.2 shall be the lesser of the capacities determined for flexure and deflection according to the formulas in Table 2306.1.4.

2306.2 Wind provisions for walls.

2306.2.1 Wall stud bending stress increase. The AF&PA NDS fiber stress in bending (F_b) design values for sawn lumber wood studs resisting out of plane wind loads shall be increased by the factors in Table 2306.2.1, in lieu of the 1.15 repetitive member factor. These increases take into consideration the load sharing and composite actions provided by the wood structural panels as defined in Section 2302.1. The increases shall apply where the studs are designed for bending and are spaced no more than 16 inches (406 mm) o.c., covered on the inside with a minimum of $1/2$-inch (12.7 mm) gypsum board fastened in accordance with Table 2306.4.5 and sheathed on the exterior with a minimum of $3/8$-inch (9.5 mm) wood structural panel sheathing. All panel joints shall occur over studs or blocking and shall be attached using a minimum of 8d common nails spaced a maximum of 6 inches o.c. (152 mm) at panel edges and 12 inches o.c. (305 mm) at intermediate framing members.

TABLE 2306.1.4
ALLOWABLE LOADS FOR LUMBER DECKING

PATTERN	ALLOWABLE AREA LOAD[a,b]	
	Flexure	Deflection
Simple span	$\sigma_b = \dfrac{8F'_b}{l^2}\dfrac{d^2}{6}$	$\sigma_\Delta = \dfrac{384\Delta E'}{5l^4}\dfrac{d^3}{12}$
Two-span continuous	$\sigma_b = \dfrac{8F'_b}{l^2}\dfrac{d^2}{6}$	$\sigma_\Delta = \dfrac{185\Delta E'}{l^4}\dfrac{d^3}{12}$
Combination simple- and two-span continuous	$\sigma_b = \dfrac{8F'_b}{l^2}\dfrac{d^2}{6}$	$\sigma_\Delta = \dfrac{131\Delta E'}{l^4}\dfrac{d^3}{12}$
Cantilevered pieces intermixed	$\sigma_b = \dfrac{20F'_b}{3l^2}\dfrac{d^2}{6}$	$\sigma_\Delta = \dfrac{105\Delta E'}{l^4}\dfrac{d^3}{12}$
Controlled random layup		
Mechanically laminated decking	$\sigma_b = \dfrac{20F'_b}{3l^2}\dfrac{d^2}{6}$	$\sigma_\Delta = \dfrac{100\Delta E'}{l^4}\dfrac{d^3}{12}$
2-inch decking	$\sigma_b = \dfrac{20F'_b}{3l^2}\dfrac{d^2}{6}$	$\sigma_\Delta = \dfrac{100\Delta E'}{l^4}\dfrac{d^3}{12}$
3-inch and 4-inch decking	$\sigma_b = \dfrac{20F'_b}{3l^2}\dfrac{d^2}{6}$	$\sigma_\Delta = \dfrac{116\Delta E'}{l^4}\dfrac{d^3}{12}$

For SI: 1 inch = 25.4 mm.

a. σ_b = Allowable total uniform load limited by bending.
   $\sigma\Delta$ = Allowable total uniform load limited by deflection.
b. d = Actual decking thickness.
   l = Span of decking.
   F'_b = Allowable bending stress adjusted by applicable factors.
   E' = Modulus of elasticity adjusted by applicable factors.

TABLE 2306.2.1
WALL STUD BENDING STRESS INCREASE FACTORS

STUD SIZE	SYSTEM FACTOR
2 × 4	1.5
2 × 6	1.35
2 × 8	1.25
2 × 10	1.2
2 × 12	1.15

2306.3 Wood diaphragms.

2306.3.1 Wood structural panel diaphragms. Wood structural panel diaphragms are permitted to resist horizontal forces using the allowable shear capacities set forth in Table 2306.3.1 or 2306.3.2. The allowable shear capacities are permitted to be calculated by principles of mechanics without limitations by using values for fastener strength in the AF&PA NDS, structural design properties for wood structural panels based on DOC PS-1 and DOC PS-2 or wood structural panel design properties given in the *APA Panel Design Specification* (PDS).

2306.3.2 Shear capacities modifications. The allowable shear capacities in Tables 2306.3.1 and 2306.3.2 for horizontal wood structural panel diaphragms shall be increased 40 percent for wind design.

2306.3.3 Diagonally sheathed lumber diaphragms. Diagonally sheathed lumber diaphragms shall be nailed in accordance with Table 2306.3.3.

2306.3.4 Single diagonally sheathed lumber diaphragms. Single diagonally sheathed lumber diaphragms shall be constructed of minimum 1-inch (25 mm) thick nominal sheathing boards laid at an angle of approximately 45 degrees (0.78 rad) to the supports. The shear capacity for single diagonally sheathed lumber diaphragms of southern pine or Douglas fir-larch shall not exceed 300 plf (4378 N/m) of width. The shear capacities shall be adjusted by reduction factors of 0.82 for framing members of species with a specific gravity equal to or greater than 0.42 but less than 0.49 and 0.65 for species with a specific gravity of less than 0.42, as contained in the AF&PA NDS.

2306.3.4.1 End joints. End joints in adjacent boards shall be separated by at least one stud or joist space and

TABLE 2306.3.3
DIAGONALLY SHEATHED LUMBER DIAPHRAGM NAILING SCHEDULE

SHEATHING NOMINAL DIMENSION	NAILING TO INTERMEDIATE AND END-BEARING STUDS		NAILING AT THE SHEAR PANEL BOUNDARIES	
	Type, size and number of nails per board			
	Common nails	Box nails	Common nails	Box nails
1 × 6	2 - 8d	3 - 8d	3 - 8d	5 - 8d
1 × 8	3 - 8d	4 - 8d	4 - 8d	6 - 8d
2 × 6	2 - 16d	3 - 16d	3 - 16d	5 - 16d
2 × 8	3 - 16d	4 - 16d	4 - 16d	6 - 16d

there shall be at least two boards between joints on the same support.

2306.3.4.2 Single diagonally sheathed lumber diaphragms. Single diagonally sheathed lumber diaphragms made up of 2-inch (51 mm) nominal diagonal lumber sheathing fastened with 16d nails shall be designed with the same shear capacities as shear panels using 1-inch (25 mm) boards fastened with 8d nails, provided there are not splices in adjacent boards on the same support and the supports are not less than 4 inch (102 mm) nominal depth or 3 inch (76 mm) nominal thickness.

2306.3.5 Double diagonally sheathed lumber diaphragms. Double diagonally sheathed lumber diaphragms shall be constructed of two layers of diagonal sheathing boards at 90 degrees (1.57 rad) to each other on the same face of the supporting members. Each chord shall be considered as a beam with uniform load per foot equal to 50 percent of the unit shear due to diaphragm action. The load shall be assumed as acting normal to the chord in the plan of the diaphragm in either direction. The span of the chord or portion thereof shall be the distance between framing members of the diaphragm, such as the joists, studs and blocking that serve to transfer the assumed load to the sheathing. The shear capacity of double diagonally sheathed diaphragms of Southern pine or Douglas fir-larch shall not exceed 600 plf (8756 kN/m) of width. The shear capacity shall be adjusted by reduction factors of 0.82 for framing members of species with a specific gravity equal to or greater than 0.42 but less than 0.49 and 0.65 for species with a specific gravity of less than 0.42, as contained in the AF&PA NDS. Nailing of diagonally sheathed lumber diaphragms shall be in accordance with Table 2306.3.3.

2306.3.6 Gypsum board diaphragm ceilings. Gypsum board diaphragm ceilings shall be in accordance with Section 2508.5.

2306.4 Shear walls. Panel sheathing joints in shear walls shall occur over studs or blocking. Adjacent panel sheathing joints shall occur over and be nailed to common framing members (see Section 2305.3.1 for limitations on shear wall bracing materials).

2306.4.1 Wood structural panel shear walls. The allowable shear capacities for wood structural panel shear walls shall be in accordance with Table 2306.4.1. These capacities are permitted to be increased 40 percent for wind

design. Shear walls are permitted to be calculated by principles of mechanics without limitations by using values for nail strength given in the AF&PA NDS and wood structural panel design properties given in the *APA Panel Design Specification*.

2306.4.2 Lumber sheathed shear walls. Single and double diagonally sheathed lumber diaphragms are permitted using the construction and allowable load provisions of Sections 2306.3.4 and 2306.3.5.

2306.4.3 Particleboard shear walls. The design shear capacity of particleboard shear walls shall be in accordance with Table 2306.4.3. Shear panels shall be constructed with particleboard sheets not less than 4 feet by 8 feet (1219 mm by 2438 mm), except at boundaries and changes in framing. Particleboard panels shall be designed to resist shear only, and chords, collector members and boundary elements shall be connected at all corners. Panel edges shall be backed with 2-inch (51 mm) nominal or wider framing. Sheets are permitted to be installed either horizontally or vertically. For $^3/_8$-inch (9.5 mm) particleboard sheets installed with the long dimension parallel to the studs spaced 24 inches (610 mm) o.c, nails shall be spaced at 6 inches (152 mm) o.c. along intermediate framing members. For all other conditions, nails of the same size shall be spaced at 12 inches (305 mm) o.c. along intermediate framing members. Particleboard panels less than 12 inches (305 mm) wide shall be blocked. Particleboard shall not be used to resist seismic forces in structures in Seismic Design Category D, E or F.

2306.4.4 Fiberboard shear walls. The design shear capacity of fiberboard shear walls shall be in accordance with Table 2306.4.4. The fiberboard sheathing shall be applied vertically or horizontally to wood studs not less than 2 inch (51 mm) in nominal thickness spaced 16 inches (406 mm) o.c. Blocking not less than 2 inch (51 mm) nominal in thickness shall be provided at horizontal joints. Fiberboard shall not be used to resist seismic forces in structures in Seismic Design Category D, E or F.

2306.4.5 Shear walls sheathed with other materials. Shear capacities for walls sheathed with lath, plaster or gypsum board shall be in accordance with Table 2306.4.5. Shear walls sheathed with lath, plaster or gypsum board shall be constructed in accordance with Chapter 25 and Section 2306.4.5.1. Walls resisting seismic loads shall be subject to the limitations in Section 12.2.1 of ASCE 7.

TABLE 2306.3.1

ALLOWABLE SHEAR (POUNDS PER FOOT) FOR WOOD STRUCTURAL PANEL DIAPHRAGMS WITH FRAMING OF DOUGLAS FIR-LARCH, OR SOUTHERN PINE[a] FOR WIND OR SEISMIC LOADING[h]

PANEL GRADE	COMMON NAIL SIZE OR STAPLE[f] LENGTH AND GAGE	MINIMUM FASTENER PENETRATION IN FRAMING (inches)	MINIMUM NOMINAL PANEL THICKNESS (inch)	MINIMUM NOMINAL WIDTH OF FRAMING MEMBERS AT ADJOINING PANEL EDGES AND BOUNDARIES[g] (inches)	BLOCKED DIAPHRAGMS — Fastener spacing (inches) at diaphragm boundaries (all cases) at continuous panel edges parallel to load (Cases 3, 4), and at all panel edges (Cases 5, 6)[b]				UNBLOCKED DIAPHRAGMS	
					6	4	2½[c]	2[c]	Case 1 (No unblocked edges or continuous joints parallel to load)	All other configurations (Cases 2, 3, 4, 5 and 6)[b]
					Fastener spacing (inches) at other panel edges (Cases 1, 2, 3 and 4)[b]				Fasteners spaced 6" max. at supported edges[b]	
					6	6	4	3		
Structural I Grades	6d (2" × 0.113")	1¼	5/16	2	185	250	375	420	165	125
				3	210	280	420	475	185	140
	1½ 16 Gage	1		2	155	205	310	350	135	105
				3	175	230	345	390	155	115
	8d (2½" × 0.131")	1⅜	3/8	2	270	360	530	600	240	180
				3	300	400	600	675	265	200
	1½ 16 Gage	1		2	175	235	350	400	155	115
				3	200	265	395	450	175	130
	10d (3" × 0.148")	1½	15/32	2	320	425	640	730	285	215
				3	360	480	720	820	320	240
	1½ 16 Gage	1		2	175	235	350	400	155	120
				3	200	265	395	450	175	130
Sheathing, single floor and other grades covered in DOC PS 1 and PS 2	6d (2" × 0.113")	1¼	5/16	2	170	225	335	380	150	110
				3	190	250	380	430	170	125
	1½ 16 Gage	1		2	140	185	275	315	125	90
				3	155	205	310	350	140	105
	6d (2" × 0.113")	1¼	3/8	2	185	250	375	420	165	125
				3	210	280	420	475	185	140
	8d (2½" × 0.131")	1⅜		2	240	320	480	545	215	160
				3	270	360	540	610	240	180

(continued)

TABLE 2306.3.1—continued
ALLOWABLE SHEAR (POUNDS PER FOOT) FOR WOOD STRUCTURAL PANEL DIAPHRAGMS WITH FRAMING OF DOUGLAS FIR-LARCH, OR SOUTHERN PINE[a] FOR WIND OR SEISMIC LOADING[h]

PANEL GRADE	COMMON NAIL SIZE OR STAPLE[f] LENGTH AND GAGE	MINIMUM FASTENER PENETRATION IN FRAMING (inches)	MINIMUM NOMINAL PANEL THICKNESS (inch)	MINIMUM NOMINAL WIDTH OF FRAMING MEMBERS AT ADJOINING PANEL EDGES AND BOUNDARIES[g] (inches)	BLOCKED DIAPHRAGMS				UNBLOCKED DIAPHRAGMS	
					Fastener spacing (inches) at diaphragm boundaries (all cases) at continuous panel edges parallel to load (Cases 3, 4), and at all panel edges (Cases 5, 6)[b]				Fasteners spaced 6" max. at supported edges[b]	
					6	4	2½[c]	2[c]	Case 1 (No unblocked edges or continuous joints parallel to load)	All other configurations (Cases 2, 3, 4, 5 and 6)
					Fastener spacing (inches) at other panel edges (Cases 1, 2, 3 and 4)[b]					
					6	6	4	3		
	1½ 16 Gage	1	3/8	2	160	210	315	360	140	105
				3	180	235	355	400	160	120
	8d (2½" × 0.131")	1⅜	7/16	2	255	340	505	575	230	170
				3	285	380	570	645	255	190
Sheathing, single floor and other grades covered in DOC PS 1 and PS 2 (continued)	1½ 16 Gage	1		2	165	225	335	380	150	110
				3	190	250	375	425	165	125
	8d (2½" × 0.131")	1⅜	15/32	2	270	360	530	600	240	180
				3	300	400	600	675	265	200
	10d[d] (3" × 0.148")	1½		2	290	385	575	655	255	190
				3	325	430	650	735	290	215
	1½ 16 Gage	1	19/32	2	160	210	315	360	140	105
				3	180	235	355	405	160	120
	10d[d] (3" × 0.148")	1½		2	320	425	640	730	285	215
				3	360	480	720	820	320	240
	1¾ 16 Gage	1		2	175	235	350	400	155	115
				3	200	265	395	450	175	130

(continued)

TABLE 2306.3.1-continued
ALLOWABLE SHEAR (POUNDS PER FOOT) FOR WOOD STRUCTURAL PANEL DIAPHRAGMS WITH FRAMING OF DOUGLAS FIR-LARCH, OR SOUTHERN PINE[a] FOR WIND OR SEISMIC LOADING[h]

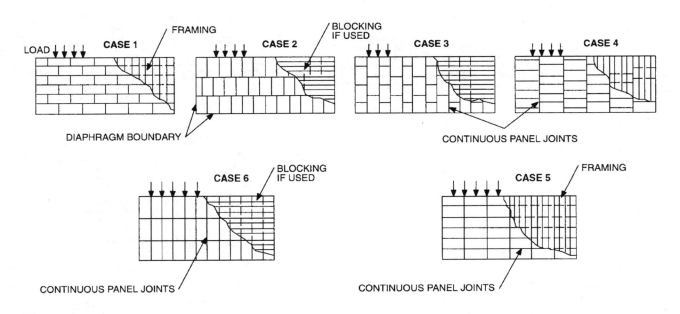

For SI: 1 inch = 25.4 mm, 1 pound per foot = 14.5939 N/m.

a. For framing of other species: (1) Find specific gravity for species of lumber in AF&PA NDS. (2) For staples find shear value from table above for Structural I panels (regardless of actual grade) and multiply value by 0.82 for species with specific gravity of 0.42 or greater, or 0.65 for all other species. (3) For nails find shear value from table above for nail size for actual grade and multiply value by the following adjustment factor: Specific Gravity Adjustment Factor = [1-(0.5 - SG)], where SG = Specific Gravity of the framing lumber. This adjustment factor shall not be greater than 1.

b. Space fasteners maximum 12 inches o.c. along intermediate framing members (6 inches o.c. where supports are spaced 48 inches o.c.).

c. Framing at adjoining panel edges shall be 3 inches nominal or wider, and nails shall be staggered where nails are spaced 2 inches o.c. or $2^1/_2$ inches o.c.

d. Framing at adjoining panel edges shall be 3 inches nominal or wider, and nails shall be staggered where both of the following conditions are met: (1) 10d nails having penetration into framing of more than $1^1/_2$ inches and (2) nails are spaced 3 inches o.c. or less.

e. 8d is recommended minimum for roofs due to negative pressures of high winds.

f. Staples shall have a minimum crown width of $^7/_{16}$ inch and shall be installed with their crowns parallel to the long dimension of the framing members.

g. The minimum nominal width of framing members not located at boundaries or adjoining panel edges shall be 2 inches.

h. For shear loads of normal or permanent load duration as defined by the AF&PA NDS, the values in the table above shall be multiplied by 0.63 or 0.56, respectively.

TABLE 2306.3.2
ALLOWABLE SHEAR (POUNDS PER FOOT) FOR WOOD STRUCTURAL PANEL BLOCKED DIAPHRAGMS UTILIZING MULTIPLE ROWS OF FASTENERS (HIGH LOAD DIAPHRAGMS) WITH FRAMING OF DOUGLAS FIR-LARCH OR SOUTHERN PINE[a] FOR WIND OR SEISMIC LOADING[b, g, h]

PANEL GRADE[c]	COMMON NAIL SIZE OR STAPLE[f] GAGE	MINIMUM FASTENER PENETRATION IN FRAMING (inches)	MINIMUM NOMINAL PANEL THICKNESS (inch)	MINIMUM NOMINAL WIDTH OF FRAMING MEMBER AT ADJOINING PANEL EDGES AND BOUNDARIES[e]	LINES OF FASTENERS	BLOCKED DIAPHRAGMS Cases 1 and 2[d]					
						Fastener Spacing Per Line at Boundaries (inches)					
						4		2½		2	
						Fastener Spacing Per Line at Other Panel Edges (inches)					
						6	4	4	3	3	2
Structural I grades	10d common nails	1½	15/32	3	2	605	815	875	1,150	-	-
				4	2	700	915	1,005	1,290	-	-
				4	3	875	1,220	1,285	1,395	-	-
			19/32	3	2	670	880	965	1,255	-	-
				4	2	780	990	1,110	1,440	-	-
				4	3	965	1,320	1,405	1,790	-	-
			23/32	3	2	730	955	1,050	1,365	-	-
				4	2	855	1,070	1,210	1,565	-	-
				4	3	1,050	1,430	1,525	1,800	-	-
	14 gage staples	2	15/32	3	2	600	600	860	960	1,060	1,200
				4	3	860	900	1,160	1,295	1,295	1,400
			19/32	3	2	600	600	875	960	1,075	1,200
				4	3	875	900	1,175	1,440	1,475	1,795
Sheathing single floor and other grades covered in DOC PS 1 and PS 2	10d common nails	1½	15/32	3	2	525	725	765	1,010	-	-
				4	2	605	815	875	1,105	-	-
				4	3	765	1,085	1,130	1,195	-	-
			19/32	3	2	650	860	935	1,225	-	-
				4	2	755	965	1,080	1,370	-	-
				4	3	935	1,290	1,365	1,485	-	-
			23/32	3	2	710	935	1,020	1,335	-	-
				4	2	825	1,050	1,175	1,445	-	-
				4	3	1,020	1,400	1,480	1,565	-	-
	14 gage staples	2	15/32	3	2	540	540	735	865	915	1,080
				4	3	735	810	1,005	1,105	1,105	1,195
			19/32	3	2	600	600	865	960	1,065	1,200
				4	3	865	900	1,130	1,430	1,370	1,485
			23/32	4	3	865	900	1,130	1,490	1,430	1,545

For SI: 1 inch = 25.4 mm, 1 pound per foot = 14.5939 N/m.

a. For framing of other species: (1) Find specific gravity for species of framing lumber in AF&PA NDS. (2) For staples, find shear value from table above for Structural I panels (regardless of actual grade) and multiply value by 0.82 for species with specific gravity of 0.42 or greater, or 0.65 for all other species. (3) For nails, find shear value from table above for nail size of actual grade and multiply value by the following adjustment factor: Specific Gravity Adjustment Factor = [1- (0.5 - SG)], where SG = Specific gravity of the framing lumber. This adjustment factor shall not be greater than 1.

b. Fastening along intermediate framing members: Space fasteners a maximum of 12 inches on center, except 6 inches on center for spans greater than 32 inches.

c. Panels conforming to PS 1 or PS 2.

d. This table gives shear values for Cases 1 and 2 as shown in Table 2306.3.1. The values shown are applicable to Cases 3, 4, 5 and 6 as shown in Table 2306.3.1, providing fasteners at all continuous panel edges are spaced in accordance with the boundary fastener spacing.

e. The minimum nominal depth of framing members shall be 3 inches nominal. The minimum nominal width of framing members not located at boundaries or adjoining panel edges shall be 2 inches.

f. Staples shall have a minimum crown width of $^7/_{16}$ inch, and shall be installed with their crowns parallel to the long dimension of the framing members.

g. High load diaphragms shall be subject to special inspection in accordance with Section 1704.6.1.

h. For shear loads of normal or permanent load duration as defined by the AF&PA NDS, the values in the table above shall be multiplied by 0.63 or 0.56, respectively.

TABLE 2306.4.1
ALLOWABLE SHEAR (POUNDS PER FOOT) FOR WOOD STRUCTURAL PANEL SHEAR WALLS WITH FRAMING OF DOUGLAS FIR-LARCH OR SOUTHERN PINE[a] FOR WIND OR SEISMIC LOADING[b, h, i, j, l]

PANEL GRADE	MINIMUM NOMINAL PANEL THICKNESS (inch)	MINIMUM FASTENER PENETRATION IN FRAMING (inches)	PANELS APPLIED DIRECT TO FRAMING — NAIL (common or galvanized box) or staple size[k]	6	4	3	2[e]	PANELS APPLIED OVER 1/2" OR 5/8" GYPSUM SHEATHING — NAIL (common or galvanized box) or staple size[k]	6	4	3	2[e]
Structural I Sheathing	5/16	1 1/4	6d (2" × 0.113" common, 2" × 0.099" galvanized box)	200	300	390	510	8d (2 1/2" × 0.131" common, 2 1/2" × 0.113" galvanized box)	200	300	390	510
		1	1 1/2 16 Gage	165	245	325	415	2 16 Gage	125	185	245	315
	3/8	1 3/8	8d (2 1/2" × 0.131" common, 2 1/2" × 0.113" galvanized box)	230[d]	360[d]	460[d]	610[d]	10d (3" × 0.148" common, 3" × 0.128" galvanized box)	280	430	550[f]	730
		1	1 1/2 16 Gage	155	235	315	400	2 16 Gage	155	235	310	400
	7/16	1 3/8	8d (2 1/2" × 0.131" common, 2 1/2" × 0.113" galvanized box)	255[d]	395[d]	505[d]	670[d]	10d (3" × 0.148" common, 3" × 0.128" galvanized box)	280	430	550[f]	730
		1	1 1/2 16 Gage	170	260	345	440	2 16 Gage	155	235	310	400
	15/32	1 3/8	8d (2 1/2" × 0.131" common, 2 1/2" × 0.113" galvanized box)	280	430	550	730	10d (3" × 0.148" common, 3" × 0.128" galvanized box)	280	430	550[f]	730
		1	1 1/2 16 Gage	185	280	375	475	2 16 Gage	155	235	300	400
	15/32	1 1/2	10d (3" × 0.148" common, 3" × 0.128" galvanized box)	340	510	665[f]	870	–	–	–	–	–
Sheathing, plywood siding[g] except Group 5 Species	5/16 or 1/4[c]	1 1/4	6d (2" × 0.113" common, 2" × 0.099" galvanized box)	180	270	350	450	8d (2 1/2" × 0.131" common, 2 1/2" × 0.113" galvanized box)	180	270	350	450
		1	1 1/2 16 Gage	145	220	295	375	2 16 Gage	110	165	220	285
	3/8	1 3/8	8d (2 1/2" × 0.131" common, 2 1/2" × 0.113" galvanized box)	200	300	390	510	8d (2 1/2" × 0.131" common, 2 1/2" × 0.113" galvanized box)	200	300	390	510
		1	1 1/2 16 Gage	220[d]	320[d]	410[d]	530[d]	2 16 Gage	260	380	490[f]	640
	7/16	1 3/8	8d (2 1/2" × 0.131" common, 2 1/2" × 0.113" galvanized box)	240[d]	350[d]	450[d]	585[d]	10d (3" × 0.148" common, 3" × 0.128" galvanized box)	260	380	490[f]	640
		1	1 1/2 16 Gage	155	230	310	395	2 16 Gage	140	210	280	360
	15/32	1 3/8	8d (3" × 0.148" common, 3" × 0.128" galvanized box)	260	380	490	640	10d (3" × 0.148" common, 3" × 0.128" galvanized box)	260	380	490[f]	640
		1	1 1/2 16 Gage	310	460	600[f]	770	–	–	–	–	–
	19/32	1 1/2	10d (3" × 0.148" common, 3" × 0.128" galvanized box)	340	510	665[f]	870	–	–	–	–	–
		1	1 3/4 16 Gage	185	280	375	475	–	–	–	–	–
	5/16[c]	1 1/4	Nail Size (galvanized casing) 6d (2" × 0.099")	140	210	275	360	Nail Size (galvanized casing) 8d (2 1/2" × 0.113")	140	210	275	360
	3/8	1 3/8	8d (2 1/2" × 0.113")	160	240	310	410	10d (3" × 0.128")	160	240	310[f]	410

Notes to Table 2306.4.1

For SI: 1 inch = 25.4 mm, 1 pound per foot = 14.5939 N/m.

a. For framing of other species: (1) Find specific gravity for species of lumber in AF&PA NDS. (2) For staples find shear value from table above for Structural I panels (regardless of actual grade) and multiply value by 0.82 for species with specific gravity of 0.42 or greater, or 0.65 for all other species. (3) For nails find shear value from table above for nail size for actual grade and multiply value by the following adjustment factor: Specific Gravity Adjustment Factor = [1-(0.5 - SG)], where SG = Specific Gravity of the framing lumber. This adjustment factor shall not be greater than 1.

b. Panel edges backed with 2-inch nominal or wider framing. Install panels either horizontally or vertically. Space fasteners maximum 6 inches on center along intermediate framing members for $^3/_8$-inch and $^7/_{16}$-inch panels installed on studs spaced 24 inches on center. For other conditions and panel thickness, space fasteners maximum 12 inches on center on intermediate supports.

c. $^3/_8$-inch panel thickness or siding with a span rating of 16 inches on center is the minimum recommended where applied direct to framing as exterior siding.

d. Allowable shear values are permitted to be increased to values shown for $^{15}/_{32}$-inch sheathing with same nailing provided (a) studs are spaced a maximum of 16 inches on center, or (b) panels are applied with long dimension across studs.

e. Framing at adjoining panel edges shall be 3 inches nominal or wider, and nails shall be staggered where nails are spaced 2 inches on center.

f. Framing at adjoining panel edges shall be 3 inches nominal or wider, and nails shall be staggered where both of the following conditions are met: (1) 10d (3" × 0.148") nails having penetration into framing of more than $1^1/_2$ inches and (2) nails are spaced 3 inches on center.

g. Values apply to all-veneer plywood. Thickness at point of fastening on panel edges governs shear values.

h. Where panels applied on both faces of a wall and nail spacing is less than 6 inches o.c. on either side, panel joints shall be offset to fall on different framing members, or framing shall be 3-inch nominal or thicker at adjoining panel edges and nails on each side shall be staggered.

i. In Seismic Design Category D, E or F, where shear design values exceed 350 pounds per linear foot, all framing members receiving edge nailing from abutting panels shall not be less than a single 3-inch nominal member, or two 2-inch nominal members fastened together in accordance with Section 2306.1 to transfer the design shear value between framing members. Wood structural panel joint and sill plate nailing shall be staggered in all cases. See Section 2305.3.11 for sill plate size and anchorage requirements.

j. Galvanized nails shall be hot dipped or tumbled.

k. Staples shall have a minimum crown width of $^7/_{16}$ inch and shall be installed with their crowns parallel to the long dimension of the framing members.

l. For shear loads of normal or permanent load duration as defined by the AF&PA NDS, the values in the table above shall be multiplied by 0.63 or 0.56, respectively.

TABLE 2306.4.3
ALLOWABLE SHEAR FOR PARTICLEBOARD SHEAR WALL SHEATHING[b]

PANEL GRADE	MINIMUM NOMINAL PANEL THICKNESS (inch)	MINIMUM NAIL PENETRATION IN FRAMING (inches)	PANELS APPLIED DIRECT TO FRAMING				
			Nail size (common or galvanized box)	Allowable shear (pounds per foot) nail spacing at panel edges (inches)[a]			
				6	4	3	2
M-S "Exterior Glue" and M-2 "Exterior Glue"	$^3/_8$	$1^1/_2$	6d	120	180	230	300
	$^3/_8$	$1^1/_2$	8d	130	190	240	315
	$^1/_2$			140	210	270	350
	$^1/_2$	$1^5/_8$	10d	185	275	360	460
	$^5/_8$			200	305	395	520

For SI: 1 inch = 25.4 mm, 1 pound per foot = 14.5939 N/m.

a. Values are not permitted in Seismic Design Category D, E or F.

b. Galvanized nails shall be hot-dipped or tumbled.

TABLE 2306.4.4
ALLOWABLE SHEAR VALUES (plf) FOR WIND OR SEISMIC LOADING ON SHEAR WALLS OF FIBERBOARD SHEATHING BOARD CONSTRUCTION FOR TYPE V CONSTRUCTION ONLY[a,b,c,d,e,f,g,h]

THICKNESS AND GRADE	FASTENER SIZE	SHEAR VALUE (pounds per linear foot) 3-INCH NAIL SPACING AROUND PERIMETER AND 6-INCH AT INTERMEDIATE POINTS
$^1/_2$" Structural	No. 11 gage galvanized roofing nail $1^1/_2$" long, $^7/_{16}$" head	125[g]
$^{25}/_{32}$" Structural	No. 11 gage galvanized roofing nail $1^3/_4$" long, $^7/_{16}$" head	175[g]

For SI: 1 inch = 25.4 mm, 1 pound per foot = 14.5939 N/m.

a. Fiberboard sheathing diaphragms shall not be used to brace concrete or masonry walls.

b. Panel edges shall be backed with 2 inch or wider framing of Douglas fir-larch or Southern pine.

c. Fiberboard sheathing on one side only.

d. Fiberboard panels are installed with their long dimension parallel or perpendicular to studs.

e. Fasteners shall be spaced 6 inches on center along intermediate framing members.

f. For framing of other species: (1) Find specific gravity for species of lumber in AF&PA NDS and (2) Multiply the shear value from the above table by 0.82 for species with specific gravity of 0.42 or greater, or 0.65 for all other species.

g. The same values can be applied when staples are used as described in Table 2304.9.1.

h. Values are not permitted in Seismic Design Category D, E or F.

TABLE 2306.4.5
ALLOWABLE SHEAR FOR WIND OR SEISMIC FORCES FOR SHEAR WALLS OF LATH AND PLASTER OR GYPSUM BOARD WOOD FRAMED WALL ASSEMBLIES

	TYPE OF MATERIAL	THICKNESS OF MATERIAL	WALL CONSTRUCTION	FASTENER SPACING[b] MAXIMUM (inches)	SHEAR VALUE[a,e] (plf)	MINIMUM FASTENER SIZE[c,d,j,k]
1.	Expanded metal or woven wire lath and portland cement plaster	$^7/_8$"	Unblocked	6	180	No. 11 gage $1^1/_2$" long, $^7/_{16}$" head 16 Ga. Galv. Staple, $^7/_8$" legs
2.	Gypsum lath, plain or perforated	$^3/_8$" lath and $^1/_2$" plaster	Unblocked	5	100	No. 13 gage, $1^1/_8$" long, $^{19}/_{64}$" head, plasterboard nail 16 Ga. Galv. Staple, $1^1/_8$" long 0.120" Nail, min. $^3/_8$" head, $1^1/_4$" long
3.	Gypsum sheathing	$^1/_2$" × 2' × 8'	Unblocked	4	75	No. 11 gage, $1^3/_4$" long, $^7/_{16}$" head, diamond-point, galvanized
		$^1/_2$" × 4'	Blocked[f]	4	175	
			Unblocked	7	100	16 Ga. Galv. Staple, $1^3/_4$" long
		$^5/_8$" × 4'	Blocked	4" edge/ 7" field	200	6d galvanized 0.120" Nail, min. $^3/_8$" head, $1^3/_4$" long
4.	Gypsum board, gypsum veneer base or water-resistant gypsum backing board	$^1/_2$"	Unblocked[f]	7	75	5d cooler ($1^5/_8$" × .086") or wallboard 0.120" nail, min. $^3/_8$" head, $1^1/_2$" long 16 Gage Staple, $1^1/_2$" long
			Unblocked[f]	4	110	
			Unblocked	7	100	
			Unblocked	4	125	
			Blocked[g]	7	125	
			Blocked[g]	4	150	
			Unblocked	8/12[h]	60	No.-6 $1^1/_4$" screws[i]
			Blocked[g]	4/16[h]	160	
			Blocked[f,g]	4/12[h]	155	
			Blocked[g]	8/12[h]	70	
			Blocked[g]	6/12[h]	90	
		$^5/_8$"	Unblocked[f]	7	115	6d cooler ($1^7/_8$" × 0.092") or wallboard 0.120" Nail, min. $^3/_8$" head, $1^3/_4$" long 16 Gage Staple, $1^1/_2$" legs, $1^5/_8$" long
			Unblocked[f]	4	145	
			Blocked[g]	7	145	
			Blocked[g]	4	175	
			Blocked[g] Two-ply	Base ply: 9 Face ply: 7	250	Base ply-6d cooler ($1^7/_8$" × 0.092") or wallboard $1^3/_4$" × 0.120" Nail, min. $^3/_8$" head $1^5/_8$" 16 Ga. Galv. Staple $1^5/_8$" 16 Gage Galv. Staple Face ply-8d cooler ($2^3/_8$" × 0.113") or wallboard 0.120" Nail, min. $^3/_8$" head, $2^3/_8$" long 15 Ga. Galv. Staple, $2^1/_4$" long
			Unblocked	8/12[h]	70	No. 6-$1^1/_4$" screws[i]
			Blocked[g]	8/12[h]	90	

For SI: 1 inch = 25.4 mm, 1 foot = 304.8 mm, 1 pound per foot = 14.5939 N/m.

a. These shear walls shall not be used to resist loads imposed by masonry or concrete construction (see Section 2305.1.5). Values shown are for short-term loading due to wind or seismic loading. Walls resisting seismic loads shall be subject to the limitations in Section 12.2.1 of ASCE 7. Values shown shall be reduced 25 percent for normal loading.

b. Applies to fastening at studs, top and bottom plates and blocking.

c. Alternate fasteners are permitted to be used if their dimensions are not less than the specified dimensions. Drywall screws are permitted to substitute for the 5d ($1^5/_8$" × 0.086"), and 6d ($1^7/_8$" × 0.092")(cooler) nails listed above, and No. 6 $1^1/_4$ inch Type S or W screws for 6d ($1^7/_8$" × 0.092) (cooler) nails.

d. For properties of cooler nails, see ASTM C 514.

e. Except as noted, shear values are based on a maximum framing spacing of 16 inches on center.

f. Maximum framing spacing of 24 inches on center.

g. All edges are blocked, and edge fastening is provided at all supports and all panel edges.

h. First number denotes fastener spacing at the edges; second number denotes fastener spacing at intermediate framing members.

i. Screws are Type W or S.

j. Staples shall have a minimum crown width of $^7/_{16}$ inch, measured outside the legs, and shall be installed with their crowns parallel to the long dimension of the framing members.

k. Staples for the attachment of gypsum lath and woven-wire lath shall have a minimum crown width of $^3/_4$ inch, measured outside the legs.

2306.4.5.1 Application of gypsum board or lath and plaster to wood framing.

2306.4.5.1.1 Joint staggering. End joints of adjacent courses of gypsum board shall not occur over the same stud.

2306.4.5.1.2 Blocking. Where required in Table 2306.4.5, wood blocking having the same cross-sectional dimensions as the studs shall be provided at joints that are perpendicular to the studs.

2306.4.5.1.3 Fastening. Studs, top and bottom plates and blocking shall be fastened in accordance with Table 2304.9.1.

2306.4.5.1.4 Fasteners. The size and spacing of fasteners shall be set forth in Table 2306.4.5. Fasteners shall be spaced not less than $^3/_8$ inch (9.5 mm) from edges and ends of gypsum boards or sides of studs, blocking and top and bottom plates.

2306.4.5.1.5 Gypsum lath. Gypsum lath shall be applied perpendicular to the studs. Maximum allowable shear values shall be as set forth in Table 2306.4.5.

2306.4.5.1.6 Gypsum sheathing. Four-foot-wide (1219 mm) pieces of gypsum sheathing shall be applied parallel or perpendicular to studs. Two-foot-wide (610 mm) pieces of gypsum sheathing shall be applied perpendicular to the studs. Maximum allowable shear values shall be as set forth in Table 2306.4.5.

2306.4.5.1.7 Other gypsum boards. Gypsum board shall be applied parallel or perpendicular to studs. Maximum allowable shear values shall be as set forth in Table 2306.4.5.

SECTION 2307
LOAD AND RESISTANCE FACTOR DESIGN

2307.1 Load and resistance factor design. The structural analysis and construction of wood elements and structures using load and resistance factor design shall be in accordance with AF&PA NDS.

2307.1.1 Wood structural panel shear walls. In Seismic Design Category D, E or F, where shear design values exceed 490 pounds per foot (7154 N/m), all framing members receiving edge nailing from abutting panels shall not be less than a single 3-inch (76 mm) nominal member or two 2-inch (51 mm) nominal members fastened together in accordance with AF&PA NDS to transfer the design shear value between framing members. Wood structural panel joint and sill plate nailing shall be staggered in all cases. See Section 2305.3.11 for sill plate size and anchorage requirements.

SECTION 2308
CONVENTIONAL LIGHT-FRAME CONSTRUCTION

2308.1 General. The requirements of this section are intended for conventional light-frame construction. Other methods are permitted to be used, provided a satisfactory design is submitted showing compliance with other provisions of this code. Interior nonload-bearing partitions, ceilings and curtain walls of conventional light-frame construction are not subject to the limitations of this section. Alternatively, compliance with AF&PA WFCM shall be permitted subject to the limitations therein and the limitations of this code. Detached one- and two-family dwellings and multiple single-family dwellings (townhouses) not more than three stories above grade plane in height with a separate means of egress and their accessory structures shall comply with the *Residential Code of New York State*.

2308.1.1 Portions exceeding limitations of conventional construction. When portions of a building of otherwise conventional construction exceed the limits of Section 2308.2, these portions and the supporting load path shall be designed in accordance with accepted engineering practice and the provisions of this code. For the purposes of this section, the term "portions" shall mean parts of buildings containing volume and area such as a room or a series of rooms.

2308.2 Limitations. Buildings are permitted to be constructed in accordance with the provisions of conventional light-frame construction, subject to the following limitations, and to further limitations of Sections 2308.11 and 2308.12.

1. Buildings shall be limited to a maximum of three stories above grade. For the purposes of this section, for buildings in Seismic Design Category D or E as determined in Section 1613, cripple stud walls shall be considered to be a story.

   Exception: Solid blocked cripple walls not exceeding 14 inches (356 mm) in height need not be considered a story.

2. Maximum floor-to-floor height shall not exceed 11 feet 7 inches (3531 mm). Bearing wall height shall not exceed a stud height of 10 feet (3048 mm).

3. Loads as determined in Chapter 16 shall not exceed the following:

   3.1. Average dead loads shall not exceed 15 psf (718 N/m^2) for combined roof and ceiling, exterior walls, floors and partitions.

   Exceptions:

   1. Subject to the limitations of Sections 2308.11.2 and 2308.12.2, stone or masonry veneer up to the lesser of 5 inches (127 mm) thick or 50 psf (2395 N/m^2) and installed in accordance with Chapter 14 is permitted to a height of 30 feet (9144 mm) above a noncombustible foundation, with an additional 8 feet (2438 mm) permitted for gable ends.

   2. Concrete or masonry fireplaces, heaters and chimneys shall be permitted in accordance with the provisions of this code.

   3.2. Live loads shall not exceed 40 psf (1916 N/m^2) for floors.

3.3. Ground snow loads shall not exceed 50 psf (2395 N/m²).

4. Wind speeds shall not exceed 100 miles per hour (mph) (44 m/s) (3-second gust).

Exception: Wind speeds shall not exceed 110 mph (48.4 m/s) (3-second gust) for buildings in Exposure Category B.

5. Roof trusses and rafters shall not span more than 40 feet (12 192 mm) between points of vertical support.

6. The use of the provisions for conventional light-frame construction in this section shall not be permitted for Occupancy Category IV buildings assigned to Seismic Design Category B, C, D, E or F, as determined in Section 1613.

7. Conventional light-frame construction is limited in irregular structures in Seismic Design Category D or E, as specified in Section 2308.12.6.

2308.2.1 Basic wind speed greater than 100 mph (3-second gust). Where the basic wind speed exceeds 100 mph (3-second gust), the provisions of either AF&PA WFCM, or the SBCCI SSTD 10 are permitted to be used.

2308.2.2 Buildings in Seismic Design Category B, C, D or E. Buildings of conventional light-frame construction in Seismic Design Category B or C, as determined in Section 1613, shall comply with the additional requirements in Section 2308.11.

Buildings of conventional light-frame construction in Seismic Design Category D or E, as determined in Section 1613, shall comply with the additional requirements in Section 2308.12.

2308.3 Braced wall lines. Buildings shall be provided with exterior and interior braced wall lines as described in Section 2308.9.3 and installed in accordance with Sections 2308.3.1 through 2308.3.4.

2308.3.1 Spacing. Spacing of braced wall lines shall not exceed 35 feet (10 668 mm) o.c. in both the longitudinal and transverse directions in each story.

2308.3.2 Braced wall panel connections. Forces shall be transferred from the roofs and floors to braced wall panels and from the braced wall panels in upper stories to the braced wall panels in the story below by the following:

1. Braced wall panel top and bottom plates shall be fastened to joists, rafters or full-depth blocking. Braced wall panels shall be extended and fastened to roof framing at intervals not to exceed 50 feet (15 240 mm) between parallel braced wall lines.

Exception: Where roof trusses are used, lateral forces shall be transferred from the roof diaphragm to the braced wall by blocking of the ends of the trusses or by other approved methods.

2. Bottom plate fastening to joist or blocking below shall be with not less than 3-16d nails at 16 inches (406 mm) o.c.

3. Blocking shall be nailed to the top plate below with not less than 3-8d toenails per block.

4. Joists parallel to the top plates shall be nailed to the top plate with not less than 8d toenails at 6 inches (152 mm) o.c.

In addition, top plate laps shall be nailed with not less than 8-16d face nails on each side of each break in the top plate.

2308.3.3 Sill anchorage. Where foundations are required by Section 2308.3.4, braced wall line sills shall be anchored to concrete or masonry foundations. Such anchorage shall conform to the requirements of Section 2308.6 except that such anchors shall be spaced at not more than 4 feet (1219 mm) o.c. for structures over two stories in height. The anchors shall be distributed along the length of the braced wall line. Other anchorage devices having equivalent capacity are permitted.

2308.3.3.1 Anchorage to all-wood foundations. Where all-wood foundations are used, the force transfer from the braced wall lines shall be determined based on calculation and shall have a capacity greater than or equal to the connections required by Section 2308.3.3.

2308.3.4 Braced wall line support. Braced wall lines shall be supported by continuous foundations.

Exception: For structures with a maximum plan dimension not over 50 feet (15 240 mm), continuous foundations are required at exterior walls only.

2308.4 Design of elements. Combining of engineered elements or systems and conventionally specified elements or systems is permitted subject to the following limits:

2308.4.1 Elements exceeding limitations of conventional construction. When a building of otherwise conventional construction contains structural elements exceeding the limits of Section 2308.2, these elements and the supporting load path shall be designed in accordance with accepted engineering practice and the provisions of this code.

2308.4.2 Structural elements or systems not described herein. When a building of otherwise conventional construction contains structural elements or systems not described in Section 2308, these elements or systems shall be designed in accordance with accepted engineering practice and the provisions of this code. The extent of such design need only demonstrate compliance of the nonconventional elements with other applicable provisions of this code and shall be compatible with the performance of the conventionally framed system.

2308.5 Connections and fasteners. Connections and fasteners used in conventional construction shall comply with the requirements of Section 2304.9.

2308.6 Foundation plates or sills. Foundations and footings shall be as specified in Chapter 18. Foundation plates or sills resting on concrete or masonry foundations shall comply with Section 2304.3.1. Foundation plates or sills shall be bolted or anchored to the foundation with not less than $^1/_2$-inch-diameter (12.7 mm) steel bolts or approved anchors. Bolts shall be embedded at least 7 inches (178 mm) into concrete or masonry, and spaced not more than 6 feet (1829 mm) apart. There shall be a minimum of two bolts or anchor straps per piece with one bolt or anchor strap located not more than 12 inches (305 mm) or less than 4 inches (102 mm) from each end of each piece. A properly sized nut and washer shall be tightened on each bolt to the plate.

2308.7 Girders. Girders for single-story construction or girders supporting loads from a single floor shall not be less than 4 inches by 6 inches (102 mm by 152 mm) for spans 6 feet (1829 mm) or less, provided that girders are spaced not more than 8 feet (2438 mm) o.c. Spans for built-up 2-inch (51 mm) girders shall be in accordance with Table 2308.9.5 or 2308.9.6. Other girders shall be designed to support the loads specified in this code. Girder end joints shall occur over supports.

Where a girder is spliced over a support, an adequate tie shall be provided. The ends of beams or girders supported on masonry or concrete shall not have less than 3 inches (76 mm) of bearing.

2308.8 Floor joists. Spans for floor joists shall be in accordance with Table 2308.8(1) or 2308.8(2). For other grades and or species, refer to the *AF&PA Span Tables for Joists and Rafters*.

2308.8.1 Bearing. Except where supported on a 1-inch by 4-inch (25.4 mm by 102 mm) ribbon strip and nailed to the adjoining stud, the ends of each joist shall not have less than $1^1/_2$ inches (38 mm) of bearing on wood or metal, or less than 3 inches (76 mm) on masonry.

2308.8.2 Framing details. Joists shall be supported laterally at the ends and at each support by solid blocking except where the ends of the joists are nailed to a header, band or rim joist or to an adjoining stud or by other means. Solid blocking shall not be less than 2 inches (51mm) in thickness and the full depth of the joist. Notches on the ends of joists shall not exceed one-fourth the joist depth. Holes bored in joists shall not be within 2 inches (51 mm) of the top or bottom of the joist, and the diameter of any such hole shall not exceed one-third the depth of the joist. Notches in the top or bottom of joists shall not exceed one-

sixth the depth and shall not be located in the middle third of the span.

Joist framing from opposite sides of a beam, girder or partition shall be lapped at least 3 inches (76 mm) or the opposing joists shall be tied together in an approved manner.

Joists framing into the side of a wood girder shall be supported by framing anchors or on ledger strips not less than 2 inches by 2 inches (51 mm by 51 mm).

2308.8.2.1 Engineered wood products. Cuts, notches and holes bored in trusses, structural composite lumber, structural glue-laminated members or I-joists are not permitted except where permitted by the manufacturer's recommendations or where the effects of such alterations are specifically considered in the design of the member by a registered design professional.

2308.8.3 Framing around openings. Trimmer and header joists shall be doubled, or of lumber of equivalent cross section, where the span of the header exceeds 4 feet (1219 mm). The ends of header joists more than 6 feet (1829 mm) long shall be supported by framing anchors or joist hangers unless bearing on a beam, partition or wall. Tail joists over 12 feet (3658 mm) long shall be supported at the header by framing anchors or on ledger strips not less than 2 inches by 2 inches (51 mm by 51 mm).

2308.8.4 Supporting bearing partitions. Bearing partitions parallel to joists shall be supported on beams, girders, doubled joists, walls or other bearing partitions. Bearing partitions perpendicular to joists shall not be offset from supporting girders, walls or partitions more than the joist depth unless such joists are of sufficient size to carry the additional load.

2308.8.5 Lateral support. Floor, attic and roof framing with a nominal depth-to-thickness ratio greater than or equal to 5:1 shall have one edge held in line for the entire span. Where the nominal depth-to-thickness ratio of the framing member exceeds 6:1, there shall be one line of bridging for each 8 feet (2438 mm) of span, unless both edges of the member are held in line. The bridging shall consist of not less than 1-inch by 3-inch (25 mm by 76 mm) lumber, double nailed at each end, of equivalent metal bracing of equal rigidity, full-depth solid blocking or other approved means. A line of bridging shall also be required at supports where equivalent lateral support is not otherwise provided.

2308.8.6 Structural floor sheathing. Structural floor sheathing shall comply with the provisions of Section 2304.7.1.

2308.8.7 Under-floor ventilation. For under-floor ventilation, see Section 1203.3.

TABLE 2308.8(1)
FLOOR JOIST SPANS FOR COMMON LUMBER SPECIES (Residential Sleeping Areas, Live Load = 30 psf, L/Δ = 360)

JOIST SPACING (inches)	SPECIES AND GRADE		DEAD LOAD = 10 psf				DEAD LOAD = 20 psf		
		2x6	2x8	2x10	2x12	2x6	2x8	2x10	2x12
		(ft. - in.)	(ft. - in.)	(ft. - in.)	(ft. - in.)	(ft. - in.)	(ft. - in.)	(ft. - in.)	(ft. - in.)
					Maximum floor joist spans				
12	Douglas Fir-Larch SS	12-6	16-6	21-0	25-7	12-6	16-6	21-0	25-7
	Douglas Fir-Larch #1	12-0	15-10	20-3	24-8	12-0	15-7	19-0	22-0
	Douglas Fir-Larch #2	11-10	15-7	19-10	23-0	11-6	14-7	17-9	20-7
	Douglas Fir-Larch #3	9-8	12-4	15-0	17-5	8-8	11-0	13-5	15-7
	Hem-Fir SS	11-10	15-7	19-10	24-2	11-10	15-7	19-10	24-2
	Hem-Fir #1	11-7	15-3	19-5	23-7	11-7	15-2	18-6	21-6
	Hem-Fir #2	11-0	14-6	18-6	22-6	11-0	14-4	17-6	20-4
	Hem-Fir #3	9-8	12-4	15-0	17-5	8-8	11-0	13-5	15-7
	Southern Pine SS	12-3	16-2	20-8	25-1	12-3	16-2	20-8	25-1
	Southern Pine #1	12-0	15-10	20-3	24-8	12-0	15-10	20-3	24-8
	Southern Pine #2	11-10	15-7	19-10	24-2	11-10	15-7	18-7	21-9
	Southern Pine #3	10-5	13-3	15-8	18-8	9-4	11-11	14-0	16-8
	Spruce-Pine-Fir SS	11-7	15-3	19-5	23-7	11-7	15-3	19-5	23-7
	Spruce-Pine-Fir #1	11-3	14-11	19-0	23-0	11-3	14-7	17-9	20-7
	Spruce-Pine-Fir #2	11-3	14-11	19-0	23-0	11-3	14-7	17-9	20-7
	Spruce-Pine-Fir #3	9-8	12-4	15-0	17-5	8-8	11-0	13-5	15-7
16	Douglas Fir-Larch SS	11-4	15-0	19-1	23-3	11-4	15-0	19-1	23-0
	Douglas Fir-Larch #1	10-11	14-5	18-5	21-4	10-8	13-6	16-5	19-1
	Douglas Fir-Larch #2	10-9	14-1	17-2	19-11	9-11	12-7	15-5	17-10
	Douglas Fir-Larch #3	8-5	10-8	13-0	15-1	7-6	9-6	11-8	13-6
	Hem-Fir SS	10-9	14-2	18-0	21-11	10-9	14-2	18-0	21-11
	Hem-Fir #1	10-6	13-10	17-8	20-9	10-4	13-1	16-0	18-7
	Hem-Fir #2	10-0	13-2	16-10	19-8	9-10	12-5	15-2	17-7
	Hem-Fir #3	8-5	10-8	13-0	15-1	7-6	9-6	11-8	13-6
	Southern Pine SS	11-2	14-8	18-9	22-10	11-2	14-8	18-9	22-10
	Southern Pine #1	10-11	14-5	18-5	22-5	10-11	14-5	17-11	21-4
	Southern Pine #2	10-9	14-2	18-0	21-1	10-5	13-6	16-1	18-10
	Southern Pine #3	9-0	11-6	13-7	16-2	8-1	10-3	12-2	14-6
	Spruce-Pine-Fir SS	10-6	13-10	17-8	21-6	10-6	13-10	17-8	21-4
	Spruce-Pine-Fir #1	10-3	13-6	17-2	19-11	9-11	12-7	15-5	17-10
	Spruce-Pine-Fir #2	10-3	13-6	17-2	19-11	9-11	12-7	15-5	17-10
	Spruce-Pine-Fir #3	8-5	10-8	13-0	15-1	7-6	9-6	11-8	13-6

(continued)

TABLE 2308.8(1)—continued
FLOOR JOIST SPANS FOR COMMON LUMBER SPECIES (Residential Sleeping Areas, Live Load = 30 psf, L/Δ = 360)

JOIST SPACING (inches)	SPECIES AND GRADE	DEAD LOAD = 10 psf				DEAD LOAD = 20 psf			
		2x6	2x8	2x10	2x12	2x6	2x8	2x10	2x12
		(ft. - in.)	(ft. - in.)	(ft. - in.)	(ft. - in.)	(ft. - in.)	(ft. - in.)	(ft. - in.)	(ft. - in.)
		Maximum floor joist spans							
19,2	Douglas Fir-Larch SS	10-8	14-1	18-0	21-10	10-8	14-1	18-0	21-0
	Douglas Fir-Larch #1	10-4	13-7	16-9	19-6	9-8	12-4	15-0	17-5
	Douglas Fir-Larch #2	10-1	12-10	15-8	18-3	9-1	11-6	14-1	16-3
	Douglas Fir-Larch #3	7-8	9-9	11-10	13-9	6-10	8-8	10-7	12-4
	Hem-Fir SS	10-1	13-4	17-0	20-8	10-1	13-4	17-0	20-7
	Hem-Fir #1	9-10	13-0	16-4	19-0	9-6	12-0	14-8	17-0
	Hem-Fir #2	9-5	12-5	15-6	17-1	8-11	11-4	13-10	16-1
	Hem-Fir #3	7-8	9-9	11-10	13-9	6-10	8-8	10-7	12-4
	Southern Pine SS	10-6	13-10	17-8	21-6	10-6	13-10	17-8	21-6
	Southern Pine #1	10-4	13-7	17-4	21-1	10-4	13-7	16-4	19-6
	Southern Pine #2	10-1	13-4	16-5	19-3	9-6	12-4	14-8	17-2
	Southern Pine #3	8-3	10-6	12-5	14-9	7-4	9-5	11-1	13-2
	Spruce-Pine-Fir SS	9-10	13-0	16-7	20-2	9-10	13-0	16-7	19-6
	Spruce-Pine-Fir #1	9-8	12-9	15-8	18-3	9-1	11-6	14-1	16-3
	Spruce-Pine-Fir #2	9-8	12-9	15-8	18-3	9-1	11-6	14-1	16-3
	Spruce-Pine-Fir #3	7-8	9-9	11-10	13-9	6-10	8-8	10-7	12-4
24	Douglas Fir-Larch SS	9-11	13-1	16-8	20-3	9-11	13-1	16-2	18-9
	Douglas Fir-Larch #1	9-7	12-4	15-0	17-5	8-8	11-0	13-5	15-7
	Douglas Fir-Larch #2	9-1	11-6	14-1	16-3	8-1	10-3	12-7	14-7
	Douglas Fir-Larch #3	6-10	8-8	10-7	12-4	6-2	7-9	9-6	11-0
	Hem-Fir SS	9-4	12-4	15-9	19-2	9-4	12-4	15-9	18-5
	Hem-Fir #1	9-2	12-0	14-8	17-0	8-6	10-9	13-1	15-2
	Hem-Fir #2	8-9	11-4	13-10	16-1	8-0	10-2	12-5	14-4
	Hem-Fir #3	6-10	8-8	10-7	12-4	6-2	7-9	9-6	11-0
	Southern Pine SS	9-9	12-10	16-5	19-11	9-9	12-10	16-5	19-11
	Southern Pine #1	9-7	12-7	16-1	19-6	9-7	12-4	14-7	17-5
	Southern Pine #2	9-4	12-4	14-8	17-2	8-6	11-0	13-1	15-5
	Southern Pine #3	7-4	9-5	11-1	13-2	6-7	8-5	9-11	11-10
	Spruce-Pine-Fir SS	9-2	12-1	15-5	18-9	9-2	12-1	15-0	17-5
	Spruce-Pine-Fir #1	8-11	11-6	14-1	16-3	8-1	10-3	12-7	14-7
	Spruce-Pine-Fir #2	8-11	11-6	14-1	16-3	8-1	10-3	12-7	14-7
	Spruce-Pine-Fir #3	6-10	8-8	10-7	12-4	6-2	7-9	9-6	11-0

Check sources for availability of lumber in lengths greater than 20 feet.

For SI: 1 inch = 25.4 mm, 1 foot = 304.8 mm, 1 pound per square foot = 47.8 N/m².

TABLE 2308.8(2)
FLOOR JOIST SPANS FOR COMMON LUMBER SPECIES (Residential Living Areas, Live Load = 40 psf, L/Δ = 360)

JOIST SPACING (inches)	SPECIES AND GRADE		DEAD LOAD = 10 psf				DEAD LOAD = 20 psf			
			2x6	2x8	2x10	2x12	2x6	2x8	2x10	2x12
			Maximum floor joist spans							
			(ft. - in.)	(ft. - in.)	(ft. - in.)	(ft. - in.)	(ft. - in.)	(ft. - in.)	(ft. - in.)	(ft. - in.)
12	Douglas Fir-Larch	SS	11-4	15-0	19-1	23-3	11-4	15-0	19-1	23-3
	Douglas Fir-Larch	#1	10-11	14-5	18-5	22-0	10-11	14-2	17-4	20-1
	Douglas Fir-Larch	#2	10-9	14-2	17-9	20-7	10-6	13-3	16-3	18-10
	Douglas Fir-Larch	#3	8-8	11-0	13-5	15-7	7-11	10-0	12-3	14-3
	Hem-Fir	SS	10-9	14-2	18-0	21-11	10-9	14-2	18-0	21-11
	Hem-Fir	#1	10-6	13-10	17-8	21-6	10-6	13-10	16-11	19-7
	Hem-Fir	#2	10-0	13-2	16-10	20-4	10-0	13-1	16-0	18-6
	Hem-Fir	#3	8-8	11-0	13-5	15-7	7-11	10-0	12-3	14-3
	Southern Pine	SS	11-2	14-8	18-9	22-10	11-2	14-8	18-9	22-10
	Southern Pine	#1	10-11	14-5	18-5	22-5	10-11	14-5	18-5	22-5
	Southern Pine	#2	10-9	14-2	18-0	21-9	10-9	14-2	16-11	19-10
	Southern Pine	#3	9-4	11-11	14-0	16-8	8-6	10-10	12-10	15-3
	Spruce-Pine-Fir	SS	10-6	13-10	17-8	21-6	10-6	13-10	17-8	21-6
	Spruce-Pine-Fir	#1	10-3	13-6	17-3	20-7	10-3	13-3	16-3	18-10
	Spruce-Pine-Fir	#2	10-3	13-6	17-3	20-7	10-3	13-3	16-3	18-10
	Spruce-Pine-Fir	#3	8-8	11-0	13-5	15-7	7-11	10-0	12-3	14-3
16	Douglas Fir-Larch	SS	10-4	13-7	17-4	21-1	10-4	13-7	17-4	21-0
	Douglas Fir-Larch	#1	9-11	13-1	16-5	19-1	9-8	12-4	15-0	17-5
	Douglas Fir-Larch	#2	9-9	12-7	15-5	17-10	9-1	11-6	14-1	16-3
	Douglas Fir-Larch	#3	7-6	9-6	11-8	13-6	6-10	8-8	10-7	12-4
	Hem-Fir	SS	9-9	12-10	16-5	19-11	9-9	12-10	16-5	19-11
	Hem-Fir	#1	9-6	12-7	16-0	18-7	9-6	12-0	14-8	17-0
	Hem-Fir	#2	9-1	12-0	15-2	17-7	8-11	11-4	13-10	16-1
	Hem-Fir	#3	7-6	9-6	11-8	13-6	6-10	8-8	10-7	12-4
	Southern Pine	SS	10-2	13-4	17-0	20-9	10-2	13-4	17-0	20-9
	Southern Pine	#1	9-11	13-1	16-9	20-4	9-11	13-1	16-4	19-6
	Southern Pine	#2	9-9	12-10	16-1	18-10	9-6	12-4	14-8	17-2
	Southern Pine	#3	8-1	10-3	12-2	14-6	7-4	9-5	11-1	13-2
	Spruce-Pine-Fir	SS	9-6	12-7	16-0	19-6	9-6	12-7	16-0	19-6
	Spruce-Pine-Fir	#1	9-4	12-3	15-5	17-10	9-1	11-6	14-1	16-3
	Spruce-Pine-Fir	#2	9-4	12-3	15-5	17-10	9-1	11-6	14-1	16-3
	Spruce-Pine-Fir	#3	7-6	9-6	11-8	13-6	6-10	8-8	10-7	12-4

(continued)

TABLE 2308.8(2)—continued
FLOOR JOIST SPANS FOR COMMON LUMBER SPECIES (Residential Living Areas, Live Load = 40 psf, L/Δ = 360)

JOIST SPACING (inches)	SPECIES AND GRADE		DEAD LOAD = 10 psf				DEAD LOAD = 20 psf			
			2x6	2x8	2x10	2x12	2x6	2x8	2x10	2x12
			(ft. - in.)	(ft. - in.)	(ft. - in.)	(ft. - in.)	(ft. - in.)	(ft. - in.)	(ft. - in.)	(ft. - in.)
			Maximum floor joist spans							
19.2	Douglas Fir-Larch	SS	9-8	12-10	16-4	19-10	9-8	12-10	16-4	19-2
	Douglas Fir-Larch	#1	9-4	12-4	15-0	17-5	8-10	11-3	13-8	15-11
	Douglas Fir-Larch	#2	9-1	11-6	14-1	16-3	8-3	10-6	12-10	14-10
	Douglas Fir-Larch	#3	6-10	8-8	10-7	12-4	6-3	7-11	9-8	11-3
	Hem-Fir	SS	9-2	12-1	15-5	18-9	9-2	12-1	15-5	18-9
	Hem-Fir	#1	9-0	11-10	14-8	17-0	8-8	10-11	13-4	15-6
	Hem-Fir	#2	8-7	11-3	13-10	16-1	8-2	10-4	12-8	14-8
	Hem-Fir	#3	6-10	8-8	10-7	12-4	6-3	7-11	9-8	11-3
	Southern Pine	SS	9-6	12-7	16-0	19-6	9-6	12-7	16-0	19-6
	Southern Pine	#1	9-4	12-4	15-9	19-2	9-4	12-4	14-11	17-9
	Southern Pine	#2	9-2	12-1	14-8	17-2	8-8	11-3	13-5	15-8
	Southern Pine	#3	7-4	9-5	11-1	13-2	6-9	8-7	10-1	12-1
	Spruce-Pine-Fir	SS	9-0	11-10	15-1	18-4	9-0	11-10	15-1	17-9
	Spruce-Pine-Fir	#1	8-9	11-6	14-1	16-3	8-3	10-6	12-10	14-10
	Spruce-Pine-Fir	#2	8-9	11-6	14-1	16-3	8-3	10-6	12-10	14-10
	Spruce-Pine-Fir	#3	6-10	8-8	10-7	12-4	6-3	7-11	9-8	11-3
24	Douglas Fir-Larch	SS	9-0	11-11	15-2	18-5	9-0	11-11	14-9	17-1
	Douglas Fir-Larch	#1	8-8	11-0	13-5	15-7	7-11	10-0	12-3	14-3
	Douglas Fir-Larch	#2	8-1	10-3	12-7	14-4	7-5	9-5	11-6	13-4
	Douglas Fir-Larch	#3	6-2	7-9	9-6	11-0	5-7	7-1	8-8	10-1
	Hem-Fir	SS	8-6	11-3	14-4	17-5	8-6	11-3	14-4	16-10[a]
	Hem-Fir	#1	8-4	10-9	13-1	15-2	7-9	9-9	11-11	13-10
	Hem-Fir	#2	7-11	10-2	12-5	14-4	7-4	9-3	11-4	13-1
	Hem-Fir	#3	6-2	7-9	9-6	11-0	5-7	7-1	8-8	10-1
	Southern Pine	SS	8-10	11-8	14-11	18-1	8-10	11-8	14-11	18-1
	Southern Pine	#1	8-8	11-5	14-7	17-5	8-8	11-3	13-4	15-11
	Southern Pine	#2	8-6	11-0	13-1	15-5	7-9	10-0	12-0	14-0
	Southern Pine	#3	6-7	8-5	9-11	11-10	6-0	7-8	9-1	10-9
	Spruce-Pine-Fir	SS	8-4	11-0	14-0	17-0	8-4	11-0	13-8	15-11
	Spruce-Pine-Fir	#1	8-1	10-3	12-7	14-7	7-5	9-5	11-6	13-4
	Spruce-Pine-Fir	#2	8-1	10-3	12-7	14-7	7-5	9-5	11-6	13-4
	Spruce-Pine-Fir	#3	6-2	7-9	9-6	11-0	5-7	7-1	8-8	10-1

Check sources for availability of lumber in lengths greater than 20 feet.

For SI: 1 inch = 25.4 mm, 1 foot = 304.8 mm, 1 pound per square foot = 47.8 N/m^2.

a. End bearing length shall be increased to 2 inches.

2308.9 Wall framing.

2308.9.1 Size, height and spacing. The size, height and spacing of studs shall be in accordance with Table 2308.9.1 except that utility-grade studs shall not be spaced more than 16 inches (406 mm) o.c., or support more than a roof and ceiling, or exceed 8 feet (2438 mm) in height for exterior walls and load-bearing walls or 10 feet (3048 mm) for interior nonload-bearing walls.

2308.9.2 Framing details. Studs shall be placed with their wide dimension perpendicular to the wall. Not less than three studs shall be installed at each corner of an exterior wall.

Exception: At corners, two studs are permitted, provided wood spacers or backup cleats of $^3/_8$-inch-thick (9.5 mm) wood structural panel, $^3/_8$-inch (9.5 mm) Type M "Exterior Glue" particleboard, 1-inch-thick (25 mm) lumber or other approved devices that will serve as an adequate backing for the attachment of facing materials are used. Where fire-resistance ratings or shear values are involved, wood spacers, backup cleats or other devices shall not be used unless specifically approved for such use.

2308.9.2.1 Top plates. Bearing and exterior wall studs shall be capped with double top plates installed to provide overlapping at corners and at intersections with other partitions. End joints in double top plates shall be offset at least 48 inches (1219 mm), and shall be nailed with not less than eight 16d face nails on each side of the joint. Plates shall be a nominal 2 inches (51 mm) in depth and have a width at least equal to the width of the studs.

Exception: A single top plate is permitted, provided the plate is adequately tied at joints, corners and intersecting walls by at least the equivalent of 3-inch by 6-inch (76 mm by 152 mm) by 0.036-inch-thick (0.914 mm) galvanized steel that is nailed to each wall or segment of wall by six 8d nails or equivalent, provided the rafters, joists or trusses are centered over the studs with a tolerance of no more than 1 inch (25 mm).

2308.9.2.2 Top plates for studs spaced at 24 inches (610 mm). Where bearing studs are spaced at 24-inch (610 mm) intervals and top plates are less than two 2-inch by 6-inch (51 mm by 152 mm) or two 3-inch by 4-inch (76 mm by 102 mm) members and where the floor joists, floor trusses or roof trusses that they support are spaced at more than 16-inch (406 mm) intervals, such joists or trusses shall bear within 5 inches (127 mm) of the studs beneath or a third plate shall be installed.

2308.9.2.3 Nonbearing walls and partitions. In nonbearing walls and partitions, studs shall be spaced not more than 28 inches (711 mm) o.c. and are permitted to be set with the long dimension parallel to the wall. Interior nonbearing partitions shall be capped with no less than a single top plate installed to provide overlapping at corners and at intersections with other walls and partitions. The plate shall be continuously tied at joints by solid blocking at least 16 inches (406 mm) in length and equal in size to the plate or by $^1/_2$-inch by $1^1/_2$-inch (12.7 mm by 38 mm) metal ties with spliced sections fastened with two 16d nails on each side of the joint.

2308.9.2.4 Plates or sills. Studs shall have full bearing on a plate or sill not less than 2 inches (51 mm) in thickness having a width not less than that of the wall studs.

2308.9.3 Bracing. Braced wall lines shall consist of braced wall panels that meet the requirements for location, type and amount of bracing as shown in Figure 2308.9.3, specified in Table 2308.9.3(1) and are in line or offset from each other by not more than 4 feet (1219 mm). Braced wall panels shall start not more than $12^1/_2$-feet (3810 mm) from each end of a braced wall line. Braced wall panels shall be clearly indicated on the plans. Construction of braced wall panels shall be by one of the following methods:

1. Nominal 1-inch by 4-inch (25 mm by 102 mm) continuous diagonal braces let into top and bottom plates and intervening studs, placed at an angle not more than 60 degrees (1.0 rad) or less than 45 degrees (0.79 rad) from the horizontal and attached to the framing in conformance with Table 2304.9.1.

2. Wood boards of $^5/_8$ inch (15.9 mm) net minimum thickness applied diagonally on studs spaced not over 24 inches (610 mm) o.c.

TABLE 2308.9.1
SIZE, HEIGHT AND SPACING OF WOOD STUDS

| STUD SIZE (inches) | BEARING WALLS | | | | NONBEARING WALLS | |
| | Laterally unsupported stud height[a] (feet) | Supporting roof and ceiling only | Supporting one floor, roof and ceiling | Supporting two floors, roof and ceiling | Laterally unsupported stud height[a] (feet) | Spacing (inches) |
		Spacing (inches)				
2 × 3[b]	-	-	-	-	10	16
2 × 4	10	24	16	-	14	24
3 × 4	10	24	24	16	14	24
2 × 5	10	24	24	-	16	24
2 × 6	10	24	24	16	20	24

For SI: 1 inch = 25.4 mm, 1 foot = 304.8 mm.

a. Listed heights are distances between points of lateral support placed perpendicular to the plane of the wall. Increases in unsupported height are permitted where justified by an analysis.

b. Shall not be used in exterior walls.

3. Wood structural panel sheathing with a thickness not less than $^5/_{16}$ inch (7.9 mm) for a 16-inch (406 mm) stud spacing and not less than $^3/_8$ inch (9.5 mm) for a 24-inch (610 mm) stud spacing in accordance with Tables 2308.9.3(2) and 2308.9.3(3).

4. Fiberboard sheathing panels not less than $^1/_2$ inch (12.7 mm) thick applied vertically or horizontally on studs spaced not over 16 inches (406 mm) o.c. where installed with fasteners in accordance with Section 2306.4.4 and Table 2306.4.4.

SEISMIC DESIGN CATEGORY	MAXIMUM WALL SPACING (feet)	REQUIRED BRACING LENGTH, b
A, B and C	35"-0"	Table 2308.9.3(1) and Section 2308.9.3
D and E	25"-0"	Table 2308.12.4

For SI: 1 foot = 304.8 mm.

FIGURE 2308.9.3
BASIC COMPONENTS OF THE LATERAL BRACING SYSTEM

5. Gypsum board [sheathing $\frac{1}{2}$-inch-thick (12.7 mm) by 4-feet-wide (1219 mm) wallboard or veneer base] on studs spaced not over 24 inches (610 mm) o.c. and nailed at 7 inches (178 mm) o.c. with nails as required by Table 2306.4.5.

6. Particleboard wall sheathing panels where installed in accordance with Table 2308.9.3(4).

7. Portland cement plaster on studs spaced 16 inches (406 mm) o.c. installed in accordance with Section 2510.

8. Hardboard panel siding where installed in accordance with Section 2303.1.6 and Table 2308.9.3(5).

For cripple wall bracing, see Section 2308.9.4.1. For Methods 2, 3, 4, 6, 7 and 8, each panel must be at least 48 inches (1219 mm) in length, covering three stud spaces where studs are spaced 16 inches (406 mm) apart and

TABLE 2308.9.3(1)
BRACED WALL PANELS[a]

SEISMIC DESIGN CATEGORY	CONDITION	CONSTRUCTION METHODS[b,c]								BRACED PANEL LOCATION AND LENGTH[d]
		1	2	3	4	5	6	7	8	
A and B	One story, top of two or three story	X	X	X	X	X	X	X	X	Located in accordance with Section 2308.9.3 and not more than 25 feet on center.
	First story of two story or second story of three story	X	X	X	X	X	X	X	X	
	First story of three story	-	X	X	X	X[e]	X	X	X	
C	One story or top of two story	-	X	X	X	X	X	X	X	Located in accordance with Section 2308.9.3 and not more than 25 feet on center.
	First story of two story	-	X	X	X	X[e]	X	X	X	Located in accordance with Section 2308.9.3 and not more than 25 feet on center, but total length shall not be less than 25% of building length[f].

For SI: 1 inch = 25.4 mm, 1 foot = 304.8 mm.

a. This table specifies minimum requirements for braced panels that form interior or exterior braced wall lines.

b. See Section 2308.9.3 for full description.

c. See Sections 2308.9.3.1 and 2308.9.3.2 for alternative braced panel requirements.

d. Building length is the dimension parallel to the braced wall length.

e. Gypsum wallboard applied to framing supports that are spaced at 16 inches on center.

f. The required lengths shall be doubled for gypsum board applied to only one face of a braced wall panel.

TABLE 2308.9.3(2)
EXPOSED PLYWOOD PANEL SIDING

MINIMUM THICKNESS[a] (inch)	MINIMUM NUMBER OF PLIES	STUD SPACING (inches) Plywood siding applied directly to studs or over sheathing
$\frac{3}{8}$	3	16[b]
$\frac{1}{2}$	4	24

For SI: 1 inch = 25.4 mm.

a. Thickness of grooved panels is measured at bottom of grooves.

b. Spans are permitted to be 24 inches if plywood siding applied with face grain perpendicular to studs or over one of the following: (1) 1-inch board sheathing, (2) $\frac{7}{16}$-inch wood structural panel sheathing or (3) $\frac{3}{8}$-inch wood structural panel sheathing with strength axis (which is the long direction of the panel unless otherwise marked) of sheathing perpendicular to studs.

TABLE 2308.9.3(3)
WOOD STRUCTURAL PANEL WALL SHEATHING[b] (Not Exposed to the Weather, Strength Axis Parallel or Perpendicular to Studs Except as Indicated Below)

MINIMUM THICKNESS (inch)	PANEL SPAN RATING	STUD SPACING (inches)		
			Nailable sheathing	
		Siding nailed to studs	Sheathing parallel to studs	Sheathing perpendicular to studs
$\frac{5}{16}$	12/0, 16/0, 20/0 Wall–16" o.c.	16	—	16
$\frac{3}{8}$, $\frac{15}{32}$, $\frac{1}{2}$	16/0, 20/0, 24/0, 32/16 Wall–24" o.c.	24	16	24
$\frac{7}{16}$, $\frac{15}{32}$, $\frac{1}{2}$	24/0, 24/16, 32/16 Wall–24" o.c.	24	24[a]	24

For SI: 1 inch = 25.4 mm.

a. Plywood shall consist of four or more plies.

b. Blocking of horizontal joints shall not be required except as specified in Sections 2306.4 and 2308.12.4.

covering two stud spaces where studs are spaced 24 inches (610 mm) apart.

For Method 5, each panel must be at least 96 inches (2438 mm) in length where applied to one face of a panel and 48 inches (1219 mm) where applied to both faces.

All vertical joints of panel sheathing shall occur over studs and adjacent panel joints shall be nailed to common framing members. Horizontal joints shall occur over blocking or other framing equal in size to the studding except where waived by the installation requirements for the specific sheathing materials.

Sole plates shall be nailed to the floor framing and top plates shall be connected to the framing above in accordance with Section 2308.3.2. Where joists are perpendicular to braced wall lines above, blocking shall be provided under and in line with the braced wall panels.

2308.9.3.1 Alternative bracing. Any bracing required by Section 2308.9.3 is permitted to be replaced by the following:

1. In one-story buildings, each panel shall have a length of not less than 2 feet 8 inches (813 mm) and a height of not more than 10 feet (3048 mm). Each panel shall be sheathed on one face with $^3/_8$-inch-minimum-thickness (9.5 mm) wood structural panel sheathing nailed with 8d common or galvanized box nails in accordance with Table 2304.9.1 and blocked at wood structural panel edges. Two anchor bolts installed in accordance

TABLE 2308.9.3(4)
ALLOWABLE SPANS FOR PARTICLEBOARD WALL SHEATHING (Not Exposed to the Weather, Long Dimension of the Panel Parallel or Perpendicular to Studs)

GRADE	THICKNESS (inch)	STUD SPACING (inches)	
		Siding nailed to studs	Sheathing under coverings specified in Section 2308.9.3 parallel or perpendicular to studs
M-S "Exterior Glue"	$^3/_8$	16	—
and M-2 "Exterior Glue"	$^1/_2$	16	16

For SI: 1 inch = 25.4 mm.

TABLE 2308.9.3(5)
HARDBOARD SIDING

SIDING	MINIMUM NOMINAL THICKNESS (inch)	2 × 4 FRAMING MAXIMUM SPACING	NAIL SIZE[a,b,d]	NAIL SPACING	
				General	Bracing panels[c]
1.Lap siding					
Direct to studs	$^3/_8$	16" o.c.	8d	16" o.c.	Not applicable
Over sheathing	$^3/_8$	16" o.c.	10d	16" o.c.	Not applicable
2.Square edge panel siding					
Direct to studs	$^3/_8$	24" o.c.	6d	6" o.c. edges; 12" o.c. at intermediate supports	4" o.c. edges; 8" o.c. at intermediate supports
Over sheathing	$^3/_8$	24" o.c.	8d	6" o.c. edges; 12" o.c. at intermediate supports	4" o.c. edges; 8" o.c. at intermediate supports
3.Shiplap edge panel siding					
Direct to studs	$^3/_8$	16" o.c.	6d	6" o.c. edges; 12" o.c. at intermediate supports	4" o.c. edges; 8" o.c. at intermediate supports
Over sheathing	$^3/_8$	16" o.c.	8d	6" o.c. edges; 12" o.c. At intermediate supports	4" o.c. edges; 8" o.c. at intermediate supports

For SI: 1 inch = 25.4 mm.

a. Nails shall be corrosion resistant.

b. Minimum acceptable nail dimensions:

	Panel Siding (inch)	Lap Siding (inch)
Shank diameter	0.092	0.099
Head diameter	0.225	0.240

c. Where used to comply with Section 2308.9.3

d. Nail length must accomodate the sheathing and penetrate framing 1 $^1/_2$ inches.

with Section 2308.6 shall be provided in each panel. Anchor bolts shall be placed at each panel outside quarter points. Each panel end stud shall have a tie-down device fastened to the foundation, capable of providing an approved uplift capacity of not less than 1,800 pounds (8006 N). The tie-down device shall be installed in accordance with the manufacturer's recommendations. The panels shall be supported directly on a foundation or on floor framing supported directly on a foundation that is continuous across the entire length of the braced wall line. This foundation shall be reinforced with not less than one No. 4 bar top and bottom.

Where the continuous foundation is required to have a depth greater than 12 inches (305 mm), a minimum 12-inch by 12-inch (305 mm by 305 mm) continuous footing or turned down slab edge is permitted at door openings in the braced wall line. This continuous footing or turned down slab edge shall be reinforced with not less than one No. 4 bar top and bottom. This reinforcement shall be lapped 15 inches (381 mm) with the reinforcement required in the continuous foundation located directly under the braced wall line.

2. In the first story of two-story buildings, each wall panel shall be braced in accordance with Section 2308.9.3.1, Item 1, except that the wood structural panel sheathing shall be provided on both faces, three anchor bolts shall be placed at one-quarter points, and tie-down device uplift capac-

ity shall not be less than 3,000 pounds (13 344 N).

2308.9.3.2 Alternate bracing wall panel adjacent to a door or window opening. Any bracing required by Section 2308.9.3 is permitted to be replaced by the following when used adjacent to a door or window opening with a full-length header:

1. In one-story buildings, each panel shall have a length of not less than 16 inches (406 mm) and a height of not more than 10 feet (3048 mm). Each panel shall be sheathed on one face with a single layer of $^3/_8$ inch (9.5 mm) minimum thickness wood structural panel sheathing nailed with 8d common or galvanized box nails in accordance with Figure 2308.9.3.2. The wood structural panel sheathing shall extend up over the solid sawn or glued-laminated header and shall be nailed in accordance with Figure 2308.9.3.2. A built-up header consisting of at least two 2 x 12s and fastened in accordance with Item 24 of Table 2304.9.1 shall be permitted to be used. A spacer, if used, shall be placed on the side of the built-up beam opposite the wood structural panel sheathing. The header shall extend between the inside faces of the first full-length outer studs of each panel. The clear span of the header between the inner studs of each panel shall be not less than 6 feet (1829 mm) and not more than 18 feet (5486 mm) in length. A strap with an uplift capacity of not less than 1,000 pounds (4,400 N) shall fasten the header to the inner studs opposite the sheathing. One anchor bolt not less than $^5/_8$ inch (15.9

For SI: 1 foot = 304.8 mm; 1 inch = 25.4 mm; 1 pound = 4.448 N.

FIGURE 2308.9.3.2
ALTERNATE BRACED WALL PANEL ADJACENT TO A DOOR OR WINDOW OPENING

mm) diameter and installed in accordance with Section 2308.6 shall be provided in the center of each sill plate. The studs at each end of the panel shall have a tie-down device fastened to the foundation with an uplift capacity of not less than 4,200 pounds (18 480 N).

Where a panel is located on one side of the opening, the header shall extend between the inside face of the first full-length stud of the panel and the bearing studs at the other end of the opening. A strap with an uplift capacity of not less than 1,000 pounds (4400 N) shall fasten the header to the bearing studs. The bearing studs shall also have a tie-down device fastened to the foundation with an uplift capacity of not less than 1,000 pounds (4400 N).

The tie-down devices shall be an embedded strap type, installed in accordance with the manufacturer's recommendations. The panels shall be supported directly on a foundation that is continuous across the entire length of the braced wall line. This foundation shall be reinforced with not less than one No. 4 bar top and bottom.

Where the continuous foundation is required to have a depth greater than 12 inches (305 mm), a minimum 12-inch by 12-inch (305 mm by 305 mm) continuous footing or turned down slab edge is permitted at door openings in the braced wall line. This continuous footing or turned down slab edge shall be reinforced with not less than one No. 4 bar top and bottom. This reinforcement shall be lapped not less than 15 inches (381 mm) with the reinforcement required in the continuous foundation located directly under the braced wall line.

2. In the first story of two-story buildings, each wall panel shall be braced in accordance with Item 1 above, except that each panel shall have a length of not less than 24 inches (610 mm).

2308.9.4 Cripple walls. Foundation cripple walls shall be framed of studs not less in size than the studding above with a minimum length of 14 inches (356 mm), or shall be framed of solid blocking. Where exceeding 4 feet (1219 mm) in height, such walls shall be framed of studs having the size required for an additional story.

2308.9.4.1 Bracing. For the purposes of this section, cripple walls having a stud height exceeding 14 inches (356 mm) shall be considered a story and shall be braced in accordance with Table 2308.9.3(1) for Seismic Design Category A, B or C. See Section 2308.12.4 for Seismic Design Category D or E.

2308.9.4.2 Nailing of bracing. Spacing of edge nailing for required wall bracing shall not exceed 6 inches (152 mm) o.c. along the foundation plate and the top plate of the cripple wall. Nail size, nail spacing for field nailing and more restrictive boundary nailing requirements shall be as required elsewhere in the code for the specific bracing material used.

2308.9.5 Openings in exterior walls.

2308.9.5.1 Headers. Headers shall be provided over each opening in exterior-bearing walls. The spans in Table 2308.9.5 are permitted to be used for one- and two-family dwellings. Headers for other buildings shall be designed in accordance with Section 2301.2, Item 1 or 2. Headers shall be of two pieces of nominal 2-inch (51 mm) framing lumber set on edge as permitted by Table 2308.9.5 and nailed together in accordance with Table 2304.9.1 or of solid lumber of equivalent size.

2308.9.5.2 Header support. Wall studs shall support the ends of the header in accordance with Table 2308.9.5. Each end of a lintel or header shall have a length of bearing of not less than $1^1/_2$ inches (38 mm) for the full width of the lintel.

2308.9.6 Openings in interior bearing partitions. Headers shall be provided over each opening in interior bearing partitions as required in Section 2308.9.5. The spans in Table 2308.9.6 are permitted to be used. Wall studs shall support the ends of the header in accordance with Table 2308.9.5 or 2308.9.6, as appropriate.

2308.9.7 Openings in interior nonbearing partitions. Openings in nonbearing partitions are permitted to be framed with single studs and headers. Each end of a lintel or header shall have a length of bearing of not less than $1^1/_2$ inches (38 mm) for the full width of the lintel.

2308.9.8 Pipes in walls. Stud partitions containing plumbing, heating or other pipes shall be so framed and the joists underneath so spaced as to give proper clearance for the piping. Where a partition containing such piping runs parallel to the floor joists, the joists underneath such partitions shall be doubled and spaced to permit the passage of such pipes and shall be bridged. Where plumbing, heating or other pipes are placed in or partly in a partition, necessitating the cutting of the soles or plates, a metal tie not less than 0.058 inch (1.47 mm) (16 galvanized gage) and $1^1/_2$ inches (38 mm) wide shall be fastened to each plate across and to each side of the opening with not less than six 16d nails.

2308.9.9 Bridging. Unless covered by interior or exterior wall coverings or sheathing meeting the minimum requirements of this code, stud partitions or walls with studs having a height-to-least-thickness ratio exceeding 50 shall have bridging not less than 2 inches (51 mm) in thickness and of the same width as the studs fitted snugly and nailed thereto to provide adequate lateral support. Bridging shall be placed in every stud cavity and at a frequency such that no stud so braced shall have a height-to-least-thickness ratio exceeding 50 with the height of the stud measured between horizontal framing and bridging or between bridging, whichever is greater.

2308.9.10 Cutting and notching. In exterior walls and bearing partitions, any wood stud is permitted to be cut or notched to a depth not exceeding 25 percent of its width. Cutting or notching of studs to a depth not greater than 40 percent of the width of the stud is permitted in nonbearing partitions supporting no loads other than the weight of the partition.

TABLE 2308.9.5
HEADER AND GIRDER SPANS[a] FOR EXTERIOR BEARING WALLS (Maximum Spans for Douglas Fir-Larch, Hem-Fir, Southern Pine and Spruce-Pine-Fir[b] and Required Number of Jack Studs)

HEADERS SUPPORTING	SIZE	GROUND SNOW LOAD (psf)[e]											
		30						50					
		Building width[c] (feet)											
		20		28		36		20		28		36	
		Span	NJ[d]	Span	NJ[d]	Span	NJ[d]	Span	NJ[d]	Span	NJ[d]	Span	NJ[d]
Roof & Ceiling	2-2×4	3-6	1	3-2	1	2-10	1	3-2	1	2-9	1	2-6	1
	2-2×6	5-5	1	4-8	1	4-2	1	4-8	1	4-1	1	3-8	2
	2-2×8	6-10	1	5-11	2	5-4	2	5-11	2	5-2	2	4-7	2
	2-2×10	8-5	2	7-3	2	6-6	2	7-3	2	6-3	2	5-7	2
	2-2×12	9-9	2	8-5	2	7-6	2	8-5	2	7-3	2	6-6	2
	3-2×8	8-4	1	7-5	1	6-8	1	7-5	1	6-5	2	5-9	2
	3-2×10	10-6	1	9-1	2	8-2	2	9-1	2	7-10	2	7-0	2
	3-2×12	12-2	2	10-7	2	9-5	2	10-7	2	9-2	2	8-2	2
	4-2×8	9-2	1	8-4	1	7-8	1	8-4	1	7-5	1	6-8	1
	4-2×10	11-8	1	10-6	1	9-5	2	10-6	1	9-1	2	8-2	2
	4-2×12	14-1	1	12-2	2	10-11	2	12-2	2	10-7	2	9-5	2
Roof, Ceiling & 1 Center-Bearing Floor	2-2×4	3-1	1	2-9	1	2-5	1	2-9	1	2-5	1	2-2	1
	2-2×6	4-6	1	4-0	1	3-7	2	4-1	1	3-7	2	3-3	2
	2-2×8	5-9	2	5-0	2	4-6	2	5-2	2	4-6	2	4-1	2
	2-2×10	7-0	2	6-2	2	5-6	2	6-4	2	5-6	2	5-0	2
	2-2×12	8-1	2	7-1	2	6-5	2	7-4	2	6-5	2	5-9	3
	3-2×8	7-2	1	6-3	2	5-8	2	6-5	2	5-8	2	5-1	2
	3-2×10	8-9	2	7-8	2	6-11	2	7-11	2	6-11	2	6-3	2
	3-2×12	10-2	2	8-11	2	8-0	2	9-2	2	8-0	2	7-3	2
	4-2×8	8-1	1	7-3	1	6-7	1	7-5	1	6-6	1	5-11	2
	4-2×10	10-1	1	8-10	2	8-0	2	9-1	2	8-0	2	7-2	2
	4-2×12	11-9	2	10-3	2	9-3	2	10-7	2	9-3	2	8-4	2
Roof, Ceiling & 1 Clear Span Floor	2-2×4	2-8	1	2-4	1	2-1	1	2-7	1	2-3	1	2-0	1
	2-2×6	3-11	1	3-5	2	3-0	2	3-10	2	3-4	2	3-0	2
	2-2×8	5-0	2	4-4	2	3-10	2	4-10	2	4-2	2	3-9	2
	2-2×10	6-1	2	5-3	2	4-8	2	5-11	2	5-1	2	4-7	3
	2-2×12	7-1	2	6-1	3	5-5	3	6-10	2	5-11	3	5-4	3
	3-2×8	6-3	2	5-5	2	4-10	2	6-1	2	5-3	2	4-8	2
	3-2×10	7-7	2	6-7	2	5-11	2	7-5	2	6-5	2	5-9	2
	3-2×12	8-10	2	7-8	2	6-10	2	8-7	2	7-5	2	6-8	2
	4-2×8	7-2	1	6-3	2	5-7	2	7-0	1	6-1	2	5-5	2
	4-2×10	8-9	2	7-7	2	6-10	2	8-7	2	7-5	2	6-7	2
	4-2×12	10-2	2	8-10	2	7-11	2	9-11	2	8-7	2	7-8	2

(continued)

TABLE 2308.9.5—continued
HEADER AND GIRDER SPANS[a] FOR EXTERIOR BEARING WALLS (Maximum Spans for Douglas Fir-Larch, Hem-Fir, Southern Pine and Spruce-Pine-Fir[b] and Required Number of Jack Studs)

HEADERS SUPPORTING	SIZE	GROUND SNOW LOAD (psf)[e]											
		30						50					
		Building width[c] (feet)											
		20		28		36		20		28		36	
		Span	NJ[d]	Span	NJ[d]	Span	NJ[d]	Span	NJ[d]	Span	NJ[d]	Span	NJ[d]
Roof, Ceiling & 2 Center-Bearing Floors	2-2×4	2-7	1	2-3	1	2-0	1	2-6	1	2-2	1	1-11	1
	2-2×6	3-9	2	3-3	2	2-11	2	3-8	2	3-2	2	2-10	2
	2-2×8	4-9	2	4-2	2	3-9	2	4-7	2	4-0	2	3-8	2
	2-2×10	5-9	2	5-1	2	4-7	3	5-8	2	4-11	2	4-5	3
	2-2×12	6-8	2	5-10	3	5-3	3	6-6	2	5-9	3	5-2	3
	3-2×8	5-11	2	5-2	2	4-8	2	5-9	2	5-1	2	4-7	2
	3-2×10	7-3	2	6-4	2	5-8	2	7-1	2	6-2	2	5-7	2
	3-2×12	8-5	2	7-4	2	6-7	2	8-2	2	7-2	2	6-5	3
	4-2×8	6-10	1	6-0	2	5-5	2	6-8	1	5-10	2	5-3	2
	4-2×10	8-4	2	7-4	2	6-7	2	8-2	2	7-2	2	6-5	2
	4-2×12	9-8	2	8-6	2	7-8	2	9-5	2	8-3	2	7-5	2
Roof, Ceiling & 2 Clear Span Floors	2-2×4	2-1	1	1-8	1	1-6	2	2-0	1	1-8	1	1-5	2
	2-2×6	3-1	2	2-8	2	2-4	2	3-0	2	2-7	2	2-3	2
	2-2×8	3-10	2	3-4	2	3-0	3	3-10	2	3-4	2	2-11	3
	2-2×10	4-9	2	4-1	3	3-8	3	4-8	2	4-0	3	3-7	3
	2-2×12	5-6	3	4-9	3	4-3	3	5-5	3	4-8	3	4-2	3
	3-2×8	4-10	2	4-2	2	3-9	2	4-9	2	4-1	2	3-8	2
	3-2×10	5-11	2	5-1	2	4-7	3	5-10	2	5-0	2	4-6	3
	3-2×12	6-10	2	5-11	3	5-4	3	6-9	2	5-10	3	5-3	3
	4-2×8	5-7	2	4-10	2	4-4	2	5-6	2	4-9	2	4-3	2
	4-2×10	6-10	2	5-11	2	5-3	2	6-9	2	5-10	2	5-2	2
	4-2×12	7-11	2	6-10	2	6-2	3	7-9	2	6-9	2	6-0	3

For SI: 1 inch = 25.4 mm, 1 foot = 304.8 mm, 1 pound per square foot = 47.8 N/m².

a. Spans are given in feet and inches (ft-in).

b. Tabulated values are for No. 2 grade lumber.

c. Building width is measured perpendicular to the ridge. For widths between those shown, spans are permitted to be interpolated.

d. NJ - Number of jack studs required to support each end. Where the number of required jack studs equals one, the header is permitted to be supported by an approved framing anchor attached to the full-height wall stud and to the header.

e. Use 30 pounds per square foot ground snow load for cases in which ground snow load is less than 30 pounds per square foot and the roof live load is equal to or less than 20 pounds per square foot.

TABLE 2308.9.6
HEADER AND GIRDER SPANS[a] FOR INTERIOR BEARING WALLS (Maximum Spans for Douglas Fir-Larch, Hem-Fir, Southern Pine and Spruce-Pine-Fir[b] and Required Number of Jack Studs)

| HEADERS AND GIRDERS SUPPORTING | SIZE | BUILDING WIDTH[c] (feet) | | | | | |
| | | 20 | | 28 | | 36 | |
		Span	NJ[d]	Span	NJ[d]	Span	NJ[d]
One Floor Only	2-2×4	3-1	1	2-8	1	2-5	1
	2-2×6	4-6	1	3-11	1	3-6	1
	2-2×8	5-9	1	5-0	2	4-5	2
	2-2×10	7-0	2	6-1	2	5-5	2
	2-2×12	8-1	2	7-0	2	6-3	2
	3-2×8	7-2	1	6-3	1	5-7	2
	3-2×10	8-9	1	7-7	2	6-9	2
	3-2×12	10-2	2	8-10	2	7-10	2
	4-2×8	9-0	1	7-8	1	6-9	1
	4-2×10	10-1	1	8-9	1	7-10	2
	4-2×12	11-9	1	10-2	2	9-1	2
Two Floors	2-2×4	2-2	1	1-10	1	1-7	1
	2-2×6	3-2	2	2-9	2	2-5	2
	2-2×8	4-1	2	3-6	2	3-2	2
	2-2×10	4-11	2	4-3	2	3-10	3
	2-2×12	5-9	2	5-0	3	4-5	3
	3-2×8	5-1	2	4-5	2	3-11	2
	3-2×10	6-2	2	5-4	2	4-10	2
	3-2×12	7-2	2	6-3	2	5-7	3
	4-2×8	6-1	1	5-3	2	4-8	2
	4-2×10	7-2	2	6-2	2	5-6	2
	4-2×12	8-4	2	7-2	2	6-5	2

For SI: 1 inch = 25.4 mm, 1 foot = 304.8 mm.

a. Spans are given in feet and inches (ft-in).

b. Tabulated values are for No. 2 grade lumber.

c. Building width is measured perpendicular to the ridge. For widths between those shown, spans are permitted to be interpolated.

d. NJ - Number of jack studs required to support each end. Where the number of required jack studs equals one, the headers are permitted to be supported by an approved framing anchor attached to the full-height wall stud and to the header.

2308.9.11 Bored holes. A hole not greater in diameter than 40 percent of the stud width is permitted to be bored in any wood stud. Bored holes not greater than 60 percent of the width of the stud are permitted in nonbearing partitions or in any wall where each bored stud is doubled, provided not more than two such successive doubled studs are so bored.

In no case shall the edge of the bored hole be nearer than $5/8$ inch (15.9 mm) to the edge of the stud.

Bored holes shall not be located at the same section of stud as a cut or notch.

2308.10 Roof and ceiling framing. The framing details required in this section apply to roofs having a minimum slope of three units vertical in 12 units horizontal (25-percent slope) or greater. Where the roof slope is less than three units vertical in 12 units horizontal (25-percent slope), members

supporting rafters and ceiling joists such as ridge board, hips and valleys shall be designed as beams.

2308.10.1 Wind uplift. Roof assemblies shall have rafter and truss ties to the wall below. Resultant uplift loads shall be transferred to the foundation using a continuous load path. The rafter or truss to wall connection shall comply with Tables 2304.9.1 and 2308.10.1. Wood structural panel sheathing and fastening designed to transfer resultant forces across horizontal framing joints shall constitute an acceptable continuous load path as an alternative to the use of anchorage devices when calculated by principles of mechanics using values of fastener strength and shear resistance.

2308.10.2 Ceiling joist spans. Allowable spans for ceiling joists shall be in accordance with Table 2308.10.2(1) or 2308.10.2(2). For other grades and species, refer to the *AF&PA Span Tables for Joists and Rafters.*

TABLE 2308.10.1
REQUIRED RATING OF APPROVED UPLIFT CONNECTORS (pounds)[a,b,c,e,f,g,h]

BASIC WIND SPEED (3-second gust)	ROOF SPAN (feet)							OVERHANGS (pounds/feet)[d]
	12	20	24	28	32	36	40	
85	-72	-120	-145	-169	-193	-217	-241	-38.55
90	-91	-151	-181	-212	-242	-272	-302	-43.22
100	-131	-281	-262	-305	-349	-393	-436	-53.36
110	-175	-292	-351	-409	-467	-526	-584	-64.56

For SI: 1 inch = 25.4 mm, 1 foot = 304.8 mm, 1 mile per hour = 1.61 km/hr, 1 pound = 0.454 Kg, 1 pound/foot = 14.5939 N/m.

a. The uplift connection requirements are based on a 30-foot mean roof height located in Exposure B. For Exposure C or D and for other mean roof heights, multiply the above loads by the adjustment coefficients below.

	Mean Roof Height (feet)									
Exposure	15	20	25	30	35	40	45	50	55	60
B	1.00	1.00	1.00	1.00	1.05	1.09	1.12	1.16	1.19	1.22
C	1.21	1.29	1.35	1.40	1.45	1.49	1.53	1.56	1.59	1.62
D	1.47	1.55	1.61	1.66	1.70	1.74	1.78	1.81	1.84	1.87

b. The uplift connection requirements are based on the framing being spaced 24 inches on center. Multiply by 0.67 for framing spaced 16 inches on center and multiply by 0.5 for framing spaced 12 inches on center.

c. The uplift connection requirements include an allowance for 10 pounds of dead load.

d. The uplift connection requirements do not account for the effects of overhangs. The magnitude of the above loads shall be increased by adding the overhang loads found in the table. The overhang loads are also based on framing spaced 24 inches on center. The overhang loads given shall be multiplied by the overhang projection and added to the roof uplift value in the table.

e. The uplift connection requirements are based upon wind loading on end zones as defined in Figure 6-2 of ASCE 7. Connection loads for connections located a distance of 20 percent of the least horizontal dimension of the building from the corner of the building are permitted to be reduced by multiplying the table connection value by 0.7 and multiplying the overhang load by 0.8.

f. For wall-to-wall and wall-to-foundation connections, the capacity of the uplift connector is permitted to be reduced by 100 pounds for each full wall above. (For example, if a 500-pound rated connector is used on the roof framing, a 400-pound rated connector is permitted at the next floor level down).

g. Interpolation is permitted for intermediate values of basic wind speeds and roof spans.

h. The rated capacity of approved tie-down devices is permitted to include up to a 60-percent increase for wind effects where allowed by material specifications.

2308.10.3 Rafter spans. Allowable spans for rafters shall be in accordance with Table 2308.10.3(1), 2308.10.3(2), 2308.10.3(3), 2308.10.3(4), 2308.10.3(5) or 2308.10.3(6). For other grades and species, refer to the *AF&PA Span Tables for Joists and Rafters.*

2308.10.4 Ceiling joist and rafter framing. Rafters shall be framed directly opposite each other at the ridge. There shall be a ridge board at least 1-inch (25 mm) nominal thickness at ridges and not less in depth than the cut end of the rafter. At valleys and hips, there shall be a single valley or hip rafter not less than 2-inch (51 mm) nominal thickness and not less in depth than the cut end of the rafter.

2308.10.4.1 Ceiling joist and rafter connections. Ceiling joists and rafters shall be nailed to each other and the assembly shall be nailed to the top wall plate in accordance with Tables 2304.9.1 and 2308.10.1. Ceiling joists shall be continuous or securely joined where they meet over interior partitions and fastened to adjacent rafters in accordance with Tables 2308.10.4.1 and 2304.9.1 to provide a continuous rafter tie across the building where such joists are parallel to the rafters. Ceiling joists shall have a bearing surface of not less than 1¹/₂ inches (38 mm) on the top plate at each end.

Where ceiling joists are not parallel to rafters, an equivalent rafter tie shall be installed in a manner to provide a continuous tie across the building, at a spacing of not more than 4 feet (1219 mm) o.c. The connections shall be in accordance with Tables 2308.10.4.1 and 2304.9.1, or connections of equivalent capacities shall be provided. Where ceiling joists or rafter ties are not provided at the top of the rafter

support walls, the ridge formed by these rafters shall also be supported by a girder conforming to Section 2308.4.

Rafter ties shall be spaced not more than 4 feet (1219 mm) o.c. Rafter tie connections shall be based on the equivalent rafter spacing in Table 2308.10.4.1. Where rafter ties are spaced at 32 inches (813 mm) o.c., the number of 16d common nails shall be two times the number specified for rafters spaced 16 inches (406 mm) o.c., with a minimum of 4-16d common nails where no snow loads are indicated. Where rafter ties are spaced at 48 inches (1219 mm) o.c., the number of 16d common nails shall be two times the number specified for rafters spaced 24 inches (610 mm) o.c., with a minimum of 6-16d common nails where no snow loads are indicated. Rafter/ceiling joist connections and rafter/tie connections shall be of sufficient size and number to prevent splitting from nailing.

2308.10.4.2 Notches and holes. Notching at the ends of rafters or ceiling joists shall not exceed one-fourth the depth. Notches in the top or bottom of the rafter or ceiling joist shall not exceed one-sixth the depth and shall not be located in the middle one-third of the span, except that a notch not exceeding one-third of the depth is permitted in the top of the rafter or ceiling joist not further from the face of the support than the depth of the member.

Holes bored in rafters or ceiling joists shall not be within 2 inches (51 mm) of the top and bottom and their diameter shall not exceed one-third the depth of the member.

TABLE 2308.10.2(1)
CEILING JOIST SPANS FOR COMMON LUMBER SPECIES (Uninhabitable Attics Without Storage, Live Load = 10 pounds psf, L/Δ = 240)

CEILING JOIST SPACING (inches)	SPECIES AND GRADE		DEAD LOAD = 5 pounds per square foot			
			Maximum ceiling joist spans			
			2 × 4	2 × 6	2 × 8	2 × 10
			(ft. - in.)	(ft. - in.)	(ft. - in.)	(ft. - in.)
12	Douglas Fir-Larch	SS	13-2	20-8	Note a	Note a
	Douglas Fir-Larch	#1	12-8	19-11	Note a	Note a
	Douglas Fir-Larch	#2	12-5	19-6	25-8	Note a
	Douglas Fir-Larch	#3	10-10	15-10	20-1	24-6
	Hem-Fir	SS	12-5	19-6	25-8	Note a
	Hem-Fir	#1	12-2	19-1	25-2	Note a
	Hem-Fir	#2	11-7	18-2	24-0	Note a
	Hem-Fir	#3	10-10	15-10	20-1	24-6
	Southern Pine	SS	12-11	20-3	Note a	Note a
	Southern Pine	#1	12-8	19-11	Note a	Note a
	Southern Pine	#2	12-5	19-6	25-8	Note a
	Southern Pine	#3	11-6	17-0	21-8	25-7
	Spruce-Pine-Fir	SS	12-2	19-1	25-2	Note a
	Spruce-Pine-Fir	#1	11-10	18-8	24-7	Note a
	Spruce-Pine-Fir	#2	11-10	18-8	24-7	Note a
	Spruce-Pine-Fir	#3	10-10	15-10	20-1	24-6
16	Douglas Fir-Larch	SS	11-11	18-9	24-8	Note a
	Douglas Fir-Larch	#1	11-6	18-1	23-10	Note a
	Douglas Fir-Larch	#2	11-3	17-8	23-0	Note a
	Douglas Fir-Larch	#3	9-5	13-9	17-5	21-3
	Hem-Fir	SS	11-3	17-8	23-4	Note a
	Hem-Fir	#1	11-0	17-4	22-10	Note a
	Hem-Fir	#2	10-6	16-6	21-9	Note a
	Hem-Fir	#3	9-5	13-9	17-5	21-3
	Southern Pine	SS	11-9	18-5	24-3	Note a
	Southern Pine	#1	11-6	18-1	23-1	Note a
	Southern Pine	#2	11-3	17-8	23-4	Note a
	Southern Pine	#3	10-0	14-9	18-9	22-2
	Spruce-Pine-Fir	SS	11-0	17-4	22-10	Note a
	Spruce-Pine-Fir	#1	10-9	16-11	22-4	Note a
	Spruce-Pine-Fir	#2	10-9	16-11	22-4	Note a
	Spruce-Pine-Fir	#3	9-5	13-9	17-5	21-3

(continued)

TABLE 2308.10.2(1)—continued
CEILING JOIST SPANS FOR COMMON LUMBER SPECIES (Uninhabitable Attics Without Storage, Live Load = 10 pounds psf, L/Δ = 240)

CEILING JOIST SPACING (inches)	SPECIES AND GRADE		DEAD LOAD = 5 pounds per square foot			
			Maximum ceiling joist spans			
			2 × 4	2 × 6	2 × 8	2 × 10
			(ft. - in.)	(ft. - in.)	(ft. - in.)	(ft. - in.)
19.2	Douglas Fir-Larch	SS	11-3	17-8	23-3	Note a
	Douglas Fir-Larch	#1	10-10	17-0	22-5	Note a
	Douglas Fir-Larch	#2	10-7	16-7	21-0	25-8
	Douglas Fir-Larch	#3	8-7	12-6	15-10	19-5
	Hem-Fir	SS	10-7	16-8	21-11	Note a
	Hem-Fir	#1	10-4	16-4	21-6	Note a
	Hem-Fir	#2	9-11	15-7	20-6	25-3
	Hem-Fir	#3	8-7	12-6	15-10	19-5
	Southern Pine	SS	11-0	17-4	22-10	Note a
	Southern Pine	#1	10-10	17-0	22-5	Note a
	Southern Pine	#2	10-7	16-8	21-11	Note a
	Southern Pine	#3	9-1	13-6	17-2	20-3
	Spruce-Pine-Fir	SS	10-4	16-4	21-6	Note a
	Spruce-Pine-Fir	#1	10-2	15-11	21-0	25-8
	Spruce-Pine-Fir	#2	10-2	15-11	21-0	25-8
	Spruce-Pine-Fir	#3	8-7	12-6	15-10	19-5
24	Douglas Fir-Larch	SS	10-5	16-4	21-7	Note a
	Douglas Fir-Larch	#1	10-0	15-9	20-1	24-6
	Douglas Fir-Larch	#2	9-10	14-10	18-9	22-11
	Douglas Fir-Larch	#3	7-8	11-2	14-2	17-4
	Hem-Fir	SS	9-10	15-6	20-5	Note a
	Hem-Fir	#1	9-8	15-2	19-7	23-11
	Hem-Fir	#2	9-2	14-5	18-6	22-7
	Hem-Fir	#3	7-8	11-2	14-2	17-4
	Southern Pine	SS	10-3	16-1	21-2	Note a
	Southern Pine	#1	10-0	15-9	20-10	23-11
	Southern Pine	#2	9-10	15-6	20-1	23-11
	Southern Pine	#3	8-2	12-0	15-4	18-1
	Spruce-Pine-Fir	SS	9-8	15-2	19-11	25-5
	Spruce-Pine-Fir	#1	9-5	14-9	18-9	22-11
	Spruce-Pine-Fir	#2	9-5	14-9	18-9	22-11
	Spruce-Pine-Fir	#3	7-8	11-2	14-2	17-4

For SI: 1 inch = 25.4 mm, 1 foot = 304.8 mm, 1 pound per square foot = 47.8 N/m^2.

a. Span exceeds 26 feet in length. Check sources for availability of lumber in lengths greater than 20 feet.

TABLE 2308.10.2(2)
CEILING JOIST SPANS FOR COMMON LUMBER SPECIES (Uninhabitable Attics With Limited Storage, Live Load = 20 pounds per square foot, $L/\Delta = 240$)

CEILING JOIST SPACING (inches)	SPECIES AND GRADE	DEAD LOAD = 10 pounds per square foot			
		Maximum ceiling joist spans			
		2 × 4 (ft. - in.)	2 × 6 (ft. - in.)	2 × 8 (ft. - in.)	2 × 10 (ft. - in.)
12	Douglas Fir-Larch SS	10-5	16-4	21-7	Note a
	Douglas Fir-Larch #1	10-0	15-9	20-1	24-6
	Douglas Fir-Larch #2	9-10	14-10	18-9	22-11
	Douglas Fir-Larch #3	7-8	11-2	14-2	17-4
	Hem-Fir SS	9-10	15-6	20-5	Note a
	Hem-Fir #1	9-8	15-2	19-7	23-11
	Hem-Fir #2	9-2	14-5	18-6	22-7
	Hem-Fir #3	7-8	11-2	14-2	17-4
	Southern Pine SS	10-3	16-1	21-2	Note a
	Southern Pine #1	10-0	15-9	20-10	Note a
	Southern Pine #2	9-10	15-6	20-1	23-11
	Southern Pine #3	8-2	12-0	15-4	18-1
	Spruce-Pine-Fir SS	9-8	15-2	19-11	25-5
	Spruce-Pine-Fir #1	9-5	14-9	18-9	22-11
	Spruce-Pine-Fir #2	9-5	14-9	18-9	22-11
	Spruce-Pine-Fir #3	7-8	11-2	14-2	17-4
16	Douglas Fir-Larch SS	9-6	14-11	19-7	25-0
	Douglas Fir-Larch #1	9-1	13-9	17-5	21-3
	Douglas Fir-Larch #2	8-9	12-10	16-3	19-10
	Douglas Fir-Larch #3	6-8	9-8	12-4	15-0
	Hem-Fir SS	8-11	14-1	18-6	23-8
	Hem-Fir #1	8-9	13-5	16-10	20-8
	Hem-Fir #2	8-4	12-8	16-0	19-7
	Hem-Fir #3	6-8	9-8	12-4	15-0
	Southern Pine SS	9-4	14-7	19-3	24-7
	Southern Pine #1	9-1	14-4	18-11	23-1
	Southern Pine #2	8-11	13-6	17-5	20-9
	Southern Pine #3	7-1	10-5	13-3	15-8
	Spruce-Pine-Fir SS	8-9	13-9	18-1	23-1
	Spruce-Pine-Fir #1	8-7	12-10	16-3	19-10
	Spruce-Pine-Fir #2	8-7	12-10	16-3	19-10
	Spruce-Pine-Fir #3	6-8	9-8	12-4	15-0

(continued)

TABLE 2308.10.2(2)—continued
CEILING JOIST SPANS FOR COMMON LUMBER SPECIES (Uninhabitable Attics With Limited Storage, Live Load = 20 pounds per square foot, $L/\Delta = 240$)

CEILING JOIST SPACING (inches)	SPECIES AND GRADE		DEAD LOAD = 10 pounds per square foot			
			2 × 4	2 × 6	2 × 8	2 × 10
			Maximum ceiling joist spans			
			(ft. - in.)	(ft. - in.)	(ft. - in.)	(ft. - in.)
19.2	Douglas Fir-Larch	SS	8-11	14-0	18-5	23-4
	Douglas Fir-Larch	#1	8-7	12-6	15-10	19-5
	Douglas Fir-Larch	#2	8-0	11-9	14-10	18-2
	Douglas Fir-Larch	#3	6-1	8-10	11-3	13-8
	Hem-Fir	SS	8-5	13-3	17-5	22-3
	Hem-Fir	#1	8-3	12-3	15-6	18-11
	Hem-Fir	#2	7-10	11-7	14-8	17-10
	Hem-Fir	#3	6-1	8-10	11-3	13-8
	Southern Pine	SS	8-9	13-9	18-1	23-1
	Southern Pine	#1	8-7	13-6	17-9	21-1
	Southern Pine	#2	8-5	12-3	15-10	18-11
	Southern Pine	#3	6-5	9-6	12-1	14-4
	Spruce-Pine-Fir	SS	8-3	12-11	17-1	21-8
	Spruce-Pine-Fir	#1	8-0	11-9	14-10	18-2
	Spruce-Pine-Fir	#2	8-0	11-9	14-10	18-2
	Spruce-Pine-Fir	#3	6-1	8-10	11-3	13-8
24	Douglas Fir-Larch	SS	8-3	13-0	17-1	20-11
	Douglas Fir-Larch	#1	7-8	11-2	14-2	17-4
	Douglas Fir-Larch	#2	7-2	10-6	13-3	16-3
	Douglas Fir-Larch	#3	5-5	7-11	10-0	12-3
	Hem-Fir	SS	7-10	12-3	16-2	20-6
	Hem-Fir	#1	7-6	10-11	13-10	16-11
	Hem-Fir	#2	7-1	10-4	13-1	16-0
	Hem-Fir	#3	5-5	7-11	10-0	12-3
	Southern Pine	SS	8-1	12-9	16-10	21-6
	Southern Pine	#1	8-0	12-6	15-10	18-10
	Southern Pine	#2	7-8	11-0	14-2	16-11
	Southern Pine	#3	5-9	8-6	10-10	12-10
	Spruce-Pine-Fir	SS	7-8	12-0	15-10	19-5
	Spruce-Pine-Fir	#1	7-2	10-6	13-3	16-3
	Spruce-Pine-Fir	#2	7-2	10-6	13-3	16-3
	Spruce-Pine-Fir	#3	5-5	7-11	10-0	12-3

For SI: 1 inch = 25.4 mm, 1 foot = 304.8 mm, 1 pound per square foot = 47.8 N/m².

a. Span exceeds 26 feet in length. Check sources for availability of lumber in lengths greater than 20 feet.

TABLE 2308.10.3(1)
RAFTER SPANS FOR COMMON LUMBER SPECIES (Roof Live Load = 20 pounds per square foot, Ceiling Not Attached to Rafters, $L/\Delta = 180$)

RAFTER SPACING (inches)	SPECIES AND GRADE		DEAD LOAD = 10 pounds per square foot					DEAD LOAD = 20 pounds per square foot				
			Maximum rafter spans									
			2 × 4	2 × 6	2 × 8	2 × 10	2 × 12	2 × 4	2 × 6	2 × 8	2 × 10	2 × 12
			(ft. - in.)	(ft. - in.)	(ft. - in.)	(ft. - in.)	(ft. - in.)	(ft. - in.)	(ft. - in.)	(ft. - in.)	(ft. - in.)	(ft. - in.)
12	Douglas Fir-Larch	SS	11-6	18-0	23-9	Note a	Note a	11-6	18-0	23-5	Note a	Note a
	Douglas Fir-Larch	#1	11-1	17-4	22-5	Note a	Note a	10-6	15-4	19-5	23-9	Note a
	Douglas Fir-Larch	#2	10-10	16-7	21-0	25-8	Note a	9-10	14-4	18-2	22-3	25-9
	Douglas Fir-Larch	#3	8-7	12-6	15-10	19-5	22-6	7-5	10-10	13-9	16-9	19-6
	Hem-Fir	SS	10-10	17-0	22-5	Note a	Note a	10-10	17-0	22-5	Note a	Note a
	Hem-Fir	#1	10-7	16-8	21-10	Note a	Note a	10-3	14-11	18-11	23-2	Note a
	Hem-Fir	#2	10-1	15-11	20-8	25-3	Note a	9-8	14-2	17-11	21-11	25-5
	Hem-Fir	#3	8-7	12-6	15-10	19-5	22-6	7-5	10-10	13-9	16-9	19-6
	Southern Pine	SS	11-3	17-8	23-4	Note a	Note a	11-3	17-8	23-4	Note a	Note a
	Southern Pine	#1	11-1	17-4	22-11	Note a	Note a	11-1	17-3	21-9	25-10	Note a
	Southern Pine	#2	10-10	17-0	22-5	Note a	Note a	10-6	15-1	19-5	23-2	Note a
	Southern Pine	#3	9-1	13-6	17-2	20-3	24-1	7-11	11-8	14-10	17-6	20-11
	Spruce-Pine-Fir	SS	10-7	16-8	21-11	Note a	Note a	10-7	16-8	21-9	Note a	Note a
	Spruce-Pine-Fir	#1	10-4	16-3	21-0	25-8	Note a	9-10	14-4	18-2	22-3	25-9
	Spruce-Pine-Fir	#2	10-4	16-3	21-0	25-8	Note a	9-10	14-4	18-2	22-3	25-9
	Spruce-Pine-Fir	#3	8-7	12-6	15-10	19-5	22-6	7-5	10-10	13-9	16-9	19-6
16	Douglas Fir-Larch	SS	10-5	16-4	21-7	Note a	Note a	10-5	16-0	20-3	24-9	Note a
	Douglas Fir-Larch	#1	10-0	15-4	19-5	23-9	Note a	9-1	13-3	16-10	20-7	23-10
	Douglas Fir-Larch	#2	9-10	14-4	18-2	22-3	25-9	8-6	12-5	15-9	19-3	22-4
	Douglas Fir-Larch	#3	7-5	10-10	13-9	16-9	19-6	6-5	9-5	11-11	14-6	16-10
	Hem-Fir	SS	9-10	15-6	20-5	Note a	Note a	9-10	15-6	19-11	24-4	Note a
	Hem-Fir	#1	9-8	14-11	18-11	23-2	Note a	8-10	12-11	16-5	20-0	23-3
	Hem-Fir	#2	9-2	14-2	17-11	21-11	25-5	8-5	12-3	15-6	18-11	22-0
	Hem-Fir	#3	7-5	10-10	13-9	16-9	19-6	6-5	9-5	11-11	14-6	16-10
	Southern Pine	SS	10-3	16-1	21-2	Note a	Note a	10-3	16-1	21-2	Note a	Note a
	Southern Pine	#1	10-0	15-9	20-10	25-10	Note a	10-0	15-0	18-10	22-4	Note a
	Southern Pine	#2	9-10	15-1	19-5	23-2	Note a	9-1	13-0	16-10	20-1	23-7
	Southern Pine	#3	7-11	11-8	14-10	17-6	20-11	6-10	10-1	12-10	15-2	18-1
	Spruce-Pine-Fir	SS	9-8	15-2	19-11	25-5	Note a	9-8	14-10	18-10	23-0	Note a
	Spruce-Pine-Fir	#1	9-5	14-4	18-2	22-3	25-9	8-6	12-5	15-9	19-3	22-4
	Spruce-Pine-Fir	#2	9-5	14-4	18-2	22-3	25-9	8-6	12-5	15-9	19-3	22-4
	Spruce-Pine-Fir	#3	7-5	10-10	13-9	16-9	19-6	6-5	9-5	11-11	14-6	16-10

(continued)

TABLE 2308.10.3(1)—continued
RAFTER SPANS FOR COMMON LUMBER SPECIES (Roof Live Load = 20 pounds per square foot, Ceiling Not Attached to Rafters, $L/\Delta = 180$)

RAFTER SPACING (inches)	SPECIES AND GRADE		DEAD LOAD = 10 pounds per square foot					DEAD LOAD = 20 pounds per square foot				
			2 × 4	2 × 6	2 × 8	2 × 10	2 × 12	2 × 4	2 × 6	2 × 8	2 × 10	2 × 12
			Maximum rafter spans									
			(ft.-in.)	(ft.-in.)	(ft.-in.)	(ft.-in.)	(ft.-in.)	(ft.-in.)	(ft.-in.)	(ft.-in.)	(ft.-in.)	(ft.-in.)
19.2	Douglas Fir-Larch	SS	9-10	15-5	20-4	25-11	Note a	9-10	14-7	18-6	22-7	Note a
	Douglas Fir-Larch	#1	9-5	14-0	17-9	21-8	25-2	8-4	12-2	15-4	18-9	21-9
	Douglas Fir-Larch	#2	8-11	13-1	16-7	20-3	23-6	7-9	11-4	14-4	17-7	20-4
	Douglas Fir-Larch	#3	6-9	9-11	12-7	15-4	17-9	5-10	8-7	10-10	13-3	15-5
	Hem-Fir	SS	9-3	14-7	19-2	24-6	Note a	9-3	14-4	18-2	22-3	25-9
	Hem-Fir	#1	9-1	13-8	17-4	21-1	24-6	8-1	11-10	15-0	18-4	21-3
	Hem-Fir	#2	8-8	12-11	16-4	20-0	23-2	7-8	11-2	14-2	17-4	20-1
	Hem-Fir	#3	6-9	9-11	12-7	15-4	17-9	5-10	8-7	10-10	13-3	15-5
	Southern Pine	SS	9-8	15-2	19-11	25-5	Note a	9-8	15-2	19-11	25-5	Note a
	Southern Pine	#1	9-5	14-10	19-7	23-7	Note a	9-3	13-8	17-2	20-5	24-4
	Southern Pine	#2	9-3	13-9	17-9	21-2	24-10	8-4	11-11	15-4	18-4	21-6
	Southern Pine	#3	7-3	10-8	13-7	16-0	19-1	6-3	9-3	11-9	13-10	16-6
	Spruce-Pine-Fir	SS	9-1	14-3	18-9	23-11	Note a	9-1	13-7	17-2	21-0	24-4
	Spruce-Pine-Fir	#1	8-10	13-1	16-7	20-3	23-6	7-9	11-4	14-4	17-7	20-4
	Spruce-Pine-Fir	#2	8-10	13-1	16-7	20-3	23-6	7-9	11-4	14-4	17-7	20-4
	Spruce-Pine-Fir	#3	6-9	9-11	12-7	15-4	17-9	5-10	8-7	10-10	13-3	15-5
24	Douglas Fir-Larch	SS	9-1	14-4	18-10	23-4	Note a	8-11	13-1	16-7	20-3	23-5
	Douglas Fir-Larch	#1	8-7	12-6	15-10	19-5	22-6	7-5	10-10	13-9	16-9	19-6
	Douglas Fir-Larch	#2	8-0	11-9	14-10	18-2	21-0	6-11	10-2	12-10	15-8	18-3
	Douglas Fir-Larch	#3	6-1	8-10	11-3	13-8	15-11	5-3	7-8	9-9	11-10	13-9
	Hem-Fir	SS	8-7	13-6	17-10	22-9	Note a	8-7	12-10	16-3	19-10	23-0
	Hem-Fir	#1	8-4	12-3	15-6	18-11	21-11	7-3	10-7	13-5	16-4	19-0
	Hem-Fir	#2	7-11	11-7	14-8	17-10	20-9	6-10	10-0	12-8	15-6	17-11
	Hem-Fir	#3	6-1	8-10	11-3	13-8	15-11	5-3	7-8	9-9	11-10	13-9
	Southern Pine	SS	8-11	14-1	18-6	23-8	Note a	8-11	14-1	18-6	22-11	Note a
	Southern Pine	#1	8-9	13-9	17-9	21-1	25-2	8-3	12-3	15-4	18-3	21-9
	Southern Pine	#2	8-7	12-3	15-10	18-11	22-2	7-5	10-8	13-9	16-5	19-3
	Southern Pine	#3	6-5	9-6	12-1	14-4	17-1	5-7	8-3	10-6	12-5	14-9
	Spruce-Pine-Fir	SS	8-5	13-3	17-5	21-8	25-2	8-4	12-2	15-4	18-9	21-9
	Spruce-Pine-Fir	#1	8-0	11-9	14-10	18-2	21-0	6-11	10-2	12-10	15-8	18-3
	Spruce-Pine-Fir	#2	8-0	11-9	14-10	18-2	21-0	6-11	10-2	12-10	15-8	18-3
	Spruce-Pine-Fir	#3	6-1	8-10	11-3	13-8	15-11	5-3	7-8	9-9	11-10	13-9

For SI: 1 inch = 25.4 mm, 1 foot = 304.8 mm, 1 pound per square foot = 47.9 N/m².
a. Span exceeds 26 feet in length. Check sources for availability of lumber in lengths greater than 20 feet.

TABLE 2308.10.3(2)
RAFTER SPANS FOR COMMON LUMBER SPECIES (Roof Live Load = 20 pounds per square foot, Ceiling Not Attached to Rafters, $L/\Delta = 240$)

RAFTER SPACING (inches)	SPECIES AND GRADE		DEAD LOAD = 10 pounds per square foot					DEAD LOAD = 20 pounds per square foot				
			2 × 4	2 × 6	2 × 8	2 × 10	2 × 12	2 × 4	2 × 6	2 × 8	2 × 10	2 × 12
			(ft. - in.)	(ft. - in.)	(ft. - in.)	(ft. - in.)	(ft. - in.)	(ft. - in.)	(ft. - in.)	(ft. - in.)	(ft. - in.)	(ft. - in.)
			Maximum rafter spans									
12	Douglas Fir-Larch	SS	10-5	16-4	21-7	Note a	Note a	10-5	16-4	21-7	Note a	Note a
	Douglas Fir-Larch	#1	10-0	15-9	20-10	Note a	Note a	10-0	15-4	19-5	23-9	Note a
	Douglas Fir-Larch	#2	9-10	15-6	20-5	25-8	Note a	9-10	14-4	18-2	22-3	25-9
	Douglas Fir-Larch	#3	8-7	12-6	15-10	19-5	22-6	7-5	10-10	13-9	16-9	19-6
	Hem-Fir	SS	9-10	15-6	20-5	Note a	Note a	9-10	15-6	20-5	Note a	Note a
	Hem-Fir	#1	9-8	15-2	19-11	25-5	Note a	9-8	14-11	18-11	23-2	Note a
	Hem-Fir	#2	9-2	14-5	19-0	24-3	Note a	9-2	14-2	17-11	21-11	25-5
	Hem-Fir	#3	8-7	12-6	15-10	19-5	22-6	7-5	10-10	13-9	16-9	19-6
	Southern Pine	SS	10-3	16-1	21-2	Note a	Note a	10-3	16-1	21-2	Note a	Note a
	Southern Pine	#1	10-0	15-9	20-10	Note a	Note a	10-0	15-9	20-10	25-10	Note a
	Southern Pine	#2	9-10	15-6	20-5	Note a	Note a	9-10	15-1	19-5	23-2	Note a
	Southern Pine	#3	9-1	13-6	17-2	20-3	24-1	7-11	11-8	14-10	17-6	20-11
	Spruce-Pine-Fir	SS	9-8	15-2	19-11	25-5	Note a	9-8	15-2	19-11	25-5	Note a
	Spruce-Pine-Fir	#1	9-5	14-9	19-6	24-10	Note a	9-5	14-4	18-2	22-3	25-9
	Spruce-Pine-Fir	#2	9-5	14-9	19-6	24-10	Note a	9-5	14-4	18-2	22-3	25-9
	Spruce-Pine-Fir	#3	8-7	12-6	15-10	19-5	22-6	7-5	10-10	13-9	16-9	19-6
16	Douglas Fir-Larch	SS	9-6	14-11	19-7	25-0	Note a	9-6	14-11	19-7	24-9	Note a
	Douglas Fir-Larch	#1	9-1	14-4	18-11	23-9	Note a	9-1	13-3	16-10	20-7	23-10
	Douglas Fir-Larch	#2	8-11	14-1	18-2	22-3	25-9	8-6	12-5	15-9	19-3	22-4
	Douglas Fir-Larch	#3	7-5	10-10	13-9	16-9	19-6	6-5	9-5	11-11	14-6	16-10
	Hem-Fir	SS	8-11	14-1	18-6	23-8	Note a	8-11	14-1	18-6	23-8	Note a
	Hem-Fir	#1	8-9	13-9	18-1	23-1	Note a	8-9	12-11	16-5	20-0	23-3
	Hem-Fir	#2	8-4	13-1	17-3	21-11	25-5	8-4	12-3	15-6	18-11	22-0
	Hem-Fir	#3	7-5	10-10	13-9	16-9	19-6	6-5	9-5	11-11	14-6	16-10
	Southern Pine	SS	9-4	14-7	19-3	24-7	Note a	9-4	14-7	19-3	24-7	Note a
	Southern Pine	#1	9-1	14-4	18-11	24-1	Note a	9-1	14-4	18-10	22-4	Note a
	Southern Pine	#2	8-11	14-1	18-6	23-2	Note a	8-11	13-0	16-10	20-1	23-7
	Southern Pine	#3	7-11	11-8	14-10	17-6	20-11	6-10	10-1	12-10	15-2	18-1
	Spruce-Pine-Fir	SS	8-9	13-9	18-1	23-1	Note a	8-9	13-9	18-1	23-0	Note a
	Spruce-Pine-Fir	#1	8-7	13-5	17-9	22-3	25-9	8-6	12-5	15-9	19-3	22-4
	Spruce-Pine-Fir	#2	8-7	13-5	17-9	22-3	25-9	8-6	12-5	15-9	19-3	22-4
	Spruce-Pine-Fir	#3	7-5	10-10	13-9	16-9	19-6	6-5	9-5	11-11	14-6	16-10

(continued)

TABLE 2308.10.3(2)—continued
RAFTER SPANS FOR COMMON LUMBER SPECIES (Roof Live Load = 20 pounds per square foot, Ceiling Not Attached to Rafters, $L/\Delta = 240$)

RAFTER SPACING (inches)	SPECIES AND GRADE		DEAD LOAD = 10 pounds per square foot					DEAD LOAD = 20 pounds per square foot				
			2 × 4	2 × 6	2 × 8	2 × 10	2 × 12	2 × 4	2 × 6	2 × 8	2 × 10	2 × 12
			(ft. - in.)	(ft. - in.)	(ft. - in.)	(ft. - in.)	(ft. - in.)	(ft. - in.)	(ft. - in.)	(ft. - in.)	(ft. - in.)	(ft. - in.)
			Maximum rafter spans									
19.2	Douglas Fir-Larch	SS	8-11	14-0	18-5	23-7	Note a	8-11	14-0	18-5	22-7	Note a
	Douglas Fir-Larch	#1	8-7	13-6	17-9	21-8	25-2	8-4	12-2	15-4	18-9	21-9
	Douglas Fir-Larch	#2	8-5	13-1	16-7	20-3	23-6	7-9	11-4	14-4	17-7	20-4
	Douglas Fir-Larch	#3	6-9	9-11	12-7	15-4	17-9	5-10	8-7	10-10	13-3	15-5
	Hem-Fir	SS	8-5	13-3	17-5	22-3	Note a	8-5	13-3	17-5	22-3	25-9
	Hem-Fir	#1	8-3	12-11	17-1	21-1	24-6	8-1	11-10	15-0	18-4	21-3
	Hem-Fir	#2	7-10	12-4	16-3	20-0	23-2	7-8	11-2	14-2	17-4	20-1
	Hem-Fir	#3	6-9	9-11	12-7	15-4	17-9	5-10	8-7	10-10	13-3	15-5
	Southern Pine	SS	8-9	13-9	18-1	23-1	Note a	8-9	13-9	18-1	23-1	Note a
	Southern Pine	#1	8-7	13-6	17-9	22-8	Note a	8-7	13-6	17-2	20-5	24-4
	Southern Pine	#2	8-5	13-3	17-5	21-2	24-10	8-4	11-11	15-4	18-4	21-6
	Southern Pine	#3	7-3	10-8	13-7	16-0	19-1	6-3	9-3	11-9	13-10	16-6
	Spruce-Pine-Fir	SS	8-3	12-11	17-1	21-9	Note a	8-3	12-11	17-1	21-0	24-4
	Spruce-Pine-Fir	#1	8-1	12-8	16-7	20-3	23-6	7-9	11-4	14-4	17-7	20-4
	Spruce-Pine-Fir	#2	8-1	12-8	16-7	20-3	23-6	7-9	11-4	14-4	17-7	20-4
	Spruce-Pine-Fir	#3	6-9	9-11	12-7	15-4	17-9	5-10	8-7	10-10	13-3	15-5
24	Douglas Fir-Larch	SS	8-3	13-0	17-2	21-10	Note a	8-3	13-0	16-7	20-3	23-5
	Douglas Fir-Larch	#1	8-0	12-6	15-10	19-5	22-6	7-5	10-10	13-9	16-9	19-6
	Douglas Fir-Larch	#2	7-10	11-9	14-10	18-2	21-0	6-11	10-2	12-10	15-8	18-3
	Douglas Fir-Larch	#3	6-1	8-10	11-3	13-8	15-11	5-3	7-8	9-9	11-10	13-9
	Hem-Fir	SS	7-10	12-3	16-2	20-8	25-1	7-10	12-3	16-2	19-10	23-0
	Hem-Fir	#1	7-8	12-0	15-6	18-11	21-11	7-3	10-7	13-5	16-4	19-0
	Hem-Fir	#2	7-3	11-5	14-8	17-10	20-9	6-10	10-0	12-8	15-6	17-11
	Hem-Fir	#3	6-1	8-10	11-3	13-8	15-11	5-3	7-8	9-9	11-10	13-9
	Southern Pine	SS	8-1	12-9	16-10	21-6	Note a	8-1	12-9	16-10	21-6	Note a
	Southern Pine	#1	8-0	12-6	16-6	21-1	25-2	8-0	12-3	15-4	18-3	21-9
	Southern Pine	#2	7-10	12-3	15-10	18-11	22-2	7-5	10-8	13-9	16-5	19-3
	Southern Pine	#3	6-5	9-6	12-1	14-4	17-1	5-7	8-3	10-6	12-5	14-9
	Spruce-Pine-Fir	SS	7-8	12-0	15-10	20-2	24-7	7-8	12-0	15-4	18-9	21-9
	Spruce-Pine-Fir	#1	7-6	11-9	14-10	18-2	21-0	6-11	10-2	12-10	15-8	18-3
	Spruce-Pine-Fir	#2	7-6	11-9	14-10	18-2	21-0	6-11	10-2	12-10	15-8	18-3
	Spruce-Pine-Fir	#3	6-1	8-10	11-3	13-8	15-11	5-3	7-8	9-9	11-10	13-9

For SI: 1 inch = 25.4 mm, 1 foot = 304.8 mm, 1 pound per square foot = 47.9 N/m².

a. Span exceeds 26 feet in length. Check sources for availability of lumber in lengths greater than 20 feet.

TABLE 2308.10.3(3)
RAFTER SPANS FOR COMMON LUMBER SPECIES (Ground Snow Load = 30 pounds per square foot, Ceiling Not Attached to Rafters, $L/\Delta = 180$)

RAFTER SPACING (inches)	SPECIES AND GRADE		DEAD LOAD = 10 pounds per square foot					DEAD LOAD = 20 pounds per square foot				
			2 × 4	2 × 6	2 × 8	2 × 10	2 × 12	2 × 4	2 × 6	2 × 8	2 × 10	2 × 12
			Maximum rafter spans									
			(ft. - in.)	(ft. - in.)	(ft. - in.)	(ft. - in.)	(ft. - in.)	(ft. - in.)	(ft. - in.)	(ft. - in.)	(ft. - in.)	(ft. - in.)
12	Douglas Fir-Larch	SS	10-0	15-9	20-9	Note a	Note a	10-0	15-9	20-1	24-6	Note a
	Douglas Fir-Larch	#1	9-8	14-9	18-8	22-9	Note a	9-0	13-2	16-8	20-4	23-7
	Douglas Fir-Larch	#2	9-5	13-9	17-5	21-4	24-8	8-5	12-4	15-7	19-1	22-1
	Douglas Fir-Larch	#3	7-1	10-5	13-2	16-1	18-8	6-4	9-4	11-9	14-5	16-8
	Hem-Fir	SS	9-6	14-10	19-7	25-0	Note a	9-6	14-10	19-7	24-1	Note a
	Hem-Fir	#1	9-3	14-4	18-2	22-2	25-9	8-9	12-10	16-3	19-10	23-0
	Hem-Fir	#2	8-10	13-7	17-2	21-0	24-4	8-4	12-2	15-4	18-9	21-9
	Hem-Fir	#3	7-1	10-5	13-2	16-1	18-8	6-4	9-4	11-9	14-5	16-8
	Southern Pine	SS	9-10	15-6	20-5	Note a	Note a	9-10	15-6	20-5	Note a	Note a
	Southern Pine	#1	9-8	15-2	20-0	24-9	Note a	9-8	14-10	18-8	22-2	Note a
	Southern Pine	#2	9-6	14-5	18-8	22-3	Note a	9-0	12-11	16-8	19-11	23-4
	Southern Pine	#3	7-7	11-2	14-3	16-10	20-0	6-9	10-0	12-9	15-1	17-11
	Spruce-Pine-Fir	SS	9-3	14-7	19-2	24-6	Note a	9-3	14-7	18-8	22-9	Note a
	Spruce-Pine-Fir	#1	9-1	13-9	17-5	21-4	24-8	8-5	12-4	15-7	19-1	22-1
	Spruce-Pine-Fir	#2	9-1	13-9	17-5	21-4	24-8	8-5	12-4	15-7	19-1	22-1
	Spruce-Pine-Fir	#3	7-1	10-5	13-2	16-1	18-8	6-4	9-4	11-9	14-5	16-8
16	Douglas Fir-Larch	SS	9-1	14-4	18-10	23-9	Note a	9-1	13-9	17-5	21-3	24-8
	Douglas Fir-Larch	#1	8-9	12-9	16-2	19-9	22-10	7-10	11-5	14-5	17-8	20-5
	Douglas Fir-Larch	#2	8-2	11-11	15-1	18-5	21-5	7-3	10-8	13-6	16-6	19-2
	Douglas Fir-Larch	#3	6-2	9-0	11-5	13-11	16-2	5-6	8-1	10-3	12-6	14-6
	Hem-Fir	SS	8-7	13-6	17-10	22-9	Note a	8-7	13-6	17-1	20-10	24-2
	Hem-Fir	#1	8-5	12-5	15-9	19-3	22-3	7-7	11-1	14-1	17-2	19-11
	Hem-Fir	#2	8-0	11-9	14-11	18-2	21-1	7-2	10-6	13-4	16-3	18-10
	Hem-Fir	#3	6-2	9-0	11-5	13-11	16-2	5-6	8-1	10-3	12-6	14-6
	Southern Pine	SS	8-11	14-1	18-6	23-8	Note a	8-11	14-1	18-6	23-8	Note a
	Southern Pine	#1	8-9	13-9	18-1	21-5	25-7	8-8	12-10	16-2	19-2	22-10
	Southern Pine	#2	8-7	12-6	16-2	19-3	22-7	7-10	11-2	14-5	17-3	20-2
	Southern Pine	#3	6-7	9-8	12-4	14-7	17-4	5-10	8-8	11-0	13-0	15-6
	Spruce-Pine-Fir	SS	8-5	13-3	17-5	22-1	25-7	8-5	12-9	16-2	19-9	22-10
	Spruce-Pine-Fir	#1	8-2	11-11	15-1	18-5	21-5	7-3	10-8	13-6	16-6	19-2
	Spruce-Pine-Fir	#2	8-2	11-11	15-1	18-5	21-5	7-3	10-8	13-6	16-6	19-2
	Spruce-Pine-Fir	#3	6-2	9-0	11-5	13-11	16-2	5-6	8-1	10-3	12-6	14-6

(continued)

TABLE 2308.10.3(3)—continued
RAFTER SPANS FOR COMMON LUMBER SPECIES (Ground Snow Load = 30 pounds per square foot, Ceiling Not Attached to Rafters, $L/\Delta = 180$)

RAFTER SPACING (inches)	SPECIES AND GRADE		DEAD LOAD = 10 pounds per square foot					DEAD LOAD = 20 pounds per square foot				
			Maximum rafter spans									
			2 × 4	2 × 6	2 × 8	2 × 10	2 × 12	2 × 4	2 × 6	2 × 8	2 × 10	2 × 12
			(ft. - in.)	(ft. - in.)	(ft. - in.)	(ft. - in.)	(ft. - in.)	(ft. - in.)	(ft. - in.)	(ft. - in.)	(ft. - in.)	(ft. - in.)
19.2	Douglas Fir-Larch	SS	8-7	13-6	17-9	21-8	25-2	8-7	12-6	15-10	19-5	22-6
	Douglas Fir-Larch	#1	7-11	11-8	14-9	18-0	20-11	7-1	10-5	13-2	16-1	18-8
	Douglas Fir-Larch	#2	7-5	10-11	13-9	16-10	19-6	6-8	9-9	12-4	15-1	17-6
	Douglas Fir-Larch	#3	5-7	8-3	10-5	12-9	14-9	5-0	7-4	9-4	11-5	13-2
	Hem-Fir	SS	8-1	12-9	16-9	21-4	24-8	8-1	12-4	15-7	19-1	22-1
	Hem-Fir	#1	7-9	11-4	14-4	17-7	20-4	6-11	10-2	12-10	15-8	18-2
	Hem-Fir	#2	7-4	10-9	13-7	16-7	19-3	6-7	9-7	12-2	14-10	17-3
	Hem-Fir	#3	5-7	8-3	10-5	12-9	14-9	5-0	7-4	9-4	11-5	13-2
	Southern Pine	SS	8-5	13-3	17-5	22-3	Note a	8-5	13-3	17-5	22-0	25-9
	Southern Pine	#1	8-3	13-0	16-6	19-7	23-4	7-11	11-9	14-9	17-6	20-11
	Southern Pine	#2	7-11	11-5	14-9	17-7	20-7	7-1	10-2	13-2	15-9	18-5
	Southern Pine	#3	6-0	8-10	11-3	13-4	15-10	5-4	7-11	10-1	11-11	14-2
	Spruce-Pine-Fir	SS	7-11	12-5	16-5	20-2	23-4	7-11	11-8	14-9	18-0	20-11
	Spruce-Pine-Fir	#1	7-5	10-11	13-9	16-10	19-6	6-8	9-9	12-4	15-1	17-6
	Spruce-Pine-Fir	#2	7-5	10-11	13-9	16-10	19-6	6-8	9-9	12-4	15-1	17-6
	Spruce-Pine-Fir	#3	5-7	8-3	10-5	12-9	14-9	5-0	7-4	9-4	11-5	13-2
24	Douglas Fir-Larch	SS	7-11	12-6	15-10	19-5	22-6	7-8	11-3	14-2	17-4	20-1
	Douglas Fir-Larch	#1	7-1	10-5	13-2	16-1	18-8	6-4	9-4	11-9	14-5	16-8
	Douglas Fir-Larch	#2	6-8	9-9	12-4	15-1	17-6	5-11	8-8	11-0	13-6	15-7
	Douglas Fir-Larch	#3	5-0	7-4	9-4	11-5	13-2	4-6	6-7	8-4	10-2	11-10
	Hem-Fir	SS	7-6	11-10	15-7	19-1	22-1	7-6	11-0	13-11	17-0	19-9
	Hem-Fir	#1	6-11	10-2	12-10	15-8	18-2	6-2	9-1	11-6	14-0	16-3
	Hem-Fir	#2	6-7	9-7	12-2	14-10	17-3	5-10	8-7	10-10	13-3	15-5
	Hem-Fir	#3	5-0	7-4	9-4	11-5	13-2	4-6	6-7	8-4	10-2	11-10
	Southern Pine	SS	7-10	12-3	16-2	20-8	25-1	7-10	12-3	16-2	19-8	23-0
	Southern Pine	#1	7-8	11-9	14-9	17-6	20-11	7-1	10-6	13-2	15-8	18-8
	Southern Pine	#2	7-1	10-2	13-2	15-9	18-5	6-4	9-2	11-9	14-1	16-6
	Southern Pine	#3	5-4	7-11	10-1	11-11	14-2	4-9	7-1	9-0	10-8	12-8
	Spruce-Pine-Fir	SS	7-4	11-7	14-9	18-0	20-11	7-1	10-5	13-2	16-1	18-8
	Spruce-Pine-Fir	#1	6-8	9-9	12-4	15-1	17-6	5-11	8-8	11-0	13-6	15-7
	Spruce-Pine-Fir	#2	6-8	9-9	12-4	15-1	17-6	5-11	8-8	11-0	13-6	15-7
	Spruce-Pine-Fir	#3	5-0	7-4	9-4	11-5	13-2	4-6	6-7	8-4	10-2	11-10

For SI: 1 inch = 25.4 mm, 1 foot = 304.8 mm, 1 pound per square foot = 47.9 N/m^2.

a. Span exceeds 26 feet in length. Check sources for availability of lumber in lengths greater than 20 feet.

TABLE 2308.10.3(4)
RAFTER SPANS FOR COMMON LUMBER SPECIES (Ground Snow Load = 50 pounds per square foot, Ceiling Not Attached to Rafters, L/Δ = 180)

RAFTER SPACING (inches)	SPECIES AND GRADE		DEAD LOAD = 10 pounds per square foot					DEAD LOAD = 20 pounds per square foot				
			2 × 4	2 × 6	2 × 8	2 × 10	2 × 12	2 × 4	2 × 6	2 × 8	2 × 10	2 × 12
			(ft.-in.)	(ft.-in.)	(ft.-in.)	(ft.-in.)	(ft.-in.)	(ft.-in.)	(ft.-in.)	(ft.-in.)	(ft.-in.)	(ft.-in.)
			Maximum rafter spans									
12	Douglas Fir-Larch	SS	8-5	13-3	17-6	22-4	26-0	8-5	13-3	17-0	20-9	24-10
	Douglas Fir-Larch	#1	8-2	12-0	15-3	18-7	21-7	7-7	11-2	14-1	17-3	20-0
	Douglas Fir-Larch	#2	7-8	11-3	14-3	17-5	20-2	7-1	10-5	13-2	16-1	18-8
	Douglas Fir-Larch	#3	5-10	8-6	10-9	13-2	15-3	5-5	7-10	10-0	12-2	14-1
	Hem-Fir	SS	8-0	12-6	16-6	21-1	25-6	8-0	12-6	16-6	20-4	23-7
	Hem-Fir	#1	7-10	11-9	14-10	18-1	21-0	7-5	10-10	13-9	16-9	19-5
	Hem-Fir	#2	7-5	11-1	14-0	17-2	19-11	7-0	10-3	13-0	15-10	18-5
	Hem-Fir	#3	5-10	8-6	10-9	13-2	15-3	5-5	7-10	10-0	12-2	14-1
	Southern Pine	SS	8-4	13-0	17-2	21-11	Note a	8-4	13-0	17-2	21-11	Note a
	Southern Pine	#1	8-2	12-10	16-10	20-3	24-1	8-2	12-6	15-9	18-9	22-4
	Southern Pine	#2	8-0	11-9	15-3	18-2	21-3	7-7	10-11	14-1	16-10	19-9
	Southern Pine	#3	6-2	9-2	11-8	13-9	16-4	5-9	8-5	10-9	12-9	15-2
	Spruce-Pine-Fir	SS	7-10	12-3	16-2	20-8	24-1	7-10	12-3	15-9	19-3	22-4
	Spruce-Pine-Fir	#1	7-8	11-3	14-3	17-5	20-2	7-1	10-5	13-2	16-1	18-8
	Spruce-Pine-Fir	#2	7-8	11-3	14-3	17-5	20-2	7-1	10-5	13-2	16-1	18-8
	Spruce-Pine-Fir	#3	5-10	8-6	10-9	13-2	15-3	5-5	7-10	10-0	12-2	14-1
16	Douglas Fir-Larch	SS	7-8	12-1	15-10	19-5	22-6	7-8	11-7	14-8	17-11	20-10
	Douglas Fir-Larch	#1	7-1	10-5	13-2	16-1	18-8	6-7	9-8	12-2	14-11	17-3
	Douglas Fir-Larch	#2	6-7	9-9	12-4	15-1	17-6	6-2	9-0	11-5	13-11	16-2
	Douglas Fir-Larch	#3	5-0	7-4	9-4	11-5	13-2	4-8	6-10	8-8	10-6	12-3
	Hem-Fir	SS	7-3	11-5	15-0	19-1	22-1	7-3	11-5	14-5	17-8	20-5
	Hem-Fir	#1	6-11	10-2	12-10	15-8	18-2	6-5	9-5	11-11	14-6	16-10
	Hem-Fir	#2	6-7	9-7	12-2	14-10	17-3	6-1	8-11	11-3	13-9	15-11
	Hem-Fir	#3	5-0	7-4	9-4	11-5	13-2	4-8	6-10	8-8	10-6	12-3
	Southern Pine	SS	7-6	11-10	15-7	19-11	24-3	7-6	11-10	15-7	19-11	23-10
	Southern Pine	#1	7-5	11-7	14-9	17-6	20-11	7-4	10-10	13-8	16-2	19-4
	Southern Pine	#2	7-1	10-2	13-2	15-9	18-5	6-7	9-5	12-2	14-7	17-1
	Southern Pine	#3	5-4	7-11	10-1	11-11	14-2	4-11	7-4	9-4	11-0	13-1
	Spruce-Pine-Fir	SS	7-1	11-2	14-8	18-0	20-11	7-1	10-9	13-8	16-8	19-4
	Spruce-Pine-Fir	#1	6-8	9-9	12-4	15-1	17-6	6-2	9-0	11-5	13-11	16-2
	Spruce-Pine-Fir	#2	6-8	9-9	12-4	15-1	17-6	6-2	9-0	11-5	13-11	16-2
	Spruce-Pine-Fir	#3	5-0	7-4	9-4	11-5	13-2	4-8	6-10	8-8	10-6	12-3

(continued)

TABLE 2308.10.3(4)—continued
RAFTER SPANS FOR COMMON LUMBER SPECIES (Ground Snow Load = 50 pounds per square foot, Ceiling Not Attached to Rafters, L/Δ = 180)

RAFTER SPACING (inches)	SPECIES AND GRADE		DEAD LOAD = 10 pounds per square foot					DEAD LOAD = 20 pounds per square foot				
			2 × 4	2 × 6	2 × 8	2 × 10	2 × 12	2 × 4	2 × 6	2 × 8	2 × 10	2 × 12
			(ft.-in.)	(ft.-in.)	(ft.-in.)	(ft.-in.)	(ft.-in.)	(ft.-in.)	(ft.-in.)	(ft.-in.)	(ft.-in.)	(ft.-in.)
			Maximum rafter spans									
19,2	Douglas Fir-Larch	SS	7-3	11-4	14-6	17-8	20-6	7-3	10-7	13-5	16-5	19-0
	Douglas Fir-Larch	#1	6-6	9-6	12-0	14-8	17-1	6-0	8-10	11-2	13-7	15-9
	Douglas Fir-Larch	#2	6-1	8-11	11-3	13-9	15-11	5-7	8-3	10-5	12-9	14-9
	Douglas Fir-Larch	#3	4-7	6-9	8-6	10-5	12-1	4-3	6-3	7-11	9-7	11-2
	Hem-Fir	SS	6-10	10-9	14-2	17-5	20-2	6-10	10-5	13-2	16-1	18-8
	Hem-Fir	#1	6-4	9-3	11-9	14-4	16-7	5-10	8-7	10-10	13-3	15-5
	Hem-Fir	#2	6-0	8-9	11-1	13-7	15-9	5-7	8-1	10-3	12-7	14-7
	Hem-Fir	#3	4-7	6-9	8-6	10-5	12-1	4-3	6-3	7-11	9-7	11-2
	Southern Pine	SS	7-1	11-2	14-8	18-9	22-10	7-1	11-2	14-8	18-7	21-9
	Southern Pine	#1	7-0	10-8	13-5	16-0	19-1	6-8	9-11	12-5	14-10	17-8
	Southern Pine	#2	6-6	9-4	12-0	14-4	16-10	6-0	8-8	11-2	13-4	15-7
	Southern Pine	#3	4-11	7-3	9-2	10-10	12-11	4-6	6-8	8-6	10-1	12-0
	Spruce-Pine-Fir	SS	6-8	10-6	13-5	16-5	19-1	6-8	9-10	12-5	15-3	17-8
	Spruce-Pine-Fir	#1	6-1	8-11	11-3	13-9	15-11	5-7	8-3	10-5	12-9	14-9
	Spruce-Pine-Fir	#2	6-1	8-11	11-3	13-9	15-11	5-7	8-3	10-5	12-9	14-9
	Spruce-Pine-Fir	#3	4-7	6-9	8-6	10-5	12-1	4-3	6-3	7-11	9-7	11-2
24	Douglas Fir-Larch	SS	6-8	10-3	13-0	15-10	18-4	6-6	9-6	12-0	14-8	17-0
	Douglas Fir-Larch	#1	5-10	8-6	10-9	13-2	15-3	5-5	7-10	10-0	12-2	14-1
	Douglas Fir-Larch	#2	5-5	7-11	10-1	12-4	14-3	5-0	7-4	9-4	11-5	13-2
	Douglas Fir-Larch	#3	4-1	6-0	7-7	9-4	10-9	3-10	5-7	7-1	8-7	10-0
	Hem-Fir	SS	6-4	9-11	12-9	15-7	18-0	6-4	9-4	11-9	14-5	16-8
	Hem-Fir	#1	5-8	8-3	10-6	12-10	14-10	5-3	7-8	9-9	11-10	13-9
	Hem-Fir	#2	5-4	7-10	9-11	12-1	14-1	4-11	7-3	9-2	11-3	13-0
	Hem-Fir	#3	4-1	6-0	7-7	9-4	10-9	3-10	5-7	7-1	8-7	10-0
	Southern Pine	SS	6-7	10-4	13-8	17-5	21-0	6-7	10-4	13-8	16-7	19-5
	Southern Pine	#1	6-5	9-7	12-0	14-4	17-1	6-0	8-10	11-2	13-3	15-9
	Southern Pine	#2	5-10	8-4	10-9	12-10	15-1	5-5	7-9	10-0	11-11	13-11
	Southern Pine	#3	4-4	6-5	8-3	9-9	11-7	4-1	6-0	7-7	9-0	10-8
	Spruce-Pine-Fir	SS	6-2	9-6	12-0	14-8	17-1	6-0	8-10	11-2	13-7	15-9
	Spruce-Pine-Fir	#1	5-5	7-11	10-1	12-4	14-3	5-0	7-4	9-4	11-5	13-2
	Spruce-Pine-Fir	#2	5-5	7-11	10-1	12-4	14-3	5-0	7-4	9-4	11-5	13-2
	Spruce-Pine-Fir	#3	4-1	6-0	7-7	9-4	10-9	3-10	5-7	7-1	8-7	10-0

For SI: 1 inch = 25.4 mm, 1 foot = 304.8 mm, 1 pound per square foot = 47.9 N/m².

a. Span exceeds 26 feet in length. Check sources for availability of lumber in lengths greater than 20 feet.

TABLE 2308.10.3(5)
RAFTER SPANS FOR COMMON LUMBER SPECIES (Ground Snow Load = 30 pounds per square foot,
Ceiling Attached to Rafters, L/Δ = 240)

RAFTER SPACING (inches)	SPECIES AND GRADE		DEAD LOAD = 10 pounds per square foot					DEAD LOAD = 20 pounds per square foot				
			2 × 4	2 × 6	2 × 8	2 × 10	2 × 12	2 × 4	2 × 6	2 × 8	2 × 10	2 × 12
			(ft.-in.)	(ft.-in.)	(ft.-in.)	(ft.-in.)	(ft.-in.)	(ft.-in.)	(ft.-in.)	(ft.-in.)	(ft.-in.)	(ft.-in.)
12	Douglas Fir-Larch	SS	9-1	14-4	18-10	24-1	Note a	9-1	14-4	18-10	24-1	Note a
	Douglas Fir-Larch	#1	8-9	13-9	18-2	22-9	Note a	8-9	13-2	16-8	20-4	23-7
	Douglas Fir-Larch	#2	8-7	13-6	17-5	21-4	24-8	8-5	12-4	15-7	19-1	22-1
	Douglas Fir-Larch	#3	7-1	10-5	13-2	16-1	18-8	6-4	9-4	11-9	14-5	16-8
	Hem-Fir	SS	8-7	13-6	17-10	22-9	Note a	8-7	13-6	17-10	22-9	Note a
	Hem-Fir	#1	8-5	13-3	17-5	22-2	25-9	8-5	12-10	16-3	19-10	23-0
	Hem-Fir	#2	8-0	12-7	16-7	21-0	24-4	8-0	12-2	15-4	18-9	21-9
	Hem-Fir	#3	7-1	10-5	13-2	16-1	18-8	6-4	9-4	11-9	14-5	16-8
	Southern Pine	SS	8-11	14-1	18-6	23-8	Note a	8-11	14-1	18-6	23-8	Note a
	Southern Pine	#1	8-9	13-9	18-2	23-2	Note a	8-9	13-9	18-2	22-2	Note a
	Southern Pine	#2	8-7	13-6	17-10	22-3	Note a	8-7	12-11	16-8	19-11	23-4
	Southern Pine	#3	7-7	11-2	14-3	16-10	20-0	6-9	10-0	12-9	15-1	17-11
	Spruce-Pine-Fir	SS	8-5	13-3	17-5	22-3	Note a	8-5	13-3	17-5	22-3	Note a
	Spruce-Pine-Fir	#1	8-3	12-11	17-0	21-4	24-8	8-3	12-4	15-7	19-1	22-1
	Spruce-Pine-Fir	#2	8-3	12-11	17-0	21-4	24-8	8-3	12-4	15-7	19-1	22-1
	Spruce-Pine-Fir	#3	7-1	10-5	13-2	16-1	18-8	6-4	9-4	11-9	14-5	16-8
16	Douglas Fir-Larch	SS	8-3	13-0	17-2	21-10	Note a	8-3	13-0	17-2	21-3	24-8
	Douglas Fir-Larch	#1	8-0	12-6	16-2	19-9	22-10	7-10	11-5	14-5	17-8	20-5
	Douglas Fir-Larch	#2	7-10	11-11	15-1	18-5	21-5	7-3	10-8	13-6	16-6	19-2
	Douglas Fir-Larch	#3	6-2	9-0	11-5	13-11	16-2	5-6	8-1	10-3	12-6	14-6
	Hem-Fir	SS	7-10	12-3	16-2	20-8	25-1	7-10	12-3	16-2	20-8	24-2
	Hem-Fir	#1	7-8	12-0	15-9	19-3	22-3	7-7	11-1	14-1	17-2	19-11
	Hem-Fir	#2	7-3	11-5	14-11	18-2	21-1	7-2	10-6	13-4	16-3	18-10
	Hem-Fir	#3	6-2	9-0	11-5	13-11	16-2	5-6	8-1	10-3	12-6	14-6
	Southern Pine	SS	8-1	12-9	16-10	21-6	25-1	8-1	12-9	16-10	21-6	Note a
	Southern Pine	#1	8-0	12-6	16-6	21-1	25-7	8-0	12-6	16-2	19-2	22-10
	Southern Pine	#2	7-10	12-3	16-2	19-3	22-7	7-10	11-2	14-5	17-3	20-2
	Southern Pine	#3	6-7	9-8	12-4	14-7	17-4	5-10	8-8	11-0	13-0	15-6
	Spruce-Pine-Fir	SS	7-8	12-0	15-10	20-2	24-7	7-8	12-0	15-10	19-9	22-10
	Spruce-Pine-Fir	#1	7-6	11-9	15-1	18-5	21-5	7-3	10-8	13-6	16-6	19-2
	Spruce-Pine-Fi	#2	7-6	11-9	15-1	18-5	21-5	7-3	10-8	13-6	16-6	19-2
	Spruce-Pine-Fi	#3	6-2	9-0	11-5	13-11	16-2	5-6	8-1	10-3	12-6	14-6

(continued)

TABLE 2308.10.3(5)—continued
RAFTER SPANS FOR COMMON LUMBER SPECIES (Ground Snow Load = 30 pounds per square foot, Ceiling Attached to Rafters, L/Δ = 240)

RAFTER SPACING (inches)	SPECIES AND GRADE		DEAD LOAD = 10 pounds per square foot					DEAD LOAD = 20 pounds per square foot				
			2 × 4	2 × 6	2 × 8	2 × 10	2 × 12	2 × 4	2 × 6	2 × 8	2 × 10	2 × 12
			(ft. -in.)	(ft. -in.)	(ft. -in.)	(ft. -in.)	(ft. -in.)	(ft. -in.)	(ft. -in.)	(ft. -in.)	(ft. -in.)	(ft. -in.)
			Maximum rafter spans									
19.2	Douglas Fir-Larch	SS	7-9	12-3	16-1	20-7	25-0	7-9	12-3	15-10	19-5	22-6
	Douglas Fir-Larch	#1	7-6	11-8	14-9	18-0	20-11	7-1	10-5	13-2	16-1	18-8
	Douglas Fir-Larch	#2	7-4	10-11	13-9	16-10	19-6	6-8	9-9	12-4	15-1	17-6
	Douglas Fir-Larch	#3	5-7	8-3	10-5	12-9	14-9	5-0	7-4	9-4	11-5	13-2
	Hem-Fir	SS	7-4	11-7	15-3	19-5	23-7	7-4	11-7	15-3	19-1	22-1
	Hem-Fir	#1	7-2	11-4	14-4	17-7	20-4	6-11	10-2	12-10	15-8	18-2
	Hem-Fir	#2	6-10	10-9	13-7	16-7	19-3	6-7	9-7	12-2	14-10	17-3
	Hem-Fir	#3	5-7	8-3	10-5	12-9	14-9	5-0	7-4	9-4	11-5	13-2
	Southern Pine	SS	7-8	12-0	15-10	20-2	24-7	7-8	12-0	15-10	20-2	24-7
	Southern Pine	#1	7-6	11-9	15-6	19-7	23-4	7-6	11-9	14-9	17-6	20-11
	Southern Pine	#2	7-4	11-5	14-9	17-7	20-7	7-1	10-2	13-2	15-9	18-5
	Southern Pine	#3	6-0	8-10	11-3	13-4	15-10	5-4	7-11	10-1	11-11	14-2
	Spruce-Pine-Fir	SS	7-2	11-4	14-11	19-0	23-1	7-2	11-4	14-9	18-0	20-11
	Spruce-Pine-Fir	#1	7-0	10-11	13-9	16-10	19-6	6-8	9-9	12-4	15-1	17-6
	Spruce-Pine-Fir	#2	7-0	10-11	13-9	16-10	19-6	6-8	9-9	12-4	15-1	17-6
	Spruce-Pine-Fir	#3	5-7	8-3	10-5	12-9	14-9	5-0	7-4	9-4	11-5	13-2
24	Douglas Fir-Larch	SS	7-3	11-4	15-0	19-1	22-6	7-3	11-3	14-2	17-4	20-1
	Douglas Fir-Larch	#1	7-0	10-5	13-2	16-1	18-8	6-4	9-4	11-9	14-5	16-8
	Douglas Fir-Larch	#2	6-8	9-9	12-4	15-1	17-6	5-11	8-8	11-0	13-6	15-7
	Douglas Fir-Larch	#3	5-0	7-4	9-4	11-5	13-2	4-6	6-7	8-4	10-2	11-10
	Hem-Fir	SS	6-10	10-9	14-2	18-0	21-11	6-10	10-9	13-11	17-0	19-9
	Hem-Fir	#1	6-8	10-2	12-10	15-8	18-2	6-2	9-1	11-6	14-0	16-3
	Hem-Fir	#2	6-4	9-7	12-2	14-10	17-3	5-10	8-7	10-10	13-3	15-5
	Hem-Fir	#3	5-0	7-4	9-4	11-5	13-2	4-6	6-7	8-4	10-2	11-10
	Southern Pine	SS	7-1	11-2	14-8	18-9	22-10	7-1	11-2	14-8	18-9	22-10
	Southern Pine	#1	7-0	10-11	14-5	17-6	20-11	7-0	10-6	13-2	15-8	18-8
	Southern Pine	#2	6-10	10-2	13-2	15-9	18-5	6-4	9-2	11-9	14-1	16-6
	Southern Pine	#3	5-4	7-11	10-1	11-11	14-2	4-9	7-1	9-0	10-8	12-8
	Spruce-Pine-Fir	SS	6-8	10-6	13-10	17-8	20-11	6-8	10-5	13-2	16-1	18-8
	Spruce-Pine-Fir	#1	6-6	9-9	12-4	15-1	17-6	5-11	8-8	11-0	13-6	15-7
	Spruce-Pine-Fir	#2	6-6	9-9	12-4	15-1	17-6	5-11	8-8	11-0	13-6	15-7
	Spruce-Pine-Fir	#3	5-0	7-4	9-4	11-5	13-2	4-6	6-7	8-4	10-2	11-10

For SI: 1 inch = 25.4 mm, 1 foot = 304.8 mm, 1 pound per square foot = 47.9 N/m².

a. Span exceeds 26 feet in length. Check sources for availability of lumber in lengths greater than 20 feet.

TABLE 2308.10.3(6)
RAFTER SPANS FOR COMMON LUMBER SPECIES (Ground Snow Load = 50 pounds per square foot, Ceiling Attached to Rafters, $L/\Delta = 240$)

RAFTER SPACING (inches)	SPECIES AND GRADE		DEAD LOAD = 10 pounds per square foot					DEAD LOAD = 20 pounds per square foot				
			Maximum rafter spans									
			2 × 4	2 × 6	2 × 8	2 × 10	2 × 12	2 × 4	2 × 6	2 × 8	2 × 10	2 × 12
			(ft.-in.)	(ft.-in.)	(ft.-in.)	(ft.-in.)	(ft.-in.)	(ft.-in.)	(ft.-in.)	(ft.-in.)	(ft.-in.)	(ft.-in.)
12	Douglas Fir-Larch	SS	7-8	12-1	15-11	20-3	24-8	7-8	12-1	15-11	20-3	24-0
	Douglas Fir-Larch	#1	7-5	11-7	15-3	18-7	21-7	7-5	11-7	14-1	17-3	20-0
	Douglas Fir-Larch	#2	7-3	11-3	14-3	17-5	20-2	7-1	10-5	13-2	16-1	18-8
	Douglas Fir-Larch	#3	5-10	8-6	10-9	13-2	15-3	5-5	7-10	10-0	12-2	14-1
	Hem-Fir	SS	7-3	11-5	15-0	19-2	23-4	7-3	11-5	15-0	19-2	23-4
	Hem-Fir	#1	7-1	11-2	14-8	18-1	21-0	7-1	10-10	13-9	16-9	19-5
	Hem-Fir	#2	6-9	10-8	14-0	17-2	19-11	6-9	10-3	13-0	15-10	18-5
	Hem-Fir	#3	5-10	8-6	10-9	13-2	15-3	5-5	7-10	10-0	12-2	14-1
	Southern Pine	SS	7-6	11-0	15-7	19-11	24-3	7-6	11-10	15-7	19-11	24-3
	Southern Pine	#1	7-5	11-7	15-4	19-7	23-9	7-5	11-7	15-4	18-9	22-4
	Southern Pine	#2	7-3	11-5	15-0	18-2	21-3	7-3	10-11	14-1	16-10	19-9
	Southern Pine	#3	6-2	9-2	11-8	13-9	16-4	5-9	8-5	10-9	12-9	15-2
	Spruce-Pine-Fir	SS	7-1	11-2	14-8	18-9	22-10	7-1	11-2	14-8	18-9	22-4
	Spruce-Pine-Fir	#1	6-11	10-11	14-3	17-5	20-2	6-11	10-5	13-2	16-1	18-8
	Spruce-Pine-Fir	#2	6-11	10-11	14-3	17-5	20-2	6-11	10-5	13-2	16-1	18-8
	Spruce-Pine-Fir	#3	5-10	8-6	10-9	13-2	15-3	5-5	7-10	10-0	12-2	14-1
16	Douglas Fir-Larch	SS	7-0	11-0	14-5	18-5	22-5	7-0	11-0	14-5	17-11	20-10
	Douglas Fir-Larch	#1	6-9	10-5	13-2	16-1	18-8	6-7	9-8	12-2	14-11	17-3
	Douglas Fir-Larch	#2	6-7	9-9	12-4	15-1	17-6	6-2	9-0	11-5	13-11	16-2
	Douglas Fir-Larch	#3	5-0	7-4	9-4	11-5	13-2	4-8	6-10	8-8	10-6	12-3
	Hem-Fir	SS	6-7	10-4	13-8	17-5	21-2	6-7	10-4	13-8	17-5	20-5
	Hem-Fir	#1	6-5	10-2	12-10	15-8	18-2	6-5	9-5	11-11	14-6	16-10
	Hem-Fir	#2	6-2	9-7	12-2	14-10	17-3	6-1	8-11	11-3	13-9	15-11
	Hem-Fir	#3	5-0	7-4	9-4	11-5	13-2	4-8	6-10	8-8	10-6	12-3
	Southern Pine	SS	6-10	10-9	14-2	18-1	22-0	6-10	10-9	14-2	18-1	22-0
	Southern Pine	#1	6-9	10-7	13-11	17-6	20-11	6-9	10-7	13-8	16-2	19-4
	Southern Pine	#2	6-7	10-2	13-2	15-9	18-5	6-7	9-5	12-2	14-7	17-1
	Southern Pine	#3	5-4	7-11	10-1	11-11	14-2	4-11	7-4	9-4	11-0	13-1
	Spruce-Pine-Fir	SS	6-5	10-2	13-4	17-0	20-9	6-5	10-2	13-4	16-8	19-4
	Spruce-Pine-Fir	#1	6-4	9-9	12-4	15-1	17-6	6-2	9-0	11-5	13-11	16-2
	Spruce-Pine-Fir	#2	6-4	9-9	12-4	15-1	17-6	6-2	9-0	11-5	13-11	16-2
	Spruce-Pine-Fir	#3	5-0	7-4	9-4	11-5	13-2	4-8	6-10	8-8	10-6	12-3

(continued)

TABLE 2308.10.3(6)—continued
RAFTER SPANS FOR COMMON LUMBER SPECIES (Ground Snow Load = 50 pounds per square foot, Ceiling Attached to Rafters, $L/\Delta = 240$)

RAFTER SPACING (inches)	SPECIES AND GRADE		DEAD LOAD = 10 pounds per square foot					DEAD LOAD = 20 pounds per square foot				
			Maximum rafter spans									
			2 × 4	2 × 6	2 × 8	2 × 10	2 × 12	2 × 4	2 × 6	2 × 8	2 × 10	2 × 12
			(ft.-in.)	(ft.-in.)	(ft.-in.)	(ft.-in.)	(ft.-in.)	(ft.-in.)	(ft.-in.)	(ft.-in.)	(ft.-in.)	(ft.-in.)
19.2	Douglas Fir-Larch	SS	6-7	10-4	13-7	17-4	20-6	6-7	10-4	13-5	16-5	19-0
	Douglas Fir-Larch	#1	6-4	9-6	12-0	14-8	17-1	6-0	8-10	11-2	13-7	15-9
	Douglas Fir-Larch	#2	6-1	8-11	11-3	13-9	15-11	5-7	8-3	10-5	12-9	14-9
	Douglas Fir-Larch	#3	4-7	6-9	8-6	10-5	12-1	4-3	6-3	7-11	9-7	11-2
	Hem-Fir	SS	6-2	9-9	12-10	16-5	19-11	6-2	9-9	12-10	16-1	18-8
	Hem-Fir	#1	6-1	9-3	11-9	14-4	16-7	5-10	8-7	10-10	13-3	15-5
	Hem-Fir	#2	5-9	8-9	11-1	13-7	15-9	5-7	8-1	10-3	12-7	14-7
	Hem-Fir	#3	4-7	6-9	8-6	10-5	12-1	4-3	6-3	7-11	9-7	11-2
	Southern Pine	SS	6-5	10-2	13-4	17-0	20-9	6-5	10-2	13-4	17-0	20-9
	Southern Pine	#1	6-4	9-11	13-1	16-0	19-1	6-4	9-11	12-5	14-10	17-8
	Southern Pine	#2	6-2	9-4	12-0	14-4	16-10	6-0	8-8	11-2	13-4	15-7
	Southern Pine	#3	4-11	7-3	9-2	10-10	12-11	4-6	6-8	8-6	10-1	12-0
	Spruce-Pine-Fir	SS	6-1	9-6	12-7	16-0	19-1	6-1	9-6	12-5	15-3	17-8
	Spruce-Pine-Fir	#1	5-11	8-11	11-3	13-9	15-11	5-7	8-3	10-5	12-9	14-9
	Spruce-Pine-Fir	#2	5-11	8-11	11-3	13-9	15-11	5-7	8-3	10-5	12-9	14-9
	Spruce-Pine-Fir	#3	4-7	6-9	8-6	10-5	12-1	4-3	6-3	7-11	9-7	11-2
24	Douglas Fir-Larch	SS	6-1	9-7	12-7	15-10	18-4	6-1	9-6	12-0	14-8	17-0
	Douglas Fir-Larch	#1	5-10	8-6	10-9	13-2	15-3	5-5	7-10	10-0	12-2	14-1
	Douglas Fir-Larch	#2	5-5	7-11	10-1	12-4	14-3	5-0	7-4	9-4	11-5	13-2
	Douglas Fir-Larch	#3	4-1	6-0	7-7	9-4	10-9	3-10	5-7	7-1	8-7	10-0
	Hem-Fir	SS	5-9	9-1	11-11	15-2	18-0	5-9	9-1	11-9	14-5	16-8
	Hem-Fir	#1	5-8	8-3	10-6	12-10	14-10	5-3	7-8	9-9	11-10	13-9
	Hem-Fir	#2	5-4	7-10	9-11	12-1	14-1	4-11	7-3	9-2	11-3	13-0
	Hem-Fir	#3	4-1	6-0	7-7	9-4	10-9	3-10	5-7	7-1	8-7	10-0
	Southern Pine	SS	6-0	9-5	12-5	15-10	19-3	6-0	9-5	12-5	15-10	19-3
	Southern Pine	#1	5-10	9-3	12-0	14-4	17-1	5-10	8-10	11-2	13-3	15-9
	Southern Pine	#2	5-9	8-4	10-9	12-10	15-1	5-5	7-9	10-0	11-11	13-11
	Southern Pine	#3	4-4	6-5	8-3	9-9	11-7	4-1	6-0	7-7	9-0	10-8
	Spruce-Pine-Fir	SS	5-8	8-10	11-8	14-8	17-1	5-8	8-10	11-2	13-7	15-9
	Spruce-Pine-Fir	#1	5-5	7-11	10-1	12-4	14-3	5-0	7-4	9-4	11-5	13-2
	Spruce-Pine-Fir	#2	5-5	7-11	10-1	12-4	14-3	5-0	7-4	9-4	11-5	13-2
	Spruce-Pine-Fir	#3	4-1	6-0	7-7	9-4	10-9	3-10	5-7	7-1	8-7	10-0

For SI: 1 inch = 25.4 mm, 1 foot = 304.8 mm, 1 pound per square foot = 47.9 N/m².

TABLE 2308.10.4.1
RAFTER TIE CONNECTIONS[g]

RAFTER SLOPE	TIE SPACING (inches)	NO SNOW LOAD				GROUND SNOW LOAD (pound per square foot)							
						30 pounds per square foot				50 pounds per square foot			
						Roof span (feet)							
		12	20	28	36	12	20	28	36	12	20	28	36
		Required number of 16d common (3½" × 0.162") nails[a,b] per connection[c,d,e,f]											
3:12	12	4	6	8	10	4	6	8	11	5	8	12	15
	16	5	7	10	13	5	8	11	14	6	11	15	20
	24	7	11	15	19	7	11	16	21	9	16	23	30
	32	10	14	19	25	10	16	22	28	12	27	30	40
	48	14	21	29	37	14	32	36	42	18	32	46	60
4:12	12	3	4	5	6	3	5	6	8	4	6	9	11
	16	3	5	7	8	4	6	8	11	5	8	12	15
	24	4	7	10	12	5	9	12	16	7	12	17	22
	32	6	9	13	16	8	12	16	22	10	16	24	30
	48	8	14	19	24	10	18	24	32	14	24	34	44
5:12	12	3	3	4	5	3	4	5	7	3	5	7	9
	16	3	4	5	7	3	5	7	9	4	7	9	12
	24	4	6	8	10	4	7	10	13	6	10	14	18
	32	5	8	10	13	6	10	14	18	8	14	18	24
	48	7	11	15	20	8	14	20	26	12	20	28	36
7:12	12	3	3	3	4	3	3	4	5	3	4	5	7
	16	3	3	4	5	3	4	5	6	3	5	7	9
	24	3	4	6	7	3	5	7	9	4	7	10	13
	32	4	6	8	10	4	8	10	12	6	10	14	18
	48	5	8	11	14	6	10	14	18	9	14	20	26
9:12	12	3	3	3	3	3	3	3	4	3	3	4	5
	16	3	3	3	4	3	3	4	5	3	4	5	7
	24	3	3	5	6	3	4	6	7	3	6	8	10
	32	3	4	6	8	4	6	8	10	5	8	10	14
	48	4	6	9	11	5	8	12	14	7	12	16	20
12:12	12	3	3	3	3	3	3	3	3	3	3	3	4
	16	3	3	3	3	3	3	3	4	3	3	4	5
	24	3	3	3	4	3	3	4	6	3	4	6	8
	32	3	3	4	5	3	5	6	8	4	6	8	10
	48	3	4	6	7	4	7	8	12	6	8	12	16

For SI: 1 inch = 25.4 mm, 1 foot = 304.8 mm, 1 pound per square foot = 47.8 N/m².

a. 40d box (5" × 0.162") or l6d sinker (3¼" × 0.148") nails are permitted to be substituted for 16d common (3½" × 0.16") nails.

b. Nailing requirements are permitted to be reduced 25 percent if nails are clinched.

c. Rafter tie heel joint connections are not required where the ridge is supported by a load-bearing wall, header or ridge beam.

d. When intermediate support of the rafter is provided by vertical struts or purlins to a load-bearing wall, the tabulated heel joint connection requirements are permitted to be reduced proportionally to the reduction in span.

e. Equivalent nailing patterns are required for ceiling joist to ceiling joist lap splices.

f. Connected members shall be of sufficient size to prevent splitting due to nailing.

g. For snow loads less than 30 pounds per square foot, the required number of nails is permitted to be reduced by multiplying by the ratio of actual snow load plus 10 divided by 40, but not less than the number required for no snow load.

2308.10.4.3 Framing around openings. Trimmer and header rafters shall be doubled, or of lumber of equivalent cross section, where the span of the header exceeds 4 feet (1219 mm). The ends of header rafters more than 6 feet (1829 mm) long shall be supported by framing anchors or rafter hangers unless bearing on a beam, partition or wall.

2308.10.5 Purlins. Purlins to support roof loads are permitted to be installed to reduce the span of rafters within allowable limits and shall be supported by struts to bearing walls. The maximum span of 2-inch by 4-inch (51 mm by 102 mm) purlins shall be 4 feet (1219 mm). The maximum span of the 2-inch by 6-inch (51 mm by 152 mm) purlin shall be 6 feet (1829 mm), but in no case shall the purlin be smaller than the supported rafter. Struts shall not be smaller than 2-inch by 4-inch (51 mm by 102 mm) members. The unbraced length of struts shall not exceed 8 feet (2438 mm) and the minimum slope of the struts shall not be less than 45 degrees (0.79 rad) from the horizontal.

2308.10.6 Blocking. Roof rafters and ceiling joists shall be supported laterally to prevent rotation and lateral displacement in accordance with the provisions of Section 2308.8.5.

2308.10.7 Engineered wood products. Prefabricated wood I-joists, structural glued-laminated timber and structural composite lumber shall not be notched or drilled except where permitted by the manufacturer's recommendations or where the effects of such alterations are specifically considered in the design of the member by a registered design professional.

2308.10.8 Roof sheathing. Roof sheathing shall be in accordance with Tables 2304.7(3) and 2304.7(5) for wood structural panels, and Tables 2304.7(1) and 2304.7(2) for lumber and shall comply with Section 2304.7.2.

2308.10.8.1 Joints. Joints in lumber sheathing shall occur over supports unless approved end-matched lumber is used, in which case each piece shall bear on at least two supports.

2308.10.9 Roof planking. Planking shall be designed in accordance with the general provisions of this code.

In lieu of such design, 2-inch (51 mm) tongue-and-groove planking is permitted in accordance with Table 2308.10.9. Joints in such planking are permitted to be randomly spaced, provided the system is applied to not less than three continuous spans, planks are center matched and end matched or splined, each plank bears on at least one support, and joints are separated by at least 24 inches (610 mm) in adjacent pieces.

2308.10.10 Wood trusses. Wood trusses shall be designed in accordance with Section 2303.4.

2308.10.11 Attic ventilation. For attic ventilation, see Section 1203.2.

2308.11 Additional requirements for conventional construction in Seismic Design Category B or C. Structures of conventional light-frame construction in Seismic Design Category B or C, as determined in Section 1613, shall comply with Sections 2308.11.1 through 2308.11.3, in addition to the provisions of Sections 2308.1 through 2308.10.

2308.11.1 Number of stories. Structures of conventional light-frame construction shall not exceed two stories in height in Seismic Design Category C.

2308.11.2 Concrete or masonry. Concrete or masonry walls or masonry veneer shall not extend above the basement.

Exceptions:

1. Masonry veneer is permitted to be used in the first two stories above grade plane or the first three stories above grade plane where the lowest story has concrete or masonry walls in Seismic Design Category B, provided that structural use panel wall bracing is used and the length of bracing provided is one- and one-half times the required length as determined in Table 2308.9.3(1).

2. Masonry veneer is permitted to be used in the first story above grade plane or the first two stories above grade plane where the lowest story has concrete or masonry walls in Seismic Design Category B or C.

3. Masonry veneer is permitted to be used in the first two stories above grade plane in Seismic Design Categories B and C, provided the following criteria are met:

    3.1. Type of brace per Section 2308.9.3 shall be Method 3 and the allowable shear capacity in accordance with Table 2306.4.1 shall be a minimum of 350 plf (5108 N/m).

    3.2. The bracing of the top story shall be located at each end and at least every 25 feet (7620 mm) o.c. but not less than 40 percent of the braced wall line. The bracing of the first story shall be located at each end and at least every 25 feet (7620 mm) o.c. but not less than 35 percent of the braced wall line.

    3.3. Hold-down connectors shall be provided at the ends of braced walls for the second floor to first floor wall assembly with an allowable design of 2,000 pounds (8896 N). Hold-down connectors shall be provided at the ends of each wall segment of the braced walls for the first floor to foundation with an allowable design of 3,900 pounds (17 347 N). In all cases, the hold-down connector force shall be transferred to the foundation.

    3.4. Cripple walls shall not be permitted.

2308.11.3 Framing and connection details. Framing and connection details shall conform to Sections 2308.11.3.1 through 2308.11.3.3.

TABLE 2308.10.9
ALLOWABLE SPANS FOR 2-INCH TONGUE-AND-GROOVE DECKING

SPAN[a] (feet)	LIVE LOAD (pound per square foot)	DEFLECTION LIMIT	BENDING STRESS (f) (pound per square inch)	MODULUS OF ELASTICITY (E) (pound per square inch)
		Roofs		
4	20	1/240 1/360	160	170,000 256,000
	30	1/240 1/360	210	256,000 384,000
	40	1/240 1/360	270	340,000 512,000
4.5	20	1/240 1/360	200	242,000 305,000
	30	1/240 1/360	270	363,000 405,000
	40	1/240 1/360	350	484,000 725,000
5.0	20	1/240 1/360	250	332,000 500,000
	30	1/240 1/360	330	495,000 742,000
	40	1/240 1/360	420	660,000 1,000,000
5.5	20	1/240 1/360	300	442,000 660,000
	30	1/240 1/360	400	662,000 998,000
	40	1/240 1/360	500	884,000 1,330,000
6.0	20	1/240 1/360	360	575,000 862,000
	30	1/240 1/360	480	862,000 1,295,000
	40	1/240 1/360	600	1,150,000 1,730,000
6.5	20	1/240 1/360	420	595,000 892,000
	30	1/240 1/360	560	892,000 1,340,000
	40	1/240 1/360	700	1,190,000 1,730,000
7.0	20	1/240 1/360	490	910,000 1,360,000
	30	1/240 1/360	650	1,370,000 2,000,000
	40	1/240 1/360	810	1,820,000 2,725,000

(continued)

2308.11.3.1 Anchorage. Braced wall lines shall be anchored in accordance with Section 2308.6 at foundations.

2308.11.3.2 Stepped footings. Where the height of a required braced wall panel extending from foundation to floor above varies more than 4 feet (1219 mm), the following construction shall be used:

1. Where the bottom of the footing is stepped and the lowest floor framing rests directly on a sill bolted to the footings, the sill shall be anchored as required in Section 2308.3.3.

2. Where the lowest floor framing rests directly on a sill bolted to a footing not less than 8 feet (2438 mm) in length along a line of bracing, the line shall be considered to be braced. The double plate of the cripple stud wall beyond the segment of footing extending to the lowest framed floor shall be spliced to the sill plate with metal ties, one on each side of the sill and plate. The metal ties shall not be less than 0.058 inch [1.47 mm (16 galvanized gage)] by 1.5 inches (38 mm) wide by 48 inches (1219 mm) with eight 16d common nails on each side of the splice location (see Figure 2308.11.3.2). The metal tie shall have

TABLE 2308.10.9—continued
ALLOWABLE SPANS FOR 2-INCH TONGUE-AND-GROOVE DECKING

SPAN[a]	LIVE LOAD		BENDING STRESS (f)	MODULUS OF ELASTICITY (E)
(feet)	(pound per square foot)	DEFLECTION LIMIT	(pound per square inch)	(pound per square inch)
Roofs				
7.5	20	1/240 1/360	560	1,125,000 1,685,000
	30	1/240 1/360	750	1,685,000 2,530,000
	40	1/240 1/360	930	2,250,000 3,380,000
8.0	20	1/240 1/360	640	1,360,000 2,040,000
	30	1/240 1/360	850	2,040,000 3,060,000
Floors				
4 4.5 5.0	40	1/360	840 950 1,060	1,000,000 1,300,000 1,600,000

For SI: 1 inch = 25.4 mm, 1 foot = 304.8 mm, 1 pound per square foot = 0.0479 kN/m², 1 pound per square inch = 0.00689 N/mm².

a. Spans are based on simple beam action with 10 pounds per square foot dead load and provisions for a 300-pound concentrated load on a 12-inch width of decking. Random layup is permitted in accordance with the provisions of Section 2308.10.9. Lumber thickness is $1^1/_2$ inches nominal.

For SI: 1 inch = 25.4 mm, 1 foot = 304.8 mm.

FIGURE 2308.11.3.2
STEPPED FOOTING CONNECTION DETAILS

a minimum yield of 33,000 pounds per square inch (psi) (227 MPa).

3. Where cripple walls occur between the top of the footing and the lowest floor framing, the bracing requirements for a story shall apply.

2308.11.3.3 Openings in horizontal diaphragms. Openings in horizontal diaphragms with a dimension perpendicular to the joist that is greater than 4 feet (1.2 m) shall be constructed in accordance with the following:

1. Blocking shall be provided beyond headers.

2. Metal ties not less than 0.058 inch [1.47 mm (16 galvanized gage)] by 1.5 inches (38 mm) wide with eight 16d common nails on each side of the header-joist intersection shall be provided (see Figure 2308.11.3.3). The metal ties shall have a minimum yield of 33,000 psi (227 MPa).

2308.12 Additional requirements for conventional construction in Seismic Design Category D or E. Structures of conventional light-frame construction in Seismic Design Category D or E, as determined in Section 1613, shall conform to Sections 2308.12.1 through 2308.12.9, in addition to the requirements for Seismic Design Category B or C in Section 2308.11.

2308.12.1 Number of stories. Structures of conventional light-frame construction shall not exceed one story in height in Seismic Design Category D or E.

2308.12.2 Concrete or masonry. Concrete or masonry walls or masonry veneer shall not extend above the basement.

Exception: Masonry veneer is permitted to be used in the first story above grade plane in Seismic Design Category D, provided the following criteria are met:

1. Type of brace in accordance with Section 2308.9.3 shall be Method 3 and the allowable shear capacity in accordance with Table 2306.4.1 shall be a minimum of 350 plf (5108 N/m).

2. The bracing of the first story shall be located at each end and at least every 25 feet (7620 mm) o.c. but not less than 45 percent of the braced wall line.

3. Hold-down connectors shall be provided at the ends of braced walls for the first floor to foundation with an allowable design of 2,100 pounds (9341 N).

4. Cripple walls shall not be permitted.

2308.12.3 Braced wall line spacing. Spacing between interior and exterior braced wall lines shall not exceed 25 feet (7620 mm).

2308.12.4 Braced wall line sheathing. Braced wall lines shall be braced by one of the types of sheathing prescribed by Table 2308.12.4 as shown in Figure 2308.9.3. The sum of lengths of braced wall panels at each braced wall line shall conform to Table 2308.12.4. Braced wall panels shall be distributed along the length of the braced wall line and start at not more than 8 feet (2438 mm) from each end of the braced wall line. Panel sheathing joints shall occur over studs or blocking. Sheathing shall be fastened to studs, top and bottom plates and at panel edges occurring over blocking. Wall framing to which sheathing used for bracing is applied shall be nominal 2 inch wide [actual $1^1/_2$ inch (38 mm)] or larger members.

Cripple walls having a stud height exceeding 14 inches (356 mm) shall be considered a story for the purpose of this section and shall be braced as required for braced wall lines in accordance with Table 2308.12.4. Where interior braced wall lines occur without a continuous foundation below, the length of parallel exterior cripple wall bracing

PLYWOOD SHEATHING

DIAPHRAGM OPENING

8 NAILS
4 NAILS
4 NAILS

METAL TIE 16GA. x 1 1/2" x 4'-0" MIN., (4 TOTAL) W/ 16-16d COMMON NAILS AS SHOWN

-OR-

METAL TIE 16GA. x 1 1/2" x (OPENING WIDTH + 4'-0") MIN., (2 TOTAL) W/ 24-16d COMMON NAILS

For SI: 1 inch = 25.4 mm, 1 foot = 304.8 mm.

FIGURE 2308.11.3.3
OPENINGS IN HORIZONTAL DIAPHRAGMS

shall be one and one-half times the lengths required by Table 2308.12.4. Where the cripple wall sheathing type used is Type S-W and this additional length of bracing cannot be provided, the capacity of Type S-W sheathing shall be increased by reducing the spacing of fasteners along the perimeter of each piece of sheathing to 4 inches (102 mm) o.c.

TABLE 2308.12.4
WALL BRACING IN SEISMIC DESIGN CATEGORIES D AND E
(Minimum Length of Wall Bracing per each 25 Linear Feet of Braced Wall Line[a])

CONDITION	SHEATHING TYPE[b]	$S_{DS} < 0.50$	$0.50 \leq S_{DS} < 0.75$	$0.75 \leq S_{DS} \leq 1.00$	$S_{DS} > 1.00$
One story	G-P[c]	10 feet 8 inches	14 feet 8 inches	18 feet 8 inches	25 feet 0 inches
	S-W	5 feet 4 inches	8 feet 0 inches	9 feet 4 inches	12 feet 0 inches

For SI: 1 inch = 25.4 mm, 1 foot = 304.8 mm.

a. Minimum length of panel bracing of one face of the wall for S-W sheathing or both faces of the wall for G-P sheathing; h/w ratio shall not exceed 2:1. For S-W panel bracing of the same material on two faces of the wall, the minimum length is permitted to be one-half the tabulated value but the h/w ratio shall not exceed 2:1 and design for uplift is required.

b. G-P = gypsum board, fiberboard, particleboard, lath and plaster or gypsum sheathing boards; S-W = wood structural panels and diagonal wood sheathing.

c. Nailing as specified below shall occur at all panel edges at studs, at top and bottom plates and, where occurring, at blocking: For $^1/_2$-inch gypsum board, 5d (0.113 inch diameter) cooler nails at 7 inches on center; For $^5/_8$-inch gypsum board, No. 11 gage (0.120 inch diameter) at 7 inches on center; For gypsum sheathing board, $1^3/_4$ inches long by $^7/_{16}$-inch head, diamond point galvanized nails at 4 inches on center; For gypsum lath, No. 13 gage (0.092 inch) by $1^1/_8$ inches long, $^{19}/_{64}$-inch head, plasterboard at 5 inches on center; For Portland cement plaster, No. 11 gage (0.120 inch) by $1^1/_2$ inches long, $^7/_{16}$- inch head at 6 inches on center; For fiberboard and particleboard, No. 11 gage (0.120 inch) by $1^1/_2$ inches long, $^7/_{16}$-inch head, galvanized nails at 3 inches on center.

2308.12.5 Attachment of sheathing. Fastening of braced wall panel sheathing shall not be less than that prescribed in Table 2308.12.4 or 2304.9.1. Wall sheathing shall not be attached to framing members by adhesives.

2308.12.6 Irregular structures. Conventional light-frame construction shall not be used in irregular portions of structures in Seismic Design Category D or E. Such irregular portions of structures shall be designed to resist the forces specified in Chapter 16 to the extent such irregular features affect the performance of the conventional framing system. A portion of a structure shall be considered to be irregular where one or more of the conditions described in Items 1 through 6 below are present.

1. Where exterior braced wall panels are not in one plane vertically from the foundation to the uppermost story in which they are required, the structure shall be considered to be irregular [see Figure 2308.12.6(1)].

   Exception: Floors with cantilevers or setbacks not exceeding four times the nominal depth of the floor

joists [see Figure 2308.12.6(2)] are permitted to support braced wall panels provided:

1. Floor joists are 2 inches by 10 inches (51 mm by 254 mm) or larger and spaced not more than 16 inches (406 mm) o.c.

2. The ratio of the back span to the cantilever is at least 2:1.

3. Floor joists at ends of braced wall panels are doubled.

4. A continuous rim joist is connected to the ends of cantilevered joists. The rim joist is permitted to be spliced using a metal tie not less than 0.058 inch (1.47 mm) (16 galvanized gage) and $1^1/_2$ inches (38 mm) wide fastened with six 16d common nails on each side. The metal tie shall have a minimum yield of 33,000 psi (227 MPa).

5. Joists at setbacks or the end of cantilevered joists shall not carry gravity loads from more than a single story having uniform wall and roof loads, nor carry the reactions from headers having a span of 8 feet (2438 mm) or more.

2. Where a section of floor or roof is not laterally supported by braced wall lines on all edges, the structure shall be considered to be irregular [see Figure 2308.12.6(3)].

   Exception: Portions of roofs or floors that do not support braced wall panels above are permitted to extend up to 6 feet (1829 mm) beyond a braced wall line [see Figure 2308.12.6(4)].

3. Where the end of a required braced wall panel extends more than 1 foot (305 mm) over an opening in the wall below, the structure shall be considered to be irregular. This requirement is applicable to braced wall panels offset in plane and to braced wall panels offset out of plane as permitted by the exception to Item 1 above in this section [see Figure 2308.12.6(5)].

   Exception: Braced wall panels are permitted to extend over an opening not more than 8 feet (2438 mm) in width where the header is a 4-inch by 12-inch (102 mm by 305 mm) or larger member.

4. Where portions of a floor level are vertically offset such that the framing members on either side of the offset cannot be lapped or tied together in an approved manner, the structure shall be considered to be irregular [see Figure 2308.12.6(6)].

   Exception: Framing supported directly by foundations need not be lapped or tied directly together.

5. Where braced wall lines are not perpendicular to each other, the structure shall be considered to be irregular [see Figure 2308.12.6(7)].

6. Where openings in floor and roof diaphragms having a maximum dimension greater than 50 percent of the distance between lines of bracing or an area greater than 25 percent of the area between orthogonal pairs of braced wall lines are present, the structure shall be considered to be irregular [see Figure 2308.12.6(8)].

2308.12.7 Anchorage of exterior means of egress components. Exterior egress balconies, exterior exit stairways and similar means of egress components shall be positively anchored to the primary structure at not over 8 feet (2438 mm) o.c. or shall be designed for lateral forces. Such attachment shall not be accomplished by use of toenails or nails subject to withdrawal.

2308.12.8 Steel plate washers. Steel plate washers shall be placed between the foundation sill plate and the nut. Such washers shall be a minimum of 0.229 inch by 3 inches by 3 inches (5.82 mm by 76 mm by 76 mm) in size. The hole in the plate washer is permitted to be diagonally slotted with a width of up to $^3/_{16}$ inch (4.76 mm) larger than the bolt diameter and a slot length not to exceed $1^3/_4$ inches (44 mm), provided a standard cut washer is placed between the plate washer and the nut.

2308.12.9 Anchorage in Seismic Design Category E. Steel bolts with a minimum nominal diameter of $^5/_8$ inch (15.9 mm) shall be used in Seismic Design Category E.

SECTION VIEW   SECTION VIEW

OUT OF PLANE OFFSET IN EXTERIOR BRACED WALL PANELS

FIGURE 2308.12.6(1)
BRACED WALL PANELS OUT OF PLANE

CANTILEVER/SET BACK SHALL ONLY SUPPORT ROOF AND WALL WEIGHT

SECTION THRU CANTILEVER   SECTION THRU SET BACK

4'-0" w/ 2 x 12

For SI: 1 foot = 304.8 mm.

FIGURE 2308.12.6(2)
BRACED WALL PANELS SUPPORTED BY CANTILEVER OR SET BACK

DASHED LINE INDICATES BRACED WALL LINE BELOW

THERE IS NO BRACED WALL LINE ON THIS EDGE OF THE ROOF

PLAN VIEW

FIGURE 2308.12.6(3)
FLOOR OR ROOF NOT SUPPORTED ON ALL EDGES

PLAN VIEW

ROOF OR FLOOR SHALL BE PERMITTED
TO EXTEND UP TO SIX FEET BEYOND
THE BRACED WALL LINE

NO BRACED WALL PANEL ABOVE
PERMITTED AT THIS LOCATION

For SI: 1 foot = 304.8 mm.

FIGURE 2308.12.6(4)
ROOF OR FLOOR EXTENSION BEYOND BRACED WALL LINE

REQUIRED BRACED
WALL PANEL

MORE THAN 1'-0"

EXTERIOR ELEVATION

EXTERIOR ISOMETRIC

For SI: 1 foot = 304.8 mm.

FIGURE 2308.12.6(5)
BRACED WALL PANEL EXTENSION OVER OPENING

FLOOR JOISTS
CANNOT BE
TIED DIRECTLY
TOGETHER

SECTION VIEW

SECTION VIEW

FIGURE 2308.12.6(6)
PORTIONS OF FLOOR LEVEL OFFSET VERTICALLY

PLAN VIEW

**FIGURE 2308.12.6(7)
BRACED WALL LINES NOT PERPENDICULAR**

**FIGURE 2308.12.6(8)
OPENING LIMITATIONS FOR FLOOR AND ROOF DIAPHRAGMS**

CHAPTER 24

GLASS AND GLAZING

SECTION 2401
GENERAL

2401.1 Scope. The provisions of this chapter shall govern the materials, design, construction and quality of glass, light-transmitting ceramic and light-transmitting plastic panels for exterior and interior use in both vertical and sloped applications in buildings and structures.

2401.2 Glazing replacement. The installation of replacement glass shall be as required for new installations.

SECTION 2402
DEFINITIONS

2402.1 Definitions. The following words and terms shall, for the purposes of this chapter and as used elsewhere in this code, have the meanings shown herein.

DALLE GLASS. A decorative composite glazing material made of individual pieces of glass that are embedded in a cast matrix of concrete or epoxy.

DECORATIVE GLASS. A carved, leaded or Dalle glass or glazing material whose purpose is decorative or artistic, not functional; whose coloring, texture or other design qualities or components cannot be removed without destroying the glazing material and whose surface, or assembly into which it is incorporated, is divided into segments.

SECTION 2403
GENERAL REQUIREMENTS FOR GLASS

2403.1 Identification. Each pane shall bear the manufacturer's mark designating the type and thickness of the glass or glazing material. The identification shall not be omitted unless approved and an affidavit is furnished by the glazing contractor certifying that each light is glazed in accordance with approved construction documents that comply with the provisions of this chapter. Safety glazing shall be identified in accordance with Section 2406.2.

Each pane of tempered glass, except tempered spandrel glass, shall be permanently identified by the manufacturer. The identification mark shall be acid etched, sand blasted, ceramic fired, laser etched, embossed or of a type that, once applied, cannot be removed without being destroyed.

Tempered spandrel glass shall be provided with a removable paper marking by the manufacturer.

2403.2 Glass supports. Where one or more sides of any pane of glass are not firmly supported, or are subjected to unusual load conditions, detailed construction documents, detailed shop drawings and analysis or test data assuring safe performance for the specific installation shall be prepared by a registered design professional.

2403.3 Framing. To be considered firmly supported, the framing members for each individual pane of glass shall be designed so the deflection of the edge of the glass perpendicular to the glass pane shall not exceed $^1/_{175}$ of the glass edge length or $^3/_4$ inch (19.1 mm), whichever is less, when subjected to the larger of the positive or negative load where loads are combined as specified in Section 1605.

2403.4 Interior glazed areas. Where interior glazing is installed adjacent to a walking surface, the differential deflection of two adjacent unsupported edges shall not be greater than the thickness of the panels when a force of 50 pounds per linear foot (plf) (730 N/m) is applied horizontally to one panel at any point up to 42 inches (1067 mm) above the walking surface.

2403.5 Louvered windows or jalousies. Float, wired and patterned glass in louvered windows and jalousies shall be no thinner than nominal $^3/_{16}$ inch (4.8 mm) and no longer than 48 inches (1219 mm). Exposed glass edges shall be smooth.

Wired glass with wire exposed on longitudinal edges shall not be used in louvered windows or jalousies.

Where other glass types are used, the design shall be submitted to the code enforcement official for approval.

SECTION 2404
WIND, SNOW, SEISMIC AND DEAD LOADS ON GLASS

2404.1 Vertical glass. Glass sloped 15 degrees (0.26 rad) or less from vertical in windows, curtain and window walls, doors and other exterior applications shall be designed to resist the wind loads in Section 1609 for components and cladding. Glass in glazed curtain walls, glazed storefronts and glazed partitions shall meet the seismic requirements of ASCE 7, Section 13.5.9. The load resistance of glass under uniform load shall be determined in accordance with ASTM E 1300.

The design of vertical glazing shall be based on the following equation:

$$F_{gw} \leq F_{ga} \qquad \textbf{(Equation 24-1)}$$

where:

$F_{gw}=$ Wind load on the glass computed in accordance with Section 1609.

$F_{ga}=$ Short duration load on the glass as determined in accordance with ASTM E 1300.

2404.2 Sloped glass. Glass sloped more than 15 degrees (0.26 rad) from vertical in skylights, sunrooms, sloped roofs and other exterior applications shall be designed to resist the most critical of the following combinations of loads.

$$F_g = W_o - D \qquad \textbf{(Equation 24-2)}$$
$$F_g = W_i + D + 0.5\,S \qquad \textbf{(Equation 24-3)}$$
$$F_g = 0.5\,W_i + D + S \qquad \textbf{(Equation 24-4)}$$

where:

D = Glass dead load psf (kN/m²).

For glass sloped 30 degrees (0.52 rad) or less from horizontal,

= 13 t_g (For SI: 0.0245 t_g).

For glass sloped more than 30 degrees (0.52 rad) from horizontal,

= 13 t_g cos θ (For SI: 0.0245 t_g cos θ).

F_g = Total load, psf (kN/m²) on glass.

S = Snow load, psf (kN/m²) as determined in Section 1608.

t_g = Total glass thickness, inches (mm) of glass panes and plies.

W_i = Inward wind force, psf (kN/m²) as calculated in Section 1609.

W_o = Outward wind force, psf (kN/m²) as calculated in Section 1609.

θ = Angle of slope from horizontal.

Exception: Unit skylights shall be designed in accordance with Section 2405.5.

The design of sloped glazing shall be based on the following equation:

$$F_g \leq F_{ga} \qquad \textbf{(Equation 24-5)}$$

where:

F_g = Total load on the glass determined from the load combinations above.

F_{ga} = Short duration load resistance of the glass as determined according to ASTM E 1300 for Equations 24-2 and 24-3; or the long duration load resistance of the glass as determined according to ASTM E 1300 for Equation 24-4.

2404.3 Wired, patterned and sandblasted glass.

2404.3.1 Vertical wired glass. Wired glass sloped 15 degrees (0.26 rad) or less from vertical in windows, curtain and window walls, doors and other exterior applications shall be designed to resist the wind loads in Section 1609 for components and cladding according to the following equation:

$$F_{gw} < 0.5\,F_{ge} \qquad \textbf{(Equation 24-6)}$$

where:

F_{gw} = Is the wind load on the glass computed per Section 1609.

F_{ge} = Nonfactored load from ASTM E 1300 using a thickness designation for monolithic glass that is not greater than the thickness of wired glass.

2404.3.2 Sloped wired glass. Wired glass sloped more than 15 degrees (0.26 rad) from vertical in skylights, sunspaces, sloped roofs and other exterior applications shall be designed to resist the most critical of the combinations of loads from Section 2404.2.

For Equations 24-2 and 24-3:

$$F_g < 0.5\,F_{ge} \qquad \textbf{(Equation 24-7)}$$

For Equation 24-4:

$$F_g < 0.3\,F_{ge} \qquad \textbf{(Equation 24-8)}$$

where:

F_g = Total load on the glass.

F_{ge} = Nonfactored load from ASTM E 1300.

2404.3.3 Vertical patterned glass. Patterned glass sloped 15 degrees (0.26 rad) or less from vertical in windows, curtain and window walls, doors and other exterior applications shall be designed to resist the wind loads in Section 1609 for components and cladding according to the following equation:

$$F_{gw} < 1.0\,F_{ge} \qquad \textbf{(Equation 24-9)}$$

where:

F_{gw} = Wind load on the glass computed per Section 1609.

F_{ge} = Nonfactored load from ASTM E 1300. The value for patterned glass shall be based on the thinnest part of the glass. Interpolation between nonfactored load charts in ASTM E 1300 shall be permitted.

2404.3.4 Sloped patterned glass. Patterned glass sloped more than 15 degrees (0.26 rad) from vertical in skylights, sunspaces, sloped roofs and other exterior applications shall be designed to resist the most critical of the combinations of loads from Section 2404.2.

For Equations 24-2 and 24-3:

$$F_g < 1.0\,F_{ge} \qquad \textbf{(Equation 24-10)}$$

For Equation 24-4:

$$F_g < 0.6\,F_{ge} \qquad \textbf{(Equation 24-11)}$$

where

F_g = Total load on the glass.

F_{ge} = Nonfactored load from ASTM E 1300. The value for patterned glass shall be based on the thinnest part of the glass. Interpolation between the nonfactored load charts in ASTM E 1300 shall be permitted.

2404.3.5 Vertical sandblasted glass. Sandblasted glass sloped 15 degrees (0.26 rad) or less from vertical in windows, curtain and window walls, doors, and other exterior applications shall be designed to resist the wind loads in Section 1609 for components and cladding according to the following equation:

$$F_g < 0.5\,F_{ge} \qquad \textbf{(Equation 24-12)}$$

where:

F_g = Total load on the glass.

F_{ge} = Nonfactored load from ASTM E 1300. The value for sandblasted glass is for moderate levels of sandblasting.

2404.4 Other designs. For designs outside the scope of this section, an analysis or test data for the specific installation shall be prepared by a registered design professional.

SECTION 2405
SLOPED GLAZING AND SKYLIGHTS

2405.1 Scope. This section applies to the installation of glass and other transparent, translucent or opaque glazing material installed at a slope more than 15 degrees (0.26 rad) from the vertical plane, including glazing materials in skylights, roofs and sloped walls.

2405.2 Allowable glazing materials and limitations. Sloped glazing shall be any of the following materials, subject to the listed limitations.

1. For monolithic glazing systems, the glazing material of the single light or layer shall be laminated glass with a minimum 30-mil (0.76 mm) polyvinyl butyral (or equivalent) interlayer, wired glass, light-transmitting plastic materials meeting the requirements of Section 2607, heat-strengthened glass or fully tempered glass.

2. For multiple-layer glazing systems, each light or layer shall consist of any of the glazing materials specified in Item 1 above.

Annealed glass is permitted to be used as specified within Exceptions 2 and 3 of Section 2405.3.

For additional requirements for plastic skylights, see Section 2610. Glass-block construction shall conform to the requirements of Section 2101.2.5.

2405.3 Screening. Where used in monolithic glazing systems, heat-strengthened glass and fully tempered glass shall have screens installed below the glazing material. The screens and their fastenings shall: (1) be capable of supporting twice the weight of the glazing; (2) be firmly and substantially fastened to the framing members and (3) be installed within 4 inches (102 mm) of the glass. The screens shall be constructed of a noncombustible material not thinner than No. 12 B&S gage (0.0808 inch) with mesh not larger than 1 inch by 1 inch (25 mm by 25 mm). In a corrosive atmosphere, structurally equivalent noncorrosive screen materials shall be used. Heat-strengthened glass, fully tempered glass and wired glass, when used in multiple-layer glazing systems as the bottom glass layer over the walking surface, shall be equipped with screening that conforms to the requirements for monolithic glazing systems.

Exception: In monolithic and multiple-layer sloped glazing systems, the following applies:

1. Fully tempered glass installed without protective screens where glazed between intervening floors at a slope of 30 degrees (0.52 rad) or less from the vertical plane shall have the highest point of the glass 10 feet (3048 mm) or less above the walking surface.

2. Screens are not required below any glazing material, including annealed glass, where the walking surface below the glazing material is permanently protected from the risk of falling glass or the area below the glazing material is not a walking surface.

3. Any glazing material, including annealed glass, is permitted to be installed without screens in the sloped glazing systems of commercial or detached noncombustible greenhouses used exclusively for growing plants and not open to the public, provided that the height of the greenhouse at the ridge does not exceed 30 feet (9144 mm) above grade.

4. Screens shall not be required within individual dwelling units in Groups R-2, R-3 and R-4 where fully tempered glass is used as single glazing or as both panes in an insulating glass unit, and the following conditions are met:

   4.1. Each pane of the glass is 16 square feet (1.5 m²) or less in area.

   4.2. The highest point of the glass is 12 feet (3658 mm) or less above any walking surface or other accessible area.

   4.3. The glass thickness is $^3/_{16}$ inch (4.8 mm) or less.

5. Screens shall not be required for laminated glass with a 15-mil (0.38 mm) polyvinyl butyral (or equivalent) interlayer used within individual dwelling units in Groups R-2, R-3 and R-4 within the following limits:

   5.1. Each pane of glass is 16 square feet (1.5 m²) or less in area.

   5.2. The highest point of the glass is 12 feet (3658 mm) or less above a walking surface or other accessible area.

2405.4 Framing. In Type I and II construction, sloped glazing and skylight frames shall be constructed of noncombustible materials. In structures where acid fumes deleterious to metal are incidental to the use of the buildings, approved pressure-treated wood or other approved noncorrosive materials are permitted to be used for sash and frames. Framing supporting sloped glazing and skylights shall be designed to resist the tributary roof loads in Chapter 16. Skylights set at an angle of less than 45 degrees (0.79 rad) from the horizontal plane shall be mounted at least 4 inches (102 mm) above the plane of the roof on a curb constructed as required for the frame. Skylights shall not be installed in the plane of the roof where the roof pitch is less than 45 degrees (0.79 rad) from the horizontal.

Exception: Installation of a skylight without a curb shall be permitted on roofs with a minimum slope of 14 degrees (three units vertical in 12 units horizontal) in Group R-3 occupancies. All unit skylights installed in a roof with a pitch flatter than 14 degrees (0.25 rad) shall be mounted at least 4 inches (102 mm) above the plane of the roof on a curb constructed as required for the frame unless otherwise specified in the manufacturer's installation instructions.

2405.5 Unit skylights. Unit skylights shall be tested and labeled as complying with AAMA/WDMA/CSA 101/I.S.2/A440. The label shall state the name of the manufacturer, the approved labeling agency, the product designation and the performance grade rating as specified in AAMA/WDMA/CSA 101/I.S.2/A440. If the product manufacturer has chosen to have the performance grade of the skylight rated separately for positive and negative design pressure, then the label shall state both performance grade ratings as specified in AAMA/WDMA/CSA 101/I.S.2/A440 and the skylight shall comply with Section 2405.5.2. If the skylight is not rated separately for positive and negative pressure, then the performance grade rating shown on the label shall be the performance grade rating determined in accordance with AAMA/WDMA/CSA 101/I.S.2/A440 for both positive and negative design pressure and the skylight shall conform to Section 2405.5.1.

2405.5.1 Unit skylights rated for the same performance grade for both positive and negative design pressure. The design of unit skylights shall be based on the following equation:

$$F_g \leq PG \qquad \text{(Equation 24-13)}$$

where:

F_g = Maximum load on the skylight determined from Equations 24-2 through 24-4 in Section 2404.2.

PG = Performance grade rating of the skylight.

2405.5.2 Unit skylights rated for separate performance grades for positive and negative design pressure. The design of unit skylights rated for performance grade for both positive and negative design pressures shall be based on the following equations:

$$F_{gi} \leq PG_{Pos} \qquad \text{(Equation 24-14)}$$
$$F_{go} \leq PG_{Neg} \qquad \text{(Equation 24-15)}$$

where:

PG_{Pos}=Performance grade rating of the skylight under positive design pressure;

PG_{Neg}=Performance grade rating of the skylight under negative design pressure; and

F_{gi} and F_{go} are determined in accordance with the following:

For $W_o \geq D$,

where:

W_o = Outward wind force, psf (kN/m²) as calculated in Section 1609.

D = The dead weight of the glazing, psf (kN/m²) as determined in Section 2404.2 for glass, or by the weight of the plastic, psf (kN/m²) for plastic glazing.

F_{gi} = Maximum load on the skylight determined from Equations 24-3 and 24-4 in Section 2404.2.

F_{go} = Maximum load on the skylight determined from Equation 24-2.

For $W_o < D$,

where:

W_o = Is the outward wind force, psf (kN/m²) as calculated in Section 1609.

D = The dead weight of the glazing, psf (kN/m²) as determined in Section 2404.2 for glass, or by the weight of the plastic for plastic glazing.

F_{gi} = Maximum load on the skylight determined from Equations 24-2 through 24-4 in Section 2404.2.

F_{go} = 0.

SECTION 2406
SAFETY GLAZING

2406.1 Human impact loads. Individual glazed areas, including glass mirrors, in hazardous locations as defined in Section 2406.3 shall comply with Sections 2406.1.1 through 2406.1.4.

2406.1.1 CPSC 16 CFR 1201. Except as provided in Sections 2406.1.2 through 2406.1.4, all glazing shall pass the test requirements of CPSC 16 CFR 1201, listed in Chapter 35. Glazing shall comply with the CPSC 16 CFR, Part 1201 criteria, for Category I or II as indicated in Table 2406.1.

2406.1.2 Plastic glazing. Plastic glazing shall meet the weathering requirements of ANSI Z97.1.

2406.1.3 Glass block. Glass-block walls shall comply with Section 2101.2.5.

2406.1.4 Louvered windows and jalousies. Louvered windows and jalousies shall comply with Section 2403.5.

2406.2 Identification of safety glazing. Except as indicated in Section 2406.2.1, each pane of safety glazing installed in hazardous locations shall be identified by a manufacturer's designation specifying who applied the designation, the manufacturer or installer and the safety glazing standard with which it complies, as well as the information specified in Section 2403.1. The designation shall be acid etched, sand blasted, ceramic fired, laser etched, embossed or of a type that once applied, cannot be removed without being destroyed. A label as defined in Section 1702.1 and meeting the requirements of this section shall be permitted in lieu of the manufacturer's designation.

Exceptions:

1. For other than tempered glass, manufacturer's designations are not required, provided the code enforcement official approves the use of a certificate, affidavit or other evidence confirming compliance with this code.

2. Tempered spandrel glass is permitted to be identified by the manufacturer with a removable paper designation

2406.2.1 Multilight assemblies. Multilight glazed assemblies having individual lights not exceeding 1 square foot (0.09 m²) in exposed areas shall have at least one light in the assembly marked as indicated in Section 2406.2. Other lights in the assembly shall be marked "CPSC 16 CFR 1201."

2406.3 Hazardous locations. The following shall be considered specific hazardous locations requiring safety glazing materials:

1. Glazing in swinging doors except jalousies (see Section 2406.3.1).

2. Glazing in fixed and sliding panels of sliding door assemblies and panels in sliding and bifold closet door assemblies.

3. Glazing in storm doors.

4. Glazing in unframed swinging doors.

TABLE 2406.1
MINIMUM CATEGORY CLASSIFICATION OF GLAZING

EXPOSED SURFACE AREA OF ONE SIDE OF ONE LITE	GLAZING IN STORM OR COMBINATION DOORS (Category class)	GLAZING IN DOORS (Category class)	GLAZED PANELS REGULATED BY ITEM 7 OF SECTION 2406.3 (Category class)	GLAZED PANELS REGULATED BY ITEM 6 OF SECTION 2406.3 (Category class)	DOORS AND ENCLOSURES REGULATED BY ITEM 5 OF SECTION 2406.3 (Category class)	SLIDING GLASS DOORS PATIO TYPE (Category class)
9 square feet or less	I	I	No requirement	I	II	II
More than 9 square feet	II	II	II	II	II	II

For SI: 1 square foot = 0.0929m².

5. Glazing in doors and enclosures for hot tubs, whirlpools, saunas, steam rooms, bathtubs and showers. Glazing in any portion of a building wall enclosing these compartments where the bottom exposed edge of the glazing is less than 60 inches (1524 mm) above a standing surface.

6. Glazing in an individual fixed or operable panel adjacent to a door where the nearest exposed edge of the glazing is within a 24-inch (610 mm) arc of either vertical edge of the door in a closed position and where the bottom exposed edge of the glazing is less than 60 inches (1524 mm) above the walking surface.

Exceptions:

1. Panels where there is an intervening wall or other permanent barrier between the door and glazing.

2. Where access through the door is to a closet or storage area 3 feet (914 mm) or less in depth. Glazing in this application shall comply with Section 2406.3, Item 7.

3. Glazing in walls perpendicular to the plane of the door in a closed position, other than the wall towards which the door swings when opened, in one- and two-family dwellings or within dwelling units in Group R-2.

7. Glazing in an individual fixed or operable panel, other than in those locations described in preceding Items 5 and 6, which meets all of the following conditions:

7.1. Exposed area of an individual pane greater than 9 square feet (0.84 m²);

7.2. Exposed bottom edge less than 18 inches (457 mm) above the floor;

7.3. Exposed top edge greater than 36 inches (914 mm) above the floor; and

7.4. One or more walking surface(s) within 36 inches (914 mm) horizontally of the plane of the glazing.

Exception: Safety glazing for Item 7 is not required for the following installations:

1. A protective bar 1½ inches (38 mm) or more in height, capable of withstanding a horizontal load of 50 pounds plf (730 N/m) without contacting the glass, is installed on the accessible sides of the glazing 34 inches to 38 inches (864 mm to 965 mm) above the floor.

2. The outboard pane in insulating glass units or multiple glazing where the bottom exposed edge of the glass is 25 feet (7620 mm) or more above any grade, roof, walking surface or other horizontal or sloped (within 45 degrees of horizontal) (0.78 rad) surface adjacent to the glass exterior.

8. Glazing in guards and railings, including structural baluster panels and nonstructural in-fill panels, regardless of area or height above a walking surface.

9. Glazing in walls and fences enclosing indoor and outdoor swimming pools, hot tubs and spas where all of the following conditions are present:

9.1. The bottom edge of the glazing on the pool or spa side is less than 60 inches (1524 mm) above a walking surface on the pool or spa side of the glazing; and

9.2. The glazing is within 60 inches (1524 mm) horizontally of the water's edge of a swimming pool or spa.

10. Glazing adjacent to stairways, landings and ramps within 36 inches (914 mm) horizontally of a walking surface; when the exposed surface of the glass is less than 60 inches (1524 mm) above the plane of the adjacent walking surface.

11. Glazing adjacent to stairways within 60 inches (1524 mm) horizontally of the bottom tread of a stairway in any direction when the exposed surface of the glass is less than 60 inches (1524 mm) above the nose of the tread.

Exception: Safety glazing for Item 10 or 11 is not required for the following installations where:

1. The side of a stairway, landing or ramp which has a guardrail or handrail, including balusters or in-fill panels, complying with the provisions of Sections 1013 and 1607.7; and

2. The plane of the glass is greater than 18 inches (457 mm) from the railing.

2406.3.1 Exceptions. The following products, materials and uses shall not be considered specific hazardous locations:

1. Openings in doors through which a 3-inch (76 mm) sphere is unable to pass.

2. Decorative glass in Section 2406.3, Item 1, 6 or 7.

3. Glazing materials used as curved glazed panels in revolving doors.

4. Commercial refrigerated cabinet glazed doors.

5. Glass-block panels complying with Section 2101.2.5.

6. Louvered windows and jalousies complying with the requirements of Section 2403.5.

7. Mirrors and other glass panels mounted or hung on a surface that provides a continuous backing support.

2406.4 Fire department access panels. Fire department glass access panels shall be of tempered glass. For insulating glass units, all panes shall be tempered glass.

SECTION 2407
GLASS IN HANDRAILS AND GUARDS

2407.1 Materials. Glass used as a handrail assembly or a guard section shall be constructed of either single fully tempered glass, laminated fully tempered glass or laminated heat-strengthened glass. Glazing in railing in-fill panels shall be of an approved safety glazing material that conforms to the provisions of Section 2406.1.1. For all glazing types, the minimum nominal thickness shall be $^1/_4$ inch (6.4 mm). Fully tempered glass and laminated glass shall comply with Category II of CPSC 16 CFR 1201, listed in Chapter 35.

2407.1.1 Loads. The panels and their support system shall be designed to withstand the loads specified in Section 1607.7. A safety factor of four shall be used.

2407.1.2 Support. Each handrail or guard section shall be supported by a minimum of three glass balusters or shall be otherwise supported to remain in place should one baluster panel fail. Glass balusters shall not be installed without an attached handrail or guard.

2407.1.3 Parking garages. Glazing materials shall not be installed in handrails or guards in parking garages except for pedestrian areas not exposed to impact from vehicles.

SECTION 2408
GLAZING IN ATHLETIC FACILITIES

2408.1 General. Glazing in athletic facilities and similar uses subject to impact loads, which forms whole or partial wall sections or which is used as a door or part of a door, shall comply with this section.

2408.2 Racquetball and squash courts.

2408.2.1 Testing. Test methods and loads for individual glazed areas in racquetball and squash courts subject to impact loads shall conform to those of CPSC 16 CFR, Part 1201, listed in Chapter 35, with impacts being applied at a height of 59 inches (1499 mm) above the playing surface to an actual or simulated glass wall installation with fixtures, fittings and methods of assembly identical to those used in practice.

Glass walls shall comply with the following conditions:

1. A glass wall in a racquetball or squash court, or similar use subject to impact loads, shall remain intact following a test impact.

2. The deflection of such walls shall not be greater than $1^1/_2$ inches (38 mm) at the point of impact for a drop height of 48 inches (1219 mm).

Glass doors shall comply with the following conditions:

1. Glass doors shall remain intact following a test impact at the prescribed height in the center of the door.

2. The relative deflection between the edge of a glass door and the adjacent wall shall not exceed the thickness of the wall plus $^1/_2$ inch (12.7 mm) for a drop height of 48 inches (1219 mm).

2408.3 Gymnasiums and basketball courts. Glazing in multipurpose gymnasiums, basketball courts and similar athletic facilities subject to human impact loads shall comply with Category II of CPSC 16 CFR 1201, listed in Chapter 35.

SECTION 2409
GLASS IN ELEVATOR HOISTWAY

2409.1 Glass in elevator enclosures. Glass in elevator enclosures shall be laminated glass conforming to ANSI Z97.1 or 16 CFR Part 1201. Markings as specified in the applicable standard shall be on each separate piece of glass and shall remain visible after installation.

CHAPTER 25

GYPSUM BOARD AND PLASTER

SECTION 2501
GENERAL

2501.1 Scope.

2501.1.1 General. Provisions of this chapter shall govern the materials, design, construction and quality of gypsum board, lath, gypsum plaster and cement plaster.

2501.1.2 Performance. Lathing, plastering and gypsum board construction shall be done in the manner and with the materials specified in this chapter, and when required for fire protection, shall also comply with the provisions of Chapter 7.

2501.1.3 Other materials. Other approved wall or ceiling coverings shall be permitted to be installed in accordance with the recommendations of the manufacturer and the conditions of approval.

SECTION 2502
DEFINITIONS

2502.1 Definitions. The following words and terms shall, for the purposes of this chapter and as used elsewhere in this code, have the meanings shown herein.

CEMENT PLASTER. A mixture of portland or blended cement, portland cement or blended cement and hydrated lime, masonry cement or plastic cement and aggregate and other approved materials as specified in this code.

EXTERIOR SURFACES. Weather-exposed surfaces.

GYPSUM BOARD. Gypsum wallboard, gypsum sheathing, gypsum base for gypsum veneer plaster, exterior gypsum soffit board, predecorated gypsum board or water-resistant gypsum backing board complying with the standards listed in Tables 2506.2, 2507.2 and Chapter 35.

GYPSUM PLASTER. A mixture of calcined gypsum or calcined gypsum and lime and aggregate and other approved materials as specified in this code.

GYPSUM VENEER PLASTER. Gypsum plaster applied to an approved base in one or more coats normally not exceeding $^1/_4$ inch (6.4 mm) in total thickness.

INTERIOR SURFACES. Surfaces other than weather-exposed surfaces.

WEATHER-EXPOSED SURFACES. Surfaces of walls, ceilings, floors, roofs, soffits and similar surfaces exposed to the weather except the following:

1. Ceilings and roof soffits enclosed by walls, fascia, bulkheads or beams that extend a minimum of 12 inches (305 mm) below such ceiling or roof soffits.

2. Walls or portions of walls beneath an unenclosed roof area, where located a horizontal distance from an open exterior opening equal to at least twice the height of the opening.

3. Ceiling and roof soffits located a minimum horizontal distance of 10 feet (3048 mm) from the outer edges of the ceiling or roof soffits.

WIRE BACKING. Horizontal strands of tautened wire attached to surfaces of vertical supports which, when covered with the building paper, provide a backing for cement plaster.

SECTION 2503
INSPECTION

2503.1 Inspection. Lath and gypsum board shall be inspected in accordance with Section 109.3.5.

SECTION 2504
VERTICAL AND HORIZONTAL ASSEMBLIES

2504.1 Scope. The following requirements shall be met where construction involves gypsum board, lath and plaster in vertical and horizontal assemblies.

2504.1.1 Wood framing. Wood supports for lath or gypsum board, as well as wood stripping or furring, shall not be less than 2 inches (51 mm) nominal thickness in the least dimension.

Exception: The minimum nominal dimension of wood furring strips installed over solid backing shall not be less than 1 inch by 2 inches (25 mm by 51 mm).

2504.1.2 Studless partitions. The minimum thickness of vertically erected studless solid plaster partitions of $^3/_8$-inch (9.5 mm) and $^3/_4$-inch (19.1 mm) rib metal lath or $^1/_2$-inch-thick (12.7 mm) long-length gypsum lath and gypsum board partitions shall be 2 inches (51 mm).

SECTION 2505
SHEAR WALL CONSTRUCTION

2505.1 Resistance to shear (wood framing). Wood-framed shear walls sheathed with gypsum board, lath and plaster shall be designed and constructed in accordance with Section 2306.4 and are permitted to resist wind and seismic loads. Walls resisting seismic loads shall be subject to the limitations in Section 12.2.1 of ASCE 7.

2505.2 Resistance to shear (steel framing). Cold-formed steel-framed shear walls sheathed with gypsum board and constructed in accordance with the materials and provisions of Section 2210.5 are permitted to resist wind and seismic loads. Walls resisting seismic loads shall be subject to the limitations in Section 12.2.1 of ASCE 7.

SECTION 2506
GYPSUM BOARD MATERIALS

2506.1 General. Gypsum board materials and accessories shall be identified by the manufacturer's designation to indicate compliance with the appropriate standards referenced in this section and stored to protect such materials from the weather.

2506.2 Standards. Gypsum board materials shall conform to the appropriate standards listed in Table 2506.2 and Chapter 35 and, where required for fire protection, shall conform to the provisions of Chapter 7.

TABLE 2506.2
GYPSUM BOARD MATERIALS AND ACCESSORIES

MATERIAL	STANDARD
Accessories for gypsum board	ASTM C 1047
Adhesives for fastening gypsum wallboard	ASTM C 557
Exterior soffit board	ASTM C 931
Fiber-reinforced gypsum panels	ASTM C 1278
Glass mat gypsum backing panel	ASTM C 1178
Glass mat gypsum substrate	ASTM C 1177
Gypsum backing board and gypsum shaftliner board	ASTM C 442
Gypsum ceiling board	ASTM C 1395
Gypsum sheathing	ASTM C 79
Gypsum wallboard	ASTM C 36
Joint reinforcing tape and compound	ASTM C 474; C 475
Nails for gypsum boards	ASTM C 514, F 547, F 1667
Predecorated gypsum board	ASTM C 960
Steel screws	ASTM C 954; C 1002
Steel studs, load bearing	ASTM C 955
Steel studs, nonload bearing	ASTM C 645
Standard specification for gypsum board	ASTM C 1396
Testing gypsum and gypsum products	ASTM C 22; C 472; C 473
Water-resistant gypsum backing board	ASTM C 630

2506.2.1 Other materials. Metal suspension systems for acoustical and lay-in panel ceilings shall conform with ASTM C 635 listed in Chapter 35 and Section 13.5.6 of ASCE 7 for installation in high seismic areas.

SECTION 2507
LATHING AND PLASTERING

2507.1 General. Lathing and plastering materials and accessories shall be marked by the manufacturer's designation to indicate compliance with the appropriate standards referenced in this section and stored in such a manner to protect them from the weather.

2507.2 Standards. Lathing and plastering materials shall conform to the standards listed in Table 2507.2 and Chapter 35 and, where required for fire protection, shall also conform to the provisions of Chapter 7.

TABLE 2507.2
LATH, PLASTERING MATERIALS AND ACCESSORIES

MATERIAL	STANDARD
Accessories for gypsum veneer base	ASTM C 1047
Blended cement	ASTM C 595
Exterior plaster bonding compounds	ASTM C 932
Gypsum base for veneer plasters	ASTM C 588
Gypsum casting and molding plaster	ASTM C 59
Gypsum Keene's cement	ASTM C 61
Gypsum lath	ASTM C 37
Gypsum plaster	ASTM C 28
Gypsum veneer plaster	ASTM C 587
Interior bonding compounds, gypsum	ASTM C 631
Lime plasters	ASTM C 5; C 206
Masonry cement	ASTM C 91
Metal lath	ASTM C 847
Plaster aggregates	
Sand	ASTM C 35; C 897
Perlite	ASTM C 35
Vermiculite	ASTM C 35
Plastic cement	ASTM C 1328
Portland cement	ASTM C 150
Steel screws	ASTM C 1002; C 954
Steel studs and track	ASTM C 645; C 955
Welded wire lath	ASTM C 933
Woven wire plaster base	ASTM C 1032

SECTION 2508
GYPSUM CONSTRUCTION

2508.1 General. Gypsum board and gypsum plaster construction shall be of the materials listed in Tables 2506.2 and 2507.2. These materials shall be assembled and installed in compliance with the appropriate standards listed in Tables 2508.1 and 2511.1, and Chapter 35.

TABLE 2508.1
INSTALLATION OF GYPSUM CONSTRUCTION

MATERIAL	STANDARD
Gypsum board	GA-216; ASTM C 840
Gypsum sheathing	ASTM C 1280
Gypsum veneer base	ASTM C 844
Interior lathing and furring	ASTM C 841
Steel framing for gypsum boards	ASTM C 754; C 1007

2508.2 Limitations. Gypsum wallboard or gypsum plaster shall not be used in any exterior surface where such gypsum construction will be exposed directly to the weather. Gypsum wallboard shall not be used where there will be direct exposure to water or continuous high humidity conditions. Gypsum sheathing shall be installed on exterior surfaces in accordance with ASTM C 1280.

2508.2.1 Weather protection. Gypsum wallboard, gypsum lath or gypsum plaster shall not be installed until weather protection for the installation is provided.

2508.3 Single-ply application. Edges and ends of gypsum board shall occur on the framing members, except those edges and ends that are perpendicular to the framing members. Edges and ends of gypsum board shall be in moderate contact except in concealed spaces where fire-resistance-rated construction, shear resistance or diaphragm action is not required.

2508.3.1 Floating angles. Fasteners at the top and bottom plates of vertical assemblies, or the edges and ends of horizontal assemblies perpendicular to supports, and at the wall line are permitted to be omitted except on shear resisting elements or fire-resistance-rated assemblies. Fasteners shall be applied in such a manner as not to fracture the face paper with the fastener head.

2508.4 Joint treatment. Gypsum board fire-resistance-rated assemblies shall have joints and fasteners treated.

Exception: Joint and fastener treatment need not be provided where any of the following conditions occur:

1. Where the gypsum board is to receive a decorative finish such as wood paneling, battens, acoustical finishes or any similar application that would be equivalent to joint treatment.

2. On single-layer systems where joints occur over wood framing members.

3. Square edge or tongue-and-groove edge gypsum board (V-edge), gypsum backing board or gypsum sheathing.

4. On multilayer systems where the joints of adjacent layers are offset from one to another.

5. Assemblies tested without joint treatment.

2508.5 Horizontal gypsum board diaphragm ceilings. Gypsum board shall be permitted to be used on wood joists to create a horizontal diaphragm ceiling in accordance with Table 2508.5.

2508.5.1 Diaphragm proportions. The maximum allowable diaphragm proportions shall be $1^1/_2$:1 between shear resisting elements. Rotation or cantilever conditions shall not be permitted.

2508.5.2 Installation. Gypsum board used in a horizontal diaphragm ceiling shall be installed perpendicular to ceiling framing members. End joints of adjacent courses of gypsum board shall not occur on the same joist.

2508.5.3 Blocking of perimeter edges. All perimeter edges shall be blocked using a wood member not less than 2-inch by 6-inch (51 mm by 159 mm) nominal dimension. Blocking material shall be installed flat over the top plate of the wall to provide a nailing surface not less than 2 inches (51 mm) in width for the attachment of the gypsum board.

2508.5.4 Fasteners. Fasteners used for the attachment of gypsum board to a horizontal diaphragm ceiling shall be as defined in Table 2508.5. Fasteners shall be spaced not more than 7 inches (178 mm) on center (o.c.) at all supports, including perimeter blocking, and not more than $^3/_8$ inch (9.5 mm) from the edges and ends of the gypsum board.

2508.5.5 Lateral force restrictions. Gypsum board shall not be used in diaphragm ceilings to resist lateral forces imposed by masonry or concrete construction.

TABLE 2508.5
SHEAR CAPACITY FOR HORIZONTAL WOOD FRAMED GYPSUM BOARD DIAPHRAGM CEILING ASSEMBLIES

MATERIAL	THICKNESS OF MATERIAL (MINIMUM) (inches)	SPACING OF FRAMING MEMBERS (MAXIMUM) (inches)	SHEAR VALUE[a,b] (plf of ceiling)	MIMIMUM FASTENER SIZE
Gypsum board	$^1/_2$	16 o.c.	90	5d cooler or wallboard nail; $1^5/_8$-inch long; 0.086-inch shank; $^{15}/_{64}$-inch head[c]
Gypsum board	$^1/_2$	24 o.c.	70	5d cooler or wallboard nail; $1^5/_8$-inch long; 0.086-inch shank; $^{15}/_{64}$-inch head[c]

For SI: 1 inch = 25.4 mm, 1 pound per foot = 14.59 N/m.

a. Values are not cumulative with other horizontal diaphragm values and are for short-term loading due to wind or seismic loading. Values shall be reduced 25 percent for normal loading.

b. Values shall be reduced 50 percent in Seismic Design Categories D, E and F.

c. $1^1/_4$-inch, No. 6 Type S or W screws are permitted to be substituted for the listed nails.

SECTION 2509
GYPSUM BOARD IN SHOWERS AND WATER CLOSETS

2509.1 Wet areas. Showers and public toilet walls shall conform to Sections 1210.2 and 1210.3.

2509.2 Base for tile. Cement, fiber-cement or glass mat gypsum backers in compliance with ASTM C 1178, C 1288 or C 1325 and installed in accordance with manufacturer recommendations shall be used as a base for wall tile in tub and shower areas and wall and ceiling panels in shower areas. Water-resistant gypsum backing board shall be used as a base for tile in water closet compartment walls when installed in accordance with GA-216 or ASTM C 840 and manufacturer recommendations. Regular gypsum wallboard is permitted under tile or wall panels in other wall and ceiling areas when installed in accordance with GA-216 or ASTM C 840.

2509.3 Limitations. Water-resistant gypsum backing board shall not be used in the following locations:

1. Over a vapor retarder in shower or bathtub compartments.

2. Where there will be direct exposure to water or in areas subject to continuous high humidity.

3. On ceilings where frame spacing exceeds 12 inches (305 mm) o.c. for $^1/_2$-inch-thick (12.7 mm) water-resistant gypsum backing board and more than 16 inches

(406 mm) o.c. for $^5/_8$-inch-thick (15.9 mm) water-resistant gypsum backing board.

SECTION 2510
LATHING AND FURRING FOR CEMENT PLASTER (STUCCO)

2510.1 General. Exterior and interior cement plaster and lathing shall be done with the appropriate materials listed in Table 2507.2 and Chapter 35.

2510.2 Weather protection. Materials shall be stored in such a manner as to protect such materials from the weather.

2510.3 Installation. Installation of these materials shall be in compliance with ASTM C 926 and ASTM C 1063.

2510.4 Corrosion resistance. Metal lath and lath attachments shall be of corrosion-resistant material.

2510.5 Backing. Backing or a lath shall provide sufficient rigidity to permit plaster applications.

2510.5.1 Support of lath. Where lath on vertical surfaces extends between rafters or other similar projecting members, solid backing shall be installed to provide support for lath and attachments.

2510.5.2 Use of gypsum backing board.

2510.5.2.1 Use of gypsum board as a backing board. Gypsum lath or gypsum wallboard shall not be used as a backing for cement plaster.

Exception: Gypsum lath or gypsum wallboard is permitted, with a water-resistive barrier, as a backing for self-furred metal lath or self-furred wire fabric lath and cement plaster where either of the following conditions occur:

1. On horizontal supports of ceilings or roof soffits.
2. On interior walls.

2510.5.2.2 Use of gypsum sheathing backing. Gypsum sheathing is permitted as a backing for metal or wire fabric lath and cement plaster on walls. A water-resistive barrier shall be provided in accordance with Section 2510.6.

2510.5.3 Backing not required. Wire backing is not required under expanded metal lath or paperbacked wire fabric lath.

2510.6 Water-resistive barriers. Water-resistive barriers shall be installed as required in Section 1404.2 and, where applied over wood-based sheathing, shall include a water-resistive vapor-permeable barrier with a performance at least equivalent to two layers of Grade D paper.

Exception: Where the water-resistive barrier that is applied over wood-based sheathing has a water resistance equal to or greater than that of 60-minute Grade D paper and is separated from the stucco by an intervening, substantially nonwater-absorbing layer or drainage space.

2510.7 Preparation of masonry and concrete. Surfaces shall be clean, free from efflorescence, sufficiently damp and rough for proper bond. If the surface is insufficiently rough,

approved bonding agents or a portland cement dash bond coat mixed in proportions of not more than two parts volume of sand to one part volume of portland cement or plastic cement shall be applied. The dash bond coat shall be left undisturbed and shall be moist cured not less than 24 hours.

SECTION 2511
INTERIOR PLASTER

2511.1 General. Plastering gypsum plaster or cement plaster shall not be less than three coats where applied over metal lath or wire fabric lath and not less than two coats where applied over other bases permitted by this chapter.

Exception: Gypsum veneer plaster and cement plaster specifically designed and approved for one-coat applications.

2511.1.1 Installation. Installation of lathing and plaster materials shall conform with Table 2511.1.1 and Section 2507.

TABLE 2511.1.1
INSTALLATION OF PLASTER CONSTRUCTION

MATERIAL	STANDARD
Gypsum plaster	ASTM C 842
Gypsum veneer plaster	ASTM C 843
Interior lathing and furring (gypsum plaster)	ASTM C 841
Lathing and furring (cement plaster)	ASTM C 1063
Portland cement plaster	ASTM C 926
Steel framing	ASTM C 754; C 1007

2511.2 Limitations. Plaster shall not be applied directly to fiber insulation board. Cement plaster shall not be applied directly to gypsum lath or gypsum plaster except as specified in Sections 2510.5.1 and 2510.5.2.

2511.3 Grounds. Where installed, grounds shall ensure the minimum thickness of plaster as set forth in ASTM C 842 and ASTM C 926. Plaster thickness shall be measured from the face of lath and other bases.

2511.4 Interior masonry or concrete. Condition of surfaces shall be as specified in Section 2510.7. Approved specially prepared gypsum plaster designed for application to concrete surfaces or approved acoustical plaster is permitted. The total thickness of base coat plaster applied to concrete ceilings shall be as set forth in ASTM C 842 or ASTM C 926. Should ceiling surfaces require more than the maximum thickness permitted in ASTM C 842 or ASTM C 926, metal lath or wire fabric lath shall be installed on such surfaces before plastering.

2511.5 Wet areas. Showers and public toilet walls shall conform to Sections 1210.2 and 1210.3. When wood frame walls and partitions are covered on the interior with cement plaster or tile of similar material and are subject to water splash, the framing shall be protected with an approved moisture barrier.

SECTION 2512
EXTERIOR PLASTER

2512.1 General. Plastering with cement plaster shall not be less than three coats where applied over metal lath or wire fabric lath and not less than two coats where applied over masonry, concrete or gypsum board backing as specified in Section 2510.5. If the plaster surface is to be completely covered by veneer or other facing material, or is completely concealed by another wall, plaster application need be only two coats, provided the total thickness is as set forth in ASTM C 926.

2512.1.1 On-grade floor slab. On wood framed or steel stud construction with an on-grade concrete floor slab system, exterior plaster shall be applied in such a manner as to cover, but not to extend below, the lath and paper. The application of lath, paper and flashing or drip screeds shall comply with ASTM C 1063.

2512.1.2 Weep screeds. A minimum 0.019-inch (0.48 mm) (No. 26 galvanized sheet gage), corrosion-resistant weep screed with a minimum vertical attachment flange of $3^1/_2$ inches (89 mm) shall be provided at or below the foundation plate line on exterior stud walls in accordance with ASTM C 926. The weep screed shall be placed a minimum of 4 inches (102 mm) above the earth or 2 inches (51 mm) above paved areas and be of a type that will allow trapped water to drain to the exterior of the building. The water-resistive barrier shall lap the attachment flange. The exterior lath shall cover and terminate on the attachment flange of the weep screed.

2512.2 Plasticity agents. Only approved plasticity agents and approved amounts thereof shall be added to portland cement. When plastic cement or masonry cement is used, no additional lime or plasticizers shall be added. Hydrated lime or the equivalent amount of lime putty used as a plasticizer is permitted to be added to cement plaster or cement and lime plaster in an amount not to exceed that set forth in ASTM C 926.

2512.3 Limitations. Gypsum plaster shall not be used on exterior surfaces.

2512.4 Cement plaster. Plaster coats shall be protected from freezing for a period of not less than 24 hours after set has occurred. Plaster shall be applied when the ambient temperature is higher than 40°F (4°C), unless provisions are made to keep cement plaster work above 40°F (4°C) during application and 48 hours thereafter.

2512.5 Second-coat application. The second coat shall be brought out to proper thickness, rodded and floated sufficiently rough to provide adequate bond for the finish coat. The second coat shall have no variation greater than $^1/_4$ inch (6.4 mm) in any direction under a 5-foot (1524 mm) straight edge.

2512.6 Curing and interval. First and second coats of cement plaster shall be applied and moist cured as set forth in ASTM C 926 and Table 2512.6.

TABLE 2512.6
CEMENT PLASTERS[a]

COAT	MINIMUM PERIOD MOIST CURING	MINIMUM INTERVAL BETWEEN COATS
First	48 hours[a]	48 hours[b]
Second	48 hours	7 days[c]
Finish	-	Note c

a. The first two coats shall be as required for the first coats of exterior plaster, except that the moist-curing time period between the first and second coats shall not be less than 24 hours. Moist curing shall not be required where job and weather conditions are favorable to the retention of moisture in the cement plaster for the required time period.

b. Twenty-four-hour minimum interval between coats of interior cement plaster. For alternate method of application, see Section 2512.8.

c. Finish coat plaster is permitted to be applied to interior portland cement base coats after a 48-hour period.

2512.7 Application to solid backings. Where applied over gypsum backing as specified in Section 2510.5 or directly to unit masonry surfaces, the second coat is permitted to be applied as soon as the first coat has attained sufficient hardness.

2512.8 Alternate method of application. The second coat is permitted to be applied as soon as the first coat has attained sufficiently rigidity to receive the second coat.

2512.8.1 Admixtures. When using this method of application, calcium aluminate cement up to 15 percent of the weight of the portland cement is permitted to be added to the mix.

2512.8.2 Curing. Curing of the first coat is permitted to be omitted and the second coat shall be cured as set forth in ASTM C 926 and Table 2512.6.

2512.9 Finish coats. Cement plaster finish coats shall be applied over base coats that have been in place for the time periods set forth in ASTM C 926. The third or finish coat shall be applied with sufficient material and pressure to bond and to cover the brown coat and shall be of sufficient thickness to conceal the brown coat.

SECTION 2513
EXPOSED AGGREGATE PLASTER

2513.1 General. Exposed natural or integrally colored aggregate is permitted to be partially embedded in a natural or colored bedding coat of cement plaster or gypsum plaster, subject to the provisions of this section.

2513.2 Aggregate. The aggregate shall be applied manually or mechanically and shall consist of marble chips, pebbles or similar durable, moderately hard (three or more on the Mohs hardness scale), nonreactive materials.

2513.3 Bedding coat proportions. The bedding coat for interior or exterior surfaces shall be composed of one-part portland cement, one-part Type S lime and a maximum of three parts of graded white or natural sand by volume. The bedding coat for interior surfaces shall be composed of 100 pounds (45.4 kg) of neat gypsum plaster and a maximum of 200 pounds (90.8 kg) of graded white sand. A factory-prepared bedding coat for interior or exterior use is permitted. The bedding coat for exterior surfaces shall have a minimum compressive strength of 1,000 pounds per square inch (psi) (6895 kPa).

2513.4 Application. The bedding coat is permitted to be applied directly over the first (scratch) coat of plaster, provided the ultimate overall thickness is a minimum of $^7/_8$ inch (22 mm), including lath. Over concrete or masonry surfaces, the overall thickness shall be a minimum of $^1/_2$ inch (12.7 mm).

2513.5 Bases. Exposed aggregate plaster is permitted to be applied over concrete, masonry, cement plaster base coats or gypsum plaster base coats installed in accordance with Section 2511 or 2512.

2513.6 Preparation of masonry and concrete. Masonry and concrete surfaces shall be prepared in accordance with the provisions of Section 2510.7.

2513.7 Curing of base coats. Cement plaster base coats shall be cured in accordance with ASTM C 926. Cement plaster bedding coats shall retain sufficient moisture for hydration (hardening) for 24 hours minimum or, where necessary, shall be kept damp for 24 hours by light water spraying.

CHAPTER 26

PLASTIC

SECTION 2601
GENERAL

2601.1 Scope. These provisions shall govern the materials, design, application, construction and installation of foam plastic, foam plastic insulation, plastic veneer, interior plastic finish and trim and light-transmitting plastics. See Chapter 14 for requirements for exterior wall finish and trim.

SECTION 2602
DEFINITIONS

2602.1 General. The following words and terms shall, for the purposes of this chapter and as used elsewhere in this code, have the meanings shown herein.

FOAM PLASTIC INSULATION. A plastic that is intentionally expanded by the use of a foaming agent to produce a reduced-density plastic containing voids consisting of open or closed cells distributed throughout the plastic for thermal insulating or acoustical purposes and that has a density less than 20 pounds per cubic foot (pcf) (320 kg/m³).

LIGHT-DIFFUSING SYSTEM. Construction consisting in whole or in part of lenses, panels, grids or baffles made with light-transmitting plastics positioned below independently mounted electrical light sources, skylights or light-transmitting plastic roof panels. Lenses, panels, grids and baffles that are part of an electrical fixture shall not be considered as a light-diffusing system.

LIGHT-TRANSMITTING PLASTIC ROOF PANELS. Structural plastic panels other than skylights that are fastened to structural members, or panels or sheathing and that are used as light-transmitting media in the plane of the roof.

LIGHT-TRANSMITTING PLASTIC WALL PANELS. Plastic materials that are fastened to structural members, or to structural panels or sheathing, and that are used as light-transmitting media in exterior walls.

PLASTIC, APPROVED. Any thermoplastic, thermosetting or reinforced thermosetting plastic material that conforms to combustibility classifications specified in the section applicable to the application and plastic type.

PLASTIC GLAZING. Plastic materials that are glazed or set in frame or sash and not held by mechanical fasteners that pass through the glazing material.

REINFORCED PLASTIC, GLASS FIBER. Plastic reinforced with glass fiber having not less than 20 percent of glass fibers by weight.

THERMOPLASTIC MATERIAL. A plastic material that is capable of being repeatedly softened by increase of temperature and hardened by decrease of temperature.

THERMOSETTING MATERIAL. A plastic material that is capable of being changed into a substantially nonreformable product when cured.

SECTION 2603
FOAM PLASTIC INSULATION

2603.1 General. The provisions of this section shall govern the requirements and uses of foam plastic insulation in buildings and structures.

2603.2 Labeling and identification. Packages and containers of foam plastic insulation and foam plastic insulation components delivered to the job site shall bear the label of an approved agency showing the manufacturer's name, the product listing, product identification and information sufficient to determine that the end use will comply with the code requirements.

2603.3 Surface-burning characteristics. Unless otherwise indicated in this section, foam plastic insulation and foam plastic cores of manufactured assemblies shall have a flame spread index of not more than 75 and a smoke-developed index of not more than 450 where tested in the maximum thickness intended for use in accordance with ASTM E 84. Loose fill-type foam plastic insulation shall be tested as board stock for the flame spread index and smoke-developed index.

Exceptions:

1. Smoke-developed index for interior trim as provided for in Section 2604.2.

2. In cold storage buildings, ice plants, food plants, food processing rooms and similar areas, foam plastic insulation where tested in a thickness of 4 inches (102 mm) shall be permitted in a thickness up to 10 inches (254 mm) where the building is equipped throughout with an automatic fire sprinkler system in accordance with Section 903.3.1.1. The approved automatic sprinkler system shall be provided in both the room and that part of the building in which the room is located.

3. Foam plastic insulation that is a part of a Class A, B or C roof-covering assembly provided the assembly with the foam plastic insulation satisfactorily passes FM 4450 or UL 1256. The smoke-developed index shall not be limited for roof applications.

4. Foam plastic insulation greater than 4 inches (102 mm) in thickness shall have a maximum flame spread index of 75 and a smoke-developed index of 450 where tested at a minimum thickness of 4 inches (102 mm), provided the end use is approved in accordance with Section 2603.9 using the thickness and density intended for use.

5. Flame spread and smoke-developed indexes for foam plastic interior signs in covered mall buildings provided the signs comply with Section 402.15.

2603.4 Thermal barrier. Except as provided for in Sections 2603.4.1 and 2603.9, foam plastic shall be separated from the interior of a building by an approved thermal barrier of 0.5-

inch (12.7 mm) gypsum wallboard or equivalent thermal barrier material that will limit the average temperature rise of the unexposed surface to not more than 250°F (120°C) after 15 minutes of fire exposure, complying with the standard time-temperature curve of ASTM E 119. The thermal barrier shall be installed in such a manner that it will remain in place for 15 minutes based on FM 4880, UL 1040, NFPA 286 or UL 1715. Combustible concealed spaces shall comply with Section 717.

2603.4.1 Thermal barrier not required. The thermal barrier specified in Section 2603.4 is not required under the conditions set forth in Sections 2603.4.1.1 through 2603.4.1.13.

2603.4.1.1 Masonry or concrete construction. A thermal barrier is not required for foam plastic installed in a masonry or concrete wall, floor or roof system where the foam plastic insulation is covered on each face by a minimum of 1 inch (25 mm) thickness of masonry or concrete.

2603.4.1.2 Cooler and freezer walls. Foam plastic installed in a maximum thickness of 10 inches (254 mm) in cooler and freezer walls shall:

1. Have a flame spread index of 25 or less and a smoke-developed index of not more than 450, where tested in a minimum 4 inch (102 mm) thickness.

2. Have flash ignition and self-ignition temperatures of not less than 600°F and 800°F (316°C and 427°C), respectively.

3. Have a covering of not less than 0.032-inch (0.8 mm) aluminum or corrosion-resistant steel having a base metal thickness not less than 0.0160 inch (0.4 mm) at any point.

4. Be protected by an automatic sprinkler system. Where the cooler or freezer is within a building, both the cooler or freezer and that part of the building in which it is located shall be sprinklered.

2603.4.1.3 Walk-in coolers. In nonsprinklered buildings, foam plastic having a thickness that does not exceed 4 inches (102 mm) and a maximum flame spread index of 75 is permitted in walk-in coolers or freezer units where the aggregate floor area does not exceed 400 square feet (37 m²) and the foam plastic is covered by a metal facing not less than 0.032-inch-thick (0.81 mm) aluminum or corrosion-resistant steel having a minimum base metal thickness of 0.016 inch (0.41 mm). A thickness of up to 10 inches (254 mm) is permitted where protected by a thermal barrier.

2603.4.1.4 Exterior walls-one-story buildings. For one-story buildings, foam plastic having a flame spread index of 25 or less, and a smoke-developed index of not more than 450, shall be permitted without thermal barriers in or on exterior walls in a thickness not more than 4 inches (102 mm) where the foam plastic is covered by a thickness of not less than 0.032-inch-thick (0.81 mm) aluminum or corrosion-resistant steel having a base

metal thickness of 0.0160 inch (0.41 mm) and the building is equipped throughout with an automatic sprinkler system in accordance with Section 903.3.1.1.

2603.4.1.5 Roofing. Foam plastic insulation under a roof assembly or roof covering that is installed in accordance with the code and the manufacturer's instructions shall be separated from the interior of the building by wood structural panel sheathing not less than 0.47 inch (11.9 mm) in thickness bonded with exterior glue, with edges supported by blocking, tongue-and-groove joints or other approved type of edge support, or an equivalent material. A thermal barrier is not required for foam plastic insulation that is a part of a Class A, B or C roof-covering assembly, provided the assembly with the foam plastic insulation satisfactorily passes FM 4450 or UL 1256.

2603.4.1.6 Attics and crawl spaces. Within an attic or crawl space where entry is made only for service of utilities, foam plastic insulation shall be protected against ignition by 1.5-inch-thick (38 mm) mineral fiber insulation; 0.25-inch-thick (6.4 mm) wood structural panel, particleboard or hardboard; 0.375-inch (9.5 mm) gypsum wallboard, corrosion-resistant steel having a base metal thickness of 0.016 inch (0.4 mm) or other approved material installed in such a manner that the foam plastic insulation is not exposed. The protective covering shall be consistent with the requirements for the type of construction.

2603.4.1.7 Doors not required to have a fire protection rating. Where pivoted or side-hinged doors are permitted without a fire protection rating, foam plastic insulation, having a flame spread index of 75 or less and a smoke-developed index of not more than 450, shall be permitted as a core material where the door facing is of metal having a minimum thickness of 0.032-inch (0.8 mm) aluminum or steel having a base metal thickness of not less than 0.016 inch (0.4 mm) at any point.

2603.4.1.8 Exterior doors in buildings of Group R-2 or R-3. In occupancies classified as Group R-2 or R-3, foam-filled exterior entrance doors to individual dwelling units that do not require a fire-resistance rating shall be faced with wood or other approved materials.

2603.4.1.9 Garage doors. Where garage doors are permitted without a fire-resistance rating and foam plastic is used as a core material, the door facing shall be metal having a minimum thickness of 0.032-inch (0.8 mm) aluminum or 0.010-inch (0.25 mm) steel or the facing shall be minimum 0.125-inch-thick (3.2 mm) wood. Garage doors having facings other than those described above shall be tested in accordance with, and meet the acceptance criteria of, DASMA 107.

> **Exception:** Garage doors using foam plastic insulation complying with Section 2603.3 in detached and attached garages associated with one- and two-family dwellings need not be provided with a thermal barrier.

2603.4.1.10 Siding backer board. Foam plastic insulation of not more than 2,000 British thermal units per square feet (Btu/sq. ft.) (22.7 MJ/m²) as determined by NFPA 259 shall be permitted as a siding backer board with a maximum thickness of 0.5 inch (12.7 mm), provided it is separated from the interior of the building by not less than 2 inches (51 mm) of mineral fiber insulation or equivalent or where applied as insulation with re-siding over existing wall construction.

2603.4.1.11 Interior trim. Foam plastic used as interior trim in accordance with Section 2604 shall be permitted without a thermal barrier.

2603.4.1.12 Interior signs. Foam plastic used for interior signs in covered mall buildings in accordance with Section 402.15 shall be permitted without a thermal barrier. Foam plastic signs that are not affixed to interior building surfaces shall comply with Chapter 8 of the *Fire Code of New York State*.

2603.4.1.13 Type V construction. Foam plastic spray applied to a sill plate and header of Type V construction is subject to all of the following:

1. The maximum thickness of the foam plastic shall be $3^1/_4$ inches (82.6 mm).

2. The density of the foam plastic shall be in the range of 1.5 to 2.0 pcf (24 to 32 kg/m³).

3. The foam plastic shall have a flame spread index of 25 or less and an accompanying smoke-developed index of 450 or less when tested in accordance with ASTM E 84.

2603.5 Exterior walls of buildings of any height. Exterior walls of buildings of Type I, II, III or IV construction of any height shall comply with Sections 2603.5.1 through 2603.5.7. Exterior walls of cold storage buildings required to be constructed of noncombustible materials, where the building is more than one story in height, shall also comply with the provisions of Sections 2603.5.1 through 2603.5.7. Exterior walls of buildings of Type V construction shall comply with Sections 2603.2, 2603.3 and 2603.4.

2603.5.1 Fire-resistance-rated walls. Where the wall is required to have a fire-resistance rating, data based on tests conducted in accordance with ASTM E 119 shall be provided to substantiate that the fire-resistance rating is maintained.

2603.5.2 Thermal barrier. Any foam plastic insulation shall be separated from the building interior by a thermal barrier meeting the provisions of Section 2603.4, unless special approval is obtained on the basis of Section 2603.9.

Exception: One-story buildings complying with Section 2603.4.1.4.

2603.5.3 Potential heat. The potential heat of foam plastic insulation in any portion of the wall or panel shall not exceed the potential heat expressed in Btu per square feet (mJ/m²) of the foam plastic insulation contained in the wall assembly tested in accordance with Section 2603.5.5. The potential heat of the foam plastic insulation shall be determined by tests conducted in accordance with NFPA 259 and the results shall be expressed in Btu per square feet (mJ/m²).

Exception: One-story buildings complying with Section 2603.4.1.4.

2603.5.4 Flame spread and smoke-developed indexes. Foam plastic insulation, exterior coatings and facings shall be tested separately in the thickness intended for use, but not to exceed 4 inches (102 mm), and shall each have a flame spread index of 25 or less and a smoke-developed index of 450 or less as determined in accordance with ASTM E 84.

Exception: Prefabricated or factory-manufactured panels having minimum 0.020-inch (0.51 mm) aluminum facings and a total thickness of 0.25 inch (6.4 mm) or less are permitted to be tested as an assembly where the foam plastic core is not exposed in the course of construction.

2603.5.5 Test standard. The wall assembly shall be tested in accordance with and comply with the acceptance criteria of NFPA 285.

Exception: One-story buildings complying with Section 2603.4.1.4.

2603.5.6 Label required. The edge or face of each piece of foam plastic insulation shall bear the label of an approved agency. The label shall contain the manufacturer's or distributor's identification, model number, serial number or definitive information describing the product or materials' performance characteristics and approved agency's identification.

2603.5.7 Ignition. Exterior walls shall not exhibit sustained flaming where tested in accordance with NFPA 268. Where a material is intended to be installed in more than one thickness, tests of the minimum and maximum thickness intended for use shall be performed.

Exception: Assemblies protected on the outside with one of the following:

1. A thermal barrier complying with Section 2603.4.

2. A minimum 1 inch (25 mm) thickness of concrete or masonry.

3. Glass-fiber-reinforced concrete panels of a minimum thickness of 0.375 inch (9.5 mm).

4. Metal-faced panels having minimum 0.019- inch-thick (0.48 mm) aluminum or 0.016-inch- thick (0.41 mm) corrosion-resistant steel outer facings.

5. A minimum 0.875 inch (22.2 mm) thickness of stucco complying with Section 2510.

2603.6 Roofing. Foam plastic insulation meeting the requirements of Sections 2603.2, 2603.3 and 2603.4 shall be permitted as part of a roof-covering assembly, provided the assembly with the foam plastic insulation is a Class A, B or C roofing assembly where tested in accordance with ASTM E 108 or UL 790.

2603.7 Plenums. Foam plastic insulation shall not be used as interior wall or ceiling finish in plenums except as permitted in Section 2604 or when protected by a thermal barrier in accordance with Section 2603.4.

2603.8 Protection against termites. In areas where the probability of termite infestation is very heavy in accordance with Figure 2603.8, extruded and expanded polystyrene, polyisocyanurate and other foam plastics shall not be installed on the exterior face or under interior or exterior foundation walls or slab foundations located below grade. The clearance between foam plastics installed above grade and exposed earth shall be at least 6 inches (152 mm).

Exceptions:

1. Buildings where the structural members of walls, floors, ceilings and roofs are entirely of noncombustible materials or preservatively treated wood.

2. An approved method of protecting the foam plastic and structure from subterranean termite damage is provided.

3. On the interior side of basement walls.

2603.9 Special approval. Foam plastic shall not be required to comply with the requirements of Sections 2603.4 through 2603.7 where specifically approved based on large-scale tests such as, but not limited to, NFPA 286 (with the acceptance criteria of Section 803.2), FM 4880, UL 1040 or UL 1715. Such testing shall be related to the actual end-use configuration and be performed on the finished manufactured foam plastic assembly in the maximum thickness intended for use. Foam plastics that are used as interior finish on the basis of special tests shall also conform to the flame spread requirements of Chapter 8. Assemblies tested shall include seams, joints and other typical details used in the installation of the assembly and shall be tested in the manner intended for use.

SECTION 2604
INTERIOR FINISH AND TRIM

2604.1 General. Plastic materials installed as interior finish or trim shall comply with Chapter 8. Foam plastics shall only be installed as interior finish where approved in accordance with the special provisions of Section 2603.9. Foam plastics that are used as interior finish shall also meet the flame spread index requirements for interior finish in accordance with Chapter 8. Foam plastics installed as interior trim shall comply with Section 2604.2.

[F] 2604.2 Interior trim. Foam plastic used as interior trim shall comply with Sections 2604.2.1 through 2604.2.4.

[F] 2604.2.1 Density. The minimum density of the interior trim shall be 20 pcf (320 kg/m³).

[F] 2604.2.2 Thickness. The maximum thickness of the interior trim shall be 0.5 inch (12.7 mm) and the maximum width shall be 8 inches (204 mm).

[F] 2604.2.3 Area limitation. The interior trim shall not constitute more than 10 percent of the aggregate wall and ceiling area of any room or space.

[F] 2604.2.4 Flame spread. The flame spread index shall not exceed 75 where tested in accordance with ASTM E 84. The smoke-developed index shall not be limited.

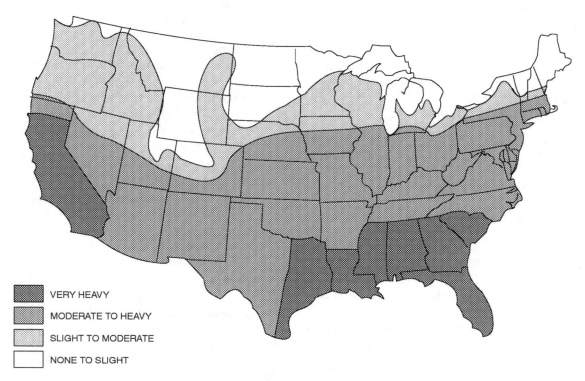

VERY HEAVY

MODERATE TO HEAVY

SLIGHT TO MODERATE

NONE TO SLIGHT

FIGURE 2603.8
TERMITE INFESTATION PROBABILITY MAP

SECTION 2605
PLASTIC VENEER

2605.1 Interior use. Where used within a building, plastic veneer shall comply with the interior finish requirements of Chapter 8.

2605.2 Exterior use. Exterior plastic veneer shall be permitted to be installed on the exterior walls of buildings of any type of construction in accordance with all of the following requirements:

1. Plastic veneer shall comply with Section 2606.4.

2. Plastic veneer shall not be attached to any exterior wall to a height greater than 50 feet (15 240 mm) above grade.

3. Sections of plastic veneer shall not exceed 300 square feet (27.9 m²) in area and shall be separated by a minimum of 4 feet (1219 mm) vertically.

    Exception: The area and separation requirements and the smoke-density limitation are not applicable to plastic veneer applied to buildings constructed of Type VB construction, provided the walls are not required to have a fire-resistance rating.

SECTION 2606
LIGHT-TRANSMITTING PLASTICS

2606.1 General. The provisions of this section and Sections 2607 through 2611 shall govern the quality and methods of application of light-transmitting plastics for use as light-transmitting materials in buildings and structures. Foam plastics shall comply with Section 2603. Light-transmitting plastic materials that meet the other code requirements for walls and roofs shall be permitted to be used in accordance with the other applicable chapters of the code.

2606.2 Approval for use. Sufficient technical data shall be submitted to substantiate the proposed use of any light-transmitting material, as approved by the code enforcement official and subject to the requirements of this section.

2606.3 Identification. Each unit or package of light-transmitting plastic shall be identified with a mark or decal satisfactory to the code enforcement official, which includes identification as to the material classification.

2606.4 Specifications. Light-transmitting plastics, including thermoplastic, thermosetting or reinforced thermosetting plastic material, shall have a self-ignition temperature of 650°F (343°C) or greater where tested in accordance with ASTM D 1929; a smoke-developed index not greater than 450 where tested in the manner intended for use in accordance with ASTM E 84, or not greater than 75 where tested in the thickness intended for use in accordance with ASTM D 2843 and shall conform to one of the following combustibility classifications:

Class CC1: Plastic materials that have a burning extent of 1 inch (25 mm) or less where tested at a nominal thickness of 0.060 inch (1.5 mm), or in the thickness intended for use, in accordance with ASTM D 635,

Class CC2: Plastic materials that have a burning rate of 2.5 inches per minute (1.06 mm/s) or less where tested at a

nominal thickness of 0.060 inch (1.5 mm), or in the thickness intended for use, in accordance with ASTM D 635.

2606.5 Structural requirements. Light-transmitting plastic materials in their assembly shall be of adequate strength and durability to withstand the loads indicated in Chapter 16. Technical data shall be submitted to establish stresses, maximum unsupported spans and such other information for the various thicknesses and forms used as deemed necessary by the code enforcement official.

2606.6 Fastening. Fastening shall be adequate to withstand the loads in Chapter 16. Proper allowance shall be made for expansion and contraction of light-transmitting plastic materials in accordance with accepted data on the coefficient of expansion of the material and other material in conjunction with which it is employed.

2606.7 Light-diffusing systems. Unless the building is equipped throughout with an automatic sprinkler system in accordance with Section 903.3.1.1, light-diffusing systems shall not be installed in the following occupancies and locations:

1. Group A with an occupant load of 1,000 or more.

2. Theaters with a stage and proscenium opening and an occupant load of 700 or more.

3. Group I-2.

4. Group I-3.

5. Exit stairways and exit passageways.

2606.7.1 Support. Light-transmitting plastic diffusers shall be supported directly or indirectly from ceiling or roof construction by use of noncombustible hangers. Hangers shall be at least No. 12 steel-wire gage (0.106 inch) galvanized wire or equivalent.

2606.7.2 Installation. Light-transmitting plastic diffusers shall comply with Chapter 8 unless the light-transmitting plastic diffusers will fall from the mountings before igniting, at an ambient temperature of at least 200°F (111°C) below the ignition temperature of the panels. The panels shall remain in place at an ambient room temperature of 175°F (79°C) for a period of not less than 15 minutes.

2606.7.3 Size limitations. Individual panels or units shall not exceed 10 feet (3048 mm) in length nor 30 square feet (2.79 m²) in area.

2606.7.4 Fire suppression system. In buildings that are equipped throughout with an automatic sprinkler system in accordance with Section 903.3.1.1, plastic light-diffusing systems shall be protected both above and below unless the sprinkler system has been specifically approved for installation only above the light-diffusing system. Areas of light-diffusing systems that are protected in accordance with this section shall not be limited.

2606.7.5 Electrical luminaires. Light-transmitting plastic panels and light-diffuser panels that are installed in approved electrical luminaires shall comply with the requirements of Chapter 8 unless the light-transmitting plastic panels conform to the requirements of Section 2606.7.2. The area of approved light-transmitting plastic materials that are used in required exits or corridors shall not exceed 30 percent of the aggregate area of the ceiling in which such panels are installed, unless the building is equipped throughout with an automatic sprinkler system in accordance with Section 903.3.1.1.

2606.8 Partitions. Light-transmitting plastics used in or as partitions shall comply with the requirements of Chapters 6 and 8.

2606.9 Bathroom accessories. Light-transmitting plastics shall be permitted as glazing in shower stalls, shower doors, bathtub enclosures and similar accessory units. Safety glazing shall be provided in accordance with Chapter 24.

2606.10 Awnings, patio covers and similar structures. Awnings constructed of light-transmitting plastics shall be constructed in accordance with the provisions specified in Section 3105 and Chapter 32 for projections. Patio covers constructed of light-transmitting plastics shall comply with Section 2606. Light-transmitting plastics used in canopies at motor fuel-dispensing facilities shall comply with Section 2606, except as modified by Section 406.5.2.

2606.11 Greenhouses. Light-transmitting plastics shall be permitted in lieu of plain glass in greenhouses.

2606.12 Solar collectors. Light-transmitting plastic covers on solar collectors having noncombustible sides and bottoms shall be permitted on buildings not over three stories in height or 9,000 square feet (836.1 m²) in total floor area, provided the light-transmitting plastic cover does not exceed 33.33 percent of the roof area for CC1 materials or 25 percent of the roof area for CC2 materials.

> **Exception:** Light-transmitting plastic covers having a thickness of 0.010 inch (0.3 mm) or less or shall be permitted to be of any plastic material provided the area of the solar collectors does not exceed 33.33 percent of the roof area.

SECTION 2607
LIGHT-TRANSMITTING PLASTIC WALL PANELS

2607.1 General. Light-transmitting plastics shall not be used as wall panels in exterior walls in occupancies in Groups A-1, A-2, H, I-2 and I-3. In other groups, light-transmitting plastics shall be permitted to be used as wall panels in exterior walls, provided that the walls are not required to have a fire-resistance rating and the installation conforms to the requirements of this section. Such panels shall be erected and anchored on a foundation, waterproofed or otherwise protected from moisture absorption and sealed with a coat of mastic or other approved waterproof coating. Light-transmitting plastic wall panels shall also comply with Section 2606.

2607.2 Installation. Exterior wall panels installed as provided for herein shall not alter the type of construction classification of the building.

2607.3 Height limitation. Light-transmitting plastics shall not be installed more than 75 feet (22 860 mm) above grade plane, except as allowed by Section 2607.5.

2607.4 Area limitation and separation. The maximum area of a single wall panel and minimum vertical and horizontal separation requirements for exterior light-transmitting plastic

wall panels shall be as provided for in Table 2607.4. The maximum percentage of wall area of any story in light-transmitting plastic wall panels shall not exceed that indicated in Table 2607.4 or the percentage of unprotected openings permitted by Section 704.8, whichever is smaller.

Exceptions:

1. In structures provided with approved flame barriers extending 30 inches (760 mm) beyond the exterior wall in the plane of the floor, a vertical separation is not required at the floor except that provided by the vertical thickness of the flame barrier projection.

2. Veneers of approved weather-resistant light-transmitting plastics used as exterior siding in buildings of Type V construction in compliance with Section 1406.

3. The area of light-transmitting plastic wall panels in exterior walls of greenhouses shall be exempt from the area limitations of Table 2607.4 but shall be limited as required for unprotected openings in accordance with Section 704.8.

2607.5 Automatic sprinkler system. Where the building is equipped throughout with an automatic sprinkler system in accordance with Section 903.3.1.1, the maximum percentage area of exterior wall in any story in light-transmitting plastic wall panels and the maximum square footage of a single area given in Table 2607.4 shall be increased 100 percent, but the area of light-transmitting plastic wall panels shall not exceed 50 percent of the wall area in any story, or the area permitted by Section 704.8 for unprotected openings, whichever is smaller. These installations shall be exempt from height limitations.

2607.6 Combinations of glazing and wall panels. Combinations of light-transmitting plastic glazing and light-transmitting plastic wall panels shall be subject to the area, height and percentage limitations and the separation requirements applicable to the class of light-transmitting plastic as prescribed for light-transmitting plastic wall panel installations.

SECTION 2608
LIGHT-TRANSMITTING PLASTIC GLAZING

2608.1 Buildings of Type VB construction. Openings in the exterior walls of buildings of Type VB construction, where not required to be protected by Section 704, shall be permitted to be glazed or equipped with light-transmitting plastic. Light-transmitting plastic glazing shall also comply with Section 2606.

2608.2 Buildings of other types of construction. Openings in the exterior walls of buildings of types of construction other than Type VB, where not required to be protected by Section 704, shall be permitted to be glazed or equipped with light-transmitting plastic in accordance with Section 2606 and all of the following:

1. The aggregate area of light-transmitting plastic glazing shall not exceed 25 percent of the area of any wall face of the story in which it is installed. The area of a single pane of glazing installed above the first story above grade plane shall not exceed 16 square feet (1.5 m²) and

TABLE 2607.4
AREA LIMITATION AND SEPARATION REQUIREMENTS FOR LIGHT-TRANSMITTING PLASTIC WALL PANELS[a]

FIRE SEPARATION DISTANCE (feet)	CLASS OF PLASTIC	MAXIMUM PERCENTAGE AREA OF EXTERIOR WALL IN PLASTIC WALL PANELS	MAXIMUM SINGLE AREA OF PLASTIC WALL PANELS (square feet)	MINIMUM SEPARATION OF PLASTIC WALL PANELS (feet)	
				Vertical	Horizontal
Less than 6	—	Not Permitted	Not Permitted	—	—
6 or more but less than 11	CC1	10	50	8	4
	CC2	Not Permitted	Not Permitted	—	—
11 or more but less than or equal to 30	CC1	25	90	6	4
	CC2	15	70	8	4
Over 30	CC1	50	Not Limited	3[b]	0
	CC2	50	100	6[b]	3

For SI: 1 foot = 304.8 mm, 1 square foot = 0.0929 m^2.

a. For combinations of plastic glazing and plastic wall panel areas permitted, see Section 2607.6.

b. For reductions in vertical separation allowed, see Section 2607.4.

the vertical dimension of a single pane shall not exceed 4 feet (1219 mm).

> **Exception:** Where an automatic sprinkler system is provided throughout in accordance with Section 903.3.1.1, the area of allowable glazing shall be increased to a maximum of 50 percent of the wall face of the story in which it is installed with no limit on the maximum dimension or area of a single pane of glazing.

2. Approved flame barriers extending 30 inches (762 mm) beyond the exterior wall in the plane of the floor, or vertical panels not less than 4 feet (1219 mm) in height, shall be installed between glazed units located in adjacent stories.

> **Exception:** Buildings equipped throughout with an automatic sprinkler system in accordance with Section 903.3.1.1.

3. Light-transmitting plastics shall not be installed more than 75 feet (22 860 mm) above grade level.

> **Exception:** Buildings equipped throughout with an automatic sprinkler system in accordance with Section 903.3.1.1.

SECTION 2609
LIGHT-TRANSMITTING PLASTIC ROOF PANELS

2609.1 General. Light-transmitting plastic roof panels shall comply with this section and Section 2606. Light-transmitting plastic roof panels shall not be installed in Groups H, I-2 and I-3. In all other groups, light-transmitting plastic roof panels shall comply with any one of the following conditions:

1. The building is equipped throughout with an automatic sprinkler system in accordance with Section 903.3.1.1.

2. The roof construction is not required to have a fire-resistance rating by Table 601.

3. The roof panels meet the requirements for roof coverings in accordance with Chapter 15.

2609.2 Separation. Individual roof panels shall be separated from each other by a distance of not less than 4 feet (1219 mm) measured in a horizontal plane.

> **Exceptions:**
>
> 1. The separation between roof panels is not required in a building equipped throughout with an automatic sprinkler system in accordance with Section 903.3.1.1.
>
> 2. The separation between roof panels is not required in low-hazard occupancy buildings complying with the conditions of Section 2609.4, Exception 2 or 3.

2609.3 Location. Where exterior wall openings are required to be protected by Section 704.8, a roof panel shall not be installed within 6 feet (1829 mm) of such exterior wall.

2609.4 Area limitations. Roof panels shall be limited in area and the aggregate area of panels shall be limited by a percentage of the floor area of the room or space sheltered in accordance with Table 2609.4.

> **Exceptions:**
>
> 1. The area limitations of Table 2609.4 shall be permitted to be increased by 100 percent in buildings equipped throughout with an automatic sprinkler system in accordance with Section 903.3.1.1.
>
> 2. Low-hazard occupancy buildings, such as swimming pool shelters, shall be exempt from the area limitations of Table 2609.4, provided that the buildings do not exceed 5,000 square feet (465 m^2) in area and have a minimum fire separation distance of 10 feet (3048 mm).
>
> 3. Greenhouses that are occupied for growing plants on a production or research basis, without public access, shall be exempt from the area limitations of Table 2609.4 provided they have a minimum fire separation distance of 4 feet (1220 mm).
>
> 4. Roof coverings over terraces and patios in occupancies in Group R-3 shall be exempt from the area limitations of Table 2609.4 and shall be permitted with light-transmitting plastics.

TABLE 2609.4
AREA LIMITATIONS FOR LIGHT-TRANSMITTING PLASTIC ROOF PANELS

CLASS OF PLASTIC	MAXIMUM AREA OF INDIVIDUAL ROOF PANELS (square feet)	MAXIMUM AGGREGATE AREA OF ROOF PANELS (percent of floor area)
CC1	300	30
CC2	100	25

For SI: 1 square foot = 0.0929 m².

SECTION 2610
LIGHT-TRANSMITTING PLASTIC SKYLIGHT GLAZING

2610.1 Light-transmitting plastic glazing of skylight assemblies. Skylight assemblies glazed with light-transmitting plastic shall conform to the provisions of this section and Section 2606. Unit skylights glazed with light-transmitting plastic shall also comply with Section 2405.5.

Exception: Skylights in which the light-transmitting plastic conforms to the required roof-covering class in accordance with Section 1505.

2610.2 Mounting. The light-transmitting plastic shall be mounted above the plane of the roof on a curb constructed in accordance with the requirements for the type of construction classification, but at least 4 inches (102 mm) above the plane of the roof. Edges of light-transmitting plastic skylights or domes shall be protected by metal or other approved noncombustible material, or the light-transmitting plastic dome or skylight shall be shown to be able to resist ignition where exposed at the edge to a flame from a Class B brand as described in ASTM E 108 or UL 790.

Exceptions:

1. Curbs shall not be required for skylights used on roofs having a minimum slope of three units vertical in 12 units horizontal (25-percent slope) in occupancies in Group R-3 and on buildings with a nonclassified roof covering.

2. The metal or noncombustible edge material is not required where nonclassified roof coverings are permitted.

2610.3 Slope. Flat or corrugated light-transmitting plastic skylights shall slope at least four units vertical in 12 units horizontal (4:12). Dome-shaped skylights shall rise above the mounting flange a minimum distance equal to 10 percent of the maximum span of the dome but not less than 3 inches (76 mm).

Exception: Skylights that pass the Class B Burning Brand Test specified in ASTM E 108 or UL 790.

2610.4 Maximum area of skylights. Each skylight shall have a maximum area within the curb of 100 square feet (9.3 m²).

Exception: The area limitation shall not apply where the building is equipped throughout with an automatic sprinkler system in accordance with Section 903.3.1.1 or the building is equipped with smoke and heat vents in accordance with Section 910.

2610.5 Aggregate area of skylights. The aggregate area of skylights shall not exceed $33^1/_3$ percent of the floor area of the room or space sheltered by the roof in which such skylights are installed where Class CC1 materials are utilized, and 25 percent where Class CC2 materials are utilized.

Exception: The aggregate area limitations of light-transmitting plastic skylights shall be increased 100 percent beyond the limitations set forth in this section where the building is equipped throughout with an automatic sprinkler system in accordance with Section 903.3.1.1 or the building is equipped with smoke and heat vents in accordance with Section 910.

2610.6 Separation. Skylights shall be separated from each other by a distance of not less than 4 feet (1219 mm) measured in a horizontal plane.

Exceptions:

1. Buildings equipped throughout with an automatic sprinkler system in accordance with Section 903.3.1.1.

2. In Group R-3, multiple skylights located above the same room or space with a combined area not exceeding the limits set forth in Section 2610.4.

2610.7 Location. Where exterior wall openings are required to be protected in accordance with Section 704, a skylight shall not be installed within 6 feet (1829 mm) of such exterior wall.

2610.8 Combinations of roof panels and skylights. Combinations of light-transmitting plastic roof panels and skylights shall be subject to the area and percentage limitations and separation requirements applicable to roof panel installations.

SECTION 2611
LIGHT-TRANSMITTING PLASTIC INTERIOR SIGNS

2611.1 General. Light-transmitting plastic interior wall signs shall be limited as specified in Sections 2611.2 through 2611.4. Light-transmitting plastic interior wall signs in covered mall buildings shall comply with Section 402.15. Light-transmitting plastic interior signs shall also comply with Section 2606.

2611.2 Aggregate area. The sign shall not exceed 20 percent of the wall area.

2611.3 Maximum area. The sign shall not exceed 24 square feet (2.23 m²).

2611.4 Encasement. Edges and backs of the sign shall be fully encased in metal.

CHAPTER 27

ELECTRICAL

SECTION 2701
GENERAL

2701.1 Scope. This chapter governs the electrical components, equipment and systems used in buildings and structures covered by this code. Electrical components, equipment and systems shall be designed and constructed in accordance with the provisions of NFPA 70.

[F] SECTION 2702
EMERGENCY AND STANDBY POWER SYSTEMS

[F] 2702.1 Installation. Emergency and standby power systems required by this code or the *Fire Code of New York State* shall be installed in accordance with this code, NFPA 110 and 111.

[F] 2702.1.1 Stationary generators. Emergency and standby power generators shall be listed in accordance with UL 2200.

[F] 2702.2 Where required. Emergency and standby power systems shall be provided where required by Sections 2702.2.1 through 2702.2.20.

[F] 2702.2.1 Group A occupancies. Emergency power shall be provided for voice communication systems in Group A occupancies in accordance with Section 907.2.1.2.

[F] 2702.2.2 Smoke control systems. Standby power shall be provided for smoke control systems in accordance with Section 909.11.

[F] 2702.2.3 Exit signs. Emergency power shall be provided for exit signs in accordance with Section 1011.5.3.

[F] 2702.2.4 Means of egress illumination. Emergency power shall be provided for means of egress illumination in accordance with Section 1006.3.

[F] 2702.2.5 Accessible means of egress elevators. Standby power shall be provided for elevators that are part of an accessible means of egress in accordance with Section 1007.4.

[F] 2702.2.6 Accessible means of egress platform lifts. Standby power in accordance with this section or ASME A18.1 shall be provided for platform lifts that are part of an accessible means of egress in accordance with Section 1007.5.

[F] 2702.2.7 Horizontal sliding doors. Standby power shall be provided for horizontal sliding doors in accordance with Section 1008.1.3.3.

[F] 2702.2.8 Semiconductor fabrication facilities. Emergency power shall be provided for semiconductor fabrication facilities in accordance with Section 415.8.10.

[F] 2702.2.9 Membrane structures. Standby power shall be provided for auxiliary inflation systems in accordance with Section 3102.8.2. Emergency power shall be provided for exit signs in temporary tents and membrane structures in accordance with the *Fire Code of New York State.*

[F] 2702.2.10 Hazardous materials. Emergency or standby power shall be provided in occupancies with hazardous materials in accordance with Section 414.5.4.

[F] 2702.2.11 Highly toxic and toxic materials. Emergency power shall be provided for occupancies with highly toxic or toxic materials in accordance with the *Fire Code of New York State.*

[F] 2702.2.12 Organic peroxides. Standby power shall be provided for occupancies with silane gas in accordance with the *Fire Code of New York State.*

[F] 2702.2.13 Pyrophoric materials. Emergency power shall be provided for occupancies with silane gas in accordance with the *Fire Code of New York State.*

[F] 2702.2.14 Covered mall buildings. Standby power shall be provided for voice/alarm communication systems in covered mall buildings in accordance with Section 402.13.

[F] 2702.2.15 High-rise buildings. Emergency and standby power shall be provided in high-rise buildings in accordance with Sections 403.10 and 403.11.

[F] 2702.2.16 Underground buildings. Emergency and standby power shall be provided in underground buildings in accordance with Sections 405.9 and 405.10.

[F] 2702.2.17 Group I-3 occupancies. Emergency power shall be provided for doors in Group I-3 occupancies in accordance with Section 408.4.2.

[F] 2702.2.18 Airport traffic control towers. Standby power shall be provided in airport traffic control towers in accordance with Section 412.1.5.

[F] 2702.2.19 Elevators. Standby power for elevators shall be provided as set forth in Section 3003.1.

[F] 2702.2.20 Smokeproof enclosures. Standby power shall be provided for smokeproof enclosures as required by Section 909.20.

[F] 2702.3 Maintenance. Emergency and standby power systems shall be maintained and tested in accordance with the *Fire Code of New York State.*

CHAPTER 28

MECHANICAL SYSTEMS

SECTION 2801
GENERAL

2801.1 Scope. Mechanical appliances, equipment and systems shall be constructed, installed and maintained in accordance with the *Mechanical Code of New York State* and the *Fuel Gas Code of New York State*. Masonry chimneys, fireplaces and barbecues shall comply with the *Mechanical Code of New York State* and Chapter 21 of this code.

CHAPTER 29

PLUMBING SYSTEMS

SECTION 2901
GENERAL

[P] 2901.1 Scope. The provisions of this chapter and the *Plumbing Code of New York State* shall govern the erection, installation, alteration, repairs, relocation, replacement, addition to, use or maintenance of plumbing equipment and systems. Plumbing systems and equipment shall be constructed, installed and maintained in accordance with the *Plumbing Code of New York State*.

SECTION 2902
MINIMUM PLUMBING FACILITIES

[P] 2902.1 Minimum number of fixtures. Plumbing fixtures shall be provided for the type of occupancy and in the minimum number shown in Table 2902.1 Types of occupancies not shown in Table 2902.1 shall be considered individually by the code enforcement official. The number of occupants shall be determined by this code. Occupancy classification shall be determined in accordance with Chapter 3.

[P] TABLE 2902.1
MINIMUM NUMBER OF REQUIRED PLUMBING FIXTURES[a] (See Sections 2902.2 and 2902.3)

NO.	CLASSIFICATION	OCCUPANCY	DESCRIPTION	WATER CLOSETS (URINALS SEE SECTION 419.2 OF THE PLUMBING CODE OF NEW YORK STATE) MALE	FEMALE	LAVATORIES MALE	FEMALE	BATHTUBS/ SHOWERS	DRINKING FOUNTAINS (SEE SECTION 410.1 OF THE PLUMBING CODE OF NEW YORK STATE)	OTHER[f]
1	Assembly (see Sections 2902.2, 2902.4 and 2902.4.1)	A-1[d]	Theaters and other buildings for the performing arts and motion pictures	1 per 125	1 per 65	1 per 200	1 per 200	—	1 per 500	1 service sink
		A-2[d]	Nightclubs, bars, taverns, dance halls and buildings for similar purposes	1 per 40	1 per 40	1 per 75	1 per 75	—	1 per 500	1 service sink
			Restaurants, banquet halls and food courts	1 per 75	1 per 75	1 per 200	1 per 200	—	1 per 500	1 service sink
		A-3[d]	Auditoriums without permanent seating, art galleries, exhibition halls, museums, lecture halls, libraries, arcades and gymnasiums	1 per 125	1 per 65	1 per 200	1 per 200	—	1 per 500	1 service sink
			Passenger terminals and transportation facilities	1 per 500	1 per 500	1 per 750	1 per 750	—	1 per 1,000	1 service sink
			Places of worship and other religious services[e].	1 per 150	1 per 75	1 per 200	1 per 200	—	1 per 1,000	1 service sink
		A-4	Coliseums, arenas, skating rinks, pools and tennis courts for indoor sporting events and activities	1 per 75 for the first 1,500 and 1 per 120 for the remainder exceeding 1,500	1 per 40 for the first 1,500 and 1 per 60 for the remainder exceeding 1,500	1 per 200	1 per 150	—	1 per 1,000	1 service sink
		A-5	Stadiums, amusement parks, bleachers and grandstands for outdoor sporting events and activities	1 per 75 for the first 1,500 and 1 per 120 for the remainder exceeding 1,500	1 per 40 for the first 1,500 and 1 per 60 for the remainder exceeding 1,500	1 per 200	1 per 150	—	1 per 1,000	1 service sink

(continued)

[P] TABLE 2902.1—continued
MINIMUM NUMBER OF REQUIRED PLUMBING FIXTURES[a]

| NO. | CLASSIFICATION | OCCUPANCY | DESCRIPTION | WATER CLOSETS (URINALS SEE SECTION 419.2 OF THE *PLUMBING CODE OF NEW YORK STATE*) | | LAVATORIES | | BATHTUBS/ SHOWERS | DRINKING FOUNTAINS (SEE SECTION 410.1 OF THE *PLUMBING CODE OF NEW YORK STATE*) | OTHER[f] |
				MALE	FEMALE	MALE	FEMALE			
2	Business (see Sections 2902.2, 2902.4 and 2902.4.1)	B	Buildings for the transaction of business, professional services, other services involving merchandise, office buildings, banks, light industrial and similar uses	1 per 25 for the first 50 and 1 per 50 for the remainder exceeding 50	1 per 25 for the first 50 and 1 per 50 for the remainder exceeding 50	1 per 40 for the first 80 and 1 per 80 for the remainder exceeding 80	1 per 40 for the first 80 and 1 per 80 for the remainder exceeding 80	—	1 per 100	1 service sink
3	Educational	E	Educational facilities	1 per 50	1 per 50	1 per 50	1 per 50	—	1 per 100	1 service sink
4	Factory and industrial	F-1 and F-2	Structures in which occupants are engaged in work fabricating, assembling or processing of products or materials	1 per 100	1 per 100	1 per 100	1 per 100	See Section 411 of the *Plumbing Code of New York State*	1 per 400	1 service sink
5	Institutional	I-1	Residential care	1 per 10	1 per 10	1 per 10	1 per 10	1 per 8	1 per 100	1 service sink
		I-2	Hospitals, ambulatory nursing home patients[b]	1 per room[c]	1 per room[c]	1 per room[c]	1 per room[c]	1 per 15	1 per 100	1 service sink per floor
			Employees, other than residential care[b]	1 per 25	1 per 25	1 per 35	1 per 35	—	1 per 100	—
			Visitors, other than residential care	1 per 75	1 per 75	1 per 100	1 per 100	—	1 per 500	—
		I-3	Prisons[b]	1 per cell	1 per cell	1 per cell	1 per cell	1 per 15	1 per 100	1 service sink
		I-3	Reformatories, detention centers and correctional centers[b]	1 per 15	1 per 15	1 per 15	1 per 15	1 per 15	1 per 100	1 service sink
		I-4	Adult day care and child care	1 per 15	1 per 15	1 per 15	1 per 15	—	1 per 100	1 service sink
6	Mercantile (see Sections 2902.2, 2902.4, 2902.4.1 and 2902.4.2)	M	Retail stores, service stations, shops, salesrooms, markets and shopping centers	1 per 500	1 per 500	1 per 750	1 per 750	—	1 per 1,000	1 service sink
7	Residential	R-1	Hotels, motels, boarding houses (transient)	1 per sleeping unit	1 per sleeping unit	1 per sleeping unit	1 per sleeping unit	1 per sleeping unit	—	1 service sink
		R-2	Dormitories, fraternities, sororities and boarding house (not transient)	1 per 10	1 per 10	1 per 10	1 per 10	1 per 8	1 per 100	1 service sink
		R-2	Apartment house	1 per dwelling unit	1 per dwelling unit	1 per dwelling unit	1 per dwelling unit	1 per dwelling unit	—	1 kitchen sink per dwelling unit; 1 automatic clothes washer connection per 20 dwelling units

(continued)

[P] TABLE 2902.1—continued
MINIMUM NUMBER OF REQUIRED PLUMBING FIXTURES[a]

| NO. | CLASSIFICATION | OCCUPANCY | DESCRIPTION | WATER CLOSETS (URINALS SEE SECTION 419.2 OF THE *PLUMBING CODE OF NEW YORK STATE*) | | LAVATORIES | | BATHTUBS/ SHOWERS | DRINKING FOUNTAINS (SEE SECTION 410.1 OF THE *PLUMBING CODE OF NEW YORK STATE*) | OTHER[f] |
				MALE	FEMALE	MALE	FEMALE			
7	Residential	R-3	One- and two-family dwellings	1 per dwelling unit	1 per dwelling unit	1 per dwelling unit	1 per dwelling unit	1 per dwelling unit	—	1 kitchen sink per dwelling unit; 1 automatic clothes washer connection per dwelling unit
		R-4	Residential care/ assisted living facilities	1 per 10	1 per 10	1 per 10	1 per 10	1 per 8	1 per 100	1 service sink
8	Storage (see Sections 2902.2, 2902.4 and 2902.4.1)	S-1 S-2	Structures for the storage of goods, warehouses, storehouses and freight depots, low and moderate hazard	1 per 100	1 per 100	1 per 100	1 per 100	See Section 411 of the *Plumbing Code of New York State*	1 per 1,000	1 service sink

a. The fixtures shown are based on one fixture being the minimum required for the number of persons indicated or any fraction of the number of persons indicated. The number of occupants shall be determined by this code.

b. Toilet facilities for employees shall be separate from facilities for inmates or patients.

c. A single-occupant toilet room with one water closet and one lavatory serving not more than two adjacent patient sleeping units shall be permitted where such room is provided with direct access from each patient room and with provisions for privacy.

d. The occupant load for seasonal outdoor seating and entertainment areas shall be included when determining the minimum number of facilities required.

e. Fixtures located in adjacent buildings under the ownership or control of the church or other place of worship shall be made available during periods the church or other place of worship is occupied.

f. See *Plumbing Code of New York State* for exceptions.

[P] 2902.1.1 Unisex toilet and bath fixtures. Fixtures located within unisex toilet bathing rooms complying with Chapter 11 of this Code are permitted to be included in determining the minimum required number of fixtures for assembly and mercantile occupancies.

[P] 2902.2 Separate facilities. Where plumbing fixtures are required, separate facilities shall be provided for each sex.

Exceptions:

1. Separate facilities shall not be required for dwelling units and sleeping units.

2. Separate facilities shall not be required in structures or tenant spaces with a total occupant load, including both employees and customers, of 15 or less.

3. Separate facilities shall not be required in mercantile occupancies in which the maximum occupant load is 50 or less.

[P] 2902.3 Number of occupants of each sex. The occupant load shall be composed of 50 percent of each sex.

[P] 2902.4 Required public toilet facilities. Customers, patrons and visitors shall be provided with public toilet facilities in structures and tenant spaces intended for public utilization. The accessible route to public facilities shall not pass through kitchens, storage rooms, closets or similar spaces. Employees shall be provided with toilet facilities in all occu-

pancies. Employee toilet facilities shall be either separate or combined employee and public toilet facilities.

[P] 2902.4.1 Location of toilet facilities in occupancies other than covered malls. In occupancies other than covered malls, the required public and employee toilet facilities shall be located not more than one story above or below the space required to be provided with toilet facilities and the path of travel to such facilities shall not exceed a distance of 500 feet (152 m).

Exception: The location and maximum travel distances to required employee facilities in factory and industrial occupancies are permitted to exceed that required by this section, provided that the location and maximum travel distance are approved.

[P] 2902.4.2 Location of toilet facilities in covered malls. In covered mall buildings, the required public and employee toilet facilities shall be located not more than one story above or below the space required to be provided with toilet facilities, and the path of travel to such facilities shall not exceed a distance of 300 feet (91 440 mm). In covered mall buildings, the required facilities shall be based on total square footage, and facilities shall be installed in each individual store or in a central toilet area located in accordance with this section. The maximum travel distance to the central toilet facilities in covered mall buildings shall be measured from the main entrance of any store or tenant space. In covered mall buildings, where employees' toilet facilities are not provided in the individual store, the maximum travel distance shall be measured from the employees' work area of the store or tenant space.

[P] 2902.4.3 Pay facilities. Where pay facilities are installed, such facilities shall be in excess of the required minimum facilities. Required facilities shall be free of charge.

[P] 2902.5 Signage. A legible sign designating the sex shall be provided in a readily visible location near the entrance to each toilet facility. Signs for accessible toilet facilities shall comply with ICC/ANSI A117.1.

CHAPTER 30

ELEVATORS AND CONVEYING SYSTEMS

SECTION 3001
GENERAL

3001.1 Scope. This chapter governs the design, construction, installation, alteration and repair of elevators and conveying systems and their components.

3001.2 Referenced standards. Except as otherwise provided for in this code, the design, construction, installation, alteration, repair and maintenance of elevators and conveying systems and their components shall conform to ASME A17.1, ASME 18.1, ASME A90.1, ASME B20.1, ALI ALCTV, and ASCE 24 for construction in flood hazard areas established in Section 1612.3. Frequency of tests and inspections of equipment shall be in accordance with Appendix N, Table-1 of ASME A17.1 and the requirements of the other standards as applicable.

3001.3 Accessibility. Passenger elevators required to be accessible by Chapter 11 shall conform to ICC/ANSI A117.1.

3001.4 Change in use. A change in use of an elevator from freight to passenger, passenger to freight, or from one freight class to another freight class shall comply with Part 8, Section 8.7 of ASME A17.1.

SECTION 3002
HOISTWAY ENCLOSURES

3002.1 Hoistway enclosure protection. Elevator, dumbwaiter and other hoistway enclosures shall be shaft enclosures complying with Section 707.

3002.1.1 Opening protectives. Openings in hoistway enclosures shall be protected as required in Chapter 7.

Exception: The elevator car doors and the associated hoistway enclosure doors at the floor level designated for recall in accordance with Section 3003.2 shall be permitted to remain open during Phase I Emergency Recall Operation.

3002.1.2 Hardware. Hardware on opening protectives shall be of an approved type installed as tested, except that approved interlocks, mechanical locks and electric contacts, door and gate electric contacts and door-operating mechanisms shall be exempt from the fire test requirements.

3002.2 Number of elevator cars in a hoistway. Where four or more elevator cars serve all or the same portion of a building, the elevators shall be located in at least two separate hoistways. Not more than four elevator cars shall be located in any single hoistway enclosure.

3002.3 Emergency signs. An approved pictorial sign of a standardized design shall be posted adjacent to each elevator call station on all floors instructing occupants to use the exit stairways and not to use the elevators in case of fire. The sign shall read: IN FIRE EMERGENCY, DO NOT USE ELEVA-TOR. USE EXIT STAIRS. The emergency sign shall not be required for elevators that are part of an accessible means of egress complying with Section 1007.4.

3002.4 Elevator car to accommodate ambulance stretcher. Where elevators are provided in buildings four or more stories above grade plane or four or more stories below grade plane, at least one elevator shall be provided for fire department emergency access to all floors. The elevator car shall be of such a size and arrangement to accommodate an ambulance stretcher 24-inch by 84-inch (610 mm by 2134 mm), with not less than 5-inch (127 mm) radius corners in the horizontal, open position and shall be identified by the international symbol for emergency medical services (star of life). The symbol shall not be less than 3 inches (76 mm) high and shall be placed inside on both sides of the hoistway door frame.

3002.5 Emergency doors. Where an elevator is installed in a single blind hoistway or on the outside of a building, there shall be installed in the blind portion of the hoistway or blank face of the building, an emergency door in accordance with ASME A17.1.

3002.6 Prohibited doors. Doors, other than hoistway doors and the elevator car door, shall be prohibited at the point of access to an elevator car unless such doors are readily openable from the car side without a key, tool, special knowledge or effort.

3002.7 Common enclosure with stairway. Elevators shall not be in a common shaft enclosure with a stairway.

3002.8 Glass in elevator enclosures. Glass in elevator enclosures shall comply with Section 2409.1.

[F] SECTION 3003
EMERGENCY OPERATIONS

[F] 3003.1 Standby power. In buildings and structures where standby power is required or furnished to operate an elevator, the operation shall be in accordance with Sections 3003.1.1 through 3003.1.4.

[F] 3003.1.1 Manual transfer. Standby power shall be manually transferable to all elevators in each bank.

[F] 3003.1.2 One elevator. Where only one elevator is installed, the elevator shall automatically transfer to standby power within 60 seconds after failure of normal power.

[F] 3003.1.3 Two or more elevators. Where two or more elevators are controlled by a common operating system, all elevators shall automatically transfer to standby power within 60 seconds after failure of normal power where the standby power source is of sufficient capacity to operate all elevators at the same time. Where the standby power source is not of sufficient capacity to operate all elevators at the same time, all elevators shall transfer to standby power in sequence, return to the designated landing and disconnect from the standby power source. After all elevators have been returned to the designated level, at least one elevator shall remain operable from the standby power source.

[F] 3003.1.4 Venting. Where standby power is connected to elevators, the machine room ventilation or air conditioning shall be connected to the standby power source.

[F] 3003.2 Fire-fighters' emergency operation. Elevators shall be provided with Phase I emergency recall operation and Phase II emergency in-car operation in accordance with ASME A17.1.

SECTION 3004
HOISTWAY VENTING

3004.1 Vents required. Hoistways of elevators and dumbwaiters penetrating more than three stories shall be provided with a means for venting smoke and hot gases to the outer air in case of fire.

Exceptions:

1. In occupancies of other than Groups R-1, R-2, I-1, I-2 and similar occupancies with overnight sleeping quarters, venting of hoistways is not required where the building is equipped throughout with an approved automatic sprinkler system installed in accordance with Section 903.3.1.1 or 903.3.1.2.

2. Sidewalk elevator hoistways are not required to be vented.

3004.2 Location of vents. Vents shall be located at the top of the hoistway and shall open either directly to the outer air or through noncombustible ducts to the outer air. Noncombustible ducts shall be permitted to pass through the elevator machine room, provided that portions of the ducts located outside the hoistway or machine room are enclosed by construction having not less than the fire protection rating required for the hoistway. Holes in the machine room floors for the passage of ropes, cables or other moving elevator equipment shall be limited so as not to provide greater than 2 inches (51 mm) of clearance on all sides.

3004.3 Area of vents. Except as provided for in Section 3004.3.1, the area of the vents shall not be less than $3^{1}/_{2}$ percent of the area of the hoistway nor less than 3 square feet (0.28 m²) for each elevator car, and not less than $3^{1}/_{2}$ percent nor less than 0.5 square feet (0.047 m²) for each dumbwaiter car in the hoistway, whichever is greater. Of the total required vent area, not less than one-third shall be permanently open. Closed portions of the required vent area shall consist of openings glazed with annealed glass not greater than 0.125 inch (3.2 mm) in thickness.

Exception: The total required vent area shall not be required to be permanently open where all the vent openings automatically open upon detection of smoke in the elevator lobbies or hoistway, upon power failure and upon activation of a manual override control.

3004.3.1 Reduced vent area. Where mechanical ventilation conforming to the *Mechanical Code of New York*

State is provided, a reduction in the required vent area is allowed provided that all of the following conditions are met:

1. The occupancy is not in Group R-1, R-2, I-1 or I-2 or of a similar occupancy with overnight sleeping quarters.

2. The vents required by Section 3004.2 do not have outside exposure.

3. The hoistway does not extend to the top of the building.

4. The hoistway and machine room exhaust fan is automatically reactivated by thermostatic means.

5. Equivalent venting of the hoistway is accomplished.

3004.4 Plumbing and mechanical systems. Plumbing and mechanical systems shall not be located in an elevator shaft.

Exception: Floor drains, sumps and sump pumps shall be permitted at the base of the shaft provided they are indirectly connected to the plumbing system.

SECTION 3005
CONVEYING SYSTEMS AND LIFTS

3005.1 General. Escalators, moving walks, conveyors, and lifts shall comply with the provisions of this section.

3005.2 Escalators and moving walks. Escalators and moving walks shall comply with ASME A17.1 and shall be constructed of approved noncombustible and fire-retardant materials. This requirement shall not apply to electrical equipment, wiring, wheels, handrails and the use of $^{1}/_{28}$-inch (0.9 mm) wood veneers on balustrades backed up with noncombustible materials.

3005.2.1 Enclosure. Escalator floor openings shall be enclosed with shaft enclosures complying with Section 707.

3005.2.2 Escalators. Where provided in below-grade transportation stations, escalators shall have a clear width of 32 inches (815 mm) minimum.

Exception: The clear width is not required in existing facilities undergoing alterations.

3005.3 Platform lifts and stairway lifts. Platform lifts and stairway lifts shall comply with ASME A18.1.

3005.4 Belt manlifts. Belt manlifts shall comply with ASME A90.1.

3005.5 Conveyors. Conveyors and related eqipment shall comply with ASME B20.1.

3005.5.1 Enclosure. Conveyors and related equipment connecting successive floors or levels shall be enclosed with fire barrier walls and approved opening protectives complying with the requirements of Section 3002 and Chapter 7.

3005.5.2 Conveyor safeties. Power-operated conveyors, belts and other material-moving devices shall be equipped with automatic limit switches which will shut off the power in an emergency and automatically stop all operation of the device.

SECTION 3006
MACHINE ROOMS AND MACHINERY SPACES

3006.1 Access. An approved means of access shall be provided to elevator machine rooms and machinery spaces.

3006.2 Venting. Elevator machine rooms that contain solid-state equipment for elevator operation shall be provided with an independent ventilation or air-conditioning system to protect against the overheating of the electrical equipment. The system shall be capable of maintaining temperatures within the range established for the elevator equipment.

3006.3 Pressurization. The elevator machine room serving a pressurized elevator hoistway shall be pressurized upon activation of a heat or smoke detector located in the elevator machine room.

3006.4 Machine rooms and machinery spaces. Elevator machine rooms and machinery spaces shall be enclosed with fire barriers complying with Section 706 or horizontal assemblies complying with Section 711 having a fire-resistance rating not less than the required rating of the hoistway enclosure served by the machinery. Openings shall be protected with assemblies having a fire-protection rating not less than that required for the hoistway enclosure doors.

3006.5 Shunt trip. Where elevator hoistways or elevator machine rooms containing elevator control equipment are protected with automatic sprinklers, a means installed in accordance with NFPA 72, Section 6.15.4, Elevator Shutdown, shall be provided to disconnect automatically the main line power supply to the affected elevator prior to the application of water. This means shall not be self-resetting. The activation of sprinklers outside the hoistway or machine room shall not disconnect the main line power supply.

3006.6 Plumbing systems. Plumbing systems shall not be located in elevator equipment rooms.

CHAPTER 31

SPECIAL CONSTRUCTION

SECTION 3101
GENERAL

3101.1 Scope. The provisions of this chapter shall govern special building construction including membrane structures, temporary structures, pedestrian walkways and tunnels, awnings and canopies, marquees, signs, and towers and antennas.

SECTION 3102
MEMBRANE STRUCTURES

3102.1 General. The provisions of this section shall apply to air-supported, air-inflated, membrane-covered cable and membrane-covered frame structures, collectively known as membrane structures, erected for a period of 180 days or longer. Those erected for a shorter period of time shall comply with the *Fire Code of New York State*. Membrane structures covering water storage facilities, water clarifiers, water treatment plants, sewage treatment plants, greenhouses and similar facilities not used for human occupancy, are required to meet only the requirements of Sections 3102.3.1 and 3102.7.

3102.2 Definitions. The following words and terms shall, for the purposes of this section and as used elsewhere in this code, have the meanings shown herein:

AIR-INFLATED STRUCTURE. A building where the shape of the structure is maintained by air pressurization of cells or tubes to form a barrel vault over the usable area. Occupants of such a structure do not occupy the pressurized area used to support the structure.

AIR-SUPPORTED STRUCTURE. A building wherein the shape of the structure is attained by air pressure and occupants of the structure are within the elevated pressure area. Air-supported structures are of two basic types:

Double skin. Similar to a single skin, but with an attached liner that is separated from the outer skin and provides an airspace which serves for insulation, acoustic, aesthetic or similar purposes.

Single skin. Where there is only the single outer skin and the air pressure is directly against that skin.

CABLE-RESTRAINED, AIR-SUPPORTED STRUCTURE. A structure in which the uplift is resisted by cables or webbings which are anchored to either foundations or dead men. Reinforcing cable or webbing is attached by various methods to the membrane or is an integral part of the membrane. This is not a cable-supported structure.

MEMBRANE-COVERED CABLE STRUCTURE. A nonpressurized structure in which a mast and cable system provides support and tension to the membrane weather barrier and the membrane imparts stability to the structure.

MEMBRANE-COVERED FRAME STRUCTURE. A nonpressurized building wherein the structure is composed of a rigid framework to support a tensioned membrane which provides the weather barrier.

NONCOMBUSTIBLE MEMBRANE STRUCTURE. A membrane structure in which the membrane and all component parts of the structure are noncombustible.

3102.3 Type of construction. Noncombustible membrane structures shall be classified as Type IIB construction. Noncombustible frame or cable-supported structures covered by an approved membrane in accordance with Section 3102.3.1 shall be classified as Type IIB construction. Heavy timber frame-supported structures covered by an approved membrane in accordance with Section 3102.3.1 shall be classified as Type IV construction. Other membrane structures shall be classified as Type V construction.

> **Exception:** Plastic less than 30 feet (9144 mm) above any floor used in greenhouses, where occupancy by the general public is not authorized, and for aquaculture pond covers is not required to meet the fire propagation performance criteria of NFPA 701.

3102.3.1 Membrane and interior liner material. Membranes and interior liners shall be either noncombustible as set forth in Section 703.4 or meet the fire propagation performance criteria of NFPA 701 and the manufacturer's test protocol.

> **Exception:** Plastic less than 20 mil (0.5 mm) in thickness used in greenhouses, where occupancy by the general public is not authorized, and for aquaculture pond covers is not required to meet the fire propagation performance criteria of NFPA 701.

3102.4 Allowable floor areas. The area of a membrane structure shall not exceed the limitations set forth in Table 503, except as provided in Section 506.

3102.5 Maximum height. Membrane structures shall not exceed one story nor shall such structures exceed the height limitations in feet set forth in Table 503.

> **Exception:** Noncombustible membrane structures serving as roofs only.

3102.6 Mixed construction. Membrane structures shall be permitted to be utilized as specified in this section as a portion of buildings of other types of construction. Height and area limits shall be as specified for the type of construction and occupancy of the building.

3102.6.1 Noncombustible membrane. A noncombustible membrane shall be permitted for use as the roof or as a skylight of any building or atrium of a building of any type of construction provided it is at least 20 feet (6096 mm) above any floor, balcony or gallery.

3102.6.1.1 Membrane. A membrane meeting the fire propagation performance criteria of NFPA 701 shall be permitted to be used as the roof or as a skylight on buildings of Type IIB, III, IV and V construction, provided it is at least 20 feet (6096 mm) above any floor, balcony or gallery.

3102.7 Engineering design. The structure shall be designed and constructed to sustain dead loads; loads due to tension or inflation; live loads including wind, snow or flood and seismic loads and in accordance with Chapter 16.

3102.8 Inflation systems. Air-supported and air-inflated structures shall be provided with primary and auxiliary inflation systems to meet the minimum requirements of Sections 3102.8.1 through 3102.8.3.

3102.8.1 Equipment requirements. This inflation system shall consist of one or more blowers and shall include provisions for automatic control to maintain the required inflation pressures. The system shall be so designed as to prevent overpressurization of the system.

3102.8.1.1 Auxiliary inflation system. In addition to the primary inflation system, in buildings exceeding 1,500 square feet (140 m^2) in area, an auxiliary inflation system shall be provided with sufficient capacity to maintain the inflation of the structure in case of primary system failure. The auxiliary inflation system shall operate automatically when there is a loss of internal pressure and when the primary blower system becomes inoperative.

3102.8.1.2 Blower equipment. Blower equipment shall meet the following requirements:

1. Blowers shall be powered by continuous-rated motors at the maximum power required for any flow condition as required by the structural design.

2. Blowers shall be provided with inlet screens, belt guards and other protective devices as required by the code enforcement official to provide protection from injury.

3. Blowers shall be housed within a weather-protecting structure.

4. Blowers shall be equipped with backdraft check dampers to minimize air loss when inoperative.

5. Blower inlets shall be located to provide protection from air contamination. The location of inlets shall be approved.

3102.8.2 Standby power. Wherever an auxiliary inflation system is required, an approved standby power-generating system shall be provided. The system shall be equipped with a suitable means for automatically starting the generator set upon failure of the normal electrical service and for automatic transfer and operation of all of the required electrical functions at full power within 60 seconds of such service failure. Standby power shall be capable of operating independently for a minimum of 4 hours.

3102.8.3 Support provisions. A system capable of supporting the membrane in the event of deflation shall be provided for in air-supported and air-inflated structures having an occupant load of 50 or more or where covering a swimming pool regardless of occupant load. The support

system shall be capable of maintaining membrane structures used as a roof for Type I construction not less than 20 feet (6096 mm) above floor or seating areas. The support system shall be capable of maintaining other membranes at least 7 feet (2134 mm) above the floor, seating area or surface of the water.

SECTION 3103
TEMPORARY STRUCTURES

3103.1 General. The provisions of this section shall apply to structures erected for a period of less than 180 days. Tents and other membrane structures erected for a period of less than 180 days shall comply with the *Fire Code of New York State*. Those erected for a longer period of time shall comply with applicable sections of this code.

3103.1.1 Permit required. Temporary structures that cover an area in excess of 120 square feet (11.16 m^2), including connecting areas or spaces with a common means of egress or entrance which are used or intended to be used for the gathering together of 10 or more persons, shall not be erected, operated or maintained for any purpose without obtaining a permit from the code enforcement official.

3103.2 Construction documents. A permit application and construction documents shall be submitted for each installation of a temporary structure. The construction documents shall include a site plan indicating the location of the temporary structure and information delineating the means of egress and the occupant load.

3103.3 Location. Temporary structures shall be located in accordance with the requirements of Table 602 based on the fire-resistance rating of the exterior walls for the proposed type of construction.

3103.4 Means of egress. Temporary structures shall conform to the means of egress requirements of Chapter 10 and shall have a maximum exit access travel distance of 100 feet (30 480 mm).

SECTION 3104
PEDESTRIAN WALKWAYS AND TUNNELS

3104.1 General. This section shall apply to connections between buildings such as pedestrian walkways or tunnels, located at, above or below grade level, that are used as a means of travel by persons. The pedestrian walkway shall not contribute to the building area or the number of stories or height of connected buildings.

3104.2 Separate structures. Connected buildings shall be considered to be separate structures.

Exceptions:

1. Buildings on the same lot in accordance with Section 503.1.2.

2. For purposes of calculating the number of Type B units required by Chapter 11, structurally connected buildings and buildings with multiple wings shall be considered one structure.

3104.3 Construction. The pedestrian walkway shall be of noncombustible construction.

Exceptions:

1. Combustible construction shall be permitted where connected buildings are of combustible construction.

2. Fire-retardant-treated wood, in accordance with Section 603.1, Item 1.3 shall be permitted for the roof construction of the pedestrian walkway where connected buildings are a minimum of Type I or II construction.

3104.4 Contents. Only materials and decorations approved by the code enforcement official shall be located in the pedestrian walkway.

3104.5 Fire barriers between pedestrian walkways and buildings. Walkways shall be separated from the interior of the building by fire-barrier walls with a fire-resistance rating of not less than 2 hours. This protection shall extend vertically from a point 10 feet (3048 mm) above the walkway roof surface or the connected building roof line, whichever is lower, down to a point 10 feet (3048 mm) below the walkway and horizontally 10 feet (3048 mm) from each side of the pedestrian walkway. Openings within the 10-foot (3048 mm) horizontal extension of the protected walls beyond the walkway shall be equipped with devices providing a $^3/_4$-hour fire protection rating in accordance with Section 715.

Exception: The walls separating the pedestrian walkway from a connected building are not required to have a fire-resistance rating by this section where any of the following conditions exist:

1. The distance between the connected buildings is more than 10 feet (3048 mm), the pedestrian walkway and connected buildings, except for open parking garages, are equipped throughout with an automatic sprinkler system in accordance with NFPA 13 and the wall is constructed of a tempered, wired or laminated glass wall and doors subject to the following:

    1.1. The glass shall be protected by an automatic sprinkler system in accordance with NFPA 13 and the sprinkler system shall completely wet the entire surface of interior sides of the glass wall when actuated.

    1.2. The glass shall be in a gasketed frame and installed in such a manner that the framing system will deflect without breaking (loading) the glass before the sprinkler operates.

    1.3. Obstructions shall not be installed between the sprinkler heads and the glass.

2. The distance between the connected buildings is more than 10 feet (3048 mm) and both sidewalls of the pedestrian walkway are at least 50 percent open with the open area uniformly distributed to prevent the accumulation of smoke and toxic gases.

3. Buildings are on the same lot in accordance with Section 503.1.2.

4. Where exterior walls of connected buildings are required by Section 704 to have a fire-resistance rating greater than 2 hours, the walkway shall be equipped throughout with an automatic sprinkler system installed in accordance with NFPA 13.

The previous exceptions shall apply to pedestrian walkways having a maximum height above grade of three stories or 40 feet (12 192 mm), or five stories or 55 feet (16 764 mm) where sprinklered.

3104.6 Public way. Pedestrian walkways over a public way shall also comply with Chapter 32.

3104.7 Egress. Access shall be provided at all times to a pedestrian walkway that serves as a required exit.

3104.8 Width. The unobstructed width of pedestrian walkways shall not be less than 36 inches (914 mm). The total width shall not exceed 30 feet (9144 mm).

3104.9 Exit access travel. The length of exit access travel shall not exceed 200 feet (60 960 mm).

Exceptions:

1. Exit access travel distance on a pedestrian walkway equipped throughout with an automatic sprinkler system in accordance with NFPA 13 shall not exceed 250 feet (76 200 mm).

2. Exit access travel distance on a pedestrian walkway constructed with both sides at least 50 percent open shall not exceed 300 feet (91 440 mm).

3. Exit access travel distance on a pedestrian walkway constructed with both sides at least 50 percent open, and equipped throughout with an automatic sprinkler system in accordance with NFPA 13, shall not exceed 400 feet (122 m).

3104.10 Tunneled walkway. Separation between the tunneled walkway and the building to which it is connected shall not be less than 2-hour fire-resistant construction and openings therein shall be protected in accordance with Table 715.4.

SECTION 3105
AWNINGS AND CANOPIES

3105.1 General. Awnings or canopies shall comply with the requirements of this section and other applicable sections of this code.

3105.2 Definition. The following term shall, for the purposes of this section and as used elsewhere in this code, have the meaning shown herein.

RETRACTABLE AWNING. A retractable awning is a cover with a frame that retracts against a building or other structure to which it is entirely supported.

3105.3 Design and construction. Awnings and canopies shall be designed and constructed to withstand wind or other lateral loads and live loads as required by Chapter 16 with due allowance for shape, open construction and similar features that relieve the pressures or loads. Structural members shall be protected to prevent deterioration. Awnings shall have frames of noncombustible material, fire-retardant-treated wood, wood of Type IV size, or 1-hour construction with combustible or noncombustible covers and shall be either fixed, retractable, folding or collapsible.

3105.4 Canopy materials. Canopies shall be constructed of a rigid framework with an approved covering that meets the fire propagation performance criteria of NFPA 701 or has a flame spread index not greater than 25 when tested in accordance with ASTM E 84.

SECTION 3106
MARQUEES

3106.1 General. Marquees shall comply with this section and other applicable sections of this code.

3106.2 Thickness. The maximum height or thickness of a marquee measured vertically from its lowest to its highest point shall not exceed 3 feet (914 mm) where the marquee projects more than two-thirds of the distance from the property line to the curb line, and shall not exceed 9 feet (2743 mm) where the marquee is less than two-thirds of the distance from the property line to the curb line.

3106.3 Roof construction. Where the roof or any part thereof is a skylight, the skylight shall comply with the requirements of Chapter 24. Every roof and skylight of a marquee shall be sloped to downspouts that shall conduct any drainage from the marquee in such a manner so as not to spill over the sidewalk.

3106.4 Location prohibited. Every marquee shall be so located as not to interfere with the operation of any exterior standpipe, and such that the marquee does not obstruct the clear passage of stairways or exit discharge from the building or the installation or maintenance of street lighting.

3106.5 Construction. A marquee shall be supported entirely from the building and constructed of noncombustible materials. Marquees shall be designed as required in Chapter 16. Structural members shall be protected to prevent deterioration.

SECTION 3107
SIGNS

3107.1 General. Signs shall be designed, constructed and maintained in accordance with this code.

SECTION 3108
RADIO AND TELEVISION TOWERS

3108.1 General. Subject to the provisions of Chapter 16 and the requirements of Chapter 15 governing the fire-resistance ratings of buildings for the support of roof structures, radio and television towers shall be designed and constructed as herein provided.

3108.2 Location and access. Towers shall be located and equipped with step bolts and ladders so as to provide ready access for inspection purposes. Guy wires or other accessories shall not cross or encroach upon any street or other public space, or over above-ground electric utility lines, or encroach upon any privately owned property without written consent

of the owner of the encroached-upon property, space or above-ground electric utility lines.

3108.3 Construction. Towers shall be constructed of approved corrosion-resistant noncombustible material. The minimum type of construction of isolated radio towers not more than 100 feet (30 480 mm) in height shall be Type IIB.

3108.4 Loads. Towers shall be designed to resist wind loads in accordance with TIA/EIA-222. Consideration shall be given to conditions involving wind load on ice-covered sections in localities subject to sustained freezing temperatures.

> **3108.4.1 Dead load.** Towers shall be designed for the dead load plus the ice load in regions where ice formation occurs.

> **3108.4.2 Wind load.** Adequate foundations and anchorage shall be provided to resist two times the calculated wind load.

3108.5 Grounding. Towers shall be permanently and effectively grounded.

SECTION 3109
SWIMMING POOL ENCLOSURES AND SAFETY DEVICES

3109.1 General. Swimming pools shall comply with the requirements of this section and other applicable sections of this code. The requirements of this section and of the other applicable sections of this code shall be in addition to, and not in replacement of or substitution for, the requirements of other applicable federal, state and local laws and regulations, including, but not necessarily limited to, (a) the requirements of Subpart 6-1 (Swimming pools) of Title 10 of the Official Compilation of Codes, Rules and Regulations of the State of New York (NYCRR), where applicable, and (b) the requirements of section 8003 (Federal swimming pool and spa drain cover standard) of Title 15 of the United States Code, where applicable.

3109.2 Definitions. The following words and terms shall, for the purposes of this section, and as used elsewhere in this code, have the meanings shown herein.

BARRIER, TEMPORARY. An approved temporary fence, permanent fence, the wall of a permanent structure, any other structure, or any combination thereof that prevents access to the swimming pool by any person not engaged in the installation or construction of the swimming pool during its installation or construction.

SUBSTANTIAL DAMAGE. For the purpose of determining compliance with the pool alarm provisions of this Section, damage of any origin sustained by a swimming pool whereby the cost of restoring the swimming pool to its before-damaged condition would equal or exceed 50 percent of the market value of the swimming pool before the damage occurred.

SUBSTANTIAL MODIFICATION. For the purpose of determining compliance with the pool alarm provisions of this Section, any repair, alteration, addition or improvement of a swimming pool, the cost of which exceeds 50 percent of the market value of the swimming pool before the improvement or repair is started. If a swimming pool sustained substantial damage, any repairs are considered substantial improvement regardless of the actual repair work performed.

SWIMMING POOLS. Any structure, basin, chamber or tank which is intended for swimming, diving, recreational bathing or wading and which contains, is designated to contain, or is capable of containing water more than 24 inches (610 mm) deep at any point. This includes in-ground, aboveground and on-ground pools; indoor pools; hot tubs; spas; and fixed-in-place wading pools.

3109.3 Public swimming pools. Public swimming pools shall be completely enclosed by a fence at least 4 feet (1290 mm) in height or a screen enclosure. Openings in the fence shall not permit the passage of a 4-inch-diameter (102 mm) sphere. The fence or screen enclosure shall be equipped with gates.

3109.3.1 Gates. Gates shall comply with the following requirements.

3109.3.1.1 Self-closing; opening configuration. All gates shall be self-closing. In addition, if the gate is a pedestrian access gate, the gate shall open outward, away from the pool.

3109.3.1.2 Self-latching; location of latch handle. All gates shall be self-latching, with the latch handle located within the enclosure (i.e., on the pool side of the enclosure) and at least 40 inches (1016 mm) above grade. In addition, if the latch handle is located less than 54 inches (1372 mm) from the bottom of the gate, the latch handle shall be located at least 3 inches (76 mm) below the top of the gate, and neither the gate nor barrier shall have any opening greater than 0.5 inch (12.7) within 18 inches (457 mm) of the latch handle.

3109.3.1.3 Locking. All gates shall be securely locked with a key, combination or other child proof lock sufficient to prevent access to the swimming pool through such gate when the swimming pool is not in use or supervised.

3109.4 Residential swimming pools. Residential swimming pools shall comply with Sections 3109.4.1 through 3109.4.3.

Exception: A swimming pool with a power safety cover or a spa with a safety cover complying with ASTM F1346.

3109.4.1 Barrier height and clearances. The top of the barrier shall be at least 48 inches (1219 mm) above grade measured on the side of the barrier that faces away from the swimming pool. The maximum vertical clearance between grade and the bottom of the barrier shall be 2 inches (51 mm) measured on the side of the barrier that faces away from the swimming pool. Where the top of the pool structure is above grade, the barrier is authorized to be at ground level or mounted on top of the pool structure, and the maximum vertical clearance between the top of the pool structure and the bottom of the barrier shall be 4 inches (102 mm).

3109.4.1.1 Openings. Openings in the barrier shall not allow passage of a 4-inch-diameter (102 mm) sphere.

3109.4.1.2 Solid barrier surfaces. Solid barriers which do not have openings shall not contain indentations or protrusions except for normal construction tolerances and tooled masonry joints.

3109.4.1.3 Closely spaced horizontal members. Where the barrier is composed of horizontal and vertical members and the distance between the tops of the horizontal members is less than 45 inches (1143 mm), the horizontal members shall be located on the swimming pool side of the fence. Spacing between vertical members shall not exceed 1.75 inches (44 mm) in width. Where there are decorative cutouts within vertical members, spacing within the cutouts shall not exceed 1.75 inches (44 mm) in width.

3109.4.1.4 Widely spaced horizontal members. Where the barrier is composed of horizontal and vertical members and the distance between the tops of the horizontal members is 45 inches (1143 mm) or more, spacing between vertical members shall not exceed 4 inches (102 mm). Where there are decorative cutouts within vertical members, spacing within the cutouts shall not exceed 1.75 inches (44 mm) in width.

3109.4.1.5 Chain link dimensions. Maximum mesh size for chain link fences shall be a 2.25 inch square (57 mm square) unless the fence is provided with slats fastened at the top or the bottom which reduce the openings to no more than 1.75 inches (44 mm).

3109.4.1.6 Diagonal members. Where the barrier is composed of diagonal members, the maximum opening formed by the diagonal members shall be no more than 1.75 inches (44 mm).

3109.4.1.7 Gates. Gates shall comply with the requirements of Sections 3109.4.1.1 through 3109.4.1.6 and with the following requirements.

3109.4.1.7.1 Self-closing; opening configuration. All gates shall be self-closing. In addition, if the gate is a pedestrian access gate, the gate shall open outward, away from the pool.

3109.4.1.7.2 Self-latching; location of latch handle. All gates shall be self-latching, with the latch handle located within the enclosure (i.e., on the pool side of the enclosure) and at least 40 inches (1016 mm) above grade. In addition, if the latch handle is located less than 54 inches (1372 mm) from the bottom of the gate, the latch handle shall be located at least 3 inches (76 mm) below the top of the gate, and neither the gate nor barrier shall have any opening greater than 0.5 inch (12.7) within 18 inches (457 mm) of the latch handle.

3109.4.1.7.3 Locking. All gates shall be securely locked with a key, combination or other child proof lock sufficient to prevent access to the swimming pool through such gate when the swimming pool is not in use or supervised.

3109.4.1.8 Dwelling wall as a barrier. Where a wall of a dwelling serves as part of the barrier, one of the following shall apply:

1. Doors with direct access to the pool through that wall shall be equipped with an alarm that produces an audible warning when the door and/or its screen, if present, are opened. The alarm shall be listed in accordance with UL 2017. The audible alarm shall activate within 7 seconds and sound continuously for a minimum of 30 seconds after the door and/or its screen, if present, are opened and be capable of being heard throughout the house during normal household activities. The alarm shall automatically reset under all conditions. The alarm shall be equipped with a manual means, such as touchpad or switch, to temporarily deactivate the alarm for a single opening. Such deactivation shall last for not more than 15 seconds. In dwellings not required to be Accessible, Type A or Type B units, the deactivation switch shall be located 54 inches (1372 mm) or more above the threshold of the door. In dwellings required to be Accessible, Type A or Type B units, the deactivation switch(es) shall be located at 54 inches (1372 mm) maximum and 48 inches minimum above the threshold of the door.

2. The pool shall be equipped with a power safety cover that complies with ASTM F 1346.

3. Other means of protection, such as self-closing doors with self-latching devices, which are approved by the administrative authority, shall be accepted so long as the degree of protection afforded is not less than the protection afforded by Section 3109.4.1.8, Item 1 or 2.

3109.4.1.9 Pool structure as barrier. Where an aboveground pool structure is used as a barrier or where the barrier is mounted on top of the pool structure, and the means of access is a ladder or steps, then the ladder or steps either shall be capable of being secured, locked or removed to prevent access, or the ladder or steps shall be surrounded by a barrier which meets the requirements of Sections 3109.4.1.1 through 3109.4.1.8. When the ladder or steps are secured, locked or removed, any opening created shall not allow the passage of a 4-inch-diameter (102 mm) sphere.

3109.4.2 Indoor swimming pools. Walls surrounding indoor swimming pools shall not be required to comply with Section 3109.4.1.8.

3109.4.3 Prohibited locations. Barriers shall be located so as to prohibit permanent structures, equipment or similar objects from being used to climb the barriers.

3109.5 Temporary Barriers. An outdoor swimming pool, including an in-ground, above-ground or on-ground pool, hot tub or spa shall be surrounded by a temporary barrier during installation or construction and shall remain in place until a permanent fence in compliance with Section 3109.3 is provided for public swimming pools, or a barrier in compliance with Section 3109.4 is provided for residential pools.

Exceptions:

1. Above-ground or on-ground residential swimming pools where the pool structure is the barrier in compliance with Section 3109.4.1.9.

2. Spas or hot tubs with a safety cover which complies with ASTM F 1346, provided that such safety cover is in place during the period of installation or construction of such hot tub or spa. The temporary removal of a safety cover as required to facilitate the installation or construction of a hot tub or spa during periods when at least one person engaged in the installation or construction is present is permitted.

3109.5.1 Height. The top of the temporary barrier shall be at least 48 inches (1219) above grade measured on the side of the barrier which faces away from the swimming pool.

3109.5.2 Replacement by a permanent barrier. A temporary barrier shall be replaced by a complying permanent barrier within either of the following periods:

1. 90 days of the date of issuance of the building permit for the installation or construction of the swimming pool; or,

2. 90 days of the date of commencement of the installation or construction of the swimming pool.

3109.5.2.1 Replacement extension. Subject to the approval of the code enforcement official, the time period for completion of the permanent barrier may be extended for good cause, including, but not limited to, adverse weather conditions delaying construction.

3109.6 Entrapment protection. Entrapment protection shall be provided in compliance with Section 3109.6.1 or 3109.6.2.

3109.6.1 Suction entrapment avoidance. Suction outlets shall be designed and installed in accordance with ANSI/APSP-7.

3109.6.2 Entrapment avoidance. Suction outlets shall be designed to protect the pool user against entrapment. The term ''main drain'' means a submerged suction outlet typically located at the bottom of a pool or spa to conduct water to a recirculating pump. The term ''unblockable drain'' means a drain of any size and shape that a human body cannot sufficiently block to create a suction entrapment hazard such as an 18 inch by 23 inch (457 mm by 584 mm) drain grate or larger, or an approved long channel drain.

3109.6.2.1 Suction fittings. All pool and spa suction outlets shall be provided with a cover that conforms to ASME A112.19.8.

3109.6.2.2 Anti-entrapment devices or systems. Pools with a single main drain other than an unblockable drain shall be equipped with one or more of the following devices or systems designed to prevent entrapment by pool drains.

1. **Safety vacuum release system.** A safety vacuum release system, capable of providing vacuum release at a suction outlet caused by a high vacuum occurrence due to a suction outlet flow blockage, that ceases operation of the pump, reverses the circulation flow, or otherwise provides a vacuum release at a suction outlet when a blockage is detected and has been determined to comply with ASME/ANSI A112.19.17 or ASTM F2387 by an accredited independent testing laboratory.

2. **Suction–limiting vent system.** A suction-limiting vent system with a tamper-resistant atmospheric opening.

3. **Gravity drainage system.** A gravity drainage system that utilizes a collector tank.

4. **Automatic pump shut-off system.** An automatic pump shut-off system.

5. **Drain disablement.** A device or system that disables the drain.

6. **Other systems.** Any approved system determined to be equally effective as, or better than, the systems described in Section 3109.6 at preventing or eliminating the risk of injury or death associated with pool drainage systems.

3109.6.2.3 Multiple main drains. When two or more main drains are installed, a minimum of two suction outlets per pump with drain cover centers at least 3 feet apart must be provided. If the minimum spacing distance or two suction per pump requirement cannot be met, the drain shall be considered a single main drain.

3109.7 Swimming Pool and Spa Alarms

3109.7.1 Applicability. A swimming pool or spa installed, constructed or substantially modified after December 14, 2006, shall be equipped with an approved pool alarm.

Exceptions:

1. A hot tub or spa equipped with a safety cover which complies with ASTM F 1346.

2. A swimming pool (other than a hot tub or spa) equipped with an automatic power safety cover which complies with ASTM F 1346.

Pool alarms shall comply with ASTM F 2208 and shall be installed, used and maintained in accordance with the manufacturer's instructions and this section.

3109.7.2 Multiple alarms. A pool alarm must be capable of detecting entry into the water at any point on the surface of the swimming pool. If necessary to provide detection capability at every point on the surface of the swimming pool, more than one pool alarm shall be provided.

3109.7.3 Alarm activation. Pool alarms shall activate upon detecting entry into the water and shall sound poolside and inside the building.

3109.7.4 Prohibited alarms. The use of personal immersion alarms shall not be construed as compliance with this section.

CHAPTER 32

ENCROACHMENTS INTO THE PUBLIC RIGHT-OF-WAY

SECTION 3201
GENERAL

3201.1 Scope. The provisions of this chapter shall govern the encroachment of structures into the public right-of-way.

3201.2 Measurement. The projection of any structure or portion thereof shall be the distance measured horizontally from the lot line to the outermost point of the projection.

3201.3 Other laws. The provisions of this chapter shall not be construed to permit the violation of other laws or ordinances regulating the use and occupancy of public property.

3201.4 Drainage. Drainage water collected from a roof, awning, canopy or marquee, and condensate from mechanical equipment shall not flow over a public walking surface.

SECTION 3202
ENCROACHMENTS

3202.1 Encroachments below grade. Encroachments below grade shall comply with Sections 3202.1.1 through 3202.1.3.

3202.1.1 Structural support. A part of a building erected below grade that is necessary for structural support of the building or structure shall not project beyond the lot lines, except that the footings of street walls or their supports which are located at least 8 feet (2438 mm) below grade shall not project more than 12 inches (305 mm) beyond the street lot line.

3202.1.2 Vaults and other enclosed spaces. The construction and utilization of vaults and other enclosed space below grade shall be subject to the terms and conditions of the authority or legislative body having jurisdiction.

3202.1.3 Areaways. Areaways shall be protected by grates, guards or other approved means.

3202.2 Encroachments above grade and below 8 feet in height. Encroachments into the public right-of-way above grade and below 8 feet (2438 mm) in height shall be prohibited except as provided for in Sections 3202.2.1 through 3202.2.3. Doors and windows shall not open or project into the public right-of-way.

3202.2.1 Steps. Steps shall not project more than 12 inches (305 mm) and shall be guarded by approved devices not less than 3 feet (914 mm) high, or shall be located between columns or pilasters.

3202.2.2 Architectural features. Columns or pilasters, including bases and moldings shall not project more than 12 inches (305 mm). Belt courses, lintels, sills, architraves, pediments and similar architectural features shall not project more than 4 inches (102 mm).

3202.2.3 Awnings. The vertical clearance from the public right-of-way to the lowest part of any awning, including valances, shall be 7 feet (2134 mm) minimum.

3202.3 Encroachments 8 feet or more above grade. Encroachments 8 feet (2438 mm) or more above grade shall comply with Sections 3202.3.1 through 3202.3.4.

3202.3.1 Awnings, canopies, marquees and signs. Awnings, canopies, marquees and signs shall be constructed so as to support applicable loads as specified in Chapter 16. Awnings, canopies, marquees and signs with less than 15 feet (4572 mm) clearance above the sidewalk shall not extend into or occupy more than two-thirds the width of the sidewalk measured from the building. Stanchions or columns that support awnings, canopies, marquees and signs shall be located not less than 2 feet (610 mm) in from the curb line.

3202.3.2 Windows, balconies, architectural features and mechanical equipment. Where the vertical clearance above grade to projecting windows, balconies, architectural features or mechanical equipment is more than 8 feet (2438 mm), 1 inch (25 mm) of encroachment is permitted for each additional 1 inch (25 mm) of clearance above 8 feet (2438 mm), but the maximum encroachment shall be 4 feet (1219 mm).

3202.3.3 Encroachments 15 feet or more above grade. Encroachments 15 feet (4572 mm) or more above grade shall not be limited.

3202.3.4 Pedestrian walkways. The installation of a pedestrian walkway over a public right-of-way shall be subject to the approval of local authority having jurisdiction. The vertical clearance from the public right-of-way to the lowest part of a pedestrian walkway shall be 15 feet (4572 mm) minimum.

3202.4 Temporary encroachments. Where allowed by the local authority having jurisdiction, vestibules and storm enclosures shall not be erected for a period of time exceeding 7 months in any one year and shall not encroach more than 3 feet (914 mm) nor more than one-fourth of the width of the sidewalk beyond the street lot line. Temporary entrance awnings shall be erected with a minimum clearance of 7 feet (2134 mm) to the lowest portion of the hood or awning where supported on removable steel or other approved noncombustible support.

CHAPTER 33

SAFEGUARDS DURING CONSTRUCTION

SECTION 3301
GENERAL

3301.1 Scope. The provisions of this chapter shall govern safety during construction and the protection of adjacent public and private properties.

3301.2 Storage and placement. Construction equipment and materials shall be stored and placed so as not to endanger the public, the workers or adjoining property for the duration of the construction project.

SECTION 3302
CONSTRUCTION SAFEGUARDS

3302.1 Remodeling and additions. Required exits, existing structural elements, fire protection devices and sanitary safeguards shall be maintained at all times during remodeling, alterations, repairs or additions to any building or structure.

Exceptions:

1. When such required elements or devices are being remodeled, altered or repaired, adequate substitute provisions shall be made.

2. When the existing building is not occupied.

3302.2 Manner of removal. Waste materials shall be removed in a manner which prevents injury or damage to persons, adjoining properties and public rights-of-way.

SECTION 3303
DEMOLITION

3303.1 Construction documents. Construction documents and a schedule for demolition must be submitted when required by the code enforcement official. Where such information is required, no work shall be done until such construction documents or schedule, or both, are approved.

3303.2 Pedestrian protection. The work of demolishing any building shall not be commenced until pedestrian protection is in place as required by this chapter.

3303.3 Means of egress. A party wall balcony or horizontal exit shall not be destroyed unless and until a substitute means of egress has been provided and approved.

3303.4 Vacant lot. Where a structure has been demolished or removed, the vacant lot shall be filled and maintained to the existing grade or in accordance with the ordinances of the jurisdiction having authority.

3303.5 Water accumulation. Provision shall be made to prevent the accumulation of water or damage to any foundations on the premises or the adjoining property.

3303.6 Utility connections. Service utility connections shall be discontinued and capped in accordance with the approved rules and the requirements of the authority having jurisdiction.

SECTION 3304
SITE WORK

3304.1 Excavation and fill. Excavation and fill for buildings and structures shall be constructed or protected so as not to endanger life or property. Stumps and roots shall be removed from the soil to a depth of at least 12 inches (305 mm) below the surface of the ground in the area to be occupied by the building. Wood forms which have been used in placing concrete, if within the ground or between foundation sills and the ground, shall be removed before a building is occupied or used for any purpose. Before completion, loose or casual wood shall be removed from direct contact with the ground under the building.

3304.1.1 Slope limits. Slopes for permanent fill shall not be steeper than one unit vertical in two units horizontal (50-percent slope). Cut slopes for permanent excavations shall not be steeper than one unit vertical in two units horizontal (50-percent slope). Deviation from the foregoing limitations for cut slopes shall be permitted only upon the presentation of a soil investigation report acceptable to the code enforcement official.

3304.1.2 Surcharge. No fill or other surcharge loads shall be placed adjacent to any building or structure unless such building or structure is capable of withstanding the additional loads caused by the fill or surcharge. Existing footings or foundations which can be affected by any excavation shall be underpinned adequately or otherwise protected against settlement and shall be protected against later movement.

3304.1.3 Footings on adjacent slopes. For footings on adjacent slopes, see Chapter 18.

3304.1.4 Fill supporting foundations. Fill to be used to support the foundations of any building or structure shall comply with Section 1803.5. Special inspections of compacted fill shall be in accordance with Section 1704.7.

SECTION 3305
SANITARY

3305.1 Facilities required. Sanitary facilities shall be provided during construction, remodeling or demolition activities in accordance with the *Plumbing Code of New York State*.

SECTION 3306
PROTECTION OF PEDESTRIANS

3306.1 Protection required. Pedestrians shall be protected during construction, remodeling and demolition activities as required by this chapter and Table 3306.1. Signs shall be provided to direct pedestrian traffic.

3306.2 Walkways. A walkway shall be provided for pedestrian travel in front of every construction and demolition site unless the authority having jurisdiction authorizes the sidewalk to be fenced or closed. Walkways shall be of sufficient width to accommodate the pedestrian traffic, but in no case shall they be less than 4 feet (1219 mm) in width. Walkways shall be provided with a durable walking surface. Walkways shall be accessible in accordance with Chapter 11 and shall be designed to support all imposed loads and in no case shall the design live load be less than 150 pounds per square foot (psf) (7.2 kN/m²).

3306.3 Directional barricades. Pedestrian traffic shall be protected by a directional barricade where the walkway extends into the street. The directional barricade shall be of sufficient size and construction to direct vehicular traffic away from the pedestrian path.

3306.4 Construction railings. Construction railings shall be at least 42 inches (1067 mm) in height and shall be sufficient to direct pedestrians around construction areas.

3306.5 Barriers. Barriers shall be a minimum of 8 feet (2438 mm) in height and shall be placed on the side of the walkway nearest the construction. Barriers shall extend the entire length of the construction site. Openings in such barriers shall be protected by doors which are normally kept closed.

3306.6 Barrier design. Barriers shall be designed to resist loads required in Chapter 16 unless constructed as follows:

1. Barriers shall be provided with 2-inch by 4-inch (51 mm by 102 mm) top and bottom plates.

2. The barrier material shall be a minimum of $^3/_4$-inch (19.1 mm) boards or $^1/_4$-inch (6.4 mm) wood structural use panels.

3. Wood structural use panels shall be bonded with an adhesive identical to that for exterior wood structural use panels.

4. Wood structural use panels $^1/_4$ inch (6.4 mm) or $^5/_{16}$ inch (23.8 mm) in thickness shall have studs spaced not more than 2 feet (610 mm) on center (o.c.).

5. Wood structural use panels $^3/_8$ inch (9.5 mm) or $^1/_2$ inch (12.7 mm) in thickness shall have studs spaced not more than 4 feet (1219 mm) o.c., provided a 2-inch by 4-inch (51 mm by 102 mm) stiffener is placed horizontally at midheight where the stud spacing exceeds 2 feet (610 mm) o.c.

6. Wood structural use panels $^5/_8$ inch (15.9 mm) or thicker shall not span over 8 feet (2438 mm).

3306.7 Covered walkways. Covered walkways shall have a minimum clear height of 8 feet (2438 mm) as measured from the floor surface to the canopy overhead. Adequate lighting shall be provided at all times. Covered walkways shall be designed to support all imposed loads. In no case shall the design live load be less than 150 psf (7.2 kN/m²) for the entire structure.

Exception: Roofs and supporting structures of covered walkways for new, light-frame construction not exceeding two stories in height are permitted to be designed for a live load of 75 psf (3.6kN/m²) or the loads imposed on them, whichever is greater. In lieu of such designs, the roof and supporting structure of a covered walkway are permitted to be constructed as follows:

1. Footings shall be continuous 2-inch by 6-inch (51 mm by 152 mm) members.

2. Posts not less than 4 inches by 6 inches (102 mm by 152 mm) shall be provided on both sides of the roof and spaced not more than 12 feet (3658 mm) o.c.

3. Stringers not less than 4 inches by 12 inches (102 mm by 305 mm) shall be placed on edge upon the posts.

4. Joists resting on the stringers shall be at least 2 inches by 8 inches (51 mm by 203 mm) and shall be spaced not more than 2 feet (610 mm) o.c.

5. The deck shall be planks at least 2 inches (51 mm) thick or wood structural panels with an exterior exposure durability classification at least $^{23}/_{32}$ inch (18.3 mm) thick nailed to the joists.

6. Each post shall be knee braced to joists and stringers by 2-inch by 4-inch (51 mm by 102 mm) minimum members 4 feet (1219 mm) long.

7. A 2-inch by 4-inch (51 mm by 102 mm) minimum curb shall be set on edge along the outside edge of the deck.

3306.8 Repair, maintenance and removal. Pedestrian protection required by this chapter shall be maintained in place and kept in good order for the entire length of time pedestrians may be endangered. The owner or the owner's agent, upon the completion of the construction activity, shall immediately remove walkways, debris and other obstructions and leave such public property in as good a condition as it was before such work was commenced.

TABLE 3306.1
PROTECTION OF PEDESTRIANS

HEIGHT OF CONSTRUCTION	DISTANCE FROM CONSTRUCTION TO LOT LINE	TYPE OF PROTECTION REQUIRED
8 feet or less	Less than 5 feet	Construction railings
	5 feet or more	None
More than 8 feet	Less than 5 feet	Barrier and covered walkway
	5 feet or more, but not more than one-fourth the height of construction	Barrier and covered walkway
	5 feet or more, but between one-fourth and one-half the height of construction	Barrier
	5 feet or more, but exceeding one-half the height of construction	None

For SI: 1 foot = 304.8 mm.

3306.9 Adjacent to excavations. Every excavation on a site located 5 feet (1524 mm) or less from the street lot line shall be enclosed with a barrier not less than 6 feet (1829 mm) high. Where located more than 5 feet (1524 mm) from the street lot line, a barrier shall be erected when required by the code enforcement official. Barriers shall be of adequate strength to resist wind pressure as specified in Chapter 16.

SECTION 3307
PROTECTION OF ADJOINING PROPERTY

3307.1 Protection required. Adjoining public and private property shall be protected from damage during construction, remodeling and demolition work. Protection must be provided for footings, foundations, party walls, chimneys, skylights and roofs. Provisions shall be made to control water runoff and erosion during construction or demolition activities. The person making or causing an excavation to be made shall provide written notice to the owners of adjoining buildings advising them that the excavation is to be made and that the adjoining buildings should be protected. Said notification shall be delivered not less than 10 days prior to the scheduled starting date of the excavation.

SECTION 3308
TEMPORARY USE OF STREETS, ALLEYS AND PUBLIC PROPERTY

3308.1 Storage and handling of materials. The temporary use of streets or public property for the storage or handling of materials or of equipment required for construction or demolition, and the protection provided to the public shall comply with the provisions of the authority having jurisdiction and this chapter.

3308.1.1 Obstructions. Construction materials and equipment shall not be placed or stored so as to obstruct access to fire hydrants, standpipes, fire or police alarm boxes, catch basins or manholes, nor shall such material or equipment be located within 20 feet (6096 mm) of a street intersection, or placed so as to obstruct normal observations of traffic signals or to hinder the use of public transit loading platforms.

3308.2 Utility fixtures. Building materials, fences, sheds or any obstruction of any kind shall not be placed so as to obstruct free approach to any fire hydrant, fire department connection, utility pole, manhole, fire alarm box or catch basin, or so as to interfere with the passage of water in the gutter. Protection against damage shall be provided to such utility fixtures during the progress of the work, but sight of them shall not be obstructed.

SECTION 3309
FIRE EXTINGUISHERS

[F] 3309.1 Where required. All structures under construction, alteration or demolition shall be provided with not less than one approved portable fire extinguisher in accordance with Section 906 and sized for not less than ordinary hazard as follows:

1. At each stairway on all floor levels where combustible materials have accumulated.

2. In every storage and construction shed.

3. Additional portable fire extinguishers shall be provided where special hazards exist, such as the storage and use of flammable and combustible liquids.

3309.2 Fire hazards. The provisions of this code and the *Fire Code of New York State* shall be strictly observed to safeguard against all fire hazards attendant upon construction operations.

SECTION 3310
EXITS

3310.1 Stairways required. Where a building has been constructed to a height greater than 50 feet (15 240 mm) or four stories, or where an existing building exceeding 50 feet (15 240 mm) in height is altered, at least one temporary lighted stairway shall be provided unless one or more of the permanent stairways are erected as the construction progresses.

3310.2 Maintenance of exits. Required means of egress shall be maintained at all times during construction, demolition, remodeling or alterations and additions to any building.

Exception: Approved temporary means of egress systems and facilities.

3310.3 Stairway floor number signs. Temporary stairway floor number signs shall be provided in accordance with the requirements of Section 1020.1.6.

[F] SECTION 3311
STANDPIPES

3311.1 Where required. Buildings four stories or more in height shall be provided with not less than one standpipe for use during construction. Such standpipes shall be installed where the progress of construction is not more than 40 feet (12 192 mm) in height above the lowest level of fire department access. Such standpipe shall be provided with fire department hose connections at accessible locations adjacent to usable stairs. Such standpipes shall be extended as construction progresses to within one floor of the highest point of construction having secured decking or flooring.

3311.2 Buildings being demolished. Where a building is being demolished and a standpipe exists within such a building, such standpipe shall be maintained in an operable condition so as to be available for use by the fire department. Such standpipe shall be demolished with the building but shall not be demolished more than one floor below the floor being demolished.

3311.3 Detailed requirements. Standpipes shall be installed in accordance with the provisions of Chapter 9.

Exception: Standpipes shall be either temporary or permanent in nature, and with or without a water supply, provided that such standpipes conform to the requirements of Section 905 as to capacity, outlets and materials.

3311.4 Water supply. Water supply for fire protection, either temporary or permanent, shall be made available as soon as combustible material accumulates.

SECTION 3312
AUTOMATIC SPRINKLER SYSTEM

[F] 3312.1 Completion before occupancy. In buildings where an automatic sprinkler system is required by this code, it shall be unlawful to occupy any portion of a building or structure until the automatic sprinkler system installation has been tested and approved, except as provided in Section 110.3.

[F] 3312.2 Operation of valves. Operation of sprinkler control valves shall be permitted only by properly authorized personnel and shall be accompanied by notification of duly designated parties. When the sprinkler protection is being regularly turned off and on to facilitate connection of newly completed segments, the sprinkler control valves shall be checked at the end of each work period to ascertain that protection is in service.

CHAPTER 34
RESERVED

CHAPTER 35

REFERENCED STANDARDS

This chapter lists the standards that are referenced in various sections of this document. The standards are listed herein by the promulgating agency of the standard, the standard identification, the effective date and title, and the section or sections of this document that reference the standard. The application of the referenced standards shall be as specified in Section 102.4.

*Denotes standards that are incorporated by reference into 19 NYCRR Part 1221.

Margin markings have not beem made in this chapter. The date of the referenced standards denotes new standards from 2007.

AA

Aluminum Association
900 - 19th Street N.W., Suite 300
Washington, DC 20006

Standard reference number	Title	Referenced in code section number
*ADM 1-00	Aluminum Design Manual: Part 1-A Aluminum Structures, Allowable Stress Design; and Part 1-B- Aluminum Structures, Load and Resistance Factor Design of Buildings and Similar Type Structures	1604.3.5, 2002.1
*ASM 35-00	Specifications for Aluminum Sheet Metal Work in Building Construction (Fourth Edition)	2002.1

AAMA

American Architectural Manufacturers Association
1827 Waldon Office Square, Suite 550
Schaumburg, IL 60173

Standard reference number	Title	Referenced in code section number
1402-86	Standard Specifications for Aluminum Siding, Soffit and Fascia	1404.5.1
* AAMA/WDMA/CSA 101/IS2/A440-08	Specifications for Windows, Doors and Unit Skylights	1714.5.1, 2405.5

ACI

American Concrete Institute
P.O. Box 9094
Farmington Hills, MI 48333-9094

Standard reference number	Title	Referenced in code section number
*216.1-97	Standard Method for Determining Fire Resistance of Concrete and Masonry Construction Assemblies	Table 720.1(2), 721.1
*318-05	Building Code Requirements for Structural Concrete	1604.3.2, Table 1704.3, 1704.4.1, Table 1704.4, 1708.3, 1805.4.2.6, 1805.9, 1808.2.23.1.1, 1808.2.23.2,1808.2.23.2.1, 1809.2.2.2.2, 1809.2.3.2, 1809.2.3.2.2, 1810.1.2.2, 1812.8,1901.2, 1901.3, 1901.4, 1902.1, 1903.1, 1904.1, 1904.2.1, 1904.2.2, 1904.2.3, 1904.3, 1904.4, 1905.1.1, 1905.2, 1905.3, 1905.4, 1905.5, 1905.6.2, 1905.6.3, 1905.6.4, 1905.6.5, 1905.7, 1905.8, 1905.9, 1905.10, 1905.11, 1905.12, 1905.13, 1906.1, 1906.2, 1906.3, 1906.4, 1907.1, 1907.2, 1907.3, 1907.4, 1907.5, 1907.6, 1907.7.1, 1907.7.2, 1907.7.3, 1907.7.4, 1907.7.5, 1907.8, 1907.9, 1907.10, 1907.11, 1907.12, 1907.13, 1908, 1908.1, 1908.1.1, 1908.1.2, 1908.1.3, 1908.1.4, 1908.1.5, 1908.1.6, 1908.1.7, 1908.1.8, 1908.1.9, 1908.1.10, 1908.1.11, 1908.1.12, 1908.1.13, 1908.1.14, 1908.1.15, 1908.1.16, 1909.1, 1909.3, 1909.4, 1909.5, 1909.6, 1912.1, 2108.3, 2205.3
*530-05	Building Code Requirements for Masonry Structures	1405.5, 1405.5.2, 1405.9, 1604.3.4, 1704.5, 1704.5.1, Table 1704.5.1, 1704.5.2, 1704.5.3, Table 1704.5.3, 1708.1.1, 1708.1.2, 1708.1.3, 1708.1.4, 1812.7,

ACI—continued

2101.2.2, 2101.2.3, 2101.2.4, 2101.2.5, 2101.2.6, 2103.13.6, 2106.1, 2106.1.1,
2106.1.1.1, 2106.1.1.2, 2106.1.1.3, 2106.3, 2106.4, 2106.5, 2106.6, 2107.1, 2107.2,
2107.3, 2107.4, 2107.5, 2107.6, 2107.7, 2107.8, 2108.1, 2108.2, 2108.3, 2108.4, 2109.1, 2109.2.3.1, 2109.7.3

Standard reference number	Title	Referenced in code section number
*530.1-05	Specifications for Masonry Structures	1405.5.1, Table 1704.5.1, Table 1704.5.3, 1805.5.2.2, 2103.13.7, 2104.1, 2104.1.1, 2104.3, 2104.4

AF&PA

American Forest & Paper Association
1111 19th St, NW Suite 800
Washington, DC 20036

Standard reference number	Title	Referenced in code section number
WCD No. 4-89	Wood Construction Data-Plank and Beam Framing for Residential Buildings	2306.1.2
*WFCM-01	Wood Frame Construction Manual for One- and Two-family Dwellings	1609.1.1, 1609.1.1.1, 2301.2, 2308.1, 2308.2.1
*PWF-07	Permanent Wood Foundation Design Specification	1805.4.6, 1807.2, 2304.9.5
*NDS-05	National Design Specification (NDS) for Wood Construction with 2005 Supplement	721.6.3.2, 1715.1.1, 1715.1.4, 1805.4.5, 1809.1.4, 2302.1, 2304.12, 2306.1, 2306.2.1, 2306.3.1, Table 2306.3.1, Table 2306.3.2, Table 2306.4.1, Table 2306.4.4, 2306.3.4, 2306.3.5, 2306.4.1, 2307.1, 2307.1.1
AF&PA-93	Span Tables for Joists and Rafters	2306.1.1, 2308.8, 2308.10.2, 2308.10.3
SDPWS-05	AF&PA Supplement Special Design Provisions for Wind and Seismic	2305.1

AHA

American Hardwood Association
1210 West N.W. Highway
Palatine, IL 60067

Standard reference number	Title	Referenced in code section number
A135.4-04	Basic Hardboard	1404.3.1, 2303.1.6
A135.5-04	Prefinished Hardboard Paneling	2303.1.6, 2304.6.2
A135.6-98	Hardboard Siding	1404.3.2, 2303.1.6

AISC

American Institute of Steel Construction
One East Wacker Drive, Suite 3100
Chicago, IL 60601-2001

Standard reference number	Title	Referenced in code section number
*341-05	Seismic Provisions for Structural Steel Buildings, including Supplement No. 1 dated 2006	1613.6.2, 1707.2, 1708.4, 2205.2.1, 2205.2.2, 2205.3, 2205.3.1
*360-05	Specification for Structural Steel Buildings	721.5.2.2.1, 1604.3.3, Table 1704.3, 2203.2, 2205.1, 2205.3

AISI

American Iron and Steel Institute
1140 Connecticut Avenue
Suite 705
Washington, DC 20036

Standard reference number	Title	Referenced in code section number
*NAS-01	North American Specification for the Design of Cold-formed Steel Structural Members, including 2004 Supplement	1604.3.3, 2209.1, 2210.1
*General-04	Standard for Cold-formed Steel Framing-General Provisions	1604.3.3, 2210.1
*Header-04	Standard for Cold-formed Steel Framing-Header Design	2210.2
*Lateral-04	Standard for Cold-formed Steel Framing-Lateral Design	2210.5, 2210.5.1

AISI—continued

*PM-01	Standard for Cold-formed Steel Framing-Prescriptive Method for One- and Two-family Dwellings, including 2004 Supplement 2210.6
*Truss-04	Standard for Cold-formed Steel Framing-Truss Design 1604.3.3, 2210.3
*WSD-04	Standard for Cold-formed Steel Framing-Wall Stud Design 2210.4

AITC

American Institute of Timber Construction
Suite 140
7012 S. Revere Parkway
Englewood, CO 80112

Standard reference number	Title	Referenced in code section number
AITC Technical Note 7-96	Calculation of Fire Resistance of Glued Laminated Timbers. 721.6.3.3
*AITC 104-03	Typical Construction Details 2306.1
*AITC 110-01	Standard Appearance Grades for Structural Glued Laminated Timber 2306.1
*AITC 113-01	Standard for Dimensions of Structural Glued Laminated Timber 2306.1
AITC 117-04	Standard Specifications for Structural Glued Laminated Timber of Softwood Species 2306.1
AITC 119-96	Standard Specifications for Structural Glued Laminated Timber of Hardwood Species 2306.1
AITC 200-04	Manufacturing Quality Control Systems Manual for Structural Glued Laminated Timber. 2306.1
ANSI/AITC A 190.1-02	Structural Glued Laminated Timber 2303.1.3, 2306.1

ALI

Automotive Lift Institute
P.O. Box 85
Courtland, NY 13045

Standard reference number	Title	Referenced in code section number
*ALI ALCTV-2006	Standard for Automotive Lifts-Safety Requirements for Construction, Testing and Validation (ANSI) 3001.2, 1011.3

ANSI

American National Standards Institute
25 West 43rd Street, Fourth Floor
New York, NY 10036

Standard reference number	Title	Referenced in code section number
A13.1-07	Scheme for the Identification of Piping Systems 415.8.6.4
*A108.1A-99	Installation of Ceramic Tile in the Wet-set Method, with Portland Cement Mortar 2103.10
*A108.1B-99	Installation of Ceramic Tile, quarry Tile on a Cured Portland Cement Mortar Setting Bed with Dry-set or Latex-portland Mortar 2103.10
*A108.4-99	Installation of Ceramic Tile with Organic Adhesives or Water-cleanable Tile-setting Epoxy Adhesive. 2103.10.6
*A108.5-99	Installation of Ceramic Tile with Dry-set Portland Cement Mortar or Latex-portland Cement Mortar. 2103.10.1, 2103.10.2
*A108.6-99	Installation of Ceramic Tile with Chemical-resistant, Water Cleanable Tile-setting and -grouting Epoxy 2103.10.3
*A108.8-99	Installation of Ceramic Tile with Chemical-resistant Furan Resin Mortar and Grout 2103.10.4
*A108.9-99	Installation of Ceramic Tile with Modified Epoxy Emulsion Mortar/Grout 2103.10.5
*A108.10-99	Installation of Grout in Tilework 2103.10.7
*A117.1-03	ICC/ANSI Accessible and Usable Buildings and Facilities 406.2.2, 907.9.1.4, 1007.6.5, 1010.1, 1010.6.5, 1010.9, 1011.3, 1101.2, 1102.1, 1103.2.14, 1106.1.1, 1106.7, 1107.2, 1107.2.1, 1107.2.2, 1108.2.2, 1109.1, 1109.2.1.1, 1109.2.2, 1109.3, 1109.4, 1109.8, 1607.7, 2902.5, 3001.3
A118.1-99	American NationalStandard Specifications for Dry-set Portland Cement Mortar 2103.10.1
A118.3-99	American National Standard Specifications for Chemical-resistant, Water-cleanable Tile-setting and -grouting Epoxy and Water Cleanable Tile-setting Epoxy Adhesive 2103.10.3
A118.4-99	American National Standard Specifications for Latex-portland Cement Mortar. 2103.10.2
A118.5-99	American National Standard Specifications for Chemical Resistant Furan Mortar and Grouts for Tile Installation 2103.10.4

ANSI—continued

A118.6-99	American National Standard Specifications for Cement Grouts for Tile Installation..............2103.10.7
A118.8-99	American National Standard Specifications for Modified Epoxy Emulsion Mortar/Grout.........2103.10.5
A136.1-99	American National Standard Specifications for Organic Adhesives for Installation of Ceramic Tile.........
2103.10.6A137.1-88	American National Standard Specifications for Ceramic Tile...............................2103.5
A208.1-99	Particleboard...2303.1.7, 2303.1.7.1
Z 97.1-84 (R1994)	Safety Glazing Materials Used in Buildings-Safety Performance Specifications and Methods of Test (Reaffirmed 1994)............................2406.1.2, 2409.1

APA

APA - Engineered Wood Association
7011 South 19th Street
Tacoma, WA 98466-5333

Standard reference number	Title	Referenced in code section number
*APA PDS-08	Panel Design Specification.....................2306.1, 2306.3.1, 2306.4.1
*APA PDS Supplement 1-90 (R95)	Design and Fabrication of Plywood Curved Panels (revised 1995)............................2306.1
*APA PDS Supplement 2-92 (R98)	Design and Fabrication of Plywood-lumber beams (revised 1998)...........................2306.1
*APA PDS Supplement 3-90 (R96)	Design and Fabrication of Plywood Stressed-skin Panels (revised 1996)......................2306.1
*APA PDS Supplement 4-90 (R93)	Design and Fabrication of Plywood Sandwich Panels (revised 1993).........................2306.1
*APA PDS Supplement 5-08	Design and Fabrication of All-plywood Beams (revised 2008).............................2306.1
*EWS R540-07	Builders Tips: Proper Storage and Handling of Glulam Beams.............................2306.1
*EWS S475-07	Glued Laminated Beam Design Tables....................................2306.1
*EWS S560-06	Field Notching and Drilling of Glued Laminated Timber Beams............................2306.1
*EWS T300-07	Glulam Connection Details...2306.1
*EWS X440-08	Product Guide-Glulam..2306.1
EWS X450-01	Glulam in Residential Construction -Western Edition...........................2306.1

APSP

The Association of Pool and Spa Professionals
2111 Eisenhower Avenue
Alexandria, VA 22314

Standard reference number	Title	Referenced in code section number
*ANSI/APSP-7 2006	American National Standard for Suction Entrapment Avoidance in Swimming Pools, Wading Pools, Spas, Hot Tubs, and Catch Basins.................................3109.6.1

ASAE

American Society of Agricultural Engineers
2950 Niles Road
St. Joseph, MI 49085-9659

Standard reference number	Title	Referenced in code section number
EP 484.2 (1998)	Diaphragm Design of Metal-clad, Post-frame Rectangular Buildings........................2306.1
*EP 486.1 (2000)	Shallow-post Foundation Design......................................2306.1
EP 559 (1997)	Design Requirements and Bending Properties for Mechanically Laminated Columns.............2306.1

ASCE

American Society of Civil Engineers
1801 Alexander Bell Drive
Reston, VA 20191-4400

Standard reference number	Title	Referenced in code section number
*3-91	Structural Design of Composite Slabs	1604.3.3, 2209.2
*5-05	Building Code Requirements for Masonry Structures	1405.5, 1405.5.2, 1405.9, 1604.3.4, 1704.5, 1704.5.1, Table 1704.5.1, 1704.5.2, 1704.5.3, Table 1704.5.3, 1708.1.1, 1708.1.2, 1708.1.3, 1708.1.4, 1812.7, 2101.2.2, 2101.2.3, 2101.2.4, 2101.2.5, 2101.2.6, 2103.13.6, 2106.1, 2106.1.1, 2106.1.1.1, 2106.1.1.2, 2106.1.1.3, 2106.3, 2106.4, 2106.5, 2106.6, 2107.1, 2107.2, 2107.3, 2107.4, 2107.5, 2107.6, 2107.7, 2170.8, 2108.1, 2108.2, 2108.3, 2108.4, 2109.1, 2109.2.3.1, 2109.7.3
*6-05	Specifications for Masonry Structures	1405.5.1, Table 1704.5.1, Table 1704.5.3, 1805.5.2.2, 2103.13.7, 2104.1, 2104.1.1, 2104.3, 2104.4
*7-05	Minimum Design Loads for Buildings and Other Structures including Supplement No. 1 and excluding Chapter 14 and Appendix 11A	1602.1, 1604.3, 1604.10, 1605.1, 1605.2.2, 1605.3.1.2, 1605.3.2, 1605.4, 1607.11.1, 1608.1, 1608.2, 1609.1.1, 1609.1.2, 1609.3, 1609.5.1, 1609.5.3, 1611.2, 1612.2, 1613.1, 1613.2, Table 1613.5.3(1), Table 1613.5.3(2), 1613.5.6, 1613.5.6.1, 1613.5.6.2, 1613.6, 1613.6.1, 1613.6.2, 1702.1, 1801.2.1, 1802.2.7, 1908.1.3, 2109.1.1 2205.2.1, 2205.3, 2205.3.1, 2208.1, 2305.1.5, 2305.2.5, 2305.3.1, 2306.4.5, Table 2306.4.5, Table 2308.10.1, 2404.1, 2505.1, 2505.2, 2506.2.1
8-02	Standard Specification for the Design of Cold-formed Stainless Steel Structural Members	1604.3.3, 2209.1
19-96	Structural Applications of Steel Cables for Buildings	2207.1, 2207.2
*24-05	Flood Resistant Design and Construction	1203.3.2, 1612.4, 1612.5, 3001.2
29-05	Standard Calculation Methods for Structural Fire Protection	721.1
*32-01	Design and Construction of Frost Protected Shallow Foundations	1805.2.1

ASME

American Society of Mechanical Engineers
Three Park Avenue
New York, NY 10016-5990

Standard reference number	Title	Referenced in code section number
A13.1-07	Scheme for Identification of Piping Systems	415.8.6.4
*A17.1-07	Safety Code for Elevators and Escalators	1007.4, 1607.8.1, 3001.2, 3001.4, 3002.5, 3003.2, 3005.2
*A18.1-05	Safety Standard for Platform Lifts and Stairway Chairlifts	1109.7, 2702.2.6, 3001.2, 3005.3
*A90.1-03	Safety Standard for Belt Manlifts	3001.2, 3005.4
A112.19.8-07	Suction Fittings for Use in Swimming Pools, Wading Pools, Spas, Hot Tubs and Whirlpool Bathing Appliances	3109.6.2.1
A112.19.17-02	Manufactured Safety Vacuum Release Systems (SVRS) for Residential and Commercial Swimming Pool, Spa, Hot Tub and Wading Pool	3109.6.2.2
B16.18-01	Cast Copper Alloy Solder Joint Pressure Fittings	909.13.1
B16.22-01	Wrought Copper and Copper Alloy Solder Joint Pressure Fittings	909.13.1
*B20.1-03	Safety Standard for Conveyors and Related Equipment	3001.2, 3005.5
B31.3-02	Process Piping	415.8.6.1

ASTM

ASTM International
100 Barr Harbor Drive
West Conshohocken, PA 19428-2959

Standard reference number	Title	Referenced in code section number
A 6/A 6M- 04a	Specification for General Requirements for Rolled Steel, Structural Steel Bars, Plates, Shapes, and Sheet Piling	Table 1704.3
A 36/A 36M-04	Specification for Carbon Structural Steel	1809.3.1, 2103.13.5
A 82-02	Specification for Steel Wire, Plain, for Concrete Reinforcement	2103.13.5, 2103.13.6
A 123/A 123M-02	Specification for Zinc (Hot-dip Galvanized) Coating on Iron and Steel Products	2103.13.7.2
A 153-03	Specification for Zinc Coating (Hot-dip) on Iron and Steel Hardware	2103.13.7.2, 2304.9.5

ASTM—continued

A 185-02	Specification for Steel Welded Wire Reinforcement, Plain for Concrete	2103.13.4, 2103.13.5
A 240-04	Standard Specification for Chromium and Chromium-nickel Stainless Steel Plate, Sheet and Strip for Pressure Vessels and for General Applications	Table 1507.4.3(1), 2103.13.5
A 252-98 (2002)	Specification for Welded and Seamless Steel Pipe Piles	1809.3.1, 1810.6.1, 1810.8.2
A 283/A 283M-03	Specification for Low and Intermediate Tensile Strength Carbon Steel Plates	1809.3.1, 1810.6.1
A 307-03	Specification for Carbon Steel Bolts and Studs, 60,000 psi Tensile Strength	1911.1, 2103.13.5
A 416/A 416M-02	Specification for Steel Strand, Uncoated Seven-wire for Prestressed Concrete	1809.2.3.1, 2103.13.6
A 421/A 421M-02	Specification for Uncoated Stress-relieved Steel Wire for Prestressed Concrete	2103.13.6
*A 435/A 435M- 90 (2001)	Specification for Straight-beam Ultrasonic Examination of Steel Plates	1708.4
A 463/A 463M-02a	Specification for Steel Sheet, Aluminum-coated, by the Hot Dip Process	Table 1507.4.3(2)
A 480/A480M-02	Specification for General Requirements for Flat-rolled Stainless and Heat-resisting Steel Plate, Sheet, and Strip	2103.13.5
A 496-02	Specification for Steel Wire, Deformed for Concrete Reinforcement	2103.13.3
A 497-01	Specification for Steel Welded Reinforcement Deformed, for Concrete	2103.13.4
A 510-03	Specification for General Requirements for Wire Rods and Coarse Round Wire, Carbon Steel	2103.13.6
A 568/A 568M-03	Specification for Steel, Sheet, Carbon, and High-strength, Low-alloy, Hot-rolled and Cold-rolled, General Requirements for	Table 1704.3
A 572/A 572M-04	Specification for High-strength Low-alloy Columbium-vanadium Structural Steel	1809.3.1
A 588/A 588M-04	Specification for High-strength Low-alloy Structural Steel with 50 ksi (345 Mpa) Minimum Yield Point to 4 inches (100 mm) Thick	1809.3.1
A 615/A 615M-04a	Specification for Deformed and Plain Billet-steel Bars for Concrete Reinforcement	1708.3, 1810.8.2, 1908.1.5, 2103.13.1, 2103.13.6
A 641/A 641M-03	Specification for Zinc-coated (Galvanized) Carbon Steel Wire	2103.13.7.1
A 653/A 653M-04a	Specification for Steel Sheet, Zinc-coated Galvanized or Zinc-iron Alloy-coated Galvannealed by the Hot-dip Process	Table 1507.4.3(1), Table 1507.4.3(2), 2103.13.7.1
A 690-00a	Standard Specification for High Strength Low-alloy Steel H-piles and Sheet Piling for Use in Marine Environments	1809.3.1
A 706/A 706M-04a	Specification for Low-alloy Steel Deformed and Plain Bars for Concrete Reinforcement	1704.4.1, Table 1704.3, 1908.1.5, 2103.13.1, 2103.13.6, 2108.3
A 722/A 722M- 98 (2003)	Specification for Uncoated High-strength Steel Bar for Prestressing Concrete	1810.8.2, 2103.13.6, 2106.1.1.3.1
A 755/A 755M-04	Specification for Steel Sheet, Metallic-coated by the Hot-dip Process and Prepainted by the Coil-coating Process for Exterior Exposed Building Products	Table 1507.4.3(1), Table 1507.4.3(2)
A 767/A 767M-00b	Specification for Zinc-coated (Galvanized) Steel Bars for Concrete Reinforcement	2103.13.1
A 775/A 775M-04	Specification for Epoxy-coated Steel Reinforcing Bars	2103.13.1
A 792/A 792M-03	Specification for Steel Sheet, 55% Aluminum-zinc Alloy-coated by the Hot-dip Process	Table 1507.4.3(1), Table 1507.4.3(2)
A 875/A 875M-02a	Standard Specification for Steel Sheet Zinc-5 percent, Aluminum Alloy-coated by the Hot-dip Process	Table 1507.4.3(2)
A 884-02	Specification for Epoxy-coated Steel Wire and Welded Wire Fabric for Reinforcement	2103.13.7.3
A 898/A 898M- 91 (2001)	Specification for Straight Beam Ultrasonic Examination of Rolled Steel Shapes	1708.4
A 899-91 (2002)	Specification for Steel Wire Epoxy-coated	2103.13.7.3
A 913/A 913M-04	Specification for High-strength Low-alloy Steel Shapes of Structural Quality, Produced by Quenching and Self-tempering Process (QST)	1809.3.1
A924-04	Standard Specification for General Requirements for Steel Sheet, Metallic-coated by the Hot-dip Process	Table 1507.4.3(1)
A 951-02	Specification for Masonry Joint Reinforcement	2103.13.2
A 992-04a	Standard Specification for Structural Shapes	1809.3.1
A 996/A 996M-04	Specification for Rail-steel and Axle-steel Deformed Bars for Concrete Reinforcement	2103.13.1, 2103.13.6
A1008/A1008M-04b	Specification for Steel, Sheet, Cold-rolled, Carbon, Structural, High-strength Low-alloy and High-strength Low-alloy with Improved Formability	2103.13.5
B 42-02e01	Specification for Seamless Copper Pipe, Standard Sizes	909.13.1
B 43-04	Specification for Seamless Red Brass Pipe, Standard Sizes	909.13.1
B 68-02	Specification for Seamless Copper Tube, Bright Annealed (Metric)	909.13.1
B 88-03	Specification for Seamless Copper Water Tube	909.13.1
B 101-02	Specification for Lead-coated Copper Sheet and Strip for Building Construction	Table 1404.5.3, Table 1507.2.9.2, Table 1507.4.3(1)
B 209-04	Specification for Aluminum and Aluminum Alloy Steel and Plate	Table 1507.4.3(1)
B 251-02e01	Specification for General Requirements for Wrought Seamless Copper and Copper-alloy Tube	909.13.1
B 280-03	Specification for Seamless Copper Tube for Air Conditioning and Refrigeration Field Service	909.13.1
B 370-03	Specification for Cold-rolled Copper Sheet and Strip for Building Construction	1404.5.2, Table 1507.2.9.2, Table 1507.4.3(1)

ASTM—continued

B 695-00	Standard Specification for Coatings of Zinc Mechanically Deposited on Iron and Steel	2304.9.5
C 5-03	Specification for Quicklime for Structural Purposes	Table 2507.2
C 22/C 22M-00	Specification for Gypsum	Table 2506.2
C 27-98 (2002)	Specification for Standard Classification of Fireclay and High-alumina Refractory Brick	2111.5, 2111.8
C 28/C 28M-00e01	Specification for Gypsum Plasters	Table 2507.2
C 31/31M-03a	Practice for Making and Curing Concrete Test Specimens in the Field.	Table 1704.4
C 33-03	Specification for Concrete Aggregates. 721.3.1.4, 721.4.1.1.3
C 34-03	Specification for Structural Clay Load-bearing Wall Tile 2103.2
C 35-95 (2001)	Specification for Inorganic Aggregates for Use in Gypsum Plaster. . . . . .Table 2507.2
C 36/C 36M-03	Specification for Gypsum Wallboard . . . . Figure 721.5.1(2), Figure 721.5.1(3), Table 2506.2
C 37/C 37M-01	Specification for Gypsum Lath. . . . . .Table 2507.2
C 55-03	Specification for Concrete Brick . . . . Table 721.3.2, 2103.1, 2105.2.2.1.2
C 56-96 (2001)	Specification for Structural Clay Non-load Bearing Tile. 2103.2
C 59/C 59M-00	Specification for Gypsum Casting and Molding Plaster. . . . . .Table 2507.2
C 61/C 61M-00	Specification for Gypsum Keene's Cement . . . . .Table 2507.2
C 62-04	Specification for Building Brick (Solid Masonry Units Made from Clay or Shale) 1805.5.2.2, 2103.2, 2105.2.2.1.1
C 67-03ae01	Test Methods of Sampling and Testing Brick and Structural Clay Tile. 721.4.1.1.1, 2104.5, 2105.2.2.1.1, 2109.8.1.1
C 73-99a	Specification for Calcium Silicate Face Brick (Sand-lime Brick) . . . . .Table 721.3.2, 2103.1
C 79/C79M-04a	Specification for Treated Core and Nontreated Core Gypsum Sheathing Board. . . . . .Table 2506.2
C 90-03	Specification for Loadbearing Concrete Masonry Units . . . . . Table 721.3.2, 1805.5.2.2, 2103.1, 2105.2.2.1.2
C 91-03a	Specification for Masonry Cement. . . . . .Table 2103.8(1), Table 2507.2
C 94/C 94M-04	Specification for Ready-mixed Concrete 109.3.1
C109/C109M-02	Standard Test Method for Compressive Strength of Hydraulic Cement Mortars (Using 2-in. or [50-mm] Cube Specimens) 2103.11.1
C 126-99	Specification for Ceramic Glazed Structural Clay Facing Tile, Facing Brick, and Solid Masonry Units .2103.2
C 140-03	Test Method Sampling and Testing Concrete Masonry Units and Related Units 721.3.1.2, 2105.2.2.1.2
C 150-04	Specification for Portland Cement . . . . .Table 2103.8(1), Table 2507.2
C 172-04	Practice for Sampling Freshly Mixed Concrete . . . . .Table 1704.4
C 199-84 (2000)	Test Method for Pier Test for Refractory Mortars 2111.5, 2111.8, 2113.12
C 206-03	Specification for Finishing Hydrated Lime . . . . .Table 2507.2
C 207-04	Specification for Hydrated Lime for Masonry Purposes . . . . Table 2103.8(1)
C 208-95 (2001)	Specification for Cellulosic Fiber Insulating Board . . . . .Table 1508.2, 2303.1.5
C 212-00	Specification for Structural Clay Facing Tile. 2103.2
C 216-04a	Specification for Facing Brick (Solid Masonry Units Made from Clay or Shale) 1805.5.2.2, 2103.2, 2105.2.2.1.1
C 270-04	Specification for Mortar for Unit Masonry. . . . . .2103.8, Table 2103.8(2)
C 315-02	Specification for Clay Flue Linings . . . . 2113.11.1, Table 2113.16(1)
C 317/C 317M-00	Specification for Gypsum Concrete 1914.1
C 330-04	Specification for Lightweight Aggregates for Structural Concrete 721.1.1
C 331-04	Specification for Lightweight Aggregates for Concrete Masonry Units 721.3.1.4, 721.4.1.1.3
C 406-00	Specification for Roofing Slate. 1507.7.4
C 442/C 442M-04	Specification for Gypsum Backing Board and Coreboard and Gypsum Shaftliner Board. . . . . . .Table 2506.2
C 472- 99 (2004)	Specification for Standard Test Methods for Physical Testing of Gypsum, Gypsum Plasters and Gypsum Concrete. . . . . .Table 2506.2
C 473-03	Test Method for Physical Testing of Gypsum Panel Products. . . . . .Table 2506.2
C 474-02	Test Methods for Joint Treatment Materials for Gypsum Board Construction . . . . .Table 2506.2
C 475/ C475M-02	Specification for Joint Compound and Joint Tape for Finishing Gypsum Wallboard . . . . .Table 2506.2
C 476-02	Specification for Grout for Masonry. 2103.12, 2105.2.2.1.1, 2105.2.2.1.2, 2105.2.2.1.3
C 503-03	Specification for Marble Dimension Stone (Exterior) 2103.4
C 514-01	Specification for Nails for the Application of Gypsum Board. . . . . Table 720.1(2), Table 720.1(3), Table 2306.4.5, Table 2506.2
C 516-02	Specifications for Vermiculite Loose Fill Thermal Insulation 721.3.1.4, 721.4.1.1.3
C 547-03	Specification for Mineral Fiber Pipe Insulation . . . . Table 720.1(2), Table 720.1(3)
C 549-02	Specification for Perlite Loose Fill Insulation 721.3.1.4, 721.4.1.1.3
C 552-03	Standard Specification for Cellular Glass Thermal Insulation. . . . . .Table 1508.2
C 557-03	Specification for Adhesives for Fastening Gypsum Wallboard to Wood Framing . . . . .Table 2506.2
C 568-03	Specification for Limestone Dimension Stone 2103.4
C 578-04	Standard Specification for Rigid, Cellular Polystyrene Thermal Insulation . . . . .Table 1508.2
C 587-02	Specification for Gypsum Veneer Plaster. . . . . .Table 2507.2
C 588/C 588M-01	Specification for Gypsum Base for Veneer Plasters. . . . . .Table 2507.2
C 595-03	Specification for Blended Hydraulic Cements . . . . .Table 2103.8(1), Table 2507.2
C 615-03	Specification for Granite Dimension Stone 2103.4
C 616-03	Specification for Quartz Dimension Stone 2103.4
C 629-03	Specification for Slate Dimension Stone 2103.4

ASTM—continued

C 630/C 630M-03	Specification for Water-resistant Gypsum Backing Board	Table 2506.2
C 631-95a (2000)	Specification for Bonding Compounds for Interior Gypsum Plastering	Table 2507.2
*C 635-00	Specification for the Manufacturer, Performance and Testing of Metal Suspension Systems for Acoustical Tile and Lay-in Panel Ceilings	803.9.1.1, 2506.2.1
C 636-04	Practice for Installation of Metal Ceiling Suspension Systems for Acoustical Tile and Lay-in Panels	803.9.1.1
C 645-04	Specification for Nonstructural Steel Framing Members	Table 2506.2, Table 2507.2
C 652-04a	Specification for Hollow Brick (Hollow Masonry Units Made from Clay or Shale)	1805.5.2.2, 2103.2, 2105.2.2.1.1
C 728-97E1	Standard Specification for Perlite Thermal Insulation Board	Table 1508.2
C 744-99	Specification for Prefaced Concrete and Calcium Silicate Masonry Units	2103.1
C 754-04	Specification for Installation of Steel Framing Members to Receive Screw-attached Gypsum Panel Products	Table 2508.1, Table 2511.1
C 836-03	Specification for High-solids Content, Cold Liquid-applied Elastomeric Waterproofing Membrane for Use with Separate Wearing Course	1507.15.2
*C 840-01	Specification for Application and Finishing of Gypsum Board	Table 2508.1, 2509.2
C 841-03	Specification for Installation of Interior Lathing and Furring	Table 2508.1, Table 2511.1
C 842-99	Specification for Application of Interior Gypsum Plaster	Table 2511.1, 2511.3, 2511.4
C 843-99e01	Specification for Application of Gypsum Veneer Plaster	Table 2511.1
C 844-99	Specification for Application of Gypsum Base to Receive Gypsum Veneer Plaster	Table 2508.1
C 847-00	Specification for Metal Lath	Table 2507.2
C 887-79a (2001)	Specification for Packaged, Dry Combined Materials for Surface Bonding Mortar	1807.2.2, 2103.9
C 897-00	Specification for Aggregate for Job-mixed Portland Cement-based Plasters	Table 2507.2
C 926-98a	Specification for Application of Portland Cement Based-plaster	2109.8.4.6, 2510.3, Table 2511.1, 2511.3, 2511.4, 2512.1, 2512.1.2, 2512.2, 2512.6, 2512.8.2, 2512.9, 2513.7
C 931/C 931M-04	Specification for Exterior Gypsum Soffit Board	Table 2506.2
C 932-03	Specification for Surface-applied Bonding Agents for Exterior Plastering	Table 2507.2
C 933-04	Specification for Welded Wire Lath	Table 2507.2
*C 946-91 (2001)	Specification for Practice for Construction of Dry-stacked, Surface-bonded Walls	2103.9, 2109.2.3.2
C 954-00	Specification for Steel Drill Screws for the Application of Gypsum Panel Products or Metal Plaster Bases to Steel Studs from 0.033 inch (0.84 mm) to 0.112 inch (2.84 mm) in Thickness	Table 2506.2, Table 2507.2
C 955-03	Standard Specification for Load-bearing Transverse and Axial Steel Studs, Runners Tracks, and Bracing or Bridging, for Screw Application of Gypsum Panel Products and Metal Plaster Bases	Table 2506.2, Table 2507.2
C 956-04	Specification for Installation of Cast-in-place Reinforced Gypsum Concrete	1914.1
C 957-04	Specification for High-solids Content, Cold Liquid-applied Elastomeric Waterproofing Membrane with Integral Wearing Surface	1507.15.2
C 960/ C960M-04	Specification for Predecorated Gypsum Board	Table 2506.2
C1002-01	Specification for Steel Self-piercing Tapping Screws for the Application of Gypsum Panel Products or Metal Plaster Bases to Wood Studs or Steel Studs	Table 2506.2, Table 2507.2
C1006-84 (2001)	Test Method for Splitting Tensile Strength of Masonry Units	2103.11.1
*C1007-00	Specification for Installation of Load Bearing (Transverse and Axial) Steel Studs and Related Accessories	Table 2508.1, Table 2511.1
C1019-03	Test Method of Sampling and Testing Grout	2105.2.2.1.1, 2105.2.2.1.2, 2105.2.2.1.3
C1029-02	Specification for Spray-applied Rigid Cellular Polyurethane Thermal Insulation	1507.14.2
C1032-04	Specification for Woven Wire Plaster Base	Table 2507.2
C1047-99	Specification for Accessories for Gypsum Wallboard and Gypsum Veneer Base	Table 2506.2, Table 2507.2
C1063-03	Specification for Installation of Lathing and Furring to Receive Interior and Exterior Portland Cement Based Plaster	2109.8.4.6, 2510.3, Table 2511.1, 2512.1.1
C 1072-00a	Standard Text Method for Measurement of Masonry Flexural Bond Strength	2103.11.1
C1088-02	Specification for Thin Veneer Brick Units Made from Clay or Shale	2103.2
C1167-03	Specification for Clay Roof Tiles	1507.3.4
C1177/C1177M-04	Specification for Glass Mat Gypsum Substrate for Use as Sheathing	Table 2506.2
C1178/C1178M-04	Specification for Glass Mat Water-resistant Gypsum Backing Panel	Table 2506.2, 2509.2
C1186-02	Specification for Flat Nonasbestos Fiber Cement Sheets	1404.10
C1261-04	Specification for Firebox Brick for Residential Fireplaces	2111.5, 2111.8
C1278/C 1278M-03	Specification for Fiber-reinforced Gypsum Panels	Table 2506.2
C1280-04	Specification for Application of Gypsum Sheathing	Table 2508.1, 2508.2
*C1283-00e01	Practice for Installing Clay Flue Liners	2113.12
C1288-01	Standard Specification for Discrete Nonasbestos Fiber-cement Interior Substrate Sheets	2509.2
C1289-03	Standard Specification for Faced Rigid Cellular Polyisocyanurate Thermal Insulation Board	Table 1508.2
C1314-03b	Test Method for Compressive Strength of Masonry Prisms	2105.2.2.2.2, 2105.3.1, 2105.3.2
C1325-04	Standard Specification for Nonasbestos Fiber-mat Reinforced Cement Interior Substrate Sheets	2509.02

ASTM—continued

C1328-03a	Specification for Plastic (Stucco Cement)	Table 2507.2
C1329-04	Specification for Mortar Cement	Table 2103.8(1)
C1386-98	Specification for Precast Autoclaved Aerated Concrete (PAAC) Wall Construction Units	2102.1, 2103.3, 2105.2.2.1.3
C1395/1395M-04	Specification for Gypsum Ceiling Board	Table 2506.2
C1396/C1396M-04	Standard Specifications for Gypsum Board	Table 2506.2
C1405-00a	Standard Specification for Glazed Brick (Single Fired, Solid Brick Units)	2103.2
C1492-03	Standard Specification for Concrete Roof Tile	1507.3.5
D 25-99E01	Specification for Round Timber Piles	1809.1.1, 2303.1.11
D 41-94 (2000) e01	Specification for Asphalt Primer Used in Roofing, Dampproofing and Waterproofing	Table 1507.10.2
D 43-00	Coal Tar Primer Used in Roofing, Dampproofing and Waterproofing	Table 1507.10.2
D 56-02a	Test Method for Flash Point By Tag Closed Tester	307.2
D 86-04b	Test Method for Distillation of Petroleum Products at Atmospheric Pressure	307.2
D 93-02a	Test Method for Flash Point By Pensky-Martens Closed Cup Tester	307.2
D 225-04	Specification for Asphalt Shingles (Organic Felt) Surfaced with Mineral Granules	1507.2.5
D 226-97a	Specification for Asphalt-saturated Organic Felt Used in Roofing and Waterproofing	1404.2, 1507.2.3, 1507.3.3, 1507.5.3, 1507.6.3, 1507.7.3, Table 1507.8, 1507.8.3, 1507.9.3, 1507.9.4, Table 1507.10.2
D 227-03	Specification for Coal-tar-saturated Organic Felt Used in Roofing and Waterproofing	Table 1507.10.2
D 312-00	Specification for Asphalt Used in Roofing	Table 1507.10.2
D 422-63 (2002)	Test Method for Particle-size Analysis of Soils	1802.3.2
D 450-96 (2000)e01	Specification for Coal-tar Pitch Used in Roofing, Dampproofing and Waterproofing	Table 1507.10.2
D 635-03	Test Method for Rate of Burning and/or Extent and Time of Burning of Self-Supporting Plastics in a Horizontal Position	2606.4
D1143-81 (1994) E01	Test Method for Piles Under Static Axial Compressive Load	1808.2.8.3
D1227-00	Specification for Emulsified Asphalt Used as a Protective Coating for Roofing	Table 1507.10.2, 1507.15.2
D1557-02	Test Method for Laboratory Compaction Characteristics of Soil Using Modified Effort [56,000 ft-lb/ft3 (2,700 KN m/m 3)]	1803.5
D1586-99	Specification for Penetration Test and Split-barrel Sampling of Soils	1613.5.5
D1761-88 (2000) e01	Test Method for Mechanical Fasteners in Wood	1715.1.1, 1715.1.2, 1715.1.3
D1863-03	Specification for Mineral Aggregate Used on Built-up Roofs	Table 1507.10.2
D1929-96 (2001)e01	Test Method for Determining Ignition Properties of Plastics	402.15.4, 406.5.2, 1407.11.2.1, 2606.4
D1970-01	Specification for Self-adhering Polymer Modified Bituminous Sheet Materials Used as Steep Roof Underlayment for Ice Dam Protection	1507.2.4, 1507.2.9.2, 1507.3.9, 1507.5.6, 1507.8.7, 1507.9.8
D2166-00	Test Method for Unconfined Compressive Strength of Cohesive Soil	1613.5.5
D2178-97a	Specification for Asphalt Glass Felt Used in Roofing and Waterproofing	Table 1507.10.2
D2216-98	Test Method for Laboratory Determination of Water (Moisture) Content of Soil and Rock by Mass	1613.5.5
D2487-00	Practice for Classification of Soils for Engineering Purposes (Unified Soil Classification System)	Table 1610.1, 1802.3.1
D2626-04	Specification for Asphalt Saturated and Coated Organic Felt Base Sheet Used in Roofing	1507.3.3, Table 1507.10.2
D2822-91 (97)e01	Specification for Asphalt Roof Cement	Table 1507.10.2
D2823-90 (97) e1	Specification for Asphalt Roof Coatings	Table 1507.10.2
D2843-99 (2004)	Test for Density of Smoke from the Burning or Decomposition of Plastics	2606.4
D2850-03a	Test Method for Unconsolidated, Undrained Triaxial Compression Test on Cohesive Soils	1613.5.5
D2898-94 (1999)	Test Methods for Accelerated Weathering of Fire-Retardant-Treated Wood for Fire Testing	1505.1, 2303.2.1, 2303.2.3
D3019-e01(Supp)	Specification for Lap Cement Used with Asphalt Roll Roofing, Nonfibered, Asbestos Fibered and Nonasbestos Fibered	Table 1507.10.2
D3161-03b	Test Method for a Wind Resistance of Asphalt Shingles (Fan Induced Method)	1504.1.1, 1507.2.5
D3200-74 (2000)	Standard Specification and Test Method for Establishing Recommended Design Stresses for Round Timber Construction Poles	2303.1.11
D3201-94 (2003)	Test Method for Hygroscopic Properties of Fire-retardant-treated Wood and Wood-based Products	2303.2.4
D3278-96e1	Test Methods for Flash Point of Liquids by Small Scale Closed-cup Apparatus	307.2
D3462-04	Specification for Asphalt Shingles Made from Glass Felt and Surfaced with Mineral Granules	1507.2.5
D3468-99	Specification for Liquid-applied Neoprene and Chlorosulfonated Polyethylene Used in Roofing and Waterproofing	1507.15.2
D3679-04	Specification for Rigid Poly [Vinyl Chloride (PVC) Siding]	1404.9, 1405.13
D3689-90 (1995)	Method for Testing Individual Piles Under Static Axial Tensile Load	1808.2.8.5
D3737-03	Practice for Establishing Allowable Properties for Structural Glued Laminated Timber (Glulam)	2303.1.3
D3746-85 (2002)	Test Method for Impact Resistance of Bituminous Roofing Systems	1504.7
D3747-79 (2000)e1	Specification for Emulsified Asphalt Adhesive for Adhering Roof Insulation	Table 1507.10.2
D3909-97b	Specification for Asphalt Roll Roofing (Glass Felt) Surfaced with Mineral Granules	1507.2.9.2, 1507.6.4, Table 1507.10.2

ASTM—continued

D 3957-03	Standard Practices for Establishing Stress Grades for Structural Members Used in Log Buildings	2303.1.10
D4022-94 (2000)e01	Specification for Coal Tar Roof Cement, Asbestos Containing	Table 1507.10.2
D4272-03	Test Method for Total Energy Impact of Plastic Films by Dart Drop	1504.7
D4318-00	Test Methods for Liquid Limit, Plastic Limit and Plasticity Index of Soils	1613.5.5, 1802.3.2
D4434-04	Specification for Poly (Vinyl Chloride) Sheet Roofing	1507.13.2
D4479-00	Specification for Asphalt Roof Coatings-Asbestos-free	Table 1507.10.2
D4586-00	Specification for Asphalt Roof Cement, Asbestos-free	Table 1507.10.2
D4601-98	Specification for Asphalt-coated Glass Fiber Base Sheet Used in Roofing	Table 1507.10.2
D4637-04	Specification for EPDM Sheet Used in Single-ply Roof Membrane	1507.12.2
D4829-03	Test Method for Expansion Index of Soils	1802.3.2
D4869-04	Specification for Asphalt-saturated (Organic Felt) Underlayment Used in Steep Slope Roofing	1507.2.3, 1507.5.3, 1507.6.3, 1507.7.3, 1507.8.3, 1507.9.3
D4897-01	Specification for Asphalt-coated Glass Fiber Venting Base Sheet Used in Roofing	Table 1507.10.2
D4945-00	Test Method for High-strain Dynamic Testing of Piles	1808.2.8.3
D4990-97a	Specification for Coal Tar Glass Felt Used in Roofing and Waterproofing	Table 1507.10.2
D5019-96e01	Specification for Reinforced Nonvulcanized Polymeric Sheet Used in Roofing Membrane	1507.12.2
D5055-04	Specification for Establishing and Monitoring Structural Capacities of Prefabricated Wood I-Joists	2303.1.2
D5456-03	Specification for Evaluation of Structural Composite Lumber Products	2303.1.9
D5516-03	Test Method of Evaluating the Flexural Properties of Fire-retardant-treated Softwood Plywood Exposed to the Elevated Temperatures	2303.2.2.1
D5643-94 (2000)e01	Specification for Coal Tar Roof Cement, Asbestos-free	Table 1507.10.2
D5664-02	Test Methods for Evaluating the Effects of Fire-retardant Treatment and Elevated Temperatures on Strength Properties of Fire-retardant-treated Lumber	2303.2.2.2
D5665-99a	Specification for Thermoplastic Fabrics Used in Cold-applied Roofing and Waterproofing	Table 1507.10.2
D5726-98	Specification for Thermoplastic Fabrics Used in Hot-applied Roofing and Waterproofing	Table 1507.10.2
D6083-97a	Specification for Liquid Applied Acrylic Coating Used in Roofing	Table 1507.10.2, 1507.15.2
D6162-00A	Specification for Styrene Butadiene Styrene (SBS) Modified Bituminous Sheet Materials Using a Combination of Polyester and Glass Fiber Reinforcements	1507.11.2
D6163-00 E01	Specification for Styrene-Butadiene-Styrene (SBS) Modified Bituminous Sheet Materials Using Glass Fiber Reinforcements	1507.11.2
D6164-00	Specification for Styrene-Butadiene-Styrene (SBS) Modified Bituminous Sheet Metal Materials Using Polyester Reinforcements	1507.11.2
D6222-02	Specification for Atactic Polypropylene (APP) Modified Bituminous Sheet Materials Using Polyester Reinforcements	1507.11.2
D6223-02	Specification for Atactic Polypropylene (APP) Modified Bituminous Sheet Materials Using a Combination of Polyester and Glass Fiber Reinforcements	1507.11.2
D6298-00	Specification for Fiberglass Reinforced Styrene-Butadiene-Styrene (SBS) Modified Bituminous Sheets with a Factory Applied Metal Surface	1507.11.2
D6305-02e01	Practice for Calculating Bending Strength Design Adjustment Factors for Fire-retardant-treated Plywood Roof Sheathing	2303.2.2.1
D6380-01E1	Standard Specification for Asphalt Roll Roofing (Organic) Felt	1507.2.9.2, 1507.3.3, 1507.6.4
D6381-03	Standard Test Method for Measurement of Asphalt Shingle Mechanical Uplift Resistance	1504.2.1, Table 1504.2.1, 1609.5.2
D6694-01	Standard Specification for Liquid-applied Silicone Coating Used in Spray Polyurethane Foam Roofing	1507.15.2
D6754-02	Standard Specification for Ketone Ethylene Ester Based Sheet Roofing	1507.13.2
D6757-02	Standard Specification for Inorganic Underlayment for Use with Steep Slope Roofing Products	1507.2.3
D6841-03	Standard Practice for Calculating Design Value Treatment Adjustment Factors for Fire-retardant-treated Lumber	2303.2.2.2
D6878-03	Standard Specification for Thermoplastic Polyolefin Based Sheet Roofing	1507.13.2
E 72-02	Standard Test Methods of Conducting Strength Tests of Panels for Building Construction	2103.11.1
E 84-05	Test Methods for Surface Burning Characteristics of Building Materials	402.10, 402.15.4, 406.5.2, 410.3.5.3, 703.4.2, 719.1, 719.4, 802.1, 803.1, 803.5, 803.6.1, 806.5, 1407.9, 1407.10.1, 2303.2, 2603.3, 2603.4.1.13, 2603.5.4, 2604.2.4, 2606.4, 3105.4
E 90-04	Test Method for Laboratory Measurement of Airborne Sound Transmission Loss of Building Partitions and Elements	1207.2
E 96-00	Test Method for Water Vapor Transmission of Materials	202, 1203.2
E 108-04	Test Methods for Fire Tests of Roof Coverings	1505.1, 2603.6, 2610.2, 2610.3

ASTM—continued

E 119-08a	Test Methods for Fire Tests of Building Construction and Materials	. . 410.3.5.2, 703.2, 703.2.1, 703.2.3, 703.3, 704.7, 704.9, 706.2.1, 706.7, 711.3.2, 712.3.1, 712.4.1.1, 713.1, 713.4, 714.7, 715.2, 716.5.2, 716.5.3, 716.6.1, 716.6.2, Table 720.1(1), 1407.10.2, 2103.2, 2603.4, 2603.5.1
E 136-99e01	Test Method for Behavior of Materials in a Vertical Tube Furnace at 750°C	. . . . 703.4.1
E 328-02	Methods for Stress Relaxation for Materials and Structures	. . . . 2103.13.6
E 330-02	Test Method for Structural Performance of Exterior Windows, Curtain Walls and Doors by Uniform Static Air Pressure Difference	. . . . 1714.5.2
E 331-00	Test Method for Water Penetration of Exterior Windows, Skylights, Doors and Curtain Walls by Uniform Static Air Pressure Difference	. . . . .1403.2
E 492-04	Test Method for Laboratory Measurement of Impact Sound Transmission Through Floor-ceiling Assemblies Using the Tapping Machine	. . . . .1207.3
E 518-03	Standard Test Methods for Flexural Bond Strength of Masonry	. . . . .2101.3.11.1
E 519-07	Standard Test Method for Diagonal Tension (Shear) in Masonry Assemblages	. . . . 2103.11.1
E 605-00	Test Method for Thickness and Density of Sprayed Fire-resistive Material (SFRM) Applied to Structural Members	. . . . 1704.10.3, 1704.10.3.1, 1704.10.3.2, 1704.10.4
E 681-04	Test Methods for Concentration Limits of Flammability of Chemical Vapors and Gases	. . . . .307.2
E 736-00	Test Method for Cohesion/Adhesion of Sprayed Fire-resistive Materials Applied to Structural Members	. . . . 1704.10.5
E 814-02	Test Method of Fire Tests of Through-penetration Firestops	. . . . 702.1, 712.3.1.2, 712.4.1.1.2
E 970-00	Test Method for Critical Radiant Flux of Exposed Attic Floor Insulation Using a Radiant Heat Energy Source	. . . . 719.3.1
E1300-04e01	Practice for Determining Load Resistance of Glass in Buildings	. . . . .2404.1, 2404.2, 2404.3.1, 2404.3.2, 2404.3.3, 2404.3.4, 2404.3.5
E1592-01	Test Method for Structural Performance of Sheet Metal Roof and Siding Systems by Uniform Static Air Pressure Difference	. . . . 1504.3.2
*E1602-01	Guide for Construction of Solid Fuel-burning Masonry Heaters	. . . . .2112.2
E1886-04	Test Method for Performance of Exterior Windows, Curtain Walls, Doors and Storm Shutters Impacted by Missiles and exposed to Cyclic Pressure Differentials	. . . . . 1609.1.2
E1966-00	Test Method for Fire-resistant Joint Systems	. . . . 702.1, 713.3
E1996-04	Specification for Performance of Exterior Windows, Glazed Curtain Walls, Doors and Storm Shutters Impacted by Windborne Debris in Hurricanes	. . . . .1609.1.2, 1609.1.2.1
E 2307-04	Standard Test Method for Determining Fire Resistance of Perimeter Fire Barrier Systems Using Intermediate-scale, Multistory Test Apparatus	. . . . .713.4
F 547-01	Terminology of Nails for Use with Wood and Wood-based Materials	. . . . .Table 2506.2
F1346-91 (1996)	Performance Specification for Safety Covers and Labeling Requirements for All Covers for Swimming Pools, Spas and Hot Tubs	. . . . .3109.4, 3109.4.1.8, 3109.5, 3109.7.1
F1667-03	Specification for Driven Fasteners: Nails, Spikes and Staples	. . . . Table 720.1(2), Table 720.1(3), 1507.2.6, 2303.6, Table 2506.2
F2208-08	Standard Specification for Pool Alarms	. . . . 3109.7.1
F2387-04	Standard Specification for Manufactured Safety Vacuum Release Systems (SVRS) for Swimming Pools, Spas and Hot Tubs	. . . . .3109.6.2.2
G 152-04	Practice for Operating Open Flame Carbon Arc Light Apparatus for Exposure of Nonmetallic Materials	. . . . .1504.6
G 154-00A	Practice for Operating Fluorescent Light Apparatus for UV Exposure of Nonmetallic Materials	. . . . . .1504.6
G 155-04	Practice for Operating Xenon Arc Light Apparatus for Exposure of Nonmetallic Materials	. . . . .1504.6

AWCI

The Association of the Wall and Ceiling Industries International
513 West Broad Street, Suite 210
Falls Church, VA 22046

Standard reference number	Title	Referenced in code section number
*12-B-04 Second Edition	Technical Manual 12-B Standard Practice for the Testing and Inspection of Field Applied Thin-Film Intumescent Fire-Resistive Materials; an Annotated Guide, Second Edition	. . . . .1704.11

AWPA

American Wood-Preservers' Association
P.O. Box 5690
Grandbury, TX 76049

Standard reference number	Title	Referenced in code section number
C1-00	All Timber Products-Preservative Treatment by Pressure Processes	1505.6
M4-02	Standard for the Care of Preservative-treated Wood Products	1809.1.2, 2303.1.8
	USE CATEGORY SYSTEM: User	
U1-04	Specification for Treated Wood Except Section 6, Commodity Specification H	1403.5, Table 1507.9.5, 1805.4.5, 1805.4.6, 1805.7.1, 1809.1.2, 2303.1.8, 2304.11.2, 2304.11.4, 2304.11.6, 2304.11.7

AWS

American Welding Society
550 N.W. LeJeune Road
Miami, FL 33126

Standard reference number	Title	Referenced in code section number
D1.1-04	Structural Welding Code-Steel	Table 1704.3, 1704.3.1, 1708.4
D1.3-98	Structural Welding Code-Sheet Steel	Table 1704.3
D1.4-98	Structural Welding Code-Reinforcing Steel	Table 1704.3, Table 1704.4, 2107.6

BHMA

Builders Hardware Manufacturers' Association
355 Lexington Avenue, 17th Floor
New York, NY 10017-6603

Standard reference number	Title	Referenced in code section number
A 156.10-05	American National Standard for Power Operated Pedestrian Doors.	1008.1.3.2
*A 156.19-02	Standard for Power Assist and Low Energy Power Operated Doors	1008.1.3.2

CGSB

Canadian General Standards Board
222 Queens Street
14th Floor, Suite 1402
Ottawa, Ontario, Canada KIA 1G6

Standard reference number	Title	Referenced in code section number
37-GP-52M (1984)	Roofing and Waterproofing Membrane, Sheet Applied, Elastomeric.	1504.7, 1507.12.2
37.54-95	Polyvinyl Chloride Roofing and Waterproofing Membrane	1507.13.2
37-GP-56M (1980)	Membrane, Modified, Bituminous, Prefabricated and Reinforced for Roofing- with December 1985 Amendment.	1507.11.2

CPSC

Consumer Product Safety Commission
4330 East West Highway
Bethesada, MD 20814-4408

Standard reference number	Title	Referenced in code section number
16 CFR Part 1201(1984)	Safety Standard for Architectural Glazing Material	2406.1.1, 2406.2.1, 2407.1, 2408.2.1, 2408.3
16 CFR Part 1209 (1979)	Interim Safety Standard for Cellulose Insulation	719.6

CPSC—continued

16 CFR Part 1404 (1984)	Cellulose Insulation 719.6	
16 CFR Part 1500 (2010)	Hazardous Substances and Articles; Administration and Enforcement Regulations 307.2	
*16 CFR Part 1500.44 (2001)	Method for Determining Extremely Flammable and Flammable Solids 307.2	
16 CFR Part 1507 (2001)	Fireworks Devices 307.2	
16 CFR Part 1630 (2007)	Standard for the Surface Flammability of Carpets and Rugs 804.4.1	

CSA

Canadian Standards Association
5060 Spectrum Way, Suite 100
Mississauga, Ontario, L4W 5N6 Canada

Standard reference number	Title	Referenced in code section number
*AAMA/WDMA/CSA 101/I.S.2/A440-08	Specifications for Windows, Doors and Unit Skylights 1714.5.1, 2405.5	

CSSB

Cedar Shake and Shingle Bureau
P.O. Box 1178
Sumas, WA 98295-1178

Standard reference number	Title	Referenced in code section number
CSSB-97	Grading and Packing Rules for Western Red Cedar Shakes and Western Red Shingles of the Cedar Shake and Shingle Bureau . . . . Table 1507.8.4, Table 1507.9.5	

DASMA

Door and Access Systems Manufacturers
Association International
1300 Summer Avenue
Cleveland, OH 44115-2851

Standard reference number	Title	Referenced in code section number
107-98 (03)	Room Fire Test Standard for Garage Doors Using Foam Plastic Insulation .2603.4.1.9	

DOC

U.S. Department of Commerce
National Institute of Standards and Technology
100 Bureau Drive Stop 3460
Gaithersburg, MD 20899

Standard reference number	Title	Referenced in code section number
PS-1-95	Construction and Industrial Plywood . . . . .2303.1.4, 2304.6.2, Table 2304.7(4), Table 2304.7(5), 2306.3.1, Table 2306.3.1, Table 2306.3.2	
PS-2-92	Performance Standard for Wood-based Structural-use Panels . . . . .2303.1.4, 2304.6.2, Table 2304.7(5), Table 2306.3.1, 2306.3.1, Table 2306.3.2	
PS 20-99	American Softwood Lumber Standard 1809.1.1, 2302.1, 2303.1.1	

DOL

U.S. Department of Labor
c/o Superintendent of Documents
U.S. Government Printing Office
Washington, DC 20402-9325

Standard reference number	Title	Referenced in code section number
29 CFR Part 1910.1000	Air Contaminans	902.1

DOTn

U.S. Department of Transportation
c/o Superintendent of Documents
U.S. Government Printing Office
Washington, DC 20402-9325

Standard reference number	Title	Referenced in code section number
49 CFR-2009	Specification of Transportation of Explosive and Other Dangerous Articles, UN 0335,UN 0336 Shipping Containers	307.2
49 CFR Parts 173.137 (2009)	Shippers-General Requirements for Shipments and Packaging-Class 8-Assignment of Packing Group	307.2

FEMA

Federal Emergency Management Agency
Federal Center Plaza
500 C Street S.W.
Washington, DC 20472

Standard reference number	Title	Referenced in code section number
*FIA-TB11-01	Crawlspace Construction for Buildings Located in Special Flood Hazard Areas.	1807.1.2.1

FM

Factory Mutual
Standards Laboratories Department
1151 Boston-Providence Turnpike
Norwood, MA 02062

Standard reference number	Title	Referenced in code section number
4450 (1989)	Approval Standard for Class 1 Insulated Steel Deck Roofs-with Supplements through July 1992	1504.3.1, 1508.1, 2603.3, 2603.4.1.5
4470 (1992)	Approval Standard for Class 1 Roof Covers	1504.3.1, 1504.7
*4880 (2001)	American National Standard for Evaluating Insulated Wall or Wall and Roof/Ceiling Assemblies, Plastic Interior Finish Materials, Plastic Exterior Building Panels, Wall/Ceiling Coating Systems, Interior and Exterior Finish Systems	2603.4, 2603.9

GA

Gypsum Association
810 First Street N.E. #510
Washington, DC 20002-4268

Standard reference number	Title	Referenced in code section number
GA 216-04	Application and Finishing of Gypsum Board	Table 2508.1, 2509.2
GA 600-03	Fire-Resistance Design Manual, 17th Edition . . . . Table 720.1(1), Table 720.1(2), Table 720.1(3)

HPVA

Hardwood Plywood Veneer Association
1825 Michael Faraday Drive
Reston, VA 20190-5350

Standard reference number	Title	Referenced in code section number
HP-1-2000	The American National Standard for Hardwood and Decorative Plywood 2303.3, 2304.6.2	

ICC

International Code Council
5203 Leesburg Pike, Suite 600
Falls Church, VA 22041

Standard reference number	Title	Referenced in code section number
*ICC/ANSI A117.1-03	Accessible and Usable Buildings and Facilities 406.2.2, 907.9.1.4,1007.6.5, 1010.1, 1010.6.5, 1010.9, 1011.3, 1101.2, 1102.1, 1103.2.14, 1106.1.1, 1106.7, 1107.2, 1107.2.1, 1107.2.2, 1108.2.2, 1109.1, 1109.2.1.1, 1109.2.2, 1109.3, 1109.4, 1109.8, 1607.7, 2902.5, 3001.3	
*ICC 300-02	ICC Standard on Bleachers, Folding and Telescopic Seating and Grandstands. 1025.1.1	
ECCCNYS-10	Energy Conservation Construction Code of New York State 101.4.7, 1203.3.2, 1301.1.1, 1403.2, 1403.7	
EBCNYS-10	Existing Building Code of New York State 101.4.8, 102.3, 102.8, 1009.3, 1103.2.2, 1107.7.1.3, 1107.7.1.4, 1510.1, 1613.3	
FCNYS-10	Fire Code of New York State . . . . . 101.4.6, 102.8, 103.4, 105.1, 201.3, 307.1, 307.1.1, 307.2, Table 307.1(1), Table 307.1(2), 404.2, 406.5.1, 406.6.1, 410.3.6, 411.1, 412.4.1, 413.1, 414.1.1, 414.1.2, 414.1.2.1, 414.2, 414.2.5, Table 414.2.5(1), Table 414.2.5(2), 414.3, 414.5, 414.5.1, Table 414.5.1, 414.5.2, 414.5.4, 414.5.5, 414.6, 415.1, 415.2, 415.3, 415.3.1, Table 415.3.1, Table 415.3.2, 415.6, 415.6.1, 415.6.1.4, 415.6.2, 415.6.2.3, 415.6.2.5, 415.6.2.7, 415.6.2.8, 415.6.2.9, 415.6.3, 415.6.3.3.3, 415.6.3.5, 415.6.4, 415.7, 415.8.1, 415.8.2.7, 415.8.5.1, 415.8.7.2, 415.8.9.3, 415.8.10.1, 416.1, 420.1, 420.7, 501.3, 501.4, 704.8.2, 706.1, 901.2, 901.3, 901.5, 901.6.2, 903.2.6.1, 903.2.11, Table 903.2.13, 903.5, 904.2.1, 905.1, 905.3.6, 906.1, 907.2.5, 907.2.12.2, 907.2.14, 907.2.16, 907.14, 907.19, 909.20, 910.2.2, Table 910.3, 1001.3, 1203.4.2, 1203.5, 2603.4.1.12, 2702.1, 2702.2.9, 2702.2.11, 2702.2.12, 2702.2.13, 2702.3, 3102.1, 3103.1, 3309.2,	
FGCNYS-10	Fuel Gas Code of New York State . . . . 101.4.2, 201.3, Table 307.1(1), 415.6.3, 2113.11.1.2, 2113.15, 2801.1	
MCNYS-10	Mechanical Code of New York State . 101.4.3, 201.3, 307.1, Table 307.1(1), 406.4.2, 406.6.3, 406.6.5, 409.3, 412.4.6, 414.1.2, 414.3, 415.6.1.4, 415.6.2, 415.6.2.8, 415.6.3, 415.6.4, 415.8.11.1, 416.3, 420.5, 603.1, 603.1.1, 603.1.2, 707.2, 716.2.2, 716.5.4, 716.6.1, 716.6.2, 716.6.3, 717.5, 719.1,719.7, 903.2.12.1, 904.2.1, 904.11, 908.6, 909.1, 909.10.2, 1015.5, 1017.4.1, 1203.1, 1203.2.1, 1203.4.2, 1203.4.2.1, 1203.5, 1209.3, 2304.5, 2801.1, 3004.3.1, 3401.3, 3410.6.7.1, 3410.6.8, 3410.6.8.1	
PCNYS-10	Plumbing Code of New York State . . . . 101.4.4, 201.3, 415.6.4, 603.1.2, 717.5, 903.3.5, 912.5, 1006.3, 1206.3.3, 1503.4, 1807.4.3, 2901.1, Table 2902.1, 3305.1	
PMCNYS-10	Property Maintenance Code of New York State. . . . . 101.4.5, 102.6, 103.3, 3401.3, 3410.3.2.	
RCNYS-10	Residential Code of New York State 101.2, 308.2, 308.3, 308.5, 310.1, 2308.1	
*SBCCI SSTD 10-99	Standard for Hurricane Resistant Residential Construction 1609.1.1, 1609.1.1.1, 2308.2.1	
SBCCI SSTD 11-97	Test Standard for Determining Wind Resistance of Concrete or Clay Roof Tiles. 1715.2.1, 1715.2.2	

ISO

International Standards Organization
ISO Central Secretariat1, rue de Varembee, Case postale 56
CH-1211 Geneva 20, Switzerland

Standard reference number	Title	Referenced in code section number
ISO 8115-86	Cotton Bales-Dimensions and Density. . . . . Table 415.8.2.1.1	

NAAMM

National Association of Architectural
Metal Manufacturers
8 South Michigan Ave
Chicago, IL 60603

Standard reference number	Title	Referenced in code section number
FP 1001-97	Guide Specifications for Design of Metal Flag Poles	1609.1.1

NCMA

National Concrete Masonry Association
2302 Horse Pen Road
Herndon, VA 22071-3499

Standard reference number	Title	Referenced in code section number
TEK 5-84 (1996)	Details for Concrete Masonry Fire Walls	Table 720.1(2)

NFPA

National Fire Protection Association
1 Batterymarch Park
Quincy, MA 02269

Standard reference number	Title	Referenced in code section number
*11-05	Standard for Low, Medium and High Expansion Foam	904.7
*12-08	Carbon Dioxide Extinguishing Systems	904.8, 904.11
*12A-04	Halon 1301 Fire Extinguishing Systems	904.9
*13-07	Installation of Sprinkler Systems 707.2, 903.3.1.1, 903.3.2, 903.3.5.1.1, 903.3.5.2, 904.11, 905.3.4, 907.8, 3104.5, 3104.9	
*13D-07	Installation of Sprinkler Systems in One-and Two-family Dwellings and Manufactured Homes. 903.3.1.3, 903.3.5.1.1	
*13R-07	Installation of Sprinkler Systems in Residential Occupancies Up to and Including Four Stories in Height 903.3.1.2, 903.3.5.1.1, 903.3.5.1.2, 903.4	
*14-07	Installation of Standpipe and Hose System 905.2, 905.3.4, 905.4.2, 905.8	
*16-07	Installation Foam-water Sprinkler and Foam-water Spray Systems	904.11
*17-09	Dry Chemical Extinguishing Systems. 904.6, 904.11	
*17A-09	Wet Chemical Extinguishing Systems. 904.5, 904.11	
*30-08	Flammable and Combustible Liquids Code.	415.3
*31-06	Installation of Oil-burning Equipment.	2113.15
*32-07	Dry Cleaning Plants 415.6.4	
*40-07	Storage and Handling of Cellulose Nitrate Film	409.1
*61-08	Prevention of Fires and Dust Explosions in Agricultural and Food Product Facilities 415.6.1	
*70-08	National Electric Code. 603.1.3, 904.3.1, 907.5, 909.11, 909.12.1, 909.16.3, 1205.4.1, 2701.1, 2701.1	
*72-07	National Fire Alarm Code 901.6, 903.4.1, 904.3.5, 907.2, 907.2.1.1, 907.2.2.1, 907.2.7.2, 907.2.9.1.3.1, 907.2.10, 907.2.10.4, 907.2.11.2, 907.2.11.3, 907.2.12.2.3, 907.2.12.3, 907.4, 907.5, 907.9.2, 907.10, 907.14, 907.16, 907.17, 911.1, 3006.5	
*80-07	Fire Doors and Fire Windows 508.2.2.1, 715.4, 715.4.5, 715.4.6.1, 715.4.7.2, 715.5, 715.5.4, 1008.1.3.3	
*85-07	Boiler and Combustion System Hazards Code 415.6.1	
	(Note: NFPA 8503 has been incorporated into NFPA 85)	
*92B-05	Smoke Management Systems in Malls, Atria and Large Spaces	909.8
*101-06	Life Safety Code 1025.6.2	
*105-03	Standard for the Installation of Smoke Door Assemblies 405.4.2, 715.4.3.1, 909.20.4.1	
*110-05	Emergency and Standby Power Systems.	2702.1
*111-05	Stored Electrical Energy Emergency and Standby Power Systems	2702.1
*120-04	Standard for Fire Prevention and Control in Coal Mines 415.6.1	
*211-06	Chimneys, Fireplaces, Vents and Solid Fuel-burning Appliances	2112.5
*230-03	Standard for the Fire Protection of Storage	507.3
*252-03	Standard Methods of Fire Tests of Door Assemblies 715.3, 715.4.1, 715.4.2, 715.4.3, 715.4.4.1	
*253-00	Test for Critical Radiant Flux of Floor Covering Systems Using a Radiant Heat Energy Source. 402.11.1, 406.6.4, 804.2, 804.3	

NFPA—continued

*257-00	Standard for Fire Test for Window and Glass Block Assemblies	715.3, 715.4.3.2, 715.5, 715.5.1, 715.5.2, 715.5.8.1
*259-03	Test Method for Potential Heat of Building Materials	2603.4.1.10, 2603.5.3
*265-07	Method of Fire Tests for Evaluating Room Fire Growth Contribution of Textile Wall Coverings on Full Height Panels and Walls	803.6.2, 803.6.2.1
*268-01	Standard Test Method for Determining Ignitibility of Exterior Wall Assemblies Using a Radiant Heat Energy Source	1406.2.1, 1406.2.1.1, 1406.2.1.2, 2603.5.7
*285-98	Standard Method of Test for the Evaluation of Flammability Characteristics of Exterior Nonload-bearing Wall Assemblies Containing Combustible Components	1407.10.4, 2603.5.5
*286-06	Standard Method of Fire Test for Evaluating Contribution of Wall and Ceiling Interior Finish to Room Fire Growth	402.15.4, 803.2, 803.2.1, 803.5, 803.6.3, 2603.4, 2603.9
*288-01	Standard Methods of Fire Tests of Floor Fire Door Assemblies in Fire-resistance-rated Floor Systems	711.8
*303-06	Fire Protection Standards for Marinas and Boatyards	905.3.7
*409-04	Aircraft Hangars	412.2.6, 412.4.5
*418-01	Standard for Heliports	412.5.5
*484-06	Combustible Metals, Metal Powders and Metal Dust	415.6.1
*651-98	Machining and Finishing of Aluminum and the Production and Handling of Aluminum Products	415.6.1
*654-06	Standard for the Prevention of Fire and Dust Explosions from the Manufacturing, Processing and Handling of Combustible Particulate Solids	415.6.1
*655-07	Prevention of Sulfur Fires and Explosions	415.6.1
*664-07	Prevention of Fires Explosions in Wood Processing and Woodworking Facilities	415.6.1
*701-04	Standard Methods of Fire Tests for Flame-propagation of Textiles and Films	402.11.1, 410.3.6, 801.1.2, 806.1, 806.1.2, 806.2, 3102.3, 3102.3.1, 3102.6.1.1, 3105.4
*704-07	Standard System for the Identification of the Hazards of Materials for Emergency Response	414.7.2, 415.2
*750-06	Water Mist Fire Protection Systems	904.12
*1124-06	Code for the Manufacture, Transportation, Storage and Retail Sale of Fireworks and Pyrotechnic Articles	415.3.1
*2001-08	Clean Agent Fire Extinguishing Systems	904.10

PCI

Precast Prestressed Concrete Institute
209 W. Jackson Boulevard, Suite 500
Chicago, IL 60606-6938

Standard reference number	Title	Referenced in code section number
MNL 124-89	Design for Fire Resistance of Precast Prestressed Concrete	721.2.3.1
*MNL 128-01	Recommended Practice for Glass Fiber Reinforced Concrete Panels	1903.2

PTI

Post-Tensioning Institute
1717 W. Northern Avenue, Suite 114
Phoenix, AZ 85021

Standard reference number	Title	Referenced in code section number
PTI-2004	Standard Requirements for Analysis of Shallow Concrete Foundations on Expansive Soils, First Edition	1805.8.2
PTI-2004 1805.8.2	Standard Requirements for Design of Shallow Post-tensioned Concrete Foundation on Expansive Soils	

RMI

Rack Manufacturers Institute
8720 Red Oak Boulevard, Suite 201
Charlotte, NC 28217

Standard reference number	Title	Referenced in code section number
RMI (2002)	Specification for Design, Testing and Utilization of Industrial Steel Storage Racks	2208.1

SJI

Steel Joist Institute
3127 10th Avenue, North
Myrtle Beach, SC 29577-6760

Standard reference number	Title	Referenced in code section number
JG-1.1-05	Standard Specification for Joist Girders	1604.3.3, 2206.1
K-1.1-05	Standard Specification for Open Web Steel Joists, K-Series	1604.3.3, 2206.1
LH/DLH-1.1-05	Standard Specification for Longspan Steel Joists, LH Series and Deep Longspan Steel Joists, DLH Series	1604.3.3, 2206.1

SPRI

Single-Ply Roofing Institute
77 Rumford Ave.
Suite 3-B
Walthem, MA 02453

Standard reference number	Title	Referenced in code section number
*ES-1-03	Wind Design Standard for Edge Systems Used with Low Slope Roofing Systems	1504.5
*RP-4-02	Wind Design Guide for Ballasted Single-ply Roofing Systems	1504.4

TIA

Telecommunications Industry Association
2500 Wilson Boulevard
Arlington, VA 22201-3834

Standard reference number	Title	Referenced in code section number
TIA/EIA-222-F-96	Structural Standards for Steel Antenna Towers and Antenna Supporting Structures	1609.1.1, 3108.4

TMS

The Masonry Society
3970 Broadway, Unit 201-D
Boulder, CO 80304-1135

Standard reference number	Title	Referenced in code section number
0216-97	Standard Method for Determining Fire Resistance of Concrete and Masonry Construction Assemblies	Table 720.1(2), 721.1
*402-05	Building Code Requirements for Masonry Structures	1405.5, 1405.5.2, 1405.9, 1604.3.4, 1704.5, 1704.5.1, Table 1704.5.1, 1704.5.2, 1704.5.3, Table 1703.4.5.3, 1708.1.1, 1708.1.2, 1708.1.3, 1708.1.4, 1805.5.2, 1812.7, 2101.2.2, 2101.2.3, 2101.2.4, 2101.2.5, 2101.2.6, 2103.13.6, 2106.1, 2106.1.1, 2106.1.1.1, 2106.1.1.2, 2106.1.1.3, 2106.3, 2106.4, 2106.5, 2106.6, 2107.1, 2107.2, 2107.3, 2107.4, 2107.5, 2107.6, 2107.7, 2107.8, 2108.1, 2108.2, 2108.3, 2108.4, 2109.1, 2109.2.3.1, 2109.7.3
*602-05	Specification for Masonry Structures	1405.5.1, Table 1704.5.1, Table 1704.5.3, 1805.5.2.2, 2103.13.7, 2104.1, 2104.1.1, 2104.3, 2104.4

TPI

Truss Plate Institute
583 D'Onofrio Drive, Suite 200
Madison, WI 53719

Standard reference number	Title	Referenced in code section number
*TPI 1-2002	National Design Standards for Metal-plate-connected Wood Truss Construction	2303.4.2, 2306.1

UL

Underwriters Laboratories, Inc.
333 Pfingsten Road
Northbrook, IL 60062-2096

Standard reference number	Title	Referenced in code section number
10A-98	Tin Clad Fire Doors-with Revisions through March 2003	715.4
10B-97	Fire Tests of Door Assemblies-with Revisions through October 2001	715.4.2
10C-98	Positive Pressure Fire Tests of Door Assemblies-with Revisions through November 2001	715.4.1, 715.4.3
14B-98	Sliding Hardware for Standard Horizontally Mounted Tin Clad Fire Doors- with Revisions through July 2000	715.4
14C-99	Swinging Hardware for Standard Tin Clad Fire Doors Mounted Singly and in Pairs	715.4
94-96	Test for Flammability of Plastic Materials for Parts in Devices and Appliances	402.11.1
103-01	Factory-built Chimneys, for Residential Type and Building Heating Appliances	717.2.5
127-99	Factory-built Fireplaces-with Revisions through November1999	717.2.5, 2111.11
199E-04	Outline of Investigation for Fire Testing of Sprinklers and Water Spray Nozzles for Protection of Deep Fat Fryers	904.11.4.1
217-97	Single and Multiple Station Smoke Alarms-with revisions through January 2004	907.2.10
268-96	Smoke Detectors for Fire Protective Signaling Systems-with Revisions through January 1999	407.6, 907.2.6.2
300-96	Fire Testing of Fire Extinguishing Systems for Protection of Restaurant Cooking Areas - with Revisions through December 1998	904.11
555-99	Fire Dampers-with Revisions through January 2002	716.3
555C-96	Ceiling Dampers	716.3, 716.6.2.1
555S-99	Smoke Dampers-with Revisions through January 2002	716.3, 716.3.1.1
580-94	Test for Uplift Resistance of Roof Assemblies-with Revisions through February 1998	1504.3.1, 1504.3.2
641-95	Type L Low-temperature Venting Systems-with Revisions through April 1999	2113.11.1.4
710B-04	Recirculating Systems	904.11
790-04	Tests for Fire Resistance of Roof Covering Materials-with Revisions through July 1998	1505.1, 2603.6, 2610.2, 2610.3
793-03	Standards for Automatically Operated Roof Vents for Smoke and Heat	910.3.1
864-03	Standards For Control Units and Accessories for Fire Alarm Signaling Systems- with Revisions through October 2003	909.12
*1040-96	Fire Test of Insulated Wall Construction-with Revisions through April 2001	1407.10.3, 2603.4, 2603.9
1256-02	Fire Test of Roof Deck Construction	1508.1, 2603.3, 2603.4.1.5
*1479-03	Fire Tests of Through-penetration Fire stops –with Revisions through August 2008	712.3.1.2, 712.4.1.1.2, 712.5
1482-98	Solid-fuel Type Room Heater-with Revisions through January 2000	2112.2, 2112.5
1715-97	Fire Test of Interior Finish Material –with Revisions through October 2002	1407.10.2, 1407.10.3, 2603.4, 2603.9
1777-04	Chimney Liners-with Revisions through July 1998	2113.11.1, 2113.19
1784-95	Air Leakage Tests of Door Assemblies	707.14.1, 710.5.2, 715.4.3.1, 715.4.5.1, 715.4.5.3
1897-98	Uplift Tests for Roof Covering Systems-with Revisions through November 2002	1504.3.1
1975-96	Fire Test of Foamed Plastics Used for Decorative Purposes	402.10, 402.11.1, 402.15.5
2017-2000	Standards for General-purpose Signaling Devices and Systems-with Revisions through June 2004	3109.4.1.8
2079-98	Tests for Fire Resistance of Building Joint Systems	702.1, 713.3, 713.6
2200-98	Stationary Engine Generator Assemblies (Revisions through July 2004)	2702.1.1
2390-04	Test Method for Measuring the Wind Uplift Coefficients for Asphalt Shingles	1504.2.1, 1609.5.2

ULC

Underwriters Laboratories of Canada
7 Crouse Road
Scarborough, Ontario, Canada M1R3A9

Standard reference number	Title	Referenced in code section number
CAN/ULC S102.2-1988	Standard Method of Test for Surface Burning Characteristics of Flooring, Floor Coverings and Miscellaneous Materials and Assemblies with 2000 Revisions	719.4

USC

United States Code
c/o Superintendent of Documents
U.S. Government Printing Office
Washington, DC 20402-9325

Standard reference number	Title	Referenced in code section number
18 USC Part 1, Ch.40	Importation, Manufacture, Distribution and Storage of Explosive Materials 307.2	

WDMA

Window and Door Manufacturers Association
410 N. Michigan Avenue, Suite 2200
Chicago, IL 60611

Standard reference number	Title	Referenced in code section number
*AAMA/WDMA/CSA 101/I.S.2/A440-08	Specifications for Windows, Doors and Unit Skylights 1714.5.1, 2405.5	

WRI

Wire Reinforcement Institute, Inc.
203 Loudon Street, S.W.
2nd Floor, Suite 203C
Leesburg, VA 22075

Standard reference number	Title	Referenced in code section number
WRI/CRSI-81	Design of Slab-on-ground Foundations-with 1996 Update 1805.8.2	

APPENDIX A
RESERVED

APPENDIX B

RESERVED

APPENDIX C
RESERVED

APPENDIX D

RESERVED

APPENDIX E

SUPPLEMENTARY ACCESSIBILITY REQUIREMENTS

SECTION E101
GENERAL

E101.1 Scope. The provisions of this appendix shall control the supplementary requirements for the design and construction of facilities for accessibility to physically disabled persons.

E101.2 Design. Technical requirements for items herein shall comply with this code and ICC A117.1.

SECTION E102
DEFINITIONS

E102.1 General. The following words and terms shall, for the purposes of this appendix, have the meanings shown herein.

CLOSED-CIRCUIT TELEPHONE. A telephone with a dedicated line such as a house phone, courtesy phone or phone that must be used to gain entrance to a facility.

MAILBOXES. Receptacles for the receipt of documents, packages or other deliverable matter. Mailboxes include, but are not limited to, post office boxes and receptacles provided by commercial mail-receiving agencies, apartment houses and schools.

TRANSIENT LODGING. A building, facility or portion thereof, excluding inpatient medical care facilities and long-term care facilities, that contains one or more dwelling units or sleeping units. Examples of transient lodging include, but are not limited to, resorts, group homes, hotels, motels, dormitories, homeless shelters, halfway houses and social service lodging.

SECTION E103
ACCESSIBLE ROUTE

E103.1 Raised platforms. In banquet rooms or spaces where a head table or speaker's lectern is located on a raised platform, an accessible route shall be provided to the platform.

SECTION E104
SPECIAL OCCUPANCIES

E104.1 General. Transient lodging facilities shall be provided with accessible features in accordance with Sections E104.2 and E104.3. Group I-3 occupancies shall be provided with accessible features in accordance with Sections E104.3 and E104.4.

E104.2 Accessible beds. In rooms or spaces having more than 25 beds, five percent of the beds shall have a clear floor space complying with ICC A117.1.

E104.2.1 Sleeping areas. A clear floor space complying with ICC A117.1 shall be provided on both sides of the

accessible bed. The clear floor space shall be positioned for parallel approach to the side of the bed.

Exception: This requirement shall not apply where a single clear floor space complying with ICC A117.1 positioned for parallel approach is provided between two beds.

E104.3 Communication features. Communication features complying with ICC A117.1 shall be provided in accordance with Sections E104.3.1 through E104.3.4.

E104.3.1 Transient lodging. In transient lodging facilities, sleeping units with accessible communication features shall be provided in accordance with Table E104.3.1. Units required to comply with Table E104.3.1 shall be dispersed among the various classes of units.

E104.3.2 Group I-3. In Group I-3 occupancies at least 2 percent, but no fewer than one of the total number of general holding cells and general housing cells equipped with audible emergency alarm systems and permanently installed telephones within the cell, shall comply with Section E104.3.4.

E104.3.3 Dwelling units and sleeping units. Where dwelling units and sleeping units are altered or added, the requirements of Section E104.3 shall apply only to the units being altered or added until the number of units with accessible communication features complies with the minimum number required for new construction.

E104.3.4 Notification devices. Visual notification devices shall be provided to alert room occupants of incoming telephone calls and a door knock or bell. Notification devices shall not be connected to visual alarm signal appliances. Permanently installed telephones shall have volume controls and an electrical outlet complying with ICC A117.1 located within 48 inches (1219 mm) of the telephone to facilitate the use of a TTY.

E104.4 Partitions. Solid partitions or security glazing that separates visitors from detainees in Group I-3 occupancies shall provide a method to facilitate voice communication. Such methods are permitted to include, but are not limited to, grilles, slats, talk-through baffles, intercoms or telephone handset devices. The method of communication shall be accessible to individuals who use wheelchairs and individuals who have difficulty bending or stooping. Hand-operable communication devices, if provided, shall comply with Section E106.3.

SECTION E105
OTHER FEATURES AND FACILITIES

E105.1 Portable toilets and bathing rooms. Where multiple single-user portable toilet or bathing units are clustered at a single location, at least 5 percent, but not less than one toilet unit or bathing unit at each cluster, shall comply with ICC

A117.1. Signs containing the International Symbol of Accessibility and complying with ICC A117.1 shall identify accessible portable toilets and bathing units.

Exception: Portable toilet units provided for use exclusively by construction personnel on a construction site.

E105.2 Laundry equipment. Where provided in spaces required to be accessible, washing machines and clothes dryers shall comply with this section.

E105.2.1 Washing machines. Where three or fewer washing machines are provided, at least one shall comply with ICC A117.1. Where more than three washing machines are provided, at least two shall comply with ICC A117.1.

E105.2.2 Clothes dryers. Where three or fewer clothes dryers are provided, at least one shall comply with ICC A117.1. Where more than three clothes dryers are provided, at least two shall comply with ICC A117.1.

E105.3 Depositories, vending machines, change machines and similar equipment. Where provided, at least one of each type of depository, vending machine, change machine and similar equipment shall comply with ICC A117.1.

Exception: Drive-up-only depositories are not required to comply with this section.

E105.4 Mailboxes. Where mailboxes are provided in an interior location, at least 5 percent, but not less than one, of each type shall comply with ICC A117.1. In residential and institutional facilities, where mailboxes are provided for each dwelling unit or sleeping unit, mailboxes complying with ICC A117.1 shall be provided for each unit required to be an Accessible unit.

E105.5 Automatic teller machines and fare machines. Where automatic teller machines or self-service fare vending, collection or adjustment machines are provided, at least one machine of each type at each location where such machines are provided shall be accessible. Where bins are provided for envelopes, wastepaper or other purposes, at least one of each type shall be accessible.

E105.6 Two-way communication systems. Where two-way communication systems are provided to gain admittance to a building or facility or to restricted areas within a building or facility, the system shall comply with ICC A117.1.

SECTION E106
TELEPHONES

E106.1 General. Where coin-operated public pay telephones, coinless public pay telephones, public closed-circuit telephones, courtesy phones or other types of public telephones are provided, accessible public telephones shall be provided in accordance with Sections E106.2 through E106.5 for each type of public telephone provided. For purposes of this section, a bank of telephones shall be considered two or more adjacent telephones.

E106.2 Wheelchair-accessible telephones. Where public telephones are provided, wheelchair-accessible telephones complying with ICC A117.1 shall be provided in accordance with Table E106.2.

Exception: Drive-up-only public telephones are not required to be accessible.

TABLE E104.3.1
DWELLING OR SLEEPING UNITS WITH ACCESSIBLE COMMUNICATION FEATURES

TOTAL NUMBER OF DWELLING OR SLEEPING UNITS PROVIDED	MINIMUM REQUIRED NUMBER OF DWELLING OR SLEEPING UNITS WITH ACCESSIBLE COMMUNICATION FEATURES
1	1
2 to 25	2
26 to 50	4
51 to 75	7
76 to 100	9
101 to 150	12
151 to 200	14
201 to 300	17
301 to 400	20
401 to 500	22
501 to 1,000	5% of total
1,001 and over	50 plus 3 for each 100 over 1,000

E106.3 Volume controls. All public telephones provided shall have volume control complying with ICC A117.1.

E106.4 TTYs. TTYs complying with ICC A117.1 shall be provided in accordance with Sections E106.4.1 through E106.4.9.

E106.4.1 Bank requirement. Where four or more public pay telephones are provided at a bank of telephones, at least one public TTY shall be provided at that bank.

Exception: TTYs are not required at banks of telephones located within 200 feet (60 960 mm) of, and on the same floor as, a bank containing a public TTY.

E106.4.2 Floor requirement. Where four or more public pay telephones are provided on a floor of a privately owned building, at least one public TTY shall be provided on that floor. Where at least one public pay telephone is provided on a floor of a publicly owned building, at least one public TTY shall be provided on that floor.

E106.4.3 Building requirement. Where four or more public pay telephones are provided in a privately owned building, at least one public TTY shall be provided in the building. Where at least one public pay telephone is provided in a publicly owned building, at least one public TTY shall be provided in the building.

E106.4.4 Site requirement. Where four or more public pay telephones are provided on a site, at least one public TTY shall be provided on the site.

E106.4.5 Rest stops, emergency road stops, and service plazas. Where a public pay telephone is provided at a public rest stop, emergency road stop or service plaza, at least one public TTY shall be provided.

E106.4.6 Hospitals. Where a public pay telephone is provided in or adjacent to a hospital emergency room, hospital recovery room or hospital waiting room, at least one public TTY shall be provided at each such location.

E106.4.7 Transportation facilities. Transportation facilities shall be provided with TTYs in accordance with Sections E109.2.5 and E110.2 in addition to the TTYs required by Sections E106.4.1 through E106.4.4.

E106.4.8 Detention and correctional facilities. In detention and correctional facilities, where a public pay telephone is provided in a secured area used only by detainees or inmates and security personnel, then at least one TTY shall be provided in at least one secured area.

E106.4.9 Signs. Public TTYs shall be identified by the International Symbol of TTY complying with ICC A117.1. Directional signs indicating the location of the nearest public TTY shall be provided at banks of public pay telephones not containing a public TTY. Additionally, where signs provide direction to public pay telephones, they shall also provide direction to public TTYs. Such signs shall comply with ICC A117.1 and shall include the International Symbol of TTY.

E106.5 Shelves for portable TTYs. Where a bank of telephones in the interior of a building consists of three or more public pay telephones, at least one public pay telephone at the bank shall be provided with a shelf and an electrical outlet in accordance with ICC A117.1.

Exceptions:

1. In secured areas of detention and correctional facilities, if shelves and outlets are prohibited for purposes of security or safety shelves and outlets for TTYs are not required to be provided.

2. The shelf and electrical outlet shall not be required at a bank of telephones with a TTY.

SECTION E107
SIGNAGE

E107.1 Signs. Required accessible portable toilets and bathing facilities shall be identified by the International Symbol of Accessibility.

E107.2 Designations. Interior and exterior signs identifying permanent rooms and spaces shall be tactile. Where pictograms are provided as designations of interior rooms and spaces, the pictograms shall have tactile text descriptors. Signs required to provide tactile characters and pictograms shall comply with ICC A117.1.

Exceptions:

1. Exterior signs that are not located at the door to the space they serve are not required to comply.

2. Building directories, menus, seat and row designations in assembly areas, occupant names, building addresses and company names and logos are not required to comply.

3. Signs in parking facilities are not required to comply.

4. Temporary (seven days or less) signs are not required to comply.

5. In detention and correctional facilities, signs not located in public areas are not required to comply.

E107.3 Directional and informational signs. Signs that provide direction to, or information about, permanent interior spaces of the site and facilities shall contain visual characters complying with ICC A117.1.

TABLE E106.2
WHEELCHAIR-ACCESSIBLE TELEPHONES

NUMBER OF TELEPHONES PROVIDED ON A FLOOR, LEVEL OR EXTERIOR SITE	MINIMUM REQUIRED NUMBER OF WHEELCHAIR-ACCESSIBLE TELEPHONES
1 or more single unit	1 per floor, level and exterior site
1 bank	1 per floor, level and exterior site
2 or more banks	1 per bank

Exception: Building directories, personnel names, company or occupant names and logos, menus and temporary (seven days or less) signs are not required to comply with ICC A117.1.

E107.4 Other signs. Signage indicating special accessibility provisions shall be provided as follows:

1. At bus stops and terminals, signage must be provided in accordance with Section E108.4.

2. At fixed facilities and stations, signage must be provided in accordance with Sections E109.2.2 through E109.2.2.3.

3. At airports, terminal information systems must be provided in accordance with Section E110.3.

SECTION E108
BUS STOPS

E108.1 General. Bus stops shall comply with Sections E108.2 through E108.5.

E108.2 Bus boarding and alighting areas. Bus boarding and alighting areas shall comply with Sections E108.2.1 through E108.2.4.

E108.2.1 Surface. Bus boarding and alighting areas shall have a firm, stable surface.

E108.2.2 Dimensions. Bus boarding and alighting areas shall have a clear length of 96 inches (2440 mm) minimum, measured perpendicular to the curb or vehicle roadway edge, and a clear width of 60 inches (1525 mm) minimum, measured parallel to the vehicle roadway.

E108.2.3 Connection. Bus boarding and alighting areas shall be connected to streets, sidewalks or pedestrian paths by an accessible route complying with Section 1104.

E108.2.4 Slope. Parallel to the roadway, the slope of the bus boarding and alighting area shall be the same as the roadway, to the maximum extent practicable. For water drainage, a maximum slope of 1:48 perpendicular to the roadway is allowed.

E108.3 Bus shelters. Where provided, new or replaced bus shelters shall provide a minimum clear floor or ground space complying with ICC A117.1, Section 305, entirely within the shelter. Such shelters shall be connected by an accessible route to the boarding area required by Section E108.2.

E108.4 Signs. New bus route identification signs shall have finish and contrast complying with ICC A117.1. Additionally, to the maximum extent practicable, new bus route identification signs shall provide visual characters complying with ICC A117.1.

Exception: Bus schedules, timetables and maps that are posted at the bus stop or bus bay are not required to meet this requirement.

E108.5 Bus stop siting. Bus stop sites shall be chosen such that, to the maximum extent practicable, the areas where lifts or ramps are to be deployed comply with Sections E108.2 and E108.3.

SECTION E109
TRANSPORTATION FACILITIES AND STATIONS

E109.1 General. Fixed transportation facilities and stations shall comply with the applicable provisions of Section E109.2.

E109.2 New construction. New stations in rapid rail, light rail, commuter rail, intercity rail, high speed rail and other fixed guideway systems shall comply with Sections E109.2.1 through E109.2.8.

E109.2.1 Station entrances. Where different entrances to a station serve different transportation fixed routes or groups of fixed routes, at least one entrance serving each group or route shall comply with Section 1104 and ICC A117.1.

E109.2.2 Signs. Signage in fixed transportation facilities and stations shall comply with Sections E109.2.2.1 through E109.2.2.3.

E109.2.2.1 Tactile signs. Where signs are provided at entrances to stations identifying the station or the entrance, or both, at least one sign at each entrance shall be tactile. A minimum of one tactile sign identifying the specific station shall be provided on each platform or boarding area. Such signs shall be placed in uniform locations at entrances and on platforms or boarding areas within the transit system to the maximum extent practicable. Tactile signs shall comply with ICC A117.1.

Exceptions:

1. Where the station has no defined entrance but signs are provided, the tactile signs shall be placed in a central location.

2. Signs are not required to be tactile where audible signs are remotely transmitted to handheld receivers, or are user or proximity actuated.

E109.2.2.2 Identification signs. Stations covered by this section shall have identification signs containing visual characters complying with ICC A117.1. Signs shall be clearly visible and within the sightlines of a standing or sitting passenger from within the train on both sides when not obstructed by another train.

E109.2.2.3 Informational signs. Lists of stations, routes and destinations served by the station which are located on boarding areas, platforms or mezzanines

shall provide visual characters complying with ICC A117.1 Signs covered by this provision shall, to the maximum extent practicable, be placed in uniform locations within the transit system.

E109.2.3 Fare machines. Self-service fare vending, collection and adjustment machines shall comply with ICC A117.1, Section 707. Where self-service fare vending, collection or adjustment machines are provided for the use of the general public, at least one accessible machine of each type provided shall be provided at each accessible point of entry and exit.

E109.2.4 Rail-to-platform height. Station platforms shall be positioned to coordinate with vehicles in accordance with the applicable provisions of 36 CFR, Part 1192. Low-level platforms shall be 8 inches (250 mm) minimum above top of rail.

Exception: Where vehicles are boarded from sidewalks or street level, low-level platforms shall be permitted to be less than 8 inches (250 mm).

E109.2.5 TTYs. Where a public pay telephone is provided in a transit facility (as defined by the Department of Transportation) at least one public TTY complying with ICC A117.1, Section 704.4, shall be provided in the station. In addition, where one or more public pay telephones serve a particular entrance to a transportation facility, at least one TTY telephone complying with ICC A117.1, Section 704.4, shall be provided to serve that entrance.

E109.2.6 Track crossings. Where a circulation path serving boarding platforms crosses tracks, an accessible route complying with ICC A117.1 shall be provided.

Exception: Openings for wheel flanges shall be permitted to be $2^1/_2$ inches (64 mm) maximum.

E109.2.7 Public address systems. Where public address systems convey audible information to the public, the same or equivalent information shall be provided in a visual format.

E109.2.8 Clocks. Where clocks are provided for use by the general public, the clock face shall be uncluttered so that its elements are clearly visible. Hands, numerals and digits shall contrast with the background either light-on-dark or dark-on-light. Where clocks are mounted overhead, numerals and digits shall comply with ICC A117.1, Section 703.2.

SECTION E110
AIRPORTS

E110.1 New construction. New construction of airports shall comply with Sections E110.2 through E110.4.

E110.2 TTYs. Where public pay telephones are provided, at least one TTY shall be provided in compliance with ICC A117.1, Section 704.4. Additionally, if four or more public pay telephones are located in a main terminal outside the security areas, a concourse within the security areas or a baggage claim area in a terminal, at least one public TTY complying with ICC A117.1, Section 704.4, shall also be provided in each such location.

E110.3 Terminal information systems. Where terminal information systems convey audible information to the public, the same or equivalent information shall be provided in a visual format.

E110.4 Clocks. Where clocks are provided for use by the general public, the clock face shall be uncluttered so that its elements are clearly visible. Hands, numerals and digits shall contrast with their background either light-on-dark or dark-on-light. Where clocks are mounted overhead, numerals and digits shall comply with ICC A117.1, Section 703.2.

SECTION E111
REFERENCED STANDARDS

DOJ 36 CFR Part 1192	Americans with Disabilities Act (ADA) Accessibility Guidelines for Transportation Vehicles (ADAAG). Washington, D.C.: Department of Justice, 1991	E109.2.4, E109.3.2
DOJ 28 CFR Part 36	Americans with Disabilities Act (ADA). Washington, D.C.: Department of Justice, 1991	E109.4
ICC/ANSI *A117.1-03	Accessible and Usable Buildings and Facilities	E101.2, E104.2, E104.2.1, E104.3, E104.3.1, E104.3.4, E105.1, E105.2.1, E105.2.2, E105.3, E105.4, E105.6, E106.2, E106.3, E106.4, E106.4.9, E106.5, E107.2, E107.3, E108.3, E108.4, E109.2.1, E109.2.2.1, E109.2.2.2, E109.2.2.3, E109.2.3
16 USC Sec. 470	National Historic Preservation Act	E111.2, E111.3, E111.3.2

APPENDIX F
RODENT PROOFING

SECTION F101
GENERAL

F101.1 General. Buildings or structures and the walls enclosing habitable or occupiable rooms and spaces in which persons live, sleep or work, or in which feed, food or foodstuffs are stored, prepared, processed, served or sold, shall be constructed in accordance with the provisions of this section.

F101.2 Foundation wall ventilation openings. Foundation wall ventilator openings shall be covered for their height and width with perforated sheet metal plates no less than 0.070 inch (1.8 mm) thick, expanded sheet metal plates not less than 0.047 inch (1.2 mm) thick, cast iron grills or grating, extruded aluminum load-bearing vents or with hardware cloth of 0.035 inch (0.89 mm) wire or heavier. The openings therein shall not exceed $^1/_4$ inch (6.4 mm).

F101.3 Foundation and exterior wall sealing. Annular spaces around pipes, electric cables, conduits, or other openings in the walls shall be protected against the passage of rodents by closing such openings with cement mortar, concrete masonry or noncorrosive metal.

F101.4 Doors. Doors on which metal protection has been applied shall be hinged so as to be free swinging. When closed, the maximum clearance between any door, door jambs and sills shall not be greater than $^3/_8$ inch (9.5 mm).

F101.5 Windows and other openings. Windows and other openings for the purpose of light or ventilation located in exterior walls within 2 feet (610 mm) above the existing ground level immediately below such opening shall be covered for their entire height and width, including frame, with hardware cloth of at least 0.035 inch (0.89 mm) wire or heavier.

F101.5.1 Rodent-accessible openings. Windows and other openings for the purpose of light and ventilation in the exterior walls not covered in this chapter, accessible to rodents by way of exposed pipes, wires, conduits and other appurtenances, shall be covered with wire cloth of at least 0.035 inch (0.89 mm) wire. In lieu of wire cloth covering, said pipes, wires, conduits and other appurtenances shall be blocked from rodent usage by installing solid sheet metal guards 0.024 inch (0.61 mm) thick or heavier. Guards shall be fitted around pipes, wires, conduits or other appurtenances. In addition, they shall be fastened securely to and shall extend perpendicularly from the exterior wall for a minimum distance of 12 inches (305 mm) beyond and on either side of pipes, wires, conduits or appurtenances.

F101.6 Pier and wood construction.

F101.6.1 Sill less than 12 inches above ground. Buildings not provided with a continuous foundation shall be provided with protection against rodents at grade by providing either an apron in accordance with Section F101.6.1.1 or a floor slab in accordance with Section 101.6.1.2.

F101.6.1.1 Apron. Where an apron is provided, the apron shall not be less than 8 inches (203 mm) above, nor less than 24 inches (610 mm) below, grade. The apron shall not terminate below the lower edge of the siding material. The apron shall be constructed of an approved nondecayable, water-resistant rodentproofing material of required strength and shall be installed around the entire perimeter of the building. Where constructed of masonry or concrete materials, the apron shall not be less than 4 inches (102 mm) in thickness.

F101.6.1.2 Grade floors. Where continuous concrete grade floor slabs are provided, open spaces shall not be left between the slab and walls, and openings in the slab shall be protected.

F101.6.2 Sill at or above 12 inches above ground. Buildings not provided with a continuous foundation and which have sills 12 or more inches (305 mm) above the ground level shall be provide with protection against rodents at grade in accordance with any of the following:

1. Section F101.6.1.1 or F101.6.1.2;

2. By installing solid sheet metal collars at least 0.024 inch (0.6 mm) thick at the top of each pier or pile and around each pipe, cable, conduit, wire or other item which provides a continuous pathway from the ground to the floor; or

3. By encasing the pipes, cables, conduits or wires in an enclosure constructed in accordance with Section F101.6.1.1.

APPENDIX G
RESERVED

APPENDIX H

RESERVED

APPENDIX I

PATIO COVERS

SECTION I101
GENERAL

I101.1 General. Patio covers shall be permitted to be detached from or attached to dwelling units. Patio covers shall be used only for recreational, outdoor living purposes and not as carports, garages, storage rooms or habitable rooms. Openings shall be permitted to be enclosed with insect screening, approved translucent or transparent plastic not more that 0.125 inch (3.2 mm) in thickness, glass conforming to the provisions of Chapter 24 or any combination of the foregoing.

SECTION I102
DEFINITIONS

I102.1 General. The following word and term shall, for the purposes of this appendix, have the meaning shown herein.

PATIO COVERS. One story structures not exceeding 12 feet (3657 mm) in height. Enclosure walls shall be permitted to be of any configuration, provided the open or glazed area of the longer wall and one additional wall is equal to at least 65 percent of the area below a minimum of 6 feet 8 inches (2032 mm) of each wall, measured from the floor.

SECTION I103
EXTERIOR OPENINGS

I103.1 Light, ventilation and emergency egress. Exterior openings required for light and ventilation shall be permitted to open into a patio structure. However, the patio structure shall be unenclosed if such openings are serving as emergency egress or rescue openings from sleeping rooms. Where such exterior openings serve as an exit from the dwelling unit, the patio structure, unless unenclosed, shall be provided with exits conforming to the provision of Chapter 10.

SECTION I104
STRUCTURAL PROVISIONS

I104.1 Design loads. Patio covers shall be designed and constructed to sustain, within the stress limits of this code, all dead loads plus a minimum vertical live load of 10 pounds per square foot (0.48 kN/m^2) except that snow loads shall be used where such snow loads exceed this minimum. Such patio covers shall be designed to resist the minimum wind and seismic loads set forth in this code.

I104.2 Footings. In areas with a frost depth of zero, a patio cover shall be permitted to be supported on a concrete slab on grade without footings, provided the slab conforms to the provisions of Chapter 19 of this code, is not less than $3^1/_2$ inches (89 mm) thick and further provided that the columns do not support loads in excess of 750 pounds (3.36 kN) per column.

APPENDIX J

RESERVED

APPENDIX K
RESERVED

APPENDIX L

ASSISTIVE LISTENING SYSTEMS PERFORMANCE STANDARDS

SECTION L101
GENERAL

L101.1 Scope. The provisions of this appendix shall control the performance standards of assistive listening systems.

SECTION L102
INDUCTION LOOP SYSTEM

L102.1 Induction loop system specifications.

1. If the ambient electromagnetic noise (generally caused by lighting regulation systems or major power supplies) produces a field strength exceeding 30mA/meter at frequencies that would decrease the signal-to-noise ratio specified in Item 4, then it is recommended that, unless the noise can be reduced, an induction loop system not be considered.

2. If the eletromagnetic signal produced by a nearby induction loop system spills over into a new user area being considered for a different induction loop system and produces an average magnetetic field strength exceeding 15 mA/meter, then it is recommended that, unless the use of each system can be scheduled so as not to occur simultaneously, an induction loop system not be considered in the new area.

3. Given an input signal to the amplifier that has a constant level over a minimum frequency range of 100 Hz to 8,000 Hz, the measured frequency response of the magnetic field generated by the induction loop system over that range shall not vary by more than +/-3 decibels from the value of 1,000 Hz. In actual usage, graphic equalization of the output signal is allowed.

4. Given an output power level equal to the average value specified in Item 6, the minimum signal-to-noise ratio of the program signal carried by the electromagnetic field shall be at least 30 decibels.

5. Given a 1,000 Hz input signal to the amplifier that has a level sufficient to produce the minimum signal-to-noise ratio specified in Item 4, the harmonic distortion between the input signal and the program signal carried by the electromagnetic field shall not vary by more than 5 percent over the field strength range specified in Item 6.

6. Given a 1,000 Hz sinusoidal input signal, at a level equal to the long-time average level of a speech signal, the average value of the magnetic field strength generated within the user area by the loop shall equal 100mA/meter +/-3 decibels.

   The maximum value of the magnetic field strength for a system set to the above recommended average value shall be 400 mA/meter (derived on the basis that the difference of the maximum short-time average level between a speech signal - approximately 0.125 seconds and the long-time average level is approximately 12 decibels).

   Both measurements shall be made 48 inches (1219 mm) above floor level at any point within the user area.

7. If a hand-held receiver with[in] earphone is used, the specifications in Items 3, 4 and 5 shall apply. Additionally, the sound pressure level generated by the receiver and earphone shall be at least 80 decibels.

   The maximum high-frequency average sound pressure level generated by the receiver earphone shall not exceed 130 decibels.

8. The system must have inputs capable of accepting signals at line level and microphone level and must be capable of interfacing with existing public address systems or stand alone.

9. Any stand-alone devices powered by 110-120 volt AC used as part of the system must have been tested by an approved laboratory.

10. All input and output wiring must comply with NFPA 70. Output wiring may be enclosed in nonmetallic raceways or molding.

11. The installation of all stand-alone components of the system must comply with all state and local codes.

SECTION L103
INFRARED SYSTEM

L103.1 Infrared system specifications

1. If the ambient infrared light (generally caused by other infrared light-generating devices or direct sunlight) produces interference, it is recommended that, unless the interfering infrared light can be reduced, infrared systems not be considered.

2. Given an input signal to the transmitter within the range of levels specified in Item 6 over a minimum frequency range of 200 Hz to 8,000 Hz, the measured frequency response of the output signal generated by the receiver and transducer over that range shall not vary by more than +/-5 decibels from the value at 1,000 Hz. In actual usage, graphic equalization of the output signal is allowed.

3. Given an output signal to the transmitter within the range of levels specified in Item 6, the minimum signal-to-noise ratio of the output generated by the receiver and transducer shall be 35 decibels at all frequencies specified in Item 2.

4. Given an output signal of 1,000 Hz to the transmitter at a level sufficient to produce the minimum signal-to-noise ratio specified in Item 3, the harmonic distortion produced by the receiver and transducer shall not be more than 5 percent.

5. Given a 1,000 Hz sinusoidal input signal at a level within the range specified in Item 6, the following are the possible transducers:

 5.1 If using a neckloop as an output transducer, generate a magnetic field strength of at least 150 mA/meter. The peak field strength shall not exceed 600 mA/meter. Measurements shall be made at the geometric center of the plane of the neckloop.

 5.2 If using a silhouette as an output transducer, generate a magnetic field strength of at least 50 mA/meter (the peak field strength shall not exceed 200 mA/meter). Measurements shall be made at a distance of 10 centimeters from the silhouette.

 5.3 If using a miniature earphone as an output transducer, generate a sound pressure level of at least 80 decibels. The maximum high-frequency average sound pressure level shall not exceed 130 decibels.

 5.4 If a direct input cable is used between the output of the receiver and the input of the hearing aid boot or shoe, generate a minimum voltage range of 2 mV to 800 mV and match a boot/shoe input impedance of 50 ohms or greater. The plugs at either end shall be molded 2-pin, 3-pin and/or 3.5-millimeter mini-plug (stereo or mono).

6. The system must have inputs capable of accepting signals at line level and microphone level and must be capable of interfacing with existing public address systems or stand alone.

7. The minimum light level of the transmitted infrared carrier signal must be sufficient so that a receiver can produce the specifications in Items 2, 3, 4 and 5 at any point within the user area.

8. Any stand-alone devices powered by 110-120 volt AC used as part of the system must be tested by an approved laboratory.

9. All input wiring must comply with NFPA 70.

10. The installation of all stand-alone components of the system must comply with all state and local codes.

SECTION L104
FM SYSTEM

L104.1 FM system specifications.

1. If an ambient FM signal (generally caused by other agencies on the same frequency or major power supplies) produces interference, it is recommended that, unless the frequency can be changed, an FM system not be considered.

2. Given an input signal to the transmitter within the range of levels specified in Item 6 over a minimum frequency range of 100 Hz to 8,000 Hz, the measured frequency response of the output signal generated by the receiver and a transducer over that range shall not vary by more than +/-5 decibels from the value at

1,000 Hz. In actual usage, graphic equalization of the output signal is allowed.

3. Given an input signal to the transmitter within the range of levels specified in Item 6, the minimum signal-to-noise ratio of the output generated by the receiver and transducer shall be 35 decibels at all frequencies specified in Item 2.

4. Given an input signal to the transmitter at 1,000 Hz at a level sufficient to produce the minimum signal-to-noise ratio specified in Item 3, the total harmonic distortion between the input signal and the program signal produced by the receiver and transducer shall not be more than 10 percent.

5. Given a 1,000 Hz sinusoidal input signal at a level within the range specified in Item 6, the following are among the possible transducers:

 5.1 If using a neckloop as an output transducer, generate a magnetic field strength of at least 150 mA/meter. The peak field strength shall not exceed 600 mA/meter. Measurements shall be made at the geometric center of the plane of the neckloop.

 5.2 If using a silhouette as an output transducer, generate a magnetic field strength of at least 50 mA/meter. The peak field strength shall not exceed 200 mA/meter. Measurements shall be made at a distance of 10 centimeters from the silhouette.

 5.3 If using a miniature earphone as an output transducer, generate a sound pressure level of at least 80 decibels. The maximum high-frequency average sound pressure level shall not exceed 130 decibels.

 5.4 If a direct input cable is used between the output of the receiver and the input of the hearing aid boot or shoe, generate a minimum voltage range of 2 mV to 800 mV and match a boot/shoe input impedance of 50 ohms or greater. The plugs at either end shall be molded 2-pin, 3-pin and/or 3.5-millimeter mini-plug (stereo or mono).

6. The system must have inputs capable of accepting signals at line level and microphone level and must be capable of interfacing with existing public address systems or stand alone.

7. The minimum sensitivity of the receiver shall be at least 2 uV at 12 decibels SINAD. The maximum RF signal generated by the transmitter shall not exceed 8,000 uV/meter at 30 meters.

8. Any stand-alone devices powered by 110-120 volt AC used as part of the system must be tested by an approved laboratory.

9. All input wiring must comply with NFPA 70.

10. The installation of all stand-alone components of the system must comply with all state and local codes.

11. The frequencies used by the transmitter should be in compliance with applicable FCC rules.

NEW YORK STATE AGENCIES WITH CONSTRUCTION REGULATIONS OR CONSTRUCTION AUTHORITY

The following is a list of New York State Agencies with construction related regulations or construction authority that complement the requirements of the *Uniform Fire Prevention and Building Code*. These listed requirements are not enforceable by a code enforcement official unless empowered by other law, statute, ordinance or regulation. Note: This list may not be all-inclusive and is subject to change; it is published as a courtesy to enforcers, designers and the public.

Adirondack Park Agency 562

Commission on Quality of Care & Advocacy for Persons with Disabilities 562

Office of Alcoholism and Substance Abuse Services 563

      A. Occupancy Classification Table 563

Office of Children & Family Services 564

      A. Foster Care Occupancy Classification Table 565

      B. Child Day Care Occupancy Classification Table 566

Department of Correctional Services 567

Dormitory Authority of the State of New York 567

Education Department 568

Energy Research and Development Authority 569

Department of Environmental Conservation 569

Office of General Services—Design and Construction Contract Administration 571

Department of Health 571

      A. Adult Residential Care Occupancy Classification Table 575

Division of Housing and Community Renewal 577

Department of Labor 577

Office of Mental Health 579

      A. Occupancy Classification Tables 579

Metropolitan Transit Authority 580

Office of Parks, Recreation and Historic Preservation 580

Office for People with Developmental Disabilities 581

      A. Occupancy Classification Tables 581

Public Service Commission 582

Power Authority 582

State University Construction Fund 582

Department of State 583

Thruway Authority & Canal Corporation 583

Adirondack Park Agency

P.O. Box 99
1133 NYS Route 86
Ray Brook, NY 12977
Phone: 518-891-4050
Fax: 518-891-3938
www.apa.state.ny.us

The APA is responsible for maintaining the protection of the forest preserve and overseeing development proposals of the privately owned lands within the Adirondack Park

Applicable Regulations:

The Adirondack Park Agency administers the Adirondack Park Agency Act (Executive Law, article 27), the Freshwater Wetlands Act (Environmental Conservation Law, article 24) within the Adirondack Park and, for private lands within the Adirondack Park, the Wild Scenic and Recreational Rivers System Act (Environmental Conservation Law, article 15, title 27).
http://www.apa.state.ny.us/Regulations/index.html

Commission on Quality of Care
& Advocacy for Persons with Disabilities

401 State Street
Schenectady, NY 12305
Phone: 518-388-1281
Fax: 518-388-1276
www.cqcapd.state.ny.us

In 2005 the NYS Commission on Quality of Care for the Mentally Disabled and the NYS Office of Advocate for Persons with Disabilities were merged to form a new agency: the NYS Commission on Quality of Care and Advocacy for Persons with Disabilities. Through its Advocacy and Outreach Division the Commission promotes the inclusion of people with disabilities in all aspects of community life by supporting policies which ensure that people with disabilities have every opportunity to be productive and participating citizens able to exercise all of the rights and responsibilities accorded all New Yorkers. Implementation of progressive legislation and regulations protecting the equal rights of persons with disabilities is but one of the tools used by the Commission to help achieve this goal. Implementation and refinement of the accessibility requirements of the New York State Uniform Fire Prevention and Building Code are but one example of many such activities.

In addition to providing information and technical assistance on a variety of disability related subjects, the Commission also provides information and technical assistance regarding the accessibility requirements of the New York State Fire Prevention and Building Code, the Americans with Disabilities Act Accessibility Guidelines to local codes enforcement officers, architects, disability advocates and the public at large and the nondiscrimination provisions and accessibility provisions of the Fair Housing Amendments Act of 1988.

OASAS

Office of Alcoholism and Substance Abuse Services

1450 Western Avenue
Albany, NY 12203
General Info: 518-473-3460
http://www.oasas.state.ny.us/

About OASAS

The New York State Office of Alcoholism and Substance Abuse Services (OASAS) plans, develops and regulates structured addiction treatment and prevention system. OASAS licenses and regulates more than 1,200 addiction treatment providers statewide and operates 13 Addiction Treatment Centers. The agency also provides funding for approximately 300 prevention providers at 1,700 education and prevention programs based in schools and communities throughout the state. Additionally, in July 2005, the agency assumed responsibility for overseeing the outreach, prevention, treatment, training and certification related to compulsive gambling services.

Applicable Regulations:

Chemical Dependence Services
Part 814 General Facility Requirements

Individual programs and modalities are governed by the regulatory requirements found in Title 14 and may have other specific facility requirements within the Part 800 series. Please see the link below for additional information:

http://www.oasas.state.ny.us/regs/index.cfm

Office of Alcoholism and Substance Abuse Services
Occupancy Classifications for the Codes of New York State

Modality	Reference	OASAS	Comments/Qualifications/Exceptions
Chemical Dependence Crisis Services	Part 816	I-2	In hospitals/incapacitated patients (see 816.5(a)(1)).
Chemical Dependence Residential Rehab for Youth	Part 817	R-2; R-4	R-2=permanent boarding houses with stays less than 30 days, R-4 = 5 - 16 beds.
Chemical Dependence Inpatient Rehabilitation	Part 818	R-2; R-4	R-2=permanent boarding houses with stays less than 30 days, R-4 = 5 - 16 beds.
Chemical Dependence Residential Services	Part 819	R-2; R-4	R-2=permanent boarding houses with stays less than 30 days, R-4 = 5 - 16 beds.
Residential Chemical Dependency for Youth	Part 820	R-2; R-4	R-2=permanent boarding houses with stays less than 30 days, R-4 = 5 - 16 beds.
Non-med Supervised Chemical Dependence Outpatient	Part 821	B	Clinic/Professional Office Services
Chemical Dependence Outpatient	Part 822	B	Clinic/Professional Office Services
Outpatient Chemical Dependency for Youth	Part 823	B	Clinic/Professional Office Services

Office of Children & Family Services (OCFS)

Capital View Office Park
52 Washington Street
Rensselaer, New York 12144-2796
Phone: (518) 473-7793
Fax: (518) 486-7550
http://www.ocfs.state.ny.us

The New York State Office of Children and Family Services (OCFS) is charged by State Law to regulate, license/register and monitor those child care settings that meet the State definition of child day care. At the current time there are approximately 18,800 regulated facilities that are licensed or registered under the auspice of OCFS. The types of licensed and registered care are day care centers (outside of New York City); School Age Child Care Programs (statewide) that provide supervision for children before and after school and outside normal school hours; group family day care (statewide) which can care for up to 14 children in a provider's home; and registered family day care programs that can provide care to a maximum of 8 children in a provider's home.

Applicable Regulations:

Day Care Regulations

* Child Day Care Definitions, Enforcement & Hearings (Part 413)

* School Age Child Care (Part 414)

* Group Family Day Care Homes (Part 416)

* Family Day Care Homes (Part 417)

* Child Day Care Centers (Subpart 418-1)

* Small Day Care Centers (Subpart 418-2)

http://www.ocfs.state.ny.us/main/chilecare/daycare_regs.asp

Child Day Care occupancy classifications
18 NYCRR 413: Definitions, Enforcement and Hearings

Family day care homes 3 - 6 children + 2 school age children 6 weeks - 12 years 18 NYCRR 417	**Residential Code** if: One or two family dwellings or Multiple single family (townhouses) @ three stories or less
	R-3 - one- or two-family dwelling if: Dwelling not residential code
	R-2 - permanent multiple dwellings
Group family day care homes 7-12 children + 2 school age children 6 weeks to 12 years 18 NYCRR 416	**Residential Code** if: One or two family dwellings or Multiple single family (townhouses) @ three stories or less
	R-3 - one- or two-family dwelling if: Dwelling not residential code
	R-2 - permanent multiple dwellings
Child day care center 7 or more children 6 weeks - 12 years 18 NYCRR 418-1	**I-4** - institutional 5 or more; 2 $\frac{1}{2}$ years or less
	E - educational if: 5 - 100 children, 2 $\frac{1}{2}$ years or less; where the rooms for such children are located on the level of exit discharge with each room having a door directly to the exterior
	E - educational older than 2 $\frac{1}{2}$ years
School-age day care 6 years - 12 years 18 NYCRR 414	**E** - educational older than 2 $\frac{1}{2}$ years
Small day care center Less than10 children 18 NYCRR 418-2	**I** or **E**

Day care in a residence requires a remote second means of egress which can be an emergency escape and rescue window of not less than 24 inches by 24 inches. Day care in E or I occupancy requires 35 square foot per person and one toilet room per 15 persons, distributed throughout the space (one per day care room). The Certificate of Occupancy shall state the appropriate occupancy classification.

Child Welfare Division occupancy classifications

INSTITUTIONAL facility for 13 or more children operated by a child care agency 18 NYCRR 442.5(i)	**I-1**
GROUP RESIDENCE institution for not more than 25 children operated by an authorized agency 18 NYCRR 448.3(b)(10)(xvi)	**I-1**
GROUP RESIDENCE for mothers and babies 18 NYCRR 442.17	**I-2**
GROUP HOME family-type home for not less than seven, nor more than twelve, children who are at least 5 years of age, operated by an authorized agency (except min. age not applicable to siblings in the same facility nor mother in same facility) 18 NYCRR 448.3(b)(10)(xvi)	**R-4** or **Residential Code** if: One or two family dwellings or Multiple single family (townhouses) @ three stories or less
AGENCY BOARDING HOME family-type home for not more than six children, operated by an authorized agency (except for more than six brothers and sisters of the same family) 18 NYCRR 447.2(b)(4)(xvii)	**Residential Code** if: One or two family dwellings or Multiple single family (townhouses) @ three stories or less
	R-3 - One or two family dwelling if: Dwelling not residential code
AGENCY BOARDING HOME transitional housing: ages 16 through 21 18 NYCRR 447.2(b)(4)(xvii)	**Residential Code** or **R-3** as above, or **R-2** - permanent multiple dwelling
SUPERVISED INDEPENDENT LIVING family-type home for not more than three children who reside in the community 18 NYCRR 447.2(b)(4)(xvii)	**Residential Code** if: One or two family dwellings or Multiple single family (townhouses) @ three stories or less
	R-3 - One or two family dwelling if: Dwelling not residential code
	R-2 - permanent multiple dwelling
Limited Service Facility	**I-3 Institutional**
Secured Facility	**I-3 Institutional**

Each occupancy is required to have an annual inspection by the local fire authority or the insurance carrier.
The Certificate of Occupancy shall state the appropriate occupancy classification.

Domestic Violence Occupancy Classifications

18 NYCRR Part 452 & 453

DOMESTIC VIOLENCE SAFE DWELLING *self-contained residence for nine or fewer adults and children, to provide temporary shelter*	*Residential Code if: One or two family dwellings or Multiple single family (townhouses) @ three stories or less*
	R-3 one or two family dwelling if: Dwelling not residential code
DOMESTIC VIOLENCE SHELTER *congregate residential facility for 10 or more adults and their children, for temporary shelter, for victims and their minor children*	*Residential Code if: One or two family dwellings or Multiple single family (townhouses) @ three stories or less*
	R-3 one or two family dwelling if: Dwelling not residential code
	R-2 multiple dwelling, including dormitory style dwellings

Department of Correctional Services

Building 2
1220 Washington Ave
Albany, New York 12226-2050
(518) 457-8126
http://www.docs.state.ny.us/

The Department of Correctional Services is responsible for the confinement and habilitation of approximately 65,000 inmates held at 70 state correctional facilities.

Dormitory Authority of the State of New York

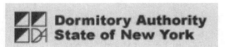

515 Broadway
Albany, New York 12207-2964
518-257-3000
Fax: 518-257-3100
www.dasny.org

The Dormitory Authority of the State of New York is a public benefit corporation that finances and constructs a variety of facilities for New York State agencies, municipal agencies, educational and not-for-profit institutions, independent hospitals, independent colleges, court facilities and Facilities for the Aged.

In accordance with Part 1204 of Title 19 of the Official Compilation of Codes, Rules and Regulations of the State of New York, the Dormitory Authority is designated as a construction permitting agency and is responsible for the administration and enforcement of the New York State Uniform Fire Prevention and Building Code (Uniform Code) with respect to certain construction activities it undertakes.

Projects in the following New York State programs are subject to the Dormitory Authority's Construction Permitting Program:

* Department of Health (DOH)

* Office of Alcohol and Substance Abuse Services (OASAS) (state operated facilities only)

* Office of Mental Health (OMH)

* Office of Mental Retardation and Developmental Disabilities (OMRDD)

* State Education Department (SED)

* State University of New York (SUNY)

There may be extenuating circumstances requiring certain other projects be included in the program. In such cases, the Dormitory Authority Code Compliance Unit will make a determination.

Where the Dormitory Authority participates in the construction of a new building or existing building, and where upon its completion such building will be in the custody of an entity **other** than a state agency, administration and enforcement of the Uniform Code will be the responsibility of the code enforcement agency generally performing those functions at the location of the work.

Education Department

89 Washington Avenue
Albany, New York 12234
Phone: (518) 474-3852
http://www.nysed.gov/

New York State Education Law Section 408 requires the Commissioner of Education to review and approve the plans and specifications for any capital construction project for a public school district outside of New York City. The New York City Board of Education is responsible for approval of capital construction projects in New York City. Additionally, Department of State regulations place the responsibility for enforcement of the New York State Uniform fire Prevention and Building Code, in public school buildings, with the Education Department.

Education Law Section 409 allows the Commissioner to adopt regulations to assure the health and safety of students and staff in relation to proper heating, lighting, ventilation, sanitation and health, fire and accident protection. To this end the Education Department has been adopting regulations and reviewing plans and specifications since 1904.

The regulations applicable to public schools, which are in addition to the NYS Uniform Code, can be found in the Commissioners Regulations Part 155 and the State Education Department's Manual of Planning Standards. These standards along with a host of additional information concerning health and safety in public schools can be found on the State Education Department Office of Facilities Planning's web site, www.emsc.nysed.gov/facplan./publications/mps1998.pdf

For Additional information and technical assistance please call the NYSED Office of Facilities Planning at 518-474-3906.

Office of Facilities Planning,
Room 1060 EBA Education Building, Albany, NY 12234
Tel. (518) 474-3906 Fax (518) 486-5918
WEBSITE http://www.nysed.gov/fmis/facplan/

Applicable Regulations:

Laws, Regulations and Policies Relating to Public and Non-Public Schools in New York State, pertaining to Facilities Planning
http://www.emsc.nysed.gov/facplan/LawsRegs.htm

Additional Information:

The Office of the Professions
Phone: 518-474-3817
Title VIII - The Professions
Article 145 Engineering and land surveying
Article 147 Architecture
Article 148 Landscape architecture
Article 161 Interior design
http://www.op.nysed.gov/

Energy Research and Development Authority

17 Columbia Circle
Albany, New York 12203-6399
toll-free 1-866-NYSERDA
http://www.nyserda.org

Executive Order 111

"All agencies and departments over which the Governor has Executive authority, and all public benefit corporations and public authorities the heads of which are appointed by the Governor (hereinafter referred to as "State agencies and other affected entities"), shall seek to achieve a reduction in energy consumption by all buildings they own, lease or operate of 35 percent by 2010 relative to 1990 levels. All State agencies and other affected entities shall establish agency-wide reduction targets and associated schedules to reach this goal and shall also be responsible for establishing peak electric demand reduction targets for each state facility by 2005 and 2010."

http://www.nyserda.org/programs/exorder111.asp

Department of Environmental Conservation

625 Broadway
Albany, NY 12233
Phone: 518-402-8651
http://www.dec.ny.gov

DEC plays a key role in enhancing the quality of life and economic well-being of New Yorkers. The department manages natural resources and protects environmental quality to improve public health and increase the economic benefits that flow from new technologies and environmentally sound development. DEC public services make New York State an attractive place for business, tourism and recreation.

Natural Resources and Water Quality Programs
DEC manages the state's natural resources to provide healthy, abundant populations of fish and wildlife, clean lakes and rivers, thriving forests and safe, productive mines and wells.

Mineral Resources (518) 402-8076
Activities: regulates and monitors the drilling and production of oil, natural gas and solution salt; the underground storage of natural gas and liquefied petroleum gas; and the extraction of rocks and minerals, including reclamation of affected land.

Water (518) 402-8233
Activities: protects water quality in lakes, rivers, aquifers and coastal areas by regulating wastewater discharges, monitoring water bodies and controlling surface runoff; provides technical assistance and education; manages freshwater resources; and helps prevent flood damage and beach erosion.

Air and Waste Management Programs
DEC protects land, air and water through pollution control and prevention, waste reduction, and cleanup of hazardous spills and sites.

Air Resources (518) 402-8452
Activities: regulates, permits and monitors sources of air pollution; forecasts ozone and stagnation events; educates the public about reducing air pollution; and researches atmospheric dynamics, pollution and emission sources.

Environmental Remediation (518) 402-9706
Activities: manages the Inactive Hazardous Waste Disposal Site Remediation Program and the Construction Grants Program for wastewater treatment facilities; manages and promotes the Environmental Restoration (Brownfields) Program, the Voluntary Cleanup Program, and the Spill Prevention and Response Program; and regulates petroleum and chemical bulk storage facilities, underground storage tanks and major oil storage facilities.

Solid and Hazardous Materials (518) 402-8651

Activities: Carries out regulatory programs; encourages waste reduction, reuse and recycling for solid and hazardous waste facilities and generators of hazardous waste; promotes sound management, including waste reduction, reuse and recycling; provides technical and compliance assistance for waste disposal and generation; controls disposal of radioactive materials and application of pesticides; and provides cancer researchers with a database on pesticide application and sales.

Applicable Regulations:

Laws, Regulations and Policies Relating to:
>   Chapter III- Air Resources Parts 200-317
>   Chapter IV- Quality Services Parts 320-486
>   Chapter V - Resource Management Services Parts 500-614
>   Chapter VI - General Regulations Parts 615-624
>   Chapter X - Division of Water Resources Parts 649-941

http://www.dec.ny.gov/regulations/regulations.html

DEC Stormwater Information
http://www.dec.ny.gov/chemical/8468.html

State Pollutant Discharge Elimination System (SPDES)

General Permit for stormwater discharges from Construction Activity

Pursuant to Section 402 of the Clean Water Act ("CWA"), stormwater discharges from certain construction activities to waters of the United States are unlawful unless they are authorized by a NPDES (National Pollutant Discharge Elimination System) permit or by a state permit program. New York's SPDES (State Pollutant Discharge Elimination System) is a NPDES-approved program with permits issued in accordance with the Environmental Conservation Law ("ECL"). Discharges of pollutants to all other "Waters of New York State" such as groundwaters are also unlawful unless they are authorized by a SPDES permit. A discharger, owner, or operator may obtain coverage under this general permit by submitting a Notice of Intent ("NOI") to the Department. Copies of this General Permit and the NOI for New York are available by calling (518) 402-8109 or at any Department of Environmental Conservation (the Department) regional office. Forms Related to the SPDES General Permit for Stormwater Discharges are available at: http://www.dec.ny.gov/chemical/43133.html

Local Programs of a Regulated MS4

Under the federal Phase II stormwater program, many cities, villages, towns, and other public entities in New York State which are located within "Urbanized Areas" as defined by the U.S. Census and who operate a Municipal Separate Storm Sewer System ("MS4") will be required to obtain SPDES permit coverage for stormwater discharges under their jurisdiction and control (see 40CFR Part 122 §122.26.32). Additionally, MS4s may be designated by the Department as regulated MS4s. Among other requirements, the Phase 2 NPDES stormwater regulations require regulated MS4s to address stormwater runoff from construction activities. Construction activities covered under this general permit, which are subject to stormwater runoff controls of a regulated MS4, will also need to comply with the MS4's controls.

Tools for Planning, Design and Implementation of the Stormwater Construction Permit
http://www.dec.ny.gov/chemical/8694.html

Office of General Service Design And Construction Contract Administration

35th Floor, Room 3564
Corning Tower, Empire State Plaza
Albany, NY 12242
Tel: 518-474-0200
Fax: 518-486-1650
www.ogs.state.ny.us

NYS OFFICE OF GENERAL SERVICES
DESIGN AND CONSTRUCTION GROUP
Serving New York

The New York State Office of General Services manages and leases real property, designs and builds facilities, and delivers a wide array of support services.

New York State Department of Health

Corning Tower
Empire State Plaza,
Albany, NY 12237
http://www.nyhealth.gov

Applicable Regulations:

In addition to the requirements set forth in Title 19 NYCRR, Department of Health, Bureau of Community Environmental Health and Food Protection (CEHFP) and Bureau of Water Supply Protection (BWSP) have additional requirements that can be found at: http://www.health.state.ny.us/nysdoh/phforum/nycrr10.htm

Subpart 5-1 for Public Water Systems
Subpart 6-1 for Swimming Pools
Subpart 6-2 for Bathing Beaches
Subpart 6-3 for Recreational Aquatic Spray Grounds
Subpart 7-1 for Temporary Residences (Hotels/Motels/Cabin Colonies)
Subpart 7-2 for Children's Camps
Subpart 7-3 for Campgrounds
Subpart 7-4 for Mass Gatherings
Part 14 for Food Service Establishments
Part 15 for Migrant Farmworker Housing
Part 17 for Mobile Home Parks
Appendix 5B for Standards for Individual Water Supply
Appendix 75A for Wastewater Treatment Standards – Individual Household Systems

Program: **Public Water Systems**
Regulatory Authority: Subpart 5-1 of the State Sanitary Code *(10 NYCRR Part 5)*

Provides for regulation of the design, operation and maintenance of public water systems and their sources. Applies to public water systems as defined in Subpart 5-1.1 and covers source water quality, drinking water standards, design and approval for water system infrastructure, treatment requirements, monitoring, operations, cross connection control, water supply emergency plans, public education and notification. Requires notification and approval before any modifications are made to public water systems.

Provides the minimum standards for construction, renovation, development and abandonment of drinking water wells used for drinking, culinary and/or food processing purposes.

Program: **Public Swimming Pools and Bathing Beaches and Recreational Aquatic Spray Grounds**
Regulatory Authority: Subparts 6-1 (Swimming Pools), 6-2 (Bathing Beaches) and 6-3 (Recreational Aquatic Spray Grounds) of the State Sanitary Code *(10 NYCRR Part 6)*

Swimming Pool – A structure, together with buildings and appurtenances used in connection therewith, intended for bathing, swimming or diving purposes, made of concrete, masonry, metal or other impervious material, located either indoors or outdoors.

Bathing Beach – A bathing place together with any buildings or appurtenances, and the water and land areas used in connection therewith, at a pond, lake, stream or other body of fresh or salt water which is used for bathing or swimming with the express or implied permission or consent of the owner or lessee of the premises or which is operated for a fee or any other consideration or which is openly advertised as a place for bathing or swimming.

Recreational Aquatic Spray Ground – Also known as "spray grounds", are the buildings and appurtenances used in conjunction with a spray pad in which sprayed water is continually drained and collected in a treatment and recirculation system.

This program contains the design criteria for new construction or modification, fencing requirements, supervision/lifeguard standards, pool water chemistry and treatment; and water quality at all pools, spas and beaches available to the general public, except those owned and/or maintained by an individual for use of family or friends.

Other State agencies that may have additional regulatory oversight include Department of Labor and Department of Environmental Conservation.

Program: **Temporary Residences**
　　　　Regulatory Authority: Subpart 7-1 of the State Sanitary Code *(10 NYCRR Part 7)*

Temporary Residence – A tract or tracts of land and any hotel, motel, cabin colony, building, camping unit other structures including worker housing that may be pertinent to its use, maintained primarily for overnight occupancy by persons who are provided at least some part or portion of the use of the facilities.

This program contains provisions that regulate temporary residences (hotel, motels, cabin colonies) providing accommodations for 11 or more guests for at least 60 hours in a calendar year, including requirements for fire safety, food service, water supply and sewage disposal. Facilities located in cities having a population of 125,000 or more which receive all water from a public water supply and discharge all sewage in a public sewer system are exempt.

Other State agencies that may have additional regulatory oversight include, Department of Labor, Department of Environmental Conservation.

Program: **Children's Camps**
　　　　Regulatory Authority: Subpart 7-2 of the State Sanitary Code *(10 NYCRR Part 7)*

Children's Overnight Camp – A property consisting of a tract of land and any tents, vehicles, buildings or other structures that may be pertinent to its use, any part of which may be occupied by persons under 18 years of age for the purpose of outdoor or indoor organized activities and on which provisions are made for overnight occupancy of children.

Summer Day Camp – A property consisting of a tract of land and any tents, vehicles, building, or other structures that may be pertinent to its use, any part of which may be occupied on a scheduled basis at any time between June 1 and September 15 in any year by children under 16 years of age, under general supervision, primarily for the purpose of outdoor organized group activities for a period of less than twenty-four hours on any day the property is so occupied, and/or which no provisions are made for overnight occupancy by such children.

Until April 1, 2011, a children's overnight camp shall mean a property consisting of a tract of land and any tents, vehicles, buildings or other structures that may be pertinent to its use, any part of which may be occupied by persons under 18 years of age for the purpose of outdoor or indoor organized activities and on which provisions are made for overnight occupancy of children.

On April 1, 2011, a summer day camp shall mean a property consisting of a tract of land and any tents, vehicles, buildings, or other structures that may be pertinent to its use, any part of which may be occupied on a scheduled basis at any time between June 1 and September 15 in any year by children under 16 years of age, under general supervision, for the purpose of indoor or outdoor organized group activities, involving nonpassive recreational activities with significant risk of injury, as defined in subdivision 7-2.2(1) of this Subpart, for a period of less than twenty-four hours on any day the property is so occupied, and/or which no provisions are made for overnight occupancy by such children.

Traveling Summer Day Camp – A summer day camp which regularly operates in a period between May 15 and September 15, and which regularly transports children under 16 years of age on a regular schedule to a facility, site or property, including any tract of land, beach, park, stadium, building, tents or other structures pertinent to its use and primarily for the purpose of organized group activity.

This program contains provisions for camper supervision, activity safety, fire safety, housing, water supply, sewage disposal, food preparation, transportation and medical safety.

Other State agencies that may have additional regulatory requirements, State Education Department, Department of Environmental Conservation.

Program: Campgrounds
> Regulatory Authority: Subpart 7-3 of the State Sanitary Code *(10 NYCRR Part 7)*

Campground – Any parcel or tract of land including buildings or other structures, under the control of any person, where five or more campsites are available for temporary or seasonal occupancy.

This program includes standards for the water supply, sewage disposal, food service; fire safety and design, operation and maintenance at facilities operating more than 60 hours in any calendar year available to the public, not including those regulated by another State agency.

Other State agencies that may have additional regulatory oversight include Department of Environmental Conservation, Department of Labor.

Program: Mass Gathering
> Regulatory Authority: Subpart 7-4 of the State Sanitary Code *(10 NYCRR Part 7)*

Mass Gathering – A gathering that is likely to attract 5,000 people or more and continue for 24 hours or more but shall not include a temporary residence under permit.

This program contains provisions that regulate food service, water supply and sewage disposal, overnight camping as well as security, transportation, medical care, noise control and site lighting at the sight of the mass gathering.

Other State agencies that may have additional regulatory oversight include, Department of Labor, New York State Police and Department of Transportation.

Program: Food Protection
> Regulatory Authority: Subparts 14-1, 14-2, 14-4, 14-5 of the State Sanitary Code *(10 NYCRR Part 14)*

Food Service Establishment – (Subpart 14 -1) – A place where food is prepared and intended for individual portion service and includes the site at which the individual portions are provided, whether consumption occurs on or off the premises. The term excludes food processing establishments, retail food stores, private homes where food is prepared or served for family consumption, and food service operations where a distinct group mutually provides, prepares, serves and consumes the food such as a "covered-dish supper" limited to a congregation, club or fraternal organization.

Temporary Food Service Establishment – (Subpart 14-2) A place where food is prepared or handled and served to the public, with or without charge, and which operates at a fixed location in conjunction with a single even or celebration of not more than 14 consecutive days duration.

This program provides standards to regulate food service establishments, school and institutional food services, temporary food service establishments, mobile food pushcarts (Subpart 14-4) and vending machines (Subpart 14-5) for food and beverages.

Other State agencies that may have additional regulatory oversight include Department of Agriculture and Markets and Department of Environmental Conservation.

Program: Migrant Farmworker Housing
> Regulatory Authority: Part 15 of the State Sanitary Code *(10 NYCRR Part 15)*

Migrant Farmworker Housing – Facilities occupied by five or more persons, one of whom are employed to perform farm activities.

This program provides standards for housing, water and sewage disposal/treatment, food service, fire safety, laundry and bathing facilities for housing occupied by migrant laborers of whom are employed to perform farm activities of a seasonal or temporary nature. This program does not include housing at facilities that provide year round employment such as dairy farms.

Other State agencies that may have additional regulatory requirement include Department of Labor, Department of Environmental Conservation, and Division of Housing and Community Renewal. The United States Department of Labor may also have additional requirements for migrant housing.

Program: **Mobile Home Parks**

Regulatory Authority: Part 17 of the State Sanitary Code *(10 NYCRR Part 17)*

Mobile Home Park – A property consisting of a tract of land maintained by an operator for placement of 5 or more mobile homes and/or manufactured homes, and buildings or other structures that may be pertinent to their use, any part of which may be occupied by persons for residential purposes other than recreation, traveling or vacationing and who are provided services or facilities necessary for their use of the property.

Other State agencies that may have additional regulatory oversight include the Department of Environmental Conservation and Division of Housing and Community Renewal. The U.S. Department of Housing and Urban Development may also have additional requirements for mobile home parks.

Program: **Standards for Individual Water Supply and Individual Sewage Treatment Systems**

Regulatory Authority: Part 75 of the State Sanitary Code (10 NYCRR Part 75)

Provides minimum standards and implementation procedures for residential water supply and wastewater treatment systems when a municipal system is not available. Procedures and jurisdiction for issuance of waivers by the Department and local health departments are provided. Appendix 75A (below) is referenced as the minimum standard for residential onsite wastewater treatment systems.

Program: **Wastewater Treatment Standards – Individual Household Systems**

Regulatory Authority: Appendix 75A of the State Sanitary Code *(10 NYCRR Part 75)*

Provides for minimum standards for the design of residential on-site wastewater treatment systems that are not otherwise regulated by the Department of Environmental Conservation (DEC) under Article 17 of the Environmental Conservation Law. By interagency agreement, onsite wastewater treatment systems at residences and some commercial facilities (those requiring Health Department permits to operate) are addressed under 10 NYCRR Part 75, Appendix 75A, and 1988 DEC Design (Commercial Systems) Standards for Wastewater Treatment Works..

Program: **Approval of Reality Subdivisions**

Regulatory Authority: Part 74 of the State Sanitary Code (10 NYCRR Part 74)

Provides for regulation of the design and construction of sewerage and water facilities for realty subdivisions. Health Department review and approval is required to address community sewerage, individual onsite wastewater treatment and disposal. public water, and individual water supply systems.

Additional Information:
Bureau of Community Environmental Health and Food Protection
547 River Street
Flanigan Square Room 515
Troy, New York 12180-2216
1-800-458-1158 ext. 27600

Bureau of Water Supply Protection
547 River Street
Flanigan Square Room 400
Troy, New York 12180-2216
1-800-458-1158 ext. 27650

Licensed Health Care Facilities

Construction requirements set forth by the Department of Health for Article 28 licensed health care facilities, Title 10 NYCRR by visiting NYSDOH website at www.health.state.ny.us

Part 711 for General Standards of Construction

Part 712 for Standards of Construction for New Hospitals

Part 713 for Standards of Construction for Nursing Homes

Part 715 for Standards of Construction for New Diagnostic or Treatment Centers

Part 716 for Standards of Construction for New Rehabilitation Facilities

Part 717 for Standards of Construction for New Hospice Facilities and Units

For Article 28 Licensed Health Care facilities, the following base occupancies apply per the *Building Code of New York State*. The Department of Health may apply additional requirements specific to the program and scope of services provided:

Acute Care Hospitals	Institutional I-2
Nursing Homes:	Institutional I-2
Diagnostic or Treatment:	Business Occupancy

DOH Adult Residential Care occupancy classifications

Effective February 23, 2005 - Chapter 2 of the Laws of 2004; Public Health Law Article 46-b

All Assisted Living Residences shall be licensed by NYSDOH

Division of Home and Community Based Care

Public Health Law section 4651, subdivision 15 defines the term "enhanced assisted living certificate" as a certificate issued by the Department which authorizes an ALR to provide aging in place by retaining residents who desire to continue to age in place and who: (a) are chronically chairfast and usable to transfer; or chronically require physical assistance of another person to transfer; (b) chronically require physical assistance of another person to walk; (c) chronically require physical assistance of another person to climb or descend stairs; (d) are dependent on medical equipment and require more than intermittent or occasional assistance from medical personnel; or (e) has chronic unmanaged urinary or bowel incontinence.

18 NYCRR Parts 485 through 488;

Assisted Living Residences (ALR); Enriched Assisted Living Residences (EALR) and Special Needs Assisted Living Residences (SNALR)

Adult Home and Adult Home-Based ALR, EALR & SNALR (16 or more residents)	I-1
Adult Home and Adult Home-Based ALR, EALR & SNALR (5 to 16 residents)	R-4
Enriched Housing and Enriched Housing-Based ALR, EALR & SNALR (16 or more residents)	I-1
Enriched Housing and Enriched Housing-Based ALR, EALR & SNALR (5 to 16 residents)	R-4

Programmatically, dementia patients in the early stages of the condition are permitted to reside in any of these occupancies. These individuals are expected to retain the skills required to stay in these kinds of occupancies for a longer period of time, thus delaying the progression of the condition. It is the responsibility of the regulating agency, to require these clients to be transferred to a facility which better suits their needs when it becomes necessary. Therefore, alterations to these occupancies for use by dementia patients do not constitute a change in occupancy classification.

Building Code of New York State (BCNYS) Section 310.1 states in part:

Group R-4 occupancies shall meet the requirements for construction as defined for Group R-3, except as otherwise provided for in this code, or shall comply with the *Residential Code of New York State* in accordance with Section 101.2. RCNYS Section 101.2 provides the RCNYS is applicable to detached one- and two-family dwellings not more than three stories in height and townhouses not more than three stories in height. For one- and two-family dwellings four stories of more in height, BCNYS R-3 construction is appropriate.

The Certificate of Occupancy shall state either R-4 or I-1 occupancy classification, as appropriate.

Additional Information:
Bureau of Architectural and Engineering Facilities Planning
Hedley Building 6th Floor
533 River Street
Troy, New York 12180-2216
(518) 402-0964

Day Programs

New York State (NYS) law provides general standards under which some adult day programs operate, and the NYS Department of Health (DOH) is responsible for quality assurance of adult day programs. The standards to which the services must adhere relate to admission, assessment, staffing qualifications, and patients rights. There are three types of adult day care programs:

Adult day health care (ADHC) provides medically supervised services for individuals with physical and mental impairments. The program is available through the Medicaid state plan and also serves private pay participants. All ADHC programs are operated by nursing homes, otherwise known as residential care facilities (RCFs), although they are not necessarily located at the nursing home. ADHC program operators must submit a certificate of need (CON) application and obtain written approval from the Department, and must comply with the pertinent provisions in Title 10, NYS Health Rules and Regulations. An RCF must be approved as a provider of specialized services by the Department to provide ADHC services for acquired immune deficiency syndrome (AIDS)/human immunodeficiency virus (HIV) registrants.

Day programs, which provide personal care, supervision, and other services, serve nonresidents in certified adult care facilities (adult homes, residences for adults, or enriched housing programs) and must comply with the pertinent provisions in Title 18, NYS Health Rules and Regulations. The operator of an adult care facility must obtain written approval from the Department to provide services to nonresidents, which is granted only when the Department finds that a consistently high level of care is being provided to residents of the facility.

Social adult day services (SADS) programs provide a variety of long-term care services to a group of individuals with functional limitations--due to either physical or cognitive impairments--in a congregate setting in accordance with an individualized plan of care. Social adult day services are not regulated unless the program is located in a certified adult care facility, where it will be subject to the facility's relevant requirements. Currently, there are over 200 social adult day programs in NYS supported by a wide array of sources with no dedicated funding stream. In 2004, the New York Legislature created an elder law for New York, which included provisions for the promulgation of rules and regulations to establish standards and requirements with regard to the operation of all social adult day care programs receiving funding from the State Office for the Aging. An analysis is underway regarding the projected costs and benefits of establishing uniform standards and requirements for SADS.
10 NYCRR 425, 713-2.13, 711.2

Division of Housing and Community Renewal (DHCR)

Hampton Plaza
38-40 State Street
Albany, NY 12207
Phone: 518-402-3728
http://www.dhcr.state.ny.us

The Division of Housing and Community Renewal is responsible for the supervision, maintenance and development of affordable low- and moderate-income housing in New York State. The Division performs a number of activities in fulfillment of this mission, including:

Housing Operations - Oversight and regulation of the State's public and publicly assisted rental housing;

Community Development - Administration of housing development and community preservation programs, including State and Federal grants and loans to housing developers to partially finance construction or renovation of affordable housing; and

Rent Administration - Administration of the rent regulation process for more than one million rent-regulated apartments in both New York City, and those localities in the counties of Albany, Erie, Nassau, Rockland, Schenectady, Rensselaer and Westchester subject to rent laws.

Additional Information:

http://www.dhcr.state.ny.us/general/dhcrpub.htm

NYS Department of Labor

W. Averell Harriman State Office Campus
Building 12
Albany, NY 12240
Phone: 518-457-9000
www.labor.state.ny.us

Engineering Services Unit

The Engineering Services Unit is responsible for the review and approval of permit applications for places of public assembly, ski tows, tramways, elevators and escalators, large tents for 300 or more occupants, bleachers, window cleaning scaffolds and other devices. The Unit develops standards to conduct safety and health activities mandated by law, reviews variance requests and reviews design plans submitted by public employers to the Hazard Abatement Board. For additional information about Engineering Services Unit visit us at www.labor.state.ny.us/business_ny/employer_responsibilities/safety_health.html

Applicable regulations:
Listing of DOL Laws and Regulations that Effect NYS UFP & BC

The synopsis only covers the section of Laws and codes that overlap with building code requirements.

Title 12 NYCRR
Industrial Code Rule 4, "Construction, Installation, Inspection and Maintenance of Low pressure Boilers; Construction of Unfired Pressure Vessels."
Part 4-6 contains requirements for construction of boiler rooms with clearance requirements greater than most manufacturers' minimums. DOL currently issues variances for clearances less than required in CR but greater than manufacturers' specifications. Also includes requirements for boiler room egress. Biennial inspections required by certified boiler inspectors, conducted by authorized insurance companies or the jurisdiction.

Industrial Code Rule 14, "Construction, Installation, Inspection and Maintenance of High pressure Boilers; Construction of Unfired Pressure Vessels."
Part 14-1.10 contains requirements for platforms and ladders to gain access to remote areas of the boiler and controls. Variances are issued under certain conditions to allow portable approved ladders in lieu of platforms.

Part-2.2 contains requirements for minimum clearances of the boilers from building walls or partition for proper care, maintenance and inspection, which may be greater than the manufacturers' minimums. DOL currently issues variances for clearances less than required in CR but greater than manufacturers' specifications in order to maintain satisfactory accessibility. Annual inspections required by certified boiler inspector, conducted by authorized insurance companies or the jurisdiction.

Industrial Code Rule 8, "Construction, Guarding, Equipment, Maintenance and Operation of Elevators, Dumbwaiters, Escalators, Hoists and Hoistways in Factories and Mercantile Establishments."

This code rule was last updated in 1923, so many sections are obsolete (no one under 18 can be employed as an elevator operator). As per title ICR 8 only applies to factories and mercantile establishments. Requires filing of plans with DOL and issuance of approval of plans by DOL.

Industrial Code Rule 36, "Places of Public Assembly"

Covers areas of public assembly, including theaters, moving picture houses, assemble halls, with capacity of 150 persons. Specifies requirements for egress, construction, railings, wall decorations/hangings, bleachers, tents, etc. Includes both indoor and outdoor public assembly. Requires filing of plans with DOL or local enforcing authority, inspection of premises, and certificate of compliance.

Industrial Code Rule 39, "Possession, Handling, Storage, & Transportation of Explosives"

Covers the manufacture, ownership, possession, storage, use transportation, purchase, sale or gift of explosives. Specifies requirements for the construction of magazines used to store explosives. Also provides requirements for the placement of magazines in proximity to other structures and public transportation. (Also, regulated by NYS Penal Law Section 405).

Industrial Code Rule 45, "Amusement Devices, Viewing Stands and Tents at Carnival, Fairs, and Amusement Parks"

Provides requirements for viewing stands and tents, other temporary structures where an admission fee is usually charged. Permit is required prior to use of such in NYS. Annual inspections required.

Industrial Code Rule 56, "Asbestos"

Requires asbestos survey prior to any demolition activities on buildings, with specific exceptions. Provides requirements for asbestos abatement.

http://www.labor.state.ny.us/workerprotection/safetyhealth/DOSH_CODE_RULES.shtm

New York State Office of Mental Health

44 Holland Avenue
Albany, New York 12229
Phone: 1-800-597-8481
http://www.omh.state.ny.us/

New York State Office of Mental Health

A system of mental health care for New Yorkers

New York State has a large, multifaceted mental health system that serves more than 500,000 individuals each year. The Office of Mental Health (OMH) operates psychiatric centers across the State, and also regulates, certifies and oversees more than 2,500 programs, which are operated by local governments and nonprofit agencies. These programs include various inpatient and outpatient programs, emergency, community support, residential and family care programs.

Applicable Regulations:

Part 584 - Operation of Residential Treatment Facilities for Children and Youth
http://www.omh.state.ny.us/omhweb/policy/policy.htm

Office of Mental Health Occupancy Classifications

COMMUNITY RESIDENCE
(as defined in Mental Hygiene Law)
including: INDIVIDUAL RESIDENTIAL ALTERNATIVE

	Residential code if:
Residential for 14 persons or fewer: one-family or two-family	**One or two family dwellings or Multiple single family (townhouses) @ three stories or less**
	R3 - one or two family dwelling if: Dwelling not residential code
Residential for 14 persons or fewer: when located in a permanent multiple dwelling	R2 - permanent multiple dwelling
Residential for 15 people or more: permanent multiple dwelling	R2 - permanent multiple dwelling

PSYCHIATRIC CENTERS

	I-2 - Institutional

DAY HABILITATION

Nonresidential for day training facility, clinic treatment facility, & day treatment facility	B - business
Nonresidential Sheltered Workshop certified as a day training facility	B - business

Metropolitian Transit Authority - MTA New York

Metropolitan Transportation Authority (MTA) NYC Transit is a self permitting agency.

Administration and enforcement of the NYS Uniform Fire Prevention and Building Code is indicated in Program Management Guideline (PMG) #322 and circulated to all designers at the commencement of work. A code compliance checklist is provided and completed by each design discipline at contract completion.

The principal Code Compliance Manager can be reached at 1-212-878-7000

http://www.mta.nyc.ny.us

The MTA - New York City Transit (NYCT), a New York State agency, builds and maintains all forms of structures to support its vast transit system infrastructure.

The MTA complies with the Uniform Fire Prevention and Building Code of New York State and its Referenced Standards.

New York State Office of Parks, Recreation and Historic Preservation

Empire State Plaza
Agency Building 1
Albany NY, 12238
(518) 474-0456
(518) 486-1899 TDD
http://nysparks.state.ny.us/

New York State Historic Preservation Office
Peebles Island Resource Center
P.O. Box 189
Waterford, NY 12188-0189
(518) 237-8643
http://nysparks.state.ny.us/shpo/

New York's State Historic Preservation Office (SHPO) helps communities identify, evaluate, preserve, and revitalize their historic, archeological, and cultural resources. The SHPO administers programs authorized by both the National Historic Preservation Act of 1966 and the New York State Historic Preservation Act of 1980. These programs, including the Statewide Historic Resources Survey, the New York State and National Registers of Historic Places, the federal historic rehabilitation tax credit, the Certified Local Government program, the state historic preservation grants program, state and federal environmental review, and a wide range of technical assistance, are provided through a network of teams assigned to territories across the state. The SHPO works with governments, the public, and educational and not-for-profit organizations to raise historic preservation awareness, to instill in New Yorkers a sense of pride in the state's unique history and to encourage heritage tourism and community revitalization.

New York State and National Registers Information

http://nysparks.state.ny.us.shpo/register/index.htm

Office for People with Developmental Disabilities

44 Holland Avenue
Albany, NY 12229
518-473-9689
http://www.omr.state.ny.us/

The New York State Office for People with Developmental Disabilities and its local governments have a responsibility for the prevention and early detection of mental retardation and developmental disabilities and for the comprehensively planned provision of services including care, treatment, habilitation and rehabilitation of their citizens with mental retardation and developmental disabilities.

Applicable Regulations:

Mental Hygiene Law, Chapter 676, Title C
The Mental Retardation & Developmental Disabilities Act

http://www.omr.state.ny.us/regs/index.jsp

COMMUNITY RESIDENCE
(as defined in Mental Hygiene Law)
including: INDIVIDUAL RESIDENTIAL ALTERNATIVE

Residential for 14 persons or fewer: one-family or two-family	Residential code if: One or two family dwellings or Multiple single family (townhouses) @ three stories or less
	R3 - one or two family dwelling if: Dwelling not residential code
Residential for 14 persons or fewer: when located in a permanent multiple dwelling	R2 - permanent multiple dwelling
Residential for 15 persons or more: permanent multiple dwelling	R2 - permanent multiple dwelling

DEVELOPMENTAL CENTERS

	I-2 - Institutional

DAY HABILITATION

Nonresidential for day training facility, clinic treatment facility, & day treatment facility	B - business
Nonresidential Sheltered Workshop certified as a day training facility	B - business

Public Service Commission

Empire State Plaza
Agency Building 3
Albany, NY 12223-1350
Phone: (518) 474-7080
www.dps.state.ny.us

The Department of Public Service has a broad mandate to ensure that all New Yorkers have access to reliable and low-cost utility services. The Department is the staff arm of the Public Service Commission. The Commission regulates the state's electric, gas, steam, telecommunications, and water utilities. The Commission also oversees the cable industry. The Commission is charged by law with responsibility for setting rates and ensuring that adequate service is provided by New York's utilities. In addition, the Commission exercises jurisdiction over the siting of major gas and electric transmission facilities and has responsibility for ensuring the safety of natural gas and liquid petroleum pipelines.

Applicable Regulations:

Article 7A – Home insulation and energy conservation act

Power Authority

30 South Pearl Street,
Albany, N.Y.,12207-3425
Our corporate switchboard can be
reached at (914) 681-6200.

The New York Power Authority (NYPA) is one of the largest state-owned power organizations, operating 17 generating facilities and more than 1,400 circuit-miles of transmission lines.

New York Power Authority sells power to government agencies; to community-owned electric systems and rural electric cooperatives; to job-producing companies; to private utilities for resale-without profit—to their customers; and to neighboring states, under federal requirements.

NYPA provides a variety of energy-related services to businesses and municipalities.

State University Construction Fund

353 Broadway
Albany, New York 12246
www.sucf.suny.edu

In addition to the requirements set forth in the current edition of the Building Code of New York State, the State University Construction Fund (SUCF) requires additional safeguards for all buildings and accessory structures (including equipment and mechanical services) constructed with its funds on SUNY campuses. A full description of these additional safeguards can be found at http://www.sucf.suny.edu/design/bulletin.shtml

Department of State

41 State Street
Albany, New York 12231
www.dos.state.ny.us

Division of Code Enforcement and Administration
Phone (518)-474-4073

The Codes Division provides a variety of services related to New York's Uniform Fire Prevention and Building Code and State Energy Conservation Construction Code. The Division provides technical assistance, administers variances, delivers educational courses, oversees the enforcement practices of local governments and serves as secretariat to the State Fire Prevention and Building Code Council.

Thruway Authority and Canal Corporation

200 Southern Blvd., P.O. Box 189
Albany, NY 12201-0189
www.thruway.state.ny.us

In addition to the requirements set forth in 19 NYCRR, the New York State Uniform Fire Prevention and Building Code, the Authority/Corporation requires that new buildings, accessory structures, and structures related to buildings be designed in compliance with the Americans with Disabilities Act Accessibility Guidelines (ADAAG) and the Code of Federal Regulations, Occupational Safety and Health Standards (29 CFR 1910) where the Authority/Corporation is the owner and occupant. The Authority/Corporation leases land to both the public and private sector. Public and private entities should contact one of the following offices for additional information.

NYS Thruway Authority/NYS Canal Corporation
Administrative Headquarters
Department of Maintenance Engineering
Bureau of Facilities and Code Administration
Construction Permitting Unit
200 Southern Blvd. P.O. Box 189
Albany, NY 12201-0189
Phone (518) 436-2953

Division Offices

NYS Thruway Authority/NYS Canal Corp.
Code Enforcement Official
New York Division
4 Executive Blvd.
Suffern, NY 10901
Phone (845) 918-2627

NYS Thruway Authority/NYS Canal Corp.
Code Enforcement Official
Syracuse Division
Suite 250, 2nd Fl.
290 Elwood Davis Rd.
Liverpool, NY 13083-2104
Phone (315) 438-2397

NYS Thruway Authority/NYS Canal Corp.
Code Enforcement Official
Albany Division
270 Mt. Hope Drive
Albany, NY 12209
Phone (518) 471-5316

NYS Thruway Authority/NYS Canal Corp.
Code Enforcement Official
Buffalo Division
455 Cayuga Rd., Suite 800
Cheektowaga, NY 14225
Phone (716) 635-6276

INDEX

A

ACCESS OPENINGS
Attic................................. 1209.2
Crawl space 1209.1
Doors 711.3.2
Fire damper 716.4
Fire department 402.16
Mechanical appliances................ 1209.3
Refuse/laundry chutes 707.13.3

ACCESSIBILITY .... Chapter 11
Airports E110
Assembly seating 1108.2, 1109.10
Bus stops E108
Detectable warnings.................... 1109.9
Detention and correctional facilities 1103.2.13,
1107.5.5, 1108.4.2, E101.1
Dining areas 1108.2.8
Dwelling units 1107
Egress................................1007
Elevators 1007.2.1, 1007.4,
1109.6, 3001.3
Employee work areas........907.9.1.2, 1103.2.3,
1104.3.1
Entrances 1105
Escalators............................. 1003.7
Existing buildings 1103.2.2
Historic buildings..................... 3409.9
Judicial facilities 1108.4
Lifts...........................1007.5, 1109.7
Maintenance.........................1003.2.9
Parking and passenger loading facilities 1106
Performance areas....................1108.2.7
Platform, raised...................... E103.1
Ramps 1010
Recreational facilities 1109.14
Route 1104, 1107.4,
Scoping................. 1101, 1103.1, E101.1
Service facility....................... 1109.12
Signage..........................1110, E107
Sleeping units..........................1107
Storage 1108.3, 1109.8
Telephone.............................E106
Toilet and bathing facilities........1109.2, E105.1
Transient lodging 1103.2.11, 1107.6.1,
E104.1
Transportation facilities and stations E109

ACCESSIBLE MEANS OF EGRESS 1007

ADMINISTRATION .... Chapter 1

ADOBE CONSTRUCTION 2102.1, 2109.8

AEROSOLS........307.1, 307.2, 311.2, 414.1.2.1,
414.2.5, 907.2.16

AGRICULTURAL BUILDINGS (GROUP U) 312.1,
1103.2.5, Appendix C

AIR CONDITIONING (see MECHANICAL)... 101.4.3,
2801.1, 3006.2

AIR INTAKES (YARDS OR COURTS) 1206.3.2

AIRCRAFT HANGARS 412.2
Aircraft paint hangars 412.4, 507.8
Basements 412.2.2
Construction exterior walls 412.2.1
Heliports and helistops 412.5
Residential........................412.3, 907.2.21
Unlimited height....................... 504.1

AIRCRAFT-RELATED OCCUPANCIES.........412
Airport traffic control towers 412.1, 907.2.22
Egress 412.1.3
Fire detection systems
automatic 412.1.4, 907.2.22
Standby power 412.1.5, 2702.2.18
Type of construction 412.1.2

AISLE................................ 1002.1
Assembly seating 1025
Bleachers.......................... 1025.1.1
Check-out 1109.12.2
Converging 1025.9.3
Egress 1014.4
Folding and telescopic seating 1025.1.1
Grandstands 1025.1.1
Obstructions 1025.9.6
Tents 3103.4
Walking surfaces.................... 1025.11
Width 1025.9.1

ALARM SYSTEMS, EMERGENCY............ 908

ALARMS, FIRE (see FIRE ALARM AND DETECTION SYSTEMS)

ALARMS, VISIBLE 907.9.1

ALARMS, VOICE
High-rise buildings.................. 907.2.12.2

ALLOWABLE STRESS DESIGN 1602.1
Load combinations 1605.3
Masonry design................. 2101.2.1, 2107
Wood design................... 2301.2, 2306

ALTERNATIVE MATERIALS, DESIGN AND METHODS 104.11

ALTERNATING TREAD DEVICES 1009.9
Construction 1009.9.2
Galleries, catwalks and gridirons 1015.6.1

ALUMINUM .... 1404.5.1, 1604.3.5, Chapter 20

AMUSEMENT BUILDING, SPECIAL. 411
  Emergency voice/alarm
    communications system 411.6
  Exit marking 411.7
  Fire detection, automatic 411.3
  Interior finish. 411.8
  Smoke detection system 907.2.11
  Sprinklers, automatic 411.4

AMUSEMENT PARK STRUCTURES 303

**ANCHOR STORE (see COVERED MALL
  BUILDINGS)**. 402.2
  Construction type. 402.6
  Means of egress. 402.4.3.1
  Occupant load .402.4.1.3

ANCHORAGE. 1604.8
  Braced wall line sills. 2308.3.3
  Concrete. 1911, 1912
  Concrete walls 1604.8.2
  Conventional light-frame
    construction. 2308.11.3.1,
     2308.12.7, 2308.12.9
  Decks. 1604.8.3
  Empirical design of masonry 2109.7
  Masonry walls 1604.8.2, 2106.2
  Perforated shear walls. 2305.3.8.2
  Seismic anchorage for
    masonry chimneys 2113.4
  Seismic anchorage for
    masonry fireplaces 2111.4
  Wood sill plates 2305.3.11, 2308.3.3

APARTMENT HOUSES 310.1

APPEALS. 107.3

**ARCHITECT (see definition for REGISTERED
  DESIGN PROFESSIONAL)**

ARCHITECTURAL TRIM 1406.2.2

AREA, BUILDING. . . . . Chapter 5
  Enclosed parking garage. 509.2, 509.3, 509.4
  Limitations 503, 505
  Membrane structures. 3102.4
  Mezzanines 505.2
  Mixed construction types 3102.6
  Mixed occupancy 508
  Modifications 506
  Open parking garage. 509.2, 509.3,
    509.4, 509.7, 509.8
  Residential aircraft hangars. 412.3.6,
  Unlimited 503.1.3, 506.2.1, 507

**AREA FOR ASSISTED RESCUE, EXTERIOR (see
  EXTERIOR AREAS FOR ASSISTED RESCUE)**

AREA OF REFUGE 1007.6

ASSEMBLY OCCUPANCY (GROUP A) . . . 303, 1025
  Accessory. 508.3.1
  Aisles 1025.9

Bleachers (see BLEACHERS)
  Egress, special provisions 1008.1.9
  Fire alarms 907.2.1
  Folding and telescopic seating. 1025.1.1
  Grandstands (see GRANDSTANDS)
  Interior finishes . . . . Table 803.5
  Live load . . . . Table 1607.1
  Motion picture theaters 507.10
  Panic hardware. 1008.1.9
  Seating, fixed (see SEATING, FIXED)
  Seating, smoke-protected. 1025.6.2
  Sprinklers 507.3, 507.6, 507.10, 903.2.1
  Standby power systems 2702.2.1
  Standpipes 905.3.2

**ASSISTED LIVING (see RESIDENTIAL CARE/
  ASSISTED LIVING FACILITIES)**

ATRIUM 404
  Automatic sprinkler protection 404.3
  Enclosure 404.5
  Fire alarm system 907.2.13
  Interior finish 404.7
  Smoke control. 404.4, 909
  Standby power 404.6
  Use 404.2

ATTIC 202
  Access 1209.2
  Combustible storage. 413.2
  Draftstopping. 717.4
  Insulation. 719.3.1
  Live load . . . . Table 1607.1
  Unusable space fire protection. 711.3.3
  Ventilation. 1203.2

AUDITORIUM 303.1
  Accessibility 1108.2
  Foyers and lobbies 1025.4
  Interior balconies and galleries. 1025.5
  Motion picture projection rooms 409
  Stages and platforms 410

**AUTOMOBILE PARKING GARAGE (see GARAGE,
  AUTOMOBILE PARKING)** 406

AWNINGS
  Design and construction. 3105.3
  Drainage, water 3201.4
  Live load 1607.11.2.4
  Plastic. 2606.10
  Public right-of-way
    encroachments 3202.2.3, 3202.3.1

B

BALCONIES. 1014.5
  Accessibility 1108.2.3
  Construction requirements 1406.3
  Egress, means of 1014.5, 1016.3, 1025.5
  Emergency escape. 1026.1

      2010 BUILDING CODE OF NEW YORK STATE

Encroachments. .3202.3.2
Exterior .1602.1, 1016.3
Guards 1013
Interior. 1025.5
Live load . . . . Table 1607.1
Projection .704.2, 1406.3
Travel distance 1016.3

BARBECUES 2801

BARRIERS, VEHICLE. 406.2.4, 1602.1, 1607.7.3

BASEMENT (see UNDERGROUND BUILDINGS)
Aircraft hangars 412.2.2
Area modification 506.1
Considered a story 502.1
Emergency escape. 1026
Flood loads. 1612.2
Height modifications for 509.2, 509.3,
509.4, 509.5
Prohibited 415.4, 415.5,
415.6.3.5, 415.8.5.2.2, 418.1
Rodentproofing. . . . . .Appendix F
Sprinklers 903.2.10.1
Waterproofing and dampproofing. 1807

BASEMENT WALLS
Concrete . . . . .Table 1904.2.2, 1909.6.1
Soil loads 1610.1
Waterproofing and dampproofing. 1807

BASIC WIND SPEED 1609.3

BAY AND ORIEL WINDOWS 1406.4

BLEACHERS. 303.1
Accessibility 1108.2
Egress. 1025.1.1
Occupant load. 1004.7

**BLOCK (see CONCRETE BLOCK, and
GLASS UNIT MASONRY)**

BOILER ROOM
Exits 1015.3

BOLTS. 2204.2
Anchors. 1912, 1913, 2103.13.5, 2204.2.1
High strength, steel. 1704.3.3

BONDING, MASONRY . . . 2103.9, 2109.6, 2109.7.2.1

BRACED WALL LINE. 2302.1, 2308.3
Bracing 2308.3
Seismic requirements. 2308.12.3, 2308.12.4
Sill anchorage. .2308.3.3
Spacing. 2308.3.1
Support 2308.3.4

BRACED WALL PANEL. 2302.1, 2308.9.3
Alternative bracing 2308.9.3.1, 2308.9.3.2
Connections 2308.3.2

BRICK (see MASONRY)
Calculated fire resistance 721.4
Foundations. 1805.5
Veneer. 1405.5, 1405.9

BUILDING
Access, fire department 402.16
Area (see AREA, BUILDING) . . . . .Chapter 5
Demolition 3303
Existing 101.4.5
Height (see HEIGHT, BUILDING). . . . . . .Chapter 5
Occupancy classification. . . . . .Chapter 3

BUILT-UP ROOFS. 1507.10

BUSINESS OCCUPANCY (GROUP B) 304
Aisles. 1014.4.1
Educational above 12th grade 304.1
Fire alarm 907.2.2
Parking under 509.2, 509.7, 509.8

C

CABLES, STEEL STRUCTURAL 2207

**CALCULATED FIRE RESISTANCE (see FIRE
RESISTANCE, CALCULATED) CANOPIES** 3105
Live load 1607.11.2.4
Materials 3105.4
Motor vehicle service stations. 406.5.2

CANOPIES 3105
Live load 1607.11.2.4
Materials 3105.4
Motor vehicle service stations. 406.5.2

CARPET
Floor covering 804.2
Textile wall coverings 803.6
Textile ceiling finish. 803.6

CATWALKS
Means of egress 410.3.2, 1015.6.1
Sprinklers. 410.6

CEILING
Height 409.2, 909.20.4.3, 1205.2.2, 1208.2
Interior finish 803
Penetration of fire resistant
assemblies 707, 712.4, 716.2, 716.6
Suspended acoustical. 803.9.1.1

CELLULOSE NITRATE FILM 409.1, 903.2.4.3

CERAMIC TILE
Material requirements 2103.5
Mortar 2103.10

CHILD CARE (see DAY CARE) 305.2, 308.3.1,
308.5.2, 407.1

CHIMNEYS 2102.1, 2111
    Factory-built 717.2.5

CHURCHES
  (see RELIGIOUS WORSHIP, PLACES OF)

CIRCULAR STAIRS (see CURVED STAIRWAYS)

CLAY ROOF TILE 1507.3
    Testing 1715.2

COAL POCKETS 415.6.1.6

COLD STORAGE,
  FOAM PLASTIC INSULATION 2603.3, 2603.5
    Thermal barrier. 2603.4, 2604.1

COLD-FORMED STEEL 2202.1, 2209
    Special inspection for seismic resistance . . .1707.4
    Light-frame construction 2210

COMBUSTIBLE DUSTS 415.6.1

COMBUSTIBLE LIQUIDS 415.6.2

COMBUSTIBLE MATERIAL
    High-pile stock or rack storage 413.1, 910.2.2
    In concealed spaces 413.2, 717.5
    In Type I and Type II 603, 805.1
    On exterior side of exterior wall 1406

COMBUSTIBLE PROJECTIONS 704.2, 1406.3

COMBUSTIBLE STORAGE 413, 910.2.2

COMMON PATH OF EGRESS TRAVEL 1014.3

COMPARTMENTATION
    Underground buildings. 405.4

COMPRESSED GAS 307.2, 415.8.7.2.2

CONCEALED SPACES 413.2, 717

CONCRETE . . . . Chapter 19
    Anchorage 1911, 1912
    Calculated fire resistance. 721.2
    Conduits embedded in 1906
    Construction documents 1901.4
    Construction joints 1906
    Curing. 1905.11
    Durability 1904
    Exposure conditions. 1904
    Footings 1805.4.2
    Formwork 1906
    Foundation walls .1805.5
    Materials. 1704.4.1, 1903
    Mixing. 1905
    Pipe columns, concrete-filled. 1915
    Pipes embedded in 1906
    Placing 1905
    Plain, structural 1909
    Proportioning 1905.2
    Quality 1905
    Reinforced gypsum concrete. 1914
    Reinforcement 1907

    Rodentproofing .Appendix F
    Roof tile. .1507.3, 1715.2
    Shotcrete. 1913
    Slab, minimum 1910
    Special inspections . . . . .1704.4, Table 1704.4
    Specifications 1903
    Strength testing. 1704.4.1, 1905.6
    Wood support 2304.12

CONCRETE MASONRY
    Calculated fire resistance 721.3
    Construction 2104
    Design. 2101.2
    Materials 2103.1
    Surface bonding 2109.2.3
    Testing 2105.2.2.1.2
    Wood support 2104.1.6, 2304.12

CONCRETE ROOF TILE 1507.3
    Wind resistance 1609.5.3, 1715.2

CONDOMINIUM (see APARTMENT HOUSES)

CONDUIT, PENETRATION PROTECTION 711.5,
                              712.3, 1020.1.1

CONFLICTS IN CODE 102.1

CONSTRUCTION DOCUMENTS 202, 1603
    Concrete construction. 1901.4
    Design load bearing capacity 1802.6
    Fire alarm and detection systems 907.1.1
    Fire-resistant-joint systems. 713
    Floor live load 1603.1.1
    Masonry 2101.3
    Penetrations 712
    Roof assemblies 1503
    Roof live load 1603.1.2
    Roof snow load .1603.1.3
    Seismic 1603.1.5
    Soil classification. 1802.6
    Special loads. .1603.1.7
    Systems and components 1603.1.8
    Wind load 1603.1.4

CONSTRUCTION JOINTS
    Concrete. 1906.4
    Shotcrete. 1913.7

CONSTRUCTION, PUBLIC
  PROPERTY . . . . Chapter 32

CONSTRUCTION TYPES . . . . Chapter 6
    Automobile
      parking garage . . . . .Table 406.3.5, 509.2,
                  509.3, 509.4, 509.7, 509.8
    Classification. 602
    Combustible material in Type I and Type II
      construction 603
    Covered mall buildings 402.6
    Fire resistance . . . . .Table 601, Table 602
    Highrise 403. 3.1
    Underground buildings 405.2

CONTRACTOR'S RESPONSIBILITIES . . 901.5, 1706

CONTROL AREA 414.2

CONVENTIONAL LIGHT-FRAME
    CONSTRUCTION 2301.2, 2302.1, 2308
    Additional seismic requirements. 2308.11,
        2308.12
    Braced wall lines. 2308.3
    Connections and fasteners 2308.5
    Design of elements. 2308.4
    Floor joists 2308.8
    Foundation plates or sills 2308.6
    Girders 2308.7
    Limitations. 2308.2
    Roof and ceiling framing. 2308.10
    Wall framing 2308.9

CORNICES
    Live load . . . . Table 1607.1
    Masonry 2104.2.1
    Projection 704.2, 1406.3
    Draftstopping 717.2.6

CORRIDOR 1017
    Dead end 1017.3
    Elevation change 1003.5
    Headroom. 1003.2, 1003.3.1
    HPM service 903.2.4.2
    Live load . . . . Table 1607.1
    Walls. 708.1, 1017.1
    Width. 1017.2

CORRIDOR PROTECTION, EXIT ACCESS
    Construction,
      fire protection. . . . . . 708.1, Table 1017.1, 1017.5
    Doors 715.4
    Interior finish . . . . Table 803.5, 804.4
    Opening protectives . . . . Table 715.4
    Return and exhaust air 716.5.4.1

CORROSIVES. 414.3

COURTS 1206

COVERED MALL BUILDINGS 402
    Emergency voice/alarm system 907.2.20
    Standby power 2702.2.14
    Standpipe system 905.3.3

COVERED WALKWAY. 3306.7

CONVEYING SYSTEMS 3005

CRAWL SPACE
    Access 1209.1
    Drainage. 1807.1.2
    Ventilation. 1203.3

CRIPPLE WALL 2302.1, 2308.9.4

CRYOGENIC FLUIDS . . . . Table 307.1, 307.2,
    Table 414.5.1, Table 415.8.2.1.1

CURVED STAIRWAYS. 1009.7

D

DAMPERS (see FIRE DAMPERS and SMOKE
    DAMPERS) . . . . 716.2 - 716.5

DAMPPROOFING AND WATERPROOFING 1807
    Required 1807.2, 1807.3
    Subsoil drainage system. 1807.4

DAY CARE 305.2, 308.5
    Adult care 308.5.1
    Child care 308.5.2
    Egress   308.5.2, Table 1004.1.1,
        Table 1015.1, Table 1019.2

DEAD END 1017.3

DEAD LOAD 1602.1, 1606
    Footing design load. 1805.4.1.1

DECK. 1602.1
    Anchorage. 1604.8.3

DEFLECTIONS 1604.3.1
    Framing supporting glass 2403.3
    Preconstruction load tests. 1714.3.2
    Wood diaphragms. 2305.2.2
    Wood shear walls 2305.3.2, 2305.3.8.2.9

DEMOLITION. 3303

DESIGN STRENGTH. 1602.1, 2102.1
    Conformance to standards 1710.1
    New materials 1710.2

DESIGNATED SEISMIC SYSTEM 1702.1
    Seismic qualification 1708.5
    Special inspection 1707.9

DIAPHRAGMS. 1602.1, 2102.1, 2302.1
    Empirical masonry. 2109.2.1.2
    Fexible. 1613.6.1
    Special inspection 1704.6.1, 1707.3
    Wood. 2305.2, 2306.3

DOORS 1008
    Access-controlled 1008.1.3.4
    Emergency escape 1026
    Fire (see OPENING
      PROTECTIVES). 715.4, 1020.1.1
    Glazing 715.4.6, 1405.12
    Hardware (see LOCKS AND
      LATCHES) 1008.1.8
    Horizontal sliding. 1008.1.3.3
    Landings 1008.1.5
    Operation. 1008.1.8
    Panic and fire exit hardware 1008.1.9
    Power operated. 1008.1.3.2
    Revolving. 1008.1.3.1
    Security grilles 1008.1.3.5
    Side swinging 1008.1.2
    Smoke barrier 709.5
    Structural testing, exterior 1714.5

Thresholds 1003.5, 1008.1.4, 1008.1.6
Width 1008.1.1

DRAFTSTOPPING
Attics. 717.4
Floor-ceiling assemblies 717.3

DRY CLEANING PLANTS 415.6.4

DRYING ROOMS 417

DUCTS AND AIR TRANSFER
OPENINGS 704.14, 706.10, 716

DUMBWAITERS 707.14

E

EARTHQUAKE LOADS (see SEISMIC) 1613
Construction documents 1603.1.5
Seismic design category 1613.2
Site class 1613.2, 1613.5.2
Site classification for seismic design 1613.5.5
Site coefficients 1613.2, 1613.5.3
Wind and seismic detailing 1604.10

EAVES (see COMBUSTIBLE PROJECTIONS and
CORNICES)

EDUCATIONAL OCCUPANCY (GROUP E) 305
Day care. 305.2
Egress, special provisions 1008.1.9
Fire alarm 907.2.3
Live load. . . . . .Table 1607.1
Manual fire alarm boxes. 902.23, 907.3
Panic hardware 1008.1.9
Special occupancy separation. 508.3.1,
Table 508.3.3
Sprinkler system. 903.2.2

EGRESS (see MEANS OF EGRESS) . . . . Chapter 10

ELECTRICAL . . . . Chapter 27

ELEVATOR . . . . Chapter 30
Accessibility 1007.2.1, 1007.4,
1109.6, 3001.3
Car size 3002.4
Construction 707.14
Conveying systems 3005
Emergency operations. 3002.3, 3002.5, 3003
High-rise 403.9
Hoistway enclosures 3002, 3005.3.1, 3009.2.1
Hoistway venting 3004
Lobby 707.14.1, 1007.4
Machine rooms. . . . . Table 1607.1, 3006
Means of egress. 1003.7, 1007.2.1, 1007.4
Number of elevator cars in hoistway 3002.2
Personnel and material hoists 3005.4
Seismic requirements 1613
Shaft enclosure 707.14
Signs 1007.7
Standby power. 2702.2.5, 2702.2.19

EMERGENCY COMMUNICATIONS
Area of refuge 1007.6.3

EMERGENCY EGRESS OPENINGS 1026
Window wells 1026.5

EMERGENCY LIGHTING 1006

EMERGENCY POWER
Exit signs. 1011.5.3, 2702.2.3
Group I-3. . . . . .408.4.2, 2702.2.17
Hazardous. 414.5.4, 415.8.10
High-rise 403.11, 2702.15
Means of egress illumination 1006.3
Underground buildings 405.10

EMPIRICAL DESIGN OF
MASONRY 2101.2.4, 2109
Adobe construction. 2109.8
Anchorage. 2109.7
Bond 2109.6
General 2109.1
Compressive stress requirements 2109.3
Lateral stability 2109.2
Lateral support 2109.4
Quality assurance. 1708.1
Special Inspection. 1704.5
Thickness of masonry. 2109.5

EMPLOYEE
Accessibility for work areas 907.9.1.2,
1103.2.3, 1104.3.1

ENCLOSED, WALKWAY 3104

ENCROACHMENTS INTO THE
PUBLIC RIGHT OF WAY . . . . Chapter 32

END-JOINTED LUMBER 2303.1.1

ENERGY EFFICIENCY . . . . Chapter 13

ENGINEER (see definition for REGISTERED
DESIGN PROFESSIONAL)

EQUIVALENT OPENING FACTOR . . . . . Figure 704.7

ESCALATORS 3005
Floor opening protection. 707.2
Illumination 2702.2.4
Means of egress. 1003.7

ESSENTIAL FACILITIES
(see OCCUPANCY CATEGORY). 1602.1

EXCAVATION, GRADING AND FILL 1803

EXISTING BUILDING
Accessibility 1103.2.2
Rodentproofing . . . . .Appendix F

EXIT (see MEANS OF EGRESS) . . . . Chapter 10
Aisles 1014.4
Aisles with tables 1014.4.3
Boiler rooms 1015.3
Construction 706.1

Corridors 1017
Courts 1024.5
Discharge 1024
Enclosure 1020.1
Fire resistance 706.3. 1020
Furnace rooms 1015.3
Horizontal 1022
Illumination 1006.1
Incinerator rooms 1015.3
Interior finish . . . . Table 803.5
Mezzanines 505.3, 1004.6
Number, minimum 1019.1
Passageway 1021
Path, common 1014.3
Refrigerated rooms or spaces 1015.5
Refrigeration machinery rooms 1015.4
Signs 1011
Travel distance 1016
Underground buildings 405.8

EXIT ACCESS
(see MEANS OF EGRESS) 1014-1017

EXIT DISCHARGE
(see MEANS OF EGRESS) 1024

EXIT PASSAGEWAY
(see MEANS OF EGRESS) 1021

EXIT SIGNS 1011
Accessibility 1007.6.4, 1007.6.5,
1007.7, 1007.8.3, 1011.3
Special amusement buildings 411.7

EXPLOSIVES . . . . Table 414.5.1, Table 415.3.1,
Table 415.3.2

EXPOSURE CATEGORY (see WIND LOAD) . 1609.4

EXTERIOR AREAS FOR
ASSISTED RESCUE 1007.8

EXTERIOR WALLS
(see WALLS, EXTERIOR) . . . . 704, Chapter 14

F

FACTORY OCCUPANCY (GROUP F) 306
Dead end corridor 1017.3
Low hazard occupancy 306.3
Moderate hazard occupancy 306.2
Smoke and heat vents 910.2
Travel distance 1016.1

FARM BUILDINGS . . . . Appendix C

FASTENING, WOOD CONSTRUCTION 2304.9

FENCES 312.1

FIBERBOARD 2302.1, 2303.1.5
Shear wall 2306.4.4

FILL MATERIAL 1803.5

FINGER-JOINTED LUMBER
(see END-JOINTED LUMBER)

FIRE ALARM AND DETECTION SYSTEMS
Aerosol storage 907.2.16
Assembly 907.2.1
Audible alarm 907.9.2
Battery room 907.2.23
Construction documents 907.1.1
Covered mall 907.2.20
High-rise 907.2.12
Lumber mills 907.2.17
Occupancy requirements 907.2
Special amusement buildings 907.2.11
Underground buildings 907.2.18, 907.2.19
Visible alarm 907.9.1

FIRE ALARM BOX, MANUAL 907.3

FIRE BARRIERS 706

FIRE COMMAND CENTER 403.8, 911

FIRE DAMPERS 716.2-716.5

FIRE DEPARTMENT ACCESS 402.16

FIRE DETECTION SYSTEM, AUTOMATIC
Airport traffic control towers 412.1.4
High-rise buildings 403.5
Institutional occupancy 407.2.1, 407.2.3, 407.6
Special amusement buildings 411.3

FIRE DOOR
(see OPENING PROTECTIVES) 715, 1020.1.1

FIRE EXTINGUISHERS, PORTABLE 906

FIRE EXTINGUISHING SYSTEMS,
NONWATER BASED 904

FIRE PARTITION 708, 716.5.4

FIRE PROTECTION
Alarm, audible 907.9.2
Alarm, emergency systems 908
Alarms, visible 907.9.1
Explosion control 414.5.1, 911
Fire extinguishers, portable 906
Glazing, rated 715.2
Smoke and heat vents 910
Smoke control systems 909

FIRE PROTECTION SYSTEMS 901.2

FIRE RESISTANCE
Calculated 721
Conditions of restraint 703.2.3
Ducts and air transfer openings 716
Joint systems 713
Prescriptive 720
Ratings . . . . Chapter 6, 703, 704.5, 706
Tests 703
Thermal and sound insulating materials 719.1

FIRE RESISTANCE, CALCULATED 721
   Clay brick and tile masonry 721.4
   Concrete assemblies 721.2
   Concrete masonry .721.3
   Steel assemblies 721.5
   Wood assemblies. .721.6

FIRE-RETARDANT-TREATED WOOD 2303.2
   Awnings 3105.3
   Balconies 1406.3
   Canopies 3105.3
   Concealed spaces .717.5
   Fastening 2304.9.5
   Fire wall vertical continuity. 705.6
   Partitions 603.1
   Platforms 410.4
   Roof construction . . . . Table 601, 705.6, 1505
   Shakes and shingles 1505.6
   Veneer 1405.4

FIRE SEPARATION DISTANCE . . . . . Table 602, 702
   Exterior walls 1406.2.1.1

**FIRE SHUTTER (see OPENING
PROTECTIVES)** 715.4, 715.4.8,
715.4.9, Table 715.5

FIRE WALLS 705
   Combustible framing 705.7
   Exterior intersecting walls 705.5.1
   Fire-resistance rating 705.4
   Materials. 705.3
   Openings, protected. 705.8
   Structural stability. .705.2

FIRE WINDOWS (see OPENING PROTECTIVES)

FIREBLOCKING. 717.2
   Chimneys. 717.2.5, 2113.20
   Fireplaces. 2111.12
   Wood construction 717.2.1, 717.2.7, 1406.2.4
   Wood stairs 717.2.4

FIREPLACES, FACTORY-BUILT 2111.13.1

FIREPLACES, MASONRY 2111
   Combustibles 2111.11
   General provisions 2111
   Hearth extension 2111.9, 2111.10
   Steel units. 2111.5.1

FIREWORKS 307.2, 307.3

FLAMESPREAD. . . . . .802, Table 803.5

FLAMMABLE FINISHES 416
   Fire protection 416.4

**FLAMMABLE AND
COMBUSTIBLE LIQUIDS** 415.6.2

FLAMMABLE SOLIDS. 307.5, 415

FLASHING 1503.2, 1507.3.9,
1507.5.6, 1507.7.6, 1507.8.7, 1507.9.8

   Roof 1503.2
   Wall, veneer 1405.3, 1405.11.7

FLOOD-RESISTANT CONSTRUCTION
   Accessibility 1107.7.5
   Flood loads 1602.1, 1603.1, 1612,
3001.2, 3102.7
   Flood resistance 1403.5, 1403.6
   Grading and fill 1803.4, 1807.1.2.1
   Interior finishes 801.1.3
   Ventilation, under floor 1203.3.2

FLOOR/CEILING (see FLOOR CONSTRUCTION)

**FLOOR CONSTRUCTION (see FLOOR
CONSTRUCTION, WOOD)**
   Draftstopping. 717.3
   Fire resistance 711
   Live loads 1607.3, 1607.4
   Materials. . . . . .Chapter 6
   Penetration of
fire-resistant assemblies 711.5, 712

FLOOR CONSTRUCTION, WOOD
   Beams and girders 2304.11.2.1, 2308.7
   Bridging/blocking 2308.8.5, 2308.10.6
   Diaphragms 2305.2
   Fastening schedule. 2304.9.1
   Framing. 602.4.2, 2304.4
   Joists. 2308.8
   Sheathing 2304.7

FLOOR COVERING 804.1, 804.2

FLOOR FINISH, INTERIOR 804

FLOOR LEVEL AT DOORS 1008.1.4

FLOOR LOADS
   Construction documents. 1603.1.1
   Live 1607.3, 1607.4
   Posting 1603.3

**FLOOR OPENING PROTECTION (see VERTICAL
OPENING PROTECTION)**

FOAM PLASTICS 402.15.5
   Attics 719.3.1, 2603.4.1.6
   Cold storage 2603.4.1.2
   Crawl space 2603.4.1.6
   Density mall signs. 402.15.5.1
   Doors 2603.4.1.7
   Exterior walls of multistory buildings. 2603.5
   Interior finish 801.2.2, 2603.9, 2604
   Label/identification 2603.2
   Roofing 2603.4.1.5
   Siding backer board 2603.4.1.10
   Stages and platform scenery 410.3.6
   Surface burning characteristics 2603.3
   Thermal barrier requirements. . . . 2303.4, 2603.5.2
   Thickness 402.15.5.2
   Trim. 806.3, 2604
   Walk-in coolers 2603.4.1.3

FOLDING AND TELESCOPIC SEATING 1025.1.1
    Accessibility 1108.2
    Egress. 1025.1.1
    Occupant load. 1004.7

FOOD COURT. 402.2
    Occupant load. 402.4.1.4

FOOTINGS AND FOUNDATIONS 1805

FORMWORK, CONCRETE. 1906

FOUNDATION
    Basement wall loads. 1610
    Footing design 1801.2, 1805.4.1
    Pier 1808, 1812
    Pile (see PILE FOUNDATIONS) 1808, 1809,
                                1810, 1811
    Required for wood buildings. 2308.6
    Rodentproofing. . . . . .Appendix F
    Soils investigation (see SOILS AND
       FOUNDATIONS) 1802.2, 1802.4
    Special inspections. 1704.4, 1704.8, 1704.9
    Waterproofing and dampproofing. 1807

FOYERS
    Assembly occupancy 1025.4
    Covered mall. 402.1

FRATERNITIES. 310

FROST PROTECTION 1805.2.1

FURNACE ROOMS. 1015.3

G

GALLERIES
    Means of egress. 1015.6.1, 1025.5
    Sprinklers 410.6

GARAGE, AUTOMOBILE PARKING 406.2
    Accessible provisions 1105.1.1,
                         1106.11, 1110.1
    Barriers, vehicle 406.2.4, 1607.7.3
    Beneath other occupancies 509
    Construction type 406.3.3,
    Enclosed. 406.4
    Guards 406.2.3
    Live load . . . . Table 1607.1
    Occupancy separation 508.3.3, 509
    Occupant load. . . . . Table 1004.1.1
    Open. 406.3
    Sprinklers 903.2.9
    Underground. 405

GARAGE, REPAIR 406.6
    Floor surface. 406.6.4
    Gas-detection system. 406.6.6, 908.5
    Sprinklers 903.2.8.1
    Ventilation. 406.6.3

GARAGES, TRUCK AND BUS
    Live load 1607.6
    Sprinklers. 903.2.9.1

**GARAGES AND CARPORTS,
  PRIVATE** 406.1, 508.2
    Area limitations 406.1.2

GATES. 1008.2

GIFT SHOPS 407.2.4

GIRDERS
    Fire resistance. Table 601
    Materials . . . . .Chapter 6
    Wood construction. 2304.11.2.1, 2308.7

GLASS (see GLAZING)

GLASS BLOCK (see GLASS UNIT MASONRY)

GLAZING
    Athletic facilities. 2408
    Doors 709.5, 715.4.3.2, 1405.12, 1714.5
    Fire doors 715.4.4.1, 715.4.6
    Fire windows 714.5, 715.5
    Handrails and guards 1013.1, 2406.3, 2407
    Identification 2403.1, 2406.2
    Impact loads 2406.1, 2408.2.1
    Impact resistance 1609.1.2
    Jalousies 2403.5
    Label/identification. . . 715.4.5.1, 715.4.6.3, 715.5.8
    Loads. 2404
    Louvered windows 2403.5
    Nonwired 715.5.4
    Opening protectives 715.2
    Railings 2407
    Replacement. 2401.2, 3405
    Safety 715.4.6.4, 2406
    Skylights 2405
    Sloped 2404.2, 2405
    Swimming pools 2406.3
    Supports 2403.2
    Testing. 1714.5, 2406.1.1, 2408.2.1
    Veneer. 1405.11
    Vertical. 2404.1
    Wired. 715.5.3

GLASS UNIT MASONRY 2102.1, 2110
    Atrium enclosure 404.5
    Design method 2101.2.5
    Fire resistance. 2110.1.1
    Hazardous locations 2406.1.3, 2406.3.1
    Material requirements 2103.6
    Placing. 2104.1.2.4

GRADE (PLANE). 502

GRADE, LUMBER (see LUMBER) 2302.1

GRAIN ELEVATORS. 415.6.1.5

GRANDSTANDS 303.1, 1025.1.1
    Accessibility 1108.2
    Exit signs 1011
    Live load. . . . . .Table 1607.1
    Occupant load 1004.7

GREENHOUSES
    Area . . . . Table 503
    Classification of 312.1
    Deflections . . . . .Table 1604.3
    Membranes 3102.1
    Plastic. 2606.11
    Roof live load 1607.11.2.1
    Sloped glazing 2405

GRIDIRON
    Means of egress. 1015.6.1
    Sprinklers 410.6

GRINDING ROOMS 415.6.1.2

GROSS LEASABLE AREA
(see COVERED MALL BUILDINGS) 402

GROUND SNOW LOADS 1608.2

GROUT 712.3.1, 712.4.1, 2103.12

GUARDS. 1013
    Bleachers 1025.1.1
    Equipment platform 505.5.3
    Folding and telescopic seating 1025.1.1
    Glazing. .2406.3, 2407
    Grandstands. 1025.1.1
    Loads 1607.7
    Mechanical equipment. 1013.5
    Opening limitations. 1013.3
    Parking garage. 406.2.4
    Ramps 1010.10
    Residential 1013.2
    Screen porches .1013.4

GUTTERS. 1503.4.1

GYMNASIUMS
    Live load. . . . . .Table 1607.1
    Occupant load 1004.1
    Occupancy separation 508.3.1

GYPSUM. . . . . Chapter 25
    Aggregate, exposed. 2513
    Board . . . . Chapter 25
    Concrete, reinforced 1914
    Construction. 2508
    Diaphragms 2508.5
    Draftstopping 717.3.1
    Exterior soffit . . . . .Table 2506.2
    Fastening 2306.4.5.1.4,
                    Table 2306.4.5, 2508.1
    Fire resistance 721.2.1.4, 721.6.2
    Fire-resistant joint treatment 2508.4
    Inspection. 2503
    Lath 2507, 2510

    Lathing and furring for cement plaster . . .718, 2510
    Lathing and plastering 2507
    Materials. 2506
    Plaster, interior 2511
    Plaster, exterior. .2512
    Shear wall construction. . .2306.4.5, 2308.9.3, 2505
    Sheathing .2304.6.1
    Showers and water closets. 2509
    Stucco. 2510
    Veneer base 2507.2
    Veneer plaster 2507.2
    Vertical and horizontal assemblies. 2504
    Wallboard . . . . Table 2506.2
    Water-resistant backing board 2506.2, 2509. 2

H

HANDRAILS 1009.10, 1607.7
    Assembly aisles 1025.13
    Alternating tread devices 1009.9
    Bleachers 1025.1.1
    Folding and telescopic seating 1025.1.1
    Glazing 2407
    Grandstands 1025.1.1
    Graspability. 1012.3
    Guards 1013.2
    Loads 1607.7
    Projection 1012.5
    Ramps. 1010.8
    Stairs. 1009.10

HARDBOARD. 1404.3.2, 2302.1, 2303.1.6

HARDWOOD
    Fastening 2304.9
    Quality. 2303.3
    Veneer 1404.3.2

HAZARDOUS MATERIALS 414
    Control areas 414.2
    Explosion control . . . . 414.5.1, Table 414.5.1,
                                415.8.5.4
    Special provisions. 415.4, 415.5
    Sprinklers . . . . .Table 414.2.5(1),
              Table 414.2.5(2), 415.5.2, 415.6.2.4
    Ventilation 414.3, 415.6.2.8,
           415.8.2.6, 415.8.4.3, 415.8.5.7, 415.8.6.3
    Weather protection 414.6.1

HEAD JOINT, MASONRY 2102.1
    Bonding pattern .2109.6.5
    Thickness 2104.1.2.1

HEADER, MASONRY (BONDER) 2102.1

HEADROOM 1003.3.1, 1008.1.1, 1009.2, 1010.5.2

HEALTH CARE (see INSTITUTIONAL I-1 and
INSTITUTIONAL I-2)
    Clinics 304
    Hospitals 308

HEALTH-HAZARD MATERIALS 307.2

HEAT VENTS 910

HEATING (see MECHANICAL)
    Aircraft hangars 412.2.4
    Parking garages 406.2.8
    Repair garages 406.6.5

HEIGHT, BUILDING . . . . Chapter 5
    Limitations. 503
    Mixed construction types 509.1
    Modifications. 504
    Roof structures 504.3

HEIGHT, STORY 502.1

HIGH PILED COMBUSTIBLE STORAGE 413,
                  907.2.14, 910.2.2

HIGH-HAZARD OCCUPANCY (GROUP H) . . 307, 415
    Classification. 307
    Combustible liquids .415.6.2
    Control areas 414.2
    Conveyors. 415.6.1.3
    Corrosives. . . . . Table 414.2.5(1), 414.3
    Cryogenic fluids . . . . Table 414.5.1,
                   Table 415.8.2.1.1
    Dispensing, use and handling 414.7.2
    Dry cleaning (see DRY CLEANING PLANTS)
    Emergency alarm systems 908.1, 908.2
    Exceptions 307.1
    Exempt 307.1
    Explosives. . . . . Table 414.5.1, Table 415.3.1
    Factory industrial F-1 moderate
      hazard occupancy 306.2
    Factory industrial F-2 low
      hazard occupancy 306.3
    Fire alarm, manual .901.6.3
    Flammable liquids. .415.6.2
    Flammable solids . . . . 307.2, Table 307.1(1)
    Grinding rooms 415.6.1.2
    Group H-1 . . . . 307.3
    Group H-2 . . . . 307.4
    Group H-3 . . . . .307.5, 415.7
    Group H-4 . . . . .307.6. 415.7
    Group H-5 . . . . .307.7, 415.8
    Health-hazard materials 415.2,
               Table 414.2.5(1), 415.4,
          415.8.6.2, Table 415.8.2.1.1
    Height 415.4, 415.5
    Interior finishes 416.2.1, 416.3.1
    Irritants . . . . . . Table 414.2.5(1), Table 415.8.2.1.1
    Liquid, highly toxic and toxic. 415.7.3, 908.3
    Location on property. 415.3
    Multiple hazards 307.8
    Organic peroxides . . . . .Table 415.3.2
    Oxidizers, liquid and solid. 415.5.1
    Pyrophoric materials. 415.4.1, 415.5.1
    Sensitizers . . . . .Table 415.8.2.1.1
    Separation from other
      occupancies . . . . .Table 415.3.1, 415.6.3.4.1

Solids, highly toxic and toxic 415.7.3,
             Table 415.8.2.1.1, 908.3
Special provisions H-1, H-2, H-3 . . . . 415.4, 415.5
Sprinklers. 415.5.2, 415.6.2.4, 415.8.6.3,
    415.8.9, 415.8.10.1, 415.8.11, 704.8.1, 903.2.4
Standby power systems 2702.2.10-2702.2.13
Storage and dispensing 414.1, 414.5, 414.6
Tank protection 415.6.2.2, 415.6.2.3
Unstable materials . . . . .Table 414.2.5(1),
    Table 414.5.1, Table 415.3.2, 415.5.1, 415.8
Water-reactive materials . . . . .Table 415.3.2,
    415.5, 415.5.1, 415.5.2, 415.8, Table 415.8.2.1.1

HIGH-RISE BUILDINGS 403
    Automatic fire detection. 403.5, 907.2.12
    Automatic sprinkler system 403.2
    Elevators 403.9
    Fire command station 403.8
    Fire department communication 403.7
    Smokeproof enclosure 1020.1.7
    Sprinklers. 403.2
    Stairway door operation 403.12
    Standby power, light and
      emergency systems 403.10, 2702.2.15
    Voice alarm 403.6, 907.2.12
    Zones. 907.8.2

HORIZONTAL EXIT. 1022
    Doors. 1022.3
    Fire resistance. 1022.2
    Institutional I-3 occupancy. 408.2, 1022.1
    Institutional I-2 occupancy. 1022.1

HORIZONTAL FIRE SEPARATION 704
    Combustible projections 704.2

HOSE CONNECTIONS (see STANDPIPES, REQUIRED)

HURRICANE SHUTTERS 1609.1.2

**HURRICANE PRONE REGIONS
(see WIND LOADS)** 1609.2

I

IDENTIFICATION, REQUIREMENTS FOR
    Glazing 2403.1, 2406.4
    Inspection certificate 1702.1
    Label, information required on 1703.5.3
    Pier and pile materials. 1808.2.20
    Preservative-treated wood 2303.1.8.1
    Structural Steel 2203.1

IMPACT LOAD 1602.1, 1607.8

INCINERATOR ROOMS 1015.3

INDUSTRIAL (see FACTORY OCCUPANCY)

INSPECTIONS
    Approval required 1704.1
    EIFS. 1704.12

Fabricators 1704.2
Lath or gypsum board 2503
Pier. 1704.9
Pile 1704.8, 1808.2
Reinforcing steel 1704.4
Seismic. 1707
Special 109.3.9, 1704.13
Sprinklers 904.4
Steel, structural 1704.3
Steel framing, cold-formed. 1704.3
Welding 1704.3.1, 2204.1
Wood, structural. 1704.6

INSTITUTIONAL I-1 . . . . .308.2
Accessibility 1107.5.1
Emergency egress. 1026
Fire alarm. 907.2.6.1
Visible alarms. 907.9.1.3
Sprinklers 903.2.5, 903.3.2

INSTITUTIONAL I-2 . . . . .308.3
Accessibility 1107.5.2, 1107.5.3, 1107.5.4
Combustible decorations 806.1
Corridor width. 1017.2
Exterior exit stair 1023.2
Fire alarm and detection 907.2.6
Special requirements 407
Sprinklers 903.2.5, 903.3.2
Suites 1014.2
Openings in smoke barriers. 909.5.2, 709.5

INSTITUTIONAL I-3 . . . . .308.4
Accessibility 1103.2.13, 1107.5.5
Exit sign exemption 1011.1
Openings in smoke barriers. 909.5.2
Special requirements 408

INSTITUTIONAL I-4 . . . . .308.5
Accessibility 1103.2.12
Corridor rating 1017.1
Fire alarm. 907.2.6
Sprinklers 903.2.5

INSTITUTIONAL OCCUPANCY (GROUP I) 308
Adult care. 308.5.1
Child care. 308.3.1, 308.5.2
Group I-1 . . . . .308.2
Group I-2 . . . . .308.3, 407
Group I-3 . . . . .308.4, 408
Group I-4 day care facilities 308.5
Sprinkler system, automatic. 903.2.5

INSULATION
Concealed 719.2
Duct insulation 719.1
Exposed. 719.3
Fiberboard 2303.1.5.2, 2303.1.5.3
Foam plastic (see FOAM PLASTICS). 719.1
Roof 719.5
Thermal 719

INTERIOR ENVIRONMENT

Lighting 1205
Rodentproofing . . . . .Appendix F
Sound transmission .1207
Space dimensions 1208
Temperature control .1204
Ventilation. 1203.4
Yards or courts 1206.2, 1206.3

INTERIOR FINISHES . . . . Chapter 8
Acoustical ceiling systems 803.9
Application 803.4, 804.4
Atriums 404.7
Decorative materials. 801.1.2, 806
Floor finish 804
Foam plastic insulation 2603.3, 2603.4
Foam plastic trim 806.3
Light-transmitting plastics 2606
Signs. 402.15, 2611
Wall and ceiling finishes 803

J

JOINT
Concrete construction joints 1906.4
Gypsum board 2306.4.5.1.1, 2508.4
Lumber sheathing. 2308.10.8.1
Masonry reinforcement. 2103.13.2, 2109.7.2.3
Shotcrete. 1913.7
Structural plain concrete. 1909.3
Waterproofing 1807.3.3

JOINTS, FIRE-RESISTANT SYSTEMS 713

K

KIOSKS. 402.10

L

LABORATORIES
Classification of. 304.1, 508.2
Hazardous materials. 414
Incidental use . . . . Table 508.2

**LAMINATED TIMBER,
STRUCTURAL GLUED.** 602.4, 2302.1

LANDINGS
Doors 1008.1.5
Ramp 1010.6
Stair. 1009.4, 3403.4

LATH, METAL OR WIRE . . . . .Table 2507.2

LAUNDRIES . . . . .304.1, 306.2, Table 508.2

LAUNDRY CHUTE 707.13, 903.2.10.2

LIBRARIES
Classification, other than school. 303.1

Classification, school 508.3.1
Live load . . . . Table 1607.1

LIGHT, REQUIRED 1205.1

LIGHTING, EMERGENCY (see EMERGENCY LIGHTING)

LIGHTS, PLASTIC CEILING DIFFUSERS 2606.7

LINTEL
Adobe 2109.8.4.7
Fire resistance 714.6
Masonry 2104.1.5
Masonry, wood support 2304.12

LIQUEFIED PETROLEUM GAS 415.6.3

LIVE LOADS 1602.1, 1607
Construction documents. 1603.1.1
Posting of 1603.3

LOAD COMBINATIONS 1605
Strength design or load and
resistance factor design. 1605.2
Allowable stress design 1605.3
Special seismic load combinations 1605.4

LOADS 1602.1
Combinations 1605
Dead 1602.1, 1606
Flood. 1603.1.6, 1612
Impact. 1602.1, 1607.8
Live 1603.1.1, 1603.3, 1607
Pile foundation 1808, 1811
Rain. 1611
Seismic 1603.1.5, 1613
Snow. 1603.1.3, 1608
Soil lateral 1610
Structural . . . . Chapter 16
Wind 1603.1.4, 1609

LOBBIES
Assembly occupancy 1025.4
Elevator. 707.14.1, 1007.2.1, 1007.4

LOCKS AND LATCHES 1008.1.8.3
Delayed egress locks 1008.1.8.6
Institutional I-3 occupancy 408.4

LUMBER
General provisions . . . . Chapter 23
Quality standards 2303

M

MAINTENANCE
Accessibility 3409.2

MALL (see COVERED MALL BUILDINGS)

MANUAL FIRE ALARM BOX 907.3

MARQUEES 3106, H113

Live load . . . . Table 1607.1

MASONRY
Adhered veneer. 1405.9
Adobe 2109.8
Anchorage 1604.8.2, 2106.2, 2109.7
Anchored veneer. 1405.5
Ashlar stone 2102.1
Autoclaved aerated concrete (AAC) 2102.1,
2103.3
Bond 2109.6
Cavity wall 2109.4.2
Chimneys 2113
Cold weather construction. 2104.3
Compressive stress requirements 2109.3
Construction 2104, 2109.8.4
Construction documents 2101.3
Corbelled 2104.2
Dampproofing 1807
Design, methods 2101.2, 2107-2109
Fire resistance, calculated 721.3.2, 721.3.4
Fireplaces 2101.3.1, 2111
Floor anchorage 1604.8.2, 2109.7.3
Foundation walls 1805.5
Foundations, adobe 2109.8.4.3
Glass unit. 2101.2.5, 2103.5, 2110
Grouted 2102.1
Headers (see BONDING, MASONRY). . . 2109.6.2
Hollow units 2104.1.2.2
Hot weather construction 2104.4
Inspection, special. 1704.5
Joint reinforcement 2103.13.2,
2108.9.2.2, 2109.7.2.3
Lateral stability. 2109.2
Lateral support 2106.2, 2109.4
Materials 2103
Parapet walls. 2109.5.4
Penetrations 712, 712.3.1
Quality assurance 1708.1, 2105
Rodentproofing . . . . Appendix F
Roof anchorage. 1604.8.1, 2106.2, 2109.7.3
Rubble stone 2102
Running bond 2109.6.5
Seismic provisions. 2106
Serviceability 1604.3.4
Shear walls 2106.1.1
Solid. 2104.1.2.3, 2109.6.2.1
Stack bond 2109.6.5.2
Stone 2103.4, 2109.8
Support (see also MASONRY,
Lateral support) 2304.12
Surface bonding 2103.9
Test procedures 1708.1, 2105.2.2.2
Thickness 2109.5
Tie, wall 2104.1.3, 2109.6.3
Veneer. 2101.2.6, 2308.11.2
Wall, composite 2102.1
Wall, hollow 2102.1
Wall, intersecting. 2109.7.2
Wall anchorage 1604.8.2, 2109.7

Waterproofing. 1807
Weepholes. 2104.1.8
Wetting brick 2104.5
Wythe defined 2102.1

MATERIALS
Alternates. 103.3
Aluminum. . . . . Chapter 20
Concrete. . . . . Chapter 19
Glass and glazing. . . . . Chapter 24
Gypsum . . . . Chapter 25
Masonry . . . . Chapter 21
Noncombustible. 703.4
Plastic. . . . . Chapter 26
Steel . . . . Chapter 22
Testing (see TESTING) 1715
Wood . . . . Chapter 23

MEANS OF EGRESS. . . . . Chapter 10
Accessible 1007
Aircraft hangers, residential. 412.3.3
Aisles 1014.4
Assembly 1007.1, 1025
Atrium. 404.8
Bleachers 1025.1.1
Capacity 1005.1
Child care facilities (see Day care facilities)
Ceiling height 1003.2
Corridors. 1017
Covered mall buildings. 402.4
Day care facilities. . . . . . . 308.5.2, Table 1004.1.1,
         Table 1015.1, Table 1019.2
Doors 1008
Elevation change .1003.5
Elevators 1003. 7
Emergency escape and rescue. 1026
Emergency lighting values. 1006.4, 3410.6.15
Enclosures under stairways. 1009.5.3
Escalators 1003.7
Existing buildings 3409.6, 3410.5, 3410.6.11
Exit (see EXIT). 1018-1023
Exit access. 1014-1017
Exit discharge. 1024
Exit doors 1018.2
Exit signs 1011
Fire escapes. . . . 412.5.4, 1019.1.2, Table 1607.1
Floor surface 1003.4
Gates 1008.2
Grandstands. 1025.1.1
Guards 1013
Handrails 1012
Headroom 1003.1, 1008.1.1 1009.2, 1010.5.2
High Hazard Group H 415.8.4.4
Helistops. 412.5.4, 1019.1.2
Horizontal exits. 1022
Illumination 1006
Institutional Group I-2. . . . . 407.4.2
Institutional Group I-3. . . . . .408.2, 408.3,
         408.5, 408.6.3
Mezzanines 505.3, 505.4, 1004.6, 1007.1
Minimum width. .1005.1

Moving walk 1003.7
Number 1019.1
Occupant load. 1004.1
Parking 406.3.8
Passageway 1021
Path of egress travel, common. 1014.3
Protruding objects. 1003.3, 1005.2
Ramps. 1010, 1023
Seating at tables. 1014.4.3
Seating, fixed 1007.1, 1025
Single exit 1015.1.1, 1019.2
Special amusement 411.2
Stage. 410.3.3, 410.5.3, 1015.6
Stairways 1009, 1020.1, 1023
Temporary structures 3103.4
Travel distance 1016.1, 1025.7
Turnstile 1008.3
Underground buildings 405.5.1, 405.8
Vertical exit enclosures. 1020.1
Width. . . . . . 1005.1, Table 1005.1, 1025.6, 1025.8

MECHANICAL (see AIR CONDITIONING, HEATING, REFRIGERATION, AND VENTILATION)
Air transfer openings. 704.14, 705.11,
         706.10, 716.5
Chimneys (see CHIMNEYS) 2113
Code . . . . Chapter 28
Equipment on roof 1509, 1510.2
Factory-built fireplace 2111.13.1
Fireplaces 2111.1
Room separation . . . . Table 508.2, 508.2.2
Seismic inspection and testing. 1707.8,
         1707.9, 1708.5
Smoke control systems 909
Systems . . . . 1613.2, Chapter 28

MECHANICALLY LAMINATED DECKING . . 2304.8.3

MEMBRANE ROOF COVERINGS 1507.11,
         1507.12, 1507.13

MEMBRANE STRUCTURES 2702.2.9, 3102

MENTAL HOSPITALS 308.3

MERCANTILE OCCUPANCY (GROUP M)
Aisles 1014.4.1, 1014.4.2
Area 503, 505, 506, 507
Classification. 309
Height 504
Interior finishes . . . . Table 803.5
Live load . . . . Table 1607.1
Sprinkler system, automatic 903.2.6

METAL
Aluminum . . . . Chapter 20
Roof coverings 1504.3.2, 1507.5
Steel . . . . Chapter 22
Veneer 1404.5

MEZZANINES. 505
Accessibility 1104.4, 1108.2.3, 1108.2.8
Area limitations 505.2, 505.5.1

Egress. 505.3, 505.4, 1004.6, 1007.1
Guards 1013.1
Height 505.1
Stairs. . . . . 707.2(9), 1009.9, 1020.1

MIRRORS . . . . 1008.1, 2406.3.1(7)

MIXED OCCUPANCY (see OCCUPANCY
    SEPARATION)

MOISTURE PROTECTION 1403.2, 1503,
                                    2303.2.3, 2304.11

MONASTERIES. 310.1

MORTAR 2102.1
    Ceramic tile. 2103.5
    Compressive stresses,
        masonry. . . . . Table 2103.8(2)
    Dampproofing. 1807
    Fire resistance 712.3.1, 712.4.1
    Glass unit masonry. 2110.6
    Material. 2103.8
    Placing 2104.1.2
    Rodentproofing. . . . . .Appendix F
    Surface-bonding. 2102.1, 2103.9

MOTELS 310.1

MOTION PICTURE PROJECTION ROOMS. 409
    Construction 409.2
    Exhaust air 409.3.2
    Lighting control 409.4
    Projection room. 409.3
    Supply air 409.3.1
    Ventilation. 409.3

MOTOR FUEL-DISPENSING SYSTEM 406.5

MOTOR VEHICLE FACILITIES 304, 311, 406

MOVING WALKS 3005.2
    Means of egress. 1003.7

N

NAILING 2302.1, 2303.6, 2304.9

NONCOMBUSTIBLE BUILDING MATERIAL. . . 703.4

NURSING HOMES 308.3

O

OCCUPANCY
    Accessory. 508.3.1
    Atriums 404.2
    Change. 3406, 3409.4
    Floor loads . . . . Table 1607.1
    Special . . . . .Chapter 4

OCCUPANCY CATEGORY. 1602.1, 1604.5
    Multiple occupancies. 508, 1604.5.1

OCCUPANCY CLASSIFICATION
    Covered mall buildings 402
    HPM. 415.8
    Mixed. 508.3
    Mixed occupancy values 406, 508.2.1,
                                            Table 508.2
    Special. . . . . .Chapter 4

OCCUPANCY SEPARATION
    Covered mall building 402.7
    Incidental use areas 508.2, 706.3.6
    Mixed. 508
    Parking garages . . . . .Table 508.3.3(c),
                                        406.1.4, 406.2.7
    Repair garages 406.6.2
    Required fire resistance . . . . Table 508.3.3
    Residential aircraft hangars 412.3.2

OCCUPANT LOAD
    Covered mall building 402.4.1
    Determination of 1004.1
    Increased. 1004.2
    Outdoors 1004.8
    Seating, fixed. 1004.7
    Signs 1004.3

OFFICE BUILDINGS
    Classification. 304
    Live loads . . . . Table 1607.1

OPENING PROTECTION, EXTERIOR WALLS . 704.1

OPENING PROTECTION, FLOORS (see VERTICAL
    OPENING PROTECTION)

OPENING PROTECTIVES 715
    Automatic-closing devices. 715.4.7, 909.5.2
    Fire door and
        shutter assemblies 704.8.2, 715.4
    Fire windows 715.5
    Glazing 715.5
    Glass unit masonry (see GLASS UNIT
        MASONRY) 2110.1.1
    Interior walls 708.6
    Required fire resistance 715.5
    Self-closing 715.4.7

ORGANIC COATINGS .418

ORGANIC PEROXIDES 307.4, 307.5

OXIDIZERS, LIQUID AND SOLID. 307.2

P

PANIC HARDWARE .1008.1.9

PARAPET, EXTERIOR WALL 704.11, 2109.5.4
  Construction. 704.11.1
  Fire wall 705.6
  Height. 704.11.1

PARKING, ACCESSIBLE 1106, 1110.1,
  3409.4, 3409.7

PARKING GARAGES (see GARAGE, AUTOMOBILE PARKING). 406.2
  Barriers, vehicle 406.2.4, 1602.1, 1607.7.3
  Classification 406.2.1
  Guards 406.2.3, 2407.1.3
  Height, clear. 406.2.2
  Live loads. . . . . .Table 1607.1
  Mixed separation 406.2.7

PARKING GARAGES, OPEN 406.3
  Area and height 406.3.5
  Construction type. 406.3.3
  Stairs and exits. 406.3.8
  Standpipes 406.3.9

PARKING GARAGES, ENCLOSED 406.4
  Heights and areas 406.4.1
  Ventilation. 406.4.2

PARTICLEBOARD 2302.1
  Draftstopping 717.3.1
  Fastening 2304.9
  Moisture protection. 1403.2, 1405.2
  Quality 2303.1.7
  Shear walls. 2306.4.3
  Veneer 1405.4
  Wall bracing 2308.9.3

PARTITIONS
  Materials. 602.4.6, 603.1
  Occupancy, specific. 708.1
  Structural 1607.5, 1607.13

PARTITIONS, FIRE 708
  Construction, general. 703
  Continuity. 508.2.2.1, 708.4
  Exterior walls . . . . Table 602, 704.5, 708.5
  Fire-resistance rating of walls . . . . . 603.1(8), 708.3
  Joint treatment gypsum 2508.4
  Joints 713
  Opening protection. 715
  Rated glazing 715.5

PASSAGEWAY, EXIT (see EXIT) 1021.1

PASSENGER STATIONS 303

PATIO COVERS. 2606.10

PEDESTRIAN
  Protection at construction site 3306
  Walkways and tunnels. 3104

PENETRATION-FIRESTOP SYSTEM
  Fire-rated walls. 712.3.2
  Fire-rated horizontal assemblies 712.4.1.2

PENETRATIONS 712
  Fire partitions 708.7
  Fire-resistant assemblies 712.3
  Nonfire-resistant assemblies 712.4.2

PERLITE . . . . Table 720.1(1), Table 2507.2

PIER FOUNDATIONS. 1808, 1812
  Special inspections. 1704.9, 1707.5

PILE FOUNDATIONS 1808
  Base piles, enlarged concrete 1808.1, 1810.2
  Caisson. 1808.1, 1810.7
  Composite. 1811
  Concrete, cast-in-place. 1810
  Concrete, precast 1809.2
  Concrete-filled steel pipe and tube. 1808.1,
  1810.6
  Drilled or augered uncased 1810.3
  Driven 1809, 1810.4
  Micropiles 1808.1, 1810.8
  Pile load, allowable. 1808.2.8
  Seismic design 1808.2.23,
  1809.2.2.2.1-1809.2.3.2.2
  Special inspections. 1704.8
  Steel, structural. 1809.3
  Steel-cased. 1808.1, 1810.5
  Timber. 1808.1, 1809.1

PIPES
  Embedded in concrete 1906.3
  Embedded in fire protection 714.3
  Insulation covering 719.7
  Penetration protection. 712, 1020.1.2
  Under platform 410.4

PLAIN CONCRETE (see CONCRETE) 1909

PLASTER
  Fire-resistance requirements 718
  Gypsum. 718.1, 718.2
  Portland cement . . . . 718.5, Table 2507.2,
  Table 2511.1.1

PLASTIC. . . . . Chapter 26
  Approval for use 2606.2
  Finish and trim, interior. 2604
  Light-transmitting panels. 2607
  Roof panels. 2609
  Signs. 402.15, 2611
  Thermal barrier 2603.4
  Veneer 1404.8, 2605
  Walls, exterior 2603.4.1.4, 2603.5

PLASTIC, FOAM
  Insulation (see FOAM PLASTICS). 2603
  Interior finish 2604
  Malls 402.15.5

PLASTIC, LIGHT-TRANSMITTING
  Awnings and patio covers. 2606.10
  Bathroom accessories 2606.9
  Exterior wall panels. 2607

Glazing 2608
Greenhouses 2606.11
Light-diffusing systems 2606.7
Roof panels 2609
Signs, interior 2611
Skylight 2610
Solar collectors 2606.12
Structural requirements 2606.5
Unprotected openings 2608.1, 2608.2
Veneer, exterior . . . . . . 603.1(12), 603.1(14), 2605
Wall panels 2607

PLATFORM
(see STAGES AND PLATFORMS) 410
Construction 410.4
Temporary 410.4.1

PLATFORM LIFTS, WHEELCHAIR 1007.2,
1007.5, 1009.1, 1109.7

PLENUM
Underground buildings 907.2.18.1

PLUMBING
Facilities, minimum 2902
Fixtures . . . . Table 2902.1
Residential aircraft hangars 412.3.5

PLYWOOD 2302.1
Bracing 2308.9.3
Decorative 2303.3
Design requirements 2301
Diaphragm 2305.2, 2306.3
Fastening 2304.9
Fire-retardant treated . . . . 2303.2|
Preservative-treated 2303.1.8.1, 2304.11
Quality 2303
Roof sheathing 2304.7, 2308.10.8
Seismic shear panels 2305.1.5,
2305.3, 2308.12.4
Standards 2306.1
Veneer 1405.4

PRESCRIPTIVE FIRE RESISTANCE 720

PRESERVATIVE-TREATED WOOD 2302.1
Fastenings 2304.9.5
Quality 2303.1.8
Required 1403.5, 2304.11
Shakes, roof covering 1507.9.5, 1507.9.7

PROJECTION ROOMS
Motion picture 409

PROJECTIONS, COMBUSTIBLE 704.2.3, 1406.3

PROPERTY LINE (see FIRE SEPARATION
DISTANCE) 704.3

PROSCENIUM
Opening protection 410.3.5
Wall 410.3.4

PUBLIC ADDRESS SYSTEM

Covered mall building 402.14, 2702.2.14
Special amusement buildings 411.6
Underground buildings 405.7

PUBLIC PROPERTY . . . . Chapter 32, Chapter 33

PUBLIC RIGHT OF WAY
Encroachments . . . . Chapter 32

PYROPHORIC MATERIALS . . . . 307.4, Table 307.1(1)

R

RAILING (see GUARDS and HANDRAILS)

RAMPS 1010.1
Assembly occupancy 1025.11
Construction 1010.7
Existing buildings 3409.8.5
Parking garage 406.2.5
Slope 1010.2

REFERENCED STANDARDS . . . . Chapter 35
Applicability   102.5
Fire resistance   703.2
List   Chapter 35
Organizations   Chapter 35

REFORMATORIES 308.4

REFRIGERATION (see MECHANICAL)
Machinery room 1015.4

REFUGE AREAS (see AREA OF REFUGE and AREA
FOR ASSISTED RESCUE, EXTERIOR)

REFUSE CHUTE 707.13

REINFORCED CONCRETE (see CONCRETE)
General 1901.2
Inspections 1704.4

REINFORCEMENT
Concrete 1907, 1913.4, 1915.4
Glass block 2110.7
Masonry 2103.13

RELIGIOUS WORSHIP, PLACES OF
Classification 303, 305.1
Door operations 1008.1.8.3
Egress 1025
Fire alarm 907.2.1
Interior finishes . . . . Table 803.5
Balcony enclosure 1025.5.1
Unlimited area 507.6

RESIDENT HOUSING AREA, INSTITUTIONAL I-3
OCCUPANCY
Accessibility 1103.2.13, 1107.5.5,
1108.4.2, E104.3, E104.4
Fire detection 907.2.6.3.3
Occupant load 1004.1
Subdivision 408.7

**RESIDENTIAL CARE/ASSISTED LIVING
FACILITIES**...............................308.1
   Accessibility 1107.5.1, 1107.5.2,
                    1107.6.4, 3409.8.7
   Fire alarms................. 907.2.6, 907.9.1.3
   Separations .... Table 508.2, Table 508.3.3
   Smoke alarms 907.2.10.1.3
   Sprinklers..................... 903.2.5, 903.3.2

RESIDENTIAL OCCUPANCY (GROUP R) 310
   Accessibility 1107.6
   Area .... Chapter 5
   Doors 1008.1
   Draftstopping 717.4.2
   Emergency escape 1026.1
   Height............................. Chapter 5
   Interior finishes.....................Table 803.5
   Live load.........................Table 1607.1
   Parking under............................ 509
   Partitions 708.1
   Smoke alarms 907.2.10
   Sprinklers 903.2.7
   Visible alarms.......................907.9.1.3

RETAINING WALLS. **1806**

**REVIEWING STANDS (see BLEACHERS and
GRANDSTANDS)** 1025.1.1
   Live load.........................Table 1607.1

RISERS, STAIR (see STAIRWAY CONSTRUCTION)
   Alternating tread device 1009.9.2
   Assembly 1025.6.1, 1025.11
   Closed 1009.3.3
   General...............................1009.3
   Spiral 1009.8
   Uniformity........................... 1009.3.2

RODENTPROOFING .... Appendix F

ROLL ROOFING. 1507.6

ROOF ACCESS 1009.11.1

ROOF ASSEMBLIES AND ROOFTOP STRUCTURES
   Cooling towers 1509.4
   Drainage.............................1503.4
   Fire classification 1505
   Height modifications....................504.3
   Impact resistance......................1504.7
   Materials............................ 1506
   Parapet walls 1503.3
   Penthouses 1509.2
   Tanks 1509.3
   Towers, spires, domes and cupolas 1509.5
   Weather protection. 1503
   Wind resistance 1504.1, 1609.5

ROOF CONSTRUCTION
   Construction walkways 3306.7
   Coverings (see ROOF COVERINGS).... 1609.5.2
   Deck.............................. 1609.5.1
   Draftstopping 717

   Fire resistance ....Table 601
   Fireblocking........................... 717.2
   Live loads ....Table 1607.1, 1607.11
   Materials..........................Chapter 6
   Penetration of fire resistant assemblies 711.5
   Rain loads............................1611
   Roof structures 504.3, 1509
   Slope, minimum ....Chapter 15
   Snow load....................1603.1.3, 1608
   Wood (see ROOF CONSTRUCTION, WOOD)

ROOF CONSTRUCTION, WOOD 602.4.5
   Anchorage to masonry 1604.8.2, 2109.7.3.3
   Attic access............................ 1209.2
   Ceiling joists 2308.10.2
   Diaphragms 2305.2, 2306.3.2
   Fastening schedule.................... 2304.9
   Framing............... 2304.10.3, 2308.10
   Plank-and-beam 2306.1.2
   Rafters 2306.1
   Sheathing 2304.7, 2308.10.8
   Ventilation, attic. 1203.2
   Wind uplift.........................2308.10.1
   Wood trusses 2308.10.10

ROOF COVERINGS 1507
   Asphalt shingles 1507.2
   Built up 1507.10
   Clay tile............................ 1507.3
   Concrete tile 1507.3
   Fire resistance 1505
   Flashing 1503.2, 1507.3.9, 1507.5.6
   Impact resistance 1504.7
   Insulation............................1508
   Liquid applied coating............... 1507.15
   Membrane...........................3102
   Metal panels 1507.4
   Metal shingles...................... 1507.5
   Modified bitumen 1507.11
   Plastics, light-transmitting panels 2609
   Reroofing 1510
   Roll 1507.6
   Single-ply 1507.12
   Slate shingles 1507.7
   Sprayed polyurethane foam 1507.14
   Thermoplastic single-ply............... 1507.13
   Wind loads 1504.1, 1609.5
   Wood shakes 1507.9
   Wood shingles 1507.8

ROOF DRAINAGE 1503.4

**ROOF PROTECTION FROM ADJACENT
CONSTRUCTION** 3307.1

ROOF REPLACEMENT/RECOVERING 1510

ROOF VENTS..........................1016.2

ROOM DIMENSIONS 1208

ROOMING HOUSE 310

S

SAFEGUARDS DURING CONSTRUCTION . . . . Chapter 33
Adjoining property protection 3307
Construction 3302
Demolition 3303
Exits 3310
Fire extinguishers 3309
Protection of pedestrians 3306
Sanitary facilities 3305
Site work 3304
Sprinkler system, automatic 3312
Standpipes 3311
Temporary use of streets, alleys,
    and public property 3308

SAFETY GLAZING 715.4.6.4, 2406

SCHOOLS (see EDUCATIONAL OCCUPANCY)

SEATING, FIXED
Accessibility 1108.2
Bleachers (see BLEACHERS)
Grandstands (see GRANDSTANDS)
Live load . . . . Table 1607.1
Occupant load 1004.7

SECURITY GRILLES 1008.1.3.5

SEISMIC 1613
Loads 1613
Masonry 2106
Piers or piles 1808.2.23
Steel 2205
Soils investigation 1802.2.6, 1802.2.7
Structural observations 1707, 1709
Structural testing 1708
Ties, concrete footings 1805.4.2.2
Ties, pile foundation 1808.2.23
Wood 2305, 2308.11, 2308.12

SERVICE STATION (see MOTOR FUEL-DISPENSING FACILITIES)

SHAFT (see SHAFT ENCLOSURE and VERTICAL OPENING PROTECTION) 702

SHAFT ENCLOSURE (see VERTICAL OPENING PROTECTION) 707
Construction 707.11, 707.12
Elevators 707.14
Fire-resistance rating 707.4
High-rise buildings 403.3.2
Materials 707.3
Penetrations 707.8, 716.5.3
Refuse and laundry chutes 707.13
Required 707.2

SHEAR WALL
Gypsum board and plaster 2505
Masonry 2102.1, 2106.1.1, 2109.2.1
Wood 2302.1, 2305.3, 2306.4

SHEATHING
Clearance from earth 2304.11.2.2
Fastening 2304.9
Fiberboard 2306.4.4
Floor 2304.7, 2308.8.6
Gypsum 2306.4.5.1.6
Moisture protection 2304.11.2.2
Particleboard 2306.4.3
Roof 2304.7
Roof sheathing 2308.10.8
Wall 2304.6.1, 2308.9.3
Wood structural panels 2303.1.4

SHOPPING CENTERS 309

SHOTCRETE 1913

SHUTTERS, FIRE (see OPENING PROTECTIVES) 715.4

SIGNS 3107
Accessibility 1007.6, 1007.7,
    1011.3, 1110, E107, E109.2.2
Area of refuge, accessible 1007.6.4, 1007.6.5,
    1110.1, 1110.3
Area for assisted rescue, exterior 1007.8.3,
    1110.3
Covered mall building 402.15
Doors 1008.1.8, 1008.1.8.3
Elevators 1109.6, 1110.2
Exit 1011.1, 2702.2.3
Floor loads 1603.3
Occupant content, assembly 1004.3
Parking spaces 1110.1
Plastic 2611
Stair identification 1020.1.6, 1110.2, 1110.3
Standpipe control valve 905.7.1

SITE WORK 3304

SKYLIGHTS
Light, required 1205.1
Plastic 2610
Protection from adjacent construction 3307.1

SLAB, COMPOSITE STEEL DECK/CONCRETE 2209.2

SLAB ON GROUND, CONCRETE . 1910, 2304.11.2.4

SLATE SHINGLES 1507.7

SMOKE BARRIERS 709, 716.5.5
Construction 709.4, 909.5
Doors 709.5, 715.4, 909.5.2

Duct penetration. 716.5.5
Fire-resistance rating 709.3
Materials. 709.2
Openings .709.5, 909.5.2
Penetrations. 709.6
Required. 407.4, 408.6
Walls. 709.4

SMOKE CONTROL 909
Atrium buildings 404.4
Covered mall building 402.9
High-rise. 1020.1.7
Special inspections 1704.14
Stages 410.3.7.2
Standby power systems. 2702.2.2
Systems 909
Underground buildings. 405.5

SMOKE DAMPERS 716.2-716.5
Smoke barriers. 716.5.4, 716.5.5

SMOKE DETECTORS
Covered mall 907.2.20
High-rise buildings 403.5, 907.2.12
HPM. 415.8.9
Institutional I-2 . . . . .407.6
Multiple-station. 907.2.10
Residential aircraft hangars 907.2.21
Residential occupancies 907.2.10.1
Single-station. 907.2.10
Smoke activated doors 715.4.7.3
Special amusement buildings 411.5
Underground buildings. 907.2.18

SMOKE EXHAUST SYSTEMS
Underground buildings. 405.5, 907.2.18, 909.2

SMOKE PARTITIONS 407.3, 710
Materials. 710.2
Fire-resistance rating 710.3
Continuity 710.4
Openings 710.5
Penetration and joint 710.6
Ducts and air transfer openings. 710.7
Smoke and draft control doors. 710.5.2

SMOKE VENTS 410.3.7.1, 910, 1016.2

SMOKEPROOF ENCLOSURES 1020.1.7
Design 909.20

SNOW LOAD 1608
Glazing. 2404

SOILS AND FOUNDATIONS . . . . Chapter 18
Classification 1802.3
Depth of footings 1805.2
Excavation, grading and fill 1803
Expansive. 1802.3.2, 1805.8
Footings and foundations. 1805
Footings on or adjacent to slopes 1805.3
Foundation walls .1805.5
Foundations, pile and pier 1808

Grading. 1803.3
Investigation 1802
Investigation, pile and pier 1802.2.4
Investigation, seismic 1802.2.6,1802.2.7
Loadbearing values 1804
Soil boring and sampling 1802.5
Soil lateral load 1610
Special inspection. 1704.7
Testing, piles. 1808.2.8.3

SOUND TRANSMISSION 1207

SPECIAL CONSTRUCTION . . . . Chapter 31

SPECIAL INSPECTIONS (see
INSPECTIONS) . . . . Chapter 17
Continuous 1702.1
Periodic 1702.1
Statement 1705

SPIRAL STAIRS. 1009.8
Stages. 410.5.3

SPRAY-APPLIED
FIRE RESISTANT MATERIALS. 1702.1
Inspection 1704.10
Steel column calculated
fire resistance. 721.5.2.2

SPRINKLER SYSTEMS, AUTOMATIC 903
Exempt locations 903.3.1.1.1
Substitute for fire rating . . . . Table 601(e)

SPRINKLERS, REQUIRED 903
Aircraft hangars .412.2.6
Aircraft paint hangars 412.5
Atrium building 404.3
Basements 903.2.10.1
Covered mall building. 402.8
Garages 406.3.10, 903.2.8
Hazardous occupancies 903.2.4
High-rise buildings 403.2
Incinerator rooms . . . . Table 508.2
Laundry chutes, refuse chutes, termination rooms
and incinerator rooms 707.13, 903.2.10.2
Multistory buildings 903.2.10.3
Spray finishing booth 416.4
Supervision
(see SPRINKLERS, SUPERVISION) 903.4
Underground buildings 405.3

SPRINKLERS, SUPERVISION. 903.4
Service 901.6
Underground buildings 405.3

STAGES AND PLATFORMS 410
Alternating tread stairway. 410.5.3
Dressing rooms. 410.5
Egress. 410.5.3, 1015.6
Fire barrier wall. .410.5.1
Floor finish and floor covering 804.4
Platform, temporary 410.4.1
Platform construction 410.4

Proscenium curtain. 410.3.5
Proscenium wall 410.3.4
Roof vents. 410.3.7.1
Scenery. 410.3.6
Smoke control. 410.3.7.2
Sprinkler system, automatic 410.6
Standpipes 410.7
Ventilation. 410.3.7

STAIRWAY (see ALTERNATING TREAD DEVICES, STAIRWAY CONSTRUCTION and STAIRWAY ENCLOSURE)
Exterior exitway 1023.1, 1024.1
Discharge barrier 1020.1.6
Width, minimum 1009.1

STAIRWAY CONSTRUCTION
Aisle 1025.9
Alternating tread 1009.9
Circular (see Curved)
Curved 1009.7
Elevators. 3002.7
Enclosure under 1009.5.3
Fireblocking 717.2.4
Handrails. 1009.10
Headroom. 1009.2
Illumination 1205.4
Landings 1009.4
Live load . . . . Table 1607.1
Seismic anchorage. 2308.12.7
Spiral. 408.3.3, 1009.8
Treads and risers 1009.3
Width. 1009.1
Winders. 1009.3.1

STAIRWAY ENCLOSURE 1020.1
Access 1020.1.7.2
Construction 1020.1.2
Discharge 1024.1
Elevators within. 3002.7
Fire-resistant construction 1020.1
Penetrations 1020.1.2
Space below, use 1009.5.3
Ventilation. 1020.1.3

STANDBY POWER
Atriums 404.6
Covered mall building. 402.13
Elevators. 3003.1
Hazardous occupancy 414.5.4
High-rise 403.10
Underground buildings 405.9

STANDPIPE AND HOSE SYSTEMS (see STANDPIPES, REQUIRED) 905
Dry 905.8
Hose connection location 905.1, 905.4-905.6
Cabinet locks 905.7.2

STANDPIPES, REQUIRED
Assembly 905.3.2, 905.5.1
Covered mall buildings. 905.3.3

During construction 905.10
Stages 905.3.4
Underground buildings 405.11, 905.3.5

STEEL . . . . .Chapter 22
Bolting 2204.2
Cable structures 2207
Calculated fire resistance 721.5
Cold-formed. 2202.1, 2210
Conditions of restraint 703.2.3
Deck/concrete composite slabs 2209.2
Identification and protection 2203
Joists 2202.1, 2206
Open web joist. 2206
Parapet walls 1503.3
Piles. 1809.3
Reinforcement, concrete 1907
Seismic provisions. 2205.2
Storage racks 2208
Structural 2205
Welding 2204.1

STONE VENEER. 1405.6
Slab-type 1405.7

STORAGE OCCUPANCY (GROUP S) 311
Area. . . . . .Chapter 5
Automobile parking garage 406
Floor loads. . . . . .Table 1607.1
Hazard storage, Group S-1, moderate 311.2
Hazard storage, Group S-2, low 311.3
Height . . . . .Chapter 5
High piled combustible 413
Interior finishes . . . . Table 803.5
Smoke and heat vents 910.2
Sprinkler system, automatic 903.2.9
Travel distance increase 1016.2

STRENGTH
Design requirements. 1604.2
Masonry. 2102.1
Nominal 1602.1
Required 1602.1

STRENGTH DESIGN. 1602.1, 1604.1
Masonry. 2101.2.2, 2108

STRUCTURAL DESIGN . . . . .Chapter 16
Aluminum . . . . .Chapter 20
Concrete . . . . .Chapter 19
Foundations. . . . . .Chapter 18
Masonry. . . . . .Chapter 21
Steel . . . . .Chapter 22
Wood . . . . .Chapter 23

STRUCTURAL TESTS AND SPECIAL INSPECTIONS . . . . .Chapter 17
Alternative test procedure 1711
Approvals. 1703
Contractor responsibilities. 1706
Design strengths of materials 1710
General 1701

In-situ load tests 1713
Material and test standards 1715
Preconstruction load tests 1714
Special inspections 1704, 1707
Statement of special inspections 1705
Structural observations 1709
Structural testing 1708
Test safe load 1712

STRUCTURAL OBSERVATION 1702.1, 1709

STUCCO 2512

SWIMMING POOL, GLASS 2406.3

SWIMMING POOL, ENCLOSURES 3109
Gates, access 3109.3.1, 3109.4.1.7
Public 3109.3
Residential 3109.4

T

TELEPHONE EXCHANGES 304

**TELESCOPIC SEATING (see FOLDING AND
   TELESCOPIC SEATING)**

TEMPORARY STRUCTURES 3103

TENANT SEPARATION
Covered mall buildings 708.1

TENTS
Standby power 2702.2.8

TERMITES, PROTECTION FROM 2304.11

TERRA COTTA 1405.8

TESTING
Concrete 1905.6.2.4, 1905.6.5
Fire-resistant materials 703.2
Glazing 2406, 2408.2.1
Roof tile 1715.2
Seismic 1708
Smoke control 909.3
Soils 1802
Sprinklers 904.4
Structural . . . . Chapter 17

**THEATERS (see PROJECTION ROOMS and
   STAGES AND PLATFORMS)** 303

**THERMAL BARRIER, FOAM PLASTIC
   INSULATION** 2603.4, 2603.5.2

**THERMAL- AND SOUND-INSULATING
   MATERIALS** 719
Cellulose loose-fill insulation 719.6
Loose-fill insulation .719.4
Roof insulation 719.5

THROUGH-PENETRATIONS
Air ducts 716.6.1
Fire barriers 706.8

Fire rated walls 712.3.1
Fire-rated horizontal assemblies 712.4.1
Firestop system 712.3.1.2, 712.4.1.2

TILE 2102.1
Ceramic (see CERAMIC TILE)

TOILETS
Accessible 1109.2
Fixture count . . . . Table 2902.1
Grab bars 1607.7.2
Location 2902.4, 2902.5, 2902.6
Rooms openings 1210.5
Unisex .1109.2.1, 2902.1.1

TOWERS
Airport traffic control 412.1
Construction 3108.3
Dead load 3108.4.1
Grounding 3108.5
Location and access 3108.2
Radio 3108
Television 3108
Wind load 3108.4.2

TOWERS, COOLING .1509.4

TOXIC MATERIALS
Classification 307.6
Gas detection system 908.3
Separation 415.7.3

TRAVEL DISTANCE
Area of refuge 1007.6
Atrium 404.8
Balcony, exterior 1016.3
Common path of travel 1013.3
Factory-industrial occupancy, increase 1016.2
Mall 402
Mall tenant space .402.4.4
Measurement 1016.1
Storage occupancy, increase 1016.2

TREADS, STAIR (see STAIRWAY CONSTRUCTION)

TREATED WOOD 2302.1
Stress adjustments 2306.1.3

TRUSSES 2303.4
Fire resistance 714.2.3
Materials . . . . Chapter 6
Metal-plate-connected parallel wood 2303.4.2

TUNNELED WALKWAY 3104

TURNSTILES 1008.3

U

UNDERGROUND BUILDINGS 405
Compartmentation 405.4
Construction type 405.2
Elevators 405.4.3

Emergency power loads. 405.10
Exits 405.8
Fire alarm systems 405.6
Public address 405.7
Smoke exhaust. 405.5.2
Smokeproof enclosure 1020.1.7
Sprinkler system, automatic 405.3
Standby power 405.9.1, 2702.2.16
Standpipe system. 405.11
Voice alarms. 907.2.19

UNLIMITED AREA BUILDINGS 507

UNSTABLE MATERIALS 307.3

UNUSABLE SPACE 711.3.3

USE AND OCCUPANCY. . . . . Chapter 3
Accessory 508.3.1
Incidental . . . . 508.2, Table 508.2
Mixed 508.3

UTILITY AND MISCELLANEOUS OCCUPANCY (GROUP U) 312
Egress illumination 1011.2
Sprinkler system, automatic 903.2.10

V

VEHICLE BARRIERS 406.2.4, 1602.1, 1607.7.3

VEHICLE SHOW ROOMS. 304

VENEER
Glazing 1405.11
Cement plaster 1405.14
Fastening 1405.16
Fiber cement siding 1405.15
Masonry, adhered. 1405.9
Masonry, anchored. 1405.5
Metal 1405.10
Plastic 2605
Slab-type. 1405.7
Stone. 1405.6
Terra cotta 1405.8
Vinyl 1405.13
Wood 1405.4

VENTILATION (see MECHANICAL)
Attic. 1203.2
Bathrooms 1203.4.2.1
Crawl space 1203.3
Elevator hoistways 3004
Enclosed parking garages 406.4.2
Exhaust, hazardous 1203.5
Exhaust, HPM. 415.8.10.2
Exit enclosure 1020.7.1
Fabrication areas, HPM 415.8.2.6
Hazardous, storage and dispensing. 414.3
High-rise 1020.1.7
HPM service corridors 415.8.4.3
Mechanical 1203.1

Natural. 1203.4
Projection rooms 409.3
Repair garages 406.6.3
Smokeproof enclosures 909.20.3, 909.20.5
Stages 410.3.7
Under-floor ventilation 1203.3

VERTICAL OPENING PROTECTION
Atriums 404.5
Duct penetrations 716.1
Elevators 707.14
Institutional I-3 occupancy. 408.5
Shaft enclosure 707

VESTIBULES, EXIT DISCHARGE 1024.1

VINYL
Expanded 802, 803.7
Rigid 1405.13

VOICE ALARM (see also ALARMS, VOICE)
Amusement buildings, special 411.6
Covered mall buildings 402.14
High-rise buildings. 907.2.12
Underground buildings 907.2.19.1

W

WALKWAY, COVERED, ENCLOSED AND TUNNELED WALLBEARING 3104
Fire resistance. . . . . Table 601
Live load . . . . Table 1607.1
Materials per construction type . . . . .Chapter 6
Opening protection 715

WALL, EXTERIOR 704
Bearing . . . . .Chapter 6
Coverings 1405
Fire-resistance ratings. 704.5, 1403.4
Flashing, veneered walls. 1405.3
Foam plastic insulation 2603.4.1.4, 2603.5
Light-transmitting plastic panels 2607
Materials 704.4, 1406
Nonbearing . . . . .Chapter 6
Opening protection 704
Projections. 704.2
Structural stability 704.6
Veneer (see VENEER)
Weather resistance 1403.2, 1405.2
Weather resistant barriers. 1405.2

WALL, FIRE (see FIRE WALLS)

WALL, FIRE RESISTANT, PENETRATIONS . . . 712.3

WALL, FOUNDATION. 1805.5
Dampproofing and waterproofing 1807

WALL, INTERIOR
Opening protection 715

WALL, INTERIOR NONBEARING (see PARTITIONS)

WALL, MASONRY 2102.1
    Lateral stability 2109.2
    Lateral support 2109.4, 2106
    Shear 2109.2.1
    Wood contact 2304.11.2.3, 2304.11.2.5

WALL, PARAPET. 704.11, 1503.3, 2109.5.4

WALL, PARTY (see FIRE WALLS)

WALL, RETAINING 1806, 2304.11.7

WALL, VENEERED (see VENEER). . . . . . Chapter 14

WALL, WOOD CONSTRUCTION
    Bracing 2308.9.3
    Cutting, notching, boring 2308.9.10
    Exterior framing 2308.9
    Fastening schedule 2304.9
    Framing 2304.3, 2308.9
    Interior bearing partition 2308.9.1
    Interior nonbearing partition 2308.9.2.3
    Openings 2308.9.5, 2308.9.6, 2308.9.7
    Shear walls. 2305.3, 2306.4
    Sheathing (see SHEATHING)
    Studs 2308.9.1
    Top plates .2308.9.2.1

WATER-REACTIVE MATERIALS . . . . .Table 307.1(1)

WEATHER, COLD
    Concrete construction 1905.12
    Masonry construction. 2104.3

WEATHER, HOT
    Concrete construction 1905.13
    Masonry construction. 2104.4

WEATHER PROTECTION
    Exterior walls .1405.2
    Roofs 1503

WEEP HOLES 2104.1.8

WELDING 2204.1
    Materials, verification of
      steel reinforcement 1704.4.1
    Special inspections 1704.3.1, 1707.2
    Splices of reinforcement in masonry 2107.6,
                                      2108.3

WIND LOAD 1609
    Basic wind speed 1609.3
    Construction documents 1603.1.4
    Exposure category. 1609.4
    Glazing. 2404
    Glass block. 2110.3.1
    Hurricane-prone regions 1609.2
    Provisions for walls 2306.2
    Roofs 1504.1, 1609.5, 2308.10.1
    Seismic detailing 1604.10
    Testing 1715.2.2
    Wind-borne debris region. 1609.2

WINDERS, STAIR (see STAIRWAY CONSTRUCTION)

WINDOW
    Emergency egress 1026
    Exterior, structural testing. 1714.5
    Glass (see GLAZING) 1405.12
    Operable. 1109.13.1
    Required, light and ventilation 1205.2
    Wells 1026.5

WOOD . . . . Chapter 23
    Allowable stress design 2306
    Assemblies, calculated fire resistance 721.6
    Bracing, walls 2308.9.3
    Ceiling framing 2308.10
    Connections and fasteners. 2304.9
    Contacting concrete, masonry
      or earth. 2304.11.4
    Decay, protection against. 2304.11
    Diaphragms 2305.2, 2306.3
    Draftstopping. 717.3, 717.4
    End-jointed lumber 2303.1.1
    Fiberboard. 2303.1.5, 2306.4.4
    Fire-retardant treated 2303.2
    Fireblocking. 717.2
    Floor and roof framing (see FLOOR
      CONSTRUCTION, WOOD). 2304.4
    Floor sheathing 2304.7
    Foundation 1805.4.6, 2308.3.3.1
    Grade, lumber. 2303.1.1
    Hardboard. 2303.1.6
    Heavy timber construction 2304.10
    Hurricane shutters 1609.1.2
    I-joist 2303.1.2
    Inspection, special 1704.6, 1707.3
    Lateral force-resisting systems. 2305
    Light-frame construction, conventional. 2308
    Load and resistance factor design 2307
    Moisture content 2303.1.8.2, 2303.2.5
    Nails and staples 2303.6
    Particleboard shear walls 2306.4.3
    Plywood, hardwood 2303.3
    Preservative treated 1403.5, 2303.1.8
    Roof framing (see
      ROOF CONSTRUCTION, WOOD) 2304.4
    Roof sheathing 2304.7
    Seismic provisions 2305, 2306,
                         2308.11, 2308.12
    Shear walls 2305.3, 2306.4
    Standards and quality, minimum 2303
    Structural panels. 2302.1, 2303.1.4
    Supporting concrete or masonry 2304.12
    Termite, protection against. 2304.11
    Trusses 2303.4
    Veneer . . . . .Chapter 14
    Wall framing (see WALL,
      WOOD CONSTRUCTION) 2304.3
    Wall sheathing 2304.6
    Wind provisions 2306.2

WOOD SHINGLES AND SHAKES 1507.8, 1507.9

WOOD STRUCTURAL PANELS
   (see WOOD) 2302.1, 2303.1.4
   Diaphragms 2306.3.2
   Shear walls 2306.4.1
   Sheathing 2304.6.1

Y

YARDS OR COURTS 1206